Business Law:
Text and Cases

Third Edition

Business Law: Text and Cases

TOWNES LORING DAWSON, B.B.A., B.S., M.B.A., LL.B., J.D., Ph.D.

Professor of Business Law, University of Maryland
Member of Maryland, District of Columbia and
Texas Bars, and admitted to practice before the
Federal District Courts, United States Court of
Appeals and the United States Supreme Court

EARL WINIFIELD MOUNCE, M.A., LL.M., LL.D.

Late Professor of Law and Labor, University of
Maryland. Member of Maryland, Missouri and
United States Supreme Court Bars.

D. C. HEATH AND COMPANY
Lexington, Massachusetts Toronto London

Preface

Many interesting and unusual cases have been added to this third edition, bringing the text up-to-date while retaining its original approach to teaching business law, that is, reinforcing the legal text with lively cases for students to relate to their own experiences. This approach to teaching business law evolved out of many years of classroom experience where the authors found retention and learning was made easier for students when cases were discussed along with the rules of law.

In this text, the aspects of law that fall within the realm of business law are set forth as accurately and as lucidly as possible. Emphasis is placed on the development of these rules, giving historical background and the manner in which economic conditions and social philosophy have caused changes in the law through the years. Quite aside from the pedagogical reasons for this emphasis, it is of the highest practical importance for prospective businessmen and laymen to realize that law is far from static and that it is in their best interest to stay current with changes that occur.

While the text serves to inform students of the rules of law and how they are constructed, the cases provide illustrations of how the legal mind works in applying the rules to specific situations. By studying the techniques of legal analysis illustrated in the cases, the student will develop his own powers of analysis and legal reasoning so that his study of law becomes of practical value. Gradually he will begin to apply these techniques of reasoning to the day-to-day legal problems that will arise in the conduct of his own business and personal life. Though many cases are recent, no premium has been placed on recentness for its own sake, as we have found from our classroom experience that many older cases have proven to be particularly enlightening to students.

Review cases are included at the end of most chapters to provide the student with an opportunity to apply what he has learned. For each case the citation is supplied so that the student, when in doubt, may research a particular case himself.

The Uniform Commercial Code has now been adopted by all states except Louisiana and reference is made to the provisions of that code throughout. An appendix contains the complete text of the Uniform Commercial Code and the Uniform Partnership Act. An index of cases precedes the general index.

Acknowledgment to reproduce the Uniform Partnership Act and the Uniform Commercial Code is gratefully made to The American Law Institute and to the National Conference of Commissioners on United States Laws.

TOWNES L. DAWSON

Contents

Appendix

Business Law:
Text and Cases

Introduction

part I

START

ISTANBUL
MON. NIGHT

Legal
Backgrounds

1

IMPORTANCE OF A KNOWLEDGE OF LAW
AND ITS SCOPE

The study of law involves an inquiry into one of the great fields of human knowledge. Like religion, science, and the arts, it had its origin far back in the annals of the human race, and its history is a record of one of man's major achievements. At the same time the study of law is of enormous practical value, for law is a vital and ever-present force in modern life and no one is beyond its influence and effect. It is not only on those relatively rare occasions when we buy a house or make a will or are involved in an automobile accident that we come into contact with the law. On the contrary, every time we purchase a newspaper or a candy bar, take a suit to the cleaner, ride a bus, write a check, or eat a meal in a restaurant, our actions are regulated and controlled by a number of vital legal principles. Furthermore, everyone is presumed to know the law: "Ignorance of the law excuseth no man." Hence it is well worth while to spend some time in gaining at least a general knowledge of the law. Such knowledge will make one more aware of his legal rights and duties and better able to protect his interests in his business transactions.

Just how important is law to us as individuals?

When a person is born, the law requires that the attending midwife or physician fill out a birth certificate. After birth, the law requires that the parents support the child. If not, there are certain penalties prescribed for not doing so. As the child matures, there are juvenile laws that govern his activities, and when he decides to take the fatal step, that is, get married, he must meet certain legal requirements. For example, the boy in many jurisdictions has to be 18 to 21 years of age to marry without parental consent, and the girl is usually required to be 16 to 18 years of age. After the honeymoon is over, and the parties decide they want a divorce, the law prescribes the grounds that must be met, and if those grounds are not met, the parties cannot be divorced. But if the grounds are met and the divorce is granted, the property rights of the parties are decided according to law. For example, the husband may be required to pay child support in the event there are children and/or alimony to the wife when prescribed by law. After several marriages and divorces, a party gets old and lies down and dies; a death certificate must be issued by the attending physician. He is then usually taken to a local morgue, which is zoned according to law, and the attendants in the mortuary have passed examinations for a mortician as required by law. Thereafter, the deceased is usually taken to a graveyard, which is zoned, again according to law, and he is buried to the depth prescribed by law, usually six feet under.

All may not be over yet. If the deceased has property and/or money, his estate must be administered by the probate or orphans' court, which usually takes one to three years, and should the deceased have more than $60,000, a federal estate tax return must be filed. So you see, the law is with us from birth, through marriage, divorce, death, and almost to resurrection!

It is obvious that the man who operates a business enterprise needs an even more thorough knowledge of the law than the person not so engaged. Every day that he carries on his business he is confronted with problems growing out of contracts, agency, negotiable instruments, property rights, insurance, bailments, and even the possibility of tort liability rising from his own activities or those of his agents and employees. If he operates his business as a partnership or corporation, he is continually confronted with special laws governing those types of business enterprises. The possibility of costly error is constantly before him.

Furthermore the man who operates a business today is faced with a more formidable problem in understanding the law than the businessman of past generations. Our economy is becoming progressively more complex, and our business enterprises are becoming more and more subject to government regulation. The modern businessman must try to acquaint himself with the law that has to do with such diverse matters as interstate commerce, taxation, labor relations, social security, workmen's compensation, and many others, as they apply to his particular business. This involves a general knowledge of the jurisdiction and procedures of the various federal and state agencies and commissions that administer these specialized fields of law. He need not become an expert in all of these fields, or even in any one of them, but he should be sufficiently aware of their scope to be able to operate his business within their confines and to know when he should seek the services of a competent attorney. Experience has fully demonstrated that a lawyer can often obtain more satisfactory results for his client if the client himself has some knowledge of the law. In the first place, such a client is more likely to have preserved necessary evidence; in the second place, he knows at what point he should seek the services of an attorney. Like the doctor, the lawyer is often called in too late to save the "patient."

DEFINITION OF LAW

The legal historians Pollock and Maitland say: "The law may be taken for every purpose, save that of strictly philosophical inquiry, to be the sum of the rules administered by the courts of justice." [1] Much the same definition is contained in Justice Holmes's comment that to him law was merely "a statement of the circumstances in which the public force will be brought to bear upon man through the courts." [2] Attempts to frame a more philosophical definition have been numerous, but none has been generally accepted. At the outset of our study, therefore, we shall define the term *law*, as it is to be used in this book,[3] as the body of rules of human conduct which the courts recognize and enforce. These rules deal with the relation of persons to other persons and to the state. They may emanate from a congress or a parliament, from an emperor or a dictator, or from the previous decisions of the courts themselves. Whatever their ultimate source, when the courts will take cognizance of them and enforce them they are "the law," and all who come within their jurisdiction are bound by them.

Law falls into two great divisions. One part of it deals with the legal rights and duties of persons; this part is called *substantive law*. For example, if A buys a car, the substantive law gives him certain rights with respect to the car. But these rights would not amount to much if the law did not also provide a means of protecting them and a remedy in case they are violated. That part of the law which deals with remedies and with the methods and procedures for the enforcement of legal rights and duties is called *procedural* or *adjective law*. Thus if A's car is stolen and damaged by B, the procedural law provides A with an appropriate remedy against B and with the legal machinery of courts and court proceedings to secure it. Our concern in this book will be chiefly with substantive

---

[1] *History of the English Law* (Cambridge, 1911), p. xxv.

[2] *American Banana Co. v. United Fruit Co.*, 213 U. S. 347, 356.

[3] Sometimes called *positive law* or *jural law*, to differentiate it from various other senses of the word, as for example in the expressions "scientific law," "moral law," "the laws of economics."

law, but some important aspects of procedural law will also be described, particularly in this introductory section.

It must be kept in mind that the law differs from jurisdiction to jurisdiction. The law of the United States is not the law of France, nor is the law of Maryland the law of New York. Moreover, within any one jurisdiction the law is not static; on the contrary, it may be said to be dynamic, changing, to some degree, from generation to generation. For law tends to reflect what the people feel will best serve their needs and desires; and as these change, the law gradually follows suit, through new legislation and court decisions. Thus the law in the United States today is not the same as it was in 1865, or in 1900, or even in 1950. On the other hand, the law also manifests under ordinary circumstances a strongly conservative tendency which makes for stability and continuity. As we shall soon see, many features of our present-day law had their origin centuries ago.

ORIGIN AND DEVELOPMENT OF LAW

The birth of law long antedated the beginning of recorded history. It is perhaps safe to assume that the crudest forms of social organization gave rise rather promptly to the need for regulation, and that sooner or later law began to evolve to fill that need. At all events, the earliest civilizations of which we have records possessed bodies of law already far removed from the primitive.

Since the beginning of recorded history a number of distinct systems of law have been produced. Professor Wigmore [1] enumerates sixteen such legal systems: Egyptian, Mesopotamian, Chinese, Hindu, Hebrew, Greek, Maritime, Roman, Keltic, Germanic, Church (Canon), Japanese, Mohammedan, Slavic, Romanesque, and Anglican. The earliest of these, the Egyptian, can be traced back at least as far as 4000 B.C.; the Mesopotamian, to about 3500 B.C.; the Chinese, to 3000 B.C. The first two of these have long since vanished; the third still flourishes today, and is thus the oldest legal system in existence. By contrast the Mohammedan legal system, which is the basic law for at least a quarter of a billion people today, goes back only to 600 A.D.

A study of the earlier systems of law shows a close relationship between law and religion. This is reflected in recurring traditions of the divine origin of the law. The Egyptians, for example, ascribed their first body of law to their deity Thot; the Hindus, whose legal system originated in India around 400 B.C., believed that their god Manu had given them their first laws. The Hebrew legal system, which had its formative period

[1] John H. Wigmore, *A Panorama of the World's Legal Systems* (Washington, D. C., Washington Law Book Co., 1936), p. 4.

around 1200 B.C., is the most familiar example of the influence of religion upon the origin and development of the law; but an equally striking instance is the Mohammedan law, which similarly makes no distinction between religious and jural law. Even in the most secular systems of law certain areas reflect strongly the moral convictions of the people.

In other areas their economic, political, and social circumstances have always been mirrored. The Hebrew system reflected the nomadic life of the people; by contrast, the Mesopotamian system, formulated by the Babylonians and Assyrians of the regions around the Tigris and Euphrates rivers, was the product of a society which developed extensive business and commerce, and it gives evidence of the use of such legal instruments as deeds, leases, loan agreements, bills of sale, and the like. The so-called Greek legal system reflected the political disunity and the democratic political institutions of the Greek city-states; the Roman system, by contrast, was shaped by the needs and pressures of a farflung but closely unified empire.

It would be highly enlightening if we could survey the salient features of each of these legal systems in turn, but space permits only an account of the two which today are dominant in western Europe, Great Britain, and North and South America: the two named in Professor Wigmore's list as Romanesque and Anglican, but more generally known as the *Roman civil law* and the *English common law*.

What is called the Roman civil law stems back ultimately to the legal system of ancient Rome. The Romans were the great lawgivers of antiquity. They gave to the world the first fully developed systems of substantive and procedural law and created a highly developed court system, ranging from courts with minor or limited jurisdiction to courts of final resort. Some of the greatest judges, jurisconsults, and legal scholars of all time were produced under the Roman legal system.

All this came gradually, of course. The first known body of Roman law, called the Twelve Tables (c. 450 B.C.), was a rather crude codification of customary law. But as Rome expanded from a city-state, first conquering all of Italy and later most of the then known world, the necessity for some uniform system of law to hold the empire together gave full scope to Roman legal genius. From time to time great codes were promulgated by the Roman emperors. They were usually the products of commissions appointed by the emperor to study existing law, bring it up to date, and give it systematic form. Upon completion the resulting code was put into effect by imperial decree, after which all judges throughout the empire were required to enforce it in the courts of law. The greatest of the Roman codes, and one of the most important legal productions of all time, was the Code Justinian (528–535 A.D.), put together by a commission of legal experts at the instigation of the emperor whose name it bears.

During the centuries of chaos after the fall of Rome, the ancient Roman law as finally embodied in the Code Justinian was largely forgotten. Among the Germanic invaders, certain codes of law appeared, such as the Salic Law of the Franks (around 500), the Code of the Lombards (659), and the Forum Judicum of the Goths of Spain (around 650). But in the eleventh century, with the emergence of greater economic and political stability in western Europe, a new interest in learning appeared; and in the universities which came to be established, law was one of the subjects which received fresh attention. The Code Justinian was resurrected, and students of law took a deep interest in it. Eventually new codes of law were drawn up and adopted which represented a merging of the Germanic law with the Roman law of antiquity. This union produced what is now known as the Roman civil law.

Today the system of law which originated in this way prevails in all of western continental Europe and in Scotland. It is also the basic law throughout South and Central America (except British Guiana, Honduras, and the Canal Zone), Mexico, Cuba, the Province of Quebec, and our own state of Louisiana. It has also left its mark on many areas of Asia. Probably more people today live under the Roman civil law than under any other system of law.

The outstanding characteristic of the Roman civil law, as distinguished from the English common law, is its formal codification. It is presumed to be entirely contained in a code, ordinarily prepared by a commission of legal scholars and then made "the law of the land" by official decree. Whatever is not in the code is not enforceable in the courts. The task of a judge, under the code, is simply to find and apply the proper provisions as individual cases arise.

The English common law, on the other hand, developed largely out of the customs and traditions of the English people as interpreted and applied by the courts of law. In other words, the common law is largely the work of the courts, and is found in the cases decided by the courts. It is today the basic law throughout the British Empire and the United States and its possessions, with the exception, already pointed out, of Scotland, Quebec, and Louisiana.

The remainder of this chapter is devoted to a brief survey of the sources and early development of the English common law. It should be said at the outset that the term "common law" is used by the courts and legal authorities with a variety of meanings. In its broadest sense—the sense in which we have just been using it—the term denotes the entire system of Anglo-American law, in contrast to other systems of law, such as the

Roman civil law or the Mohammedan law. In a narrower sense, it is used to designate the *case law*, or law developed by the courts in their decisions (sometimes called also the *judge-made law*), in contrast to *statutory law*, or law enacted by the legislative branch of a government, such as the English Parliament, our own Congress, or a state legislature. (The case law is sometimes referred to as the *unwritten law*, while the statutory law is referred to as the *written law*.) Again, the term is used in contradistinction to such special areas of the law as ecclesiastical law, the law merchant, or even equity law. When this distinction is intended, the "common law" is looked upon merely as the product of the decisions of the common law courts. Finally, in writings on the law of the United States the term is often used to designate the law of England, both written and unwritten, as it existed and was recognized in this country at the time of the Revolutionary War—in other words, the law which we inherited from England, as distinguished from the developments and changes which it has undergone since that time.

BEGINNINGS OF THE COMMON LAW

ORIGIN AND DEVELOPMENT

The early history of the common law takes us back to the years immediately after the Norman Conquest in 1066. When William the Conqueror seized the English throne, he found in existence two principal types of local courts, the *hundred moot* and the *shire moot*. The hundred moot (so called from the name of a political subdivision of the shire or county) had jurisdiction over most types of cases, both civil and criminal. Its "judges" were originally the whole body of freeholders within the hundred, but their number was later reduced to twelve or some multiple of twelve. It ordinarily met monthly. The shire moot or county court was composed of leading churchmen and secular officials of the county, and met twice a year. It was actually a court of appeals, since it heard only cases which had first been tried in the hundred moot. Cases could be appealed from a shire moot to the king.

The procedure in these courts was very different from modern court procedure. The applicable law, which was said to be based upon the customs and traditions of the people, was announced in advance by the judges. The outcome of the case did not, however, depend upon the presentation of evidence in the modern legal sense of the word. The disposition of both criminal and civil cases was determined either by *ordeal* or by *compurgation*. The ordeal, which was conducted by a priest, was in effect an appeal to God to indicate how the case should be decided. The accused or defendant was subjected to some physical test, the results of which determined the verdict. For example, he might be bound and thrown into water. If he sank, he was deemed innocent, because the water consented to receive him; if he floated, he was adjudged guilty. Or he was required to thrust his arm into boiling water, or to submit to being burned by hot metal. If the wound healed normally, he was deemed innocent; if it became infected, he was deemed guilty. In compurgation the decision was based upon the oaths of the parties and of others, called *compurgators* or *oath-helpers*, who swore not to the truth or falsity of the alleged facts but to the veracity of the party they were aiding, somewhat in the manner of character witnesses.

William the Conqueror did not attempt to uproot the existing Anglo-Saxon law; on the contrary, he recognized it as the law of his new subjects, and he allowed the local courts to carry on their customary procedures. But as a part of the strong centralized government which he immediately began to set up he established the *Curia Regis*, or King's Court, composed of the leading men of the realm and possessed of broad political and judicial authority. This was the beginning of a system of royal courts which gradually overshadowed the local courts and absorbed their work.

Until the time of Magna Carta (1215) the Curia Regis followed the king wherever he went, and court did not convene at any definite time or place. This practice proved most inconvenient for litigants, and in consequence one of the provisions of Magna Carta was that "common pleas," or civil suits between private individuals, should be separated from the other judicial work of the Curia Regis and heard in a court permanently established at Westminster Hall in London. Next the royal justices began to "go on circuit" from county to county, holding court in each county at rather regular intervals.

Like the judges of the Anglo-Saxon courts, these judges of the royal courts found their law in the customs and traditions of the people. It soon became their practice to prepare written accounts of their decisions, which were then assembled in volumes known as the *Year Books* and thus made available to all the judges. A judge with a case before him for adjudication could refer to earlier decisions for "guidance" and have the benefit of the work of previous judges. Eventually this practice of referring to previous decisions and following them became an important and distinctive feature of the common law. It became known as the doctrine of *stare decisis* (to stand on the decided cases). No decree of the king or act of Parliament required the judges to follow this "rule of precedent"; the judges imposed the practice upon themselves, and with relatively few exceptions it has been followed by the courts [1] down to the present

---

[1] For stare decisis in the American courts see the next chapter.

day. This custom tended early to make the law "common" or uniform throughout all England, and it may well have been the source of the name "common law."

The uniformity and stability of the law administered by the royal courts was one of the major reasons for the gradual absorption by them of the work of the hundred moots and shire moots. Another was the adoption by the royal courts of a new means of trying cases, namely by *trial* or *petit jury* whose function was to determine the truth or falsity of the alleged facts of a given case. The superiority of this method to compurgation and ordeal became clear to a steadily increasing number of people, and since the local courts failed to adopt it, litigants gradually abandoned recourse to them and took their cases to the royal courts. By 1300 trial by jury had almost completely superseded the earlier methods.

COMMON LAW ACTIONS

The common law courts made available three legal remedies: (1) money damages, (2) recovery of possession of personal property, and (3) recovery of possession of real property. These remedies were secured through the use of certain *actions* brought through the process of writs secured from the court. Each writ set forth the nature and subject matter of the action to be brought and gave the court jurisdiction of the case. It also placed upon the sheriff the duty of compelling the defendant to appear in court. For many years these writs were granted when needed and the courts were not averse to granting a new type of writ if conditions demanded it. All told there were probably some thirty or forty different forms of action created, with the objective of making available, under proper circumstances, the three common law remedies.

The common law actions used to secure money damages and to recover possession of personal property were broadly classified as *contract* (*ex contractu*) *actions* and *tort* (*ex delicto*) *actions*. The principal contract actions were covenant, assumpsit, debt, and account. The principal tort actions were detinue, replevin, trespass, case, and trover.

An action of *covenant* was used if the plaintiff was suing for money damages for the alleged breach of a contract under seal. This was the first contract action devised by the common law courts. An action of *assumpsit* was used where action was brought for money damages for the alleged breach of a simple contract, not under seal. An action of *debt* was brought to recover a specific or liquidated sum of money alleged to be due to the plaintiff by the defendant, e.g., a suit on a note. An action of *account* was used to compel the defendant to compute mutual accounts between the plaintiff and himself. The action would lie only where some relation existed between the parties which obligated the defendant to advise the plaintiff of the status of their business relationship, such as in the case of a principal and agent, a trustee and his cestui que trust (beneficiary), or a guardian and ward.

An action of *detinue* was used to recover specific personal property which had been rightfully obtained but was wrongfully detained or withheld. An action of *replevin* was used to secure the possession of personal property where the plaintiff was able to prove both a wrongful taking and a wrongful withholding of his property by the defendant. An action of *trespass* was used to secure money damages from the defendant for trespass to the person, to the personal property, or to the real property of the plaintiff. If the trespass was to the person of the plaintiff, the action was termed *trespass vi et armis* (with force and arms); if to his personal property, it was called *trespass de bonis asportatis* (for goods which have been carried away); if to his real property, it was *trespass quare clausum fregit* (because he has broken the close). An action of *trespass on the case*, or simply *case*, as it was generally called, was used where the injury was indirect. The action of case was used in any case of indirect injury either to the person of the plaintiff or to his real or personal property. This action was also used to recover damages in cases of fraud, libel, slander, waste, malicious prosecution, infringement of patents, copyrights, and trade-marks. The action of *trover* was brought to recover money damages for the conversion of personal property. In order to recover, the plaintiff had to show that he had either a general or special ownership in the property and was also entitled to immediate possession.

There were various actions to recover possession of real property, but the one which gradually came to be principally used was the action of *ejectment*.

It will be seen from this brief summary that the procedures and techniques provided for securing redress in the common law courts eventually became extremely technical and complicated. Excessive emphasis tended to be placed upon meeting formal requirements, and this tended to lessen the usefulness of the common law courts as agencies of justice. Reform of this obstacle was long in coming, and it is interesting to note that it was finally initiated in the United States. In 1848 the state of New York discarded the old common law system of pleading and provided for a new system known as *code pleading*. Under this system there is but one form of action, called a *civil action*, so that it is no longer necessary for the success of the plaintiff's case that he secure a particular type of writ. Most of the states have followed the lead of New York by adopting code pleading, and similar reforms have been made in the English system of procedure. It should be understood that this change was only in the procedural law and in no way affected the substantive law.

EQUITY COURTS AND JURISDICTION

ORIGIN AND DEVELOPMENT

Eventually a point was reached where the common law courts ceased to accommodate themselves to changing conditions. The process of granting new writs to meet new needs came practically to an end. Unless one of the existent writs covered a given case and provided the precise remedy required by the plaintiff, he was unable to obtain relief. So far as providing new remedies was concerned, the common law had come to a standstill by the early years of the fourteenth century. It was this stagnancy that led to the creation of the equity courts.

Since litigants were unable to secure from the courts the relief they felt entitled to, they began to appeal to the king, who under the law was the source of all justice. At first the king himself dealt with some of these appeals, but it soon became impossible for him to attend personally to all of them, and he began to refer them to his Chancellor, who was regarded as his personal representative.

The Chancellor's training was usually in the Roman and Canon Law, and it might have been expected that he would adopt the principles of those systems of law in his handling of cases, but he did not do so; though he did not avail himself of the services of the petit jury, he made no attempt to inject into the legal system the principles of the continental systems. He did, however, establish certain basic rules to guide him in the handling of the cases that came before him. He early established the principle that he would not grant relief unless it could be shown either that no remedy at law existed, or, if one did exist, that it was inadequate. This is still a basic principle of equity law. The principle was also established that whereas the law courts acted *in rem* (upon the matter), the equity courts acted *in personam* (upon the person). This means that a law court, in awarding the plaintiff a judgment against the defendant, merely handed down a decision that the defendant owed the plaintiff a specified amount of money in the way of damages; it did not command the defendant to pay the plaintiff. But if a court of equity decided in favor of the complainant and against the respondent, it issued a decree ordering the respondent to do or not to do a certain thing. If he failed to comply with the decree, he was in contempt of court and might be fined or sent to jail, or both. This distinction between law and equity still exists.

The development of the courts of chancery (or equity courts, as we call them), with a completely new jurisdiction, separate and apart from the common law courts, came about slowly and by very gradual steps. The Court of Chancery was not created by royal decree or by an act of Parliament. The king, in referring appeals and complaints of litigants to the Chancellor, had no preconceived idea of creating a separate series of courts alongside the common law courts. But the Chancellor performed his judicial task so well that by the end of the fourteenth century the Court of Chancery was generally recognized as a separate court with a more or less defined jurisdiction. Since that time the chancery courts have gradually broadened their jurisdiction (not without opposition on the part of the common law courts) until today they preside over a wide and very important area of human relations.

In this country equity courts existed side by side with the law courts until about the middle of the nineteenth century, when some of the states began to "fuse" their law and equity courts; that is, they provided that law and equity cases should be tried by the same court. The fusion made no change in the legal and equitable remedies available. At the present time only four or five states have separate law and equity courts.

MAXIMS OF EQUITY

The equity courts early developed certain comprehensive precepts or principles out of which grew the entire system of equity jurisprudence. These maxims may be looked upon as the foundation stones upon which was erected the whole structure of equity law. Among the most important of these maxims are the following: Equity will not suffer a wrong without a remedy; Equity looks to the intent, rather than to the form; He who comes into equity must come with clean hands; He who seeks equity must do equity; Equity follows the law; Where there are equal equities, the first in time shall prevail; Equity aids the vigilant, not those who slumber on their rights.

EQUITABLE REMEDIES

An equity court will not grant relief to a complainant unless it is shown either that no remedy exists at law, or, if there is a remedy, that the remedy is inadequate. Consequently, if a suit is filed in an equity court wherein the complainant asks for money damages, the equity court will deny relief, since there exists an adequate remedy at law. However, if the complainant asks for equitable relief and the court finds that the complainant is entitled both to equitable relief and to money damages, it will grant both the equitable relief and money damages. The equity court does not feel that it would be equitable to dismiss the complaint as to money damages and require the complainant to file a separate suit, on the law side of the court, for money damages.

There exist today a large number of equitable remedies, and it would require more space than is here available to give an adequate notion of the breadth and comprehensiveness of the jurisdiction of equity courts. But several equitable remedies that will be encountered in the cases as our study of business law progresses may be briefly described here. (Some of them will be more fully discussed later.) It should be understood that the granting of these remedies and the other equitable remedies is within the sound discretion of the court; however, its exercise of discretion is not subject to its own whim or caprice but is based upon well-established and recognized principles of equity law.

Injunctions. The injunction is one of the most important forms of equitable relief and was one of the first to be devised and developed by the chancery courts. Its principal uses have been to protect property rights and to prevent public and private wrongs or injury. If a court of equity issues an injunction against the defendant, it orders him to refrain from, or to discontinue, a certain action. The injunction has been used to prevent the commission of waste to property, to prevent trespass to property, to prevent public and private nuisances, to prevent the infringement of patents, copyrights, and trade-marks, to protect the purchaser of the good will of a business, to restrain a corporation or its officers from committing illegal or ultra vires acts, and to enforce negative covenants in contracts. More recently the injunction has been used in labor disputes.

Specific performance of contracts. In general, courts of equity will grant specific performance of contracts (1) where the subject matter of the contract is of such a special nature, or of such a peculiar value, that money damages awarded by a court of law would be inadequate, or (2) where, because of the nature of the subject matter of the contract, the awarding of money damages would be impracticable.

Reformation and rescission of contracts. Under certain circumstances, courts of equity will decree the reformation of legal instruments, such as contracts and deeds, to conform with the real intentions of the parties; or they will decree the complete rescission of such instruments on grounds of mistake, fraud, misrepresentation, duress, or undue influence.

Foreclosure of mortgages. A mortgage is given on property to secure a debt or obligation, which is usually evidenced by a note. In case of a default in the payment of the note, the holder of the note may file a bill in equity to foreclose the equity of redemption of the debtor or mortgagor

Accountings. The common law action of account had such a limited application that it did not furnish adequate remedies in a great number of cases. In such cases the courts of equity stepped in and made available a remedy by permitting suits for an accounting. Today suits for an accounting in equity are used in the settlement of affairs between executor, or administrator, and the devisees and legatees under a will, or the heirs at law; between beneficiaries and trustees in the case of trust estates; and especially in the winding up of a partnership.

Bills to remove cloud from title. Under certain circumstances a party may file a bill in equity to remove a cloud from the title to property— usually real property, though some courts have held that this relief is also applicable to personal property, as in the case of a void chattel mortgage or the fraudulent issue of corporate stock. The most common use of this remedy is in cases brought to cancel deeds which have been obtained through fraud and in cases brought to cancel invalid mortgages. It may also be used in establishing and clearing the title of one who holds real property through adverse possession.[1]

Partition suits. Two or more persons may hold property as co-owners, each owning a part interest in the entire property (a so-called *undivided interest*). If one of the co-owners wishes to withdraw his share of the property and is unable to reach an agreement with the other co-owner or co-owners, he may go into equity and ask that the property be divided among the co-owners according to their interests. Usually, if an actual division of the property between the co-owners is not feasible or just, the court will order a sale of the property and divide the proceeds among the co-owners.

EXTRAORDINARY REMEDIES

In addition to legal and equitable remedies, certain remedies for use in special situations where no other remedy was adequate were made available through writs emanating from the king as the source of all justice. Because these writs were issued by royal prerogative, they were called prerogative writs. These special remedies were carried over into our own system of law, and in this country they are more properly referred to as extraordinary legal remedies. In general, these remedies are used against public officials, courts, municipal and private corporations, and holders of special franchises. It will be useful in our study to have some knowledge of two of these writs, mandamus and quo warranto.

A *writ of mandamus* is issued by a law court and is directed to a corporation, a public official, or a court of inferior jurisdiction, commanding the performance of some public duty specified in the writ. For example, if a petition for articles of incorporation is denied by the Secretary of State, those who are attempting to incorporate may ask for a writ of mandamus against the Secretary of State. If the court finds that all requirements for incorporation have been met by the petitioners, it will grant the writ ordering the Secretary of State to issue the articles of incorporation.

A *writ of quo warranto* is issued by a law court to the holder of a public office or the holder of a public franchise, directing the party to appear be-

---

[1] Adverse possession is discussed in Chapter 24.

fore the court and show by what authority he or it holds such office or franchise. In the case of public officials it is used in election contest cases. In the case of a corporation holding a public franchise it is often used at the start of *ouster* proceedings, where the corporation is charged with misusing, or failing to use, its franchise.

ECCLESIASTICAL LAW

Important segments of our present-day law had their origin in the ecclesiastical law of England, administered by separate courts of the church.

Canon laws or church laws have had a profound effect and great influence on our court system. Often church law and lay law run almost parallel; that is, if the act done is immoral, it is also illegal. But at times the two do not run quite parallel. For example, adultery is a very serious offense in the eyes of the church, but only a minor violation according to the laws of some states. In Maryland, it is only a $10 fine, while in the state of New York, it is not illegal at all. After prolonged conflict and rivalry with the royal courts, reflecting the late medieval struggle between church and state that occurred throughout much of western Europe, the ecclesiastical courts of England finally established for themselves a rather well-defined jurisdiction. They not only heard cases pertaining to strictly ecclesiastical matters and cases of every kind involving clergymen, but they also had jurisdiction over cases arising out of marriage contracts and wills, which were considered to pertain to spiritual matters. This jurisdiction they maintained until about the middle of the nineteenth century, when they were divested of all authority save over matters that affect the Church of England. Probate and divorce were assigned to a newly created division of the high court of justice, together with admiralty cases.

In the United States the various states have separate courts to handle probate matters. In some states they are called probate courts; in others, orphans' courts, surrogates' courts, or registers' courts. Courts of law have jurisdiction over the granting of divorces.

THE LAW MERCHANT

What is commonly known as the law merchant (from Latin *lex mercatoria*) was the mercantile law of the Middle Ages. It has been rather aptly referred to as "private international law" because it involved the private business dealings of merchants of many countries and was applicable to all of them alike, regardless of nationality. It was a product of growth over many centuries. It seems to have been in the process of development among the merchants of Italy, France, and some other countries of western Europe as early as the eleventh century, and it was generally understood and used among the merchants of England in the early part of the thirteenth century.

The law merchant developed gradually out of the usages and customs of the merchants. Through long experience they learned what seemed to them to be the most advantageous and satisfactory methods of carrying on trade and commerce, and they wanted their business dealings and transactions to be regulated and controlled by these customary usages. When they attended the great international fairs in the various countries of western Europe and England, they found the local laws and courts ill adapted to their needs. Nor does it appear that the local courts, especially in England, had any desire in the beginning to assume jurisdiction over the disputes of these merchants. The English common law courts had grown up in a feudal, agricultural economy; the judges knew little or nothing of the customs and practices of the international merchants and were not equipped to adjudicate their controversies. Moreover the procedures in the courts were cumbersome and slow. The great fairs lasted only a short time, and the merchants needed "speedy justice," which the common law and equity courts of England were in no position to give. Similar conditions existed on the Continent. The upshot was that the merchant guilds provided for the establishment of special fair courts to hear and adjudicate the disputes of the merchants.

The common law courts of England eventually absorbed the law merchant by assuming jurisdiction over all such controversies, and the fair courts eventually went out of existence. This transition, however, came about slowly, and it was not till the middle of the eighteenth century that it was practically completed. Separate courts for the law merchant never existed in this country, but here, as in England, the principles of law which developed under that system have had a profound and lasting effect. Many of the basic principles of our law of contracts, sales, agency, negotiable instruments, surety and guaranty, partnerships, and insurance were established in the formative years of the law merchant.

The American System of Law

2

It would be a serious mistake to infer from the title of this chapter that the American people have created an entirely new legal system. On the contrary, the law under which we live today developed from the English system which has been sketched in the preceding chapter. That system of law was brought to this country in the seventeenth century by English colonists and maintained its continuity without any sharp break after the American Revolution. Consequently the American law still resembles the law of England so closely that for purposes of comparison with other systems the two are united under the single comprehensive name of Anglo-American law. Nevertheless, since the time of our political separation from England, the law in both countries has undergone independent development and modification, so that the American system of law now has many distinctive features which mark it off from its parent.

The three major sources of the law administered by our courts today are our federal and state constitutions, legislative enactments, and court decisions. In this chapter we shall first consider the principal characteristics of the law arising from each of these sources, and then we shall examine briefly three special areas of the law with which students of business law need at least a nodding acquaintance—administrative law, criminal law, and tort law.

CONSTITUTIONAL LAW

At the apex of our legal system stands our constitutional law, set forth in the federal Constitution and in the constitutions of the various states. The written constitution is probably America's greatest contribution to the science of government and law. While there was some historical precedent for it in the charters of some of the colonies, it did not achieve its full flowering until the people of the original thirteen states adopted the federal Constitution and put it into effect in 1789.

Though the constitutional law is the supreme law of the land, it can be changed by the people, who brought it into being in the first place. Our governmental system is based upon the concept that the people are sovereign; that is, that all authority emanates, directly or indirectly, from them. In the Constitution of the United States they set up a government to serve as their agent in carrying out their will. But they did not confer upon it an absolute grant of power. The framers of the Constitution had had recent experience with arbitrary government, and they were wary about granting too much power even to a government of their own creation. They therefore delegated to it only a portion of the power at their disposal; and to prevent dangerous concentration of the delegated power they divided it among three separate and coordinate branches, the legislative, the executive, and the judicial. Furthermore, they placed beyond the control of the government certain basic and "unalienable" rights to which they believed every individual entitled. These rights cannot be curtailed or withdrawn except by the people themselves through the amending process. Thus Congress cannot, by the enactment of a statute, enlarge or redistribute the powers of government or take away the fundamental rights of the people. Acts of Congress must conform to the Constitution.

Under the Tenth Amendment "the powers not delegated to the United States by the Constitution, nor prohibited by it to the states, are reserved to the states respectively, or to the people." The present state constitutions are based upon the same underlying principles as the federal Constitution. Enactments of the state legislature must conform to the state constitution as well as to the federal Constitution.

The Constitution does not expressly provide what shall be done if Congress passes a law that violates the Constitution. The country was brought face to face with this problem in 1803 in the famous case of *Marbury v. Madison*,[1] in which it became necessary for the Supreme Court to decide whether it would recognize the clause in the Constitution which expressly delimits the original jurisdiction [2] of the Supreme Court or the provision in the Judiciary Act of 1789 in which Congress had attempted to enlarge the Court's original jurisdiction. Chief Justice Marshall held unequivocally that the act of Congress was unconstitutional and void. In theory, at least, since that memorable decision, the Supreme Court of the

---

[1] Cranch (U. S.) 137, 2 L. Ed. 60 (1803).

[2] I.e. the Court's right to try cases in the first instance, as contrasted with its *appellate jurisdiction,* its right to hear appeals in cases tried in the first instance by lower courts.

United States has stood as the guardian of our fundamental rights as embodied in the federal Constitution. In the same way it protects the Constitution from any unconstitutional act that may be passed by a state legislature or any unconstitutional ordinance that may emanate from a city council.

This principle has been carried over to the various states so that the state supreme courts guard their respective state constitutions from the enactment of unconstitutional legislation by the state legislatures and city councils.

STATUTORY LAW

NATURE AND ORIGIN

Next in order of authority to the federal and state constitutions are the federal statutes, enacted by Congress, and the state statutes, enacted by the state legislatures. As we have just seen, federal statutes must conform to the federal Constitution, and state statutes must conform to both the federal Constitution and to the constitution of the state in which it is enacted.

Statutory law, in its modern sense of law enacted by the legislative branch of a government, had its beginning in England in the fourteenth century with the establishment of Parliament. However, important actions taken by the king and his council began to be referred to as statutes a century before the appearance of Parliament. The English law brought to this country by the early colonists was in part statutory law.

UNIFORM STATUTES

With fifty separate state legislatures enacting laws and fifty separate court systems interpreting them, the statutory laws of the various states are naturally far from uniform. This lack of uniformity was not a serious inconvenience in the earlier days of the Republic; but with the geographical expansion of the nation, the appearance of new states, the development of transportation, and the ever-increasing volume of interstate business, it grew into more and more of a problem, especially for businessmen. In the 1890's a movement developed to induce the states to adopt uniform statutes; actively supported by the American Bar Association, it led to the creation of the National Conference of Commissioners on Uniform State Law, which undertook the work of preparing model statutes and recommending their adoption by the states. Model uniform statutes have been prepared covering most of the areas of the law that are usually included in a course in business law, as well as others. All told, some eighty-five or ninety model statutes have been prepared by the commissioners. Only one of these—the Uniform Negotiable Instruments Law—has been adopted by all the states, but several other important ones have been adopted by a large number of states.

UNIFORM COMMERCIAL CODE

For a number of years it has been felt by professors of law and the bench and bar that the uniform acts dealing with commercial transactions should be revised in order "to keep in step with modern commercial practices." Such a revision was made possible by a large grant from the Maurice and Laura Falk Foundation of Pittsburgh. The project was undertaken jointly by the American Law Institute and the National Conference of Commissioners on Uniform State Law. The work was begun on January 1, 1945, completed in 1952, and is known as the Uniform Commercial Code. The latest edition is referred to as the 1966 Official Edition.

The following uniform statutes are incorporated in the Uniform Commercial Code: Uniform Sales Act, Uniform Negotiable Instruments Law, Uniform Bills of Lading Act, Uniform Warehouse Receipts Act, Uniform Stock Transfer Act, Uniform Conditional Sales Act, Uniform Trust Receipts Act, Uniform Written Obligations Act, and Uniform Fiduciaries Act. The Uniform Commercial Code not only modernizes and expands the material in these earlier uniform statutes but also makes a fresh approach to it which is described as follows in the Comments on the text:

"The concept of the present Act is that 'commercial transactions' is a single subject of the law, notwithstanding its many facets. A single transaction may very well involve a contract for sale, followed by a sale, the giving of a check or draft for a part of the purchase price, and the acceptance of some form of security for the balance. The check or draft may be negotiated and will ultimately pass through one or more banks for collection. If the goods are shipped or stored the subject matter of the sale may be covered by a bill of lading or warehouse receipt or both. Or it may be that the entire transaction was made pursuant to a letter of credit either domestic or foreign. Obviously, every phase of commerce involved is but a part of one transaction, namely, the sale of and payment for goods. If, instead of goods in the ordinary sense, the transaction involved stocks and bonds, some of the phases of the transaction would obviously be different. Others would be the same. In addition, there are certain additional formalities incident to the transfer of stocks and bonds from one owner to another.

"This Act purports to deal with all the phases which may ordinarily arise in the handling of a commercial transaction, from start to finish." [1]

The first state to adopt the Uniform Commercial Code was Pennsyl-

[1] Uniform Commercial Code, official draft, Text and Comments Edition, 1952, p. 2.

vania, where it went into effect on July 1, 1954. Thereafter, all states except Louisiana have followed suit and adopted the Code.

CITY ORDINANCES

A city or municipal corporation is a political subdivision of the state. It owes its legal existence to the state, and it possesses only the power or authority that has been delegated to it by the state. The legal basis of any city government is its charter.

The authority to make local laws or *ordinances* is vested in the city council. Such ordinances must conform to federal and state constitutional and statutory law. They cover many matters of vital importance to businessmen, such as the protection of life and property, traffic, sanitation and health, zoning, housing, building codes, billboards and signs, licensing, filling stations, handbills, elevators, and so on.

CASE LAW

We have already seen in Chapter 1 that much of our law is found not in constitutions and statutes but in the decisions of our appellate courts. The courts are frequently confronted with cases involving issues to which no constitutional provision or statute is applicable. Under our system of law the courts do not dismiss such cases; instead, they turn to our common or case law for guidance.[1] Following the principle of stare decisis the attorneys search for a precedent in the case law of the jurisdiction in which the case arose. If the particular issues in the case have never been adjudicated in that jurisdiction, then the search is carried to the case law of the surrounding jurisdictions. Though the court will not feel bound by stare decisis to follow pertinent holdings which may turn up in the case law of other jurisdictions, it will nevertheless give them "much weight" in arriving at a decision in the case at bar. Where no American precedents are found, our courts have at times examined British and Canadian decisions for guidance. If no precedents are found anywhere, the court will use its own best judgment and hand down a decision, perhaps upon the basis of "customs and traditions of the people," or upon the basis of "equity and justice."

Thereafter when similar cases arise, courts in the same jurisdiction will feel bound by stare decisis to apply the rule of law established in the earlier case. After such a rule of law has been recognized and applied in a num-

---

[1] It should be understood that the following remarks apply to both law and equity cases. As we have already seen, equity is an important part of our present-day American system of law, and our equity courts have always followed stare decisis.

ber of cases, it becomes firmly established in our common or case law. At times, to be sure, both our federal courts and our state courts have broken with precedent. In particular the U. S. Supreme Court has refused to follow stare decisis on a number of occasions in the past few years. But it has been severely criticized for doing so, both by judges in the lower courts and by attorneys. It is contended that since so much of our law comes from the decisions of our courts, the Supreme Court's failure to follow previous decisions tends to "unsettle the law," so that neither judges attempting to "apply" the law in a given case nor attorneys advising clients can be sure "what the law is." It is generally felt by the courts that if the rule of law is misconceived, or if changed economic, social, or political conditions require a change in it, then it is the duty of the legislature to make the change through statutory enactment.

Our case law is "inferior" to our constitutional and statutory law. If it conflicts with either it must give way.

ADMINISTRATIVE LAW

The framers of the Constitution, as we have seen, based the new governmental machinery on the concept of the separation of powers. To the legislative branch of the government (Congress) they assigned the function of making the laws; to the executive branch (the President), the function of enforcing the laws; to the judicial branch (the courts), the function of interpreting the laws. The underlying theory was that Congress would enact the laws and the executive branch would see that they were carried out. If the executive branch felt that someone had violated the law, he would be charged with the alleged violation, and the courts would then interpret the law and determine whether the defendant had violated it. Under this plan our courts could decide only "cases and controversies" as they were brought before them. They could not give advance opinions as to the rights and duties of individuals in various situations that might arise under the law, and thus anticipate or prevent infractions of it.

During the early years of the Republic, when our economic organization was simple and government regulation of business and social life was at a minimum, this system was adequate to the demands made upon it. But after the Civil War a period of great national expansion began. New states were admitted to the Union, population increased by leaps and bounds, great cities arose, a vast and complicated industrial system emerged, and powerful labor and agricultural organizations were brought into being. These changes brought in their wake enormous new economic and social problems; and demands began to be made upon the federal and state governments for aid in solving them. In response to these demands, new and far-reaching laws were enacted. It was soon found, however, that the old system, whereby the legislature enacted a law and the executive branch enforced its provisions through the courts, was inadequate in dealing with such new and pressing problems as railway rates, fair trade practices, wages and hours, compensation for industrial accidents, the regulation of public utilities and insurance companies, and a host of other matters. Both Congress and the state legislatures found that it was often impossible, in attempting to deal with a problem of the scope of these, to draft a statute sufficiently detailed and comprehensive to provide for every type of case that might arise under the statute. The handling of many of these problems required the services of experts in a variety of specialized fields of knowledge; moreover, it usually required a "day-by-day administration" of the statutes, not merely an adjudication of a dispute or conflict in the courts.

In an attempt to find a solution within the confines of the concept of the separation of powers, Congress and the state legislatures began to enact broad general statutes and to provide within those statutes for the setting up of boards and commissions to administer and enforce them. Such a statute would set forth in broad terms the general purposes and objectives of the act, set up *standards* to guide the administrative board or commission, and give it authority to issue rules and regulations for the effective carrying out of its duties and to hear and settle disputes that might arise under such rules and regulations. An example of one of these great statutes was the Act of 1887 which provided for the regulation of railroads engaged in interstate commerce. That act set forth in general terms the policies of the government in regard to the regulation of the interstate activities of railroads, and then set up the Interstate Commerce Commission to administer the act and carry out those policies. This general pattern has since been followed in the enactment of a large number of important statutes.

Such statutes have been charged with unconstitutionality on two scores. It was at first objected that to endow administrative agencies with authority to make their own rules and regulations was an "unwarranted delegation" by Congress of its legislative function to an administrative agency. This objection has been fairly well overcome by placing in the statutes adequate "standards" to guide the administrative agencies. It has also been charged that to permit these agencies to "hear and settle" controversies involving the determination of private rights is an encroachment upon the function of the judiciary. This objection has been overcome by providing, within the statutes themselves, for appeals to the courts on questions of law. It is said that administrative boards and commissions do not "try" cases and controversies and render judgments; they merely hold "hearings" and issue orders, directives, and awards, which may be appealed to the courts for final adjudication. Hence it is contended that these administrative agencies do not usurp the function of the judiciary, but perform merely quasi-judicial functions.

The rules and regulations of the administrative agencies, the thousands of decisions made by them, their orders, directives, and awards, together with thousands of court opinions dealing with appeals from the decisions of the agencies and with petitions by the agencies to the courts for enforcement of their orders and directives, are the core of the relatively new branch of law called administrative law. It has immense influence on the operation and management of business enterprises in our country today, for no business can fail to come within the ambit of one or more of the various federal and state administrative agencies. The federal agencies, in addition to the Interstate Commerce Commission, include the Federal Trade Commission, the Federal Reserve Board, the Securities and Exchange Commission, the National Labor Relations Board, the Federal Communications Commission, the Civil Aeronautics Board, the Food and Drug Administration, and others. Among the most important of the state administrative agencies are public service commissions, insurance commissions, workmen's compensation commissions, and securities commissions.

CRIMINAL LAW

DEFINITION AND NATURE

The inclusion of a brief account of criminal law is justified not only by the importance of criminal law in the American legal system but also by the fact that at times questions relating to it confront the businessman in his own sphere of activity. Is the principal liable for the crime of his agent if it is committed within the scope of the agent's employment? Is one partner liable for a crime committed by another partner while engaged in partnership business? Can a corporation commit a crime? Such questions demonstrate that at least a superficial understanding of the law of crimes is necessary in the study of business law.

A crime may be defined as an offense against the state or the public, an offense so flagrant that the state takes cognizance of it and prosecutes the offender. To quote Dean Miller, it is "the commission or omission of an act which the law forbids or commands under pain of a punishment to be imposed by the state by a proceeding in its own name." [1] For example, if A is guilty of criminally assaulting B, he has done more than injure B; he has also "offended" the whole public. In other words, his act consti-

---

[1] Justin Miller, *Criminal Law* (St. Paul, Minn., West Publishing Co., 1931), p. 16.

tutes a threat to the whole group. Hence, not only may B bring a civil action against A for money damages for injury to his person, but the state may proceed against him and prosecute him for his criminal act. B's civil action against A would be titled *B v. A*. The criminal action against A would be titled *The State v. A, The Commonwealth v. A, The People v. A*, depending upon the practice in the given state.

Crimes are often divided into common law crimes and statutory crimes. In many states today, however, the criminal law is wholly statutory, the state legislatures having embodied the common law crimes in their criminal statutes or codes side by side with new types of crime which were not classed as criminal acts at common law. All federal crimes are statutory. Since the federal government possesses only those powers which are expressly or impliedly given to it by the Constitution, the only acts regarded as crimes against the United States are those which are made crimes by constitutional provision or by statutes enacted by Congress under the Constitution.

A crime at common law must contain both a *criminal act* [1] and *criminal intent;* the act without the intent is not a crime. If A deliberately kills B, he has committed a crime; if he kills him accidentally and through no fault of his own, his act is not a crime. It should be noted, however, that if B is killed through the gross negligence or wanton recklessness of A, even though A did not intend his death specifically, A will be held criminally liable for B's death. In such a case the law construes "intent" as applying not only to an immediate action but to its natural consequences.

Not every statutory crime must include criminal intent. Certain statutes —frequently, for example, those regulating the operation of motor vehicles—are so framed that performance of a forbidden act, with or without intent, constitutes criminal violation.

State of Connecticut v. Brown

161 Conn. 219, 286 A (2d) 304 (1971)
Supreme Court of Connecticut

Defendant, who was indicted for murder in the first degree, entered plea of guilty to murder in the second degree and subsequently moved for permission to withdraw plea. The Superior Court . . . denied the application and the Supreme Court . . . set aside judgment and remanded. On trial to jury . . . , defendant was convicted of first-degree murder and he appealed. The Supreme Court . . . held no error.

HOUSE, C. J. James Brown was indicted by a grand jury on May 29, 1967, for the crime of murder in the first degree in that on May 12, 1967, he did wilfully, deliberately and with premeditation and malice aforethought shoot and kill Charlotte Bland in violation of § 53–9 of the General Statutes. Initially

---

1 "Act" here includes failure to perform an act when there is a duty to perform it.

the defendant pleaded not guilty but, on October 18, 1967, he entered a plea of guilty to murder in the second degree. He subsequently moved for permission to withdraw this plea and the motion was denied by the trial court. On appeal this court held that it was error to deny the motion. The judgment was set aside and the case was remanded for further proceedings. . . . Thereafter, the defendant pleaded not guilty to the indictment. He was tried by a jury of twelve which returned a verdict of guilty of murder in the first degree. After a hearing held in accordance with the provisions of § 53-10 of the General Statutes, the jury recommended a sentence of life imprisonment, which was imposed. On this appeal the sole assignment of error is the claim that the court erred in denying the defendant's motion to set aside the verdict of guilty of murder in the first degree. It is the basic claim of the defendant that the state failed to prove beyond a reasonable doubt the necessary elements of the crime of murder in the first degree. Such a claim is tested by the evidence printed in the appendices to the briefs and such exhibits as are made a part of the record. . . . If the verdict is one which twelve honest jurors acting fairly, intelligently and reasonably could have reached on the evidence submitted to them, then the verdict cannot be disturbed. . . .

From the evidence the jury could have found the following facts: The defendant, aged forty-seven, with a wife and four children living in North Carolina, came to Stamford in 1966 and established an illicit sexual relationship with Miss Bland, whom he regarded as "his woman." On the night of May 11, 1967, Miss Bland with a friend, Helen Brown, who lived at the same address as the defendant, spent several hours with two men visiting bars and restaurants in Stamford and Portchester, New York. The women returned home about 4 A.M., on May 12, and Miss Bland, who was driving, stopped her car in front of the apartment house in which the defendant lived to let Miss Brown out. As Miss Bland was preparing to drive away, the defendant, who had been sitting on the porch waiting for her, walked over to the car and shot at her seven times. The shots came in two bursts. Three of the bullets struck Miss Bland and she died of exsanguination resulting from massive hemorrhages in the space surrounding the heart and both lungs caused by a bullet wound in the chest. After the shooting, the defendant returned to his apartment, gave the pistol to Louise Adams and said to her: "Mom, call the police. I just killed Charlotte." She placed the pistol on a dresser and made a telephone call to the police department. The defendant took the telephone from her, identified himself to the desk sergeant at police headquarters and related the circumstances of the shooting. While the defendant was still telephoning, a policeman arrived at the apartment and the defendant stated to him: "The gun is over here." The officer took possession of the pistol which was lying on the dresser. A ballistic expert testified that the pistol was a semi-automatic type which meant that the trigger had to be squeezed to discharge each bullet. Tests disclosed that seven cartridges found at the scene of the shooting and two bullets removed from the body of Charlotte Bland had been fired from the pistol.

There was also evidence that around 11 P.M., before the 4 A.M. shooting, the defendant borrowed an alarm clock from one of his cotenants and was walking in and out of the house and back and forth in the hall for about two hours. . . . On cross-examination, the defendant admitted that he did not go to bed because he wanted to talk to Miss Bland and that, with his gun in his pocket, he sat on the front porch waiting for her to come home.

On this evidence, the jury were amply justified in concluding that the state had proved beyond a reasonable doubt the essential elements of the crime of murder in the first degree. Of particular significance is the evidence that the defendant was incensed that Miss Bland was "running around," that with a loaded pistol in his pocket he sat for hours on his front porch waiting for her appearance and when she did arrive he fired seven rounds of bullets at her, pulling the trigger for each of the seven rounds which were fired in two bursts, separated by a short interval. "The length of time necessary to deliberate, or to form a specific intent to kill, need only be time enough to form a wilful, premeditated and specific intent to kill before the killing, and if there be such time, it is sufficient, no matter how long or how short it may be." . . .

Upon the evidence, the conclusion of the jury that the defendant was malice aforethought formed a wilful, deliberate intent to kill Charlotte Bland, and did so, was reasonable and logical.

There is no error.

CLASSIFICATION OF CRIMES

Crimes at common law are classified as (1) treason, (2) felonies, and (3) misdemeanors. Treason is defined by the federal Constitution as follows: "Treason against the United States shall consist only in levying war against them, or in adhering to their enemies, giving them aid and comfort."[1] At common law, felonies were those types of crimes which were usually punishable by death. The criminal's property was also forfeited to the king. All other crimes were called misdemeanors. Our modern criminal statutes usually specify whether a crime is a felony or a misdemeanor. Generally, a crime punishable by death or by imprisonment in the state penitentiary is a felony. Murder, arson, rape, and grand larceny are examples of felonies. A crime punishable by a fine or a sentence to the county jail is a misdemeanor. Trespass, simple assault, petty larceny, and disorderly conduct are generally classed as misdemeanors.

There is disagreement as to whether violations of police regulations and city ordinances should be designated as crimes. Some courts and legal writers contend that such violations are misdemeanors; others, while agreeing that they are crimes, argue that they should be assigned to a fourth class, inferior to misdemeanors. Still others would remove them from the category of crimes altogether. Special designations, such as "public torts" and "petty offenses," have been suggested for them.

Crimes may be committed against (1) the person, (2) the habitation,

[1] Article III, Section III.

(3) property, and (4) the public peace, health, and welfare. Crimes against the person include assault, battery, false imprisonment, kidnapping, mayhem, rape, and homicide. Crimes against the habitation are burglary and arson. Crimes against property include larceny, robbery, embezzlement, receiving stolen goods, forgery, and obtaining money or goods under false pretenses. Crimes against public peace, health, and welfare include breach of the peace, forcible entry and detainer, riots and unlawful assemblies, libel, bigamy, adultery, and nuisance.

ILLEGAL SEARCH AND SEIZURE AND SELF-INCRIMINATION

Evidence obtained by illegal search and seizure is inadmissible upon proper objection by defense counsel, and a person may not be compelled to testify against himself. Both are based upon constitutional grounds.

The Fourth Amendment reads:

The right of the people to be secure in their persons, houses, papers and effects, against unreasonable searches and seizures, shall not be violated, and no warrants shall issue, but upon probable cause, supported by oath or affirmation, and particularly describing the place to be searched, and the persons or things to be seized.

Part of the Fifth Amendment reads:

No person . . . shall be compelled in any criminal case to be a witness against himself.

United States of America v. James Edward Ward

Criminal No. 7-075 (1973)
The United States District Court for the District of Maryland
For U.S.: Michael E. Barr
For Defendant: Townes L. Dawson

MEMORANDUM AND ORDER

NORTHROP, C. J. The defendant has moved this Court to suppress evidence obtained from his residence during a warrantless search on April 28, 1972, and to dismiss the indictment. The validity of the search hinges on a question of whether or not the defendant's estranged wife could consent to the search. It appears that the defendant and his wife first met in 1951, and they entered into a common-law relationship in the District of Columbia in April, 1952. In November, 1962, they moved to Chillum, Maryland. During November, 1970, the defendant's wife told him that she intended to leave him. She stated at the hearing that they had never gotten along, and that her husband had begun to drink heavily. Finally, Mrs. Ward left her husband on January 23, 1971, after a violent fight, during which she was physically beaten and verbally abused.

While the wife had an equal interest in the house as a tenant by the entirety, she stated that she had only returned on a few occasions after this incident, because she considered her husband to be violent.

It was shown at the hearing that Mrs. Ward had a male friend, and that some time prior to the search they had driven to an open field to talk. Shortly after they arrived they heard a noise in the trunk, and upon investigating found that the defendant was hiding there. Mrs. Ward's male companion shot the defendant, with the bullet entering the defendant's spleen.

Then, on the evening prior to the contested search, Mrs. Ward's male companion [a different one] was shot and killed in a car while Mrs. Ward was present. The next morning, April 28, 1972, at approximately 7:30 A.M., the defendant was arrested at his place of employment and taken to the Forrestville Police Station, Prince George's County, Maryland. Later that morning the police approached Mrs. Ward and asked for her consent to search the defendant's residence. She gave her consent readily, and accompanied the police to the house. The police then began an extensive search that lasted for approximately nine hours, during which they seized a footlocker, various books and papers, parts of a machine gun and various chemical items. At no time prior to the conclusion of the search did the authorities obtain a search warrant or the consent of the defendant.

The defendant's estranged wife . . . returned to the premises on a couple of occasions subsequent to her estrangement, although she had not been there for several months. She also stated that the defendant had changed all of the locks to the house, and that he was the only person with a key.

It is well-established that the burden is on the Government to show that exceptional circumstances existed to justify a warrantless search of a dwelling. *Vale v. Louisiana*, 399 U.S. 30, 90 S. Ct. 1969 (1970). However, consent to such a search may be sufficient to justify the warrantless search. The question presented to this Court is the sufficiency of the consent of the defendant's estranged common-law wife under the circumstances.

The Fourth Amendment prohibition against unlawful search and seizure is a personal right. *Simmons v. United States*, 390 U.S. 377, 389, 88 S. Ct. 967 (1968); *Anderson v. United States*, 399 F. (2d) 753, 755 (10th Cir. 1968). It is also true that it is a personal right with property right overtones. *Anderson v. United States, supra*. In effect, the law is that the Fourth Amendment right is personal, but when two persons have a property interest in the property to be searched, the waiver of the Fourth Amendment right of one party may be binding on the other party. *United States v. Airdo*, 380 F. (2d) 103 (7th Cir. 1967); *United States v. Eldridge*, 302 F. (2d) 463 (4th Cir. 1962). Consent to a search can be binding even though there was probable cause and sufficient time to obtain a search warrant. *Bumper v. State of North Carolina*, 391 U.S. 543, 88 S. Ct. 1788.

The question remains, when two persons have co-existent interests in the property searched, under what circumstances will the consent of one party be binding on the other? It is well-established that the search must be reasonable under the circumstances. . . .

Therefore, this Court in determining the reasonableness of the search in this situation adopts the test used by the court in *United States v. Martinez*. . . . The first factor to be considered is the legal and possessory rights to the premises and items searched. While it is clear that Mrs. Ward had established residence elsewhere, and had not lived at the residence in question for a considerable length of time, she was a tenant by the entirety. Thus the Court concludes that Mrs. Ward did have legal and possessory rights in the premises searched, but it is clear that she had no rights in the items searched that were not a part of the dwelling itself. This would include footlockers, drawers to furniture that were not her own personal property, cardboard boxes and the like.

The second consideration is the relationship of the third party to the subject of the search. While Mrs. Ward was the defendant's common-law wife, they certainly did not have a typical marriage relationship. It is clear that the events which led to their separation, and their violent confrontations subsequent to the separation, had established a strong animosity between them. It is also significant that she was clearly aware of the fact that the defendant was a prime suspect in the murder of her male companion.

Finally, the circumstances of the search as they objectively appeared to the police at the time of the search must be considered. While the police had reason to believe that Mrs. Ward had equal rights in the premises, her relationship with the man Mr. Ward was suspected of murdering should have made them question her capacity to consent to a search of the premises. In addition, the police had sufficient time to obtain a search warrant without the danger that evidence could be removed from the house since the defendant was already in police custody.

Having weighed all of these factors the Court concludes that Mrs. Ward's consent to the entry and search of the premises was not sufficient, and that the search constituted a violation of the defendant's constitutional right against unlawful searches and seizures.

The defendant's contentions in support of his motion to suppress his confession which was given after he was confronted with the items seized from his house are equally compelling. Since these items were illegally seized, and it is clear that the confession was given only after he was confronted with the items, this confession must be viewed as a product of the illegal search also.

The defendant has further moved that the Court dismiss Counts 2 and 3 of the indictment on the basis that the M. P. Beretta Model 38/42, 9-mm submachine gun, serial number 7385, is not within the ambit of Title 26, United States Code, Section 5861 (c). At the hearing Special Agent Marcus J. Davis of the Bureau of Tobacco, Alcohol and Illegal Firearms, testified that the gun did not have a stock or bolt and that in such a condition it was not capable of firing. The cases involving similar contentions have held that testimony by witnesses and the results of firing tests are the bases which the Court should rely on in determining whether or not the gun is sufficiently operable to come within the provisions of the statute. *United States v. Williams*, 427 F. (2d) 1031, 1033 (9th Cir. 1970); *United States v. Melancon*, 462 F. (2d) 82, 95 (5th Cir. 1972). Under 26 U.S.C. § 5845 (b) "the term 'machinegun' means any weapon that shoots, is designed to shoot, or can be readily restored to shoot, automatically more than one shot, without manual loading, by a single function of the trigger. The term shall also include . . . any combination of parts from which a machinegun can be assembled if such parts are in the possession or under the control of a person." In the case at bar no evidence was introduced to show that the defendant had the stock or the bolt in his possession or under his control. The failure to establish this fact is even more significant when one considers the length of time involved in the search of the defendant's dwelling house. When the Court views the definition of a machine gun contained in Section 5845 (b) and the testimony of Special Agent Davis it is clear that the weapon in question does not fall within the scope of the statute.

For the reasons stated herein, it is this 20th day of August, 1973, ordered:

1. That the defendant's motion to suppress the evidence obtained as a result of the search of his residence on April 28, 1972 be, and the same hereby is, granted;

2. That the defendant's motion to suppress his confession be, and the same hereby is, granted;

3. That the defendant's motion to dismiss Counts 2 and 3 of the indictment be, and the same hereby is, granted. . . .

TORT LAW

NATURE OF TORTS

A tort (from Latin *torquere,* to twist or wrench aside) is a private or civil wrong or injury, done to an individual or a specific group of individuals, in contrast to a crime, which is said to injure the public or society as a whole. When a crime is committed, the state steps in to prosecute and punish the wrongdoer. When a tort is committed, the state takes no judicial notice of it, but it does provide appropriate remedies to the injured party if he cares to avail himself of them. As we saw in the preceding section, certain offenses, for example criminal assault, may be both crimes and torts, rendering the offender subject both to civil liability to the person injured and to penalties imposed by the state.

Our tort law may be said to be based upon a *right-duty relationship* between individual members of society. We as individuals under the law have many rights and duties that are recognized and enforced by the courts. These rights and duties are of varying origin. Some of them we create for ourselves by voluntarily entering into certain relationships with other persons. An employment contact is a simple example. No one is required by law to enter into such a relationship, but once it has been created by mutual agreement, the law will recognize the legal rights of the parties to it, and if one of the parties violates his duties, the law provides a remedy to the other party. It is with rights and duties of this kind that our study of business law will be chiefly concerned. The rights and duties involved in tort law have a different source. They do not depend upon our own choice but are "imposed by law" upon all members of our society. An example is the right to the safety of one's own person, with the correlative duty to respect the safety of another. The law recognizes that an individual has many such rights in his relations with others and that, under usually rather well-defined circumstances, other persons have a duty to respect them. Anyone who fails to do so has committed a "wrong" or tort, and the law provides a remedy to the injured party.

This safeguarding of rights and imposing of duties had its origin very early in the common law. As we saw in Chapter 1, the common law courts developed for use in tort cases a number of actions, such as trespass, replevin, and trover, which were collectively called ex delicto actions.

KINDS OF TORTS

In general, under tort law, one is entitled to (1) the safety of his person, and freedom from fear of bodily harm; (2) the safety of his property, both real and personal, from trespass or conversion; (3) his good reputation, and that it be not defamed; (4) freedom from interference in his business relations; (5) freedom from interference in his domestic relations. If one interferes with the safety of another's person, he is probably liable for assault, battery, or false imprisonment, depending upon the circumstances of the case. If he interferes with the safety of another's property, he is probably liable in trespass or conversion. If he defames another's reputation, he is liable for libel or slander. If he interferes with another's business relations, he is probably liable in an action for deceit, slander of title, or inducement of a breach of contract. If he interferes in another's domestic relations, he will probably be liable in an action of tort for damages.

LIBEL AND SLANDER

Associated Press v. Walker

393 S. W. (2d) 671 (1965)

Judgment for Plaintiff. Defendant Appealed. Affirmed.

PER CURIAM. This is a libel suit. The parties will be designated as they were in the court . . . or The Associated Press as the A. P. and Walker by name.

The . . . two statements . . . which were complained of by Walker as being libelous and which form the basis of special issues submitted by the Court were: (1) "Walker, who Sunday led a charge of students against federal marshals on the Ole Miss Campus" (October 2, 1962 report), and (2) "Walker assumed command of the crowd" (October 3, 1962 report). For the sake of brevity these two statements will hereinafter be referred to as the "charge" and "command" statements respectively.

In answer to special issues one through four, the jury found that the "charge" statement was not "substantially true," did not constitute fair comment, was not made in good faith and was actuated by malice. It found to the same effect in response to similar issues five through eight concerning the "command" statement.

. . . the jury found damages in the sum of $500,000.00 and . . . found that exemplary damages should be awarded and in the amount of $300,000.00.

Based upon the verdict of the jury, judgment was entered for Walker and against the A. P. in the sum of $500,000. The judgment recited that there is no evidence to support the jury's findings of malice and $300,000 for exemplary damages.

Appellant contends that the court erred in rendering judgment for appellee rather than it because (1) as a matter of law the evidence conclusively established that the "charge" and "command" statements were substantially true; (2) each statement was a fair comment about a matter of public concern published for general information and thus privileged under the provisions of Art. 5432, *Vernon's Ann. Civ. St.;* (3) such statements made without malice are protected by the First and Fourteenth Amendments to the Constitution of the United States; (4) over objection appellee was permitted to testify that he did not assume command; (5) it held as a matter of law that the "charge" and "command" statements were libelous rather than submitting issues as to each; (6) the evidence conclusively established as a matter of law that the "charge" and "command" statements were made in good faith with reference to matters it had a duty to report to its members and thence to the public; (7) the amount of damages found was so grossly excessive as to be patently wrong and unjust and the findings in response to the damage issue No. 9 and to special issues one, two, three, five, six and seven are so against the weight and preponderance of the evidence as to be manifestly wrong and unjust and thus inefficient to support such answers; and (8) the evidence conclusively established as a matter of law that the jury was guilty of material error.

Throughout the trial Walker maintained the firm position that because of his opposition to the use of Federal troops within a State, and his personal knowledge of the deviation between the occurrences at Little Rock where he was indeed in command and the newspaper stories of those occurrences, that he was at Oxford to see for himself at firsthand what was actually going on. He maintained that he did not assume command of the crowd, did not lead a charge, and did not participate in the rioting. He was present for the sole purpose of observing. The jury saw him, observed his demeanor, heard what he said, and believed him.

Having considered each of the appellant's points of error and the cross-points raised by the appellee and having concluded what each should be they are each and all accordingly overruled, and the judgment of the trial court is affirmed.

INVASION OF PRIVACY

Hamberger v. Eastman
206 A. (2d) 239 (1965)
Supreme Court of New Hampshire

These were companion suits for invasion of privacy. The Court, MORRIS, J., reserved and transferred case to Supreme Court without ruling. Remanded.

The plaintiffs, husband and wife, brought companion suits for invasion of their privacy against the defendant who owned and rented a dwelling house to the plaintiffs. The plaintiffs allege that the defendant installed and concealed "a listening and recording device" in their bedroom, which was in the dwelling house rented to them by the defendant and that this device was connected to the defendant's adjacent residence by wires "capable of transmitting and recording any sounds and voices originating in said bedroom."

The declaration in the suit by the husband reads as follows:

"In a plea of the case, for that the defendant is the owner of a certain dwelling house located at Gilford, County of Belknap, and State of New Hampshire, which was, and still is, occupied by the plaintiff and his family as a dwelling house on a weekly rental basis; that said dwelling house is located adjacent to and abutting other land of the defendant whereon the defendant maintains his place of residence, together with his place of business.

"That, sometime during the period from October, 1961, to October 15, 1962, the defendant, wholly without the knowledge and consent of the plaintiff, did willfully and maliciously invade the privacy and sanctity of the plaintiff's bedroom, which he shared with his wife in their dwelling house, by installing and concealing a listening and recording device in said bedroom; that this listening and recording device, which was concealed in an area adjacent to the bed occupied by the plaintiff and his wife was attached and connected to the defendant's place of residence by means of wires capable of transmitting and recording any sounds and voices originating in said bedroom.

"That, on or about October 15, 1962, plaintiff discovered the listening and recording device which defendant had willfully and maliciously concealed in his bedroom, and the plaintiff, ever since that time and as a direct result of the actions of the defendant, has been greatly distressed, humiliated, and embarrassed and has sustained and is now sustaining, intense and severe mental suffering and distress, and has been rendered extremely nervous and upset, seriously impairing both his mental and physical condition, and that the plaintiff has sought, and still is under, the care of a physician; that large sums have been, and will be in the future, expended for medical care and attention; that because of his impaired mental and physical condition, the plaintiff has been and still is unable to properly perform his normal and ordinary duties as a father and as a husband, and has been unable to properly perform his duties at his place of employment, and has been otherwise greatly injured."

The declaration in the suit by the wife is identical, with appropriate substitutes of the personal pronoun, and omission of the allegation of inability to perform duties at her place of employment.

In both actions the defendant moved to dismiss on the ground that on the facts alleged, no cause of action is stated. The Court (Morris, J.) reserved and transferred the cases to the Supreme Court without ruling.

KENISON, C. J. The question presented is whether the right of privacy is recognized in this state. There is no controlling statute and no previous decision in this jurisdiction which decides the question. Inasmuch as invasion of the right of privacy is not a single tort but consists of four distinct torts, it is probably more concrete and accurate to state the issue in the present case to be whether this state recognizes that intrusion upon one's physical and mental solitude or seclusion is a tort. The most recent, as well as the most comprehensive, analysis of the problem is found in Prosser, *Torts*, s. 112 (3d ed. 1964).

In capsule summary the invasion of the right of privacy developed as an independent and distinct tort from the classic and famous article by Warren and Brandeis, "The Right to Privacy," 4 *Harv. L. Rev.* 193.

The four kinds of invasion comprising the law of privacy include: (1) intrusion upon the plaintiff's physical and mental solitude or seclusion; (2) public disclosure of private facts; (3) publicity which places the plaintiff in a false light in the public eye; (4) appropriation, for the defendant's benefit or advantage, of the plaintiff's name or likeness. In the present case, we are concerned only with the tort of intrusion upon the plaintiffs' solitude or seclusion.

The tort of intrusion upon the plaintiff's solitude or seclusion is not limited to a physical invasion of his home or his room or his quarters. As Prosser points out, the principle has been carried beyond such physical intrusion "and extended to eavesdropping upon private conversations by means of wire tapping and microphones."

If the peeping Tom, the big ear and the electronic eavesdropper (whether ingenious or ingenuous) have a place in the hierarchy of social values, it ought not to be at the expense of a married couple minding their own business in the seclusion of their bedroom who have never asked for or by their conduct deserved a potential projection of their private conversations and actions to their landlord or to others. Whether actual or potential such "publicity with respect to private matters of purely personal concern is an injury to personality. It impairs the mental peace and comfort of the individual and may produce suffering more acute than that produced by a mere bodily injury." III Pound, *Jurisprudence* 58 (1959). The use of parabolic microphones and sonic wave devices designed to pick up conversations in a room without entering it and at a considerable distance away makes the problem far from fanciful. Dash, Schwartz & Knowlton, *The Eavesdroppers*, pp. 346–358 (1959).

. . . For the purposes of the present case it is sufficient to hold that the invasion of the plaintiffs' solitude or seclusion, as alleged in the pleadings, was a violation of their right of privacy and constituted a tort for which the plaintiffs may recover damages to the extent that they can prove them. "Certainly, no right deserves greater protection, for, as Emerson has well said, 'solitude, the safeguard of mediocrity, is to genius the stern friend.'" Ezer, "Intrusion on Solitude: Herein of Civil Rights and Civil Wrongs," 21 *Law in Transition* 63, 75 (1961).

The motion to dismiss should be denied.
Remanded.
All concurred.

Many torts arise out of negligence. Under certain circumstances A and B owe to each other the duty to use care. If A and B are driving their automobiles and are ten miles apart, neither owes to the other a duty to drive carefully. But as they approach each other on the highway and attempt to pass each other, then a duty to use due care arises on the part of both A and B. If either fails in this duty, with the result that the other is injured, the negligent party is liable in tort for his negligence. The degree of care required in all such cases is that of the ordinarily prudent man.

ILLEGALITY

Katko v. Briney
183 N. W. (2d) 657 (1971)
Supreme Court of Iowa

This was an action for damages resulting from injury suffered by trespassing plaintiff when he triggered a spring gun placed in uninhabited house by defendants. The Mahaska District Court, Harold Fleck, Jr., gave judgment for plaintiff for both actual and punitive damages, and defendants appealed. The Supreme Court . . . affirmed.

MOORE, C. J. The primary issue presented here is whether an owner may protect personal property in an unoccupied boarded-up farm house against trespassers and thieves by a spring gun capable of inflicting death or serious injury.

We are not here concerned with a man's right to protect his home and members of his family. Defendants' home was several miles from the scene of the incident.

Plaintiff's action is for damages resulting from serious injury caused by a shot from a 20-gauge spring shotgun set by defendants in a bedroom of an old farm house which had been uninhabited for several years. Plaintiff and his companion, Marvin McDonough, had broken and entered the house to find and steal old bottles and dated fruit jars which they considered antiques.

At defendants' request plaintiff's action was tried to a jury consisting of residents of the community where defendants' property was located. The jury returned a verdict for plaintiff and against defendants for $20,000 actual and $10,000 punitive damages.

After careful consideration of defendants' motions for judgment notwithstanding the verdict and for new trial, the experienced and capable trial judge overruled them and entered judgment on the verdict. Thus we have this appeal by defendants.

I. In this action our review of the record as made by the parties in the lower court is for the correction of errors at law. We do not review actions at law de novo. Rule 334, *Rules of Civil Procedure.* Findings of fact by the jury are binding upon this court if supported by substantial evidence.

II. Most of the facts are not disputed. In 1957 defendant Bertha L. Briney inherited her parents' farm land in Mahaska and Monroe Counties. Included was an 80-acre tract in southwest Mahaska County where her grandparents and parents had lived. No one occupied the house thereafter. Her husband, Edward, attempted to care for the land. He kept no farm machinery thereon. The outbuildings became dilapidated.

For about 10 years, 1957 to 1967, there occurred a series of trespassing and housebreaking events with loss of some household items, the breaking of windows and "messing up of the property in general." The latest occurred June 8, 1967, prior to the event on July 16, 1967 herein involved.

Defendants through the years boarded up the windows and doors in an attempt to stop the intrusions. They had posted "no trespass" signs on the land several years before 1967. The nearest one was 35 feet from the house. On June 11, 1967 defendants set "a shotgun trap" in the north bedroom. After Mr. Briney cleaned and oiled his 20-gauge shotgun, the power of which he was well aware, defendants took it to the old house where they secured it to an iron bed with the barrel pointed at the bedroom door. It was rigged with wire from the doorknob to the gun's trigger so it would fire when the door was opened. Briney first pointed the gun so an intruder would be hit in the stomach but at Mrs. Briney's suggestion it was lowered to hit the legs. He admitted he did so "because I was mad and tired of being tormented" but "he did not intend to injure anyone." He gave no explanation of why he used a loaded shell and set it to hit a person already in the house. Tin was nailed over the bedroom window. The spring gun could not be seen from the outside. No warning of its presence was posted.

Plaintiff lived with his wife and worked regularly as a gasoline station attendant in Eddyville, seven miles from the old house. He had observed it for several years while hunting in the area and considered it as being abandoned. He knew it had long been uninhabited. In 1967 the area around the house was covered with high weeds. Prior to July 16, 1967 plaintiff and McDonough had been to the premises and found several old bottles and fruit jars which they took and added to their collection of antiques. On the latter date about 9:30 P.M. they made a second trip to the Briney property. They entered the old house by removing a board from a porch window which was without glass. While McDonough was looking around the kitchen area plaintiff went to another part of the house. As he started to open the north bedroom door the shotgun went off striking him in the right leg above the ankle bone. Much of his leg, including part of the tibia, was blown away.

The overwhelming weight of authority, both textbook and case law, supports the trial court's statement of the applicable principles of law.

Prosser on Torts, Third Edition, pages 116–118, states:

". . . the law has always placed a higher value upon human safety than upon mere rights in property, it is the accepted rule that there is no privilege to use any force calculated to cause death or serious bodily injury to repel the threat to land or chattels, unless there is also such a threat to the defendant's personal safety as to justify a self-defense. . . . spring guns and other man-killing devices are not justifiable against a mere trespasser, or even a petty thief. They are privileged only against those upon whom the landowner, if he were present in person would be free to inflict injury of the same kind."

In *Hooker v. Miller*, 37 Iowa 613, we held defendant vineyard owner liable for damages resulting from a spring gun shot although plaintiff was a trespasser and there to steal grapes . . .

The jury's findings of fact including a finding defendants acted with malice and with wanton and reckless disregard, as required for an allowance of punitive or exemplary damages, are supported by substantial evidence. We are bound thereby.

This opinion is not to be taken or construed as authority that the allowance of punitive damages is or is not proper under circumstances such as exist here. We hold only that question of law not having been properly raised cannot in this case be resolved.

Study and careful consideration of defendants' contentions on appeal reveal no reversible error.

Affirmed.

CONTRIBUTORY NEGLIGENCE.   Contributory negligence is the breach of a duty by the plaintiff to exercise due care for his own safety in respect to an occurrence about which he complains. It is usually a complete defence to the plaintiff's cause of action.

Hodges v. Nofsinger
183 So. (2d) 14 (1966)

This was an action against automobile driver to recover for injuries sustained by passenger–owner when driver kissed her and automobile veered across the road into a canal. The Circuit Court for Dade County entered final judgment on a verdict for plaintiff, and defendant appealed. The District Court of Appeal, Swann, J., held that conflicting evidence as to whether passenger–owner cooperated in kiss or was so surprised that she did not have time to protest or object presented issue for jury as to contributory negligence of passenger–owner.

Judgment affirmed.

SWANN, J. The defendant, Gary C. Hodges, appeals from a final judgment entered for the plaintiff, Mary Nofsinger, after a jury trial, in the sum of $7,500.00. The sole question on appeal is whether the plaintiff was guilty of contributory negligence, as a matter of law, thereby precluding her from any recovery from the defendant in this cause.

The parties have referred to this as the "kissing case." The defendant's version of the facts on appeal are as follows. The parties had seen each other many times prior to the accident. The plaintiff was a single woman, about twenty-five years of age, and the defendant was a member of the United States

Air Force, stationed at Homestead, Florida at the time the accident occurred. On that day, the defendant and a friend went to the plaintiff's house. The friend had to return to the base early, but the defendant wanted to stay and the plaintiff agreed to take him back to the base in her automobile later in the evening.

At about 8:oo P.M. they departed for Homestead with the defendant driving the plaintiff's car and the plaintiff sitting close to him on the front seat, "about the middle of the car." She testified that the defendant drove normally, and made the following answers to questions propounded at trial:

*   *   *

"Q   From the time you got onto Allapattah Drive up to the time of the accident, describe what happened.

"A   Well, we were just driving along Allapattah, and Gary kissed me, and we went off the road into the canal."

*   *   *

"Q   You didn't protest or object, or push Gary away at all during the kissing, did you?

"A   No, I didn't."

*   *   *

" 'A   The kissing occurred for a number of seconds, and we hit right then. I mean there was no pause in between.' "

*   *   *

"Q   [By Counsel] Would you please tell me, please, isn't it a fact that you did kiss fully on the mouth?

"A   The kiss was fully on the mouth."

*   *   *

"Q   And the kiss continued for a number of seconds, didn't it?
"A   I felt at the time that it did.
"Q   And it endured up to the time of the accident?
"A   Yes."

*   *   *

"Q   This wasn't the first time you kissed, was it?
"A   No."

*   *   *

The defendant contends that on these facts and circumstances the plaintiff cooperated in the kissing, with a reckless disregard for her safety, and was therefore guilty of contributory negligence as a matter of law.

The plaintiff sets forth the facts in a different light than those of the defendant. The plaintiff contends, and submitted to the jury, the same preliminary factual situation as the defendant. The essential difference in the evidence of the parties is summarized as follows. The defendant was driving in a normal manner, looking straight ahead, and suddenly, without any prior conversation or warning, the defendant kissed the plaintiff. This surprised her and she did not react or cooperate. She did not have an opportunity to protest or object to the defendant's kissing her before the car veered across the road through a guard rail and into a canal, which resulted in her injuries.

It is apparent from the testimony that there are conflicts in the evidence as to the issue of contributory negligence; that is, whether the plaintiff cooperated in the kiss, or whether she was so surprised that she did not have time in which to protest or object to the actions of the defendant. The conflicting evidence on this issue was properly submitted to the jury to be resolved by it. *Dearie v. Johnston*, Fla. 1958, 104 So. (2d) 3; *Reiss v. 1550 Collins Corp.*, Fla. App. 1964, 161 So. (2d) 572; *Goldstein v. Great Atlantic & Pacific Tea Company*, Fla. App. 1962, 142 So. (2d) 115.

On appeal by the defendant from a final judgment based on a jury verdict, all testimony and proper inferences therefrom are required to be construed most favorably to the plaintiff. *F. W. Woolworth Company v. Stevens*, Fla. App. 1963, 154 So. (2d) 201. Inasmuch as we are required to construe the testimony and proper inferences therefrom most favorably to the plaintiff, we cannot say on appeal that the plaintiff was guilty of contributory negligence, as a matter of law.

For the reasons stated, the judgment appealed from is therefore
Affirmed.

MALICIOUS PROSECUTION. Malicious prosecution is of very ancient origin and is brought for the recovery of damages to person, property or reputation resulting from the institution, maliciously and without probable cause, of a suit, civil or criminal, which has terminated in favor of the defendant therein.

Thomas v. E. J. Korvette, Inc.
329 F. Supp. 1163 (1971)
United States District Court

This was an action by former employee against former employer for false arrest, malicious prosecution and defamation of character. The jury found in favor of plaintiff. On defendant's motion for judgment n. o. v. and for a new trial . . . Court . . . held that damages . . . were excessive . . . and should not exceed $150,000, and question of proper relationship between actual and punitive damages was somewhat clouded; plaintiff would be permitted, if he so desired, to file a remittitur "under protest," and to seek review of the court's exercise of discretion in disposing of issue of excessiveness.

FULLAM, D. J. The plaintiff was employed as security manager of the King of Prussia store of the defendant when, on November 12, 1965, the defendant caused him to be arrested and prosecuted on a charge of larceny by employee. This criminal charge was later dismissed at a Justice of the Peace hearing, and the present action for false arrest, malicious prosecution and defamation of character followed.

Liability issues were tried first. The jury expressly found that there was no probable cause for plaintiff's arrest and prosecution, that the defendant was motivated by malice, and that certain disputed defamatory statements were made. Additional evidence was then presented on the damage issues, and the jury awarded compensatory damages in the sum of $250,000, and punitive damages in the sum of $500,000, making a total award of $750,000. The defendant has moved for judgment n. o. v. and for a new trial.

Plaintiff's evidence was substantially as follows: after serving as a police officer for fifteen years with a distinguished record, he was employed by the defendant as a security officer and later, on the basis of merit, was promoted to the position of security manager of the King of Prussia store. On November 12, 1965, at about 11:30 A.M., he went to the toy department to obtain a certain "getaway chase" game for his child's forthcoming birthday. He had previously been advised that a shipment of these games was anticipated shortly, and he therefore inquired of the manager of the toy department. The manager went to a backroom and obtained one of the games, and handed it to the plaintiff. As the plaintiff was on his way toward the cash register in the toy department, where he intended to pay for his purchase, he spotted a woman who had previously been identified to him as a suspected shoplifter, and determined to follow her. His pursuit of the suspected shoplifter led him to the vicinity of the front door of the store. The plaintiff's automobile happened to be parked nearby, so, as a matter of convenience, he put his package in the trunk of his car, and returned to the interior of the store. Thereafter, his attention was diverted by reason of other pressing matters, and he forgot about the game until about 2:30 P.M., when he returned to the toy department, made another purchase, advised a cashier of his former purchase, and paid for both articles at the same time, whereupon he took his second purchase out to his automobile and placed it in the trunk on top of the former purchase. At that time, the sales slip for both purchases was still attached to the second purchase by a gummed tape.

It appears that a Mr. Brown, assistant manager of the store, had observed the plaintiff taking a package out through the front door and placing it in his automobile. He called the matter to the attention of his superiors, and, ultimately, the security manager of one of the defendant's other stores was called in to investigate. Plaintiff was called into the security office at about 3:30 or 4 o'clock that afternoon and confronted with the accusation of Mr. Brown. He readily agreed that he had placed the packages in his car, but claimed that they were paid for. He was escorted to his automobile, and the packages were removed, but no sales slip was then attached, and he was unable to substantiate his purchase by means of a sales slip. The packages were then "confiscated" and the investigation continued inside the store.

Plaintiff testified that he identified the cashier to whom he had made payment for the purchases; she was interviewed and corroborated his statement. Nevertheless, because the sales slip could not be produced, plaintiff's explanation was not accepted. He thereupon became angry and resigned his position. The police were called, and he was placed under arrest.

The matter was scheduled for a preliminary hearing six days later, on November 18, 1965. In the meantime, plaintiff testified he had found the missing sales slip in the trunk of his car, in the well which held the spare tire. (The sales slip does not precisely correspond to the correct pricing of the two games; plaintiff contends that the cashier must have erred in ringing up the sale.) Plaintiff did not produce the sales slip or advise the defendant's representatives of its existence until some time during the preliminary hearing on November 18, 1965. At the conclusion of the hearing, the Justice of the Peace dismissed the charges, but ordered the plaintiff to pay the costs.

There was evidence (disputed) that during the interval between plaintiff's arrest and the preliminary hearing, Mr. Smith, the security agent investigating the matter, told at least one of the cashiers that the plaintiff had "over a thousand dollars worth of toys." There was also evidence that the defendant, during the same interval, circulated to all of its store security managers a notice advising them of plaintiff's arrest, in rather extravagant terms; however, the jury expressly found that the defendant did not abuse its privilege on this occasion.

Plaintiff testified that, since his arrest, he has been utterly unable to obtain employment in the security field. He obtained employment as a salesman of cosmetics, but, while engaged in this occupation, was asked to leave one of the defendant's stores, on the ground that he was a "security risk." In February, 1969, a prospective employer, checking with the defendant for references, was told: "If you want a thief working for you, go ahead."

As can be seen from the foregoing recitation, the case involved many issues:

(1) Whether there was probable cause for the original arrest;

(2) Whether there was probable cause for continuing to press the prosecution at the Magistrate's hearing on November 18, 1965;

(3) Whether the alleged statements to the cashier amounted to actionable slander;

(4) Whether the letter to the security managers was libelous, and whether there was an abuse of the privileged occasion there involved;

(5) Whether evidence of the alleged derogatory statements in February of 1969 was admissible, either (a) as evidence of malice in connection with the earlier incident, or (b) as an independently actionable defamation.

. . . The evidence established that, up to the date of trial, plaintiff had sustained the following pecuniary losses:

Bail bond	$ 65.00
Attorney fee	350.00
Employment agency fee	310.00
Wages lost between jobs	950.00
TOTAL	$1,675.00

In addition, plaintiff claimed loss of future earning capacity by reason of his inability to obtain employment in the security field. The difficulty with this assertion is that he has been earning more as a salesman than he was earning at Korvette's. However, there was evidence that employment in the security field, other than at Korvette's, would pay approximately $600 per year more than plaintiff's present income.

Obviously, plaintiff did sustain substantial general damages for such intangibles as injury to feelings, humiliation, embarrassment, damage to reputation, etc. His life has been substantially changed as a result of the arrest. Exclusion from his chosen field of endeavor, which he very much enjoyed and in which he was quite successful, is an element of damage of considerable magnitude, even though incapable of precise measurement.

Giving all these factors their appropriate weight, however, I find it impossible to justify an award of $250,000 as representing actual damages sustained by the plaintiff. In my judgment, the most that a reasonable jury could have awarded under these circumstances is $100,000, and even that may be generous.

On the issue of punitive damages, there are several points to be discussed. Defendant contends that it was error to admit into evidence the $155,600,000 net worth of Spartan Industries, Inc., the successor to E. J. Korvette, Inc., defendant. Defendant concedes, of course, that under Pennsylvania law the net worth of the defendant is admissible as an aid in determining punitive damages.

MEMORANDUM AND AMENDED ORDER. On July 6, 1971, in disposing of post-trial motions in this case, I entered an order denying defense motions on the liability issues, but providing that a new trial on damages would be granted unless plaintiff filed a remittitur, reducing the total verdict from $750,000 to $150,000. Plaintiff now seeks an amendment to that order, adding the following language:

". . . however, the plaintiff's filing of the remittitur shall not be construed to mean that the plaintiff agrees with the court's judgment, and should the defendant thereafter file a notice of appeal, the plaintiff shall have ten (10) days thereafter in which to file a cross-appeal, said cross-appeal preserving to the plaintiff his right to challenge the court's discretion in ordering the remittitur."

Amendment to order permitted.

Many torts arise out of negligence. Under certain circumstances A and B owe to each other the duty to use care. If A and B are driving their automobiles and are ten miles apart, neither owes to the other a duty to drive carefully. But as they approach each other on the highway and attempt to pass each other, then a duty to use due care arises on the part of both A and B. If either fails in this duty, with the result that the other is injured, the negligent party is liable in tort for his negligence. The degree of care required in all such cases is that of the ordinarily prudent man.

FEDERAL TORT CLAIMS ACT

Since the state is sovereign, it may not be sued except by its own consent. By the Federal Tort Claims Act of 1946[1] the United States gave its

con ent to be sued, under certain specified conditions, for the torts of its
ager ts and employees.

The Act provides that suit for claims of any amount may be brought
agai ist the government in the U. S. District Courts. The District Court of
the district where the plaintiff resides or where the act or omission complained of occurred has exclusive jurisdiction, with or without a jury,
"to iear, determine, and render judgment on any claim against the United
States, for money only, . . . on account of damage to or loss of property,
or cn account of personal injury or death caused by the negligence or
wrongful act or omission of any employee of the Government while
acting within the scope of his office or employment, under circumstances
where the United States, if a private person, would be liable to the claimant ior such damage, loss, injury or death in accordance with the law of
the place where the act or omission occurred. . . . The United States
shall be liable in respect of such claim to the same claimants, in the same
manner, and to the same extent as a private individual under like circumstances, except that the United States shall not be liable for interest prior
to judgment, or for punitive damages." The judgment of the District
Court is subject to review by the U. S. Courts of Appeals or the U. S.
Court of Claims. The final judgment in such an action constitutes a complete bar to any action by the claimant, by reason of the same subject
matter, against the agent or employee of the United States whose act or
omission gave rise to the claim.

If the claim is for $1000 or less, the claimant may, if he prefers, present
it fcr settlement to the federal agency involved. The Act confers authority upon the head of each executive department or other federal
agency to "consider, ascertain, adjust, determine, and settle" any such
claim. Awards are paid out of funds appropriated by Congress for such
purpose. The acceptance by the claimant of any such award constitutes a
complete release by him of any claim against the United States and against
the agent or employee whose act or omission gave rise to the claim.

Every claim of either sort must be brought within two years after it
accrues.

Joyce v. United States
329 F. Supp. 1242 (1971)
United States District Court

Postal employee brought action under the Federal Tort Claims Act for injuries sustained when he was struck on the head by large bar of soap which
came from window of the United States court house and post office building

---

[1] U. S. Code, Title 28, Ch. 20 (1947); U. S. Code, Supp. *TV* (1951), Ch. 171.

while employee was on his way to work. . . . [Plaintiff granted judgment for $35,474.03.] After trial, the United States presented motion to amend its answer so as to question the jurisdiction of the Court on the ground that the Federal Employee's Compensation Act was applicable. . . .

Motion denied; judgment for plaintiff.

GOURLEY, D. J. The plaintiff, a postal employee, was on his way to work when a large bar of soap came from a window of the United States Courthouse and Post Office Building, and struck the plaintiff on the head. The accident occurred on one of the busy street intersections in the business district of the City of Pittsburgh, Pennsylvania, some 300 to 350 feet from where the plaintiff would have entered the Federal Building for the performance of his duties. The site of the injury was on a public sidewalk owned by the City, available for use by many thousands of persons each day. The only part of the sidewalk owned by the United States was 9¼ inches from the bottom of the building and it is not disputed that no person could walk on this small area.

Unquestionably, employment is the reason or the cause for the workman's journey between his home and place of business. An employer, however, has never been held responsible for injuries to an employee, absent a contractual provision, on a portal to portal basis, or from the doorsteps of a home to the entranceway of the business enterprise. Liability for an injury on the premises of an employer is a compromise between the extreme of no coverage whatsoever and coverage for the whole journey. If such a compromise has any significance, the injured employee should, at least, be on his employer's premises for coverage to exist. Sidewalk maintenance and safe passageway requirements, which by local City Ordinance all abutting property owners have a duty to provide, do not make the sidewalk the premises of the employer. Furthermore, the law seems to be settled and it is generally taken for granted that workmen's compensation coverage was not intended to protect the employee against all perils of that journey. See *1 Larson Workmen's Compensation Law*, 1968 Ed., § 15.11, p. 195. *O'Keeffe v. Smith, etc., Associates*, 380 U. S. 359, 85 S. Ct. 1012, 13 L. Ed. 2d 895 (1964) is not applicable here. In *O'Keeffe* an employee who had been transported to Korea and drowned while more than 30 miles from his job site on his off day, was found to be covered under the provisions of the Longshoreman's and Harbor Worker's Compensation Act, 33 U. S. C. A. § 901, et seq., because the conditions of his employment created a "zone of special danger." No reason or basis exists to conclude that the vicinity of Grant Street and Seventh Avenue in Pittsburgh, Pennsylvania, the area where the plaintiff was injured, constitutes a "zone of special danger." Very simply stated, the public sidewalk, under the circumstances which existed in this case, was not the premises of the employer. This is particularly true in this proceeding since there was no right to control said public thoroughfare which was for all pedestrian use.

No sound or real basis exists to conclude or accept the thesis of the United States since there is no substantial question presented of coverage under the Federal Employee's Compensation Act.

If the Court is in error in concluding that coverage does not exist for the reasons stated, the Motion of the Government raising the jurisdictional question must be denied for additional reasons.

I must state my awareness that the general rule permits jurisdiction to be raised at any time in the trial and appellate courts. *Norton v. Larney*, 266 U.S. 511, 45 S. Ct. 145, L. Ed. 413.

However, the general rule is subject to the exception that raising a question of this nature is discretionary with the Court where the defendant has had time and opportunity on many occasions to do so and be heard.

Where a defendant chooses to participate fully in discovery, pretrial and in the preparation and formulation of the issues for trial, said litigant has no right to amend its answer to deny jurisdiction. Indeed, for the Court to permit the amendment under the circumstances herein set forth it would be an abuse of discretion. *Di Frischia v. New York Central Railroad Company*, 279 F. 2d 141 (3 Cir. 1960); *Klee v. Pittsburgh and West Virginia Railway Company*, 22 F. R. D. 252 (W. D. Pa. 1958), and *Kreger v. Ryan Brothers, Inc.*, 308 F. Supp. 727 (W. D. Pa. 1970).

In this proceeding the defendant participated throughout the full and complete preparation for and trial of this proceeding without giving any consideration to the Federal Employee's Compensation defense. This included pleadings, motions, pretrial conferences, discovery, arguments and trial. The action was filed on February 25, 1970, and trial commenced May 20, 1971. . . . .

The Court will adjudicate the merits of the cause of action under the Federal Tort Claims Act since jurisdiction exists.

To restate briefly the facts—

The case involves a United States Postal employee enroute to work who, while walking along the sidewalk adjacent to the United States Post Office and Courthouse Building, was struck on the top of the head by a bar of soap coming from a window in the said building located approximately fifty feet above street level. As a result of this blow to the head, he sustained severe injuries.

Pennsylvania law is settled that where a falling object is thrown onto the street from within a building in such a way that it must have been propelled by a human agency, prima facie evidence exists that a wilful or negligent act occurred on the part of someone, and this is especially true where the owner of the building, or the person charged with fault through its employees or agents had exclusive control of the object which occasioned the injury. *Tallarico v. Autenreith et al.*, 347 Pa. 170, 31 A. (2d) 906 (1943).

The evidence is undisputed in this proceeding that the United States of America had exclusive control of the building; that the soap thrown or propelled from the lavatory on the third floor was the property of the United States, and no evidence has been offered to establish or show any fault on the part of the plaintiff. In fact, employees of the United States were working in the lavatory area from where the soap was propelled a very short time before the accident.

There is no possible contributory negligence on the part of the plaintiff and the circumstances under which the accident occurred have been confirmed by other employees of the United States who witnessed the whole or part of the incidents which gave rise to the accident and injuries. No further discussion need be given relative to liability and consideration must be most carefully given to the most unusual injuries, mental and physical, expenses, damages and material impairment of the plaintiff's economic horizon.

Indeed plaintiff is a most unusual and dedicated type of individual who extends himself in his employment far beyond the norm of most people. As indicated he has suffered most grievous harm and injury, with extreme discomfort, pain, suffering and inconvenience. He has incurred substantial medical expense for medication and hospitalization, and will incur such expense in the future. Moreover, there can be no doubt that as a result of the injuries sustained, the range of plaintiff's economic horizons has been drastically curtailed. Motion denied; judgment for plaintiff.

Court
Systems

3

We have a dual system of courts in the United States, comprising (1) the federal system and (2) the state system. The line of demarcation between the jurisdictions of these two systems is broadly determined by the Tenth Amendment to the Constitution, in accordance with which the federal judiciary possesses only the jurisdiction which is specifically delegated to it in the Constitution, all other jurisdiction being reserved to the state courts. The specific delegation of jurisdiction to the federal court system is set forth in Article III, Section II, subsection 1 of the Constitution, which provides: "The judicial power shall extend to all cases, in law and equity, arising under this Constitution, the laws of the United States, and treaties made, or which shall be made, under their authority;—to all cases affecting ambassadors, other public ministers and consuls;—to all cases of admiralty and maritime jurisdiction;—to controversies to which the United States shall be a party;—to controversies between two or more states;—between a state and citizens of another state; [1]—between citizens of different states;—between citizens of the same state claiming lands under grants of different states, and between a state, or the citizens thereof, and foreign states, citizens or subjects." The jurisdiction over all types of controversies not enumerated in the foregoing section resides in the state court system.

While certain types of cases may be appealed from the highest state courts to the federal courts, it would be entirely incorrect to visualize our state courts as generally inferior to the federal courts. Actually, with respect to most types of cases that fall within the jurisdiction of the state

[1] The Eleventh Amendment (1798) withdrew from the federal judiciary jurisdiction over "any suit in law or equity, commenced or prosecuted against one of the United States by citizens of another state, or by citizens or subjects of any foreign state."

courts, the state supreme courts have final jurisdiction. It is more proper to think of the federal and state court systems as existing side by side, except for the relatively few instances in which cases may be appealed from the state courts to the federal courts.

The word "jurisdiction" means the authority of a court to hear and decide cases. No court has authority to try all types of cases. For example, some courts have only original jurisdiction, others only appellate jurisdiction (though some have both). In a few states some courts have only equity jurisdiction, while others have only jurisdiction over law cases. There are courts that have only jurisdiction over criminal cases, or divorce cases, or probate cases, or juvenile cases. A particular type of case may fall within the exclusive jurisdiction of one court or within the concurrent jurisdiction of more than one.

FEDERAL COURT SYSTEM

There are two general types of federal courts, (1) constitutional courts and (2) legislative courts.

The constitutional courts are those established by authority of Article III, Section I of the Constitution, which provides that "The judicial power of the United States shall be vested in one Supreme Court, and in such inferior courts as Congress may from time to time ordain and establish." Their judicial power is limited to the decision of "cases and controversies." The constitutional courts are the U. S. District Courts, the U. S. Courts of Appeals, and the U. S. Supreme Court.

The legislative courts are those set up by Congress to aid in the execution and administration of specific statutes, under the authority granted it by Article I, Section VIII, subsection 18 of the Constitution. The following are legislative courts: the U. S. Court of Claims, the U. S. Customs Court, and the U. S. Court of Customs and Patent Appeals.

The judges of all the aforementioned courts are appointed by the President, by and with the advice and consent of the Senate, to serve during good behavior.

CONSTITUTIONAL COURTS

U. S. DISTRICT COURTS. At the present time (1974), the country is divided into eighty-five judicial districts, each with a U. S. District Court. No district cuts across state lines; each state has at least one District Court, and some have two, three, or four. For the convenience of litigants, many of the districts have been divided into two or more divisions. Each District Court has from one to eighteen district judges, depending upon the amount of work in the district. There are, as of 1974, 400 district judgeships authorized. Usually only one judge is required to hear and decide a case in a District Court, but in some types of cases three judges are required. Each District Court has a clerk, a district attorney, a marshal, several U. S. Commissioners, and a number of referees in bankruptcy, probation officers, and court reporters.

The U. S. District Courts are courts of original jurisdiction. Their jurisdiction includes the following types of cases:

(1) All civil actions arising under the Constitution, laws, or treaties of the United States wherein the matter in controversy exceeds the sum or value of $10,000, exclusive of interest and costs.

(2) All civil actions between citizens of different states (diversity of citizenship) wherein the matter in controversy exceeds the sum or value of $10,000, exclusive of interest and costs.[1]

(3) Any civil case of admiralty or maritime jurisdiction.

(4) Cases involving the federal tax laws.

(5) All matters and proceedings in bankruptcy.

(6) All cases involving the anti-trust laws.

(7) All cases involving patents, copyrights, and trade-marks.

(8) Any civil action commenced by the United States against any national banking association.

(9) All offenses against the laws of the United States.[2]

It will be observed from the foregoing list that the U.S. District Courts have broad jurisdiction over civil, equity, and criminal cases. These courts are the trial courts of the federal court system. Unlike the U. S. Courts of Appeals and the U. S. Supreme Court, in which only matters of law are reviewed, they use juries in the trial of cases.

Cases from the U.S. District Courts are usually reviewable by the U. S. Courts of Appeals. In a few cases, such as where an act of Congress has been held unconstitutional, the appeal is directly to the U. S. Supreme Court.

U. S. COURTS OF APPEALS.   The U. S. Courts of Appeals were created by an act of Congress in 1891 to relieve the Supreme Court of considering all appeals in cases originally decided by the U. S. District Courts. At present (1974) they number eleven. The country is divided into ten circuits, each with a U. S. Court of Appeals; and there is also the U. S. Court of Appeals for the District of Columbia. Each of these courts has from three to nine circuit judges. In 1974 there were ninety-seven judgeships authorized. A justice of the U. S. Supreme Court is assigned to each Court of Appeals largely for supervisory purposes. Usually three judges hear a

---

[1] In the first two groups of cases the federal and state courts have concurrent jurisdiction. If the plaintiff files his case in the state court, the defendant may remove it to the federal court. Where the amount involved is less than $10,000 the state courts have exclusive jurisdiction.

[2] U. S. Code, Supp. IV (1951), Ch. 85.

case, though two constitute a quorum. The court may sit en banc, in which case all judges are present.

The U. S. Courts of Appeals are intermediate appellate courts. They hear appeals from all final decisions of the U. S. District Courts, except in a few cases where the law provides for a direct review by the U. S. Supreme Court; and cases decided by them may be appealed to the U. S. Supreme Court. They also review and enforce orders of many federal administrative agencies, such as the National Labor Relations Board, the Interstate Commerce Commission, and the Federal Trade Commission. The Courts of Appeals have no original jurisdiction.

U. S. SUPREME COURT.   As we have seen, the Constitution specifically provides for "one Supreme Court"; and in accordance with this provision the U. S. Supreme Court was created in 1789. The Supreme Court comprises a Chief Justice and eight associate justices.

Its officers, appointed by the Court, are the clerk, three deputy clerks, the reporter, the marshal, and the librarian.

The term of the Supreme Court begins the first Monday in October and continues as long as the business before the Court requires. Six members constitute a quorum and may decide a case by a simple majority. On the average the Court passes upon about 1500 cases every year. Most of these cases are disposed of by the brief decision that the subject matter is either not proper or not of sufficient importance to warrant court review. However, the Court decides between 150 and 200 cases on their merits. These are usually cases in which there is great public interest and where some important constitutional question is involved.

The Supreme Court is specifically granted both original and appellate jurisdiction by Article III, Section II, subsection 2 of the Constitution. It is given original jurisdiction "in all cases affecting ambassadors, other public ministers and consuls, and those in which a state shall be a party." Pursuant to this provision, the Court has original and exclusive jurisdiction of (1) all controversies between two or more states and (2) all actions or proceedings against ambassadors or other public ministers of foreign states or their domestic servants, not inconsistent with the law of nations. It has original but not exclusive jurisdiction of (1) all actions or proceedings brought by ambassadors or other public ministers of foreign states or to which consuls or vice consuls of foreign states are parties, (2) all controversies between the United States and a state, and (3) all actions or proceedings by a state against the citizens of another state or against aliens. The Supreme Court has appellate jurisdiction in the following types of cases and controversies: (1) cases involving the constitutionality of acts of Congress, (2) cases in the Courts of Appeals that may be reviewed by the U. S. Supreme Court, (3) cases reviewed from the

Court of Claims, (4) cases reviewed from the Court of Customs and Patent Appeals, and (5) cases reviewed from the state courts. The review of a case by the U. S. Supreme Court is a privilege and not a right.

LEGISLATIVE COURTS

U. S. COURT OF CLAIMS.   The U. S. Court of Claims was established by an act of Congress in 1855, to provide a means to determine the validity of certain kinds of claims against the United States. Prior to the creation of this court, relief in such cases could be had only by special acts of Congress. This court decides suits filed with it against the United States and determines claims referred to it by Congress and the executive branch. It also hears certain claims filed under the Federal Tort Claims Act.

The Court of Claims consists of a chief judge and four associate justices. Three judges constitute a quorum. The Court has eleven commissioners, a clerk, a bailiff, and three assistants. It is located in Washington, D. C.

U. S. CUSTOMS COURT.   The U. S. Customs Court was created in 1926. It reviews appraisals of imported merchandise and all decisions of collectors of customs, including orders on rates of duty, exclusion of merchandise, and so on.

The Court is made up of nine judges. The offices of the Court and the official station of its judges are in New York City. However, for the convenience of importers who have customs controversies in other import cities the Chief Judge arranges for hearings where such controversies arise, assigning to the hearings the various judges of the Court. The Court itself is divided into three Divisions, each composed of a panel of three judges.

U. S. COURT OF CUSTOMS AND PATENT APPEALS.   The U. S. Court of Customs and Patent Appeals was created in 1910 to decide certain questions arising under the customs law. In 1929 it was given jurisdiction to review certain patent and trade-mark cases. It reviews decisions of the Customs Court on classification and duties upon imported merchandise, and decisions of the Patent Office, as well as legal questions in the findings of the Tariff Commission as to unfair practices in import trade.

The Court is made up of a chief judge and four associate judges; there are also a clerk, a marshal, a reporter, and certain minor assistants. The Court sits en banc in Washington, D. C.

STATE COURT SYSTEM

Like the U. S. Constitution, each state constitution contains an article dealing with the establishment of a state court system. Within the confines of these articles the various state legislatures have set up systems of courts for the respective states. Since each state has the constitutional authority to provide the kind of court system it prefers, there is considerable variation in the state court systems. However, this variation is largely in minor details, as the following discussion indicates.

Some states have three levels of courts, and some have four. At the bottom, there is a type of tribunal usually called the justice of the peace court or magistrate's court. Just above this is the trial court. At the top there is an appellate court of last resort. In the states with four levels of courts there is in addition an intermediate appellate court between the trial court and the court of last resort.

JUSTICE OF THE PEACE COURTS

The justice of the peace court, or magistrate's court, traces its origin back to medieval England. It is of very limited jurisdiction, not only territorially but as to subject matter and amount involved. Territorially it is usually limited to matters arising within a town, township, city, or ward, or adjacent township or ward. It has jurisdiction over minor contract and tort cases, such as suits for the breach of contracts, suits for rent, actions on notes and open accounts, civil actions for damages for assault and battery, actions growing out of automobile accidents, landlord-tenant cases, and so on, but only if the amount involved does not exceed a specified maximum, ranging from perhaps $200 to $300 in rural areas to possibly $1000 in some metropolitan areas. Usually the justice courts may try misdemeanor cases, but their connection with felony cases is limited to giving preliminary hearings. They have no jurisdiction over equity cases, divorce cases, or cases to try title to real estate.

The trial of a case in the justice court is often very informal. The "rules of evidence" are often disregarded. While juries may be used in the trial of cases, their use is often waived. These courts are not courts of record. All decisions may be appealed to the trial court. When this is done the case is tried de novo, that is, as if it had never been tried in the justice court at all.

In many cities the customary work of the justice of the peace court is divided according to the nature of the cases and handled by special courts, known by other names, such as police courts, small claims courts, traffic courts, or recorder's courts.

TRIAL COURTS

Just above the justice of the peace courts come the trial courts, variously called circuit courts, district courts, superior courts, county courts, or courts of common pleas. These courts have both appellate and original jurisdiction. Their appellate jurisdiction includes appeals from such courts as the justice courts, the probate or orphans' courts, and such special courts (if any exist in the jurisdiction) as the police court, the small claims court, and so on. Their most important jurisdiction is their original jurisdiction over civil, equity, and criminal cases. They have complete equity jurisdiction; they can try felony and misdemeanor cases; they have jurisdiction over all types of civil actions not otherwise given to minor courts in the judicial hierarchy; they can grant divorces and try title to real estate.

The judges of these courts are usually elected by popular vote, but in a few states they are appointed by the governor or by the state legislature. The term of office ranges from four to six years.

The judge of a trial court is aided in his work by both the petit jury and the grand jury. The petit jury serves in the trial of both civil and criminal cases. The grand jury is used only in criminal cases. It is not a trial jury; its function is to investigate situations in which persons are accused of crimes, to determine whether there is sufficient evidence to warrant holding the accused for trial. If the grand jury finds enough evidence to constitute a prima facie case against the accused, he is tried before a judge and a petit jury. The work of the trial court also calls for the services of a number of other officials, such as the prosecuting attorney,[1] the clerk of the court and his deputies, the sheriff and his deputies, the court reporter, and the coroner. The court clerk is especially important, since it is his office in which all pleadings must be filed and from which all warrants, writs, processes, subpoenas, etc. must emanate.

Cases decided by the trial courts may be appealed to the proper appellate courts.

INTERMEDIATE APPELLATE COURTS

Some states[2] have intermediate appellate courts between their trial courts and their court of last resort. They have various names, as circuit courts of appeals, superior courts, and so on. In some states there is only one such court; other states are divided into two or three areas, with an intermediate appellate court in each.

These courts were created to relieve the highest state court of some of its burden of work. Though a few have been given some original jurisdic-

---

[1] In some states he is known as the state's attorney or the district attorney.

[2] Such as Alabama, California, Georgia, Illinois, Indiana, Maryland, Missouri, New York, Ohio, Tennessee, and Texas.

tion, most of them have only appellate jurisdiction. The cases which they usually hear are those appealed from the trial courts. In general, any case decided in an intermediate appellate court may be appealed to the highest state court.

STATE SUPREME COURTS

Every state has a court which it designates as its highest court, or court of last resort. Most of the states call their highest court the supreme court. Kentucky, Maryland, and New York call it the Court of Appeal; Massachusetts and Maine have given it the name of Supreme Judicial Court.

There are from three to nine judges on the various state supreme courts. In a majority of the states they are elected by popular vote. Their tenures range from two years to life on good behavior; six-year terms are the most common.

The jurisdiction of the state supreme courts is largely appellate, though most of them do have original jurisdiction to the extent of issuing prerogative writs. They work without juries, since they pass on questions of law and not of fact. The facts involved in each case are contained in the transcript of the evidence taken in the trial court and made available to them on appeal. The decision of the state supreme court is final, unless the case involves the U. S. Constitution, statutes, or treaties, in which case it may be taken to the U. S. Supreme Court.

Court
Procedure

4

PROCEEDINGS BEFORE TRIAL

PREPARING THE CASE

Lawsuits arise out of the various conflicts that occur between people in their economic and social relations with one another. In the field of business most of these conflicts arise over contracts and property rights and interests, but a rather large number result from the commission of torts. If the parties are unable to work out an amicable settlement of their difficulties, one of the parties is likely to consult his attorney. If the attorney fails to negotiate a satisfactory settlement with the other disputant, then his client will probably ask him to file suit against the other party.

In preparing his case the attorney will ask his client (the *plaintiff*) many questions concerning the nature of his complaint or grievance against the other party (the *defendant*). If the conflict arises out of a written instrument, like a contract, note, or will, the attorney will carefully study the instrument and evaluate its terms in relation to the dispute. After he has acquired all available facts in the case, and has determined which of these facts he will probably be able to establish as evidence, through witnesses and exhibits, in the event of trial, he will proceed to make a careful study of the law applicable to the facts of the case. This will require that he investigate not only his state code or statutes but also the case law of his state. As he progresses, he must try to work out a *theory* of his client's case. If his study of the facts and the law causes him to conclude that his client does not have a cause of action against the other party, then it would be useless for him to file suit for his client. To justify a suit he must first be able to work out in his own mind that his client has suffered some wrong of which the courts will take cognizance. After he has determined the nature of his client's injury, he must ascertain whether his client has a remedy at law. If he finds no adequate remedy at law available, then he must consider the possibility of an appropriate remedy in equity.

After the plaintiff's attorney has worked out a theory of his case, and has determined the specific remedy in law or equity to which he believes his client is entitled, he must determine what court has jurisdiction of the case. He will then prepare the plaintiff's first pleading and file it with the clerk of that court.

THE PLEADINGS

Probably most laymen think that a pleading is an attorney's address to the jury. This is a natural conclusion, for it is often said that lawyers *plead* their cases. In technical usage, however, the pleadings in a given case are the written statements filed with the clerk of the court by the plaintiff and the defendant, stating their respective positions on the matter in controversy. The objective of the pleadings is to reach an issue in the case, for until the parties are at issue the case is not ready for trial. The pleadings advise each party as to the other's theory of the case; they inform the court as to the exact nature of the dispute; and they form the basis for the submission of evidence at the trial. It should be understood that all of the pleadings in a case are filed before the case is presented to the judge and jury for trial.

PLAINTIFF'S FIRST PLEADING. The plaintiff's first pleading is variously called a declaration, petition, or complaint. In it the plaintiff alleges the facts upon which he based his action against the defendant. He states his theory of the case and the grounds for recovery of a judgment against the defendant. He sets forth the name of the court, the county, the state, and the parties, and concludes with a prayer for relief, usually for a judgment for so many dollars and his costs. If he is to succeed in his action, he must state sufficient facts to constitute a cause of action—or, in technical language, a *prima facie case* against the defendant.

The plaintiff's attorney files the declaration in the office of the clerk of the court in which the case is to be tried. In some states the declaration must be accompanied by a *praecipe* for a *summons*, requesting the clerk to issue a summons to bring the defendant into court.[1] Usually the declaration is signed by the plaintiff's attorney, but in certain types of cases it must be signed and acknowledged by the plaintiff himself.

The *summons* is a formal notice to the defendant that the plaintiff has filed suit against him and that he must appear and defend in the action. The form, the content, and the service of the summons are all important. Failure to meet the requirements with respect to any one of them may

[1] In some states the summons may be issued by the plaintiff's attorney.

prove fatal to the plaintiff's action, for it may result in the dismissal of his declaration or petition, upon motion of the defendant. The summons must designate specifically the court, county, state, and parties. It must state the nature of the cause, the amount sued for, and the date on which the defendant is required to appear and defend. The date specified is usually known as the *return day;* its determination is governed by state statute. If the defendant fails to appear and defend himself against the plaintiff's action, the plaintiff may take a *judgment by default* against the defendant.

The summons should be addressed to the officer who is to serve it. A summons usually may be served by the sheriff, a constable, or the coroner; it is probably most often served by the sheriff or one of his deputies. When the summons is served on the defendant, he is also given a copy of the declaration, so that he may be fully informed about the nature of the action. The statutes of each state set forth the various methods of getting service on resident and non-resident defendants. In general, there are two types of service in the case of resident defendants, (1) actual service, and (2) substitute or constructive service (service by publication in a newspaper in the county).

DEMURRERS.   If the defendant wishes to avoid a judgment by default, he must either demur or plead. If he does either one of these things he has made an appearance which has the effect of preventing the plaintiff from taking a judgment by default.

A demurrer (from early French *demorrer,* to stay, delay, or abide) raises a question of law as to the legal sufficiency of the plaintiff's declaration.[1] It has nothing to do with the facts of the case. If the defendant demurs to the plaintiff's declaration, he does not admit or deny that the facts alleged in the declaration are true; he merely states, in effect, "Assuming that the facts which you allege are true, you haven't stated a cause of action against me." For example, A sues B alleging that B promised to give him $1000, but now refuses to do so. B demurs that A's allegations do not constitute a cause of action. Even if the facts are as alleged, B is not legally obligated to give A $1000. The codes of many of the states set forth the specific grounds for demurrer.[2]

Since demurrers involve only questions of law and not of fact, they are argued by counsel before the judge without a jury. Demurrers are set down for argument on what are usually called *motion days.* If the judge thinks that the plaintiff has not stated a cause of action against the defendant, he *sustains* the demurrer. Under the practice of most states the plaintiff may, upon request, secure the court's permission to amend

---

[1] Either party may demur to the other party's pleadings. This is also true in equity cases.

[2] In some states such matters are raised by *motion* rather than by demurrer.

his declaration in an effort to state a cause of action against the defendant. If the judge is of the opinion that the plaintiff has stated a cause of action against the defendant, he *overrules* the demurrer, and it then becomes incumbent upon the defendant to file an answer.

DEFENDANT'S ANSWER. If the defendant decides that the plaintiff has stated a cause of action against him, he may forgo filing a demurrer and file an answer instead. Or, if he has filed a demurrer to the plaintiff's declaration and it has been overruled, he must then file an answer if he is to avoid a judgment by default.

The defendant's answer may be in the form of (1) a general denial (traverse), (2) a special answer, or (3) an answer by way of a confession and avoidance. If the answer is in the form of a *general denial*, the parties are at issue, for the plaintiff has made certain allegations and the defendant has denied them. This raises a question of fact and not one of law. If the defendant answers by filing a *special answer*, he denies only portions of the plaintiff's allegations, and the parties are at issue on those portions. If he files an *answer by way of a confession and avoidance*, he admits the facts alleged in the plaintiff's declaration and sets up new facts or new matter. For example, if A sues B on a promissory note, B might answer by admitting the plaintiff's allegations concerning the note, and then plead, by way of defense, that he has paid the note, or that it has been outlawed by the statute of limitations.

PLAINTIFF'S REPLY OR REPLICATION. If the defendant answers by way of a confession and avoidance, the parties are not at issue, since the defendant has brought new matter into the case. In order to put the parties at issue on the facts, the plaintiff must file a reply or replication. Usually the pleadings do not go beyond the reply or replication, but they may do so. The further pleadings are known as rejoinder, surrejoinder, rebutter, and surrebutter.

DEPOSITIONS   TYPE OF WITTNESS

Depositions are often used by the parties in the preparation of their cases. A deposition is a statement, under oath, concerning the facts involved in a given case. The deposition of the parties as well as of witnesses may be taken before trial, the questions and answers being taken down by a stenographer. Depositions are used to perpetuate testimony, as in the case of a party or witness who is ill and may not be living at the time of the trial. They are also used in securing testimony of a witness outside the jurisdiction, or in prison. If a deponent is not available at the time of the trial, his deposition may be introduced as evidence at the proper time in the proceedings.

Sometimes *written interrogatories* are used in place of depositions. The attorney submits to the party or witness interrogated a list of questions concerning the case, which he is required to answer in writing under oath. Written interrogatories are less expensive than depositions and are generally more convenient to all parties concerned.

SCHEDULING THE TRIAL

TRIAL CALENDAR OR DOCKET.   After the parties have arrived at an issue as a result of their pleadings, the case is ready for trial. The clerk thereupon places the case on the trial calendar or trial docket for trial during the next term of court. The case is designated by a number which was given to it when the plaintiff's first pleading was filed. The cases that are ready for trial at a given term of court are called for trial by the judge in the order of their appearance on the docket. However, for various reasons cases are not always tried in the order in which they appear on his docket.

CONTINUANCES.   One reason for such a change of order is that sometimes a case is *continued* (that is, its trial is postponed) at the request of one of the parties. The power to grant or to refuse continuance is said to be inherent in the court and within its sound discretion. Continuances are not particularly favored by the courts, but they are granted upon occasion in the interests of justice. Grounds for granting continuances are often set out in the state statutes or codes, or in the rules of the court. Among the grounds for continuance are (1) illness of one of the parties; (2) illness of one of the attorneys; (3) illness of a vital witness, or inability to secure his presence at the time set for trial; (4) change in counsel by one of the parties, when the new counsel requests a continuance to secure more time in which to prepare for trial; (5) defective service of process, when the plaintiff requests further time in which to perfect such service. Continuances are also generally granted upon the mutual agreement of the parties and their counsels. On rare occasions a case is continued upon motion of the judge himself.

CHANGE OF VENUE.   Cases sometimes do not go to trial before the judge to whom they have been assigned, because he may grant the request of one of the parties (usually the defendant) for a *change of venue*. Where a change of venue is granted, the case is transferred to another judge in the same county, or to a judge in another county or district. Conditions under which a change of venue may be allowed are usually regulated by statute. A motion or petition for a change of venue must be in writing and must set out the grounds upon which the petition or motion is based. Such petitions usually allege that the judge is disqualified to hear the case because of his bias or prejudice, or because he is related to one of the parties to the action, or has formerly been employed as an attorney for one of the parties, or upon some similar grounds. Sometimes a change of venue is granted because of what is called "local prejudice."

WITNESSES—SUBPOENAS

After a specific date has been indicated by the court for the trial of a case, it becomes necessary for both parties to subpoena their witnesses and all documents needed in the trial of the case. From the clerk of the court which is to try the case the attorneys secure *subpoenas*,[1] which are forms containing blank spaces to be filled in by the attorneys. The subpoenas are addressed to the witnesses designated by the attorneys and command the witnesses to appear on a designated date before the named judge of a specified court to testify in the action between the plaintiff and defendant. If a witness fails to obey the command of the court, he is held to be in contempt of court.

If the attorney wishes a witness to bring along with him certain named documents, books, papers, or other physical evidence, then he uses what is called a *subpoena duces tecum*.[2]

All subpoenas are served upon the witnesses by the sheriff or one of his deputies.

TRIAL OF THE CASE

IMPANELING THE JURY

The parties in all civil and criminal cases[3] are entitled to have their cases tried by a jury called the petit or trial jury to distinguish it from the grand jury. This right may be waived, in which case the case is tried by the court, or judge, without a jury.

The statutes of the several states carefully regulate the selection and impaneling of petit juries. Every effort is used to secure the service of competent and unbiased juries, and to see that they are fairly selected. The methods used in the various states differ somewhat in details. In some states the jury list is prepared by a jury commission, in others by the county commissioners or the county court or some other method. In any event a large number of names are selected from the residents of the county, secured possibly from a tax or voters' list, and placed in a jury

[1] From Latin *sub*, under, *poena*, penalty. The chancery courts used the writ of subpoena to command the defendant, as well as witnesses, to appear in court. Even today the subpoena is often used in equity cases to require the defendant to appear and answer charges against him.

[2] *Duces tecum* means "you shall bring with you."

[3] Juries are not used in equity cases, as a rule, and the right to jury trial in equity cases is not guaranteed by the Constitution. Occasionally a jury is used in an equity case but its finding is merely advisory to the court and not binding on it.

wheel or box.[1] A person is designated by statute to reach into the box and draw a specified number of names. The persons whose names are drawn constitute a panel or venire from which the jury is drawn for each case as it comes up for trial. There are twelve jurors on a petit jury.

The attorneys have a right to question the prospective jurors and to challenge their right to serve. There are three types of challenge. (1) An attorney may *challenge the array*, i.e. the entire panel, on some such grounds as irregularities in the selection of the panel. If the judge finds the charges true, the entire panel is discharged and a new panel is called. (2) An attorney may *challenge for cause* any juror whom he considers disqualified by reason of his relationship to one of the parties or attorneys, bias in the case, lack of statutory qualifications to serve as a juror, and so on. (3) The statutes allow each side a certain number of *peremptory challenges*. In a peremptory challenge the attorney may ask that the name of a certain juror be stricken from the list without giving reason.

THE COURSE OF THE TRIAL

OPENING STATEMENTS TO THE JURY.   After the jury is impaneled and sworn, the attorneys usually make opening statements to the jury, though either side may waive its opening statement. The attorneys do not present arguments in their opening statements but merely outline the nature of the case to the jury and present certain facts which they hope to prove by their evidence.

INTRODUCTION OF EVIDENCE.   The attorneys are then ready to proceed with the introduction of evidence. The plaintiff presents his case first; that is, he has all of his witnesses testify and introduces all of his documentary evidence (exhibits) before the defendant presents his witnesses and documentary evidence. The questioning of the plaintiff's witnesses by the plaintiff's attorney is called *direct examination*. As soon as the plaintiff's attorney has completed his direct examination of a witness, the witness is turned over to the defendant's attorney for *cross-examination*. *Leading questions*, or questions so framed as to suggest the desired answer, may not be asked a witness on direct examination unless he proves to be a "hostile" witness, but they may be asked on cross-examination.

After the plaintiff's attorney has presented all of his evidence, he announces that "the plaintiff rests." At this point the attorney for the defendant may ask for a *directed verdict*. The effect of such a motion is to raise a question of law as to whether the plaintiff has made his case by his evidence. In effect the defendant says: "Even if all your evidence is true,

---

[1] They must meet prescribed qualifications as to age, sex, residence, citizenship, and so on. Some groups, such as clergymen, physicians, teachers, and government officials, are usually exempt from jury service.

still you have not proved your case against me." [1] Courts are reluctant to grant a motion for a directed verdict. They usually feel that the jury should hear the defendant's case and render a verdict on the basis of all the evidence. Occasionally, however, the motion is granted and the case is dismissed.

If the defendant is denied his request for a directed verdict, he must proceed to place his evidence before the jury. His witnesses are introduced one by one, examined, and turned over to the plaintiff's counsel for cross-examination.

In the examination of a witness either attorney may object to a question asked by the other attorney. The court will either overrule or sustain the objection. The party against whom the court rules usually *takes exception* to the court's ruling in order to preserve the objection in case of an appeal.

ARGUMENTS TO THE JURY.   After all of the evidence is in, the attorneys for the plaintiff and the defendant argue the case before the jury. Each side is allowed the same amount of time. The attorney for the plaintiff "opens" and "closes" the arguments. Attorneys must confine their arguments to the evidence in the case.

INSTRUCTIONS TO THE JURY.   As soon as the arguments of counsel are concluded, the judge instructs or charges the jury on the law applicable to the case.

VERDICT.   The jury then retires to consider its verdict. In a criminal case a verdict of guilty must be unanimous. In civil cases, in most states, nine of the twelve jurors may render a verdict. After reaching a verdict the jurors return to the court room, and in the presence of the judge, the parties, and their attorneys, the foreman reads the verdict. Upon the request of either party the jury may be *polled;* that is, each juror may be separately asked whether this is his verdict.

JUDGMENT.   On the basis of the verdict the judge renders his judgment. The wording of the judgment is important. Consequently, the judge may avail himself of the services of the attorneys in its preparation.

Occasionally the attorney for the losing party files a motion with the court for a *judgment non obstante veredicto* (notwithstanding the verdict). In behalf of such motion the attorney argues that on the basis of the evidence in the case the verdict was obviously for the wrong party.

---

[1] It will be noted that a motion for a directed verdict resembles a demurrer in important respects. In some jurisdictions, indeed, such a procedural move is called a *demurrer to the evidence,* a term handed down from the early common law. In other jurisdictions it is called a motion to exclude the evidence from the jury or a nonsuit.

Only in cases where the verdict is clearly contrary to the law and the evidence will such motion be granted.

MOTION FOR NEW TRIAL.   After the judgment in the case has finally been rendered, either party may file a written motion for a new trial. In most cases, of course, it is the losing party who does so, but if the party who has received judgment feels that the amount of the judgment is insufficient, he sometimes files such a motion. The motion is argued by the attorneys, and the judge either grants or refuses a new trial. If the motion is granted, a new trial before the same court is ordered. If the motion is denied, the movant may appeal the case to the proper appellate court.

JUDICIAL REVIEW

METHODS OF OBTAINING REVIEW

The procedures for obtaining a review of a decision in the trial court were developed early in the law. Actually, two methods of review were devised, (1) by writ of error and (2) by writ of appeal. The *writ of error* developed in the common law courts. The party who wished to have the trial of a case in the trial court reviewed filed a writ of error with the appellate court. This was looked upon as a new suit, in which the appellant brought suit not only against the other party but also against the trial court. If the writ was granted, the appellate court ordered the trial court to submit its record of the case to it. The *writ of appeal* developed in the equity courts. Review under this writ was looked upon not as a new case, but as merely a continuance of the case from the trial court to the appellate court.

At the present time some states still recognize the theoretical distinction between a writ of error and a writ of appeal, using the writ of error only in law cases and the writ of appeal in equity cases. Many states, however, permit either writ to be used in both law and equity cases. In fact, under the modern codes of civil procedure and practice a prescribed method of appeal in all cases is provided for.

In taking a case up on appeal the appellant, or plaintiff-in-error, must file an *affidavit of appeal*. He must also deposit a designated fee in the office of the clerk of the court, after which the proper writ is issued. The appellant may also be required to post an *appeal bond*.

Among the grounds for an appeal are the following: (1) that the court erred in admitting incompetent, irrelevant, and immaterial evidence offered by the appellee; (2) that the court erred in rejecting or excluding competent, relevant, and material evidence offered by the appellant; (3) that the court erred in the instructions given to the jury; (4) that the court erred in refusing to grant the appellant a directed verdict;

(5) that the verdict was against the evidence, against the weight of the evidence, and against the law under the evidence.

RECORD, BILL OF EXCEPTIONS, AND BRIEFS

The appellant is usually required to furnish a transcript of the entire record of the proceedings of the trial court. This record may have to be abstracted or summarized for the convenience of the court. The appellant will also have to prepare a *bill of exceptions* or an *assignment of errors*, listing his various objections and exceptions to the trial court's rulings during the progress of the case. In general, the appellate court refuses to rule on alleged errors unless the appellant's attorney made proper objection and took exception to the rulings of the trial court. Finally, the appellant must prepare a *brief* of his case. This brief will contain the attorney's arguments in the case, supported by citations of previous decisions.

The entire record must be printed and a number of copies filed with the court; the appellee's attorney is also entitled to several copies. The expense of preparing and printing the record is often a major factor in a party's decision not to appeal a case. It is included in the costs of the entire case, which are paid by the party who loses the case.

The appellee's attorney also prepares a brief.

ARGUMENTS AND OPINION

The appellate court hears the case without a jury. There are no witnesses, and no new evidence is taken. The function of the appellate court is to decide whether there has been material error in the proceedings of the trial court; and it bases its decision upon the record of that court.

Usually a case is set down for argument on a specified date, and the opposing counsels appear before the court and present their arguments. Sometimes, however, a case is presented upon briefs alone, without oral arguments. The court, after a careful review of the case, renders its decision and writes its opinion. Opinions of the appellate courts are preserved in permanent bound volumes or reports. It is such decisions by the state and federal appellate courts that we will study throughout later chapters of this book.

The court, in its decision or holding, may affirm the judgment of the trial court, or reverse it, or remand the case to the trial court for a new trial.

Unless a case is remanded, a decision reached by the highest appellate court having jurisdiction is final as to the issues and parties involved, and no further proceeding can be had between the parties on the same issues. The decision is said to stand *res judicata,* a thing judicially determined.

ENFORCEMENT OF THE JUDGMENT

A judgment for the plaintiff in a court of law means only that the court has decided that the defendant owes the plaintiff a certain sum of money. If the defendant fails or refuses to pay the judgment, he is not in contempt of court, as he would be if he disregarded a decree of a court of equity; nor may he be fined or thrown into jail for failing or refusing to pay the judgment. But the law does provide certain legal procedures to aid the plaintiff in recovering the amount of the judgment. It is up to the plaintiff, however, to take the initiative in putting the processes of the law in motion in his own behalf. It should be noted that the plaintiff is not always successful in securing payment, since the defendant may be what is called judgment-proof;[1] that is, he may not have sufficient property out of which to satisfy the judgment.

One aid available to the plaintiff in attempting to collect his judgment is known as a *writ of execution*. The writ is obtained from the clerk of the court that rendered the judgment and is directed to the sheriff, commanding him to levy upon sufficient property of the defendant to satisfy the judgment of the plaintiff. If the sheriff finds sufficient property available for purposes of levy, he will seize the property and sell it at public vendue or auction, in accordance with the provisions of the state statutes. At times the plaintiff is required to put up bond to indemnify the sheriff against unlawful seizure of the defendant's property. There are various statutory exemptions which exempt certain types of property from levy and execution.

A second method in aid of execution is *garnishment*. Garnishment is a statutory remedy; it was not known at common law. It may be used in the satisfaction of a judgment where property or other assets of the defendant are in the hands of third persons. For example, if the defendant is employed, the plaintiff may run a garnishment against the defendant's employer (called the *garnishee*) to obtain a portion of the defendant's wages or salary. The statutes specify what portion may be taken under garnishment—sometimes a percentage, sometimes all above a certain amount. A writ of garnishment usually runs for the life of the current term of court (though it may usually be renewed for another term); at the end of the term the garnishee is required to turn over to the court the amount of money he has withheld from the defendant's wages or salary under the garnishment. Bank accounts, accounts receivable, and goods in storage may also be reached by garnishment.

A judgment in favor of the plaintiff, if unsatisfied, may stand as a *lien* against the real property of the defendant. In some states the lien attaches

---

[1] It would be more accurate to say that the defendant may be *execution-proof*.

as soon as the judgment is rendered; while in other states in order for the plaintiff to avail himself of the benefits of the lien he must have his judgment recorded in the proper office at the court house.

If a judgment is not paid, it finally outlaws under the state's *statute of limitations*. The length of time involved varies from state to state. The defendant may also have the judgment discharged by going into bankruptcy and scheduling the judgment among his debts and obligations.

BANKRUPTCY

Kohnke v. Justice
280 So. (2d) 665 (1973)
Court of Appeals of Louisiana

Judgment debtor brought summary proceeding against judgment creditors and clerk of court to cancel money judgment obtained against him approximately 11 months prior to his discharge in bankruptcy. The . . . Distritct Court . . . refused to cancel judgment, and plaintiff appealed.

Reversed and rendered.

BAILES, J. In prior proceedings Messrs. Smith and Gisevius sued the plaintiff in rule and obtained a money judgment in their favor in the amount of $1,325. This judgment was rendered on January 31, 1971. On August 24, 1971, Mr. Kohnke, the plaintiff, filed a petition in bankruptcy and therein this judgment was listed in the debt schedule. On November 22, 1971, plaintiff was discharged of this judgment.

In the bankruptcy proceedings plaintiff listed three separate pieces of immovable property that were affected by the Smith–Gisevius judgment. The referee in bankruptcy on the petition of the trustee in bankruptcy disclaimed and abandoned any right, title and interest in said properties on the ground that there was no equity therein in favor of the bankrupt's estate by reason of the outstanding mortgages thereon.

It is these three immovable properties that are affected by the money judgment owned by defendants, Smith and Gisevius.

After the trial of the rule to show cause, the district court rejected the plaintiff's demand for cancellation of the judgment. We find the trial court committed an error of law in refusing to cancel the judgment affecting plaintiff's property.

LSA–R.S. 9:5166 under which this action was brought provides:

"Upon rule to show cause by any interested party against the clerk of court and ex officio recorder of mortgages of the several parishes and the recorder of mortgages for the parish of Orleans, the judgment creditor and a judgment debtor discharged in bankruptcy, *the court shall order the cancellation of the inscription of any dischargeable judgment rendered twelve months previously unless the judgment creditor can prove that he continues to possess a secured interest in the property affected by such judgment,* or any judgment rendered in a tort proceeding wherein the judgment debtor's liability arose out of his wilful negligence, or any judgment for taxes due or any other judgment otherwise not discharged in bankruptcy." (Emphasis added.)

According to this statute, when an interested party files a rule to show cause against the Clerk of Court and ex officio recorder of mortgages and the judgment creditor (although the statute also names the judgment debtor as a defendant against whom the rule should be brought, obviously such is not required when the judgment debtor is the interested party–plaintiff), the court shall order the cancellation of the inscription of any dischargeable judgment rendered twelve months previously *unless the judgment creditor can prove that he continues to possess a secured interest in the property affected by such judgment.* What this condition of the statute means is that the judgment creditor must prove that the property affected by his judgment is worth in dollar value an amount sufficiently in excess of existing encumbrances which prime his judgment as to afford him a secured interest in the property affected by his judgment.

On the trial of the rule to show cause in the district court only two witnesses testified. One was the plaintiff who testified that more was owed on prior existing mortgages on the property than it was worth; and the other witness was Mr. Gisevius, defendant in rule whose testimony was only about matters extraneous to this action. The defendants offered no proof of any nature whatever of the value of the property affected by their judgment. No proof was made that the defendants in rule possessed a secured interest in these properties. This is the sole issue before the court.

Under the express provisions of LSA–R.S. 9:5166, supra, the judgment creditor has the burden of proving that he continues to possess a secured interest in the property affected by such judgment. As there is not one scintilla of evidence produced by the judgment creditor, or otherwise in the record, to sustain this burden, the judgment of the trial court must be reversed.

For the foregoing reasons, the judgment appealed is reversed and there is judgment herein in favor of the plaintiff.

Reversed and rendered.

Contracts

part II

Introduction to
the Law of
Contracts

5

In our highly industrialized society the importance of a knowledge of contract law can hardly be overestimated. At the basis of almost every business transaction—even so common a one as buying food or clothing or taking a ride on a bus or street car—there is a contract which determines the legal rights and duties of the contracting parties. Many of the contracts we make from day to day are of no great importance; but some contracts, especially those which are made in the operation of a business, may involve us in serious consequences. It may take only one bad mistake in our contractual dealings with others to place us in financial difficulties. For this reason the time one spends in acquiring a knowledge of contract law will in all probability pay worthwhile dividends.

ORIGIN AND NATURE OF CONTRACTS

ORIGIN OF CONTRACTS

Both criminal and tort law preceded the beginnings of the law of contracts. The early Anglo-Saxons, prior to the Norman Conquest in 1066, had devised for themselves a crude system of criminal and tort law for the protection of their persons and property; but their economy was so primitive that there was little or no need for contract law as we know it today. The economy was predominantly agricultural, and the exchange of property was almost entirely in the form of barter. Commerce and trade were practically non-existent. It was not until after the Norman Conquest that the concept of an agreement legally enforceable in the courts came into being. Contract law developed concurrently with the development of commerce and trade and the substitution of money and credit devices for barter in the exchange of personal property.

NATURE OF CONTRACTS

The legal rights and duties which we as individuals possess in our relations with other individuals do not all spring from the same source. Some of them, as we have seen in our brief survey of tort law, are automatically and uniformly imposed upon us as members of the society in which we live. Such, for example, is our legal duty not to trespass on land belonging to someone else. There are many others, however, which we create and assume of our own free will, by entering into agreements with other individuals to do so. For example, A owns a typewriter, and the law protects him in his rights as owner. But let us suppose that A enters into an agreement with B whereby he promises to sell his typewriter to B for $50 and B promises to pay $50 to A for the typewriter. Provided the agreement meets certain requirements, A has now assumed by his own act the legal duty to hand over his typewriter to B and the legal right to receive $50 from B; B, in turn, has assumed the legal duty to pay $50 to A and the legal right to receive the typewriter from A. Such an agreement, creating legal rights and duties by the free assent of the parties, is called a contract.

When we say that a contract is an agreement that creates legal rights and duties, we mean that it is an agreement that creates rights and duties which the courts will recognize and enforce. This test of the existence of a contract is the basis of the definition in the *Restatement of the Law of Contracts:* "A contract is a promise or a set of promises for the breach of which the law gives a remedy, or the performance of which the law in some way recognizes as a duty." [1] Many of the agreements that we make are not contracts; in other words, they do not create legal rights and duties, and hence will not be enforced by the courts. If A and B make an appointment to go fishing together on a certain day, they have entered into an agreement but not into a contract. There may be a social or even a moral obligation upon each of them to live up to the agreement, but there is no legal duty to do so. Hence, if either fails to keep the appointment, no court will grant legal or equitable relief to the other. But if A says to B, "I will give you $100 cash for your television set if you will let me have possession of it immediately," and B replies, "I accept your offer," A and B have entered into an agreement which creates legal rights and duties. They have made a contract, which the courts will recognize and enforce.

It should be emphasized that a contract is voluntarily and freely entered into, and that the obligations assumed by the parties are voluntarily assumed. The parties are not compelled by law to enter into a particular contract; if they do enter it, whatever rights and duties they have under

[1] American Law Institute (1932), Sec. 1, p. 1.

the contract are derived from their own voluntary agreement. Whether or not a contract results from the negotiation of the parties depends upon the parties themselves. If they fail to meet the essential requirements of a contract, no contract will result from their negotiations. But once they have entered into a contract by their own free act, the courts will interpret and enforce it.

If an agreement is entered into as a result of fraud, misrepresentation, duress, or undue influence, it is unenforceable. The free and genuine assent of both parties is essential to the formation of a contract.

ESSENTIALS OF A CONTRACT

There are four elements essential to every contract. (1) There must be a mutual agreement voluntarily entered into by the parties. (2) The parties must have legal capacity to contract at the time they enter into the agreement. (3) The agreement must be supported by a valid or legal consideration. (4) The subject matter or objectives of the contract must be legal. These four elements must be present in every agreement in order to make it a legally enforceable contract. Indeed, the term *contract* has sometimes been defined directly in terms of these essential requirements. For example, in the case of *Justice v. Lang* [1] the court defined a contract as "a bargain or agreement voluntarily made upon good consideration, between two or more persons capable of contracting, to do, or forbear to do, some lawful act."

Not all contracts have to be in writing to be enforceable by the courts. However, under the Statute of Frauds certain types of contracts must be in writing to be enforceable. Where an agreement belonging to one of these types satisfies the four essentials but is not in writing, a contract exists but it may not be enforced.

These requirements are discussed in detail in Chapters 6–12.

CLASSIFICATION OF CONTRACTS

It has proved useful to classify contracts in various ways on the basis of one characteristic or another. The most common classifications are: (1) formal and informal (or simple) contracts; (2) express and implied contracts; (3) executed and executory contracts; (4) bilateral and unilateral contracts. In addition, some contracts are classified as unenforceable, voidable, or void.

[1] 42 N. Y. 493, 1 Am. R. 576.

FORMAL AND INFORMAL CONTRACTS

A formal contract is one which derives its validity from its form. The most common example is the *contract under seal*. Historically, this type of contract was the earliest to be recognized and enforced by the courts. It was required to be in writing and signed and to bear an affixed seal, i.e. a wafer of wax on which some distinguishing or identifying impression had been made. Nowadays when it is necessary to execute a legal instrument under seal the requirement may be met by making a pen scroll or by merely writing the word "Seal" or the letters "L. S." (for *locus sigilli*, the place of the seal) following the signatures of the signers of the instrument. Even in this form the seal is of far less importance than it was in the past, and in a number of states the efficacy of the seal has been entirely abolished by statute.[1]

A second example of a formal contract is the *recognizance*. A recognizance is an acknowledgment before some court of record or magistrate that one is bound to a certain obligation, such as paying a debt, appearing in court for trial or as a witness, or keeping the peace, subject to the condition that on performance of the specified act the obligation is discharged.

Negotiable instruments are often classified as formal contracts because their existence depends upon their meeting certain formal requirements set out in the Uniform Commercial Code. However, their validity or enforceability does not depend upon their meeting these formal requirements[2]

All other contracts, whether written or oral, are informal or simple contracts.

EXPRESS AND IMPLIED CONTRACTS

A contract is said to be an express contract if the parties to the contract expressly state their intention to contract and the terms of their agreement, either in writing or orally. A contract implied in fact is one in which the intention of the parties and the terms of the contract are not explicitly stated, either in writing or orally, but are implied by the conduct of the parties and the surrounding circumstances. To use a familiar illustration, A telephones her grocer B and says, "Please send me a pound of butter, a dozen eggs, ten pounds of potatoes, and three cans of corn." B says, "Thank you," and hangs up the receiver. Later B delivers the groceries to A. While A never said that she would pay for the groceries, there is an implied promise on her part to pay for them.

---

[1] For further details see below, p. 183.
[2] These points will be expanded in a later section.

EXECUTED AND EXECUTORY CONTRACTS

An executed contract is one that has been fully performed by both parties, so that nothing remains to be done by either party under the terms of the contract. If A goes into B's store, picks up the evening paper, and hands B a nickel, a contract results. The contract is immediately executed, since both parties have duly performed and nothing remains to be done in the future. An executory contract is one that has not yet been performed by either party. Under its terms performance is to take place at some future time. For example, A and B enter into a contract whereby A agrees to sell B his car for $800, and B agrees to buy the car for $800. It is further agreed that A is to deliver the car to B five days later, at which time B will pay A $800 in cash. Since neither party is to perform until a future date, this is an executory contract.

A contract may be partly executed and partly executory; for example, one party may have performed and the other party may not have performed, or either or both may have performed partially.

BILATERAL AND UNILATERAL CONTRACTS

A bilateral contract is one in which the parties exchange reciprocal promises. For example, A promises to sell his house to B for $20,000, and B promises to pay A $20,000 for his house. Here we have an exchange of promises, or, as it is often expressed, a promise for a promise.

In a unilateral contract there is an exchange of a promise for an act. One party promises an act or forbearance in exchange for an act on the part of the other party; in other words, the promisor's offer is so framed as to call for acceptance, not by a return promise, but by the performance of the designated act itself. No contract arises until the second party performs the act. For example, A says to B, "I will pay you $10 if you will repair my radio." If B repairs the radio, a unilateral contract comes into being. The offer of a reward supplies another common example of a unilateral contract. A places in the newspaper an advertisement promising to pay $10 to anyone who finds and returns his lost dog Trixie. B reads the advertisement; the next day he finds the dog and returns her to A. A unilateral contract results, under which A is bound to pay $10 to B.

Most business contracts are bilateral contracts.

UNENFORCEABLE, VOIDABLE, AND VOID CONTRACTS

An unenforceable contract is one that meets the four requirements of a contract but for one reason or another will not be enforced by the courts. One example, already noticed above, is an oral contract which under the Statute of Frauds would have to be in writing to be enforceable. Another is a contract which was valid when it was made but has now been outlawed by the statute of limitations.

A voidable contract is one that has full legal effect as to one of the parties but is not enforceable against the other party against his will. The second party has the option of treating the agreement as valid and subsisting, or of repudiating it. For example, a contract between A, who is of legal age, and B, who is a minor, is valid as to A but voidable as to B.

A so-called void contract is an agreement that has no legal effect because it fails to fulfill one or more of the four essential requirements of a contract. Strictly speaking, the term is a misnomer, since such an agreement never attains the status of a contract. An agreement to commit a crime would fall into this category.

QUASI–CONTRACTS

As we have seen, a contract arises out of a voluntary agreement between the parties, and the obligations arising out of it are consequently self-imposed. In addition to these normal contractual arrangements, we have also in our law what are called quasi-contracts or contracts implied in law. A quasi-contract is not a true contract, for the obligations imposed do not grow out of a voluntary agreement between the parties; instead, they are imposed by law. Under certain circumstances, where the court is of the opinion that in equity and justice the defendant should do a certain thing, it will imply a promise on his part to perform the act. The promise is obviously a fiction, but since it is implied in law the defendant is as fully bound by it as if he had expressly made it.

Quasi-contractual obligations are founded in general upon the doctrine that no one should be permitted to enrich himself unjustly at the expense of another. A typical situation is one in which the plaintiff has performed in good faith some action beneficial to the defendant, under the mistaken notion that a valid contract exists between them, and the defendant then refuses to compensate the plaintiff for the benefit he has enjoyed. Recovery in quasi-contract must be based upon proof by the plaintiff that the defendant was unjustly enriched at the plaintiff's expense. A plaintiff who can prove only that he himself has suffered expense will not be permitted to recover. Moreover, the sum which can be recovered will normally be the reasonable value of the benefits to the defendant, not the price which may be specified in the alleged contract.

The following are examples of quasi-contracts: (1) A delivers goods to B under a contract which is voidable as to B or unenforceable, but not illegal, and B makes use of the goods but refuses to pay A. A can recover in quasi-contract the value of the goods furnished to B. (2) By oral contract A agrees to work for B for two years. Under the Statute of Frauds such a contract is unenforceable if it is not in writing. A works for B for three months, and B refuses to pay him. A may recover in quasi-contract for the reasonable value of his labor for the three months. (3) A mistakenly pays to B money that B is not entitled to. When the error is discovered, B refuses to return the money. A may recover the amount in quasi-contract.

Recovery in quasi-contract is at law, not in equity, even through equitable principles seem to underlie the remedy. It is generally agreed that the existence of quasi-contracts was first recognized by Lord Mansfield in the case of *Moses v. Macferlan* in 1760.[1]

Kalavros v. Deposit Guaranty Bank & Trust Co. et al.
158 So. (2d) 740 (1963)
Supreme Court of Mississippi

These were actions, tried on one record, by decedent's sister-in-law on claim filed in decedent's estate proceedings and by sister-in-law against decedent's executors to establish that decendent had contracted to marry sister-in-law or bequeath her one-half of his estate or money equivalent thereto or to establish that sister-in-law was entitled to compensation on quantum meruit basis for services rendered decedent. The Chancery Court, Hinds County, S. V. Robertson, Jr., Chancellor, rejected claim and dismissed action against the estate, and sister-in-law appealed.

Judgment and decree affirmed.

RODGERS, J. This is action originated from a claim filed by Katherine Kalavros in the estate proceedings of Theo Grillis, deceased, and from a separate suit filed by appellant against the executors of the estate. The claims involve the same issues and were tried on one record.

The testimony and pleadings reveal that Theo Grillis was a native of Greece, born on the historic Island of Patmos, about the year 1896. He imigrated to America while yet a young man and accumulated a large estate in Mississippi. In 1929 he married Themis Kalavros, who was also a native of Greece. This marriage was terminated in 1948 when Themis Grillis lost her life as the result of an automobile accident. In 1950, Theo Grillis and Dora Allred were united in marriage, and from this union, one son, Lucas Theologue Grillis, was born. Theo Grillis and Dora Allred Grillis were divorced in 1952, and the father was awarded custody of his son. In 1956, Theo Grillis suffered a nervous breakdown and was adjudicated incompetent. The son was placed in the Methodist Orphanage. The following March, 1957, Theo Grillis was adjudicated to have been restored to his competency.

In the summer of 1958, Theo Grillis, in company with his son, visited rela-

[1] 2 Burr. 1005.

tives on the Island of Patmos in Greece, for a period of about six months. Katherine Kalavros, sister of Theo Grillis' first wife, came to visit them at the home of Theo Grillis' stepmother, and the evidence reveals overwhelmingly, that Theo Grillis and Katherine Kalavros "fell in love." Theo Grillis asked her to marry him and become the mother of his son. After Theo Grillis returned to Jackson, he wrote many letters and sent many telegrams to Katherine Kalavros indicating his desire to have her come to Jackson for the purpose of marriage. He went to great expense and effort to obtain her admission into the United States, and finally obtained for her a temporary, thirty-day, visa.

In 1961, Katherine Kalavros came to Jackson and lived in the home of Theo Grillis for a period of nine months, from January 16, 1961, to October 15, 1961. Immediately after the arrival of Katherine Kalavros, Theo Grillis filed a petition in chancery court, requesting the court to grant him the custody of his son, setting out that he had arranged for his sister-in-law, Katherine Kalavros, to come to this country from Greece to take care of his home and rear his minor son. The prayer of the petition was granted and petitioner's son, Lucas, went to live with petitioner under the care and tutelage of Katherine Kalavros.

Theo Grillis and Katherine Kalavros were devout members of the Greek Orthodox Catholic Church. The religious belief of the church prohibited a marriage between a brother-in-law and sister-in-law. The parties believed, however, this impediment might be removed under the jurisdiction of the church in the United States. Theo Grillis never succeeded in obtaining the necessary dispensation to permit their marriage in the church. He considered a civil marriage, but before this could be accomplished, he suddenly died October 15, 1961. A short time before his death, he again reaffirmed his intention to marry Katherine Kalavros as soon as he was well.

The will of Theo Grillis, executed July 7, 1958 (before Katherine Kalavros came to America) was probated on October 19, 1961. Thereafter, the claim of Katherine Kalavros was filed and the claimant's separate suit was instituted, as above set out. The suit against the estate sought to establish that Theo Grillis contracted to marry appellant or to make a will bequeathing to her one-half of his estate; or to will her a sum of money equivalent to one-half of his estate; or, in the alternative, that Katherine Kalavros was entitled to compensation for services rendered to decedent Theo Grillis on a quantum meruit basis.

The chancellor, after having heard the testimony, rejected the claim of Katherine Kalavros, and dismissed her suit against the estate of deceased.

Appellant has appealed to this Court, and assigned as error the failure of the trial court to allow her claim as set out in her original bill, and alleges particularly that the finding and decree of the trial court are contrary to the manifest weight of the evidence adduced.

The original bill alleges that the agreement and services rendered and tendered by complainant to Theo Grillis and his minor son, Lucas, and the consideration furnished him whereby she changed her whole way of life in her native land and came to the United States and served him until his death, was with a contract to marry. Moreover, it is stipulated that she carried out her part of the contract or service to the deceased Theo Grillis, and was ready, willing and able to carry out the marriage agreement. The bill of complaint, however, is not based upon a breach of promise to marry for two apparent reasons: (1) It is obvious that the deceased Theo Grillis intended to marry Katherine Kalavros as shown by his statement to complainant just prior to his death. He was making an effort to marry "in the church" at the time of his death. (2) An agreement to marry necessarily implies that the parties will live to perform the contract, and the death of either party before the breach of the contract terminates it.

The chancellor rejected the claim of appellant, holding that the facts in this case fail to establish an irrevocable contract between the parties, which required Theo Grillis to make a will devising one-half of his property to appellant. We are of the opinion that the chancellor was correct in so doing, because the evidence is not "clear, definite and certain," as is required by the rule of law heretofore recognized in cases in this State where the contract is sought to be established to make a will. . . .

The burden was upon appellant to establish her claim as set out in the original bill, and under the facts here presented, we cannot hold the chancellor was manifestly wrong, since the testimony introduced did not clearly establish her claim. . . .

The pleadings and testimony in this case show that appellant did not fully perform the alleged contract to marry Theo Grillis, because, it is said "She was prevented from completing the agreement by the death of the said Theo Grillis," and that "The untimely death of Theo Grillis prevented her compliance" with the marriage contract. The decisions of this State have followed the rule that a partial performance of an oral contract to convey land is not sufficient to take the contract out of the operation of the statute of frauds. . . .

The claim in the instant case is not based upon an alleged verbal contract to pay appellant a certain amount for services performed, as was true in the case of *Stephens v. Duckworth*, 188 Miss. 626, 196 So. 219, but rather an alleged understanding growing out of the circumstances sufficient to establish a contract "to devise unto affiant a one-half of his property."

This Court pointed out in *Wells v. Brooks*, 199 Miss. 327, 24 So. (2d) 533, that an oral promise to transfer property by will or deed, or otherwise, is within the statute of frauds, citing many cases. See also to the same effect, *Collins' Estate v. Dunn*, 233 Miss. 636, 103 So. (2d) 425.

We are of the opinion . . . that the chancellor was correct in disallowing the claim of appellant and holding that the facts and circumstances in this case were not sufficient to establish a contract to devise appellant one-half of his property. The final question for determination in the instant case is whether or not appellant is entitled to recover for services rendered Theo Grillis on a quantum meruit basis.

A recovery for services rendered on a quantum meruit basis is permitted because the law will imply a contract to pay for services where the circumstances are such as to warrant an inference of an understanding by the person performing the work, that the person receiving the services, intends to pay for it. See 58 *Am. Jur., Work and Labor*, § 3, p. 512. See also § 6, supra, p. 514, where it is said: "The general rule is that where services are rendered by one person for another, which are knowingly and voluntarily accepted, without more, the law presumes that such services were given and received in the expectation of being paid for, and implies a promise to pay their reasonable worth.

"A promise to pay for services is implied when they are rendered and received in such circumstances as authorize the party performing to entertain a reasonable expectation of payment for them by the party benefited.

In the case of *Stephens v. Duckworth*, 188 Miss. 626, 196 So. 219, this Court held that although an oral contract to convey the home of a father to his daughter, in return for care during his lifetime, was unenforceable; nevertheless, since there was a contract for services, the daughter could recover a fair value for her services on a quantum meruit basis.

Without belaboring the thesis that there is a presumption of gratuity for mutual services growing out of a family relation existing between persons living in the same household (98 *C. J. S. Work & Labor* § 16, p. 740; 58 *Am. Jur. Work and Labor*, § 11, p. 519), we have reached the conclusion that the testimony shows that the services performed by appellant were not under a contract, expressed or implied, in which it was understood that Theo Grillis would pay Katherine Kalavros for her services, but that her services were gratuitous and rendered in furtherance of the plan of the parties to marry. Death cut these plans short, leaving the estate of Theos Grillis to be administered according to his original plan and will, made before Katherine Kalavros came into his life. Courts may sometimes point out inequities and injustices created by thoughtlessness and carelessness of men, but courts do not have and should not have, power to make contracts where none exists, nor take property from one person, like Robin Hood, and give it to another.

Judgment and decree of the trial court will now be affirmed.

Affirmed.

Boone et al. v. Coe
153 Ky. 233, 154 S. W. 900 (1913)

This was an action in quasi-contract by W. H. Boone and J. T. Coe (plaintiffs) against J. F. Coe (defendant). Defendant's demurrer to plaintiffs' petition was sustained and the petition was dismissed. Plaintiffs appealed. Judgment affirmed.

Defendant was the owner of a large farm in Texas. Plaintiffs were farmers and were living in Kentucky. In the fall of 1909 defendant made a verbal contract with plaintiffs whereby he rented to them his farm in Texas for a period of twelve months, to commence from the date of plaintiffs' arrival at defendant's farm. Following the negotiation of the verbal contract plaintiffs moved their families, livestock, and other property from their home in Kentucky to the farm of defendant in Texas. It took plaintiffs fifty-five days to make the trip. Upon their arrival, on December 6, 1909, defendant refused to allow plaintiffs to occupy the house and premises. As a result, plaintiffs returned to their home in Kentucky. Plaintiffs alleged that, as a result of defendant's repudiation of the contract, they were damaged to the extent of $1,387.80, for which they prayed judgment. Defendant's demurrer to plaintiffs' petition was sustained and the petition was dismissed. Plaintiffs appealed.

CLAY, J. The Statute of Frauds, in Kentucky, provides as follows: "No action shall be brought to charge any person: (6) upon any contract for the sale of real estate, or any lease thereof, for a longer term than one year; nor, (7) upon any agreement which is not to be performed within one year from the making thereof, unless the promise, contract, agreement, representation, assurance, or ratification, or some memorandum or note thereof, be in writing, and signed by the party to be charged therewith, or by his authorized agent."

The question presented is: May the plaintiffs recover for expenses incurred and time lost on the faith of a contract that is unenforceable under the Statute of Frauds?

In the case of *Grumley et al. v. Broyles,* 58 S. W. 924, 22 Ky. 830, it was held that a tenant with a parol agreement for a lease for another year, which was within the Statute of Frauds, could not recover as damages for breach of the contract the loss sustained by him in making preparations for raising a crop. It is the general rule that damages cannot be recovered for violation of a contract within the Statute of Frauds. *Alabama Mineral Land Co. v. Jackson,* 121 Atl. 172, 77 Am. St. Rep. 46; *Dumphy v. Ryan,* 116 U. S. 497, 6 Sup. Ct. 389.

To this general rule there are certain well-recognized exceptions. Thus, it has been held that, where services have been rendered during the life of another, on the promise that the person rendering the service should receive at the death of the person served a legacy, and the contract so made is within the Statute of Frauds, a reasonable compensation may be recovered for the services actually rendered. *Grimes v. Shieve,* 6 T. B. Mon. 557. And, under a contract for personal services within the statute an action may be maintained on a quantum meruit. *Kellman v. Collins,* 9 Bus. 406; *Meyers v. Korb,* 50 S. W. 1108, 21 Ky. 163. The doctrine of these cases proceeds upon the theory that the defendant has actually received some benefits from the acts of part performance; and the law therefore implies a promise to pay. In 29 *Am. and Eng. Ency.* 836, the rule is thus stated: "Although part performance by one of the parties to a contract within the Statute of Frauds will not, at law, entitle such party to recover upon the contract itself, he may nevertheless recover for money paid by him, or property delivered, or services rendered in accordance with and upon the faith of the contract. The law will raise an implied promise on the part of the other party to pay for what has been done in the way of part performance. But this right of recovery is not absolute. . . . It must appear that defendant has actually received, or will receive, some benefit from the acts of part performance. It is immaterial that the plaintiff may have suffered a loss because he is unable to enforce his contract."

In the case under consideration the plaintiffs merely sustained a loss. Defendant received no benefit. Had he received a benefit, the law would imply an obligation to pay therefor. Having received no benefit, no obligation to pay is implied. The statute says that the contract of defendant made with the plaintiff is unenforceable. Defendant therefore had a legal right to decline to carry it out. To require him to pay plaintiffs for losses and expenses incurred on the faith of the contract, without any benefit accruing to him, would, in effect, uphold a contract upon which the statute expressly declares no action shall be brought. Judgment affirmed.

WHAT LAW GOVERNS IN CONTRACT CASES

If the facts and surrounding circumstances do not indicate a contrary intention on the part of the parties, the law of the state or country in which the contract was entered into governs. It is held that the act of entering into a contract in a given state or country indicates an intention that the law of that state or country shall govern as to the validity and interpretation of the contract. This is always the situation where the contract is to be performed in the state or country where the contract was made. On the other hand, if a contract is made in one state or country and by its terms is to be performed in another state or country, the *presumption* is that the law of the state or country where the contract is to be performed will govern. This is a rebuttable presumption, however, and a contrary intention, express or clearly implied, would overcome the presumption.

Breen v. Aetna Casualty and Surety Company
153 Conn. 633, 220 A. (2d) 254 (1966)

This was an action by Donald Breen (plaintiff) against the Aetna Casualty and Surety Company et al. (defendants). Judgment for plaintiff and defendants appealed. Judgment reversed.

This was an action on a motor vehicle liability insurance policy issued by the defendant to the plaintiff, a resident of New York.

In the early morning of January 25, 1959, the plaintiff was operating the station wagon on the Merritt Parkway in Greenwich, Connecticut, when he lost control of the car. It overturned, and Mrs. Breen, his wife, a passenger in the front seat, died almost immediately as a result of the injuries she sustained. The plaintiff was unhurt, no other car was involved, and there was no property damage except to the plaintiff's car.

SHANNON, A.J. Under Connecticut law, interspousal suits are permitted. Under New York law, they are permitted by statute, but under Sec. 167(3) of the New York Insurance Law, *McKinney's Consol. Laws*, c. 28, liability to a spouse is not covered by a motor vehicle liability insurance policy "unless express provision relating specifically thereto is included in the policy." Since there was no such express provision in the policy, Aetna made the claim that there was no coverage of this particular accident.

The New York Court of Appeals has held that (1) Sec. 167(3) of the New York Insurance Law "is mandated into and made a part of every policy of automobile liability insurance issued in * * * [New York]" and (2) the legislature intended that the statute apply "no matter where the accident occurs." As New York law is to govern, the decision of New York's highest court authoritatively determines the construction of the insurance policy in the light of the statute. *Jenkins v. Indemnity Ins. Co., supra*, 152 Conn. 255, 205 A. (2d) 780.

There is error, the judgment is set aside and the case is remanded with direction to render judgment declaring that the policy in question imposes no coverage for an interspousal suit arising in Connecticut and that the Aetna Casualty and Surety Company is neither obliged to defend the civil action brought by the defendant Lloyd W. Anthony, administrator, against the plaintiff nor to pay any judgment which may be rendered therein against the plaintiff.

Mutual
Assent I:
Offer

6

As was stated in Chapter 5, one of the four essentials of a contract is a mutual agreement voluntarily entered into by the parties. To constitute such an agreement there must be (1) an offer and (2) an acceptance of the offer. Offer is discussed in the present chapter, Acceptance in Chapter 7.

DEFINITION OF OFFER

We have seen that a contract is based upon either (1) the exchange of a promise for a promise or (2) the exchange of a promise for an act. An offer is a proposal of the exact terms of such an exchange, made by one party (called the *offeror*) to another (called the *offeree*). In an offer the offeror promises the offeree that he will perform some specified act or forbearance on condition that in exchange the offeree will promise to perform, or will actually perform, some specified act or forbearance. In more technical language the *Restatement of the Law of Contracts* defines an offer as "a promise which is in its terms conditional upon an act, forbearance or return promise being given in exchange for the promise or its performance." [1]

On analysis it will be seen that in an offer the offeror states (1) what he is willing to do and (2) what the offeree must do in exchange. The offeror may lay down in his offer any terms or conditions he wishes, however unreasonable or harsh they may seem. The offeree's protection is the fact that he is under no legal obligation whatsoever to accept the offer if he does not choose to do so. If he does not accept it, there is no contract.

[1] Vol. I, Sec. 24.

86

INTENTION TO CONTRACT

An offer must be made with contractual intent; that is, the offeror must have a serious intent to be bound by the terms of his offer if it is accepted. Similarly, an acceptance must be made with intent on the part of the offeree to be bound by the resulting contract.

It is obviously impossible for the courts to ascertain the private thoughts and intentions of the parties to an alleged contract. The test of the existence of contractual intent is therefore not subjective but objective; that is, it does not ask what the actual intentions of the parties were, but what a reasonably prudent man would have understood them to be in view of the statements and the acts of the parties. Thus, if A makes certain statements to B which a reasonably prudent man would construe as an offer, and if B, relying upon such statements, accepts the offer, A is bound. On the other hand, if a reasonably prudent man would not believe that A was seriously intending to make an offer, then A is not bound. If A makes a statement obviously in jest, or while laboring under great excitement or emotion, B is not privileged to treat it as an offer, even though under different circumstances the same statement might well be construed as an offer. Likewise, if A makes B an offer with contractual intent and B accepts it as a joke, it being obvious to a reasonably prudent man that B has no real intention of accepting the offer, no contract results.

It is often stated that before a contract can result there must be a meeting of minds, and that if the minds of the parties have not met on all the essential terms of the agreement, there is no contract. In determining whether the minds of the parties have met, the courts apply the objective test. As one court expressed it: "If, whatever a man's real intention may be, he so conducts himself that a reasonable man would believe he was assenting to the terms proposed by the other party, and the other party on that belief enters into a contract with him, the man thus conducting himself would be equally bound as if he had intended to agree to the other party's terms." [1]

Davis v. Davis
119 Conn. 194, 175 Atl. 574 (1934)

This was an action by Davis (plaintiff) against Davis (defendant) to annul a marriage. From a judgment dismissing the complaint, plaintiff appealed. There was error, and the case was remanded with direction to enter judgment for plaintiff.

Plaintiff and defendant went on an automobile ride with several other young people. It was a joyous occasion, and to add to the excitement defendant dared plaintiff to marry her. Plaintiff accepted the dare, a license for the marriage

[1] *Hughes v. Smith*, L. R., 6 Q. B., Case 607 (1871).

was procured in New York state, and the ceremony was at once performed by a justice of the peace there. Neither party intended at the time to enter into the marriage status. They returned to their respective homes after the ceremony and have never cohabited. Each was nineteen years old at the time. They were at the time of the marriage and still are residents of Connecticut. Defendant made default of appearance.

The essential claim of plaintiff was that the parties never were in fact married, despite the ceremony which was performed, because of the lack of real consent on the part of either to enter into that relationship.

MALTBIE, C.J. The consent of the parties is everywhere deemed an essential condition to the forming of the marriage relationship. A purported marriage lacking such an element as consent of the parties is, unless some statutory provision governs, void, and needs no decree of the court to make it so. Where two parties go through the form of entering into a contract, both understanding that there is no intent thereby to incur legal obligations, no contract is in fact created.

The statute in this State provides that "whenever from any cause any marriage shall be void, the Superior Court may, upon complaint, pass a decree declaring such marriage void."

"Marriage is that ceremony or process by which the relationship of husband and wife is constituted. The consent of the parties is everywhere deemed an essential condition to the forming of this relation. To this extent it is a contract. But when the relation is constituted, then all its incidents, as well as the rights and duties of the parties resulting from the relation, are absolutely fixed by law. Hence, after a marriage is entered into, the relation becomes a status, and is no longer one resting merely on contract." *Allen v. Allen*, 73 Conn. 54, 46 Atl. 242.

It is an accepted principle that where two parties go through the form of entering into a contract, both understanding that there is no intent thereby to incur legal obligations, no contract is in fact created. 1 *Williston, Contracts,* p. 23; 1 *Page, Contracts,* Par. 80. In a case very similar to the one before us, Chancellor Zabriskie applied this principle to the marriage contract in the following language: "Mere words, without any intention corresponding to them, will not make a marriage or any other civil contract. . . . But the words are the evidence of such intention, and if once exchanged, it must be clearly shown that both parties intended and understood that they were not to have effect. In this case the evidence is clear that no marriage was intended by either party; that it was a mere jest got up in exuberance of spirits to amuse the company and themselves. If this is so there was no marriage." *McClurg v. Terry*, 21 N. J. Eq. 225. It has been said that where, after such a marriage, cohabitation has followed, "the interests of society become involved and in many cases prevent the courts from interfering except in extreme cases." *Warren v. Warren,* 199 N. Y. Supp. 856, 858. We do not, however, in this case need to consider the extent to which that view is sound, for in this instance the parties separated after the ceremony and never have cohabited. Judgment for plaintiff.

Lucy et al. v. Zehmer et al.

84 S. E. (2d) 516, 196 Va. 493 (1954)

This was a suit by W. O. Lucy and J. C. Lucy (complainants) against A. H. Zehmer and Ida S. Zehmer, his wife (defendants). Decree for defendants, and complainants appealed. Reversed.

Complainants instituted this suit to have specific performance of a contract by which it was alleged the defendants had sold to W. O. Lucy for $50,000 a tract of land known as the Ferguson farm, owned by defendant A. H. Zehmer. J. C. Lucy, the other complainant, is a brother of W. O. Lucy, to whom W. O. Lucy transferred a half interest in his alleged purchase.

The instrument sought to be enforced was written by A. H. Zehmer on December 20, 1952, in these words: "We hereby agree to sell to W. O. Lucy the Ferguson farm for $50,000, title satisfactory to buyer," signed by both defendants.

The answer of A. H. Zehmer admitted that at the time mentioned W. O. Lucy offered him $50,000 cash for the farm but that he (Zehmer) considered that the offer was made in jest; that so thinking, and both he and Lucy having had several drinks, he wrote out the "memorandum" quoted above and induced his wife to sign it; that he did not deliver the memorandum to Lucy, but Lucy picked it up, read it, put it in his pocket, and attempted to offer him $5.00 to bind the bargain; that he refused to accept, and, realizing for the first time that Lucy was serious, assured him that he had no intention of selling the farm, and that the whole matter was a joke. Lucy left the premises insisting that he had purchased the farm.

On Monday, December 22nd, Lucy engaged an attorney to examine the title. The attorney reported favorably on December 31st, and on January 2nd Lucy wrote to Zehmer stating that the title was satisfactory and that he was ready to pay the purchase price in cash, and asking when Zehmer would be ready to close the deal. Zehmer replied by letter asserting that he had never agreed or intended to sell the farm. Thereupon complainants brought this suit. The issue is whether the agreement was entered into with contractual intent or was merely a joke.

BUCHANAN, J. In his testimony Zehmer claimed that he "was high as a Georgia pine," and that the transaction "was just a bunch of two doggoned drunks bluffing to see who could talk the biggest and say the most." That claim is inconsistent with his attempt to testify in great detail as to what was said and what was done. . . . The record is convincing that Zehmer was not intoxicated to the extent of being unable to comprehend the nature and consequence of the instrument he executed, and hence that instrument is not to be invalidated on that ground.

The evidence is convincing also that Zehmer wrote two agreements, the first one beginning "I hereby agree to sell"; that Lucy told him that he wanted Zehmer's wife to sign the memorandum; and that Zehmer tore up the first agreement and then made a second one which read "We hereby agree to sell." Both he and his wife signed the second memorandum.

The appearance of the contract; the fact that it was under discussion for forty minutes or more before it was signed; Lucy's objection to the first draft because it was written in the singular and he wanted Mrs. Zehmer to sign it also; the rewriting to meet that objection and the signing by Mrs. Zehmer; the discussion of what was to be included in the sale; the provision for examination of the title; the completeness of the instrument that was executed; the taking possession of it by Lucy with no request or suggestion by either of the defendants that he give it back, are facts which furnish persuasive evidence that the execution of the contract was a serious business transaction rather than a casual, jesting matter, as defendants now contend.

In the field of contracts, as generally elsewhere, "We must look to the outward expression of a person as manifesting his intention rather than his secret or unexpressed intention. The law imputes to a person an intention corresponding to the reasonable meaning of his words and acts." *First Nat. Exchange Bank of Roanoke v. Roanoke Oil Co.*, 169 Va. 99, 192 S. E. 764.

The mental assent of the parties is not requisite for a formation of a contract. If the words or other acts of one of the parties have but one reasonable meaning, his undisclosed intention is immaterial except where an unreasonable meaning which he attaches to his manifestations is known to the other party.

An agreement or mutual assent is of course essential to a valid contract but the law imputes to a person an intention corresponding to the reasonable meaning of his words and acts. So a person cannot set up that he was merely jesting when his conduct and words would warrant a reasonable person in believing that he intended a real agreement. Reversed.

TERMS OF OFFER MUST BE REASONABLY CLEAR

The terms of the offer must be sufficiently clear to indicate to the offeree with *reasonable* certainty the nature of the proposition made to him. Absolute certainty is not required. If the offer is vague and uncertain as to price, compensation, quantities, property involved, time of performance, place of performance, or the like, even though the offeree indicates that he accepts the offer it may be impossible to establish in a court of law that there was an actual agreement or meeting of minds on all the essential terms of the alleged contract. It is often said that if the parties fail to make a contract for themselves, the court will not make one for them. It is therefore of prime importance, in attempting to negotiate a contract for oneself or one's principal, to make sure that the contract contains the desired terms definitely stated.

Trouble often occurs where A has offered to pay B "a fair price" or "a fair share of the profits," or to give "reasonable recognition" to B's efforts on behalf of A. If B accepts such an offer, it is evident that the terms of the alleged contract are dangerously vague and indefinite. Whether the court will find a contract in such cases depends upon the nature of the agreement, the subject matter of the contract, the usages of the trade,[1] and the ease of determining what is "a fair price," "a fair share of the profits," or "reasonable recognition." For example, if the price of the goods involved in the transaction can be readily determined in the open market, the court will hold that there is a contract. But if prices and profits cannot be related to current market conditions, and if there is no record of previous dealings between the parties to serve as a yardstick, the court will hold that there is no contract.

In some cases where the terms are too vague and indefinite to allow recovery on the alleged contract, the plaintiff may recover in quasi-contract if he can show that the defendant has been unjustly enriched at the plaintiff's expense. A judgment in quasi-contract would be for the reasonable value of the services or property involved, not for the alleged contract price.

In cases where the agreement specifies the price or amount to be paid but fails to state whether credit is to be given, the law implies that the terms are cash.

UNIFORM COMMERCIAL CODE

Secs. 2–204, 2–305, and 2–306 of the Uniform Commercial Code state the requisites of a valid contract to sell goods, and elsewhere the Code explains rights and duties of parties in a contract to sell goods. They are elaborated upon later in Part V, Sales.

Varney v. Ditmars
111 N. E. 822, 217 N. Y. 223 (1916)

This was an action by Varney (plaintiff) against Ditmars (defendant) for breach of an alleged contract. The complaint was dismissed, and plaintiff appealed. Judgment affirmed.

Plaintiff was employed by defendant at a salary of $35 per week. Defendant said to him: "I'm going to give you $5.00 more per week if you will continue the way you have been and the first of next January I will give you a fair share of my profits." Plaintiff continued in defendant's employ and was paid $40 per week until he was discharged later in the year for alleged disloyalty and insubordination. Defendant denied that he had any agreement with plaintiff. Plaintiff sought to recover for services from just prior to the time of the alleged discharge until the following January 1st at the rate of $40 per week and also for a fair and reasonable share of the net profits of the defendant's business.

CHASE, J. The statement alleged to have been made by the defendant about giving the plaintiff a fair share of his profits is vague, indefinite and uncertain,

[1] See the Uniform Commercial Code Sec. 1–205 (2) in the Appendix.

and the amount cannot be computed from anything that was said by the parties or by reference to any document, paper or other transaction. The minds of the parties never met upon any particular share of the defendant's profits to be given the employees or upon any plan by which such share could be computed or determined. The contract so far as it related to the special promise or inducement was never consummated. It was left subject to the will of the defendant or for further negotiation.

The question whether the words "fair" and "reasonable" have a definite and enforceable meaning when used in business transactions is dependent upon the intention of the parties in the use of such words and upon the subject-matter to which they refer. In the cases of merchandising and in the purchase and sale of chattels the parties may use the words "fair and reasonable value" as synonymous with "market value." A promise to pay the fair market value of goods may be inferred from what is expressly agreed by the parties. The fair, reasonable or market value of goods can be shown by direct testimony of those competent to give such testimony. The competency to speak grows out of experience and knowledge. The testimony of such witnesses does not rest upon conjecture.

In the case of a contract for the sale of goods or for hire without a fixed price or consideration being named, it will be presumed that a reasonable price or consideration is intended and the person who enters into such a contract for goods or services is liable thereafter as on an implied contract. Such contracts are common, and when there is nothing therein to limit or prevent an implication as to the price, they are, so far as the terms of the contract are concerned, binding obligations. The contract in question, so far as it relates to a share of the defendant's profits, is not only uncertain but it is necessarily affected by so many other facts that are in themselves indefinite and uncertain that the intention of the parties is pure conjecture. A fair share of the defendant's profits may be any amount from a nominal sum to a material part according to the particular views of the person whose guess is considered. Such an executory contract must rest for performance upon the honor and good faith of the parties making it. The courts cannot aid parties in such a case when they are unable or unwilling to agree upon the terms of their own proposed contract. It is elementary in the law that, for the validity of a contract, the promise, or the agreement, of the parties to it must be certain and explicit and that their full intention may be ascertained to a reasonable degree of certainty. Their agreement must be neither vague nor indefinite, and, if thus defective, parol proof cannot be resorted to. *United Press v. New York Press Co.*, 164 N. Y. 406.

In *Butts v. Kemmerer*, 218 Pa. St. 242, the plaintiff was in the employ of the defendant at a regular salary and the defendant promised him that if there were any profits in the business he would divide them with the plaintiff "upon a very liberal basis." The action was brought to recover a part of the profits of the business and the court held that the contract was never made complete and that there was no standard by which to measure the degree of liberality with which the defendant should regard the plaintiff.

The rule stated from the United Press case does not prevent a recovery upon quantum meruit in case one party to an alleged contract has performed in reliance upon the terms thereof, vague, indefinite and uncertain though they are. In such case the law will presume a promise to pay the reasonable value of the services. Judge Gray, who wrote the opinion in the United Press case, said: "I entertain no doubt that, where work has been done, or articles have been furnished, a recovery may be based upon quantum meruit, or quantum valebat; but where a contract is of an executory character and requires performance over a future period of time, as here, and it is silent as to the price which is to be paid to the plaintiff during its term, I do not think that it possesses binding force. . . ."

The amount that the plaintiff could recover, therefore, if any, based upon the agreement to pay $40 per week would be very small, and he did not present to the court facts from which it could be computed. His employment by the defendant was conditional upon his continuing the way he had been working, getting the defendant out of his trouble and getting certain unenumerated jobs that had been in the office three years, started. There was nothing in the contract specifying the length of service except as stated. It was not an unqualified agreement to continue the plaintiff in his service until the first of January, and it does not appear whether or not the special conditions upon which the contract was made had been performed. I do not think that on the testimony as it appears before us it was error to refuse to leave to the jury the question whether the plaintiff was entitled to recover anything at the rate of $40 per week. The judgment should be affirmed, with costs.

Wilhelm Lubrication Co. v. Brattrud
197 Minn. 626, 268 N. W. 634 (1936)

This was an action by Wilhelm Lubrication Co. (plaintiff) against one Brattrud (defendant) for breach of an alleged contract for failure to accept delivery of 11,500 gallons of lubricating oil. Judgment for plaintiff, and defendant appealed. Reversed and remanded.

On January 24, 1934, plaintiff and defendant entered into an agreement which read as follows:

"The above seller hereby sells and agrees to hold in its storage for the purchaser, and the above purchaser hereby buys, the merchandise described below, which shall be shipped to purchaser at Waseka, Minn., on August 1, 1934, unless ordered sooner.

Quantity	Description	Per Gallon
5000 gals.	Worthmore motor oil SAE 10-70	21–31¢
3000 gals.	Betterlube motor oil SAE 10-70	26–36¢
2000 gals.	Costal motor oil SAE 10-70	18.5–28.5¢
1500 gals.	Penzalube motor oil	34–44¢

As per price list 34 attached."

Approximately three weeks after the making of the above agreement, defendant repudiated the same. Plaintiff treated the contract as breached, and brought this action for damages.

The principal question involved is whether or not the terms of the agreement were so indefinite as to be unenforceable.

DEVANEY, C.J. In considering the question as to whether or not the terms of the agreement were so indefinite as to be unenforceable it is necessary to explore the meaning of the terms used in the contract. Defendant, Brattrud, agreed to take a total of 11,500 gallons of oil of the different brands listed. The technical term SAE 10–70 opposite each item in the contract signifies seven weights of oil. The lightest of these groups is designated SAE 10; the heaviest SAE 70; the intervening ones are 20, 30, 40, 50, 60. The price varies with the weight. Thus, for example, under this contract, defendant agreed to take 5000 gallons of "Worthmore motor oil" of any weight he should choose from 10 to 70. The price for SAE 10 was 21¢ per gallon, and the price for SAE 70 was 31¢ per gallon. The same applies to the other brands of oil that defendant agreed to take. The total quantity of each brand of oil purchased was definite. Defendant, however, had the right under the contract to specify any weight of oil he wished within the weights listed. The weight controlled the price, the price of each weight being definite. But until the defendant chose a particular weight, the price he was obligated to pay under the contract was not ascertained. Nor was there any agreement as to how many gallons of each weight defendant was to take. As to these matters there had been no meeting of minds or expression of mutual assent of the parties to the contract. There was and could be no agreement as to these elements until the defendant indicated his wants within the specified limits of the alleged contract. This indefiniteness and uncertainty in the contract is, in our opinion, fatal to plaintiff's cause of action. The subject matter of a contract of sale must be definite as to quantity and price. The reason for this requirement is obvious when we consider the question of damages. As the contract now stands with respect to the oil defendant agreed to take, the application of any measure of damages, which in case of breach of such contract must be based partly on the contract price, is impossible. Here the quantity of each brand to be taken and the contract price thereof cannot be determined until the defendant places an order. This was never done. The agreement was repudiated before any order was placed. The court or jury cannot be allowed to speculate as to the measure of damages, and there is no sound authority for taking an average or arbitrary price as the contract price in a case of this kind. This, in effect, would be inserting a new term in the contract, thereby remaking the agreement for the parties, which is beyond the power of a court or jury. *Wheeling Steel & Iron Co. v. Evans*, 97 Md. 305, 55 Atl. 373. Reversed and remanded.

[NOTE: Certain portions of the agreement, which involve other points of law, are not included in this abstract.]

INVITATION TO DEAL OR NEGOTIATE

In the making of a contract there are often a number of preliminary negotiations or dealings before either party finally makes a firm offer. These preliminary dealings are commonly referred to as "dickering." Each party is trying to feel out the other party and to induce him to make an offer, for there is usually an advantage in getting the other party to commit himself first. In such situations both parties must be on their guard against interpreting as an offer what is merely a preliminary statement. A and B may be negotiating with each other for the sale of A's house to B. In their preliminary negotiations B may ask A how much he will take for the house. If A replies, "Well, I have always said that I would not take less than $15,000 for the house," A has not made an offer to B to sell him the house for $15,000. His statement is merely an *invitation to deal or negotiate*. He is really inviting B to make him an offer.

Just where dickering ends and a firm offer comes into being is often difficult to determine. Borderline situations frequently wind up in the courts, where each must be decided upon its merits in the light of the facts, the intentions of the parties, and the usages and customs of the trade or business. However, certain general rules have become established.

ADVERTISEMENTS OF GOODS

The general rule is that advertisements of goods and services in newspapers and magazines, over the radio or on television, or in circulars, mail-order catalogs, and trade letters are not offers but merely invitations to deal, intended to elicit offers from others. For example, the A company advertises in the newspaper a sale of men's suits at $50. If B enters the store, states that he has come to accept the offer made in the advertisement, and demands a suit at the price quoted, no contract results. Actually, B is the offeror, and a contract will not arise until the store accepts his offer. If the store does not have a suit in B's size, or if for some reason it does not wish to deal with him, it may reject his offer, and he would have no cause of action against the store.

The same rule applies to quotations of prices in response to inquiries and to estimates of the cost of performing particular jobs.

It should be understood that firm offers can be made by any of the above-mentioned methods if there is clear evidence that the statements are intended and understood by the parties to be offers.

BIDS ON CONSTRUCTION WORK

An advertisement for bids on construction work is generally held to be an invitation to deal. Any bids submitted are offers, and the bidders are offerors. However, if the advertisement expressly states that the contract will be let to the lowest bidder without reservation, the advertisement is treated as a firm offer, and the bidder who submits the lowest bid is entitled to the contract.

AUCTION SALES

In the sale of property by auction, the statements of the auctioneer (who is the agent of the seller or vendor) are merely invitations for offers (bids) from the persons present at the sale. The bidders are the offerors, and no sale is made until the fall of the auctioneer's hammer, which indicates his acceptance of one of the offers. The general rule is that the auctioneer can withdraw an article from sale at any time before the hammer falls; in other words, he is permitted, like any other offeree, to reject any and all offers made to him. But if the sale has been announced or advertised to be "without reserve," the auctioneer is not permitted to withdraw the property after a bid has been made.

A bidder may always withdraw a bid before the hammer has fallen.[1]

Carlill v. Carbolic Smoke Ball Company
1 Q. B. 256 (1893)

This was an appeal from a decision of Hawkins, J.

The defendants, who were the proprietors and vendors of a medical preparation called "The Carbolic Smoke Ball," inserted in the *Pall Mall Gazette* of November 13, 1891, and in other newspapers, the following advertisement: "100l. reward will be paid by the Carbolic Smoke Ball Company to any person who contracts the increasing epidemic influenza, colds, or any disease caused by taking cold, after having used the ball three times daily for two weeks according to the printed directions supplied with each ball. 1000l. is deposited with the Alliance Bank, Regent Street, shewing our sincerity in the matter."

The plaintiff, a lady, on the faith of this advertisement, bought one of the balls at a chemist's, and used it as directed, three times a day, from November 20, 1891, to January 17, 1892, when she was attacked by influenza. Hawkins, J., held that she was entitled to recover the 100l. The defendants appealed.

. . . The limitation "during the prevalence of the epidemic" is inadmissible, for the advertisement applies to colds as well as influenza. The limitation "during use" is excluded by the language "after having used." The third is, "within a reasonable time," and that is probably what was intended; but it cannot be deduced from the words; so the fair result is that there was no legal contract at all.

. . . It is contended that it is not binding. In the first place, it is said that it is not made with anybody in particular. Now that point is common to the words of this advertisement and to the words of all other advertisements

---

[1] The Uniform Commercial Code Sec. 2–328 governs sale of goods by auction.

offering rewards. They are offers to anybody who performs the conditions named in the advertisement, and anybody who does perform the condition accepts the offer. In point of law this advertisement is an offer to pay 100*l.* to anybody who will perform these conditions, and the performance of the conditions is the acceptance of the offer. That rests upon a string of authorities, the earliest of which is *Williams v. Carwardine*, which has been followed by many other decisions upon advertisements offering rewards.

But then it is said, "Supposing that the performance of the conditions is an acceptance of the offer, that acceptance ought to have been notified." Unquestionably, as a general proposition, when an offer is made, it is necessary in order to make a binding contract, not only that it should be accepted, but that the acceptance should be notified. But is that so in cases of this kind. I apprehend that they are an exception to that rule, or, if not an exception, they are open to the observation that the notification of the acceptance need not precede the performance. This offer is a continuing offer. It was never revoked, and if notice of acceptance is required—which I doubt very much, for I rather think the true view is that which was expressed and explained by Lord Blackburn in the case of *Brogden v. Metropolitan Ry. Co.*—if notice of acceptance is required, the person who makes the offer gets the notice of acceptance contemporaneously with his notice of the performance of the condition. If he gets notice of the acceptance before his offer is revoked, that in principle is all you want. I, however, think that the true view, in a case of this kind, is that the person who makes the offer shows by his language and from the nature of the transaction that he does not expect and does not require notice of the acceptance apart from notice of the performance.

We, therefore, find here all the elements which are necessary to form a binding contract enforceable in point of law. Affirmed.

Lovett v. Frederick Loesser & Co.
207 N. Y. Supp. 735, 123 Misc. Rep. 81 (1924)

This was an action by Charles H. Lovett (plaintiff) against Frederick Loesser & Co. (defendant) to recover damages for breach of an alleged contract. Defendant filed a motion for judgment on the pleadings, dismissing the complaint on the ground that it does not state facts sufficient to constitute a cause of action. Motion granted.

The complaint alleged that on September 19, 1924, the defendant advertised in a New York newspaper that it would sell, deliver, and install certain standard makes of radio receivers at 25 to 50 per cent off the advertised list prices. Among the sets thus advertised were De Forest D-12 reflex radiophone receiving sets. The complaint further alleged that on September 20, 1924, plaintiff attempted to buy two of the De Forest sets on the terms and conditions named in defendant's advertisement, but that defendant repudiated its offer to sell; that thereupon on September 22nd plaintiff unconditionally accepted defendant's offer and tendered his certified check for the amount of the list price of the De Forest sets, less 25 per cent.

The complaint demanded judgment for the damages suffered by plaintiff by reason of the alleged breach of defendant's contract to sell said sets.

Plaintiff's theory is that the offer of defendant contained in the advertisement ripened into a contract by his acceptance thereof.

SPIEGELBERG, J. I am of opinion that the plaintiff sets forth no cause of action. The defendant's advertisement is nothing but an invitation to enter into negotiations, and is not an offer which may be turned into a contract by a person who signifies his intention to purchase some of the articles mentioned in the advertisement. In *Georgian Company v. Bloom*, 27 Ga. App. 468, 108 S. E. 813, the court says: "A general advertisement in a newspaper for the sale of an indefinite quantity of goods is a mere invitation to enter into a bargain, rather than an offer."

"Frequently negotiations for a contract are begun between parties by general expressions of willingness to enter into a bargain upon stated terms and yet the natural construction of the words and conduct of the parties is rather that they were inviting offers, or suggesting the terms of a possible future bargain, than making positive offers. Especially is this likely to be true when the words in question are in the form of an advertisement. Thus, if goods are advertised for sale at a certain price, it is not an offer, and no contract is formed by the statement of an intending purchaser that he will take a specified quantity of the goods at that price. The construction is rather favored that such an advertisement is a mere invitation to enter into a bargain rather than an offer." 1 Williston, *Cont.* 32, 33. To the same effect see 13 C. J. 289.

As stated by Professor Williston (*supra,* at p. 35), a positive offer may be made by an advertisement or general notice, and the only general test is the inquiry whether the facts show that some performance was promised in positive terms in return for something requested. But this is not the situation here. This is the ordinary case of an advertisement which extends an invitation to all persons that the advertiser is ready to receive offers for the goods upon the terms stated.

In re Hilliard's Estate

Appeal of George S. Lipman

117 A. (2d) 728, 383 Pa. 63 (1955)

This was a petition by George S. Lipman (complainant) against the Estate of Mary M. J. Hilliard (defendant) for specific performance of an alleged contract. Decree for defendant, and complainant appealed. Decree affirmed.

Mary M. J. Hilliard, the deceased, was the owner of premises No. 204 South Homestead Avenue, Pittsburgh. Under her will she named the Union National Bank of Pittsburgh and Thomas A. Robinson executors, giving them full power of sale of the real estate. On July 2, 1954, C. W. Doyle, an employee in the real estate division of the corporate fiduciary, mailed a circular letter to twenty-eight individuals, including seventeen real estate brokers. The letter advised each of the addressees that the property in question was then available for purchase. The premises were described and the tax assessment was given. The letter stated: "The property is being placed on the market at an asking price of $60,000, subject to a reasonable offer. All offers are subject to the approval of the co-executors. . . ." The letter also stated: "We will recognize as the broker in any transaction that person who first submits an offer on behalf of a purchaser, provided said offer is acceptable to the co-executors, a satisfactory agreement of sale executed, and the sale closed in accordance with the terms of the agreement. We will be glad to discuss the sale of this property with you at any time at your convenience."

C. L. Totten Company, real estate brokers, received one of the letters on July 6, 1954. F. X. Totten of that company came to the bank, met Ralph F. Torrence, its real estate officer, and stated that George S. Lipman, his client, had authorized him to pay $2,000 as hand money and to inform the bank that Lipman "was ready to buy the property for $60,000 cash, as was asked." The real estate officer testified, without contradiction: "I told [the broker] that I would take that offer with his check; that it was in accordance with the terms of our letter, subject to approval by the co-executors, including our Trust Investment Committee; that letters of a similar nature had been written to many real estate agents, and that as a fiduciary I had to give them a chance to see what they would do; and that I would present that offer to the Trust Investment Committee and the co-executor, and that it would probably be a while before I would have the answer."

The check was accepted and deposited in the escrow account of the bank. On July 8, 1954, the real estate officer wrote to the broker to acknowledge the receipt of the check, and stated, among other things: "May I advise that we have deposited this check with the understanding that such action does not denote acceptance of this offer. . . ."

Thereafter the co-fiduciary received a substantially higher offer for the property from another broker. This fact was communicated to the C. L. Totten Company with an inquiry whether Dr. Lipman would increase his offer. The bank was informed by Mr. Totten that his client refused to increase the offer. On July 26, 1954, the bank advised the broker by letter that the co-executors rejected Dr. Lipman's offer. This suit was then filed asking for a decree of specific performance of the alleged contract. The issue was whether or not a contract resulted from the foregoing negotiations.

STEARNE, J. Appellant contends that under the circular letter of July 2, 1954, C. L. Totten Company became the agent of the co-fiduciaries of the estate, and that the acceptance by the agent of the $2,000 deposit resulted in the formation of an enforceable agreement between the co-fiduciaries of the estate and the appellant for the sale of the premises at $60,000. The circular letter, however, unequivocally stipulated that all offers were subject to the approval of the co-executors, and that no broker would be recognized unless offers submitted were acceptable to the co-executors and a satisfactory agreement of sale executed. Therefore, the circular letter merely constituted an invitation to bid or negotiate. Since appellant's offer was not accepted by the co-executors, and no agreement of sale executed, no contract was ever consummated. *Upsal Street Realty Co. v. Rubin*, 326 Pa. 327, 192 A. 481. An offer is distinguishable from preliminary negotiations for a contract. *Restatement, Contracts*, sections 25 and 26. Decree affirmed.

Moulton v. Kershaw and Another
59 Wis. 316, 18 N. W. 172 (1884)

This was an action by J. H. Moulton (plaintiff) against C. J. Kershaw and another (defendants). The defendants demurred to the complaint, and from an order overruling their demurrer defendants appealed. Reversed and remanded.

The complaint alleged that defendants were dealers in salt in Milwaukee; that plaintiff was a dealer in salt in La Crosse, and accustomed to buy in large quantities, which fact was known to defendants; that on September 19, 1882, defendants wrote plaintiff the following letter: "Dear Sir: In consequence of a rupture in the salt trade, we are authorized to offer Michigan fine salt, in full carload lots of 80 to 95 bbls., delivered at your city, 85¢ per bbl. to be shipped per C. & N. W. R. R. Co. only. At this price it is a bargain, as the price in general remains unchanged. Shall be pleased to receive your order."

Plaintiff replied to this letter on September 20 by sending the following telegram: "Your letter of yesterday received. You may ship me two thousand (2,000) barrels Michigan fine salt, as offered in your letter. Answer."

The complaint further alleged that "On September 21, 1882, defendants attempted to withdraw said offer contained in their letter of September 19, 1882. Plaintiff thereupon demanded of defendants the delivery to him of 2,000 barrels of Michigan fine salt, in accordance with the terms of said offer, accepted by plaintiff as aforesaid, and offered to pay them therefor in accordance with said terms. . . . Nevertheless, defendants utterly refused to deliver the same, or any part thereof, by reason whereof plaintiff sustained damages to the amount of eight hundred dollars."

The counsel for plaintiff claimed that the letter of defendants was an offer to sell to plaintiff, on the terms mentioned, any reasonable quantity of Michigan fine salt that he might see fit to order, not less than one carload. The counsel for defendants claimed that the letter was not an offer to sell any specific quantity of salt, but simply a letter such as a businessman would send out to customers or those with whom he desired to trade, soliciting their patronage.

The only question presented is whether defendants' letter, and the telegram sent by plaintiff in reply thereto, constituted a contract for the sale of 2,000 barrels of Michigan fine salt by defendants to plaintiff at the price named in the letter.

TAYLOR, J. As the only communications between the parties, upon which a contract can be predicated, are the letter and the reply of the respondent [Moulton], we must look to them, and nothing else, in order to determine whether there was a contract in fact. We are not at liberty to help out the written contract, if there be one, by adding by parol evidence additional facts to help out the writing so as to make out a contract not expressed therein. . . . Rather than introduce an element of uncertainty into the contract, we deem it much more reasonable to construe the letter as a simple notice to those dealing in salt that the appellants were in a condition to supply that article for the price named, and requesting the person to whom it was addressed to deal with them. This case is one where it is eminently proper to heed the injunction of Justice Fuller in the opinion in *Lyman v. Robinson*, 14 Allen, 254: "That care should always be taken not to construe as an agreement letters which the parties intended only as preliminary negotiations."

We hold that the letter of the appellants in this case was not an offer. If the letter had said to the respondent we will sell you all the Michigan fine salt you will order, at the price and on the terms named, then it is undoubtedly the law that the appellants would have been bound to deliver any reasonable amount the appellant might have ordered, possibly any amount, or make good their default in damages. . . . We, however, place our opinion upon the language of the letter of the appellants, and hold that it cannot be fairly construed into an offer to sell the respondent any quantity of salt he might order, nor any reasonable amount he might see fit to order. The language is not such as a businessman would use in making an offer to sell to an individual a definite amount of property. The word "sell" is not used. They say, "We are authorized to offer Michigan fine salt," etc., and volunteer an opinion that at the terms stated it is a bargain. They do not say, we offer to sell to you. They use general language proper to be addressed generally to those who were interested in the salt trade. It is clearly in the nature of an advertisement or business circular, to attract the attention of those interested in that business to the fact that good bargains in salt could be had by applying to them, and not as an offer by which they were to be bound, if accepted, for any amount the persons to whom it was addressed might see fit to order. We think the complaint fails to show any contract between the parties.

Berkeley Unified School District v. James I. Barnes Construction Co.

112 F. Supp. 396 (1953)

This was an action by the Berkeley Unified School District of Alameda County (plaintiff) against the James I. Barnes Construction Co. and the Seaboard Surety Co. (defendants) for breach of an alleged contract. Judgment for plaintiff.

Plaintiff, by advertisement in a newspaper, invited the submission of bids for the construction of two public school buildings in Berkeley, California. This invitation prescribed the following requirements for all bids: (1) bids could be submitted only upon "bid forms" prepared by plaintiff; (2) each bid was required to be accompanied by a bid bond (drafted by plaintiff) and a cashier's check or certified check in the amount of $25,000; (3) bids were required to be made in accordance with a designated set of plans and specifications; (4) minimum wage standards were specified for labor to be employed on the project to which the bid applied.

Defendant contractor submitted a bid, offering to construct the school buildings for the sum of $1,377,700. This bid was in accordance with the requirements set out in the advertisement for bids and was accompanied by a certified check for $25,000 and the required bid bond, executed by defendants, the contractor as principal and the surety company as surety. The bid itself was a mimeographed form, which had been prepared by plaintiff, containing blanks to be filled in by the bidder.

Thereafter, plaintiff opened all sealed bids which had been submitted, determined that the bid of defendant was the lowest responsible bid, and passed a resolution accepting such bid and awarding the contract to defendant. Plaintiff then notified defendant construction company that it had been awarded the contract and tendered, for execution, a formal contract embodying all the terms specified in the advertisement for bids and the bid submitted by the defendant. Defendant refused to execute the tendered contract or to furnish performance bonds as required by the invitation for bids by law. Subsequently, plaintiff again advertised for sealed bids to be submitted for the proposed construction. From the bids submitted in response to this second advertisement, that of a firm called Moore & Roberts, Inc., was determined to be the lowest responsible bid and the contract was awarded to that firm. Moore & Roberts, Inc. then executed a formal contract with plaintiff. The bid of Moore & Roberts, Inc. exceeded that of defendant contractor, and because of this fact plaintiff alleged damages. Defendants contended that the complaint failed to state a cause for which relief could be granted, since the parties were not to be bound until the formal contract was executed by the parties.

CARTER, D.J. The general rule is that where a public body advertises for bids, a good and binding contract is formed when the public body, acting by responsible officers, accept a written bid of a bidder. However, the defendant contractor contends that it was not within the contemplation of the parties that a contract should be formed until the execution of the formal document referred to in the advertisement for bids and the bid itself. It is true that parties to an agreement may make its reduction to a formal writing and the execution of such writing a condition precedent to its effectiveness notwithstanding complete agreement to all its terms. However, the general rule is that though the parties contemplate the ultimate execution of a more formal writing, the acceptance of a bid or offer results in a binding contract when none of the material terms remain unsettled or require future determination.

No question is raised as to the lack of agreement between the parties as to any material provision of the contract. The only question is as to whether or not the execution of the formal document was a condition precedent to the formation of the contract. Courts are disinclined to construe the stipulations of a contract as condition precedent unless so compelled by language plainly expressed. *San Diego Const. Co. v. Mannix*, 175 Cal. 548, 166 P. 325. Not only does the language of the bid state that the bidder has "examined the form of contract which he will be required to sign," but it also states that if the bidder is awarded the contract he "will execute the contract for this work and perform all the terms, covenants, and conditions of said contract. . . ." Thus there is a clear promise in the bid to perform the construction if the contract is awarded. The promise "to execute a contract" under the circumstances is no more than a promise to sign the formal document which would contain all of the terms and conditions previously agreed to by the parties.

The construction contended for by the defendant contractor would leave a bidder whose competitive bid has been accepted by a public corporation free to determine, after such acceptance, whether he would revoke his bid or not. The view is almost uniform that a bid submitted to a municipal corporation in response to an advertisement constitutes an irrevocable offer. Since defendant contractor's bid constituted an irrevocable offer to the school district, all that was required to form a contract was a valid acceptance. The governing board of a school district determined that the defendant contractor had submitted the lowest responsible bid and accepted that bid by a resolution. No other limitation existing as to the power of that board to make a contract, that resolution, when communicated to the defendant contractor, was effective to accept the bid and to form a contract. Judgment for plaintiff.

COMMUNICATION OF OFFER

A mere intention to make an offer is not an offer. To be effective, an offer must be communicated to the offeree. If A writes a letter to B offering to sell his house to B for $20,000, and then decides not to mail the letter, no offer has been made to B. If he mails the letter and it is lost in the mail, so that the offer never reaches B, there is again no offer.

The communication of the offer must be made by the offeror or by his agent. A third party cannot make proper communication of offer. For example, A happens to mention to B that he has made up his mind to offer C $200 for his horse. B is not A's agent. B tells C what A has told him, and C writes to A and states that he accepts A's offer. A would not be bound, since there was not a proper communication of his offer.

Offers may be made or communicated by the spoken word, by letter, by telegram, by handbills, by advertisement in a newspaper or magazine, by announcement over the radio or on television, or by an act or gesture. Any of these methods may be used by either the offeror or his agent.

The question whether there has been proper communication of offer often arises in connection with insurance policies, bills of lading, warehouse receipts, railway or steamship tickets, baggage checks, and parking-lot checks. There is lack of uniformity in the decisions of the courts concerning these types of cases. Most courts, however, hold that if the legal instrument involved purports to be a contract, e.g. an insurance policy, a bill of lading, a warehouse receipt, or an express receipt, and if the offeree accepts the instrument, even though he does not read it, there has been sufficient communication of the offer and the offeree is bound thereby. In such cases the law places upon the offeree the duty to read, since he knows or should know that he is becoming a party to a contract. The decisions are not uniform in regard to railway and steamship tickets. While many courts hold that such tickets are contracts and that the purchaser is bound by any terms printed on them, other courts have held that they are mere tokens or receipts. It is usually held that a baggage-room check or a parking-lot ticket is looked upon by the holder (bailor) as an identification check only, and not as evidence of a contract which probably attempts to place a limit upon the extent of the liability of the check-room or parking lot (bailee). In such cases the courts place upon the bailee the responsibility and duty of calling the attention of the bailor to any terms and conditions under which the bailee accepts possession of the property. Such terms must be communicated.

Mayor, etc., of Jersey City v. Town of Harrison et al.
72 N. J. L. 185, 62 Atl. 765 (1905)

This was an action by the Mayor and Aldermen of Jersey City (plaintiff) against the town of Harrison (defendant) to enforce an alleged contract. Judgment for defendant, and plaintiff brought error. Judgment affirmed.

On July 7, 1903, the following resolution was adopted by the town council of Harrison: "Resolved, that the president of the common council and the town clerk of the said town be, and they are hereby, authorized to execute on behalf of the said town, and in common with the municipal authorities of Jersey City, for a new water supply for the said town to be furnished by the said Jersey City on the same terms and conditions and for a similar period of time as are contained in a certain contract made on the 31st day of July, 1885, between the mayor and aldermen of Jersey City and the said town of Harrison. . . ." This resolution was adopted by a unanimous vote of the town council of Harrison. But there was nothing in the record to show that the council directed that the resolution should be transmitted to Jersey City, or gave anyone authority to present the resolution to Jersey City for its action thereon. The authorities of Jersey City, in some way not explained, procured a certified copy of the resolution, and thereupon caused to be prepared and executed a paper purporting and claimed to be a contract as was called for by the resolution. The paper was presented to the town council of Harrison, and a demand was made on behalf of Jersey City that it should be executed by the officials of the town of Harrison who were named in the resolution. It had not been so executed when the town council of Harrison adopted a rescinding resolution, thereby revoking the resolution of July 7, 1903.

Plaintiff contended that the resolution of the town of Harrison and the acts of Jersey City thereon constituted an offer and an acceptance, and therefore a contract between the parties; and that defendant could not avoid this contract by repealing or rescinding the resolution.

Defendant denied that a contract existed.

MAGIE, CH. No contract exists between the parties. A proposition for a contract, to be competent to be accepted, must be communicated to the party with whom the contract is proposed. It will not be sufficient that the latter acquire knowledge of it, unless the knowledge is acquired with the express or implied intention of the proposing party. The proposition, in this case, had not been communicated by the town of Harrison to Jersey City. An owner of land, contemplating the sale thereof, might direct his stenographer or other agent to draft a contract for sale to a particular person on specified terms. If the owner has not communicated, or intended to communicate, the proposed contract to that person, the latter, having acquired knowledge thereof, could not, by acceptance, bring the owner into a contractual relation of sale. The owner might leave his uncommunicated draft in his agent's hands without liability, and retract his agency and abandon his plan at any time. Until communication there is no effective proposal which could be accepted. *Potter v. Hollister*, 45 N. J. Eq. 509, 18 Atl. 204. In like manner, the resolution, never having been communicated to Jersey City by any act of the town of Harrison, did not constitute a proposal, and could not be raised to a binding contract by an acceptance. Judgment affirmed.

Miller v. United States
62 F. Supp. 327 (1945)

This was an action by Anthony P. Miller and Anthony P. Miller, Inc. (plaintiffs) against the United States (defendant), to recover a sum of money alleged to be due under a war housing project. Judgment for plaintiffs.

On October 10, 1942, the Federal Public Housing Authority invited bids for the construction of a war housing project at Hatboro, Pennsylvania. The invitation stated that bids would be opened at the Authority's office at 270 Broadway at 2 P.M. on October 22. Plaintiffs were engaged in the general contracting business. On October 21, they mailed a letter from Atlantic City, New Jersey, which was their principal place of business, to the Authority, containing a bid of $693,000. This letter arrived in time for the opening of bids.

The instructions to bidders contained a provision that telegraphic modifications of bids already submitted in writing would be considered if received by the Authority prior to the hour set for the opening of bids. This provision, which was usual in invitations, was often made use of by bidders, including plaintiffs, when bidding on Government contracts. It enabled them to set their final bids on the basis of late offers received by them from prospective sub-contractors, and of late information concerning prices. Plaintiffs, having received later offers from subcontractors justifying a reduction of their mailed bid, sent a telegram at 12:43 P.M. on October 22 reducing their bid by $50,000. This telegram was not delivered to the Authority until about 3 P.M. the same day.

At 2:00 P.M., on October 22, the bids, of which there were five, were opened by a Mr. Skinner in the conference room of the Authority's office in New York, and the amounts of the bids were read aloud to those present. Plaintiffs' bid of $693,000 was lowest. A Mr. Hager of Philadelphia, had been requested by plaintiffs to attend the opening to observe and report what happened. After the bids had been read, Hager called plaintiffs over the telephone and advised them that their bid of $693,000 was the low bid. He was asked by plaintiffs to find out whether their telegram modifying their bid had been received. He returned to the room where the bids had been opened, and was told by Skinner that he had not heard of any such telegram. Hager then returned to the public telephone and reported to plaintiffs what he had learned. He was told to go back and tell Skinner to disregard the telegram when it arrived as it had been sent "in error."

On November 6 the Authority wrote to plaintiffs that it had accepted their bid of $693,000 as reduced by their telegram, and that a contract setting the price at $643,000 was being prepared for plaintiffs' signatures. On November 12 plaintiffs and the Authority signed such a contract, but pursuant to discussion, inserted in the contract the following provision: "Notwithstanding anything to the contrary herein, it is mutually understood and agreed by and between the parties hereto that neither the execution of this contract nor any action taken thereunder, nor the recital of the contract sum herein, shall constitute or be construed as a waiver by the contractors of any right which the said contractors might have to establish, by such lawful process as the said contractors shall deem expedient, the true contract price to be the sum of $693,000 being the amount of the written bid submitted. The Government grants the aforesaid right of action and shall not interpose the defense of waiver or estoppel."

The construction called for by the contract has been completed. Plaintiffs are now suing for the $50,000 involved in the telegram.

Plaintiffs assert that, since their telegram reducing their bid had not been received by the Authority by two o'clock, the hour set for opening bids, and since section 9 (1) of the instructions to bidders said "unless specifically authorized, telegraphic bids will not be considered, but modifications by telegraph of bids already submitted will be considered if received prior to the hour set for opening," the Authority had no right to consider their telegraphic modification, just as they would have had no right to have it considered if their original bid had not been the low bid. The Government urges that the quoted provision was inserted for the benefit of the Government; that it could, at its option, either insist upon it or waive it; and that since plaintiffs' bid in writing was already low, and hence no other bidder could complain, there was no reason why the Government could not accept a still lower, though belated, offer from the already low bidder.

MADDEN, J. We think that the plaintiffs did not make an effective offer to reduce their written bid. They dispatched a telegram intended to make such an offer, but when they learned that the telegram had been delayed and that their written bid of $693,000 was low, they formed the intention to withdraw the offer contained in the telegram, and communicated that intention to the intended offeree, the Authority, before their offer reached it. An offer is not made until it has been communicated to the offeree, and until it is made it may be withdrawn, or obliterated, by a communication expressing an intent to do so. If the willingness to contract on the basis of words previously dispatched no longer exists, and if the absence of that willingness has been brought home to the person to whom the words were dispatched, the words, when they later arrive, are empty of the substance necessary to the meeting of the minds of parties in a contract. We have found that the plaintiffs' oral message, withdrawing the offer to reduce their bid, was delivered through Hage to Skinner before the telegram was delivered to the Authority. There was, therefore, no offer to reduce the bid, made either on time or late, which the Authority could accept, either under the particular procedures by which Government contracts are made, or under ordinary contract law.

We consider that the plaintiffs' bid was $693,000. That was, therefore, the price which the Authority promised to pay for the work. It follows that the plaintiff may recover $50,000. It is so ordered.

Healey v. New York Central and H. R. R. Co.
153 App. Div. 516, 138 N. Y. Supp. 287 (1912); affirmed, 210 N. Y. 646, 105 N. E. 1086 (1914)

This was an action by William J. Healey (plaintiff) against the New York Central & Hudson River Railroad Co. (defendant). Judgment for plaintiff, and defendant appealed. Affirmed.

This action was brought to recover the value of a handbag and contents, which plaintiff checked at the parcel room of defendant at its station in Albany. Defendant gave plaintiff a cardboard coupon, two by three inches in size, upon the face of which was printed:

New York Central Lines
New York Central & Hudson River Railroad Company
Duplicate coupon.
N.B.—See Conditions on back.

Received _____

Delivered _____

Upon the back of the coupon was printed, among other things, the following: "The depositor in accepting this duplicate coupon expressly agrees that the Company shall not be liable to him or her for any loss or damage of any piece to an amount exceeding TEN DOLLARS. W. M. Skinner, General Baggage Agent." The words assuming to limit the liability of defendant were in fine print, with the exception of the words "TEN DOLLARS." Plaintiff, upon receiving the coupon, put it in his pocket without reading it, and without his attention having been called to the limitation of liability printed thereon. When he returned for his handbag it was discovered that, through a mistake of the persons in charge of the parcel room, the coupons had been mismatched, and plaintiff's handbag had been delivered to another person. It has never been found, and its value, with the contents, was $70.10. Upon defendant's refusal to pay plaintiff more than $10 for the loss plaintiff filed this suit.

Plaintiff contended that the terms of the offer were not communicated to him, and that therefore no contract existed whereby defendant's liability was limited to $10. Defendant, on the other hand, maintained the existence of a contract whereby its liability is limited to the sum of $10.

LYON, J. The unreasonable condition printed upon the coupon, attempting to limit the liability of the defendant to not exceeding $10, is void. Had notice been given by the defendant to the plaintiff of the condition limiting the liability of the defendant, and the plaintiff then seen fit to enter into such a bailment contract, a contract would have resulted. But no notice whatever was given to the plaintiff of the existence of this condition, neither was there anything connected with the transaction which would tend in any way to suggest to a reasonably prudent man, or lead him to suspect, the existence of such a special contract, or tend to put him on guard or on inquiry relative thereto. The coupon was presumptively intended as between the parties to serve the special purpose of affording a means of identifying the parcel left by the plaintiff. In the mind of the plaintiff the little piece of cardboard, which he undoubtedly hurriedly slipped into his pocket without any reasonable opportunity to read it, and hastened away without any suggestion having been made upon the part of the parcel-room clerk as to the statements in fine print thereon, did not rise to the dignity of a contract by which he agreed that in the event of loss of the parcel, even through the negligence of the defendant's employees themselves, he would accept therefore a sum which would be but a small fraction of the actual value. The plaintiff having no knowledge of the existence of the special contract limiting the liability of the defendant to an amount not exceeding $10, and not being chargeable with such knowledge, is not bound thereby. Judgment for plaintiff affirmed with costs.

DURATION AND TERMINATION OF OFFER

An offer may be terminated (1) by revocation by the offeror; (2) by the expiration of a period of time specified in the offer; (3) by the expiration of a reasonable time when no time limit is specified in the offer;

(4) by rejection by the offeree; (5) by the death or insanity of either the offeror or the offeree; (6) by bankruptcy; (7) by the death or loss of the subject matter of the contemplated contract; (8) by the offer's becoming illegal; (9) by acceptance by the offeree.

REVOCATION BY THE OFFEROR. The general rule is that an offer other than that for the sale or contract to sell goods may be revoked or withdrawn by the offeror at any time prior to its acceptance. This is true even when the offeror has expressly promised that the offer will remain open for a specified time. A mere promise to keep an offer, other than for the sale of goods, open for a specified time, if unsupported by consideration, is a "naked promise" or *nudum pactum*, and is unenforceable. For example, A offers to sell investment securities to B for $400. B asks A to hold the offer open for him for ten days, and A agrees to do so. Nevertheless, A may, if he chooses, revoke the offer, prior to B's acceptance, at any time during the ten days.

There are two exceptions to the foregoing rule. (1) If an offer is made by an instrument under seal,[1] it may not be revoked during the period specified. (2) If the offeree has paid the offeror some valuable consideration, e.g. $10, to keep the offer open for a specified period, the offer may not be revoked during that period. An agreement whereby the offeree pays the offeror something to keep the offer open for a specified time is called an *option contract*, and the courts will enforce it. The Uniform Commercial Code Sec. 205 states that an offer by a merchant to buy or sell goods in a signed writing which by its terms gives assurance that it will be held open is not revocable, for lack of consideration.

An offeror revokes an offer by notifying the offeree that he has withdrawn the offer. The revocation does not become effective until notification has actually reached the offeree.

When an offer has been made to the public generally, the offeror may revoke it by the same means which he used in making the offer. For example, if he used a newspaper to advertise a reward for the return of his lost watch, he may withdraw the offer at any time before acceptance by placing a notice to that effect in the same paper. This notice of revocation would be effective even if the watch was subsequently returned by someone who had read the offer but had not heard of the revocation.

In the case of offers which look to the formation of unilateral contracts —that is, offers which call for acceptance by means of an act rather than a promise, like the reward offer just mentioned—a special question arises when the act called for by the offer requires a considerable time to perform and the offeree has started to perform before the offer is revoked.

---

[1] In states which have not abolished by statute the common law effect of the seal. The Uniform Commercial Code Sec. 203 makes a seal inoperative when affixed to a contract or an offer to buy or sell goods.

In such cases no contract results until performance of the required act is complete, and the offeror may therefore revoke his offer at any time before completion of the act. However, under certain circumstances the offeree may recover in quasi-contract for the reasonable value of any benefits which the offeror has derived from the part performance.

EXPIRATION OF THE TIME DESIGNATED IN THE OFFER. If an offer specifies a termination date and is not revoked by the offeror or rejected or accepted by the offeree before that date, it terminates automatically on the date specified. An attempted acceptance after that date is ineffectual.

At times the offeror does not specify a termination date for his offer but does limit the duration of the offer in some way. For example, he may stipulate for an answer "by return mail," or for "prompt wire acceptance," or for "immediate acceptance." The question arises in such cases, just how much time has the offeree to accept the offer? The general rule is that the offeree has a reasonable time under the circumstances. What is a reasonable time depends upon such factors as the nature of the subject matter of the offer, the state of the market, the exact wording of the offer, and the means by which the offer was communicated. Such matters would bear upon the vital element of intent. For example, a letter containing an offer to sell farm land and specifying an answer "by return mail" would give the offeree a longer time in which to accept than would a telegram offering to sell stock listed on the New York Stock Exchange and specifying that the offeree must reply "immediately" or "by immediate wire acceptance." In the case of the offer to sell farm land, in a community where, we will assume, there is little fluctuation in the value of land, the stipulation for an answer "by return mail" would doubtless be met by posting a letter during the course of the day, or, if the letter containing the offer had arrived late in the afternoon, by posting a letter the first thing the next morning. Such a stipulation is generally held not to be limited strictly to the next mail out. However, where an offer to sell stock is made by telegraph and it is stipulated that the offeree must reply "immediately" or "by prompt wire acceptance," a reasonable time for acceptance is very short. Stock values fluctuate rapidly on the market, and a reasonable time where they are involved would be held to be only a few minutes or at most an hour or so. The same principles apply where the subject matter of the offer is perishable goods. The fact that the offeror uses a telegram instead of a letter in making his offer and specifies acceptance by the same means indicates his intent as to the urgency of the matter. The time and method of acceptance become a part of his offer.

EXPIRATION OF A REASONABLE TIME.   If no time is specified in the offer, the offer terminates at the end of a reasonable time. No offer will remain open indefinitely. In determining what is a reasonable time in a given case, the courts will take into consideration such matters as the nature of the subject matter of the offer, the state of the market, the exact wording of the offer, and the means by which the offer was communicated.

REJECTION BY THE OFFEREE.   An offer terminates when it is rejected by the offeree. He cannot later accept the offer unless it is renewed by the offeror.

Rejection of an offer by the offeree may come about by his direct statement that he will not accept the offer, or by his making a counter-offer or attempting to make a conditional or qualified acceptance. If A says to B, "I will sell you my car for $1000," and B replies, "I am sorry but I am not interested in your offer," B has flatly rejected A's offer. If to the same offer B replies, "I think you are too high but I will give you $800 for your car," B has rejected A's offer with a counter-offer. If A says to B, "I will sell you my car for $1000 cash upon delivery," and B replies, "I will accept your offer if you will let me keep the car in your garage until spring without any charge," B has rejected A's offer with a conditional acceptance. As we have seen, an offeror may lay down any terms and conditions he wishes in his offer; and a contract does not result unless and until the offeree accepts unconditionally the terms of the offer. However, a mere inquiry or a request for interpretation of some detail of the offer is not held to be a rejection of the offer.

When an offeree rejects an offer with a counter-offer or a conditional acceptance, the positions of the parties are reversed: the offeree becomes the offeror, and the offeror becomes the offeree. A contract would not result unless the original offeror consented to the new terms and conditions set forth in the original offeree's counter-offer or conditional acceptance.

DEATH OR INSANITY OF EITHER PARTY.   In all the foregoing cases termination is brought about by the voluntary acts of the parties themselves. There are in addition several situations in which an offer is terminated automatically and without notice by some circumstance outside the control of the parties. In such cases the offer is said to terminate *by operation of law.*

If either party dies or becomes insane before acceptance of the offer, the offer is terminated by operation of law. After the death of the offeree, the executor or administrator of his estate cannot accept the offer unless it is renewed by the offeror; similarly, after the death of the offeror, his estate is not bound by an attempted acceptance, even though the offeree is ignorant of the death of the offeror when he comunicates his acceptance. The rule is based on the concept that there can be no meeting of minds of the parties when one of them has died or become insane.

BANKRUPTCY.   The general rule is that the bankruptcy of either party will terminate the offer by operation of law. However, the bankruptcy of the offeree does not terminate the offer if his bankruptcy will have no effect upon his ability to perform the contract if he accepts the offer.

DEATH OR LOSS OF THE SUBJECT MATTER.   The death or destruction of the property which was the subject of the offer automatically terminates the offer by operation of law. This rule is based upon the impossibility of performance. For example, A offers to sell B a horse which he has out on his farm. The next day B accepts A's offer. In the interval the horse has been killed by lightning, though neither party knows this. The offer terminated with the death of the horse, and no contract arises as a result of B's attempted acceptance.

ILLEGALITY.   If an offer is legal when made but becomes illegal before acceptance, the offer terminates by operation of law at the time it becomes illegal. Such a situation may occur as the result of new legislation or the issuance of an executive order by the President. For example, before Pearl Harbor A offered to sell B a new automobile. The President later issued an executive order prohibiting the sale of new cars to the general public. A's offer automatically terminated upon the issuance of the executive order.

ACCEPTANCE OF THE OFFER.   If the offeree accepts the offer, it terminates and a contract arises.

Bosshardt & Wilson Co. v. Crescent Oil Co., Ltd.
171 Pa. St. 109 (1895)

This was an action in assumpsit by the Bosshardt & Wilson Co. (plaintiff) against the Crescent Oil Co., Ltd. (defendant) to recover damages for breach of an alleged contract. Plaintiff appealed from an order of the court entering nonsuit against it. Affirmed.

On July 31, 1893, defendant wrote the plaintiff a letter containing an offer to furnish him with crude oil for two years. The letter concluded with this statement: "We extend to you a refusal of making the contract on the above basis for the term of sixty days from this date. Should it not be accepted in writing on or before that time, the above is to become null and void, and without effect between us." On September 19th plaintiff notified defendant verbally that it accepted defendant's offer contained in its letter of July 31st. On September 25th defendant wrote to plaintiff as follows: "We wish to advise you that we withdraw our offer of July 31st." Plaintiff, replying to this letter on September 27th, wrote as follows: "We hereby notify you that we will accept and will fully carry out the option and contract given to us by your company letter dated July 31, 1893. . . . We hereby repudiate your attempted withdrawal of said option and contract as expressed in your letter to us, dated September 25, 1893."

Plaintiff alleged the existence of a contract and the breach thereof and asked judgment for damages in the amount of the profits lost, in the amount of $119,250.

Defendant maintains that no contract resulted from the correspondence between the parties.

McCOLLUM, J. The plaintiff seeks to hold the defendant to its contract by an alleged verbal acceptance made prior to September 25th. This verbal acceptance failed to result in a contract. The defendant expressly declared that the acceptance should be in writing, and, in my judgment, nothing else than a written acceptance was sufficient to bind the defendant. We conclude that the learned court below did not err in refusing to take off the nonsuit. Judgment for the defendant affirmed.

UNIFORM COMMERCIAL CODE

In regard to the sale of goods, Secs. 2–206 and 2–207 of the Code provide that an offer may stipulate the terms of acceptance, and if unambiguously indicated by the language or circumstances will be binding on the offeree.

Johnson v. Whitney Metal Tool Company
342 Ill. App. 258, 96 N. E. (2d) 372 (1950)

This was a suit by Mildred C. Johnson (plaintiff) against Whitney Metal Tool Company (defendant) for specific performance of an alleged contract. Decree for plaintiff, and defendant appealed. Decree reversed and cause dismissed.

At a meeting of the board of directors of the Whitney Metal Tool Co., held on February 26, 1942, a resolution was adopted giving appellee, Mildred C. Johnson, an option to purchase a substantial amount of the unissued stock of the company at a par value of $10 per share. The resolution recited that the option was being granted "as a reward for her many years of faithful devotion and loyalty to the interests of the company" and directed John Jensen, the then president of the company, to report back to the board of directors Mrs. Johnson's decision as to the amount of stock she desired. On April 30, 1942, the board of directors met, and the record of that meeting recites: "Mr. Jensen reported that he had interviewed Mildred C. Johnson on the option extended to her in regard to purchasing of stock and reports she has decided to take 250 shares at a par value of $10 per share; the stock to be issued to her in block of 50 shares each upon the payment to the company of $500 for each block."

Plaintiff testified that after the board meeting of April 30, 1942, she talked with Mr. Jensen about the purchase of the stock. She testified that she told Mr. Jensen that she was unable, at the time, to pay for the stock and that "I would have to have some time, perhaps a couple of years," because she had purchased a home and did not want to take on any other obligations at the time, "unless I could get them to take my note or perhaps borrow the money at the bank and put up the stock for collateral." She testified that neither of these proposals was acceptable to defendant company.

During the period from 1942 to the date of the filing of this suit in 1947 the business of defendant prospered. The par value of its stock was $48 per share in 1942. In 1947 it was $120 per share. In February 1947 plaintiff tendered a certified check for $2500 to defendant and demanded that it issue to her 250 shares of the company's stock. This, defendant declined to do.

DOVE, J. What the record shows in this case is that the board of directors of appellant, on February 26, 1942, gave the appellee an option to purchase an undetermined number of shares of its stock at $10 per share. Appellee was informed of this offer and decided to take 250 shares at $10 per share. The minutes of the meeting of April 30, 1942, recite these facts and then show that by the unanimous action by the board of directors appellee was given this privilege. When informed of this action, there were two courses open to her. She could accept the offer as made or she could reject it. She testified that she told the president of the company that she didn't want to take on the purchase of that stock at that time and that she was unable to pay for it. This was an unequivocal rejection of the offer, the effect of which was to leave "the matter as if no offer had ever been made." It was after this that she made the company two counter-offers or counter-proposals. One was that she would give the company a note for the purchase price of the stock. This was declined. The other proposal was that the company issue and deliver to her the stock and she would negotiate a loan at a bank and use the stock as collateral security, and this proposal was also declined by the company.

No contract is complete without the mutual assent of the parties. A contract is made by an offer and an acceptance, and an offer imposes no obligations until it is accepted according to its terms. So long as the offer has been neither accepted nor rejected, the negotiation remains open and imposes no obligation upon either party. The one may decline to accept or the other may withdraw his offer and either rejection or withdrawal leaves the matter as if no offer had ever been made. 6 R. C. L. 603–4. An assent to an offer is an act of the mind. If the party making an offer does not require an immediate response, and the offer itself seems to contemplate acceptance, assent of the other party will be implied, in the absence of a revocation, from his acting pursuant to it within a reasonable time. The assent to the offer must be substantially as made. There must be no variance between the acceptance and the offer. *Maclay v. Harvey*, 90 Ill. 525, 32 Am. Rep. 35. An acceptance upon terms varying from those offered is a rejection of the offer and puts an end to the negotiations unless the party who made the original offer revives it or assents to the modification suggested. The other party, having once rejected the offer, cannot afterwards revive it by tendering an acceptance of it. The acceptance must be unequivocal and unconditional. If to the acceptance of a proposal a condition be affixed by a party to whom the offer is made, or any modification or change in the offer be made or requested, there is a rejection of the offer. Having in effect rejected the offer by his conditional acceptance, the offeree cannot subsequently bind the offeror by an unconditional acceptance. Every person has the right to dictate the terms upon which he will contract and the proposer may limit the time for acceptance. Unless the time is limited, the proposition is open until it is accepted or rejected, provided an answer is given within a reasonable time. An acceptance after the time limited in the offer, or, in the absence of an express limitation, after the lapse of a reasonable time, will not bind the party making the offer and imposes no obligation upon him. The offer, unless sooner withdrawn, stands during the time limited, or, if there is no express limitation, during a reasonable time. Until the end of that time the offer is regarded as being constantly repeated. After that there is no offer, and properly considered nothing to withdraw. The time having expired, there is nothing which the acceptor can do to revive the offer, or produce an extension of time.

An option is a unilateral undertaking lacking the mutual elements of a contract. It confers a privilege or right to elect to buy, but it does not impose any obligation to buy.

Applying the foregoing legal principles to the facts as they appear in this record, it is apparent that the decree of the lower court was erroneous for two reasons. First, appellant granted appellee an option or privilege to purchase 250 shares of stock in block of 50 shares each upon the payment to the company of $500 for each block. When advised of this action by the company, she declined to accept it. Her declination of the offer as made left the matter as if no offer had been made. Her counter-offers or proposals were both rejected by the company. This, too, left the matter as if no offer had been made. Second, if, however, appellee had not rejected the offer as submitted to her, she was required to accept the offer as made within a reasonable time. This she did not do. It was not until February 21, 1947, that her attorneys informed the appellant of the acceptance and tendered the purchase price of the stock. This was not within a reasonable time under the facts and circumstances disclosed by this record.

Brunner-Booth Fotochrome Corp. v. Kaufman
18 A. D. (2d) 160, 238 N. Y. S. (2d) 26 (1963)

This was an action by Brunner-Booth Fotochrome Corp. (plaintiff) against Sara Kaufman et al., (defendants). Judgment for plaintiff and defendants appealed. Judgment affirmed.

On January 21, 1961, Fotochrome, Inc. and Brunner-Booth Photo Co. entered into an asset purchase agreement whereby Fotochrome, Inc. purchased all of the assets of Brunner-Booth Photo Co. Attached to the asset purchase agreement was a separate list of ten insurance policies to be conveyed absolutely without qualification on the closing date to Fotochrome, Inc. or its assignee. The list included the two policies here involved.

On October 15, 1960, Brunner-Booth Photo Co. made an offer to Kaufman to sell to him the two said insurance policies on his life for their cash surrender value. Kaufman, on April 4, 1961, sold all his interest in said organization to Nadalino, a wholly-owned subsidiary of Brunner-Booth Photo Co., for the sum of $166,000, giving a general release for himself and his heirs. On said date, Brunner-Booth also sold all its interest to said purchaser.

STEVENS, J. Kaufman died April 24, 1961. At no time while alive did Kaufman or anyone in his behalf express any interest in purchasing the policies, nor did he demand any option rights, pay any consideration therefor, nor was any memo concerning the same made.

. . . All papers were then submitted to New York Life Insurance Company, which without knowledge of the sale and based upon the papers submitted to it, certified the transfer of the policies to the executrix on June 19, 1961. . . . The policies had a cash surrender value of $15,709.25 on April 4, 1961, the date of the closing. The proceeds of the policies, $77,040.32, are the subject of this submission and the issue is, which party is entitled thereto.

The rights of the beneficiary under the policies became fixed as of the time of Kaufman's death (*Fink v. Fink*, 171 N. Y. 616, 64 N. E. 506), and, the option not having been exercised, the policy or its proceeds could not validly have been transferred without the consent of the owner-beneficiary, the plaintiff herein. Even the resolution executed in May 1961, and signed by the board of directors of the seller, Brunner-Booth Photo Co., could not serve to transfer an interest in the title to the policies or the proceeds thereof, for the seller then had nothing to transfer.

There are sufficient facts presented necessary to the determination of the controversy.

Judgment for plaintiff, upon the law and the facts, in the sum of $77,040.32 without costs.

Fisher Iron & Steel Co. v. Elgin J. E. Railway Co.
101 Fed. (2d) 373 (1939)

This is an action by the Fisher Iron & Steel Co. (plaintiff) against the Elgin, Joliet & Eastern Railway Co. (defendant), for breach of an alleged contract to sell an abandoned railroad track owned by defendant. From an order sustaining a motion to dismiss the amended complaint, plaintiff appealed. Affirmed.

Defendant wrote a letter to plaintiff, dated June 17, 1937, in which it indicated to plaintiff that it was the owner of an abandoned stretch of railroad track which it was desirous of selling, and that it would welcome an offer from plaintiff for the purchase of same. On June 21, 1937, plaintiff wrote to defendant and stated that it had made an inspection of the railroad track and that it offered to purchase same for $10,000. In this letter plaintiff enclosed a certified check in the amount of $1000 as evidence of good faith. The letter then went on to state that "in view of the fact that we have tendered you our herein enclosed certified check we must ask that our offer be given some final answer on or before June 28th." Defendant did nothing further about the matter until August 17, 1937, when it wrote a letter to plaintiff in which it returned the certified check for $1000.

It is the theory of plaintiff that there was an implied acceptance of plaintiff's offer by defendant continuing to retain plaintiff's check for an unreasonable time.

TREANOR, J. There could not have been any acceptance of plaintiff's offer after June 28th, either impliedly or otherwise. In fact after that date there was no offer remaining which defendant could have accepted. Plaintiff had in its offer expressly limited the time within which an acceptance could be made. After that time plaintiff was no longer bound by its offer, and even if the defendant had expressly accepted, such acceptance could not have been binding upon the plaintiff. The situation was no different than it would have been had plaintiff on June 28th notified the defendant that its offer was withdrawn.

In *Waterman v. Banks*, 144 U. S. 394, the rule is thus stated: "There can be no question but that when an offer is made for a time limited in the offer itself, no acceptance afterwards will make it binding. Any offer without consideration may be withdrawn at any time before acceptance; and an offer which in its terms limits the time of acceptance is withdrawn by the expiration of the time."

Under the situation presented in this case we think the enclosure of the certified check did not alter the legal rights of the parties. That was entirely voluntary on the part of the plaintiff and did not extend the time of the offer from that expressly stated, and its retention by the defendant, under such circumstances, could not obligate the defendant to the acceptance of an offer which by its very terms had ceased to exist. After that time plaintiff had a right to demand and obtain the return of its check given in connection with its offer to purchase, which by its own terms was no longer in existence.

Judgment affirmed.

REVIEW CASES

1. On Dec. 15th Ramsey leased certain real property to Armstrong, giving him a 30–day option from date to buy the property. Armstrong at once entered into negotiations with a bank for a loan to be used in buying the property, but the loan was not granted until Jan. 23rd. On Jan. 19th Ramsey agreed to sell the property to Herndon. As soon as the loan was granted, Armstrong attempted to exercise his option, whereupon Herndon

filed suit for specific performance of his contract with Ramsey. Judgment for whom? (Herndon v. Armstrong et al., 148 Ore. 602, 38 P.(2d) 44)

2. Harsh wrote the Nebraska Seed Co. that he had 1,800 bushels of millet seed, of which he mailed the company a sample. He stated: "I want $2.25 per cwt. for this seed F. O. B. Lowell, Nebraska." The company at once telegraphed Harsh: "Accept your offer, millet like sample two-twenty-five per hundred. Wire how soon can load." It also sent a letter confirming this telegram and adding: "We have booked purchase of your 1,800 bushels of millet seed, to be fully equal to sample you sent us." Harsh refused to deliver the seed, and the company brought suit. Judgment for whom? (Nebraska Seed Co. v. Harsh, 98 Neb. 89, 152 N. W. 310)

3. Fonseca engaged passage on a Cunard liner from Liverpool to Boston. Near the top of his ticket, which was a sheet of paper of large quarto size, appeared in bold type "Passenger's Contract Ticket." On the side margin was this notice. "All passengers are requested to take notice that the owners of the ship do not hold themselves responsible for . . . loss, detention, or damage to luggage." On the back was a similar disclaimer of liability for damage to luggage by whatever cause, including negligence of the company's employees. Fonseca's attention was not called in any way to these provisions. During the voyage his trunk was entirely ruined owing to the negligence of the company's employees, and he sued for damages. Was he entitled to a judgment? (Fonseca v. Cunard Steamship Co., 153 Mass. 553)

4. On Dec. 8th the Columbus Rolling Mill Co. wrote the Minneapolis & St. Louis Railway Co.: "For iron rails, we will sell 2,000 to 5,000 tons of 50 lb. rails for $54 per gross ton for spot cash, F. O. B. cars at our mill, March delivery. . . ." On Dec. 16th the railway company sent the following telegram to the mill: "Please enter our order for 1,200 tons rails, March delivery, as per your favor of the eighth." The mill replied by telegraph: "We cannot fill your order at present at that price." On Dec. 19th the railway company sent the following telegram: "Please enter an order for 2,000 tons rails, as per your letter of the eighth." The mill refused to fill the order, and the railway company brought suit. Judgment for whom? (Minneapolis & St. Louis Railway Co. v. Columbus Rolling Mill Co., 119 U. S. 149, 30 L. Ed. 376)

5. Bromley and another submitted a bid to McHugh for the erection of a building, enclosing as required a certified check for 5 per cent of their bid. Their bid was the lowest submitted but was too high for McHugh. He therefore cut down the original specifications for the building and asked Bromley and his associate to furnish new figures, which they did. Meanwhile their check was returned to them and accepted without demur. Later McHugh made other arrangements for the construction of the building, whereupon they brought suit. Were they entitled to a judgment? (Bromley v. McHugh, 122 Wash. 361, 210 P. 809)

6. Allen wrote to various large shippers of freight that the Interstate Commerce Commission would hold important hearings on proposed freight classifications and that copies of the official reports could be furnished, at established rates, to anyone wishing to order in advance. Bissinger & Co. ordered one copy. The reports were sent in installments as the hearings

proceeded. After several months Bissinger & Co. wrote to Allen: "We are in receipt of another allotment of your I. C. C. report and want to say to you that this is something that we cannot use at all. . . . In ordering these from you in the first place we expected to find the information we wanted in one volume and did not think we were going to get a full library." Allen accepted cancellation of their order for future installments but refused to take back the reports already furnished, and thereafter rendered a statement for $1,047.50 to cover their cost. Bissinger & Co. refused to pay and when sued contended that the minds of the parties had never met on the subject matter of the alleged contract. Holding? (Allen v. Bissinger & Co., 82 Utah 226, 219 P. 539, 31 A. L. R. 376)

Mutual
Assent II:
Acceptance

7

As we have seen, the process of negotiating a contract is begun when the offeror makes and communicates an offer to the offeree. It is concluded when the offeree accepts the offer, in the terms of the offer, and (in cases where notice of acceptance is required) communicates the fact of his acceptance to the offeror. By accepting the offer the offeree assents to the terms of the offer, with full intent to be bound by them.

ACCEPTANCE MUST BE IN TERMS OF OFFER

The general rule is that acceptance must be absolute and unconditional and in the terms of the offer. We have seen that it is the privilege of the offeror to lay down in his offer any terms and conditions he wishes. If the offeree wishes to accept the offer, he must unequivocally assent to all such terms and conditions before the offer can become a binding promise and a contract arise. If the offer calls for a promise, the offeree must accept by making the specified promise; if he makes the promise, a bilateral contract will result. If the offer calls for an act, or a forbearance to act, the offeree must accept by performing the specified act or forbearance; if he does so, a unilateral contract will arise.

We learned in the common law if the offeree attempts to accept with qualifications or conditions, not only does no contract arise but the offer is terminated, so that any later attempt at acceptance by the offeree would be ineffectual. This holds not only for terms expressly stated by the offeror but for implied terms as well. For example, A writes to B, who lives in another city, offering to sell him his securities for $50 cash. B writes to A in reply: "I accept your offer. Bring the securities here next Monday and I will give you the money." B's attempted acceptance is not valid, for A's silence as to the place of delivery and payment will as a rule be held to imply that delivery and payment are to be made at his residence, not B's. On the other hand, where B makes his acceptance conditional upon some term which is already present by implication in the offer, his acceptance is valid. For example, A offers to sell B a tract of land for $15,000 cash, and B replies, "I will accept your offer on condition that you furnish good title to the land." B's reply will not be regarded as a conditional acceptance, for the law implies that any seller of property must furnish good title unless he provides otherwise in his offer. B will therefore be held to have accepted in the terms of A's offer.

UNIFORM COMMERCIAL CODE

In contracts for the sale of goods some important changes have been made in the general rule that acceptance must be absolute and unconditional and in terms of the offer. The Code in Sec. 2–207 provides that there may be an acceptance of an offer even though the acceptance states terms additional to or different from those offered. These provisions are discussed later in Part V, Sales.

Litterio & Company, Inc. v. Glassman Construction Company, Inc.
319 F. (2d) 736 (1963)
United States Court of Appeals

This was an action by prime contractor against subcontractor to recover difference between amount of bids by subcontractor and the bid of another company which actually did the work. The United States District Court for the District of Columbia. . . . granted summary judgment for the prime contractor, and the subcontractor appealed. Reversed and remanded.

FAHY, C.J. Appellant, N. Litterio & Company, Inc., defendant in the District Court, was sued there by Glassman Construction Company, Inc., appellee, for $17,706, the difference between the amount of a bid by Litterio to Glassman to do certain brick and masonry work and the bid by another company which actually did the work when Glassman was awarded the prime contract to construct a school building. Glassman's bid for the prime contract, which it performed, was $1,539,000. Motion of Glassman for summary judgment for $17,706 was granted, and Litterio's motion for summary judgment was denied. These motions were decided on the pleadings, depositions and statements filed under the rules applicable to summary judgment proceedings. On the basis of the data thus before the District Court we pass upon the appeal by Litterio.

The Litterio bid was prepared by Mr. Hammer, an estimator in the employ of Litterio, and communicated orally by Hammer to Glassman on the latter's oral request. Upon receiving the bid Glassman advised Hammer it seemed low and asked that it be rechecked. This was done by Hammer and confirmed by telephone. Glassman's evidence tends to show that it then advised Hammer that since the bid he submitted was lowest it was being used by Glassman in its bid for the prime contract, and if Glassman received that contract Litterio would be given the subcontract for the brick and masonry work. When the prime contract was awarded to it Glassman sent Litterio a written proposed subcontract for the brick and masonry work to be done for the amount of Litterio's bid. The proposal contained various terms which, so far as the record shows, had not theretofore been the basis of any communication between the parties, including a provision that it was not valid unless signed and returned within ten days. The President of Litterio in the meantime had returned to the City, from which he had been absent when Hammer submitted the bid. The President concluded the bid was based on mistaken calculations and was too low. Litterio did not sign and return the proposed subcontract. Arrangements were then made by Glassman with the next lowest bidder among those newly solicited for the brick and masonry work.

In Hedden the bid of the subcontractor was used by the contractor who obtained the prime contract, as Glassman says it did in our case, but the subcontract offered differed in several particulars from "the General Conditions and General Requirements" contained in the specifications. Pointing this out, and noting the absence of any evidence of what the local trade custom was with respect to oral bids, the court held the subcontractor not bound by its bid, saying:

"[T]he foregoing variances constitute a counter-offer. This court has long adhered to the position of 1 Restatement, Contracts, § 60 (1932), that 'a reply to an offer, though purporting to accept it, which adds qualifications or requires performance of conditions, is not an acceptance but is a counter-offer.' . . . Assuming, as we must, that Lupinsky phoned a proposal to plaintiffs, his bid constituted an offer to perform the job for a specified amount in accordance with the specific provisions of the General Conditions and Requirements contained in the specifications. When plaintiffs sent the sub-contract to defendant with terms in variance with those in the specifications, they were actually submitting a counter-offer for his acceptance. Lupinsky chose not to accept and, consequently, no contract resulted."

. . . Summary judgment was not available to Glassman on the ground of promissory estoppel; and, as we have said, no bilateral contractual basis for the judgment existed. Since, however, Litterio's own motion for summary judgment was not advanced on the basis of Glassman's failure to prove justifiable reliance upon the Litterio bid, but rather on the theory that no agreement existed, it would not be appropriate for this court to direct the entry of summary judgment for Litterio. We shall reverse and remand so that the case may go to trial, having in mind that ordinarily an estoppel is a question of fact. . . .

The remand will also provide Litterio with the opportunity at trial to establish its claim of lack of authority in Hammer to have made the bid on Litterio's part, and, also, the absence of damage to Glassman should it appear either that Glassman did not use the Litterio figure in its own bid for the prime contract or that Glassman suffered no real loss when it obtained another subcontractor to do the brick and masonry work. These issues of agency and damages were disputed issues of material fact when the case was before the District Court on the motions for summary judgment. See *Fed.R.Civ.P.* 56(c).

Reversed and remanded for further proceedings consistent with this opinion.

Anderson et al. v. Stewart
149 Neb. 660, 32 N. W. (2d) 140 (1948)

This was an action by Alma Anderson and Clyde Anderson (plaintiffs) against Hallie Stewart (defendant) for specific performance of an alleged contract to convey real property. From the decree dismissing plaintiffs' bill of complaint, plaintiffs appealed. Affirmed.

Defendant was the owner of the real estate involved. The property was located at Imperial, Nebraska. On February 23, 1946, defendant entered into a lease with plaintiffs renting to them this property for the period from March 25, 1946, to March 25, 1947. This lease contained the following provision: "Lease subject to sale with the option to parties of the second part to purchase same." This provision was understood by the parties to give plaintiffs the first opportunity to buy the property if the defendant should decide to sell during the term of the lease. Having decided to sell, the defendant, in accordance with this understanding, wrote a letter on July 6, 1946, from her home in Eagle, Neb., to Mrs. Anderson, advising her as follows: "I have decided to sell. In the contract we have is a statement that I am to give you folks the first opportunity to buy, so what do you wish to do?" On July 30, 1946, defendant wrote to Mrs. Anderson: "I hereby withdraw my offer and the place is not for sale at any price." This letter was received by Mrs. Anderson on July 31, 1946. However, on July 30, 1946, Mrs. Anderson wrote to defendant as follows: "We have decided to exercise our option and are enclosing deed which, when you have signed it before a notary, will you please send to the Farmers & Merchants Bank, where the $6500 is on deposit. Do you have an abstract?" This letter was mailed by Mrs. Anderson July 31, 1946, at Imperial, Neb., before she recived the letter of defendant dated July 30, 1946.

WENKE, J. "Revocation of an offer may be made by a communication from the offeror received by the offeree which states or implies that the offeror no longer intends to enter into the proposed contract, if the communication is received by the offeree before he has exercised his power of creating a contract by acceptance of the offer." *Restatement, Contracts,* Sec. 41, p. 49.

We find the acceptance was mailed before the letter withdrawing the offer was received, therefore a contract was entered into *if the acceptance was unconditional,* for, as set forth in 55 *Am. Jur., Vendor and Purchaser,* Sec. 16, p. 483: "The acceptance of an offer to buy or sell real estate must be an unconditional acceptance of the offer as made; otherwise no contract is formed. There must be no substantial variation between the offer and acceptance. If the acceptance differs from the offer or is coupled with any condition that varies or adds to the offer, it is not an acceptance, but is a counter-proposition. Thus, it is held that an acceptance specifying a different place for the delivery of the conveyance or payment of the price from that stated in the offer or implied as a matter of law is not a sufficient unconditional acceptance."

It will be observed that while the offer made no reference thereto, the acceptance directed the defendant to send the deed to the Farmers & Merchants Bank at Imperial, Neb., and that payment of the purchase price would be made there. It might be argued that the language used in the letter of July 30, 1946, merely requested that the deed be sent to the bank and did not require that it be done as a condition of their acceptance; however, a letter of Mrs. Anderson to defendant dated July 31, 1946, mailed immediately following receipt of defendant's letter withdrawing the offer, and her subsequent letter of August 6, 1946, clearly show that plaintiffs did intend defendant should be required to send the deed to the bank as a requirement of their acceptance and did intend that the money should be paid there where they said it was on deposit.

"If no place for payment is specified in the offer, where the negotiations are carried on by correspondence, it is implied that payment is to be made to the vendor in the city where he resides." 66 C. J., Vendor and Purchaser, Sec. 61, p. 524, note 23b.

The plaintiffs, not having unconditionally accepted the offer before it was withdrawn, cannot have it enforced. Decree affirmed.

ACCEPTANCE MUST BE RESPONSIVE TO OFFER

An acceptance must be genuinely responsive to an offer. A sends a letter to B in which he offers to sell his house to B for $20,000. Before receiving this letter B writes a letter to A in which he offers to buy A's house for $20,000. B's letter is not an acceptance of A's offer, since it was written before A's offer was communicated to B and therefore cannot be responsive to A's offer. Hence no contract arises from the exchange of letters.

The question whether an acceptance is responsive to the terms of an offer sometimes arises in cases where a reward has been offered for the return of lost property or for information leading to the arrest and conviction of a criminal. The general rule is that the recovery of such a reward is based upon the existence of a contract. Hence the plaintiff, in order to recover, must show that an offer was made and communicated to him and that he accepted in the terms of the offer and in response to it. An offer to pay a reward looks to the creation of a unilateral contract through the performance of a designated act, and the person who claims the reward for performing the act must show that he knew of the offer when he performed the act and that he performed it in response to the offer; otherwise no contract exists and he cannot recover the reward. A few courts have recognized an exception to this rule where the offer has been made by the government for the apprehension and conviction of a criminal. In such cases the reward is regarded not as a contractual obligation but as a bounty paid by the government. The exception seems to be based upon sound public policy.

Glover v. Jewish War Veterans of the United States, Post No. 58
D. C. Munic. App. 68 A. (2d) 233 (1949)

This was an action by Mary Glover (plaintiff) against the Jewish War Veterans of the United States, Post No. 58, a body corporate (defendant), to recover a reward. Judgment for the defendant, and plaintiff appealed. Affirmed.

The controversy grew out of the murder on June 5, 1946, of Maurice L. Bernstein, a local pharmacist. The following day, June 6th, Post No. 58, Jewish War Veterans of the United States, communicated to the newspapers an offer of a reward of $500 "to the person or persons furnishing information resulting in the apprehension and conviction of the persons guilty of the murder of Maurice L. Bernstein." Notice of the reward was published in the newspaper on June 7th. A day or so later Jesse James Patton, one of the men suspected of the crime, was arrested and the police received information that the other murderer was Reginald Wheeler and that Wheeler was the "boy friend" of a daughter of Mary Glover, plaintiff and claimant in the present case. On the evening of June 11th the police visited Mary Glover, who in answer to questions informed them that her daughter and Wheeler had left the city on June 5th. She told the officers she didn't know exactly where the couple had gone, whereupon the officers asked for the names of relatives whom the daughter might be visiting. In response to such questions she gave the names and addresses of several relatives, including one at Ridge Spring, South Carolina, which was the first place visited by the officers and where Wheeler was arrested in company with plaintiff's daughter on June 13th. Wheeler and Patton were subsequently convicted of the crime. According to the testimony of both plaintiff and her husband plaintiff knew nothing of the offer of the reward at the time she furnished the foregoing information to the police officers.

The issue in the case is whether a person giving information leading to the arrest of a murderer without any knowledge that a reward has been offered for such information by a non-governmental organization is entitled to collect the reward.

CLAGGETT, J. We have concluded that the trial court correctly instructed the jury to return a verdict for defendant. While there is some conflict in the decided cases on the subject of rewards, most of such conflict has to do with rewards offered by governmental officers and agencies. So far as rewards offered by private individuals and organizations are concerned, there is little conflict on the rule that questions regarding such rewards are to be based upon the law of contracts.

Since it is clear that the question is one of contract law, it follows that, at least so far as private rewards are concerned, there can be no contract unless the claimant when giving the desired information knew of the offer of the reward and acted with the intention of accepting such offer; otherwise the claimant gives the information not in the expectation of receiving a reward but rather out of a sense of public duty or other motive unconnected with the reward. "In the nature of the case," according to Professor Williston, "it is impossible for an offeree actually to assent to an offer unless he *knows* of its existence." After stating that courts in some jurisdictions have decided to the contrary, Williston adds, "It is impossible, however, to find in such a case (that is, in a case holding to the contrary) the elements generally held in England and America necessary for the formation of a contract. If it is clear the offeror intended to pay for the service, it is equally certain that the person rendering the service performed it voluntarily and not in return for a promise to pay. If one person expects to buy, and the other to give, there can hardly be found mutual assent. These views are supported by the great weight of authority, and in most jurisdictions a plaintiff in the sort of case under discussion is denied recovery."

The American Law Institute in its *Restatement of the Law of Contracts* follows the same rule, thus: "It is impossible that there should be an acceptance unless the offeree knows of the existence of the offer."

Affirmed.

WHO MAY ACCEPT AN OFFER

An offer which is made to a specific person may be accepted only by that person or his authorized agent. This is a fair and just rule of law, for one should not be required to contract with a person with whom he does not care to contract. For example, A says to B, "I will sell you my car for $800 cash." C is standing by and hears A make this offer to B. Before B can reply, C says, "I accept your offer." A would not be bound, since he did not make the offer to C. A may have some personal reason why he does not care to sell the car to C; or he may have some question about C as a credit risk. The protection offered by this rule is particularly important in offers of employment, since in such cases the offeree has usually been selected because of his personal qualifications.

The rule cannot be evaded by the offeree's assignment of the offer to a third party, since an offer may not be assigned.[1] This is true even though the offeree has purchased an option from the offeror. An offer is personal to the offeree.

An offer which has been made to the public may, as a general rule, be accepted by any person who hears about it and who accepts in the terms of the offer.

[1] Assignment is discussed in detail in Chapter 13.

Rease v. Kittle et al.

56 W. Va. 269, 49 S. E. 150 (1904)

This was an action by F. P. Rease (plaintiff) against C. B. Kittle and others (defendants) for specific performance of an alleged contract. Decree for plaintiff, and defendant O. C. Womelsdorf appealed. Reversed.

Kittle executed and delivered to J. E. Howell a contract which read as follows: "That the aforesaid Kittle has this day agreed to give the aforesaid Howell an option on a certain tract of land, hereinafter described and bounded, containing 50 acres, for the sum of $47.50 per acre, of which $1.00 cash in hand is paid, the receipt of which is hereby acknowledged. Now, if the aforesaid Howell pays the aforesaid Kittle the aforesaid sum of money before the expiration of five years from this date, the aforesaid Kittle binds himself to make the aforesaid Howell a general warranty deed for the aforesaid tract of land. And it is further agreed that, in case the aforesaid Howell fail to pay the aforesaid Kittle the aforesaid sum of money before the expiration of five years from this date, then this contract is to be void."

Before the expiration of the time limit fixed by the foregoing paper, Kittle conveyed the land to O. C. Womelsdorf by deed dated September 2, 1899, reciting a cash consideration of $1000. On February 12, 1900, Howell executed and delivered to F. P. Rease a paper purporting to assign all his right to purchase said land, and all rights pertaining to said option. On November 16, 1900, Rease sent his agent to Kittle to close the option and pay the purchase price of the land; but the latter refused to accept the money or to make a deed. Immediately afterwards Rease brought this suit in equity to compel specific performance of the alleged contract, making Kittle, Womelsdorf, and Howell defendants, and the court granted the relief prayed for.

The principal question is whether a continuing offer in writing to sell land, irrevocable because based upon a valuable consideration, and made to a particular person, vests in that person an equitable title to the land, which he can convey to a third person, or is capable of assignment to such third person.

POFFENBARGER, J. A contract of this kind is in no sense a sale of the land, and vests no equitable title in the optionee. It amounts at the most to an irrevocable privilege of purchase. It is unlike an accepted offer of sale, which constitutes a contract of sale, giving mutuality of remedy to both parties, by which either may enforce the specific performance of it. "An option contract to purchase is but a continuing offer to sell, and conveys no interest in the property." *Caldwell v. Frazier*, 68 Pac. 1076.

Although based upon a consideration, it is but an offer, a privilege extended, differing from an ordinary offer only in this: that it is not revocable, because based upon a valuable consideration. An assignment of it, therefore, passes no interest in the property to which it relates. Hence Howell's assignment to Rease could carry nothing except the continuing offer to him. It was not made to the world at large, nor does the contract say it was made to J. E. Howell and his assigns. Whether, if it did, he might turn it over to another, there is no occasion to say. The offer is personal to him. The authorities say that an offer made to a particular person can be turned into a contract by him alone. "When an offer is made to a particular person, it can be accepted by him alone, and is not assignable to another." 9 *Cyc.* 255.

"A party has a right to select and determine with whom he will contract. It may be of importance to him who performs the contract, as when he contracts with another to paint a picture, or write a book, or when he relies upon the character or qualities of an individual, or has, as in this case, reasons why he does not wish to deal with a particular party." *Boston Ice Co. v. Potter,* 123 Mass. 28, 25 Am. Rep. 9.

The decree complained of must be reversed, the demurrer sustained, and the bill dismissed with costs.

HOW AN ACCEPTANCE MAY BE MADE

An acceptance may be either express or implied. An express acceptance is one explicitly made by the offeree, orally or in writing. An implied acceptance is one implied from the conduct of the offeree.

Not infrequently the question rises whether acceptance may be implied by silence. The general rule is that mere silence on the part of the offeree does not constitute acceptance. If A makes an offer to B by letter and B does not reply, B's silence may not be construed as an acceptance. The courts have also held that A may not, by his unilateral action, put B in such a position as to make silence an acceptance on his part. For example, A writes to B: "I have sent you by parcel post twelve beautiful neckties. These neckties regularly sell for $2.50 each, but I am offering all twelve neckties to you for only $15. If I do not hear from you in ten days I shall consider that you have accepted my offer and shall expect to receive your check for $15 within a few days." If B does not reply and does not make use of the ties, no contract is consummated by his silence; the law does not require him to go to the trouble of returning the ties to A, or of notifying A that he refuses to accept them. One party is not privileged, under the law, to foist a contract upon another without his consent. However, if B wears the ties, his use of them constitutes an implied acceptance of the offer and he becomes liable upon an implied contract.

The foregoing rule is subject to certain exceptions. For instance, if the parties agree that silence may be treated as acceptance, the courts will enforce the agreement. Or if because of a previous course of dealing between the parties, or because of the particular relationship between them, the offeree owes the offeror a duty to "speak" if he does not wish to accept, his failure to speak will be held to be acceptance.

Austin v. Burge
150 Mo. App. 283, 137 S. W. 618 (1911)

This was an action brought by O. D. Austin (plaintiff) against Charles Burge (defendant) on an account for the subscription price of a newspaper. Judgment for defendant, and plaintiff appealed. Reversed.

Plaintiff was the publisher of a newspaper in Butler, Missouri. Defendant's father-in-law subscribed for the paper, to be sent to defendant for two years, and paid for it at that time. It then continued to be sent to defendant through the mail for several years more. On two occasions defendant paid a bill presented for the subscription price, but each time he directed that it be stopped. Defendant testified that, notwithstanding his order to stop sending the paper, it was continued, and that he received it and read it.

ELLISON, J. It is certain that one cannot be forced into contractual relations with another, and that, therefore, he cannot, against his will, be made a debtor of a newspaper publisher. But it is equally certain that he may cause contractual relations to arise by necessary implication from his conduct. The law in respect to contractual indebtedness for a newspaper is not different from that relating to other things which have not been made the subject of an express agreement. Thus, one may not have ordered supplies for his table, or other household necessities, yet if he continue to receive and use them, under circumstances where he has no right to suppose they were a gratuity, he will be held to have agreed, by implication, to pay their value. In this case defendant admits that, notwithstanding he ordered the paper discontinued at the time when he paid a bill for it, yet plaintiff continued to send it, and he continued to take it from the post office to his home. This was an acceptance and use of the property, and, there being no pretense that a gratuity was intended, an obligation arose to pay for it.

The preparation and publication of a newspaper involves much mental and physical labor, as well as an outlay of money. One who accepts the paper, by continuously taking it from the post office, receives a benefit and pleasure arising from such labor and expenditure as fully as if he had appropriated any other product of another's labor, and by such act he must be held liable for the subscription price. On the defendants' own evidence plaintiff should have recovered. Judgment reversed.

Hendrickson v. International Harvester Company of America
135 Atl. 702 (1927)

This was an action by Peter Hendrickson (plaintiff) against the International Harvester Co. (defendant). Judgment for plaintiff, and defendant brings exceptions. Judgment affirmed.

In this action of contract plaintiff seeks to recover damages on account of defendant's failure to deliver to him an eight-foot broadcast seeder.

On June 28, 1921, defendant's sales representatives went to plaintiff's farm and proposed to sell him any farm machinery he might require. He finally made an arrangement with them to exchange a drill seeder which he then owned for an eight-foot broadcast seeder, the same to be delivered to him the following spring. One of defendant's agents produced a blank form and made out the order for the broadcaster. The form was signed by plaintiff. By its terms it was subject to the approval of defendant. The order was forwarded to defendant and bore the date of June 28, 1921. Defendant retained the order received from its agent until this action was filed. During this time it did not indicate that it either accepted or rejected the offer of plaintiff to buy the eight-foot seeder.

The lower court charged the jury that the fact that defendant kept the order without approving it or notifying plaintiff of its disapproval would amount to an acceptance.

POWERS, J. True it is that it takes two to make a bargain, and that silence gives consent in these cases only when there is a duty to speak. And true it is that it is frequently said that one is ordinarily under no obligation to do or say anything concerning a proposition which he does not choose to accept; yet we think that, when one sends out an agent to solicit orders for his goods, authorizing such agent to take such orders subject to his (the principal's) approval, fair dealings and the exigencies of modern business require us to hold that he shall signify to the consumer within a reasonable time from the receipt of the order his rejection of it, or suffer the consequences of having his silence operate as an approval. We are aware that there are authorities to the contrary, but the rule we adopt is supported by *Cole-McIntyre-Norfleet Co. v. Holloway*, 141 Tenn. 679; *Peterson v. Graham-Brown Shoe Co.*, 210 S. W. 737; and *Bluegrass Cordage Co. v. Luthy*, 98 Ky. 583, and is in general harmony with *Porter v. Evert's Est.*, 81 Vt. 512, 71 A. 722, holding that acceptance may be evidenced and communicated by conduct.

Judgment affirmed.

Cohen et al. v. Johnson et al.

91 F. Supp. 231 (1950)

This was an action by Morris Cohen and others, trading as co-partners under the name of Rochester Fuel & Feed Company (plaintiffs) against Frank Johnson and another (defendants) for breach of an alleged contract. Judgment for defendants.

Plaintiffs assert that a valid, definitive, binding contract of purchase and sale of coal was created when Morris Cohen and defendants executed a certain paper on July 1, 1947; failing therein, plaintiffs assert that such a contract may be implied in fact from plaintiffs' letter to defendants dated July 3, 1947, and defendants' conduct subsequent thereto.

Morris Cohen, after inspecting defendants' plant and product on July 1,

1947, advised them that he desired to purchase some of their coal during the 1947–48 burning season. After discussing the amounts of coal defendants would likely have available, defendants quoted plaintiffs a price per ton of $8.75 for stove and chestnut, and $7 for pea coal. Cohen wrote some notes on the top sheet of defendants' desk memorandum pad, signed his name thereto, removed the sheet, and asked defendants to sign their name thereto. Defendants refused to sign, advising Cohen that they did not make a practice of doing so, that they were only quoting prices, and suggested that the word "quotation" be written across the top of the page. After Cohen complied with this suggestion, defendants affixed their signatures under his and he took the paper.

On July 3, 1947, plaintiffs wrote to defendants and said: "I am glad to place an order with you. . . . Coal is to be shipped as ordered by us. . . . We will pay for the coal upon receipt of invoice. Initial purchase of 10,000. . . . Will lead to a continuous volume of business. Arrange to ship . . . July, 8 cars stove coal, 8 cars of chestnut, and 4 cars of pea coal." Defendants made no reply to plaintiffs' letter but proceeded to fill the order for the 20 cars of coal mentioned in plaintiffs' letter of July 3rd. The 20 cars did not constitute 10,000 tons of coal.

On July 21st plaintiffs wrote to defendants and asked them to ship 10 cars of coal for August delivery. The wages of coal miners were increased late in July and the price of coal was increased. Defendants notified plaintiffs of this price increase. Shortly thereafter plaintiffs acknowledged receipt of the new price quotations and then placed an order for 20 cars of coal for September delivery, but insisted that all shipments be made at July 1st prices. Since defendants had already delivered the 10 cars for the August delivery, it billed the plaintiffs for these cars at the July 1st prices. However, it refused to fill the order for September delivery at that price. Thereupon plaintiffs filed this action alleging a contract to buy and sell 10,000 tons of coal at the July 1st price, that all of this amount had not yet been delivered, and that hence defendants had breached their contract. Defendants contended that they had never accepted plaintiffs' offer to buy 10,000 tons of coal.

MURPHY, J. There was no contract entered into by the parties on July 1, 1947, for the purchase and sale of 10,000 tons of coal. The memorandum above referred to merely constituted a quotation of price and not an offer. When price quotations are made it is not considered in the coal industry as an offer of sale but as an invitation to trade or to submit orders, which may or may not be accepted. Acceptance is indicated by shipping the coal. Therefore, the memorandum may not be construed as a contract. Whatever plaintiffs' intent may have been as to making an offer to purchase 10,000 tons of coal, in the letter of July 3rd, the offer was not accepted by the defendants. Defendants' silence and other conduct were not sufficient to indicate an acceptance of plaintiffs' offer to purchase 10,000 tons of coal. So, no contract resulted from plaintiffs' letter of July 3rd. Likewise, defendants had a right to refuse to accept plaintiffs' order for September delivery, it being only an offer to buy.

While an offer may be accepted by conduct, to be a contract an offer must be accepted. An offeree has a right to make no reply to an offer, and his silence and inaction cannot be construed as an assent to the offer. Plaintiffs' letter being contrary to and beyond the prior understanding, defendants' silence had no effect since they obviously declined to recognize the overall offer to buy 10,000 tons of coal, but construed it as an offer to purchase 20 cars of coal, which they proceeded to accept by making delivery. There was no implied contract here to accept plaintiffs' offer to purchase 10,000 tons of coal. But it did accept the offer for 20 cars of coal for July delivery. Therefore, defendants did not breach any contract when they refused to accept the order for 20 cars for September delivery. Judgment for defendants.

COMMUNICATION OF ACCEPTANCE

ACCEPTANCE OF A BILATERAL OFFER

If the offer is a bilateral offer, i.e. an offer looking to the formation of a bilateral contract, the acceptance by the offeree must be communicated to the offeror or his authorized agent. A mere decision upon the part of the offeree to accept will not produce a contract. Where the parties are dealing face to face or by telephone, B may simply state to A that he accepts A's offer, whereupon the contract is consummated. Where the negotiation is carried out by other means, such as letters or telegrams, various questions arise as to the precise time at which the contract comes into being.

If the offeror specifies in his offer a method or means by which the offeree shall communicate his reply, a contract arises as soon as the acceptance is transmitted to the specified agency. For example, if A makes an offer by letter and specifies an acceptance by return mail, a contract is consummated the moment B drops his letter of acceptance, properly addressed and stamped, in the mailbox, even though through some mistake A never receives the letter. But suppose that B sends his acceptance by telegram instead of letter. Would a contract result? And if so, when would it come into being? Though courts have sometimes held that under such circumstances the offeree has not accepted in the terms of the offer, the better view is that a contract would result but not until A actually received B's acceptance.[1] The distinction as to the time when the contract arises is based on what is sometimes called the *agency theory*, to the effect that the means of communication (whether post office department, telephone company, telegraph company, or some other) is the agent of

[1] See *Restatement of the Law of Contracts*, Sec. 68: "An acceptance inoperative when dispatched only because the offeree uses means of transmission which he was not authorized to use is operative when received, if received by the offeror within the time within which an acceptance sent in an authorized manner would probably have been received by him."

whichever party has chosen it. If the offeror has chosen it and thus made it his authorized agent, an acceptance handed to it has the same legal effect as an acceptance handed to him. But if it is the agent of the offeree, then the acceptance does not become valid until it has come into the hands of the offeror.

If the offeror does not specify the means by which the offeree is to communicate his acceptance, it is implied that the offeree may use the same means in communicating his acceptance that the offeror used in communicating his offer. A letter of acceptance in reply to an offer made by letter, or a telegram of acceptance in reply to an offer made by telegram, will create a contract as soon as it is deposited for transmission. If the offeree chooses a means of communication different from that employed by the offeror, then no contract arises until the acceptance is received by the offeror.

The foregoing rules help to solve the problem that arises when a letter of acceptance and a letter revoking an offer "cross in the mail." For example, on May 1st A posts a letter in which he makes an offer to B. B receives the letter on May 2nd, and at 10 A.M. on May 3rd he posts a letter of acceptance, which reaches A at 10 A.M. on May 4th. Meanwhile, at 9 A.M. on May 3rd A posts a letter revoking his offer, and the letter reaches B at 9 A.M. on May 4th. Is there a contract? The answer is that a contract came into being when B posted his letter of acceptance at 10 A.M. on May 3rd. When an offer made by letter is accepted by letter, a contract arises when the letter of acceptance is posted, while a letter revoking an offer is not effective until it is received by the offeree. These general rules tend to work to the disadvantage of the offeror, but this effect is offset by the offeror's privilege of so framing his offer as to make the formation of the proposed contract dependent upon his actual receipt of the acceptance.

As was stated in Chapter 5, the general rule is that in the operation of contracts the substantive law of the place where the contract is made applies. The foregoing discussion will answer questions as to what law applies when the offeror and the offeree reside in different states. If the contract becomes effective as soon as B transmits his acceptance to the local post office or telegraph office for delivery to A, the law of B's state applies. If the circumstances are such that no contract arises until B's acceptance is actually received by A, the law of A's state applies. Where the telephone is used to transmit an acceptance from B in one state to A in another, the law of B's state applies.

Once an acceptance has been communicated to the offeror and a contract has come into being, the acceptance cannot be revoked without liability. But in cases where an interval exists between the time when the promisee dispatches his acceptance and the time when the contract comes into being, the acceptance may be revoked during that interval. A makes an offer to B by letter, and B posts a letter of acceptance to A. B then changes his mind and wires A to disregard his letter. Even though the telegram arrives first, B is bound, since a contract was formed when he posted his letter. But if A stipulated in his offer that no contract was to arise until he had B's acceptance in his hands, then a telegram of revocation that reached him before B's letter of acceptance would be effective.

UNIFORM COMMERCIAL CODE

In regard to the sale of goods, Sec. 2–206 of the Code alters the above mode of acceptance to the effect that if no means of acceptance is specified in the offer, the acceptance may be in any manner and by any medium reasonable under the circumstances. This is further discussed in this volume in Part V, Sales.

Geary v. Great Atlantic & Pacific Tea Co.
366 Ill. 625, 10 N. E. (2d) 350 (1937)

This was an action by Jean S. Geary, assignee of the Foreman Trust & Savings Bank, receiver (plaintiff) against Great Atlantic and Pacific Tea Co. (defendant). Judgment for plaintiff in the municipal court of Chicago; defendant appealed to the Appellate Court, judgment reversed; plaintiff appealed. Judgment of the Appellate Court reversed and judgment of the municipal court affirmed.

On February 25, 1931, defendant, then in possession of the premises, wrote to the Foreman Trust & Savings Bank as follows: "Herewith original and duplicate copies of renewal lease for one year commencing May 1, 1931, at a monthly rental rate of $125 with one one-year renewal privilege at $135.00 per month."

On March 2nd the Foreman Bank, having executed the lease sent by defendant with its letter of February 25th, mailed them to defendant with the following letter: "We are pleased to advise you that the court authorized us to execute a lease with your Company from May 1, 1931, for a period of one year at a monthly rental rate of $125. We are returning herewith the two leases signed." On the same day, March 7, 1931, at 1:30 P.M., defendant mailed a letter to plaintiff in which it advised that it was withdrawing its offer. When defendant mailed its letter of revocation it did not know of the mailing of the executed leases by plaintiff.

STONE, J. The rule of law is that a contract is ordinarily effected by offer and acceptance, and when an offer is made by letter and the offeree posts his acceptance, the contract is complete, notwithstanding a revocation or withdrawal of the offeree is mailed before the letter of acceptance is received. Withdrawal of an offer is not effectual until communicated, and an acceptance prior to a communicated withdrawal completes the contract, and so, where an offer is accepted by posting a letter of acceptance before notice of the withdrawal of the offer is received, the contract is completed.

The facts in this case show a negotiation instigated by the defendant, a submission of an offer by it and with it a renewal lease on a form prepared by it. This can be construed to be an offer to renew the lease. When the acceptance of that offer was mailed before receiving notice of an intention to withdraw the offer, the contract closed.

Judgment for the plaintiff.

Walrus Manufacturing Co. v. New Amsterdam Casualty Co.

184 F. Supp. 214 (1960)

United States District Court

This was an action by Illinois subcontractor against foreign insurance company which was surety on contractor's performance bond. Surety moved to dismiss. Motion denied.

POOS, D.J. Plaintiff brings suit against defendant to recover on a performance bond issued by it in Pennsylvania to United Construction Company. The United Construction Company is not a party to this proceeding. It is a resident of Pittsburgh, Pennsylvania. On September 19, 1957, the United Construction Company had a contract to provide the necessary labor and material for the installation of certain equipment in a school building in Pennsylvania. The contract to supply the equipment was signed by plaintiff, a resident of Illinois, in Decatur, Illinois, and was sent to The United Construction Company at Pittsburgh, Pennsylvania, who signed the contract on its part and returned it to plaintiff by United States mail on October 2, 1957.

Particular notice is taken that plaintiff is a citizen of Illinois and that plaintiff signed its subcontract in Illinois, the contract having been sent there by the agent of "United," the United States mail was agent to deliver the contract to plaintiff, and by so doing authorized the U. S. Mail as its agent to receive the contract executed by plaintiff after signature. The minute the plaintiff signed the contract and deposited it in the mail, it became a binding contract executed by plaintiff at the exact time it was placed in the United States Mail at Decatur, Illinois. This contract without dispute in this record was delivered to "United" in Pittsburgh. In the *American Law Institute Restatement of the Law, Contracts*, Sec. 69, p. 71, the rule applicable to this factual situation is announced as follows:

"An acceptance is authorized to be sent by the means used by the offeror or customary in similar transactions at the time when and the place where the offer is received, unless the terms of the offer or surrounding circumstances known to the offeree otherwise indicate."

The illustration cited is:

"1. A makes B an offer by mail. B promptly mails an acceptance. There is a contract as soon as B's letter is mailed."

In addition to this "United" signed the contract and returned it to Decatur, Illinois, place of plaintiff's residence. This put plaintiff's manufacturing process into motion in Illinois, the materials were fabricated in Illinois and shipped in interstate commerce to Pennsylvania and the defendant on default of payment by "United" under the terms of its bond became liable.

For the reasons herein set out the motion to dismiss is denied, and defendant is ruled to plead within 20 days from this date.

ACCEPTANCE OF A UNILATERAL OFFER

A unilateral offer calls for acceptance by the performance of a specified act or forbearance. We have already seen in Chapter 6 that such an offer can be accepted only by complete performance of the designated act or forbearance. The question sometimes rises whether the offeree is required to notify the offeror that he has accepted the offer. It is generally held that notice is not necessary to consummate the contract, which is brought into being as soon as performance is complete; but there are certain cases in which failure to give notice has the effect of discharging the offeror of any liability under the existing contract.

No notice is required if the circumstances are such that the offeror could naturally or normally know or observe that the offeree has accepted the offer by performance or forbearance. If he could not easily have such knowledge, then the offeree's failure to notify the offeror within a reasonable time that he has accepted the offer would relieve the offeror of any liability under the contract.

The time needed for performance also has important bearing upon whether notice is necessary to safeguard the offeree's interests under the contract. If the offer calls for an act or a series of acts that require considerable time for performance, the courts generally hold that the offeree must give notice. For example, if A offers B $50,000 to manufacture for him a complicated piece of machinery which will require five or six months for construction, then B is required to notify A when he has performed. If, however, the offer calls for an act that can be performed at once or within a short time, no notice of performance is required. For example, if a retailer places an order with a wholesaler for certain merchandise, and the wholesaler fills the order within a day or so by placing the merchandise in the hands of a carrier for transmission to the retailer, he has done all that he need do by way of acceptance. Filling of the order by the seller (offeree) immediately or within a reasonable time is acceptance, and the receipt of the bill of lading or the notice of the arrival of the goods by the buyer (offeror) is sufficient notice of compliance with the terms of the offer (*Crook v. Cowan*, 642 N. C. 743).

Notice that the offeree has acted on the offer is generally required in the case of offers of guaranty of credit. For example, A writes to B as follows: "If you will make a loan of $500 to C, I will guarantee that he will repay the loan when due; and if he does not pay you, I will." If B accepts A's offer by extending the loan to C, the law requires that he notify A of this fact. If B fails to give such notice to A, A is not bound. The reason for this requirement is that A should be in a position to protect himself. Some courts hold that if the offeror (A) learns through some other reliable source that the offeree (B) has extended the loan, the offeror will be bound. Other authorities hold that the notice must come from the offeree himself.

In all cases where a unilateral offer has been accepted, the safest procedure for the offeree is to give the offeror written notice of his acceptance.

UNIFORM COMMERCIAL CODE

Sec. 2–206 of the Code states that "(1) Unless otherwise unambiguously indicated by the language or circumstances an order or other offer to buy goods for prompt or current shipment shall be construed as inviting acceptance either by prompt promise to ship or by the prompt or current shipment. . . ."

Simmons v. United States
308 F. (2d) 160 (1962)

This was an action by William Simmons and Viola Simmons (plaintiffs) against United States of America (defendant). Judgment for defendant and plaintiffs appealed. Judgment affirmed.

This is an action by an income taxpayer for recovery of an alleged overpayment of income taxes, where the taxpayer received a cash prize of $25,000 for catching a certain tagged fish placed in Chesapeake Bay by a brewery company. The United States District Court (Maryland), at Baltimore, Roszel C. Thomsen, Chief Judge, 199 F. Supp. 673, on defendant's motion for summary judgment, entered judgment for the government, and an appeal was taken.

SOBELOFF, C.J. Catching Diamond Jim III was essentially a matter of luck. The case might be different if, for example, Simmons had at considerable risk to himself captured and destroyed a killer whale terrorizing the Maryland seashore. That could have been regarded as a genuine civic achievement. But catching this fish cannot reasonably be so denominated, for the only community interest in the event was one of idle curiosity. The character of this fortuitous event is not raised to a civic level by being linked to an advertising campaign aimed at selling beer. Far from resembling a Nobel or Pulitzer prizewinner, Mr. Simmons fits naturally in the less-favored classification the legislators reserved for beneficiaries of "giveaway" programs.

The taxpayer alleges that he was at least entitled to have a jury decide whether the $25,000.00 payment to him was a gift, excluded from gross income by section 102. It suffices to repeat that it is the function of the trier of fact to determine the basic facts and from these to infer the motivations of the donor. This does not mean, however, that in an appropriate case a district judge may not make a decision on summary judgment. Where, from the facts stipulated and submitted on affidavit, when viewed in the light most favorable to the tax-payer, it plainly appears that a jury could not reasonably infer that the payments were motivated "out of affection, respect, admiration, charity or like impulses," or from a "detached or disinterested generosity," or from similar sentiments, summary judgment for the Government is the correct disposition. Such is the present case.

The established fact is that there was no personal relationship between Simmons and the brewery to prompt it to render him financial assistance. Nor was it impelled by charitable impulses toward the community, for the prize was to be paid to whoever caught the fish, regardless of need or affluence. Rather, the taxpayer has apparently rendered the company a valuable service, for, by catching the fish and receiving the award amid fanfare, he brought to the company the publicity the Fishing Derby was designed to generate.

Moreover, under accepted principles of contract law on which we may rely in the absence of pertinent Maryland cases, the company was legally obligated to award the prize once Simmons had caught the fish and complied with the remaining conditions precedent. The offer of a prize or reward for doing a specified act, like catching a criminal, is an offer for a unilateral contract. For the offer to be accepted and the contract to become binding, the desired act must be performed with knowledge of the offer. The evidence is clear that Simmons knew about the Fishing Derby the morning he caught Diamond Jim III. It is not fatal to his claim for refund that he did not go fishing for the express purpose of catching one of the prize fish. So long as the outstanding offer was known to him, a person may accept an offer for a unilateral contract by rendering performance, even if he does so primarily for reasons unrelated to the offer. Consequently, since Simmons could require the company to pay him the prize, the case is governed by *Robertson v. United States*, 343 U. S. 711, 713–714, 72 S. Ct. 994, 96, L. Ed. 1237 (1952). There, the Supreme Court held that, since the sponsor of a contest for the best symphonies submitted was legally obligated to award prizes in accordance with his offer, the payment made was not a gift to the recipient.

Judgment affirmed.

AGREEMENTS LATER TO BE REDUCED TO WRITING

On occasion the parties, having arrived at an understanding as to the terms of their proposed contract, decide to reduce their agreement to a written instrument. The question sometimes arises whether the parties are bound by the agreement before this written instrument is executed and signed by them. Of course, if the contract is one that is required to be in writing under the Statute of Frauds, no question arises where the pre-liminary negotiations are oral; in such a case the parties are not bound until the contract is in writing and signed. But what if the preliminary negotiations are contained in a series of letters or telegrams which would in themselves meet the legal requirement of written form? And what of cases in which written form is not required?

The answer in both these types of situation depends upon the intent of the parties as evidenced by what they said and did during the preliminary negotiations. If the facts in a given case show that the parties agreed upon all the essential terms of the contract in advance of the formal writing, so that nothing remained to be done except to set down those terms in the written instrument, the courts generally hold that the parties became bound when they arrived at their agreement. In such cases the courts find that the parties intended to be bound by the preliminary agreement and looked upon the written contract as a mere memorandum of that agreement. On the other hand, if the facts of a given case indicate that the parties did not intend to be bound until their preliminary agreement had been reduced to writing, then it will be held that they did not become bound before the execution of the written instrument.

Tradeways Incorporated v. Chrysler Corporation
342 F. (2d) 350 (1965)
United States Court of Appeals

This was an action by sales promotion service company against automobile manufacturer for breach of contract. The United States District Court, after jury trial, rendered judgment for plaintiff on its claim and for defendant on its counterclaim, and both parties appealed.

Judgment on plaintiff's claim reversed with instructions to dismiss the complaint; judgment on counterclaim affirmed.

SWAN, J. This is an action for breach of contract. Federal jurisdiction rests on diversity, plaintiff being a New York corporation with its principal place of business in New York and defendant, a corporation of Delaware, with its principal place of business in Michigan.

Plaintiff was engaged in the business of rendering sales promotional services to large corporations. Its complaint alleged that plaintiff entered into an express, bilateral, oral contract with defendant on November 22, 1955, and that defendant broke its contract obligations. Defendant counter-claimed for $12,480.12, the unpaid balance of a $15,000 advance made by defendant to plaintiff as part of the transaction. The case was tried before Judge Murphy and a jury in January 1964. The jury's verdict awarded plaintiff damages in the amount of $108,000. Judge Murphy directed entry of a judgment in favor of defendant on its counterclaim.

As a preliminary argument Chrysler asks us to dismiss the complaint on the grounds that Tradeways failed to prosecute its case with proper dispatch. The original complaint was filed on October 29, 1958. Four amended complaints were submitted between January 3, 1959 and February 18, 1960. The case was dismissed twice for lack of prosecution during 1960 and 1961. Twice it was restored to the calendar with Chrysler's consent. . . . Mr. Taylor had discussed the cost to the defendant and had stated two alternative price terms. The first alternative was that one part of the program could be purchased for $130,000 and the other part for between $35,000 and $40,000. The second was that each participating dealer would purchase the program for $180, to be paid at the rate of $15 per month. It is well settled that no contract can be formed if agreement has not been reached on an essential element, and price is certainly such an element. . . . Moreover, Chrysler told Mr. Taylor they wanted the proposal in writing. No agreement could bind Chrysler until the parties settled on a written document. . . . Four or five days after the presentation of the program on November 22, defendant's employee, Mr. Blount, telephoned Mr. Taylor that Tradeways was "selected" but Taylor did not know whether payment alternative No. 1 or No. 2 was accepted, and in any event it is apparent that the telephone conversation was not intended to supersede the requirement that Tradeways' offer be in writing, and therefore it cannot be considered to be the agreement from which Chrysler's obligations are measured. . . . The well recognized doctrine is that the existence of other exceptions to the statute of frauds [do] not take a contract out of the statute if performance is to continue beyond one year—the one-year rule of § 31(1) is still applicable. 2 *Corbin on Contracts* § 469 (1950); 3 *Williston on Contracts* § 501, at 613–615 (3d ed. 1960). Therefore, the statute of frauds would bar the introduction of any evidence relating to the alleged oral agreement of November 22, as there exists no memorandum signed by Chrysler embodying the terms of that agreement.

With regard to the counterclaim, judgment was ordered entered in favor of Chrysler for $12,480.12, which, by Tradeways' admission, was the unpaid balance of a $15,000 advance made by Chrysler to Tradeways under the terms of the written contract. We find no error with respect to this judgment and accordingly affirm.

Judgment on Tradeways' claim is reversed with instructions to dismiss the complaint. Judgment on Chrysler's counterclaim is affirmed.

REVIEW CASES

1. In a word-building contest run by the People's Monthly Co., the sum of $1,000 was offered for the largest list of correct words made from the word DETERMINATION. Scott submitted the largest number of correct words but failed to comply fully with all the rules of the contest. She sued for the prize money. Ruling? (Scott v. People's Monthly Co., 209 Iowa 503, 228 N. W. 263)

2. The Springfield Y. M. C. A. invited architects to submit plans for a proposed building, reserving the right to reject any and all designs submitted. Benton was among those who submitted plans. The committee thereafter voted that Benton be chosen architect, and two members of the committee

later unofficially informed him of this action. The vote remained on the books for forty days and was then rescinded. Benton brought an action against the Y. M. C. A., alleging the existence of a contract and the breach thereof. Judgment for whom? (Benton v. Springfield Y. M. C. A., 170 Mass. 534, 49 N. E. 928)

3. Kempner, who lived in Hot Springs, mailed a letter on Jan. 30th to Cohn, who lived in Little Rock, offering to sell him a lot on specified terms. The letter reached Cohn on Feb. 2d. On Feb. 7th Cohn deposited in the mail a letter accepting Kempner's offer. The same day Kempner wrote Cohn that he had changed his mind and would not sell the lot. Cohn sued Kempner for breach of contract. What holding? (Kempner v. Cohn, 47 Ark. 519, 1 S. W. 869)

4. Hobbs sued the Massasoit Whip Co. to recover on a shipment of eelskins. The skins had not been ordered by the company, but on four or five previous occasions Hobbs had sent skins to it, and they had been received and paid for. Hobbs knew that the company used such skins in its business and that they must be in good condition and over 22 inches long. He testified that the skins in question had fulfilled these conditions, and that the company had not sent him any notice of rejection. The company denied that a contract existed. Judgment for whom? (Hobbs v. Massasoit Whip Co., 158 Mass. 194, 33 N. E. 495)

5. Cline sent a letter, dated Jan. 29th, to Caldwell, offering to pay him $6,000 cash and to deed to him his land on Indian Creek in exchange for Caldwell's land known as the McKinsey farm, and stating, "I will give you eight days to accept or reject the offer." Caldwell received the letter on Feb. 2d, and on Feb. 8th he wired Cline as follows: "Land deal is made. Prepare deed to me. See letter." The telegram reached Cline on Feb. 9th. He refused to carry out the agreement, and Caldwell instituted a suit in equity for specific performance. Cline contended (1) that the offer and acceptance were too vague and uncertain, (2) that the acceptance was not made within the time specified in the offer, and (3) that since the offer was made by letter, the acceptance could be made only by letter. Judgment for whom? (Caldwell v. Cline, 109 W. Va. 565) 156 S. E. 55

6. Lomax wrote Rothchild Bros. the following letter: "I hereby agree to stand as surety for Watson to you on any credit which you may extend to him not exceeding $500, and hereby guarantee the payment of such account to that amount. Leroy Lomax." Rothchild Bros. sold liquor to Watson on credit to the amount of $976.63, of which $500 was extended on the faith of the guaranty. No notice was given to Lomax. Watson became insolvent, and his unpaid balance was $807.93. Lomax refused to pay the $500 demanded by Rothchild Bros. under the guaranty, and Rothchild Bros. brought suit. Judgment for whom? (Rothchild Bros. v. Lomax, 75 Ore. 395, 146 P. 479)

7. Gordon offered to sell certain realty to Arthur for $1,500. On March 3rd Arthur wrote to Gordon: "We consider this land to be worth $600 in cash, and if you are agreeable to sell out to us at that figure we will remit amount with deed for your signature." Gordon replied on March 23d: "Yours of March 3d received, containing bid of $600, which I am sorry to say I can-

not accept. When you can give me $1,000 send me your deed and money."
On June 22d Arthur wrote Gordon: "I am not willing to give you any
more than $750. If you are willing to accept this sum, advise me immediately
and the deed will be sent for your signature." Gordon never replied to this
letter. On June 28th Arthur's agent wrote Gordon: "I am directed by Mr.
Arthur to accept your offer of March 23d." To this Gordon replied on
July 5th: "I have turned my business over to Hugh White and he will trade
with you and then send me deed. Upon presentation of deed from him, will
sign and send back through Citizens Bank, Nevada, Missouri." On July 21st
Gordon and his wife conveyed the land to C. B. White. Arthur thereupon
filed suit against Gordon, asking for specific performance. Ruling? (Arthur
v. Gordon et al., 37 F. 558)

Mutual Assent III: Genuineness of Assent

8

We have seen that a contract can result only from an agreement between the parties which is voluntarily entered into. The minds of the parties must meet on all the essential terms of the agreement, and the assent to these terms by both parties must be unforced and free, so that their obligations under the contract are willingly assumed. Anything which interferes with these requirements will prevent an agreement from culminating in a valid contract.

It may appear on the face of an agreement that the parties assented to its terms and conditions, and the words used may seem to show clearly the contractual intent of the parties; nevertheless equity will go beyond the words of the agreement to determine whether the apparent assent is genuine assent.

Among the conditions which may prevent the agreement from being genuine and voluntarily arrived at, and which thereby destroy the apparent assent, are: (1) mistake, (2) innocent misrepresentation, (3) fraud, (4) duress, and (5) undue influence. Where one of these is found to have been operative in the formation of an agreement, the agreement will be held to be void or voidable, depending upon the circumstances.

MISTAKE

As a general rule, a party who has freely and unequivocally assented to the terms of a contract cannot later escape from its obligations simply by proving that his assent was based on a mistake, so that he finds himself in a situation different from the one he contemplated when he gave his assent. However, there are certain situations in which the courts will recognize that a misunderstanding or misconception has interfered with genu-

143

ineness of assent and is therefore grounds for rescission of the agreement. These situations arise (1) where the parties, though supposing that they have the same thing in mind, actually mean different things, or (2) where one or both of the parties, while meaning the same thing, form untrue conclusions as to the subject matter of the agreement.

In the first type of situation, the minds of the parties do not meet on the subject matter of the agreement. For example, A agrees to sell B a house which he owns on Walnut Street. About half of Walnut Street is known as East Walnut Street and the other half as West Walnut Street. A owns a house on East Walnut Street and another on West Walnut Street. When he agreed to sell a house to B, A had in mind his house on East Walnut Street; but B had in mind the house on West Walnut Street. In such a case, if neither party is at fault, the court would hold that no contract was formed.

In the second type of situation, the parties mean the same thing, but one or both parties enter into the agreement under some misconception about the subject matter. Where the mistake is unilateral, i.e. held by only one of the parties, the general rule is that no relief will be granted. For example, A, a contractor, submits his bid for the erection of a certain building, and the contract is later awarded to him. He then discovers that he made a mistake in his computations and that his bid was therefore lower than it should have been. A would ordinarily be unable to obtain equitable relief for his unilateral mistake. However, there are various exceptions to this rule. For example, if at the time of the agreement the other party was aware of A's mistake and wrongfully kept silent, A could probably have the contract rescinded. Likewise, in certain "hardship cases," where great injustice would otherwise result, courts will grant equitable relief where the mistake is by one party only.

In the case of mutual mistakes, i.e. mistakes common to both parties, the courts will often grant equitable relief by way of rescission of the contract. The general rule is that relief will be granted only if the mutual mistake concerns a *material fact*—that is, a fact sufficiently important to induce one or both parties to enter into the agreement—and only if it relates to the past or present. If the mistake relates to probable future happenings, no relief will be granted. A party to a contract may not avoid it merely by proving that it turned out to be more burdensome or less profitable than the parties expected when they entered into it. On the same principle, a mutual mistake as to the *quality* or *value* of the subject matter will not render the agreement void. Thus, A sells B a painting for $10, which both believe to be a fair price; but when B takes the painting to a dealer for resale, he discovers that it is worth $1000. A is bound by his contract.

A mutual mistake as to the existence of the subject matter at the time the agreement was entered into will warrant the rescission of the agreement. For example, if A agrees to sell B an automobile which, without the knowledge of either, has been destroyed by fire a few hours earlier, the agreement would be void and could be rescinded. A mutual mistake as to the quantity of the subject matter would have the same effect. For example, A agrees to sell B 10,000 bushels of wheat in a certain elevator for $22,000, and both A and B believe that the elevator contains 10,000 bushels of wheat. If it proved to contain only 8,000 bushels, B would be entitled to go into equity and rescind the agreement; alternatively, A would be unable to get specific performance of the agreement.

In spite of ignorance of the law or a mistake as to the meaning of the law, as applicable to the contract involved, the courts of equity generally refuse to grant relief, whether the mistake is unilateral or mutual. The general rule is that ignorance of the law is no excuse for the mistake, since everyone is presumed to know the law. This does not, however, apply to the law of another state or a foreign country. Furthermore, it is held that where the nonexistence of a right is involved, the mistake is not a mistake of law but a mistake of fact, and the court of equity will rescind the contract. This may be illustrated by a case where A thought that he had the legal title to a certain house and lot and agreed to sell the property to B. Later, when it was discovered that he did not have good title to the property, upon application to the court of equity the contract was rescinded.

Slenderella Systems, Inc. v. Gerber
163 A. (2d) 1960
Municipal Court of Appeals for the District of Columbia

This was an action on contract for weight-reducing course of treatment. Defendant counterclaimed for rescission because of alleged impossibility of performance and mutual mistake of fact. The Municipal Court for the District of Columbia . . . found for defendant, and plaintiff appealed.

ROVER, C.J. Appellant sued on a contract signed by appellee for a weight-reducing course of treatment according to the Slenderella system. The amount sued for was $290, being the balance due on a contract which was dated June 2, 1958, under which appellee agreed to pay $300 in installments and on which she made a $10 deposit.

The evidence showed appellee had long suffered from a back ailment and had been under a doctor's care for that condition since March 12, 1957. She also suffered from a weight problem and on the advice of some friends visited a Slenderella salon to inquire about their weight-reducing plan. She was given a complimentary treatment to illustrate the Slenderella method. This method consists primarily of manipulating and massaging parts of the body, including the back, by vibratory and oscillatory machinery. Before the complimentary treatment appellee was interviewed by the salon manager who inquired about her health in general. Appellee told the manager about her back ailment. After the treatment appellee was induced to take a weight-reducing course consisting of 150 treatments at a total cost of $300. She stated the salon manager told her the treatments would be helpful in firming her muscles, and that she herself thought that they would probably do her back some good.

Several days after the complimentary treatment appellee's back hurt so much that it was difficult for her to get up and move about. She visited her doctor and in the course of the consultation told him about the reducing treatment she had taken. He advised her against taking such treatments. At trial the doctor testified that appellee's back condition was chronic in the sense that it would be recurrent and continuing but not necessarily painful all the time. He stated that the vibratory machine used in this reducing method would aggravate appellee's condition and would be detrimental to her health if the treatments were continued. The court found for appellee, rescinded the contract due to impossibility of performance and mutual mistake of fact, and granted her counterclaim ordering restitution of the $10 down payment.

Appellant contends that appellee is bound by the language of the contract: "We rely on your representations that you are of full legal age, in good health, not pregnant, and know of no reason that would prevent you from starting and completing this slenderizing course." However, appellee did advise the salon manager of her back condition at the time of the complimentary treatment. The manager did not testify at trial, having been reassigned to appellant's Philadelphia salon. Consequently the court was correct in drawing any proper inference from appellant's failure to call its agent who had negotiated the contract. That left appellee's claim that she told the manager of her back condition uncontradicted and thus no representation of good health was made contrary to the provisions of the contract.

Appellant next assigns as error the failure of the court to find that appellee knew of her back injury and assumed the risk of incapacity to perform. Impossibility of performance due to illness is grounds for discharging a contract where the services are of a personal nature and unable to be performed for or by another. Appellee here did not so clearly assume the risk of such incapacity as to come under the exception to the rule and be bound thereby. Knowledge alone does not indicate an assumption of the risk of incapacity where appellee, at the inducement of appellant, contracted for treatments with the belief that her back condition would not be aggravated by the reducing plan, but could even prove to be benefited by it. The treatment proved to be extremely painful resulting in appellee's inability to perform under the contract; but this reflects more of a mutual mistake of fact as to the possible effect these treatments might have on her than does the blind willingness to proceed with them in spite of her condition. Since appellant knew of appellee's condition the court was forced either to accept this view or conclude that appellant knowingly allowed appellee to contract for treatments which could be injurious to her health.

With the exception of the down payment, this contract was wholly executory. To return the parties to their respective statuses worked no hardship on either of them. The counterclaim to rescind was timely and we find no error in the disposition by the court.

Affirmed.

Wood v. Boynton and Another
64 Wis. 265, 25 N. W. 42 (1885)

This was an action by Wood (plaintiff) against Boynton and another (defendants) to recover possession of an uncut diamond. Judgment for defendants, and plaintiff appealed. Affirmed.

Defendants were partners in the jewelry business. Plaintiff owned a small stone, of the nature and value of which she was ignorant. On December 28, 1883, she sold the stone to defendants for $1.00. Afterwards it was ascertained that the stone was a rough diamond worth about $700. After learning this fact plaintiff tendered defendants the $1.00 and ten cents as interest, and demanded a return of the stone to her. Defendants refused to deliver the stone, and thereupon plaintiff brought this action.

Plaintiff testified that she had thought the stone might be a topaz. She further testified, "Before I sold the stone I had no knowledge whatever that it was a diamond." Mr. Samuel B. Boynton, defendant to whom the stone was sold, testified that at the time he bought the stone he had never seen an uncut diamond, and that "I had no idea this was a diamond, and it never entered my mind at the time."

Plaintiff contended that there was a mutual mistake as to the kind or species of the thing sold and this justified a rescission. On the other hand, defendants argued that a mutual mistake as to the quality or value of the thing sold is no ground for a rescission of a contract; that a contract for the sale of a thing, the extent or value of which is understood to be unknown to both parties, or which is from its nature or character doubtful or uncertain, is valid and binding.

TAYLOR, J. This evidence clearly shows that the plaintiff sold the stone to the defendants and delivered it for a consideration of one dollar. The title to the stone passed by the sale and delivery to the defendants. How has that title been divested and again vested in the plaintiff? The contention of the learned counsel for the plaintiff is that the title became vested in the plaintiff by the tender to the defendant of the purchase money, with interest, and the demand of a return of the stone to her. Unless such tender and demand revested the title in the plaintiff, she cannot maintain her action.

The only question in the case is whether there was anything in the sale which entitled the plaintiff to rescind the sale and so revest the title in her. The only reasons we know for rescinding a sale and revesting the title in the vendor so that he may maintain an action at law for the recovery of the possession against the vendee are (1) that the vendee was guilty of some fraud in procuring a sale to be made to him; and (2) that there was a mistake made by the vendor in delivering an article which was not the article sold—a mistake in fact as to the identity of the thing sold with the thing delivered upon the sale. This last is not in reality a rescission of the sale made, as the thing delivered was not the thing sold, and no title ever passed to the vendee by such delivery. In this case there can be no just grounds for alleging that she was induced to make the sale by any fraud or unfair dealings on the part of the defendant. Both were entirely ignorant at the time of the character of the stone and of its intrinsic value. Mr. Boynton was not an expert in uncut diamonds, and had made no examination of the stone except to take it in his hand and look at it before he made the offer of one dollar. The plaintiff had the stone in her possession for a long time and it appears from her own statement that she had made some inquiry as to its nature and qualities. If she chose to sell it without further investigation as to its intrinsic value to a person who was guilty of no fraud or unfairness which induced her to sell it for a small sum, she cannot repudiate the sale because it is afterwards ascertained that she made a bad bargain. *Kennedy v. Panama, etc., Mail Co.*, L. R. 2 Q. B. 580.

There is no pretense of any mistake as to the identity of the thing sold. It was produced by the plaintiff and exhibited to the defendant before the sale was made, and the thing sold was delivered to the vendee when the purchase price was paid.

When this sale was made the value of the thing sold was open to the investigation of both parties; neither knew its intrinsic value, and, so far as the evidence in this case shows, both supposed the price paid was adequate. How can fraud be predicated upon such a sale, even though after-investigation showed that the intrinsic value of the thing sold was hundreds of times greater than the price paid?

The general rule of law is that, in the absence of fraud or warranty, the value of the property sold, as compared with the price paid, is no ground for a rescission of a sale. *Wheat v. Cross*, 31 Md. 99; *Lambert v. Heath*, 15 Mess. and W. 487; *Bryant v. Pember*, 45 Vt. 487.

Judgment for defendants affirmed.

INNOCENT MISREPRESENTATION

In the negotiation of a contract the parties frequently make descriptive statements about the subject matter of the contemplated contract. The law presumes that the parties will exercise common sense in interpreting such statements. Remarks that fall into the category of "puffing," "dealer's talk," "commendatory statements," or mere opinion must not be seriously relied upon by the other party in making up his mind about entering into the contract. For example, A, a retail furniture dealer, says to B, a customer, "This living-room suite is the best buy in town." Under the law B is not privileged to give serious consideration to this statement, for a reasonable man would recognize it as "seller's talk." However, if the statement made by A is an affirmation of a material fact involving the subject matter, and if it induces B to enter into the contract, A would be bound by his representations. If A tells B that the living-room suite is solid walnut, his statement is an affirmation of a material fact; and if B, in good faith, relies upon it in entering the contract, A would be bound by his statement. Particularly is this true if the facts contained in the statement are peculiarly within the knowledge of the party who makes them, and the other party has no knowledge of them himself and no adequate opportunity to verify them.

When misrepresentation of a material fact by one party has influenced another party to enter a contract, the contract may be rescinded in a court of equity by the party who has been misled, even though the party who made the false representation made it innocently and without knowledge that it was false. Such a contract is not absolutely void but it is voidable at the option of the injured party. If the contract is still executory the equity court will not grant specific performance to the party that misrepresented the fact. The misrepresentation may also form the basis for an action for damages.

Bates v. Cashman
119 N. E. 663, 230 Mass. 167 (1918)

This was a suit by N. C. Bates (plaintiff) against Daniel Cashman (defendant). Bill dismissed.

Plaintiff brought this suit to recover for the breach of a written contract to buy the stocks and bonds of the Newburyport Cordage Company. The securities were the means by which to convey control of land with a factory and machinery. Defendant contended that he was induced to sign the contract by false representations by plaintiff and that, therefore, he was not bound.

It was found by the master that during the negotiations preceding the contract, plaintiff represented that a right of way, which was a substantial factor of value in the real estate, was owned by the Newburyport Cordage Company and could not be interfered with. This representation, though made in good faith by plaintiff, was not true. Defendant relied upon such innocent representation and would not have signed the contract if he had known that it was false.

RUGG, C.J. A person seasonably may rescind a contract to which he has been induced to become a party in reliance upon false though innocent misrepresentations respecting a cognizable material fact made as of his own knowledge by the other party to the contract. The wrong in such a representation consists in stating as a fact that which is not known positively to be a fact. It is no excuse for making such a statement as of one's own knowledge that it was believed to be true or that the true state of affairs had been forgotten. It is wrongful to state a fact as true of one's own knowledge when he has no such knowledge.

In view of the express finding of fact by the master, this principle of law is decisive against the right of the plaintiff to recover. Bill dismissed.

FRAUD

Fraud, as distinguished from innocent misrepresentation, is characterized by deliberate deception or by representation made without regard to whether it is true or false. The courts have been hesitant to lay down a precise definition of fraud, for to formulate the exact requirements that must be met to constitute fraud would merely invite the crafty and cunning to accomplish their ends by showing through some fine distinction between the precise definition and their acts, that they have not actually committed a fraud. However, the general understanding of the term, as recognized by the courts, is made evident by their decisions. On the basis of these decisions, the elements of fraud may be stated as follows: (1) There must be misrepresentation or nondisclosure of a material fact. (2) The misrepresentation must be either deliberately false or made with reckless disregard of the truth or falsity of the statement. (3) The false statement must be made with an intent that the other party shall rely upon it as true. (4) The other party must actually rely upon it as true. (5) The other party must suffer injury as a result of such reliance.

Fraudulent misrepresentation can be made not only by means of deliberate misstatements but also through nondisclosure or deceptive partial disclosure of a material fact or facts when there is a duty to speak or to make full disclosure. Usually there is no legal obligation for one party to tell the other everything he knows about the matter under negotiation. As long as the parties are dealing at arm's length, each party is expected, under the law, to look after his own interests by informing himself as to the facts involved. Under such circumstances silence alone is not held to be fraud. But silence (or partial disclosure) does constitute an element of fraud when there is a duty to speak, as where a fiduciary or confidential relationship exists, e.g. between principal and agent, guardian and ward, attorney and client, and trustee and cestui que trust (beneficiary). Concealment and half-truths are in the same category as affirmative misstatements knowingly made. The law requires that both parties to the negotiation act in good faith.

To be fraudulent, the representation must relate to a present or past state of fact. A general statement as to the value of property, or the expression of an opinion as to future happenings or circumstances, is not considered a statement of fact, and hence if untrue does not constitute fraud. For example, if A says to B, "This car is worth twice what I am asking you for it," his statement is not regarded as a statement of fact. But if A says to B, "I paid $1500 for this car, but I am willing to sell it to you for only $800," his statement that he paid $1500 for the car purports to be a statement of fact, and if he paid less for the car his statement may be fraudulent.

In order to establish fraud, the innocent party must show not only that he relied upon the false statement, but also that he was justified in doing so. Here the courts apply the "reasonable man" test. The question whether the injured party acted prudently is a question of fact and one for the jury to decide.

Finally, in order to recover damages the injured party must show that he was injured by having entered into the contract in reliance upon the false statements made by the other party.

A number of remedies for fraud are available; the action chosen by the injured party will depend on the circumstances of the given case. He may go into equity and ask that the contract be rescinded and that he be allowed to recover anything he has paid. Or, if the contract is executory, he may refuse to perform it, and, if sued, set up the fraud as a defense. Finally, if the contract is executed on his part, he may elect to treat the contract as valid and sue in a court of law for money damages for the fraud and deceit practiced upon him.

Craun v. Craun

168 A. (2d) 898, 300 F. (2d) 737 (1962)

United States Court of Appeals

District of Columbia Circuit

This was an action for annulment of a ceremonial marriage. The Municipal Court for the District of Columbia dismissed wife's complaint and wife appealed. The Municipal Court of Appeals. . . . affirmed and wife was allowed an appeal. Judgment reversed and case remanded with instructions.

BASTIAN, J. This is an appeal allowed by this court from a decision of the Municipal Court of Appeals . . . dismising appellant's (wife) complaint for annulment of her ceremonial marriage to appellee on the ground of fraud. Appellee filed an answer to the complaint but did not appear at the trial of the case, although he was represented there by counsel. Neither he nor counsel appeared at the hearing in the Municial Court of Appeals or at the hearing in this court; nor was a brief filed on his behalf in either court.

Two witnesses, as well as appellant, testified in appellant's behalf in the Municipal Court. The following facts appear without contradiction:

Appellant followed her parents from West Virginia to Washington in September 1958, leaving behind her the wreckage of a marriage contracted when she was seventeen years of age and dissolved four years later by a divorce secured by her for nonsupport. She went to work at Sherrill's Bakery in Southeast Washington and shortly thereafter met appellee in a nearby restaurant, where her mother worked as a waitress. After dating for approximately two months, they decided to get married. During the course of their courtship appellee represented to appellant that he was steadily employed; that he had been so employed with his present employer for seven years; and that he had a furnished apartment into which they could move after the wedding. Appellant accepted on faith the truth of these statements and made no independent inquiry to determine their validity.

On November 3, 1958, appellee, accompanied by a couple named Smith called for appellant as she was getting off work. The four of them then drove to Forestville, Maryland, where they participated in a double wedding ceremony. Immediately after this ceremony the party began the drive back to Washington. In the course of conversation appellant was advised by appellee that he was not then employed and that he had not been employed for some time; that he had no furnished quarters rented for them but that, in fact, he expected appellant to live in an apartment consisting of one bedroom, living room and kitchen and occupied by the Smiths and two other unmarried couples who were living together meretriciously. Appellant refused to accept such living accommodations and insisted on being taken to her home; she was then informed by appellee that he did not want to see her again until she was willing to live with him where he wanted. The marriage was never consummated.

Appellant subsequently learned that at the time of the marriage appellee had a criminal record (six disorderly charges and one conviction for petit larceny). She testified under oath at the trial of this case that had she known all of these facts prior to the ceremony she would never have consented to the marriage.

Relief was denied appellant by the Municipal Court and the Municipal Court of Appeals mainly on the basis that she had made no premarital investigation of appellee's background. Those courts reasoned that, since appellant was no neophyte to the marital experience, she should have been on her guard concerning the representations of her intended husband. In other words, it was thought that the disillusionment occasioned by the failure of her first marriage should have made her more cautious about contracting her second.

The present marriage was contracted in Maryland. The Maryland courts have said that fraud which goes to the very essence of the marriage contract will render the contract voidable at the request of the innocent party. Further, the requirements as to the degree of fraud necessary to set aside a marriage are less exacting when the marriage has not been consummated. Of the essence of the marriage contract are the rights and duties pertaining to marital cohabitation.

Applying these principles to the instant case, we find that the appellee revealed to appellant, almost immediately after the wedding ceremony, that he expected her to spend the bridal night in a one bedroom apartment already occupied by the Smiths and two other couples who were not married. It certainly cannot be disputed, if we are to be civilized, that there are certain sectors of living which demand privacy; and consummation of a marriage is one phase of life in the private sector.

Moreover, appellee's fraud in this respect was not limited to the first night of the marriage. He placed no time limit on the living conditions he expected appellant to share with him. As far as he was concerned, those living conditions were to continue for an unspecified period of time. In effect, the fraud perpetrated by appellee upon appellant consisted of the misrepresentation or concealment of the fact that their marital cohabitation was scheduled to take place in circumstances akin to communal concubinage. The principle of togetherness has not yet ingratiated itself so pervasively into the fabric of our society that we are inclined to gainsay the conclusion that fraud of this character, if promptly denounced upon discovery by the innocent party, can vitiate a marriage where the proof is clear and convincing. Certain it is, there is no public interest to be promoted by maintaining such a union, either in form or substance. In any event, the idea violates our conception of the basic fundamentals of marriage. We think the concealment of such a warped design for conjugal existence as proposed by appellee in the instant case constituted fraud piercing to the heart of the marital compact, particularly when viewed in the light of other facts presented here.

Upon discovery of the living arrangements envisaged by her spouse, appellant immediately protested. In the face of appellee's adamant insistence that she either live with him on his terms or not at all, she chose to do the latter. She returned to her own home the same evening she was married, and the marriage was never consummated. In such circumstances we think appellant is entitled to an annulment of her marriage. We quite agree with the following language quoted from the dissenting opinion of the Municipal Court of Appeals:

"In these circumstances I think it was unrealistic to deny relief to this plaintiff on the ground 'that the public has a direct interest in [the marriage] as an institution of transcendent importance to social welfare.' It was even more unrealistic to deny relief because plaintiff did not launch a premarital investigation of her husband's financial status and criminal record. Nor is there much appeal in the trial court's suggestion of the much less savory remedy of a suit for divorce on the ground of adultery."

The judgment is reversed and the case is remanded with instructions to direct the reinstatement of appellant's complaint and to dispose of it in accordance with this opinion.

So ordered.

Progressive Life Insurance Co. v. James
8 S. E. (2d) 191, 62 Ga. App. 387 (1940)

This was an action by H. Brady James (plaintiff) against Progressive Life Insurance Co. (defendant). Judgment for plaintiff, and defendant appealed. Affirmed.

Plaintiff brought suit on a policy of insurance in which his wife was named as the insured, and he as the beneficiary. The sole defense of defendant, as shown by its answer, was that plaintiff had executed a release which completely discharged it from any and all liability on the policy. The jury returned a verdict in favor of plaintiff for $250 as principal and $55.68 as interest.

Plaintiff testified in part: "I signed the release on the policy the day my wife was buried, and the occasion of my signing was that Mr. Cooper (the agent of defendant who solicited and delivered the policy) said he had to have it to get the insurance. When he gave me the dollar and I signed the paper Mr. Cooper said he had to have some showing for the company, and he was going to take the paper to Atlanta and collect the $250. He said he would have to have the release before he could get the money. . . . I signed the release after I had surrendered the policy. . . . I have never read the release. When the application was made out Mr. Cooper asked me to sign it, and I did. I have known Mr. Cooper for several years. . . . Mr. Cooper had told me that they were not going to pay; but, when I signed that release he told me he was going to get the money for me anyhow. He didn't attempt to explain how he was going to get it, but said he had to have the release. . . . He simply misled me."

The sole question is, did the evidence show a signed release by plaintiff that discharged defendant company from any liability on the policy?

BROYLES, C.J. The testimony of the plaintiff clearly establishes that he was inexperienced in insurance matters, and that he was literally following the requests of Cooper, the agent, as though he were a child, in first complying with his request to sign his wife's name to the application after Cooper had filled it out, and also in delivering the policy and the signed release settlement after the death of his wife. If Cooper, the general agent of the company, had not procured the signature of the plaintiff to the release settlement, there could be no question as to the company's liability to pay the indemnity named in the policy. That plaintiff was misled by Cooper is therefore obvious. It is therefore our opinion that the case comes within the exception stated in the following rule of law: "It is a fundamental principle that one who can read must read; and the signing of a paper would be a waiver of representations alone as to the contents thereof. However, such representations as to the contents of a paper, coupled with a trick or artifice to procure the signing of same, may constitute such fraud as would relieve the signer of the obligation thereunder." *Gossett Sons v. Wilder*, 46 Ga. App. 651, 168 S. E. 903. Judgment for plaintiff affirmed.

General Motors Acceptance Corporation v. Blanco

181 Neb. 562, 149 N. W. (2d) 516 (1967)

Supreme Court of Nebraska

This was an action by General Motors Acceptance Corporation (plaintiff) against Joe Blanco and Bobby Blanco (defendants). Judgment for plaintiff and defendants appealed. Judgment affirmed.

This is a replevin action brought by General Motors Acceptance Corporation, hereinafter referred to as plaintiff, against Joe and Bobby Blanco, defendants. Bobby Blanco did not sign the contract involved herein, but is a defendant because the certificate of title to the automobile, which is the subject of the contract, shows title in Joe Blanco or Bobby Blanco. Any interest Bobby may have depends upon the title of her husband and no reference will be made to her hereafter. Joe Blanco will be referred to as defendant.

SPENCER, J. A short description of the contract is necessary to an understanding of the case. On the front side of the contract, immediately following the title in solid capitals, "CONDITIONAL SALE CONTRACT," is the following sentence: "The undersigned seller hereby sells, and undersigned buyer or buyers, jointly and severally hereby purchase(s), subject to the terms and conditions set forth below *and upon the reverse side hereof,* the following property, delivery and acceptance of which in good order are hereby acknowledged by buyer, viz.: * * *." (Italics supplied.) Here follows a description of the vehicle. Following that are eight numbered paragraphs which set forth the price, insurance premium, and terms of the transaction. The remainder of the face of the instrument above the signature line is an explanation of insurance provisions.

The following then appears: "Executed in quadruplicate, copy of which was delivered to, and receipt is acknowledged by, buyer, this 21 day of _____ July _____, 1964

(DO NOT DATE ON SUNDAY)

"A Buyer Signs in Ink   Joe Blanco (Sgd.)

2038   12th,   Mitchell, Nebraska

(STREET)   (TOWN)   (POSTAL ZONE)   (STATE)

"B Co-Buyer Signs in Ink   _____

(STREET)   (TOWN)   (POSTAL ZONE)   (STATE)

"Seller Signs in Ink   Kramer Motors, Inc.

By   John A. Plaster (Sgd.)

(TITLE)   (ADDRESS)"

Following the signatures is the assignment and transfer of the instrument to the plaintiff.

It is to be noted that we italicized "and upon the reverse side hereof," appearing in the first paragraph of the contract. We did this to indicate that these words are in boldface type to contrast them from the rest of the sentence, although the size of the type is the same.

On the reverse side of the instrument, under the title "Provisions," are 12 numbered sections, some of which have several paragraphs. The type is small but readable. Provision No. 1 is as follows: "For the purpose of securing payment of the obligation hereunder, seller reserves title, and shall have a security interest, in said property until said obligation is fully paid in cash."

We have heretofore, in *Blanco v. General Motors Acceptance Corp.*, fully and adequately described the transaction and set out sufficient of the defendant's allegations and assumptions that no purpose will be served by repetition herein. Suffice it to say that defendant's argument is bottomed upon the premise that the language of the contract is so unintelligible, vague, ambiguous, so contrary to public policy, and so consciously loaded in favor of the plaintiff, that its execution constituted a fraud on the defendant, and that fraud vitiated or rendered the contract void.

Defendant tries to make much of the fact that he did not read the reverse side of the contract. Generally in the absence of fraud, one who does not choose to read a contract before signing it cannot later relieve himself of its burdens.

The only question to be determined herein is the right to possession. The trial court properly found the right of possession in plaintiff. Affirmed.

DURESS

Duress is defined in Section 492 of the *Restatement of the Law of Contracts* as "any wrongful act of one person that compels a manifestation of apparent assent by another to a transaction without his volition, or any wrongful threat of one person by words or other conduct that induces another to enter into a transaction under the influence of such fear as precludes him from exercising free will and judgment, if the threat was intended or should reasonably have been expected to operate as an inducement." When duress has been exercised in the negotiation of a legal instrument, the instrument is *voidable* at the option of the injured party.

Under the early common law a person was required to exercise a high degree of resistance to ulterior pressures and influences of others in business relationships. The standard set up by the early courts was that of a constant and courageous man. Later the courts reduced the requirement of resistance to that of a person of ordinary firmness. Modern courts reject these yardsticks and examine each case upon its individual merits, taking into consideration such factors as the age, sex, and mental capacity of the injured party, the relations of the parties, and the nature of the act or threat. If the violence or threat of violence is found to have been sufficient to overcome the free exercise of the individual's will power, it is held that duress was present. No one is deprived of the protection of the law simply because he is timid or because a more courageous person would not have yielded to the duress.

Duress may be exercised by personal violence or threat of personal violence, imprisonment or threat of imprisonment, threat to one's property or to his wife, child, or other close relative. Modern courts have even extended the application of the law concerning duress to acts or threats to one's business.

Owings v. Owings

(141 Md. 416) 118 A. 858 (1922)

Court of Appeals of Maryland

ADKINS, J. In the bill of complaint filed in this case the appellant asks for annulment of his marriage to the appellee on the ground that he was forcibly and without his consent married to the appellee, and that at the time of the marriage appellant was in such a mental condition that he was entirely unconscious of what was being done, and was incapable of entering into a valid marriage contract. . . .

[The] appellant and appellee became acquainted in December, 1920, while they were employed at Springfield Hospital; he as attendant and she as nurse. . . . They became attached to each other, . . . and she became pregnant early in June, whereupon he promised to marry her, and appointed a day in June, but gave some excuse for not keeping this appointment, and suggested a postponement until July. On July 22, 1922, appellee and her mother went to Catonsville to see appellant to find out what he was going to do. He requested them to get a marriage license, saying he was busy and could not well leave his work, promising to come to appellee's home to be married at 5 o'clock on the afternoon of Saturday, July 23d. He did not come. . . . Appellee's brothers, Henry and Irvin Blum . . . in passing Mr. Shipley's place . . . noticed appellant's car in the yard, and correctly surmised that he was calling on Miss Iva Shipley. Stopping there Peter Blum knocked at the door, and Miss Shipley answered. He asked for George, and George went outside with him. There appears to have been quite a dispute and considerable . . . scrimmage, in the course of which George declined to go with them to be married, and ran to his car, on the side where there was no door, which, according to Peter, made him suspect that George was reaching over for his pistol, whereupon Peter drew his and flourished it in the air. . . . [The] Blums deny George's story that he was hit on the head and rendered unconscious, and that he was taken to Westminster in that condition of mind, and went through the ceremony obvious to all that was going on. He is corroborated only by the testimony of his roommate, Zimmerman, that when he got back to Catonsville he had a knot on his head as big as a hen egg, and his trousers were torn, and he had no hat. . . .

There does not seem to be much doubt that at Shipley's George protested against entering into the marriage state that night, and that he would have gotten away if some pressure had not accompanied the arguments that were used to make him see his duty.

In the case of *Seyer v. Seyer*, 37 N. J. Eq. 210, the Vice Chancellor said: "It may be said that when the court is satisfied that antenuptial incontinence has taken place, the charge of threat or menace unlawful, or fraud or duress, must be most fully and satisfactorily established before the court will annul the marriage."

But, even if it could be found from the evidence, either that the marriage was contracted, as he contends, while appellant was not in a mental condition to give valid assent to it, or was induced by fear of bodily harm, in neither event would such a finding avail him anything, because voluntary consummation is established by the overwhelming weight of the testimony. That he went with his wife to her home after the ceremony and spent the night with her in her room is sworn to by six or seven witnessees and contradicted by no one except the appellant. . . . A marriage contract, which when entered into was voidable merely, may be ratified by the parties by cohabitation as husband and wife after the condition which made it voidable has ceased to exist. . . . Certainly there was no such restraint upon the appellant in this case as to compel him to consummate the marriage. He admits that consciousness returned before they left Westminster. . . .

The principle that application for nullification in case of duress must be made promptly and before a consummation of the marriage by voluntary cohabitation is recognized in *Ridgely v. Ridgely*, 79 Md. 307, 29 Atl. 597, 25 *L. R. A.* 800.

The application was not made in this present case until after appellant had been indicted for failure to support his wife. [In essence the court said to George Owings "you have tarried too long."]

Decree affirmed, with costs to appellee.

UNDUE INFLUENCE

Undue influence exists when the will of the promisor is influenced or dominated by the stronger personality or will of another to such an extent that his assent cannot be said to be genuine. Like duress, it is a form of coercion; but while in the case of duress the promisor yields his assent because of fear, in undue influence he yields because his will cannot hold out against the dominating personality or the superior position of the other party.

Undue influence commonly arises (1) where the promisor is old or in ill health; (2) where the promisor is mentally incapacitated; (3) where the promisor is in a position of financial distress or physical helplessness or dependency; (4) where a confidential or fiduciary relationship exists, such as trustee and cestui que trust, guardian and ward, attorney and client; or (5) where the so-called "parental relationship" exists, as between parent and child, husband and wife, brother and sister. When the relationship between the parties is one of confidence and trust, there is a presumption of undue influence. This presumption is rebuttable, but it does throw upon the promisee or grantee or devisee the burden of proof that no undue influence was exerted by him.

The courts do not hold that reasonable persuasion or arguments addressed to the promisor by the promisee are per se undue influence so long as the promisor reaches a decision upon the basis of his own judgment. But if the promisee exerts such influence upon the promisor that the latter is unable to resist and consequently acts against his own judgment in the matter, the court will hold that undue influence exists.

Contracts and comparable legal instruments, such as wills, deeds, and mortgages, that result from undue influence are not void but voidable at the option of the injured party.

Clement v. Smith
293 Mich. 393, 292 N. W. 243 (1940)

This was a bill in equity by Augusta Day Clement (plaintiff) against William L. Smith (defendant) to set aside a deed and collateral contract and for other relief. Decree for plaintiff, and defendant appealed. Affirmed.

Plaintiff, a widow over 70 years of age, owned and made her home in a small house in Croswell, Michigan. Her son was a farmer and lived near Sanilack, Michigan. She lived alone and saw her son only occasionally. Defendant and his wife were old friends of plaintiff. Defendant frequently came to Croswell, and while there he stayed as a guest in plaintiff's home. Sometimes defendant's wife accompanied him. There was no blood relationship, but there was a feeling of kinship because plaintiff's father was a brother of defendant's first wife's father. Plaintiff also visited defendant at his home in Detroit. At the time of the event in question, plaintiff was in poor health, her eyesight was defective, and her memory was weak. She trusted defendant implicitly in all her affairs. He did many odd jobs at her house to make her more comfortable. In 1935 plaintiff executed a warranty deed to her home, naming defendant as grantee, reserving a life estate in herself. The deed was deposited in escrow with an attorney. Plaintiff testified that she always understood that she could withdraw the deed whenever she so wished. Defendant agreed in writing to pay the medical bills for her last illness and for her burial and also to erect a headstone on her grave. This agreement was executed on November 4, 1935. The deed was recorded on January 14, 1938. About a year later plaintiff filed a bill of complaint to set aside the conveyance and cancel the agreement on the ground that execution thereof was induced by defendant's overreaching influence and abuse of confidence placed in him. The trial judge concluded that plaintiff was of weak mentality, that she placed her trust in defendant, and that he took advantage of her confidence and obtained the conveyance for a grossly inadequate consideration. Relief was decreed in accordance with the prayer of the bill.

BUTZEL, J. It is said that equity will set aside a conveyance executed for a grossly inadequate consideration when there is great weakness of mind in the person executing it from age, sickness, or any other cause which would not amount to an absolute disqualification. *Allore v. Jewell*, 94 U. S. 506; *Bilman v. Kolarik*, 234 Mich. 689. Though the grantor may have been capable of understanding the nature of a business transaction, if there was inability fairly to appreciate its consequences which resulted in overlooking many considerations which would lead to sounder judgment, there is an exposure to imposition by those in confidence. Where the confidence has been abused, as under the facts before us, equity will not stand by with folded arms. *Seeley v. Price*, 14 Mich. 541. The conclusion of the trial court was fortified by the fact that the conveyance left plaintiff without any security for her future support, for her life estate in the property would be practically unmarketable. It has been said that such facts demonstrate beyond question "either incapacity or dishonest intent, or both." *Thorn v. Thorn*, 51 Mich. 167. The decree is affirmed.

UNIFORM COMMERCIAL CODE

Sec. 1–107 of the Code states that "any claim or right arising out of an alleged breach can be discharged in whole or in part without consideration by a written waiver or renunciation signed and delivered by the aggrieved party."

If the court finds a contract or any clause in a contract for the sale of goods to be unconscionable, it may refuse to enforce it. Section 2–302 of the Code provides: (1) If the court as a matter of law finds the contract or any clause of the contract to have been unconscionable at the time it was made, the court may refuse to enforce the contract, or it may enforce the remainder of the contract without the unconscionable clause, or it may so limit the application of any unconscionable clause as to avoid any unconscionable result. (2) When it is claimed or appears to the court that the contract or any clause thereof may be unconscionable, the parties shall be afforded a reasonable opportunity to present evidence as to its commercial setting, purpose, and effect to aid the court in making the determination.

In *Hume v. U.S.*, 132 U. S. 406, 10 S. Ct. 134, the court said, "an unconscionable bargain or contract is one which no man in his senses, not under delusion, would make, on the one hand, and which no fair and honest man would accept, on the other."

This principle has been applied in both law and equity, not only for the sale of goods but in other transactions as well.

REVIEW CASES

1. Tolles' agent and Newton executed an agreement by which Tolles agreed to sell and Newton to buy the Tolles farm, "a certain parcel of land situated in Nashua . . . containing about 200 acres." Upon payment of the purchase price, Newton took possession of the farm and shortly thereafter found that it contained only about 135 acres. Failing to adjust the matter with Tolles, Newton filed suit in equity asking that the agreement be rescinded and his money refunded. Holding? (Newton v. Tolles, 66 N. H. 136, 19 A. 1092)

2. Raffles entered into a purported contract with Wichelhaus for the sale of cotton. The cotton was to arrive aboard the ship *Peerless* from Bombay. There were two ships by the name of *Peerless* sailing from Bombay. Raffles had in mind the *Peerless* sailing from Bombay in October, while Wichelhaus had in mind the *Peerless* sailing from Bombay in December. Was there a binding contract? (Raffles v. Wichelhaus, 6 Eng. Rul. Cas. 198, 159 Eng. Rep. 375)

3. Ackerman was informed by Halsell, a representative of the Williamson-Halsell-Frazier Co., that his son had embezzled about $4,000 of the company's money, that Halsell had a warrant for the son's arrest, that a deputy sheriff was waiting in the next room to serve the warrant, and that unless the father signed the notes and mortgage in question, the son would be arrested, tried, and sent to prison. The father signed the notes and mortgage, but when they came due he refused to pay. The company sued to foreclose on the mortgage and recover on the notes. Judgment for whom? (Williamson-Halsell-Frazier Co. v. Ackerman et al., 77 Kan. 502, 94 P. 807)

4. Randall through his agent sold goods to Bauman, who stated that he had $3,000 in his business, consisting of merchandise and book accounts, and that he had $300 in cash. On the strength of these representations Randall extended credit and shipped the goods. Actually Bauman was indebted in his business to the amount of $2,000. A creditor of Bauman took judgment against him and levied upon the goods in question by having the sheriff seize them. Randall sued the sheriff, Newell, in replevin to recover the goods. Judgment for whom? (Newell v. Randall, 32 Minn. 171, 19 N. W. 972)

5. R. H. Leathers was ninety years old, sick, had to be carried from room to room, and needed constant attention. He lived with his nephew, who took care of him and managed all his affairs. Shortly before his death he gave most of his property to his nephew and the nephew's wife. Turner and other heirs attacked the gifts on the ground of undue influence. Ruling? (Turner et al. v. Leathers et ux., 191 Tenn. 292, 232 S. W.(2d) 269)

6. Alexander innocently misrepresented to McFadden that he owned certain patent rights, and contracted to sell them to McFadden. In fact, Alexander had only a license to use the patent rights. McFadden sued to recover the purchase money. Judgment for whom? (McFadden v. Alexander, 154 Iowa 716, 135 N. W. 396)

Capacity of
Parties

9

In order to create an agreement that is legally binding and enforceable, the parties to the agreement must have legal capacity to contract. This is the second essential of a contract.

As the requirement indicates, not all persons have full capacity to contract. Some persons have only partial capacity; some have none. If A, a person with full contractual capacity, enters into a contract with B, a person with only partial contractual capacity, the contract will be binding as to A but voidable at the option of B. If A attempts to contract with C, a person with no contractual capacity, the agreement will be void.

The requirement of legal capacity to contract applies only to the parties themselves. For example, A contracts to buy a diamond ring from B to give to C. A and B are the parties to the contract; C's capacity to contract has no bearing on the validity of the contract.

It is presumed that all parties to an agreement have full capacity to contract. Therefore, if a defendant does not have such capacity, that fact must be set up by him by way of defense.

A person may not enter into a contract with himself. Nor may a party in his individual capacity contract with himself in a representative capacity. For example, if A is the executor of the estate of B, he may not in his individual capacity enter into a contract with himself as executor of the estate of B, to borrow money from B's estate.

The question of capacity to contract may arise with respect to any agreement to which one of the following is a party: (1) infants (i.e. minors); (2) insane persons; (3) intoxicated persons; (4) married women; (5) aliens.

INFANTS

GENERAL CONTRACTUAL CAPACITY

Under the common law an infant is a person of either sex under the age of twenty-one. With rare exceptions this is also true under the statutes of the several states. Under the statutes of a few states, however, a woman attains her majority at the age of eighteen, especially with respect to her ability to make a marriage contract; and in a few states infants, both male and female, acquire full contractual rights when they marry.

Under the common law an infant becomes of age at the beginning of the day before his twenty-first birthday. Thus, if A was born on May 2, 1928, he would be held to have reached his majority on May 1, 1949. Today the statutes of some states provide that an infant reaches his majority on his twenty-first birthday. The precise dividing line between infancy and majority is important upon occasion in determining the rights of the parties in a given business transaction.

Contrary to the view held by many people, the contracts of infants are not void but merely voidable at the election of the infant. If an infant wishes to recognize an agreement he has entered into, the agreement is enforceable; but if he elects to disaffirm the contract, his infancy is an absolute defense. The defense of infancy is available only to the infant himself, and may not be set up by the other party to the contract if he is an adult who possesses full contractual capacity. The basis for this rule of law is the assumption that persons under the age of twenty-one, because of their immaturity and lack of business experience, may be taken advantage of by scheming and unscrupulous adults, to the loss or dissipation of their property or estates; hence the law affords them special protection against the making of unwise and unfair contracts. The decisions of the courts make clear, however, that this legal protection is to be used by the infant as a shield and not as a sword.

LIABILITY FOR BUSINESS CONTRACTS

Infants are not liable on their business contracts if they elect to disaffirm them. The courts take the position that the law does not contemplate that a minor shall become the proprietor or operator of a business or occupation which involves the making of a variety of contracts. Thus, he is not liable on his contracts for the repair, improvement, or insurance of his real estate, for insurance on his own life, or for goods or merchandise purchased for a business which he is conducting.

An infant may become a member of a partnership, but his contract to become a member is voidable at his option. He may disaffirm the contract and withdraw from the firm without being liable for damages for the breach of his contract. In most states, however, his capital contribution to the partnership will be subject to the claims of partnership creditors.

Under the common law the parent is entitled to the earnings of his minor child unless the child has been emancipated. The child may be emancipated either by the parent or through prescribed statutory procedure. It should be noted, however, that emancipation of a minor does not have the effect of endowing him with full contractual capacity; his contracts are still voidable at his option.

LIABILITY FOR NECESSARIES

An infant is not liable on his contracts for necessaries, whether they be for goods or for services. However, he is liable in quasi-contract for the reasonable value (not the contract price) of such necessaries if they are actually furnished to him and he makes use of them. The Uniform Sales Act states, "Where necessaries are sold and delivered to an infant . . . he must pay a reasonable price therefor . . ." (Section 2). The law thus protects an infant against the possibility that the other party to the agreement has taken advantage of him by overcharging him. If the necessaries have not yet been accepted or received, the infant may disaffirm the contract without liability.

There is no hard and fast rule as to what goods and services constitute "necessaries." In general the courts hold that food, clothing, lodging, medical and dental attention, tools of the trade, and an elementary or vocational education are necessaries. Section 2 of the Uniform Sales Act states, "necessaries in this section means goods suitable to the condition in life of such infant or other person, and to his actual requirements at the time of delivery." Thus, an item might be considered a necessary for one infant and not for another. Moreover, an item is not a necessary if it duplicates what has already been furnished to the infant by his parents or guardian. Courts will always take into consideration the quality and quantity of the things supplied to the infant, in relation to his circumstances and needs.

The general rule is that an article or service, in order to be classed as a necessary, must be personal to the infant; that is, it must be for his own personal needs, "either those of his body, or those of his mind." For example, food and clothing bought for the use of another would not be classed as necessaries. An important exception to this rule of law is that the infant is liable for the reasonable value of necessaries furnished to his wife, and, in most states, to his children.

Schoenung v. Gallet
238 N. W. 852, 206 Wis. 52 (1931)

This was an action by Leo Schoenung (plaintiff), by his guardian ad litem, against Helen Gallet, as administratrix of the estate of Robert H. Hippe, deceased (defendant). Judgment for defendant, and plaintiff appealed. Reversed and remanded with directions.

Plaintiff, while a minor, commenced this action on March 13, 1930, to recover possession of an automobile and his promissory note for $250, which he delivered to defendant in exchange for another automobile, which plaintiff had returned to defendant.

On April 15, 1929, plaintiff, a minor, nineteen years of age, purchased from defendant an automobile for $300, for which he gave his judgment note for $250 and an automobile, which defendant accepted in trade at a valuation of $50. At that time plaintiff was an emancipated minor living with his parents on a farm, which was three miles from the city where he was employed at $75 per month in an implement business. He had been working for several years and had been permitted to keep his earnings. Between April 15 and June 6, 1929, he drove the automobile between 600 and 1000 miles on pleasure trips, and used it occasionally in going to or from his work. On June 6, 1929, he restored the automobile to defendant by leaving it at defendant's garage, and he demanded the return of his note and his former automobile. Defendant refused to accept the returned automobile and to return the plaintiff's note and his former automobile, which had been sold and which had been wrecked. The terms of the purchase were fair and reasonable, and there was nothing wrong with the automobile when plaintiff returned it on June 6th.

The lower court concluded that the automobile was necessary to plaintiff to carry on his business and employment and that he was not entitled to rescission and to recover his note and former automobile.

FRITZ, J. That plaintiff was an emancipated minor was immaterial as a matter of law in this action. Emancipation does not remove or affect a minor's incapacity to subject himself to contractual liability for things which are not necessaries. Consequently, plaintiff lacked capacity to contract for the purchase of this automobile, unless it was a necessary for him under the particular facts and circumstances of this case. In 31 *C. J.* 1077, Sec. 175, it is said: "The term 'necessaries,' as used in the law relating to the liability of infants therefor, is a relative term, somewhat flexible, except when applied to such things as are obviously requisite for the maintenance of existence, and depends on the social position and situation in life of the infant, as well as upon his own fortune and that of his parents. The particular infant must have an actual need for the article furnished; not for mere ornament or pleasure. The articles must be useful and suitable, but they are not necessaries merely because useful or beneficial. Concerning the general character of the things furnished, to be necessaries the articles must supply the infant's personal needs, either those of his body or those of his mind. However, the term 'necessaries' is not confined to merely such things as are required for a bare subsistence. There is no positive rule by means of which it may be determined what are or what are not necessaries, for what may be considered necessaries for one infant may not be necessaries for another infant whose state is different as to rank, social position, fortune, health, or other circumstances, the question being one to be determined from the particular facts and circumstances of each case."

In *Covault v. Nevitt*, 157 Wis. 113, 146 N. W. 1115, the question arose as to whether a minor who owned real estate could contract for the employment of a janitor. This court said: "It is clear that in the instant case the alleged contract could only be sustained, if at all, upon the ground that it was a contract for necessaries; and it is equally clear that such a contract is not a contract for necessaries. The general rule respecting necessaries is that they must be such as to supply the personal needs of the infant. Manifestly the contract in this case is not a contract for necessaries. . . ."

In *Wallace v. Newdale Furniture Co.*, 188 Wis. 205, 205 N. W. 819, a minor sought to recover money which she had paid as part of the purchase price for furniture, which she used for keeping roomers, and then returned during her minority to the defendant. The court said: "It has not been contended by counsel for the appellant that the articles purchased by the plaintiff were necessaries. The fact that a minor engages in business does not remove the incapacity to make general contracts, and, in the absence of statutes, purchases made in trade cannot be regarded as necessaries."

Although conditions and circumstances may exist because of which an automobile may be considered a necessary for a minor, it has thus far been held that a motor vehicle is not a necessary and that his contract for the purchase thereof is voidable. In the case at bar an automobile was not necessary for the personal use or support of plaintiff. The mere fact that his place of employment was three miles from the home of his parents, with whom he resided, did not necessitate his ownership of an automobile. Likewise, inasmuch as he lacked capacity to contract for an automobile for use in a business of his own, he was also thus incapacitated to contract for an automobile which he might occasionally have use for in performing his work for his employer. It follows that when plaintiff, during his minority, restored that automobile and the certificate of title to the defendant, he was entitled to the return of his note and his former automobile, or the value thereof.

Judgment reversed, and cause remanded, with directions to enter judgment for the recovery by plaintiff of the sum of $50, with interest from June 6, 1929, and the surrender for cancellation of plaintiff's note for $250, dated April 15, 1929.

Williams v. Buckler
264 S. W. (2d) 279 (1954)

This was an action by Charles Williams (plaintiff) against William Buckler (defendant). Judgment for defendant and plaintiff appealed. Reversed.

Plaintiff brought this action for a judgment for $2,000, the alleged value of certain farm machinery which the petition averred defendant had wrongfully converted. The petition alleged that defendant was under twenty-one years of age and was engaged in farming, and that the machinery was loaned to him to aid him in cultivating a farm so that he might earn a living for himself, wife, and child. The farm machinery consisted of a tractor, disc, and culti-packer. It was further averred in the petition that the machinery was loaned to the infant defendant in consideration of his agreement that when the machinery was not in use he would store it in the Farmers' Warehouse located in Lebanon, which was known by plaintiff to be a safe place in which to store the machinery; that defendant willfully disregarded his agreement, and when the machinery was not in use he stored it in a warehouse in Lebanon which contained bottled gas and high explosives; that the warehouse burned and destroyed the machinery to defendant's damage of $2,000.

The trial judge was of the opinion that the infant defendant could not be held liable for his tort in breaching his contract of bailment because to do so it would be necessary to base the liability upon his voidable bailment contract, as the machinery was not a necessary for which an infant may be held liable. The plaintiff appealed.

SIMS, C.J. We regard this farm machinery as a necessary for the infant defendant; therefore, he is liable on his contract. At the time he made his contract with the plaintiff, Williams, defendant was married and had a wife and child dependent upon him for support. He was supporting himself and family by tilling the soil and in order to do that in the machine age it was necessary for him to have a tractor, disc, and cultipacker. Years ago we held a work horse was necessary for an infant who was earning a living for himself and family by farming and he was liable for the reasonable value of the horse. We see a distinction between a pleasure horse and a work horse just as we see a distinction between an automobile and a farm tractor, and while a pleasure horse and an automobile cannot ordinarily be termed necessaries, we think a work horse and a tractor may be so considered.

We realize the general rule to be that an infant should not be encouraged to go into business and articles purchased by him for business purposes are not usually regarded as necessaries. But this court said in the Beeler Case, "An infant must live as well as a man." In the case at bar these farm tools are necessaries for the infant to support himself and family and he is liable for their reasonable value.

Generally, if the bailed property is used for a different purpose from that which was intended by the parties, or for a longer period or in a different manner or place than the parties intended, the bailee is not only responsible for all damages, but if a loss occurs, although by an inevitable casualty, he will generally be held liable therefor; nor is infancy a defense. As long as the infant keeps within the terms of the bailment, he is not liable for damages to the property, but when he willfully departs from the object of the bailment and puts the property to an unauthorized use, or puts it in an unauthorized place, as was done in the instant case, the bailment is immediately terminated and there is a conversion of the property for which the infant is liable the same as if he had taken the property in the first place without permission. *Vermont Acceptance Corp. v. Wiltshire*, 103 Vt. 219, 153 A. 199.

DISAFFIRMANCE OF CONTRACT

In general, an infant may disaffirm his contract at any time before he reaches his majority or within a reasonable time thereafter. But after he has once disaffirmed the contract, he may not change his mind and ratify it.

In disaffirming his contract an infant is not required to use any set method. Disaffirmance may be expressly stated, either orally or in writing; or it may be implied by the infant's behaving in such a manner as to make clear his intention not to be bound by the contract.

The problem of disaffirmance is simple if the contract is wholly executory, i.e. if neither party has performed. In that case, all the infant need do is to disaffirm the contract. Since he has not given any consideration to the other party, he is entitled to nothing upon disaffirmance; nor has the other party any cause of action against him.

A more serious problem arises where the contract has been executed by both parties and the infant then decides to disaffirm the contract and demands a return of the consideration which he has given to the other party. The decisions of the courts in such cases are not uniform in all respects. Practically all courts agree that if the infant is in a position to restore the consideration which he has received from the other party, or any part of it, he must do so as a prerequisite to disaffirmance. If he has used, dissipated, disposed of, or even squandered the consideration which he received, or if it has depreciated in value, most courts hold that he is still entitled to secure the return of the consideration which he gave the other party; some, however, have held that such loss must be taken into consideration in determining the amount which the other party to the contract will be required to pay or return to the infant.

If the contract is executed and the infant fails to disaffirm it within a reasonable time after he reaches his majority, he is deemed to have ratified it. The right of the infant to disaffirm his executed contract extends to his heirs, personal representatives, and guardian, in case of his death. On the other hand, if the contract is executory, the infant's failure or omission to ratify when he reaches his majority, or in a reasonable time thereafter, is not held to be a ratification of the contract; he does not become bound until and unless he definitely ratifies the contract. However, some courts have modified this rule by holding that if the infant has received something of value under the contract, he should be held to the bargain if he retains the consideration and does not disaffirm within a reasonable time after he reaches his majority.

A special rule governs contracts involving real property. An infant may not disaffirm such a contract until he has attained his majority; then he may either disaffirm it or ratify it. In most of the states "a reasonable time" in which to disaffirm a contract is longer in the case of real property than in the case of personal property.

Disaffirmance sometimes raises questions concerning the rights of third parties. For example, A, a minor, sells his typewriter to B, an adult, for $100 cash. Soon thereafter B sells the typewriter to C, an innocent purchaser for value and without notice. Then A disaffirms his contract and demands the return of the typewriter from C. Is C required to return the typewriter to A? Under the common law C would be required to return the typewriter to A, but not under the Uniform Sales Act. Section 24 of the Uniform Sales Act provides: "Where the seller of goods has a voidable title thereto, but his title has not been avoided at the time of the sale, the buyer acquires a good title to the goods, provided he buys them in good faith, for value, and without notice of the seller's defect of title."

Cassella v. Tiberio

150 Ohio St. 27, 80 N. E. (2d) 426, 5 A. L. R. (2d) 1 (1948)

This was an action by Lena Cassella (plaintiff) against Lee, Rosa, and Louis Tiberio (defendants) upon a cognovit note. Plaintiff took judgment by confession, and Lee and Louis Tiberio filed separate petitions to vacate the judgment. From the judgment in favor of Louis Tiberio, plaintiff appealed to the Court of Appeals, which affirmed the judgment. Plaintiff appealed. Judgment affirmed.

On April 20, 1933, Lee Tiberio, Rosa Tiberio, his wife, and Louis Tiberio, his son, the latter then being nineteen years of age, affixed their signatures to a cognovit note in the sum of $4,024.22, payable to the order of Giuseppe Cassella. The consideration for such note was loans of money previously made to Lee Tiberio by Giuseppe Cassella. Thereafter, the note was sold and transferred to Lena Cassella, niece of Giuseppe, who took judgment thereon by confession on August 21, 1939, in the Court of Common Pleas against the three Tiberios. The judgment became dormant and Lena Cassella moved for an order of revivor. The Tiberios were directed to show cause why the judgment should not be revived. Objection was made by Louis Tiberio for the reason (1) that he had signed the note as a witness only, and (2) that he was a minor when he affixed his signature thereto. The court overruled the objections and ordered the judgment revived. Thereafter, Louis Tiberio filed a petition to vacate the judgment. The court, upon hearing, decided the matter in his favor and entered an order vacating the original judgment. Lena Cassella (plaintiff) appealed to the Court of Appeals, which affirmed the judgment. She then appealed to the Supreme Court of Ohio.

ZIMMERMAN, J. In 27 *American Jurisprudence* 808, under the general heading "Infants," it is categorically stated that "the great weight of authority is to the effect that omission to disaffirm within a reasonable time does not ratify an executory contract, provided the former infant does not retain possession of the consideration. . . . It seems, however, that an executed contract voidable on the ground of infancy is deemed to be ratified by the failure of the former infant to disaffirm it within a reasonable time after reaching majority."

Certainly, a written and signed promise to pay money comes within the classification of an executory contract so far as the promisor is concerned. Most of the authorities that have come to our attention and that deal squarely with the subject are of the following import: Except for a limited class of contracts considered binding, as for necessaries, etc., the contract of an infant is voidable, and this is so as to both executed and executory contracts, but with different applications of the term "voidable." Thus, to say that the executed contract of an infant is voidable means that it is binding until disaffirmed by some act demonstrating that the party refuses longer to be bound thereby. To say that the executory contract of an infant is voidable means that it is capable of being confirmed or avoided, although, until there is a definite ratification or confirmation by the infant after he becomes of age, it may not be enforced against him.

In *Nicols & Shepard Co. v. Synder*, 78 Minn. 502, 81 N. W. 516, the court said: "The contract of an infant is simply voidable, and in law there is a marked distinction between his executed contract and his contract merely executory. As to the latter he may always interpose his infancy as a defense in an action for its enforcement, and he is not bound by such a contract unless he has affirmed or ratified it, after he has arrived at maturity, by some sufficient act or deed." Such rule is particularly appropriate in a situation like the one presented by the instant case.

Looking at the matter realistically, we see no good reason why, when an infant receives something of value under a contract which is executory as to him, he should not be held to the bargain if he retains the thing and does nothing by way of disaffirmance for an appreciable length of time after reaching legal age. In our opinion the executed contract of an infant is and should be binding upon him by his failure to disaffirm it within a reasonable time after attaining majority, but where the contract is wholly executory and it is apparent the infant has received no benefit a different conclusion is in order. 43 C. J. S., Infants, p. 169, Sec. 74.

In *Brownell, Rec'r v. Adams*, 121 Neb. 304, 236 N. W. 750, the court said: "Where an infant has received some benefit during infancy, he must repudiate the contract within a reasonable time after attaining majority. . . . But not having received any benefit, and not having ratified the contract after his arrival at majority, he is not bound by the same." Other cases support the proposition that a contract which is patently of no benefit to an infant must be ratified by him after he reaches majority to render him liable thereon.

Judgment for Louis Tiberio affirmed.

RATIFICATION OF CONTRACT

As we have seen, an infant may disaffirm or avoid his contracts, except those involving real property, prior to reaching his majority. On the other hand, he may not affirm or ratify his contracts until he has attained his majority. A little reflection will make clear that this rule is in sound accord with the principle of affording protection to infants in the making of their contracts.

A few states require that ratification be in writing; elsewhere it may be either express (oral or written) or implied. If the former infant actually performs the acts called for by the contract, or accepts benefits under it, ratification is implied. Mere acknowledgment of the existence of the contract does not constitute ratification. Silence does not constitute ratification of an executory contract; but, as we have already seen, failure to disaffirm an executed contract within a reasonable time after reaching one's majority is deemed to constitute ratification.

While the cases are not uniform as to whether the former infant must know at the time when he ratifies his contract that it is voidable at his option, the majority view is that such knowledge is not necessary. The infant has now attained his majority and is presumed to know the law; he can no longer plead ignorance of the law as a defense. The rule seems sound.

The effect of ratification is to make the contract absolutely binding on the infant, and his ratification is retroactive to the time when the contract was entered into.

Rubin et al. v. Strandberg
288 Ill. 64, 122 N. E. 808 (1919)

This was an action by David M. Rubin, Ike Rubin, and Jacob L. Rubin, partners (plaintiffs) against E. P. Strandberg, Jr. (defendant). Judgment for plaintiffs, and defendant appealed. Affirmed.

On March 4, 1915, plaintiffs entered into a contract with defendant by which plaintiffs agreed to sell, and defendant agreed to purchase, certain lots for the sum of $6,000, to be paid for as follows: $1,000 in cash; the balance in monthly installments of $150 each, with interest at 6%. The $1,000 cash payment was paid; also the further payments, with interest from the date of the contract up to and including the payment on December 4, 1915.

At the time the contract was entered into, defendant was a minor. He attained his majority on October 7, 1915. The payments made in November and December were made after he was of age. No payment was made in January or February 1916. On January 3, 1916, defendant caused the contract to be recorded in the recorder's office. On February 4, 1916, defendant disaffirmed the contract and demanded that plaintiffs pay back to him the money which he had paid them. Plaintiffs refused to pay the money back and shortly thereafter filed their bill to annul and remove, as a cloud upon the title to the lots involved, the contract between plaintiffs and defendant, and in the alternative that Strandberg (defendant) be required to pay the amount due under the contract, and that upon making such payments the contract be reinstated and declared in full force and effect.

Defendant answered and filed a cross-bill, wherein he set up his infancy as a defense, alleging that he had been induced to enter into the contract by fraud and misrepresentation, and asked for the return of his payments to plaintiffs.

FARMER, J. It is not disputed that defendant was a minor when the contract was entered into, and that he attained his majority October 7, 1915; but plaintiffs contend that the payments made by defendant after he became of age, and his act in causing the contract to be recorded in January, 1916, constituted a ratification of the contract after he attained his majority. The defendant's answer to this contention is that at the time these acts were performed he did not know he had the legal right to disaffirm the contract upon attaining his majority, and that before said acts can be held to be a ratification of the contract it is necessary that the defendant should have known, at the time of their performance, that he had a right to disaffirm the contract on the ground that it was entered into during his minority.

There was a failure of the proof to sustain the allegations of the answer and cross-bill of defendant that he was induced to enter into the contract by fraud and misrepresentation, and his right to disaffirm the contract rested alone upon whether he had ratified it after becoming of age. A minor may disaffirm a contract made by him during minority within a reasonable time after attaining his majority, and he may by acts recognize the contract after becoming of age, and thereby ratify it. There can be no doubt that the acts of the defendant after attaining his majority in making the monthly payments and causing the contract to be recorded, were a ratification of the contract, unless the law is, as contended by defendant, that it was essential, in order to constitute said acts a ratification, that he knew at the time he performed the acts that the law authorized him to disaffirm the contract.

In this case the proof failed to show that defendant had been induced by fraud or misrepresentation to enter into the contract. He had no reason for disaffirming it except that he had changed his mind. His change of mind was not the result of any discovery of the truth of facts which had been fraudulently misrepresented to him by plaintiffs and upon which he relied in making the contract. He simply concluded that he had made an unprofitable contract, and sought to disaffirm solely because he was a minor when it was made. He defaulted in the January, 1916 payment, and on the day the February payment was due notified plaintiffs of his election to disaffirm. He then would have had the legal right to disaffirm the contract, if he had not previously, and since attaining his majority, ratified it. The payments in November and December 1915, evidenced his intention to comply with his contract and were a ratification of it, unless, as contended, he did not then know the law authorized him to disaffirm it. In our opinion defendant's acts after becoming of age must be regarded as done in the light of the knowledge of his legal right to disaffirm; that he was presumed to know the law, and cannot be heard to say that he was ignorant of his legal right in that respect and performed the alleged acts of ratification in ignorance of that right. Upon this particular question the authorities are not altogether in accord, but in our opinion the more logical reasoning sustains that proposition. *Wharton on Contracts* says: "Hence the better opinion is that a ratification made by a person of sound mind of arriving at his majority will be held valid, if untainted with fraud or undue influence, though the party making it was not at the time aware that it bound him in law."

Judgment for plaintiff affirmed.

MISREPRESENTATION OF AGE

The fact that an infant has misrepresented his age in order to secure a contract which he could not otherwise have obtained will not later prevent him from setting up his infancy as a defense if he is *sued on the contract*, and in many states will not prevent him from disaffirming the contract.[1] However, infants are in general liable for their *torts*; consequently, in most states the other party to the contract could recover in a tort action for deceit.

It is evident that businessmen should use extreme caution in dealing with infants. In fact, it is advisable not to deal with an infant at all, but to contract directly with his parent or guardian.

Rice v. Boyer
108 Ind. 472, 9 N. E. 420 (1886)

This was an action by Rice (plaintiff) against Boyer (defendant) to recover on a promissory note. Defendant demurred and the demurrer was sustained. Plaintiff appealed. Reversed, with instructions to overrule the demurrer to the complaint.

Plaintiff sold a buggy and a set of harness to defendant on credit. Defendant executed a promissory note to plaintiff and secured same with a chattel mortgage on the buggy. Upon default in the payment of the note plaintiff brought this suit. Plaintiff alleged in his complaint that defendant falsely and fraudulently represented that he was 21 years of age, whereas he had not yet attained the age of 21.

---

[1] California, Idaho, North Dakota, and South Dakota have enacted statutes which prevent an infant from disaffirming his contract where he has misrepresented his age. See Williston, *Contracts*, Vol. I, sec. 230.

Defendant set up as a defense his infancy and demurred to plaintiff's complaint.

ELLIOTT, C.J. The material and controlling question in the case is this: Will an action to recover the actual loss sustained by the plaintiff lie against an infant who has obtained property on the faith of a false and fraudulent representation that he is of full age? There is stubborn conflict in the authorities on this question. Our judgment, however, is that, where the infant does fraudulently and falsely represent that he is of full age, he is liable in action ex delicto (in tort) for the injury resulting from his tort. This result does not involve a violation of the principle that an infant is not liable where the consequence would be an indirect enforcement of his contract; for the recovery is not upon the contract, as that is treated as of no effect, nor is he made to pay the contract price of the article purchased by him, as he is only held to answer for the actual loss caused by his fraud. In holding him responsible for the consequences of his wrong, an equitable conclusion is reached, and one which strictly harmonizes with the general doctrine that an infant is liable for his torts. Nor does our conclusion invalidate the doctrine that an infant has no power to deny his disability; for it concedes this, but affirms that he must answer for his positive fraud.

Our conclusion that an infant is liable in tort for the actual loss resulting from a false and fraudulent representation of his age is well sustained by authority, although, as we have said, there is a fierce conflict, and it is strongly entrenched in principle. In *Neff v. Landis*, 1 Atl. Rep. 177, the court said: "It cannot be doubted that a minor who under such circumstances obtains the property of another, by pretending to be of full age and legally responsible, when in fact he is not, is guilty of false pretense, for which he is answerable under the criminal law." If it be true, as asserted in the case from which we have quoted, that an infant who falsely and fraudulently represents himself to be of full age is amenable to the criminal law, it must be true that he is responsible in an action of tort to the person whom he has wronged.

It is laid down as a general rule by all text writers that infants are liable for their torts; but many of these writers, when they come to consider such a question as we have here, are sorely perplexed by the early English decisions, and by subtle refinement attempt to discriminate between pure torts and torts connected with contracts, and to create an artificial class of actions. Their reasoning is not satisfactory. Aside from mere personal torts, it is scarcely possible to conceive a tort not in some way connected with a contract, and yet all the authorities agree that the liability of infants is not confined to mere personal torts.

It seems to us that an infant is liable, to the extent of the loss actually sustained, for his tort, where recovery can be had without giving effect to the contract. Any other rule would, in many cases, suffer a person guilty of positive fraud to escape loss, although his fraud had enabled him to secure and make way with the property of one who had trusted in good faith to his representation, and had exercised due care and diligence. We are unwilling to sanction any rule which will enable an infant, who obtained the property of another by falsely and fraudulently representing himself to be of full age, to enjoy the fruits of his fraud, either by keeping the property himself, or selling it to another, and, when asked to pay its just and reasonable value, successfully plead his infancy. Such a rule would make the defense of infancy both a shield and a sword, and this is a result which the principles of justice forbid, for they require that it should be merely a shield of defense.

Judgment reversed, with instructions to overrule the demurrer to the complaint.

R. J. Goerke Co. v. Nicolson
5 N. J. Supp. 412, 69 A. (2d) 326 (1949)

This was an action by R. J. Goerke Co. (plaintiff) against Florence Nicolson (defendant). Judgment for plaintiff, and defendant appealed. Affirmed.

On November 5, 1946, defendant made personal application to plaintiff's credit manager, Mary Zack, to open a charge account. Defendant furnished credit data to the said credit manager, which data were incorporated in a printed application. The application contained the further provision that the applicant expressly represented that she was of full legal age. The application was signed by Florence R. Nicolson, defendant, and was witnessed by Mary Zack.

Between November 15, 1946, and November 27, 1946, there were charges to that amount in the sum of $493.15. A credit of $100 was made on January 8, 1947, leaving a balance of $393.15.

Defendant having failed and refused to pay the balance due on her account, plaintiff brought this action on March 22, 1947. Defendant did not appear on the return day, March 28, 1947. On April 1, 1947, a judgment by default was entered in favor of plaintiff. Subsequently, defendant's salary was garnisheed.

On or about February 1, 1948, the court below reopened the judgment for the purpose of taking testimony as to whether the judgment should be set aside. The entire case was tried on its merits. Defendant set up as a defense that she was an infant. She testified that she did not recall being asked if she was of full age or of having read the provision concerning age in the application. Mary Zack testified that she asked defendant if she were of full age and received an affirmative reply. She also testified that she read the provision concerning age to defendant. At the conclusion of the hearing the court held for plaintiff.

DONGES, J. In *La Rosa v. Nichols*, 92 N. J. L. 375, 105 A. 201, the court said: "It seems anomalous indeed that youths of sufficient age and capacity, although less than 21 years old, may be convicted of crime, and be held liable for their torts, and yet not be liable on their contracts, when apparently of sufficient capacity to make them, and when they procure their making by fraud."

In the instant case, it does not appear that the infant returned any of the articles purchased. There is ample and competent evidence in the record to indicate that the defendant misrepresented herself to be of full age and that she appeared to the credit manager to be an adult. Under circumstances such as these, an infant will not be permitted to use as a sword her plea of infancy which in fact was given her as a shield.

The appeal dismissed with costs.

INSANE PERSONS

In determining the nature of the liability of insane persons on their contracts, the courts make a distinction between cases involving persons who have been judicially determined to be insane and cases where no such determination has been made. The contracts of a person who has been judicially declared insane by a court of competent jurisdiction (usually a probate court) are absolutely void. This is also the rule in regard to his deeds, mortgages, will, negotiable instruments, and comparable instruments. On the other hand, the general rule is that the contracts of an insane person who has not been judicially declared insane are voidable only. While he may not ratify or disaffirm such contracts during his insanity, he may do so when he regains his sanity, or in some lucid interval. If he is adjudged insane after the making of such contract, the contract may be ratified or disaffirmed by his guardian or conservator. The privilege of ratification and disaffirmance of an insane person's contracts is also given upon his death to his personal representative or heirs.

If the sane party to the contract acts fairly and in good faith, not knowing that the other party is insane, and if such other party has not been judicially declared insane, and if the contract is executed, most courts refuse to allow the insane party to avoid the contract unless he can return to the other party the consideration which he has received, or its equivalent. But if the same party knows (or should know, in terms of the "reasonable man" test) that the party with whom he is dealing is mentally incompetent, the contract is voidable at the option of the insane person, his guardian, or his personal representative.

The rule in regard to necessaries purchased by mentally incompetent persons is the same as in the case of infants. While the other party to the agreement may not recover on the agreement, the insane person is liable in quasi-contract for the reasonable value of the necessaries furnished to him, or to his wife or dependent children. Section 2 of the Uniform Sales Act states, "Where necessaries are sold and delivered to a person who by reason of mental incapacity . . . is incompetent to contract, he must pay a reasonable price therefor." To be considered mentally incompetent, one must be unable to understand the terms of his contract and their general nature and consequences.

As to the rights of innocent third parties, the rules of law are the same in the case of insane persons as in the case of infants. The common law gives the innocent third party no protection, but the Uniform Sales Act, Section 24, provides, "Where the seller of goods has a voidable title thereto, but his title has not been avoided at the time of the sale, the buyer acquires a good title to the goods, provided he buys them in good faith, for value, and without notice of the seller's defect of title."

Fissel v. Gordon et al.
83 Ohio App. 349, 83 N. E. (2d) 525 (1948)

This was an action by Charles Fissel (plaintiff) against Stanley Gordon and others (defendants). Judgment for defendants, and plaintiff appealed. Affirmed.

Plaintiff conveyed an undivided one-half interest in certain real estate to defendant, Stanley Gordon, on March 18, 1941. This action is one to have the conveyance and subsequent successive conveyances by Gordon to Lovita Giffert and by her to Martha L. Johnson and Grace Cox set aside, and the title of plaintiff quieted, and for an accounting of rents and for damages.

PER CURIAM. The sole ground alleged in the petition is that at the time the plaintiff executed the deed to Stanley Gordon he was of unsound mind and lacked mental capacity to contract and execute a deed. There is no allegation or proof that Lovita Giffert at the time she acquired title knew of any defect in the title of Gordon, and, unless the deed from Gordon to her was totally void, she acquired a title that was free of any equity which the plaintiff might have had to rescind the conveyances and recover the title and possession of the property. The conveyance to Martha L. Johnson and Grace Cox was made during the pendency of this action, and, of course, they took title subject to whatever judgment might be entered in this action; but, if Lovita Giffert's title was free of the claim of the plaintiff, their title would be equally so.

We have weighed the evidence in this case and have been unable to find any substantial evidence that in 1941 when the deed to Gordon was executed the plaintiff lacked mental capacity to execute a deed. At that time he was transacting every other form of business, contracts of employment, depositing in and withdrawing money from a building association, etc., and performing all other acts that would normally be performed by a sane person in his environment. There is a failure of proof of lack of mental capacity.

It might be added that a deed executed by an insane person is not void unless the person is so bereft of reason as to make him incapable of giving even an imperfect assent to the transaction. It is voidable. And mere weakness of mind, in the absence of fraud or undue influence, is not a ground for declaring a deed either void or voidable. The title of Lovita Giffert would, therefore, be free of any claim of the plaintiff and she could transmit such title to her grantees, notwithstanding the pendency of this action. That would prevent the plaintiff from recovering the real estate, and would leave nothing to be considered except the claim for a personal judgment, and, as to that there is no allegation of fraud or undue influence against any of the defendants and no substantial evidence to that effect.

INTOXICATED PERSONS

In general, the position of an intoxicated person with regard to his contracts is the same as that of an insane person. If a person enters into a contract when he is so intoxicated that he is incapable of comprehending the nature of his acts, the contract is voidable at his option. If he is only slightly intoxicated, he will be bound by the agreement. In some few states intoxication is not recognized as a ground for avoiding a contract; but if it can be shown that the other party to the agreement fraudulently induced and encouraged the party to become intoxicated in order to secure his apparent consent to an unfair agreement, such agreement may be set aside by a court of equity.

Usually an intoxicated person may ratify or disaffirm his contract when he becomes sober, if he does so within a reasonable time. Failure to disaffirm the contract within a reasonable time is generally held to be ratification. If he elects to disaffirm his contract within a reasonable time, the courts hold, with rare exception, that his ability to do so is dependent upon his returning to the other party to the contract any consideration which he has received.

As in the case of minors and insane persons, an intoxicated person is liable in quasi-contract for necessaries furnished him or his family.

MARRIED WOMEN

At common law a single woman who had reached her majority could contract as fully as a man of legal age, but if she married she lost completely her capacity to make valid contracts. Upon her marriage all her personal property became the property of her husband, and, while her real property did not become his absolute property, he did acquire an interest in the nature of a life estate in all her realty. (This interest was not the same as the husband's right of "curtesy," since that right became consummate only if a child was born alive and if the wife predeceased the husband.) Equity recognized, however, that trust estates could be set up for married women, in which their husbands had no right or interest and over which they had no control. For example, a father could set up a separate estate in trust for the use and benefit of his married daughter, and she could enjoy the income from this separate estate without legal interference by her husband. A married woman could also purchase necessaries on the credit of her husband, if he failed to supply same, and he would be liable for such purchases. Married women were also liable for their torts at common law, as under present-day statutes.

The common law contractual disability of married women has been largely removed by statutes in all the states. However, the statutes of some states place certain limitations upon a married woman's capacity to contract. For example, a few states provide by statute that the wife may not contract with her husband, or that she may not become a surety for him, or that she may not form a partnership with her husband. Such rules are thought to lead to domestic tranquillity and also to give a wife better protection as to her separate estate from a domineering husband.

Rollings v. Gunter
211 Ala. 671, 101 So. 446 (1924)

This was a bill in equity by Robert Rollings (plaintiff) against A. C. Gunter and wife (defendants) seeking to have declared valid a mortgage executed by the defendants. Decree for defendants, and plaintiff appealed. Affirmed.

Robert Rollings contracted with A. C. Gunter to sell him 40 acres of land for $2000. At first it was agreed upon as a cash deal. When preparing to close the deal Gunter advised Rollings he could not get the money just then but was promised it within six months. Gunter thereupon offered to give a mortgage, including another 40 acres of land, as additional security. Gunter informed his wife that he had purchased the land, and had her get the deed to the other 40 to be mortgaged as additional security. The parties all met at the office of the attorney selected to prepare the papers. The attorney there discovered and informed Rollings that the title to the land proposed as security was in Bettie Gunter, the wife of A. C. Gunter. All parties being present, the attorney asked to whom the property was being sold, and was told A. C. Gunter. The attorney then advised that the sale should be to Bettie Gunter; that she could not give a valid mortgage on her lands to secure her husband's debt. The attorney then asked to whom they wanted the deed made. The husband suggested to make it to the husband and wife jointly. The wife, by silence at least, acquiesced. The deed was so drawn and executed, and a joint and several note for the entire purchase money secured by mortgage on both forties drawn and executed therefor. The wife signed by mark. Possession of the land purchased was delivered to the defendants. No part of the purchase money was ever paid. Thereupon the plaintiff filed this bill in equity to have declared valid the mortgage executed by the defendants and to regain possession of the land in question.

The sole question was whether the mortgage given on the lands of the wife, and by her sought to be canceled, under her cross-bill, was given by her as security for the debt of her husband.

BOULDIN, J. Under our statutes the wife has full legal capacity to contract as if she were sole, except as otherwise provided by law. The husband and wife may contract with each other subject to the rules governing contracts between persons standing in confidential relations, "but the wife shall not, directly or indirectly, become the surety for her husband." *Code,* 1907, Sec. 4497.

It has been held that the wife may convey her property to her husband; she may sell it in direct payment of the husband's debt; she may borrow money to be used in payment of the husband's debt; she may, by novation, satisfy her husband's debt by giving her own primary obligation in lieu thereof; she may join her husband in creating a joint debt or liability. In all cases, she is bound, except when she undertakes to bind herself or property solely as the surety of her husband. No matter what the form of the transaction, if the husband is the real debtor, and the sole purpose is to secure his debt, the wife is not bound. *Myers v. Sternberg,* 206 Ala. 457, 90 So. 302.

The statute expresses a public policy to shield the property of the wife against the moral duress inherent in the relation of husband and wife, inducing her by the influence of the husband, or of third persons, or even of her own inclinations, to help the husband or promote his interests by becoming surety for his debt.

The relation of principal and surety is of the essence of this inquiry. Here there is no question that the debt was contracted, in the first instance, by the husband. The wife was not involved until the time came to secure the debt. As we weigh the frank statement of Mrs. Gunter and that of Mr. Rollings on cross-examination, in connection with all the evidence, we have a conviction that this is a case our statute is designed to cover—the protection of a wife's property against an indirect method of binding it for the husband's debt.

The decree of the trial court denying relief to the plaintiff, and awarding relief to the defendant, Bettie Gunter, under her cross-bill for cancellation of the mortgage as a cloud upon title, is affirmed.

ALIENS

In time of peace aliens have practically the same capacity to contract as citizens. An important exception to this rule is that under the statutes of a few states persons of certain designated nationalities may not acquire and own real property; consequently, their contracts to buy real estate would be absolutely void.

In time of war an enemy alien may not enter into any new contracts, except that if he is living in this country he may generally contract for bare necessities, such as food, lodging, and clothing. Moreover, his right to sue upon any contract legally negotiated before the war started is suspended during hostilities, but is restored when the war ends.

CONTRACTUAL CAPACITY OF SOVEREIGN STATES

The United States government and the governments of the several states have authority to contract. This is a prerogative of sovereignty. They may also maintain suits in courts of law. The question then arises, may the United States and the several states be sued on their contracts? The answer is that by reason of their sovereignty they may not be sued against their will; but they may, and often do, consent to be sued. The circumstances under which they will consent to be sued are laid down either by constitutional provisions or by statutory enactment.

REVIEW CASES

1. Ryan, a minor, purchased from Smith a barber shop with furnishings, to be used as his sole means of earning a living. Shortly after the sale Ryan repudiated the contract and brought an action to recover the money he had paid Smith. Should the judge rule that the articles purchased were necessities? (Ryan v. Smith, 165 Mass. 303, 43 N. E. 109)

2. Inman, a minor, was a Cambridge undergraduate, the son of a well-to-do architect. Nash sold him a quantity of expensive clothing and later sued him for the purchase price, contending that the clothes were necessities suitable to Inman's station in life. Inman's father testified that his son was adequately furnished with suitable clothing. Ruling? (Nash v. Inman, 2 K. B., 1 Br. Rul. Cas. 143)

3. Myers, a minor, purchased a car from Hurley Motor Co., misrepresenting his age as 24. He defaulted in his payments, and the car was repossessed in accordance with the terms of the contract. Upon attaining his majority he disaffirmed the contract and sued the company for return of $406, the amount he had paid on the car. The company filed a counterclaim for $525, the cost of restoring the car to the same condition as when it was sold to Myers: Holding? (Myers v. Hurley Motor Co., 273 U. S. 18, 47 Sup. Ct. 227)

4. Sears was adjudged mentally incompetent, and thereafter borrowed money from his son-in-law, Kay, for attorney's fees and other costs to have himself declared competent. The court refused to adjudge him sane. Sears died, and Mrs. Kay was appointed administratrix of her father's estate. She refused to reimburse her husband from the estate for his loan to her father. Kay sued. Holding? (Kay v. Kay, 53 Ariz. 336, 89 P.(2d) 496)

5. Josiah Boyden sold to William Boyden and another, both minors, a horse and a plow, taking a note in payment. The horse was disposed of after one of the boys became of age, and the plow was kept by them for three years

after the second reached his majority, without any attempt to return it. Josiah Boyden then sued on the note. Can the defendants maintain the contention that they never ratified the contract? (Boyden v. Boyden, 9 Metc. (Mass.) 519)

6. Port Huron Co. refused to sell machinery on credit to Myers alone but sold it to Myers and wife jointly, with the wife's property securing the sale by a mortgage. The machinery was not paid for, and Steernberg, trustee for the company, filed suit to foreclose the mortgage on the wife's separate property. Defense: a wife cannot become surety for her husband. Ruling? (Sternberg v. Myers, 90 So. 302, 206 Ala. 457)

7. Hardy, receiver for Newsom, sued McKaig to get possession of land sold by McKaig to Newsom. McKaig in his defense swore that Newsom had administered drink to him that deprived him of his reason, in consequence of which he had signed a deed to Newsom for the land. Was the deed valid? (McKaig v. Hardy, 196 Ga. 582, 27 S. E.(2d) 11)

Consideration

10

THE NATURE OF CONSIDERATION

The third essential of a legally enforceable contract is consideration. To be enforceable, a promise must be supported by a valid consideration, unless the promise is under seal. It follows that every agreement must be supported by a consideration, unless under seal.[1]

Many promises that people make do not create legal obligations to perform such promises, and hence are not enforceable in a court of law. The existence or non-existence of consideration in any given case determines whether or not a legal obligation is created between the parties. If consideration is present, a legal obligation arises; if consideration is not present, at most only a social or moral obligation is created. If A promises to take B to lunch at his club but later fails to do so, B would have no cause of action against A, since B has given A no legal consideration for his promise. If A promises to give $100 to B and later refuses to do so, A would not be liable to B, since consideration is again lacking. A's promise to make the gift was not supported by anything done or promised by B in return, and hence it was merely a "naked promise" or nudum pactum, not recognized by the courts. Thus, gratuitous promises are unenforceable, though after a gift is executed the donor is bound.

---

[1] The Uniform Commercial Code Sec. 203 makes a seal inoperative when affixed to a contract or an offer to buy or sell goods.

LOVE AND AFFECTION

Collins v. Collins
194 Misc. 65, 88 N. Y. S. (2d) 136 (1949)
City Court of New York

This was an action on contract for support by Agnes Collins against Edmund Collins. On motion to dismiss amended complaint for insufficiency on its face.

Motion granted.

CARLIN, J. This motion to dismiss the amended complaint for insufficiency on its face, which was heretofore granted by default, has been, by consent, restored to the calendar and is now considered on the merits.

This is an action, as shown in the complaint, by a mother, allegedly aged and destitute, against her son. It is set forth in the complaint that the defendant, the son, agreed to pay to the plaintiff, the mother, the sum of $50 per month for her support and that the agreement was based upon "good and valuable consideration." The defendant demanded a bill of particulars and plaintiff served one, in which the consideration for such agreement is stated to be "love and affection." This application to dismiss the amended complaint, under Rule 112, *Rules of Civil Practice*, is predicated upon the complaint as limited by the bill of particulars.

"Love and affection" is not a sufficient consideration to support an executory contract. The case would be different if an executed deed, assignment or mortgage were involved; if in fact the transaction were accomplished.

The plaintiff relies upon *Calhoun v. Calhoun*, 49 App. Div. 520, 63 N. Y. S. 601, but that action was founded upon a mortgage which had been executed and delivered. It is true that it was stated in the opinion that love and affection or the moral obligation to support, constituted a sufficient consideration. But such statement was unnecessary to the decision, which could have rested either upon the fact that the mortgage in suit had been delivered and the transaction was therefore executed; or upon the fact that the defendant had undertaken to support the plaintiff, his mother, partly at least, because she had conveyed a farm to him. The view expressed in that opinion that love and affection alone, or a moral obligation to support, is a sufficient consideration is not, wherever an executory agreement is involved, in accord with the rule in this state. Cf. *Whitaker v. Whitaker*, 52 N. Y. 368, 11 *Am. Rep.* 711; *Wilbur v. Warren*, 104 N. Y. 192, 10 N. E. 263; Clark, *New York Law of Contracts*, Vol. 1, p. 517, footn. 46.

It appears dehors the pleadings, that the plaintiff is not a resident of New York, but of Pennsylvania. Any rights which she might have had, if she had been a resident, under Section 101, Social Welfare Law, are therefore not germane to a consideration of this case. Also, cf. *Matter of Salm's Guardianship*, 171 Misc. 367, 371, 12 N. Y. S. (2d) 678, 683.

As plaintiff does not, upon any suggested theory, have a good cause of action against the defendant, the complaint should be dismissed without leave to plead over.

The motion under Rule 112, R. C. P., to dismiss the amended complaint, as amplified by the bill of particulars, for insufficiency, is granted. Judgment of dismissal may be entered in favor of the defendant.

Execution of judgment for costs is stayed for 30 days after service of notice of entry upon the attorney for the plaintiff.

The theory of consideration underlying most contracts is called the *bargain theory*. In this theory, consideration for a promise is regarded as the price bargained for and given in exchange for the promise. In a unilateral contract, the price bargained for by the promisor as consideration for his promise is a specified act or forbearance by the promisee. By performing the act or forbearance called for, the promisee purchases the promise of the promisor. Until such performance there is no consideration and hence no contract. In a bilateral contract, where mutual promises are exchanged, each party purchases the promise of the other by giving a return promise.

To constitute valid consideration, the price paid for a promise must cost the promisee a *legal detriment*. He must assume some legal obligation that he was not bound to assume; or he must surrender some legal right that he was not bound to surrender. If A promises B $100 and B merely promises that he will accept it with thanks, B's promise is not valid consideration, for it commits him to no new legal duty. But if A promises to pay B $100 for his typewriter and B promises to turn over the typewriter to A for $100, B's promise to surrender his legal title to his typewriter is valid consideration for A's promise to pay him $100. Or suppose that B has filed suit against A in the belief that he has just grounds for legal action against him. A promises him $100 if he will dismiss his suit, and he promises to do so. B's promise to surrender his legal right to sue constitutes adequate consideration for A's promise to pay him $100. On the other hand, if B had no real cause of action against A, his promise not to sue would not constitute valid consideration. One suffers no legal detriment by promising to forbear some act which he has no legal right to perform, or to do something that he is legally obligated to do in any case.

The doctrine of consideration developed under the common law and is unknown to the other great systems of law. No date can be cited for its origin, but it is believed to have had its beginning in the common law actions of debt and case (assumpsit), and thus to have originated in the procedural law. An action of debt was brought upon the theory that the defendant (debtor) had money or property that belonged to the plaintiff, which the plaintiff brought the action to recover; in other words, upon the theory that the defendant (debtor) had received benefit from the transaction and should therefore pay the plaintiff. On the other hand, an action on the case was brought upon the theory that the plaintiff (promisee) had suffered a legal detriment, since he had given the promise asked for by the promisor and the promisor had afterward refused to perform his promise. Out of these two concepts developed the idea that consideration could be established by showing a legal benefit to the promisor *and* a legal detriment to the promisee. Today most courts take the position that the only thing which must be proved to show consideration is a legal detriment to the promisee. Whether the promisor has benefited from the promise or act of the promisee is immaterial.

The general rule of law is that there is no presumption of consideration in the case of simple contracts. However, the statutes of a few states, such as California, Iowa, Kansas, and Missouri, provide that in the case of contracts in writing there is a rebuttable presumption of consideration; the same rule holds for negotiable instruments. If consideration is to become an issue in such cases, it must be set up by way of defense by the party primarily liable on the instrument.

UNIFORM COMMERCIAL CODE

Sec. 1–203 of the Code imposes on the parties an obligation of good faith in the performance or enforcement of every contract within the Act.

Sec. 2–205 of the Code provides that an offer in writing to buy or sell goods, giving assurance it will be kept open, is binding between merchants, although not supported by consideration; and by Sec. 2–209, an agreement modifying a contract for the sale of goods needs no consideration to be binding. However, by Sec. 2–302, if the contract or parts thereof are unconscionable, they will not be enforced, even though supported by consideration.

Hamer v. Sidway

124 N. Y. 538, 27 N. E. 256 (1891)

This was an action by Hamer (plaintiff) against Sidway, executor of the estate of William E. Story, Sr. (defendant). Judgment for defendant, and plaintiff appealed. Reversed.

The plaintiff presented a claim to the executor of the estate of William E. Story, Sr., for $5,000. The plaintiff acquired this claim through several assignments from William E. Story, 2d. The claim being rejected by the executor, this action was brought.

William E. Story, Sr. was the uncle of William E. Story, 2d. William E. Story, Sr., on March 20, 1869, in the presence of the family and guests, promised his nephew that if he would refrain from drinking, using tobacco, swearing, and playing cards or billiards for money until he became 21 years of age, he would pay him the sum of $5,000. The nephew assented thereto, and fully performed the conditions inducing the promise. When the nephew arrived at the age of 21 years, on January 31, 1875, he wrote to his uncle informing him that he had performed his part of the agreement, and had thereby become entitled to the sum of $5,000. The uncle received the letter and a few days later, on February 6th, wrote to the nephew to the effect that he "had no doubt" that the nephew had performed his part of the agreement and that he, the uncle, had the money in the bank for him. The nephew received the letter and thereafter consented that the money should remain with the uncle until the nephew should care to make use of it. The uncle died without having turned the money over to his nephew. In the meantime the nephew had assigned the claim to his wife, who soon thereafter assigned it to the plaintiff.

The defendant contended that the contract was without consideration and that the promise of the nephew to refrain from the use of liquor and tobacco was not a detriment to him but actually benefited him.

PARKER, J. Courts "will not ask whether the thing which forms the consideration does in fact benefit the promisor or a third party, or is of any substantial value to anyone. It is enough that something is promised, done, forborne, or suffered by the party to whom the promise is made as consideration for the promise made to him." Anson, *Contracts*, p. 63. "In general a waiver of any legal right at the request of another party is a sufficient consideration for a promise." Parsons, *Contracts*, p. 444. "Any damage, or suspension, or forbearance of a right will be sufficient to sustain a promise." Kent, *Comm.* (12th Ed.), p. 465. Pollock, in his work on Contracts, p. 166, after citing the definition given by the Exchequer, already quoted, says: "The second branch of this judicial description is really the most important one. 'Consideration' means not so much that one party is profiting as that the other abandons some legal right in the present, or limits his legal freedom of action in the future, as an inducement for the promise of the first." Now, applying this rule to the facts before us, the promisee (nephew) used tobacco, occasionally drank liquor, and he had a legal right to do so. That right he abandoned for a period of years upon the strength of the promise of the promisor (uncle) that for such forbearance he would give him $5,000. We need not speculate on the effort which may have been required to give up the use of those stimulants. It is sufficient that he restricted his lawful freedom of action within certain prescribed limits upon the faith of the uncle's agreement, and now, having fully performed the conditions imposed, it is of no moment whether such performance actually proved a benefit to the promisor, and the court will not inquire into it; but, were it proper subject of inquiry, we see nothing in this record that would permit a determination that the uncle was not benefited in a legal sense.

In *Talbott v. Stemmons*, 12 S. W. 297, the step-grandmother of the plaintiff made with him the following agreement: "I do promise to give my grandson, Albert R. Talbott, $500 at my death if he will never take another chew of tobacco or smoke another cigar during my life, from this date up to my death." The executor of Mrs. Stemmons demurred to the complaint on the ground that the agreement was not based on a sufficient consideration. In the opinion of the court it was said that "the right to use and enjoy the use of tobacco was a right that belonged to the plaintiff, and not forbidden by law. The abandonment of its use may have saved him money, or contributed to his health; nevertheless, the surrender of that right caused the promise, and having the right to contract with reference to the subject-matter, the abandonment of the use was a sufficient consideration to uphold the promise."

Judgment for the plaintiff.

Langer v. Superior Steel Corporation
161 A. 571, 105 Pa. Sup. 579 (1932)

This was an action by William F. Langer (plaintiff) against the Superior Steel Corporation (defendant) to recover damages for breach of an alleged contract. Judgment for defendant, and plaintiff appealed. Reversed.

Plaintiff alleged that he was entitled to recover certain monthly payments provided for in the following letter: "August 31, 1927. Mr. William F. Langer. Dear Sir: As you are retiring from active duty with this company, as Superintendent of the Annealing Department, on August 31st, we hope that it will give you some pleasure to receive this official letter of commendation for your long and faithful service with the Superior Steel Corporation. The directors have decided that you will receive a pension of $100 per month as long as you live and preserve your present attitude of loyalty to the Company and its officers and are not employed in any competitive occupation. We sincerely hope that you will live long to enjoy it and that this and the other evidences of the esteem in which you are held by your fellow employees and which you will to-day receive with this letter, will please you as much as it does us to bestow them. Cordially yours, Frank R. Frost, President."

Defendant paid the sum of $100 per month for approximately four years, when plaintiff was notified that the Company no longer intended to continue the payments.

The issue raised is whether the letter created a gratuitous promise or an enforceable contract.

BALDRIDGE, J. It is frequently a matter of great difficulty to differentiate between promises creating legal obligations and mere gratuitous agreements. Each case depends to a degree upon its peculiar facts and circumstances. Was this promise supported by a sufficient consideration, or was it but a condition attached to a gift? If a contract was created, it was based on a consideration, and must have been the result of an agreement bargained for in exchange for a promise. It was held in *Presbyterian Board of Foreign Missions v. Smith*, 209 Pa. 363, 58 A. 689, that "a test of good consideration is whether the promisee, at the instance of the promisor, has done, forborne, or undertaken to do anything real, or whether he has suffered any detriment, or whether, in return for the promise, he has done something that he was not bound to do, or has promised to do some act, or has abstained from doing something." Mr. Justice

Sadler pointed out in *York Metal & Alloys Co. v. Cyclops S. Co.*, 280 Pa. 585, 124 A. 752, that a good consideration exists if one refrains from doing anything that he has a right to do, "whether there is any actual loss or detriment to him or actual benefit to the promisor or not."

The plaintiff, in his statement, which must be admitted as true, alleged that he refrained from seeking employment with any competitive company, and that he complied with the terms of the agreement. By so doing, has he sustained any detriment? Was his forbearance sufficient to support a good consideration? Prof. Williston, on Contracts, Sec. 112, says: "It is often difficult to determine whether words of condition in a promise indicate a request for consideration or state a mere condition in a gratuitous promise. An aid, though not a conclusive test, in determining which construction of the promise is more reasonable is an inquiry whether the happening of the condition will be a benefit to the promisor. If so, it is a fair inference that the happening was requested as a consideration."

It is reasonable to conclude that it is to the advantage of the defendant if the plaintiff, who had been employed for a long period of time as its superintendent in the annealing department, and who, undoubtedly, had knowledge of the methods used by the employer, is not employed by a competitive company; otherwise, such a stipulation would have been unnecessary. That must have been the inducing reason for inserting that provision . . . By receiving the monthly payments, he impliedly accepted the conditions imposed, and was thus restrained from doing that which he had a right to do. This was a sufficient consideration to support a contract. Reversed.

Stonestreet v. Southern Oil Co.
37 S. E. (2d) 676 (1946)

This was an action by C. C. Stonestreet (plaintiff) against the Southern Oil Co. (defendant) to recover half the cost of digging a water well on land leased to defendant by plaintiff. Judgment for plaintiff, and defendant appealed. Reversed.

On October 24, 1934, plaintiff and his wife leased to defendant a lot for a filling station for a term of ten years with privilege of buying at any time during the term of the lease at the price of $5,000. The lease contained the following stipulation: "Said Stonestreet and wife agree to furnish lessee with water for the station insofar as they are able to do so with their present water supply. In case said lessors' well fails to supply ample water, they are not to be responsible, and the lessee will be required to make its own arrangements for securing water."

In June, 1935, the lessee needed more water; whereupon plaintiff and defendant engaged C. W. Fisher to drill a well on the premises, each party agreeing to pay one-half the cost. The Southern Oil Co. paid its half amounting to $329, and plaintiff credited Fisher with a like amount on his grocery bill.

It is alleged by plaintiff that at the time C. W. Fisher was engaged to drill the well, under a written contract signed by all the parties, it was further agreed orally between plaintiff and defendant that if the lessee exercised its option to buy the premises defendant "would repay plaintiff his one-half paid for boring said well, but if defendant did not exercise the option to buy, then the well would belong to plaintiff and he would not be reimbursed the one-half he had paid." Defendant denied the alleged oral agreement, and pleaded the Statute of Frauds, satisfaction by the deed of conveyance, and no consideration for the alleged oral agreement to reimburse plaintiff.

On cross-examination, plaintiff testified: "While they were digging the well Mr. Brinson (defendant's representative) came down and talked to me and promised me, in the event he took the property under the option, to pay me back whatever I put into it. He promised to pay me back the $329 if he exercised the option. I did not give him anything in money or property or make any promises in return for his promise to pay me back my one-half of the cost of digging the well. I did not promise him any money, didn't give him any money, I didn't think I had to. I thought he was an honest man."

Defendant exercised its option, under the contract, to purchase the property.

STACY, C.J. Passing the initial pleas of the Statute of Frauds and satisfaction by the deed of conveyance when the defendant exercised its option, it would seem that under the facts appearing of record, as distinguished from the allegations in the complaint, the defendant's plea of no consideration has been made out and constitutes a bar to the plaintiff's case.

It may be stated as a general rule that "consideration" in the sense the term is used in legal parlance, as affecting the enforceability of simple contracts, consists of some benefit or advantage to the promisor, or of some loss or detriment to the promisee. *Exum v. Lynch*, 188 N. C. 392, 125 S. E. 15. *Cherokee County v. Meroney*, 173 N. C. 653, 92 S. E. 616.

It has been held that "there is a consideration if the promisee, in return for the promise, does anything legal which he is not bound to do, or refrains from doing anything which he has a right to do, whether there is any actual loss or detriment to him or actual benefit to the promisor or not." 17 *C. J. S., Contracts*, Sec. 74, p. 426; *Spencer v. Bynum*, 169 N. C. 119, 85 S. E. 216. On the other hand, a mere promise, without more, lacks a consideration and is unenforceable. 17 *C. J. S., Contracts*, Sec. 87, pp. 434-5.

It is said that when one receives a naked promise and such promise is not kept, he is no worse off than he was before the promise was made. He gave nothing for it, loses nothing by it, and upon its breach he suffers no recoverable damage. For example, A promises to give B a horse at Christmastime, or to leave him a legacy in his will, and does neither. There being no consideration for the promise, B would have no cause of action against A or his estate. A bare promise, made without consideration, creates no legal rights and imposes no legal obligation. Its fulfillment is a matter of grace or favor on the part of the one making the promise.

In the instant case the promise on the part of the defendant to reimburse the plaintiff "his one-half paid for boring said well" was not more than a gratuity. Plaintiff promised nothing and gave nothing in return for the defendant's promise. The agreement to dig the well was in writing and its terms stated. Plaintiff lost nothing by the promise. His rights and obligations were fixed and determined by the written agreement.

Judgment reversed.

MUTUALITY OF OBLIGATION

In a bilateral contract, where the consideration for the promise of one party is the promise of the other party, the promise of each party must impose upon him a legal duty. Otherwise the agreement is said to lack mutuality and is void for lack of consideration. A little reflection will show that this rule follows logically from the definition of consideration. If A and B exchange promises such that A obligates himself absolutely to perform but B does not, B's promise not only imposes no legal duty upon him but it fails to fulfill the requirements for consideration and hence does not bind A's promise either. Consequently it is said that both parties must be bound or neither will be bound.

Let us suppose that A promises to buy from B all the ice he wishes to order during the year at a price of 40¢ a hundred, and B promises to furnish A with all the ice he orders at the specified price. Analysis of this agreement shows that, while B has made a binding promise to A, A has not made a binding promise to B. If B fails to furnish ice at the contract price in response to orders by A, A would have a cause of action against B. But B would have no cause of action against A if A failed to order ice, since A's promise does not bind him to order any ice at all. The agreement therefore lacks mutuality and does not give rise to an enforceable contract. But if A promises to buy from B at 40¢ a hundred all the ice he needs for his soda fountain during the year, and B promises to sell A all the ice he orders during the year at the specified price, mutuality exists. Even under circumstances where it is not certain that A will need any ice at all, many courts hold that A's promise to buy from B all the ice he may need during the year is adequate consideration for B's exchange promise, since it imposes on A the duty not to order ice from any other company during the year.

Oscar Schlegel Mfg. Co. v. Peter Cooper's Glue Factory
231 N. Y. 479, 132 N. E. 148 (1921)

This was an action by the Oscar Schlegel Mfg. Co. (plaintiff) against Peter Cooper's Glue Factory (defendant) to recover damages for an alleged breach of contract. A judgment for plaintiff for a substantial amount was affirmed by the Appellate Division, and defendant appealed. Reversed and complaint dismissed.

The complaint alleged that on or about December 9, 1915, the parties entered into a written agreement by which defendant agreed to sell and deliver to plaintiff, and plaintiff agreed to purchase from defendant, all its "requirements" of special BB glue for the year 1916, at the price of nine cents per pound. It also alleged the terms of payment, the manner in which the glue was to be packed, the place of delivery, the neglect and refusal of defendant to make certain deliveries, and the damages sustained, for which judgment was demanded.

It was contended by defendant that it was not liable since no contract existed because of lack of mutuality.

McLAUGHLIN, J. I am of the opinion that the judgment appealed from should be reversed, upon the ground that the alleged contract, for the breach of which a recovery was had, was invalid since it lacked mutuality. The contract was invalid since a consideration was lacking. Mutual promises or obligations of parties to a contract, either express or implied, may furnish the requisite consideration. The defect in the alleged contract here under consideration is that it contains no express consideration, nor are there any mutual promises of the parties to it from which such consideration can be fairly inferred. The plaintiff, it will be observed, did not agree to do or refrain from doing anything. It was not obligated to sell a pound of defendant's glue or to make any effort in that direction. It did not agree not to sell other glue in competition with defendant's. The only obligation assumed by it was to pay nine cents a pound for such glue as it might order. Whether it should order any at all rested entirely with it. If it did not order any glue, then nothing was to be paid. The agreement was not under seal, and therefore fell within the rule that a promise not under seal made by one party, with none by the other, is void. Unless both parties to a contract are bound, so that either can sue the other for a breach, neither is bound. *Grossman v. Schenker*, 206 N. Y. 466, 100 N. E. 39; *Levin v. Dietz*, 194 N. Y. 376, 87 N. E. 454. Had the plaintiff neglected or refused to order any glue during the year 1916, defendant could not have maintained an action to recover damages against it, because there would have been no breach of the contract. In order to recover damages, a breach had to be shown, and this could not have been established by a mere failure on the part of the plaintiff to order glue, since it had not promised to give such orders.

There are certain contracts in which mutual promises are implied: Thus, where the purchaser, to the knowledge of the seller, has entered into a contract for the resale of the article purchased (*Shipman v. Straitsville Central Mining Co.*, 158 U. S. 356); where the purchaser contracts for his requirements of an article necessary to be used in the business carried on by him (*Wells v. Alexander*, 130 N. Y. 642); or, for all the cans needed in a canning factory (*Dailey Co. v. Clark Can Co.*, 128 Mich. 591, 87 N. W. 761); all the lubrication oil for party's use (*Manhattan Oil Co. v. Richardson Lubrication Co.*, 113 Fed. 923); all the coal needed for a foundry during a specified time (*Minnesota Lumber Co. v. Whitebreast Coal Co.*, 160 Ill. 85); all the iron required during a certain period for a furnace (*National Furnace Co. v. Keystone Mfg. Co.*, 110 Ill. 427); and all the ice required in a hotel during a certain season (*Great Northern Railway Co. v. Witham*, L. R. 9 C. P. 16). In cases of this character, while the quantity of the article contracted to be sold is indefinite, nevertheless there is a certain standard mentioned in the agreement by which such quantity can be determined by an approximately accurate forecast. In the contract under consideration there is no standard mentioned by which the quantity of glue to be furnished can be determined with any approximate degree of accuracy.

The judgments of the Appellate Division and trial court should be reversed, and the complaint dismissed, with costs in all courts. Judgment for the defendant.

Tucson Federal Savings and Loan Association v. Aetna Investment Corp.
274 Ariz. 163, 254 P. (2d) 423 (1952)

This was an action by the Aetna Investment Corporation (plaintiff) against the Tucson Federal Savings & Loan Association (defendant). Judgment for plaintiff, and defendant appealed. Affirmed.

Aetna Investment Corporation, an Arizona company, is engaged in the insurance business with its principal place of business in Phoenix, Arizona. The Tucson Federal Savings & Loan Association is a federal savings and loan association organized and existing under the Home Owners Loan Act of 1933, and carrying on its business in Tucson. Under its charter and regulations of the Federal Home Loan Bank, by whom it is supervised, the Tucson Federal is required to obtain fire and extended coverage insurance as collateral security on all mortgage loans made by it. Tucson Federal on November 30, 1941, entered into a written agreement with Aetna Investment Corporation to provide this coverage. The contract, which recites a consideration of mutual promises, was to run for a ten-year period, and it obligated Tucson Federal to purchase exclusively from Aetna all policies of insurance needed in connection with its business, to be paid for at the rate at which said policies of insurance and bonds are written in Pima County, Arizona. Aetna agreed on its part to secure such insurance and bonds as "may be needful or required by Tucson Federal."

For nearly five years the parties operated under this agreement but with a change in the directorate of Tucson Federal its board of directors on September 16, 1946, revoked and rescinded, effective immediately, the prior agreement. Suit by Aetna followed, seeking damages.

By its answer Tucson Federal admitted the execution of the written agreement and that since September 16, 1946, it had refused to comply with same. It then alleged certain affirmative defenses. One of these defenses was that the agreement was not a valid and enforceable contract because it lacked consideration.

UDALL, C.J. Following the trial upon the merits before the court sitting without a jury, the court found as a fact that the agreement was entirely honest and fair, that there was an adequate consideration for the same; and, that as a direct and proximate result of Tucson Federal's breach of the agreement, Aetna had been damaged in the sum of $10,000.

It is claimed that there was no consideration for the agreement, in that Aetna was only promising to do what it would be legally bound to do whenever it accepted a policy application and premium from an owner and hence there was no mutuality in this contract as between Aetna and Tucson Federal. We believe that an examination of the agreement itself clearly indicates that each party to the agreement promised to conduct itself in a particular manner for a period of ten years. Tucson Federal promised to procure from Aetna all insurance policies of every description needed by it in the conduct of its mortgage loan business, and Aetna agreed on its part to furnish, at the standard prices, all such policies. Prior to this agreement Tucson Federal was under no legal obligation to acquire any insurance from Aetna, and by the same token Aetna was under no obligation to furnish any insurance to Tucson Federal. The moment the agreement was signed each party had a legal benefit and a legal detriment accrue to it which is legal consideration. *Federal Rubber Co. v. Pruett*, 55 Ariz. 76, 98 P. (2d) 849.

PAST CONSIDERATION

To constitute valid consideration for a promise, the promisee's act, forbearance, or return promise must be given in response to the promisor's promise; it must be the price actually bargained for and paid for the promisor's promise. Hence it cannot precede the promisor's promise. As it is often expressed, a past consideration will not support a present promise. "Past consideration" is therefore a misnomer, since what it denotes is not consideration at all.

Past consideration must be carefully distinguished from consideration for an implied promise which is subsequently expressed. If a person performs a service for another, at the other's request and under circumstances wherein neither party understands such performance to be gratuitous, a subsequent promise to pay a specific sum for the service will bind the promisor. For example, A asks B to repair the roof of his house but says nothing about compensating B. There is nothing in the transaction or in the previous relationship of A and B to create a presumption that the work is to be gratuitous. After B has completed the job, A promises to pay him $50 on the first of the following month, but when the time comes he refuses to pay. B files suit, and A sets up as a defense "past consideration." Under such circumstances the court would hold A liable on his promise. B's work was consideration for A's implied promise to pay B what the job was worth, and his later promise to pay $50 was a statement of what the sum should be—a matter which would otherwise be determined by a jury.

Brown v. Addington
114 Ind. App. 404, 52 N. E. (2d) 640 (1944)

This was an action by Francis W. Brown, administrator of the estate of William E. Brown, deceased (plaintiff), against Claude L. Addington (defendant). Judgment for defendant, and plaintiff appealed. Affirmed.

Defendant, a nephew of plaintiff's decedent, became homeless when eight years old. Although under no legal obligation to do so, the said decedent took defendant into his own home where, during the ensuing six years, the decedent fed, clothed, educated in the public schools, and otherwise cared for defendant, without remuneration. For many years thereafter defendant, when not employed, spent much of his time in the decedent's home and paid nothing for food and shelter. By July 20, 1929, the decedent had reached an advanced age and became apprehensive that he might not have sufficient means to provide for his needs during the remainder of his life. He thereupon requested defendant, in consideration of the board and lodging furnished, to assist him during his old age by payment to him of $100 per year for the remainder of his life. This defendant agreed to do, and thereupon signed the following written statement:

"I, Claude L. Addington, remembering and appreciating the many favors and acts of kindness, rendered to me, during the years that have passed, by my beloved uncle, William E. Brown, and desiring to express my gratitude to him in something more than empty words, hereby promise and pledge that I will pay to my said uncle, William E. Brown, the sum of One Hundred Dollars ($100) during each year that the said William E. Brown shall live. Payment to be made on or about the first day of January of each said year, beginning the year 1930. (Signed) Claude L. Addington."

Addington failed to make the payments set out in this statement. Upon the death of William E. Brown this action was brought by his administrator.

Defendant set up as a defense past consideration; that the promise was a mere promise to pay money in recognition of past favors and kindnesses prompted by the natural love and affection defendant held for the decedent during his life.

CRUMPACKER, J. If a person has been benefited in the past by some act or forbearance for which he incurred no legal liability and "afterwards, whether from good feeling or interested motives, he makes a promise to the person by whose act or forbearance he has benefited, and that promise is made on no other consideration than the past benefit, it is gratuitous and cannot be enforced; it is based on motive and not on consideration." 17 C. J. S., Contracts, p. 470, Sec. 116. Although natural love and affection is sufficient consideration for an executed contract, it is generally held insufficient to support an executory contract. *Galbraith v. Galbraith*, 99 Ind. App. 563, 193 N. E. 707, *West v. Cavins, Executor*, 74 Ind. App. 265.

By the great weight of authority a past consideration, if it imposed no legal obligation at the time it was furnished, will support no promise whatever. A past consideration is insufficient, even though of benefit to the promisor, where the services rendered or things of value furnished were intended and expected to be gratuitous. *In re Greene*, D. C., 1930, 45 F. (2d) 428, *Ernst v. Campbell*, 235 Mich. 301, 209 N. W. 78.

Judgment for defendant affirmed.

ADEQUACY OF CONSIDERATION

The general rule is that the courts will not inquire into the adequacy of consideration unless there is evidence of fraud, duress, or undue influence in the transaction. The courts take the position that a very slight legal detriment to the promisee is a sufficient consideration to support a contract if the parties genuinely intend such to constitute consideration. This rule of law is based upon the feeling of the courts that the parties to a contract should be permitted to determine for themselves what consideration will be exacted and paid; if they have agreed upon its adequacy, the courts are not prone to question it. The Supreme Court of the state of Washington, in commenting upon this situation, declared: "The courts . . . do not inquire into the adequacy of the consideration. This, in the absence of fraud or overreaching, is solely the business of the parties. The courts inquire only into the legality of the consideration, not whether the party to be bound made an improvident bargain." [1] If there is evidence of fraud, duress, or undue influence, the courts will inquire into the entire transaction, but the basic concern of such inquiry is whether fraud, duress, or undue influence existed, and not whether the consideration is adequate. Such inquiry most commonly takes place in cases (1) where unequal sums of money are agreed to be exchanged at the same time and place, or (2) where unequal quantities of fungible goods [2] are agreed to be exchanged at the same time and place.

In a variety of contractual situations the sum of $1.00 is agreed upon between the parties as adequate consideration to bind the bargain; and one frequently sees in written instruments such a statement as "In consideration of $1.00 to me in hand paid, the receipt of which is hereby acknowledged, I promise to . . ." or "In consideration of $1.00 and other valuable consideration, I promise to. . . ." The consideration of $1.00 is generally held to be valid consideration if the parties understand and in-

---

[1] *Nelson v. Brassington*, 64 Wash. 180.
[2] Goods of which any unit is considered equal to any other unit, such as grain, flour, sugar, and liquids of all kinds.

tend it to be consideration, and if it is given for anything other than money. But the $1.00 must actually be paid. Although a few courts have held otherwise, the great weight of authority is to the effect that the mere recitation of the consideration of $1.00 in a written instrument, without actual payment of the sum, is not sufficient.

Allen v. Allen
133 A. (2d) 116 (1957)
Municipal Court of Appeals for the District of Columbia

These were actions by one brother and by administrator of another brother against sister and third brother for shares in proceeds of sales of realty as promised by sister and third brother under written contract with mother. The Municipal Court for the District of Columbia, Civil Division, found that the agreement was a simple contract not under seal, ruled that the consideration was grossly inadequate, and entered judgment for defendants, and plaintiffs appealed. . . . Affirmed.

HOOD, A.J. In 1898 by deed of conveyance from an aunt, appellees, who are brother and sister, became tenants in common of certain improved real estate. The conveyance was subject to the condition that appellees provide their father and mother a comfortable home on the premises for as long as they lived, unless the mother became the wife of another husband. By 1938 the father had died and the family consisted of appellees, their mother, and three brothers who were born after the 1898 conveyance. In that year appellees at the request of the mother, enter into a written agreement with her whereby "in consideration of the sum of One ($1.00) Dollar to them paid by Julia A. Allen (the mother), the receipt whereof is hereby acknowledged," they promised and agreed that in the event of the sale of the property during their lifetime, they would divide the proceeds equally among themselves and their three brothers.

The mother died in 1951 and in 1953 appellees sold the property for $15,000. These suits were then brought by one of the three brothers, one suit being on his own behalf and the other as administrator of a deceased brother's estate, each claiming one-fifth share of the $15,000. The original 1938 agreement had either been lost or misplaced, but a copy thereof was received in evidence. While the agreement recited that appellees and the mother "have hereunto set their hands and seals," the copy did not disclose anything purporting to be a seal after the signatures of the parties.

The trial court found that the agreement was a simple contract not under seal, and ruled that the consideration of one dollar was "grossly inadequate" to support the contract. Judgment was entered for the appellees and these appeals followed.

Appellant first argues that since the agreement of 1938 recited that it was executed under seal, appellees are estopped from contending that it was otherwise, and that the trial court was in error in holding it was a simple contract. Under the circumstances of this case, where only a copy of the agreement was presented to the court and such copy disclosed nothing purporting to be a seal and merely recited that the parties had affixed their hands and seals, there was a factual question to be determined by the court whether or not the original was executed under seal. We cannot hold that the finding that the instrument was a simple contract was erroneous.

Appellant next argues that it was error for the trial court to question the adequacy of the consideration recited in the agreement. In ruling that the consideration was grossly inadequate, the trial court relied on our case of *Sloan v. Sloan*, D. C. Mun. App., 66 A. (2) 799, wherein we held that, although generally a court will not inquire as to the adequacy of the consideration, where there is an agreement to exchange unequal sums of money and the sums are grossly disproportionate, the agreement will not receive the sanction of the courts. We agree with appellant that the Sloan case is inapplicable here. This was not an exchange of unequal sums of money. Appellees' promise was that should the property be sold during their lifetime they would divide the proceeds equally with their three brothers. If the property were not sold, they were not bound to pay anything; and they were not obligated to sell unless they so desired.

However, we think the trial court's denial of recovery was sound for another reason, and in the discussion of this reason will be found the answer to appellant's final contention that the recital of receipt of one dollar consideration estopped appellees from showing the real consideration or lack thereof.

The testimony was that the one dollar mentioned in the agreement as consideration was never paid by the mother to appellees and they received no consideration whatever for signing, that they signed in order to please their mother, and that one of appellees even paid the lawyer's fee of $10 for preparing the agreement. We think it is plain from this testimony, and implicit in tie trial court's reference to the "stated payment of One ($1.00) Dollar" as the only consideration, that the one dollar not only was not paid but was never intended to be paid.

As stated in the Sloan case, adequacy of consideration is not required; and if one dollar is intended as the consideration and paid and accepted as such, it is sufficient consideration. However, a stated consideration which is a mere pretense and not a reality is not sufficient; because if in fact no consideration was intended and none given, recital of a consideration cannot make the promise enforceable. *Restatement, Contracts* § 82; *Corbin on Contracts* § 130; *Williston on Contracts* (Rev. Ed.) § 115(b).

The recital in the agreement of a consideration and acknowledgment of payment thereof was evidence that such consideration was agreed upon by the parties and that payment was actually made; but such evidence was not conclusive. Recital of consideration in an unsealed instrument may be contradicted by parol evidence. On the evidence here the court found no actual but only a stated consideration. We conclude, therefore, that the promise of the appellees was without consideration and unenforceable.

Affirmed.

Colburn v. Mid-State Homes, Inc.

266 So. (2d) 865 (1972)

Supreme Court of Alabama

This was a bill in equity by mortgagors against mortgagee's assignee seeking to restrain foreclosure of the mortgage and praying its cancellation and that title to described property be quieted in them on grounds the mortgage was null and void and not duly executed. The Circuit Court, in Equity, . . . denied requested relief, and complainants appealed. . . . Affirmed.

McCALL, J. The chancellor's final decree denied complainants the relief prayed for in their bill of complaint. They appeal from the rendition of that decree.

The appellants, who are husband and wife, filed their bill in equity against the respondent Mid-State Homes, Inc., who is the appellee and was the sole party respondent in the cause. The appellee is the assignee of Jim Walter Corporation, under a written assignment, dated September 7, 1967, of an installment promissory note and real property mortgage, executed to the latter corporation to secure the purchase price of a "shell home." The appellants executed the note and mortgage on August 25, 1967.

The bill charges that the "mortgage is null, void, and of no effect, and complainants deny the due execution of said alleged mortgage." The appellants contend that the agent of the Jim Walter Corporation, who closed the purchase transaction, never explained to them that it was a mortgage that they were executing before him or that he was a notary public engaged in taking their acknowledgments to the mortgage; that he falsely certified that they voluntarily executed the instrument; that it was not proper for him as an employee of Jim Walter Corporation to certify their acknowledgments; that the manner in which the certificate of acknowledgment was executed rendered it ineffectual to convey their homestead rights in the property; and that the actual value of the "shell home" was greatly less than the amount of the indebtedness covered by the mortgage.

In their bill, the appellants pray for an order restraining foreclosure, for a cancellation of the mortgage, and for title to the real property described in the mortgage to be quieted in them.

The answer admits that the appellants own the mortgaged property, but own it subject to the appellee's rights as assignees of the unpaid note and security mortgage. The appellee denies the invalidity of the mortgage.

The mortgage and the acknowledgment thereto purport on their face to be in due form, complete and regular in all particulars, including the subscription to the mortgage by the appellants, and the certification of its execution by the notary public.

Each appellant admits having voluntarily signed before Jim Walter's agent, who is now shown to be a notary public, an instrument that they identified at the trial as the mortgage in question. However, they deny knowing at the time of signing that they were executing a mortgage or that the person before whom they signed was a notary public. The notary public handed the note and mortgage to the appellants separately, at different times and places, for the purpose of having them subscribe their names thereto, and, at his request each signed the mortgage in his presence. They asked no questions concerning the papers. The appellants admit that they were to pay 144 installments of money in consecutive monthly installments of $67.40 each as the purchase price, and the agent had told them the total purchase price of the house, though they did not recall it at the trial. They might readily have calculated it from information they had by multiplying the number of installments by the amount of each monthly payment. There was testimony by appellant Colburn that Jim Walter Corporation's agent said they wanted five acres as security and he thought he and his wife agreed to that. He further testified that before signing the papers a man came out and surveyed their property, though he could not say whether he paid for the survey or not. What the appellants considered they were signing on the occasion does not appear from the evidence.

After the appellants signed the papers presented to them, Jim Walter Corporation constructed them a house on the five acre tract conveyed by the mortgage.

There is no merit in appellants' contention that the mortgage is null, void, and of no effect.

An efficacious acknowledgment not only renders the instrument self-proving, if seasonably recorded, but it also imports a verity against which none can be heard to complain, unless it is for duress or fraud. It is a quasi-judicial, if not judicial, act of an officer, and his certificate cannot be questioned, if his jurisdiction was obtained, except on the grounds above noted. *Vizard v. Robinson,* 181 Ala. 349, 353, 61 So. 959; *Morris v. Bank of Attalla,* 153 Ala. 352, 357, 45 So. 219. In *Ford v. Fauche,* 272 Ala. 348, 351, 131 So. 2d 852, 854, it is stated:

". . . [W]hen a certifying officer acquires jurisdiction by having the grantor and the instrument before him, the resulting certificate of acknowledgment is conclusive of the facts therein stated in the absence of fraud or duress. *Weldon v. Bates,* supra [229 Ala. 169, 155 So. 560]; *Woolen v. Taylor,* 249 Ala. 455, 31 S. 2d 320. . . ."

*   *   *

Aside from the above, it may well be that the relief sought by appellants should be denied for another reason. Although there was no pleading or direct proof on the point, for aught that appears, appellee, Mid-State Homes, Inc., was a bona fide purchaser for value of the installment note and mortgage and would not be affected by the alleged irregularities, if such they were.

The instrument of assignment, which was introduced into evidence, recites that value was paid for the assignment to Mid-State Homes, Inc. And, there were neither allegations in the bill, nor statements in the evidence, to the effect that Mid-State had notice, actual or constructive, at the time of the purchase of the note and mortgage, of any then existing infirmities, defects, or defenses claimed by appellants against the mortgagee. Indeed, it is virtually impossible that appellee could have had any such notice, for appellants made timely payments under the mortgage without protest as to its validity for over three years (all but a few weeks of which was after the assignment to Mid-State) before any of the defenses involved in this suit were raised.

The Uniform Commercial Code, Tit. 7A, §§ 1–101 through 10–104, which applies in this case, provides in § 3–302(1) as follows:

"(1) A holder in due course is a holder who takes the instrument (a) for value; and (b) in good faith; and (c) without notice that it is overdue or has been dishonored or of any defense against or claim to it on the part of any person."

The law on the question of whether or not equities and defenses against the mortgagee may be set up against the assignee of the note and mortgage seems clearly settled against appellants. In this state, equities and defenses which would be available against the mortgagee cannot ordinarily be raised against a bona fide purchaser for value before maturity and without notice. And, the holder in due course of a negotiable note secured by a mortgage takes the mortgage subject to only those defenses which could be raised by the mortgagor against the note itself.

In *Hawley v. Bibb*, 69 Ala. 52, 57, we find the following comment on the subject written by Chief Justice Brickell:

". . . A bona fide holder of the bill . . . can not be affected by the illegality of consideration, which would render it void as between the immediate parties. Illegality of consideration affects the right and title of bona fide holders, only when by statute the invalidity of the instrument is pronounced, and it is made void in the hands of every holder, whether he has notice of the illegality or not.—*Saltmarsh v. Tuthill*, 13 Ala. 390.

The appellants acknowledge that Jim Walter Corporation built the house or "shell home" on the five acre tract. They do not complain that the vendor failed to construct the same type of house as selected by them, or that the workmanship was faulty, or that they did not receive exactly what they bargained for in every respect. The appellants simply say that the value of the house they bought is not as great as the amount they agreed to pay for it.

The accepted general rule is that the mere inadequacy of consideration, alone, is insufficient to vitiate a contract or conveyance, otherwise valid. *Decker v. Decker*, 253 Ala. 345. . . .

The appellants entered into a contract on August 25, 1967, to pay $9,705.60 for the erection of a "shell home" on their land. They paid the installments, when and as they came due until January 1971, when a dispute arose over a charge for insurance. Now, after adhering to the contract for nearly four years, they attack it for inadequacy of consideration by asserting that the house they bought was only worth $2,000. We think their complaint on this score comes too late, there being no evidence of fraud. ". . . The slightest consideration is sufficient to support the most onerous obligation; the inadequacy, as has been well said, is for the parties to consider at the time of making the agreement, and not for the court when it is sought to be enforced. . . ." 17 *C. J. S.* Contracts § 127, p. 843.

For the reasons stated we are of the opinion that the final decree of the trial court is due to be affirmed. We so hold.

Affirmed.

A PROMISE TO PERFORM AN EXISTING OBLIGATION

We have seen above that doing or promising to do what one is already legally bound to do does not constitute a valid consideration, since it lacks the requirement of legal detriment. This is the general rule, whatever the source of the obligation.

It has been held that one who occupies a public office cannot offer as consideration a performance of a duty to which his office obligates him in any case. For example, A offers a reward for the apprehension and conviction of the murderer of B. C, the sheriff of the county in which the murder was committed, arrests X and gives testimony leading to X's conviction on the murder charge. C is not legally entitled to the reward, for he did nothing more than he was legally bound to do under the law as the sheriff of the county, and hence his act did not constitute consideration for A's promise.

Another type of situation which falls under the general rule may be illustrated by a building contract. A enters into a contract with B to build a house for B for $15,000. After A has done some work on the house, he comes to the conclusion that he will lose money under his contract, and he informs B that he will not complete the house unless B will pay him $2,500 more. B tells A to go on with the job and promises to pay him the additional $2,500. Under normal circumstances, A may not collect the extra $2,500 from B when the house is completed, since A gave no new or additional consideration for B's promise to pay the extra $2,500. A suffered no legal detriment in completing the house, since he was already legally bound to complete it for the original contract price of $15,000. The fact that the contract turned out to be an unprofitable one for A did not alter his obligation to carry out his part of it. However, A could probably have recovered on the new agreement if he had promised to do something not called for by the original contract, such as putting in an extra fireplace or an extra closet or so. Such a promise would have constituted the fresh consideration required to purchase B's promise. It would also have been possible for A and B to come to a mutual agreement to discharge the old contract providing for a compensation of $15,000 and to substitute for it a new contract providing for a compensation of $17,500. The parties to an unexecuted contract may at any time mutually agree to release or discharge each other under the contract, and their mutual promises will provide adequate consideration. After such a release and discharge of the old contract, the parties may legally enter into a new contract containing any terms they may mutually agree upon.

An important exception to the general rule illustrated above is recognized by many courts in cases where performance by one of the parties to the contract becomes more burdensome than was contemplated by the parties, owing to exceptional and unforeseen circumstances. This exception may be illustrated by another building contract. Let us assume that A agrees to build a house for B for $20,000. According to the terms of the contract A agrees to construct a full basement at least seven feet deep. Soon after A starts to excavate for the basement he unexpectedly runs into solid rock, and he sees that completion of the basement will incur an additional cost of $1,000. He notifies B that he will not continue with the work unless B agrees to pay him $1,000 extra, and B agrees to make such additional payment. If, after the house is completed, B refuses to pay the additional $1,000, most courts would hold that B is bound under the new agreement. It is difficult to find any new consideration in such a case, but it would seem that equity and justice might well justify the courts in treating this type of case as an exception to the general rule.

Leggett et al. v. Vinson
155 Miss. 411, 124 So. 472 (1929)

This was an action by M. W. Vinson (plaintiff) against L. Ford Leggett et al. (defendants). Judgment for plaintiff, and defendants appealed. Reversed.

Plaintiff was a building contractor. He and defendants, Dr. Leggett and wife, entered into a written contract whereby plaintiff agreed to build a house for defendants for the sum of $3,950. After plaintiff had been working on the house for about seven weeks he discovered that he could not complete the work at the price fixed in the written contract without suffering considerable loss. He informed Dr. Leggett of this fact, whereupon, plaintiff testified, Dr. Leggett said: "Go ahead and complete the job like we started and I will pay you time and pay the bills." Plaintiff alleged in his declaration that "the defendant was to pay the plaintiff the sum of 50¢ per hour for the time employed in and about the performance of the contract, and was also to pay the plaintiff, upon the completion of the building, for all material of every kind and description used by him in the erection of the building. . . ."

When the building was completed defendants paid plaintiff the complete contract price, as provided for in the written contract, in the amount of $3,950, but refused to pay plaintiff the additional amount claimed by plaintiff to be due under the alleged oral contract. Plaintiff brought this action to recover $2,200.89, which he claimed that defendant owed him under the alleged oral agreement.

Defendants maintained that plaintiff, under the alleged oral contract, assumed no burdens or obligations other than those already imposed by the written contract, and that therefore the oral agreement, if made, was without consideration.

COOK, J. While there is some authority to the contrary, the great weight of authority seems to establish as the general rule the proposition that a promise to do that which a party is already legally bound to do is not sufficient consideration to support a promise by the other party to the contract to give the former an additional compensation or benefit, and such a promise cannot be legally enforced although the other party has completed his contract in reliance upon it; and with this general rule, prior decisions of this court are in accord.

In the case of *Ayres v. Railroad Co.*, 52 Iowa 478, 3 N. W. 522, a contractor threatened to stop construction because it was unprofitable, and the railroad company agreed to pay the debts incurred by the contractor if he would continue, and after the performance of the contract in reliance on this promise, it was sought to enforce the promise, but the court said: "An agreement to do what one is already under a legal obligation to do does not constitute a consideration for a contract."

Where A and B have entered into a bilateral agreement, it not infrequently happens that one of the parties, becoming dissatisfied with the contract, refuses to perform or to continue performance unless a larger compensation than that provided in the original agreement is promised him. Especially common is the situation where a builder or contractor undertakes work in return for a promised price, and afterwards finding the contract unprofitable, refuses to fulfill his agreement, but is induced to fulfill it by the promise of added compensation. On principle the second agreement is invalid, for the performance by the recalcitrant contractor is no legal detriment to him whether actually given or promised, since, at the time the second agreement was entered into, he was already bound to do the work; nor is the performance under the second agreement a legal benefit to the promisor, since he was already entitled to have the work done. In such situations and others identical in principle, the great weight of authority supports this conclusion.

Some of the cases supporting the general rule, as herein approved, recognize as an exception to this rule cases where a party refused to complete his contract on account of exceptional circumstances or unforeseen difficulties and burdens which would justify such party in rescinding the contract, but it will be unnecessary for us to here consider any question of exceptions, if any, to the general rule, for the reason that there is in the record now before us no evidence of any exceptional circumstances or unforeseen and substantial difficulties that would justify the defendant in rescinding the contract. Mere inadequacy of the contract price which is the result of an error of judgment on the part of the contractor is insufficient, and nothing more is made to appear in this record.

It is undoubtedly true that the parties to a contract may modify it, or waive their rights under it, and ingraft new terms upon it, and in such case the promise of one party will be sufficient consideration for the promise of the other. But where the promise of one is merely a repetition of a subsisting legal promise, and the duties, obligations, and burdens imposed upon such party by the contract are in no way varied, altered, or changed, there is no consideration for the promise of the other. Such is the case made by the plaintiff's proof, and therefore the alleged promise of the defendant was without consideration.

Judgment for defendants.

Schwartzreich v. Bauman-Busch, Inc.
131 N. E. 887, 231 N. Y. 196 (1921)

This was an action by Louis Schwartzreich (plaintiff) against Bauman-Busch, Inc. (defendant). Judgment for plaintiff, and defendant appealed. Affirmed.

On August 31, 1917, plaintiff and defendant entered into an agreement under which defendant agreed to employ plaintiff as a designer of coats and wraps. Under the terms of the agreement "The employment herein shall commence on November 21, 1917, and shall continue for twelve months thereafter. The party of the second part (plaintiff herein) shall receive a salary of $90 per week, payable weekly." In October plaintiff was offered more money by another concern. Mr. Bauman, an officer of defendant company, hearing about the offer, had a conversation with plaintiff concerning the matter. During this conversation Mr. Bauman offered plaintiff $100 per week if he would remain with defendant. Plaintiff thereupon agreed to stay with defendant. Mr. Bauman then dictated to his stenographer a new contract, dated October 17, 1917, in the exact words of the first contract and running for the same period, the salary being $100 per week instead of $90 per week, as under the August 31st contract. The contract was duly executed by both parties and witnessed. Simultaneously with the signing of this new contract plaintiff's copy of the old contract was left with Mr. Bauman and the signatures were torn off.

Plaintiff remained in defendant's employ until the following December, when he was discharged. He brought this action on the contract of October 17th for his damages.

The defense was that there was no consideration for the new contract since plaintiff was already bound under his agreement of August 31, 1917, to do the same work for the same period of time at $90 per week.

CRANE, J. It has been repeatedly held that a promise made to induce a party to do that which he is already bound by contract to perform is without consideration. But the cases in this state, while enforcing this rule, also recognize that a contract may be canceled by mutual consent and a new one made.

Any change in an existing contract, such as a modification of the rate of compensation, or a supplemental agreement, must have a new consideration to support it. In such a case the contract is continued, not ended. Where, however, an existing contract is terminated by consent of both parties and a new one executed in its place and stead, we have a different situation and the mutual promises are again a consideration. Very little difference may appear in a mere change of compensation in an existing and continuing contract and a termination of one contract and the making of a new one for the same time and work, but at an increased compensation. There is, however, a marked difference in principle. Where the new contract gives any new privilege or advantage to the promisee, a consideration has been recognized, though in the main it is the same contract. If this were not the rule, parties having once made a contract would be prevented from changing it no matter how willing and desirous they might be to do so, unless the terms conferred an additional benefit to the promisee.

All concede that an agreement may be rescinded by mutual consent and a new agreement made thereafter on any terms to which the parties may assent. "A rescission followed shortly afterwards by a new agreement in regard to the same subject-matter would create the legal obligations provided in the subsequent agreement." Williston, *Contracts*, Vol. I, Sec. 130a.

Judgment for plaintiff affirmed.

PAYMENT OF A LARGER SUM BY A LESSER SUM

It has long been the rule of law that the payment of a lesser sum in satisfaction of a larger sum, the sum being *liquidated*, i.e. not indefinite or in dispute, is not sufficient to discharge the debt. For example, A owes B $1000 which is past due. A is unable or unwilling to pay the debt. B agrees to accept payment of $500 in full settlement of the debt, and in accordance with his agreement A pays B $500. B then files suit for the balance of $500. B may recover the balance. This rule, which is generally believed to have had its origin in 1602 in *Pinnel's Case*, 5 Coke, K. B. 117, is clearly in accord with the principles of consideration already studied. In making part payment the debtor has done nothing that he was not already legally bound to do in his original contract, and has therefore paid the creditor nothing by way of consideration for the creditor's promise to take less than the full amount of the debt.

Though the courts have generally followed the rule, many of them have felt that it is often harsh and inequitable in its results and that it may defeat the clear intentions of the parties. Consequently, most courts have not hesitated to seize upon the most trivial act or distinction to find consideration. In *Pinnel's Case* itself, the court, after stating that "the payment of a lesser sum on the day due in satisfaction of a greater sum cannot be a satisfaction of the whole," went on to say: "The gift of a horse, a hawk, or a peppercorn in satisfaction is good, for it shall be intended

that these articles are as valuable to the creditor as the money itself."
Later courts have followed and extended this lead. If the obligation is paid
ahead of time, or at a different place, or in a different manner, or in property other than money, or by a lesser sum together with other property,
or if the debtor forgoes his legal right to go into bankruptcy as an alternative to settlement in full, the debt will be held to be discharged on the
ground that new consideration has been given. Some courts have based
decisions contrary to the rule on the theory of an executed gift. For
example, if A, who holds B's note for $100, accepts $50 from B in payment of the debt and surrenders the note to him, or destroys or cancels
the note, it will be held that A has made B an executed gift of the unpaid
balance of the debt.

A few courts have felt so strongly that the rule is unjust and inequitable
that they have been willing to reject it completely. Under the statutes of
some states the rule has been changed so that the acceptance of a lesser
sum in satisfaction of a larger sum, where the debt is liquidated and not in
dispute, discharges the debt.[1]

The rule of law is different where the amount owed is indefinite or in
dispute. For example, Dr. A performs an appendectomy on B without
advance agreement on the fee. After the operation Dr. A presents B with a
bill for $300, and B refuses to pay it on the ground that it is excessive.
Under these circumstances it is clear that B owes Dr. A something for his
services, but the amount due is in dispute. Such a sum is said to be *un-
liquidated*. If Dr. A agrees to accept $250 as full settlement of the obliga-
tion and B pays the $250, this is full accord and satisfaction of the debt.
Consideration here is found in the surrender by the parties of their legal
right to have the sum determined by a court of law. Moreover, if B, upon
receiving Dr. A's bill for $300, sends him a check for $250, marked "Payment in full for appendectomy," and Dr. A cashes the check and then
sues B for the balance of $50 which he claims is still due, he would not be
able to recover, even if he drew a line through the words "Payment in
full for appendectomy" before cashing the check. By cashing the check
Dr. A would be held to have accepted B's offer of settlement of an un-
liquidated debt.

Melroy v. Kemmerer
218 Pa. 381, 67 Atl. 699, 11 L. R. A., N. S. 1018 (1907)

This was an action of assumpsit by Melroy & Bachman, a partnership (plaintiff) against Charles R. Kemmerer (defendant) for goods sold and delivered.
Judgment for plaintiff, and defendant appealed. Reversed.

[1] Alabama, Georgia, Maine, North Carolina, North Dakota, Oregon, South Dakota,
Tennessee, and Virginia.

Defendant had purchased certain goods and merchandise from plaintiff on open account. Defendant became insolvent and contemplated going into bankruptcy. Certain conferences were held between plaintiff and defendant whereby an agreement was reached that if defendant would not go into bankruptcy but would pay plaintiff 30% of the amount due him, plaintiff would accept such payment as payment in full of the entire debt. In compliance with this agreement defendant paid plaintiff the agreed amount of 30% of the indebtedness. Following this payment plaintiff brought this action to recover the balance of 70% of the original debt. It was not disputed that defendant was insolvent when the 30% agreement was made.

It was the contention of plaintiff that acceptance of a part of an amount due cannot affect the satisfaction of the whole debt.

Defense set up by defendant was that he had paid plaintiff the 30%, as agreed, and that this payment was a good accord and satisfaction of the whole claim because at the time the payment was made plaintiff had dissuaded him from going into bankruptcy.

MITCHELL, C.J. The exact point is whether the debtor's relinquishment of his intention to such a discharge in bankruptcy and his payment of the 30% instead constituted a sufficient consideration to bind the creditor to the agreement. On that point we have no doubt. A valuable consideration may consist in some right, interest, or benefit to one party, or some loss, detriment, or responsibility resulting actually or potentially to the other. "If there is any advantage to the creditor the law will not weigh the adequacy of the consideration." *Fowler v. Smith*, 153 Pa. 639.

It was said in *Ebert v. Johns*, 206 Pa. 395, that the rule that the acceptance of a smaller sum for a debt presently due, though agreed and expressed to be payment in full, is not a good accord and satisfaction, was a deduction of scholastic logic and was always regarded as more logical than just, and hence any circumstance of variation is sufficient to take a case out of the rule. As illustrations of such circumstances of variation, it has been held that payment a day or even an hour before the debt is due, or at a different place, or of a certainty in amount where the amount of the debt is uncertain, or payment of even a part by a third person, or additional security of any kind such as the indorsement of a note by a third person, or payment in chattels or any thing other than money, will be a good discharge of the whole by way of accord and satisfaction. *Fuller v. Kemp*, 138 N. Y. 231.

The rule itself is founded on the want of consideration for the agreement. As a part can never be equal to the whole, payment of a part of a debt presently due gives the creditor nothing that he was not entitled to and deprives the debtor of nothing he was not bound to part with before, and therefore there is no consideration. The logic is unimpeachable, but it fails to take into consideration the practical importance of the difference between the right to a thing and the actual possession of it. As said in *Ebert v. Johns*, 206 Pa. 395, "To a merchant with a note coming due, $5,000 before three o'clock today which will save his commercial credit may well be worth more than $20,000 tomorrow after his note has gone to protest." If the debt is not due till tomorrow the payment of the lesser sum under all the cases will be a good consideration and a full accord and satisfaction. But if the debt was due yesterday but the debtor can only pay part today, the benefit to the creditor of getting that part now rather than the whole when it is too late, is just as great, and whatever conclusion the scholastic logic and theoretical reasoning may lead to, the importance of the practical result is a matter for the creditor to decide for himself, and having so decided and got the benefit of it, justice and common honesty ought to hold him to his agreement.

The accord in this case was good on both sides. By it the creditors got a sum certain, instead of the chances of an uncertain dividend in bankruptcy; the debtor accepted the responsibility of paying a sum certain whether his assets were sufficient or not, and gave up his right to a release of his full assets, and to a discharge from his whole debt without regard to the sufficiency of his present assets. On principle and on authority, therefore, the agreement in the present case was binding.

Judgment reversed.

Levine v. Blumenthal
186 A. 457, 117 N. J. L. 23 (1936)

This was an action by William Levine (plaintiff) against Anne Blumenthal and another (defendants). Judgment for plaintiff, and defendants appealed. Affirmed.

On April 18, 1931, plaintiff leased to defendants, for the retail merchandising of women's wearing apparel, store premises situated in Paterson, N. J. The term was two years, to commence on May 1, 1931, with an option of renewal for the further period of three years. The rent reserved was $2,100 for the first year and $2,400 for the second year, payable in equal monthly installments in advance. In the month of April, 1932, before the expiration of the first year of the term, defendants advised plaintiff that "it was absolutely impossible for them to pay any increase in rent; that their business had so fallen down that they had great difficulty in meeting the present rent of $175 per month; that if plaintiff insisted upon the increase called for in the lease, they would be forced to remove from the premises." Defendants maintained that plaintiff "agreed to allow them to remain under the same rental until business improved." Plaintiff alleged that he merely agreed to accept the payment of $175 each month "on account." For eleven months of the second year rent was paid by defendant, and accepted by plaintiff, at the rate of $175 per month. The option of renewal was not exercised; and defendants surrendered the premises at the expiration of the term, leaving the last month's rent unpaid. This action was brought to recover the unpaid balance of the rent reserved by the lease for the second year—$25 per month for eleven months, and $200 for the past month.

HEHER, J. It is elementary that the subsequent agreement to impose the obligation of a contract must rest upon a new and independent consideration. The rule was laid down in very early times that even though a part of a matured liquidated debt or demand has been given and received in full satisfaction thereof, the creditor may yet recover the remainder. The payment of a part was not regarded in law as a satisfaction of the whole, unless it was in virtue of an agreement supported by a consideration. *Pinnel's Case*, 5 Coke 117, a, 77 Eng. Reprint 237; *Fitch v. Sutton*, 5 East. 230; Williston *Contracts,* Sec. 120 et seq. The principle is firmly imbedded in our jurisprudence that a promise to do what the promisor is already legally bound to do is an unreal consideration. It has been criticized, at least in some of its special applications, as "mediaeval" and wholly artificial, a rule that operates to defeat the "reasonable bargains of business men." 12 *Harvard Law Review,* 515; *Brooks v. White,* 43 Mass. 283. But these strictures are not well grounded. They reject the basic principle that a consideration, to support a contract, consists either of a benefit to the promisor or a detriment to the promisee— a doctrine that has always been fundamental in our conception of consideration.

Any consideration for the new undertaking, however insignificant, satisfies this rule. For instance, an undertaking to pay part of the debt before maturity, or at a place other than where the obligor was legally bound to pay, or to pay in property, regardless of its value, or to effect a composition with creditors by the payment of less than the sum due, has been held to constitute a consideration sufficient in law. The test is whether there is an additional consideration adequate to support an ordinary contract, and consisting of something which the debtor was not legally bound to do or give.

So tested, the secondary agreement at issue is not supported by a valid consideration; and it therefore created no legal obligation. General economic adversity, however disastrous it may be in its individual consequences, is never a warrant for judicial abrogation of this primary principle of the law of contracts.

Judgment affirmed.

Rye v. Phillips
230 Minn. 567, 282 N. W. 459 (1938)

This was an action by Gullick N. Rye (plaintiff) against Ben Phillips (defendant) on a note. From an order denying defendant's motion for a new trial, defendant appealed. Order reversed.

Plaintiff, as indorsee, brought this suit against defendant, as the maker of the note sued upon. Defendant set up as his defense a release or an accord and satisfaction. More specifically, defendant introduced evidence of a composition settlement of the note by which he agreed to turn over to plaintiff certain livestock in payment of same. The value of the livestock was less than the balance due on the note but was accepted by plaintiff as full settlement of same.

Plaintiff filed a motion in the trial court for a directed verdict. This motion was granted upon the ground that "a mere promise of a creditor to receive, and of the debtor to pay, a sum less than the debt in full satisfaction of it is without consideration and binds neither party."

STONE, J. The doctrine thus invoked is one of the relics of antique law which should have been discarded long ago. It is evidence of the former capacity of lawyers and judges to make the requirement of consideration an overworked shibboleth rather than a logical and just standard of actionability.

In *Oien v. St. Paul City Ry. Co.*, 198 Minn. 363, 270 N. W. 1, we made such observations concerning it that the bar should have been advised thereby that we were ready to label the proposition as a museum piece of the law and shelve it accordingly. As Mr. Dunnell suggests, *Minn. Dig.*, 1932 Supp., Sec. 39, the doctrine may have sprouted from "a mistake in reporting," in *Pinnel's Case*, in 1602. It is characterized as "an artificial and groundless rule which has been consistently condemned." Its true status is accurately stated in *Selected Readings on the Law of Contracts* (Macmillan, 1931), 325, as follows: "And the rule is commonly thought to be a corollary of the doctrine of consideration. But this is a total misconception. The rule is older than the doctrine of consideration and is simply the survival of a bit of formal logic of the mediaeval lawyers." The law has been changed by statute in at least ten states. But, being a judge-made rule, judges are just as competent to get rid of it as the legislature.

There is more than one ground of logic and good law upon which this old and indefensible rule may be discarded. There is no reason why a person should be prevented from making an executed gift of incorporeal as well as corporeal property. Why should a receipt in full for the entire debt not be taken in a proper case as sufficient evidence of an executed gift of the unpaid portion of the debt? Again, where there is proof, or on adequate evidence a finding, that a completed legal act such as a waiver has set a matter at rest, why is it necessary to search for any consideration?

The modern view is that a new promise to pay a debt barred by the Statute of Limitations or discharge in bankruptcy is binding without consideration. In that field at least, judges have recognized the futility of their former efforts to create a synthetic consideration where there is no actual consideration.

We have no hesitation in saying that the answer pleads a defense. It avers a new contract between the plaintiff and defendant. Furthermore, it shows that the agreement was executed. Insofar as defendant agreed to turn over livestock, he assumed new obligations which were not his as maker of the note. Hence, it is immaterial whether the obligation substituted by the new contract for the old one under the note would or would not be the latter's equivalent in money value. For these reasons it was reversible error to exclude defendant's offered evidence in support of his defense and to direct a verdict for plaintiff. Order reversed.

SUBSCRIPTION AGREEMENTS

Some interesting legal problems concerning consideration arise in cases involving what are generally called subscription agreements. It is not an uncommon occurrence for subscriptions to be taken to benefit charitable, educational, religious, and other institutions, and it is likewise not uncommon for some of the subscribers to fail or refuse to pay their subscriptions. If the promisee or donee institution sues the subscriber, the most common defense is lack of consideration. From the standpoint of the bargain theory, the donee institution has paid nothing for the subscriber's promise to make a gift, and the promise is therefore unenforceable. However, in general the courts have attempted to find some other theory as a basis for requiring a subscriber to honor and pay his subscription. They seem to feel that it is good public policy to do so.

Some courts find consideration in the mutual promises of the subscribers, but this theory is not very satisfactory, since the promises run between the subscribers themselves and not between the subscribers and the donee institution. A much sounder basis for the enforcement of subscription agreements is a theory which is often called the *injurious reliance theory*. Under this theory, a subscriber's promise to pay money is regarded as an offer, which, like other offers, may be revoked by the offeror at any time before acceptance. Like other offers, too, it terminates with the offeror's death; his estate would not be bound by an attempted acceptance after his death, nor could the subscription be legally paid by the executor or administrator of his estate. Acceptance takes place when the offeree institution, relying upon the offer, obligates itself contractually to a third party or parties—for example, for the construction of a building, or for the purchase of land or other property, or for any purpose for which the subscription was promised. As soon as the institution assumes such liability in reliance upon the subscriber's promise, a contract arises and the subscriber is bound.

Furman University v. Waller et al.
124 S. C. 68, 117 S. E. 356 (1923)

This was an action by Furman University (plaintiff) against Coleman B. Waller and another as administrators of the estate of C. A. C. Waller, deceased (defendants). From a judgment for plaintiff entered on a directed verdict, defendants appealed. Affirmed.

This was an action to enforce a subscription for $10,000 made by the late C. A. C. Waller to "The Baptist Seventy-five Million Campaign." The deceased signed a subscription card wherein he agreed to pay $10,000, all of which was to be designated to Furman University, a Baptist institution. In the agreement the donor agreed to pay $100 upon signing the subscription, and the balance in stated installments. He made the initial payment of $100 and died before any of the installments became due.

In reliance upon the various subscriptions to the "Baptist Seventy-five Million Campaign," money was borrowed by Furman University and many improvements were made. The campaign closed on December 7, 1919, and a contract for the erection of a new dormitory was entered into on December 30, 1919. The dormitory and other building were erected and land was purchased for that and other purposes of enlargement. The faculty and the students were doubled in members. All of this was done on the strength of the subscriptions in this campaign.

Defendants' first and main contention is that the evidentiary facts adduced and relied upon by plaintiff are insufficient to establish a binding legal obligation. They say that the subscription of Waller was a nudum pactum, a mere naked promise to give something in the future, unsupported by a valuable consideration and unenforceable in law or equity.

MARION, J. In *Currie v. Misa*, L. R., 10 Exch., 153, the court said: "A valuable consideration, in the sense of the law, may consist either in some right, interest, profit, or benefit accruing to the one party, or some forbearance, detriment, loss, or responsibility given, suffered, or undertaken by the other."

"In a very few of the earliest cases, as will be observed, a narrow view was taken, and an agreement of this character to pay money to a charitable fund was regarded as purely gratuitous, a nudum pactum, a promise without consideration, and unenforceable on any legal ground; thus leaving the performance of the agreement to the conscience and sense of honor of the individual subscriber. But the courts soon receded from this position, and perhaps out of regard for public policy, and a desire to give greater stability and security to institutions thus largely dependent on donations from the public, began to look to other subscriptions to the same fund for a consideration for the one in question—or to acts performed by the promisee on the faith of the subscription as constituting a consideration for it; and generally the tendency has been to uphold the subscription as valid and enforceable wherever that was possible." 48 L. R. A. (N. S.) 783.

In the case of *Young Men's Christian Association v. Estill*, 48 L. R. A. (N. S.) 783, the court said: "A promise to donate money to a charitable purpose is gratuitous and unenforceable unless some consideration therefor exists. Such a promise amounts to nothing more than a voluntary offer which may be withdrawn before being acted upon. But if, on the faith of the promise, the promisee, before withdrawal of the promise, expends money and incurs enforceable liabilities in furtherance of the enterprise the promisor intended to promote, the consideration is supplied and the promise is rendered valid and binding."

A subscription for a charitable purpose will be considered gratuitous and as merely a continuing offer to make a gift, which may be withdrawn and is unenforceable until accepted and acted upon by the promisee in such a manner as to establish mutuality of obligation as between the promisor and the promisee. Where the promisee has, before withdrawal, accepted the subscription, and has expressly, or by clear implication, agreed to apply the promised contribution to the purpose for which it was subscribed, and has thereby assumed the discharge of an obligation which may be enforced in law or in equity, the element of valuable consideration to support the promisor's agreement is supplied by the enforceable covenant of the promisee; there is then a promise for a promise; and therefrom springs a valid and enforceable contract.

Where, in the absence of a formal acceptance or promise or covenant on the part of the promisee to assume the performance of an enforceable obligation, the promisee or beneficiary on the faith of the subscription and before its withdrawal has expended money or incurred liabilities in furtherance of the enterprise or undertaking that the promisor intended to promote, the reciprocal promise or covenant on the part of the promisee required to supply the element of consideration will be implied, or the expense incurred or liabilities assumed will be regarded as in the nature of an executed consideration induced by the request impliedly contained in the subscription offer.

Judgment for plaintiff.

MORAL CONSIDERATION

While some of the earlier cases held that a moral obligation constituted sufficient consideration to support a promise, it is well settled today that moral consideration does not constitute valid consideration. For example, A rescues B from a burning building, and B later expresses his gratitude by promising to give A $1000. A's act of rescue would of course not constitute consideration, for it was not performed in response to B's promise; yet it would appear that B was morally bound to pay A the promised reward. Nevertheless the courts would hold that he was not legally bound, since a moral obligation is not valid consideration. This rule may seem very harsh, but the alternative would involve the courts in endless uncertainty and dispute concerning moral judgments, or else would result in making all promises enforceable on the ground that every promise creates a moral obligation upon the promisor to carry it out.

Exceptions to the preceding rule have been recognized by the courts in certain well-defined situations where equity and justice or sound public policy requires that a promise be held enforceable but where consideration cannot be shown under the bargain theory. Where an obligation has become outlawed by the statute of limitations and the debtor afterwards promises to pay the debt, the courts will hold the debtor to his promise. Similarly, where a debt has been discharged by a bankruptcy proceeding and the debtor afterwards promises to pay the discharged debt, the courts will hold the debtor to his promise.[1] In both cases the discharge of the debt came about by operation of law and not by the action of the parties. These exceptions are based on the theory that the outlawing of the debt under the statute of limitations or discharge in bankruptcy does not actually discharge the obligation but merely bars recovery by the creditor; by his new promise the debtor has waived his defense and is therefore morally bound to comply with his new promise.

It is possible under the law for a debtor to enter into what is known as a *composition agreement* with his creditors, whereby the creditors agree to discharge the debtor of his obligations if he will pay them a lesser sum, as agreed upon in the composition agreement. It is difficult to find any new consideration running between the debtor and his creditors to support the agreement; nevertheless the courts do recognize and enforce such agreements. The courts generally profess to find consideration for the promises of the creditors to accept less than the full amount owed them in the mutual promises of the creditors themselves. Another theory finds consideration in the fact that the debtor has purchased the promises of his creditors by forgoing his right to go through bankruptcy. Occasionally it has been said that such agreements may be upheld upon the theory of an executed gift of the balance, or even upon a third-party beneficiary theory.[2] Whatever the theory adopted, the courts do enforce composition agreements.

If a debtor, having been relieved of his obligations as a result of a composition agreement, afterwards promises to pay the balance due one of his creditors, his promise would not be enforceable without some new consideration on the creditor's part. At first glance it would appear that such a promise should follow the same rule that applies to promises made by debtors whose debts have been discharged in bankruptcy proceedings. However, the courts make a distinction between the two cases. It is said, as we have seen, that a discharge in bankruptcy does not wipe out the debt; it simply creates, by operation of law, protection of the debtor against a suit on the debt by the creditors, which protection the debtor may waive if he likes. A composition agreement, on the other hand, discharges the debt, not by operation of law, but by the contract of the parties; the composition agreement wipes out the obligation completely, and any new promise by the debtor to pay the debt looks to a new contract and would require a new consideration to support it.

---

[1] Most states require by statute that a new promise to pay a debt outlawed by the statute of limitations be in writing; and a number of states make the same requirement for a new promise to pay an obligation discharged in bankruptcy.

[2] See section entitled Third-Party Beneficiaries in Chapter 13 of this text.

Mills v. Wyman

20 Mass. (3 Pick. 207) (1825–26)

This was an action by Daniel Mills (plaintiff) against Seth Wyman (defendant) to recover on an alleged contract. The court directed a nonsuit, and plaintiff appealed. Affirmed.

Levi Wyman, the son of the defendant, Seth Wyman, left his home in Massachusetts and went to sea. Several years later, and when he was 25 years of age, he returned from a voyage. He suddenly became ill in Hartford, Conn., and was financially unable to take care of himself. Plaintiff, Daniel Mills, took him into his home, where he boarded and nursed him from February 5th to February 20, 1821, when Levi Wyman died. On February 24th, defendant Seth Wyman, Levi's father, wrote a letter to plaintiff (Mills) in which he promised to pay him for the expenses incurred in caring for his son. Later defendant refused to pay plaintiff, as promised, and this action was brought. Plaintiff was nonsuited and thereupon appealed.

PARKER, J. General rules of law established for the protection and security of honest and fair-minded men, who may inconsiderately make promises without any equivalent, will sometimes screen men of a different character from engagements which they are bound in foro conscientiae to perform. This is a defect, inherent in all human systems of law. The rule that a mere verbal promise, without any consideration, cannot be enforced, is universal in its application, and cannot be departed from to suit particular cases in which a refusal to perform such a promise may be disgraceful.

The promise declared on in this case appears to have been made without any legal consideration. The kindness and services toward the sick son of the defendant were not bestowed at his request. The son was in no respect under the care of the defendant. He was twenty-five years old, and had long left his father's family. On his return from a foreign country, he fell sick among strangers, and the plaintiff acted the part of the good Samaritan, giving him shelter and comfort until he died. The defendant, his father, on being informed of this event, influenced by a transient feeling of gratitude, promised in writing to pay the plaintiff for the expenses he had incurred. But he has determined to break his promise, and is willing to have this case appear on record as a strong example of particular injustice sometimes necessarily resulting from the operation of general rules.

It is said a moral consideration is a sufficient consideration to support an express promise; and some authorities lay down the rule thus broadly; but upon examination of the cases we are satisfied that the universality of the rule cannot be supported, and that there must have been some preexisting obligation, which has become inoperative by positive law, to form a basis for an effective promise. The case of debts barred by the Statute of Limitations, of debts incurred by infants, and of debts of bankrupts, are generally put for illustration of the rule. Express promises founded on such preexisting obligations may be enforced; there is good consideration for them; they merely remove an impediment created by law to the recovery of debts honestly due, but which public policy protects the creditors from being compelled to pay. In all these cases there was originally a quid pro quo; and, according to the principles of natural justice, the party receiving ought to pay; but the legislature has said he shall not be coerced; then comes the promise to pay the debt that is barred, or the promise of the man to pay the debt of the infant, or the promise of the discharged bankrupt to restore his creditor what by the law he has lost. In all these cases there is a moral obligation founded upon an antecedent valuable consideration. These promises therefore had a sound legal basis. They are not promises to pay something for nothing; not naked pacts; but the voluntary revival or creation of obligations which before existed in natural law, but which had been dispensed with, not for the benefit of the party obliged solely, but principally for the public convenience.

The general position, that moral obligation is a sufficient consideration for an express promise, is to be limited in its application to cases where at some time or other a good or valuable consideration has existed. Otherwise, a moral obligation does not constitute a valid consideration. Judgment affirmed.

Herrington v. Davitt
220 N. Y. 162, 115 N. E. 476, 1 A. L. R. 1700 (1917)

This was an action by Etta F. Herrington (plaintiff) against Ida K. Davitt and others (defendants). From a judgment for plaintiff at the Trial Term, affirmed by the Appellate Division, defendants appealed. Affirmed.

The action was upon a promissory note made by defendants' testator. After the note was delivered, the maker was adjudged a bankrupt, and thereunder received his discharge. A composition was effected, under the provisions of the Bankruptcy Act, between the bankrupt and his creditors. Plaintiff duly accepted the offer of the composition and the 20 per cent of the face value of the note payable under it. Defendants' testator thereafter wrote a letter to plaintiff as follows: "My dear Sister: Your letter received. Was somewhat surprised at its contents. In regard to your claim against me you will be paid every dollar of it with interest as soon as I sell the mill. If anything happens to me the farm is in my name and you will be paid. I have left orders to that effect. . . . Yours truly, A. W. Davitt." The claim mentioned in the letter was the note now sued upon.

COLLINS, J. The action was properly brought upon the note. For the purpose of the remedy, the original debt might still be considered the cause of action. *Dusenbury v. Hoyt*, 53 N. Y. 521, 13 Am. Rep. 543. It might, had the plaintiff so elected, have been brought upon the new promise. The note was a debt provable in the bankruptcy proceedings. The legal obligation which it created or evidenced was, by virtue of the confirmation of the composition offer and the discharge in the proceedings, discharged by force of the statute, and the remedy of the plaintiff, existing at the time the discharge was granted to recover her debt by action, was barred. The right of action is given by a new and efficacious promise. The practice of bringing the action upon the original demand is, however, sanctioned by usage. The discharge in bankruptcy is, under such practice, regarded as a discharge of the debt sub modo only, and the new promise as a waiver of the bar to the recovery of the debt created by the discharge. The new promise with such other facts as are essential to constitute it a valid cause of action may, however, be alleged.

Under our statute a promise to pay a debt discharged in bankruptcy must be in writing. The letter, in this case, is a sufficient writing. It constituted a distinct and unqualified promise to pay the debt.

The rule of law is well-nigh universal that such a promise made has an obligating and validating consideration in the moral obligation of the debtor to pay. The debt is not paid by the discharge in bankruptcy. It is due in conscience, although discharged in law, and this moral obligation, uniting with the subsequent promise to pay, creates a right of action.

Judgment affirmed.

CONTRACTS UNDER SEAL

In the early days of the common law, before the doctrine of consideration came into being, a seal was used as evidence of intent on the part of the contracting parties. At first only contracts under seal were enforceable. As the doctrine of consideration developed, the courts began to enforce both written and oral contracts that were not under seal, if they were supported by sufficient consideration. A contract under seal was enforced by an action of covenant; a contract not under seal, whether written or oral, was enforced by an action of assumpsit.

The purpose of the seal was to furnish proof that the parties intended to become legally bound by their agreement. The solemn act of placing a seal upon the agreement was thought to be adequate assurance that the parties intended without doubt to enter into the agreement. After the doctrine of consideration became established, the chief effect of the seal was to dispense with the necessity of proving consideration. The courts held either that the seal imported consideration or else that it took the place of consideration. In either case the presence of consideration was unrebuttable.

Today a number of the states have abolished the efficacy of the private seal. In some states, however, the seal retains its common law effect. In these jurisdictions, some courts say that the presence of the seal imports consideration, while others hold that it renders consideration unnecessary.

UNIFORM COMMERCIAL CODE

The Code makes seals inoperative in a contract for sale or an offer to buy or sell goods. Sec. 2–203 of the Code provides: "The affixing of a seal to a writing evidencing a contract for sale or as offer to buy or sell goods does not constitute the writing a sealed instrument and the law with respect to the sealed instruments does not apply to such a contract or offer."

McGowan v. Beach
242 N. C. 73, 86 S. E. (2d) 763 (1955)

This was an action by Mrs. Lois Sanders McGowan (plaintiff) against Benjamin Beach, administrator of the estate of Wade H. McGowan, deceased (defendant). Judgment for plaintiff, and defendant appealed. Affirmed.

This was a civil action by plaintiff to recover from the estate of Wade H. McGowan (who died April 6, 1951, leaving surviving him his widow, plaintiff herein, but no lineal descendants) the sum of $15,000, together with interest.

Plaintiff alleges in her complaint that on January 2, 1945, Wade H. McGowan (her husband) borrowed from her the sum of $15,000, and as evidence of such indebtedness executed under seal his memorandum in words and figures as follows: "January 2, 1945. I owe my wife Lois McGowan $15,000. W. H. McGowan. (Seal)." On the back of this instrument is recorded the payment of $150 as interest. Plaintiff introduced this instrument in evidence, as plaintiff's exhibit A. Defendant Beach, the administrator, denied the execution of the instrument by the decedent and refused to pay same. Thereupon plaintiff filed this action.

The jury found that W. H. McGowan signed the instrument and delivered it to plaintiff for a valuable consideration, and upon the basis of the jury's verdict the court found for plaintiff. Defendant appealed.

DENNY, J. It is stated in 12 *Am. Jur.,* Contracts Under Seal, section 74, p. 567: "At common law a promise under seal, but without any consideration, is binding because no consideration is required in such a case, or, as is sometimes said, because the seal imports or gives rise to a presumption of consideration. It has been said that the solemnity of a sealed instrument imports consideration, or, to speak more accurately, estops a covenantor from denying a consideration except for fraud."

Whether we construe the instrument under consideration to be a nonnegotiable note, a due bill, or merely an acknowledgment by W. H. McGowan of a debt to his wife in the sum of $15,000, the fact that it was executed under seal, which, in the absence of proof to the contrary, imports a consideration, makes the instrument sufficient as an acknowledgment of such debt.

When one unqualifiedly acknowledges a debt as a subsisting obligation, the law will imply a promise to pay. Judgment affirmed.

REVIEW CASES

1. Marshall entered into a composition agreement with his creditors whereby they accepted partial payment as full settlement of their claims. Afterward

Marshall agreed orally to pay the balance due on Garrison's original claim, and later executed a note for the amount due. Garrison, a party to the composition agreement, did not give any new consideration for the note. The note was not paid, and Garrison brought suit. Judgment for whom? (Garrison v. Marshall, 117 Kan. 722, 233 P. 119)

2. Mrs. Sanders executed a subscription pledge which stated in part: "In consideration of my interest in Christian missions and of the securing by the board of other pledges for its work, and for value received, I hereby promise to pay to the board the sum of $5,000, which shall become due and payable one day after my death out of my estate." Mrs. Sanders died, leaving all her property by will to her children. The board had performed no act in reliance upon her pledge. The board sued. Holding? (Board of Home Missions of M. E. Church v. Manley, 19 P.(2d) 21)

3. King sued to recover the balance claimed to be due for construction of a roadbed for the Duluth Railway Co. In the course of the work King found that because of difficulties arising from severe winter weather he would lose about $30,000 if he carried out the contract then in effect. He notified the company that he would not complete the contract unless he was paid $30,000 more. The company agreed, but when the work was finished it refused to pay the $30,000. Judgment for whom? (King v. Duluth Railway Co., 61 Minn. 482, 63 N. W. 1105)

4. An officer of the Indian Refining Co. called separately into his office certain long-time employees of the company and promised to pay each for the rest of his life at half his salary then in effect. The payments were made for a time, but later they were stopped, and Plowman and others sued, alleging the existence of contracts. Consideration for the contracts, it was contended, arose out of the relationship then existing, the desire of the company to provide for the future welfare of these aging employees, and the provision in the agreements that the employees would call at the office for their checks each payday. The defense was that the payments were gratuitous. Judgment for whom? (Plowman v. Indian Refining Co., 20 F. Supp. 1)

5. Graves promised to pay Silver et al. "a sum of money that would be satisfactory to them" if they would dismiss an appeal contesting a will in which all were interested. The appeal was dismissed but Graves refused to settle. Silver et al. brought an action for breach of contract. Ruling? (Silver et al. v. Graves, 210 Mass. 26, 95 N. E. 948)

6. Middleton signed a contract with Holecroft, in part as follows: "I propose to employ you to work for me for 15 months at my option . . . $300 per month. . . . If I fail to offer you work . . . you are free to seek employment elsewhere." Holecroft worked 5½ hours and then quit. Middleton sued to recover damages for breach of contract. Ruling? (Middleton v. Holecroft, 270 S. W.(2d) 90)

7. The testator by will created a trust valued at $3,000,000 for his son and bequeathed $1,000 to his adopted son. The adopted son assigned to the son for $100,000 all his interest in the testator's estate, agreeing that he would not contest the will in a legal action. Later the adopted son brought suit to set aside the assignment, relying in part on inadequacy of consideration. Holding? (Peyton v. Peyton, 271 S. W.(2d) 493)

8. Myers Store, Inc. breached a contract for the purchase of shoe polish from Wurzburg Bros. The amount to be paid in damages for the breach was in dispute. Myers Store sent Wurzburg Bros. a check along with a letter saying "paid in full." Wurzburg Bros. cashed the check but notified Myers Store that they intended to sue for freight costs in addition. Were they entitled to a judgment? (Myers Store, Inc. v. Wurzburg Bros., 21 S. W.(2d) (Ark.) 969)

Legality of Subject Matter

11

THE NATURE OF ILLEGALITY

The fourth essential of a valid contract is legality of the subject matter. An agreement is not valid and enforceable unless the consideration, purposes, and objectives of the agreement and the intentions of the parties are legal. Thus, if an agreement has as its objective the violation of a statute or of the common law, or if the performance of the agreement is deemed by the court to be against public policy, it will be held to be illegal and unenforceable.

In dealing with illegal agreements, the courts state that some are unenforceable because they violate specific statutes, some because they violate the common law, some because they contravene the "public policy" of the state. Broadly speaking, however, all such agreements are unenforceable because they contravene what is considered to be sound public policy. This is so because public policy is reflected in the statutory and case law of a given jurisdiction as well as in the current decisions of the courts. Conceptions of what is sound public policy vary from place to place, and also from one period to another within any one place, for they are shaped by the changing views of the people on vital social and economic questions. Under the early English common law, for example, wagering agreements were not unenforceable because of illegality, but today they are generally held to be against public policy in every state in the United States.

It is recognized everywhere that if the objectives of an agreement are illegal, the agreement is illegal and unenforceable even though the parties were not aware, when they arrived at their agreement, that it was illegal. For example, A agrees to act as B's agent in selling certain corporation stocks. There is a statute that makes the selling of stocks without a broker's license a misdemeanor. A and B are not aware of this statute, and A has therefore not obtained the required license. The agreement is nevertheless illegal and may not be enforced. If, however, it is possible, under the terms of an agreement, for the agreement to be performed in either a legal or an illegal manner, and if one of the parties, without the knowledge of the other, intends to perform in an illegal manner, it is generally held that the innocent party may enforce the agreement.

As a general rule, even if one party to an agreement knows, or has good reason to believe, that the other party intends to use the subject matter of the contract for illegal purposes, such fact will not make the agreement illegal. Thus, if A sells B a deck of playing cards, knowing or having reason to believe that B will use the cards illegally for gambling, A's knowledge will not void the agreement unless A is to participate in some way in the illegal undertaking. An important exception to this rule arises when the contemplated illegal purpose is a heinous crime. For example, if A sells a revolver to B, knowing that B intends to use it to murder C, the agreement would be illegal and unenforceable.

Illegal agreements encompass a broad range of subject matter. Among the many types that have been held to be unenforceable because of illegality are agreements to stifle bidding at public sales, agreements to hinder, delay, or defraud creditors in the collection of their claims, agreements to promote immorality, agreements to influence wrongfully the actions and decisions of public officials, agreements that tend to obstruct the course of justice, and agreements of attorneys to split fees with laymen, and agreements in perpetual restraint of marriage or remarriage.

Shackleton v. Food Machinery and Chemical Corp.

166 F. Supp. 636 (1958)

United States District Court

The court held that where corporation agreed to pay mother of plaintiff a royalty on each machine sold during her life and upon her death like royalties to the daughter provided she shall not have theretofore remarried and plaintiff survived her mother and machines had been since sold by the corporation, since the condition subsequent restraining the daughter's remarriage was void under Illinois law it was entirely inoperative and the daughter retained her right to the royalties unaffected by that condition.

Defendant's motion for summary judgment denied.

PLATT, C.J. Plaintiff, Dorothy Sells Landsheft Shackelton, a citizen of Michigan, filed suit to enforce the provisions of Clause 6 of a written contract executed October 26, 1928, between her brothers, Ogden, Millar and Neal Sells, and John Bean Manufacturing Company, predecessor of defendant, Food Machinery and Chemical Corporation, an organization incorporated in

Delaware. By the language of the contract the Sells brothers obligated them-selves individually to transfer all the outstanding shares of Sprague-Sells, a family corporation, in consideration of $224,985, 2,778 shares of fully paid no par common stock of John Bean Company, and a provision for employment of Sells brothers upon specified terms. The First Trust and Savings Bank of Chicago, Illinois, was nominated escrowee. Clause 6 recites:

"In addition to such purchase price The Bean Company agrees to pay Mrs. Lottie Sells, the mother of the Individuals, a royalty of $25 for each corn-husking machine sold by it or any of its subsidiaries during her life. Upon her death like royalties on sales of such machines thereafter shall be paid to her daughter, Dorothy S. Landsheft, provided she shall not have theretofore remarried; such royalties to be paid to her until her death or remarriage."

From the pleadings, affidavits and depositions the following facts appear. Ogden Sells negotiated the contract on behalf of his brothers and managed to secure Clause 6 as a part of the consideration. At the time the contract was made in 1928, plaintiff was 30 years of age and living with her mother. Though she had been informed of the provisions of the contract after it was executed, she nevertheless remarried in 1944, one year prior to the death of her mother. The defendant's Sprague-Sells Division, located at Hoopeston, Illinois, manu-factures nearly all of the defendant's cornhuskers, and it was this Division which paid to Lottie Sells, the royalties accruing during her lifetime. Upon these essential facts there is no dispute, and both parties have presented a motion for summary judgment.

Plaintiff maintains that the conditions of Clause 6 restraining her remarriage are in violation of public policy, and that the court should strike them and leave the agreement to pay royalties in force. Since there is no provision for the payment of royalties to another should she remarry, plaintiff further con-tends that the conditions of Clause 6 violate the "in terrorem" rule and are therefore void upon this additional ground. Defendant on the other hand contends that Clause 6 embodies a condition precedent that plaintiff shall not have remarried prior to the death of her mother, and a condition subsequent or limitation which alone recites whatever provision may be in total restraint of marriage. Since plaintiff did remarry prior to the death of her mother, it is urged that she did not comply with the condition precedent, that her rights are therefore barred, and that the question of the validity of the condition sub-sequent or limitation is thus made moot. The defendant further insists that if the condition against remarriage becomes relevant it is not against public policy. In support of this position, defendant attempts to convince the court that the rule with regard to restraints upon marriage varies from that applicable to the case of remarriage.

. . . Clause 6 contains two conditions precedent; royalties are payable only if husking machines be sold by the defendant, and then only in the event that plaintiff is living at the death of her mother. The life interest created in the mother was to be followed by a similar but contingent interest in Dorothy. It is apparent from the terms of the instrument that the contracting parties, insofar as Dorothy is concerned, had but a single purpose in view; no royalties were to be paid to her in the event of her remarriage. Although there are separate phrases it is obvious that the parties attempted to express but one condition in two different ways in order to accomplish the same effect. Though the purportedly separate conditions are separated by a semicolon, punctuation in a contract while it may shed light on the meaning of the parties is not necessarily controlling. *Allen v. United States Fidelity & Guaranty Co.*, 1915, 269 Ill. 234, 109 N. E. 1035. The effect intended was to impose a perpetual restraint upon Dorothy's remarriage, and it is this intention of the parties that is given effect rather than the words which are used. This court will "look at the substance rather than the form of contracts, and seek for the real intention of the parties, from a consideration of all parts of the contract. The intention thus ascertained is the essence of the contract, and to this legal effect is given." *Smith v. Riddell*, 1877, 87 Ill. 165, 169.

To follow the construction of Clause 6 as defendant suggests would be to allow indirectly the imposition of a perpetual restraint upon remarriage which is condemned as against public policy if attempted directly.

Since the parties intended to impose but one condition, which is in total restraint of marriage, it is necessary for the court to determine whether that condition is precedent or subsequent.

"When there is a doubt in regard to the meaning of words implying a condition, courts do not construe them as precedent. The words 'conditions precedent' used in a deed by the grantor do not necessarily make the conditions precedent. (Citing a case.) Whether a condition in a deed is precedent or subsequent is a question of intention and not of phrase or form. . . . [If the condition upon which the estate depends] does not necessarily precede the vesting of the estate but may accompany or follow it, the condition is subsequent."

In *Winterland v. Winterland*, 1945, 389 Ill. 384, 388, 59 N. E. 2d 661, 663, it is reported that:

"The rule in this State is that the principles applicable to the vesting of real estate apply generally in the case of personal property."

In view of these holdings this court feels compelled to hold that the parties intended to impose an absolute and perpetual restraint of remarriage by means of a condition subsequent, and that the condition thus expressed is absolutely null and void as violative of the public policy of Illinois. Since plaintiff survived her mother and husking machines have been since sold by defendant, there has been full compliance with the only conditions precedent intended by the parties. The contingencies having obtained, plaintiff's rights have vested. Because the condition subsequent restraining plaintiff's remarriage is void, it is entirely inoperative and plaintiff retains her right to the royalties unaffected by that condition. *Eureka College v. Bondurant*, 1919, 289 Ill. 289, 124 N. E. 652.

There are decisions in other states holding that the prohibition of perpetual restraint upon marriage is not applicable in the case of remarriage.

Defendant's motion for summary judgment is therefore denied; the provisions of Clause 6 as construed by this court entitles the plaintiff to the royalties which have accrued and which may hereafter accrue.

Final order may be submitted in accordance with the views expressed herein.

Since the general effect of illegality is to prevent an agreement from ever becoming a contract at all, the courts usually refuse to grant either party to the agreement any relief. Whether the agreement is executory, executed, or partly executed, they generally leave the parties where they found them. There are certain exceptions, however. If the parties are not *in pari delicto*, i.e. not equally guilty, the courts at times take the position that it is good public policy to grant some degree of legal or equitable relief to the less guilty party. This exception is illustrated in cases where one party has induced the other to enter into an illegal agreement by fraud, undue influence, or duress. If an agreement contains several promises, some of which are legal and some illegal, the courts will enforce the legal promises (provided, of course, that they meet the requirements of a contract) if they are separable from the illegal. This situation is illustrated by an employment contract containing an illegal restrictive covenant (to be discussed later in this chapter). If, before the performance of an illegal agreement, one of the parties repents of the bargain and wishes to terminate it, he may usually recover any consideration he has given. For example, A and B bet on the outcome of a ball game and place their bets in the hands of C, as stakeholder. If A decides to withdraw before the game has been played, he may recover his money from C.

Wechsler v. Novak et al.
26 So. (2d) 884, 157 Fla. 703 (1946)

This was an action by Jack Wechsler (plaintiff) against Ben and Bella Novak, husband and wife, and others (defendants). Judgment for defendants, and plaintiff appealed. Affirmed.

Plaintiff in his declaration alleged, in part, that on or about June 5, 1943, defendants were engaged in operating the Atlantis Hotel at Miami Beach, Florida, and the hotel at the time was leased to the United States Army and that defendants were desirous of having the hotel returned to civilian use; that on June 20, 1943, defendants employed plaintiff to obtain information and assist in securing the return of the hotel to civilian use; defendants promised and agreed in consideration of the services to be performed and money spent and subsequent services to be performed in the event the Atlantis Hotel was returned to civilian use that they would pay plaintiff the sum of $10,000.

Plaintiff rendered certain services to defendants at their request. He appeared before the United States Army Real Estate Board in Washington, D. C., on four different occasions; and assisted defendants in securing information as to the possibilities of having the hotel released from the Army. On November 12, 1943, plaintiff notified defendants that the hotel would be returned to civilian use and they would receive within a few days an official notice thereof through proper authorities of the United States Army. On December 12, 1943, the hotel was returned to defendants. Afterwards defendants refused to pay plaintiff the compensation agreed upon for his services, and plaintiff filed this action.

Among other defenses set up by defendants was the following: "The original agreement sued upon is contrary to public policy, illegal and void in that plaintiff was therein seeking compensation for exerting influence upon public officials of the United States government."

CHAPMAN, C.J. The inherent and inalienable right of every man to enter into contracts or refuse so to contract is not only recognized but well established. Competent persons have the utmost liberty of contracting and when these agreements are shown to be voluntarily and freely made and entered into, then the courts usually will uphold and enforce them. The general right to contract is subject to the limitation that the agreement must not violate the Federal or state constitutions or state statutes or ordinances of a city or town or some rule of the common law. Individuals have never been allowed to stipulate for iniquity. The doctrine relating to illegal agreements is founded on a regard for the public welfare and therefore each contract must have a lawful purpose. 12 *Am. Jur.* 642, par. 149.

Agreements entered into against the public interest or contrary to the public policy of a state or nation usually are by the courts held illegal and void. The legality of agreements to influence administrative and executive officers or departments is to be determined in each case by weighing all the elements involved and then deciding whether the agreement promotes corrupt means to accomplish an end or to bring influence to bear on public officials of a nature other than the advancement of the best interests of the government. Agreements employing one to secure government contracts or concessions, etc., may be without taint on the face and yet illegal and unenforceable. 12 *Am. Jur.* 709, par. 206.

A contract involving the use of personal influence with public executive or administrative officers or the heads of departments in order to induce them to grant favors or privileges, as a general rule, is regarded as against public policy. Many courts hold such agreements invalid on the theory of their tendency to induce corrupt means in the influencing of public officials and especially is it true in those cases where compensation is contingent on success.

It must be admitted by the parties here that at the time (June 20, 1943) the agreement was entered into, the United States government was engaged in a bitter and desperate war with powerful enemies; that many points in Florida had by the Federal government been fortified and otherwise prepared against possible invasion by the public enemy; cautious measures were continuously exercised for protection of the American people; our troops were housed in tourist hotels at Miami Beach. The opportunities for self-aggrandizement and personal gain were secondary objects. The agreement sued upon has not only violated the rule against public policy and is therefore void, but it is reasonable to concede that the shifting of our troops from the Atlantis Hotel could have given an invading enemy an advantage not anticipated. If the plaintiff had the power or influence to obtain a return of the Atlantis Hotel, then by analogy other hotels on the Miami Beach likewise could be returned. Thus the prosecution of the war indirectly could be adversely affected. Judgment for defendants affirmed.

Harbison v. Shirley et al.
139 Iowa 605, 117 N. W. 963, 19 L. R. A., N. S. 662 (1908)

This was an action by John Harbison (plaintiff) against M. D. Shirley and W. V. Silvers (defendants). Judgment for plaintiff, and defendants appealed. Affirmed.

On March 30, 1903, plaintiff leased to defendants certain premises to be used as a cigar store and a restaurant. Plaintiff exacted from defendants a bond in the penal sum of $500, conditioned in substance, that the defendants should engage in no unlawful business upon the premises, and that plaintiff should be held harmless from any expenditure, injunction, or assessment under the prohibitory laws of the State.

Defendants caused or permitted intoxicating liquors to be sold upon the premises and a tax of $150 was levied and assessed against the property, and plaintiff was compelled to pay the same in order to discharge his property from the lien. He, thereupon, brought this action against defendants to recover the amount of $150, with interest.

The only defense which was relied on was that the lease was made for the purpose of permitting one Shipley to sell liquors on the said premises in violation of the law, and that plaintiff was frequently in the building and knew the character of business that was being conducted by the said Shipley "at the time the lease was renewed and at the time the bond was given." Defendant Silvers was a liquor dealer and Shirley was one of his traveling salesmen. They did not give their personal attention to the conduct of the business on plaintiff's premises. Shipley had conducted the business for defendants during the summer of 1903, and had sold intoxicating liquors on the premises in violation of the law. It was contended by defendants that these circumstances were sufficient to warrant the jury in finding that plaintiff knew at the time he executed the extension of the lease that defendants intended to sell intoxicating liquors in violation of the law. Upon this premise, defendants contended, as a matter of law, that the bond was void, and that plaintiff could not recover.

EVANS, J. We cannot concur in the defendants' position—neither of fact nor of law. The authorities are not altogether in harmony as to the rule which renders a contract void when it is entered into by one of the parties with the intent to violate the law, and where such intent is known or suspected by the other party. The great weight of authority, however, is that mere knowledge or suspicion on the part of the lessor that the lessee intends to violate the law upon the property will not of itself render a contract void. In order to defeat a recovery for rent by the lessor, it must be shown that he participated in some degree, however slight, in the wrongful purpose and intended that the property should be so used. Mere indifference on his part as to the intended use of the property is not sufficient. If the lessor in any way aids the lessee in his unlawful design, such participation will render the contract void. His relation to the unlawful purpose must be in some degree active, rather than merely passive. If he does any act in aid of the unlawful purpose, however slight, it is sufficient participation on his part to defeat recovery. But, until there be some degree of connivance shown, a contract will not be avoided. *Tracy v. Talmadge,* 14 N. Y. 162; *Chamberlin v. Fisher,* 117 Mich. 428, 75 N. W. 931.

Under the evidence in this case the most that can be said is that the plaintiff feared or suspected that intoxicating liquors might be sold upon the premises. There is no testimony indicating any connivance on his part. The lease expressly forbade the use of the premises for any unlawful purpose. It is argued by the defendant that this was a mere pretense to cover up the real purpose; but, the evidence does not warrant such contention. The defendant, Shirley, testified to his conversation with the plaintiff as follows: "Mr. Harbison said that he did not want anything sold in there that would be a nuisance. He said: 'You want it for restaurant purposes. All right, take it for restaurant purposes.'" This oral statement is in harmony with the prohibition of the lease, and indicated no ulterior purpose on the part of the plaintiff. There was no other evidence on the question. The burden was upon the defendants to prove their affirmative defense. They have wholly failed to do so.

Judgment affirmed.

AGREEMENTS TO COMMIT CRIMES AND TORTS

Any agreement which has for its objective or purpose the commission of a crime or inducing the commission of a crime is illegal and unenforceable. This is so whether the crime is a common law crime or one created by statute. Thus, if A agrees to give B $100 if he will criminally assault C, and B, in compliance with his agreement with A, assaults C, B could not recover the $100 which A promised him. Or if A says to B, "I will give you $50 if you will steal an automobile for me" and B steals an automobile and turns it over to A, B may not recover a judgment against A for the $50. The services of the court are not available to those who wish to enforce illegal agreements.

Likewise, an agreement which has as its objective or purpose the commission of a tort is illegal and unenforceable: for example, an agreement to defraud a third person or to injure his property or reputation, or to infringe his patent, or to breach his contract, or an agreement whereby A assigns his property to B in order to defeat his creditors.

Robey v. Sun Record Company
242 F. (2d) 684 (1957)

This was an action by Sun Record Company, Inc. (plaintiff) against Donald D. Robey (defendant). Judgment for plaintiff and defendant appealed. Judgment affirmed.

Herman Parker, known as "Little Junior," was a blues and rhythm singer with a limited reputation in and around Memphis, Tennessee. On June 18, 1953, he and four others known as "The Blue Flames," a group of instrumental musicians, made a contract with Sun Record Company, Inc., a Tennessee corporation having its principal place of business in that State. The Blue Flames are not involved in the matters before us. By the contract Parker agreed to record eight phonograph record sides and more if Sun should require. The agreement gave Sun the exclusive services of Parker in the record making field and contained an express covenant that, during the life of the agreement, he would not record for anyone else. The contract was for the period of a year, and Sun had the option to extend the term for an additional year. The renewal option was exercised. Four records (eight record sides) were made. The first of these, with "Feelin' Good" on one side and "Fussin' and Fightin' Blues" on the other, was released on July 18, 1953, and soon became listed as one of the top blues and rhythm records in popularity and sales.

On September 4, 1953, the appellant, Robey, a resident of Texas, entered into a contract with Parker. It had, in substance, the same terms as Parker's prior contract with Sun except that the amount which Parker was to receive for his services was somewhat more and the term was for a longer period. In November of 1953 Sun released the second of the Parker records and its initial sales were good. Sun did not then know but soon thereafter learned of the contract between Parker and Robey. On December 3, 1953, Sun advised Robey that Parker was under contract to it. Robey was then making or preparing to make the first of his Parker records. He declined to recognize the contract of Parker with Sun and thereafter made and released several Parker records. Sun brought suit in the United States District Court against Robey for wrongful interference with the contractual relationship between Parker and Sun and for wrongfully inducing the breach by Parker of his contract with Sun. The case was tried without a jury, findings of fact and conclusions of law were made, and judgment was entered in favor of Sun and against Robey for $17,500.00 actual damages. Exemplary damages were denied. A motion was made to set aside the judgment, for a new trial, and to amend the findings of fact. After denial of the motion this appeal was brought.

JONES, C.J. The contentions of the appellant, Robey, are (a) that the findings of the trial court, essential to its judgment, are unsupported by, or at least contrary to, the great weight of the evidence, (b) that the court erroneously awarded damages for anticipated profits which were speculative and conjectural both as to existence and amount, (c) that the trial court's failure to find the formulae by which the $17,500.00 award was settled upon is a procedural error in violation of the requirement of specific fact findings, (d) that the introduction of trade journals to prove the facts stated therein was error, (e) that the undisputed evidence shows that appellee failed to mitigate its damages, and (f) that the contract between Sun Record Co., Inc. and Parker was not valid and no liability existed for inducing a breach thereof.

This is a typical case calling for the application of the rule that recovery may be had for the wrongful procurement of a breach of contract by one not a party to it. The doctrine has roots in the medieval Ordinance of Labourers, 1349, 23 Edw. III Ch. 1. The leading English case and the one from which our present jurisprudence stems is *Lumley v. Gye*, 1853, 2 El. & Bl. 216, 118 *Eng. Rep.* 749, 1 *Eng. Rul. Cas.* 707. In Texas the rule was introduced in 1903 by *Raymond v. Yarrington*, 96 Tex. 443, 72 S. W. 580, 73 S. W. 800, 62 *L. R. A.* 962, 97 *Am. St. Rep.* 914, where *Lumley v. Gye* and a number of other cases are reviewed. The rule was announced that a person who induces a party to a contract to break it, intending thereby to injure another person or get a benefit for himself, commits an actionable wrong. From *Temperton v. Russell*, 1893, 1 Q. B. Div. 715, the Supreme Court of Texas quoted with approval the following, "I presume that the principle is this, viz., that the contract confers certain rights on the person with whom it is made, and not only binds the parties to it by the obligation entered into, but also imposes on all the world the duty of respecting that contractual obligation." The courts of Texas have applied the rule in many circumstances. 25 *Tex. Jur.*, 31 et seq., *Interference* Sec. 2.

Judgment affirmed.

REGULATORY STATUTES AND ORDINANCES

A state has broad and far-reaching police power through which it may pass laws designed to safeguard the health, safety, morals, and general well-being of its people. Under this power all the states have enacted many regulatory statutes concerning the practice of various professions and the carrying on of business and commerce; and the various municipalities, through their delegated authority from the states, have adopted many regulatory ordinances similarly intended to protect the public.

A second type of statute or ordinance springs from the power of the states and municipalities to tax for the purpose of raising revenue. One common method of raising revenue is to require that one who wishes to practice a given profession or to conduct a certain type of business must first obtain a license or certificate and pay a specified fee to the state or city involved. Failure to secure the required license usually subjects the offender to the payment of a fine.

So far as contract law is concerned, the important question is the effect of such statutes and ordinances upon agreements which are in violation of them. Are such agreements illegal? For example, all states have statutes which require lawyers to secure a license to practice law. In order to secure such license a person must meet certain specified requirements as to education, training, experience, and character. A is a senior in law school but has not been admitted to the bar and therefore is not licensed to practice law in the state. A enters into an agreement with B whereby A agrees to draw up a will for B for a fee of $50. If A prepares a perfectly satisfactory will for B and delivers it to B, and B refuses to pay A the agreed $50, and A sues B, can A recover?

In answering this question it should be noted in the first place that many of the statutes and ordinances specifically provide that all agreements which violate them shall be void and unenforceable. In these cases no question arises. Where such provision is lacking, the courts look to the intent of the statute or ordinance, either as explicitly stated or as implied by its nature, history, and background. If the court is of the opinion that a statute was enacted for the protection of the public, it will hold that agreements in contravention of the statute are void. If, on the other hand, it concludes that the particular statute was intended solely to raise revenue, then it will hold that contracts entered into in contravention of the statute are legal and enforceable. It is generally held that this is true even though the statute imposes a penalty for violation. The mere imposition of a penalty is only prima facie evidence of an intention to make contravening agreements void.

Wood v. Krepps
168 Cal. 382, 143 P. 691 (1914)

This was an action by Luther B. Wood (plaintiff) against J. E. Krepps and another (defendants). Judgment for plaintiff, and defendants appealed. Affirmed.

This action was brought to foreclose a chattel mortgage given as security for the payment of a promissory note for $1,000, executed by defendants in favor of plaintiff.

The answer of defendants set up that at the time of the execution of the note and mortgage plaintiff was engaged in the city of Los Angeles in carrying on the business of pawnbroking and the business of lending money on personal security and on personal property; and as a special defense against the right of plaintiff to recover, alleged that plaintiff had not, at the time of the execution of the note and mortgage, procured a license, as required by an ordinance of the city of Los Angeles, to authorize him to carry on the business of pawnbroking, or the business of lending money on personal security and upon personal property in which he was engaged.

LORINGAN, J. Whether the imposition of a penalty under a statute or ordinance is intended to be prohibitory or not is to be determined from a consideration of its nature and terms, and in determining this, certain rules have been established which are generally recognized. The general doctrine now well settled by the authorities is that when the object of the statute or ordinance, in requiring a license for the privilege of carrying on a certain business, is to prevent improper persons from engaging in that particular business, or is for the purpose or regulating it for the protection of the public morals, health, or general well-being, the imposition of the penalty amounts to a prohibition against doing the business without a license, and a contract made by an unlicensed person in violation of the statute or ordinance is void. On the other hand, it is equally well settled, though it must be admitted that there are some few authorities to the contrary, that when the object of the statute or ordinance, in imposing a license to conduct a harmless and legitimate business, is solely for the purpose of yielding a public revenue, and not for the purpose of protection, contracts made in the conduct of such business are valid, notwithstanding a penalty is imposed for a failure to obtain a license to conduct it. This was the purpose—municipal revenue solely—which the municipality had in view by requiring a license for carrying on the business of loaning money on personal property or the personal property brokerage business in which plaintiff was engaged, and out of which the note and mortgage here involved arose. There is no law in this state making the business of loaning money on personal property illegal. It is a legitimate branch of commercial business which the state has only regulated to the extent of fixing the maximum rate of interest. The business itself, however, is not affected. It is neither malum in se nor malum prohibitum. The ordinance does not pretend to proscribe or prohibit the business. Anyone may carry it on, the only condition attached to doing so being that the person engaged in it must obtain a license. The only penalty imposed is that if he does not obtain a license he will not only be subject to a civil action at the instance of the city, but likewise to a penalty in a criminal proceeding for doing business without having obtained it. The carrying on of the business itself is not prohibited; it is only the carrying on of it without a license. The prohibition runs against the person engaged in it without a license, not against the business itself. The ordinance does not declare that a contract, made by any one in the conduct of the various businesses for which licenses are provided to be procured under the ordinances, shall, if a license is not obtained, be invalid; nor is there any provision therein indicating in the slightest that this failure was intended to affect in any degree the right of contract. The primary purpose of the ordinance was to secure revenue.

Judgment affirmed.

Knight Drug Co. v. Naismith
38 S. E. (2d) 87 (1946)

This was an action by J. A. Naismith (plaintiff) against the Knight Drug Co. (defendant) for work and services allegedly performed as an accountant. Defendant's demurrer to plaintiff's petition was overruled, and defendant brought error. Affirmed.

J. A. Naismith brought an action on account against defendant. The petition alleged that defendant corporation was indebted to plaintiff in the sum of $150 for work done and services performed as shown by the following itemized statement of the account: "Balancing and correcting; posting and footing and making adjusted entries in books of the Knight Drug Co. (three months) last quarter 1944–$50; preparing and compiling 1944 State and Federal income tax returns and schedules for the Knight Drug Co. (including amended Federal returns)–$100; total–$150."

Defendant demurred to the petition on the ground that plaintiff's petition does not allege that plaintiff had, prior to the services he alleged he performed, obtained a license for the year 1945 from the Georgia Board of Accountancy nor that he had obtained from the proper authority in Chatham County and the City of Savannah, a license or paid the tax required as a condition precedent to a recovery in this action.

The state statutes of Georgia required that any person who engages in the practice of public accounting in Georgia would have to apply for registration with the State Board of Accountancy, and, if found qualified, upon the payment of the prescribed fee would receive a license. Sec. 84–9902 provided that "If any person shall hold himself out as having received a certificate provided for in Ch. 84–2 on the subject of certified public accountants, or shall assume to practice thereunder as a certified public accountant, or use the initials 'C. P. A.' without having received such certificate, or, if the same shall have been revoked he shall be guilty of a misdemeanor . . ."

SUTTON, J. The account sued on was for balancing and posting the books of the defendant for the last three months in 1944, and for preparing and compiling 1944 state and federal income tax returns for the defendant. The part of its demurrer, which the defendant here insists the court erred in overruling, is to the effect that the plaintiff "does not allege that he had, previous to the service he alleges he performed, obtained a license for the year 1945 from the Georgia State Board of Accountancy, nor that he had applied to said Board for registration." There was no necessity for any such allegations in the plaintiff's petition, as the petition does not show that the plaintiff was engaged in the profession of public accounting, as defined by the statute, so as to be required to obtain a license from the State Board of Accountancy, or to register with said Board. The defendant contends in its brief that Code, Sec. 84–215, is applicable to the plaintiff. This section provides, in part, "It shall be unlawful: For any person other than a certified public accountant, certified and registered as provided by this Chapter, to practice *as a certified public accountant,* or *hold himself out as,* or *assume to practice as* a certified public accountant, or use the term 'Certified Public Accountant,' or the abbreviation 'C. P. A.' . . . ."

The plaintiff's petition does not show that he was practicing as a certified public accountant and that he maintained an office for such purpose in this State, or that he used the style or title of public accountant. It is within the legitimate province of a bookkeeper to balance and post books, without obtaining a license as a certified public accountant, or registering as a public accountant. Also, a person other than a public accountant or certified public accountant may legally prepare state and federal income tax returns for another, without registering as a public accountant or obtaining a license as a certified public accountant.

The petition does not show on its face that the plaintiff was engaged in the profession of public accounting, as defined by the statute, so as to be required to obtain a license or certificate, or that if he was, he had not complied with the law. Therefore, the petition was not subject to demurrer. These are matters of defense, and they were not presented by the defendant, by way of defense. If it had been shown that the plaintiff held himself out as a public accountant or a "C. P. A." and had not complied with the statute in securing a license then he would have been in violation of the statute and the agreement would have been void and unenforceable.

The general rule is that where the object of the statute, requiring the payment of a license fee, or compliance with other provisions, as a condition precedent to carrying on or engaging in a business or profession, is to exact qualifications of the applicant or otherwise furnish protection to the public, even though the object of the statute may also include revenue, the inhibition implied from a penalty invalidates contracts made by persons defined in the regulatory measure. However, in the case at bar, it has not been shown, by way of defense, that the plaintiff violated the applicable statute, since it was not shown, by way of defense, that he held himself out as a public accountant or C. P. A. Therefore, the plaintiff's petition sets out a cause of action and was not subject to the defendant's demurrer.

Judgment for the plaintiff.

USURIOUS AGREEMENTS

Interest is the compensation received by the lender of money from the borrower for the use of such money. At common law no limitations were placed upon the amount of interest a lender could exact for the loan of his money; but most states now have statutes which limit the interest rate. The statutes usually specify two rates of interest, namely, the *legal rate* and the *lawful* or *maximum contract rate*. In some states they are the same. The legal rate is the rate allowed in the absence of specific agreement between the parties, for example on court judgments. In most states the legal rate is 6 per cent, but there is some variation from state to state; for example, in North Dakota it is 4 per cent, in California and Georgia 7 per cent. The lawful or maximum contract rate is the maximum that a lender is allowed by law to charge a borrower under a contract. It varies in the several states from 6 to 30 per cent; in a few states no maximum is established by law. The charging of a rate of interest in excess of the lawful or maximum contract rate is called *usury*.

Penalties are prescribed by statute for charging usurious rates of interest. The statutes vary from state to state, but in general they may be divided into three classes. (1) In a few states the whole transaction is made void, and the lender forfeits both the principal and the interest. (2) In some states the lender merely forfeits the excess interest above the *legal* rate of interest. Thus, in a state where the legal rate is 6 per cent and the lawful or maximum contract rate is 8 per cent, a lender who has charged 10 per cent would be able to recover judgment for the entire principal plus 6 per cent interest. (3) In a number of states the lender may recover his entire principal but forfeits all of the interest. This seems to be the most equitable and effective type of statute.

In most states the usury statutes do not apply to loans to corporations. Corporations may therefore contract for any rate of interest they are willing to pay.

Various means have been used to circumvent the usury statutes. One of the most common methods is to require the payment of "service charges" or "handling charges" in addition to the maximum contract rate of interest. Such additional charges will be held legal if they are in payment of legitimate services furnished by the lender, such as necessary legal fees, recording fees, fees for investigation, charges for securing insurance, and the like. Otherwise they are held to be illegal and in violation of the usury statutes.

One who is lending his own money may not circumvent the usury statutes by charging a "commission" or a "bonus" for the loan, in addition to interest. A loan broker, i.e. one who is in the business of securing loans for others, is entitled to charge a commission for his services in arranging a loan.

Not many years ago a person with little or no credit who suddenly found himself in need of money for an emergency was often unable to obtain a loan at the lawful rate, since loans to poor credit risks involve such a high percentage of loss that lenders are unwilling to enter into them at the same rate charged to good risks. Necessitous persons often had no recourse except to "loan sharks," who are ingenious in evading the usury laws. To find some means of offering protection to both borrowers and honest lenders under such circumstances, the Russell Sage Foundation a few years ago made an exhaustive study of the problem and finally drafted a model statute known as the Uniform Small Loan Law, to guide states in the enactment of legislation. Thirty-six states and the District of Columbia have since enacted Small Loan Laws. Under these statutes licensed lenders are permitted to lend small amounts (usually limited to $300 a customer) at a higher rate of interest than the general usury laws permit. The rate varies from state to state; the average seems to be in the neighborhood of $2\frac{1}{2}$ to 3 per cent a month on the unpaid balance. A few states set no limit.

Planters' National Bank of Virginia v. Wysong & Miles Co. et al.

177 N. C. 380, 99 S. E. 199, 12 A. L. R. 1416 (1919)

This was an action by the Planters' National Bank of Virginia (plaintiff) against the Wysong & Miles Co. (defendant). Verdict and judgment for plaintiff, and both plaintiff and defendant appealed. Error on plaintiff's appeal. No error on defendant's appeal.

Plaintiff brought this action to recover of defendant the amount of three promissory notes aggregating $10,349.54. Plaintiff asked judgment for the face value of the notes with interest from maturity, at the rate of 6 per cent per annum.

Defendant in its answer admitted the making of the three notes but counterclaimed for $7,161.37, which it alleged represented usurious interest charged by plaintiff.

The evidence showed that when plaintiff extended loans to defendant it permitted defendant to check against such amount to the extent of 80 per cent of the amount borrowed, but retained the balance of 20 per cent against which defendant could not draw checks.

WALKER, J. If a bank loans $2,000 at 6 per cent interest, with the understanding and agreement that it shall retain $500 of the amount as a deposit of the borrower in the bank, which shall not be subject to his check or his withdrawal of it but remain on general deposit in the bank, it is evident that the bank is charging and receiving $7\frac{1}{2}$ per cent interest, or $1\frac{1}{2}$ per cent in excess of the maximum legal rate. The transaction has not even the merit of having an ingenious device to hide or conceal the usury, for it is perfectly apparent what the legal effect is, as the borrower is paying 6 per cent on $2,000 when he is to receive only $1,500. The usury is plain and palpable, and there can be no doubt of the intent, on the part of the bank, to violate the law against payment of excessive interest, or usury. There are, generally speaking, four elements of usury: (1) a loan or forbearance of money, either express or implied; (2) upon an understanding that the principal shall be or may be returned; (3) and that for such loan or forbearance a greater profit than is authorized by law shall be paid or agreed to be paid; (4) entered into with an intention to violate the law. The fourth element may be implied if all the others are expressed on the face of the contract; the other three must be established by a sufficiency of evidence. The transaction in question clearly embraces all of these elements. The usury is indisputable.

29 *Am. & Eng. Ency.* (2d Ed.) p. 509, states that "in the case of loans or discounts by a bank at the highest legal rate of interest, a provision that the proceeds of the loan or discount or any part thereof shall be kept as a deposit in the bank during the period or a portion of the period of the loan renders

the transaction usurious, for the reason that the borrower thus pays interest on money which he does not receive or have use of."

[COMMENT: Several issues were involved in the case. On the foregoing issue of usury the court held that plaintiff was entitled to judgment on the three notes but that defendant was entitled to credit for the usurious interest charged.]

WAGERING AGREEMENTS

A wager, in the legal sense, is an agreement between two or more parties whereby they promise to pay money or transfer some other form of property upon the determination of some uncertain or future event. For example, A and B are playing cards. A wagers or bets B $10 that he (A) will win the next game, and B bets A $10 that A will not win the next game. Each has assumed a risk of losing something, depending upon the outcome of the next game. In the foregoing example the determining event is created by the parties themselves, but this is by no means always true; for instance, the wager may turn on the outcome of a Presidential election. However, the risk involved in the wager is created by the parties themselves, and the assumption of the risk is the subject matter of the agreement. Consideration is found in the mutual promises of the parties to pay money or transfer other property upon the determination of the event. Hence each party must assume the risk of losing something. If A bets B $100 that Jones will win the election and B does not bet A that Jones will lose the election, by promising to pay A some agreed amount if Jones wins, there would be no wagering agreement.

Under the English common law, wagering agreements were held to be valid and enforceable. In other words, it was held that the consideration in a wagering agreement was legal, and that only illegality of subject matter would prevent the agreement from being enforced. In this country the courts have, as a general rule, held wagering agreements illegal. At the present time most of the states have statutes which either prohibit or strictly limit and regulate all forms of wagering, betting, and gambling. A few states have statutes that permit pari-mutuel betting, if carried on strictly in accordance with certain prescribed standards set up by statute. The Maryland statute, for example, provides: "The Racing Commission shall have full power to prescribe rules, regulations, and conditions under which all horse races shall be conducted within the state of Maryland. Said Commission may make rules governing, restricting, or regulating betting on such races and may fix, regulate, and condition the rate of charge by the licensee for admission, or for the performance of any service, or for the sale of any article on the premises of such licensee, and may regulate the size of the purse, stake, or reward to be offered for the conduct of such races." [1]

In general, risk-bearing contracts such as insurance and hedging contracts are legal and enforceable, since their enforcement is held to be socially and economically desirable. While such contracts, strictly speaking, are wagers upon some future event, they are valid if certain conditions are present. The principal requirement for the validity of an insurance contract is that the insured must have an insurable interest in the life or property insured; otherwise the agreement is void, as against public policy. The reasoning behind this rule of law is plain. If, for example, the law would permit A to insure a house in which he had no insurable interest, the fact that he had nothing to lose if the house burned might induce him to commit the crime of arson.

In defining just what constitutes an insurable interest in a life or in property, it may be said in general that if the insured would sustain serious financial or other loss as a result of the death or destruction of the life or property insured, the insured would have an insurable interest in same. In the case of life insurance, a husband may insure the life of his wife, the wife may insure the life of her husband, a parent may insure the life of his child, a child may insure the life of his parent, an employer may insure the life of his employee, one partner may insure the life of another partner, and a creditor may insure the life of his debtor to the amount of the debt. But in this country A may not insure the life of B if B is not related to A and in no way under a contractual relation with A. Similar rules apply to property insurance. The owner of property may insure it against fire, windstorm, or other form of loss or damage. Likewise, a mortgagee has an insurable interest in the property upon which he holds a mortgage. It has also been held that the holder of an option to buy property has an insurable interest in the property.

In the case of life insurance, the insured must have an insurable interest in the life insured when the contract is entered into, but he need not have such interest when the policy becomes due and payable. In the case of property insurance, the insured must have an insurable interest in the property insured both at the time when the contract is entered into and at the time of the loss or damage.

Whether a contract dealing in "futures" is legal and enforceable depends upon the intent of the parties when the contract is consummated. If the parties intend that the grain or commodity contracted for is actually to be delivered at the specified future time, the agreement is valid and enforceable. It has been held that such a contract is valid even if it

[1] Article 78B, Section 11.

contains an option as to the time of delivery. But if the parties do not intend that delivery of the commodity shall be made on the future date, but only a settlement based upon the difference between the contract price and the market price on that date, the agreement is deemed to be a "bucket shop" transaction and therefore illegal. Determining the real intentions of the parties usually requires a careful examination of all available evidence, such as written contracts, letters and telegrams, past dealings, storage facilities, and the like.

Guyman v. Burlingame
36 Ill. 201 (1864)

Error to Circuit Court of *Randolph* County.

Debt brought by defendant in error against plaintiff in error and Seaburn J. Moore (the former only being served with process), upon a promissory note of which the following is a copy:

"Thirty days after date, we, or either of us, promise to pay A. H. Burlingame, or bearer, one hundred and sixty dollars, for value received, providing Abraham Lincoln receives the electoral votes of the state of Illinois. Eden, Oct. 15, 1860.

"Noah Guyman. [SEAL]

"S. J. Moore.   [SEAL]"

The summons by which the suit was commenced was indorsed as follows:

"I hereby appoint R. H. Jenkins special bailiff to execute this writ, April 9th, 1861. M. S. McCormick, Shff. R. C., Ills."

"I have executed the within writ by reading to the within named Noah Guyman, Seaburn Moore not in my county. April 12th, 1861. M. S. McCormick, sheriff of R. C., Ill., by R. H. Jenkins, speciall bailiff."

The questions for determination are sufficiently stated in the opinion.

Nelson & Sanders, for plaintiff in error. H. K. S. O'Melveny, for defendant in error.

BREESE, J. Two questions are presented by this [203*] record. First, Can the ordinary process of a circuit court be executed by a special bailiff, under the appointment *pro hac vice* of the sheriff? And next, Was the note sued on a bet on an election authorized by law?

At common law, several kinds of bailiffs were recognized, and among them sheriff's bailiffs, who are regarded as servants to sheriffs of counties, to execute writs, warrants, etc., for whose misdemeanors or defaults the sheriffs were answerable. Sheriffs had under them an under-sheriff, bailiffs, jailor, etc., for all of whom they were answerable. *Jacobs' Law Dict.*, title, "Sheriffs."

We do not suppose our statute respecting sheriffs and coroners has taken away or in any manner abridged this common law power of the sheriff to appoint a special bailiff, on an emergency, his appointment being indorsed on the writ. We believe it is the general practice. It seems a power necessary for him to possess in order to the due performance of the various duties devolving on him, which he cannot perform in person. And as all their acts are done in the name of the sheriff, and for which he is answerable, no injury can result to the public, but much good, by the proper exercise [204*] of this power.

On the other point we are constrained to hold, on the authority of the case of *Gordon v. Casey*, 23 Ill. 71, that the note sued on was, to all intents and purposes, a bet on an election authorized by the laws of this state, and consequently void.

The judgment, for this reason, must be reversed.

Judgment reversed.

Las Vegas Hacienda, Inc. v. Gibson
359 P. (2d) 85 (1961)

This is an action by George Gibson (plaintiff) against Las Vegas Hacienda, Inc. (defendant). Judgment for plaintiff and defendant appealed. Judgment affirmed.

Respondent [plaintiff] commenced this action in the lower court to recover the sum of $5,000 based on the following transaction.

Appellant [defendant] made a public offer to pay $5,000 to any person who, having paid 50¢ for the opportunity of attempting to do so, shot a hole in one on its golf course. There were certain specified conditions in connection with said offer.

The lower court found from the evidence that the respondent complied with said conditions, that he shot a hole in one, and that appellant refused to abide by its offer. It further determined that this transaction was a valid contract enforceable at law and not a gambling contract. Judgment was entered in favor of respondent in the sum of $5,000 plus interest and costs. Appeal is from said judgment.

McNAMEE, J. On this appeal we are not concerned with any factual matters, the lower court properly having resolved such matters in favor of respondent.

Appellant specified the following two errors:

1. The court below erred in not holding that the alleged contract on which the action is based was a wagering contract and therefore unenforceable.

2. The court below erred in finding that the shooting of a "hole in one" is a feat of skill and not a feat of chance.

Although gambling, duly licensed, is a lawful enterprise in Nevada (*Nevada Tax Commission v. Hicks*, 73 Nev. 115, 310 P. (2d) 852), an action will not lie for the collection of money won in gambling. *Weisbrod v. Fremont Hotel*, 74 Nev. 227, 326 P. (2d) 1104. It is therefore necessary to determine whether the transaction between appellant and respondent in this case constituted a gaming contract.

It is generally held, in the absence of a prohibitory statute, that the offer of a prize to a contestant therefor who performs a specified act is not invalid as being a gambling transaction. *Porter v. Day*, 71 Wis. 296, 37 N. W. 259. The offer by one party of specified compensation for the performance of a certain act as a proposition to all persons who may accept and comply with its conditions constitutes a promise by the offeror. The performance of that act is the consideration for such promise. The result is an enforceable contract. *Robertson v. United States*, 343 U. S. 711, 72 S. Ct. 994, 96 L. Ed. 1237. There is no statute in Nevada prohibiting such offers.

A prize or premium differs from a wager in that in the former, the person offering the same has no chance of gaining back the thing offered, but, if he abides by his offer, he must lose; whereas in the latter, each party interested therein has a chance of gain and takes a risk of loss. *Toomey v. Penwell*, 76 Mont. 166, 245 P. 943, 45 A. L. R. 993; *Pompano Horse Club v. State*, 93 Fla. 415, 111 So. 801, 52 A. L. R. 51.

Ballentine's Law Dictionary, 2d Ed., p. 1002, defines premium as "a reward or recompense for some act done. It is known who is to give before the event. It is not to be confounded with a bet or wager, for in a wager, it is not known who is to give until after the event."

Inasmuch as the contesting for a prize offered by another, which the one offering must lose in the event of compliance with the terms and conditions of his offer is not gambling, it was not error to hold that the said contract was valid and enforceable.

The test of the character of a game is not whether it contains an element of chance or an element of skill, but which is the dominating element. *People ex rel. Ellison v. Lavin*, 179 N. Y. 164, 71 N. E. 753, 66 L. R. A. 601. It was within the province of the trial court to determine this question. *Brown v. Board of Police Commissioners*, 58 Cal. App. (2d) 473, 136 P. (2d) 617.

Affirmed.

AGREEMENTS IN CONTRAVENTION OF STATUTE AGAINST PUBLIC POLICY AND TO INFLUENCE GOVERNMENTAL ACTION

At times agreements are entered into whereby one of the parties promises, for a consideration, to use his personal influence in attempting to secure (or prevent) the enactment of certain legislation, whether by Congress or a state legislature or a city council. Such agreements are popularly known as *lobbying contracts*. In any such case, if objectionable methods, such as bribery or political pressure, are used in procuring the objectives of the agreement, the agreement is illegal and void. There is a federal statute which aims at regulating the activities of lobbyists by establishing certain standards under which lobbying may legally be carried on. One may enter into a valid contract to carry on investigations, assemble data, prepare petitions and arguments to be presented before legislative committees, and engage in other such unobjectionable activities in order to influence legislation. But the use of corrupt methods will make a lobbying agreement illegal and unenforceable.

Much the same rule applies to agreements under the terms of which one party promises, for a consideration, to use his influence in negotiating a contract for the other party with a government department or agency. Such an agreement is void if corrupt or illegal methods are used in carrying it out; otherwise it is, as a general rule, valid and subsisting.

Ewing v. National Airport Corporation
115 F. (2d) 859 (1940)
Circuit Court of Appeals, Fourth Circuit

This was an action by Orman W. Ewing against the National Airport Corporation for services rendered in securing the passage of a bill by Congress for elimination of a road separating two airport landing fields. From a judgment for defendant, notwithstanding a verdict for plaintiff, the plaintiff appeals.

Affirmed.

NORTHCOTT, C.J. This is an action brought by Orman W. Ewing, appellant, here referred to as the plaintiff, against the appellee National Airport Corporation, here referred to as the defendant, in the District Court of the United States for Eastern District of Virginia, at Alexandria. The complaint was filed in February, 1939, and a trial was had before a jury in April, 1940.

The object of the action was to recover for services rendered in securing the passage of a bill through Congress for the elimination of what was known as a Military Road which separated two airport landing fields. These fields constituted the Washington Airport, operated by the defendant, in the State of Virginia, just across the Potomac River from Washington, District of Columbia. The running of this road through the landing fields caused great inconvenience in the operation of the airport and it was also alleged that the operation of the airport constituted a menace to the general public using the road.

The officials of the defendant corporation, desiring to have the road closed and abandoned, entered into an agreement with the plaintiff, who was a former member of the National Committee of one of the major parties, for the State of Utah, to secure the passage of legislation for the abandonment of the Military Road. The plaintiff after talking with the Vice-President and General Manager of the Washington Airport went to New York to see the President of the National Aviation Corporation, which corporation owned all the stock of the defendant company and, after some negotiations, which were closed either in New York or on plaintiff's return to Washington (there is some conflict in the evidence on this point, which is immaterial), plaintiff entered into the service of the defendant corporation and was paid $500 a month for his expenses and services.

A bill providing for the abandonment of the road upon the defendants paying $25,000 to Arlington County, Virginia, with which to build a new road, was passed by both Houses of Congress but was vetoed by the President. Later another bill was introduced and passed by Congress and signed by the President.

The plaintiff claiming that he was to be paid an additional sum if successful in his efforts to have the road abandoned, demanded of the defendant $10,000, which the defendant refused to pay and the plaintiff brought this action.

At the close of plaintiff's evidence at the trial defendant moved for a directed verdict on the ground that the contract sued on was a lobbying contract and not enforceable at law. The court overruled the motion which was renewed at the end of the trial. Upon this latter motion the court reserved decision. The jury returned a verdict in favor of the plaintiff for $8,750. Thereupon the defendant moved to set aside the verdict and in arrest of judgment. The judge below, after hearing argument, entered an order setting aside the verdict and entered judgment for the defendant on the ground that the contract was a lobbying contract and not enforceable. From this action this appeal was brought.

The sole question involved on this appeal is whether the court was right in holding that the contract sued on was a lobbying contract and therefore unenforceable.

There is practically no conflict in the authorities which all hold to the effect that no court will lend its asistance in any way toward carrying out the terms of an illegal contract; that a contract to secure the passage of legislation by any other means than the use of reason and presentation of facts, making arguments and submitting them orally or in writing, is invalid as a "lobbying contract."

The decision of the United States Courts and of the Supreme Court of Appeals of Virginia are in accord on this principle. In the case of *Campbell County v. Howard & Lee*, 133 Va. 19, 112 S. E. 876, 889, the court said: "The authorities very generally hold that a contract to pay for services to be performed in the endeavor to obtain or defeat legislation by other means than the use of argument addressed to the reason of the legislators, such as, for example, for the exertion of personal or political influence apart from the appeal to reason as applied to the consideration of the merits or demerits of the legislation in question, is an illegal contract."

* * *

In the case of *John W. Burke, Executor of Nicholas P. Trist v. Linus M. Child*, 88 U. S. 441, 21 Wall. 441, 452, 22 L. Ed. 623, the court said:

". . . The taint lies in the stipulation for pay. Where that exists, it affects fatally, in all its parts, the entire body of the contract. In all such cases, potior conditio defendentis. Where there is turpitude, the law will help neither party.

"The elder agent in this case is represented to have been a lawyer of ability and high character. The appellee is said to be equally worthy. This can make no difference as to the legal principles we have considered, nor in their application to the case in hand. The law is no respecter of persons."

* * *

In *Elliott on Contracts*, Vol. 2, p. 329, the author says: "The validity of a contract for procuring legislation is usually determined by the consideration as to whether or not it calls for or contemplates personal solicitation of or pressure brought to bear upon a member or members of a legislative body. If personal influence or personal solicitation is used or is contemplated by the contract, instead of open and fair argument, it is void."

* * *

Contingent fees for services in securing the passage of legislation are especially regarded with disfavor by the courts. *Marshall v. B. & O. Railroad Company*, 16 How. 314, 14 L. Ed. 953; *Providence Tool Company v. Norris*, supra.

A study of plaintiff's evidence given at the trial, and of letters admittedly written by him to the officers of the defendant corporation, shows conclusively that the plaintiff in securing the passage of the legislation in question used personal and political influence. As a former member of a national political committee he was in Washington doing lobbying work. He promised certain senators to exert political influence for them in their home states in return for their help in the passage of the legislation he was favoring. He repeatedly admitted this in the letters he wrote and in the testimony he gave in the trial of the case. While the legislation may have been meritorious and while the plaintiff may have done nothing more than return personal favors for help in securing the passage of the bill he was advocating, he may not come into a court and enforce payment for his services before the Congress.

The judge below was clearly right in setting aside the verdict and entering judgment for the defendant.

Affirmed.

Wasserman v. Weisner

36 Misc. (2d) 916, 234 N. Y. S. (2d) 128 (1962)

Supreme Court, New York

This was an action on behalf of children by their mother as guardian ad litem against her husband for damages for breach of alleged contract of husband to marry mother, adopt children, create trust of one million dollars for each, support, maintain, and educate them, and provide suitably for them in his will if they would forsake support, maintenance, and education benefits from their natural father and accept husband in propria patria as their father, wherein the husband filed motion to dismiss the amended complaint for insufficiency. The Supreme Court, . . . held that alleged breach did not entitle the children to recover; consideration for the agreement was illegal, unenforceable, and contrary to public policy and morale as tending to support a claim for alienation of affections.

Motion granted with leave to amend.

NEWMAN, J. Defendant moves . . . to dismiss the amended complaint on the ground of legal insufficiency.

The three infant plaintiffs are children of the guardian ad litem by a former marriage. The complaint alleges that some time before the marriage of the defendant and the guardian, that Seymour Wasserman (the guardian's then husband and the natural father of the infant plaintiffs) agreed in writing with the guardian, by a separation agreement and trust indenture, to provide for their children (the infant plaintiffs herein). Continuing, the complaint alleges that, in consideration of the guardian's marriage to defendant and of the infant plaintiffs' agreement to forsake any support, maintenance and education benefits from their natural father, and their acceptance of defendant "in propria patria and as their father," defendant offered to adopt them; to create a trust of one million dollars for each of the infant plaintiffs; to support, maintain and educate them; and to provide suitably for them in his will.

Further, it is alleged that in reliance upon defendant's representations of "great wealth" and his offer, as above set forth, the infant plaintiffs became estranged from their natural father; refused to accept moneys from him for their support; refused to permit him to visit them; and have accepted and treated this defendant as their father in their natural father's place and stead.

As a result of defendant's asserted failure to support them or to create or maintain a trust and a provision in his will for their benefit, the infant plaintiffs seek $1,000,000. as exemplary damages; $3,000,000. as compensatory damages; and accruing damages at the rate of $1,000. a week for the breach of the alleged "agreement" of support.

In the court's opinion, this action as pleaded in the amended complaint, may not be maintained as a matter of law. The consideration for the alleged agreement sued upon is illegal, unenforceable and contrary to public policy and morale in that such contract, in effect, tends to support a claim for alienation of affections outlawed by Article 2–A of the Civil Practice Act.

No person may maintain an action to enforce any right based upon an agreement to marry and a subsequent breach thereof. The applicable statute may not be circumvented merely by instituting this action in the names of the infant children, rather than in the name of the guardian individually (*Katz v. Katz*, 197 Misc. 412, 95 N. Y. S. (2d) 863). The infant plaintiffs here, at best, are in the position of third-party beneficiaries, and possess no greater right to enforce the alleged contract than the actual parties thereto.

Moreover, a court of equity, in the absence of most compelling and unusual circumstances, should not lend its aid to encourage or enforce an agreement which seeks to have infant children forsake, refuse to see or visit, and become completely estranged from their own natural father, who had expressed his willingness to care for and educate them properly.

. . . Here, if the infant plaintiffs endeavor to rely on promises purportedly made by them on considerations based on the promise of their mother to marry the defendant, then they are confronted by Article 2–A of the Civil Practice Act and by *Katz v. Katz*, supra. Accordingly the motion to dismiss the complaint is granted, with leave to plaintiffs to serve an amended complaint within twenty days after service of a copy of this order, with notice of entry.

CONTRACTS LIMITING LIABILITY FOR NEGLIGENCE

The extent to which one is to be liable for his negligence under a proposed contract may be more important to him than any other term of the proposed contract. Generally, the degree of liability that a contracting party will assume is as much subject to negotiation as is the price or the quantity or the quality of the thing contracted for. If A is unwilling to assume the usual liabilities involved in the proposed contract, and if B is willing to enter into the proposed contract under conditions whereby A's liability is waived or limited, and if the parties contract upon such understanding, the contract would generally be held to be valid. There is, however, an important exception to this rule. Where the rights of the public are involved, a contract under which one of the parties is exempt from liability *to the public* for his negligence would be held to be against public policy, and therefore void. If A owes a duty to the public at large to use due care, it is legally impossible for him to relieve himself of that liability by negotiating a contract with B whereby B agrees, for a consideration, to exempt A from such liability. In conformity with this rule of law the courts have held that common carriers, innkeepers, and public warehousemen may not contract away their responsibility to the public to exercise due care.

Smith v. Kennedy
195 So. (2d) 820 (1966)

This is an action by Jo Fay Kennedy and William Oliver Kennedy (plaintiffs) against Dollie K. Smith et al. (defendants). Judgment for plaintiffs and defendants appealed. Judgment affirmed.

Mrs. Jo Fay Kennedy sued the defendants for damages for personal injuries consisting of burns on her neck, head and back, suffered while she was getting a permanent wave. The complaints were in two counts. Count One in each case charged simple negligence. Count Two alleged wanton injury.

Defendants pleaded the general issue, assumed risk, contributory negligence and a hold harmless agreement signed by the plaintiff Jo Fay Kennedy.

The plaintiffs' demurrers were sustained to the defendants' pleas II, III, IV and V. The cases were submitted to the jury under both counts of the complaint. The jury returned a verdict against the defendants for Mrs. Jo Fay Kennedy for $1,000.00, and in favor of William Oliver Kennedy for $500.00. Motions for new trial were denied. Defendants appeal.

PRICE, J. On July 23, 1962, before the work performed on the plaintiff by the defendants was begun, the plaintiff and defendants entered into the following agreement:

HOLD HARMLESS AGREEMENT
(Student Operator Beauty School)

July 23, 1962

I, Mrs. W. O. Kennedy, residing at Trussville, Alabama, Route I, Box 735 do hereby acknowledge that I am fully aware that Birmingham Beauty College is a school for beauty culture and cosmetology, that the operators in this school are not being held out as skilled and trained operators, that for this reason, a reduction in the prices customarily charged is being made for this work. Therefore, in consideration of the reduction in price given in this work, it is agreed and understood that I will in no wise hold the above named school, its proprietors, officers or agents, or any of its operators liable or accountable for any injury or damage that may occur to me as a result of work performed on me in this school.

Witness: Robbie Reed—signed: Mrs. W. O. Kennedy

Under Alabama law a party may not by contract absolve himself from liability for the negligence of himself or his servants. *Housing Authority of Birmingham Dist. v. Morris*, 244 Ala. 557, 14 So. (2d) 527; *Gulf M. & O. R. Co. v. Scott*, 32 Ala. App. 326, 27 So. (2d) 150.

Mrs. Kennedy's hair was first shampooed, cut and then rolled up on rollers. Then the operator put something from a bottle on her hair. The bottle was like a tube, with a little old thing on it. The girl mashed it and the solution ran onto her head. She waited a few minutes, ran cold water on her head and then put something else on it. The solution ran down her neck and back, onto her forehead and into her face. Witness kept wiping her forehead with a kleenex to keep it from getting into her eyes. She could feel it running down her back and the top of her slip, her brassiere, the top, neck, shoulders and back of the old dress and the thin towel were saturated with the solution. Her back came in contact with the back of the chair she was sitting in. She kept telling the operator the solution was running down her back and also told her it was burning, but the operator said it wouldn't hurt her. Later that day she went to Leeds Hospital for treatment.

Dr. Erwin testified he saw Mrs. Kennedy in the emergency room of the Leeds Hospital on the night of July 23rd. She was suffering from "second degree chemical burns of the neck, completely around and extends from the hairline to the shoulder on the sides posteriorily and from the chin to the clavicle." Mrs. Kennedy still had some redness and pustules, small areas of infection, when he saw her on August 6th.

Judgment affirmed.

SUNDAY AGREEMENTS

Most states today have statutes concerning the making of contracts on Sunday, but situations not covered by statute follow the common law rule that contracts made on Sunday are valid and enforceable. Generalizations about Sunday agreements are difficult not only because of the wide variation in the statutory provisions but also because of the variation in the court decisions of the several states concerning the interpretation of certain common provisions in the Sunday contract laws. For instance, some of the statutes prohibit labor or business of one's "ordinary calling," others prohibit "servile work or labor," and still others prohibit "all work or labor" on Sunday. The courts have not always agreed upon what is meant by such phrases. One court, discussing the term "common labor" in relation to the signing of a promissory note, said: "Will it be said that written contracts are embraced by it because writing is manual labor? The fact is not so in a large majority of cases. By far the most numerous written agreements are promissory notes. To write such a note requires some manual exertion, but not labor, in the proper or common signification of the word."

A few helpful generalizations may nevertheless be made concerning the law applicable to Sunday contracts. (1) Practically all the Sunday statutes expressly except from their prohibition "works of necessity or charity." Of course, the courts have not always agreed, in specific cases, upon the interpretation of these terms, but there is rather general agreement that whatever is requisite in order to preserve or protect the life or health of a person or to preserve property from immediate danger of destruction may properly be considered "necessary," and there has been little difficulty experienced in determining what constitutes "charity." (2) The prohibition of the statutes usually applies both to contracts made on Sunday and to contracts which, under their terms, require prohibited work on Sunday, even though they are made on a secular day. (3) It is generally held that although an agreement made on Sunday may be void as between the parties to the agreement, an innocent purchaser or assignee, without notice, is protected. For example, A gives B a promissory note on Sunday, and the giving of the note is void under the Sunday statutes, yet if B negotiates the note to C, who is an innocent purchaser for value and without notice, A could not set up against C the defense that the note was void because it was made on Sunday. (4) Both engagements to marry and marriages are valid if made on Sunday. (5) While a Sunday contract which is illegal under the statutes may not be ratified on a subsequent secular day, in a majority of the states such contract may be "adopted" on such a day, in which case it would be valid. Most courts take the position that if a Sunday contract is made void by statute, then there is nothing to be ratified; but the effect of "adopting" the contract is actually to make a new contract. (6) An agreement which is finally reached in full on a secular day is not void merely because some of its terms were agreed upon on Sunday. (7) If a transaction is entered into on Sunday in violation of the statute and if both parties completely perform the agreement, most courts hold that the parties are bound.

Whether negotiable instruments, deeds, mortgages, insurance policies, and so on are valid and enforceable if made on Sunday depends upon the exact wording of the statute, the courts' interpretation of the statute, and the facts involved in the given case. If the statute expressly prohibits the making of all agreements on Sunday, there is little doubt that all such instruments would be void. But if the statute merely prohibits "work and labor" on Sunday, many courts have held that the execution of such instruments is valid. It would appear that if a given statute specifically permits a certain type of business to be conducted on Sunday, e.g. a restaurant or a drug store, then a check given by a purchaser in payment for food or other merchandise sold to him would be valid. On the other hand, a check given in the performance of a Sunday contract that is made void by statute would be illegal.

It is not uncommon for a state statute to prohibit work and labor on Sunday and then to specify certain exceptions. For example, the statutes of one state specify in one section: "No person whatsoever shall work or do any bodily labor on the Lord's Day, commonly called Sunday . . . ," and in another section provide: "No person in this State shall sell, dispose of, barter or deal in, or give away articles of merchandise on Sunday, except retailers, who may sell and deliver on said day tobacco, cigars, cigarettes, candy, sodas and soft drinks, ice, ice cream, ices and other confectionery, milk, bread, fruits, gasoline, oils and greases. . . ."

Greene v. Birkmeyer
8 N. Y. 217, 73 A. (2d) 728 (1950)

This was an action by John F. Greene (plaintiff) against Paul J. Birkmeyer (defendant). Judgment for plaintiff, and defendant appealed. Reversed.

On Sunday, December 5, 1948, plaintiff agreed to buy land provided he were able to borrow on it a certain sum. At the same time he deposited $500 with the vendor on account of the purchase. Plaintiff sued for the return of the $500, alleging that he was unable to obtain the mortgage, also that he refused to fulfill the contract because it was made upon the Sabbath. The District Court was of the opinion that, since the contract was made on Sunday, plaintiff had a right to disaffirm and recover his deposit. Judgment followed accordingly, and defendant appealed.

The state statute, R. S. 2:207–1, N. J. S. A., provided in part: "No traveling, worldly employment or business, ordinary or servile labor or work either upon land or water, except *works of necessity or charity* . . . shall be done, performed, used or practiced by any person within this State on the Christian Sabbath, or first day of the week, commonly called and hereinafter designated as Sunday."

BIGELOW, J. It is, of course, apparent that the bargain for the real estate and the deposit of $500 thereon were business dealings forbidden by the statutes. That a contract made on Sunday will not be enforced or a transaction on that day will not be given effect, is abundantly established. An action cannot be maintained for the amount due on a promissory note made on Sunday. *Reeves v. Butcher*, 31 N. J. L. 224. Or for an accounting of commissions upon a contract made on Sunday. *Gennert v. Wuestner*, 53 N.J. Eq. 513, 48 A. 818. A notice to a tenant, given on Sunday, that after the expiration of his term, the rent will be increased to a certain amount, is without effect and the tenant, remaining in possession, is liable only at the old rate. *Canno v. Ryan*, 49 N. J. L. 314, 8 A. 293. One who, on Sunday, repairs a boiler pursuant to a contract, even though made on a week day, cannot recover. *Telfer v. Lambert*, 79 N. J. L. 299, 75 A. 779 (1910). A release under seal, executed and delivered on a Sunday is not a good defense. *Hamilton v. Standard Metal Co.*, 81 N. J. L. 247, 79 A. 1031 (1911). One who, on a Sunday, sells his Irish setter and is paid part of the price, cannot maintain replevin for his dog.

On the other hand, a loan made on Sunday is not an illegal consideration, in the sense that it will not support an express promise to pay made on a subsequent day. *Brewster v. Banta*, 66 N. J. L. 367, 49 A. 718. Likewise, one who buys vegetables on Sunday and, on a secular day, gives his check in payment, is liable on his check. *Rosenblum v. Schachner*, 84 N. J. L. 525, 87 A. 99. A bailor can hold a bailee answerable for failure to return her jewelry, although the bailment was made on Sunday.

It is the rule in many states that where money has been paid on a contract which is illegal, the party making the payment may repudiate the contract, provided it still remains executory, and may recover the money, even though the parties are in pari delicto. *Greenberg v. Evening Post Association*, 91 Conn. 371, 99 A. 1037; *Harrington v. Bochenski*, 140 Md. 24, 116 A. 836 (1922). See *C. J. S., Contracts*, Sec. 275, and *Restatement, Contracts*, Sec. 605.

With respect to illegal contracts in general, we take it that the law in New Jersey will not aid one guilty party to recapture a payment that he has made to the other. "The law leaves the parties to an illegal transaction where it finds them; it will not actively help either, and therefore such a law cannot be invoked to imply a promise in favor of a particeps criminis to pay money due on a contract which such law itself denounces as invalid." *Reeves v. Butcher*, supra.

The plaintiff in the action before us was himself guilty of violating the express command of the statute. The law will not help him out of the situation in which his own illegal conduct has placed him, and so the judgment must be reversed.

CONTRACTS IN RESTRAINT OF TRADE

At one time any agreement in restraint of trade was absolutely void under the common law. When this rule of law was established by the English courts, economic life was dominated by the philosophy of laissez faire, which held that governmental control over the economy should be held to the minimum, that prices should be established upon the basis of free competition, and that natural and juristic persons should not be permitted to enter into contracts relative to business and employment that would have as their effect the restraint of trade and commerce. Owing to the vast economic changes that have taken place over the past hundred years or so, this rule of law has been modified until today the prevailing rule is that such agreements are valid and enforceable so long as they do not *unreasonably* restrain trade and commerce. What is "unreasonable" restraint is determined by the courts, in each case, upon the facts involved.

Broadly speaking, contracts in restraint of trade fall under two general classifications: (1) contracts wherein one of the parties to the contract agrees not to compete with the other party in the future; and (2) contracts wherein the parties enter into an agreement to stifle competition, control prices, and monopolize trade and commerce.

AGREEMENTS NOT TO COMPETE

One type of agreement not to compete is frequently found in contracts to sell business enterprises. In such contracts the seller often covenants not to compete with the purchaser, either directly or indirectly, in the future. Or a partner who sells his interest in the partnership business to the remaining partner or partners may covenant not to compete with the partnership in the future. The general rule applicable to such restrictive covenants is that if the restraint placed upon the seller is not greater than is necessary to protect the buyer in his investment, the agreement is valid and enforceable. This rule works to the benefit of the seller as well as of the buyer. If A could not make a valid contract to sell his business to B and covenant not to compete with B, B would not be willing to pay much for the good will of A's business.

A covenant in which A, selling his grocery store in X, agrees never again to engage in the grocery business, would clearly be unenforceable. Such a broad restriction, unlimited both as to time and as to place (territory), is obviously unnecessary to protect the buyer in his purchase of the good will of A's business. If A covenants not to operate a similar business in X for the next three years, and if X is a village, the agreement would probably be deemed valid and enforceable, since it is reasonably limited both as to time and as to place. A could operate a grocery business at any place other than X, and after three years he could even operate such a business in X. But if X is a city and A is operating a small neighborhood business, the very same terms would, no doubt, be held to be unreasonable, since A could perfectly well operate another such store in a different part of the city without jeopardizing B's business.

A second type of restrictive covenant is sometimes placed in employment contracts. For example, A has developed certain methods and techniques which are highly valuable in his business and which he carefully guards against falling into the hands of his competitors. He employs B with the intention of training him in these methods and techniques. In his employment contract B promises that if he leaves A's employ he will not set up a competitive business nor take employment with A's competitors. Reasonable restrictions of this type are considered beneficial not only to the employer but to the employee and to the economic and social system in general. If A could not enforce such a covenant, he might feel that he should not run the risk of disclosing his trade secrets even to an employee, in which case he might decide not to take an employee into his business; yet without adequate personnel in his establishment the growth of his business would be severely retarded. Hence the law permits reasonable restrictive covenants in employment contracts. Such covenants are governed by approximately the same rules of law that apply to contracts for the sale of a business, though the courts are perhaps a little less lenient in approving restrictive covenants in employment contracts. In any event, the restraint must not be greater than is necessary to protect the employer in the conduct of his business.

MONOPOLIES

Under the common law of England a contract that has for its objective the establishment of a monopoly is simply unenforceable. In the United States, such an agreement, both at common law and under the anti-trust laws, not only is unenforceable but also renders the parties to the agreement liable to indictment for the commission of a crime, if they have the ability and the intention to monopolize the market and if the restraint upon commerce and business is unreasonable.

Anti-trust legislation has been passed both by Congress and by the states. The basic federal statute is the Sherman Anti-Trust Act of 1890. Section I of this Act made illegal "every contract, combination in the form of trust or otherwise, or conspiracy in restraint of trade or commerce among the several states, or with foreign nations." The Act also declared that "every person who shall monopolize, or attempt to monopolize, or combine or conspire with any other person or persons to monopolize, any part of the trade or commerce among the several states, or with foreign nations, shall be deemed guilty of a misdemeanor." The Clayton Act of 1914 strengthened the Sherman Act by specifically invalidating certain monopolistic practices. It prohibited discrimination in price between different purchasers of commodities, exclusive dealing agreements, and tying contracts where the effect was substantially to lessen competition or to tend to create a monopoly in any line of commerce. The Robinson-Patman Act of 1936, the Miller-Tydings Act of 1937, and other statutes have made further amendments. Most of the states have anti-trust laws which follow in general the pattern of the federal law.

Most of the states have enacted resale price maintenance laws, or the so-called Fair Trade Laws. In general, these laws provide that price-maintenance contracts are legal.

Tawney et al. v. Mutual System of Maryland, Inc.
47 A. (2d) 372 (Md.) (1946)

This was an action by the Mutual System of Maryland, Inc., and another (plaintiffs) against Charles W. Tawney, Marian V. Brewer, the Tawney Loan Service, Inc., and others (defendants) for an injunction and an accounting. Decree for plaintiff, and defendants appealed. Decree affirmed in part, reversed in part, and case remanded.

Plaintiff's bill alleged that the respondents, Tawney and Brewer, entered into employment contracts with the complainants, whereby the employees agreed: (J) to keep secret the names of or any information relative to any past, present or prospective borrowers from and customers of their employers; (K) to refrain from using any information relative to such borrowers and customers and not to persuade any such borrowers or customers to do anything that might be to the disadvantage of their employers; (L) to so keep secret and to so refrain for a period of three years from the date of termination of the employment; and (M) to refrain from engaging directly or indirectly in any business competitive with that of their employers in the Baltimore City trading area for a period of two years from the date of termination of the employment. The bill alleged that Tawney, who was employed as manager of Mutual, and Brewer, who was employed as cashier, resigned in June, 1945, and immediately engaged in a competing business under the style and name of the Tawney Loan Service, Inc., and that they systematically solicited borrowers and customers of Mutual, making use of the confidential information gained from their previous employment.

There was little dispute as to the facts. Prior to his employment by Mutual, Tawney had been engaged in the small loan business in Baltimore, first with Household Finance Co., for about six years, and later with Lincoln Loan Service, Inc., as manager, for about three years. He had graduated from the School of Business Administration, University of Maryland, in 1931. The respondent, Brewer, was cashier of Lincoln Loan Service, Inc., and came with Mutual in a similar capacity shortly after the new branch was opened. In June, 1945, the respondents executed a certificate of incorporation. The Tawney Loan Service, Inc., leased an office only two blocks from Mutual's office, and commenced business. From June 19, 1945 through July 10, 1945, when a temporary restraining order became effective, 101 open accounts of Mutual customers, totaling $18,994.99, were paid off by The Tawney Loan Service, Inc. Of these, 38, totaling $6,963.47 had been originally acquired by Mutual through purchase of other small loan companies.

The appellants (defendants) contended (1) that the restrictive covenants contained in the employment contracts were against public policy and invalid, and (2) that if the covenants were valid in part, the appellees were entitled only to such relief as is necessary for the protection of their business.

HENDERSON, J. The *Restatement, Contracts,* Sec. 514, declares that "a bargain in restraint of trade is illegal if the restraint is unreasonable." Sec. 515 declares that "a restraint of trade is unreasonable . . . if it (a) is greater than is required for the protection of the person for whose benefit the restraint is imposed, or (b) imposes undue hardships upon the person restricted, or . . . (e) is based on a promise to refrain from competition and is not ancillary . . . to an existing employment or contract of employment." Conversely, Sec. 516 (f) declares that a bargain not to compete "within such territory and during such time as may be reasonably necessary for the protection of the employer or principal, without imposing undue hardship on the employee or agent," is reasonable.

The elements to be considered are thus stated in *May v. Young,* 125 Conn. 1, 2 A. (2d) 385: "Of the principal considerations affecting the validity of restrictive covenants on grounds of public policy, one is injury to the public by being deprived of the restricted party's industry or services; the other the injury to the party himself by being precluded from pursuing his occupation and thus being prevented from supporting himself and family. But if neither of these evils ensue and if the contract is founded on a valid consideration and a reasonable ground of belief to the other party, it is free from objection, and may be enforced."

In the case at bar it is sought to enforce a restriction beyond the time when new employees might reasonably become acquainted with existing customers, and apply it to the whole trading area of Baltimore and environs, wherein there are several hundred thousand people with whom the employer has no contact whatever, and to a business where the occasional financial need of the customer, rather than the recurrent calls of the supplier, is the prime incentive. We think this goes beyond what is necessary to protect the good will of the employer, and works an undue hardship upon the employees, who would be excluded from engaging in the business for which they are specially fitted by long training and experience. Moreover, the effect of enforcing the clause (M) would be to stifle competition in a field where the existence of competition is clearly in the public interest.

We think, however, that the covenants contained in clauses (J), (K) and (L) of the contract, are severable and enforceable in terms. The relief should not exceed what is there called for, because such covenants must be strictly construed. We shall therefore remand the case in order that the decree may be modified so as to enforce the covenants contained in clauses (J), (K) and (L) of the contracts, but not clause (M). We sustain that portion of the decree that directs an accounting.

REVIEW CASES

1. Gardner sold commercial fertilizer to Reed, who breached the contract. In the ensuing suit Reed denied liability on the ground that Gardner had failed to comply with the requirements of the Mississippi Code as a seller of commercial fertilizer, and particularly the requirement for registration as a dealer therein, the purchase of stamps, the payment of inspection fees, and the giving of notice to the Commissioner of Agriculture of the shipments. Holding? (Gardner v. Reed, 207 Miss. 306, 42 So.(2d) 206)

2. Layfield became insolvent, and his lumber mill and residence were decreed to be sold. He and his wife entered into an agreement with Fallon et al., some of his creditors, that if Fallon et al. refrained from bidding at the sale and thus permitted the Layfields to buy the property at a low price, the Layfields would execute a deed of trust along with notes in favor of Fallon et al. to secure their claims. After the sale at a very low price to the Layfields, they refused to execute the deed of trust and notes, and Fallon et al. sued. Ruling? (Fallon et al. v. Layfield et al., 94 W. Va. 175, 119 S. E. 172)

3. Bell gave Rush a note bearing 8 per cent interest, but they agreed that Bell would pay Rush 2 per cent per month on the note. The legal rate in Indiana was 8 per cent per annum. Bell sued Rush to recoup money paid in excess of the legal rate. Ruling? (Bell v. Rush, 98 Ind. App. 303, 189 N. E. 181)

4. Fitch, while married, agreed to marry Coates, who knew that Fitch was a married man. After Fitch's wife died he refused to marry Coates, and she sued him for breach of promise. Judgment for whom? (Fitch v. Coates, 167 S. W. (2d) 478)

5. Malone drove into a parking lot, paid the fee, turned his car over to an attendant, and received a ticket, which he put into his pocket without reading it. The ticket stated that the management assumed no responsibiliy of any kind for cars parked in the lot. The employee, after parking the car, left the keys in it. Later a thief, posing as Malone's brother, persuaded the attendant to let him have the car. It was customary to present the identification stub before receiving the car. The thief had no stub and no authority to take the car. Malone sued for the value of his automobile. Ruling? (Malone v. Santora, 135 Conn. 286, 64 A. (2d) 51)

6. Oscanyan, Consul-General of Turkey and residing in this country, made a contract with the Arms Co. whereby he was to receive a certain commission on arms sold to his government by the company. His job was to influence an agent sent from Turkey to examine the arms. As a result of Oscanyan's influence, sales of arms were made to Turkey, and he brought an action to recover his commission. Holding? (Oscanyan v. Arms Co., 103 U. S. 261, 26 L. Ed. 539)

Contracts Required to Be in Writing

12

HISTORY AND PROVISIONS OF THE STATUTE OF FRAUDS

We have seen in the foregoing chapters that a contract results when the four essential requirements of a contract have been met. However, certain types of contracts, despite the fact that they satisfy the four requirements, are not enforceable in the courts unless they are in writing.

Experience with parol (oral) contracts taught the English people that such contracts frequently opened the door to fraud and perjured testimony. It was easy for A to sue B for the breach of an alleged oral contract and prove the agreement by his own and his friends' perjured testimony. To provide at least a partial remedy for this situation (and for others that frequently gave rise to fraud) the English Parliament enacted in 1677 what became known as the Statute of Frauds (29 Charles II, Chap. 3). Sections 4 and 17 of the statute dealt with contracts and set forth certain types of contracts which were required to be in writing to be enforced. It should be clearly understood that the Statute of Frauds did not make written form a "fifth essential" for the creation of a valid contract in these cases; rather, it made written evidence of the existence of the contract a condition precedent to the right to sue on it. In other words, if the agreement had fulfilled the four essential conditions but was not in writing, it was a contract but unenforceable. As it has been expressed, the statute did not go to the existence of a contract but merely affected the matter of procedure or proof.[1]

The statute referred only to executory contracts and not to executed contracts.[2] If A and B entered into an oral agreement which was required

[1] *McLellan v. McLellan*, 65 Me. 500.
[2] *Bucknam v. Nash*, 12 Me. 474; *Webster v. La Compte*, 74 Md. 249, 22 A. 232.

under the Statute of Frauds to be in writing and if both fully performed the agreement, both parties were bound. This was logical in view of the fact that the effect of the statute was not to make certain oral agreements void, but merely to make them unenforceable. Further, the statute was a matter of defense: that is, if the defendant wished to take advantage of it he had to set it up as a defense; otherwise, the court would enforce the agreement.[1]

The English Statute of Frauds has generally been accepted, with slight variations, by the various states of this country, either by constitutional provision or by statutory enactment, so that at present it is basically the law in our country.

Sec. 4 of the statute provides:

> No action shall be brought,
>   (1) whereby to charge any executor or administrator upon any special promise to answer for damages out of his own estate;
>   (2) or whereby to charge the defendant upon any special promise to answer for the debt, default, or miscarriage of another person;
>   (3) or to charge any person upon any agreement made in consideration of marriage;
>   (4) or upon any contract or sale of land, tenements, or hereditaments, or any interest in or concerning them;
>   (5) or upon any agreement that is not to be performed within the space of one year from the making thereof;
> UNLESS the agreement upon which such action shall be brought, or some memorandum or note thereof, shall be in writing and signed by the party to be charged therewith, or some other person thereunto by him lawfully authorized.

Sec. 17 reads as follows:

> Be it further enacted that no contract for the sale of any goods, wares, or merchandise for the price of ten pounds sterling, or upwards, shall be allowed to be good, except (a) the buyer shall accept part of the goods so sold, and actually receive the same; (b) or give something in earnest to bind the bargain, or in part payment; (c) or that some note or memorandum in writing of the said bargain be made and signed by the parties to be charged by such contract, or their agents thereunto lawfully auauthorized.

A contract may fall within more than one section or subsection of the statute or it may appear to be excluded by one section but be included by another. For example, a contract to sell personal property for less than the prescribed statutory amount would not be required to be in writing

[1] *Middlesex Co. v. Osgood*, 4 Gray 447; *Lawrence v. Chase*, 54 Mass. 196, *Adams v. Patrick*, 30 Vt. 516.

under Sec. 17; but if under its terms it could not be performed within one year, it would be unenforceable under Sec. 4 (5) unless it was in writing.

UNIFORM COMMERCIAL CODE

The Code in Sec. 2–201 has made a substantial change in the formal requirements relating to the Statute of Frauds for contracts to sell goods. The Code in Sec. 8–319 states the requirements for a binding contract for the sale of securities, and Sec. 9–203 states the essentials for an enforceable security agreement. Sec. 1–206 provides a Statute of Frauds for kinds of personal property not otherwise covered by the Code.

SEC. 4 (1). PROMISE BY EXECUTOR OR ADMINISTRATOR

The legal effect of Sec. 4 (1) is that an executor or administrator of an estate is not bound by a promise to pay personally a claim against the estate unless his promise to pay is in writing and signed by him. In addition to the requirement of a writing, the promisee (creditor) would also have to prove that he gave the promisor (executor or administrator) consideration. To illustrate, B is the executor of A's estate. During A's lifetime C had extended credit to him in the amount of $500, and after A's death C presents his claim to B as executor. B promises that if there are insufficient funds in A's estate to pay the debt, he himself will pay the $500 out of his own property. If C gives consideration for B's promise, the court will enforce the promise if it is in writing, but will refuse to enforce it if it is not in writing. Under such circumstances A's promise to C at the time when the debt was contracted is called an original or primary promise, and B's promise to C is called a collateral or secondary promise.

Romano v. Brown
125 N. J. L. 293, 15 A. (2d) 818 (1940)

This was an action by Anthony R. Romano (plaintiff) against Adele M. Brown (defendant). Judgment for plaintiff, and defendant appealed. Affirmed.

Andrew L. Brown during his lifetime operated a funeral parlor as a single proprietor. Plaintiff from time to time sold Brown merchandise, and at the time of the death of Brown, on December 22, 1931, he owed plaintiff the sum of $724.80. His wife, Adele M. Brown, the defendant in this action, was appointed administratrix of her husband's estate. She continued to operate the business as A. Brown Estate.

Plaintiff alleged in his petition that upon the death of Andrew L. Brown he and defendant entered into a contract whereby she agreed to become per-

sonally liable for the obligation of Andrew L. Brown to plaintiff in consideration that he would extend credit to her in her operation of the business. He
testified at the trial that between December 22, 1931, and February 11, 1935, he
extended credit to her to the extent of $2,850.25 and that she had paid on this
account $2,127.35, leaving a balance due of $722.90. Plaintiff asked judgment
for the amount of $724.80, which was owed to him by Andrew L. Brown at
the time of his death, and which plaintiff claimed that defendant had personally obligated herself to pay, and for $722.90, which represented the bal-
ance owed by defendant for the credit which had been extended to her during
her operation of the business.

Defendant contended that she had not personally agreed to become liable
for the payment of her husband's debt; that the promise made was as administratrix of her husband's estate; and that since the promise was oral it was
not enforceable under Sec. 4 (1) of the Statute of Frauds.

CAMPBELL, J. The contention of the defendant is that the contract of assumption was in violation of the Statute of Frauds because it was an oral
promise to pay the debt of another. It is well settled that where the oral promise upon which suit is brought is an original one, and not merely a collateral
undertaking, it need not be in writing. The determinative test is to whom was
the credit, in fact, given. If there was proof in support of the plaintiff's contention that the credit was, in fact, given to the defendant, Adele M. Brown
personally, then the jury might find that the promise was an original one.
Under the facts proven in this case the question whether the agreement was
original or collateral was factual and required submission to the jury. And
where the promise to pay the debt of another is founded upon a new consideration and this consideration passed between the parties to the promise,
and gives the promisor a benefit which he did not enjoy before, and would
not have possessed but for the promise, it will be regarded as an original promise and enforceable though not in writing. *Federal Wire Co. v. Jabberwock
Country Club*, 120 N. J. 334, 199 A. 594. The evidence sustains the finding of
the jury that the plaintiff extended the credit to the defendant, upon her individual promise, and was not extended to the estate of Andrew L. Brown,
upon the oral promise of the defendant, as administratrix of the estate. Judgment for plaintiff affirmed.

SEC. 4 (2). PROMISE TO ANSWER FOR DEBT OF ANOTHER

Sec. 4 (2) is applicable to "any special promise to answer for the debt,
default, or miscarriage of another person." Contracts falling under this
subsection are made up of two parts: (1) a primary or original promise or
obligation; (2) a secondary or collateral promise or obligation. The primary or original promise or obligation is unconditional and need not be
in writing under Sec. 4 (2). The secondary or collateral promise or obli-

gation is conditional and must be in writing under Sec. 4 (2). A contract arising out of such a secondary or collateral promise is called a *guaranty contract*. There are three parties involved in such a contract: the creditor, the principal debtor, and the guarantor of the debt. If A and B go into C's grocery store and A buys on credit certain groceries, promising to pay C on the first of the following month, A's promise is a primary or original promise and is not covered by Sec. 4 (2). Now let us suppose that when A gives his order, C refuses to let him have the groceries because he thinks that A is not a good credit risk. If B says, "Let him have the groceries and I will pay for them on the first of next month," B's promise to C is another example of a primary or original promise, since C extends credit to him and not to A. But suppose that B says, "Let him have the groceries and if he does not pay for them on the first of next month, I will." There are now two parts to the transaction: the primary promise of A (principal debtor) to C (creditor), and the secondary or collateral promise of B (guarantor) to C. B's promise to C is a guaranty contract and must be in writing to be enforceable.

A guaranty contract must not be confused with another type of contract involving three parties, namely a *novation contract*. In a guaranty contract the principal debtor remains primarily liable after the promise of the guarantor is made. If the debtor does not continue to be liable on his promise after the third party makes his promise, but instead the third party is *substituted* for him and he is discharged from his liability, a novation takes place. Novation contracts do not fall under Sec. 4 (2). They are held to be primary promises. To illustrate, A owes C $100 for groceries purchased during the month. B owes the same amount to A. B promises to pay C $100 in consideration of A's releasing him from his debt to A. If C agrees to the arrangement, a novation results, by which B is substituted for A in the contract with C, and consequently A is released from all liability. To be valid, a novation agreement must have the assent of all the parties.

Indemnity contracts do not fall under Sec. 4 (2). An indemnity contract is an agreement whereby the promisor promises to indemnify the promisee against loss or liability which he may incur as the result of some given act, event, or transaction. For example, A buys from B, an insurance company, an indemnity contract on his automobile under which B contracts, among other things, to make good any loss A may suffer as the result of injuring some third party by negligent operation of the automobile. Although B's obligation is contingent upon injury to a third party, its promise to A is clearly a primary promise and need not be in writing under Sec. 4 (2), though as a practical matter such contracts are usually put in writing.

To fall under Sec. 4 (2) the guarantor's promise must obligate his own estate. If B places certain money in A's hands, to be paid to C when C completes a certain job for B, and A promises C that he will pay him when the job is completed, A's promise is a primary promise and need not be in writing under Sec. 4 (2). If A in the meantime uses the money for other purposes, he would still be liable to C on his promise.

If A, in promising B that he will discharge C's debt if C does not pay, has in view primarily his own benefit and only incidentally the discharge of the debt, his promise would be held to be a primary promise and not to come under Sec. 4 (2). For example, if A (mortgagee) holds a mortgage on B's (mortgagor) house, and C contracts to buy the house from B and orally agrees to pay the mortgage, if B does not pay it, C would be bound by his promise, even though it was not put in writing. It is held that the promise of the promisor (C) created an original or independent debt which does not require a writing. In such a case A could recover from C on a third-party beneficiary theory. A would be a creditor beneficiary.[1]

Dunn v. Rostock et al.
59 N. E. (2d) 48, 74 Ohio App. 311 (1944)

This was an action by one Dunn (plaintiff) against Otto Rostock and wife (defendants), on a contract for labor upon a residence. Judgment for plaintiff, and defendants appealed. Reversed and remanded.

Defendant Grace Rostock owned a lot in the city of Cincinnati. She entered into a contract with one Jones to erect a residence thereon. Jones engaged the plaintiff to do, or furnish carpenters to do, some or all of the carpenter work at $1.25 per hour. While the work was in progress and at a time when $159 was due and unpaid, plaintiff reached the conclusion that Jones could not build the house for the contract price and became apprehensive about being paid for the carpenter work. He went to the house and told his employees to quit work, but before they had left the premises defendant Otto Rostock, the husband of Grace Rostock, appeared and, according to plaintiff, asked plaintiff to stay on the job. Plaintiff testified that Rostock told him: "You leave your men on, go ahead and finish. I will guarantee that you will get every cent that is coming to you." Rostock denied making this statement, but did testify that he said: "I wouldn't pull the men off. I will promise you that I will pay from this time on."

One of the defenses was that the promise sued on was to answer for the debt, default and miscarriage of another, which, to be enforceable, was required to be in writing under Section 8621, General Code (Sec. 4 (2), Statute of Frauds), and that, as there was a failure to prove any such written promise, there was a failure of proof of the kind required by the statute.

The trial court concluded that the Statute of Frauds was inapplicable and

[1] See section entitled Third-Party Beneficiaries in Chapter 13 of this text.

instructed the jury that: "A contract of this kind, if you find there was a valid contract, according to the testimony of the plaintiff, such as he has testified to, need not be in writing, and it is for you to say what if any contract was made between the plaintiff and defendants." The jury returned a verdict against Otto Rostock and he appealed. The issue raised by the appeal was whether any reasonable construction of the testimony would bring the promise within the statute as a collateral promise to answer for the default of another.

MATTHEWS, J. Now, it is clear that a contract was made between the plaintiff and Otto Rostock. Was it an absolute independent promise by Otto Rostock, or was it a collateral special promise to answer for the default of Jones? Only in the event that the uncontradicted evidence proved an independent promise was the court justified in charging that it need not be in writing. If there was evidence, even though controverted, that it was a promise collateral to that of Jones, it became an issue of fact to be decided by the jury.

The test in every case of this kind is whether the parties intended to make an absolute and independent contract or a conditional or collateral one. Ordinarily, the parties have not so stated in express terms, and the trier of the facts is driven to the drawing of inferences from facts and circumstances to determine intent.

The conflicting evidence as to the exact words and the facts and circumstances hereinbefore set forth, furnished ample basis for reasonable difference as to the intent of the parties. There was present, therefore, an issue of fact for decision by the trier of the facts, which in this case was the jury. The function of the court was to formulate this issue and submit it to the jury for decision, under proper instructions. For these reasons the judgment is reversed and the cause remanded for further proceedings according to law.

SEC. 4 (3). AGREEMENTS IN CONSIDERATION OF MARRIAGE

Sec. 4 (3) is applicable to "any agreement made in consideration of marriage." This subsection does not apply to mutual promises to marry (engagements). If A and B become engaged their mutual promises to marry need not, so far as Sec. 4 (3) is concerned, be in writing to be enforceable. It should be noted, however, that if they agree to marry each other on a date later than one year in the future, their agreement comes under Sec. 4 (5), which is discussed below. Incidentally, a number of the states have enacted statutes which outlaw breach of promise or "love-balm" suits.

Sec. 4 (3) applies to promises to make a settlement of property or to pay money in consideration of marriage. Such agreements are generally called ante-nuptial contracts. For example, A promises to marry B, and, in consideration of A's promise, B orally promises to marry A and to settle $10,000 upon A. B's promise to settle the money falls under Sec. 4 (3); since it was oral it is not enforceable, nor will it become so if A and B actually marry. To be enforceable it must be put in writing.

Brock v. Button
187 Wash. 27, 59 P. (2d) 761 (1936)

This was an action by Margaret J. Brock (plaintiff) against C. A. Button (defendant) for damages for the breach of an alleged contract to marry. Judgment for defendant, and plaintiff appealed. Affirmed.

The parties were well acquainted with each other and each was the parent of one or more children by a former marriage. Each had procured a divorce. Defendant gave plaintiff many presents, and they were together frequently and often talked of marriage. Plaintiff testified that "around the first of May, 1931" they entered into an agreement to marry. At that time defendant had several unmarried daughters and a son living with him. The son was about fourteen years of age. In plaintiff's cross-examination she testified that when she and defendant agreed to be married it was understood by the parties that the marriage would take place when defendant's son finished high school. She further testified that the son would not get out of high school "for at least three years."

There was no writing or memorandum of the agreement. In September, 1934, more than three years after the engagement, the son finished high school. A few months thereafter plaintiff asked defendant when they would get married, and he then told her that he would not marry her; thereupon this action was commenced.

MITCHELL, J. The agreement falls within the inhibition of Rem. Rev. Stat., Sec. 5825, subd. 1, as follows: "In the following cases specified in this section, any agreement, contract or promise shall be void, unless such agreement, contract, or promise, or some note or memorandum thereof, be in writing and signed by the party to be charged therewith, or by some person thereunto by him lawfully authorized, that is to say: (1) every agreement that by its terms is not to be performed in one year from the making thereof." No specified date was fixed in the marriage agreement, and it clearly appears from the plaintiff's testimony and from the surrounding circumstances discussed and understood by the parties that, by the terms of the agreement, they did not agree or intend that their marriage should take place within one year from the making of the agreement. The agreement provided that the marriage should take place when the boy went to college, which would be at least three years after the making of the agreement.

The plaintiff further contends that the oral, mutual promises to marry are valid under the third subsection of sec. 5825, which requires "every agreement, promise or undertaking made upon consideration of marriage, except mutual promises to marry," to be in writing to be valid. We do not so understand that language. It is plain that this provision covers those kinds of agreements and promises made in consideration of marriage other than mutual promises of marriage. That is, in enumerating agreements and promises made in consideration of marriage, which are required to be in writing to be enforceable, the words "except mutual promises to marry" do not mean that the latter kind of agreements are valid and enforceable if not in writing.

The Supreme Court of Nebraska, in the case of *Barge v. Haslam*, 63 Neb. 296, 88 N. W. 516, said:. "The weight of authority seems to be in favor of the proposition that mutual promises to marry are within the inhibition of the provision of the Statute of Frauds avoiding contracts which by their terms are not to be performed within a year."

"The contracts most usually held to fall within the provision requiring contracts in consideration of marriage to be in writing are antenuptial agreements between the intended spouses for a settlement on the wife. It included, however, prior to the married women's property acts, agreements that the wife shall enjoy her property as her separate estate free from any claim on the part of the husband by reason of his common law marital rights, such agreements being in the nature of agreements by the husband to settle property upon the wife. This is also true as regards an agreement by an intended spouse in consideration of the marriage to renounce the interest in the estate of the other spouse to which he or she would be entitled as the survivor. As a general rule, mutual promises of marriage are not regarded as within the provision. Some of the statutes expressly excluded from their operation mutual promises of marriage." 25 *R. C. L.*, Statute of Frauds, sec. 272. This is precisely what has been done in this state. They are excepted, that is, excluded, from this clause of the statute (subsection 1).

Affirmed.

SEC. 4 (4). CONTRACTS FOR SALE OF LAND OR INTEREST IN LAND

Sec. 4 (4) provides that "No action shall be brought . . . (4) upon any contract or sale of lands, tenements, or hereditaments, or any interest in or concerning them, . . . unless the agreement upon which such action shall be brought, or some memorandum or note thereof, shall be in writing, and signed by the party to be charged therewith, or some other person thereunto by him lawfully authorized." This subsection applies to contracts that have to do with the sale of real estate, or an interest therein, as distinguished from personal property.

It is not always easy to draw a precise line between real and personal property, and hence between contracts that fall under Sec. 4 (4) and those that do not. What is regarded as realty in one situation may be regarded as personalty in another. For example, "land" within the meaning of this section ordinarily includes not only the surface of the earth but everything that is firmly attached to it, such as a building; hence a contract for the sale of a dwelling house or an apartment house or a factory must ordinarily be in writing to be enforceable. But suppose that A owns a house and lot, and that he comes to an agreement with B to sell him the house on condition that within thirty days B is to move it from the lot, to which A is to retain title. The courts have generally held that the sale of the house apart from the lot is a sale of personal property and hence need not be in writing under Sec. 4 (4).

UNIFORM COMMERCIAL CODE

Under Sec. 2–107 of the Code, a contract for the sale of timber, minerals or the like or a structure or its materials to be removed from realty is a contract for the sale of goods if they are to be severed by the seller. For example, if A sells B standing trees to be severed by A, it would be a contract for the sale of goods. On the other hand, if A sells standing timber to B to be severed and removed by B, it would be a contract for the sale of realty and would come under Sec. 4 (4) of the Statute of Frauds. A contract for the sale apart from the land of growing crops or other things attached to realty and capable of severance without material harm thereto is a contract for the sale of goods whether the subject matter is to be severed by the buyer or by the seller even though it forms part of the realty at the time of contracting.

The distinction between real and personal property will be treated at greater length in Part IV, below. Detailed discussion of the various types of interest in land is also reserved for that section. Here it may be said in general that contracts coming under Sec. 4 (4) must involve a substantial interest in the land, not merely arrangements that are preliminary to the acquisition of such an interest. For example, most courts would hold that a contract to lend money to buy real estate or to pay for searching the title to real estate would not fall under Sec. 4 (4); nor would a contract for the building of a house. Long-term leases, mortgages, and easements are held to be interests in land, but a lease for a year or less is usually held not to be an interest in land.

We have already seen that the Statute of Frauds does not govern executed contracts. In the case of partly executed oral contracts for the sale of land, courts of law will grant only relief in quasi-contract to the purchaser, but under certain circumstances courts of equity will grant specific performance of the contract to the purchaser. Thus, if the purchaser or grantee under an oral agreement takes possession of the property and makes improvements on it, the equity court will often grant specific performance. For example, A and B enter into an oral contract whereby A agrees to sell, and B to buy, a certain city lot. Under the agreement B is to make a down payment and to pay the balance in twenty-four equal installments, after which A is to deliver to B a properly executed warranty deed to the lot. B makes the required down payment, takes possession, and proceeds to erect a house on the lot. B makes his monthly payments, as agreed. When he makes his final payment A refuses to deliver to him the promised warranty deed and threatens to file an ejectment suit against B. B thereupon files a bill in equity asking for specific performance of the oral contract and asks the court to decree that A execute and deliver the promised warranty deed. If the court finds that B has fully performed his part of the agreement, it will decree that A execute and deliver the warranty deed to B; in other words, the court of equity will grant specific performance of the oral contract. Courts of equity will not permit the Statute of Frauds to be used as an instrument of fraud. Some courts have granted specific performance of such oral contracts if the grantee has taken possession and paid a part or all of the purchase price, in reliance upon the agreement, even though he has not made any "valuable" improvements on the land.

Martin v. Underhill
265 N. C. 669, 144 S. E. (2d) 872 (1965)
Supreme Court of North Carolina

This was an action by J. D. Martin (plaintiff) against C. L. Underhill (defendant). Judgment for plaintiff and defendant appealed. No error (judgment affirmed).

This is a suit to have the defendant declared constructive trustee of a tract of land in Wake County and of certain farm equipment, and to compel him to convey the same to the plaintiff and to account for rents and profits therefrom.

LAKE, J. The jury found that the defendant agreed with the plaintiff to take title to the property in trust for the plaintiff and to convey it to him upon payment of the purchase price and the fee of $500. The court thereupon entered judgment that the defendant took title to the property as constructive trustee for the plaintiff and ordered him to convey it to the plaintiff upon the latter's tender of the amount found by the court to be due, the parties having agreed that the amount, if any, to be so tendered might be found by the court. From such judgment the defendant appeals assigning as error the refusal of the court to grant his motion for judgment as of nonsuit, the refusal of the court to set aside the verdict as contrary to the weight of the evidence and the action of the court in entering the said judgment.

Construing the evidence as we must upon a motion for judgment of nonsuit, it indicates no intention on the part of the defendant, at the time of this agreement, to attend the sale or bid upon the property for his own account. The purpose of the agreement was not to prevent or discourage him from doing so. There is no indication that the plaintiff had any knowledge of any change of intent on the part of the defendant until after the sale was completed and he called upon the defendant for a deed in accordance with their agreement.

It is well settled in this State that such an agreement to acquire the legal title to land and to hold it in trust for a person other than the grantor is not within the Statute of Frauds and such parol trust is enforceable. *Paul v. Neece*, 244 N. C. 565, 94 S. E. (2d) 596, and others. *Rush v. McPherson*, 176 N. C. 562, 97 S. E. 613; *Allen v. Gooding*, 173 N. C. 93, 91 S. E. 694; *Avery v. Stewart*, 136 N. C. 426, 48 S. E. 775, 68 L. R. A. 776; *Owens v. Williams*, 130 N. C. 165, 41 S. E. 93; *Cobb v. Edwards*, 117 N. C. 245, 23 S. E. 241; *Lee, North Carolina Law of Trusts* (2d ed.), 67, 68.

In order to establish that the grantee in a deed, absolute upon its face, holds title subject to such a parol trust, the evidence of the agreement so to hold it must be clear, cogent and convincing, *McCorkle v. Beatty*, 226 N. C. 338, 38 S. E. (2d) 102, but whether the evidence has that convincing quality is a question for the jury upon proper instructions from the court, the rule as to the sufficiency of the proof to withstand a motion for judgment of nonsuit being the same as in other cases. *Cunningham v. Long*, 186 N. C. 526, 120 S. E. 81; *Hendren v. Hendren*, 153 N. C. 505, 69 S. E. 506; *Gray v. Jenkins*, 151 N. C. 80, 65 S. E. 644. The court properly instructed the jury as to the degree of proof required to establish the alleged trust and the jury found in favor of the plaintiff.

No error.

Lindsey v. Hornady

223 S. W. (2d) 768, 215 Ark. 797 (1949)

This was an action by L. E. Hornady (plaintiff) against Joe Lindsey and another (defendants) to quiet title to land. Decree for plaintiff, and defendants appealed. Decree reversed.

This was a controversy between rival purchasers of 150 acres of timberland, formerly owned by the nineteen heirs of T. A. Neely. The Chancellor ruled in complainant Hornady's favor in this action to quiet his title to the land. The defendants contend that the Chancellor erred in refusing to sustain their claim to an undivided nineteen forty-seconds interest in the property.

In early July, 1946, both Hornady and the two defendants were negotiating with the Neely heirs for the purchase of this timberland. On July 10th Hornady made an oral contract with four of the heirs, by which he agreed to buy the property for $3,500. This agreement was subject to these conditions: (1) That the other adult heirs agree to the sale; (2) that Hornady institute probate proceedings for the sale of the interest of the nine minor heirs; (3) that Hornady be the successful bidder at the probate sale; and (4) that after the conveyance Hornady reconvey the land without the timber to Henry Neely, one of the heirs, for $1,000. Hornady prepared a warranty deed to be signed by all the adult heirs. Four of them signed and acknowledged it on July 10th. The deed was then left in the custody of a notary public, with the understanding that the other adult heirs would come in and sign it if they agreed to the sale. The notary was not authorized to deliver the deed to the grantee; on the contrary, after everyone had signed he was to deliver it to one of the grantors, who was to retain it until the sale was completed and the consideration paid.

On July 20th all the other grantors except Henry Neely called at the notary public's office and signed the deed. Thus the matter stood until early in September, when Carl Neely became dissatisfied with what he considered to be the slow progress of the probate proceeding. He borrowed the deed from the notary and in company with the defendant Lindsey submitted it to his attorney for an opinion as to whether he was bound by his oral agreement with Hornady. The attorney advised that the oral contract was unenforceable and that Neely was free to sell to the defendants if he wished. Acting on that advice Carl Neely conveyed his interest to the defendants, who promptly recorded the deed. Between then and September 21st several other Neely heirs also became dissatisfied and sold their interests to the defendants. By these deeds the defendants acquired the nineteen forty-seconds interest they now assert.

Hornady was the highest bidder at the probate sale and received the guardian's deed on September 24th. In October Henry Neely signed the original deed and it was delivered to Hornady. Checks for the purchase price were sent to the various heirs, but those who had already sold to the defendants refused to accept the tender. Hornady then brought this suit against the defendants to quiet title and to cancel the deed to them. By cross complaint the defendants sought partition.

SMITH, J. We think Carl Neely's attorney was right in his view of the law. Although the heirs may have been morally bound by their agreement with Hornady, the Statute of Frauds renders the contract unenforceable. The deed itself was the only writing signed by the vendors. To satisfy the requirements of the statute a written memorandum must state the consideration and all other essential terms of the agreement. *St. L., I. M. & S. Ry. Co. v. Beidler*, 45 Ark. 17. Here the deed recited a consideration of $1.00 and made no mention whatever of those terms of the contract having to do with the probate provisions and the reconveyance to Henry Neely. It was therefore not sufficient to take the agreement out of the statute.

Here the notary acted as the grantors' agent in retaining the deed and was instructed to return it to one of the grantors. These facts also answer the alternative contention; for delivery of a deed to the grantor's agent, to be held by him until the purchase money is paid, cannot be treated as a delivery to the grantee. *American Central Fire Ins. Co. v. Arndt*, 129 Ark. 309, 195 S. W. 1075.

SEC. 4 (5). AGREEMENTS NOT TO BE PERFORMED WITHIN ONE YEAR

Sec. 4 (5) provides that "No action shall be brought . . . (5) upon any agreement that is not to be performed within the space of one year from the making thereof; . . . unless the agreement upon which such action shall be brought, or some memorandum or note thereof, shall be in writing, and signed by the party to be charged therewith, or some other person thereunto by him lawfully authorized."

Sec. 4 (5) has been interpreted by the courts to cover only contracts that are incapable, under their terms, of being completely performed within one year from the time they were entered into. The fact that a contract is not likely, or not expected, to be performed within one year will not put the contract under this subsection, so long as it is capable of being performed within one year. Even if a given oral contract is not in fact performed within one year, it is enforceable if its terms are such that it could conceivably have been performed within one year.

A contract which, under its terms, is not to be performed within one year, but which provides that one of the parties has an option under which he may perform within a year, if he should elect to do so, is enforceable even though not in writing. For example, A buys a house and lot from B and agrees to pay B in five equal annual installments; but the contract provides further that A may pay the entire amount due any time he chooses. Since the contract may be performed within one year, it does not fall under Sec. 4 (5), though it does fall under Sec. 4 (4).

If the performance of an agreement is dependent upon some contingency capable of occurring within a year, the agreement is enforceable even though it is oral. For example, if A orally agrees to pay B $500 upon the death of C, the contract is enforceable no matter how long C lives, since he might have died within a year. The same thing is true if A agrees to support C for the rest of his life.[1] But if A orally agrees to pay B $500 if he will not go to Europe within the next eighteen months, and B promises not to do so, the contract could not be performed within a year and hence would be unenforceable.

It is generally held that the one-year period in a contract starts to run on the day when the contract is entered into and not the day on which performance is to begin. Thus, if A contracts with B on January 1 to work for B for one year, beginning January 5, the contract must be in writing to be enforceable. Under the statutes of a number of the states it is provided that leases for a term not exceeding one year need not be in writing to be enforceable.

Warren v. Charm Fashions, Inc., et al.
82 N. Y. S. (2d) 476 (1948)

This was an action by Murray Warren (plaintiff) against Charm Fashions, Inc., and Budget Shops, Inc. (defendants). Judgment for plaintiff.

---

[1] It should be observed, however, that if A orally agrees to work for B for three years, the contract would not be enforceable. Even though it might be *terminated* within a year by the death of A or B, it could not be fully performed within a year.

This was an action on an oral contract of employment, alleged by plaintiff to have been made on April 14, 1947, for a term of one year commencing on that date. Defendants, however, assert that the contract was made on March 30, 1947, two weeks before plaintiff began work under the contract, and that the contract was therefore unenforceable under Sec. 5 (5).

It was not disputed that on March 30th the parties discussed the question of plaintiff's employment, defendant corporation being represented by its president and its vice-president. Nor is it disputed that at that time plaintiff was employed elsewhere, and that he was to be employed by defendant, if at all, sometime in the future. There is conflict in the evidence, however, as to when the contract was entered into, and as to whether it was to be for a term of one year or a hiring at will. There is no doubt that, with the exception of the question of salary, the terms of the contract were virtually agreed upon on March 30th.

Plaintiff testified that during the course of negotiations on March 30th it was agreed to reduce the agreement to writing; that on April 15th, when he reported for work, he was disappointed to learn that the contract had not been prepared; that when he demurred, Mr. Schwartz, defendant's president, shook hands with him and assured him that he had a contract until April 14, 1948—the year following.

Schwartz denied that there was any understanding that the contract was to be reduced to writing, but admitted that, except for the salary, the terms of employment were agreed upon on March 30th, and that on April 14th, when plaintiff appeared for work, the question of salary was fully settled.

BENEVENGA, J. The evidence is that, while negotiations for the contract were started on March 30th, the terms and conditions of employment were not definitely and completely agreed upon until April 14th, when the question of salary was finally settled, and plaintiff was assured that he had a contract for a year beginning on that day.

It is well settled that, in order that there may be a valid and enforceable contract, there must be a meeting of the minds of the contracting parties upon all the essential terms and conditions of the contract. "There is no contract so long as any essential element is open to negotiation." *Varney v. Ditmars*, 217 N. Y. 223, 111 N. E. 822. If the contract is indefinite and incomplete in respect to any material term or condition, or still open to negotiation, as, for instance, as to salary or compensation, then there is no valid and enforceable contract.

It is important to distinguish between preliminary negotiations leading to a contract and the completed contract itself. There is no meeting of minds of the parties until all the essential terms and conditions of the contract have been definitely and completely agreed upon. 1 *Williston on Contracts*, Sec. 27, 28. Applying these principles, it has been held that a contract is not deemed made within the meaning of statutes similar to the Personal Property Law, sec. 31, supra, until there has been a definite meeting of minds of the contracting parties upon all the essential terms and conditions of the contract. It is clear, therefore, that the contract of employment here involved was not made and completed until April 14th, when the plaintiff reported for work, and the question of salary was finally agreed upon. Prior to that time there was no contract, but only preliminary negotiations which finally culminated in the contract.

The cases cited by the defendant held that an oral contract of employment to commence on a future day is within the Statute of Frauds and unenforceable; that, to take the contract out of the operation of the statute, it is necessary that there be a renewal of the contract in express terms within the year, and that it is not sufficient that the contract be merely "restated or confirmed without modification." While the principles laid down here are well settled, they are inapplicable to the situation here presented. Here, the contract was not made on March 30th, and restated and confirmed without modification on April 14th. On the contrary, preliminary negotiations leading to the contract were started on March 30th, and the contract was not made and completed until April 14th. Therefore, by its terms the contract was for one year and does not have to be in writing to be enforceable.

MEMORANDUM AND SIGNATURE

Sec. 4 provides that the five classes of contracts which we have just been studying are not enforceable "unless the agreement upon which such action shall be brought, or some memorandum or note thereof, shall be in writing, and signed by the party to be charged therewith, or some other person thereunto by him lawfully authorized."

If an agreement which falls under the provisions of Sec. 4 is fully embodied in a written, signed contract, there can be little question that the requirements of a "writing" have been met. In other cases, however, various questions arise as to what will constitute a sufficient memorandum or note and what is meant by the word "signed."

The courts have held, without dissent, that the requirement of a writing may be met by a series of papers, such as letters, telegrams, and cablegrams, if they clearly set forth (1) the parties to the contract, (2) the subject matter of the contract, and (3) the terms and conditions of all the promises constituting the contract and by whom the promises are made. If they fail in respect to any one of these conditions, they do not constitute a sufficient memorandum. The courts are not in agreement as to whether the memorandum must also show the consideration supporting the contract, but in a majority of the states it is now required, either by statute or by the decisions of the courts, that it must do so.

While the memorandum may consist of a number of separate papers or documents, the courts require that it must be shown from the papers and documents themselves that they are connected and involve the same agreement. Such a showing may not be made by parol evidence. Such connection may be shown by reference within one document to another; for example, A writes to B: "Referring to your letter of September 1, 1954, in which you offer to sell me 100 bushels of hybrid seed corn for $5.50 per bushel, for immediate delivery, will say that I am pleased to accept your offer. . . ."

Sec. 4 requires that the memorandum be signed only by "the party to be charged therewith or by some other person thereunto by him lawfully authorized." This fact has given rise to considerable confusion and conflict in the decisions of the courts in certain cases in which the plaintiff has not signed and has not fully performed, but the majority of the courts have held that the requirements of Sec. 4 have been met if the defendant has signed.

It is not necessary that the signature be at the end of the memorandum. It may appear in the body or even at the top of the memorandum. The signature may be by mark or initials, or it may be printed, stamped, or typed, so long as it is clearly intended as the signature of the party involved. A few of the state statutes require that such memoranda be "subscribed to"; where such a statute exists, the signature must be a formal signature and affixed at the end of the memorandum.

The signature of an authorized agent is as binding as that of his principal. In most instances his authority to sign for his principal does not have to be established by an instrument in writing (i.e. a power of attorney); but in a few instances, such as land contracts, the agent must have written authority to sign on behalf of his principal.

Central Shoe Co. v. J. P. Conn & Co.
133 So. 126, 160 Miss. 151 (1931)

This was an action by the Central Shoe Co. (plaintiff) against J. P. Conn & Co. and another (defendants). Judgment for defendant, and plaintiff appealed. Reversed.

Plaintiff brought this action against J. P. Conn & Co. on an open account, and against J. P. Conn on an alleged guaranty for the payment of the account for shoes sold by plaintiff to defendant J. P. Conn & Co. There was a judgment against J. P. Conn & Co. for the amount sued for, and a judgment in favor of J. P. Conn personally. From the latter judgment, in favor of J. P. Conn, plaintiff appealed.

J. P. Conn & Co. was a corporation, and J. P. Conn was president of the company. J. Z. Wilson was in charge of the business, and was purchaser for the company, J. P. Conn having nothing to do with the buying. In May, 1929, a Mr. Ford, plaintiff's agent, secured from Mr. Wilson a written order for some shoes. In receipt of the order, the plaintiff, finding the credit standing of

J. P. Conn & Co. not satisfactory, wrote a letter to that effect, requesting that J. P. Conn guarantee the payment of the order. Two days later, plaintiff wired Conn: "Will you please wire us guaranty order 244 for 26 dozen. Thanks." Conn replied by wire: "I guarantee order 244 for 26 dozen." Thereupon the shoes so ordered were immediately shipped to J. P. Conn & Co. Shortly afterwards J. P. Conn & Co. ordered another lot of shoes from the plaintiff, consisting of 24 dozen pairs, and, as in the first order, the shoes and prices were listed. The plaintiff, by letter, requested that J. P. Conn guarantee this order. The order had been secured by Mr. Ford, plaintiff's salesman, from Mr. Wilson. Plaintiff's letter requested that J. P. Conn confirm Ford's statement "to the effect of guaranteeing payment at the maturity date of orders just recently received." J. P. Conn received this letter, and returned it to the plaintiff, with the following, written at the bottom, and signed by him: "I will comply with your request as stated above. August 15, 1929. Yours very truly, J. P. Conn."

The question in the case is whether or not, under the Statute of Frauds, the telegrams and letter referred to constituted a sufficient memorandum in writing to bind appellee, J. P. Conn, for the payment of the account of J. P. Conn & Co. sued on.

Over appellant's objection, the court admitted evidence that J. P. Conn did not intend, by the telegrams and letter, to guarantee the payment of the account, but only intended, as president of J. P. Conn & Co., to ratify the action of Wilson in purchasing the shoes for the company.

ANDERSON, J. We are of the opinion that the telegrams and letter, together with the parol evidence, were sufficient to bind J. P. Conn for the debt of J. P. Conn & Co. under Sec. 4 of the Statute of Frauds.

The written memorandum or contract is not required by the statute to be in one writing; it may be in several different writings necessarily connected with each other. If a paper signed by the party sought to be charged makes such reference to another writing as that, construing them together, all the terms of the bargain are expressed, it is sufficient under the statute, and parol evidence is admissible to identify the papers referred to and apply the reference. *Wilkinson v. Taylor Mfg. Co.*, 67 Miss. 231, 7 So. 356.

Here we have the written order of J. P. Conn & Co. for the shoes, setting out in detail the number of pairs of shoes ordered and the prices and the dates of the orders. Then there are the telegrams and letter referred to, by the terms of which J. P. Conn guaranteed the payment of the orders. We think the telegrams and the letter and the orders for the shoes point to each other with sufficient certainty. But, in addition to the evidence to that effect which they bear on their face, J. P. Conn testified in the case, and admitted that the telegrams and the letters referred to the account sued on; but, as stated, he testified that there was no purpose on his part to guarantee the payment of the account, but only to certify to Wilson's authority to buy the shoes for J. P. Conn & Co. The latter testimony was clearly incompetent, because it went to contradict the plain terms of the contract, as embodied in the telegrams and letter.

Appellant's request for a directed verdict against J. P. Conn should have been granted. Reversed and judgment here for appellant.

Cohen v. Arthur Walker & Co.
192 N. Y. Supp. 228 (1922)

This was an action by Jacob Cohen (plaintiff) against Arthur Walker & Co., Inc. (defendant). From a judgment in favor of defendant, dismissing the complaint, plaintiff appealed. Reversed and remanded.

Plaintiff sued to recover damages for failure to deliver certain merchandise. The only question involved in this appeal was the sufficiency of plaintiff's proof of the two orders set forth in his cause of action, and whether these orders constituted sufficient memoranda in writing to satisfy the Statute of Frauds. These orders were not signed by plaintiff but were on the printed blanks of defendant and contained the details of the orders and the printed name of defendant. The proof showed that these orders were filled out by defendant and sent to plaintiff by mail; that thereafter and during February and March following the receipt of the written orders, plaintiff spoke to defendant's vice president several times, and demanded delivery of the goods called for in the orders.

Defendant, in its answer, set up as a defense the Statute of Frauds and alleged that there was no "memorandum in writing subscribed by the defendant in this action, the party to be charged therewith."

PER CURIAM. The present Statute of Frauds does not require the memorandum to be "subscribed" by the party to be charged. It is sufficient if that party or his authorized agent signs the same. Section 85, Personal Property Law (Consol. Law, c. 41).

It is now well settled that under the present Statute of Frauds the printed name of the party sought to be charged, at the top or in the body of the memorandum is sufficient to comply with the Statute of Frauds. *Cohen v. Wolgel*, 107 Misc. Rep. 505, 176 N. Y. S. 764; *Pearlberg v. Levisohn*, 112 Misc. Rep. 96, 182 N. Y. S. 615. The defendant having filled out these orders by its duly authorized officer, Mr. Smith, the vice president, that constituted an appropriation of the printed name of the defendant as its signature of these transactions.

This proof established a prima facie case and required the submission of the case to the jury. The dismissal of the complaint was therefore error, and the judgment should be reversed.

Reversed and a new trial ordered.

CONTRACTS FOR THE SALE OF GOODS

UNIFORM COMMERCIAL CODE

Sec. 2–201 of the Code provides that a contract for the sale of goods for the price of $500 or more is not enforceable unless there is some writing sufficient to indicate that a contract for sale has been made between the parties and signed by the party against whom enforcement is sought or by his authorized agent or broker. A writing is not insufficient because it omits or incorrectly states a term agreed upon, but the contract is enforceable only to the extent of the quantity of goods shown in such writing. If between merchants there is an oral contract for the sale of goods and one writes to the other confirming the contract, and does not receive a reply in ten days objecting to the contents of the confirmation, it satisfies the requirements of the Statute of Frauds and the parties are bound.

A contract for, say, the sale of a color television set for $550 clearly falls within a statute which fixes a value of $500 or more. But what if the agreement involves the sale of a number of items, none exceeding $50 but totaling more than $500? If the purchase of the items involved one transaction, that is, if the items were all purchased or agreed to be purchased at the same time, clearly the contract would fall under the code and would be required to be in writing; the fact that a separate price was agreed upon for each article would be immaterial. If each item was purchased separately and involved a separate transaction, then probably none of the transactions would be required to be in writing. The problem of determining whether a single transaction or a series of transactions took place is a question of fact to be determined by the jury under the evidence.

The Code does not cover contracts for "work and labor," i.e. employment contracts, though such contracts may be required to be in writing under Sec. 4 (5). It is not always clear whether a contract is for the sale of goods or for "work and labor." This problem often arises in the case of a contract to sell future goods, i.e. goods that are not both existing and identified at the time the contract is entered into, but to be identified, made, or manufactured at a later date. Take the case of the dentist who enters into a contract with a patient to make him a set of artificial teeth. Probably the actual material for the teeth is not worth more than $50, yet under the contract the dentist is to be paid $550. Is this a contract for the sale of personal property or one for work and labor? Or a retailer enters into a contract with a manufacturer for certain merchandise, to be delivered in sixty days. The manufacturer does not have the merchandise in stock at the time the contract is entered into, but expects to manufacture it and have it ready for delivery within sixty days. In manufacturing the merchandise the manufacturer will use certain materials and will apply to the materials considerable labor. Doubtless most of the contract price will go to pay the manufacturer's labor bill. Is this a contract for the sale of goods or a contract for work and labor?

There are three rules that are applied to such contracts, namely, the English, the New York, and the Massachusetts rules. Under the English rule it is held that such a contract is for the sale of goods and falls under Sec. 17. The New York rule is just the opposite; it holds that if the goods are not in existence when the contract is entered into but are made afterwards, the contract is a contract for work and labor and falls under Sec. 4 (5). A few states follow one or the other of these rules, but the great majority follow a third rule, the so-called Massachusetts rule, which has been embodied in the Uniform Commercial Code. In the words of Sec. 2–201 (3) (a) of the Code, "if the goods are to be specially manufactured for the buyer and are not suitable for sale to others in the ordinary course of the seller's business," then the contract is for work and labor and comes under Sec. 4 (5); otherwise the contract is for the sale of goods and comes under Sec. 2–201 of the Code.

Sec. 2–201 provides that a contract for the sale of goods in excess of the statutory amount ($500) need not be in writing to be enforceable if payment has been made and accepted or if the goods have been received and accepted or if a party against whom enforcement is sought admits in his pleading, testimony, or otherwise in court that a contract for the sale of goods was made. However, liability on the contract does not go beyond the quantity of goods admitted.

While these requirements seem, upon first reading, to be quite clear, nevertheless they have given the courts considerable difficulty in specific cases. Just what acts constitute "acceptance" and what acts constitute "receipt"? Must either precede the other? Is symbolic delivery enough, or does the clause require actual physical delivery? In general, it may be said that the buyer's assent to becoming the owner of the goods constitutes acceptance. While receipt would generally involve physical possession, in a number of situations there may be receipt of the goods without actual physical possession; for example, the placing of the goods in a warehouse and the issuance of a warehouse receipt to the buyer would satisfy the requirement. Likewise, in the case of bulky goods there may be delivery and receipt of the goods by symbolic delivery.

To meet the requirements as to payment it is not required that money be given; any object of value given by the buyer to the seller is sufficient. In most states the payment may be given after the contract has been entered into. A check does not constitute "value" until it has actually been honored and paid by the drawee-bank, unless the seller accepts the check as payment of a part of the contract price.

Driggs v. Busch et al.
152 Mich. 53, 115 N. W. 986, 15 L. R. A., N. S. 654 (1908)

This was an action by Hue H. Driggs (plaintiff) against Levi Bush and William Dean (defendants) for breach of a contract for the sale of hay. Judgment for plaintiff, and defendants appealed. Affirmed.

Plaintiff was a buyer of hay. Through his agents, Homer B. McWilliams and John Van Horn, he made a contract with defendants, who owned and operated two farms, and who were the joint owners of a hay crop thereon. Under this contract plaintiff agreed to purchase 24 tons of hay or more, at the option of defendants. The contract was by parol, and as appeared by the testimony offered on behalf of plaintiff, was as follows: "Mr. Dean said, 'I want $10 a ton, and you bale the hay.' We finally bought all the hay for $10 a ton and we were to do the baling and we were to take the hay to the first cars we could get at Globeville after the hay was baled."

The testimony of the other witness for plaintiff does not vary materially from this, he stating: "We were to pay him $10 a ton for it, and we were to pay for the baling."

It was also a part of the agreement that defendants were to draw the hay to Globeville and place the same on board cars. After the contract was made, plaintiff sent balers to the premises of defendants, who baled the hay, defendants being present and assisting in the work. The price paid for baling the hay was $1.10 per ton, or $35.55, that being the regular price for such services. Defendants subsequently refused performance of the contract and this action was brought to recover damages for the breach. Plaintiff was permitted to recover in the lower court the difference between the purchase price of the hay and its actual market price at the date when delivery was contemplated. Defendants brought error and contended that the contract was unenforceable under the Statute of Frauds, and this presented the principal question for the consideration of the court. [The statutory minimum was $50.]

MONTGOMERY J. The circuit judge was of the opinion that when the hay was baled by the plaintiff's agents upon the premises of the defendants and with their cooperation, this constituted such a delivery and acceptance as would answer the requirements of the Statute of Frauds.

We are not concerned with the correctness of the reasoning of the circuit judge if the correct result was reached. The question occurs, therefore, whether the expenditure of $1.10 per ton upon this hay, which remained the property of the defendants, which expenditure was received and accepted by them, and was made in pursuance of the contract between the parties, was such a payment as answered the requirements of the statute. It is contended that the thing in earnest must be actually paid and received by the seller. This we fully accept. But there can be no doubt in this case that the service of baling this hay was received and accepted by these defendants, and if this was done at a time while the hay remained their property, and such service was received in pursuance of the contract made between the parties, we can conceive of no valid objection to treating this as a part payment of the consideration which was to pass from the plaintiff to the defendant at a time prior to the passing of the title of the hay to plaintiff. This being so, there has been a payment by the plaintiff and a receipt by the defendants of a part of the consideration. It was the hay in its improved form as baled hay which, according to the theory of the defendants, was to pass from the defendants to the plaintiff, and if this can be accepted as true, which it doubtless is, it cannot be successfully contended that the defendants have not received the value of services performed by the plaintiff in pursuance of this contract. It is not necessary that the payment upon the contract be in money. *Kuhns v. Gates*, 92 Ind. 66; *Howe v. Jones*, 57 Iowa 130.

Any work done upon the hay in baling the same passed a present benefit from the purchaser to the seller, and as it was done in pursuance of the contract it could be nothing else than payment upon the contract.

Judgment affirmed.

The defendants in the above case admitted in court that a contract was made for the sale of goods (hay) in the amount alleged by plaintiff, but contended the contract was unenforceable under the Statute of Frauds. Thus, if this case had been decided under the U. C. C., Sec. 2–201, the defendants would have been bound to the full amount of the oral contract by admitting same in court.

Moore v. Camden Marble & Granite Co.
80 Ark. 274, 96 S. W. 1063 (1906)

This was an action by the Camden Marble & Granite Co. (plaintiff) against Dave Moore (defendant). Judgment for plaintiff, and defendant appealed. Affirmed.

Defendant gave a verbal order to plaintiff for a tombstone to be made and set up in the burial ground, but refused to accept it when complete and ready for delivery. In this action against him brought by plaintiff to recover $40, the agreed price of the tombstone, he pleaded the Statute of Frauds.

The sole question for determination was whether the contract in question was one for the sale of goods, wares, and merchandise, and therefore within the Statute of Frauds, or one for work and labor to be done and materials to be furnished, which is not within the statute.

McCULLOCH, J. In England and Canada the rule seems to be settled that, where under the contract the title to a chattel is to be transferred from one person to another, it is a contract for sale of goods within the meaning of the Statute, regardless of the previous condition of the product or the amount of labor and talent to be expended in producing or constructing it.

A majority of the American courts have followed the Massachusetts rule to the effect that an agreement by one to construct an article especially for, or according to the plan of, another, whether at an agreed price or not, although the transaction is to result in a sale of the article, is a contract for work and labor, and not within the statute; but, if the article to be made and delivered is of a kind which the producer usually has for sale in the course of his business, it is a contract for the sale of goods and must be in writing.

Now, in the case at bar, the facts as found by the jury were that the plaintiff operated a marble yard and took orders for completed tombstones according to patterns and designs in a catalogue. It is not shown by the evidence the precise condition the material out of which the plaintiff constructed the tombstone was in when the order was given, but the plaintiff and another witness introduced by him testified in general terms that he made the tombstone after defendant gave the order for it according to the design selected, and cut the inscription upon it which the defendant selected. It was constructed in accordance with the design selected by the defendant, and the names and dates were inscribed thereon as he directed. This brought the case within the rule announced, and the court properly refused to instruct the jury that the contract was within the Statute of Frauds. Affirmed.

REVIEW CASES

1. Taylor, a warehouseman, went to the farm of Foster, who was picking apples that were mortgaged to Beede. Beede was present. Taylor, who was to provide storage for the apples, told Beede that he would look to him for the rent if Foster was unable to pay. Beede agreed. The rent came due, and both Foster and Beede refused to pay. At the trial Beede set up the Statute of Frauds as a defense. Was the defense good? (Beede v. Foster, 88 N. H. 131, 185 A. 168)

2. Castle telephoned Swift & Co. and offered to buy 200 cases of eggs at 36½¢ a dozen if Swift & Co. would "put them in the butter cooler" and "hold them until I order them out." Swift's agent accepted the offer, put the eggs in the cooler, and billed them to Castle. The next day Castle telephoned again and said that "the egg deal is off." The eggs were sold to someone else, and the company sued to recover its losses. Castle denied liability on his oral agreement because the amount involved exceeded the statutory minimum. Ruling? (Castle v. Swift & Co., 132 Md. 631, 104 A. 187)

3. By oral agreement Robnolte sold to Kohart for cash a house on the Robnolte farm. More than a year later Kohart attempted to remove the building. Robnolte objected and brought this suit asking for an injunction and damages. The time when the house was to be removed was in dispute. Robnolte asserted that the contract provided definitely for removal within a year from the date of sale. Kohart asserted that the house was to be removed as soon as he could secure a house mover, and that he had been hindered in the removal by the fact that a tenant of Robnolte was occupying the house. Does the Statute of Frauds apply to this case? (Robnolte v. Kohart, 81 Ohio App. 1, 76 N. E.(2d) 913)

4. Irving, a salesman for the Goodimate Co., agreed to move to Boston if his commission was increased from 4 per cent to 5 per cent. Rubin Lipsky, an authorized agent for the company, agreed by letter to begin paying the higher rate after Irving had lived in Boston for a year. The letter bore no other signature than the typewritten words "The Goodimate Co." The symbol "RL/s" was typed in the lower lefthand corner of the page. The additional commission was not paid, and Irving brought an action to recover it. The company pleaded the Statute of Frauds in that the letter was not signed by the company. Holding? (Irving v. Goodimate Co., 70 N. E.(2d) 414)

5. Sutton orally agreed to sell to Wright & Sanders 100,000 cubic yards of gravel to be excavated from his land at the rate of at least 1,000 yards a month, and all to be removed within five years. Sutton sued for breach of contract and damages, and Wright & Sanders set up Sec. 4 (4) and Sec. 4 (5) of the Statute of Frauds as defenses. Holding? (Sutton v. Wright & Sanders, 280 S. W. (Tex.) 908)

6. Paine orally promised Roderick that if she would marry him he would give her an automobile. She married him, received the automobile, and later divorced him. She then discovered that the car was heavily mortgaged. To prevent foreclosure of the mortgage she paid off the obligation, and then brought suit against Paine to collect the amount expended on the mortgage. Ruling? (Roderick v. Paine, 121 Me. 420, 117 A. 575)

7. Evans, executrix of the estate and sole beneficiary, by oral contract hired Gabbett and another, attorneys at law, to defend a claim against the estate, agreeing to pay them a fee of $500. The work was done but the fee was not paid, and suit was brought to collect it. Evans contended that the contract was unenforceable under Sec. 4 (1) of the Statute of Frauds. Ruling? (Gabbett v. Evans, 184 Mo. App. 283, 166 S. W. 635)

Rights of
Third Parties

13

The legal effect of the formation of a contract is the creation of a *chose in action,* i.e. a right on the part of each party to sue if the other party breaches the contract. A person's rights under a contract are held by the courts to be property, just as much as his land or his house is; and they are fully protected under the Constitution.

Ordinarily only the parties to a contract have rights under the contract. Under certain circumstances, however, an outside party may acquire rights under a contract either (1) by assignment or (2) as a third-party beneficiary.

THE NATURE OF ASSIGNMENT

The term *assignment* in a broad sense means a transfer by one party to another of the ownership of property of any kind, whether real or personal; but in this section it is used in the narrower sense of a transfer, by one of the parties to a contract, of his rights under the contract to a third or "outside" party, i.e. a person not a party to the contract. The party who transfers the rights is called the *assignor;* the recipient of the rights is called the *assignee.*

The early common law courts held that a contract created a personal relationship, and that hence a party to the contract could not assign or transfer either his rights or his duties to a third party without the consent of the other party to the contract. Later the courts of equity began to recognize that in certain types of contracts a party could transfer or assign his *rights* under the contract to a third person without the consent of the other party to the contract. This, in general, is the law today. On the other hand, a party to a contract may not assign his *duties* under a contract, though in certain types of contracts, as we shall see below, duties may be *delegated*.

Most assignments are contractual in nature, the assignee paying the assignor a valuable consideration for the assignment. Assignments may, however, be gratuitous. If A owes B $500 under a contract and B wishes to make a gift of the obligation to C, he may do so merely by assigning to C his right to the $500. If he actually makes the assignment, it becomes an executed gift and may not be revoked; but a bare promise to make an assignment is not enforceable by the prospective assignee. Naturally, in the business world most assignments arise out of contract.

Generally an assignment may be made without meeting any formal requirements. It may be either oral or in writing, so long as it is clear that the assignor intends to make an assignment. Some state statutes, however, require that certain types of assignment—for example, assignment of wages—must be in writing.

WHAT RIGHTS MAY BE ASSIGNED

The general rule is that a party may assign all his rights under a contract without the consent of the other party to the contract, unless the contract is made non-assignable by its terms. Certain exceptions to this general rule are discussed in the following paragraphs.

ASSIGNMENT OF PERSONAL RIGHTS AND SERVICES. A contract for personal services may not be assigned by either party. If A employs B as his private secretary, he is not permitted to assign to C his right to B's services as a private secretary, nor may B assign to another secretary D his right to work for A. The same principles of law would apply in the case of contracts for the services of doctors, lawyers, artists, architects, and engineers. These rules have also been extended to contracts for the services of unskilled workers. A common laborer X might be willing to work at a specified wage for the A Corporation but not for the B Corporation, because of differences in the nature of the work, the location of the work, or the credit standing of the firms. Consequently, the A Corporation may not assign its contractual rights to X's services to the B Corporation without X's consent. Nor may X assign his rights under the contract to his friend Y, who is also a common laborer.

ASSIGNMENT OF WAGES. Without question an employee may assign his right to wages that have been earned. He may also assign his right to future wages if he is working under a contract of employment, even though the term of his employment is uncertain. But he may not assign a mere expectancy, i.e. wages that he hopes to earn if he is successful in securing employment.

Most states have statutes which carefully regulate the assignment of wages and salaries. These statutes generally require that such assignments be in writing. They also often place a limit upon the percentage of wages that may be assigned and require that the spouse sign the instrument. For example, in Maryland, Sec. 11 of Art. 8 provides: "No assignment of wages or salary shall be valid so as to vest in the assignee any beneficial interest, either in law or in equity, unless such assignment be in writing, signed by the assignor and acknowledged in person by him or her before a justice of the peace in and for the city and county, as the case may be, in which the assignor resides, and entered on the same day by said justice of the peace upon his docket; and unless further, within three days from the execution and acknowledgment of said assignment, a true and complete copy thereof, together with the certificates of its acknowledgment, be served upon the person, firm or corporation by whom said wages or salary are due or to become due, in the same manner that the summons in chancery is now required by law to be served; provided, however, that no assignment of wages or salary by a married person shall be valid unless the same is also executed and acknowledged as above by the assignor's wife or husband, as the case may be."

ASSIGNMENT OF CLAIMS FOR MONEY. Generally, any claim for money due under a valid contract, including wages and salaries, may be assigned. If A owes B $100 under a contract, B may assign his right to the $100 to C. This is true even though the $100 is not yet due to B. Suppose that A, a contractor, has entered into a contract with B to build B a house for $15,000. Later A needs $3,000 to complete the house, and he asks the X Bank for a loan of $3,000. He may assign his rights under his contract with B as security for the loan of $3,000 by the X Bank, even though under his contract with B he is not entitled to any payment until he has completed performance.

PARTIAL ASSIGNMENT. Under the common law a creditor may not assign a *part* of the debt due him under his contract. The reason given for this rule is that a debtor has a right to pay his debt in full to the creditor, and that to permit the creditor to assign a part of the debt to a third person might subject the debtor to two or more lawsuits. In equity, however, a partial assignment is valid, since the debtor would not be subjected to the possibility of two or more suits; if the debtor is sued by either the creditor or his assignee, the court of equity will join the other in such suit and adjudicate the entire controversy in a single proceeding.

Paige v. Faure
229 N. Y. 114, 127 N. E. 898 (1920)

This was an action by H. Ray Paige (plaintiff) against Alexander Faure (defendant). Judgment for plaintiff, and defendant appealed. Reversed and complaint dismissed.

On December 12, 1914, defendant, a dealer in automobile tires, entered into a contract with plaintiff and one Lindner. By the terms of the contract Faure (defendant) gave Paige and Lindner the exclusive agency in the United States, except the cities of Boston and New York, to sell automobile tires by and for him and bearing his name. Among other things Faure agreed to consign tires to Paige and Lindner, title to remain in Faure, and they were to account to Faure for sales made each month. Later Lindner sold his interest in the contract to Paige. Under the terms of the contract Paige and Lindner had an option to renew the contract for another year upon giving a 30-day notice prior to the expiration date of the contract. Plaintiff (Paige) gave defendant (Faure) such 30-day notice, but defendant refused to renew the contract with plaintiff, and plaintiff brought this suit alleging breach of the contract.

McLAUGHLIN, J. The principal question involved is whether the contract was assignable without Faure's consent; in other words, did Lindner's assignment to Paige of all his interest in the contract justify Faure in refusing, at the request of Paige, to renew the contract another year? I am of the opinion that it did. Faure entered into a contract, not with Paige, but with Paige and Lindner. He was to have the benefit of the services of both, not one, in the sale of his product. He agreed to give credit to both, not one, and it may very well be, except for Lindner, he would not have executed the contract at all.

The general rule is that rights arising out of a contract cannot be transferred if they are coupled with liabilities or if they involve a relationship of personal credit and confidence.

In the case of *Hardy Implement Co. v. South Bend Iron Works*, 129 Mo. 222, 31 S. W. 599, the defendant entered into a contract with a firm composed of two persons, Hardy and Mason, for the sale of plows manufactured by it, to which a credit was to be given and certain discount advantages offered. Mason withdrew from the firm and transferred and assigned his interest in the contract to the plaintiff. The defendant refused to ship to the plaintiff the goods called for by the contract. Action was brought to recover damages alleged to have been sustained. A demurrer was interposed to the complaint, which was sustained, the court stating that when an executory contract is made between two parties and one of them consists of two persons, composing a partnership, and one of those partners withdraws from the firm, which is thereby dissolved, it is for the party who contracted with the firm to say whether the contract shall proceed or not. The principle upon which the rule is predicated is that a party cannot be forced to accept a contract which he did not, in the first instance, make, and to which he did not subsequently assent.

Judgment reversed and complaint dismissed.

UNIFORM COMMERCIAL CODE

Sec. 2–210 of the Code refers to assignment of rights under contracts to sell goods and the rights and duties of the primary obligor, the assignor, and the assignee. The Code in Article 9 refers to any transaction intended to create a security interest in personal property or fixtures. Sec. 9–102 deals with items such as goods, documents, instruments, general intangibles, sale of accounts, contract rights, and chattel paper.

Sec. 9–104 excludes certain transactions from coverage under the Code such as security interest under the Ship Mortgage Act of 1920, sale of accounts, contract rights, or chattel paper which is for the purpose of collection only, or a transfer of a contract right to an assignee who is also to do the performance under the contract. For further discussion see Chapter 26, Secured Transactions.

State Street Furniture Co. v. Armour & Co.
345 Ill. 160, 177 N. E. 702 (1931)

This was an action by the State Street Furniture Co. (plaintiff) against Armour & Co. (defendant). Judgment for plaintiff and defendant appealed. Affirmed.

Plaintiff sued defendant to recover a judgment for certain wages assigned to plaintiff by one of defendant's employees. Defendant set up as a defense a written contract between defendant and the employee to the effect that in consideration of employment by defendant the employee agreed not to make an assignment of his wages. Defendant proved that prior to the date of the assignment it had given written notice to numerous firms, including plaintiff, that it had entered into such a contract with all of its employees and would no longer honor wage assignments. It was, therefore, the contention of defendant that because of such contract and notice the subsequent assignment of wages without its consent was null and void.

ORR, J. The principal question presented is whether, by reason of the employment contract, the assignment of wages was void, since the written consent of the defendant was not obtained thereto. The determination of this question is of great importance to all mercantile firms which sell goods on the installment plan.

The right of an employee to make an assignment of his wages has long been recognized in this state, and the privilege of using and contracting for the disposal of wages is both a liberty and a property right. *Massie v. Cessna,* 239 Ill. 352, 88 N. E. 152. "Property" includes every interest in any and every thing subject to the ownership of man, and the right to dispose of that interest is a property right. *Bailey v. People,* 190 Ill. 76, 80 N. E. 98. The relationship between employer and employee with respect to unpaid wages is that of debtor and creditor, and the right of the employee to those wages is a chose in action and as such may be assigned. This court has not only held that assignments of wages may be enforced as to past services, but also sanctioned such assignments as to wages to be earned in the future under an existing employment if such assignment is made for a valuable consideration and untainted with fraud. *Mallin v. Wenham*, 209 Ill. 252. 70 N. E. 564.

Wage assignments are also expressly recognized and the rights of wage earners sought to be protected by different statutory provisions in this state.

The contract relied upon to defeat the judgment in this case contained no absolute denial of the employee's right to make an assignment of his wages. It only specified that such wages should not be assigned without the written consent of Armour & Co. and that unless such consent was obtained the assignment should be null and void. It is not necessary to have the consent of the employer to make a valid assignment of wages, where the assignment is of the entire claim.

The fact that the defendant sent out a circular notifying the plaintiff and others that it would not consent to an assignment of wages given by any of its employees is of no legal effect; as such consent was not necessary to the validity of the assignment. Since the consent of the employer was not necessary to make the assignment valid, the withholding of consent cannot make the assignment void, otherwise the power to withhold consent would be the power to destroy valuable property rights.

This is a suit by an assignee of wages due from the assignor's employer. The relationship of the parties to this suit is that of debtor and creditor, since the assignee stands in the shoes of the employee as to the latter's wages due from the employer. There was no privity of contract between the assignee and the employer. They were relying upon two separate contracts with the employee, to each of which one or the other was not a party. The contract of the employee with Armour & Co. not to assign his wages without its consent was not binding upon the assignee, who was not a party to the agreement. After a contract has been fully executed and nothing remains to be done except to pay the money, the claim becomes a chose in action, which is assignable and enforceable under section 18 of the Practice Act. Judgment affirmed.

Seligman & Latz, Inc. et al. v. Noonan
104 N. Y. S. (2d) 35, 201 Misc. 96 (1951)

This was a suit by Seligman & Latz, Inc. and another (plaintiffs) against Richard Noonan (defendant). Decree for defendant, and plaintiffs appealed. Affirmed.

This action was brought by Seligman & Latz, Inc. and Seligman & Latz Rochester Corporation to enjoin the defendant from entering the employ of a rival beauty parlor in violation of a covenant contained in a contract of employment.

On August 12, 1949, Sidney Seligman, Edward K. Latz, and Israel A. Latz, a partnership doing business under the firm name of Seligman & Latz, entered into a contract with the defendant. This contract recited that the partnership operated various beauty and hairdressing salons throughout the United States and Canada wherein beauty treatments of the internationally advertised and world famous Antoine of Paris are given; that the only operators employed in these Antoine Beauty Salons are those who have been especially trained in the highly distinctive Antoine methods and techniques and who have been taught the unique Antoine types and methods of hairdress either by Antoine himself or at the Antoine Training School operated by the partnership; that the defendant is seeking employment as an Antoine operator and desires to receive training as such; that by virtue of such training the defendant will become possessed of knowledge of the unique techniques and methods of giving Antoine Hairdress and beauty culture treatments and of fashioning the distinctive Antoine styles. By the terms of the agreement, the partnership agreed to train the defendant in the Antoine Training School conducted by them and thereafter to employ him as an Antoine operator at a salary of $40 per week plus commissions. The defendant undertook and agreed to exert his best efforts in the performance of his duties, not to engage in any business or profession, not to give any lectures, talks, advice or instructions except at the written request of the partnership, and further agreed that upon termination of his employment by the partnership, he would not for a period of one year thereafter be employed in, conduct or be associated in any way with any other beauty or hairdressing establishment located one mile from any Antoine Beauty Salon.

The complaint alleges that this contract was subsequently assigned by the partnership to plaintiff, Seligman & Latz, Inc.; that the defendant attended a school operated by Seligman & Latz, Inc., and there received his instruction, and that thereafter, defendant entered the employ of plaintiff, Seligman & Latz Rochester Corporation, which operates a beauty salon in the store of B. Forman Company, Rochester, New York, under supervision and control of plaintiff, Seligman & Latz, Inc. The complaint further alleges that on or about October 16, 1950, defendant left the employ of Seligman & Latz Rochester Corporation and entered the employ of or became associated with another beauty salon located at an address which is within one mile of the place of business of Seligman & Latz Rochester Corporation. The complaint contains no allegation that the assignment of the contract from the partnership to the plaintiff, Seligman & Latz, Inc. was with the knowledge, consent, or approval of the defendant.

ROBERTS, J. The plaintiff claims the right to enforce the contract as the assignee of the partnership. Its right to seek enforcement of the covenant in the contract depends upon whether or not the contract is assignable. The weight of authority seems clearly to hold that a bilateral contract involving the performance of personal services cannot be assigned by either party without the consent of the other. *Paige v. Faure*, 229 N. Y. 114, 127 N. E. 898, *Avenue Z Wet Wash Laundry Co., Inc. v. Yarmush*, 221 N. Y. S. 788.

It is significant that contracts for personal services which contemplate that the services are to be performed personally by one of the parties, terminate upon the death of either of the parties to the contract. A right which does not survive is ordinarily not capable of assignment; at least, survivability is one of the tests of assignability.

Contracts involving the element of personal confidence and credit are also held not to be assignable without the consent of the other party.

The plaintiffs cite certain cases which it is claimed sustain the validity of the assignment here involved. In *Devlin v. Mayor of City of New York*, 63 N.Y. 8, the court upheld an assignment of a contract for cleaning the streets of New York City. Obviously the contracting party did not himself undertake personally to do the work of cleaning the streets. The court held that this was not a contract for personal services within the rule which is stated in the following language: ". . . Contracts other than such as are personal in their character, as promises to marry or engagements for personal services requiring skill, science or peculiar qualifications, may be assigned. . . ."

The contract here before the court involves not only the training and instruction of the defendant by the three men constituting the partnership but it also involves personal services to be rendered by the defendant to the partnership. These services were to consist of his employment as an operator in an Antoine Beauty Salon where according to the contract the only operators involved "Are those who have been specially trained in the highly distinctive Antoine methods and techniques and taught the unique Antoine types and methods of headdress, . . . and these operators are commonly known to the public and among the trade as Antoine operators." The contract not only required the defendant to render personal services, it required him to render such services because of the special skill and peculiar qualifications which he was to possess through the special training the partnership was to furnish. Under the foregoing authorities, such a contract is not assignable and hence cannot here be enforced by the assignee.

NOTICE OF ASSIGNMENT

In order to complete an assignment it is not necessary for the assignee to notify the debtor of the assignment. Upon the completion of the assignment both the assignor and the assignee, as between themselves, are bound by the assignment. However, important reasons exist which make it essential that the assignee give the debtor immediate notice of the assignment in order to protect his rights under the assignment. The most important of these reasons are as follows:

(1) *To protect himself in case of payment to assignor.* If the assignee fails to give the debtor notice of the assignment, the debtor may make payment or render performance to the assignor and thus discharge his obligations under the contract. For example, A (debtor-obligor) owes B (creditor-obligee) $1,000 under a certain contract. B assigns his right to

receive the $1,000 to C (assignee), but C fails to give A notice of the assignment. A, not knowing of the assignment, proceeds to pay B, thus discharging his obligation under the contract. C's only recourse would be against B.

(2) *To protect himself against successive assignments.* By giving notice to the debtor (obligor), the assignee protects himself from the legal hazards of successive assignments. For example, A (debtor-obligor) owes B (creditor-obligee) $1,000 under a certain contract. B assigns his right to receive the $1,000 to C (assignee), but C fails to give A notice of the assignment. Shortly thereafter B assigns the same rights to D (second assignee), and D immediately notifies A of the assignment. If A pays D, the debt is discharged. Assume that A does not pay D, and both C and D claim that they are entitled to payment from A. Which party is correct in his contention? The English courts and many of the American courts hold that the assignee who first gives notice to the debtor has priority. On the other hand, a number of the American state courts hold that the first assignee has priority. The United States Supreme Court takes this position unless the equities are on the side of the assignee who first gave notice of the assignment. The courts that give priority to the first assignee take the position that after the creditor assigned his rights under the contract to the first assignee, he had nothing left to assign to the second assignee. The courts that favor the assignee who first gave notice take the position that the difficulties rose from the negligence of the first assignee in failing to give notice, and that he should therefore be the one to suffer.

Unless a statute prescribes a specific method of giving notice of assignment, the notice may be either oral or in writing; but caution requires that it be given in writing.

Rosenblatt v. Credit Discount Company, et al.
98 P. (2d) 747, 37 Cal. App. (2d) 108 (1940)

This was an action by Harry Rosenblatt (plaintiff) against the Credit Discount Company and others (defendants). Judgment for plaintiff, and defendants appealed. Affirmed.

This action was brought to obtain a determination of the priority of plaintiff's claim to certain accounts receivable as against the claim of defendants to the same accounts receivable.

The material facts were not in dispute. The original owner of the accounts receivable assigned the accounts for value to both plaintiff and defendants. The assignment to defendants was prior in point of time, but defendants gave no notice of the assignment to the debtors. During the negotiations of plaintiff with the assignor, defendants made inquiry of the debtors and ascertained the correctness of the assignor's statement of the accounts. Plaintiff entered into his transaction with the assignor without any notice of the assignment to defendants. He immediately gave notice to the debtors of his assignment. The only question involved is that of the priority between the claims of plaintiff and defendants.

SPENCE, J. It is conceded by all parties that the settled rule in this jurisdiction is that found in *Graham Paper Co. v. Pembroke*, 127 Cal. 117, 56 P. 627, 44 L. R. A. 632, which rule has been followed by the [California] Supreme Court in numerous cases. The rule as tersely stated is as follows: "As between two bona fide assignees for value the one who first gives notice to the debtor acquires priority." Defendants argue for a contrary rule, claiming that the settled rule in this jurisdiction should be discarded. We are not impressed with defendants' argument. The rule of the above-mentioned cases appears to be in accord with the majority view (see 31 *A. L. R.* 876), and it was adopted after a careful consideration of the conflict of authority in other jurisdictions. But even if we were impressed with defendants' argument, we would feel impelled to follow the rule thus firmly settled by the decisions of our Supreme Court.

LEGAL POSITION OF ASSIGNOR AND ASSIGNEE

POSITION OF THE ASSIGNOR

If B, an obligee under a contract with A, assigns his rights to C for a valuable consideration, and if A then fails or refuses to perform, is B liable to C? The answer to this vital question depends upon the facts of the given case. The law applicable to such cases is as follows:

(1) The assignor of a right under a contract impliedly warrants (a) that the right which he purports to assign exists and is valid, and is not subject to defenses; and (b) that he will do nothing that will prevent the assignee from obtaining performance under the original contract. (2) However, the assignor does not impliedly warrant that the obligor will perform his obligation under the contract; that is, he does not warrant the obligor's solvency or ability to pay or perform. He does not guarantee to the assignee the payment of the debt or the performance of the obligation.

Under the assignor's first warranty he impliedly warrants to the assignee that the obligor has no defenses which he could set up as valid reasons for failing or refusing to perform under the contract, such as failure of consideration, breach of warranty, fraud, illegality, payment, infancy, or some set-off or counterclaim. Consequently, if in a given case it could be shown that the obligor had one or more of these defenses, the assignor would be liable to the assignee for breach of his implied warranty that no such defenses existed. For example, B claims that A is indebted to him under a certain contract to the extent of $500. B assigns his claim to C. C makes demand upon A for payment, and A refuses to pay. C files suit against A and A sets up one of the aforementioned defenses, e.g. fraud. If the defense is valid and C is unable to recover from A, he may recover from B on his implied warranty that the claim was not subject to defenses.

Under his second warranty the assignor warrants that he will do nothing that will prevent the assignee from obtaining performance under the original contract. Therefore, the assignor would be liable to the assignee (1) if he should accept payment or performance from the original obligor, or (2) if he should make a second assignment of his rights under the contract and the second assignee should obtain performance from the obligor.

The assignor does not impliedly warrant that the obligor will perform his obligations under the original contract. Consequently, if the obligor refuses to perform or pay, without having a valid defense, or if he is insolvent and unable to pay, the assignor would not be liable to the assignee.

POSITION OF THE ASSIGNEE

The assignee takes under the assignment only the rights possessed by the assignor. The assignee is said to "step into the shoes of the assignor." Consequently, any defense that the obligor could have set up against the obligee (assignor) if the obligee had not assigned his rights under the contract, he may set up against the assignee.

Sinclair Refining Co. v. Rosier
104 Kan. 719, 180 Pac. 807 (1919)

This was an action by the Sinclair Refining Co. (plaintiff) against W. Lacy Rosier, doing business as the Hutchinson Oil Co. (defendant). Judgment for defendant, and plaintiff appealed. Judgment affirmed.

Plaintiff brought this action to recover the value of a car of oil and a car of gasoline, alleged to have been sold to defendant by the Chanute Refining Co. on an open account, the balance alleged to be due being $1,516.58. This account was subsequently assigned and transferred by the Chanute Refining Co. to plaintiff. Defendant refused to pay plaintiff, claiming that $289.70 had been paid on the account. Defendant also filed a cross-demand for $1477.30 based on dealings between the Chanute Refining Co., plaintiff's assignor, and defendant. Defendant alleged in his cross-demand that he had purchased oil from time to time from the Chanute Refining Co. and had paid certain inspection fees under an inspection law that had since been declared to be invalid, and that he was entitled to a refund of said inspection fees from the Chanute Refining Co., but that he had not received such refund. Defendant, therefore, maintained that this sum of $1477.30 should be set off against plaintiff's claim.

JOHNSON, C.J. Plaintiff's objection to the rulings raises the question whether the defendant is entitled to set off his claim against the assigned account on which the action was brought. It was money had and received by the plaintiff's assignor, to which the defendant was entitled, and it certainly constituted an actionable demand as against the Chanute Refining Co. We have the question, then, whether the assignment of the account to the plaintiff cut off defenses which the defendant might have used against the plaintiff's assignor. The thing assigned was an open account, which lacks the qualities of negotiable paper, and the plaintiff took it subject to any set-off or demand which the defendant held against the assignor at the time of the transfer.

It has been determined that when demands exist between parties, one of them cannot defeat the demands of the other by an assignment. The larger demand is deemed to be satisfied up to the amount of the smaller demand.

The claim of defendant, based as it is on the fees charged against and paid by the defendant, and which were collected by plaintiff's assignor for the use and benefit of the defendant, amounted to a cross-demand, and from the time they were collected by the assignor, cross-demands existed between the original parties, and for his demand the defendant had a right of action against the plaintiff's assignor.

Although it may not be important, it is alleged that the assigned account was received by plaintiff with full knowledge of the existence of the defendant's demand. The answer of the defendant was sufficiently definite, and it set forth a good ground of defense upon the cross-demand of the defendant.

Judgment for defendant affirmed.

DELEGATION OF DUTIES

A party may not assign his duties under a contract without the consent of the other party. However, if the duties do not involve personal skill, credit, or a relation of trust and confidence, he may *delegate* them; that is, he may turn them over to someone else for actual performance, while remaining personally liable to the other party to the contract for competent performance of the duties. If A enters into a contract with B, a building contractor, to build a house, it is assumed that he has special confidence in B's skill and responsibility, and B may not assign to another his duty to build the house according to the terms of the contract and the accompanying plans and specifications. B may, however, delegate to subcontractors, normally without A's consent, certain portions of the work, such as wiring and plumbing. It is assumed that so long as such work is competently done, A will not care what individuals perform it. If the quality of the work is not satisfactory, B is responsible to A.

A party to a contract may be completely discharged of his duty to perform under a novation contract, as we have seen earlier. Such a contract requires the agreement of all three parties.

Crane Ice Cream Co. v. Terminal Freezing & Heating Co.
147 Md. 588, 128 A. 280, 39 A. L. R. 1184 (1925)

This was an action by the Crane Ice Cream Co. (plaintiff) against the Terminal Freezing & Heating Co. (defendant). Judgment for defendant, and plaintiff appealed. Affirmed.

Defendant and one W. C. Frederick entered into a contract for the delivery of ice by defendant to Frederick. Before the expiration of the contract Frederick assigned the contract to plaintiff. Defendant refused to deliver ice to the assignee (plaintiff) and the assignee brought this action on the contract against defendant for the alleged breach.

The contract imposed upon defendant the liability to sell and deliver to Frederick such quantities of ice as he might use in his business as an ice cream manufacturer to the extent of 250 tons per week, at, and for, the price of $3.25 per ton on the loading platform of Frederick.

Frederick made and sold ice cream in Baltimore, where his plant was located. The assignee (plaintiff) was a corporation engaged in the ice cream business on a large and extensive scale in the city of Philadelphia, as well as in the city of Baltimore and state of Maryland.

PARKE, J. It may be stated as a general rule that a contract cannot be enforced by or against a person who is not a party to it, but there are circumstances under which either of the contracting parties may substitute another for himself in the rights and duties of the contract without obtaining the consent of the other party to the contract. The inquiry here is whether the facts bring the case within the scope of the general rule, and the answer must be found from a consideration in detail of the relation of the parties concerned, the subject matter of the contract, its terms, and the circumstances of its formation.

The rights of the assignor (Frederick) were (1) the right to take no ice, if he used none in his business, but, if he did (2) to require defendant to deliver all the ice he might need to the extent of 250 tons per week. The duties or liabilities of the assignor included the duty (1) to pay to the defendant on every Tuesday during the continuance of the contract the stipulated price for the ice.

Whether the attempted assignment of these rights, or the attempted delegation of these duties, must fail because the rights or duties are of too personal a character, is a question of construction to be resolved from the nature of the contract and the express and presumed intention of the parties.

The character, credit, and resources of Frederick had been tried and tested by defendant before it renewed the contract. Not only had his ability to pay as agreed been established, but his fidelity to his obligations not to buy or accept any ice from any other source up to 250 tons a week had been ascertained. When Frederick went out of business and turned over his plant to plaintiff, it was no longer his business, or subject to his care, control, or maintenance, but it was the business of a stranger, whose skill, competency, and requirements of ice were altogether different from those of Frederick.

Under all the circumstances of the case, it is clear that the rights and duties of the contract were of so personal a character that the rights of Frederick cannot be assigned nor his duties delegated without defeating the intention of the parties to the original contract.

While a party to a contract may as a general rule assign all his beneficial rights, except where a personal relation is involved, his liability under the contract is not assignable inter vivos, because any one who is bound to any performance whatever or who owes money cannot by any act of his own, or by any act in agreement with any other person than his creditor or of the one to whom his performance is due, cast off his own liability and substitute another's liability. If this were not true, obligors could free themselves of their obligations by the simple expedient of assigning them. For these reasons it has been uniformly held that a man cannot assign his liabilities under a contract, but one who is bound so as to bear an unescapable liability may delegate the performance of his obligation to another, if the liability be of such a nature that its performance by another will be substantially the same thing as performance by the promisor himself. In such circumstances the performance of the third party is the act of the promisor, who remains liable under the contract and answerable in damages if the performance be not in strict fulfillment of the contract.

The analysis of the facts leaves no room for doubt that the case at bar falls into the category of those assignments where an attempt is made both to transfer the rights and to delegate the duties of the assignor under an executory bilateral contract whose terms and the circumstances made plain that the personal qualification and action of the assignor, with respect to both his benefits and burdens under the contract, were essential inducements in the formation of the contract, and further that the assignment was a repudiation of any future liability of the assignor.

We take it to be sound doctrine that, where one contracting party repudiates his obligations, the other party has the right of declining to be bound to a stranger by its terms.

Judgment affirmed.

ASSIGNMENT BY OPERATION OF LAW

Our discussion thus far has been limited to assignments that result from the action of the parties themselves. Under certain circumstances assignments of contracts may result by operation of law. Under the early common law, which provided that the title to the wife's personal property passed to her husband, such an assignment took place immediately upon marriage, but this type has been abolished by statute. Today we have two common situations in which an assignment takes place by operation of law. (1) Upon the death of a person who is possessed of personal property, the title immediately passes to his executor or administrator for the purpose of paying the just debts of the decedent. Likewise, any contracts of the decedent that are not of a personal nature, involving confidence and trust, and that may be performed as well by one person as by another, pass to the executor or the administrator. Many business contracts fall into this class, as, for example, contracts for the purchase or sale of goods, contracts for the payment of money, and building contracts. Contracts which involve the personal services of the decedent—e.g. a contract by a surgeon to perform an operation, or a contract by a lawyer to try a case—would not pass to his personal representative. (2) Bankruptcy operates to confer upon the assignee of the bankrupt his rights and liabilities under his contracts.

THIRD–PARTY BENEFICIARIES

A contract may confer benefits, either specifically or incidentally, upon a person who is not a party to the contract. The recipient of such benefits is called a *third-party beneficiary*. Third-party beneficiaries are usually classified as follows: (1) donee beneficiaries; (2) creditor beneficiaries; (3) incidental beneficiaries.

A *donee beneficiary* is not a party to the contract, he gives no consideration of any kind, and anything which he is to receive under the contract is a mere gratuity. However, if the contract, or any provision in it, is made specifically for his benefit, it is generally held that he may sue to enforce the contract. For example, A and B enter into a contract whereby A sells his store to B, and the contract contains a provision to the effect that B will continue to employ C as manager of the store for a period of one year at a salary of $500 per month. Though C is not a party to the contract between A and B, and has paid no consideration for B's promise to retain him as manager of the store for one year, yet, since this provision of the contract is made expressly for his benefit, he may enforce his rights as a donee beneficiary under the contract. If B should discharge C prior to the expiration of the one year period, C would have a cause of action against B. Probably the best example of a donee beneficiary is found in the case of life insurance. A insures his life with the X Insurance Company and names B as the beneficiary. While there is no privity of contract between the X Insurance Company and B, the courts permit B to sue on the contract, as a donee beneficiary, in case the X Insurance Company refuses to pay B upon the death of A.

In the case of a *creditor beneficiary* the debtor under one contract enters into a second contract with another party, under which the other party agrees to pay a specified amount of money to the creditor under the first contract, or to perform some act for his benefit. A good example of a creditor beneficiary is found in the case of the assumption of a mortgage. A sells his house to B for $15,000. B pays A $8,000 in cash and signs a note for the balance of $7,000. He gives A a mortgage on the house to secure the note. Later B sells the house to C, who, as a part of the purchase price, assumes and agrees to pay the note and mortgage to A. It is evident that A has paid no consideration for C's promise to pay the note and mortgage. However, the courts treat A as a creditor beneficiary, and will permit him to sue C on his promise if C refuses or fails to keep his promise to B that he will pay the debt to A.

An *incidental beneficiary* is not permitted to recover for the loss, through breach of a contract, of incidental benefits which he would have received if the contract had been performed. The reason for denying recovery to an incidental beneficiary is the fact that the contract upon which he sues was not made for his special benefit. This basic requirement must be met by any third-party beneficiary before he may recover. For example, A owns a certain lot on Cherry Street. B owns the adjoining house and lot. A enters into a contract with a contractor, C, to build a $50,000 house on A's lot. The construction of such an expensive house on A's lot would have the effect of increasing the value of B's house and lot. B would therefore be an incidental beneficiary. But since the contract between A and C was in no way intended to secure the express benefit of B, B would have no cause for action if C should breach his contract with A.

LeBallister v. Redwood Theatres, Inc., et al.
36 Pac. (2d) (Cal.) 827 (1934)

This was an action by Homer LeBallister (plaintiff) against Redwood Theatres, Inc., et al. (defendant) for the breach of an alleged contract. Judgment for defendants, and plaintiff appealed. Reversed.

Plaintiff brought this action to recover as a third-party beneficiary under an agreement entered into by defendant, Redwood Theatres, Inc., with the owners of the controlling interest in the corporation by which plaintiff was formerly employed. Defendant, Mann, guaranteed the performance of the said agreement by defendant corporation.

SPENCE, J. The question presented on this appeal is whether plaintiff was entitled, under the provisions of sec. 1559 of the Civil Code, to recover upon the contract set forth in the complaint. Said section reads as follows: "A contract, made expressly for the benefit of a third person, may be enforced by him at any time before the parties thereto rescind it." The agreement provided for the purchase by the defendant corporation of certain stock of the National Theatres Syndicate for the sum of $43,973.50 and contained the following provision: "It is further understood and agreed that in the event you accept this offer and control of the said corporation is taken over by us, we agree to retain your

Mr. Homer LeBallister, now employed by you as manager, in some suitable position for a period of one year at a salary of not less than eighty-five dollars ($85.00) per week."

The appellant contends that said contract was one made expressly for his benefit within the meaning of said section 1559 of the Civil Code and that the trial court erred in denying the recovery upon the ground stated. In our opinion this contention must be sustained. While the contract was not made solely and exclusively for appellant's benefit, it was not necessary that it should have been so made in order to entitle him to recover. *Stanton v. Santa Anna Sugar Co.*, 84 Cal. App. 206, 257 P. 907. The word "expressly" means "in an express manner; in direct or unmistakable terms; explicitly; definitely; directly." Here the respondent corporation agreed in direct and unmistakable terms to employ appellant for a definite period at a salary of not less than $85 per week. It could have done nothing more than it did do to make this provision one "expressly" for appellant's benefit. From the reading of the agreement before us we believe that the intent to benefit appellant clearly appears from its terms.

Reversed.

REVIEW CASES

1. Langel contracted to sell realty to Hurwitz and Hollander, who assigned their contract to Benedict, who in turn assigned to Betz. The assignment contained no delegation to the assignee of the performance of the assignor's duties. The date of performance was extended at Betz's request because the title company had not completed its search. On the extended date Betz did not appear and perform, although Langel appeared with the deed ready to perform. Langel filed suit against Betz for specific performance. Holding? (Langel v. Betz, 250 N. Y. 159, 164 N. E. 890)

2. DuPuy, an attorney, under written contract with Williams, agreed to perfect Williams' title to certain lots for the option of buying them at $500 each. DuPuy assigned all his rights and duties under the contract to Sloan. Sloan perfected the titles and then demanded that Williams sell the lots to him and tendered payment in full. Upon Williams' refusal Sloan filed suit for specific performance. Ruling? (Sloan v. Williams, 138 Ill. 43, 27 N. E. 531)

3. The Board of Regents of the University of Wisconsin entered into a contract with Bentley to construct an addition to a dormitory, payments to be made upon written certificates of the architects that such payments were due. The architects issued certificates to Bentley, who assigned them to Skobis Bros. et al., subcontractors. The subcontractors gave no notice of assignment to the Board of Regents. The Board paid most of the money to Bentley. Bentley made an assignment for the benefit of creditors to Ferge. Skobis Bros. et al. contended that said transactions constituted an equitable assignment to them and brought suit against Ferge and the Board of Regents. Ruling? (Skobis Bros. et al. v. Ferge et al., 102 Wis. 122, 78 N. E. 426)

4. Parlier sold to Brown and wife a tract of land, and the deed was recorded. Brown gave Parlier a note, secured by a mortgage on the land. The mortgage was recorded. Brown and wife sold and deeded the land to Miller, who agreed to pay the Parlier note. Miller died before the note was paid, and Parlier sued the administrators of his estate to compel payment. Judgment for whom? (Parlier v. Miller et al., 186 N. C. 501, 119 S. E. 898)

5. Coburn assigned the American Bridge Co. all money due under a contract he had with the City of Boston, which was given notice of the assignment. Shortly thereafter Coburn breached the contract, damaging the City of Boston. The American Bridge Co. sued the City of Boston for the amount of the contract, and the City pleaded the damages from the breach as a partial defense. Judgment for whom? (American Bridge Co. et al. v. City of Boston, 202 Mass. 374, 88 N. E. 1089)

Interpretation

14

Most contracts are performed by the contracting parties without disagreement or controversy. However, upon occasion disagreements do arise, and if the parties are unable to settle the controversy among themselves, one or the other of the parties is likely to bring the matter to court for adjudication. In one case the only issue may be whether a contract does in fact exist. In another case the parties may agree that a contract does exist but disagree as to their rights and duties under the contract. Certain rules of evidence and construction have been devised to aid the courts in arriving at a determination of such controversies.

THE PAROL EVIDENCE RULE

Of the many rules of evidence applied by courts in interpretation of contracts, space permits discussion of only one, the Parol Evidence Rule, which is incorporated in the Uniform Commercial Code, Sec. 2–202.

The Parol Evidence Rule applies only to written contracts. When the parties reduce their agreement to writing, it is presumed to contain their complete agreement. Therefore, under the rule, parol (oral) evidence will not be admitted to add to, vary, contradict, or take from the terms of the instrument. Upon reflection it would seem that this rule is proper and just. If such were not the rule, the parties to a written contract could never be quite certain as to their legal rights and duties under their contract. A contrary rule would open the way to fraud and perjury, and might, upon occasion, reduce a written agreement to the status of a mere "scrap of paper."

The rule permits oral evidence to be introduced for certain purposes: for example, (1) to show that there is no agreement at all because one of the essentials of a contract is lacking; (2) to attack the validity of the contract on grounds of mistake, misrepresentation, fraud, duress, or undue influence; and (3) to assist the court in determining the meaning of technical terms or words used in a special sense arising from the usages or customs of a particular trade or business.

The Parol Evidence Rule has no application in the proof of an oral contract. The existence or non-existence of an oral contract is determined by the words and acts of the parties under the given circumstances. If the words and acts of the parties indicate an intention to create certain rights and obligations, the parties will be bound by these manifestations, even though such finding may not correspond to the professed intentions of the parties as stated at the time of the trial. In other words, in ascertaining the intentions of the parties the court bases its judgment upon the objective intent of the parties, not their subjective intent.

Hayden v. Hoadley
94 Vt. 345, 111 A. 343 (1920)

This was an action by Howard G. Hayden and another (plaintiffs) against Melvin A. Hoadley and another (defendants). Judgment for plaintiffs, and defendants appealed. Reversed and remanded.

The parties to this action exchanged properties, and as a part of the arrangement the defendants gave the plaintiffs the following writing, which all signed: "Memorandum of agreement made this 2d day of May, A.D. 1919, by and between Melvin A. Hoadley and George A. Peck, both of Montpelier, in the county of Washington and state of Vermont, and Howard G. and Georgia V. Hayden, both of Worcester, in the county of Washington and state of Vermont, witnesseth: We, the said Hoadley and Peck, in consideration of the said Haydens having this day conveyed to us their farm in Worcester aforesaid, and whereas, we, the said Hoadley and Peck, have this day conveyed to the said Haydens certain land and premises situated on the westerly side of North street in the city of Montpelier, as and for additional consideration for such exchange of properties, bind ourselves and agree to make, without expense to said Haydens, the following repairs upon the premises conveyed to the said Haydens as aforesaid, viz.: The said Hoadley and Peck agree to straighten up and shingle the barn on said premises; to straighten up the house; to repair and paint the roof, and paint the back of said house; to repair the cellar wall; and to install a pump in said house."

It is for noncompliance with this agreement that suit is brought.

At the trial, the defendants offered to show that at the time the writing was signed it was agreed that they should have until October 1, 1919, in which to make the repairs, that only $60 need be expended therefor, and that No. 2 shingles were to be used on the barn. These offers were excluded, and the defendants excepted.

POWERS, J. The rulings were correct. The case calls for the application of a rule so often and so recently reaffirmed by this court that we need take no time in its discussion. A written contract which contains no latent ambiguity cannot be qualified, controlled, contradicted, enlarged, or diminished by any contemporaneous or antecedent understanding or agreement; and oral testimony can no more be received to vary or contradict the legal intendment of such a contract than to vary or contradict its express terms. *Kinnear & Gager Mfg. Co. v. Miner*, 88 Vt. 324, 92 A. 459; *Wood v. James*, 93 Vt. 36, 106 A. 566. The legal effect of the contract before us—it being silent as to the time of performance—was to require the repairs specified to be completed within a reasonable time. This is a provision of the contract implied by the law, and that which is so implied is as binding as that which is expressed. In legal consequence, then, this contract is just what it would be if it was therein expressly provided that the repairs were to be made within a reasonable time. To admit the testimony offered by the defendants to the effect that the parties agreed upon October 1 as the limit of the time given for the repairs would be to allow the plain legal effect of the written contract to be controlled by oral evidence. This is not permissible. The contract before us is unequivocal and complete, and to say that parol evidence can be received to fix the time of performance, on the ground that the contract is incomplete, is wholly illogical and wrong.

[NOTE: The judgment of the trial court was reversed and the case remanded on grounds other than those contained in this abstract.]

RULES OF CONSTRUCTION

Representative of the rules of construction which the courts have adopted to aid them in their interpretation of contracts are the following:

(1) In determining the rights and duties of the parties the contract is read and interpreted as a whole.

(2) A word is given its ordinary or popular meaning unless the circumstances show that a different meaning existed in the minds of the parties.

(3) Technical language is given its technical meaning, unless it is clear that the parties intended otherwise.

(4) The contract will be so interpreted as to carry out most accurately the intentions of the parties.

(5) Where a printed contract form is used and there is a conflict between the printed provisions and typed provisions, the typed provisions will control. If the form is partly typed and partly in longhand and there is a conflict between the typed provisions and those made in longhand, the longhand provisions will be taken as the true expression of the intentions of the parties.

(6) Where the amount involved in a contract is expressed both in words and in figures and they are different as to amount, the amount expressed in words will be taken as correct.

(7) Where one of the parties prepares the contract and certain terms are ambiguous, the terms will be construed most favorably to the party who did not prepare the contract.

(8) If general terms are followed by special terms, the court will assume that the special terms qualify the general terms.

Kuhn v. Stan A. Plauche Real Estate Company

249 La. 85, 185 So. (2d) 210 (1966)

Supreme Court of Louisiana

This was an action by Stan A. Plauche Real Estate Company, Inc. (plaintiff) against Jacob J. Kuhn et al. (defendants). Judgment for plaintiff and defendants appealed. Judgment reversed.

SUMMERS, J. On January 4, 1962, Matrana signed an offer to sell the property in question for "$43,000 net to owner" under credit terms providing that Matrana was to receives notes for the credit portion of the sale. No loan needed to be negotiated with others. Under this agreement Matrana was to pay the Plauche firm a commission equal to the difference between $43,000 and the actual price at which the Plauche firm could sell the property.

On the same day, in a separate instrument, the Plauche firm obtained the signature of Jacob J. Kuhn to an agreement to purchase the property for the sum of $52,000, on credit terms which were stipulated. A deposit by the purchaser of 10% of the purchase price, or $5,200, was required, which could be declared forfeited in the event the purchaser (Kuhn) failed to comply with the agreement to purchase.

Several days later Kuhn deposited the $5,200 required by the Agreement.

It then became known to the Plauche firm that Matrana had only a Bond for Deed whereby he was to purchase the property; and that since executing the Bond for Deed on October 17, 1952, his wife had died, and his two minor daughters became vested with a one-half interest in the Bond for Deed. It was necessary, therefore, in order to tender a merchantable title to the prospective purchaser (Kuhn), that Matrana, as tutor of his minor children, obtain court authorization to sell the property under the terms and conditions of the "Agreement to Purchase" signed by Kuhn and accepted by him. Accordingly a petition was addressed to the appropriate court seeking the necessary authorization. But, due to ex parte declarations of the judge to the effect that the commission was too much, and due also to the fact that the judge felt that the property was worth more than $52,000 (based on an appraisal which he had caused to be made), the petition seeking the authorization was withdrawn.

The time allowed for tendering a merchantable title under the "Agreement to Purchase" of January 4, 1962, having expired, Kuhn instituted suit against the Plauche firm and Matrana for the return of the $5,200 deposit held by Plauche. Plauche then reconvened against Kuhn and filed a cross claim against Matrana, alleging a breach of the contract by one or the other, or, alternatively, that it was entitled to a commission of $9,000, with interest, costs and attorney's fees. The reconventional demand was dismissed as to Kuhn, and there was judgment in his favor for the amount of the deposit—$5,200. Although he was represented by counsel at the time, Matrana did not appear in person or testify in his own behalf; and judgment was rendered in favor of the Plauche firm for the commission of $9,000, plus $1,500 attorneys' fees and costs.

Matrana's appeal to the Fourth Circuit resulted in an affirmance of the trial court judgment.

We granted certiorari on Matrana's application, 248 La. 438, 179 So. (2d) 275.

In his concise brief to this court Matrana's counsel argues simply that no commission was due to be paid until the act of sale took place, and, as there was no sale, no commission was due.

This position is based upon certain language of the agreement dated January 4, 1962, whereby Matrana agreed to pay all monies of the selling price above $43,000 as commission—this agreement having been incorporated by reference into the contract which Matrana accepted. The printed portion of the agreement in question, insofar as it affects Matrana's contention here, provides: "If this offer is accepted, seller agrees to pay the agent a commission of *all monies above $43,000.00* of the selling price, which commission is earned by agent when this agreement is signed by both parties and when the mortgage loan(s) if any, has been secured. Either party hereto who fails to comply with the terms of this offer, if accepted, or who fails to cooperate with Stan A. Plauche Real Estate, Inc., in securing the mortgage loan, is obligated and agrees to pay the agent's commission and all fees and costs incurred in enforcing collections and damages." (Italicized portion typewritten.)

Appearing in the document as the final stipulation after the entire printed portion is the following typewritten sentence: "*Seller agrees to pay the agent at the act of sale the amount of the commission in cash.*"

As we understand counsel's argument on behalf of Matrana this final typed sentence supersedes anything to the contrary in the printed portion of the contract. A fair reading of the sentence, he says, permits the interpretation that the commission, because it was payable "at the act of sale," was not due until the sale took place. As no sale did take place, the condition upon which the payment of the commission was predicated did not occur; and, therefore no commission could be collected.

Under elementary principles of interpretation of contracts, the written portions prevail over the printed portions when the two are in conflict; and, therefore, we find no difficulty in holding that the typewritten sentence providing that the commission would be paid "at the act of sale" supersedes the printed clause providing that the commission is earned when the offer is accepted. *Dean v. Pisciotta*, 220 La. 725, 57 So. (2d) 591 (1952) and authorities therein cited. This reasoning leaves only the provision which is typewritten remaining. As we have already observed, because the agreement is to pay the agent "at the act of sale" it is premature to demand payment before that time.

For the reasons assigned, the judgment is annulled, reversed and set aside.

Discharge

15

CONDITIONS

A promise given by a party under a contract imposes upon him a legal duty or obligation to do or refrain from doing something. Under the terms of the contract, or by implication, such an obligation may be either absolute or conditional. If the obligation is absolute, it must be performed, unless excused, and failure to perform constitutes a breach of contract. If the obligation to perform is contingent upon the happening or nonhappening of some future act or event, the promise is held to be conditional. While every contract contains a promise, not every contract contains a condition.

There are three types of conditions: (1) conditions precedent, (2) conditions subsequent, and (3) conditions concurrent.

CONDITIONS PRECEDENT

In the case of a condition precedent, the promisor obligates himself to perform a designated act or forbearance upon the happening of a specified event. He makes a conditional promise which becomes absolute when the condition is fulfilled; if it is not fulfilled, he is discharged of all liability under his promise. For example, A, a building contractor, contracts to employ B as a foreman in the construction of an apartment house if A is awarded a contract to erect the apartment house. The awarding of the contract to A is a condition precedent to his duty to employ B as a foreman. If A is not successful in securing the construction contract, he will be discharged of any liability to B under his contract of employment with B.

A common example of a condition precedent is a building contract which contains a provision that the contractor is not to receive final payment until a designated architect or engineer has approved the building and has issued a certificate that the building has been erected according to the terms and specifications of the contract. The approval and certificate of the architect or engineer constitutes a condition precedent to the legal duty of the promisor to make final payment to the contractor. As a general rule the courts will enforce such provisions. They are waived or excused only when the architect dies, becomes insane or otherwise incapacitated, is guilty of collusion or fraud, or has made a gross mistake in his calculations or facts.

CONDITIONS SUBSEQUENT

In the case of a condition subsequent, the fulfillment of a designated condition has the effect of discharging one of the parties to the contract from his duty to perform. In other words, the contracting party is under a duty to perform if the designated condition is not fulfilled; if it is, he is discharged of his liability under the contract. For example, A sells B a television set on the condition that if B does not like it he may return it within ten days and get his money back. Another common example is a lease which contains a provision that it may be terminated by 30-day written notice of either party to the other.

Manufacturers, builders, and carriers often insert in their contracts certain conditional or protective provisions which have the effect of relieving them from liability or discharging them from their contractual obligations in case of fire, windstorms, strikes, collisions, and the like. Under such contracts they are bound to perform unless one of the specified hazards or events takes place. Such conditions in contracts are conditions subsequent.

CONDITIONS CONCURRENT

If, under the terms of a contract, the performance on each side of the contract is conditional upon simultaneous performance on the other side, the conditions are concurrent. Before either party can put the other party in default, he must *make tender of performance.*[1] Such conditions may be expressly stated in the contract or implied from the nature of the contract or from usage or custom. They are common in business contracts. For example, A contracts to sell certain goods to B for cash. The delivery of the goods by A and the payment of the cash by B are concurrent conditions.

Conditions of any type may be either express or implied.

[1] See below, pp. 278–279.

Rotermund v. United States Steel Corporation

474 F. (2d) 1139 (1973)

United States Court of Appeals

This was an action by officer of materials company and against steel company seeking, inter alia, specific performance of an alleged agreement to purchase certain shares of stock in materials company from plaintiff officer. The United States District Court . . . entered summary [Judgment] in favor of defendants, and plaintiff appealed.

Affirmed.

STEPHENSON, J. The 1965 agreement provides that an option to purchase the Powell shares by USS could not be made pursuant to the terms thereof unless: (1) Powell died, or (2) Powell retired from the management of Basic, or (3) the book value of stock would become less than a specified standard. The record before us indicates that none of these conditions precedent had occurred. Thus, no present obligation to Rotermund as a third-party beneficiary had been breached, and USS, therefore, is not obligated to purchase Rotermund's stock under the 1965 agreement.

Inasmuch as the trial court based its determination of defendants' motion for summary judgment solely upon the terms of the 1965 agreement as originally drawn and relied upon by Rotermund, we hold that the trial court did not err in determining it unnecesary to decide whether the 1965 agreement could be amended without Rotermund's consent insofar as it affects his rights as a third-party beneficiary.

Rotermund's rights under the 1965 agreement are based wholly upon the rights of Powell thereunder. The 1965 agreement relied upon by Rotermund provides in Section 10 that USS would be obligated to purchase Rotermund's stock upon condition that USS first exercise its option to purchase *all* Powell's shares pursuant to the 1965 agreement. As we have determined, it is evident from this record that none of the triggering circumstances enumerated under Sections 5 and 6 had taken place: Powell had not died, nor had he retired, nor had the book value of the stock fallen below the given standard. Moreover, Section 10 of the 1968 amendment expressly states that the purchase of 25,000 shares of Powell's stock by USS would not be construed as constituting a "purchase" within the meaning of Section 10 of the 1965 agreement. Since Powell was not entitled to compel USS to purchase all his common shares of Basic stock, Rotermund is in no better position. . . . Consequently, Rotermund cannot now force upon USS a purchase of his 2,000 shares. Affirmed.

Lowe v. Copeland

125 Cal. App. 315, 13 P. (2d) 522 (1932)

This was an action by Leonard Lowe, Jr. (plaintiff) against Francis C. Copeland and others (defendants). Judgment for defendants, and plaintiff appealed. Affirmed.

This action was one for equitable relief, namely, a decree declaring the plaintiff to be the owner of certain shares of stock in defendant American Metal Products Corporation and enjoining defendants Copeland and the Cig-a-Lite Corporation from transferring certain patent rights.

Defendant Copeland was the inventor of various cigar- and cigarette-lighting devices, and the holder of certain patents and applications for patents for such devices. He organized defendant Cig-a-Lite Corporation, in which he owned a majority of the stock. On March 25, 1927, plaintiff entered into a contract with Copeland and the Cig-a-Lite Corporation by which the latter two agreed to transfer the patent rights to said devices to a corporation to be organized under the laws of Nevada, in which Copeland should own 51% of the stock and act as president. In consideration of the issuance to him of 44% of the stock of the Nevada corporation, plaintiff agreed to advance to this company in cash from time to time as needed sums not to exceed $44,000. This promise was evidenced by a note, and considered as his subscription for the stock mentioned. It was also agreed that no contract involving more than $500 should be entered into by the Nevada corporation without the approval of defendant Copeland; further, that the transfers of the patent rights to the company were to be subject to the condition that it should manufacture and sell at least 5,000 of the devices during each calendar year, and that if it failed to do so, then upon demand the said patent rights should be reassigned. The Nevada corporation was organized and the patent rights were assigned to it.

The complaint alleged that plaintiff executed and paid said note, and in accordance with said contract became the owner of said stock, which had not been issued to him, although demand therefore had been made; that good and reasonable offers were made to the Nevada corporation for the manufacture and sale of said devices, but that defendant Copeland without good cause refused to approve the same and thus obstructed and prevented the manufacture and sale of said devices by the Nevada corporation; that as a result this company failed to manufacture and sell the number of said devices agreed upon within the time fixed in the contract, following which Copeland and the Cig-a-Lite Corporation gave notice on that ground of their election to terminate the contract, and demanded a reassignment of the patent rights. The complaint contained further allegations that Copeland by virtue of his majority interest in the stock of the Nevada company controlled the action of its board of directors. Plaintiff prayed that he be declared the owner of the stock mentioned, and that Copeland and the Cig-a-Lite Corporation be restrained from reassigning the patent rights; that the Nevada corporation be relieved from the condition in said contract; and that a receiver of its business be appointed.

PER CURIAM. We are satisfied that there was sufficient evidence to support the finding that the defendant Copeland, in rejecting the offers mentioned, did not act arbitrarily or in bad faith. Fairness in business transactions is presumed, and, the question being one of fact, provable both by direct and circumstantial evidence, and there being evidence in the record which the trial court believed reasonably sufficient to support its conclusion, its finding on this issue cannot be disturbed.

That title to the patents and patent rights mentioned passed by assignment to the Nevada corporation subject to a condition subsequent is plain from the provisions of the contract, and in such cases title remains in the assignee until the forfeiture is enforced. A condition subsequent refers to a future event upon the happening of which the obligation becomes no longer binding on the party in whose favor the condition was created if he chooses to enforce it.

We have examined the evidence, and are satisfied that the findings of the court are fairly supported, and that no sufficient ground for reversing the judgment has been shown. Judgment affirmed.

THE MEANING OF DISCHARGE

When a valid contract has been created, it continues to exist until it is discharged by some happening which is held by law to be sufficient to terminate its existence. Under some circumstances the entire contract is discharged, and the obligations of both parties to the contract are terminated. Under other circumstances only one of the contracting parties is discharged of his obligations under the instrument; where this takes place, usually the injured party has a cause of action against the other party by way of damages for the breach of the contract.

Contracts may be discharged (1) by performance; (2) by agreement of the parties; (3) by impossibility of performance; (4) by operation of law.

DISCHARGE BY PERFORMANCE

If both parties to a contract fully and completely perform all of their duties in accordance with the terms of the contract, the liabilities of the parties are extinguished and the contract is discharged. If one party has performed and the other party has not performed, the contract is not discharged, but the party who has performed is discharged from his liabilities under the contract and has a cause of action against the defaulting party for breach of contract.

SUBSTANTIAL PERFORMANCE

Under the early common law, the express stipulations of the contract were required to be fully and strictly performed. However, the equity courts did not require literal performance in all types of cases. As a result, today our courts recognize and apply to many contractual situations what is known as the *doctrine of substantial performance*. In certain agreements where literal or complete performance is impossible or would result in great hardship, the courts do not require complete performance but will allow recovery of the contract price less the amount of the damages suffered by the other party by reason of the incomplete performance. However, before the courts will allow such recovery the plaintiff must show that he acted in good faith and that his deviation from the terms of the contract is not great, but, on the contrary, is capable of being remedied. The doctrine of substantial performance is particularly applicable to construction and building contracts.

The doctrine of substantial performance will not be applied to cases where it is possible to render strict or full performance. For example, if A owes B $100, his obligation is capable of full performance by his paying B the $100 when due and consequently the courts would not accept payment of $90 as substantial performance of the contract. Or if A agrees to sell B 100 shares of stock of the X Corporation, and the X Corporation's stock is listed on a stock exchange and may be obtained without difficulty, A's obligation to deliver the stock, as agreed, is capable of full performance, and therefore anything less than full performance would not suffice.

Cassinelli et al. v. Stacy
238 Ky. 827, 38 S. W. (2d) 980 (1931)

This was an action by Troy Stacy (plaintiff) against Peter Cassinelli (defendant). Judgment for plaintiff, and defendant appealed. Reversed and remanded with directions.

This action was instituted to recover the balance of $789.33, alleged to be due under a contract for the construction of a building, to be used as a theater. The contract provided that for $7,000 to be paid the plaintiff, plaintiff was to furnish the material and labor necessary to complete the building according to the plans and specifications which were made a part of the contract. In this action plaintiff alleged that he completed the building according to the terms of the contract and brought this action to recover the balance due of $789.33.

Defendant contended that the building was not constructed according to the terms of the contract and presented a counterclaim.

The evidence showed that there were a number of important deviations from the terms of the contract, and that some of the work called for in the contract was not done at all. A. L. Ware, an engineer and architect, testified in detail relative to the differences between the building called for by the plans and specifications and that which, in fact, plaintiff erected, and estimated that the building could be corrected for the sum of $2,299.00.

Plaintiff contended that there was substantial performance.

RICHARDSON, J. It cannot be said that the appellee (plaintiff) has literally performed his written contract according to the plans and specifications or that he has substantially performed it. It is established by the evidence that he did not substantially perform the written contract and erect the building according to the plans and specifications. Originally, at common law it was the rule that a literal performance with respect to building contracts was applied in such cases. This rule has been changed to the extent of allowing the equitable doctrine relating to substantial performance to be applied.

Two reasons are given by the courts for the rule that a substantial performance for a building contract will support a recovery. One is that it is next to impossible for a builder to comply with all the minute specifications in a building contract. The other is that in the erection of a building on the lot of the owner, such owner must receive the benefit of the contractor's labor and materials, and it is therefore deemed equitable to require him to pay for what he gets. *Jackson Lumber & Supply Co. v. Deaton*, 209 Ky. 239, 272 S. W. 717. The rule of substantial performance cannot be invoked where the defects in the construction or the omissions from the requirements set forth in the building contract are intentional, and not the result of an attempt in good faith to perform the contract. *Brown v. Kimball*, 203 Mass. 364, 89 N. E. 542. But an intentional omission to do certain things called for by the contract, if the contractor believes they are not required of him, and intends in good faith to do all that he has agreed to do, does not prevent the application of the doctrine of substantial performance from controlling his rights and remedies. The doctrine of substantial performance permits the builder to recover on the entire building contract if the work has been done under a building contract, but is defectively done, allowing damages for incompleteness. The measure of recovery for a breach of the contract by the builder in such event is the difference between the contract price of the building constructed according to the contract, and its reasonable value as it is at the date of completion. But, if any work or material required by the contract has been omitted, and same may be done or furnished at reasonable cost, in that event the measure of recovery is the cost of doing the work or furnishing the material so omitted

On consideration of the evidence we are convinced by the preponderance of the evidence that the lower court erred, and that the defendant, on the proven facts and principles of law enunciated in the cases, is entitled to a judgment for the reasonable cost of correcting the defects and supplying the omissions in the building. as it was constructed. The estimation of the amount necessary to accomplish this is fixed, by uncontroverted evidence, at the sum of $2,299.00. Giving plaintiff the benefit of the items which Cassinelli agreed for the plaintiff to correct and then would "pay-off," and considering his admission that he consented for "the machine booth to be moved from left to right, and the change in the placing of the front window," on this account, we reduce the amount fixed by the engineer, Ware, $299.00, thus fixing the amount of defendant's recovery, on his counterclaim, at $2,000, less $789.33, the balance claimed to be due by plaintiff on the contract.

Reversed and remanded, and judgment will be entered consistent with this opinion.

Johnson et al. v. Fehsefeldt

106 Minn. 202, 118 N. E. 707 (1908)

This was an action by Harold Johnson and others (plaintiffs) against John Fehsefeldt (defendant). Judgment for plaintiffs, and defendant appealed. Reversed.

Plaintiffs, who were owners of a threshing outfit, entered into a verbal agreement with defendant to thresh defendant's grain, for which defendant agreed to pay the sum of 10¢ a bushel for wheat, 6¢ a bushel for oats, and 15¢ a bushel for flax. Pursuant to the agreement plaintiffs threshed a portion of the crop. Before the entire crop had been threshed plaintiffs hauled their threshing machine away from defendant's premises and refused to thresh more for the reason that they were losing money. Plaintiffs filed this action to recover for the grain which they threshed. They contended that the case involved an agreement to thresh grain at so much per bushel. Defendant maintained that the agreement was to thresh all of his crop of grain.

The lower court directed a verdict for plaintiffs for the work and threshing they had done at the agreed price per bushel, and defendant brought this appeal.

JAGGARD, J. The essential question is whether the contract was entire and indivisible, in the sense that the plaintiffs could not recover upon a quantum meruit or upon the contract to the extent to which it had been performed. On principle we are of the opinion that the plaintiffs could not recover. When they found that they were operating at a loss, they had the option to complete the contract, recover the contract price, and submit to the loss, or to abandon the contract, lose the work they had done, and be subject to whatever damages might be recoverable for the breach of the contract. The fact that the plaintiffs had rendered services, the value of which defendant retained, did not entitle the plaintiffs to recover on quantum meruit because of the contract and of the inability of defendants to return the services. As the court said, in *Galvin v. Prentice*, 45 N. Y. 162, "When the contract is entire, and one party is willing to complete the performance and is not in default, no promise can be implied on his part to compensate the other party for a part performance. Certainly it must be so where the failure to fully perform is due wholly to the fault of such other party."

It would be obviously inconsistent with common justice that the plaintiffs should recover on the contract which they had substantially violated. They were in the wrong. They were not in a position to say to the defendant: "We will perform the contract we have agreed to if it proves profitable. If we find it unprofitable we will abandon it." Defendant did not agree in advance to a breach of the contract and to accept in lieu of performance the requirement that he pay the plaintiffs what they had done under the contract and for the balance to accept the right to try damages before a jury. It is well settled in this state that the failure to perform an entire contract ordinarily defeats the right to recover on the contract. Atwater, J., said in *Mason v. Heyward*,

3 Minn. 182: "Where a party willfully, or without cause, refuses to complete a contract which he has made, and upon the execution of which he has entered, courts should never interfere to protect him from the consequences of his own wrong." It is true that where, as in building contracts, there is a substantial performance, the court will not permit the owner of the land to retain the fruits of the labor and refuse to pay for it. It is equally clear, however, that where there has been an intentional failure to complete the contract, or a departure so substantial as to be incapable of a remedy, there can be no partial recovery.

"A partial performance may be a defense pro tanto, or it may sustain an action pro tanto; but this can be only in cases where the duty to be done consists of parts which are distinct and severable in their own nature, and are not bound together by expressions giving entirety to the contract. It is not enough that the duty to be done is in itself severable, if the contract contemplated it only as a whole. The mere fact that . . . the value is ascertained by the price affixed to each pound, or yard, or bushel of the quantity contracted for will not be sufficient to render the contract severable." Parsons, *Contracts*, p. 517.

Reversed and a new trial granted.

PERFORMANCE TO SATISFACTION OF PROMISEE

At times contracts provide that one of the contracting parties is to perform to the entire satisfaction of the other party. The courts have divided such contracts into two groups: (1) contracts wherein personal taste, fancy, judgment, or sensibility is involved; (2) contracts wherein operative fitness or mechanical utility is involved.

In the first group of cases, the courts quite generally take the parties at their word and require that performance be to the entire satisfaction of the promisee. However, the promisee is required to act in good faith; fraud on his part would waive the condition. His dissatisfaction must be real and not feigned. A and B enter into a contract whereby A agrees to paint B's portrait and B agrees to pay A $2,000 if the portrait is entirely satisfactory to him. When A has completed his work, B refuses to accept and pay for the portrait, for he maintains that a poor job has been done and that he is not satisfied with the work. If A should sue B for the $2,000, he could not recover unless he could show that B was not acting in good faith or was guilty of fraud. It would not aid A in his suit to obtain the testimony of other artists to the effect that a satisfactory job had been done. The test, in such a case, is not whether a good job has been done, but whether the promisee is satisfied.

Where operative fitness or mechanical utility is involved, a different test is applied, namely, that of a reasonable man. A and B enter into a contract whereby A agrees to air-condition B's house for $2,000. The contract further provides that the work is to be done to the entire satisfaction of B. After A has completed the job, B says that he is not entirely satisfied with the work and refuses to pay A, and A sues for the $2,000.

The test applied in such a case is whether a reasonable man would be satisfied with the job done by A. This is a question of fact for the jury to decide. The courts say that personal taste or fancy is not involved in such cases. Consequently, if A is able to prove, by competent witnesses, that a satisfactory job was done, and if the jury believe that a reasonable man should be satisfied, A would be able to recover a judgment for the contract price of $2,000.

Duplex Safety Boiler Co. v. Garden
101 N. Y. 387, 4 N. E. 749 (1886)

This was an action by the Duplex Safety Boiler Co. (plaintiff) against one Garden (defendant). Judgment for plaintiff, and defendant appealed. Affirmed.

Plaintiff sued to recover $700, the agreed price, as it alleged, for materials furnished and work done for defendant, at his request, upon certain boilers belonging to him. The defense set up was that the work was done under a written contract for the alteration of the boilers, and to be paid for only when defendant "was satisfied that the boilers, as changed, were a success."

The evidence showed that plaintiff completed the required work, within the specified time, and that defendant used the boilers after they were altered and repaired.

DANFORTH, J. The contention on the part of the defendant is that the plaintiff was entitled to no compensation, unless the defendant "was satisfied that the boilers, as repaired, were a success, and that this question was for the defendant alone to determine"; thus making his obligation depend upon his mental condition, which he alone could disclose. Performance must, of course, accord with the terms of the contract; but if the defendant is at liberty to determine for himself when he is satisfied, there would be no obligation, and consequently no agreement which could be enforced. It cannot be presumed that the plaintiff entered upon its work with this understanding, nor that the defendant supposed he was to be the sole judge in his own cause.

In the case before us, the work required to be done was specified, and was completed. The plaintiff repaired the boilers, and the defendant continued to use them without objection or complaint. If there was full performance on the plaintiff's part, nothing could be required, and the time for payment had arrived.

Another rule has prevailed where the object of a contract was to gratify taste, serve personal convenience, or satisfy individual preference. In either of these cases the person for whom the article is made, or the work done, may properly determine for himself—if the other party so agrees—whether it shall be accepted. One who makes a suit of clothes, or paints a portrait, may not unreasonably be expected to be bound by the opinion of his employer, honestly entertained. A different case is before us, and in regard to it no error has been shown. Judgment for the plaintiff affirmed.

TIME OF PERFORMANCE

If a contract does not provide that performance is to take place upon a certain date or within a specified time, it is implied that performance must occur within a reasonable time. What constitutes a reasonable time depends upon the nature of the subject matter of the contract. A reasonable time for the delivery of perishable goods would be much less than a reasonable time for the payment of money.

It was held at common law that if a contract fixed a definite time for performance, failure to perform on the date specified constituted a breach of the contract. Equity courts, however, modified this rule. They went back of the specific time stated in the contract to ascertain the real intentions of the parties. As a result, courts today generally hold that performance on the date specified is not per se a condition precedent, though it may be made one by the terms of the contract. It is not unusual for contracts to provide that *time is of the essence.* The courts usually recognize such express provisions as creating a condition precedent, but in some cases courts of equity have refused to do so, because they felt that the consequence would be to work hardship and injustice. On the other hand, it is not always necessary for such intent to be expressly stated in the contract. Under certain types of contracts it will be implied. This is particularly true in mercantile contracts, contracts involving perishable goods, contracts involving property of which the market value fluctuates rapidly, like corporate securities, and contracts for the payment of debts. For example, A, the owner of a retail store, places an order with B in September for a quantity of toys, to be delivered not later than November 1st. B knows that A wants the toys for the Christmas trade. The contract does not state that "time is of the essence." The toys are not delivered until January 1st. In such a case the court would imply that the parties intended that time was of the essence of the contract and would hold that A was completely discharged of his obligations under the contract. Furthermore, B would be liable to A for damages for the breach of the contract.

Neumann et al. v. Gorak et al.

11 N. W. (2d) 155, 243 Wis. 503 (1943)

This was an action by Herman E. Neumann and others (plaintiffs) against Thomas Gorak, Jr. and others (defendants) for specific performance of a contract for the sale of real estate. From a decree dismissing the complaint plaintiffs appealed. Judgment affirmed.

On October 11, 1941, plaintiffs and defendants entered into a contract for the purchase and sale of certain real estate. Plaintiffs made a down payment of $100. After reciting the terms of sale the contract provided that the transaction was "to be closed on or before November 1, 1941, or the above sum paid may be retained at their [defendants'] option. . . ." Plaintiffs had to negotiate a loan in order to complete the transaction for the purchase of defendants' property. The proceeds of the loan were not available until November 5, 1941—four days after the expiration of the contract. Plaintiffs requested an extension of the time to close the transaction but defendants refused to extend the time. On several occasions toward the end of October the real estate broker and plaintiffs' counsel called plaintiffs' attention to the expiration date of the contract and urged that they be prepared to close the transaction on or before November 1st. Plaintiffs delayed making application for the loan until October 30th.

Plaintiffs contended that if specific performance was not had they were entitled to damages for breach of contract; and that if both reliefs were denied they were entitled to recover the down payment of $100. Their principal contention was that time was not of the essence of the contract.

MARTIN, J. If time was of the essence of the contract the judgment must be affirmed. The trial court's decision and finding were grounded on the theory that time was of the essence of the contract. It is clear that the real estate broker and the plaintiffs' counsel considered time as of the essence of the contract. Counsel endeavored to get an extension of the time within which to close the transaction. In *James v. Knox*, 155 Wis. 118, 143 N. W. 1071, the court, speaking of the provision in a contract fixing the date for closing the transaction, said: "These are plain words, and clearly indicate an intention by both parties that the deal should be fully closed on or before the date specified. That both parties so understood it is also clearly manifest from the evidence of plaintiff, E. W. James, that on or before March first the defendant sought to have him sign a paper extending the time of performance of the agreement to March 11, 1912 (the date set in the contract was March 1st), which he refused to do. . . . In view of the provisions of the agreement, and the evidence, the trial court properly held that time was of the essence of the contract. . . ."

We are of the opinion that the findings of the trial court, in the case at bar, are amply sustained by the evidence. Judgment affirmed.

Sunshine Cloak & Suit Co. v. Roquette et al.
30 N. D. 143, 152 N. W. 359 (1915)

This was an action by the Sunshine Cloak & Suit Co. (plaintiff) against Roquette et al. (defendants) to recover $173.25. Judgment for defendants, and plaintiff appealed. Judgment affirmed.

The complaint alleged that on March 24, 1911, defendants purchased certain ladies' cloaks and coats to be manufactured by plaintiff, and to be delivered by August 15, 1911; that the agreed and reasonable price was $173.25, which defendants agreed to pay upon delivery; that plaintiff did manufacture and deliver the said cloaks and coats to defendants on September 28, 1911, and that defendants did not pay for them.

Defendants answered that the goods were not delivered in accordance with the contract; that they were ordered for the fall trade of 1911, and plaintiff agreed to deliver for said trade; that owing to the negligence of plaintiff the goods were delivered too late for the fall trade; and that upon receipt defendants immediately returned the cloaks and coats to plaintiff, who accepted and retained them.

Plaintiff contended that time was not of the essence of the contract; and that the date of shipment was immaterial and hence defendants were not relieved from the contract by plaintiff's late shipment, but that the remedy of defendants was to bring an action for damages sustained.

The evidence showed that the goods were shipped by plaintiff on September 28, 1911, by freight, and were not received by defendants until October 11, 1911.

CHRISTIANSON, J. It is doubtless true, as plaintiff contends, that time is never considered as of the essence of a contract, unless by its terms it is clearly so provided. In fact, that is a statutory provision in this state. However, still it is not necessary to declare in so many words "that time is of the essence of the contract," but it is sufficient if it appears that it was the intention of the parties that time should be of the essence thereof. The rule is stated in *Benjamin on Sales* as follows: "In determining whether stipulations as to the time of performing a contract of sale are conditions precedent, the court seeks simply to discover what the parties really intended, and if time appears, on a fair consideration of the language and the circumstances, to be of the essence of the contract, stipulations in regard to it will be held conditions precedent." *Benjamin on Sales* (6th Ed.), p. 539.

In the case of *Cleveland Rolling Mill Co. v. Rhodes*, 121 U. S. 255, 7 Sup. Ct. 882, 30 L. Ed. 920, the Supreme Court of the United States said: "In the contracts of merchants, time is of the essence. . . . A statement descriptive of the subject-matter or of some material incident, such as the time or place of shipment, is ordinarily to be regarded as a warranty, in the sense in which that term is used in insurance and maritime law; that is to say, a condition precedent, upon the failure or nonperformance of which the party aggrieved may repudiate the whole contract."

In 35 *Cyc.* 175, it is said: "If the contract specifies the time when delivery is to be made time is of the essence of the contract, and if delivery is not made within the time agreed on, the buyer is not liable. In such case the buyer may refuse to accept the goods, or he may receive them and rely on his right to damages for the breach, unless his acceptance is under such circumstances as to constitute a waiver of the breach."

We are satisfied that the agreement to ship by August 15th was a condition precedent, and that before plaintiff could insist upon performance, i.e., payment by the defendants, it must be able to prove that it had fulfilled this condition,—at least, substantially so. It seems obvious that shipment made on

September 28th was no substantial compliance with the agreement to make such shipment by August 15th. The purchasers were clearly within their rights in refusing to accept these goods when received; and the delay on the part of plaintiff to make shipment until September 28th was such failure to perform on its part as will prevent a recovery when the purchasers refused to accept the goods.

Judgment for defendants affirmed.

TENDER OF PERFORMANCE

A tender is an offer or attempt by one of the contracting parties to perform his part of the contract. Such tender may involve either (1) the payment of money required under the terms of the contract or (2) the performance of an act called for by the contract, such as the delivery of goods or the performance of services.

If a tender of *money*, properly made in every respect under the terms of the contract, is refused by the creditor, such tender does not discharge the debt or obligation of the debtor to pay the debt, but it will (1) stop the running of interest from the date on which the tender was made, (2) relieve the debtor from the payment of court costs if the creditor should subsequently file suit, and (3) release any security which the debtor may have given the creditor to secure the debt, such as mortgages, deeds of trust, and property pledged as collateral security. On the other hand, an attempted performance of the *acts* called for under the contract, if properly made, will have the effect of discharging the party who makes the tender of performance. For example, A and B enter into a contract whereby A agrees to sell B 100 suits of clothes and B agrees to pay A $2,500 for same, delivery to be made on April 15th. On that date A tenders delivery, but B refuses to accept and pay for the suits. A is discharged from all liability under the contract, and he also has cause of action for damages against B.

In order to make a proper tender in the payment of money due under a contract, the debtor must tender the exact amount due, and the money tendered must be *legal tender*. Under the Emergency Banking Act of 1933 all coins and paper money of the United States are declared to be legal tender. Since checks are not legal tender they do not constitute payment and do not discharge a debt unless they are accepted by the creditor as payment of the debt. Unless otherwise agreed to by the parties, acceptance of a check is conditional and does not discharge the obligation until the check is honored and paid by the drawee bank.

Steele v. Northup
143 N. W. (2d) 302 (1966)

This was an action by Emanuel E. Steele and Marjorie K. Steele, husband and wife (plaintiffs) against Harry Northup (defendant). Judgment for plaintiffs and defendant appealed. Judgment affirmed.

Plaintiffs brought an action in equity claiming they had given adequate timely notice of intent to exercise a repurchase option but performance was prevented by conduct of defendant, asked for accounting, extension of payment date, and that defendant be enjoined from forfeiting their option rights. The trial court granted relief and defendant appeals.

RAWLINGS, J. On February 4, 1962, plaintiffs talked with defendant about three hours, told him they wanted to know the amount owing so payment could be made and their farm deal settled according to the option. Part of the 1961 corn crop was still in the field. Defendant finally produced a book showing the year's receipts and disbursements but the entries were neither accurate nor complete.

Defendant says he then estimated there was about $5000 owing. In any event he admittedly could not and did not then tell plaintiffs the actual amount due. He finally told them, "we have plenty of time left before the first of March" and he would "get to work on the books in a few days."

On February 21, 1962, plaintiffs made arrangements through a bank to secure the money with which to pay defendant but were never advised by him as to the amount owing.

This action was commenced February 23, 1962. The option exercise date was extended to March 1, 1965, by order of court. Although the reason for this stay of almost three years is not disclosed we, in this case, shall assume it was unavoidable.

After an accounting the trial court ultimately concluded there was owing to defendant the sum of $3,453.48. On October 28, 1964, plaintiffs deposited this sum with the Clerk of Court, gave to defendant formal notice the option had been exercised and the amount due tendered.

On appeal defendant contends, (1) plaintiffs' option rights were forfeited by their failure to effectively act within the time agreed upon, and (2) they were not excused from tendering the purchase money prior to the agreed option expiration date. We find neither substance nor merit in these claims.

Our first question is whether plaintiffs effectively expressed an intent and desire to exercise their option rights.

Stated otherwise, did plaintiffs give defendant an unqualified, proper and timely notice of intention to redeem their property? We are satisfied defendant could only reasonably conclude plaintiffs not only meant but wanted very much to exercise the option.

The next question to be resolved is whether plaintiffs made tender of the amount due within the prescribed option period, and if not were they excused?

The factual situation need not be repeated at length. It is to us evident that under the terms and conditions of the assignment, the option and existing facts, payment was a condition subsequent.

Furthermore, it is apparent the terms of the option, together with defendant's conduct, served to excuse plaintiffs from making tender prior to the option expiration date. In fact, any attempt to effect a tender would have been futile.

It is a general rule that where performance of a contract has been made impossible the law does not require the useless formality of a tender.

It is to us apparent the trial court acted properly in relieving plaintiffs from a forfeiture of their rights under the option and extending the payment date until an accounting by defendant had been effected.

Equity will not knowingly permit a party to benefit by his own delay and mistakes, and abhors forfeitures. *Bentler v. Poulson*, Iowa, 141 N. W. (2d) 551.

There is no basis upon which to conclude other than that plaintiffs were entitled to the relief accorded them by the trial court. Costs are taxed to defendant. Affirmed.

DISCHARGE BY AGREEMENT OF THE PARTIES

There are a number of ways in which the obligations of the parties under a contract may be discharged by agreement of the parties. These methods include (1) mutual rescission, (2) substituted contract, (3) novation, and (4) waiver.

MUTUAL RESCISSION

Since a contract is an agreement voluntarily entered into by the contracting parties, it is entirely logical that they should be permitted to rescind it by mutual agreement. Such an agreement has the effect of discharging both parties of their obligations under the contract.

If the contract is bilateral and wholly executory, an agreement between the parties to discharge each other of their obligations under the contract is valid and binding upon the parties. Sufficient consideration for the new agreement is found in the mutual promises of the parties, by which each party surrenders his legal rights under the old contract. However, if the contract is bilateral and has been executed by one party, an agreement whereby the party who has performed agrees to release the other party from his contractual obligations would not be binding unless supported by some new consideration. New consideration is also required for an agreement to discharge a unilateral contract.[1]

---

[1] In states that still recognize the efficacy of the seal, a rescission agreement in writing and under seal does not require fresh consideration. Also see Sec. 1–107 of the U. C. C.

Kester v. Nelson

92 Mont. 69, 10 P. (2d) 379 (1932)

This was an action by C. H. Kester (plaintiff) against Harvey Nelson (defendant). Judgment for defendant, and plaintiff appealed. Affirmed.

This action was instituted by C. H. Kester, as administrator of the estates of C. B. Rinio and Hans Kristofferson, both deceased, against Harvey Nelson, executor of the last will and testament of James Nelson, deceased, to recover the sum of $2,182.44, the balance alleged to be due from James Nelson on a sale made to him by plaintiff's intestates of certain meat market equipment.

The complaint alleged that on May 1, 1928, plaintiff's intestates sold to James Nelson "meat market equipment consisting of an Armstrong ammonia plant, a five-horsepower electric motor, set of platform scales, two refrigerators, set beam scales, and equipment usual to a meat market . . . for which Nelson agreed to pay the sum of $2,000." Of this amount Nelson made payments from time to time aggregating $120, leaving a balance due and owing to plaintiff's intestates in the amount of $1,880.

Defendant, by answer, denied generally the averments in plaintiff's declaration, and alleged affirmatively that the property described therein was sold to James Nelson for the agreed purchase price of $1,000, and that in September, 1929, the contract was abrogated and rescinded, it being agreed in substitution that the ammonia plant, which constituted the principal item of the chattels involved, should be and remain the property of the seller, to be kept and stored by James Nelson until disposed of, and that the sum of $120 paid by James Nelson under the original contract would be accepted by plaintiff's intestates in full satisfaction for the remainder of the property. Issue was joined by reply, and the cause was tried to a jury, which rendered verdict in favor of defendant. Judgment was duly entered upon the verdict, and the cause was appealed by plaintiff.

GALEN, J. The right of the parties to an executory contract to terminate it by mutual consent exists independently of any agreement permitting them so to do; and it is immaterial whether such termination be characterized as abandonment, mutual rescission, modification, or waiver. The effect is the same, to discharge the parties from obligations previously assumed. *Ogg. v. Herman*, 71 Mont. 10, 227 p. 476.

"Persons competent to contract can as validly agree to rescind a contract already made as they could agree to make it originally. However, as a contract is made by the joint will of two parties, it can be rescinded only by the joint will of the two parties. It is obvious that one of the parties can no more rescind the contract, without the other's express or implied assent, than he alone can make it. But if the parties agree to rescind the contract, and each one gives up the provisions for his benefit, the mutual assent is complete, and the parties are then competent to make any new contract that may suit them." 6 R. C. L., Sec. 304, p. 922. "Again, a contract need not be rescinded by an express agreement to that effect. If the parties to a contract make a new and independent agreement concerning the same matter, and the terms of the latter are so inconsistent with those of the former that they cannot stand together, the latter may be construed to discharge the former." Id. Sec. 307, p. 923.

There can be no question but what a contract may be mutually abandoned or modified by the parties at any stage of performance, and each of the parties released from further obligation on account thereof; that it may be accomplished by parol, and the fact of its having been done established by evidence of the acts and declarations of the parties. *Tompkins v. Davidow,* 27 Cal. App. 27, 149 p. 788.

The modification of the contract of sale or its rescission as respects the ammonia plant was established by the testimony of witnesses as to the oral statements and declarations made by the parties in their lifetime in the presence of witnesses; and, while such testimony is not the most satisfactory, yet by reason of necessity it is admissible.

The evidence presented a question of fact for the jury to decide as to whether the contract of sale was modified or rescinded under proper instructions as to the law. The jury has resolved the question of rescission or modification in favor of the defendant, and we see no reason to disturb the verdict. Judgment affirmed.

SUBSTITUTED CONTRACT

A contract may be discharged by the entrance of the parties into a new contract which is inconsistent with the old one. Such new agreement must be supported by a valid consideration. If only some of the terms of the new contract are inconsistent with the old contract, the old contract is discharged only to the extent that the new contract is inconsistent with it. For example, A employs B, a contractor, to build a house for $12,000. When the house is half finished, B finds that, owing to the increased cost of materials and labor, he will lose money if he completes the house for $12,000. After discussing the matter, the parties enter into a new contract whereby A agrees to pay B an additional $2,000 if B will complete the house. If the new agreement is supported by sufficient consideration—if, for example, B agrees to do a little more than he agreed to do under the original contract—the original contract will be discharged to the extent to which the terms of the two contracts are inconsistent. In such cases it is probably best for the parties to rescind the old agreement by mutual assent and then to enter into a new contract.

Riverside Coal Company v. American Coal Company
107 Conn. 40, 139 Atl. 276 (1927)

This was an action by the Riverside Coal Company (plaintiff) against the American Coal Company (defendant) for the purchase price of coke sold and delivered. Judgment for plaintiff for part of the amount prayed for, and plaintiff appealed. Judgment affirmed.

The complaint alleged that on or about February 1, 1926, defendant contracted to purchase from plaintiff 1500 tons of Scotch coke, to be imported by plaintiff, at a price of $12 per ton. The coke was to be unloaded at New Haven and shipped by rail to defendant at Hartford. Delivery was to be made during the month of February. The complaint further alleged that plaintiff imported the coke and shipped it to defendant, whereby defendant became obligated to pay plaintiff $17,966.40, less an advance payment of $2,000.

Defendant denied all the allegations except that certain coke was shipped to it. Defendant alleged, as a defense, that under the contract of February 1st the coke was to arrive at Hartford sometime in February but the boat carrying the coke did not arrive at New Haven until March 8th; that a dispute arose because of the delay in arrival and on March 17th the parties executed a new contract with regard to the purchase and sale of the coke; and that under this new agreement defendant was to accept delivery of the coke at New Haven and was to pay plaintiff at the rate of $6.50 per ton for the coke.

The lower court gave judgment to plaintiff for $7,441.05, and plaintiff appealed.

HINMAN, J. The court refers to the transaction as a "novation," which term is usually used with reference to instances in which a new party is introduced into the new contract, while "substituted contract" is the designation commonly employed to cover agreements between the same parties which supersede and discharge prior contract obligations. There is, however, no distinction so far as concerns the legal effect.

We think that the language of the second contract is, of itself, clearly sufficient to place it in the category of substitute contracts. Its plain intent and effect is that instead of the February arrangement therein described, by which the plaintiff agreed to sell and the defendant agreed to buy the specified quantity of coke at $12 per ton, delivered at Hartford, the same parties agreed to sell and to buy, respectively, a like quantity, but at a price of $6.50 per ton (instead of the $12 called for by the first agreement), delivery to be at New Haven (instead of at Hartford), and making provisions concerning payment of freight, division of demurrage, and other incidents of the transaction not present in the first agreement. Being thus "made by the same parties, but containing terms inconsistent with the former contract so that the two cannot stand together," it exhibits the characteristics and responds to recognized tests indicating a substitute contract. Furthermore, we think that an intent that the agreement to so sell and buy, on the substituted terms, shall discharge the prior contract and all claims and demands growing out of it is unmistakably expressed by the language used.

The nature and effect of the second contract as alleged and claimed by the defendant is, therefore, borne out by the writing itself, to the exclusion of the interpretation claimed by the plaintiff and upon which the efficacy of its demurrer depends. Moreover, the defenses are to be tested, on demurrer, not only by the writing itself, but also by the facts which are provable under their allegations and which elucidate the making and the meaning of the writing.

As a general rule, when the new contract is in regard to the same matter and has the same scope as the earlier contract and the terms of the two are inconsistent either in whole or in a substantial part, so that they cannot subsist together, the new contract abrogates the earlier in toto and takes its place, even though there is no express agreement that the new contract shall have that effect. Judgment affirmed.

NOVATION

A novation, as we have already seen, takes place when a new party is substituted for one of the original parties to a contract. The party thus replaced is discharged of his obligations under the contract, and these are assumed instead by the substitute party. For example, A leases B's house for a year. After six months A has to leave the city and wishes to be relieved of his liability under the lease. His friend C would like to occupy the house and is willing to assume A's responsibility under the lease. A, B, and C thereupon enter into an agreement whereby B agrees to release A from all liability under the lease and to substitute C in A's place, and C agrees to assume A's liability under the lease. Under this agreement A's obligations under the lease are completely discharged. To be valid, a novation agreement must have the assent of all the parties.

WAIVER

A waiver is the voluntary relinquishment by one party of some right which he has under the contract. A waiver may be express or implied. For example, A and B enter into a contract wherein A agrees to purchase from B 12,000 tons of coal. Under the terms of the contract the coal is to be delivered in monthly installments of 1,000 tons each, delivery to be made between the 1st and 5th of each month. B makes delivery as agreed for the first five months, but in the sixth month he does not make delivery until the 25th of the month. If A accepts delivery without objection he thereby waives his right to complain later.

Pellegrene v. Luther
403 Pa. 212, 169 A. (2d) 298 (1961)

Supreme Court of Pennsylvania

This was an action by a contractor to recover under an alleged oral contract for construction of a home. From an adverse judgment of the Court of Common Pleas . . . the defendants appealed. The Supreme Court . . . held that evidence of negotiations leading up to a written contract of construction of house and of an alleged prior oral agreement to pay plaintiff for labor and material plus $500 was inadmissible action, but such inadmissibility was waived by defendant's failure to object.

Judgment affirmed.

BELL, J. Plaintiff recovered a verdict for $13,572.81, based upon an alleged *oral* contract for the construction of defendants' house, i.e., the cost of the labor and materials plus the sum of $500. Plaintiff testified that the parties agreed to cancel a written contract under the terms of which plaintiff agreed to build the house for $20,500 and to substitute the above mentioned oral contract. Defendant-husband vigorously denied any oral contract as well as plaintiff's other material evidence, and counterclaimed for damages resulting from plaintiff's breach of his written contract. A witness testified that defendant-husband admitted he owed plaintiff some money for the work on his house. If the weight of the evidence was the only question involved, the appeal could be dismissed without further discussion. However, the appeal raises material questions and alleges numerous errors concerning the parol evidence rule which was apparently misunderstood by everyone.

Plaintiff not only introduced in evidence the written contract and the attached specifications, but he likewise proved (a) all the negotiations which led up to the written contract, and (b) a parol agreement entered into by the parties which was at complete variance with the *subsequent* written contract.

The modern Pennsylvania parol evidence rule which dispelled the thick fog of confusion which enveloped the old Pennsylvania parol evidence rule, has been forged and perfected during the last 30 years. That rule, it is universally agreed, is as stated in *Bardwell v. Willis Co.*, 375 Pa. 503, 100 A. 2d 102, 103. In that case plaintiff brought an action in trespass for loss of profits suffered as a result of false and fraudulent material representations made by defendants immediately prior to or contemporaneous with the execution of the five year lease. Plaintiff further averred that he relied upon these fraudulent representations and was, because of them, induced to enter into the lease. Notwithstanding these averments, this Court sustained a demurrer by defendant and said (375 Pa. at pages 506–507, 100 A. (2d) at page 104):

"Where the alleged prior or contemporaneous oral representations or agreements concern a subject which is specifically dealt with in the written contract, and the written contract covers or purports to cover the entire agreement of the parties, the law is now clearly and well settled that in the absence of fraud, accident or mistake the alleged oral representations or agreements are merged in or superseded by the subsequent written contract, and parol evidence to vary, modify or supersede the written contract is inadmissible in evidence [unless it is averred and proved that they were omitted from the written agreement by fraud, accident or mutual mistake]: *Phillips Gas and Oil Co. v. Kline*, 368 Pa. 516, 519, 84 A. 2d 301. . . .

"The Parol Evidence Rule has had a checkered career in Pennsylvania. Now that it has been well and wisely settled we will not permit it to be evaded and undermined by such tactics. . . ."

It is clear that if plaintiff had sued on this alleged first oral agreement or on the subsequent written contract, the evidence would have been both inadmissible and futile. Plaintiff did not aver that the written contract to build the house for $20,500 was entered into, or that anything was omitted from the written agreement by fraud, accident or mistake.

Defendants erroneously contend that when parties enter into a complete written agreement, that written agreement cannot be changed by a subsequent oral agreement. The law is well settled that a written agreement can be modified by a subsequent oral agreement provided the latter is based upon a valid consideration and is proved by evidence which is clear, precise and convincing. *Betterman v. American Stores Co.*, 367 Pa. 193, 80 A. (2d) 66. . . .

In *Elliott-Lewis Corp. v. York-Shipley, Inc.*, 372 Pa. at pages 349–350, 94 A. (2d) at page 49, the Court said:

"The Parol Evidence Rule which prohibits the admission of oral evidence to vary or contradict a written contract does not apply to or prohibit a subsequent modification by parol; it applies only to prior or contemporaneous statements or agreements which induced the written agreement in question. *Grubb v. Rockey*, 366 Pa. 592, 79 A. (2d) 255. Such oral statements, representations, warranties or agreements are excluded because they have either been abandoned, or merged into and superseded by the written agreement. *Walker v. Saricks*, 360 Pa. 594, 63 A. (2d) 9. However, it is well settled that a written agreement may be modified by a subsequent (written or) oral agreement and that this modification may be shown by writings or by words or by conduct or by all three: [Citing cases]."

The oral contract which modifies or changes or cancels a prior written contact must be proved by evidence which is clear, precise and convincing. *Herr Estate*, 400 Pa. 90, 161 A. (2d) 32. . . .

While plaintiff's evidence to establish the subsequent oral contract left a great deal to be desired, we cannot say that it was not sufficient to take the case to the jury.

Evidence of the negotiations leading up to the written contract and the alleged prior oral agreement under which defendants allegedly agreed to pay plaintiff for all the labor and material of the house, plus $500—and thus varied and flew in the teeth of the subsequent written contract—was clearly inadmissible. To hold otherwise would merely allow a new and easy device to avoid the parol evidence rule and nullify the integrity and effectiveness of written contracts, which we have vigorously asserted we intend to maintain. However, defendants never objected to this evidence either when it was offered or at the conclusion of the court's charge thereon, in spite of the trial Judge's inquiry "is there anything else", to which both counsel indicated there was nothing further. Furthermore, defendants never objected to this evidence in the reasons given by them in their motion for a new trial. The inadmissibility of the evidence was therefore waived. *Bell v. Yellow Cab Co.*, 399 Pa. 332, 160 A. (2d) 437. . . .

Defendants counter-claimed for $3,765.58 for the additional amount which they were compelled to pay to complete the house when plaintiff failed to complete it and breached his written contract. The jury did not return any verdict on the counter-claim as it should have, but this was cured by defendants' silence and more particularly because the jury's finding of a verdict in favor of Pellegrene against Luthers for $13,578.81 with interest necessarily and clearly disposed of Luthers' counter-claim.

Judgment affirmed.

DISCHARGE BY IMPOSSIBILITY OF PERFORMANCE

NATURE OF IMPOSSIBILITY

It is important, in the beginning, to distinguish between impossibility of performance which occurs *before* the parties enter into an agreement and impossibility of performance which occurs *after* the negotiation of the contract. If, at the time the parties entered into their agreement, performance of the agreement was physically or legally impossible, but the parties were unaware of that fact, neither party would be liable. Actually, as we have already seen, under such circumstances a contract was never created. The legal position of the parties is different where impossibility of performance arises after the formation of the contract. Such impossibility will not, as a general rule, discharge the promisor from his obligation. The promisor may not set up as an excuse for nonperformance or for delay in performance his inability to secure necessary material, car shortage, increase in prices, strikes, fire, floods, and the like. The courts justify this rule of law on the ground that since the promisor knowingly entered into the contract, and failed to provide in the contract for such contingencies, it is only fair to the promisee that the promisor be held liable on his contract. If he failed to insert sufficient protective provisions in his contract, he has only himself to blame. While an exception is made for common carriers in the so-called act of God cases, such exceptions do not exist in the case of contracts generally. As the court said, in *Berg v. Erickson*,[1] "The general rule is that one who makes a positive agreement to do a lawful act is not absolved from liability for a failure to fulfill his covenant by a subsequent impossibility caused by an act of God, or an unavoidable accident, which, if he desired, he could make in his agreement, and thereby induce the other contracting party, in consideration of his positive covenant, to enter into and become bound by the contract." Certain exceptions will be discussed below.

City of Minneapolis v. Republic Creosoting Co. et al.
161 Minn. 178, 201 N. W. 414 (1924)

This was an action by the City of Minneapolis (plaintiff) against the Republic Creosoting Company, et al. (defendants) for damages for the alleged breach of contract. Judgment for plaintiff, and defendants appealed. Affirmed.

On December 31, 1919, plaintiff and defendants entered into a contract whereby defendants agreed to sell, furnish and deliver to plaintiff a certain quantity of creosoted wood paving blocks, at a specified price, "during the first six months of the year, 1920." Defendant failed to make delivery according to the terms of the contract, and plaintiff filed this action for damages. Defendants set up as a defense impossibility of performance, alleging the existence of a country-wide car shortage.

[1] 234 Fed. 817.

BUFFINGTON, J. There was nothing in the contract excusing defendant from punctual performance because of strikes, lockouts, a car shortage or similar hazards beyond the control of the defendant.

We assume that a country-wide car shortage did exist. We assume also defendants' willingness and ability to deliver as soon as a car supply enabled it to assemble the raw material, complete the processes of manufacture, and get the finished product to Minneapolis. At best, in defendants' case, that would have taken some months after May 10, 1920. No part of the blocks was delivered or tendered by defendants. They declined to make any effort to fill plaintiff's requisitions, professing inability to do so. The plaintiff disregarded its offer of deliveries later, and as soon as railroad service permitted, considered the contract irrevocably breached by the defendant, procured the blocks elsewhere, and at a higher price, and commenced this action for the damages arising from their increased cost.

There was no clause in the contract or specifications which expressly, or by implication, excused performance in case of a car shortage or labor trouble. It was competent for the parties so to have conditioned the contract. They did not do so. Defendants' obligation to perform was absolute. It was the defendants' business to manufacture and deliver where and as required, the commodity in question. Plaintiff was not its only customer. Supposedly, it was manufacturing and selling paving blocks in large quantities. It had a plant in Minneapolis. It might have conditioned performance upon continued and normal railroad freight service. It did not take that precaution. It must take the consequences, for performance was normally possible and the thing which prevented performance was a foreseeable contingency against which it might have protected itself, and notwithstanding which, it undertook punctual performance. *Cowley v. Davidson*, 13 Minn. 86; *Stees v. Leonard*, 20 Minn. 448. Judgment affirmed.

EXCEPTIONS TO GENERAL RULE

There are certain generally recognized exceptions to the general rule that impossibility of performance occurring subsequent to the negotiation of a contract does not discharge a party from his liability under the contract. These exceptions are: (1) impossibility imposed by law; (2) destruction of the subject matter; (3) death or incapacity of one of the parties in personal service contracts.

IMPOSSIBILITY IMPOSED BY LAW

If performance of a contract becomes legally impossible because of a change in the law, judicial interpretation, an executive order, or a declaration of war, the promisor will be excused from performance. The law will not compel a party to a contract to commit an illegal act. If the change in the law merely makes the performance of the contract more difficult, not illegal, the promisor is not exonerated. For example, A leased his storeroom to B for one year at a specified rental, with the stipulation that B was to use the storeroom only for the sale of new automobile tires. Three months after the lease was executed, the United States went to war, and an executive order was issued prohibiting the sale of new tires. B refused to pay his rent after the issuance of the executive order, and A sued B. A would be unable to recover. However, if the lease had not placed any restrictions upon the type of business B could operate in the building, even though in fact he conducted a business of selling new tires, the issuance of the executive order would not have discharged him of liability under the lease. Though it would doubtless be a hardship for him to shift to some other type of business in order to make use of the building, it would not be impossible under the contract. Such cases are generally referred to as *commercial frustration* cases.

Elsemore v. Inhabitants of Town of Hancock
18 A. (2d) 692 (1941)
Supreme Judicial Court of Maine

MURCHIE, J. The defendant brings this case before the Court on exceptions to the ruling of a Justice of the Superior Court accepting the report of a referee awarding damages of $775 to the plaintiff. Hearing was held under a rule of reference which reserved the right of exceptions to both parties as to questions of law, and the case is properly before the Court under that reservation.

The action is case to recover damages for breach of a contract under which the plaintiff alleges that he was employed to teach the high school in the defendant town during the school year 1939–1940. The alleged contract is an oral one made between the superintendent of schools and the plaintiff on the basis of authorization claimed to have been voted at a meeting of the superintending school committee held May 3, 1939. Defendant relies on the fact that said meeting was not legally convened because of the lack of proper notice to all members of the school board and that it was conducted in the absence of a member who in fact received no actual notice prior to the time for which the meeting was called. No question is raised but that if defendant is answerable in damages, the amount of the award is a proper one.

The referee found, as a matter of law, that the meeting in question was not a legal meeting.

Defendant claims that notwithstanding the contract on which plaintiff relies was entered into between the parties (if the fact shall so be determined), that contract was terminated, without liability on the part of the town, by the vote to abolish the free high school which plaintiff, under the contract, was to teach. The case contains a stipulation, entered by agreement of counsel which reads:

"It is agreed that there was a special town meeting held in the town of Hancock, July 24th, 1939. One of the articles in the warrant, to wit article 4, was 'to see if the town will vote to discontinue the High School and to transfer the unexpended balances to the secondary tuition account.' On that article it was 'Voted to discontinue the High School, and Voted unexpended balances be transferred to the secondary tuition account.' "

Under this stipulation counsel for defendant argues, as heretofore noted, that any contract to teach in the high school must be presumed to have been entered into subject to an implied understanding that the contract might be abrogated, without liability on the part of the town, by the action so taken.

The sovereignty rule has been recognized in this State in Re Guilford Water Co., 118 Me. 367 at 372, 108 A. 446, 449, where the Court said,

"The rule is general that every contract touching matters within the police power must be held to have been entered into with the distinct understanding that the continuing supremacy of the state, if exerted for the common good and welfare, can modify the contract when and as the benefit of that interest properly may require."

*   *   *

The contract here in question is one to which the defendant town became a party, through the action of that authority duly constituted by law to engage its teachers. Just as the contract came into existence by action of an agent of of the town, so the defendant claims that termination resulted, and without liabiliy, by the action of another town agency, the town meeting.

. . . There is no suggestion of a stipulated limitation that the contract, which was verbal, should be ineffective if the voters of the town should elect to discontinue the school. To hold that the sovereignty rule, which avoids a contract made either between individuals or corporations, or between an individual or corporation and a municipality, by the soverign exercise of police power, is applicable to the present facts would be a great extension of the rule for which no precedent has been called to our attention. Assuming authority to be vested in the voters of a town to discontinue a free high school at will, where no contract rights are involved, we do not believe it should be permitted as one of the parties to a valid contract to avoid its contractual obligations by such roundabout action.

Defendant offers no authority to support its claim that a town may abolish its high school, notwithstanding a contract to teach therein, except such inference as flows from the use of the word "may" in Section 91 of Chapter 19 of the revised statutes of 1930, used in connection with the authorization for towns to raise money to maintain free high schools, as against the word "shall," used in Section 16 of the same chapter, which imposes the requirement that towns raise and expend money for the support of common schools. It seems unnecessary to determine in the present case whether or not the supervision and management of free high schools, vested in the superintending school committee by the provisions of Section 90 of Chapter 19, give that committee the same control as to discontinuance of free high schools, or changes in their location, which is applicable to schools generally under Section 2 of said chapter. For the purpose of the present case, it is enough to say that the town of Hancock, which became party to a contract for teaching in its free high school, did not terminate its liability under that contract by vote at town meeting to abolish the school, and the entry must be

Exceptions overruled.

DESTRUCTION OF SUBJECT MATTER

If the parties contract with reference to a specific thing or subject matter and it is destroyed through no fault of either party, performance will be excused. Since the continued existence of the subject matter is essential to the performance of the contract, such contracts are held to contain an implied condition that destruction of the subject matter will excuse the parties from performance. For example, A and B enter into a contract whereby A agrees to sell to B, at an agreed price, his entire crop of strawberries grown upon a specific plot of ground. Because of unfavorable weather the entire crop of strawberries is destroyed. A would be excused from performance. If only a part of the strawberry crop were destroyed, B would have the option of treating the contract as canceled or of accepting partial performance on the part of A.

Where the contract does not involve a specific thing or subject matter, the destruction of the subject matter which the promisor had intended to use in performing his contract will not excuse him from performance. For example, A, a wholesaler, entered into a contract with B, a retailer, to sell B 500 men's suits of a certain description. At the time the contract was entered into, A had 500 such suits on hand in his warehouse and intended to send them to B in performance of his contract; but before he could prepare them for shipment, his warehouse burned and the suits were destroyed. Under such circumstances A would not be excused from performance, since the parties had not contracted with specific merchandise in mind. It was still possible for A to perform his part of the contract by buying the necessary suits on the market and delivering them to B. Even A's showing that he would lose money on the transaction would be no excuse for nonperformance.

These two rules of law have particular significance in the case of building contractors. For example, A employs B, a building contractor, to repair a building for him. After B has completed about half of the repair work, the building is destroyed by fire, without fault on the part of either A or B. B would be entitled to receive payment for the work which he had completed at the time of the fire, but he would not be entitled to recover damages for an alleged breach of the contract, nor would he be liable for damages for breach of contract. The continued existence of the building was essential to the performance of the contract. When it ceased to exist it became impossible for either party to perform, and consequently both parties were discharged from the duty of further performance. Likewise, in such cases the building contractor would be unable to recover the value of any materials which he might have purchased to be used in the repair of the building, even though he could show that he had purchased them for use on this particular job and that they would be of no value to him on another job.

The rule of law is different where a contractor contracts to build a new building. For example, A, a building contractor, contracts with B to build a new house for B. When the house is half completed, the structure is completely destroyed by fire. In such case A would not be discharged from his legal duty to perform the contract. This is so since it is still possible for A to carry out the terms of the contract by building a new house for B. When he contracted to build the house, he assumed the risk that the structure might be destroyed by fire. If he wished to protect himself from such a contingency, he could stipulate against such risk in his contract (if the other party were willing to agree to such a stipulation) or else insure the risk.

Sunseri et al. v. Garcia & Maggini Company
298 Pa. 249, 148 Atl. 81, 67 A. L. R. 1428 (1929)

This was an action by Salvatore Sunseri et al., copartners, trading as the Pennsylvania Macaroni Company (plaintiffs) against Garcia & Maggini Company (defendant). Judgment for plaintiffs, and defendant appealed. Affirmed.

Under a written contract plaintiffs purchased from defendant five carloads, 300 sacks each, of "Bon·Ton white graded garlic San Juan District." The contract was dated April 7, 1924, and contemplated delivery the following fall, when the crop growing in California had matured. Defendant delivered, under the contract, only half a carload, which plaintiffs refused to accept, alleging that it was not the quantity stipulated for in the contract. This action was to recover damages for the failure to deliver as the agreement required.

The controversy arose over a paragraph of the contract which read: "Liability: Seller is not responsible for delay or non-delivery or non-shipment or default in shipment in whole or in part, if prevented or interfered with by exercise of governmental authority, or by strikes, war, riots, revolutions; or for delay in transportation due to demands or embargoes of the United States Government or any other government, or non-delivery or delays through fires, flood, droughts, accidents, insurrections, blackouts, breakdown of machinery, commandeering of vessel carrying goods, or detention or delay to vessel, resulting directly or indirectly from acts of God, perils of the sea, stoppage of labor, shortage of labor, shortage of cars, or crop failure, or by any other unavoidable cause other than seller's own negligence."

SCHAFFER, J. The particular feature to be considered is that of "crop failure," appellant's defense being that it was unable to comply with its undertaking owing to a 90% failure of the crop of garlic in San Juan district, by drought.

Appellant insists that it met the requirements of its written undertaking by shipping 10% of what it had agreed to, and urges that it was error in the trial judge not to so hold. That there was a partial crop failure is not disputed. Just how much below normal it was is not established with certainty.

The only question in the case is—What is the meaning of the words "crop failure" in the contract? Their normal meaning, in business contracts, is total failure. And this is the only type of failure that the common law recognizes as an excuse for non-performance.

The provision in the contract which the defendant offers as an excuse for nonperformance provides: "The seller is not responsible for . . . nondelivery or delay through fires, floods . . . stoppage of labor, shortage of cars, or crop failure. . . ." An excuse to be available must connote an "unavoidable cause," and here there was none, for sufficient garlic could have been bought by defendants, if they had been willing to pay the market price for it. So, also, if the intention had been to cover a partial failure from an unavoidable cause, the words used would naturally have been "crop shortage," as in the case of "shortage of cars," the change in language indicating a change in meaning.

Since defendants contracted to deliver a specific quantity of garlic, they can excuse their failure so to do by proof of impossibility of performance, of which there is no evidence in this record. On the contrary, there was testimony that San Juan garlic was being offered in the fall of 1924 at high prices and plaintiffs actually bought some. It was admitted by defendants that additional garlic could have been obtained, at a price higher than that named in the contract, and that it made no endeavor to purchase any to meet its undertaking. The fact that more might have to be paid for the commodity than was contemplated when the engagement was entered into in no way absolves the defendant from its undertaking. We are not dealing with a case where there was a total failure or with one in which a grower had agreed to make delivery from a *specified tract or field* and there had been a partial crop failure. "An agreement to sell the crop of a specified piece of land is excused if there is no crop. But an agreement to sell a specified quantity of produce is not excused by the fact that the seller expected to fulfill the contract with the crop of particular land, and that crop, without fault on his part, is a failure." 3 Williston, *Contracts*, p. 3310. Affirmed.

UNIFORM COMMERCIAL CODE

Section 1–107 states that "any claim or right arising out of an alleged breach can be discharged in whole or in part without consideration by a written waiver or renunciation signed and delivered by the aggrieved party."

INCAPACITY OF A CONTRACTING PARTY TO PERFORM

In the case of an employment contract calling for the personal services of one of the parties, the death or incapacity of the party who is to render the services discharges him or his estate from all liability under the contract. Thus, if A employs B, an accountant, to work for him for one year, and B dies one month after the contract is consummated, the contract would be discharged. B's estate would not be liable to A for breach of contract, nor would A be liable to B's estate for wages for the remaining eleven months.

Sometimes difficult legal problems arise in employment contracts where the employee suffers a prolonged illness. How long must an employee be ill and off the job before the employer is discharged of his duties under the contract? It is evident that the problems raised in such cases are serious for both employee and employer. Naturally, no hard and fast rule of law can be laid down in such cases. However, it may be stated that if the illness is only temporary and of short duration, the contract is not discharged; but if it is serious in nature and extends over a considerable period of time, the contract is discharged.

It should be carefully noted that if the contract in question does not involve personal services, the death of one of the parties does not discharge the contract. All other contracts survive the death of the contracting party, unless the contract provides for its discharge on the death of one of the parties during the term of the contract. For example, A leases a house to B for one year. B dies in six months. Unless the lease (contract) provided that the death of B would excuse further performance on his part, B's estate would still be bound by the lease. Likewise, if A owes B $500, the death of A will not discharge the debt.

Kowal v. Sportswear by Revere, Inc.
222 N. E. (2d) 779 (1967)

This is an action by Sanford A. Kowal, administrator (plaintiff) against Sportswear by Revere, Inc. (defendant). Judgment for plaintiff in part and judgment for defendant in part. Plaintiff appealed. Orders for judgment reversed and judgment entered for administrator.

This is an action of contract brought by the administrator of the estate of Joseph E. Prince to recover for commissions for sales made by Prince under a written contract. The case was submitted on a statement of agreed facts. The judge ordered judgment for the defendant on the plaintiff's amended declaration and for the plaintiff (original defendant) on the declaration in set-off. The plaintiff appealed.

Prince had represented the defendant as a salesman for twenty-two years prior to his death on August 22, 1962. A written contract, drafted by the defendant and running for the calendar year, had been entered into annually. In 1961, because Prince was ill and unable fully to cover his territory, the defendant hired Sol Nadler to represent it in Prince's territory. Prince was to receive commissions on orders obtained by Nadler.

SPALDING, J. In the absence of contrary provisions, contracts are generally held to survive the death of one of the parties. But contracts which involve acts and services which can only be performed personally by the promisor or some other particular person are exceptions to this general rule. Such contracts terminate when death renders the personal performance impossible. In this case, Prince had twenty-two years' experience as the defendant's salesman. In view of the generally personal nature of a salesman's services, and particularly of Prince's long experience in his relationship with the defendant, the administrator could not have been expected to perform Prince's contractual duties satisfactorily. Prince's death having rendered the performance of his duties impossible, the defendant's obligations also ceased for failure of consideration.

There was, however, neither impossibility nor failure of consideration with respect to orders placed before Prince's death. Once Prince or Nadler had placed an order with the defendant, his services in respect to that order had been fully performed, and the defendant was obligated to pay a commission.

The commissions due Prince or his administrator under the 1962 contract should be computed on the basis of 6½ per cent of all goods shipped and paid for in respect of orders placed before Prince's death. It would appear that this amounts to $22,827. The defendant having already paid $18,435.74, the plaintiff's recovery should be $4,391.26.

The orders for judgment are reversed and judgment is to be entered for the plaintiff in the sum of $4,391.26. Interest on this amount, unless agreed to by the parties, is to be determined by the trial judge.

So ordered.

DISCHARGE BY OPERATION OF LAW

Contracts may be discharged by operation of law (1) by bankruptcy, (2) by the running of the statute of limitations, (3) by merger, or (4) as a consequence of the intentional and wrongful alteration of a written contract.

DISCHARGE IN BANKRUPTCY

We have already seen that a discharge in bankruptcy does not technically discharge the debtor of his contract obligations but merely bars action against him by his creditors. But it has the practical effect of discharging the debtor, since, if he does not later agree to perform such obligations, his discharge would be an effective defense if he were sued by any of his creditors. All bankruptcy proceedings take place in the U. S. District Courts.

STATUTE OF LIMITATIONS

All jurisdictions have what are known as statutes of limitations, the effect of which is to bar action upon contracts [1] after the cause of action has run for the specified statutory period. If suit is not brought within the statutory period, the obligation is "outlawed." The following table gives examples of the length (in years) of such periods.

	Open Accounts	Promissory Notes	Oral Contracts	Written Contracts	Contracts under Seal [2]
CALIFORNIA	4	4	2	4	4
DISTRICT OF COLUMBIA	3	3	3	3	12
FLORIDA	3	5	3	5	20
MARYLAND	3	3	3	3	12
MISSOURI	5	10	5	10	10
NEW YORK	6	6	6	6	6
TENNESSEE	6	6	6	6	6
VIRGINIA	3	5	3	5	10

The period of the statute of limitations starts to run when a cause of action accrues; that is, when one of the parties has a right to commence suit against the other. In the case of the breach of a contract, for example, a cause of action accrues when the breach occurs. In the case of failure to pay a promissory note which by its terms is due and payable upon a specified future date, the statute of limitations runs from the maturity date of the note, and not from the date the note was executed. For example, on May 1, 1953, A gives B a note for $500 which is due and payable "one year from date." If A fails to pay the note, the statute of limitations would start to run on May 1, 1954 and not on May 1, 1953. However, if the note is a demand note, the prevailing rule is that the statute starts to run on the date on which the note was executed. In the case of open accounts, the statute of limitations runs from the date of the last item of the account, regardless of whether it is a debit or a credit. For example, on May 1, 1955, A opens an account at the X Department Store and makes a $50 purchase. The statute starts to run on that date. On May 10 he makes a $10 purchase. This addition to A's account is said to "toll the statute" and to start it running again from the beginning for another full period. On June 1 A makes a $25 payment on his account, which again tolls the statute.

It is important to note that the receipt, by the holder of a note, of money accruing from the sale of collateral security does not interrupt the

---

[1] They apply also to torts, crimes, and judgments.

[2] The Uniform Commercial Code, Sec. 203, makes a seal inoperative when affixed to a contract or an offer to buy or sell goods.

running of the statute. Likewise, money received from the sale of other property in which the debtor has an interest, and applied on the obligation by the creditor, does not ipso facto toll the statute. This is so even though the debtor has consented to the sale and to the application of the money to the debt. The courts hold that such consent does not automatically make the creditor the agent of the debtor to toll the statute.

Piersma v. Seitz

10 Md. App. 439, 271 A. (2d) 199 (1970)

Court of Special Appeals of Maryland

Certiorari Granted Feb. 17, 1971

This was to Court of Appeals of Maryland a personal injury action arising out of automobile collision. The Circuit Court for Prince George's County, Roscoe H. Parker, J., rendered judgment for the plaintiff and the defendant appealed. The Court of Appeals, Murphy, C.J., held that where reissuance of summons which had been returned "non est" was not dependent upon plaintiff's counsel's request and the statute of limitations would have remained tolled had clerk performed his duty of reissuing the summons, failure of clerk to perform the wholly perfunctory duty of reissuing the summons did not cause statute of limitations to continue running in action in which plaintiff caused original summons to issue before expiration of limitations period.

Affirmed.

Martin H. Freeman, Upper Marlboro, for appellant.

Townes L. Dawson, Hyattsville, for appellee.

MURPHY, C.J. On April 19, 1965, the motor vehicles driven by appellant and appellee were involved in a collision in Prince George's County, as a result of which appellee on April 18, 1968—one day before the statute of limitations would have barred the action—sued appellant for personal injuries in the Circuit Court for Prince George's County. The summons issued for appellant was returned non est (moved) on April 25, 1968. By letter dated May 17, 1968, the Clerk of the Court so notified appellee's counsel and requested that he "issue written instructions to this office for purposes of re-issue and service by the Sheriff." Appellee's counsel did not respond to the Clerk's letter and the summons was not reissued. On November 14, 1968, the case was placed on the stet docket. Subsequently, in March of 1969, appellee located appellant living in Pennsylvania and service was effected upon her. Appellant pleaded limitations. That defense was held without merit and the case was eventually tried before a jury which awarded appellee judgment in the amount of $15,000.

Appellant claims on appeal that while the suit was filed within the statutory period of limitations, the action was discontinued as barred by limitations because the appellee did not obtain two successive returns of non est before allowing the sumomns to lie dormant. He relies on *Neel v. Webb Fly Screen*

Mfg. Co., 187 Md. 34, 48 A. (2d) 331; Maryland Rule 112, and Rule 108 of the Rules of Court of the Seventh Judicial Circuit.

It is well settled that for the purpose of preventing the running of the statute of limitations the impetration of the original writ is deemed the commencement of the suit. *Logan v. State, to Use of Nesbitt,* 39 Md. 177. At common law, where the party instituted the suit within the period of limitations but the summons proved ineffectual to bring the defendant into court, it was necessary, in order to keep the suit alive, that such summons be regularly renewed from term to term until the defendant was served; and the omission so to renew operated as a discontinuance of the action. *Hazlehurst v. Morris,* 28 Md. 67. Statutes declaratory of the common law were enacted in 1864, 1886, and 1888; "they merely established more frequent—and finally monthly —'return days' in lieu of the thrice yearly 'term days.'" *Renewal of Process and the Statute of Limitations,* 9 M. L. R. 74, 76. Subsequently, by Chapter 180 of the *Acts of 1894,* it was provided that in the courts of the City of Baltimore, where summons had been returned not executed, "the same *may* be renewed," and that "after two returns of any original writ not executed at the two succeeding return days after the writ is first issued, the same shall be permitted to lie dormant, * * *." Substantially identical provisions were subsequently enacted for the various Circuit Courts of the counties by Chapter 240 of the *Acts of 1914.*

In *Neel v. Webb Fly Screen Mfg. Co., supra,* decided in 1946, the Court of Appeals, in interpreting these statutes modifying the common law rule, held that after two ineffective issues of the summons (at two successive return days) the suit was kept alive and not barred by limitations for failure thereafter to renew the summons. The statutes interpreted in *Neel* were repealed by Chapter 399 of the *Acts of 1957;* they were in effect superseded by Maryland Rule 112 entitled "Renewal of Process—Dormant Process," which reads as follows:

"*a. Once as of Course, by Clerk.* Upon the return of the summons to a party endorsed non est, the same shall be renewed by the clerk as a matter of course, returnable to the next return day.

"*b. After Two Non Ests, to Lie Dormant.* After two returns of non est, the summons to a party shall be permitted to lie dormant, renewable only on the written order of the plaintiff to such future return day as the plaintiff may direct.

"*c. Further Renewal.* Thereafter, upon a further return of non est, said summons shall again be permitted to lie dormant, renewable only as aforesaid, the said plaintiff having the right to renew said summons to as many subsequent return days, under the same mode of procedure as may be deemed proper, until the same is executed."

The requirement that the Clerk renew the summons "as a matter of course" imposes upon him, as a matter of law, a non-discretionary, wholly automatic duty, to reissue the summons so returned non est, returnable to the next return day. The Rule can bear no other interpretation; the Clerk's duty is not, as appellant suggests, dependent upon a request of the party seeking service of the summons.

Rule 108[1] of the Seventh Judicial Circuit, under which the Clerk acted in asking appellee's counsel to provide written instructions for reissuance of the summons, reads:

"The Sheriff shall promptly make his return to the Clerk of the Court. If process has not been served, the return shall state the reason why and the Clerk of Court shall forthwith notify counsel accordingly."

We see no inconsistency between the local Rule and Maryland Rule 112. (Were there such an inconsistency, the local Rule would yield. Maryland Rule 1 f.) Nothing in the local Rule purports to permit the Clerk in Prince George's County to ignore the plain mandate of Rule 112 requiring that he reissue such summons "as a matter of course." That such a reissuance would likely result in another return of the summons endorsed non est does not mean that he can refuse to renew it unless he is provided with another address; indeed, the Rule, in requiring two successive returns of non est as a condition precedent to inhibit the bar of limitations, contemplates that such procedure will act as a double check on the Sheriff's performance in his initial undertaking to effect service. By directing such automatic reissuance of the summons, it was one plain purpose of Rule 112 to assure that once the suit was filed within the period of limitations, counsel need have no further concern that limitations would run against his client for failure on his part to renew the summons. In this connection, the Rule of court, unlike the common law, or the now repealed statutes, imposes the mandatory responsibility for reissuance upon the Clerk, rather than an optional responsibility upon counsel; and we think counsel should not be called upon to superintend the duties of the Clerk, but on the contrary, in these wholly mechanical circumstances, should be entitled to rely upon the proper performance of the Clerk's duty. Indeed, in this case, the record discloses that appellee did not have a better address for appellant than that originally supplied; that she had moved to Pennsylvania in August of 1966; and had the summons been reissued, as automatically required under the Rule, it would have been again returned non est.

The thrust of appellant's claim is that appellee's action "was barred by the statute of limitations when, under the Rules of Court, he did not as a matter of course request a reissue in response to the Clerk's letter of May 17, 1968." Since the reissuance was not dependent upon counsel's request therefor, and since the statute of limitations would have remained tolled had the Clerk followed the clear mandate of the law, it would appear to be a plain perversion of the purpose and intent underlying Rule 112 to invoke the bar of limitations upon a litigant solely by reason of the neglect and omission of the Clerk to perform the wholly perfunctory duty compelled by the Rule of reissuing the summons. *Cf. Bertonazzi v. Hillman,* Adm'x, 241 Md. 361, 216 A. (2d) 723. We think Rule 112 is so structured as to permit us to hold, on these

---

[1] It is then "renewable only on the written order of the plaintiff to such future return day as the plaintiff may direct." Id. "Thereafter, upon a further return of non est, said summons shall again be permitted to lie dormant, renewable only as aforesaid, the plaintiff having the right to renew said summons to as many subsqeuent return days, under the same mode of procedure as may be deemed proper, until the same is executed." Rule 112 c.

facts, and under these circumstances, that the conditions requisite to achieving a state of dormancy of process were, in effect, met in this case.

Judgment affirmed; appellant to pay costs.

PER CURIAM. Court of appeals adopts opinion of special court of appeals and affirms the judgment appealed from. Judgment affirmed with costs.

Nilsson et al. v. Kielman et al.
17 N. W. (2d) (S. D.) 918 (1945)

This was an action by M. T. Nilsson and E. P. Nilsson (plaintiffs) against Ethel E. Kielman and L. T. Nilsson (defendants) on a note. Upon motion of Ethel E. Kielman the trial court directed a verdict in her behalf on ground of the running of the statute of limitations. Plaintiffs appealed. Affirmed.

On February 17, 1926, defendants executed a promissory note for $4,000 payable August 1, 1926. The notes bore five endorsements of payments between the dates of December 3, 1931, and February 20, 1943. The trial court granted the motion of defendant Ethel E. Kielman for a directed verdict on the ground that as to her the action was barred by the six-year statute of limitations.

Payments of $1,121.26 on January 19, 1940, and $74.40 on February 20, 1943, endorsed on the note, are the only payments claimed to have been made within six years immediately preceding the commencement of this action. These payments resulted from the sale of a grocery store in January, 1932. Plaintiff M. T. Nilsson testified: "The endorsement of January 19, 1940, is for the equity that they (defendants) had in the house. . . . When they closed up, they traded this stock and fixtures, the balance they had, for this building. . . . Title was taken in our name. It was understood they would take this building off our hands, some time. So we held it that way until at this time he said they could not take it over. . . . So then we figured out what their credit was and gave them credit for it. The endorsement of $74.40 represents an account that we collected. When they traded the store for this building it was understood that these accounts were all to be turned over to us and as we collected them we should credit them on this note." (Defendants were divorced in October, 1940.)

Plaintiffs' claim is that the several payments started the running of the statute of limitations from the time of each payment. Defendant Ethel E. Kielman contended that it was from the date of the transfer of the property and accounts in 1932; and that the direction to collect and apply proceeds did not carry with it authority to renew or extend the debt.

ROBERTS, J. It appears from the provisions of SDC 33.0213 that an acknowledgment or promise, to be effectual to interrupt the running of the statute of limitations, must be in writing and signed by the party to be charged, but this requirement does not take away or alter the effect of a part payment. It is settled law of this state that a part payment to be effectual to interrupt the statute of limitations must have been voluntary and must have been made and accepted under circumstances consistent with an intent to pay the balance. The principle on which a part payment operates to take a debt without the statute is that the debtor by the payment intends to acknowledge the continued existence of the debt.

The agreement with reference to the amount of credit on January 19, 1940, constituted neither a new promise in writing nor a part payment as of that date. It is the fact of voluntary payment made by the debtor and not entry of credit that interrupts the running of the statute. Nor did the collection of the account amounting to $74.40 give new life to the debt. Plaintiffs were authorized to collect the accounts and apply the proceeds to payment of the debt, but this did not have the same effect as if made personally by defendants. There is no vital distinction between such a case and one where money received by the payee of a note from collateral security, such as notes and mortgages of third persons pledged by the maker, is credited on the principal note. Such payment does not interrupt the running of the statute. The underlying reason for the doctrine is that a creditor is not the agent of the debtor to such an extent as to make an act done by him in the name of the debtor operate as a new promise to himself without which element the payment cannot operate to interrupt the statute. Judgment appealed from is affirmed.

MERGER

Another type of discharge by operation of law is discharge by merger. For example A owes B $50 on an open account. B urges A to give him a note for $50 "to take the place of the open account," and A accedes to B's request. The effect of this transaction is to merge the open contract obligation into an obligation of a "higher degree or order," namely, that of a promissory note. As a result the open account obligation is extinguished or discharged, but A is now liable on the promissory note. Another example is the case of a judgment. After one party to a contract has obtained a judgment against the other party for the breach of the contract, the contractual obligation is merged in the judgment, and is therefore discharged.

ALTERATION

If one of the parties to a contract intentionally makes a material alteration of a written contract, without the consent of the other party to the instrument, such act will usually discharge the contract. For example, the intentional erasing or crossing out of a material part of the instrument would be a sufficient alteration to work a discharge. It is generally held that absence of fraudulent intent does not hinder the operation of the rule. If the alteration is intentional and fraudulent, the party who commits the alteration is usually barred from recovering upon the contract. If the alteration is intentional but not fraudulent, it destroys the efficacy of the instrument itself, but the party who innocently altered the instrument may generally recover on the original consideration.

Accidental alteration of an instrument by one of the parties has no effect upon the rights and liabilities of the parties to the instrument. It is generally held that alteration by a stranger to the contract, without the knowledge of either party to the contract, will not discharge the instrument.

Lowe v. Henson
190 S. W. (2d) 423 (1945)

This was a suit by H. L. Lowe (plaintiff) against W. A. Henson and another (defendants) for specific performance of a contract to convey land and for damages. Decree for defendants, and plaintiff appealed. Affirmed.

On March 2, 1944, Lowe went to the farm homestead of Henson and entered into a written contract with Henson and his wife for the purchase of their farm. The portion of the contract, immediately following the description of the land, material to this case, read as follows: "save and except an undivided ¼ interest, of all oil, gas and other minerals in or under said land *fully* participating. The agreed price to be paid is *$64.00* per acre, a total of *$10,240.00*."

The contract was on a printed form. The words and figures italicized above were written in the blank spaces in pencil by Lowe. The contract provided for the furnishing of an abstract, examination thereof, curing of title defects, and the deposit by Lowe of $500 earnest money in escrow in a Lubbock bank. Duplicate copies of the instrument were signed in ink by Lowe and Mr. & Mrs. Henson.

At the time the contract was made, Henson owned but one half of the minerals in the land, the other half having been reserved when he bought it. The next day the Hensons consulted an attorney relative to the effect of the contract and were informed that they were obligated to convey three fourths of the minerals. That afternoon they wrote Lowe as follows: "In drawing up the terms of the contract yesterday there was an honest error made by us. . . . We have notified your bank, pending the adjustment of these matters, to hold all papers. Sincerely yours, W. A. Henson and Dora Henson." The Hensons met Lowe at the escrow bank in Lubbock the next morning and explained the situation. The testimony as to what was actually said at this meeting is meager, but we infer that Henson took the position that Lowe should require a conveyance of only one fourth of the minerals, while Lowe's stand was that he should get one half of the minerals and an adjustment in price for the one fourth that could not be conveyed. In the course of the discussion Lowe altered both copies of the contract to read as follows: "Save and except an undivided *None* interest, of oil, gas and other minerals in or under said land participating. The agreed price to be paid is $62.50 per acre, a total of $10,000, of which amount $10,000 is to be paid in cash on delivery of the title and deed." The changes or alterations were made by erasing the figures

"$\frac{1}{4}$" and substituting the word "None," and changing the figures relative to the consideration from "$64" to "$62.50," and from "$10,240" to "$10,000." All this was done in pencil. The word "fully" was marked through in ink. The contracts were not re-executed following the change. Lowe returned one copy to the escrow holder and the other to the Hensons. The testimony of the parties to the contract is conflicting on whether the Hensons agreed to the alterations.

Thereafter Henson made no effort to comply with the contract and ignored letters from Lowe's attorney requesting him to furnish an abstract or be sued. On March 23rd Henson sold the farm to defendant Webber. On March 24, 1944, Lowe filed this suit for specific performance.

BOYCE, J. The trial court found that neither of the Hensons agreed to the alteration of the contract and concluded that appellant was not entitled to either specific performance or damages.

We think it is a legitimate conclusion that the Hensons met with Lowe at the bank for the purpose of securing to themselves the reservation of one fourth of the minerals. The fact that the contract was changed in their presence to reflect a different obligation is not in itself sufficient to establish their consent to the change. The Hensons denied that they agreed to the alterations. Their conduct following the meeting at the bank is consistent with their testimony that they did not agree to the alteration of the contract. They refused to have a deed drawn. Mr. Henson failed to furnish an abstract in the face of a letter threatening him with suit if he did not furnish it. They sold to Webber on the terms they had quoted to Lowe. We therefore hold that there is evidence to support the trial court's finding of fact. The material alteration of a written instrument made by one of the parties to it after execution and without the authority or consent of another party to it avoids the instrument as to the nonconsenting party.

Judgment affirmed.

REVIEW CASES

1. Porter sued Harrington for specific performance on a written contract for the conveyance of real estate. The contract specified that a certain amount per month was to be paid on the lots, that time was of the essence, and that Harrington had an option to cancel the contract if payments were not made on time. Late payments were accepted on many occasions, and some months no payments were made at all. After several years Harrington informed Porter that he had decided to exercise his option to cancel. Thereupon Porter tendered payment in full, which Harrington refused. Ruling? (Porter v. Harrington, 262 Mass. 203, 159 N. E. 530)

2. Halsey contracted to repair a building for Waukesha Springs Sanitarium, which employed an architect to pass upon the work. The architect had passed upon all the work completed shortly before the building burned down by accident, rendering the completion of Halsey's contract impos-

sible. Halsey presented a bill for the work done before the fire, but the architect refused to render a certificate. Halsey sued to collect, but the lower court held that the architect's certificate was a condition precedent to Halsey's recovery. Halsey appealed. What judgment? (Halsey v. Waukesha Springs Sanitarium, 125 Wis. 311)

3. Janssen contracted to dig a well satisfactory to Muller. Janssen stated just prior to making the contract that he had a good outfit and could go down to 1,500 feet if necessary. The well was dug to 1,000 feet, where sufficient water was found for household purposes, but Muller wanted it dug deeper. Janssen refused and brought this action to collect on the contract. Judgment for whom? (Janssen v. Muller, 38 S. D. 611, 162 N. W. 393)

4. Goodhue contracted with W. E. and J. W. Drew to haul for him all the wood that should be cut on a certain tract of land. They were to be paid 85¢ per cord, of which 25¢ per cord was to be withheld until the job was finished. Later Goodhue refused to pay them the amount withheld, claiming that they had not completed the contract, and they brought suit. It was ascertained that out of 8,345 cords cut, they had overlooked 7½ cords which had been concealed by snow. Judgment for whom? (Drew et al. v. Goodhue, 74 Vt. 436, 52 A. 971)

5. Moore brought an action against Norman to recover possession of personal property, which Norman had mortgaged to her to secure two promissory notes. Norman contended that the mortgages had been discharged by a tender of payment which he claimed was sufficient in amount, together with payments previously made, to satisfy the debt. The evidence showed that Norman, in tendering the money, had demanded that Moore surrender the notes; that Moore had refused to do so because she claimed that a larger amount was due; that she had offered to receive the money tendered and indorse it on the notes, but Norman had refused the offer. Judgment for whom? (Moore v. Norman, 50 Minn. 83, 53 N. W. 809)

6. Brady engaged the Matthews Construction Co. to carry out certain alterations and additions to his residence, including the rebuilding of a private chapel which required a great deal of mill and cabinet work of special design. The construction company ordered this material from the Butler-Howell Co., and it was ready for delivery when the building was destroyed by fire, without the fault of either party. Brady paid the construction company for work done and material furnished and installed before the fire, but he refused to pay the $4,407.84 for which the construction company was indebted to the Butler-Howell Co. The construction company filed an action to recover this amount. Judgment for whom? (Matthews Construction Co. v. Brady, 104 N. J. L. 438, 140 A. 433)

Breach and Remedies

16

A breach of a contract occurs whenever a party to a contract fails or refuses to perform his part of the contract. Breach usually occurs when performance is due or after it has been begun; the offending party may simply fail to perform, or he may expressly renounce the contract. At times renunciation is made before performance is due (anticipatory breach). A third means of breaching a contract is for one of the parties to commit an act which makes performance impossible.

A breach of a contract by one of the parties gives the other party a right of action for damages; under certain circumstances it also discharges him from further duty to perform under the contract.

BREACH WHEN PERFORMANCE IS DUE

In most cases where one of the parties to a contract fails in whole or in part to perform his part of the contract, the other party may treat such failure to perform as a discharge of his own obligations under the contract, and sue for damages for the breach of the contract. But in certain types of cases it is held that the breach of only a part of the contract does not discharge the other party but merely gives him a cause of action for damages for the breach, or entitles him to set up the breach as a defense in case the party who breached a portion of the contract should file action against him, alleging nonperformance. The determining consideration is whether the contract is *divisible* or *indivisible* (entire). If the contract is indivisible, a total or partial breach by one of the parties will discharge the other party from all liability under the contract and give him the right to file action for damages for the breach of the contract. If the contract is divisible, a breach of only a part of the contract will not discharge the

345

innocent party from his obligations under the contract, but it will give him a right of action for damages for the breach; or, in case he refuses to perform his part of the contract and is sued, he may set up such breach as a set-off in such action.

The courts have frequently had difficulty in determining whether a specific contract is divisible or indivisible. The intention of the parties always plays an important part in the determination. It would seem, upon an analysis of the cases, that if the contract is capable of being separated into distinct parts, or if there are a number of separate promises or undertakings, upon the part of the parties, and performance by one of the parties is not dependent upon performance by the other, the contract is divisible, unless a contrary intent on the part of the parties is clearly shown. For example, A and B were negotiating for the sale of A's house and lot to B. A also had a power lawn mower. B offered A $15,000 for the house and $100 for the mower, and A accepted the offer. Upon A's refusal to deliver the mower to B on the day of settlement, B refused to go ahead with the transaction, contending that A had breached the contract and that he (B) was therefore completely discharged of any liabilities under the contract. Since the contract was clearly divisible into two separate parts, B was wrong in his contention. A would be liable for damages for breach of part of the contract, but the entire contract would not be discharged. On the other hand, if the promises on each side are mutually dependent, and if complete performance is to be rendered by one of the parties before or simultaneously with complete performance on the part of the other party, the contract is indivisible or entire.

Producers' Coke Co. v. Hillman et al.
243 Pa. 313, 90 A. 144 (1914)

This was an action by the Producers' Coke Co. (plaintiff) against J. H. Hillman, Jr., and others, partners, doing business under the firm name of J. H. Hillman & Sons Company (defendants). Judgment for plaintiff, and defendants appealed. Reversed.

On May 10, 1912, plaintiff and defendants entered into a contract whereby plaintiff contracted to turn over to defendants substantially all the coke it produced from July 1 to December 31, 1912. Relying upon this contract defendants contracted to sell large quantities of coke to its customers, same to be delivered between July 1 and December 31, 1912. On July 20th, at the request of plaintiff, the original, or May 10th, contract was rescinded and a new contract was entered into. Under this new agreement plaintiff promised to deliver to defendants the amounts of coke which defendants had already resold to their customers. Deliveries by plaintiff to defendant, under the new, or July 20th, contract, were to be made as follows: "during July 3,780 tons;

and 2,124 tons per month for the months of August, September, October, November, and December." During the month of July plaintiff delivered to defendants about 844 tons, less than the amount called for, and failed to deliver any coke whatever during the month of August. On September 29, 1912, plaintiff filed this action to recover for the coke delivered during the month of July.

Plaintiff maintained that the contract was severable.

The contention of defendants was that the contract was entire or indivisible, and that there could be no recovery by plaintiff for any partial performance.

STEWART, J. Where a question of this kind arises it is the intention of the parties that controls, and not the divisibility of the subject, and this intention is to be collected from the words employed, where the intention can be clearly derived therefrom. When, as understood in the ordinary sense, the words do not disclose the manner and intent to which the parties intended to be bound, resort must be had to rules of construction as aids. Having regard simply to the words employed in this contract, the reference that the contract was intended to be entire would be quite as reasonable as that it was intended to be divisible. . . . The distinguishing mark of a divisible contract is that it admits of apportionment of the consideration on either side so as to correspond to the unascertained consideration on the other side. Where such a purpose appears in the contract, or is clearly deducible therefrom, it is allowed great significance when ascertaining the intentions of the parties. It is a mistake, however, to suppose that in every case it is conclusive in itself. It is determining only when there are no opposing signs or marks. Where these latter are present it becomes a question of preponderance.

Each party to this contract had a definite object in view which was so clearly expressed that there was no room for doubt by either. The plaintiff, whose sole object was to secure a cancellation of the agreement which required it to deliver to the defendants for sale its entire output of coke during the remaining months of the year, must have fully understood the object of the defendants in requiring, as a condition of their assent, a promise from the plaintiff that it would protect the defendants from liability on contracts of sale they had already entered into, by furnishing them the coke sufficient to meet their engagements, at a definite fixed price. The contract here set up is a promise by the plaintiff, on a sufficient consideration, that it would make these deliveries, not only some, but all of them, for the one definite purpose to save harmless the defendants who otherwise would be exposed to the danger of loss. These engagements by the defendants were for deliveries at specified times, in specified amounts, and at specified rates; and the promise by the plaintiff was to supply the defendants with an adequate amount of coke, to meet them all, amounting in the aggregate to 14,300 tons. There is no mistaking the end or object in view, and it is quite as apparent that to hold this contract severable, or divisible, and not entire, would defeat the object both parties had in view. The consideration paid by the defendants—surrender of their rights under the earlier contract—was based upon a contemplated entire performance by the plaintiff, for, except as this was so, the agreement accomplished nothing in the way of protection to the defendants.

The present case is a case in which the manifest purpose of the agreement would be defeated were it held to be a divisible contract, thereby allowing the plaintiff not simply to disappoint the defendants in what it was intended they should receive for a specific and express purpose, but requiring from the defendants payment for so much performance as met the pleasure, convenience, and advantage of the plaintiff. Reversed.

Zambetti v. Commodores Land Co.
102 Fla. 586, 136 So. 644 (1931)

This was a suit by Victor Zambetti (plaintiff) against the Commodores Land Company (defendant). From a final decree dismissing the bill, plaintiff appealed. Affirmed.

Defendant made a contract with plaintiff in which defendant agreed to sell and plaintiff agreed to purchase a certain lot of ground for a consideration of $6,500, payable as follows: $1500 cash on execution and delivery of contract, and the balance in three equal installments, payable one, two, and three years from date, with interest payable semiannually at 6 per cent. The contract was dated March 1, 1927, and bound the vendor (defendant) to perform the following covenants: "(a) Within sixty days after the date of this contract to let a contract for, or itself commence, the construction of, and thereafter within a reasonable time cause to be completed or to complete, the paving at its own expense with some appropriate material to a width of 24 feet of the street, if any, shown upon said plat in front of said lot, if such street has not been then already paved; and (b) Within said sixty days after the date of this contract, to let a contract for, or itself begin, the construction at its own expense of a water main under the street, if any, shown upon said plat in front of said lot. . . ."

On execution and delivery of the contract plaintiff, Zambetti, made the payment of $1500, according to the terms of the contract. The Commodores Land Co. (defendant) failing to perform the two aforementioned covenants, as agreed, plaintiff filed this bill in equity praying for the rescission of the contract and for an accounting, and asked that his down payment of $1500 be returned to him.

The case turns on the question of whether the covenants (a) and (b) are dependent or independent.

TERRELL, J. Generally, covenants to an agreement are said to be dependent when made by two parties to a deed or contract and are such that the thing covenanted to be done on the part of each enters into the whole consideration for the covenant on the other part, or where the acts or covenants of the parties are concurrent, and are to be done or performed at the same time, and neither party can maintain an action against the other without averring and proving performance on his part. Covenants for conveyance and payment of the consideration for land as do covenants by a lessee to pay rent and by a lessor to make essential improvements or repairs without which the premises would be useless are typical examples of dependent covenants. Covenants are construed to be dependent or independent according to the intentions and meaning of the parties as gleaned from all the circumstances of the case and any technical application of words should give way to such an intention.

The covenants on the part of the vendor to pave and extend the water main and the vendee to pay the purchase price did not run concurrently. The covenant to pay the purchase price ran over a period of three years, while the covenant to pave the street in front of and extend the water main to the lot involved in this litigation was to be contracted to be done within sixty days. The unpaved portion of the street in front of the lot was between three and four hundred feet long, and whether this portion was to be paved in full or only in front of the lot (which we do not here decide) is immaterial to the disposition of this cause, as from the showing in the record the cost of the paving in either event will be but a small part of the cost of the lot. The cost of executing the covenant to pave and extend the water main can be easily ascertained, and while the execution of this covenant will add to the accessibility and desirability of the lot, it will not add materially to its intrinsic value, nor will it affect a particle the value, accessibility of the lots or community generally in the vicinity of the lot in question.

The covenants provoking this litigation were to be performed at different times and there is no indication whatever in the contract that the parties considered them as dependent. By the terms of the contract the complainant could have prosecuted an action for damages against the defendant for its failure to comply with the contract and could have reduced the same to judgment long prior to the due date of his final payment. Where this can be done and his damages can be readily ascertained, his remedy at law is adequate and he cannot seek the aid of a court of equity to rescind.

The rule seems to be well settled that when covenants on the part of different parties to a contract are to be performed at different times or when covenants to make improvements are independent of covenants to purchase, or when a covenant goes only to part of the consideration on both sides and a breach of such covenant may be compensated in damages and will not defeat the purpose of the contract, the covenant is independent and an action at law may be maintained for its breach by the party or parties interested. 27 *R. C. L.* 646; *Crampton v. McLaughlin Realty Co.*, 51 Wash. 522, 99 p. 586; *Amer. Emigrant Co. v. County of Adams*, 100 U. S. 61, 25 L. Ed. 563.

For reasons announced in this opinion it is our conclusion that the covenants to pave and extend the water main were independent and in no wise dependent on the covenant to pay the purchase price, that a breach of the former is not a ground for rescission in equity, but that a full, adequate and complete remedy therefor lies in an action of law. Judgment affirmed.

ANTICIPATORY BREACH

When a party renounces a contract before the other party is entitled to performance, the breach is known as an anticipatory breach. Most courts hold that such renunciation by one of the parties discharges the other party from performance, if he so elects, and entitles him to bring an action at once for the breach, without waiting until the time fixed by the contract for performance arrives. If he does not elect to sue at once, the contract is not discharged but remains in force, in which case, if the contract is not performed by the other party when the time for performance arrives, he may sue for damages for the breach of the contract. In other words, he is not required to accept the anticipatory breach by filing suit immediately; he may refuse to do so and demand that the other party perform the contract.

To operate as an anticipatory breach, the offending party's declaration that he will not perform the contract when it becomes due must be unconditional and absolute. A mere statement that he will probably not perform or an assertion that he will not be able to perform the contract is not sufficient. His statement must contain a distinct and unequivocal refusal to perform his part of the contract.

The doctrine of anticipatory breach does not apply to contracts for the payment of a debt, such as a note. Thus, if A borrows $500 from B and signs a promissory note as evidence of the debt, same to be paid six months from date, and if A notifies B two months before the due date that he will not pay the note, A's renunciation will not entitle B to sue immediately. B must wait until the note is due; if A then refuses and fails to pay, B may file suit.

If one of the parties renounces the contract during the course of performance, the other party may treat the renunciation as an anticipatory breach and bring action for damages for the breach of the contract immediately. For example, A employs B to manufacture 600 suits at an agreed price. Under the contract B is to deliver 200 suits per month until the entire 600 suits have been delivered. During the first month B manufactures and delivers 200 suits, at which time A notifies B that he can take no more suits and informs B that he renounces the contract. If the renunciation is unequivocal and absolute, B would be privileged to treat the contract as breached and file an action for damages immediately.

Gilmore v. American Gas Machine Co.
129 N. W. (2d) 93 (Ohio) (1952)

This was an action by Jackson G. Gilmore (plaintiff) against American Gas Machine Company (defendant). Judgment for plaintiff, and defendant appealed. Affirmed.

On August 26, 1941, a written contract was executed by the parties whereby defendant agreed to manufacture certain oil burners and plaintiff was to have the exclusive selling rights during the life of the contract, which was to terminate on June 20, 1956.

On September 14, 1950, a letter was sent to plaintiff by F. A. Trow, president of defendant company, the body of which reads as follows: "This is to advise you that we (Queen Stove Works, Inc.) have acquired control of American Gas Machine Co. I understand that you have some sort of a working agreement with said company whereby they paid you a certain commission on sales made to outside concerns for burners to be fabricated by them. This letter is to advise you that we are not interested in continuing this connection with you, so you will please consider such an arrangement cancelled as of this date."

Treating this letter as a renunciation of the contract, plaintiff filed his petition herein on October 2, 1950. Plaintiff seeks to recover the profits which he claims he would have made under the contract for the balance of the term.

For its first defense defendant entered a general denial. For its second defense it alleged that it was willing to abide by the terms of the contract. For reply plaintiff alleged that defendant did not indicate its willingness to so abide by the terms of the contract until after he had filed suit, and had otherwise changed his position.

GESSAMAN, J. The letter of September 14, 1950, was a renunciation of the contract in question and could be treated by the plaintiff as such and as constituting an anticipatory breach thereof. The rule is well stated in *Builders' Supply & Fuel Co. v. Huntington & Fink Co.*, 1 Ohio Law ABST. 251, at p. 252: "A renunciation to be treated as a breach by the opposite party must be clear and unequivocal so that the party will be informed that he need not expect anything further upon the contract from the other side. . . . To make a renunciation a breach, the other party must treat it as a breach and act upon it."

The plaintiff did act upon the renunciation and thereby treated it as a breach. The attempt of the defendant's president later on to revoke and rescind the letter of September 14, 1950, was of no effect in undoing what had been done. The contract had already been renounced by the letter of September 14th. We conclude, therefore, that the action of the defendant was clear and unequivocal, that it was a renunciation of the contract and that it was treated as such and as an anticipatory breach by the plaintiff, and that he acted thereon by the filing of this suit on October 2, 1950.

[NOTE: The question as to the amount of damages allowed the plaintiff is not discussed in this abstract.]

PREVENTION OF PERFORMANCE

One of the parties to a contract may breach the contract either by committing an act which makes performance on his part impossible or by committing an act which makes performance on the part of the other party impossible. Such action may take place prior to the time of performance or during the course of performance. In either case, if the act is committed without legal justification, the injured party is privileged to treat the contract as discharged and to sue immediately for the breach of the contract. For example, on September 1st A entered into a valid contract with B to sell his automobile to B. Under the terms of the contract A agreed to assign the certificate of title and insurance to B on September 5th and to make delivery of the car on that date. On September 2nd A sold the car to C and immediately assigned the certificate of title and insurance to C and made delivery of the automobile to C. This action by A obviously made it impossible for him to perform his part of the contract with B. The effect of A's action was to breach his contract with B. B could, therefore, treat the contract as discharged and immediately sue A for damages. Again, A employs B to install a furnace in his house. Before B commences work, he and A get into an argument about another matter, and A refuses to allow B to come upon the premises to install the furnace. B sues A for damages, alleging a breach of contract. A sets up as a defense nonperformance. B could recover from A, since B's breach of the contract occurred because A prevented him from coming upon the premises.

Chatsworth 72nd Street Corp v. Rigai and Luchetti

71 Misc (2d) 647, 1336 N. Y. Supp. (2d) 604 (1972)

Civil Court of the City of New York, New York County

These were consolidated summary nonpayment proceedings. The Civil Court of the City of New York held that tenants whose illegal occupancies of basement apartments in rent controlled buildings precluded landlord from obtaining permanent certificate of occupancy for the building were not entitled to rely on the lack of certificate of occupancy as basis for refusal to pay any rent and to retain occupancy in the apartments.

Order in accordance with opinion.

SHAINSWIT, J. These two summary non-payment proceedings were tried jointly, by consent of all parties, and this opinion applies to both.

I find for landlord in each proceeding.

Both tenants are musicians, who have occupied their 2-room studio apartments, in the basement of the large, choice apartment house on 72nd Street and West End Avenue, since 1964 and 1967 at monthly rents of $85 and $100 respectively. However, neither has paid any rent since February 1971, relying on the fact that occupancy of their basement apartments is illegal.

Tenants have urged that they can remain in possession forever, without paying any rent at all, and that no one—neither the landlord, the Rent Commissioner, nor the courts—can alter this state of affairs.

On the facts and on the law, the Court rejects the tenants' posture. Turning first to the facts:

These apartments, along with at least eight others, were created by converting storage rooms in 1949, without meeting legal requirements for such conversion. Concededly, for some years landlord has been seeking to correct this illegality—if for no other reason than that, under the Multiple Dwelling Law, the illegal basement apartments prevent the issuance of a Certificate of Occupancy for the entire building. Landlord has, in fact, taken all possible steps to remedy the situation. Indeed, a temporary Certificate of Occupancy was issued by the Buildings Department on the basis of the plans filed by landlord, since they included all the legally required changes—a basement sprinkler system, fireproofing, new walls, etc. These plans involved drastic structural alterations, necessitating removal of the tenants in occupancy . . . , and all of the other basement tenants have long since vacated their apartments.

The two instant tenants, however, have successfully fought eviction. They first blocked landlord from seeking to cure the illegal condition through the simple eviction routes available for decontrolled tenants. Tenants established, in the course of lengthy proceedings, that they were subject to rent control. [Landlord had urged that the leasing to them was for commercial use; tenants answered that their occupancy was residential. Landlord then pointed out that these apartments were created by conversion from non-housing to housing use; tenants replied that such a conversion did not result in decontrol where a Certificate of Occupancy was not obtained. Tenants prevailed on both questions.]

Landlord was then at an impasse. It pointed out on the trial herein—and tenants vociferously agreed—that it could not bring Rent Commission eviction proceedings directly based on tenants' illegal occupancy. Under a 1970 ordinance, such proceedings are apparently permitted only if the Buildings Department finds the illegal situation to be one of such gravity that it issues a vacate order, or if the violation is initially created by tenant [Administrative Code of City of New York, § Y51–6.0, subd. a(3)]. Further, the temporary Certificate of Occupancy issued by the Buildings Department, based on landlord's filing of plans to correct the illegal occupancies, has expired by operation of law, because of landlord's inability to obtain possession of the two apartments within the statutory time period.

The Commissioner made that ruling precisely because of his finding that these two tenants' illegal occupancy was the sole factor preventing the issuance of a Certificate of Occupancy for the whole building; that criminal proceedings were pending because of tenants' occupancy; and that the reduction to $1 a month was helping prevent curing of the violations by encouraging tenants to remain in occupancy. . . .

Tenants here, similarly, have impeded performance of the condition stated in Section 302, i.e., obtaining the Certificate of Occupancy. They cannot be permitted to set up as a defense that very non-performance for which they are responsible.

The other defenses pleaded in tenants' answers, on the record as a whole,

I find are demonstrably without merit, and they are therefore dismissed. The relief sought by petitioner-landlord, in accordance with the Rent Commissioner's Order, is granted, with a 10 day stay.

LEGAL REMEDIES

THE UNIFORM COMMERCIAL CODE

The Code states in Sec. 1–106: "(1) The remedies provided by this Act shall be liberally administered to the end that the aggrieved party may be put in as good a position as if the other party had fully performed but neither consequential or special nor penal damages may be had except as specifically provided in this Act or by other rule of law.

"(2) Any right or obligation declared by this Act is enforceable by action unless the provision declaring it specifies a different and limited effect."

In reference to breach of a sales contract, the Code in Part 7 of Article 2 on Sales states in detail the rights and remedies of the buyer and seller, and elsewhere in the Code are found special remedies for the parties.

KINDS OF DAMAGES

The principal legal remedy available to the injured party in the case of a breach of contract is an action at law for money damages. There are three kinds of damages, (1) nominal, (2) compensatory or actual, and (3) punitive or exemplary. Nominal damages are awarded the plaintiff where he is able to show a breach of the contract on the part of the defendant, but is unable to show any actual loss or damage as a result of the breach. In such cases the plaintiff will receive a judgment for some nominal sum, such as one dollar, and the court costs will be assessed against the defendant. Compensatory damages are awarded the plaintiff in order to compensate him for losses which he has actually sustained as a result of the breach of the contract by the defendant. Punitive or exemplary damages are awarded for the purpose of punishing the defendant for fraud, malice, or gross negligence. They are awarded not in place of, but in addition to, compensatory damages. Punitive damages are usually awarded in tort cases; the only type of case in which they are awarded for breach of a contract is the breach of a promise to marry.

The enforcement of judgments for money damages has already been discussed in Chapter 4.

MEASURE OF DAMAGES

The general rule is that the plaintiff is entitled to such damages as will fairly compensate him for the losses which he has sustained as a result of the breach of the contract by the defendant. For example, if A contracts on January 1st to sell B 1000 bushels of wheat at the rate of $2.00 per bushel, payment and delivery to take place on March 1st, and if A refuses to make delivery on March 1st, because wheat is selling on the market on that date for $2.50 per bushel, the measure of damages would be the difference between the contract price, on January 1st, and the market price, on March 1st, or $.50 per bushel. The rule for determining or measuring the amount of damages in this type of case is clear and easy to apply. But the determination of damages in many other types of cases is not so easily arrived at, and the courts have adopted certain rules to guide them in making such determination. For example, they have laid down the rule that the plaintiff may be compensated only for those damages that might well have been contemplated by the parties, and that they are the natural and probable consequences of the breach of the contract. As was stated by the court, in *Hadley v. Baxendale:* [1] "Where two parties have made a contract which one of them has broken, the damages which the other party ought to recover, in respect of such breach of contract, should be such as may fairly and reasonably be considered as arising naturally, i.e., according to the usual course of things, from such breach of contract itself; or such as may reasonably be supposed to have been in the contemplation of both parties, at the time they made the contract, as the probable result of the breach of it." In a case involving the alleged loss of profits, damages will not be allowed where the alleged profits are merely hypothetical or highly speculative and incapable of actual proof or ascertainment. However, if the alleged profits are capable of being proved with reasonable certainty, damages will be allowed. For example, A leased a rooming house from B for a period of three years. At the end of the three-year period he leased the house for another three years. B breached the second lease, and A sued B for damages for the loss of contemplated profits for the balance of the term. In such case A would probably be able to recover damages, since the extent of his losses may be substantially proved on the basis of his profits during the term of his first lease. But if A had breached the first lease by refusing to give B possession of the premises, and B had sued for damages for loss of profits, the court would probably hold that the possibility of profits was so speculative and hypothetical that it would be impossible to determine with any degree of accuracy the amount of damages, if any.

[1] 9 Exch. 341, 5 Eng. Rul. Cas. 502.

Troppi v. Scarf

31 Mich. App. 240, 187 N. W. (2d) 511 (1971)

Court of Appeals of Michigan

This was an action by parents who had unwanted child against pharmacist who negligently billed prescription for birth control pills. Court dismissed the complaint and plaintiffs appealed.

LEVIN, P.J. In this case we consider the civil liability of a pharmacist who negligently supplied the wrong drug to a married woman who had ordered an oral contraceptive and, as a consequence, became pregnant and delivered a normal, healthy child.

A summary judgment was entered dismissing the complaint of the plaintiffs, John and Dorothy Troppi, on the ground that it does not state a claim upon which relief can be granted. In our appraisal of the correctness of the trial judge's ruling, we accept as true plaintiffs' factual allegations.

In August 1964, plaintiffs were the parents of seven children, ranging in age from six to sixteen years of age. John Troppi was 43 years old, his wife 37.

While pregnant with an eighth child, Mrs. Troppi suffered a miscarriage. She and her husband consulted with their physician and decided to limit the size of their family. The physician prescribed an oral contraceptive, Norinyl, as the most desirable means of insuring that Mrs. Troppi would bear no more children. He telephoned the prescription to defendant, Frank H. Scarf, a licensed pharmacist. Instead of filling the prescription, Scarf negligently supplied Mrs. Troppi with a drug called Nardil, a mild tranquilizer.

Believing that the pills she had purchased were contraceptives, Mrs. Troppi took them on a daily basis. In December 1964, Mrs. Troppi became pregnant. She delivered a well-born son on August 12, 1965.

Plaintiffs' complaint alleges four separate items of damage: (1) Mrs. Troppi's lost wages; (2) medical and hospital expenses; (3) the pain and anxiety of pregnancy and childbirth; and (4) the economic costs of rearing the eighth child.

In dismissing the complaint the judge declared that whatever damage plaintiffs suffered was more than offset by the benefit to them of having a healthy child.

Setting aside, for the moment, the subtleties of the damage question, it is at least clear that the plaintiffs have expended significant sums of money as a direct and proximate result of the defendant's negligence. The medical and hospital expenses of Mrs. Troppi's confinement and her loss of wages arose from the defendant's failure to fill the prescription properly. Pain and suffering, like that accompanying childbirth, have long been recognized as compensable injuries.

This review of the elements of tort liability points up the extraordinary nature of the trial court's holding that the plaintiffs were entitled to no recovery as a matter of law. We have here a negligent, wrongful act by the defendant, which act directly and proximately caused injury to plaintiffs.

While the reasonableness of a plaintiff's efforts to mitigate is ordinarily to be decided by the trier of fact, we are persuaded to rule, as a matter of law, that no mother, wed or unwed, can reasonably be required to abort (even if legal) or place her child for adoption. The plaintiffs are entitled to have the jurors instructed that if they find that negligence of the defendant was a cause in fact of the plaintiffs' injury, they may not, in computing the amount, if any, of the plaintiffs' damages, take into consideration the fact that the plaintiffs might have aborted the child or placed the child for adoption.

It should be clear that ascertainment of *gross* damages is a routine task. Whatever uncertainty attends the final award arises from application of the benefits rule, which requires that the trier of fact compute the dollar value of the companionship and services of an unwanted child. Placing a dollar value on these segments may well be more difficult than assessing damages for, say, Mrs. Troppi's lost wages. But difficulty in determining the amount to be subtracted from the gross damages does not justify throwing up our hands and denying recovery altogether.

Michigan law is clear that there need only be a basis for reasonable ascertainment of the amount of the damages. Where the fact of liability is proven, difficulty in determining damages will not bar recovery. . . .

Moreover, the Michigan Supreme Court has repeatedly recognized that the dollar value of a child's services and companionship is not too uncertain to be left to the judgment of the trier of fact. Beginning in 1960 with *Wycko v. Gnodtke* (1960), 361 Mich. 331, 105 N. W. (2d) 118, recovery for the wrongful death of a child was measured by considering, among other elements of damage, the value of his services and companionship. Although there was spirited dissent as to the statutory basis of this rule, subsequent cases reflected no feeling on the part of the Court that these damages were too uncertain to be entrusted to determination by the trier of fact. The recent disavowal of Wycko in *Breckon v. Franklin Fuel Company* (1970), 383 Mich. 251, 174 N. W. (2d) 836, involved a question of statutory interpretation, and not the specificity of the measure of damages.

The assessment of damages in this case is properly within the competence of the trier of fact. The element of uncertainty in the net recovery does not render the damages unduly speculative.

Reversed and remanded for trial.

MITIGATION OF DAMAGES

Though the law permits the recovery of money damages for breach of a contract, it requires that the injured party mitigate or keep down the amount of the damages as much as is reasonably possible. For example, A and B enter into a written contract whereby A employs B for a year at a monthly salary of $500. At the end of six months A discharges B, stating that business has fallen off and that he no longer needs B's services. Under such circumstances B is not warranted in remaining unemployed for the balance of the term of six months, on the assumption that he will be able to recover a judgment against A for $3,000 (six months at the rate of $500 per month). The law requires that B make a reasonable effort to mitigate the amount of damages by trying to secure the same type of employment with some other employer in the same locality.

The same rule of law applies in the case of a contract to manufacture or sell merchandise. For example, A makes a contract with B, a manufacturer of men's wear, whereby A agrees to buy 500 overcoats from B. Under the contract 300 overcoats are to be delivered to A on September 1st and the remaining 200 overcoats are to be delivered on November 1st. On September 1st B delivers the 300 overcoats and A pays for them, in accordance with the terms of the contract. At the same time A tells B that he will not need the remaining 200 overcoats and that he will refuse to accept them if delivery is tendered. Under these circumstances B would not be warranted in going ahead and manufacturing the additional 200 overcoats for the sole purpose of tendering them to A on November 1st. The law requires that B mitigate the damages by not manufacturing the additional overcoats. B would of course have a cause of action against A for damages for the breach of the contract. In addition to the profit that B would have made on the additional 200 overcoats, the measure of damages would include any expense which he could show he had incurred in preparing to manufacture the 200 overcoats, e.g., for purchase of materials with which to make the overcoats. But if B could use the materials in the manufacture of overcoats or suits for other customers (a further mitigation), he could not recover for their entire cost.

Wetzel v. Rixse
93 Okla. 216, 220 P. 607 (1923)

This was an action by F. D. Rixse and Charles B. Jenkins, partners (plaintiffs) against Eugene Wetzel (defendant). Judgment for plaintiffs, and defendant appealed. Modified and affirmed.

Plaintiffs were architects. They entered into a contract with defendant to prepare preliminary plans, drawings, and specifications for a proposed building to be built by defendant. Under the terms of the agreement plaintiffs were to receive 1 per cent of the cost of the building for drawing up the plans and specifications, another 1 per cent when the contract was let, another three-fourths of 1 per cent when the building was half completed, and another three-fourths of 1 per cent when the building was completed.

The petition alleged that the contract had been broken by defendant on or about August 29, 1919, in that defendant informed plaintiffs that he would not perform the contract and repudiated same; that they had prepared all the preliminary drawings, completed working drawings and all plans and specifications for the construction of the building, and had at all times been willing and able to perform all the services specified in said contract, and *had been damaged* in the sum of $1,820 on account of the alleged breach of the contract by defendant, for which they demanded judgment.

Defendant answered that plaintiffs had not prepared any plans which he was able to use, in that the plans, drawings, and specifications submitted involved an encroachment of the building on adjoining lots and buildings belonging to other parties on which defendant had no right to go, and that plaintiffs had failed to comply with any part of their contract. Plaintiffs replied to defendant's answer that defendant found that he did not have sufficient money available to build a three-story building; and that he changed his mind on a number of occasions concerning the whole matter.

After the alleged breach of the contract on August 29, 1919, plaintiffs submitted a number of other plans to defendant, for which they claim compensation.

FOSTER, C. While the evidence in the case is conflicting and unsatisfactory, it is admitted that the plaintiffs prepared and submitted plans involving a three-story building, and that these plans were in accordance with the contract. In these circumstances we think the evidence was sufficient to take the case to the jury and to warrant the jury in finding for the plaintiff upon the proposition that a breach of contract by the defendant had occurred by reasons of the fact that he had discovered after he let the contract that he could not erect a three-story building for the amount of money available, if they believed the testimony on this proposition.

If the trial court did not err in submitting the case to the jury, it follows that the verdict of the jury must stand, unless the jury erred in the assessment of the amount of recovery. In our judgment, the jury did so err, and the verdict and judgment for $1,100 was excessive upon the facts proven.

The plaintiff testified that when the preliminary plans were submitted, the defendant refused to accept them, because he could not construct a three-story building for $30,000. At this point there occurred a breach on the part of the defendant of his contract which discharged the plaintiffs from any further obligation on their part under the contract. Under these circumstances, we do not think that the plaintiffs were justified in preparing further plans or performing other duties under the contract. Therefore, their recovery is limited to the amount of the damage they had sustained at the time of the breach. If subsequent to this breach they completed working drawings and specifications, they did so at their peril, and can recover nothing as compensation therefor. The plaintiffs testified that the cost of a three-story building would be between $42,000 and $50,000. The contract provided as compensation for preliminary drawings 1% of the estimated cost of the building. Allowing $50,000 as the estimated cost of the building it is obvious that $500 would be the maximum sum which the jury could have properly allowed. Therefore, if the plaintiffs will file a remittitur for all in excess of the sum of $500, within thirty days, the judgment as thus modified will be affirmed; otherwise the judgment will be reversed and remanded and a new trial granted.

LIQUIDATED DAMAGES

Sometimes the parties specify in their contract an amount which shall be paid as damages in case of default or breach of the contract by one of the parties. The amount so specified is known as liquidated damages. For example, a contract between A and B, a building contractor, for the construction of an apartment house for $200,000 might contain some such clause as the following: "It is further agreed, upon the part of B, that if said apartment house is not completed and ready for occupancy on or before September 1, 1954, he will pay to A $100 per day for each and every day the said apartment house is delayed in its completion. It is agreed and understood by the contracting parties that any payment under this provision shall be looked upon as liquidated damages, and as compensation for any damages sustained by A."

The chief reason for providing for liquidated damages is the fact that in certain kinds of contracts it is often difficult, and sometimes practically impossible, to estimate, with any degree of accuracy, the actual amount of damages that would result in case one of the parties breached the contract. Such stipulations will be enforced by the courts if they are reasonable; that is, if the amount of damages stipulated bears a close approximation to the probable damages actually suffered by the injured party. It must also be clear that the amount specified is looked upon and understood by the parties as *compensation* for any damages which would be sustained in the event of the breach of the contract. If the court should be of the opinion, on the contrary that the stipulation was placed in the contract as a *penalty*, for the purpose of forcing one of the contracting parties to perform his part of the contract, it would refuse to recognize the stipulation as liquidated damages. In that case, it would be the responsibility of the jury, under proper instructions, to determine the amount of damages, if any, sustained by the plaintiff.

In the foregoing example the court would probably hold that the stipulated sum of $100 for each day the contractor was delayed in completing the apartment house was in the nature of liquidated damages, because (1) the parties expressly declared that they understood the stipulated sum to be liquidated damages and as compensation to A, and (2) the amount specified was reasonable, since the payment of $100 per day on a $200,000 investment in the apartment house could not be considered out of line. On the other hand, the same stipulation in a contract to build a house for $12,000 would no doubt be held by the court to be a penalty, since the amount would far exceed any actual damages which A might reasonably be expected to suffer by the delay of a day or a few days in the completion of the house.

Smith v. Lane
236 S. W. (2d) 214 (1951)

This was an action by Blaze H. Lane (plaintiff) against Pinkie Smith (defendant) seeking to recover the amount of liquidated damages provided for in two contracts in the total sum of $780. Judgment for plaintiff, and defendant appealed. Affirmed.

By the terms of the first contract sued on, Lane agreed to lend to Smith the sum of $500, and Smith agreed to provide a suitable place for the operation of Lane's juke boxes and coin-operated music machines in two places of business operated by him and at any other place where he might engage in a business. No other juke boxes were to be permitted to operate upon such premises, for a violation of which the sum of $500 was agreed upon as "liquidated damages, because of the inconvenience of ascertaining the actual damages and the uncertainty thereof." Smith was to receive one-half of all funds and money deposited in the juke boxes, but such payment was first to be applied to the payment of the loan until it was completely paid back to Lane.

The second contract was exactly the same as the first, except that the loan was for the sum of $280 and the liquidated damages were for the same amount.

Breach of these two contracts was alleged and a default judgment was rendered for the stipulated liquidated damages in the sum of $780. Defendant appealed, contending that the provisions for damages in the event of a breach were for penalties and not for liquidated damages, as such.

MURRAY, C.J. The provision not only referred to the damages as "liquidated damages" but further gave the reason why liquidated damages were agreed upon, to wit, "because of the inconvenience of ascertaining the actual damages and the uncertainty thereof." It is true the courts are inclined to construe such provision as one for a penalty rather than as for liquidated damages, as such, but this is true only where the defendant appears and by both allegation and proof raises the issue. Under such circumstances the burden of proof is upon the defendant.

Here the damages were indefinite and uncertain and in view of the language of the contracts and the default of the defendant, the trial court properly construed the contracts as providing for liquidated damages and not for penalties. Judgment affirmed.

EQUITABLE REMEDIES

The principal equitable remedies which are applicable to contracts are (1) specific performance, (2) injunction, and (3) rescission and reformation. It should be remembered that the granting of any type of equitable relief by a court of equity is a matter of sound discretion on the part of the court. Furthermore, courts of equity take the position that before they will grant equitable relief to the complainant he must allege and prove either that no remedy at law exists or, if such a remedy does exist, that it is inadequate in his case.

SPECIFIC PERFORMANCE

In general, courts of equity will grant specific performance of contracts (1) where the subject matter of the contract is of such a special nature or of such a peculiar value that money damages, awarded by a law court, would be inadequate, or (2) where, because of the nature of the subject matter money damages would be impracticable.

CONTRACTS TO SELL LAND.   It is firmly established that courts of equity will usually specifically enforce a contract to sell land, assuming that it is in writing and properly executed. The buyer's right to specific perform-ance is predicated upon the assumption that every piece of real estate is *unique*—that no two pieces of land are exactly alike. The seller's right to specific performance is based upon the *doctrine of mutuality* (or *mutual remedies*): the courts hold that it would not be equitable to grant the remedy of specific performance to one class of parties (buyers) and not to the other class (sellers).

CONTRACTS TO SELL PERSONAL PROPERTY.   The general rule is that courts of equity will not grant specific performance of contracts to sell personal property. The reason for this is the view, on the part of the courts, that money damages in a court of law are adequate, since similar chattels are generally available on the market, and the measure of damages, in money, is usually readily ascertainable. However, if the subject matter of the con-tract is *unique* the equity courts will grant specific performance. A chat-tel may be unique because it possesses certain sentimental value to the purchaser, or because it is rare and impossible or extremely difficult to purchase on the open market. Since the purchaser could not duplicate such a chattel on the open market, money damages are held to be inade-quate. A practical illustration today is a contract to sell shares of corporate stock. In general, such a contract will not be specifically enforced if the same class of stock of the corporation is obtainable on the market, but if it is not available, specific performance will probably be granted. Like-wise, a number of courts have granted specific performance of contracts to sell personal property, even where it was not unique, if the remedy at law (money damages) would not be adequate, owing to the fact that the seller was insolvent, or in such poor financial condition that the purchaser would probably be unable to collect a judgment for money damages. The courts of equity refuse specific performance of a building contract be-cause of the difficulty or inconvenience of enforcing a decree.

UNIFORM COMMERCIAL CODE

Section 2–716 states that the buyer has a right to specific performance where the goods are unique or in other proper circumstances, which will be discussed in greater detail in Part V, Sales.

CONTRACTS FOR PERSONAL SERVICES (EMPLOYMENT CONTRACTS). Courts of equity refuse to grant specific performance of employment contracts. Enforcement of such contracts also smacks of involuntary servitude.

Lee Builders, Inc. v. Wells et al.
95 A. (2d) 692 (Del.) (1953)

This was suit by Lee Builders, Inc., assignee of J. Rowland Morgan (plaintiff) against William F. Wells, Jr. and Catherine Wells, his wife, and Sarah E. Wells, widow (defendants). Decree for complainant, and defendants appealed. Affirmed.

On May 12, 1950, defendants and one J. Rowland Morgan entered into a written agreement for the sale by defendants to Morgan of parts of two lots with improvements, in Elsmere, Delaware, defendants retaining a part of said lots for purposes hereinafter set forth.

The agreement provided, in substance: that the purchase price was to be $19,000, of which $1,000 was paid at the time of the execution of the agreement; that plaintiff at its own expense should remove the houses thereon to that portion of the lots retained by defendants, dig a cellar and erect foundations for the houses when moved, and lay a sidewalk and driveway to conform to the new location; and that final settlement would be made on or before September 1, 1950.

Shortly after the execution of this agreement defendants became dissatisfied with the arrangement and so informed the purchaser. After some negotiation the parties, on September 1, 1950, executed a subsequent agreement, whereby it was provided that one Theodore Wells, Jr., a nephew of defendants, but not a party to this action, was to be paid an additional sum of $2,000. The time of settlement was extended to November 15, 1950. These agreements were later assigned by Morgan to plaintiff.

Difficulties again arose between the parties, largely relative to the work which was to be performed by plaintiff. Defendants again indicated their dissatisfaction with the arrangement. They informed a surveyor and a house mover whom plaintiff had sent to the property to examine the same that they were not going to comply with their obligation. Plaintiff had taken out a building permit for the construction of the building, had purchased the steel for the store building which it intended to erect on the property and had had it fabricated, at a total cost of $10,000. Complainant asked defendants to comply with their contract by giving a deed to the property and defendants refused to do so. Complainant thereupon filed this suit asking for specific performance of the contract.

BRAMHALL, C. Assuming that the signature of the defendants to the contract of May 12, 1950, may have been obtained under such circumstances that a court of equity in good conscience would not decree specific performance thereon, the fact remains that all the pertinent conditions of this contract were reaffirmed in the agreement of September 1, 1950.

It is true that specific performance will not be granted where plaintiff has an adequate remedy at law. Nevertheless, it is also true that in the case of an agreement for the sale of land, courts will assume that money damages do not constitute an adequate remedy for the breach of such contract and take jurisdiction without the necessity of an actual showing that such is the case. 49 *Am. Jur.*, Specific Performance, sec. 92, p. 107, n. 15. This principle is affirmed in the case of *F. B. Norman Co. v. E. I. du Pont de Nemours & Co.*, 12 Del. Ch. 155, 108 A. 143, in the following language: "It is almost a matter of course that a court of equity will enforce specific performance of contracts concerning land, for all land is assumed to have a peculiar value to those who contract as to it, so that damages for breach of contract is not an adequate remedy."

I find no merit in defendants' contention that there is such substantive hardship and inconvenience to defendants as to warrant this court in refusing a decree of specific performance.

INJUNCTION

The principal use of the injunction [1] in contract law is to enjoin the defendant from breaching a *negative covenant* of his contract. One of the first recorded instances of such use was the well-known case of *Lumley v. Wagner*.[2] In that case a famous singer, Johanna Wagner, had contracted to sing at the plaintiff's theater for a certain number of nights. In her contract she also agreed not to sing for anyone else during that time (a negative covenant). She broke her contract with Lumley and was preparing to sing for Gye in his theater. Lumley filed a suit in equity asking the court to grant him specific performance of his contract. The court refused to grant specific performance because it felt that it would not be feasible or practical to supervise the defendant's singing. But it did grant Lumley an injunction enjoining Wagner from breaching the negative covenant in her contract by singing for someone else.

Whether or not a court of equity will enjoin a negative covenant in a contract depends upon the circumstances of the given case. As with other equitable remedies, such relief will not be granted if the court is of the opinion that the remedy at law is adequate. In the case of an employment contract wherein the employee agrees to work for the employer and for no one else during the period of the contract, in order for the employer to enjoin the employee from breaching the negative provision of the con-

[1] See above section entitled Equitable Remedies in Chapter 1 of this text.
[2] 1 Deg. M. & G. 604 (Eng.).

tract, he usually has to prove that the services which the employee contracted to perform were unique in character, requiring special skill and ability, and that it would be extremely difficult or impossible to replace the employee. In the type of contract wherein the seller agrees to sell his product to the buyer and to no one else within a specified territory, usually the buyer may not obtain an injunction if the seller breaches his contract and sells to others; but if he alleges and proves that the financial condition of the seller is so poor that a judgment for money damages would be uncollectible, he may usually obtain injunctive relief.

Shubert Theatrical Co. v. Raft et al.
271 Fed. Rep. 827 (1921)

This was a suit in equity by the Shubert Theatrical Company (plaintiff) against George and Richard Raft (defendants). Decree for complainant, and defendants appealed. Affirmed.

Complainant was a theatrical manager and producer, and defendants were acrobatic performers. On July 8, 1919, the parties entered into a written agreement by the terms of which complainant engaged defendants to render their exclusive services to complainant for a period of one year commencing on September 1, 1919. It was agreed that defendants should appear at all times as directed by complainant during the year, and complainant guaranteed that defendants should be employed for 20 weeks in the minimum. The salary of defendants was fixed at the sum of $250 per week while appearing in the city of New York and $275 per week while on the road. It was further provided that complainant had an option on the services of defendants for the year beginning September 1, 1920, provided complainant exercised the option prior to July 1, 1920. If complainant exercised the option reserved to it, the agreement provided that the guaranty of 20 weeks should again apply for the period but that the salary should be $300 per week while appearing in the city of New York and $325 per week while appearing on the road. Defendants agreed that they would not render their services or appear publicly for any other firm or corporation, during the term of the contract, without the written consent of complainant. Defendants further agreed, in the contract, that their services were extraordinary and unique and could not be replaced.

On June 7, 1920, complainant, pursuant to its option, employed defendants for the year beginning September 1, 1920. Notwithstanding this, defendants advised complainant that they refused to perform according to their agreement. They had contracted with a rival manager to appear in a production to be presented in the city of New York. Complainant thereupon asked for an injunction to restrain defendants from performing for any manager other than complainant, or from performing in any other theater or place of public amusement, or in any other company, except that of complainant, until the expiration of the term mentioned in the agreement made between complainant and defendants. The court below granted the injunction and defendant appealed.

ROGERS, J. The testimony shows that the acrobatic performances of the defendants are unique and extraordinary. These services were to be given to the complainant exclusively, and the contract contains an express negative covenant that they would not be given under any other management during the period of the contract. By a negative covenant the covenantor promises that something shall not be done. The relief appropriate to a breach of such a contract is an injunction. The leading authority, as represents covenants for personal services, is the well-known case of *Lumley v. Wagner*, 1 Deg., M. & G. 604. In that case a famous singer agreed to sing in the opera house of the complainant for a certain time, and not to sing for anyone else during that time. As the services contracted for were those of a person possessing special and extraordinary qualifications, Lord Chancellor St. Leonards granted an injunction restraining the defendant from singing at any other theater than that belonging to the complainant. It was held that the fact that the court would have been unable to enforce specifically the defendant's affirmative covenant to sing at the plaintiff's theatre did not affect the complainant's right to an injunction to restrain a violation of the negative covenant not to sing elsewhere.

The basis upon which the decisions rest in all such cases is that the damages for the breach of such contracts cannot be estimated with any certainty, and the employer cannot by means of any damages purchase the same services from others. The injury in such cases is irreparable.

It is familiar doctrine that courts of equity do not exercise their jurisdiction to grant the remedy of an affirmative specific performance of a contract for personal services. This they decline to do because they cannot in any direct manner compel an actor to act or a singer to sing. But the rule is so established that the courts of equity may restrain by injunction the breach of a negative covenant by which an actor or a singer of unusual gifts has agreed not to act or not to sing in a specified period, except under the management of the other party to the contract. Decree affirmed.

RESCISSION AND REFORMATION

Another important equitable remedy applicable to contract law is found in the power of equity courts to order the rescission or reformation of contracts. Under certain conditions a court of equity may reform the contract so that it will conform with the real intentions of the parties. Under other situations such instruments may be completely rescinded or canceled.

In general, rescission and reformation may be decreed by a court of equity because of mistake, fraud, misrepresentation, duress, undue influence, and illegality. For example, if A secures the signature of B to a contract as a result of fraud, B may have the contract rescinded by a court of equity. And if A and B enter into a contract whereby A agrees to sell a house and lot to B, and through a mutual mistake the property is incorrectly described in the contract, either party may ask the court of equity to reform the contract so that it will represent the real intentions of the parties.

REVIEW CASES

1. Patterson and Meyerhofer executed a contract whereby Patterson was to purchase four parcels of land at a foreclosure sale and convey them to Meyerhofer for $23,000. Before the sale Meyerhofer told Patterson that she intended to buy the land at the sale on her own account, and she did so, outbidding Patterson and acquiring the land for $22,380. Patterson sued for damages of $620. Judgment for whom? (Patterson v. Meyerhofer, 204 N. Y. 96, 97 N. E. 472)

2. Hill contracted with Balkcom to teach certain children designated by Balkcom for a period of nine months for a specified sum. Hill taught the children for only 8½ months and brought suit in contract for recovery. The lower court permitted no recovery, and Hill appealed. Judgment for whom? (Hill v. Balkcom, 79 Ga. 444, 5 S. E. 200)

3. Millikin sold a barber shop to Bradshaw, agreeing not to compete in the barber business for two years in Hamlet, N. C. The contract had a liquidated damages clause for $400 in case of a breach. Millikin breached the restrictive covenant, and Bradshaw filed a bill in equity to enjoin violation of the contract. Ruling? (Bradshaw v. Millikin, 173 N. C. 432, 92 S. E. 161)

4. O'Neill sued the Supreme Council of the American Legion of Honor for breach of contract on a benefit certificate to pay O'Neill's sister, in trust for his six children, the sum of $5,000. O'Neill was to pay premiums when due, and upon his death the benefit certificate was to be collected. Thereafter the Supreme Council told O'Neill that it would pay only $2,000 to the beneficiaries after his death, and refused further premium payments from O'Neill. Ruling? (O'Neill v. Supreme Council, American Legion of Honor, 70 N. J. L. 410, 57 A. 463)

5. Zak contracted orally with Gray to purchase a lot from him for $500, and Gray agreed to permit Zak to move his cobbler shop onto the property. The shop was moved at a cost of $1,000, but Gray refused to convey title to the property unless Zak paid him $3,000. Has Zak a remedy? (Zak v. Gray, 324 Mich. 522, 37 N. W.(2d) 550)

6. Clark contracted with Marsiglia to clean and repair certain pictures for an agreed amount per picture. Before completion of the job, Clark ordered Marsiglia to stop work on the pictures, but Marsiglia continued until he had finished and then sued for the full amount of the contract, covering labor and materials used. Clark contended that he was not liable for any work done after the countermand. Holding? (Clark v. Marsiglia, 1 Denio. 317 (N. Y.), 43 Am. Dec. 670)

7. Boyarsky signed a written contract with Geremia to do painting and carpenter work on a house. The next day Boyarsky discovered an error in his

calculations and notified Geremia that he could not perform for the amount stipulated in the contract but would for another amount. Geremia refused the new proposition, awarded the contract to someone else, and brought suit for damages for breach of contract. Boyarsky asked the court to rescind the contract. Geremia had good reason to know when he entered the contract that a mistake had been made. Ruling? (Geremia v. Boyarsky et al., 107 Conn. 387, 140 A. 749)

Agency

part III

Nature and Creation of the Agency Relation

17

NATURE OF THE AGENCY RELATION

INTRODUCTION

It would be difficult to overemphasize the importance of a knowledge of agency law (and the closely related law of employer and employee) in the modern business world. Since most people earn their living either in the capacity of a principal or an employer or in that of an agent or an employee, their daily activities are constantly affected by those parts of the law. The relationship of principal and agent and that of employer and employee give rise to certain duties and liabilities, as well as rights and privileges; consequently a better understanding of these legal relationships not only puts one in a better position to protect his own interests, but enables him to perform more successfully his particular functions and duties in the business world. Failure on the part of a principal or an employer to understand such matters proves costly at times, not only in dollars and cents but in terms of the harmonious operation of his business. Similar failure on the part of an agent or employee may result in his needlessly incurring some liability; more broadly, it is likely to make him a less useful agent or employee and thus to stand in the way of his advancement on the job.

Prior to the Industrial Revolution, when the economy was basically agricultural, little "business" in the modern sense of the term was carried on. The form of the business enterprise was that of a single proprietorship: the master craftsman, who operated the business, was the "master," and the journeymen and apprentices, who lived and worked in the master craftsman's house, were the "servants." The manufacturing was commonly done in the rear of the house, the retailing from the front room adjacent to the street. Few if any "agents" existed.

With the coming of the Industrial Revolution and the factory system, great economic changes took place; and these changes were reflected in the form of the business unit. As business expanded, it was found advantageous to make use of the partnership and the corporation. The entrepreneurs needed more personnel, some to assist with the manufacturing processes, and others to help in the marketing processes by contacting prospective customers and selling the products. These vast economic changes were reflected in the law and resulted in what were known as the Law of Master and Servant (today generally called the Law of Employer and Employee) and the Law of Principal and Agent. Basically, the law regarding these two relationships is the same. In the present section, therefore, the law that applies to the relationship of principal and agent forms the basis of discussion; where it differs from the law applicable to the relationship of employer and employee, the differences will be noted.

Most of the law of agency is based upon the broad principles of contract law and tort law. Consequently, we shall draw constantly upon what we have learned about contract law and tort law. Later, when we study other areas of the law, such as the law of partnerships and corporations, we shall draw in turn upon our knowledge of agency law.

RELATIONSHIP OF PRINCIPAL AND AGENT DISTINGUISHED FROM OTHER RELATIONSHIPS

At the beginning of our study of agency law it is important to distinguish between the relationship of (1) principal and agent, (2) employer and employee,[1] and (3) employer and independent contractor.

PRINCIPAL AND AGENT. In a principal-agent relationship the agent represents his principal in business transactions with third parties. Such representation usually involves the negotiation of contracts, but it may involve negotiations that have for their purpose the modification or termination of a contract. In all such transactions the agent acts purely in a representative capacity, and the agency relationship involves the delegation of certain duties and responsibilities by the principal to the agent. Three parties are involved, namely, the principal, the agent, and the third party. In certain specialized transactions the agent may be known by some other name, such as "factor," "broker," or "attorney." A *factor* is an agent who sells goods belonging to his principal and who is entrusted with the possession of such goods. A *broker* sells for his principal but does not have

---

[1] We shall use the terms *employer* and *employee* everywhere in the text, though the corresponding *master* and *servant* will be found in some of the cases.

possession of the property which he is to sell. An *attorney in fact* is an agent who is given authority by his principal to perform a particular act not of a legal nature. An *attorney at law* by no means always acts in the capacity of an agent for his client, but he does so when he represents his client in business transactions with third parties.

EMPLOYER AND EMPLOYEE.   The relationship of employer and employee exists where one party employs another to perform purely mechanical or manual acts and services. An employee deals with things, and not with third persons, on behalf of his employer; consequently there are only two parties to such an arrangement. An employee acts, directly or indirectly, under the direction and control of his employer. Factory workers, farm hands, and clerical workers are good examples of employees.

EMPLOYER AND INDEPENDENT CONTRACTOR.   An important distinction is made between the relationship of employer and employee and that of employer and independent contractor. While an employee acts under the direction and control of the employer, an independent contractor contracts to produce a certain *result* and has full control over the means and methods which he shall use in producing the result. He is usually said to carry on an independent business. He furnishes his own tools, machines, and employees; and in some cases, though not in all, he furnishes the materials used in performing the job to be done. A good example is a building contractor who contracts to build a house conforming to the specifications laid down by his contract. His employer does not direct or control his handling of the job. The contractor may purchase the necessary materials from whom he pleases and on terms which seem desirable to himself. He may employ as many employees as he chooses to assist him in building the house. The only concern of the employer is the end result. He does insist, and he has a right to insist, that the house, when completed, shall conform to the terms of the contract.

It is important to make the distinction between an employee and an independent contractor because the tort liability of the employer differs under the two relationships. The employer is liable for the torts of his employee when committed within the scope of his employment. But he is not liable for the torts of the independent contractor or of the latter's employees. The one exception to this rule is that some courts hold the employer liable for the torts of the independent contractor in cases where the employer was negligent in employing him. Since neither employee nor independent contractor has authority to contract on the employer's behalf, the employer is not liable for the contracts of either.

Turnbull et al. v. Shelton et al.

286 P. (2d) 676 (Wash.) (1955)

This was an action by A. J. Turnbull and others (plaintiffs) against Cleo L. Shelton and others (defendants). Judgment for plaintiffs, and defendants appealed. Affirmed.

The plaintiffs, A. J. Turnbull and T. R. Lonon, were partners, and carried on business under the firm name of Columbia Asphalt Paving Company. They sued Cleo L. Shelton for $1,236, that being the amount of their bid, plus the sales tax, for laying 1040 square yards of asphalt paving on the premises belonging to the defendant Shelton.

The material facts were as follows: Shelton was building an apartment house. Tom Sager, who supposedly had connections by virtue of which he could buy at lower prices than could Shelton, purchased materials, equipment, and fixtures for the defendant Shelton, and secured bids for some phases of the work, such as that performed by the plaintiffs. In some instances, purchases and contracts were made in Sager's name. Ostensibly, Sager was from time to time a financier, a vendor of building materials, etc., an independent contractor, a joint venturer or partner. The trial court was not confused by these protean aspects and found that, in the transaction with which we are here concerned, Sager was at all times the agent of Shelton.

This action was brought by the plaintiffs against the defendant Shelton upon the theory that Sager was Shelton's agent, and, because of that relationship Shelton was liable for the payment of the sum of $1,236 to the plaintiffs.

The defendant Shelton contended that he was not liable since Sager was an independent contractor. Sager, in the meantime, went into bankruptcy.

HILL, J. An implied agency is an actual agency and can be proved from the facts and circumstances by deduction or inference; it is established by the words and conduct of the parties and by the circumstances of the particular case. *Sharpe Sign Co. v. Parrish*, 33 Wash. (2d) 883, 207 P. (2d) 758.

In *Coombs v. R. D. Bodle Co.*, 33 Wash. (2d) 280, 205 P. (2d) 888, we quoted the following definition of "agency," from 1 *Restatement, Agency*, 7, Sec. 1 (1): "Agency is the relationship which results from the manifestation of consent by one person to another that the other shall act on his behalf and subject to his control, and consent by the other so to act." In *McCarty v. King County Medical Service Corporation*, 26 Wash. (2d) 669, 175 P. (2d) 653, Judge Connelly used the same definition, emphasizing that control of the conduct of the agent is a vitally essential element in the relationship of principal and agent.

The record supports the inference that the defendant Shelton consented that Sager should act for him, in his behalf and subject to his control, and that Sager consented so to act, in consequence thereof becoming a purchasing agent and contract procurement agent in connection with the construction of the apartment house, and that he was so acting in the transaction with which we are here concerned.

The defendant asked Sager to get bids for the asphalt paving. Sager contacted the defendants and presumably others, and introduced plaintiff Turnbull to the defendant. It was from defendant that Turnbull secured the information as to the work to be done on the basis of which he made his bid. Sager advised the plaintiff that he had received their bids and that the plaintiffs were "low." Defendant directed Sager to request the plaintiffs to go ahead with the job, and was present much of the time while the work was being done.

It is contended by the defendant that a relationship of owner and independent contractor existed between Sager and himself. . . . The control exercised by the defendant over the work performed and over Sager's purchases is inconsistent with any claim that Sager was an independent contractor. In *Losli v. Foster*, 37 Wash. (2d) 220, 222 P. (2d) 824, we quoted with approval the rule that marks the dividing line between an agent and an independent contractor, as stated in 2 *Am. Jur.* 17, Agency, sec. 8: "'An independent contractor may be distinguished from an agent in that he is a person who contracts with another to do something for him, but who is not controlled or subject to the control of the other in the performance of such contract, but only as to the result. A principal, on the other hand, has the right to control the conduct of an agent with respect to matters intrusted to him.'"

The transactions with which we are here concerned . . . are clearly on the principal-agent side of that dividing line. We conclude that Sager was defendant's agent and not an independent contractor.

Glenn, Collector of Internal Revenue v. Beard
141 F. (2d) 376 (1944)

This was an action by Eleanor Beard (plaintiff) against Seldon R. Glenn, Collector of Internal Revenue (defendant), to recover taxes alleged to have been erroneously collected under the Social Security Act. Judgment for plaintiff, and defendant appealed. Affirmed.

The Collector of Internal Revenue levied and collected Social Security taxes from appellee, who, thereafter, filed a petition in the District Court for refund and was awarded a judgment therefor. The court held that appellee was not an employer; that the workers upon whose asserted employment the taxes were levied were independent contractors; and that appellee, under the statute, was not liable for the exaction.

The appellee maintained studios in Kentucky, where, for many years, she had engaged women to make comforters, quilts, and similar articles. The women did the work in their homes on farms, within a 25-mile radius of a studio. Appellee supplied materials stamped with designs, and specifications for the work agreed upon. The material and thread, together with the specifications or instructions, were delivered to the worker at the time of the signing of a contract between the worker and the appellee. The contract provided that the homeworker would work the material according to the specifications; that the work could be done at such time—within a designated period—and at such places as were agreeable to the worker, and that, futher, the worker could do the work personally or by agent of her selection. It was also provided that upon completion of the specified work and its delivery to the appellee, a certain price would be paid to the worker, who was responsible for any damage or injury to the materials while they were in her possession. There was no supervision of the work, and appellee never even called at the homes of the workers to inspect the work. Payment was made when the finished product was delivered to the appellee. Other individuals and companies were engaged in the same kind of business as appellee, and often homeworkers would be engaged in working on various materials for several such concerns at the same time, interspersing such work with their household duties. They only worked when they wanted to, and at such time in the year as farm duties permitted them.

McALLISTER, C.J. The question presented by this appeal is whether the workers in question are independent contractors, exempt from the provisions of the statute, or whether they are employees, subject to the Act.

According to the pertinent regulations of the Commissioner of Internal Revenue, promulgated under Title IX of the Social Security Act, it is provided: "In general, if an individual is subject to the control or discretion of another merely as to the result to be accomplished by the work and not as to the means and method of accomplishing the result, he is an independent contractor, not an employee." Treasury Regulation No. 90, Art. 205. The regulation is in harmony with the assumption that the Act took over the term "employee," as the common law knew it, "for it enumerates the generally accredited determinants in such cases, of which the most important is the putative employer's control over the employee's business." *Texas Co. v. Higgins*, 118 F. (2e) 636. As was said in *Ruth Bros. v. Stanbaugh's Adm'r*, 275 Ky. 677, 122 S. W. (2d) 501, "The main question in all cases of this type is whether or not the one who is claimed to be an independent contractor has contracted to do the work according to his own methods and without being subject to the control of his employer except as to the result of his work." We agree with the conclusion of the district court that the homeworkers were independent contractors and not employees. Judgment affirmed.

CAPACITY OF PARTIES

Most agencies, as we shall see, are created by contract, and they are frequently created for the negotiation of contracts. It follows that the contractual capacity of the parties is important. This raises questions as to (1) who may be a principal and (2) who may be an agent.

WHO MAY BE A PRINCIPAL. The general rule is that what one may do for himself he may do through an agent. In other words, if a person is legally competent to make a contract for himself, he is legally competent to appoint an agent to make the contract for him. There are, however, exceptions to this general rule. For instance, a person may not appoint an agent to vote for him at an election, or to make and execute his will, or to enter into the marriage relation.

If one who does not possess full legal capacity to contract appoints another as his agent, both the contract creating the agency and any contract made by the agent with third parties on behalf of the principal will be either void or voidable, depending upon the circumstances in a given case. For instance, if A, a minor, and B enter into a contract whereby B is to act as A's agent, the contract would be voidable as to A, and any contracts entered into by B on behalf of A with third parties would likewise be voidable as to A. If A, who has been judicially adjudged insane, enters into an agreement to appoint B as his agent, the agreement, together with all contracts made by B on A's behalf, would be absolutely void.

WHO MAY BE AN AGENT.   In order to act as an agent, one is not required to possess legal capacity to contract. Anyone who may, in the judgment of the principal, possess the ability to perform the undertaking may be vested with authority to represent the principal as his agent. This means that, although one may not be able to act in the capacity of a principal himself, he may serve in the capacity of an agent for another. Thus, a minor may act as an agent, and the contracts he makes on behalf of his principal, within the scope of his authority, are binding upon the principal. However, the contract between the principal and the minor agent which created the agency is voidable at the election of the minor.

The reason behind the rule that an agent need not possess full contractual capacity in order to serve as an agent is that he is merely acting in a representative capacity. The contracts which he makes on behalf of the principal are not his contracts but the contracts of his principal, made under the authority and direction of the principal. Their legal status is therefore determined by the principal's contractual capacity, not by the agent's.

Talbot v. Bowen
8 Ky. 436 (1819)

This was a suit by William P. Bowen (plaintiff) against Isham Talbot (defendant) to obtain a title to a portion of a lot of ground. Decree for plaintiff, and defendant appealed. Affirmed.

The defendant Talbot was the owner of a portion of a lot in the town of Henderson, Kentucky. He gave his minor son oral authority to act as his agent to find a buyer for this interest. Upon the basis of this authority the son contracted one Featherston and signed a contract with Featherston, on behalf of the defendant, to sell the defendant's interest in the lot. Featherston then sold and assigned his interest under the contract to the plaintiff Bowen. Bowen brought this suit in equity for specific performance of the contract.

The defendant Talbot set up as a defense the infancy of his son; that his minor son could not legally act as an agent.

OWSLEY, J. If authorized, according to the settled doctrine of the law, the defendant's son being an infant can afford no objection against the liability of the defendant Talbot; for, although the contracts of infants are not, in all cases, binding upon them, there is no doubt but, as they may act as agents, their contracts, made in that character, if otherwise unexceptionable, will be binding upon their principal. And that the son was authorized either verbally or in writing to make the sale, from the circumstances detailed in evidence, there is no room for a moment of doubt.

Upon the whole, we are satisfied that the plaintiff Bowen is entitled to a specific execution of Featherston's purchase. Judgment for plaintiff affirmed.

Manufacturers Trust Co. et al. v. Podvin et al.
10 N. J. 199, 89 A. (2d) 672 (1952)

This was a suit by the Manufacturers Trust Co. and others (plaintiffs) against Rubin Podvin and others (defendants). Decree for plaintiffs, and defendants appealed. Decree modified and affirmed.

On August 3, 1949, Salvatore Zingale was hospitalized for a long-standing mental ailment and on October 8, 1949, the New York Supreme Court adjudged him mentally incompetent and appointed the plaintiff Manufacturers Trust Company as the guardian of his person and conservator of his property. Plaintiff May Zingale, his wife, was appointed the guardian in the instant action.

On July 22, 1949, twelve days before his commitment, Zingale acquired the Hotel Davenport in Atlantic City from the defendants, Rubin Podvin and Gussie Podvin, taking title in the name of Salvatore Zingale, Inc., a corporation of this state organized for the purpose. Zingale held all of the outstanding stock of the corporation except two qualifying shares. He was named president and general manager of the corporation.

Zingale is a cobbler by trade and was born in Italy. His home is in the state of New York. He speaks broken English but is unable to read or write English. He worked as a cobbler until 1942 when he started to sell novelty jewelry. His history of mental illness dates back to 1936. He was first hospitalized in 1945, and thereafter, until his final adjudication, underwent almost continuous treatment. The uncontradicted medical testimony is that he was clearly mentally irresponsible from and after 1945 and utterly devoid of judgment or understanding and effects of his acts in the instant transaction. His conduct, however, did not always betray his infirmity. In fact, at times he appeared normal.

The defendant Rubin Podvin did not meet Zingale until sometime in May,

1949. However, fifteen months earlier Zingale, while on a vacation in Atlantic City, in some manner met Saslaff, a real estate broker with whom the Podvins had listed the hotel for sale. On February 2, 1948, Zingale signed a contract to purchase the hotel for $54,000 cash and paid $4,000 deposit. This transaction failed to be carried out owing to Zingale's inability to perform certain terms of the contract. On July 22, 1949, Zingale and the Podvins entered into a second contract, for the purchase and sale of the hotel. It is this contract that forms the basis of this action by the plaintiffs to set aside the contract and to cancel certain notes and mortgages signed by Zingale and his wife.

BRENNAN, J. The settled rule of law is that "contracts with lunatics and insane persons are invalid, subject to the qualification that a contract made in good faith with a lunatic, for a full consideration, which has been executed without knowledge of the insanity, or such information as would lead a prudent person to the belief of the incapacity, will be sustained." *Drake v. Crowell*, 40 N. J. L. 58.

The Podvins concede the general rule but deny its applicability, contending that the transaction was not with the lunatic but with the corporation. Alternatively, they urge that in any event they are not to be charged with knowledge of Zingale's incompetency, the transaction was fair, and the exception to the rule applies.

The transaction was only in form with the corporation. In actual fact it was with Zingale personally and this was fully understood by both the defendants.

Where a contracting party, during his insanity, could not personally make a valid contract, his corporate nominee in virtue of a derivative authority could not do an act for him which he could not lawfully do for himself. The defendants were put on notice of the mental incompetency of Zingale during and after the negotiation of the first contract for the purchase of the hotel. If it were assumed that the corporation acted as the agent of Zingale, still Zingale would not be bound, since a lunatic is incompetent to become a principal or to appoint an agent.

CREATION OF THE AGENCY RELATION

The relationship of principal and agent may be created by (1) contract, (2) ratification, (3) necessity or emergency, (4) the conduct of the parties, and (5) operation of law.

BY CONTRACT

Most agencies are created by contract. Where this is the case both parties are bound by the agency contract, and the principal is bound by the contracts which his agent makes with third parties, within the scope of his authority. Sometimes an agent agrees to serve without compensation, in which case a *gratuitous agency* is created. Where this situation exists, either party may terminate the agreement without incurring liability to the other party; but any contract properly negotiated by the agent with a third party before the agreement is terminated will be binding on both the principal and the third party.

In most cases no particular formality is required in the creation of an agency contract. Usually it may be either oral or written, but there are a few exceptions to this rule. Under the common law the authority to execute an instrument under seal could be conferred only by an instrument of "equal dignity and solemnity," that is, by an instrument under seal. This rule applies only in the few states which have not abolished the efficacy of the seal. But most states do require that the authority of an agent to sign a deed or mortgage to real property be in writing and be filed in the office of the recorder of deeds or the land office in the county where the property is located. Often a formal power of attorney is required in such cases. Likewise, an agency contract that cannot, under its terms, be completed within one year must be in writing under the Statute of Frauds.

BY RATIFICATION

An agency relation may be created by ratification. This may occur in two types of situations: (1) where an agent, in representing his principal, exceeds his authority; (2) where a stranger, i.e. one who has not been previously authorized to act as agent, represents that he is the agent of another person and performs an act or negotiates a contract in the other person's name. In neither of these cases would the principal or the purported principal ordinarily be bound; but if he ratifies the transaction he will be bound, and the agent or stranger will be discharged from any liability.

Ratification is deemed to be equivalent to prior authorization. For this reason its validity dates back to the time when the agent or stranger performed the act or negotiated the contract, and not to the time when the act or contract was ratified by the principal. The rights and liabilities of the parties are determined as of the date of the performance of the authorized act.

An act may not be ratified by a principal that was not in existence when the act was performed. For example, A, a promoter, is promoting the organization of the X Corporation. Prior to obtaining a charter for the corporation, A represents to B that he is the president of the X Corporation, and B leases a building to the still nonexistent X Corporation. Later A obtains a charter for the X Corporation. The X Corporation could not ratify the lease-contract. However, it could *adopt* it, in which case the contract would become effective from the date of adoption.

A valid ratification requires that the one who performed the act did so upon the representation that he was acting as the agent for another person. For example, if A falsely represents to B that he is C's agent and then negotiates a contract with B upon behalf of C, C may ratify the contract. However, if A negotiates a contract with B upon his own behalf and in his own name, C, hearing of the contract and considering it a profitable one, may not step in and ratify the contract.

In order for the principal to be bound he must ratify with full knowledge of all the material facts. If some material fact is suppressed or withheld from him, he is not bound by his ratification. However, one who ratifies an act without making a reasonable effort to learn what the true facts are, will be bound by his ratification.

For ratification to be valid and effective the principal must possess full capacity to contract. Thus, ratification by an infant or an insane principal would be voidable.

Ratification may be either express or implied. The unauthorized act may be expressly ratified by a written or an oral declaration, or it may be implied from the conduct of the principal—for example, from his acceptance of benefits under the contract. Usually no formalities are required for ratification.

BY NECESSITY OR EMERGENCY

In the case of an emergency or crisis, if an agent (and, in some instances, an employee) is unable to contact his principal (or employer) for instructions as to how to proceed in handling the emergency, the law permits him to exercise his own judgment in the matter. However, the emergency must be genuine. It has been held in a number of cases that the conductor of a train, in the case of a wreck, has implied authority to secure the services of doctors, nurses, and ambulances to care for the injured passengers.

BY CONDUCT OF THE PARTIES

Under certain circumstances a person may be bound by the acts of another who is not actually his agent, because he is legally estopped from denying that such person is his agent. Such a situation happens only when innocent third parties are involved. To illustrate, A, in dealing with C, falsely holds B out as his agent, and C, relying upon A's representations, treats B as the agent of A, and negotiates with him a contract to which he and A are the parties. If A's representation were such that a reasonably prudent person under the circumstances would have thought that B was A's agent, A will be estopped from denying that B had authority to negotiate the contract as his agent.

BY OPERATION OF LAW

It is sometimes said that an agency may be created by operation of law. For example, if a husband fails to supply necessaries for his wife, the law permits her to pledge the credit of her husband to secure such necessaries. The same rule of law applies in the case of infants. Actually, the authority of the wife or minor child to pledge the credit of the husband or father is found, not in any theory of agency, but in the legal responsibility of the husband or father to support his family.

Howland v. Tri-State Theatres Corporation
139 F. (2d) 560 (1944)

This was an action by Hugh B. Howland (plaintiff) against Tri-State Theatres Corporation (defendant). Judgment for defendant, and plaintiff appealed. Affirmed.

The defendant corporation operated a theater in Omaha, Nebraska. Plaintiff's brother was a stagehand at defendant's theater. On the occasion involved in this action, plaintiff, who was not an employee of the defendant, had called at the theater for the purpose of taking his brother home. It was the duty of the brother, as stagehand, to close the theater after the last performance for the night. This required, among other things, that he lower the asbestos fire curtain with which the stage was equipped, and then raise it to a point ten or twelve feet above the level of the stage door and leave it in that position all night. On this occasion the mechanism operating the curtain worked as usual and satisfactorily while the curtain was being lowered. However, when the stagehand attempted to raise it, the mechanism failed to work. The curtain was raised and lowered by a system of steel cables, pulleys and counterweights. The stagehand announced that he would call one Kemp, the employee of the theater who had charge of the repair and maintenance of the curtain operating mechanism. There was, however, present on the stage another employee of the defendant who was not on duty at the time. He suggested that, before Kemp was called, he and plaintiff would attempt to raise the curtain while the stagehand placed a stepladder under the curtain. The stagehand accepted the suggestion. When the attempt to raise the curtain was made, the heavy counterweight of the mechanism fell to the stage, striking and seriously injuring plaintiff.

The theory upon which plaintiff's action was founded was that, upon the invitation of appellee's stagehand on duty to assist him in the raising of the curtain, he became in that operation an employee of the appellee corporation, and, as such, entitled to a safe place in which to work.

SANBORN, J. Since a master is responsible for the negligence of his servants committed in the course of their employment, and is also under a duty of exercising reasonable care to furnish his servants with a safe place in which to work and with safe appliances for use in his work, he has the absolute right to say who his servants shall be and to fix the scope of their employment and the limits of their authority. It is not contended by the plaintiff that the defendant, or anyone having express authority from the defendant so to do, employed the plaintiff to assist in the raising of the curtain in the theater. But plaintiff contends that the defendant's stagehand, in the circumstances revealed by the evidence, had the implied authority to employ the plaintiff to assist in raising the curtain, and that plaintiff, therefore, became an employee of the defendant for the time being, and as such, entitled to a safe place in which to work. The plaintiff relies upon the well recognized rule that the law implies the authority of a servant, otherwise unauthorized, in cases of emergency arising in the course of his employment to employ necessary help in the interest of the master. *Baltimore & Ohio R. R. Co. v. Burtch*, 263 U. S. 540. The infirmity in the plaintiff's case, however, is that the evidence on his behalf failed to establish the existence of an emergency justifying the exercise by defendant's stagehand of an authority which he did not otherwise possess. The stagehand was within easy telephone communication with his superiors, the managing officers of the theater, as well as with an employee of the company whose duty it was to repair and maintain the curtain raising mechanism which had failed to work. Authority in a servant to employ another to assist him in the service of his master may only be implied when the emergency confronting the servant is a real one. It is not sufficient that the servant or the person believes that an emergency exists when in fact it does not. *Ryan v. Phipps*, 131 N. Y. S. 438. The emergency must be one which arises unexpectedly in the absence of the master, and which requires the servant to act for the immediate protection of his employer's interest. We are not aware of any case which holds that, even in an emergency, an employee without authority to employ others in the work of his master, may do so when the master is present or when he may be easily and immediately consulted. The plaintiff admits that he entered the defendant's premises as a bare licensee. In our opinion, nothing occurring after his entry was sufficient to change his status to that of an invitee or an emergency employee of the defendant.

It follows from what we have said that, there being no real emergency justifying the finding of implied authority in the defendant's stagehand for the employment of the plaintiff in the present case, he was merely a licensee, who took his license at his peril, and to whom the defendant owed no duty except to refrain from willingly or wantonly injuring him. Judgment affirmed.

Kirkpatrick v. Williams
53 N. M. 477, 211 F. (2d) 506 (1949)

This was an action by Maurine Kirkpatrick (plaintiff) against Velma Williams, doing business under the firm name and style of "Velma's Beauty College" (defendant). Judgment for defendant, and plaintiff appealed. Affirmed.

This was an action for the breach of an alleged contract, wherein plaintiff alleged that she had entered into a contract with the defendant to take a course at the defendant's beauty college and that the defendant refused to permit the plaintiff to take the course.

On Tuesday, December 23, 1947, Maurine Kirkpatrick, the plaintiff, called Velma Williams, the defendant, on the telephone and stated to her that she desired to take a beauty course in her School No. 2, located in the Rosenwald Building, at Fourth and Central Avenue, in Albuquerque. At that time she was advised by the defendant that she would be pleased to see and talk to her on the following Monday, December 29th, but could not do so before that time because of the holiday rush and because her schools would be closed from December 24th until Monday, December 29th. The plaintiff nevertheless went to School No. 2 on the afternoon of December 24th, while the defendant was absent therefrom, and told Mrs. Bernice Griego, defendant's daughter, that her mother had directed her to permit the plaintiff to register as a student and then and there handed Mrs. Griego $125 in cash for the tuition. Relying upon the plaintiff's statement, the defendant's daughter furnished her with blank registration agreements which the plaintiff filled out in her own handwriting. Mrs. Jean Campbell, an instructor, signed the agreement. Within a very short time thereafter, the defendant, upon hearing that the plaintiff was a colored woman and a graduate of a beauty college, as well as a licensed operator and the owner of a beauty shop in Albuquerque, told her that she had no facilities in her school to give postgraduate work, and then and there tendered back the money, which the plaintiff refused to accept. Plaintiff filed this action alleging the breach of a contract on the part of the defendant.

LUJAN, J. The lower court found, and such findings are supported by sufficient evidence, that there was no meeting of minds between Maurine Kirkpatrick and Velma Williams; that the alleged contract signed by Jean Campbell, as instructor, was done without authority from the defendant; and, therefore, that it was not valid or binding upon the defendant in any manner. The court further found that the defendant never ratified the act of her instructor, and that she offered and tendered a refund of the money paid out by the plaintiff to defendant's daughter, but that it was refused.

The plaintiff challenges the defendant's right in refusing to admit her as a student in her privately owned beauty college, claiming that the defendant was in a different class than the operators of private schools generally, and that she was under a duty to the public which stopped her from repudiating the admission of the plaintiff as a qualified student in such school. The plaintiff has no authority to support her contention and we are unable to find any. The schools in question are private institutions conducted by the defendant as the sole owner for private gain and are wholly supported by tuition fees paid by the students accepted for instruction. We hold the plaintiff's right to admission rested solely in the discretion of the defendant.

The plaintiff further contended that the defendant ratified the whole of her employee's contract by failing to disaffirm or repudiate it in its entirety, and by offering to perform the contract in private. The evidence does not sustain her contention. Before a principal can be held to have ratified the act of an unauthorized agent, or of an employee who assumes to act as such, it must appear, either expressly or by strong implication, that the principal intended to ratify the act, and if such intention cannot be shown, there is no ratification. The defendant on learning that the plaintiff had already graduated from a beauty college and was a licensed operator under the law of New Mexico, as well as the owner of a beauty shop in Albuquerque, advised her that she had no facilities in her school to give her postgraduate work, and then and there tendered back the money, which the plaintiff refused to accept. In *Walls v. Erupcion Mining Co.*, 36 N. W. 15, 6 F. (2d) 1921, we said it is indispensable to ratification that the party held thereto shall have had full knowledge of all material facts. We have read the entire record and find that the court's findings of fact are substantial evidence, and therefore will not disturb same. Judgment affirmed.

REVIEW CASES

1. Burford, who was engaged in the roofing and cornice business, was employed by Webb to make some repairs in the cornice of his hotel in New York. Webb pointed out the defect to Burford, who agreed to remedy it, but no price or plan for doing the work was specified. In doing the work the employees of Burford suspended a ladder from the roof of the hotel and placed planks on it to serve as a scaffold. A gust of wind caused one of these planks to fall, and it struck and injured Hexamer, who happened to be passing at the time. Hexamer brought an action against Webb to recover damages for her injury, contending that the workmen, including Burford, were Webb's employees and that they had been negligent. Judgment for whom? (Hexamer v. Webb, 101 N. Y. 377, 4 N. E. 755, 54 Am. Rep. 703)

2. Whelden, who was thinking of buying a car, went to the Ray Motor Co. and was shown a second-hand Chrysler by Chapman, an authorized salesman of the company. Chapman took Whelden for a short demonstration drive in the car, and Whelden said that it seemed to be all right but that he wanted his wife to see it. Chapman told him to drive the car to his residence and show it to her. Whelden drove off in the car, met a friend with whom he had a few drinks, and then while continuing on his way home ran into a car belonging to the Gulf Refining Co. The Gulf Refining Co. brought an action against the Ray Motor Co., based in part on the theory that Whelden was acting as the motor company's agent in selling the car to his wife. Was this contention tenable? (Gulf Refining Co. v. Ray Motor Co., 129 Me. 499, 152 A. 226)

3. Mrs. Washburn married Hedtler, who introduced her to his friends as his wife. She purchased a few articles for the house plus a fur coat from Jordan Marsh for a total cost of $213.50. Thereafter the couple separated, and Hedtler wrote Jordan Marsh Co. not to let his wife have further credit. The marriage was nullified, for Mrs. Washburn had had a living husband

at the time of her marriage to Hedtler. Jordan Marsh Co. sued Hedtler for the purchases. Ruling? (Jordan Marsh Co. v. Hedtler, 288 Mass. 43, 130 N. E. 78)

4. Moreland and Madden were engaged in buying and shipping livestock. They contracted with G. H. and W. H. McWilliams to purchase cattle for them from time to time at certain prices. The McWilliamses paid for the cattle with their own checks, but these were always taken care of at the bank by Moreland and Madden. The cattle were brought to the shipping lot owned by Moreland and Madden and were cared for there until they were shipped. At the time of shipping, their value was determined. If the price paid by the McWilliamses, following the instructions of Moreland and Madden, was below the market price, the McWilliamses were paid the difference; if above the market price, Moreland and Madden bore the loss. Judgment was rendered against the McWilliamses in an action brought against them by one Snyder, and under a writ of execution the sheriff levied upon and sold sixteen head of cattle in their possession. Moreland and Madden brought an action of conversion against the sheriff, contending that the McWilliamses were their agents and that the cattle therefore belonged to them (Moreland and Madden). The defense was that the Mc-Williamses were independent contractors and that title to the cattle was in them. Judgment for whom? (Moreland et al. v. Mason, Sheriff, et al., 45 Idaho 143, 260 P. 1035)

5. Barner was a bus driver in the employ of City Service Transit Co., a common carrier. One February night at 12:40 he left Dover for Newark, about 25 miles away, with a number of passengers who had just come off the "swing shift" at the federal arsenal. It was a very cold, windy night and the road was slippery. A mile or two from Dover, in a thinly settled area, one of the rear wheels came off the bus. Barner tried to telephone the company garage but got no answer. He then telephoned Zingler, a company foreman, at his home, and Zingler promised to send a relief bus if he could locate one. Barner waited an hour and no bus appeared. He then caught a ride back to the arsenal, made arrangements for a bus to pick up his stranded passengers, accompanied the driver back to the scene of the mishap, and superintended the transfer of the passengers. On the trip to Newark the bus went out of control and left the road, and some of the passengers were injured. They sued the transit company. The company denied liability, contending that Barner had no authority to engage a relief bus. Judgment for whom? (Sibley et al. v. City Service Transit Co., 2 N. J. 458, 66 A.(2d) 864)

Principal and Agent

18

DUTIES AND LIABILITIES OF AGENT TO PRINCIPAL

The agent, in addition to his duties specified in the contract, has certain other duties which are implied at law and the breach of which will consequently result in liability on the part of the agent. Such implied duties are a part of every employment contract, unless they are modified or eliminated by the express terms of the agreement. And it is important to observe that they apply as well to a gratuitous agent as to a paid agent.

The implied duties of agents may be conveniently listed under the following headings: (1) duty of loyalty; (2) duty to obey instructions; (3) duty to use care and skill; (4) duty to inform the principal; (5) duty to account to the principal.

DUTY OF LOYALTY

The relation between principal and agent is *fiduciary;* that is, it is one which involves trust and confidence. Hence the law requires that the agent must exercise the highest degree of good faith and loyalty in representing his principal. An agent's failure to carry out this duty may result in considerable financial loss to him.

In case of a conflict of interests, the agent's personal interest or the interest of a third party must give way to that of the principal. An agent is not permitted to take a position hostile or antagonistic to the principal, except with the full knowledge and approval of the principal. If he does so, the principal may repudiate the transaction and demand from the agent an accounting for any profits received by the agent.

An agent may not compete or interfere in any way with the business of his principal. He may not make or receive any secret profits, bonuses, or commissions; if he does so and if his act comes to the attention of the principal, the principal may require him to account for same. The fact that the agent fully carried out his contract with the principal and that the principal actually was not damaged by the agent's receipt of secret profits, bonuses, or commissions would make no difference. If a principal discovers that his agent is secretly carrying on a profitable side line during time when the agent should be working for him, he may require the agent to turn over the profits to him.

If the principal has employed the agent to sell certain property, the agent may not sell such property to himself without the knowledge and consent of his principal. Likewise, if the agent is employed to purchase property for his principal, he may not purchase it secretly for himself, either directly or indirectly through a "straw person" or "dummy." Neither may he sell his own property to the principal without his principal's full knowledge and consent.

The agent's duty of loyalty requires that he may not use confidential information, acquired from his principal during the course of his employment, for his own personal advantage, if by doing so he would injure the principal. For instance, he may not take advantage of such confidential information to compete with the principal after he leaves the principal's employment. Such confidential information includes secret formulas, processes, and lists of customers prepared during his employment. But he may make any use he wishes of skills he has acquired during the course of his employment.

Dual agency, i.e., acting as agent for both parties in the same transaction, is also prohibited without the principals' consent. For example, if A acts as agent to both B and C in negotiating a contract between them, and neither B nor C knows that he is the other's agent, the dual principals, B and C, would be privileged to repudiate the contract, and A would not be entitled to any compensation from either. If B knows of the dual agency but C does not, C may repudiate the contract, but it is binding as to B. In such case A usually may collect his commission from B but not from C. If both B and C consent to the dual agency, the contract would be valid, and A would be entitled to compensation from both B and C.

Eagle Indemnity Co. v. Cherry et al.
182 F. (2d) 298 (1950)

This was an action by George T. Cherry and others (plaintiffs) against the Eagle Indemnity Company (defendant) on a fidelity bond in the principal sum of $10,000. Judgment for plaintiffs, and defendant appealed. Affirmed.

This action was brought by Cherry, Hoag, Manthey, and Blaylock, who composed the partnership firm of Southwest Industrial Equipment Company.

The company was located at Dallas, Texas, and was engaged in the business of fabricating steel products. Jack K. Chandler was employed as general manager. In order to insure the honest and faithful performance of the duties of Chandler and the other partnership employees, the defendant issued to the partnership a fidelity bond upon payment of an agreed premium. The bond insured against ". . . Any loss of money or other property . . . belonging to the insured, or in which the insured has pecuniary interest . . . which the insured shall sustain . . . through . . . fraudulent or dishonest act or acts committed by any one or more of the employees. . . ." The bond was in full force and effect during the entire period covered by the alleged fraudulent and dishonest conduct of Chandler in or about the management of the partnership business at Dallas.

It was shown that at the time Chandler was acting in the capacity of general manager of the business of the plaintiff there was a shortage of steel, and that plant production was slowed down and many orders were unfilled because of this steel shortage. During this period it was impossible for individual buyers to purchase steel from a mill or warehouse on their own account, as the industry was then operating under an informal rationing system whereby the available steel was distributed and sold only to those persons who represented old customers of a steel plant or warehouse. It was, therefore, Chandler's duty, as general manager, to keep the business going by placing orders with the steel suppliers, so that when they procured steel they would deliver a proportionate share to Southwest Industrial Equipment Co., as an old and regular customer.

The evidence revealed conclusively that on different occasions during the months of May and June, 1947, Chandler purchased in the name of Southwest Industrial Equipment Co., from National Steel Products Co. of Houston, several carloads of sheet steel which aggregated 451,624 pounds; that, instead of taking over these steel shipments for his company, he permitted one Batson to accept delivery of the steel and dispose of it for a profit on the open market, after which the profit received was divided between Batson and Chandler; that Chandler used the name of the partnership firm for which he worked, its reputation and its facilities to procure this steel and thereafter, through Batson, he clandestinely and fraudulently diverted the steel shipments from the company of which he was general manager, to other persons and companies at an increased price, for which he was paid a share of the profits amounting to thousands of dollars. In one transaction it was shown that Chandler purchased a shipment of steel in the name of the partnership, sold it through Batson to another company for a nice personal profit, and several days later bought it back again for the use of his own company at over one and a half times its original cost. No record was kept of these fraudulent transactions by Chandler and he kept them secret from the partners who owned the company and employed him.

The principal question presented is whether there is substantial evidence to support the finding of the trial court that the action of the general manager of the partnership firm in buying and selling steel at a personal profit, when such steel was purchased in the partnership name and on the strength of its reputation and standing in the trade, was such fraud or dishonesty as would constitute a breach of the defendant's fidelity bond, and render it liable for damages thereunder.

McCORD, C.J. It is a fundamental law that an agent bears a fiduciary relationship to his principal, and owes him the duty of good faith and loyalty. 2 *Am. Jur.* 202, secs. 251, 261, and 268. By virtue of this relationship, no agent is entitled to take any unfair advantage that his position may offer him to profit, at his employer's expense, beyond the agreed compensation for his services. He should not be allowed to speculate for his own private gain adversely to the interests of his employer, or to compete with his employer's business without his knowledge or consent. Here, when Chandler, as the general manager and trusted employee of Southwest Industrial Equipment Co., purchased steel in his company's name which he would have been unable to procure on his own account, and later diverted the steel through Batson to the open market at a secret personal profit, he manifestly breached the duty of good faith which he owed to his employers. We, therefore, conclude the evidence unerringly discloses fraudulent and dishonest conduct on the part of Chandler while the fidelity bond was in full force and effect, and that such constitutes a clear breach of the terms of the bond for which the defendant is liable. 35 *Am. Jur.* 516, sec. 87; *Wardell v. Union Pacific Railroad Co.*, 103 U. S. 651.

Judgment affirmed.

Holt, State Commissioner of Finance v. Joseph F. Dickmann Real Estate Co.
140 S. W. (2d) 59 (Mo.) (1940)

This was an action by R. W. Holt, Commissioner of Finance of the state of Missouri, in charge of the liquidation of the Lowell Bank (plaintiff) against the Joseph F. Dickmann Real Estate Company (defendant). Judgment for defendant, and plaintiff appealed. Reversed.

This was an action to recover $4,500 as profits realized by the defendant, as damages suffered by the plaintiff in the purchase and resale of real estate by the defendant, as agent of the plaintiff, and $950 received by the defendant as commission, aggregating $5,450.

The plaintiff alleged that he, as State Commissioner of Finance, through his special deputy, Oscar Wibbing, in the process of liquidating the Lowell Bank, entered into an agreement with the defendant, wherein the plaintiff authorized the defendant to offer for sale certain property belonging to the Lowell Bank, and the defendant accepted such authorization and agreed to attempt to find purchasers for the said property; that the defendant was to receive "the regular commission" if he succeeded in finding a buyer for any of the property; that, on June 4, 1938, the defendant presented to the plaintiff an offer purportedly from one Cecelia Ross to buy all the property for the sum of $19,000; that the said Cecelia Ross turned out to be a "straw party," and that the real purchaser was the defendant. The plaintiff further alleged that the defendant fraudulently concealed the fact that the said Cecelia Ross was acting for the defendant in making the aforesaid offer of purchase and the defendant fraudulently concealed that the said offer was actually made by itself. It was further alleged that in ignorance of these facts the plaintiff accepted the offer, and obtained permission from the court to sell the property; that deeds to the property were executed and delivered to the said Cecelia Ross, upon the payment of the sum of $19,000; that the plaintiff thereupon paid the defendant a commission of $950; and that shortly thereafter the defendant resold the said property at a profit of $4,500. Upon learning of these facts, and that the real purchaser of the property was the defendant (who was the agent of the plaintiff), the plaintiff filed this action to obtain judgment for the amount of the profits and commission made on the resale of the property. Defendant's demurrer was sustained by the lower court, and the plaintiff brought this appeal.

SUTTON, J. Aside from the allegation respecting the payment of commissions, the gist of the petition is that defendant, being the plaintiff's agent to sell certain real estate in charge of the plaintiff, as commissioner, became the purchaser of said real estate for $19,000, through a straw party, concealing from the plaintiff that it was the real purchaser, and afterwards resold said real estate at a profit of $4,500. There was no allegation of fraud.

The use of a straw party in transferring real estate is not in itself unlawful or fraudulent. However, it is a settled rule that in the absence of full knowledge or consent on the part of his principal, an agent authorized to sell his principal's property may not either directly or indirectly himself become the purchaser, and the fact that there was no fraud or unfairness practiced on the part of the agent is immaterial to the application of the rule. In the absence of consent on the part of the principal to the agent's becoming a purchaser, following full knowledge of all the material facts, the principal may elect to rescind the sale and have the property returned or reconveyed to him, or if the agent has sold the property the principal may compel him to account for the proceeds, or he may affirm the sale and sue the agent for the profits he has realized, or seek to recover his damages.

In *Meek v. Hurst*, 223 Mo. 688, 122 S. W. 1022, which involved the alleged purchase of a farm by an agent from his principal, the court said: "The doctrine of the law that forbids an agent to buy from or sell to himself is not necessarily based on the idea that such deal in dirt is (to speak colloquially) a "dirty" deal—that is to say, resulted in an injury to or a fraud upon the principal. But it is rather based on the idea of closing the door to the temptation to commit fraud. It tends to keep the agent's eye single and clear to the rights and welfare of his principal. To allow one acting in the fiduciary relation of agent to buy from or sell to himself is dangerous; for the moral stamina of the average man is inadequate to preserve a fine glow of fidelity to his trust and confidential relation in such a transaction, and the interdiction is enforced with a strong hand in the courts of justice."

In *Benton v. Watkins*, 313 Mo. 526, 285 S. W. 407, the court said: "The rule is universal that an agent authorized to sell property for another cannot himself be the purchaser unless he discloses fully to his principal that he is the purchaser, revealing everything within his knowledge relating to the transaction."

An agent is not allowed to put himself in a position antagonistic to his principal, or speculate in the subject of the agency. The most open and disinterested dealing is required of him. Judgment reversed.

Quest v. Barge
41 S. (2d) 158 (Fla.) (1949)

This was a suit by H. F. Quest (plaintiff) against Silar B. Barge and Evannah Barge, husband and wife (defendants) for specific performance of a contract to sell realty. Decree for defendants, and plaintiff appealed. Decree affirmed.

The vendee plaintiff brought suit for specific performance of a contract to sell property. Hugh R. Neighbors, a real estate agent, was commissioned by Bevins and Weaver, copartners, operating the Harlem Bar, in Pensacola, to purchase a brick building owned by the appellee (defendant). The property was in the same block as the Harlem Bar. When Neighbors got in touch with Barge (defendant), he represented that he was in contact with some out-of-town people who desired to purchase property either in Pensacola or Mobile. To induce Barge to make his decision quickly he also represented that these out-of-town people would buy in Mobile if no suitable place were found in Pensacola in a very short time. When questioned by Barge as to the type of business they desired to operate, Neighbors said he heard or thought it was to be a second-hand store. These representations were untrue and well known to be so by Neighbors. After several visits Barge consented to sell his property for $11,000. Thereupon the contract was executed, Neighbors signing as vendee and a check representing earnest money being passed to Barge. Within several days after the signing of the contract of sale Barge learned the identity of the undisclosed principals and refused to be bound by the contract. Some five weeks later Neighbors assigned all his rights and obligations under the contract to H. F. Quest, an employee of Bevins and Weaver, and appellant here. On June 24, 1947, Quest filed a bill of complaint for specific performance of the contract of sale.

The property which was covered by the contract was a brick building. In one part of the building appellee Barge operated a cafe; the remainder was let out to other establishments. The cafe was licensed to sell beer and wines. Barge had for some time been desirous of selling whiskey on the premises, but had been unable to do so because of an ordinance of the city which prohibited more than one whiskey license to the block. The Harlem Bar, owned and operated by Bevins and Weaver, the real parties in interest to the contract, was in the same block as Barge's cafe and had the only available license to sell whiskey. Barge, Weaver and Bevins were competitors in the beer and wine trade. For some years prior to the negotiations for the purchase of Barge's property, Weaver and Bevins had rented the premises occupied by the Harlem Bar. Recently, however, landlord troubles developed for them and their rent was more than doubled. As a result, they decided to purchase their own premises. With this object in mind, Bevins and Weaver commissioned Neighbors to buy Barge's building, which resulted in the contract of sale here in litigation.

BARNES, J. The facts of the case show that Neighbors acted in the capacity of agent for both these parties to the contract. Bevins and Weaver commissioned Neighbors to purchase the Barge property for them. They did not want their identity known, so they directed Neighbors to sign the contract as vendee. Barge knew nothing of the relations between Neighbors and Bevins and Weaver. There can be little doubt that such limited knowledge of the true status of the agent Neighbors was insufficient to charge Barge with a full knowledge and consent to the double agency.

In the *American Law Institute's Restatement of Agency* the duty of the agent assuming to act as agent for both parties to a transaction is as follows: "An agent who acts for adverse principals in a transaction is subject to a duty to act with fairness to each, and to disclose to each all facts which he knows or should know would reasonably affect the judgment of each in permitting such dual agency, except as to a principal who has manifested that he knows of such facts or that he does not care to know of them."

Again, in the case of *McElroy v. Maxwell*, 101 Mo. 294, 14 S. W. 1, the same doctrine was enunciated: "There may be instances where one may be agent of the two parties; but this can occur only upon the fullest disclosure by the agent of this fact, and the fullest comprehension of it by those contracting through the medium of such agent."

It is thus the policy of the law to deny the agent and his principal the benefits of a contract executed while the agent has assumed to act for both parties without full knowledge and consent to the relation by the principal sought to be held. This rule rests upon policy and not upon the proof of injury or damage to the principal. It is not necessary for a party seeking to avoid such a contract to show that any improper advantage has been gained over him; it is at his option to repudiate or disaffirm the contract, irrespective of any proof of actual fraud.

Decree for defendants affirmed.

DUTY TO OBEY INSTRUCTIONS

It is the duty of the agent to obey and put into effect all reasonable instructions of the principal in carrying out his duties under the employment contract. He has undertaken to represent his principal in the accomplishment of certain objectives desired by the principal, and he must therefore use the means and methods specified by the principal. Even though he should be of the opinion that the principal is exercising poor judgment, or that the objectives could be better obtained by other means, he is not privileged to substitute his judgment for that of his principal. However, when there are no instructions, or when the instructions are vague, ambiguous, or indefinite, the agent may use his own discretion.

The instructions of the principal need not be express. They may be implied from the express instructions themselves, from a previous course of dealing between the agent and his principal, or from the usages or customs of the particular trade or business. But if the principal's express instructions should run counter to such habitual practice, it is the duty of the agent to follow the express instructions.

There are certain exceptions to the general rule that it is the agent's duty to obey to the letter the instructions of his principal. (1) An agent is not obliged or required to obey his principal's instructions if doing so would result in the commission of an illegal or criminal act. (2) A gratuitous agent is under no duty to obey his principal's instructions unless or until he actually undertakes to represent the principal in some business transaction. While a gratuitous agent is liable for misfeasance, he is not liable for nonfeasance. (3) In an emergency an agent may disregard his principal's instructions and use his own discretion to protect the principal's interest, if it is difficult or impractical to secure new instructions from the principal.

An agent's failure to obey and carry out faithfully his principal's instructions will subject him to an action for damages for the breach of the employment contract and for any losses suffered by the principal that were the natural and proximate result of the agent's disobedience. He will also, in most cases, forfeit any right that he may otherwise have to compensation. Of course, if his deviation from instructions is subsequently ratified by the principal, he is excused from liability.

Bentonville Ice & Cold Storage Co. et al. v. Anderson
53 S. W. (2d) 993, 186 Ark. 473 (1932)

This was an action by S. J. Anderson (plaintiff) against the Bentonville Ice & Cold Storage Co. and W. M. Zimmerman (defendants). Judgment for plaintiff, and the Bentonville Ice & Cold Storage Co. appealed. Reversed and case remanded.

For many years prior to 1930 plaintiff had been an orchardist. The defendant company for several years was operating a cold storage plant. It had been a custom for orchardists to place apples in defendant's storage plant with instructions to sell them at the prevailing market price. During those years plaintiff had placed apples in defendant's storage, and, when they were sold, defendant had remitted the proceeds of the sale, less storage charges. Plaintiff delivered certain apples to defendant during the year 1930. Thereafter defendant sold the apples to one W. M. Zimmerman, a defendant below, on credit.

Counsel for plaintiff say that in all previous years defendant had sold the apples of plaintiff for cash, and that plaintiff had never authorized the sale to be made in any other manner, and that the apples were sold on credit to an insolvent person upon an indefinite credit arrangement. Plaintiff testified that he placed his apples with the defendant company with instructions to sell them as in previous years.

The manager of the defendant company testified that the apples were of poorer quality and smaller size than usual; that he found a cash buyer for the apples, but plaintiff was not willing to accept the price offered. Plaintiff admitted that this was true. Defendant's manager also testified that plaintiff's apples remained unsold at about the close of the storage season and that the company had to sell them, that it was trying to handle the apples to the best advantage for plaintiff, and that Zimmerman, the man to whom the apples were finally sold on a credit basis, was the only buyer that could be found.

Plaintiff filed action against both defendants for $309.25, the value of the apples. Upon trial, judgment was entered in favor of plaintiff for the said amount, from which the defendant company appealed. Defendant Zimmerman did not appeal.

BUTLER, J. The evidence fails to disclose what had been the custom regarding the sale of apples during the time plaintiff had done business with the defendant or what was the financial responsibility of Zimmerman, the buyer, known to the defendant, or which, in exercise of ordinary care, it should have known. Neither was there any express direction given the defendant as to how the apples should be sold. In the absence of any proof of custom or of the express direction of the owner, an agent must be reasonably diligent and exercise reasonable care in the selection of responsible purchasers and sell the commodity for its fair value or market price for cash, or upon a reasonable term of credit, and exercise reasonable diligence in collecting the purchase money when intrusted with the collection, and properly account to the owner for all money and property which has come into its hands during and by virtue of the agency. Of course, an agent is bound to make sales in accordance with the express direction of the owner, and is liable for any damage resulting from a failure to obey the direction and instructions of the owner or for failure to exercise proper care in the absence of such direction. *Houston Rice Co. v. Reeves*, 179 Ark. 700, 17 S. W. (2d) 884.

We are of the opinion that our cases support the majority rule declared in 25 C. J., Sec. 16, p. 350, cited by the defendant, as follows: "That in the absence of specific instructions to sell only for cash, the agent had implied authority to sell upon a reasonable credit, provided he exercised due care in doing so."

The evidence is not clear as to whether or not the plaintiff instructed the defendant to sell for cash. The plaintiff himself testified: "The only terms I have recollection of is as I had done before. I simply told them to sell the apples for me, if any opportunity might come up for a sale. So far as I know, that is the instructions." Of course, if the plaintiff had instructed the defendant to sell for cash and the defendant, in violation of such instructions, sold the apples to Zimmerman on credit, if Zimmerman failed to pay the plaintiff the defendant would be liable for its failure to obey the plaintiff's instructions. The cause is reversed and remanded.

DUTY TO USE CARE AND SKILL

An agent is under a duty to use ordinary care and skill in carrying out his duties under the employment contract. By ordinary care and skill is meant the degree of care and skill that a reasonably prudent and competent person would exercise under like or similar circumstances. Whether such care or skill has been exercised is a question of fact for the jury to decide.

In some instances an agent may hold himself out as possessing certain special skills, as for example, in the case of surgeons, lawyers, accountants, and engineers. Even in these types of cases the degree of care and skill required is that possessed by an ordinarily competent person in the same special field. For example, if A holds himself out to the public as a tax attorney, he must exercise that degree of care and skill that is ordinarily used by tax attorneys in that city or locality. Merely exercising the degree of care and skill that a general practicing attorney would use is not enough. But no matter how high his claims to special expertness in tax matters, he is not required to exceed the performance of the average tax attorney.

Failure on the part of an agent to use reasonable care and skill will subject him to an action by the principal for damages for his neglect of duty.

City of East Grand Forks v. Steele et al.
121 Minn. 296, 141 N. W. 181 (1913)

This was an action by the City of East Grand Forks (plaintiff) against J. Gordon Steele and others (defendants). Both parties appealed from the trial court's ruling on defendants' demurrer. Affirmed in part, and reversed in part.

The complaint set forth four causes of actions. It was alleged that the defendants, representing themselves to be expert accountants, and able to detect any irregularities in the transactions of the city officers, contracted with the city to investigate and audit the books, accounts, and financial transactions of the city clerk, for the sum of $150. The city clerk, in addition to his ordinary duties as clerk, was also employed to collect money due the city for electric lights, water and sewer assessments, and license fees, and had given a surety bond to secure the faithful performance of these additional duties. The investigation of these collections, and of whether they had been properly accounted for, was included in the duties of the defendants. They made the investigation and audit, and in February, 1909, reported to the city that all books and accounts had been correctly kept and all funds properly accounted for. The plaintiff paid defendants the full contract price therefor. In December, 1909, defendants again contracted with the city to make a similar investigation and audit, concerning both the years 1908 and 1909, for the sum of $500. They made the investigation and audit, reported that the books were correct, and the city paid them $500 for same. In fact, the clerk had embezzled the sum of $1,984.26 during the year 1908, and the further sum of $5,339 during the year 1909, and prior to the investigation made by the defendants. The defendants failed to discover and disclose these defalcations, by reason of incompetence and negligence. They were discovered and disclosed by an investigation made by the state examiner immediately after the defendants had completed their second audit. If, in making their first audit, defendants had discovered and reported the defalcation then existing, it could have been recovered from the surety company, and the clerk would have been removed from office, and his subsequent embezzlement could not have occurred. The surety company became insolvent before the investigation made by the state examiner, and the amount of the defalcations of the clerk was wholly lost to the city.

The plaintiff sought to recover the following items, and stated each as a separate cause of action: (1) The sum of $5,339, embezzled by the clerk after the first audit and before the second audit. (2) The sum of $1,984.26, embezzled by the clerk prior to the first audit. (3) The compensation paid the defendants for making the first audit. (4) The compensation paid the defendants for making the second audit.

TAYLOR, J. This is not an action in tort, but an action to recover damages for breach of contract. The rule governing liability for breach of contract is given in the syllabus to *Sargent v. Mason*, 101 Minn. 319, 112 N. W. 255, as follows: "In an action for damages for breach of contract, the defaulting party is liable only for the direct consequence of the breach, such as usually occur from the infraction of like contracts, and within the contemplation of the parties when the contract was entered into as likely to result from its nonperformance."

The damages claimed on account of the losses resulting from the defalcation of the clerk and the insolvency of his surety are too remote to be recovered, without showing the existence of special circumstances, known to defendants, from which they ought to have known that such losses were likely to result from a failure to disclose the true condition of affairs. Such losses are neither the natural nor the proximate consequences of the failure of defendants to make a proper audit. Neither are any facts shown from which it may be inferred that a loss from either of these causes was or ought to have been contemplated, when the contract was made, as likely to result from a breach of duty on the part of the defendants. If, at the making of the contract and in the light of the knowledge then possessed by them, the parties had taken thought as to what consequences might reasonably be expected to result from its breach, there is nothing set forth in the complaint from which we can say that they ought to have foreseen or to have contemplated that the clerk was likely to commit a crime, or that his surety was likely to become insolvent, and thereby entail financial loss upon the city.

The defendants represented themselves as expert accountants, which implied that they were skilled in that class of work. In accepting employment as expert accountants, they undertook, and the plaintiff had the right to expect, that in the performance of their duties they would exercise the average ability and skill of those engaged in that branch of skilled labor. They were employed to ascertain, among other things, whether any irregularities had occurred in the financial transactions of the city clerk, and, if so, the nature and extent of such irregularities. If, from want of proper skill, or from negligence, they did not disclose the true situation, they failed to perform the duty which they had assumed, and failed to earn the compensation which the plaintiff agreed to pay them for the proper performance of such duty.

The work of an expert accountant is of such technical character and requires such peculiar skill that the ordinary person cannot be expected to know whether he performs his duties properly or otherwise, but must rely upon his report as to the thoroughness and accuracy of his work. The full contract price having been paid in the belief, induced by defendants' report, that such report disclosed fully and accurately the condition of the city's accounts, the city is entitled to recover back the amounts so paid, upon proving that, through the incompetence or the negligence of the defendants, the report was in substance misleading and false.

The order sustaining the demurrer to the first cause of action is affirmed. The order overruling the demurrer to the second cause of action is reversed. The orders overruling the demurrer to the third and fourth causes of action are affirmed.

DUTY TO INFORM PRINCIPAL

It is a general rule of law that the knowledge of the agent concerning a particular transaction is imputed to his principal; that is, the principal is charged with any material information concerning a transaction which is communicated to, or comes to the attention of, the agent in the course and within the scope of the agency. For that reason it is held to be the duty of the agent to advise his principal of any material information which comes to his attention in the process of representing his principal in a business transaction, and of any notices that he may receive from a third person with whom he has been dealing on his principal's behalf. The agent's failure to discharge such duty will subject him to the payment of damages to his principal.

This rule does not apply to the relationship of employer and employee, because an employee is employed to perform only mechanical or ministerial acts or functions, and not to represent the employer in dealing with third persons.

Prince v. Du Puy
163 Ill. 417, 45 N. E. 298 (1896)

This was an action by George A. Du Puy (plaintiff) against E. H. Prince (defendant) to set aside a deed. Judgment for plaintiff, and defendant appealed. Affirmed.

Plaintiff filed a bill in equity against defendant to set aside and cancel a deed which he contended constituted a cloud upon his title to a certain lot in Chicago. The deed had been given by Luther B. Johnson to defendant.

The lot in question had been conveyed many years before to Johnson's father, and Johnson derived his title by descent, as the only heir. The property had been sold many times for unpaid taxes, and was incumbered by four or five tax titles. Johnson had very little, if any, knowledge as to the situation or value of the lot. He lived in Vermont; Prince and Du Puy lived in Chicago. In May, 1892, Du Puy wrote to Johnson to the effect that if Johnson wished to sell the property he would like to buy it. He offered Johnson $50 for the lot. He stated that he expected to leave Chicago soon and requested an early reply. In the interval Johnson wrote to Prince, a real estate agent in Chicago, about Du Puy's offer and engaged his services to look into the matter. Among other things he stated in his letter to Prince: "I should like to find out whether the offer (of $50) is the equivalent of the value (of the property)." Three days later Prince replied by letter to Johnson that upon receiving a description of the property he would look it up and see what there was in it and would then let Johnson know. He asked that Johnson furnish him with a plat and particulars of his father's death. Johnson replied that he had no plat and could not accurately describe the property. Prince then wrote to Johnson and suggested that if Johnson would give him the name of the prospective buyer he might contact him and possibly obtain the information he needed. In reply to this letter Johnson wrote: "Yours received. It is now too late to do anything about looking up the lot's title, location, or value. Inclosed find a quitclaim deed, signed, ready for delivery to the purchaser, G. A. Du Puy, City Hall, Chicago. Please collect the $50, hand over the deed, and remit to me the proceeds after deducting your charges. As Mr. Du Puy leaves the city in a day or two, I beg you to act upon the matter at once." Prince's reply to this letter was, in part, as follows: "Your letter of July 2nd is at hand, and contents noted. It came at a time when I was very busy, as my partner had just died; so your business has been neglected. I am going to gamble a little. I think, if it is worth $50 to Mr. Du Puy, it ought to be worth nearly that much to me, and I do not care to have you lose anything by my negligence. Therefor, I inclose you a draft for $50. Yourself and wife will please sign the enclosed deed, etc. . . ." Johnson supposed that Du Puy had left the city and that the trade with him had fallen through. He therefore accepted the $50 from Prince and executed the deed and sent it back to Prince. He later found that Du Puy had not left the city, but that Prince had withheld from Du Puy the fact that he had Johnson's deed for delivery to him. Johnson thereupon demanded a reconveyance from Prince and offered to return the $50, but Prince refused to comply with the demand. The evidence showed that Du Puy would have paid a larger amount for the property rather than lose it, and that Prince knew that fact, but concealed it from Johnson. Afterwards Johnson executed and delivered a quitclaim deed to the lot to Du Puy. The evidence further showed that Prince had examined the property and obtained full information concerning it but did not so advise his principal Johnson. The property was worth three or four thousand dollars.

This action was by Du Puy against Prince to cancel and set aside the deed he got from Johnson.

CARTER, J. The evidence shows that while Prince was acting as the agent of Johnson, the owner, charged with the duty which he had undertaken for Johnson of investigating the location, value, and condition of the title of the lot in question, he (Prince) concealed from Johnson information in the premises which he had obtained in the course of his employment, and which would have been of value to Johnson before he parted with his title, and instead of reporting to his principal (Johnson) information which he had tending to show that Johnson's interest was of greater value than $50, the amount which Du Puy had offered, and that Du Puy would increase the amount of his offer, took advantage of the knowledge he had so obtained, and procured from Johnson a conveyance to himself for the same consideration. In other words, the agent took advantage of the fiduciary relation which he sustained to his principal to procure for himself the subject matter of the agency. This the law will not tolerate.

It is conceded that the law is that Du Puy had the same right to maintain such action to set aside the deed to Prince that Johnson had before he conveyed to Du Puy. We have no doubt that Johnson had such right, and that his conveyance to Du Puy operated as a disaffirmance of the sale and conveyance to Prince, and that Du Puy's bill was properly brought. Decree affirmed.

DUTY TO ACCOUNT TO PRINCIPAL

Money or other property which is entrusted to the agent by the principal, or which comes into the agent's possession on his principal's behalf, must be strictly accounted for to the principal. The agent must also account for all profits received in the process of carrying on the principal's business. Hence the law requires the agent to keep and maintain financial records sufficient to show at all times what his obligations are to his principal in the way of money, other property, or profits. Failure to do so is looked upon with disfavor by the courts and militates against the agent. The agent is required to turn over to his principal on demand, or in accordance with the terms of his employment contract, any property or money which he has received on behalf of the principal.

The agent owes a duty not to commingle his own property or money with that of his principal. A breach of this duty may result in serious loss to the agent. In case an agent mixes his principal's property with his own and then is unable to identify it and separate it from his own, the principal will get all such commingled property. The problem becomes especially serious in the case of fungible goods, such as liquids or small grain. If an agent commingles his funds with those of the principal and the funds are in some way lost, the entire loss falls on the agent. For instance, if the agent (A) deposits $1,000 of his principal's (P's) money in his own personal bank account and the bank fails, A is liable to P for the full amount of $1000. A is said to hold such money in trust for P. By depositing the money in his own bank account he has asserted dominion and control over P's money. P has no control over the money, since the bank could not legally honor and pay a check drawn by him against the account. If A had deposited the $1,000 in a separate account, and in the name of P, he would not be liable if the bank failed before P had withdrawn his money, unless P could show that A was negligent in selecting the particular bank in which he deposited P's money.

Since it is held that an agent holds his principal's property or money in trust for his principal, if the agent should use his principal's property or money, or should exchange it for other property, the principal may follow his property or money to the property thus exchanged for his property or money, and impress a constructive trust upon such property, or bring an action in trover against the agent for the conversion of his property.

Westinghouse Electric Corporation v. Lyons et al.
125 N. Y. S. (2d) 420 (1953)

This was an action by Westinghouse Electric Corporation (plaintiff) against one Lyons and others (defendants). Judgment for plaintiff.

Plaintiff was seeking a decree requiring defendants to account for moneys collected from the sale of merchandise consigned to them for sale. Beginning July 1, 1944, and annually thereafter to July 1, 1951, by virtue of duly executed contracts, defendants were designated by plaintiff as their agents for the distribution of lamps. Monthly reports were submitted to plaintiff setting forth direct sales to customers and also those to "served agents," meaning smaller agents of the plaintiff, and in the latter instances defendants were given additional compensation ranging from 5 to 6 per cent. Plaintiff now claims that defendants by falsely reporting many of their "direct sales" as sales to "served agents" obtained for themselves very substantial allowances to which they were not entitled.

Plaintiff urges that the factors essential for the relief sought appear to be present: first, a fiduciary relationship between principal and agent; second, complicated and long accounts, covering an extended period of time; third, admitted collection of moneys by defendants, during the months of November and December, 1951, for which they have not accounted; and, fourth, concealed falsifications in the reports submitted to the plaintiff from the very inception of the relationship, all without the knowledge or consent of the plaintiff.

Defendants maintain, however, that plaintiff is not entitled to an accounting, contending that (1) the written agreements between the parties were modified by parol; (2) the acceptance of defendants' monthly statements with knowledge of their falsity constituted a series of accounts stated; and (3) the alleged contracts were unenforceable because they violated the anti-trust laws.

LEVY, J. Taking the defenses in their order, I have concluded, first, that there was no waiver of the provisions of the written contracts between the parties, within the meaning of section 33-c of the Personal Property Law. Justice McNally, in granting a recent motion for summary judgment, in a replevin action against the defendants, which was subsequently affirmed by the Appellate Division, 281 App. Div. 747, 118 N. Y. (2d) 742, fortifies this conclusion and renders the matter involved res adjudicata.

As to the second defense, the plaintiff could not be bound by an account stated unless it had full knowledge or was offered an opportunity to gain such knowledge of all of the true facts and circumstances. *National Surety Co. v. President, etc., of Manhattan Co.*, 252 N. Y. 247, 169 N. E. 372.

It is well settled that a defrauded party with no knowledge of the facts is not bound simply by the acceptance of an account stated. *Hopewood Plays v. Kemper*, 263 N. Y. 380, 189 N. E. 461. Especially so is this true where a fiduciary relationship exists, as in the instant case, and this court will not lend its aid to enforce the alleged defense under such circumstances.

The defendants boldly admit not only that a special, and apparently secret, consignment ledger was kept but also that their monthly reports were false and to such an extent that even they themselves were unfamiliar with all of the details. Those admissions cast a very severe and obvious pall over the defendants' position.

The evidence adduced reveals that it was not until late in 1950, or the early part of 1951, that the plaintiff was first put on notice that one or more of its agents were operating improperly, following which it forthwith secured undeniable knowledge to this effect by secretly marking lamps which were traced subsequently to the doorstep of defendants.

It may very well be that a full and thorough audit at an earlier date might have disclosed the fraudulent practices sooner, but the audits prior to 1951 appear to have been for accountability and inventory reconciliation only and the failure, therefore, to uncover the defendants' course of conduct is understandable.

The examination before trial of Kinsey, the district manager, who executed the contracts on behalf of the plaintiff, substantiates the absence of either scienter or acquiescence by the plaintiff. Surely, the testimony of the three agents, out of at least one hundred, who themselves are defendants in pending actions by the plaintiff, that they too rendered false reports to the plaintiff, is insufficient to impute to the plaintiff knowledge of or consent to the admitted false reporting of the defendants. The motion by the plaintiff to strike out all testimony of these agents as irrelevant and immaterial is granted.

Finally, the third defense of illegality, based upon violation of anti-trust laws, has neither been sustained nor established.

In view of all of the foregoing I have concluded that an accounting, as prayed for, is warranted and justified and accordingly I so decree.

DUTIES AND LIABILITIES OF PRINCIPAL TO AGENT

The principal owes the following duties to his agent: (1) to compensate the agent, (2) to reimburse the agent, and (3) to indemnify the agent.

DUTY TO COMPENSATE

The duty of the principal to compensate his agent may be either express or implied. In most cases the amount of compensation which the agent is to receive is stated in the agency contract. Where no amount is agreed upon but the agent performs certain services for his principal and it is clear under the circumstances that he is not working gratuitously, he will be entitled to reasonable compensation. The law implies that the principal promised to pay the agent the reasonable value of his services.

Unless the principal has agreed to pay the agent in advance, the performance of the services is a condition precedent to the agent's right to be paid or the principal's duty to pay. When an agent is employed on a commission basis, as in the case of a real estate broker, a question sometimes arises, where the contract has no specific terms on the point, as to when the agent has earned his commission. If the agency contract merely provides that the agent is "to bring the parties together," that is, to find a purchaser who is ready, able, and willing to contract on the terms specified by the principal, the agent has earned his commission as soon as he has performed these services. The principal cannot deprive the agent of his commission by refusing to sign a contract with the third party, discharging the agent, and then later seeking out the third party and selling the property to him. The law gives protection to the agent in such cases. On the other hand, if the agency contract provides that the agent's commission is not due until the signing of the contract between the principal and third party, then the agent has no right to his commission until the contract has been signed. After the contract has been signed he is entitled to his commission even if for some reason the contract between the principal and the third party is not performed by the third party.

In cases where the agent is employed on a commission basis for an indefinite period, and the employment may be terminated at the will of the principal, difficult problems sometimes arise where the agent has spent considerable time and money in developing potential customers and the principal terminates the agency and later reaps the rewards of his agent's efforts. It would appear that the general rule applicable to such cases is that the agent would be entitled to reasonable compensation.

Walsh v. Isgro
1 Atl. (2d) 391, 121 N. J. L. 165 (1938)

This was an action by H. Edward Walsh (plaintiff) against Mario Isgro (defendant) to recover a judgment for commissions. Judgment for plaintiff, and defendant appealed. Affirmed.

In April, 1936, defendant was the owner of a farm which was advertised for sale. One Scurria was defendant's agent for the sale of the farm. Plaintiff, a licensed real estate broker, having had an inquiry from one Grover concerning the possible purchase of a farm, entered into negotiations with the defendant and Scurria to secure authority for the sale of the farm.

Plaintiff alleged that a contract resulted from the following correspondence:

"September 9, 1936. Mr. H. Edward Walsh, Trenton, N. J. I have discussed this matter with Mr. Isgro, who advised me he is willing to authorize you to sell his farm for a price of $14,000, agreeing to pay a commission of 7%. Please reply promptly. It is understood, however, that Mr. Isgro is not to give you the exclusive right to sell. Very truly yours, George Scurria."

"September 10, 1936. Mr. George Scurria, Philadelphia, Pa. Replying to yours of September 9th in which you say Mr. Isgro is willing to pay me 7% commission, I accept this arrangement. Kindly have Mr. Isgro send me written authorization at once. Yours very truly, H. Ed. Walsh."

On September 22, 1936, the defendant, without plaintiff's knowledge, sold the farm to Grover's wife for $10,000. On September 29, 1936, plaintiff, having learned of the sale, submitted a bill to defendant for $700, being 7% commission on the sale price. The bill not being paid, this action was started.

Upon trial, the plaintiff introduced testimony that he had shown the farm to Grover several times, submitted the price of $14,000, and in return received a counter-offer of $10,000. There was further testimony that Walsh had discussed the sale with one Scudder, who held a mortgage on the farm, and had arranged that the mortgage be continued if Grover should purchase the property.

Walsh had advised Isgro and Scurria that he had a prospective purchaser but admitted he had neither introduced Grover nor revealed his name directly to the defendant. He had told Scudder that the purchaser was Grover and asked him not to say anything about the name. Walsh further testified that he was later informed by Scudder that Scurria and Isgro were planning to "do him out of the commissions" by selling to Grover direct.

Isgro and Scurria both contended that their contact with Grover and the eventual sale to his wife had been accomplished through information obtained from Scudder.

WELLS, J. It is a strongly settled rule of law that a real estate broker, duly employed in writing, earns his commission when he finds a purchaser able and willing to comply with the terms specified in the authority thus given or when he finds a purchaser who agrees to purchase on terms satisfactory to the owner. *Ganley v. Kalikman,* 105 N. J. L. 311.

It is not disputed in the present case that the plaintiff, Walsh, had secured an offer of $10,000 from Grover, and that the defendant later sold the property to Grover's wife for this amount. Nor is it disputed that Grover was his wife's agent in the negotiations with Walsh. However, the defendant contends that Walsh was entitled to commissions only on a sale made for $14,000, the amount specified in the authorization of September 9, 1936. A study of the terms of this authorization reveals a statement of the asking price and rate of commissions, but nothing, beyond the inclusion of the sale price in the authorization, to indicate that the payment of commissions was strictly conditioned on the asking price being secured. To support the defendant's contention, we would be forced to hold that where an asking price is specified in the broker's written authority, no commission could be earned unless that price be obtained, whatever terms might later prove satisfactory to the owner in a sale to a purchaser originally procured by the broker. Such a holding would in effect overrule the principle of law stated in the case of *Ganley v. Kalikman,* supra, which we think is controlling here.

Under the terms of the contract the plaintiff was entitled to commissions if he was the procuring or efficient cause of the sale to Grover. Since the evidence was conflicting so as to raise a doubt on this point, it was properly submitted as a question of fact to be determined by the jury. The jury found that the plaintiff was the procuring or efficient cause of the sale.

The plaintiff's right of recovery is not dependent upon the knowledge of the defendant that the purchaser was procured by the activity of the plaintiff. Judgment affirmed.

DUTY TO REIMBURSE

The principal is, as a general rule, obligated to reimburse the agent for any moneys expended by him in carrying out the business of his principal. However, the agent must prove that such expenditures were made within the scope of his employment and were beneficial to the principal. The agent is not entitled to recover for unnecessary expenses resulting from his own fault or neglect, or for expenses incurred in activities not expressly or impliedly covered by his contract. To illustrate, P engages A as a selling agent, with the understanding that A is to furnish his own car but P is to furnish the gasoline and oil for the car. When A leaves for a trip over his territory, P says nothing about advancing him money with which to purchase gasoline and oil; A makes the necessary purchases, and on his return P refuses to reimburse him. A would be entitled to reimbursement. But if P, an insurance company, employed A as its agent to sell insurance, but did not agree to provide transportation, A would not be entitled to reimbursement for the use of his own car or for gasoline and oil.

Bacon v. Fourth National Bank
9 N. Y. S. 435, 28 N. Y. St. Rep. 151 (1889)

This was an action by Alexander S. Bacon (plaintiff) against the Fourth National Bank of the city of New York (defendant). Judgment for defendant.

Plaintiff brought this action to recover the full amount of a deposit in the defendant bank. Defendant acknowledged the amount of the deposit, but claimed that it was entitled to be reimbursed for money paid by it on plaintiff's account. Plaintiff had deposited with defendant in escrow a mortgage and assignment, to be forwarded to its Boston correspondent and delivered by it, on payment of a certain sum, to a person in that city. Defendant forwarded the mortgage to the Maverick National Bank, and, while the securities were in the latter's possession, an attachment was levied on them. The Maverick National Bank employed an attorney to defend the suit and paid his fees, and was reimbursed therefor by defendant. Defendant now claims that it is entitled to retain this amount out of plaintiff's deposit.

McADAM, C.J. The fees paid to the attorneys in Boston were expended under circumstances from which the law implies a request to pay for them on the part of the plaintiff. Legal advice and services may be as necessary to protect property as the aid of a physician or surgeon is to protect life. Neither may prove serviceable in some cases, in others extremely so, depending in a measure on results. Prudence requires their employment in all cases wherein property or life is imperiled. It would be negligence not to employ professional aid in cases requiring it. . . . It is elementary that an agent is not permitted to reap any of the profits of his agency properly belonging to the principal; so, on the other hand, he is entitled to be indemnified against all losses which have been innocently sustained by him on the same account. . . . It is a familiar rule that an agent has the duty of taking such steps as are reasonably necessary for the protection of his principal's interests, and for the preservation of his principal's property, and that, having made outlays for that purpose, he is entitled to reimbursements at the hands of the principal.

The expenditure, being a proper one, was legally authorized, and is a good counterclaim against the plaintiff; and, the cause of action for the balance of his demand having been legally discharged by payment into court, it follows that there must be judgment for the defendant, with costs.

DUTY TO INDEMNIFY

If an agent, while acting within the scope of his authority, and while engaged in the principal's business, suffers losses, the principal is obligated to indemnify him for such losses. For example, if the agent is required to pay damages to a third party whose rights he has innocently breached while carrying out his instructions, he is entitled to be indemnified. He is not entitled to be indemnified for losses or damage suffered if he knowingly commits an act that is illegal or in violation of some right of the third party.

Horrabin v. City of Des Moines
198 Iowa 549 (1924)

This was an action by William Horrabin (plaintiff) against the City of Des Moines (defendant). Judgment for plaintiff, and defendant appealed. Affirmed.

This case was tried below on a stipulation of facts from which it appears that plaintiff entered into a written contract with the city of Des Moines to construct a bridge over the Des Moines River. From both the contract and the stipulation it appears that the city agreed to furnish plaintiff the right of way upon which the bridge and approach should be constructed. It was stipulated that under the direction of defendant's city engineer, plaintiff entered upon certain land belonging to the Central Ice Company and built the bridge or the approach thereon, and that at that time the city did not have the right to the use, occupancy, and possession of the land, and did not acquire such right until some two years later. It was further stipulated that the Central Ice Company brought suit against both the city and plaintiff for the damages resulting from the trespass upon its property, and recovered a judgment against both defendants, which plaintiff has paid. This action, begun and tried in equity, is to recover from the city the amount so paid.

VERMILLION, J. That the city and the plaintiff were, as to the Central Ice Company, joint tort-feasors, and therefore both liable for the trespass, was settled by the judgment against them. It is familiar law that, speaking generally, as between joint wrongdoers there can be no contribution. The rule is subject to exceptions, however. The only question in the case is whether the plaintiff is, under the facts, within any recognized exception to the general rule.

Judge Cooley, after stating the general rule, observes: "But there are some exceptions to the general rule which rest upon reasons at least as forcible as those which support the rule itself. They are the cases where, although the law holds all the parties liable as wrongdoers to the injured party, yet, as between themselves, some of them may not be wrongdoers at all, and their equity to require the others to respond for all the damages may be complete. There are many such cases where the wrongs are unintentional, or where the party, by reason of some relation, is made chargeable with the conduct of others." The author cites the case of the employee of a railroad company who is directed by its officers to do an act which it turns out they had no right to do, and for doing which he is made to pay damages, and continues: "Here, if the act was a plain and manifest wrong, as would be leaving the cars to commit a battery, the servant can have no indemnity, because he must have known the act to be unlawful; but, if the act directed was one he had reason to suppose was legal and he obeyed directions on that supposition, it would ill become the railroad company to demand that he be treated as a wrongdoer when called to indemnify him against the consequences of the act its officers had directed. In such a case the servant is not, in morals, a wrongdoer at all, and his claim to indemnity would be based upon a faithful obedience to orders which he had a right to presume were rightful, nothing to the contrary appearing." *Cooley on Torts*, p. 168.

The doctrine so announced and illustrated has been often and in a great variety of situations applied by the courts in cases where, while both parties were liable to the person injured because of some breach of duty, yet, as between the wrongdoers themselves, by reason of their relations or a difference in the character of the duty under which they rested, they were not equally guilty—were not in pari delicto.

Where one is employed or directed by another to do an act not manifestly wrong, the law implies a promise of indemnity by the principal for damages resulting proximately from the good faith execution of the agency.

With these principles in mind, it seems clear that the facts of the present case bring it within an exception to the general rule that there can be no contribution or indemnity between joint tort-feasors. The plaintiff was but carrying out his contract with the city. That contract provided that the city should procure the necessary right of way for the construction of the bridge and approach. The plaintiff entered upon the land of the Central Ice Company and constructed the approach thereon, by direction of the city's engineer in charge of the work. While as between himself and the owner of the property he was a trespasser, and liable as such, as between himself and the city he was but acting in fulfillment of his contract. He had a right to assume, when directed to proceed with the work upon the premises of the Ice Company, that the city had procured the right to so use the ground. What he did was done, not for himself, but for the city, and under its direction. He is, therefore, entitled to be indemnified. Judgment for plaintiff affirmed.

AGENT'S LIEN

An agent has a lien upon the principal's property and money in his (the agent's) possession to secure his claims against his principal for compensation, reimbursement, and indemnity. The lien is possessory in nature; that is, to be valid it requires that the agent have legal possession of the principal's property. For example, an attorney has a lien upon the documents, papers, and money of his client which are in his possession, to secure the payment of his fee. If the agent voluntarily surrenders possession of the money or property to his client, he loses his lien. However, the lien is not lost if the agent should die.

REVIEW CASES

1. Steinberg leased a shop in which he conducted a lucrative business in women's wearing apparel. He hired his brother and sister to help run the shop. Before the lease expired he applied to the lessor for its renewal. During Steinberg's absence from the city, and without his knowledge, his brother and sister leased the shop from the lessor on their own account. Steinberg brought an action to procure the relief that a court of equity customarily decrees in similar actions against disloyal employees. Judgment for whom? (Steinberg v. Steinberg et al., 206 N. Y. S. 134)

2. Chandler and Preston each promised to pay Nichols a stipulated compensation for bringing them together in a business trust transaction. Preston took over as trustee, and later a dispute arose between him and Chandler. As a result, Chandler filed suit against Preston, and Nichols intervened, asking for the compensation promised him by Preston. Preston contended that since Nichols had acted as agent for both principals and had already been paid by Chandler, he was not legally entitled to additional compensation from Preston. Ruling? (Chandler v. Preston, 207 Mich. 244, 174 N. W. 205)

3. Martine's testator, as agent for Whitney, made certain investments in realty for Whitney. When the investments were made, the realty was heavily encumbered by prior mortgages, and it was later sold for less than the amount of these mortgages, so that Whitney's investment was lost. Whitney brought suit to recover from Martine's estate. Judgment for whom? (Whitney v. Martine et al., 88 N. Y. 535)

4. Mason Produce Co., a broker selling food products, was agent for Harry C. Gilbert Co. for selling a car of beans. The broker sold the car of beans and notified the Gilbert Co. to deliver them. Later the purchaser canceled the order, but the broker failed to notify the Gilbert Co. The beans were shipped and not accepted and had to be sold at a loss. The Gilbert Co. sued the Mason Co. for damages. Ruling? (Mason Produce Co. v. Harry C. Gilbert Co., 194 Ind. 462, 141 N. E. 613)

5. By a written contract Smith agreed to work for Herring-Hall-Marvin Safe Co. for a certain number of years at a stipulated salary per year. For most

of the period Smith was manager of the company's New York office, though he made trips for the company to other cities. He was then sent to Philadelphia to take up work. He went to Philadelphia in response to the company's orders, but he refused to stay there, and insisted on being employed in New York. The company canceled the contract and refused to pay Smith's salary. Smith sued for his salary for the remainder of the contract period. At the trial the company offered evidence that such transfer of agents from one city to another was frequent in the trade. Holding? (Smith v. Herring-Hall-Marvin Safe Co., 115 N. Y. S. 294)

6. Thomas contracted to work one year at a specified sum for Beaver Dam Mfg. Co. He was fired before the year was up, and brought suit to recover wages for the balance of the year. Evidence was brought to show that he had absented himself from work on various occasions, once for three weeks; that he set down a fixed amount per day in his expense account, whether he spent it or not; and that he had disobeyed instructions several times. The contract expressly gave the company the right to discharge him for such actions. If such an express agreement had not existed, could Thomas have recovered? (Thomas v. Beaver Dam Mfg. Co., 157 Wis. 427, 147 N. W. 364)

7. Isaacs bought chances on an automobile, which was to be presented to the winner at a picnic on a certain date. Isaacs offered Leake $25 to take his tickets to the picnic and receive the car for him if he was the winner. Leake agreed. One of Isaacs' tickets was the lucky one, and the car was turned over to Leake, but he refused to give it to Isaacs, maintaining that the lottery was illegal and that by the rules the winner had to be present. Isaacs sued for the car. Ruling? (Leake v. Isaacs, 262 Ky. 640, 90 S. W.(2d) 1001)

Principal and Third Party

19

Since the rights and liabilities of the principal and the third party are largely determined by the authority of the agent, it becomes necessary first to consider the origin, nature, and extent of the agent's authority.

CLASSIFICATION OF AGENTS

Considering agents from the standpoint of the scope or extent of their authority there are two types of agents, (1) general agents and (2) special agents. Under the agency agreement the principal may delegate to the agent broad authority to act in his behalf; or the authority granted may be quite narrow and limited to a particular act or undertaking. If the agent is authorized to transact generally all the business of his principal, or all his business of a certain kind or at a particular place, he is said to be a general agent. For example, the manager of a branch office or store is usually held to be a general agent. If the agent is merely authorized to perform a particular act for the principal, or to act in a single transaction, he is a special agent. For example, if A appoints B his agent to find a buyer for his house or his car, B is a special agent. Sometimes it becomes difficult, in borderline cases, to determine whether a given agent is a general agent or a special agent. However, such determination is important, since the rights and liabilities of the parties in a given case may turn upon whether the agent is a general or a special agent.

KINDS OF AUTHORITY

Broadly speaking, the authority of both general and special agents may be either (1) actual or (2) apparent or ostensible. An agent's actual authority may be either (1) express or (2) implied. His actual authority

411

emanates directly from the principal himself; his apparent or ostensible authority arises out of the doctrine of estoppel.

EXPRESS AUTHORITY.   The express authority of an agent is that authority which the principal confers upon his agent in the contract or appointment. If the contract or instrument creating the agency is in writing, the agent's authority is contained in such instrument, and may be established by reference to the instrument. Its meaning is a question of law to be determined by the court. If the contract is oral, the express authority of the agent is contained in the oral understanding of the parties. In case a dispute arises over the extent of such express authority, the proof of the intentions and understandings of the parties becomes more difficult, and is a question of fact to be determined by the jury.

The third party may not safely rely upon the statement of the agent as to the existence of the agency or the scope of his authority; in fact, such matters may not be established by the agent's statements or testimony. If the authority of the agent has been reduced to writing, as in the case of a power of attorney or an informal written contract, and the third party knows that such instrument exists, he is required to insist upon seeing the instrument in order to determine for himself the scope of the authority of the agent. If the agent's authority is express but oral, and the third party has any reason to question its nature or extent, caution would require that he check with the principal.

IMPLIED AUTHORITY.   The implied authority of the agent is largely derived from his express authority. The courts hold that the implied authority of an agent is that authority which is necessary, reasonable, and proper to put into effect his express authority. It is recognized that it is practically impossible for the parties to place in their contract every detail. For example, if P appoints A as general manager of one of his branch offices or stores, it is not necessary that P describe in complete detail the authority that he confers upon A; it is enough for him to set forth in general terms the function and duties of A. It would be implied from such express authority that A has authority to do those things that are necessary, reasonable, and proper to carry out his express grant of authority. It would also be implied that he has the authority which is customarily given to a general manager of a branch store or office. For example, even though P did not give A the express authority to employ necessary clerks and other help, it would be implied that he could do so. But it could not be implied that A had authority to perform some unusual act. For example, he could not employ someone for life, move the business to another city or section of the city, or use a portion of the profits to speculate in real estate or the stock market.

The authority of the agent may also be implied from the words or acts of the principal, from a previous course of dealing, or from the customs and usages of the trade or business in the locality.

Since a third party would be justified in assuming, in the absence of evidence to the contrary, that the agent has implied authority to do those things which are necessary, reasonable, and proper to carry out his express authority and those things which are customarily done in the particular type of agency, the principal may not limit such authority by secret instructions to his agent. Although, as between the agent and the principal, such secret instructions limiting the authority of the agent would be binding upon the agent, they would not bind a third party who has no knowledge of them. But the principal is of course at liberty to make such limitations openly; and if the third party has knowledge of them, he will be bound.

APPARENT OR OSTENSIBLE AUTHORITY. While express and implied authority trace their source to the principal, apparent authority stems from the doctrine of estoppel. If the principal holds a person out as his agent, or holds his agent out as having certain authority, and a third person relies and acts upon such representations, the principal will be bound, even though, in fact, he has never made such person his agent, or has never conferred such authority upon his agent. The same rule applies where the principal permits a person to hold himself out as his agent, or permits his agent to hold himself out as having authority that he does not possess, and does not repudiate such representations. In such cases the principal would be estopped from denying that the agent or the alleged agent had the necessary authority.

Palovik et al. v. Absher et al.
181 P. (2d) 989, 198 Okla. 671 (1947)

This was a suit by Henry J. Absher and wife (plaintiffs) against Joe Palovik and wife (defendants) for specific performance of a contract for the sale of real property. Decree for plaintiffs, and defendants appealed. Affirmed.

Defendants were the owners of a small tract of land with a house thereon, and listed the same for sale with an agent named Clingenpeel. Clingenpeel sold this property to plaintiffs under a written contract for the sum of $2,000, in which was included the assumption by plaintiffs of certain specified amounts, in monthly payments, until the balance due was paid.

Plaintiffs took possession of the property in September, 1941, and remained in possession until June 1, 1942, at which time they moved to Texas, where plaintiff Henry J. Absher was employed in a war plant. After taking possession of the property, plaintiffs made a number of payments in 1941 and 1942, but not the full amounts required under the contract. In 1943 plaintiffs sent a number of money orders to the agent Clingenpeel but Clingenpeel did not cash them and give the money to defendants because defendants had taken possession of the property and occupied it.

Plaintiff Henry J. Absher testified that his failure to make payments in accordance with the terms of the contract was due to an accidental personal injury suffered by him, and financial difficulties suffered because of such injury; that he discussed his difficulties with Clingenpeel, who defendants had advised him was in full charge of the sale of the property, and that Clingenpeel agreed to excuse his failure to make regular payments under the contract until such time as he was able to do so. During the summer of 1944 plaintiffs returned to the property and found defendants in possession, and were advised by defendants that they considered the contract cancelled for the reason that they had received no money to apply on the purchase price of the property. At this same time plaintiffs discovered that Clingenpeel had not cashed the money orders which they had sent from Texas. Plaintiffs failed to come to any agreement with defendants in the matter and filed this suit for specific performance of the contract. Plaintiffs alleged a tender of all sums due under the contract and its refusal by defendants. The trial court held in favor of plaintiffs and decreed specific performance. Defendants appealed.

OSBORN, J. The defendants contend that the agent, Clingenpeel, had no authority to waive strict performance of the contract by the plaintiffs, or to excuse their default in making payments, and that if he did, defendants were not bound thereby.

Plaintiff Henry J. Absher testified that the entire transaction between him and defendants was conducted by Clingenpeel; that about a month or two after he had moved into the premises, defendant Joe Palovik talked with him, at which time he advised Palovik that he had paid the $200 down payment to Clingenpeel, and Palovik told him that he and his wife were now living in Tulsa and that Clingenpeel would continue to handle the transaction; that he had made all the payments to Clingenpeel; and that he understood that Clingenpeel was in complete charge of the sale of the property and the collection of the money. Palovik did not deny making such statements. Neither did defendants produce any evidence to show that Clingenpeel did not have such authority, but asserted the right to rescind solely because they had received no money from Clingenpeel to apply on the contract of sale. From the evidence the trial court was justified in concluding that in the transaction Clingenpeel was the general agent of the defendants, and that as such his waiver of strict compliance with the terms of the contract was binding upon them.

In 21 *R. C. L.*, p. 853, section 32, it is said: "A general agent is usually authorized to do all acts connected with the business or employment in which he is engaged, while a special agent is only authorized to do specific acts in pursuance of particular instructions, or with restrictions necessarily implied from the acts to be done."

In *Continental Supply Co. v. Sinclair Oil & Gas Co.*, 109 Okla. 178, 235

P. 471, it was said: "In the absence of notice to the contrary, a person dealing with an admitted agent may presume that he is the general agent and that he is acting within the scope of his authority; the burden being upon the principal to show notice of any limitations upon the agent's authority."

There being sufficient evidence to justify the conclusion that Clingenpeel was the general agent of the defendants, plaintiffs were justified in believing that he had a right to bind the defendants by his waiver of strict compliance with the terms and conditions of the contract, and that his acts and conduct in that respect were binding upon the defendants.

May et al. v. Ken-Rad Corporation
131 S. W. (2d) 490 (Ky.) (1939)

This was an action by George Oliver May and others, as partners doing business under the firm name and style of Price Waterhouse & Co. (plaintiffs) against the Ken-Rad Corporation, Inc. (defendant). Judgment for defendant, and plaintiffs appealed. Reversed.

Plaintiffs brought this action to recover of defendant the sum of $2,506.40 for an audit. Defendant made application to the National Recovery Administration for a wage differential under the Electrical Code promulgated by the N. R. A. Since 1922 defendant had been engaged in manufacturing in Owensboro and was the only manufacturer of radio tubes in the South. Northern and Eastern competitors filed answers and protests against the granting of the differential. After evidence had been submitted, representatives of the N. R. A. were sent to defendant's plant and to the plants of the Hygrade-Sylvania Corporation to verify and possibly to augment the evidence by personal inspection and examination. After this was done the assistant administrator advised representatives of defendant that figures and information obtained with respect to the relative costs of production at various plants did not justify the granting of a wage differential to it. Representatives of defendant, however, insisted that data furnished or obtained from its competitors were erroneous and subsequent conferences resulted in an agreement between the representatives of the N. R. A. and defendant to have an audit made of defendant and the Hygrade-Sylvania Corporation by a firm of reputable accountants selected by the representatives of the N. R. A., the cost of the audit to be borne by defendant. This agreement was later confirmed by letter from defendant to the N. R. A., which contained suggestions as to the nature and character of the audit which should be made. Plaintiffs (Price Waterhouse & Co.) were selected by the N. R. A. to make the audit. The Hygrade-Sylvania Corporation consented to an audit of its books under an agreement with the N. R. A. that it would be confidential and open only to the inspection of representatives of the N. R. A. After the audit was made and plaintiffs filed their report with the N. R. A., the application for a differential was at first denied, but later an order was entered granting defendant a 12½% wage differential. Defendant later refused to pay plaintiffs for making the audit on the ground that the audit was not of the type and character it had authorized the N. R. A. to have made and that it did not agree to pay for an audit which it was not allowed to see and which was solely for the confidential consideration of the N. R. A.

CREAL, COMMISSIONER. The record discloses beyond question that defendant made the N. R. A. its agent to select and employ a reputable firm of accountants to make the proposed audit and that it agreed to pay for same. There was no specific agreement as to the nature or character of the audit to be made nor did defendant's letter to the N. R. A., confirming the agreement, specify the nature and character of audit which it expected or for which it would pay. . . . There was no agreement that the defendant would be furnished a copy of the audit and no suggestion in its letter that payment for the audit was conditioned upon its receiving a copy or having the privilege of inspecting it. . . . The defendant gave the N. R. A. full authority to employ accountants to make the audit without any conditions, restrictions or reservations or anything more than mere suggestions.

A principal is bound by the contract of his agent within the scope of the latter's apparent authority, although not authorized in express terms. It has been held that a principal is bound by the acts of the agent within the apparent scope of authority although the authority may be in fact limited, if one dealing with the agent is ignorant of limitations upon his authority. In the latter case it is further held that where one of two parties must suffer loss through acts of an agent the loss should fall upon the one who authorized the agent to act beyond the scope of his apparent authority.

Defendant insists that the N. R. A. could not act as agent for anyone because the National Recovery Act was unconstitutional, as was later decided. In *Talbot v. Bowen*, 8 Ky. 436, it was held in effect that one under legal disability, whose contracts may not be binding upon him, may nevertheless bind his principal. Furthermore, defendant fully recognized the agency by its letter confirming the agreement to pay for the audit; and it has been held by this court that one cannot act through another and then insist that the other is not his agent. *Roesena v. Burdette*, 208 Ky. 137, 270 S. W. 731.

It is our conclusion that the finding of the court is not sufficiently supported by the evidence; that plaintiffs were entitled to recover the sum sued upon; and that the court erred in adjudging otherwise.

AUTHORITY APPLICABLE TO CERTAIN SITUATIONS

AUTHORITY OF SALES AGENT. A number of important legal problems are connected with the authority of an agent who is employed to sell personal property. For example, does the agent have authority (1) to pass title to the property? (2) to deliver? (3) to collect? (4) to fix the price? (5) to accept in payment anything other than money? (6) to warrant title and quality of the property?

In the case of personal property the authority of the sales agent may be either actual or apparent. The mere possession of the property does not imply authority to sell and pass title to the property. However, there are certain exceptions to this rule. For instance, if the owner of goods gives possession of the goods to another and places in his hands some indicium of title, such as a warehouse receipt or a bill of lading, authority to sell may be inferred. The same would be true where a wholesaler places merchandise in the hands of a retailer under a conditional sales contract. Even though the wholesaler has retained title and has merely passed the possession of the goods to the retailer, a third person, in the regular course of business, would be privileged to assume that the retailer has authority to pass good title to him.

If an agent is entrusted with the possession of goods by his principal, he has authority to deliver and collect for them if they are sold. A good example of this situation is the case of an over-the-counter sale by a clerk in a retail store. Where the agent does not have possession of the goods, e.g., where he merely solicits orders, he has no implied authority to collect. He does, however, have implied authority to fix or state the price of the goods, and, unless the price is such as to make a reasonable man suspect error, the principal will be bound.

Authority to sell confers only authority to accept payment in money. The agent, as a general rule, does not possess implied authority to sell on credit. He usually may not accept in payment negotiable paper, whether or not it is made payable to the principal or to himself. However, since it is customary to accept checks in payment, the agent may accept a check as conditional payment. If the check is dishonored, the principal may sue on the original debt or on the check, at his election. Finally, it should be observed that the agent may have authority to accept payment in something other than money if it is expressly or impliedly given, or if it is implied from a previous course of dealing or by usage and custom.

Since in the sale of property there always exists an implied warranty of title, unless otherwise expressly stated, the agent may expressly warrant the title to the property he sells. However, most courts hold that he may not warrant the quality of the goods or property, unless it is customary to do so. An agent never has implied authority to give an unusual or extraordinary warranty.

As a general rule, the authority possessed by a real estate broker is limited to finding a prospective buyer, and does not enable him to bind the principal or actually sign the contract of sale or execute a deed. Such authority may be given, but it usually must be in writing.

AUTHORITY OF PURCHASING AGENT. Among the legal problems which arise relative to the authority of a purchasing agent are the following: (1) Has he authority to purchase on credit? (2) May he fix the price and agree upon the terms of the purchase? (3) May he make payment by executing and delivering a negotiable instrument, such as a check, note, or bill of exchange?

The authority of an agent to purchase on credit depends largely upon the nature of the agency, previous course of dealing, and usage and custom. As a rule, a general purchasing agent has authority to purchase on credit, a special agent has not. If an agent is authorized to buy, it is implied that he has authority to buy on credit unless the principal supplies him with money to pay for the goods.

The purchasing agent may fix the price and agree upon the terms of the purchase.

Usually an agent may not, unless expressly authorized, pay for goods by executing some type of negotiable instrument in the principal's name, unless such authority is implied from the nature and purposes of the agency. It has been stated that "the authority to draw, accept or indorse bills, notes, and checks will not readily be implied as an incident to the express authority of an agent." [1] Such authority may be implied if the execution of such an instrument is necessary for the accomplishment of the objectives and purposes of the agency.

AUTHORITY TO APPOINT SUBAGENTS.   The general rule is that an agent has no implied authority to appoint subagents. It is presumed that the principal will wish to select personally those who are to act for him. The agent may of course be expressly granted authority to appoint subagents or subemployees, or such authority may be implied from his express authority or from trade usage or from his previous dealings with his principal. In most cases an agent has implied authority to delegate to subagents or subemployees purely mechanical or ministerial functions which do not require the exercise of specific skills or abilities necessary to put into effect the principal objects of the agency contract. For instance, A may employ B as his attorney to represent him in the trial of a lawsuit. B does not need express authority in order to delegate some of the work involved to his secretary and to younger and less-experienced attorneys in his office; but without express authority he could not delegate to someone else the duty and responsibility of trying the case. Where such mechanical and ministerial functions are delegated to subordinates, the agent is responsible for their work and for their wages and salaries. In cases where a subagent is appointed by the agent with the consent of the principal, the subagent becomes the agent of the principal.

The foregoing rules of law do not apply to independent contractors. They may, and often do, employ subcontractors or subagents. For in-

---

[1] Francis B. Tiffany, *Handbook of the Law of Principal and Agent* (West Publishing Co., St. Paul, Minn., 1924), p. 83.

stance, the contractor who contracts to build a house customarily lets the plumbing, electrical work, and other specialized tasks to subcontractors. He may do this without the consent or approval of the employer. He is, however, responsible for the work of the subcontractors and is alone liable to them for compensation for their services.

Oleson v. Albers
130 Neb. 823, 266 N. W. 632 (1936)

This was an action by A. R. Oleson (plaintiff) against Gustav Albers (defendant). Judgment for defendant, and plaintiff appealed. Affirmed.

This was an action at law to recover the purchase price of corn owned by plaintiff and delivered to defendant by a trucker, who collected the full purchase price from defendant but did not pay plaintiff. Plaintiff alleged that defendant agreed to purchase corn belonging to plaintiff at 40¢ per bushel, and in addition to pay 2¢ per bushel for the trucking charges; that under this agreement 843 bushels of corn were delivered and accepted by defendant, and that the amount due was $337.50; and that no part of same had been paid.

Defendant filed an answer denying every allegation in the petition and alleging that defendant agreed with one George Worrell to purchase corn of him at an agreed price of 42¢ per bushel, delivered at defendant's farm; that said Worrell was engaged in the business of buying and selling corn, and was the owner and operator of a truck; that Worrell delivered corn to defendant; and that thereupon, without notice or knowledge of any right or ownership of plaintiff in and to the said corn, and upon the demand of Worrell, defendant paid him for the corn. Defendant contended that Worrell either purchased the corn from plaintiff and resold it to defendant, or that he was the agent of plaintiff in the transaction; and that plaintiff, by placing him in possession of the corn and by vesting him with the power of sale, is estopped from denying his power to receive and collect the purchase price.

Plaintiff testified that Worrell came to him and asked if he had any corn to sell and said that he had a man who wanted to buy corn, and plaintiff said that he would sell 800 or 900 bushels at 40¢ per bushel at his place. The trucker told plaintiff that he could then deliver the corn at 42¢. Worrell said he would get in touch with his man and let plaintiff know. A few days later Worrell told plaintiff that he had gotten in touch with his man and that the man would take the corn. Plaintiff asked Worrell who the man was and was told that he was Gus Albers. Worrell then took the corn and delivered it to Albers. Albers paid Worrell for the corn.

Worrell left the country immediately after being paid, and plaintiff ascertained that he had been bankrupt for several years.

PAINE, J. It is stated as the general rule, in 8 *A. L. R.* 203, that "an agent authorized to sell commodities has no implied authority to receive or collect payment therefor; but this rule is subject to several well-recognized exceptions. It is established by a long line of authorities that an agent, having possession of commodities which he is authorized to sell, has implied authority to receive or collect payment therefor."

Where a principal has, by his voluntary act, placed an agent in such a situation that a person of ordinary prudence, conversant with business usages and the nature of the particular business, is justified in presuming that such agent has authority to collect sums due to the principal, the debtor will be protected in case he relies upon the appearances of authority. It is undeniable that an agent to whom merchandise has been entrusted with authority to sell and deliver it is authorized to receive the price.

In the case at bar the plaintiff gave the trucker possession of the corn knowing that it was being sold and delivered by the trucker to the defendant. The plaintiff made no inquiry of the defendant as to what the transaction was, although both parties had telephones on the same system. It was clearly the plaintiff who placed Worrell, the trucker, in a position such that an innocent purchaser of this corn had a right to assume that the trucker was authorized to sell and collect the purchase price of the corn, and while it is unfortunate that the plaintiff was deceived in the confidence that he placed in the trucker, yet the law has many times been laid down: "Whenever one of two innocent persons must suffer by the act of a third, he who has enabled such third person to occasion the loss must sustain it." *Broom's Legal Maxims*, p. 463.

Judgment affirmed.

Johns v. Jaycox
67 Wash. 403, 121 P. 854 (1912)

This was an action by Robert Johns, doing business under the name of Standard Talking Machine Company (plaintiff) against O. P. Jaycox & Co. (defendant). Judgment for defendant, and plaintiff appealed. Reversed.

Plaintiff brought this action to recover an alleged balance due upon a written contract for 200 talking machines, sold by plaintiff to defendant through its agent, Howard. The machines were purchased to give away to defendant's customers as an advertisement. The agent signed a written warranty that defendant would sell an average of 25 records to each customer to whom a machine was given. Since defendant failed to complete its payments for the machines, plaintiff brought this action for the balance alleged to be due. Defendant set up as a defense breach of warranty of the agent, Howard.

Plaintiff contended that the warranty was never a part of the contract because the agent had no authority to make it; and that the defendant was not warranted in believing that the agent had authority to make such a warranty.

ELLIS, J. The circumstances and nature of the business should put a purchaser on inquiry. The apparent scope of the agent's ability was that of a sales agent, and it is upon the powers implied by that relation that any sound decision of this case must rest.

"The rule which is supported by the more numerous and more recent decisions is that if in the sale of that kind or class of goods which the agent is empowered to sell, it is usual in the market to give a warranty, the agent may give that warranty in order to effect a sale, and the law presumes that he has such authority; and that if an agent with express authority to sell has no actual authority to warrant, no authority can be implied where the property is of a description not usually sold with warranty. The implied power of an agent to warrant title and quality rests upon the necessity and propriety of such warranties in the sale of goods. It is not therefore to be extended to other warranties of an extraordinary sort, however impossible the agent may find it to make a sale without giving such warranties." 31 *Cyc.* 1353.

The correct principle, briefly stated, is that an agent under general employment to make sales is impliedly authorized to employ only those means for the purpose usual to the business, and that the purchaser cannot safely assume that he has authority to make any extraordinary warranty, or one beyond the usage of the business in which the agent is employed. We have been cited to no authority in which it has ever been held that an agent employed to make sales at wholesale has an implied authority by usage or custom not only to warrant the quality of the thing sold but also to warrant that the purchaser will make sales thereof at retail in any particular amount or at any given profit. A more extraordinary warranty can hardly be imagined. We can conceive of no sound principle upon which such a holding could rest. There was no evidence of any prevailing custom in the business of selling talking machines which would warrant an assumption on the purchaser's part that the warranty was authorized. The extraordinary nature of the warranty made proof of such custom essential to a recovery upon the warranty in the absence of any showing of an express authority. So far as disclosed there was no such custom. Judgment reversed.

CONTRACT LIABILITY OF PRINCIPAL AND THIRD PARTY TO EACH OTHER

In most negotiations between an agent and a third party, the agent makes clear to the third party both the fact that he is acting in a representative capacity and the identity of the principal. In this situation the principal is said to be *disclosed*. If the agent discloses to the third party that he is acting in a representative capacity but does not disclose the identity of the principal, the principal is said to be *partly disclosed*. If the agent discloses to the third party neither the existence of the agency nor the identity of the principal, the principal is *undisclosed*.

The rights and liabilities of the principal and the third party with respect to each other depend upon which one of these three situations exists in a given case.

WHERE PRINCIPAL IS DISCLOSED

LIABILITY OF PRINCIPAL TO THIRD PARTY.   In the case of a disclosed principal, the principal is liable to the third party on the contract if the agent had authority to negotiate the contract and the contract was properly executed.[1] The principal is also liable if the agent exceeds his authority and the principal subsequently ratifies his acts. In such situations the contract is that of the principal and not the agent; consequently the principal must assume complete responsibility for the contract. However, if the agent exceeds his authority in negotiating a contract and his acts are not ratified by the principal, the principal is not liable to the third party.

The liability of the principal extends to the agent's representations to the third party, during the negotiations, if they were made within the scope of the agent's authority. If the representations are those that are customarily made by agents in such transactions, the principal is liable for them even though he has not expressly authorized the agent to make such representations, and, in fact, even though he has privately instructed his agent not to make them, provided the third party is unaware of such instructions. Likewise, if the agent, in order to secure the contract, knowingly makes untrue statements such that the third party is justified in believing them and does in fact rely on them, the principal is liable, even though he has expressly instructed the agent not to make such statements. From the viewpoint of the principal these appear to be harsh rules; but they are justified by the fact that it is the principal who selected the agent, endowed him with authority, retained legal control over his activities, and presumably benefited by his acts. The courts hold that where one of two innocent parties must suffer by the wrongful acts of the agent, the one who made such acts possible should be the one to suffer. The third party has a right to assume that he may trust the principal's agent and rely upon any representations of his of the sort normally and customarily made in such transactions.

The principal is liable to the third party for any money properly paid by the third party to the agent, even though the agent has not turned the money over to the principal.

In considering the liability of the principal to the third party it must be kept in mind that the principal is bound by all material information obtained by the agent in negotiating a contract, and by all material notices received by him in the course and within the scope of the agency. Such knowledge of the agent is said to be imputed to his principal. From this fact springs the duty of the agent to communicate to his principal all such information and notices. It should be observed, however, that knowledge of the agent is not imputed to the principal if the interests of the

[1] Proper execution is discussed in the following chapter, in the section entitled Liability on Authorized Contracts.

agent are, for some reason, adverse to or in conflict with those of the principal—for example, where the agent is unfaithful to his principal and in collusion with the third party against the principal.

LIABILITY OF THIRD PARTY TO PRINCIPAL.   Where the third party negotiates a contract through the agent of a disclosed principal, the third party is liable on the contract to the principal, and not to the agent.

Maryland Casualty Co. v. Tulsa Industrial Loan & Investment Co.
83 F. (2d) 14, 105 A. L. R. 529 (1936)

This was an action by the Tulsa Industrial Loan & Investment Co. (plaintiff) against the Maryland Casualty Co. (defendant). Judgment for plaintiff, and defendant appealed. Affirmed.

This was a suit to recover on two indemnity bonds similarly conditioned and given to indemnify the plaintiff against loss suffered through larceny, theft, embezzlement, misappropriation of funds, or other fraudulent acts of its employees.

Plaintiff stated in its application for the bonds that to the best of its knowledge and belief all the employees to whom the bonds would be made applicable had always performed their duties faithfully. The applications were signed by plaintiff's secretary-treasurer, Dunn.

Prior to the time that the first application was submitted, Dunn and two employees had embezzled funds of the corporation, and they were then short in their accounts to the extent of $3,116.45. While the first bond was in force these employees appropriated to their own use $22,568.27 belonging to plaintiff. During the life of the second bond they appropriated $28,561.21. Upon discovery of these misappropriations of funds plaintiff gave proper notice to defendant. Defendant refused to pay either claim, and plaintiff brought this suit.

The defense was that the knowledge of plaintiff's agent (Dunn) was imputed to plaintiff (principal), and that therefore defendant was not liable.

BRATTON, J. Dunn was the plaintiff's agent and he knew of the embezzlements in which he and his confederates had engaged; but no officer or other agent with authority had actual knowledge of them. Was this knowledge imputed to his principal? A corporation is charged with knowledge of all material facts of which its officers or agents receive notice while acting in the course of their employment and within the scope of their authority, because it is presumed in law that such facts will be disclosed to the principal. That rule rests upon considerations of sound policy and imperative expediency; otherwise rights would frequently be impaled upon uncertainty and instability. But this rule bears a well-settled exception. It is that if in the course of his employment the agent acts for his own benefit and to defraud his principal, the latter is not charged with constructive knowledge of the uncommunicated facts in the transaction, since it is manifestly essential to the existence of such fraud that the agent concealed the facts, and consequently the ordinary presumption that he will communicate to his principal all facts concerning the business does not arise. The adverse character of his interest takes the case out of the general rule. *American Surety Co. v. Pauly*, 170 U. S. 133, 18 S. Ct. 552. There is another group of cases holding that the rational basis upon which the exception rests is that the agent acts outside the scope of his agency and for that reason his knowledge cannot be imputed to the principal. *Allen v. South Boston Ry. Co.*, 150 Mass. 200, 22 N. E. 917. Regardless of the divergence of reason underlying the exception, the courts in both groups agree that under such circumstances the knowledge of the agent is not imputed to the principal. Judgment for the plaintiff affirmed.

Haskell v. Starbird
152 Mass. 117, 142 N. E. 695 (1890)

This was an action by John Haskell (plaintiff) against Charles D. Starbird (defendant), for deceit in the sale of land. Judgment for plaintiff, and defendant appealed. Affirmed.

There was evidence that the purchase of a certain tract of land in Canada, in which purchase the plaintiff alleged himself to have been deceived, was made through one Rockwell, who acted as the agent for the defendant, and that the plaintiff was deceived by the representations made by Rockwell that the land was of the value of $1,200, contained a large amount of timber, and was adjacent to a flourishing village, which representations were false. There was also evidence that Rockwell made these representations as the agent of the defendant. Rockwell testified that the defendant made these representations to him; that he therefore made them to the plaintiff; and that, before the conveyance was made, he informed the defendant that he had so made them.

The defendant denied that he ever made any representations concerning the condition or location of the land, and offered evidence that, at the time the conveyance was made by him, he informed the plaintiff that he had never seen the land and knew nothing about it except what he had been informed.

DEVENS, J. While the statement as to the value of the land might be treated as an expression of an opinion only, those in reference to the locality of the land and the amount of timber on it were statements of fact, of importance to anyone proposing to purchase it. It does not appear that the land was readily accessible or that it contained a large amount of timber.

The jury held that the defendant, by employing Rockwell as his agent to make the sale, became responsible for the methods which he adopted in so doing. The defendant contended, however, that Rockwell was a special and not a general agent, and that, therefore, he was not liable. There is not, however, any distinction in the matter of responsibility for the fraud of an agent authorized to do business generally and an agent employed to conduct a single transaction, if in either case he is acting in the business for which he was employed by the principal, and had full authority to complete the transaction. While the principal may not have authorized the particular act, he has put the agent in his place to make the sale, and must be responsible for the manner in which he has conducted himself in doing the business which the principal intrusted to him. The rule that a principal is liable civilly for the neglect, fraud, deceit, or other wrongful act of his agent, although the principal did not in fact authorize the practice of such act, is quoted with approbation by Chief Justice Shaw in *Locke v. Stearns*, 1 Metc. 560, 35 Am. Dec. 382. That a principal is liable for the false representations of his agent, is said by the court, in *White v. Sawyer*, 16 Gray, 583, to be settled by the clear weight of authority. In the case at bar, if the false representations were made by Rockwell, they were made by him while acting within the scope of his authority in making a sale of land, which the defendant employed him to sell; and the instruction of the court properly held the defendant answerable for the damage occasioned thereby. *Lothrop v. Adams*, 133 Mass. 471. Judgment affirmed.

Beeman v. May
85 N. Y. S. (2d) 122 (1948)

This was an action by Floyd Beeman (plaintiff) against Albert J. May (defendant). Complaint dismissed and judgment for defendant.

This action was brought by the plaintiff, as purchaser, to recover a down payment of $200 which he had made to the defendant, a real estate broker, as part payment on the purchase price of real estate, on the ground that the vendor (principal) could not give good title. The plaintiff was able and willing to perform his contract with the vendor but the vendor was unable to give a good title to the property. The plaintiff never had any dealings with the vendor except through his agent, the defendant, Albert J. May. The plaintiff knew when he signed the contract and made the payment to the defendant that the defendant was acting only as an agent of the vendor.

SKERRITT, J. While the plaintiff has a cause of action against the vendor (principal) for breach of contract, he has chosen instead to sue the broker to recover the down payment. The ordinary purpose of an agent is to bring his principal into some business relationship with third persons. The rule is that where an authorized agent, acting within the scope of his authority, makes a contract in the name of a disclosed principal, the agent does not by implication incur any liability to a third person. This rule applies where the third person, who has voluntarily paid money to an agent for his known principal, seeks to regain it from the agent. In the absence of a special agreement he cannot hold the agent, though the latter has wrongfully withheld the money from his principal. *Hall v. Lauderdale*, 46 N. Y. 70.

Complaint dismissed and judgment for the defendant, with costs.

WHERE PRINCIPAL IS PARTLY DISCLOSED

LIABILITY OF PRINCIPAL TO THIRD PARTY.   Where the agent makes clear to the third party that he is acting in a representative capacity but does not identify his principal, the agent is bound, but if the third party subsequently learns the identity of the principal he may, as a general rule, hold the principal liable on the contract. However, the third party may not hold both the agent and the principal, but must make an election of one or the other.

LIABILITY OF THIRD PARTY TO PRINCIPAL.   Since the contract negotiated by the agent is in reality the contract of the principal, the principal is usually privileged to disclose his identity and claim his rights under the contract. However, this would not be true if the character, skill, or solvency of the agent was materially involved in the contract or was essential to its performance.

WHERE PRINCIPAL IS UNDISCLOSED

LIABILITY OF PRINCIPAL TO THIRD PARTY.   If an agent negotiates a contract with a third party without informing the third party that he is acting in a representative capacity and hence without disclosing the name of his principal, the agent is bound by the contract. The principal is also bound. Consequently, if the third party later discovers the existence of the agency and the identity of the principal, he may usually elect to hold either the agent or the undisclosed principal liable. This rule would not apply, however, if the contract were so drawn that the third party contracted exclusively with the agent. For instance, if the third party suspects that the person with whom he is negotiating is acting for an undisclosed principal, and if he wishes to protect himself against such a possibility, he may have it stipulated in the contract that he is contracting exclusively with the agent as the other party to the contract.

The third party is said to make his election when, with full knowledge of the identity of the principal, he indicates his intention to hold liable on the contract either the agent or the principal. His election may be either express or implied. The effect of such election of one of the two is to discharge the other. It should be noted that the filing of an action by the third party against the agent is not an election if he does not know that an agency exists or who the principal is. A question rises as to whether the third party has made his election if, after he files his action against the agent but before he has obtained judgment, he discovers the existence of the agency and the identity of the principal, yet prosecutes his action to judgment. It has been generally held that such action constitutes an election, on the ground that the third party could have dismissed his action against the agent and have proceeded against the principal; but some courts have taken a contrary position on the matter. What is the situation if the third party does not learn of the identity of the principal until after he has obtained a judgment against the agent? If he finds that he is unable to satisfy his judgment against the agent and then discovers the existence of the agency and the identity of the principal, may he bring action against the principal? While most courts hold that he may not do so, at least one court has taken a contrary view.

LIABILITY OF THIRD PARTY TO PRINCIPAL.   Unless the third party has contracted exclusively with the agent, the undisclosed principal is privileged to "come out of hiding" and claim the contract. However, if he does so he takes the contract subject to all the rights and equities of the third party against the agent.

There are at least two exceptions to this rule. (1) If the contract is under seal and is signed by the agent, the principal may not claim the contract. (2) If the instrument is a negotiable instrument and is in the name of the agent, it may not be enforced by the principal.

Capital Hardware Manufacturing Co., Inc. v. Naponiello et al.
342 Ill. App. 272, 102 N. E. (2d) 685 (1951)

This was an action by Capital Hardware Mfg. Co., Inc. (plaintiff) against Nick Naponiello and another, individually and as copartners, impleaded with Joseph Olivio, individually and doing business as West Manor Realty (defendants). Judgment for plaintiff, and Olivio appealed. Judgment reversed and cause remanded with directions.

This was an action to recover the balance due on a sale of bowling alley equipment. The transaction took place in December, 1949. The Naponiellos did not personally order the equipment. The shipments of equipment followed conversations between plaintiff's vice-president and Olivio and the electrical contractor engaged in the construction of the bowling alley. Nick Naponiello testified for plaintiff that Olivio was a partner of the general contractor. This Olivio denied. It was admitted, however, that Olivio was given more than $33,000 by Naponiello which was disbursed for labor and material used in the construction of the bowling alley. Olivio also arranged a loan of $40,000 in connection with the building of the alleys. The proceeds of this loan were deposited by the Naponiellos with attorney Anzalone, who presumably represented the lender. This money was distributed by Anzalone for the payment of bills submitted to him by Nick Naponiello.

KILEY, P.J. It is apparent that the sale was not made to the electrical contractor—he merely selected the equipment. The credit was extended to Olivio on the basis of references given plaintiff by him. The account was carried in the name of West Manor Realty. The invoices carried the name of West Manor Reality and Builders as buyer, and called for shipment to the Naponiello Bowling Alley. The bills were sent to Olivio. The shipments were received by Naponiello.

Plaintiff sought payment from Olivio. He referred plaintiff's vice-president to Anzalone, and a $300 check given on account was received from Anzalone. Nothing was paid on the bowling alley equipment by Olivio. An unrelated purchase of hardware from plaintiff by Olivio amounting to $224 was paid within thirty days of January 10, 1950, which was the date of the sale of the hardware.

The suit was commenced originally against Olivio. His defense stated, among other things, that whatever he did at plaintiff's place of business in connection with the bowling alley equipment was done voluntarily for the owner of the bowling alley, and that he told plaintiff's vice-president that payment would be made through the attorney for the owner of the bowling alley. Plaintiff then amended its statement of claim, adding a count which sued the Naponiellos as principals, and alleged purchase by their agent, Olivio.

The judgment is against ". . . Olivio individually and doing business as West Manor Realty, Nick Naponiello and Jennie Naponiello. . . ." The trial court found that Olivio was liable because for all that appeared to plaintiff, Olivio was acting for himself. The court found further that the Naponiellos were liable as principals because after the sale was made they had received the equipment and had made a payment on account for it. We need not discuss these findings. The court would have been justified in entering judgment against the Naponiellos on the testimony that, though he did not disclose the relationship at the time, Olivio was acting as their agent. The court would have been justified in entering judgment against Olivio on the testimony that he was, to all appearances, acting for himself. There can be no joint liability, however, between Olivio, as agent, and the Naponiellos, as his undisclosed principals. We conclude, therefore, that the judgment is invalid, and that the plaintiff must elect which one he shall take judgment against. Judgment reversed and the cause is remanded with directions to require plaintiff to elect whether it will take judgment against Olivio, as agent, or the Naponiellos, as principal, and to enter judgment accordingly.

Eldridge v. Finnegar
105 P. 304, 25 Kan. 28 (1909)

This was an action by George C. Eldridge, trading as the Eldridge Coal Co. (plaintiff) against C. A. Finnegar (defendant). Judgment for defendant, and plaintiff brought error. Affirmed.

George C. Eldridge, trading as the Eldridge Coal Co., sued C. A. Finnegar on account for coal sold and delivered to him. The defendant admitted the purchase of the coal but interposed a setoff.

The evidence showed that plaintiff George C. Eldridge was in the coal business and was operating under the firm name of the Eldridge Coal Co. He had in his employ one Lloyd E. Eldridge, whose duties were to solicit orders and sell coal for cash. At that time there was in the city telephone directory the following: "Eldridge Coal Company, L. E. Eldridge, proprietor." On the day the coal was sold to defendant, Lloyd Eldridge went to defendant's place of business and solicited an order of coal. It was agreed between defendant and Lloyd Eldridge that defendant would purchase a certain quantity of coal; that Eldridge would employ defendant to make him a suit of clothes; that the price of the suit would be applied on defendant's coal bill; and that defendant would then pay the balance. The coal was delivered to defendant. Lloyd Eldridge was measured for the suit, and defendant made it for Eldridge. Eldridge died before the suit was actually delivered to him, and defendant was able later to sell it to someone else for a small sum. During all this time defendant did not know that Lloyd Eldridge was actually an agent and that plaintiff George C. Eldridge was his principal and the owner of the Eldridge Coal Co.

Plaintiff contended that defendant was not entitled to have the price of the suit of clothes set off against what he owned for the coal.

Since defendant tendered into court the difference between the amount of the coal bill and what he received from the sale of the suit after the death of Lloyd Eldridge, the lower court entered judgment for defendant. Plaintiff brought this appeal.

TURNER, J. The evidence fairly discloses that the defendant believed at the time the coal was sold and delivered that he was dealing with the owner thereof, and that he had no good reason to believe otherwise. The defendant did not know the plaintiff before he presented his bill, or that he had any interest in the Eldridge Coal Co. If the purchaser of property does not know that he is dealing with the agent of the owner, and has no good reason to know this, he is justified in treating the agent as owner, and payment of the purchase price to him is a good defense to an action by the owner for the amount. The defendant dealt with the agent believing him to be the principal, and made the contract accordingly. As the principal by this action now seeks to enforce the contract, he must take it as the agent and the purchaser left it. He must take his pay as the agent agreed to receive it. As was stated by the court in *Hook et al. v. Crowe et al.*, 100 Me. 399, 61 A. 1081, "If the purchaser, in dealing with the agent, believes him to be the principal, the undisclosed principal must take the contract, if he seeks to enforce it, as his agent and the purchaser left it. If he seeks the advantages of the contract, he must suffer its burdens. He must take his pay as the agent agreed to take it." While the principal may take over the contract and enforce it, he does so subject to any equities the third party had against the agent.

Judgment for defendant affirmed.

White Tower Management Corporation v. Taglino et al.

302 Mass. 453, 19 N. E. (2d) 700 (1939)

This was a suit in equity by the White Tower Management Corporation (plaintiff) against A. A. Taglino and another (defendants) for specific performance of a written agreement for the sale of a lot. From a decree for defendants, plaintiff appealed. Affirmed.

Plaintiff sought specific performance of a written agreement entered into by defendants and one Taylor, admittedly acting in an agent's capacity, for the sale of a lot of land to Taylor by defendants. The agreement was assigned by Taylor to plaintiff. Defendants, who are husband and wife, refused to carry out the agreement on the ground that they were induced to enter into it by false and fraudulent representations made by Taylor.

The lower court found that there was inequitable conduct on the part of Taylor in the negotiations leading to the execution of the agreement "in that he knew that the defendants would not enter into such an agreement if the purchasers were to be the White Tower Management Corporation, a corporation engaged in the restaurant business, and therefore concealed from the defendants the fact that he was agent for such corporation, and by misrepresentation led the defendants to believe that one or two individuals were to purchase the premises for the erection of a dwelling house thereon." The lower court denied specific performance, and plaintiff appealed.

COX, J. The evidence as reported shows no mere concealment of the name of the purchaser (White Tower Management Corporation). From the testimony of Taylor himself, as well as from that of the defendants, it appears that while Taylor did not affirmatively state that the plaintiff was not his principal, nevertheless he did represent that two individual buyers living in the Back Bay were the purchasers. Taylor admitted that the defendants asked him whom he represented. He was not bound to answer, but if he did, he was bound to tell the truth. *Potts v. Chapin*, 133 Mass. 276. The affirmative statement that two people or a family consisting of two was the purchaser was, in the circumstances, a representation that the plaintiff was not the prospective purchaser. Taylor's answer could have been found to be a half truth, which in effect was a lie.

It could have been found from the evidence that, if the defendants had known that the plaintiff was, in fact, the prospective purchaser, they would not have entered into the agreement. The plaintiff admittedly was engaged in the restaurant business, and there was evidence that the defendants would not sell to anyone who had a business or to "restaurant people," and so stated to Taylor. The representation by Taylor was material. *Thompson v. Barry*, 184 Mass. 429, 68 N. E. 674. The plaintiff does not contend that it is not bound by Taylor's misrepresentation. Therefore, it ought not to be permitted to take the benefit of false and fraudulent representations made by its agent. *Isenbeck v. Burroughs*, 217 Mass. 537, 105 N. E. 595. Decree affirmed.

TORT LIABILITY

The general rule is that the principal is liable for the torts of his agent committed within the scope of his employment, even though the agent committed the tort with knowledge that he was acting contrary to the instructions given him by his principal. This rule is based upon the doctrine of respondeat superior. It does not relieve the agent himself from liability; in such cases both the principal and his agent are liable to the third party. The rule applies to the relationship of employer and employee as well as to the relationship of principal and agent.

Though the foregoing rule is clear and universally recognized, difficulty is often experienced in applying it to specific cases. It is not always a simple matter to determine whether the tort was committed while the agent or employee was acting within the scope of his employment. For example, A is struck and injured by an automobile which is owned by B but which is being operated by B's servant C. The injury to A was due to C's negligence. Is B liable to A for damages? If the accident occurred while C was acting within the course of his employment, B would be liable; otherwise, not. For instance, if the accident took place when C had left the course of his employment and had gone on a joy ride, B would not be liable.

The rule of respondeat superior applies not only to cases where a third person is injured as a result of the negligence of the agent or employee, but also applies to other types of torts, such as fraud, assault and battery, false imprisonment, trespass, and so on. In all such cases the principal or employer is liable if the tort is committed within the scope of the agent's or employee's employment. The fact that the principal or employer exercised all possible care in the selection of the agent or employee would be no defense.

The rule of respondeat superior is justified on the ground that the employer or principal selected and appointed the employee or agent, directed his activities, and received the benefits from his activities.

Home Telephone & Electric Co. v. Branton
7 S. W. (2d) 627 (Tex.) (1928)

This was an action by W. A. Branton (plaintiff) against the Home Telephone & Electric Company and another (defendants). Judgment for plaintiff, and defendants appealed. Affirmed in part, reversed in part, and remanded.

Appellee W. A. Branton recovered judgment in the court below against appellant Home Telephone & Electric Company for damages to a tract of land on account of the unauthorized erection thereon by appellant of a telephone pole, guy wire, and anchor. Appellee in the same suit recovered judgment against appellant and Paul Beardon for damages on account of injuries sustained by him as the result of an assault committed upon him by Paul Beardon, an employee of appellant. Both of the defendants in the court below perfected an appeal to this court, but no brief was filed for Paul Beardon.

Paul Beardon was the local manager for appellant corporation, with such duties and authority as are usually conferred upon local managers of telephone exchanges. Appellant erected a telephone line along the highway, but the particular pole, guy wire, and anchor which were the cause of the trouble between appellee and Paul Beardon were erected on and attached to appellee's land by appellant's construction crew without appellee's knowledge or consent, and in such manner as to render appellant a trespasser in erecting same thereon. Appellee went to the appellant's office to see Paul Beardon on more than one occasion, protesting against the presence of the pole, guy wire, and anchor on his premises, and requesting that they be removed. Beardon made appellee promises which were unperformed. Shortly thereafter appellee and Beardon met on the street, while Beardon was going out to lunch. An argument took place, at which time appellee Branton called Beardon a damn liar. As a result Beardon struck appellee and injured him.

HICKMAN, C.J. The question of liability of a master for assault committed by his servant has been the subject of many able opinions by the courts of our state. . . . The rule of respondeat superior applies, and renders a master liable to a third person assaulted by a servant of the master while acting within the scope of the servant's employment. The rule arises out of the relation of superior and subordinate, and must necessarily be coextensive with that relation and ceases when the relation ceases. Whenever the very nature of the employment expressly or impliedly authorizes the servant to use force, and in the exercise of that authority he negligently or willfully uses more force than is necessary to further his master's business and thereby injures a third person, the master is clearly liable. On the other hand, where the act of the servant is not in the furtherance of the master's business, or for the accomplishment of the object for which he was employed, but is performed as a resentment of insults, or in the furtherance of personal animosities of the servant, the master is not liable. *International & G. N. Ry. Co. v. Anderson*, 92 Tex. 516, 17 S. W. 1039.

Applying this test to the facts of the instant case, as disclosed by appellee's own testimony, the inquiry arises: In what manner was Paul Beardon furthering the business of appellant when he committed the assault? According to appellee's own testimony, he was struck by Beardon as an immediate resentment of an insulting epithet applied by him to Beardon. Beardon was not engaged in the erection of the telephone pole upon appellee's land, nor in the removal thereof when the assault occurred. The assault within itself was not necessary to and did not have the effect of either continuing the alleged trespass or removing it from appellee's land. While the erection of the telephone pole was the remote cause of the difficulty, it was too remote to connect appellee with it.

It is insisted by the appellee that the evidence supports the finding by the jury that appellant ratified the act of Paul Beardon in the commission by him of the assault upon appellee. We find no evidence whatever of a ratification. The fact of the failure of appellant to remove the telephone pole, and thereby discontinue the trespass, is no evidence of ratification. And it is well settled by the decisions in our state that the retention of an employee after an assault committed by him upon a third person does not constitute a ratification of the assault on the part of the master. *Texas & P. Ry. Co. v. Jones*, 29 S. W. 499.

It is therefore our order that the judgment of the trial court in favor of appellee against Paul Beardon be affirmed; that the judgment in favor of appellee against appellant on account of the trespass be affirmed; and that the judgment in favor of appellee against appellant for damages on account of the assault be reversed and rendered. Affirmed in part, and reversed and rendered in part.

Cynthia Dianne Davis, a Minor, by and through R. Scott Davis, her next of friend and Husband, Plaintiff
v.
The Hecht Company, A Body Corporate, Defendant
Civil Action Law No. 52, 123

Circuit Court for Prince George's County, Maryland

DECLARATION. Cynthia Dianne Davis, a Minor, by and through her next of friend and Husband, R. Scott Davis, and by Townes L. Dawson, her attorney sues, The Hecht Company, defendant, a body corporate, for that:

COUNT I. On or about May 24, 1972, Cynthia Dianne Davis, plaintiff, went to defendant's place of business, The Hecht Company, Prince George's Plaza, Prince George's County, Maryland, to purchase a bathing suit and other items. Said store caters to the general public. Plaintiff entered the store and purchased and paid for some items and while there tried on several bathing suits and while standing near a clothes rack a man and a woman approached her, the defendant, through said man and woman, its agents, servants and/or employees accosted plaintiff and the woman showed plaintiff a Detective's badge and said to plaintiff, "Let's Go," offering no explanation. They took her against her will to the basement floor and into a dark hallway, and plaintiff asked them, "Where are we going," but neither answered. They took her and confined her against her will in a small room and would not permit her to leave for a considerable period of time. Said unlawful detention put plaintiff in great fright, great pain, great embarrassment, and caused her severe mental anguish.

Plaintiff demands $100,000.00 actual damages and $100,000.00 punitive damages and costs.

COUNT II. On or about May 24, 1972, at The Hecht Company at Prince George's Plaza, Prince George's County, Maryland, and while being unlawfully restrained and confined against her will in said small room mentioned in Count I, the defendant through its agent, servant and/or employee, said woman mentioned in Count I, said to plaintiff, "O.K. Take off your clothes." Plaintiff in great fear and embarrassment took off her clothes against her will and without her consent. Defendant found nothing, and without plaintiff's consent, defendant's agent, servant, and/or employee dumped out plaintiff's shopping bag and found nothing, then without the consent of plaintiff searched her purse and found nothing. Said unlawful disrobing of plaintiff, unlawful dumping out and searching plaintiff's bag, and unlawful searching of plaintiff's purse, all without her consent greatly upset plaintiff and put her in great fear. To add insult to injury Defendant's agent, servant, and/or employee demanded that plaintiff undress again. Plaintiff being very frightened did as she was told, taking off her clothes again against her will. Defendant found nothing. At no time did defendant advise plaintiff of her rights. Said unlawful forcing plaintiff to undress, unlawfully dumping out her bag by defendant and defendant unlawfully searching her purse in a wanton, reckless, and malicious manner caused plaintiff great pain, great embarrassment, and severe mental anguish.

Plaintiff demands $100,000.00 actual damages and $100,000.00 punitive damages and costs.

COUNT III. On or about May 24, 1972, at the Hecht Company at Prince George's Plaza, Prince George's County, Maryland, and while being unlawfully restrained and confined against her will in said small room in the basement as mentioned in Counts I and II, the defendant through its agent, servant and/or employee, said woman mentioned in Counts I and II, said to plaintiff, "All right, where is it?" Plaintiff asked what she was looking for. The woman said, "Something white that you took into the dressing room and didn't bring out." "It wasn't there when I went to look for it." "Are you ready to level with me, what did you do with it?" Said accusation was falsely and maliciously spoken and published of plaintiff by said defendant's agent, servant and/or employee. As a result of same, plaintiff suffered great pain, great embarrassment, and severe mental anguish.

Plaintiff claims $100,000.00 actual damages and $100,000.00 punitive damages and costs.

COUNT IV. On or about May 24, 1972, at the Hecht Company at Prince George's Plaza, Prince George's County, Maryland, and while being unlawfully restrained and confined against her will and without her consent in said small room in the basement as mentioned in Counts I, II, and III, the defendant through its agent and/or servant or employee, after having forced said plaintiff to undress twice, dumping out her shopping bag without her consent, and searching her purse without her consent, said woman, defendant's agent, employee and/or servant, without said plaintiff's consent, put her hands on plaintiff unlawfully searching her and unlawfully touching her without her consent, committing assault and battery upon said plaintiff, causing said plaintiff great pain, great embarrassment, and severe mental anguish.

Plaintiff demands $100,000.00 actual damages, and $100,000.00 punitive damages and costs.

(Signed)
TOWNES L. DAWSON
Attorney for the Plaintiff
CYNTHIA DIANNE DAVIS, Plaintiff
R. SCOTT DAVIS
Next of friend and husband, Plaintiff

JURY DEMAND. Plaintiff demands trial by jury on all counts.

TOWNES L. DAWSON

PLEA. Comes now the defendant, by its attorney, Carlton L. Saunders, and for plea to the declaration filed herein states:
1. That it did not commit the wrongs alleged.
2. That it is not guilty of the wrongs alleged.

(Signed)
CARLTON L. SAUNDERS
Attorney for defendant

CERTIFICATE OF MAILING. This is to certify that on the 14th day of September, 1972 a copy of the aforegoing plea was mailed to Townes L. Dawson, Esq. at 4328 Underwood Street, Hyattsville, Maryland, attorney for plaintiffs.

The above case never went to trial, because the evidence was so strong and the young and beautiful client (plaintiff) was such an excellent witness at the deposition. The case was settled out of court for a tidy sum.

REVIEW CASES

1. The South Florida Farms Co. employed Stevenson to sell a certain tract of land, but each of the parties actually sold part of it. Stevenson claimed that he had an "exclusive sale" contract and maintained that he was entitled to a commission on all the land sold, but there was no stipulation to this effect in the contract. Stevenson brought suit for the full amount. Judgment for whom? (South Florida Farms Co. v. Stevenson, 93 So. 247)

2. Mrs. Groscup's husband, without her consent or authority, authorized Downey to sell her house, and Downey had Mrs. Mahon look at the house. About two months later Mrs. Groscup sold the house to Mrs. Mahon. Evidence was presented at the trial that Downey had abandoned trying to sell the house at the time of the sale. Mrs. Groscup refused to pay Downey, and he brought suit for his commission. Judgment for whom? (Groscup v. Downey, 105 Md. 273, 65 A. 930)

3. Foy bought certain barrel staves and heads from a stranger named Rushin, not knowing that he had a principal. The order to purchase was a verbal one, and payment was made upon delivery. Actually, Rushin was the agent of an undisclosed principal, Miles. Miles demanded that Foy pay him for the items. Foy refused, and Miles brought suit. Ruling? (Miles et al. v. Foy, 38 Ga. App. 612, 144 S. E. 802)

4. Burkovits sued Morton Gregson Co. and Kleeburger for return of over-payments for meat. Kleeburger was a salesman for Morton Gregson Co., delivering meat to Burkovits and collecting weekly. Over a period of time Kleeburger altered statements to Burkovits, and in consequence Burkovits made a large overpayment. Judgment for whom? (Burkovits v. Morton Gregson Co. et al., 112 Neb. 154, 198 N. W. 868)

5. Marshall signed a contract under seal selling certain real estate to Greene. Greene was acting as agent for Levine, but Levine's name did not appear on the sealed contract, nor did Levine sign it. Greene and Levine refused to go through with the transaction, and Marshall sued both for specific performance. Holding? (Marshall v. Greene et al., 27 F. Supp. 403)

6. Williams signed a contract with Hoffacker to purchase certain land and options, knowing there was a principal but not knowing who it was. Hoffacker breached the contract; Williams sued him and obtained an un-collectible judgment against him. Later Williams learned that the Pitts-burgh Terminal Coal Corp. was Hoffacker's principal, and filed suit against it. Judgment for whom? (Pittsburgh Terminal Coal Corp. v. Williams, 70 F.(2d) 65)

7. Gerstein sued Adams to recover damages for assault and battery. Gerstein testified that Adams' agents and employees entered her home and forcibly took a clock from her premises and committed an assault and battery upon her. The evidence further showed that when the employees of Adams took the clock, they were attempting to collect installments due thereon which had not been paid. Judgment for whom? (Gerstein v. Adams Co., 169 Wis. 504, 173 N. W. 209)

20

CONTRACT LIABILITY OF AGENT TO THIRD PARTY

LIABILITY ON AUTHORIZED CONTRACTS

If the principal authorizes his agent to make a certain contract for him, the agent is not personally liable on the contract if the principal is disclosed and the contract is properly executed. Under such circumstances the contract is the principal's contract, and the principal alone is bound to the third party. In the case of *Hall v. Lauderdale* [1] the court said: "Where the agency is disclosed and the contract relates to the matter of the agency, and is within the authority conferred, the agent will not be personally bound, unless upon clear and explicit evidence of an intention to substitute or superadd his personal liability for or to that of the principal. . . . And, where the act is within the authority, the presumption is that the agent intends to bind the principal and not himself." However, if the principal is undisclosed, the agent becomes personally liable on the contract, even though the principal has authorized the contract. This is also generally held to be the case where the principal is partly disclosed.

Where the principal is disclosed and the agent acts within the scope of his authority, no difficulty ordinarily arises in the case of oral contracts. But where a written contract is to be prepared and executed, the agent must exercise care to avoid becoming personally liable, if such is his intent. (He may, of course, agree to be personally bound, or jointly bound with his principal, if such is his understanding with his principal and the

---

[1] 46 N. Y. 74.

third party.) First, it should appear clearly in the contract itself that the agreement is between the principal and the third party. Secondly, when the agent signs on behalf of his principal, he can be certain that his principal will be bound and he himself will not be bound if he signs in the following form:

John Doe [Name of principal]
By Richard Roe, his agent

If the agent should sign "Richard Roe, agent," he would bind himself and not his principal. Nor would it be safe to sign "Richard Roe, agent of John Doe." The words "agent" and "agent of John Doe" would be held to be merely descriptio personae.

The agent should take special care in the drawing and execution of contracts under seal and negotiable instruments. In the case of a contract under seal, if the principal is not named as one of the contracting parties and the contract is signed by the agent in his own name, the agent is bound and the principal is not bound. If the principal is named in the instrument as a contracting party and the instrument is signed by the agent in his own name, it is held that neither party is bound. The same principles apply in the case of negotiable instruments. A principal may not be held liable on a negotiable instrument, nor may he maintain an action on it, unless his name appears on the instrument. If he places his own signature on the instrument he is bound. Likewise, if his agent signs for him in some form that makes clear the fact that the agent is signing in his representative capacity (e.g. in the form recommended above), the principal will be bound but the agent will not be liable. In the case of a corporation it has been held that the agent is not bound if he signs as follows: "Thomas Construction Company, Inc., by J. W. Thomas, President." If an agent places his own signature on a negotiable instrument and it does not appear on the instrument that the obligation was the principal's, parol evidence may not be introduced to show that it was the obligation of the principal. In such case the agent would be bound individually on the instrument. The Negotiable Instruments Law provides: "No person is liable on the instrument whose signature does not appear thereon, except as herein otherwise expressly provided" (Section 8). "Where the instrument contains or a person adds to his signature words indicating that he signs for or on behalf of a principal, or in a representative capacity, he is not liable on the instrument if he was duly authorized; but the mere addition of words describing him as an agent, or as filling a representative character, without disclosing his principal, does not exempt him from personal liability" (Section 20).

Shoenthal v. Bernstein
93 N. Y. S. (2d) 187, 276 App. Div. 200 (1949)

This was an action by Harry Shoenthal, as assignee of an employment contract (plaintiff) against Aaron Bernstein (defendant). Judgment for plaintiff, and defendant appealed. Reversed and a new trial ordered.

By letter dated September 14, 1946, and signed by the defendant, the plaintiff's assignor was engaged as manager of a retail store in Florence, Alabama, for a period of two years from January 1, 1947, at a salary of $10,000 per year. Plaintiff's assignor, in accordance with the terms of the contract, on January 2, 1947, entered upon and continued the performance of his duties until July 26, 1947, on which date he claims to have been discharged without just cause. The store was owned by Ruth Shops, Inc., a Mississippi corporation. The corporation was also authorized to do business in the State of Alabama under the trade name of "Jean-Ann's." The plaintiff's assignor assigned the cause of action for breach of the contract to his father, who brought this suit in this State against the defendant.

The letter on which plaintiff's cause of action was based read in part as follows:

"Executive Office
Ruth Shops—Jean-Ann's—Libby's
Columbus, Mississippi
September 14, 1946

Dear Mr. Shoenthal: This will acknowledge my visit to Decatur and our understanding for you to begin as manager of our Florence, Alabama, store on January 1, 1947, and to take over the management of the Columbus Store as soon as it is completed. . . . Your experience and background fit in nicely with our needs. We are comparatively new and are going to need all your cooperation and experience, and we, in turn, promise you our fullest cooperation. . . . Sincerely yours, (Sgd.) A. Bernstein."

Defendant claimed that he did not personally hire plaintiff's assignor; that in making the contract he acted as agent for a known principal, to wit: Ruth Shops, Inc., which owned and operated the store of which plaintiff's assignor was to be the manager; that plaintiff's assignor knew that he was being engaged by Ruth's Shops, Inc.; and, that it was the intention of the parties that the contract was to be between plaintiff's assignor and Ruth Shops, Inc.

The sole issue was whether defendant became personally liable to plaintiff's assignor or whether the corporation (which was not made a party to the action) alone was liable.

COHN, J. The writing upon which the plaintiff relies, we are persuaded, is ambiguous as to the parties intended to be bound. It does not clearly appear from the instrument itself that defendant intended to become personally liable. The writing at the very beginning shows a list of names indicating that it was sent from the executive offices of "Ruth Shops—Jean-Ann's—Libby's." In the body of the letter the plaintiff's assignor is advised: "This will acknowledge my visit to Decatur and *our* understanding for you to begin as manager of *our* Florence, Alabama, store." Later the writing states: "Your experience and background fit in nicely with *our* needs. *We* are comparatively new and are going to need your cooperation and experience and *we*, in turn, promise you *our* full cooperation." (Italics ours.) It was proper for the defendant to establish by parol evidence that the plaintiff's assignor knew before September 14, 1946, that Ruth Shops, Inc. was the principal in the transaction. This, defendant unsuccessfully attempted to show by conversations which he had with the plaintiff's assignor antedating the execution of the letter. Such testimony should not have been excluded. The plaintiff's assignor, while in the employ of Ruth Shops, Inc., filed income tax returns, social security slips, and unemployment insurance forms showing that he was in the employ of Ruth Shops, Inc., and not in defendant's employ. Plaintiff's assignor admitted that from the inception of his employment he was paid by checks of Ruth Shops, Inc. Judgment reversed and a new trial ordered.

Bean v. Pioneer Mining Company et al.
66 Cal. 451, 6 P. 86 (1885)

This was an action by one Bean (plaintiff) against the Pioneer Mining Company and John E. Mason (defendants). Judgment for defendants, and plaintiff appealed. Affirmed.

This was an action on a promissory note in which the plaintiff Bean was named as payee. The note was signed as follows: "PIONEER MINING COMPANY. John E. Mason, Supt." The note read: "We promise to pay," and not "The Pioneer Mining Company promises to pay." The seal of the corporation was not attached. The plaintiff sought to charge the defendant Mason personally on the note as well as the Pioneer Mining Co. The plaintiff contended that the words "we promise to pay" clearly established that both the corporation and Mason were liable on the note.

McKINSTRY, J. The question of liability on the note is not to be established merely by reference to rules of grammar. If the note was signed unmistakably by the company, and the company alone, we could see that the mistake which would make the collective "company" the nominative, instead of the corporate name, might easily have occurred. It must be conceded that if the note had been signed "Pioneer Mining Company, by John E. Mason, Superintendent," and the superintendent had power to execute notes of the corporation, it would be the note of the corporation, notwithstanding the words "we promise." For the purpose of showing the real party to a contract (where the contract suggests the existence of circumstances which render it doubtful), conversations of the parties to the transaction at the time of making the paper, and at the time of creating the consideration for the bill or note, are admissible as part of the res gestae. Judgment for defendant affirmed.

Mortgage Investment Co., Inc. v. Toone
17 Utah (2d) 152, 406 P. (2d) 31 (1965)
Supreme Court of Utah

This was an action by Mortgage Investment Co., Inc. (plaintiff) against Spencer W. Toone (defendant). Judgment for plaintiff and defendant appealed. Judgment affirmed.

In December, 1962, the Northwestern Investment Company and Spencer W. Toone entered into a uniform real estate contract by which the former agreed to sell and the latter agreed to buy the real property known as 3324 West 3540 South, Salt Lake City. Later in the same month, plaintiff purchased and took an assignment of the contract from Northwestern. It provides for semiannual payments of $3,925 to be made in May and October of each year. When the first payment, for May, 1963, was not made, plaintiff brought this action for that amount and subsequently, by amendment, included the October payment. At the pretrial conference it was made to appear to the court that the amount stated was delinquent and unpaid, and that the defendant had no meritorious defense thereto.

CROCKETT, J. In its brief plaintiff points to three defenses asserted by defendant: (1) lack of consideration, (2) another outstanding agreement covering the same property between the parties, and (3) that defendant signed the contract only as agent for another; and makes the following colorful characterization of them: as to (1) "ridiculous," as to (2) "preposterous," and as to (3) "unsupportable by the wildest stretch of the imagination." We are in accord with the view of the trial court as to the lack of merit in the asserted defenses, though not in the terms chosen by the plaintiff.

As to (1), this is a contract duly executed by the parties containing mutual obligations which are consideration for each other. As to (2), it is not made to appear what the claim of another contract between the parties on this property has to do with the instant one, nor how the former could affect the validity of the latter. As to (3), the contract names the defendant as purchaser, and he personally signed it without indicating that he was an agent acting for a principal. He is therefore personally bound by the contract which he signed in his individual capacity. See 3 *Am. Jur.* (2d) *Agency*, Sections 192, 575.

Judgment affirmed. Costs to plaintiff (respondent).

Lady v. Thomas
38 Cal. App. 688, 102 P. (2d) 396 (1940)

This was a suit by William E. Lady (plaintiff) against James H. Thomas, his wife, Philip L. Wilson, and others (defendants) to recover a balance due on a note and foreclosure of a trust deed securing it. From so much of a foreclosure judgment as denied the plaintiff relief against defendant Wilson, plaintiff appealed. Affirmed.

The plaintiff appealed from that portion of a judgment of foreclosure which denied him relief against an undisclosed principal in the execution of the promissory note which was secured by a trust deed. The complaint alleged, and the court found, that the defendants Mr. and Mrs. James H. Thomas, for a valuable consideration, executed a promissory note September 14, 1932, for the sum of $3,200, payable to Francis E. Dalin one year from the date thereof at 7% interest per annum payable quarterly; that the note was secured by a trust deed on certain described lots in Los Angeles, also executed by Mr. and Mrs. Thomas; that, as a part of the same transaction, the note and mortgage were immediately transferred to the plaintiff William E. Lady; that Philip L. Wilson, a codefendant, was, in fact, the undisclosed principal in the execution of the promissory note, but that his name did not appear in the note or mortgage, and no reference to such undisclosed principal was made in connection with the transaction. The court thereupon rendered judgment against Mr. and Mrs. Thomas for the aggregate sum of the principal and interest due on the note. The court directed foreclosure of the trust deed and sale of the property to satisfy the judgment. The court, however, decreed that the plaintiff take nothing against the defendant Wilson, on the theory that he was exempt from liability under section 3099 of the Civil Code, because his name did not appear on the note or mortgage, and no reference to him was made in those instruments. From the last-mentioned portions of the judgment this appeal was perfected.

THOMPSON, J. This is a suit to recover the unpaid portion of a negotiable instrument and to foreclose the trust deed executed to secure the note against not only the makers of the note but also against an undisclosed principal whose signature does not appear on the instrument, and to whom no reference is made therein. The trial court properly held that the undisclosed principal was not liable under such circumstances. Under the Uniform Negotiable Instruments Act adopted by California, it is uniformly held that a suit may not be maintained on a promissory note against an undisclosed principal whose signature does not appear thereon, unless the note is signed by use of his trade or other assumed name.

The reason for the adoption of this rule releasing a principal from liability on negotiable instruments which do not bear his name is expressed in 2 Mechem on *Agency*, as follows: "In addition to the limitation upon the principal's liability growing out of the nature of the instrument under seal, there is . . . a well recognized exception to the rule in the case of notes and bills of exchange, resting upon the law of merchants. Persons dealing with negotiable instruments are presumed to take them on the credit of the parties whose names appear upon them; and a person not a party cannot be charged upon proof that the ostensible party signed or endorsed as his agent." Judgment affirmed.

LIABILITY ON UNAUTHORIZED CONTRACTS

In the case of a disclosed principal the agent impliedly warrants to the third party (1) his own authority to represent his principal in the transaction and to make the contract, and (2) the existence and competency of his principal. If the principal is undisclosed, or partly disclosed, no such implied warranties exist.

Since the agent impliedly warrants his authority to make the contract on behalf of his disclosed principal, if he has no such authority he is liable for all losses sustained by the third party. However, most courts hold that he is not liable on the contract itself, but is liable either (1) for breach of warranty of his authority to make the contract, or (2) in a tort action for deceit, depending upon the facts of the given case. If his misrepresentation was innocent, he would be liable for the breach of his implied warranty of authority; if it was deliberate and fraudulent, he would be liable in a tort action for deceit.

An agent may relieve himself of any liability resulting from an implied warranty of his authority either (1) by stipulating in the contract that he is not responsible for any lack of authority on his part to make the contract, or (2) by making a full disclosure to the third party of all the facts concerning his authority under his contract with his principal. If such full disclosure is made, it is held, the third party is in as good a position as the agent to determine the extent of the agent's authority. In making such a disclosure the agent may show the third party his contract or power of attorney if any, or, if his agreement with his principal was oral, he may explain the nature of his authority, as agreed upon with the principal.

If it is determined, under the facts of a particular case, that the principal would not have been bound if the agent had possessed the authority claimed by the agent, or implied by law, then the agent himself would not be bound. For example, if the president of a corporation, acting as the agent of the corporation, should sign a surety contract, in the name of the corporation, without having authority to do so, and if under the law or the corporate charter the corporation had no authority to sign surety contracts, with the result that the corporation would not be bound, then the president of the corporation, acting as agent for the corporation, would not be bound.

An agent impliedly warrants that his principal exists. If one professes to be the agent of a named principal, but no such principal in fact exists, the person purporting to be the agent is liable on the contract. For example, A is a promoter and is in the process of organizing a corporation. Before he has secured the charter for the corporation, he approaches B and represents that he is the agent of the proposed corporation. Upon such representations B thinks that such corporation exists, and he leases a building to the purported corporation and names the purported corporation as the lessee in the lease. Afterwards A fails to secure a charter for the corporation. A is personally liable on the lease. Where one purports to act for a nonexistent principal, he alone is liable on the contract. The courts reason, in such cases, that a contract was entered into, and that, since there was no principal, the agent must be the other party to the contract. The same rule applies in the case of an unincorporated association. An unincorporated association (as we shall see later) has no separate legal entity or existence apart from the members of the association. Therefore, where one of its members, or a committee of the association, purports to contract on behalf of the association, since no principal exists, the member or committee who acted on behalf of the purported principal will be liable on the contract. If the third party knows that the purported principal is nonexistent, the agent is not bound.

An agent impliedly warrants that his principal has general legal capacity to contract. If his principal in fact lacks full contractual capacity—e.g. if he is a minor or has been judicially declared insane—and the agent does not so inform the third party, the agent himself is liable for any loss to the third party stemming from the principal's incapacity. However, the agent does not impliedly warrant that his principal has the legal capacity to make the particular contract. For example, an agent representing a corporation impliedly warrants that the corporation exists and has legal capacity to contract, but he does not warrant that it has authority, under its charter, to enter into a particular contract.

If the agent wrongfully obtains money from the third party, he is liable to the third party in quasi-contract. This is true even though his principal is disclosed and he has paid the money over to his principal before the third party makes demand upon him for repayment. If money is paid by the third party to the agent through mistake, the agent is not liable if he has surrendered the money to a disclosed principal before the mistake is discovered; but if he still has the money in his possession, or if he has an undisclosed principal, then the agent would be liable to the third party.

Thilmany v. Iowa Paper Bag Co. et al.
108 Ia. Rep. 357, 79 N. W. 261 (1899)

This was an action by one Thilmany (plaintiff) against the Iowa Paper Bag Co., William Daggett, and the Iowa National Bank (defendants). Judgment for defendants, and plaintiff appealed. Affirmed.

This action was to recover the purchase price of a carload of paper shipped by plaintiff to the Iowa Paper Bag Company, under a contract of purchase.

The Iowa National Bank guaranteed to plaintiff payment of the purchase price by the Iowa Paper Bag Company. The contract of guaranty was signed as follows: "Iowa National Bank, by William Daggett, V. P." Upon default in the payment of the purchase price by the Iowa Paper Bag Company, plaintiff originally brought action against the Iowa Paper Bag Company, the Iowa National Bank, and William Daggett.

Plaintiff's petition charged defendant Daggett with personal liability for the purchase price of the paper because of his having signed the contract of guaranty. Daggett demurred and his demurrer was sustained. Plaintiff then filed a separate petition against Daggett. Daggett again demurred, and his demurrer was sustained. Plaintiff appealed.

DEEMER, J. The plaintiff claims that defendant Daggett is liable on the contract of guaranty for two reasons: first, because it is his individual contract, and was intended to bind him as well as the defendant bank, and was so received and acted upon by appellant (plaintiff); second, for the reason that, if he intended said guaranty to be the obligation of the bank only, he was acting beyond the scope of his authority as vice president of the bank and failed to bind the bank, and is himself liable, as an agent who attempts to bind his principal by a contract he has no authority as such agent to make.

We turn now to the plaintiff's first proposition. The guaranty was signed "Iowa National Bank, by William Daggett, V. P." Daggett's signature clearly indicates that he signed in a representative capacity and not as an individual. To hold that the contract binds Daggett personally we must eliminate the preposition "by" and the initials "V. P.," as descriptio personae. This we cannot do.

As to the second proposition of the plaintiff, the rule has been broadly stated over and over again that when an agent contracts in excess of his authority, or acts without authority when he has none, or for any reason fails to bind his principal, he is himself bound. That this is the general rule must be conceded. But, like nearly every other general rule, it is subject to exceptions. The reason given for the general rule is that as an agent assumes to represent a principal, he cannot be heard to say that he has no authority, or that there was in fact no principal to be bound; for if he assumes to represent another he warrants that there is such another, and that he has authority to represent him. If, then, there is no principal, or the agent has no authority to act for him, an action will be laid for deceit or misrepresentation. It is apparent, however, that if the party with whom the agent contracts has notice of the facts relating to the authority of the agent, and is as fully advised as to the authority as the agent himself, there can be no action for deceit. And so the text writers have generally stated that this is an exception to the general rule. A second exception to the general rule is that the implied warranty of the agent does not relate to the power of the principal to enter into the particular contract. He simply covenants that he has authority to act for his principal and not that the act of the principal is legal and binding. Hence, it has been justly said that the contract must be one which the law would enforce against the principal, if it had been authorized by him, else the anomaly would exist of giving a right of action against an assumed agent for an unauthorized representation of his power to make the contract, when a breach of the contract itself, if it had been authorized, would have furnished no ground of action against the principal. In the present case, the action is not based upon a misrepresentation as to Daggett's authority but upon the invalidity of the contract itself as between the plaintiff and the defendant bank. There was no actionable deceit. There is no implied warranty by an agent that his principal has authority to make a contract. In the case against the defendant bank (Iowa State National Bank) we held that national banks have no authority to enter into guaranty contracts, and as the plaintiff has no right of action against the defendant bank upon a contract of guaranty, no recovery should be permitted against the agent Daggett; for this would hold every agent to a warranty of the legality of his principal's contracts. This is not the obligation of the agent. We do not think that Daggett, the agent, is personally liable, under the facts disclosed in this case, and the judgment for Daggett is affirmed.

Clark et al. v. O'Rourke et al.
111 Mich. 108, 69 N. W. 147, 66 Am. St. Rep. 389 (1896)

This was an action by Clark, Farnham & Co. (plaintiffs) against Charles O'Rourke and others (defendants). Judgment for plaintiffs, and defendants brought error. Affirmed.

This case concerns the liability of an unincorporated church organization.

In 1892 an unincorporated Catholic society was formed in Eweb, Michigan. The plaintiffs were dealers in lumber in Eweb. They furnished lumber for the building of a church for the unincorporated society. Failing to receive payment for the lumber, the plaintiffs brought this action against the building committee of the society.

The testimony on the part of the plaintiffs tended to show that the defendants were the trustees and members of the building committee; that defendant Norton went with the priest to the plaintiffs' place of business and ordered the goods and agreed to see that the bill was paid; that the account was entered on the books of the plaintiff as the "Catholic Church"; that Mr. O'Rourke was instrumental in making payments upon the account; that Mr. O'Rourke upon one occasion ordered some material and told the plaintiffs to furnish same to the contractor who was building the church, and that it would be all right and that it would be paid; that, after the lumber was furnished, a dispute arose as to the amount and the defendants wanted a reduction; and that they said that they were to take care of the bill and wanted to make arrangements to pay for it.

Mr. O'Rourke testified that he had nothing to do with the original order; and that he at one time went with the carpenter to the plaintiffs' yard and selected material for the building. The priest testified that the lumber and other materials were ordered through the building committee, which consisted of Mr. Shilling, Mr. Norton, Mr. O'Rourke, and Mr. Tredau.

There was also testimony to the effect that the church congregation planned to raise the necessary money to pay the plaintiffs through private subscriptions, and by holding socials and fairs.

The plaintiffs contended that the defendants represented no legally organized society, and, in the eyes of the law, must, therefore, be held to have contracted in their own right.

The defendants contended that the credit was extended to the congregation, as such, and not to the defendants personally, and that the plaintiffs agreed to look to certain funds to be raised by voluntary subscriptions, donations, and proceeds of fairs.

GRANT, J. The church organization had no legal existence. It could neither sue nor be sued. The members of the society were not partners. Those of the society who were actually instrumental in incurring the liabilities for it are liable as either principals or agents, having no legal principals behind them. Members of the society who either authorized or ratified the transactions are liable, while those who did not are exempt from liability. *Ash v. Gjie*, 97 Pa. St. 493; *Frednall v. Taylor*, 26 Wis. 286.

The testimony does not justify the conclusion that the plaintiffs agreed to trust to the proceeds of fairs, etc. for their pay. Plaintiffs knew that the society, as a society, was irresponsible. It is entirely natural that they should inquire as to the methods by which the money should be raised, but no inference can be drawn from it that they agreed to look to this source alone.

Neither can we accede to the proposition that there was evidence tending to show that the credit was given to this unincorporated and irresponsible society. It was natural that the plaintiffs should enter the account upon the books as they did, but a jury would not be justified in drawing the conclusion from this alone that they agreed to look to such members of this society as, they might be able to show, authorized or ratified the purchase from them. . . . The alleged principal was a myth, and the entry means no more than that the credit was given to those forming the association, or to those who stood sponsors for it, and were conducting its business and obtaining the credit. These defendants were the active managers, and with the other two members of the committee were in sole charge of the work, and under the law and the facts were properly held responsible. The law does not under any circumstances leave the creditors to search out the individual members of the society who have authorized the transaction, but holds those liable who have dealt with the creditors in the capacity of agents or principals. Affirmed.

CONTRACT LIABILITY OF THIRD PARTY TO AGENT

WHERE PRINCIPAL IS DISCLOSED

If the principal is disclosed and the agent has acted within the scope of his authority, the third party is not liable to the agent on the contract, or for its breach. This is so because the contract is the principal's contract and not that of the agent.

WHERE PRINCIPAL IS UNDISCLOSED

If the agent, acting within the scope of his authority, negotiates a contract for an undisclosed or partly disclosed principal, the third party is liable to the agent for breach of the contract. However, if the contract is a simple contract, and not a contract under seal or a negotiable instrument, the principal may make known his existence and the fact that the contract is his contract, in which case he may sue on the contract instead of the agent. The third party may not be subjected to two separate suits. The right of the principal to sue is superior to that of the agent. Consequently, if the principal sues, then suit by the agent would be barred.

Scott v. Louisville and Nashville Railroad Co.
170 Tenn. 563, 98 S. W. (2d) 90 (1936)

This was an action by Frank R. Scott (plaintiff) against the Louisville & Nashville Railroad Company (defendant). From a judgment sustaining defendant's demurrer and dismissing the action, plaintiff appealed. Affirmed.

This was an action brought by Frank R. Scott against the L. & N. Railroad Company to recover damages for the alleged breach of a contract made by him, as agent of the Rex-Jellico Coal Company, covering the sale of 34,500 tons of coal to the railroad company. It was averred in the declaration, in substance, that the railroad company breached the contract by refusing to accept and pay for 22,210 tons of coal it had agreed to take, and that the plaintiff, Scott, had and was entitled to a commission, as agent for the Rex-Jellico Coal Co., of 10¢ per ton on each and every ton of coal which he sold to the railroad company under said contract, and that by reason of this commission he had and was the owner of a property right and interest in said contract.

The aforementioned contract stated that it was "made and entered into this 9th day of May, 1934, between the Louisville & Nashville Railroad Co., Inc. and Mr. Frank R. Scott, agent, Rex-Jellico Coal Co." The contract was signed as follows:

> Louisville & Nashville Railroad Company, Inc.
> By Frank R. Scott, agent, Rex-Jellico Coal Co.

The declaration alleged that the plaintiff fully performed the contract and that the Rex-Jellico Coal Co., "for which he was acting as agent," fully complied with the same.

DE HAVEN, J. It appears from the declaration that Scott, in making the contract with the railroad company, acted in behalf and for the benefit of the Rex-Jellico Coal Co., for which he was agent. By the subject-matter of the said contract, which is the manufacture of coal by the Rex-Jellico Coal Co. and its sale to the railroad company, by the description of Scott, both in the body of the contract and in the signature, as "Agent, Rex-Jellico Coal Co.," the contract made by Scott clearly appears upon its face to have been intended to bind the Rex-Jellico Coal Co., and not Scott personally. Scott was acting for a disclosed principal, and in making the contract as agent, did not agree to become a party thereto.

In the Restatement of the Law of Agency the rule is thus stated: "Sec. 320. Unless otherwise agreed, a person making or purporting to make a contract with another as agent for a disclosed principal does not become a party to the contract."

The general rule is that one who contracts as agent cannot maintain an action in his own name and right upon the contract. *Mechem on Agency*, sec. 2022; *Story on Agency*, p. 391; 3 C. J. S., Agency, 224. However, there are exceptions to this rule. In *Herron v. Bullitt and Fairthorne*, 35 Tenn. 497, the court said: "The cases in which agents acquire rights against third persons, founded upon contracts made by them, are said to be resolvable into four classes.

"First, where the contract is made in writing, expressly with the agent, and imports to be a contract personally with him, although he may be known to act as an agent.

"Secondly, where the agent is the only known or ostensible principal, and, therefore, is, in contemplation of law, the real contracting party.

"Thirdly, where, by the usage of trade, or the general course of business, the agent is authorized to act as the owner, or as a principal contracting party, although his character as agent is known.

"Fourthly, where the agent has made a contract, in the subject-matter of which he has a special interest or property, whether he professed, at the time, to be acting for himself or not. *Story on Agency*, sec. 393."

It is obvious that Scott could not maintain this suit under either one of the first three of the above rules. Can he maintain his suit under the fourth rule? We think not. He has no special interest, or property, in the subject-matter of the contract. His only claim is for commission for making the sale of the coal. His power as agent was not coupled with an interest in the subject-matter of the contract. His interest was in the proceeds which arose from the exercise of his power as agent in making the sale.

In 3 C. J. S., Agency, sec. 226, p. 135, it is stated: ". . . Thus the liability of a third person to the agent for breach of contract does not include the loss of compensation or commission which the agent was to receive from his principal in the event of the performance of the contract by the third person."

For lack of a special interest, or property, in the subject-matter of the contract it must be held that the plaintiff has no right of action thereon. Judgment affirmed.

TORT LIABILITY

LIABILITY OF AGENT TO THIRD PARTY

We have already seen [1] that both principal and agent are liable to third parties for the torts of the agent committed within the scope of his authority. Even if the agent commits a tort innocently while following his principal's instructions he will not be excused from liability to the third party. However, if under these circumstances he is required to pay damages to the third party, he is entitled to be indemnified by his principal.[2]

As a general rule an agent or employee is not liable to third persons for his negligence where he owes no duty or responsibility to such third persons to exercise due care, and where there are no contractual relations between them. However, this rule is somewhat modified in the case of public accountants. For example, if A employs B, a C.P.A., to prepare an audit of the financial conditions of his (A's) business, and if B knows, or should know, that A plans to use such audit as a basis for securing a loan from some bank or other lending institution, B does assume certain duties and responsibilities to any such institution that should extend a loan to A upon the basis of B's audit. While B is not liable to such third persons or parties for ordinary negligence in making the audit, he is liable if his negligence is gross and of such a degree that it could support an inference of fraud. It would appear, from the court decisions, that the third person or party, in order to hold B liable for damages for his negligence in making the audit, is not required to prove actual fraud on the part of B; if the third person can prove gross negligence or facts from which fraud might be inferred, B would be liable. But his liability, if any, would be in tort and not in contract, since he has no contract with any third person or party. His contract is with his employer. There seems to be a tendency to hold public accountants more strictly responsible for the accuracy of their audits. This tendency works to the advantage of both sides. It not only offers greater protection to the lending institutions which must often rely upon such audits in deciding whether to extend credit, but also enhances the status of the public accounting profession.

---

[1] See section entitled Tort Liability in Chapter 19 of this text.
[2] See section entitled Duty to Indemnify in Chapter 18 of this text.

Sharp-Boylston Co. v. Bostick
81 S. E. (2d) 853, 90 Ga. App. 46 (1954)

This was an action by Curley Bostick (plaintiff) against Sharp-Boylston Company, a corporation (defendant). Judgment for plaintiff, and defendant appealed. Affirmed.

Plaintiff alleged substantially the following: that defendant was "the express agent for the collection of rents and the maintenance and repair of a building" in which plaintiff was injured, for the non-resident owner thereof; that for several months the front steps of this building had been in a dangerous and rotten condition, and the tenants could not use them and had repeatedly notified defendant of their defective condition; that during the month of February, 1952, defendant had certain repairs made to the roof, but failed to make any repairs to the steps, although it had actual notice of their condition from certain named tenants, and also constructive notice in that in the exercise of ordinary care, while repairing the premises in February, it should have discerned the condition of the steps. It is alleged that on or about March 26th plaintiff went to the premises to visit a named tenant; that plaintiff had no knowledge of the condition of the steps and was unable to ascertain their condition because of the darkness of night and the fact that there was no light on the house; that as he was mounting the steps one of them broke without warning under his weight, and he fell through, sustaining certain described physical injuries. The allegations of negligence are that defendant (agent) did not repair the steps after being notified of their defective condition; and that it repaired the premises in such a manner as to leave a defective and dangerous condition existing upon the premises, and left premises under its control in a defective and dangerous condition.

Defendant demurred to plaintiff's petition. The demurrer was overruled and defendant assigned this as error.

TOWNSEND, J. It is contended by the defendant (agent) that the petition here does not set out a cause of action against it for the reason that it is sought to charge the agent of the owner of the property for omissions to repair, which, at most, amounted to nonfeasance rather than misfeasance. As stated in *Owens v. Nichols*, 139 Ga. 475, 77 S. E. 635, the rule is as follows: "An agent is not ordinarily liable to third persons for nonfeasance. An agent is, however, liable to third persons for misfeasance. Nonfeasance is the total omission or failure of the agent to enter upon the performance of some distinct duty or undertaking which he has agreed with his principal to do. Misfeasance means the improper doing of an act which the agent might lawfully do; or, in other words, it is the performing of his duty to his principal in such a manner as to infringe upon the rights and privileges of third persons. Where an agent fails to use reasonable care and diligence in the performance of his duty, he will be personally responsible to a third person who is injured by such misfeasance. The agent's liability, in such cases, is not based upon the ground of his agency, but upon the ground that he is a wrongdoer. Misfeasance may involve also, to some extent, the idea of not doing, as where an agent engaged in the performance of his undertaking does not do something which it is his duty to do under the circumstances, or does not take that precaution or does not exercise that care which a due regard to the rights of others requires. All this is not doing; but it is not the not doing of that which is imposed upon the agent merely by virtue of his relation, but of that which is imposed upon him by law as a responsible individual in common with all other members of society. It is the same not doing which constitutes actionable negligence in any relation."

It is contended by the defendant that the total failure on its part to attempt to repair the front steps is a complete defense, in that its conduct amounted merely to nonfeasance, and that this case is distinguishable from that of *Hoppendietzel v. Wade*, 66 Ga. App. 132, 17 S. E. (2d) 239, in that there the defendant agent was sent out to inspect and repair a certain back porch and steps, and did actually inspect and repair a part of the steps, so that its failure to repair the top tread amounted to misfeasance for which it was liable, whereas here, although the defendant repaired the roof, it never did attempt to repair the steps. The cases are, however, further distinguishable, in that in the Wade case the agent was sent out "to inspect and repair the back porch" and steps; this was his only duty to his principal insofar as the rights of the plaintiff were concerned. Here, however, the duty to the principal, as alleged, is far more comprehensible, it being the duty of *maintenance and repair of the building*. The agent's liability must be judged, not merely by a breach of its contract to its principal; but, by the extent of the duty and responsibility to third persons which it assumed coextensive with the contract. Repairs to buildings are made not merely with a view to preserving the property, but for the further purpose of keeping them in such condition that third persons lawfully upon the premises will not suffer injury as a result of the defective condition, and this is certainly true as to rental property where the presence of tenants and their invitees must reasonably be anticipated. Judgment for plaintiff affirmed.

State Street Trust Co. v. Ernst et al.
278 N. Y. 104, 15 N. E. (2d) 416 (1938)

This was an action by the State Street Trust Co. (plaintiff) against Alwin C. Ernst et al., copartners (defendants). Judgment for defendants was affirmed by the Appellate Division, and plaintiff appealed. Reversed and remanded.

The Pelz-Greenstein Co. was organized in 1922 and was engaged in the business of financing wholesalers or mills. On January 19, 1928, the president of Pelz-Greenstein applied to plaintiff for a line of credit and a loan of $300,-000. He presented an estimated balance sheet of the business and stated that defendants, a firm of accountants, were making an audit of the condition of the company and that a balance sheet certified by the defendants would be submitted to plaintiff when it had been prepared. Plaintiff refused to grant the application for a time loan until it had received the certified balance sheet of defendants and had found that it substantially corroborated the estimated balance sheet. After defendants had submitted their certified balance sheet to Pelz-Greenstein Co., on April 2, 1929, and plaintiff had examined it, plaintiff extended the line of credit and the $300,000 loan to Pelz-Greenstein Co. Defendants admitted that they knew that their audit was to be used by Pelz-Greenstein Co. to obtain credit. On April 25, 1930, Pelz-Greenstein Co. was petitioned into bankruptcy. Plaintiff received back only a portion of its loan and brought this action for the difference.

The evidence showed that Pelz-Greenstein had made old and probably uncollectible accounts appear good by causing payments to be made to them by another corporation owned by themselves, which payments, credited to such old accounts, made it appear as if the debtors had been paying their debts. They induced one Saqui, who freely admitted his own dishonesty, to furnish false inventories and to assign to Pelz-Greenstein large numbers of false and fictitious accounts. In one account of $800,000 there were $300,000 of wholly fictitious sales. At the time Pelz-Greenstein was hopelessly insolvent.

FINCH, J. To what extent may accountants be held liable for their failure to reveal this condition? We have held that in the absence of a contractual relationship or its equivalent, accountants cannot be held liable for ordinary negligence in preparing a certified balance sheet even though they are aware that the balance sheet will be used to obtain credit. *Ultramares Corp. v. Touche*, 255 N. Y. 170. Accountants, however, may be liable to third parties, even where there is lacking deliberate or active fraud. A representation certified as true to the knowledge of the accountants when knowledge there is none, a reckless statement or an opinion based on grounds so flimsy as to lead to the conclusion that there was no genuine belief in its truth, are all sufficient upon which to base liability. A refusal to see the obvious, a failure to investigate the doubtful, if sufficiently gross, may furnish evidence leading to an inference of fraud so as to impose liability for losses suffered by those who rely on the balance sheet. In other words, heedlessness and reckless disregard of consequence may take the place of deliberate intention.

In *Ultramares Corp. v. Touche*, 255 N. Y. 170, we said with no uncertainty that negligence, if gross, or blindness, even though not equivalent to fraud, was sufficient to sustain an inference of fraud. Our exact words were: "In this connection we are to bear in mind the principle already stated in the course of this opinion that negligence or blindness, even when not equivalent to fraud, is none the less evidence to sustain an inference of fraud. At least this is so if the negligence is gross."

The defendants, however, contend that they may escape all liability by insisting that the balance sheet merely purported to reflect the condition of the books and that it did this correctly. The balance sheet, however, did not correctly reflect the condition of the company even as shown by the books. Nor is the duty of an accountant in preparing a balance sheet confined to a mere setting up of the items from the books.

The record is, indeed, replete with evidence, both oral and documentary, to make a prima facie case against the defendant. The judgment for defendants should, therefore, be reversed and remanded for a new trial.

LIABILITY OF THIRD PARTY TO AGENT

A third person who commits a tort which results in the injury of an agent is liable to the agent by way of damages, but this liability has nothing to do with the agent's status as agent; it grows out of general tort law, and it would be exactly the same in a given instance if the injured party were not an agent at all. It follows that the third party has no liability to the principal in such cases.

REVIEW CASES

1. Muller & Son, auctioneers, advertised stocks for sale in their own name, although they were representing a principal, and sold the stocks to Meyer at auction, 10 per cent down and balance to be paid next day. The receipt for the down payment was signed "Adrian H. Muller & Son, per R." Next day Meyer tendered payment and demanded the stocks, but they were not delivered. Meyer brought suit in damages. At the trial the defendants offered to show that when Meyer made the down payment he was told that the stock was being sold for the People's Trust Co., but this evidence was excluded. Judgment for Meyer, and defendants appealed. Holding? (Meyer v. Redmond et al., 205 N. Y. 478, 98 N. E. 906)

2. Chapin, agent of Newport, approached Smith for a loan from his mother. Smith told Chapin that he had no authority to act for her, but he did sign the contract for a loan in his mother's name. Because of Smith's lack of authority the loan failed to go through, and Newport sued Smith in damages resulting from his unauthorized act. Holding? (Newport v. Smith, 61 Minn. 277, 63 N. W. 734)

3. The citizens of York, Nebraska, met informally on several occasions to raise money, to appoint a trustee, and to purchase land for an orphanage. The sum of $9,750 was raised by subscription notes, and Codding was appointed trustee. He bought a tract of land from Munson for $10,000 by using the subscription notes, which he indorsed without recourse. The property was conveyed to "Anson B. Codding, trustee," who in turn conveyed it to a missionary society. A balance of $250 was not paid, and Munson sued Codding for this sum. Codding denied that he was personally liable. Ruling? (Codding v. Munson, 52 Neb. 580, 72 N. W. 846)

4. Hagan, representing himself as president of Food Shops, Inc., leased realty from Asa G. Candler, Inc. The lease was signed in the name of Food Shops, Inc., by Hagan as president. Actually, no such corporation existed. Asa G. Candler, Inc. sued Hagan for rent due under the contract. Hagan maintained that he was not personally liable on the contract. What is the nature

of Hagan's liability? (Hagan v. Asa G. Candler, Inc., 189 Ga. 250, 5 S. E.(2d) 739)

5. Whitman was an agent, selling on commission all the products of Arlington Mills. Namquit Worsted Co. signed a contract with Whitman, not knowing at the time that he represented Arlington Mills, an undisclosed principal. Namquit Worsted Co. breached the contract, and Whitman filed suit for damages against the company, who contended that Whitman could not sue because he was an agent of Arlington Mills. Judgment for whom? (Namquit Worsted Co. v. Whitman et al., 221 Fed. 49)

6. Morris was a salesman for Maytag Intermountain Co., working on a commission basis, driving his own car, paying his own expenses, and free to sell where and how he chose. He made no collections. While driving his car on business, he collided with Stockwell, who sued the company and Morris. Judgment for whom? (Stockwell v. Morris, 46 Wyo. 1, 22 P.(2d) 189)

Termination of
Agency

21

TERMINATION BY ACTS OF THE PARTIES

Most agency relationships are terminated by act of the parties themselves. Such termination may be brought about (1) by mutual agreement, (2) by accomplishment of the purposes of the agency, (3) by expiration of a period specified in the agency contract, (4) by act of either party where no time for termination is agreed upon, or (5) by act of either party before designated time for termination has arrived.

(1) *By mutual agreement.* Since the agency relationship is created by the mutual agreement or consent of the parties, it may likewise be terminated by their mutual agreement or consent. The consideration is found in the mutual promises of the parties.

(2) *By accomplishment of purposes of agency.* If an agency is created to accomplish a specific objective, the authority granted under the agency terminates upon the accomplishment of the objective. For example, if A appoints B as his agent to find a buyer for A's house, B's authority under the agency terminates automatically as soon as he succeeds in finding a buyer for the property.

(3) *By expiration of specified period.* If an agency is created to continue for a specified time, it will terminate automatically at the end of that time. The parties may, however, continue the agency relationship beyond the time specified by agreeing to such continuance. This agreement need not be express. If the agent continues to act for his principal after the specified termination date, and if the principal makes no objection, it will be implied that the agency relationship has been renewed for an additional period of like duration.

(4) *By act of either party where no time for termination is agreed upon.*

If the parties have not agreed upon a specific date for termination, an *agency at will* exists. The general rule is that an agency at will may be terminated by either the principal or the agent at his election. But the parties are required to act in good faith. For example, if P discharges his agent A, whose remuneration is in the form of commissions, and in consequence unfairly deprives A of his commissions on transactions which are about ready to be closed, P will be liable to A for damages.

(5) *By act of either party before designated time for termination has arrived.* Even though an agency has been created for a definite period still either party has the *power*, even though he may not have the *right*, to terminate the agency prior to the time specified in the contract. He cannot be prevented from terminating the agency, because the equity courts will not decree specific performance in such employment contracts and will grant injunctive relief only in rare cases, such as where the services of the agent or employee are unique and extraordinary. But when the party does not have the *right* to terminate the agency, the other party may bring an action at law for money damages for breach of the contract.

The principal's power to revoke the agent's authority has one important limitation. The principal may not revoke the agent's authority if the agent's authority is coupled with an interest. Agencies coupled with an interest are discussed later in this chapter.

The principal has both the power and the right to revoke the agent's authority for cause, i.e. for disobedience, incompetence, dishonesty, or misconduct. In such cases the principal is not liable for damages for breach of the employment contract. On the other hand, if the principal wrongfully revokes the agency and discharges the agent without cause, the agent is entitled to recover compensation for any work done prior to his discharge, plus damages for the breach of the contract. He usually may sue either immediately or after the date fixed in the contract for its termination. If he elects to sue immediately, he may recover only prospective damages which he is able to establish with reasonable certainty. If he elects to postpone filing his suit until the time fixed in the contract for its termination, he may recover the actual damages sustained by the breach of the contract.[1]

The agent has both the power and the right to renounce the agency for cause. If on the other hand, he renounces his contract without just cause, he will be liable to the principal for damages. In such case most courts hold that he may not recover for any uncompensated services rendered prior to his renunciation; some courts, however, do permit him to recover the reasonable value of his services less the amount of damages allowed the principal for the breach of the contract.

[1] See the following sections in Chapter 16: Kinds of Damages, Measure of Damages, and Mitigation of Damages.

Slonaker v. P. G. Publishing Co.
338 Pa. 292, 13 A. (2d) 48 (1940)

This was an action for breach of an alleged oral contract by Samuel M. Slonaker (plaintiff) against the P. G. Publishing Co. (defendant). The jury returned a verdict for plaintiff for $4,252.54. From a judgment for defendant notwithstanding the verdict, plaintiff appealed. Affirmed.

In 1930 Joe T. Bowman conducted a newspaper distributing business in the Dormont district of Allegheny County. He was the sole distributor there of the Pittsburgh *Post-Gazette*, a daily newspaper published by the defendant company. He offered to sell to plaintiff the part of his business which related to the *Post-Gazette*. Plaintiff visited Raymond Foudray, defendant's circulation manager, and had a conversation with him upon which he bases his cause of action in the present suit. According to plaintiff's version of the interview, he wanted to find out from Foudray "whether it would be all right to buy the news agency from Mr. Bowman." Foudray told him that he had no objections to such purchase. The plaintiff told Foudray that his motive in coming to see him was "about buying Mr. Bowman's business and the exclusive right to handle the *Post-Gazette* in Dormont." He alleged that Foudray told him that any time he wanted to resell the business he could do so and Foudray would help him sell it. A couple of weeks later plaintiff made the deal with Bowman, and for more than six years thereafter acted as sole distributor for the *Post-Gazette* in the Dormont district.

In September, 1936, plaintiff publicly advertized the business for sale. When this came to Foudray's attention he told plaintiff that he could not sell the exclusive right to handle the *Post-Gazette* in that district, and shortly afterwards the defendant company refused to sell its newspapers to plaintiff and began making distribution in the Dormont district through its own employees. The present suit was to recover the sum of $4,000 alleged by plaintiff to be the fair value of his business of which he claims that he was deprived by defendant, together with the sum of $2,000 alleged to be due for unpaid car allowance.

STERN, J. The general rule is that when a contract provides that one party shall render service to another, or shall act as his agent, or shall have exclusive sales rights within a certain territory, but does not specify a definite time or prescribe conditions which shall determine the duration of the relation, the contract may be terminated by either party at will. . . . Contracts which do not fix a definite time for the duration of the relationship which they create are sometimes construed as providing for a reasonable time or some particular period inferred from the nature and circumstances of the undertaking. But even if such principle of interpretation be applied to the alleged oral agreement in the present case, it is impossible to read into it any intention, express or implied, on the part of the defendant to contract with the plaintiff that if the latter decided to buy the Bowman agency, defendant would obligate itself to allow the plaintiff to conduct the business permanently or until he desired to re-sell it, with the necessary implication that in case of a re-sale the defendant would be bound to recognize in the purchaser a right to the continuation of the exclusive agency. Nor could the plaintiff fairly have derived from his conversation with Foudray any such implication. The court below was, therefore, right in holding that the verdict in favor of the plaintiff could not be sustained.

Judgment affirmed.

Rudolph v. Murphy & Son
237 N. W. 659, 1 Neb. 612 (1931)

This was an action by Samuel H. Rudolph (plaintiff) against Andrew Murphy & Son, Inc. (defendant), in which defendant filed cross-action. Judgment for defendant, and plaintiff appealed. Reversed and remanded.

This proceeding involved, first, an action by plaintiff to compel defendant corporation to transfer on its books to plaintiff certain shares of stock. These various certificates were in due form, were duly issued by defendant corporation, and bore suitable assignments thereon to plaintiff. Plaintiff purchased these stocks and was the owner thereof, and was prima facie entitled to have the stock transferred on the books of defendant.

Defendant filed a cross-action in the nature of an action for the specific performance of a certain oral contract made with one Baker, of which it was alleged that plaintiff had due notice prior to the purchase of the stock in controversy by him. Defendant alleged that "on or about July 1, 1927, defendant entered into an oral contract with the said C. E. Baker whereby Baker agreed, as the agent of the defendant, to solicit for said defendant the purchase of stock in defendant company, in consideration of which services defendant agreed to compensate Baker. Defendant further alleged that Baker in his own behalf, not pursuant to the contract of agency, but in violation of its terms, proceeded to purchase for and on behalf of himself the stock in suit, which was purchased by plaintiff from Baker with due notice of the terms of the oral contract of agency between defendant and Baker. As relief, defendant asked for specific performance of this contract and "that said plaintiff be required to deliver said stock to the defendant upon the payment to the plaintiff by the defendant of the amount ascertained by the court to have been paid by said plaintiff for said stock."

Plaintiff denied knowledge of the alleged oral contract between defendant and Baker prior to the purchase of the stock.

EBERLY, J. Since corporation stock is regarded as property, the owner of such shares may, as a general rule, dispose of them as he sees fit. Furthermore, we are committed to the rule: "A bona fide purchaser of the capital stock of a corporation may sue in equity to compel the corporation to enter the assignment upon its books, and to issue a new certificate therefor." *Everitt v. Farmers' & Merchants' Bank*, 82 Neb. 191, 117 N. W. 401.

If the oral contract was ever made, the facts alleged in the defendant's answer disclose that it was in fact renounced and repudiated by the agent Baker. As to the power of renunciation possessed by agents under contracts of agency, the principles applicable are: "It has already been seen also that the principal may, in general, withdraw his assent at any time, subject to liability in damages in case he does so in violation of his agreement. Substantially correlative is the situation of the agent. He may, in general, renounce his agency at any time. His power to do this, in the sense that his further performance will not be specifically enforced, is coextensive with the principal's power to revoke; but his right to do so is, like the principal's right to revoke, limited by his contracts in the premises. Where the agency is indefinite in duration the agent may, upon giving reasonable notice, sever the relation at any stage without liability to the principal, and will be entitled to compensation and reimbursement for his services and expenses up to that time. Where, however, the agency was created for a definite period, or the accomplishment of a particular result was undertaken for a valuable consideration, the agent who renounces before the expiration of that period, or before the performance of his undertaking, will be liable to his principal for the damages he may sustain thereby." 1 Mechem, *Agency*, 456, sec. 641. This is undoubtedly in principle the law in Nebraska. As to what redress the injured principal may be entitled to where a valid contract of agency is wrongfully renounced, the same authority above quoted from (Mechem) says in section 642: "The action for damages, as suggested in the last section (641), is, moreover, ordinarily the only remedy for the breach of the contract, for it is well settled, as a general rule, that courts will not undertake to enforce the specific performance of contracts for personal services; or interfere by injunction to prevent their breach." In this case there is no mutuality of contract between the litigants whatever. Baker, the alleged maker of the contract sought to be enforced, is not even a party to the proceedings.

The plaintiff has denied the alleged making of this contract of agency by the defendant with Baker, and expressly denied that he had any knowledge of that fact, if it was a fact, prior to the purchase. We are required to determine this question de novo. Even though giving due consideration to the fact that the trial court personally observed the witnesses, still we are forced to the conclusion that the evidence contained in the bill of exceptions, in view of all the admitted facts and circumstances, preponderates in favor of the plaintiff. Particularly is this true as to the fact that the plaintiff had no notice of the alleged contract in suit or prior to the purchase of the stock. It follows, therefore, that both on the question of fact as well as law the trial court erred in its determination of this case, and plaintiff is entitled to judgment as prayed. Reversed and remanded.

TERMINATION BY OPERATION OF LAW

Certain events have the effect of terminating an agency relationship by operation of law. Such termination may be brought about: (1) by the death of either principal or agent; (2) by the insanity of either principal or agent; (3) in most cases, by the bankruptcy of either party; (4) by a change in the law that makes the objectives of the agency illegal; (5) by destruction of the subject matter; (6) by dissolution of a corporate principal.

(1) *By death of either party.* The death of either the principal or the agent usually automatically terminates the agency by operation of law. This is true even though the other party has no notice or knowledge of the death of the deceased party. The one exception to this rule is where the agency is coupled with an interest; in that case the agency is not terminated by the death of either party.

The general rule is that the authority of the agent terminates immediately upon the death of the principal and that all subsequent acts of the agent are void and without effect. This is so even though the agent and the third party have no knowledge of the death of the principal. If A's agent B negotiates an agreement with C on A's behalf on Tuesday, and B and C later learn that A died on Monday, the agreement is absolutely void. However, an exception to the rule is made in the case of a bank which honors and pays a check before learning that the drawer has died. Let us suppose that A has given a third party C a check on the agent bank B, and that A has died before C presents the check to B for payment. Even though the authority of the agent bank B to pay the check terminated upon A's death, if the bank honored the check before learning of A's death it could legally debit A's account and not be liable to A's estate for same. This exception is justified solely on practical grounds. If banks were unwilling to honor any check without proof that the drawer was alive at the moment of payment, their usefulness in the business world would be greatly impaired.

Similarly, the general rule is that the death of the agent immediately terminates the agency. Therefore, the agent's estate is not liable for the unfilled portion of the agent's contract, nor is it entitled to be paid for the unexpired term. This rule is justified upon the ground of the personal relationship that existed between the agent and the principal. The agent's personal representative (executor or administrator) may not complete the agent's contract and thereby obligate the principal without the principal's consent and approval. Such consent and approval, if obtained, would be tantamount to a new contract, and extension of the original contract between the agent and the principal.

Unless the principal had authorized the agent to employ subagents on behalf of the principal, the death of the agent automatically terminates the authority of all subagents appointed by the agent.

(2) *By insanity of either party.* The law is clear, from the decided cases, that if either the principal or the agent is judicially declared insane the agency (unless it is coupled with an interest) automatically terminates. Such judicial determination is constructive notice to everyone.

The law is not so well settled in cases where the insane party has not been judicially declared insane. It would appear, however, that the principal would be bound by any contract of his insane agent, negotiated within the scope of his authority and without knowledge on the part of the third party that the agent was insane, if the terms of the contract were fair to both parties.

(3) *By bankruptcy.* The bankruptcy of the principal terminates the authority of the agent to act for the principal. As a general rule the bankruptcy of the agent terminates the agency where such bankruptcy affects the ability of the agent to execute his authority as provided for in the agency relationship; otherwise it does not terminate the agency.

(4) *By illegality because of change in law.* If performance of the objectives of an agency becomes illegal by the enactment of a law or the issuance of a government regulation or decree, the agency is automatically terminated.

(5) *By destruction of the subject matter.* The destruction of the subject matter involved in the agency relationship terminates the agency. For example, P employs A, a real estate broker, to find a buyer for his house. Before A finds a buyer, the house is destroyed by fire. The agency automatically terminates.

(6) *By dissolution of corporation.* The dissolution of a corporate principal or agent automatically terminates the agency relationship. This is true because the existence of an agency relationship requires both a principal and an agent. If one or the other no longer exists, the agency terminates.

In re Ward's Estate

(Frazer v. Ward et al.)

47 N. M. 55, 134 P. (2d) 539 (1943)

This was a proceeding in the matter of the Estate of James D. Ward, deceased. In the proceeding J. D. Frazer filed a claim against Sadie Ward, administratrix of the Estate of James D. Ward, deceased, and Sadie Ward, individually. Judgment for defendants, and plaintiff appealed. Affirmed.

Plaintiff claims that he is entitled to a broker's commission for securing a buyer for the deceased's property. The property in question was listed by the deceased Ward with plaintiff Frazer for sale at a price of $40,000 net to the deceased. In August, 1941, John F. Callioux made inquiry of one Porterfield as to the latter's knowledge of the property. Porterfield advised him that he would secure information regarding it and for that purpose contacted plaintiff and secured from him a mimeographed prospectus containing facts regarding the property and the name, address, and telephone number of the owner Ward. The owner Ward died on September 11th thereafter, and a few days later Callioux was informed of that fact when he attempted to contact Ward.

In October, 1941, Callioux purchased the property from the heirs and the administratrix Sadie Ward for $35,000. At the time the sale was made Mrs. Ward knew nothing of the listing of the property with plaintiff or of any agreement to pay a commission to him if a sale were made. Mrs. Ward owned as her separate estate 250 head of the cows sold to Callioux, in addition to her community interest in the remainder of the property.

BRICE, J. That the death of Ward revoked the plaintiff's power to sell the property, is well settled. Unless he had earned his commission before Ward's death he is without remedy. *Trickey v. Crowe*, 8 Ariz. 176, 71 P. 965, *State of Missouri v. Walker*, 125 U. S. 339.

As the plaintiff was not the agent of the administratrix and heirs and his agency for the sale of the property having been revoked by the death of Ward prior to any sale or the furnishing of a client ready, able, and willing to purchase upon the terms authorized by the contract, and his power to sell not being coupled with an interest, it follows that the plaintiff is not entitled to a commission for the sale of the property by the heirs and administratrix. The judgment is affirmed.

AGENCY COUPLED WITH AN INTEREST

A true agency coupled with an interest exists where the agent has a legal or equitable interest in the subject matter of the agency. In such an agency the grantee-agent has an interest in the estate as well as in the exercise of the power granted him by his principal. Both the interest and the power must come from the same party and exist at the same time. For example, P borrows $5,000 from A, signs a note for $5,000, and gives A a mortgage on his house to secure the note or debt. A provision is inserted in the mortgage to the effect that, if P defaults in the payment of the note, A will have the power to foreclose the mortgage, sell the property, and apply the proceeds toward the payment of the debt (note). Under these circumstances A possesses an agency coupled with an interest. In other words, A (mortgagee-agent) has a power to sell, under certain specified conditions, and his power is coupled with an interest in the subject matter of the agency agreement, namely the property offered as security for the note. An agency coupled with an interest is irrevocable by the principal during his lifetime, and is not terminated by the death of either party.

An agency coupled with an interest is to be distinguished from one coupled with an obligation, that is, one which has the purpose of securing some benefit to the agent. In such an agency the agent does not have an interest in the subject matter of the agency but merely an interest in the proceeds derived from the agency, same to be applied on a debt owed by the principal to the agent. For example, P owes A $500. P makes A his agent to sell a town lot and agrees that A may pay the $500 obligation out of the proceeds of the sale of the lot and turn over to P the excess, if any, received from the sale. In such a case it is said that the agent has an agency coupled with an obligation. Such an agency is irrevocable during the lifetime of the principal, but is generally held to terminate with the death of the principal. However, the *Restatement of the Law of Agency* holds that death of the principal does not terminate such an agency.[1]

A selling agent who receives as compensation for his services a commission on the property sold has neither an agency coupled with an interest nor an agency coupled with an obligation. His agency is the usual type of agency and is looked upon as a "naked" agency; that is, it is not coupled with any additional powers or authority. It may, therefore, be terminated at any time by either the principal or the agent, even where the agency agreement provides that it is irrevocable; but if it is terminated in violation of the agency agreement, the party who wrongfully terminates it is subject to an action for damages.

Lane Mortgage Co. v. Crenshaw et al.

269 P. 672, 93 Calif. App. 411 (1928)

This was an action by the Lane Mortgage Company (plaintiff) against C. R. L. Crenshaw and another (defendants). Judgment for defendants, and plaintiff appealed. Reversed.

In this suit the plaintiff sought injunctive relief to secure the benefits to which it alleged itself entitled under a certain written contract.

The Stolls owned a valuable lot in Los Angeles. On September 1, 1921, they entered into a 99-year lease agreement with the San Joaquin Valley Hotel Corporation. Under the lease the Hotel Company agreed to pay a rental of $1,000 per month, together with all taxes, levies, and insurance. The building to be erected on the lot was to be a modern building and was to cost not less than $250,000. Under the terms of the lease the Hotel Company was privileged to make any arrangements it found necessary to finance the undertaking and could mortgage its interest in the lease to procure the money for the con-

[1] Sec. 139.

struction of the building. Under its terms the lease could be assigned, subject to all conditions and obligations to be performed by the Hotel Company.

On December 31, 1921, the Hotel Company entered into a lease and agreement with the Lane Mortgage Company whereby the Mortgage Company was to finance the construction of the building by loaning the Hotel Company $250,000, taking mortgage bonds on the building as its security, and was to lease the entire second floor of the building for the sum of $10 for a period of 20 years commencing on October 1, 1922. The lease and agreement further provided that the Hotel Company appointed the Mortgage Company as its sole and exclusive agent for the management of the building with full authority to collect all rentals and pay all operating expenses, taxes, insurance, ground rental, *interest on bonds*, and *bonds* as they matured, out of the money collected (italics ours), and procure or write all insurance agreed upon by the Hotel Company to be carried on the building, for which services it would pay the Mortgage Company 5% of gross rentals and the regular brokerage paid insurance agents. It was stated that the agency should be irrevocable during the 20-year period, except for willful misconduct on the part of the Mortgage Company.

On December 2, 1922, the Hotel Company assigned the lease and building on the property to the defendants Crenshaw and Smailes, subject to the lease of the entire second floor to the Mortgage Company for 20 years.

The Mortgage Company, in its complaint, alleged that soon after it took possession and assumed the management of the building, defendants plotted, conspired, and made every effort to take over the management of the hotel building from plaintiff, in violation of its rights under its contract.

Defendants admitted taking over the management of the building and contended that they had a right to do so since the right and power given plaintiff in this behalf was a mere naked agency revocable by defendants at their pleasure.

Defendants denied any intention of interfering with plaintiff's right to possession of the second floor for the 20-year period free of rental.

Plaintiff contended that under the contract its agency was one coupled with an interest, and asked for injunctive relief. The trial court held that the agency of plaintiff was not one coupled with an interest and held for defendant. Plaintiff appealed.

PARKER, J. After negotiating for and agreeing upon a 20-year lease it was specifically made a part of the one and same transaction that a power should be given the Lane Company whereby it could protect and render secure and valuable the lease agreed upon. The power so given was the sole and exclusive agency to manage the building to be erected, thus giving the Lane Company the ability to protect the lease against a forfeiture of the land lease. . . . Likewise embraced within the lease was the right to collect rentals and apply the same to the extinguishment of the various obligations resting upon the Hotel Company under the lease. . . . The power thus given was declared by the trial court to be a mere naked power revocable at will by the Hotel Company or its successors, and not a power coupled with an interest as the term is understood in the law relating to principal and agent. In this holding the trial court was in error.

Concretely, a power is said to be coupled with an interest when the power forms part of a contract, and is a security for money or for the performance of any act which is deemed valuable, and is generally irrevocable in terms, or, if not so, is deemed irrevocable in law. "To impart an irrevocable quality to a power of attorney in the absence of any express stipulation, and as the result of legal principles alone, there must coexist with the power an interest in the thing or estate to be disposed of or managed under the power." *Todd v. Superior Court*, 181 Cal. 406, 184 P. 684. We think that there is hardly a case that can be made to which these principles could have a more direct and fitting application than the case at bar. The Lane Company has a 20-year lease in the entire second floor of the 12-story building which is the subject of the power. That this is an interest there can be no question. The interest does not arise only upon the execution of the power, it is a live, active, valuable interest, coupled with the power to the extent that if the power did not exist the interest would be subject to destruction or forfeiture. The lease would be totally valueless in the absence of compliance with the provisions of the original land lease. The powers granted the Lane Company in their total, amount to no more than placing in the hands of the company directly the means of preserving its said interest. This manifestly constitutes such a power as Chief Justice Marshall refers to in *Hunt v. Rousmanier*, 8 Wheat. 174, 5 P. Ed. 589, namely, a power forming part of the contract and security for the performance of an act deemed valuable. The power in the present case was expressly made irrevocable and expressly tied to the entire transaction in the creation of the leasehold interest. We would concede that if the Lane Company merely held an agency to collect rents and retain 5% commission the agency would be revocable. But the mere fact that, incidental to the execution of the coupled power, an additional interest is created in the proceeds thus derived in no sense impairs the coupling of the power and interest theretofore existing.

Judgment reversed.

NOTICE OF TERMINATION

If one of the parties to an agency relationship wishes to terminate the relationship prior to the time fixed in the agency agreement for termination, the other party is entitled to notice of such intention. Such notice, under most circumstances, is not required to be formal. Consequently, an agency which is created by a written instrument may usually be terminated by oral notice to the other party. However, the common law courts held that every instrumentality must be revoked by one of equal dignity.

Where the agency is terminated by operation of law, notice to third persons is generally not necessary; but in all other methods of termination the matter of giving proper notice to third parties becomes important to the principal. His need to protect himself by giving proper notice to third parties is greater in the case of a general agency than in the case of a special agency. In the case of a general agency the rule is that third persons who have been in the habit of dealing with the principal through a general agent have the right to presume that the agency is a continuing one unless otherwise notified by the principal.

The type of notice required in the case of third persons depends upon whether they have dealt with or extended credit to the principal through the agent. To third persons who have done so, the principal, in order to protect himself, should give *actual notice*. For third persons who have had no dealings with the principal through the agent, *constructive notice*, i.e. notice published in the newspaper, is sufficient.

Ohio Oil Company v. Smith-Haggard Lumber Company, Inc. et al.

228 Ky. 278, 156 S. W. (2d) 11 (1941)

This was a suit by the Smith-Haggard Lumber Company, Inc. and others (plaintiff) against the Ohio Oil Company (defendant) to establish mechanics' and materialmen's liens and recover a money judgment. Judgment for plaintiffs, and defendant appealed. Affirmed.

The appeal was from judgments aggregating $4,607.62 in favor of four building contractors against the Ohio Oil Company and the adjudication of mechanics' and materialmen's liens for a total of $3,751.33 on its property. Judgment for the full sum was also rendered against Warren Sayers, Inc., and liens were adjudged against its property for $856.29, but it did not appeal.

Following negotiations looking to the establishment in Lexington of a sales agency for the products of the Ohio Oil Company by Warren Sayers and an associate, on March 12, 1936, the company and Sayers entered into a contract agreeing that the company would spend not in excess of $21,000 for improving a lot it had recently purchased on the corner of South Broadway and Boliver Street, and that Sayers would bear the balance of the cost of the improvements. It was contemplated that after the improvements had been completed Sayers would buy the property. Sayers organized a corporation styled "Warren Sayers, Inc., and it purchased a 36-foot lot adjoining the oil company's property with a view to having it used in connection with and as a part of the plant.

Sayers alone, acting for his corporation and for the Ohio Oil Company, procured the services of an architect, Robert W. McMeekin. Under a written contract with the Ohio Oil Company he prepared plans and specifications for the erection of a gasoline service station and an office building, and for the remodeling of a warehouse on the premises. The plans called for the development of the Sayers lot as a part of the whole, making it appear as one, although, as we understand, there was no building on it. With the approval, if not the express authority, of the oil company, the architect procured bids for the work. When it was found that the total cost would be around $45,000, the oil company's engineer in charge, F. K. Burnap, its architect, McMeekin, and Sayers, in consultation with representatives of the Smith-Haggard Lumber Company, which had bid on the general contract, worked out a plan which omitted much of the contemplated improvements and brought the cost down to $13,000. A written contract was made by the lumber company and the oil company and a bond executed for its performance. Similar contracts were also made with certain subcontractors. During the progress of the work Burnap was in charge; but it is very clear that Sayers also was quite active in the supervision. These contracts were completed in December, 1936, and all accounts were settled by the oil company.

Early in 1937, Sayers asked the architect to obtain prices for furnishing the filling station according to the original plans. After this was done Sayers made an oral contract with the Smith-Haggard Lumber Company as a general contractor, and in the same manner it sublet portions of the work. During the progress of the work the architect was advised with and Sayers was very active in the supervision. Neither Burnap, who had supervised the original work, nor any other representative of the Ohio Oil Company was on the ground. The contractors' relations were altogether with Sayers and Mc-Meekin, the architect. When the work had been completed, in March, 1937, and bills were sent in, the Ohio Oil Company denied liability on the ground that it had not authorized the contracts either directly or indirectly. The contractors gave notice and filed statements asserting liens, as required by law. The oil company adhered to its disavowal of liability, and suit was instituted against it to judgment.

The defendant oil company had never given notice to plaintiffs that Sayers was no longer its agent in further improving the property.

STANLEY, J. This is not a case of limitation of authority of an agent. The question is of the liability of a former agent whose authority had actually terminated without the third party having reason to know it. In *Middleton v. Frances*, 257 Ky, 42, 77 S. W. (2d) 425, we adopted the following definition given in 2 C. J. 427, sec. 14: "An apparent or ostensible agent is one whom the principal either intentionally or by want of ordinary care induces third persons to believe to be his agent, although he has not, either expressly or by implication, conferred authority upon him."

The general rule is that "the acts of an agent after his authority has been revoked may bind a principal as against third persons who, in the absence of notice of the revocation of the agent's authority, rely upon its continued existence. The general rule is that the acts of an agent, within the apparent scope of his authority, are binding on the principal as against one who had formerly dealt with him through the agent and who had no notice of the revocation. This is especially so with reference to transactions initiated by the agent before the revocation of his authority." 2 *Am. Jur.*, Agency, section 44. This statement is supported by a number of Kentucky cases.

Since the defendant oil company failed to give proper notice to the plaintiffs as to the termination of Sayers' agency it is liable to the plaintiffs on their contracts for labor and material furnished. It would be inequitable and unjust to permit the defendant company to retain the benefits and escape payment therefor at the expense of the plaintiffs. It would be contrary to the spirit of the statue (mechanics' lien law) to deprive the plaintiffs of their liens. Judgment affirmed.

REVIEW CASES

1. Robertson contracted orally with Atlantic Coast Realty Co. to give it an exclusive agency contract, for twelve months, to develop and sell certain land. Before the twelve months had expired, Robertson sold the property. The company sued for profits lost because of the breach of contract. Two defenses were pleaded: that the oral contract was for the sale of land and hence was unenforceable, and that the agency agreement was revocable. What ruling? (Atlantic Coast Realty Co. v. Townsend, 124 Va. 490, 98 S. E. 684)

2. Hutchinson Coal Co. signed a non-exclusive agency agreement with Wood granting him a 10¢-per-ton commission on coal that he sold. Wood sold coal to a customer under a five-year contract. Two months before the contract expired, Wood tried several times to see the president of the coal company about price and tonnage data, so as to have a firm basis for renegotiating the contract, but was put off. The company itself negotiated a new five-year contract with the customer before the old one expired. Wood, who made no effort to renew the contract when it expired, learned about the new contract several months after it had gone into effect. He claimed his commission on all coal sold under this contract. The coal company refused payment, and Wood filed suit. Judgment for whom? (Wood v. Hutchinson Coal Co., 176 F.(2d) 682, 12 A. L. R.(2d) 352)

3. Baker authorized Wheeler to sell a tract of land for him. The same day he authorized Fairchild to sell the same land. Before the day had passed, Wheeler sold the land. The next day Fairchild, who had had no notice of the sale, contracted to sell the land to Ahern. Baker refused to convey the property to Ahern, and Ahern brought an action for damages for breach of contract. Holding? (Ahern v. Baker, 35 Minn. 98, 24 N. W. 341)

4. When Caldwell became ill he handed an envelope containing a bankbook to the superintendent of the building where he worked and said: "If anything happens to me I want Bob to have this." Caldwell died and the superintendent gave the envelope to Bob. Was there a valid gift through the superintendent as Caldwell's agent? (In re Caldwell's Estate, 180 Misc. 854, 43 N. Y. S.(2d) 773)

5. The citizens of Guthrie voted to accept an offer from a railroad company to build its road within eighteen months to Guthrie for a certain bonus. They further voted to turn over the handling of the contract to the Guthrie Club, a corporation. The bonus was raised by subscription notes of citizens and turned over to the club, which notified the railroad company of the acceptance and delivered the notes to it. Later the railroad found that it could not finish construction in the time specified and asked the Guthrie Club for an extension of time. The club and the railroad signed a new contract extending the time. The subscription notes were sold to the Federal Trust Co., and when they came due, Coyle, one of the subscribers, refused to pay his note on the ground that the Guthrie Club had no authority to agree to extend the time. The Federal Trust Co. filed suit against Coyle. Ruling? (Federal Trust Co. v. Coyle, 34 Okla. 635, 126 P. 800)

6. The owner of a $27,000 note, purchased from an insolvent bank for $32, made a contract with Flanagan whereby Flanagan was to collect, sell, or dispose of the note and divide the proceeds equally between them. Thereafter the owner of the note released Brown, who was liable on the note, from his obligation on the note. Flanagan protested and maintained that he had an agency coupled with an interest and therefore irrevocable. He brought suit against Brown to collect on the note. Holding? (Flanagan v. Brown, 70 Cal. 254)

Property

part **IV**

Personal
Property

22

The cornerstone of our economic system is the institution of private property. The firm belief of the American people that an economy based upon a system of private ownership of property will bring them the maximum return in goods and services and at the same time preserve to them their traditional rights and liberties is evidenced by their general support of the system. Fundamentally, the institution of private property provides an incentive to greater economic activity on the part of our people, since from its very nature it tends to reward individual energy and initiative.

The legal meaning of the term *property* is different from the sense in which the word is commonly used in ordinary speech. When A says, "This car is my property," he uses the word to denote the physical object itself. In a strict technical sense, however, A's property is not the object of ownership itself, but the *rights and interests* which he has in the object. If A is the absolute owner of a car, he has the right (with certain limitations to be mentioned below) to possess, to use, to enjoy, and to dispose of it as he sees fit, and these rights constitute in the legal sense his property in the car. Now, if A were pressed to explain what he means when he says that the car is his property, his explanation would doubtless tend to this same effect that the car is his to use and enjoy as he pleases; hence it might seem that the distinction has little significance. This is perhaps true where the object of ownership has physical existence; but the great importance of the legal significance of the term is that it makes possible the concept of valuable rights in intangibles. For example, the technical sense alone is applicable to a chose in action, which is property just as surely as a car is "property" in the popular sense. In the present section the popular usage is often followed for convenience, but the student should always bear in mind the technical sense of the word.

In general the owner of property may use it as he wishes. It is his to enjoy and do with as he sees fit. If he owns a house he may occupy it himself or rent it to another. He may mortgage it, sell it or even give it away. His car and his television set are at his command. However, society does impose upon the property owner certain restrictions and controls. The following are examples. (1) The owner may not use his property in such a way as unduly to injure others. Organized society, operating through its various political subdivisions, has established certain rules and regulations governing the use of private property. This is necessary in order that "rights" themselves may exist for anyone. "Rights" without corresponding "duties" would result in anarchy. For that reason, though the owner of an automobile may operate and enjoy it with a great amount of freedom, still society demands that he operate it in such a way as not to imperil the lives and property of others. Limitations are also imposed upon the owner of real property. He may not maintain a nuisance upon his property to the detriment and injury of others. Thus, by limiting owners of property to a reasonable use of their property the group as a whole is benefited. (2) The power of the various political subdivisions to tax one's property is a very definite limitation upon the use and enjoyment of his property. (3) Society, through the government, reserves the power, under certain circumstances, to divest one of his property entirely. This power, which is inherent in a sovereign state, is known as the power of *eminent domain*. However, the property owner is given reasonable protection, for such power may not be exercised unless the property is taken for a public purpose and with just compensation to the property owner. If the property owner refuses to sell the property to the government at a price named by the government, the property is taken by what is known as a condemnation proceeding. In such case a jury determines what is "just compensation." Certain public utilities, such as railroads, telephone, telegraph, and light and power companies, have been granted by the state the authority to take property under such a proceeding. (4) A fourth limitation upon the use of private property is found in what is known as the *police power* of the state. This is also an inherent power of a sovereign state and is undefined by statute. In our country there has been an historic struggle between police power, on the one hand, and, on the other, the constitutional limitations contained in the Fifth and Fourteenth Amendments and the "contract clause" of the Constitution (Article I, Section 10). This is evidenced by many court battles over state and federal statutes dealing with taxation and with social legislation, such as minimum wage laws, child labor laws, safety legislation, workmen's compensation, and similar statutes.

Wood v. Security Mutual Life Insurance Co.

112 Neb. 66, 198 N. W. 537 (1924)

This was an action by Edward A. Wood (plaintiff) against the Security Mutual Life Insurance Co. (defendant). Judgment for defendant, and plaintiff appealed. Affirmed.

On and before June 1, 1915, plaintiff conducted a barber shop in a room in the south end of the basement of defendant's building, under a written lease which was to terminate 2½ years thereafter. About June 1st defendant began to remodel and reconstruct its building, and it permitted plaintiff, under a new contract, to move into and occupy a room free of charge in the north end of its building, to be used as a barber shop, while construction work was in progress. This agreement, which was put in writing, included the following provision: "In consideration that Security Mutual Life Insurance Company will furnish to the undersigned without charge office accommodations in the Security Mutual Life Building, Lincoln, Nebraska, pending the remodeling and reconstruction of such building, the undersigned hereby agrees to hold said insurance company harmless from all liability for damage to the person or property of the undersigned or their employees pending such reconstruction. . . ."

Plaintiff contended that, while the building was going on, the room was rendered almost useless as a barber shop for a period of about a year and a half, by being filled with smoke, dust, dirt, lime, mortar, and other debris, and that his business was damaged to the extent of $10,000. He further contended that the only damage which could have been reasonably contemplated, under the foregoing agreement, was damage to visible, tangible property "which plaintiff had in his shop" and which was capable of physical custody. He insisted that the contract had no reference to his trade or business and did not, therefore, work a release of liability for damages resulting from the loss of profits or injury to his business generally.

DEAN, J. We do not think plaintiff's argument is tenable. It is to be noted that, by the language of the instrument in question, the plaintiff agreed to hold defendant harmless "from all liability for damage to the person or property" of the plaintiff. The inquiry then should be directed to what is meant, under the law, by this expression as used by the parties to their agreement. Property, in a broad sense, is defined as any valuable right or interest considered primarily as a source or element of wealth, and includes in modern legal systems practically all valuable rights. In New Jersey it was held that "a calling, business or profession, chosen and followed, is property." *State v. Chapman*, 69 N. J. L. 464, 55 A. 94. In Pennsylvania the court declared that the labor and skill of the workman, be it of high or low degree, the plant of the manufacturer, the equipment of the farmer, investments of commerce, are all, in equal sense, property. *Purvis v. Local No. 500*, 214 Pa. 348, 63 A. 585. In the Purvis case the court held, in direct terms, that a person's business is property within the meaning of the law. In Illinois it has been held: "The term 'property' includes every interest any one may have in any and every thing that is the subject of ownership by man, together with the right to freely possess, use, enjoy, and dispose of the same." *Bailey v. The People*, 190 Ill. 28, 60 N. E. 98.

The contract is plain and unambiguous and its meaning can be determined without reference to extrinsic facts. The conclusion is that, when fairly construed in all its parts, the contract contemplates a release of defendant from liability arising out of the damage of which complaint is made. Judgment affirmed.

CLASSIFICATION OF PROPERTY

Property may be variously classified as (1) public and private, (2) tangible and intangible, or (3) real and personal.

PUBLIC AND PRIVATE PROPERTY

From the viewpoint of ownership, property is divided into public and private property. Public property is property owned by the federal government, the states, and the various political subdivisions of the states, such as counties, townships, and municipalities. In some respects public property is property owned collectively by the people, through their government. The federal government owns a great amount of property, including parks, dams, and public lands, post office buildings, office buildings, military installations, etc. The states, cities, and counties also own a vast quantity of property, such as state and city parks, school buildings, court houses and city halls, eleemosynary institutions, and the like.

Private property consists of property owned by individuals, corporations, trusts, and other types of business organizations.

The use of private property for public purposes does not change the title to the property or convert it into public property.

TANGIBLE AND INTANGIBLE PROPERTY

Tangible or corporeal property consists of rights and interests in objects that have physical existence, such as a house and lot, a factory building, an automobile, furniture, or livestock. In the case of intangible or incorporeal property, the "object of ownership" has no physical existence. Common examples are leaseholds, corporation stock, and rights under a contract.

REAL AND PERSONAL PROPERTY

Real property, in the popular sense of the term, is land and all things firmly attached thereto. In a technical sense, real property constitutes all rights and interests in land (except interests that are less than a freehold estate, such as leasehold interests) and the things that are firmly attached thereto. "Land" includes not only the earth's surface but everything under the surface, such as oil, gas, and minerals, and the space above the earth.[1]

All other property is said to be personal property. Personal property includes (1) chattels real and (2) chattels personal. Chattels real are rights and interests in real property that are less than a freehold estate. The best example of a chattel real is a lease of a house or an apartment. The lease gives to the lessee an interest in the lessor's real property, but the interest constitutes less than a freehold estate. The courts have always treated such interests as personal property and have called them chattels real. Chattels personal are subdivided into (1) chattels personal corporeal and (2) chattels personal incorporeal. Chattels personal corporeal, sometimes called *choses in possession*, include all tangible personal property, such as household furniture, automobiles, livestock, grain, and merchandise. Chattels personal incorporeal, usually referred to as *choses in action*, include such intangible property as contract rights, promissory notes, bills of exchange, bonds, corporate stock, patents, and copyrights.

The distinction between real and personal property is important under a variety of circumstances. (1) It is important in case of the sale of the property, in determining whether the agreement has to be in writing under the Statute of Frauds. As we have already seen, every contract for the sale of real property must be in writing, but not every contract for the sale of personal property. (2) It is important in determining what formalities, if any, are necessary in conveying and passing title to the property. A deed must always be used when real property is conveyed. Usually a bill of sale is used in the case of personal property. (3) It is important in determining the dower interest of the widow. While a widow has a dower interest in her husband's realty, she has no dower interest in his personalty. (4) It is important in the administration and settlement of a decedent's estate. The title to the realty passes immediately to the devisees under the will, or if the decedent died intestate, to his heirs at law. The title to the personal property passes to the executor or administrator, and only after the decedent's debts are paid does any remaining property pass to the legatees under the will, or if the decedent died intestate, to the heirs at law. (5) It is important in determining how the property must be taxed.

Yet it is frequently difficult in a given factual situation to determine whether certain property is real or personal. Depending upon the circumstances, one tree, for example, may be realty and another personalty, and the same tree may shift its status with shifting circumstances. A great variety of borderline cases have turned up in the courts; and though the decisions show some lack of uniformity, certain useful general rules have been established for the determination of disputed cases.

[1] This has been somewhat modified by modern aviation law.

FRUCTUS NATURALES AND FRUCTUS INDUSTRIALES. Though by definition real property includes everything firmly attached to the land, the things that grow on the land are not all treated as realty. As we have already seen,[1] the courts have divided growing vegetation into (1) fructus naturales, which are perennial in nature and have grown and developed without the labor of man, such as trees, grass, and other natural vegetable products, and (2) fructus industriales, comprising annual crops that are planted and cultivated by man, such as corn, wheat, oats, and vegetable crops. It may be stated as a general rule of law that fructus naturales are held to be realty. Fructus industriales are considered in most cases to be personalty, but under certain circumstances they are regarded as a part of the realty. For instance, if the owner of the realty sells the property and does not reserve his garden or other "annual crops," it is held that they pass with the realty to the grantee. Likewise, some courts distinguish between growing and immature crops and those that are mature and ready to be harvested. Where such a distinction is made, it is usually held that a mature crop is personalty, whereas a growing crop—one still taking its substance from the soil—is a part of the realty.

SEVERED REALTY. Property which is realty may, by severance, become personalty. For example, trees and other fructus naturales may be changed into personalty by being cut and sold. Or a house may become personalty by being removed from the land to which it was formerly attached.

Intention usually plays an important part in determining whether the severance of a portion of the realty has the effect of converting such property into personalty. In fact, intention may bring about the change of status even in advance of actual severance. Constructive severance has been recognized in cases where, under the terms of the sale, a portion of the realty is to be removed "immediately" or within a short time. For example, if A is the owner of a house and lot and he sells the house to B under an agreement whereby A is to remove the house for B from the lot within a month, the house becomes personalty before its actual removal, since A's act in selling, and B's in buying, the house apart from the realty evidences their intention to treat the house as personalty.[2]

---

[1] See Chapter 12, Martin v. Underhill and Uniform Commercial Code, Sec. 2–107.

[2] Sec. 2–105 of the Uniform Commercial Code provides: "Goods" means all things (including specially manufactured goods) which are movable at the time of identification to the contract for sale other than the money in which the price is to be paid, investment securities (Article 8) and things in action. "Goods" also includes the unborn young of animals and growing crops and other identified things attached to realty as described in the section on goods to be served from "realty."

Rankin et al. v. Ridge et al.
53 N. Mex. 33, 201 P. (2d) 359 (1949)

This was an action by Noel Rankin and Huling Means (plaintiffs) against Robert R. Ridge and others (defendants), to recover for timber cut from their land under an oral contract. Defendants filed a cross-action. The trial court dismissed the cross-complaint, and defendants appealed. Reversed and remanded.

D. C. Gibbs was the owner of the N. H. Ranch. Prior to October 1, 1946, he entered into an oral contract with defendants, by the terms of which he sold to defendants the standing timber on parts of the ranch. Under the terms of the oral contract defendants were to pay Gibbs a specified amount for the timber and were to move a saw mill onto the land and saw and remove the merchantable timber therefrom "in a reasonably continuous manner" until all the timber had been sawed and removed. Defendants made a down payment of $250 to Gibbs. Soon thereafter they moved a saw mill onto the land and began to cut, saw, and remove the timber. On October 1, 1946, Gibbs sold his ranch to plaintiffs, but before doing so he informed them of his oral contract with defendants, and they agreed to carry out the obligations of Gibbs in said contract.

On April 8, 1947, plaintiffs notified and demanded in writing that defendants remove their machinery from the property and refrain from cutting and removing any more timber. Plaintiffs filed this action to recover the sum of $399.55, which they alleged was the balance due for timber already removed from the land.

Defendants filed a cross-complaint wherein they asked for a judgment in the amount of $24,500, which they claimed represented the amount to which they had been damaged. Upon motion of plaintiffs, defendants' cross-complaint was dismissed. Defendants appealed.

BRICE, C.J. The question is whether the trial court erred in dismissing the cross-complaint, upon the theory that the contract was within the Statute of Frauds.

It is a general rule that the sale of growing timber is within the fourth section of the Statute of Frauds, in that the trees are a part of the realty. *Putney v. Day,* 6 N. H. 430; *Elsberry v. Sexton,* 61 Fla. 162, 54 So. 592. However, according to the decisions of a majority of the courts a contract for the sale of trees to be immediately severed from the freehold by the vendee is not a sale of an interest in land. *White v. Foster,* 102 Mass. 375. It is held that the phrase "immediate severance," as before used, contemplates a severance as soon as it reasonably can be done, under the existing circumstances. *Cheatham v. Head,* 203 Ky. 489, 262 S. W. 622.

" 'Goods,' within the meaning of the Statute, are:

    (a) Chattels personal, except current money bargained for as a medium of exchange;

    (b) Crops unsevered from the land, whether mature or not at the time
when by the terms of the bargain they are to be sold, if they are of
a kind subject to yearly cultivation;

    (c) Things attached to or forming part of the realty which are agreed
to be severed therefrom before sale or promptly after the formation
of the contract.

Comment: (a) Though strictly whatever is attached to the land is part
thereof, crops which are the subject of yearly planting or cultivation, that
is fructus industriales, have been classified under the Statute as goods rather
than part of the land. On the other hand, fructus naturales while growing
are part of the land; but under circumstances stated in Clause (c) even
fructus naturales have been held withdrawn from the operation of the
provision of the Statute relating to land. Clause (c) covers also things attached to land other than fructus naturales, such as minerals or ice, or even
buildings." *Restatement of the Law of Contracts*, Sec. 200 and Comment (a).

    "In England the law has gone to great length in supporting the validity
of an oral contract to sell standing trees. In *Marshall v. Green* the court held
that 'where the thing sold is to derive no benefit from the land, and it is to
be taken away immediately, the contract is not for an interest in land.' Since
part of the trees had been taken away the section of the Statute relating to
goods was satisfied and the bargain was held to be enforceable. The same doctrine has prevailed in several of the United States, prior to the passage of the
Sales Act, and, though 'the courts of most of the American States that have
considered the question [have held] expressly that a sale of growing or standing timber is a contract concerning an interest in land,' the Sales Act, copying,
as it has, the definition of 'goods,' so far as concerns this question, from the
English statute, has adopted the English rule that any growing object attached
to the soil is to be treated as goods, if by the terms of the contract it is to be
immediately severed. A contract to cut and market timber belonging to another in return for a share of the proceeds is a contract of hire and is enforceable." *Williston on Contracts*, Sec. 516.

    "Any growth of the soil, even though not produced by annual labor, is
personalty after its actual severance from the soil by the owner of the land,
as in the case of timber cut by him. Furthermore, by the weight of authority,
there may be constructive or legal severance of vegetable products while
still growing or standing in the soil. Thus, it has been decided that, upon a
conveyance by the landowner of growing trees apart from the land, they become personalty, and the same effect has been given to an exception of the
trees on a conveyance of the land. . . ." *Tiffany on Real Property*, Sec. 595.

    The tendency of the later decisions is toward the holding that if the sale is
made upon the condition that the trees are to be "immediately severed" from
the soil, the contract is not within the fourth section of the Statute of Frauds.
This view was adopted by the authors of the Uniform Sales Act. The great
weight of authority holds that the sale of crops (fructus industriales) mature

or not, is not within the statute; also there is much authority that the sale of grass uncut, and buildings attached to the soil to be immediately removed, are not within the Statute of Frauds. In the case at bar, we conclude that the sale was that of personal property and not within the Statute of Frauds. The plaintiffs were not only aware of the defendants' contract with the plaintiffs' grantor (Gibbs), but agreed to carry out its terms as a part of the consideration for the purchase of the property.

We are of the opinion that the trial court erred in dismissing the cross-complaint. The judgment is, therefore, reversed and the cause remanded to the district court with instructions to set aside its judgment, reinstate the case upon the docket of the court, and proceed to a hearing thereof not inconsistent herewith. It is so ordered.

FIXTURES. Property that is personalty may, by attachment, become realty. When a chattel has been affixed or annexed to real property in such a way that it loses its character as personal property and becomes a part of the realty, it is called a fixture. Disagreement as to whether a chattel has been converted into a fixture not infrequently arises where real property is sold or leased. For example, A sells a house and lot to B, and the parties then disagree over whether a sundial in the yard is part of the realty and hence passes to B, or a chattel which A has the right to remove. Or C leases an apartment from D, and during his tenancy attaches shelves to the kitchen wall. When his lease expires, C wishes to remove the shelves, but D contends that they have become part of the realty and must be left in place.

The court decisions show considerable conflict as to the circumstances under which chattels become fixtures, but the general test is found in the intention of the parties. Where this has not been made explicit and must therefore be determined by inference, the courts place great reliance upon the following factors: (1) the degree or nature of annexation or attachment; (2) the adaptability of the chattel to the realty; (3) the relation of the parties.

If the chattel has been so firmly annexed to the realty that to remove it would tend to weaken the realty or cause serious damage to it, the courts generally conclude that the annexer intended that the chattel was to become part of the realty. For example, if it is imbedded in concrete, or firmly bolted to the realty, it is generally held to be a fixture. The courts have held that the following are fixtures: furnaces, boilers, steam radiators, shingles attached to a building, gas burners, chandeliers, and bathroom fixtures. The following have been held not to be fixtures: gas ranges and stoves, electric refrigerators, radios, carpets, floor lamps, electric light bulbs.

Even where the disputed object is not firmly attached, it may be held to be a fixture because of its adaptability to the particular realty. Storm windows and doors, window screens, and screened doors have been held to be fixtures on this basis.

The relation of the parties and their position with respect to the property throw considerable light upon their presumed intentions. For example, A builds a house to be occupied by himself and his family, but after living in it for five years he sells it. In such a case it is likely that if A annexed any chattels to the house during his occupancy he did so with the intention that they should become fixtures. Thus when A sells the property the courts are inclined to hold that such chattels became fixtures and therefore pass to the vendee with the rest of the realty. But where the parties are related as landlord and tenant and the tenant during his temporary occupancy has attached certain chattels to the premises, the courts are more likely to hold that the chattels retain their status as personalty, provided they may be removed without doing serious damage to the realty, and if said realty is sold, the purchaser has actual knowledge of the facts or has constructive knowledge by the tenant recording a written agreement of the understanding.

TRADE FIXTURES

Bailey v. Kruithoff
280 So. (2d) 262 (1973)
Court of Appeal of Louisiana

Purchaser of pasture land brought suit against lessee for alleged wrongful removal of fence and for pasturage. . . . Judgment for lessee, and purchase appealed. . . . Reversed and rendered.

HALL, J. Immovability by nature has been characterized as a creation of the law based on practical considerations and on inherent characteristics of the things concerned. What is a building or other construction qualifying as an immovable under Article 464 is left for judicial determination according to prevailing notions in society. Two criteria that are often mentioned in decisions of the courts are some degree of integration or attachment to the soil and some degree of permanency. *Yiannopoulos Louisiana Civil Law of Property*, Sections 42, 43, 45 and 48; *Civil Law Translations*, Aubrey & Rau, Property, Section 164; Movables and Immovables in Louisiana and Comparative Law, 22 *LLR* 517 (1962).

In this case, the fence was embedded in the ground—a few of the posts were in concrete—and thereby integrated with the soil. Pasture fences are generally regarded as permanent in nature.

The nature of a movable is generally such that its identity is not lost if it is moved from one location to another. Ordinarily, all that is necessary is to detach the object from its present location and move it elsewhere with no apparent diminution of its identification in the process. Certainly this is not true of a fence which has no identity as a fence until it has been *constructed*. Once constructed the fence becomes a component part of the land on which it is placed and as such must be regarded as an "other construction" and as an immovable by nature under Article 464. In order to move a fence it must be dismantled and its identity destroyed, which is inconsistent with any reasonable concept of a movable.

American Creosote Company v. Springer, supra, is directly in point on the law to be applied in this case. In *Springer*, the object in question was railroad trackage, which had been constructed on the property under a lease agreement whereby the railroad company remained the owner of the trackage which the landowner was obligated to return at the conclusion of the lease or pay a penalty of $12,000. The lease was not recorded. The land was sold to Springer without reference to the trackage or the lease agreement and Springer disposed of the trackage. Plaintiff as subrogee of the railroad company, sued Springer for $12,000 as the value of the trackage.

The Louisiana Supreme Court held that all the railroad trackage was an immovable by nature when constructed on the land acquired by Springer, the lease could not be considered insofar as Springer is concerned and Springer acquired the trackage free and clear of the lease obligations, as he was not a party thereto nor was the lease recorded. *McDuffie v. Walker*, 51 So. 100 (1910); LSA–Civil Code Article 2266 and 2246. The court pointed out that the law provided a means by which the railroad company could have protected its interest in the trackage, that is, by recordation of the lease.

. . . Immovables by nature form an economic unity with the ground. It was held that rationally a railroad track must be regarded as "construction" under Article 464. It is firmly incorporated into the ground and must be regarded as an immovable by nature—a component part of the land.

We conclude that the fence involved in the case before us is an "other construction" under Article 464 and an immovable by nature. The fence was a "construction" under the ordinary, common sense meaning of that word. It was embedded in the soil, incorporated into the ground, and was a component part of the land. A fence is ordinarily regarded as having a degree of permanency—not to be readily moved about.

The agreement under which defendant retained the right to remove the fence was not recorded. The fence, together with the land, passed to plaintiff free and clear of defendant's unrecorded rights. Defendant had no right to come on the property after the sale to plaintiff and remove the fence, ownership of which was then vested in the plaintiff. Defendant is thus liable for the reasonable replacement cost of the fence he removed from plaintiff's property. The evidence shows this amount is $542.30.

In relation to plaintiff's claim for damages for pasturage of defendant's cattle which remained on the property several days after the sale, we find the evidence to be sufficient to support an award for this item.

For the reasons assigned, the judgment of the trial court is reversed and it is ordered, adjudged and decreed that there be judgment in favor of the plaintiff, Convie D. Bailey, II, and against defendant, Neal Kruithoff, in the sum of $542.30, together with legal interest thereon from date of judicial demand until paid, and together with all costs of this proceeding, including the cost of appeal.

Reversed and rendered.

The courts are much more favorable to tenants in their treatment of business tenancies than they are in the case of domestic tenancies. They give as a reason for this distinction "broad public policy" and a belief that liberality in the treatment of trade fixtures "encourages trade and manufacture." However, whether the tenancy is domestic, agricultural, or for trade purposes, it is advisable for the parties to have a definite understanding as to whether the chattel which has been annexed is to retain its characteristic as a personalty or has become a fixture.

Even though the thing annexed remains personalty and may therefore be removed by the seller or the tenant, as the case may be, the right to remove it does not last indefinitely. A vendor is required to remove such property before he surrenders possession of the realty to the vendee. A tenant who leases for a definite period must remove his property before the end of the term; one who leases for an indefinite period must remove his property within a reasonable time after the termination of the tenancy.

Becwar et al. v. Bear et al.
246 P. (2d) 1110, 41 Wash. 37 (1952)

This was an action by L. M. Becwar, doing business as Becwar Produce Company (plaintiff) against C. E. Bear, doing business as Hazelwood Cold Storage Company (defendant). Judgment for plaintiff, and defendant appealed. Affirmed.

Plaintiff was a tenant of a building under a lease from defendant's grantor. There was no heating equipment in the building, and the lease provided that the lessee (plaintiff) would furnish his own heat. It was necessary for plaintiff, in the conduct of his business, to heat a portion of the building, and with the consent of his lessor he installed a boiler, an oil burner, and other equipment in the basement beneath the leased premises. When defendant purchased the premises, he assumed the lease and knew that those installations had been made by plaintiff to carry on his trade and business. Prior to the expiration of the lease, when plaintiff was about to vacate the premises, defendant notified him not to remove the equipment. The heating equipment was not attached to the building except by ordinary bolts and couplings, and could have been removed without any damage whatsoever to the building. Plaintiff did not intend to make this equipment a part of the building, and placed it on the premises for the sole purpose of carrying on his trade. The value of the property converted was $1050. It was established that defendant had been damaged in the sum of $75 because of the manner in which certain property of plaintiff, other than the heating equipment, was removed from the building.

Upon these facts, the trial court concluded that the heating installations were "trade fixtures" which plaintiff should have been permitted to remove from the premises, and judgment was entered against defendant in the sum of $975. Defendant appealed.

OLSON, J. The first "holding" attacked by the defendant is that the heating installations were trade fixtures and removable by the plaintiff. This is a conclusion. It is supported by the established facts and, therefore, not erroneous. The fact is that the plaintiff did not intend that the heating installations made while he was a tenant were to enrich the freehold by becoming a part of the building, but placed them there solely for the purpose of his trade. The intent of the party making the annexation is the cardinal inquiry in determining whether a chattel annexed to the freehold is a trade fixture or part of the realty. *Ballard v. Alaska Theatre Co.*, 93 Wash. 655, 161 P. 478. Being trade fixtures, it follows that defendant should have permitted plaintiff to remove them when his lease expired.

The defendant contends that the court erred in "failing to hold" that it was the duty of the plaintiff, as tenant, to disclose his claim to defendant, an innocent purchaser for value, before his purchase. This conclusion would not have been justified in view of the fact that, when defendant purchased the premises, he knew that plaintiff had made the heating installations to carry on his business. The facts known to the defendant were naturally and reasonably connected with, and furnished a clue to, plaintiff's intention to remove this equipment. With such knowledge, defendant is deemed to have had notice of all facts which reasonable inquiry would disclose. *Dimmel v. Morse*, 36 Wash. (2d) 344, 218 P. (2d) 334. The court was not in error, as defendant contends, in this regard. Judgment affirmed.

TITLE AND POSSESSION

It is essential in the study of property law to understand the difference between *title* and *possession*. The former term carries with it the concept of ownership. If one has title to certain real or personal property, he has dominion and control over its use and disposition; he may use it as he pleases, or he may sell it, rent it, or give it away. If A owns a house and lives in it himself, he has both title and possession. But possession does not necessarily depend upon title. One person may have title to certain property and another may have possession. If A rents his house to B, he retains title to it, but B has possession. If A leaves his suit at the tailor's to be mended, A retains title to the suit, but the tailor has possession. Or if A hires a U-Drive-It car, A has only possession; the car agency retains title.

Possession does not necessarily entail immediate physical control. If you own a watch and are wearing it, so that you have manual control of it, you are said to have *actual possession* of it. It is held that one must have both the *intent* and the *power to control* a specific piece of property, to the exclusion of all others, before he has actual possession of the property. This concept envisages the actual physical control of the property. But if possession were dependent upon such control, one could have possession of very few things, and possession would be a constantly shifting status. Hence the law recognizes what is called *legal* or *constructive possession*, founded upon one's *legal right to control* a specific piece of property, whether it be real or personal. If you leave your watch in your dormitory room while you are attending class, you no longer have actual possession of it, but you have legal or constructive possession. If A owns a large ranch on which hundreds of head of cattle are scattered, he does not have actual possession of the cattle, but he has legal or constructive possession of them.

One who has physical control over property without having possession of it is said to have *custody* of it. For example, the employee who drives a delivery truck has custody of the truck and its contents. The legal or constructive possession is in his employer.

METHODS OF ACQUIRING TITLE TO PERSONAL PROPERTY

The principal methods of acquiring title to personal property are as follows: (1) by purchase, (2) by will, (3) by inheritance (descent), (4) by gift, (5) by creation, (6) by accession, (7) by confusion, (8) by finding, (9) by appropriation, and (10) by operation of law.

BY PURCHASE

Most personal property is acquired by purchase. The principles regulating the purchase and sale of personal property are discussed in Part V of this book, under the heading "Sales."

BY WILL

The acquisition of personal property under a will is discussed in Chapter 24.

BY INHERITANCE (DESCENT)

The acquisition of personal property under the statutes of descent and distribution is explained in Chapter 24.

BY GIFT

A gift is a voluntary and gratuitous transfer of property from the donor to the donee. There are two types of gifts: (1) gifts inter vivos and (2) gifts causa mortis.[1]

A gift inter vivos is the usual type of gift, whereby the donor during his lifetime makes a gift of property, either personal or real, to the donee. If the proper requirements are met, the gift is absolute and the donor may not later demand and recover the property from the donee. The requirements are as follows: (1) The donor must possess full contractual capacity (even though a gift is not based upon contract). If, for example, the donor is an infant, or if he is insane, he may recover the property from the donee. (2) The gift must be voluntarily made with an intent to vest title to the property in the donee. The donor must surrender all present and future dominion and control over the property. (3) The donee must accept the gift. A donor is not privileged to force a donee to accept property against his will. (4) There must be a valid delivery of the property. Usually actual or manual delivery is required, but under certain circumstances the requirement may be met by symbolic or constructive delivery, e.g. by the delivery of the key to a trunk or lock box, or by the delivery of some document of title, such as a warehouse receipt, a bill of lading, or a passbook to a bank account. Delivery may also be made by a *deed of gift*. A wishes to give his piano to his daughter, who lives at home with him. If he simply tells her that she may have the piano, the gift would probably not be effective to pass title, because of lack of proper delivery. But if he should execute a deed of gift, naming his daughter as donee, the gift would be valid. If the daughter had already had possession of the piano—if, for example, she had been married and living in her own home and her father had earlier permitted her to move the piano to her home—then his statement of his intention to give her the piano would result in a valid gift.

A gift causa mortis is a gift of personal property [2] given in contemplation of death. For example, A is seriously ill and has been told by his doctor that he will not recover. Believing that he has only a short time to live, he makes a gift of certain personal property to his old friend B. Such gift would be held to be valid and good as against the administrator or executor of A's estate, assuming proper delivery of the property. But if A did not die, he would be entitled to recover the property from B. Courts also hold that the donor of a gift causa mortis may revoke the gift at any time before his death, in which case he would be entitled to the return of the property. A gift causa mortis is thus in a sense conditional and not absolute, differing in that respect from a gift inter vivos.

---

[1] Testamentary gifts, or gifts under a will, comprise a third type of gift, but in the present discussion they are listed under a separate heading.

[2] One may not make a gift causa mortis of real property.

As we have already seen, a promise to make a gift may not be enforced, since it is unsupported by consideration.

Guest v. Stone
206 Ga. 234, 56 S. E. (2d) 274 (1949)

This was an action by Mrs. Eloise Guest, as administratrix of the estate of Robert M. Montgomery (plaintiff) against Mrs. Lessie Stone and the Baxley State Bank (defendants). Judgment for defendant, and plaintiff appealed. Reversed.

This action was to recover money on a savings account in the defendant bank. The bank was permitted by agreement to pay the money into court and was relieved of further responsibility.

The deceased Montgomery was a career soldier, having been in the army for many years. He was divorced from a former wife for more than 10 years, and had a daughter. Mrs. Stone was his first cousin, and for the past eight years, when on furlough, he made his home with Mr. and Mrs. Stone, who furnished him food, lodging, and companionship. Prior to December, 1945, he had sent money to Mrs. Stone, and on that date made a savings deposit of $2,000 in the bank, the deposit being made up of $300.88 in cash, and a check from Mrs. Stone for $1,699.12, which represented the aggregate amount of money he had sent her. At the time of making this deposit, he stated to the teller receiving the deposit that he wanted Mrs. Stone to be the beneficiary of the fund in the event of his death. On the deposit slip was written: "Mrs. Lessie Stone beneficiary in case of death. . . . Robert M. Montgomery." About two days before he left Mrs. Stone's home, and before going to Germany where he died, he turned over to Mrs. Stone his savings account pass book, which it was necessary to produce in order to withdraw any money, and stated to her, "If I happen to crap out, it is all yours," and also at this time gave her a check on the bank signed by him, in which no payee was named and no amount stated, and told her, "If you need any money while I am gone go to the bank and get it." After this he made a number of deposits to the account and several withdrawals. After he delivered the pass book and blank check to Mrs. Stone and left for Germany, there were a number of deposits made by Mrs. Stone to the account, aggregating $450. Whether this was money sent to her by Montgomery, does not appear from the record. At the time when she made the first of these deposits, the teller told her that she was the beneficiary, and if anything happened to Robert Montgomery she would get the money.

ATKINSON, J. Whatever might have been the intention of the deceased or the understanding of Mrs. Stone, a solution as to the legal effect of the foregoing transactions will best be determined by an application of the process of elimination.

The original deposit of $2,000 with the notation, "Mrs. Lessie Stone beneficiary in case of death," and signed by the deceased, standing alone, is clearly testamentary, and not being executed with the formality required of a will, would convey no interest therein to her.

We next consider the circumstances of the original deposit along with the subsequent fact that the deceased gave the pass book and blank check to Mrs. Stone, stating, "If I happen to crap out, it is all yours," and, "If you need any money while I am gone, go to the bank and get it." The evidence negatives the fact that this transaction occurred during the last illness or while the deceased was in peril of death, and therefore does not meet the requirement of a gift causa mortis. Nor would it constitute a gift inter vivos. We quote from *Drake v. Wayne*, 52 Ga. App. 654, 184 S. E. 339: " 'A delivery of property subject to be reclaimed by the donor at any time prior to his death, or where full control or power over the property or fund vests in the donee only after the death of the donor, does not constitute a valid gift inter vivos.' 20 *Cyc.* p. 1211, Sec. 2. A gift inter vivos 'operates, if at all, in the donor's lifetime, immediately and irrevocably; it is a gift executed; no further act of parties, no contingency of death or otherwise, is needed to give it effect.' 20 *Cyc.* p. 1192. 'To make a valid gift, there must be a present intention to give, and a complete renunciation of right, by the giver, over the thing given, without power of revocation, and a full delivery of possession as a gift inter vivos.' *Minns v. Ross*, 42 Ga. 121."

There are certain requirements for a transfer of property rights both before and after death, and even though Montgomery desired to exercise a spirit of liberality towards Mrs. Stone, his desire could not be given effect by our courts unless it was manifested by some means recognized by law. The facts here do not establish her right to the funds, as a will, a gift causa mortis, or a gift inter vivos, . . . and accordingly the court erred in overruling the motion for a new trial. Judgment reversed.

BY CREATION

One may acquire title to personal property by creating it through his own mental and physical efforts. For example, when an artist applies his skill to a canvas and produces a painting, he has created property, and as its creator he becomes its owner. The writer, the composer, the inventor create intangible property. Article I, Section VIII of the Constitution of the United States provides that "The Congress shall have power . . . To promote the progress of science and useful arts by securing for limited times to authors and inventors the exclusive right to their respective writings and discoveries." Under the authority of this constitutional provision Congress has enacted certain statutes regulating the granting of copyrights, patents, and trade-marks. The copyright law applies not only to books and other writings but also to musical compositions, maps, diagrams, architectural plans, motion pictures, photographs, sculptures, drawings, paintings, and the like. A copyright secures to the creator of such property, and his heirs and assigns, the exclusive right to reproduce it, or to authorize its reproduction, for a period of twenty-eight years, and is renewable for a second period of the same length. Copyrights are registered in the Copyright Office in the Library of Congress. A patent for an invention is a grant by the government to the inventor, his heirs and assigns, of certain exclusive rights in his invention for the term of seventeen years; it is not renewable. The Patent Office has exclusive authority to grant letters patent to inventors. Trade-mark rights will prevent others from using the same name on the same goods, but not from making the same goods without using the trade-mark. Trade-marks which are used in interstate or foreign commerce may be registered in the Patent Office.

Flavor Corporation of America v. Kemin Industries, Inc.
358 F. Supp. 1114 (1973)
United States District Court

[This was an] trademark infringement and unfair competition action in which defendants counterclaimed on theory that plaintiff maliciously damaged defendants' business through various libelous acts of unfair competition. . . . Injunction issued, judgment accordingly.

STUART, D.J. This is a trademark infringement and unfair competition action brought by Flavor Corporation of America (FCA) against Kemin Industries, Inc. (Kemin) and its president, Rolland W. Nelson. The two companies make, among other things, flavor additives for certain animal feeds and rodenticides. Defendants deny any infringement and have, by counterclaim, asserted plaintiff maliciously damaged defendants' business through various libelous acts of unfair competition. The parties seek both injunctive relief and monetary damages, but issues relating to monetary damages have been separated and are to be tried subsequent to this trial on the issues of trademark infringement and unfair competition.

*   *   *

FCA was organized in 1946. From its inception its principal products have been various flavorings for animal feeds designed to appeal to a particular species. In 1956 it added to its product line a flavoring additive for rodenticides and rodent baits. It immediately adopted a trademark, "PESTLUR," to identify the product. In 1961 a second product, "Rodentlur," designed to attract rodent pets to feed as well as for use in rodenticides, was added. "Fishlur," a flavor additive for fish feeds and baits, was first advertised in 1961 and first sold in 1962.

From August, 1958, to December, 1961, defendant R. W. Nelson was employed by plaintiff as a regional sales manager. The last 6 weeks of his employment he was acting sales manager of the company.

Early in 1962 Nelson formed his own company, Chemical Industries, Inc. The name was later changed to Kemin. This company became a direct competitor to FCA selling the same type of products to the same classes of customers. Shortly thereafter Nelson began promoting and selling his products under trademarks such as "PIG LURE," "CATTLE LURE," "CALF LURE," "CAT LURE," "STOCK LURE," "DOG LURE," "HORSE AND PONY LURE," "TURKEY LURE," "CHICK LURE," and "RAT LURE." It should be pointed out that the main area of competition between the parties is in flavorings for animal feeds in which plaintiff's trademark is "NECTAR." Rodenticide flavorings are a very small part of the business of either company.

"PESTLUR" was registered on the Principal Register of the United States Patent Office on September 22, 1964. Plaintiff sent formal notice of infringement to defendants in October, 1964.

In 1966 defendant Kemin's predecessor, Chemical Industries, Inc., was issued a registration on the Supplemental Register for its mark "LURE," flavoring for animal feeds. FCA immediately petitioned for cancellation of said "LURE" trademark, which petition was granted by the Patent Office Trademark Trial and Appeal Board (Board) relying on the trademark registration of "PESTLUR" and previous usage of "FISHLUR" and "RODENTLUR."

Plaintiff relies heavily on its contention that Nelson adopted the "LURE" trademark in bad faith and with knowledge of prior use of the mark by FCA. Mr. Nelson denied knowledge of the PESTLUR, RODENTLUR, and FISHLUR marks.

Plaintiff introduced into evidence its 1961 price catalog which Nelson had used as a salesman listing prices for these products. One invoice showed he had received a few dollars commission on "Rodentlur" on a sale made from the home office, not by him personally. He received a copy of this invoice. Plaintiff argues: "It is incredible that a man who achieved the promotion to acting sales manager would deny knowledge of the company's products and deny knowledge of his company's price catalogs."

Although the Court was not impressed with Mr. Nelson's testimony, the Court is of the opinion the "LUR" products constituted such a minor part of plaintiff's business and Nelson's actual exposure to the term was so minimal, that in all probability he had no recollection of ever having seen the marks in connection with plaintiff's business. This conclusion is supported by the testimony of Nelson's successor as sales manager for plaintiff who testified he was unaware that plaintiff sold any products under these marks. The small dollar volume of sales is discussed later in this memorandum.

In addition, Mrs. Nelson testified she suggested the use of the word "LURE" in connection with the flavorings for animal feeds.

The Court therefore finds defendants' adoption and use of the mark "LURE" was in good faith and without knowledge that plaintiff has used "LUR" as part of a trademark.

Having found defendants' adoption of the mark was done in good faith and without knowledge of use of a similar mark by plaintiff, it follows that plaintiff is not entitled to protection in market areas independently developed by defendants. "However, defendants' right to use the same mark in territory remote from territory developed by plaintiff does not allow defendants to invade territory already occupied by plaintiff's product. Plaintiff's prior use of its trademark within a given market area entitled it to exclusive use of that mark within that area." *SweeTarts v. Sunshine, Inc.*, supra, 380 F. (2d) at 928.

The *SweeTarts* case was remanded for a factual determination of plaintiff's market area. The Court said: "Though the market penetration need not be large to entitle plaintiff to protection, *Sweet Sixteen Co. v. Sweet 16 Shop*, 15 F. (2d) 920 (8th Cir., 1926), it must be significant enough to pose the real likelihood of confusion among the consumers in that area between the products of plaintiff and the products of defendants." Supra, 380 F. (2d) at 929.

After the district court, on remand, had found sufficient market penetration in certain states, the circuit court reversed, stating that the evidence was insufficient to indicate the trademark had become generally known or identified in those states, and held plaintiff could not justly claim them in its effective market area. *SweeTarts v. Sunline, Inc.* (8th Cir., 1971), 436 F. (2d) 705, 711.

There is evidence that FCA has made a nationwide mailing of its price catalogs which listed PESTLUR, FISHLUR, and RODENTLUR. In my opinion this alone is not sufficient market penetration to entitle FCA to an injunction. In *SweeTarts*, plaintiff there had solicited business from YMCA's all over the country. 436 F. (2d) 705, 708.

*   *   *

"PESTLUR" is descriptive of the product and was registered under 15 U. S. C. § 1052(f). Such registration constitutes prima facie evidence of ownership and shifts the burden of going forward with the evidence to show that it has not acquired a secondary meaning relating to the source of the product to the "infringer."

However, the cases are clear that injunctive relief must be limited to the area in which the descriptive term has acquired a secondary meaning. . . .

Whether the burden is on FCA or Kemin, the Court finds sales of "PESTLUR" have been so minimal, sporadic, and declining in the states where it has been sold, that it has in fact not acquired a secondary meaning in any of these states and there has not been sufficient penetration into the market of any area to entitle plaintiff to the protection of injunctive relief. As there have been no sales in either Georgia or Florida since 1969, it is questionable whether injunctive relief should even be imposed in these states. However, as it has previously been held a common law trademark for PESTLUR had been established prior to registration, the Court is not inclined to find abandonment at this time.

It is obvious to the Court that the bitter feelings between the parties in this lawsuit resulted from the success of a former employee in invading the former employer's market for animal feed flavorings. This trademark infringement suit and the counterclaims are by-products of this mutual animosity.

Although neither party has conducted itself in an exemplary manner, the Court is of the opinion that plaintiff has failed to sustain its burden of proving its claim of unfair competition and defendants have likewise failed to prove their claim of libel and unfair competition.

The Clerk of Court is Ordered to issue a Writ of Injunction and enter judgment in accordance herewith.

BY ACCESSION

Title to personal property may be acquired by accession. Accession takes place when one person adds value to another person's property by the application of labor and/or material to such property. For example, A takes his automobile to B's garage for repairs. When B expends labor on the car and puts in new parts, value is added to A's car. A, being the owner of the principal property, acquires title to this additional value by accession. Again, A delivers materials to B under a contract whereby B agrees to make a dress for A out of the material. B, by applying his labor and skill to the material, adds to the value of A's material. In case of a controversy between A and B as to the ownership of the dress, it would be held that A was the owner.

Little difficulty is encountered in the foregoing types of cases, since they arise out of contract. More difficult problems are presented when A converts B's property to his own use and adds value to it by the application of labor, skill, or materials. Such conversion may be made either (1) knowingly, willfully, and intentionally or (2) honestly, innocently, and unintentionally. If the conversion is willful and intentional, the owner of the original property may either recover the property in its improved form by an action of replevin, or recover damages in an action of trover for the conversion of his property. If he sues for damages, the measure of damages will be the value of the property in its improved state and not in its form at the time of its conversion. A wrongful converter may not acquire property by accession, and he is usually unable to obtain compensation for the value which he has added to the property. Only where the amount of value added by the wrongdoer is extraordinary will he be allowed to recover anything for his labor and material.

Innocent or unintentional conversion of personal property raises more problems. Because of the confusion that exists in the cases, it is difficult, if not impossible, to state a general rule that would be applicable to the many different types of situations that may arise in cases where an innocent converter has added value to the property. It can be said, however, that the courts, in arriving at decisions in such cases, usually apply one or both of the following tests: (1) loss of identity and (2) relative value of the property before and after the addition of new value. The older cases generally held that if the property had been so changed that it lost its identity, the owner lost his property to the converter and would have to be satisfied with a judgment for money damages. The owner of the original property was usually allowed to recover the value of the property at the time of the conversion, and not in its improved state. More recent decisions seem to place greater emphasis upon the relative value test. Even though the property has not been so changed that it has lost its identity, if the value has been greatly increased by the labor and/or material of the innocent converter, the courts usually allow him to retain the property in its improved form. Of course, the owner of the original property is allowed to recover damages for the conversion of his property. The amount of damages allowed is determined by the value of the property at the time of its conversion.

Mossler Acceptance Co. v. Norton Tire Co., Inc.
70 So. (2d) (Fla.) 360 (1954)

The petitioner, Mossler Acceptance Co., seeks by certiorari to review a judgment of the circuit court affirming a judgment in favor of Norton Tire Co., Inc., in a small claims court of Dade County, Florida. Denied.

From the facts it would appear that one Bruton entered into a conditional sales contract for the purchase of an automobile from a Florida car dealer. In due course the contract was recorded in the office of the State Motor Vehicles Commission. Before all payments due on the purchase price had been paid, Bruton purchased from Norton Tire Co., Inc., under a retainer title contract, a new set of tires and tubes, giving in part payment of the purchase price the tires and tubes which had been on the car when it was purchased from the car dealer.

Subsequently Bruton defaulted on his automobile contract and the car was repossessed by Mossler Acceptance Company, the assignee of the conditional sales contract. The tire company thereupon sued Mossler Acceptance Company to recover the unpaid balance of the purchase price for the tires and tubes.

The question for decision is whether Mossler Acceptance Company obtained title to the tires and tubes that were on the car at the time of repossession.

No issue is raised as to any reciprocal rights which Mossler may have against the tire company for removing the tires originally sold with the automobile.

SEBRING, J. The principle involved in this case is that of accession, which as a general doctrine is not disputed: "Accessories added to a chattel, if so incorporated as to be incapable of severance without injury to the whole, merge in the principal thing and become subject to the rights of ownership of the conditional vendor thereof. . . ." 1 *Am. Jur.* 201. As respects this principle, in the field of automobile law the rule is stated in varying language: "Under the rules of accession when attachments on a car can be easily distinguished and separated, no change in property takes place, providing the separation can be made without injury to the automobile." Blashfield, *Cyclopedia of Automobile Law & Practice*, Vol. 7A, sec. 4687.

There can be no doubt that "the ordinary repairs upon a personal chattel . . . become accretions to, and merge in, the principal thing, and become the property of the general owner." Blashfield, sec. 4787, supra.

In recognition of this principle, it has been held in Florida that materials and labor involved in repairs to an automobile become a part of the vehicle, and that claims of persons supplying such materials or labor are subject to prior liens on the car. *Fritz v. Miami Industrial Bank*, 143 Fla. 342, 196 So. 689.

In the present case, however, there is no real question as to the priority of liens. The conditional vendor of the automobile undoubtedly has a prior lien on the vehicle, and the only issue is whether certain items as sold by conditional sale have become a part of the vehicle to which they were affixed, or whether they remain independent and separate chattels subject to their vendor's claim. In respect to this issue it is held that "where a seller of an automobile under a contract for conditional sale retakes the automobile upon default of the buyer to keep the terms of the contract, he is entitled to any tires or other replacements which a purchaser placed on the machine while it was in his possession, *provided the title to such parts passed to the purchaser when he acquired them*." Berry on Automobiles, Vol. 2, sec. 1806. "When, however, such equipment is furnished by a third person, *in whom the title remains*, they do not belong to the conditional seller upon retaking the car under a contract recognizing that such equipment is separable and not accession" (emphasis supplied). Berry, sec. 1806, supra.

Where, as in the case at bar, the controversy is between two sellers of chattels, both retaining title to secure payment of the purchase price, we think the more numerous and better reasoned cases hold that tires sold under a conditional sales agreement and placed on an automobile similarly placed do not become part of the vehicle by the principle of accession. As stated in *Goodrich Silvertone Stores v. Caesar*, 214 N. C. 85, 197 S. E. 698, "the doctrine of accession is inapplicable in cases where personal property is placed upon other personal property if the property so placed had not become an *integral* part of the property to which it was attached and could be conveniently detached. . . . We think it plain that one who attaches tires which he does not own to a motor truck which he does not own does not thereby pass title in the former to the owner of the latter."

The rules herein set forth control the present case, in our opinion, and require that writ of certiorari be denied.

BY CONFUSION

Confusion of property exists when the property of one person has been so intermixed with the property of another that it is impossible to separate or identify the property of the parties. If such confusion has been tortiously brought about by one of the parties, the interest of the other party will be protected to the extent of passing title to the whole mass to him. If it has been brought about accidentally or by mutual consent of the parties, they become tenants in common of the mass of goods in proportion to their respective contributions to the mass. For example, if 10,000 bushels of wheat belonging to A and 5,000 bushels belonging to B had been innocently mixed, A would have an undivided two-thirds interest and B an undivided one-third interest in the whole mass. Any loss resulting from such confusion would be shared by A and B in proportion to their undivided interests in the goods. However, if the confusion was due to the negligence of either party, any resultant loss would fall upon him.

BY FINDING

The finder of lost property acquires good title to the property against the whole world except the true owner of the property. By finding the lost article the finder acquires a special interest in it which is good against a subsequent finder or thief. Under the common law the finder cannot sell and transfer good title to someone, as against the true owner, even though such person be a bona fide purchaser for value. However, most states have set up a statutory procedure to be followed by a finder. Such statutes require that the finder advertise the fact that he has found the property. If the procedure set out in the statute is followed and the true owner does not appear and claim the property, the finder's title becomes absolute.

The courts attempt to distinguish beween lost, mislaid, and abandoned property. Little difficulty arises in the case of abandoned property. If A decides that he no longer cares to keep and make use of an overcoat or an old typewriter and discards the article, and later B comes along and takes possession of it, he will get good title to it. This is because A, by abandonment, gave up his title to the articles, and B, by taking possession with an intent of becoming the owner, acquired title to them.

It is more difficult to state a general rule that suffices to distinguish lost and mislaid property. A distinction is sometimes made on the basis of whether the owner parted with possession of the article knowingly or unknowingly. If A intentionally lays an article down, expecting to pick it up again shortly, or if he puts it away somewhere expecting to retrieve it later, but afterwards forgets where he put it, it is said that the article has been mislaid and not lost. But if A inadvertently and unknowingly drops an article and later, when he misses it, has no idea where he dropped it, the article is lost. Another distinction made is based upon where the article is found. If B finds a wallet on the floor in a hotel lobby, the courts hold that the wallet was lost, and B may retain possession of the wallet as against the demands of the hotel for its possession. However, if B finds the wallet on the hotel desk, the courts hold that the wallet was mislaid, and the hotel can compel B to surrender possession of the wallet. In that case it is held that the hotel has a responsibility to the owner of the wallet to protect his property which has been mislaid. The rule is based upon the presumption that the owner of mislaid property will shortly return and claim his property.

The finder of lost property is not entitled to a reward from the owner unless the owner has offered a reward to the person who finds and returns the lost article.

Silcott v. Louisville Trust Company
205 Ky. 234, 265 S. W. 612, 43 A. L. R. 28 (1924)

This was an action by one Silcott (plaintiff) against the Louisville Trust Company (defendant). Judgment for defendant, and plaintiff appealed. Affirmed.

Plaintiff rented and used a safety vault box in the defendant bank. On December 14, 1921, while plaintiff was in the safety vault department for the purpose of using his own box, he found on the floor of the vault department a $1,000 Liberty bond. He notified the agent and employee of the defendant that he had found the bond on the floor, and they agreed that plaintiff should surrender the custody of the bond to defendant for the purpose of discovering its owner, and that in the event the owner was not discovered within six months, defendant would return the bond to plaintiff. After six months plaintiff made demand for the return of the bond, which was refused, whereupon this action was filed.

Defendant denied that the bond was lost when discovered by the plaintiff.

TURNER, J. It will be observed that neither party asserts ownership to the bond, and that the only question is, as between them, which is entitled to its custody. There is a lengthy and interesting discussion in the briefs as to whether under the admitted facts the bond was lost or only mislaid. . . . We are of the opinion that it was in fact only mislaid because it was, when discovered, in the custody of the owner's agent, or at least one owing him the duty of preserving it for him.

The rule is that when a chattel is discovered at such a place, and under such circumstances as to indicate that the owner has involuntarily or accidentally parted with its custody, the finder has the right of custody as against all others except the owner, and especially where the chattel is found at a public place such as a hotel, or bank, or a business house where the public generally is invited and expected to be. In such circumstances the proprietor of the premises occupies no relationship of agent or fiduciary toward the owner, and the right of custody of the finder is, therefore, superior to his. But here the bond was found in a private room of the safety vault department of the trust company—a room to which there was admitted only a limited class of persons, that is, such persons as were patrons of that department and had boxes in the safety vault. They were in every sense the custodian of such valuables as they might have in their boxes. It might be said that they were joint custodians. From the allegations of the answer it must be true almost beyond peradventure that any chattel found in one of these private rooms in the vault, access to which was had only by persons renting the boxes, must have been the property of one of the defendant's customers, and that any property, whether left in the customer's box or left in this private room, was in a true sense in the custody of the trust company, or that at least it occupied toward its customer some fiduciary relationship which imposed upon it the duty of caring for his property, whether the owner was known or unknown. We find then that the bond when found or discovered by the plaintiff, while not in the actual custody of the owner, was in such a place as imposed a duty upon the trust company to preserve the property of the customers.

If the bond had been found by the plaintiff on the street or on the floor in a hotel, or in the public part of a banking institution or business house, or any other place where the general public is expected to be, his right to the custody as against all but the real owner would be clear; but here he finds the bond in a private room, where only a limited class of people have the right to be or can be, and that the class composed of the customers of a trust company which is the custodian not only of the private room where alone its customers may be, but of their boxes in its safety vault. We, therefore, find no difficulty in saying that the bond on the floor when picked up by the plaintiff was in the custody of the defendant as the representative or agent of one of its customers who was the owner. Judgment affirmed.

BY APPROPRIATION

Under certain circumstances one may acquire title to personal property by appropriation. This may take place in the case of wild animals, fish, bees, and other forms of wildlife. While wild animals are running at large and are existing in their "natural state" they belong to no one, unless it can be said that they belong to all the people through the state. The latter concept is well recognized in the enactment of "game laws." However, with the exception of the restrictions placed upon the acquisition of wild animals by the game laws, anyone is privileged to acquire ownership of wild animals, etc., if he is able to reduce them to his possession by actually succeeding in asserting dominion and control over them. But the title thus acquired is qualified and not absolute, for if the animals later escape and return to their natural state, title to them is lost and they are again "unowned." If they are afterward reduced to possession by someone else, he becomes their owner.

If A, while trespassing on B's land, kills or captures a wild animal, does the animal belong to A or to B? The courts of a number of states hold that it belongs to B. In some other states, however, it is held that the animal belongs to A, since he reduced it to his possession.

The foregoing discussion is not applicable to domesticated animals. The law relating to them is substantially the same as for any other chattel. The owner's title to a domesticated animal is absolute, and consequently is not lost if the animal strays from his premises and becomes lost. For example, A has fifty head of cattle in his pasture; one gets through the enclosure and A has no idea of its whereabouts. If B finds the animal on the highway or even in his own pasture, he does not become its owner. Title to the animal is still in A.

BY OPERATION OF LAW

Title to personal property may be acquired by operation of law. This takes place in the case of a foreclosure of a mortgage, a sale under execution, a tax sale, or the sale of the assets of a bankrupt by the trustee in bankruptcy.

REVIEW CASES

1. Aaron Sloin and Mildred Lavine were engaged to be married, and he gave her an engagement ring and a number of other presents of lesser value. They quarreled, and the engagement was broken off by Mildred Lavine. Aaron Sloin brought a replevin action to recover the ring and the other presents. The lower court awarded the ring to Aaron Sloin but awarded the other presents to Mildred Lavine. She appealed her case. Judgment for whom? (Sloin v. Lavine, 11 N. J. Misc. 899, 168 A. 849)

2. Flood, looking in a junk pile, found $100,500 which had been dropped by bank robbers after they had robbed the City National Bank of Clinton. Flood turned the money over to the bank and demanded the statutory reward of 10 per cent for the return of lost money. The bank denied that the money was "lost" within the meaning of the statute. Flood brought suit to recover the reward. Judgment for whom? (Gus Flood v. City National Bank of Clinton, 218 Iowa 898, 253 N. W. 509)

3. The Hobart-Lee Tie Co. entered upon the land of Sligo Furnace Co., cut trees, and made them into railroad cross-ties. They later maintained that they had made an honest mistake. Sligo Furnace Co. insisted that, regardless of the question of good faith, the measure of damages should be the value of the ties. Was this contention tenable? (Sligo Furnace Co. v. Hobart-Lee Tie Co., 153 Mo. App. 442, 134 S. W. 585)

4. Mary E. Mallory on her deathbed turned over a note to her brother, Vosburg, as a gift. The note had previously been indorsed as follows: "Pay to the order of Earl B. Mallory. (signed) Mary E. Mallory." In the presence of two witnesses Mary E. Mallory scratched out the earlier indorsement and made the note payable to Vosburg, who took it and left. Later Earl B. Mallory, her son, claimed the note. Ruling? (Vosburg v. Mallory et al., 155 Iowa 165, 135 N. W. 577)

5. In July Williford purchased from Simmons for a stipulated amount the entire crop of oranges then growing on Simmons' trees. The fruit was to be gathered in October if it was then in condition to be shipped. Williford made one part payment in July and another in October, but the fruit was

not ready for picking until the middle of November. When Williford sent his employees to begin gathering the oranges, Simmons would not permit them to come on the property. For the purpose of determining Williford's legal rights, were the oranges personalty or realty? (Simmons v. Williford, 60 Fla. 359, 53 So. 452)

6. Smyth Sales Corp. sold to La Ferra, on a recorded conditional sales contract, heating equipment to heat an apartment house. Under the terms of the sales contract the equipment was to remain personal property until it was paid for in full. It was installed in such a way that it could not be removed without great damage to the apartment house. The equipment was never paid for. Smyth Sales Corp. sued the Norfolk Building & Loan Association, which had bought the apartment house at forced sale at public auction, to replevy the heating equipment. What holding? (Smyth Sales Corp. v. Norfolk Building & Loan Association, 116 N. J. L. 293, 184 A. 204, 111 A. L. R. 357)

Bailments

23

NATURE OF A BAILMENT

Bailment relationships are extremely common occurrences, though most people do not know them by that name. If you lend a book to your friend B, or leave your suit at the cleaner's or your shoes at the cobbler's, or check your coat at a restaurant, or park your car in a parking garage, you are involved in a bailment transaction. You, the *bailor*, retain title to the chattel, but possession of it passes temporarily to another party, the *bailee*, who is obligated to return it after some special purpose is accomplished. This is what distinguishes a bailment from a sale, in which both title and possession pass from the vendor to the vendee. Several large segments of the business world are founded upon bailment: the sale of goods on consignment; a wide range of rental and storage services; and especially the vast business of transporting goods and merchandise by rail, truck, ship, and plane. In the financial world bailments are also important, especially in transactions in which corporation stocks are pledged as collateral security for bank loans.

Only personal property is subject to bailment. The term is not applicable to real property.

Many of the principles governing bailment transactions were first developed under the Roman law. The early common law courts of England borrowed some of these principles and made them a part of the common law. These have in turn become part of our own law of bailments.

The earlier English and American authorities emphasized two factors in bailment transactions: (1) delivery to the bailee, either actual or constructive; (2) possession by the bailee, either actual or constructive. Most modern bailments include these two factors. But our courts have come to recognize the existence of a bailment in some situations where there has been no delivery of the property. For instance, the courts take the position that there is a bailment in the case of a finder of lost property. It is clear that in such a case there has been no delivery by the loser to the finder; hence, the basis for holding that a bailment exists is the possession of the object by the finder under circumstances which obligate him to return it to its owner as soon as the latter's identity becomes known. A similar situation arises where A's property is blown upon B's land by a windstorm, or washed upon B's land by a flood. B is not required to take possession of such property and protect it, but if he does so the law holds that a bailment exists, though there has been no delivery. Modern authorities, therefore, stress as the essential factor of a bailment the requirement that a person hold possession under such circumstances that the law imposes an obligation to deliver to another. Where delivery has been made by the bailor to the bailee, an *actual bailment* is said to exist; where there has been no delivery, either actual or constructive, to the bailee, a *constructive bailment* exists.

Though in most cases no question rises as to whether a bailment relationship has been created between two persons, much litigation has resulted from borderline cases in which it is not clear whether possession of the property has actually shifted from one person as bailor to another as bailee. Considerable difficulty has arisen in cases where property is stolen from a customer or patron in a restaurant, barber shop, beauty parlor, amusement place, store, or the like. The fundamental rule of law applicable to such cases is that if the customer delivers possession of his property (hat, coat, umbrella, packages, etc.) to the operator of the establishment and the operator accepts dominion and control over it, a bailment exists; in such cases, if the property is lost, stolen, or damaged, the operator must bear the loss. But if possession has not passed to the operator, a bailment does not arise, and the loss is the customer's. The rule is clear enough; the problem is to apply it in the great variety of factual situations that arise.

The crucial question in such cases is whether the operator of the establishment accepted dominion and control over the property. If a customer in a restaurant checks his hat and coat in a check room provided by the management and staffed by an employee of the management, a bailment is clearly created. But if he merely places his hat and coat on an empty chair at his table, or hangs them on a wall hook near by, he retains possession of the articles and no bailment is created. Often operators of restaurants, etc., display notices to the effect that they are not liable in the event that customers' property is lost or stolen. The purpose of such notices is to make it clear that they have no intention of accepting a bailment of such property. If the notices are properly communicated or brought to the attention of the customer, he is bound by them. They become a vital part of his contract with the operator of the establishment. However, other circumstances may as effectively show that there was no intention or understanding between the parties that the operator assumed dominion and control over the property of the customer. Therefore, the posting of such notices has value only to the extent that it throws light upon the intentions of the parties as to the custody and control of the property.

Difficulty has arisen also in cases where an automobile is damaged in, or stolen from, a parking lot or parking garage. Some lack of uniformity exists in the decisions involving such cases. However, the courts do seem to agree that there is a bailment in the case of "parking garages." In those situations the evidence clearly shows an intention of the garage to accept dominion and control of the automobile. More difficulty arises where cars are merely parked on a "parking lot." Such cases are sometimes divided into two groups: (1) cases where the attendant collects the fee from the customer, gives him an identification check, and directs him to a place to park, but the customer parks his own car; (2) cases where the attendant not only collects the fee and tenders an identification check but takes charge of the car, parks it, and keeps the keys. In the first group of cases it is generally held that there is no bailment. Some courts take the position that the operator of the parking lot merely granted the customer a license to park his car on the lot. Other courts view the arrangement as a short-term lease. In the second group of cases it is generally held that a bailment relationship is created and that the operator is consequently liable if the car is damaged or stolen. It is recognized that these are broad generalizations and that intervening facts may have the effect of changing the results.

CREATION OF A BAILMENT

A bailment may be entirely gratuitous, as when A lends his car to his friend B for the day. But in the business world most bailments arise out of contract; that is, the bailor and the bailee enter into a contract which provides for the creation of a bailment. No formality is required in the creation of a bailment. If the bailment relation arises out of a contract, it is of course subject to the rules of contract law. It follows that certain bailment contracts must be in writing under the Statute of Frauds; but it is customary to place important bailment contracts in writing even in cases where there is no legal requirement to do so.

Ellish v. Airport Parking Company of America, Inc.

69 Misc. (2d) 837, 345 N. Y. S. (2) 652 (1973)

Supreme Court of New York

Motorist, who had parked her automobile at self-serve airport parking lot, brought action against operator to recover for unexplained disappearance of vehicle from lot. . . . Judgment for plaintiff, and defendants appealed.

HOPKINS, J. About to leave on a flight from John F. Kennedy International Airport . . ., the plaintiff parked her automobile in a lot operated by the defendant under an agreement with the Port of New York Authority. When she returned . . ., her automobile had disappeared. Claiming that the defendant was responsible for the loss, she brought this suit. The Civil Court granted judgment in her favor, finding that the transaction was a bailment. . . . The Appellate Term reversed and dismissed the complaint, finding that no bailment had been created. . . . Plaintiff appeals.

The plaintiff followed the directions contained in the ticket she received. In her favor, we think that the plaintiff should not be closely bound by the terms of the ticket, for plainly it was a contract of adhesion. The plaintiff was hardly in a position to bargain over the conditions of the ticket and, indeed, the condition of nonliability for theft sought to be imposed by the defendant is unenforceable under the public policy of our statute. . . . Nevertheless, it is still the fact that the plaintiff heeded the warning of the ticket to lock her automobile.

We can draw the reasonable inference from the agreed statement of facts . . . that, since the plaintiff followed the directions in the ticket, she read the other warnings which it contained to the effect that the lot was not attended and that the parking of her car was at her own risk. Thus, any expectation that the defendant would take special precautions to protect her car while she was away could not reasonably have been in her mind.

The actual operation of an airport parking lot must have been apparent to her. Thousands of automobiles were constantly entering and leaving the airport, many of which were using the parking lot that her car occupied. The plaintiff, seeing the confusion and bustle, should have realized the gigantic task which an individual check-out of each automobile would require—a task which she was aware the defendant did not undertake, since the ticket which she received did not identify her automobile.

In the absence of any proof of neglect by the defendant, then, we do not think that the defendant should be held responsible for the loss of the automobile. Other courts considering parking lots at airports have concluded as we do (*Wall v. Airport Parking Co.* of Chicago, 41 Ill. (2d) 506, 244 N. E. (2d) 190; *St. Paul Fire & Marine Ins. Co. v. Zurich Ins. Co.*, 250 So. (2d) 451 [La. App.]; *Equity Mut. Ins. Co. v. Affiliated Parking*, 448 S. W. (2d) 909 [Mo. App.]). "Self park" lots and garages have been said not to create a bailor–bailee relation (see *Weinberg v. Wayco Petroleum Co.*, 402 S. W. (2d) 597 [Mo. App.]). In many cases the retention of the keys by the motorist is considered a decisive factor preventing liability for loss (see 9 Williston, *Contracts* [3rd ed.], § 1065, pp. 1011–1023; 8 *C. J. S.* Bailments § 1, subd. b, par. [2]; anno. 7 *ALR* 3d 927).

We do not find *Dunham v. City of New York*, 264 App. Div. 732, 34 N. Y. S. (2d) 289, in which we allowed recovery for the loss of an automobile parked in a lot at the World's Fair held in 1939, a precedent requiring us to hold for the plaintiff here. In *Dunham*, though the motorist locked his car after parking it and retained the keys, an attendant gave a ticket to the motorist before parking and directed him to the space to be occupied, thereby giving the appearance of the acceptance of custody for the car. Here, instead, the defendant by its procedures of impersonal parking disclaimed any appearance of custody.

The service provided by the defendant to the plaintiff was clearly a space for her automobile to stand while she was away on her trip. That space was located in a lot where many other automobiles were similarly standing and to which the operators of the automobiles and others were given access. The plaintiff was not treated differently from the other automobile operators; nor was she led to believe that the lot would not be open to others.

The plaintiff retained as much control as possible over the automobile. She locked the car and kept the keys. She did not expect or desire the defendant to move the automobile in her absence. We are of the opinion that liability should not be determined by ancient labels and characteristics not connected with present-day practices. It is one thing for the owner of a livery stable to have to explain the disappearance of a horse from its stall to the owner, but it is not at all the same for the operator of a parking lot at a busy airport to have to explain the disappearance from the lot of one of the thousands of cars parked there daily. Unless proof of negligence is present on the part of the operator of the lot, the risk of loss must be assumed by the owner of the automobile.

We therefore affirm the order of the Appellate Term, without costs.

Order of the Appellate Term of the Supreme Court, Second and Eleventh Judicial Districts, entered May 11, 1972, affirmed, without costs.

Agricultural Insurance Co. v. Constantine
58 N. E. (2d) 658, 144 Ohio St. 275 (1944)

This was an action by the Agricultural Insurance Company (plaintiff) against Thomas Constantine, doing business as Allerton Parking (defendant). Judgment for defendant, and plaintiff appealed to the Court of Appeals. Reversed by the Court of Appeals. Certified to the Supreme Court. Judgment for plaintiff affirmed.

On May 7, 1942, Mrs. Joseph Bova, Jr. parked her car in defendant Constantine's parking lot. She left her keys in the ignition lock as she was told to do by the attendant so that he could move the car around for his convenience. When she left the car she was given a ticket upon which was printed the following: "No attendant on duty after regular closing time. Cars left after closing hours at owner's risk. This station will endeavor to protect the property of its patrons, but it is agreed that it will not be liable for loss or damage of cars, accessories or contents, from whatever cause arising." This was never read by Mrs. Bova. When Mrs. Bova returned for her car it was gone from the lot. The car was later found by the police in a damaged condition. The car was insured against fire and theft by the plaintiff Agricultural Insurance Company. The plaintiff paid $154.69 for the repair of the car and by agreement with the owner (Mr. Joseph Bova, Jr.) was subrogated to his rights. The evidence further showed that Mrs. Bova had parked her car in defendant's lot on an average of once or twice a week for five or six years previous to the day in question when the car was stolen.

The defendant contended that it was released of liability, under the terms of the parking ticket.

BELL, J. The relationship between the operator of a parking lot and the operator of a motor vehicle who parks the vehicle in such parking lot, depends upon whether the parking lot operator assumes control over and custody of the vehicle or simply grants permission to park such vehicle at a designated place upon the parking lot. If the parking lot operator assumes control over and custody of the vehicle, the relationship thereby created is that of bailor and bailee. *Sandler v. Commonwealth Station Co.*, 307 Mass. 470, 30 N. E. (2d) 389, 131 A. L. R. 1170. On the other hand, if a designated place on a parking lot is assigned to the owner without any assumption of control over or custody of the vehicle by the operator of the lot the relationship would be that of lessor and lessee *Lewis v. Ebersole*, 244 Ala. 200, 12 SO. (2d) 543.

As has been pointed out in the statement of facts, Mrs. Bova had been parking the vehicle in the parking lot of defendant on the average of twice a week for five or six years previous to the day in question, and on all occasions she left her keys in the ignition lock upon request of the lot operator so that he could move the car around for his convenience. Upon that state of facts we conclude that the defendant assumed control over the custody of the vehicle and that the relation between the parties was that of bailor and bailee.

The great weight of authority in this country is to the effect that a ticket, such as was delivered to this bailor, is a mere token for identification, and printed conditions thereon, purportedly limiting the bailee's liability, become no part of the contract, at least in the absence of anything to indicate that the bailor assented to the conditions before delivering the property to the bailee.

In 6 *American Jurisprudence* 271, Section 177, the rule is stated thus: "Special provisions, to be effective as a modification of the contract implied by law from the bailment relation, must be either a part of the original contract of bailment or contained in a valid amendatory contract. The assent of both parties is necessary to effectuate this result. One party cannot, without the assent of the other, modify such implied contract. Neither the bailor nor the bailee can afterwards impose conditions or limit his liability resulting from such bailment. . . . Modification is sometimes attempted by notice. In order that such notice may result in a modification, the terms thereof must be assented to by the other party." On page 275, Section 179, of the same text we find this language: "Although there is authority apparently to the contrary, the trend of the more recent authorities is to the view that receipt from the bailee at the time of the bailment of what is ostensibly a token for later identification of the bailed property, such as a check for a parcel left at a parcel stand or a numbered identification slip for an automobile left at a garage or parking station, does not bind the bailor as to provisions, purportedly limiting the bailee's liability, which are printed thereon, where his attention is not called to them and he has no actual knowledge at the time of the bailment that they are supposed to become part of the contract. The mere retention of such a check without such knowledge does not bind him to limitation."

From the language of the various text writers upon this subject, supported by the authorities, the following rule may be deduced: Where a bailee delivers to the bailor at the time of the bailment a token or receipt ostensibly for later identification of the bailed property, upon which there are printed conditions purportedly limiting the bailee's liability, such printed conditions become no part of the contract of bailment and the parties remain subject to the usual obligations imposed by law in the absence of anything to indicate that the bailor, either expressly or impliedly, assented to such printed conditions prior to or contemporaneously with delivery of the property to the bailee.

There is no evidence in this record to support the conclusion that the bailor ever assented to or even knew of the printed conditions upon the parking ticket. However, a more cogent reason why this bailor was not bound by those conditions is that they are contrary to law and against public policy. The general rule is well stated in 6 *Amer. Jur.* 270, Section 176, which reads, in part, as follows: "It is now apparently well settled that a bailee for hire cannot, by contract, exempt himself from liability for his own negligence or that of his agents or servants. Contracts limiting liability for negligence in bailments for hire in the course of a general dealing with the public are generally regarded as against public policy." Affirmed.

CLASSIFICATION OF BAILMENTS

Bailments are classified as (1) ordinary and (2) extraordinary. Extraordinary bailments are those involving (1) common carriers and (2) innkeepers or hotels. All others are termed ordinary. The distinction, as we shall see, is important in determining the liability of the bailee.

A second classification, which is important in determining the degree of care that must be exercised by the bailee, divides ordinary bailments into three groups: (1) bailments for the sole benefit of the bailor, (2) bailments for the sole benefit of the bailee, and (3) bailments for the mutual benefit of bailor and bailee.

ORDINARY BAILMENTS

RIGHTS AND DUTIES OF THE BAILEE. There are many kinds of ordinary bailments, and the rights and duties of the bailee depend upon the kind of bailment involved in a given case. If the bailment is a bailment for hire, such as the renting of a car, truck, or other type of personal property, the bailee has a right to use the property according to the terms of the bailment contract. If the bailment is one involving services or repairs, a laundry, cleaning establishment, or shoe-repair shop, the bailee has a right to be compensated for the services which he has performed. If the bailment is one involving the warehousing or storage of goods and merchandise, the bailee is entitled to compensation for his service, according to the terms of the contract. He is also generally entitled to a lien upon the property to secure the payment of the compensation due him.

The bailee's principal duties to the bailor are: (1) the duty to exercise proper care; (2) the duty to redeliver the property to the bailor or as otherwise provided for in the contract.

The courts generally hold that the degree of care required of the bailee depends upon the type of bailment. If the bailment is for the sole benefit of the bailor, only slight care is required; or, conversely, in order to recover from the bailee for injury, loss, or damage of the property, the bailor must prove gross negligence. For example, if A agrees to care for B's pet dog without compensation while B takes his vacation, A is required to use only slight care, and would be liable only for gross negligence. If the bailment is for the sole benefit of the bailee, he must use extraordinary care and is liable for slight negligence. This would be true, for example, where A borrows B's car under an agreement whereby A is to pay B nothing for the use of the car. The most important type of ordinary bailment in the field of business is the bailment for the mutual benefit of the bailor and the bailee, such as a bailment for hire or for storage, or the pledging of securities in the case of a loan. In this type of bailment the bailee is required to use ordinary care. Owing to the difficulty of distinguishing between slight, ordinary, and extraordinary care, some courts have recently taken the position that, regardless of the type of bailment, the bailee owes the bailor the duty to use reasonable or ordinary care under the circumstances. This seems to be a better rule, for it takes into consideration the value of the property involved. Surely it is reasonable to take more care of a valuable object than of one having little worth, and particularly if the valuable object is small, so that it might be lost easily or stolen without the difficulties that would attend the theft of a bulky object. Reasonable care of a diamond is different from reasonable care of a grand piano.

A second important duty which the bailee owes the bailor is to redeliver the property to the bailor or to some third person, according to the terms of the contract. The bailee is liable to the bailor for failure to redeliver as agreed. He is also liable for misdelivery of the property. In either case he has violated his contract with the bailor and must compensate him for his losses. Since his liability is for his breach of the contract, and not in tort, the question of his negligence is not involved, unless the property has been stolen, in which case the matter of negligence becomes important in determining whether he has used proper care.

If the bailment is one for storage or service, the bailee is not privileged to make use of the property. If he does so he is liable to the bailor for such unauthorized use. In the case of a bailment for hire, e.g. the hiring of a car or truck, the bailee is liable to third persons who are injured owing to his negligent use of the property.

Farmers' Bank of White Plains et al. v. Bailey et al.
227 Ky. 179, 12 S. W. (2d) 312 (1928)

This was an action by W. N. Bailey, et al. (plaintiffs) against the Farmers' Bank of White Plains, et al. (defendants). Judgment for defendants, and plaintiff appealed. Reversed.

W. N. Bailey and others were the owners of bonds in varying amounts aggregating about $19,500, which they deposited with the defendant bank for safekeeping. When the bonds were deposited the bank delivered to each of the owners a certificate acknowledging receipt of their bonds and reciting that the bond or bonds would be returned to the depositor on the surrender of the certificate properly indorsed. The bank, without the authority of the owners, sold the bonds and placed the proceeds in a fund known as the "emergency fund." However, the proceeds were not kept separate from the other funds of the bank, but were mingled with the funds of the bank out of which it continued thereafter to transact its banking business. Six months after the sale of the bonds the bank became insolvent and its assets were placed in the hands of the State Banking Commissioner for liquidation. When the commissioner took over, the bank had in its vault $3,037 in cash and other property of considerable value. Some of the defendants and intervenors in the suit claimed priority in their claims upon the $3,037.04.

The contention of the plaintiffs was that the relationship between them and the bank was that of bailor-bailee.

DRURY, C. As the deposits were not to be returned to the depositors in kind, but the particular bonds left with the bank for safe-keeping were to be returned to the owners on the surrender of the certificates of deposit, properly indorsed, there can be no doubt that the deposits were special and not general, and that the relation between the bank and each of the bondholders was that of bailor and bailee, and not that of debtor and creditor. Hence, when the bank fraudulently sold the bonds and converted the proceeds to its own use, the circumstances were such as to create in favor of the bond owners a constructive trust which a court of equity will enforce.

One of the most important rights of the bailor is that upon a termination of the bailment he shall have returned to him the identical thing bailed or the product thereof, or the substitute for that thing. Thus, we see that the primary duty of the bank was to return to the plaintiffs the identical bonds left with it, and the primary right of the plaintiffs was to have their identical bonds; and, after the bank had sold and converted the bonds, plaintiffs were entitled to the product of that sale. They are entitled to the $3,037.04 in the "emergency account." What were the rights of the plaintiffs to the remaining $16,462.96 worth of bonds that were not there, but which it is admitted the bank had sold, and the product of which it had used? The sale of these bonds was a wrongful conversion of the property of the plaintiff to the use of the bank, for the value of the property converted. It is admitted that these bonds were sold at par. Therefore, the bank is liable to the plaintiffs by reason of its wrongful conversion of the subject matter of the bailment, for the amount it received, to wit, $16,462.96, out of other assets of the bank.

Barrett v. Freed
35 A. (2d) 180 (D. C.) (1943)

This was an action by Bettye Freed and another (plaintiffs) against Alva Barrett, trading as Barrett's Transfer Company, and another (defendants). Judgment for plaintiffs, and defendants appealed. Affirmed.

Mr. and Mrs. Freed placed certain household furniture and personal effects with Barrett for storage at an agreed monthly rate. They obtained a policy of fire insurance covering the goods in storage. Later the goods were destroyed by fire. Plaintiffs brought this action against the defendant Barrett and the insurance company. The trial court directed a verdict for the insurance company. Plaintiffs' claim against Barrett was submitted to a jury and resulted in a verdict for $450. Defendants appealed.

Defendants contended that they were not liable for loss by fire because the warehouse receipt expressly disclaimed liability for such loss. Plaintiffs contended that the provision limiting liability was not effective in the instant case.

The warehouse receipt acknowledged receipt of the goods for storage in a warehouse located at "rear 618 I Street, N. W., Washington, D. C.," and contained this notice under the heading "Important": "Are your goods insured against fire? Read your policy and see that it covers the goods in the building in which they are stored." The insurance policy obtained by the plaintiff insured the goods while stored at 618 I Street, N. W., Washington, D. C. and limited protection to loss while the goods were stored there and not elsewhere. The goods were originally stored at that address. However, they were later removed by defendants to another address. The goods were destroyed at this latter location. No notice was given plaintiffs of the removal of the goods.

HOOD, J. The question presented is whether the removal of the goods by the defendant to a place other than that specified in the warehouse receipt avoids the provision of the receipt that he assumed no responsibility for loss by fire. We think it is clear that the contract was for storage in the warehouse at 618 I Street, N. W. Otherwise there would have been no occasion for specifying the location in the receipt. One storing goods has a right to know where the goods shall be stored. Especially is this true where the warehouseman does not assume responsibility for loss by fire. The location and type of buildings affect the risk which the owner assumes.

The defendants advised the plaintiffs to obtain insurance, and, following that advice, they insured the property at 618 I Street, N. W. By the terms of the policy the goods were covered only while stored at that address. The defendant, without notice to the plaintiffs, moved the property to another address, where it was destroyed by fire. Can the defendants, notwithstanding their unauthorized removal of the goods, rely on a condition of their receipt limiting their liability? We think not. The relationship between the parties was that of bailor and bailee. The contract of bailment called for storage at a particular place and the bailees breached their contract by removing the goods to another place. It is well established that if a bailee without authority deviates from the contract as to the place of storage and a loss occurs which would not have occurred had the property been kept at the agreed place, the bailee is liable for such loss even though he is not negligent. One cannot deliberately breach a provision of a contract and rely upon another provision of the contract in an action against him for such breach. The removal of the goods from the designated place of storage was a wilful act on the part of Barrett. Indeed, removal of the goods without notice to the owners (plaintiffs), thereby causing them to lose the protection of their insurance, was gross negligence on the part of the warehouseman (defendants). Judgment for plaintiffs affirmed.

RIGHTS AND DUTIES OF THE BAILOR. The rights and duties of the bailor, like those of the bailee, depend upon the nature of the bailment contract. Of course, he has a right to demand that the bailee treat his property with the proper degree of care under the circumstances; if the bailee fails to do so and the property is damaged, lost, or stolen, he is entitled to be indemnified. Likewise, in case of misdelivery or unauthorized delivery of the property the bailor is entitled to his damages. If the bailment is one for hire or for services, he is entitled to the contract price, or, if no definite sum has been agreed upon, to reasonable compensation. He may also sue the bailee for the conversion of his property or for any other breach of the bailment contract.

The bailor has the duty to warn the bailee of any defects in the property turned over to the bailee if he has knowledge of such defects or if through the exercise of reasonable care he could have found out about the defect. He is not liable as bailor to third parties for injuries which they sustain as the result of negligent use of the property by the bailee. This is so because the bailment relationship does not constitute the bailee the agent of the bailor.

Blankenship v. St. Joseph Fuel Oil & Mfg. Co.

360 Mo. 1171, 232 S. W. (2d) 954 (1950)

This was an action by Clifford Blankenship (plaintiff) against the St. Joseph Fuel Oil & Mfg. Company (defendant). Judgment for defendant, and plaintiff appealed. Judgment affirmed.

Plaintiff sued defendant for $50,000 damages for personal injuries arising out of the rental and use by his employer, Land Construction Company, of defendant's street-sweeping machine.

The Land Construction Company had a contract for rebuilding the streets in Fairfax, Missouri. Defendant was a subcontractor of the Land Construction Company, and plaintiff was an employee of the Land Construction Company. The Land Construction Company regraded or swept and smoothed the street so the oil would adhere; then defendant furnished, applied, and cured the oil; and then the Land Construction Company applied the gravel and rolled and broomed or swept it back and forth on the street.

Plaintiff's principal duty was scattering gravel. On the day of the injury for which he brought this action, he was operating a gravel sweeper. He testified that the "sweeper lurched, or jarred, or hit something, and this caused me to be thrown off balance and to fall sideways." He was caught in the chain and sprockets of the sweeper and severely injured. His leg was later amputated.

The sweeper was rented by the defendant, St. Joseph Fuel Oil & Mfg. Company, to the Land Construction Company. Hawkins, manager of the Land Construction Company, testified that when the construction company rented the sweeper it "took it as it was," "as is," there being no warranties or representations made by the defendant. The agreement was that the construction company had possession and full control over the supervision, operation, and maintenance of the sweeper and would return it in as good condition as received less normal wear and tear.

The plaintiff operated the sweeper for several days prior to his injury.

BOLING, J. The defendant did not owe the plaintiff the duties that a master owes a servant, as such relationship did not exist between them. Plaintiff's evidence established that the Land Construction Company held the contract to resurface the streets of Fairfax and defendant was a subcontractor furnishing and spreading the oil used on the streets. The project, while mutually beneficial, was not a joint undertaking, with plaintiff a servant of the joint contractors. Plaintiff was a third party to the contract of bailment between defendant and the Land Construction Company and his right of recovery must be based on some ground other than a breach of that contract.

Generally, a bailee has the possession, control, and supervision of the thing bailed and is liable for injuries to a third party resulting from his negligent use of the chattel; but a bailor who negligently fails to furnish a chattel reasonably fit and proper for the use intended may be answerable in tort to a third person in instances wherein his own negligence proximately contributes to the damage; for instance, where he furnishes a chattel not reasonably fit for the purpose for which hired. A bailor's tort liability is more restricted than a bailee's. The chattel here bailed, the sweeper, was not inherently dangerous.

Generally speaking, a bailor is not liable to third persons for injuries from the defective condition of a leased chattel which the bailee himself has specifically selected, as here. In the instant case under plaintiff's evidence his employer, Land Construction Company, did not rely upon any representation or warranty, express or implied, of the defendant respecting the suitability of the sweeper for any particular purpose, and none was given. Plaintiff's employer rented the sweeper time and again in 1945, 1946, and 1947, taking it "as is," knowing its condition, which was the same on all occasions, and undertaking to maintain and return it to defendant, less normal wear and tear, with defendant under no obligation whatsoever. Plaintiff's employer selected the sweeper it desired. The bailment of hiring was of the individual article, the particular sweeper, and defendant did not furnish and did not undertake to furnish an article of a particular kind capable of performing a given task, with bailee relying upon defendant's judgment. Consequently, the negligence, if any, in the selection of the article is the negligence of the bailee and not that of the bailor, the defendant.

Plaintiff's employer, the bailee, could have no claim against defendant, arising out of the unguarded condition of the chain and sprockets, and owed plaintiff the nondelegable duty of furnishing him safe tools and appliances with which to work. It follows, that its employee, the plaintiff, a stranger to the bailment, likewise has no claim.

Nash v. Lang
167 N. E. 762, 268 Mass. 407 (1929)

This was an action by Geraldine S. Nash (plaintiff) against William H. Lang (defendant). Judgment for plaintiff, and defendant appealed. Affirmed.

Plaintiff brought this action in tort to recover compensation for damages to her car due to the alleged negligence of defendant.

Plaintiff was the owner of an automobile. She lent the car to her husband a physician, to make a professional call. On the trip he collided with an automobile driven by defendant. The evidence showed that the accident was due to the negligence of both Dr. Nash and defendant.

RUGG, C.J. The question involved is whether a bailor, free from personal negligence, may recover for damage to the bailed automobile resulting from concurring acts of negligence of the bailee and of a third person. Stated in slightly different form, the question is whether the negligence of the bailee, concurring with that of a third person to injure the bailed automobile, is to be imputed by law to the innocent bailor and thus bar him from recovery for the wrong done him.

The decided weight of juridical authority is that the contributory negligence of the bailee, concurring with that of a third person to injure the bailed property, is not to be imputed to the bailor who is free from any negligence. The modern trend is strongly in that direction. *Morgan County v. Payne,* 207 Ala. 674; *Bradley v. Ashworth,* 211 Ala. 395; *Tobin v. Syfrit,* 32 Del. 274.

The owner, if not himself at fault, may recover damages for injury to his property flowing from the negligence of another even though that property be at the moment in the possession of one whose relation to it is that of bailee. The bailee is not the agent of the bailor. The law of bailments is a special branch of jurisprudence under the common law. It is founded upon express or implied contracts between the parties. The delivery of a chattel in bailment, apart from specific stipulation, confers upon the bailee the right to use and enjoy the possession free from control by the bailor, subject to the obligation to do so with care, with due regard to its nature and characteristics and its preservation in safety, and to return it in good order barring unavoidable casualties at the expiration of the bailment. The general title remains in the bailor; the bailee has a special interest for the purpose of the bailment. The bailor may maintain an action against a third person for injury to the chattel or for its conversion. Affirmed.

EXTRAORDINARY BAILMENTS

COMMON CARRIERS.   There are two types of carriers, (1) private or contract carriers and (2) common carriers. A bailment involving a private or contract carrier is an ordinary bailment. A bailment involving a common carrier is held to be an extraordinary bailment. Common carriers transport both persons and goods, but our present study is limited to bailments for the transportation of goods.

A common carrier is a person who holds himself out as being able to furnish transportation service to the public generally, without discrimination, and for proper compensation. As Judge Story once remarked: "To bring a person within the description of a common carrier, he must exercise it as a public employment; he must undertake to carry goods for persons generally, and he must hold himself out as ready to engage in the transportation of goods for hire, as a business, not as a casual occupation." A common carrier usually operates over a definite route and has a definite schedule. A private or contract carrier, on the other hand is free to choose the parties with whom he contracts and to decide under what terms he will contract with each of them.

The liability of a common carrier approaches that of an insurer. Indeed, it is often said that his liability is absolute, but actually there are limitations upon it. Under the common law the common carrier is liable to the shipper for loss of the bailed goods or damage to them, regardless of whether such loss or damage is due to negligence on the part of the carrier or its employees—unless the loss or damage resulted from (1) an act of God, (2) an act of a public enemy, (3) an act of the government, (4) an act of the shipper, or (5) the inherent vice or nature of the goods themselves. It is held that "an act of God" is a natural force "operating without human agency," such as flood, lightning, earthquake, and tornado. Fire itself, if not caused by some "natural force" such as lightning, is not held to be an act of God. In the case of flood the carrier is required to make reasonable effort to remove the goods from danger of damage or destruction. The carrier is excused from liability where the goods are taken by a public enemy in time of war. But this rule is not broad enough to cover the taking of the goods by thieves, or the destruction of the goods in the case of a riot. If the goods are taken by judicial process or commandeered by the government, the carrier is not liable. Neither is the carrier liable if the damage or destruction of the goods is a result of the fault or negligence of the shipper himself. Such loss or destruction might result from faulty packing of the goods, or to a delay in delivery due to misdirection on the part of the shipper. Finally, the carrier is excused if the damage or destruction is due to the inherent nature of the goods themselves, as where a carload of perishable foodstuff suffers normal deterioration, or where an animal which is part of a shipment of livestock is injured as a consequence of its own nature and disposition.

A common carrier may generally limit its liability by special contract with the shipper. Such limitation, however, must apply to losses due to causes beyond the control of the carrier; the carrier may not relieve itself of its liability for its own negligence or the negligence of its employees. It may also limit by special contract the amount of recovery to which a shipper is entitled in case of loss or damage to his property. Under such a contract the carrier agrees to pay the shipper an amount based upon a certain valuation placed upon his property. If the shipper desires a higher valuation placed upon his property and a higher amount of recovery in case of loss or damage to his property, he must declare such value and pay a higher rate for the services of the carrier.

INNKEEPERS OR HOTELS.   At common law an innkeeper is practically the insurer of the luggage and effects of his guests. It is difficult to find a bailment in such a relationship, since the innkeeper can hardly be said to have either actual or constructive possession of the property of his guests. Yet the common law makes the innkeeper liable for the loss or destruction of such property unless the property is destroyed by an act of God, by an act of a public enemy, or as a result of the negligence of the guest himself.

Because of the severity of the common law rule as respects innkeepers, many of the states have enacted statutes that have the effect of limiting the liability of innkeepers and hotel operators for the loss or destruction of the personal belongings of their guests. Often a copy of the applicable statute is posted on the inside of the door of each guest room in the hotel or inn. Such statutes usually provide that if a guest has valuables and wishes to hold the innkeeper to his common law liability, he must deliver such valuables to the innkeeper to keep for him in a safe place until he is ready to check out. If the guest does not comply with this requirement, then the innkeeper or hotel is liable only for ordinary negligence.

Jones v. Ferguson
27 S. W. (2d) 96, 181 Ark. 522 (1940)

This was an action by R. P. Ferguson (plaintiff) against A. Jones (defendant). Decree for plaintiff, and defendant appealed. Reversed and remanded.

Plaintiff began this action to enjoin Jones, his agents, servants, and employees from operating a motor transportation business carrying freight for compensation between Little Rock and Morrilton. Plaintiff holds a license certificate to operate a freight transportation line between Morrilton and Little Rock, and it is agreed that the license certificate is valid and in full force and effect. The license to Ferguson was granted to him prior to the time that Jones made application for a license certificate. The defendant Jones purchased a truck for the purpose of hauling freight for compensation, and applied to the Railroad Commission for a permit or license, and his request was denied. He had paid $400 on a truck before his request was denied, concluded that since his license had been denied him he could not pay for the truck, and took it back to the seller expecting to lose what he had paid. Ten citizens of Morrilton paid for the truck and entered into a contract with the defendant Jones to haul freight for them between Morrilton and Little Rock, and they agreed to pay him the regular schedule rates being charged by truck lines, so long as Jones would haul only and exclusively for them and not haul for the general public. Jones accepted these conditions and agreed to haul freight for the parties signing the contract, and agreed that he would not haul for the public. Several witnesses testified about the contract, and the evidence showed that Jones hauled freight for the persons with whom he contracted and refused to haul freight for any other persons, and did not hold himself out to the public as a common carrier.

The lower court entered a decree for a permanent injunction, as prayed for in the petition, holding that the practice of Jones in securing from certain merchants and shippers, contracts of employment to haul freight does not change the character of defendant's operations as a public carrier. Defendant appealed.

MEHAFFY, J. The only question for our consideration is whether Jones was a public or a private carrier.

A common carrier is not only one that holds itself out as engaged in the business for the public, but it is required to carry for all who offer their goods. It is a public service and is therefore subject to regulation. A private carrier is not. A private carrier does not hold itself out as engaged in the business for the public and is therefore not subject to regulation as a common carrier. The act relied on by the plaintiff does not authorize the railroad commission to regulate private carriers, but only public carriers.

The undisputed evidence in the instant case shows that the defendant did not hold himself out to the public as ready to undertake for hire the transportation of goods or passengers. His general business is not with the public; he does not solicit customers from the general public, and, therefore, under the cases cited, he does not come within the regulatory provisions of the statute.

REVIEW CASES

1. Marsh left a package, containing costume jewelry worth over $2,000, in a railroad station locker while he had lunch. On his return the package was gone. He·sued the locker company, contending that it was under a duty to keep the package safely and had negligently failed to do so. The locker was of the common type which permits the individual user to deposit a coin and withdraw the key. The company retained a right of access to remove parcels left for more than 24 hours. Judgment for whom? (Marsh et al. v. American Locker Co., Inc., 7 N. J. Super. 81, 72 A.(2d) 343)

2. Parris stored his car in a garage owned and operated by Jaquith. Through the negligence of Jaquith's employee the garage burned and Parris' car was destroyed. Parris sued for the value of his car. Jaquith denied liability on the grounds that he had posted a sign over the door of the garage which stated that the garage would not be liable in case of loss by fire. There was no evidence that Parris' attention had been called to the sign. Judgment for whom? (Parris et al. v. Jaquith, 70 Colo. 63, 197 P. 750)

3. Carpenter sued the B. & O. Railroad Co. to recover for damage to a piano, which was properly crated and in good condition when delivered to the railroad. The defense of the railroad was based on the following, written in ink on the bill of lading: "Rel val 500 per cwt," which the railroad maintained meant, when interpreted, a limitation of $5 per hundredweight on the piano. Was the railroad correct in its contention that its liability was thus limited? (Carpenter v. B. & O. Railroad Co., 22 Del. 15, 64 A. 252)

4. Apfel went into Whyte's restaurant and was escorted to a table. A waiter helped him remove his overcoat and placed it on a post near Apfel. When Apfel had finished eating, he discovered that his coat was gone. He sued to recover in damages for its loss. Was there a bailment? (Apfel v. Whyte's, Inc., 180 N. Y. Supp. 712)

5. Wallace left his father's car overnight in Nickerson's garage, receiving a claim check stub from the attendant. Weibers, who was familiar with the operations of the garage, falsified a claim check and put it on the windshield of the Wallace car, retaining the stub for himself. After the night man had come on duty, Weibers returned to the garage, exhibited the stub, and took the car. The Pontiac Insurance Co. paid Wallace $900 for the theft of the car, took assignment of Wallace's claim against Nickerson, and sued Nickerson to recoup its loss. Nickerson contended that he had not been negligent and was therefore not liable. Ruling? (Pontiac Insurance Co. v. Nickerson, 64 Utah 395, 231 P. 445)

6. Kugler delivered certain silk to Ginsberg for manufacture into waists, which Ginsberg agreed to make and deliver within two weeks. The price fixed was $39 per dozen waists. Against this price was to be credited the value of the silk at $1.25 per yard. On Kugler's books Ginsberg was charged with the silk at this price. The silk was sent to Ginsberg with a memorandum reading: "Sent to Alco Waist & Dress Co. for my use only, H. Kugler." While the silk was in Ginsberg's possession his premises were burglarized and the silk was stolen. For purposes of determining the rights of the parties, was there a bailment or a sale of the silk to Ginsberg? (Ginsberg v. Kugler, 174 N. Y. S. 143)

Real
Property

24

HISTORICAL BACKGROUND

Our present-day real property law had its origin in the feudal system of land tenure which was introduced into England by William the Conqueror after his victory at Hastings in 1066. Under this system the title to all the land in England was vested in the king as "lord paramount." While the king reserved vast estates for himself, he parceled out the rest of the land as "feuds," "fiefs," or "fees" to the great nobles of his realm. Under such grants title did not pass from the king to his subject, but certain mutual rights and duties were established between them. For the privilege of having the use of the land the grantee had to do homage and swear fealty to his lord the king and promise to perform certain services, chiefly military, for him. By this process of infeudation the grantee received not title to the land but "tenure," and hence he was the king's "tenant" [1]; that is, he held the land subject to the superior rights of the king. Upon the death of the tenant, the land usually passed to his eldest son, not on the basis of inheritance but by a repetition of the act of infeudation. Later the right of inheritance was recognized.

Those tenants who held directly from the king, called tenants-in-chief, were permitted to grant certain portions of their land to subtenants, who in turn granted some of their land to others. This process of granting land to subtenants was known as subinfeudation. At the bottom of the eco-

---

[1] The words are derived from the French (and ultimately the Latin) word meaning "to hold." Cf. Blackstone: "Almost all the real property of England is by the policy of our laws supposed to be granted by, dependent upon, and holden of, some superior lord, by and in consideration of certain services to be rendered to the lord by the tenant or possessor of this property. The thing holden is therefore styled a tenement, the possessors thereof tenants, and the manner of their possession a tenure." (*Commentaries*, p. 62.)

nomic and social scale were the serfs who actually tilled the soil. The "mesne" or intermediate tenants were tenants to the lord under whom they held and in turn were lords to those who held under them. All were tenants in relation to the king and owed fealty to him. The vast pyramid of land tenure thus created, in which the only absolute owner of land was the king himself, made possible a strong centralized government.

In the intervening centuries the medieval law of land tenure has been greatly modified, so that much real property is now privately "owned." Yet many of the terms used in our modern real property law are traceable to the feudal system of land tenure. The following are examples of such terms: fee, fee simple, landlord, tenure, tenant, tenement, hereditament, seisin, disseisin, escheat, grant, devise, dower, curtesy, alienation and eminent domain.

ESTATES IN REAL PROPERTY

When we speak of an "estate" in real property we have in mind an *interest* in the physical object, and not the physical object itself. The term "estate" has to do with the quality, nature, and extent of one's interest in a given parcel of real property.

Estates are classified, on the basis of their extent, or duration, as (1) freehold estates and (2) less than freehold estates.

FREEHOLD ESTATES

Freehold estates are of two types, (1) estates in fee simple and (2) life estates.[1]

FEE SIMPLE.   An estate in fee simple, or in fee, is the highest possible type of estate in real property. It is an inheritable estate and is not limited as to time. It is alienable, i.e., it may be sold or mortgaged, during the lifetime of the owner, and it may be devised by the owner by will. If the owner dies intestate (without leaving a will) it descends to his heirs at law. All other estates are created out of fee simple estates. For example, A owns a house and lot in fee simple. B purchases a right-of-way over the land and thus acquires an easement. C leases the property for five years, thereby acquiring a leasehold interest in the property. D rents a room from C from month to month. The interests of B, C, and D in the property have been carved out of A's fee simple estate.

At common law, in order to create a fee simple estate by grant (deed), the property had to be conveyed "to A and his heirs." The common law courts took the position that a conveyance which merely named the

---

[1] A third type, a *determinable fee,* does exist, but it is of little practical importance to business students.

grantee was insufficient to create an inheritable estate. This requirement has been somewhat relaxed by statute in many of the states. Under these statutes words "having similar effect or meaning," such as "to A in fee simple" or "to A forever" are sufficient to create a fee simple estate. The statutes of some states provide that if the property is conveyed "to A," without any "words of limitation" such as "to A and his heirs," or "to A in fee simple," it is presumed that a fee simple estate is conveyed. It is not necessary to use words of limitation in order to create an estate in fee simple by will. The intention of the testator, as evidenced by the terms of the will, governs in such cases.

LIFE ESTATES.   A life estate may be created by deed or by will. It is measured by the life of the grantee or devisee, or by the life of some other person or persons named in the instrument. A life estate is not an inheritable estate but terminates upon the death of the life tenant or other person or persons named in the instrument. For example, A, the owner in fee of a house and lot, may execute a deed in which he conveys the fee simple interest in the house and lot to his son B and reserves a life estate to himself. Or A might provide in his will that his wife shall have a life estate in the house and lot and the remainder in fee shall go to "his son and his heirs." Or A might grant a life estate in the property to B, so long as C shall live, with the provision that upon the death of C the property shall revert to A and his heirs. In this case the life estate is "for the life of another" (pur autre vie). The courts have held that a life estate is created if a grant is made to a man "so long as he continues to reside in the city of X."

Life estates are alienable, i.e., may be sold or mortgaged, but in such case the estate still terminates upon the death of the person whose life measures the duration of the estate. For example, A by his will devises a life estate to his wife B, with a remainder in fee to his son C. B may sell her estate to X, but upon her death the estate in fee simple would still come to C. If X wants to purchase the property he may purchase B's life estate and C's remainder in fee; the two estates are then merged, and X has a fee simple estate in possession.

A life tenant has the right to occupy and enjoy the property during his lifetime. However, he must not commit waste or otherwise injure or damage the property. He must use reasonable care in using the property and endeavor to keep it in substantially the same condition as when he became a life tenant of the property. He is entitled to cut firewood for his own use but not to cut and sell growing timber. He may not open a new mine but he may operate a mine which was in operation at the time he became a life tenant. He must pay the taxes on the property. If there is an outstanding mortgage on the property he must pay the interest out of the income from the property, but he is not required to pay the principal.

Sauls v. Crosby
258 So. (2d) 326 (1972)
District Court of Appeal of Florida

This is an appeal from judgment . . . denying life tenant right to cut merchantable timber and enjoy proceeds. . . . Affirmed.

RAWLS, J. On the 9th day of October 1968, appellant conveyed to appellees certain lands situated in Hamilton County, Florida, with the following reservation set forth in said conveyance: "The Grantor herein, reserves a life Estate in said property." By this appeal appellant now contends that the trial court erred in denying her, as a life tenant, the right to cut merchantable timber and enjoy the proceeds.

The English common law, which was transplanted on this continent, holds that it is waste for an ordinary life tenant to cut timber upon his estate when the sole purpose is to clear the woodlands. American courts today as a general rule recognize that an ordinary life tenant may cut timber and not be liable for waste if he uses the timber for fuel; for repairing fences and buildings on the estate; for fitting the land for cultivation; or for use as pasture if the inheritance is not damaged and the acts are conformable to good husbandry; and for thinning or other purposes which are necessary for the enjoyment of the estate and are in conformity with good husbandry.

In this jurisdiction a tenant for life or a person vested with an ordinary life estate is entitled to the use and enjoyment of his estate during its existence. The only restriction on the life tenant's use and enjoyment is that he not permanently diminish or change the value of the future estate of the remainderman. This limitation places on the "ordinary life tenant" the responsibility for all waste of whatever character.

An instrument creating a life tenancy may absolve the tenant of responsibility for waste, unless it is wanton or malicious, by stating that the life tenant has the power to consume or that the life tenant is without impeachment for waste. Thus, there is a sharp distinction in the rights of an ordinary life tenant or life tenant without impeachment for waste or life tenant who has the power to consume. An ordinary life tenant has no right to cut the timber from an estate for purely commercial reasons and so to do is tortious conduct for which the remainderman may sue immediately.

In the case of *In re Paine's Estate*, the Florida Supreme Court incidentally concerned with the timber rights of a life tenant, by dictum, noted that a life tenant without impeachment for waste could cut and sell the timber on the estate. The rule pronounced in Paine conforms with the general authorities on the subject and is limited to a life tenant with power to consume or a life tenant without impeachment for waste. It does not apply to an ordinary life tenant. In the cause sub judice, the trial court was concerned with the rights of an ordinary life tenant and correctly concluded that appellant "does not have the right to cut merchantable timber from the land involved in this suit unless the proceeds of such cutting and sale are held in trust for the use and benefit of the remaindermen. . . ."

The judgment appealed is affirmed.

LESS THAN FREEHOLD ESTATES

Estates less than freehold constitute what are generally called leasehold estates. An example is an ordinary lease of a house for a year. Such estates rise out of contract. They are not treated as real property but comprise the type of personal property called chattels real. The various kinds of leasehold estates will be discussed in the next chapter, "Landlord and Tenant."

ESTATES IN EXPECTANCY

Estates are classified, on the basis of present or future possession, into (1) estates in possession and (2) estates in expectancy. Estates in expectancy involve "future interests." The law concerning such future estates is in general beyond the scope of this study, but the student should understand the nature of the two principal types, (1) reversions and (2) remainders.

An estate in reversion is created when an owner in fee simple, upon granting a life estate to another, provides that upon the expiration of the life estate the property is to revert to himself or his heirs. In other words, an estate in reversion is a type of future interest wherein the residue of the estate is to revert to the original grantor or his heirs.

An estate in remainder is a type of future interest wherein the residue of the estate is to go to some named third person. Such a remainder may be either *vested* or *contingent*. In the case of a vested remainder the right of the person entitled to receive the future estate is certain and definite; in the case of a contingent remainder the right is uncertain and indefinite. If A, the owner in fee simple of a certain house and lot, executes a deed to the property to his son B and his heirs but reserves a life estate to himself, B's future estate is vested. If A had instead reserved a life estate to himself, with a remainder in fee to B if living at the time of A's death, otherwise in fee to C, C would have a contingent remainder.

An estate in expectancy may be created either by grant (deed) or by devise (will).

DOWER AND CURTESY

Under the common law the widow was entitled to a *dower interest* in the real property (but not the personal property) of her husband. Such interest amounted to a life estate (measured by her own life) in one third of the husband's inheritable real property.

Under the common law the husband, upon his wife's death, acquired a *right of curtesy* in his wife's inheritable real property. Such right entitled him to a life estate (measured by his own life) in all the real property of the wife of which she was seised during their marriage. There was one important qualification to this rule, namely, that there must have been a child born alive to the marriage, and capable of inheriting.

The common law rules governing dower and curtesy have undergone substantial change under modern statutes. Since there is a lack of uniformity in the various state statutes, the student should check his local statutes or code.

The statutes of some states have abolished the wife's dower interest entirely and have substituted other rights. Such statutes usually give to the widow an absolute share in the husband's real property, or, in some instances, in all his property, both real and personal. In some states she is given a child's share. Some statutes have not abolished the widow's dower rights, and permit her to elect to take either her statutory interest or her dower interest; or, if her husband has left her something by will, she may elect to take under the will, or to take her dower interest, or to take her statutory interest.

A number of states have abolished curtesy by statute. In such cases the statutes usually give to the husband an interest "in the nature of a dower." The husband and wife are generally treated alike under such statutes.

The following is a typical example. If a man dies intestate, leaving a widow and children, the widow gets one third of his estate (both real and personal), and the remainder is divided equally among the children. If he leaves a widow and parents but no children or descendants of children, the widow gets half of all the property, and the husband's parents get the other half. If his parents are not living but he has brothers or sisters or descendants of brothers or sisters, the widow gets $4,000 or its equivalent and half of the residue of the estate, and the rest goes to the brothers and sisters or their descendants. If there are no other heirs, the widow gets the entire estate. The position of the husband in his wife's estate is the same as that of the wife in the husband's estate. A husband usually may not cut off his wife by making no testamentary provision for her in his will. If he fails to provide for her in his will, she is entitled to her statutory share of his estate, which is the same as if he had died intestate. Or if he makes some provision for her in his will and she is dissatisfied, she may, within thirty days after the expiration of the notice to creditors, renounce the will and elect to take her legal share of her husband's estate. The husband has the same privileges under similar circumstances.

INTEREST IN LAND OF ANOTHER

One may have an interest in the land of another which is inconsistent with the complete freedom of use which an owner in fee normally possesses. Such interests include (1) easements, (2) profits a prendre, and (3) interests arising out of covenants in deeds.

EASEMENTS

One who owns land may possess the right to make use of adjacent land belonging to another, or to restrict the owner's use of it, in such a way as to benefit his own property. Such an interest in the land of another is called an *easement appurtenant*. For example, A and B own adjoining lots. A's lot has no direct access to the street. A therefore purchases from B a right-of-way across B's land to the street. A's interest in B's land is an easement appurtenant. To take another example, C may acquire from his neighbor D an easement of light and air over D's land. Such an easement restrains D from erecting on his land a building or other structure that would cut off light and air from C's property. In all such arrangements, the property that benefits from the easement is called the *dominant tenement* and the other property is called the *servient tenement*. If the dominant tenement is sold or devised, the easement passes with it to the buyer or devisee; it is said to "run with the land," and may not be sold or devised apart from the land. It is held to be real property. It may be created by a grant or a reservation in a deed, by devise, by contract, or by prescription.[1]

A second class of easements, called *easements in gross*, do not share many of the characteristics of easements proper. They are not appurtenant to a dominant tenement, and in general they are not transferable. To illustrate, a public utility corporation may have an easement over A's land for power lines, or the residents of a village may have a right-of-way across a corner of B's land to a public beach.

An easement should be distinguished from a *license*, which it sometimes superficially resembles. A license does not give the licensee any interest in the licensor's land, but is in the nature of a mere permission given to the licensee to come upon the licensor's land for some purpose without being a trespasser. For example, A may license B to take walks in his woodland or to go boating on his lake or to fish in his stream. The license is personal to B; he may not sell it or assign it. A may revoke it if he likes, and in any case it terminates upon the death of either A or B. Most licenses arise out of oral agreement or by implication. One is a licensee if he enters the lobby of a hotel, the elevator of a public building, or a bank or store.

---

[1] Akin to adverse possession (see section entitled By Adverse Possession in Chapter 24).

PROFITS A PRENDRE

One may have an interest in the land of another which entitles him to go upon the land and take away some part of it. For example, A may have a continuing right to go upon B's land and cut and remove timber or hay, or to mine and remove coal, or to quarry and remove stone. Such an interest is called a profit a prendre. Profits a prendre, like easements, are held to be real property. They may be created by agreement, by deed, by will, or by prescription. They may be for a term of years, or for the life or lives of a named person or persons. Though they may be appurtenant to other property, they need not be so.

COVENANTS

An interest in the land of another may be acquired by what is known as a covenant in a deed. Such interests are commonly created where lots are sold in a new subdivision in a town or city. The grantee (purchaser) of each lot may be required to agree to certain stipulations, as, for example, that he will use the lot only for residential purposes, that he will not build upon the lot a house which costs less than a designated sum, that the house shall be set back from the street a designated number of feet, and, in some instances, that he will not sell the property to anyone belonging to certain designated classes of people, e.g. to "persons not of the Caucasian race." When such restrictive covenants are placed in the deeds, the purchasers mutually contract to observe the provisions. Thus, in effect, each property owner has a limited interest in the property of the others.

It has generally been held that such restrictive covenants may be enforced. However, the United States Supreme Court recently held that the enforcement of such covenants forbidding the sale or lease of property to "persons not of the Caucasian race" is unconstitutional.

Van Sant v. Royster et al.
148 Kan. 495, 83 P. (2d) 698 (1938)

This was an action by James W. Van Sant (plaintiff) against Louise H. Royster and others (defendants). Judgment for defendants, and plaintiff appealed. Affirmed.

This was a suit to enjoin the defendants from using and maintaining an underground lateral sewer drain across plaintiff's land.

In the early part of 1904 Laura Bailey was the owner of a plot of ground in Chanute, Kansas. The plot was divided into lots, and lots 19, 20, and 4 were involved in this suit. Mrs. Bailey had a house on lot 4 and resided in same. In 1904 she constructed a private lateral drain from lot 4 to the public sewer system. The drain pipe ran across lots 19 and 20. On January 15, 1904, Mrs. Bailey conveyed lot 19 to John J. Jones by general warranty deed, with the usual covenants against encumbrances, and containing no exceptions or reservations. Jones erected a dwelling on the north 156 feet of his lot. In 1920 Jones conveyed the north 156 feet of lot 19 to Carl D. Reynolds. In 1924 Reynolds conveyed this house and lot to the plaintiff Van Sant. In 1904 Mrs. Bailey conveyed lot 20 to one Murphy, who built a house thereon and later conveyed the title to defendant Royster. The deed to Murphy was a general warranty deed, without exceptions or reservations. Defendant Gray later succeeded to the title to lot 4 upon which the old Bailey home stood at the time Mrs. Bailey sold lots 19 and 20. In March, 1936, plaintiff discovered his basement flooded with sewage, and upon investigation he found for the first time that there existed on and across his property a sewer drain extending across the property of Royster to the property of Gray. The refusal of defendants to cease draining and discharging their sewage across the plaintiff's land resulted in this suit.

The trial court found that all of the original owners of the three properties in controversy, to-wit, Laura Bailey, John J. Jones, and W. P. Murphy, had notice and knowledge of the existence of the private sewer in controversy, that all acquiesced in the use of the sewer by the said parties, that the use of the sewage system by their successors in interest had been continuous from the time of its installation to the present time—a period of more than 33 years—and had been a mutual enterprise, and that the sewer was appurtenant to the properties belonging to plaintiff and defendant Royster and that the same was necessary to the reasonable use and enjoyment of the said properties of the parties.

The drain pipe was not visible on the ground, since it was buried underground for several feet.

Plaintiff contended that the evidence failed to show that an easement was ever created in his land, and, assuming there was an easement created, as alleged, that he took the premises free from the burden of the easement for the reason that he was a bona fide purchaser without notice, actual or constructive. The defendant contended (1) that an easement was created by the dominant estate, by the deed from Mrs. Bailey to Jones, and (2) there was a valid easement by prescription.

ALLEN, J. As an easement is an interest which a person has in land in the possession of another, it necessarily follows that an owner cannot have an easement in his own land. However, an owner may make use of one part of his land for the benefit of another part, and this is frequently spoken of as a quasi-easement. "When one thus utilizes part of his land for the benefit of another part, it is frequently said that a quasi-easement exists, the part of the land which is benefited being referred to as the 'quasi-dominant tenement' and the part which is utilized for the benefit of the other part being referred to as the 'quasi-servient tenement.' If the owner of land, one part of which is subject to a quasi-easement in favor of another part, conveys the quasi-dominant tenement, an easement corresponding to such quasi-easement is ordinarily regarded as thereby vested in the grant of the land, provided, it is said, the quasi-easement is of an apparent, continuous and necessary character." Tiffany, *Real Property*, p. 1272.

The evidence makes it clear that the easement is necessary to the comfortable enjoyment of the defendants' property. If land may be used without an easement but cannot be used without disproportionate effort and expense, an easement may still be implied in favor of either the grantors or grantees on the basis of necessity alone. This is the situation found by the trial court.

Neither can it be claimed that the plaintiff purchased without notice. At the time the plaintiff purchased the property he and his wife made a careful and thorough inspection of the property. They knew the house was equipped with modern plumbing and that the plumbing had to drain into a sewer. Under the facts as found by the court we think the purchaser (plaintiff) was charged with notice of the lateral sewer. It was an apparent easement, as the term is used in the books.

"While there is some conflict of authority as to whether existing drain pipes and sewers may be properly characterized as apparent within the rule as to apparent or visible easements, the majority of the cases which have considered the question have taken the view that appearance and visibility are not synonymous, and that the fact that the pipe, sewer, or drain may be hidden underground does not negative its character as an apparent condition; at least where the appliances connected with and leading to it are obvious." 58 *A. L. R.*, p. 832. Judgment affirmed.

Shelley et ux. v. Kraemer et ux.
334 U. S. 1, 68 Sup. Ct. 836 (1948)

This was an action by one Kraemer et ux. (plaintiffs) against one Shelley et ux. (defendants). Judgment for defendants in the trial court (Missouri), and plaintiffs appealed. Reversed by the Supreme Court of Missouri. U. S. Supreme Court granted certiorari. Reversed.

This case involved the enforcement of certain restrictive covenants directed against persons not of the Caucasian race.

On February 16, 1911, thirty out of a total of thirty-nine owners of property fronting on both sides of Labadie Avenue, between Taylor Avenue and Cora Avenue, in the city of St. Louis, signed an agreement, providing in part: ". . . the said property is hereby restricted to the use and occupancy for the term of fifty years from this date, so that it shall be a condition all the time and whether recited and referred to or not in subsequent conveyances and shall attach to the land as a condition precedent to sale of the same, that hereafter no part of said property or any portion thereof shall be, for said term of fifty years, occupied by any person not of the Caucasian race, it being intended hereby to restrict the use of said property for said period of time against the occupancy as owners or tenants of any portion of said property for resident or other purpose by people of the Negro or Mongolian race."

On August 11, 1945, pursuant to a contract of sale, petitioners Shelley and wife, who were Negroes, for valuable consideration received from one Fitzgerald a warranty deed to the parcel in question. On October 9, 1945, respondents, as owners of other property subject to the terms of the restrictive covenant, brought suit in the Circuit Court of the city of St. Louis praying that petitioners Shelley and wife be restrained from taking possession of the property and that judgment be entered divesting title out of petitioners Shelley and wife and revesting title in the immediate grantor. The trial court denied the requested relief on the ground that the restrictive agreement had never become final and complete because it was the intention of the parties to that agreement that it was not to become effective until signed by all property owners in the district, and signatures of all the owners had never been obtained. The Supreme Court of Missouri reversed and directed the trial court to grant the relief for which respondents had prayed. This court granted certiorari.

MR. CHIEF JUSTICE VINSON. It cannot be doubted that among the civil rights maintained to be protected from discriminatory state action by the Fourteenth Amendment are the rights to acquire, enjoy, own and dispose of property. . . . This court has previously held unenforceable acts of state legislatures when in violation of the Fourteenth Amendment. But the present case, unlike previous cases, does not involve action by state legislatures or city councils. Where the particular patterns of discrimination, and the areas in which the restrictions are to operate, are determined, in the first instance, by the terms of agreements among private individuals, participation of the State consists in the enforcement of the restrictions so defined. The crucial issue with which we are here confronted is whether this distinction removes these cases from the operation of the prohibiting provisions of the Fourteenth Amendment. . . . That Amendment erects no shield against merely private conduct, however discriminatory or wrongful. We conclude, therefore, that the restrictive agreements standing alone cannot be regarded as violative of any rights guaranteed to petitioners by the Fourteenth Amendment. So long as the purposes of those agreements are effectuated by voluntary adherence to their terms, it would appear clear that there has been no action by the State and the provisions of the Amendment have not been violated. But here there was more. This is a case in which the purposes of the agreements were secured only by judicial enforcement by the state courts of the restrictive terms of the agreements. The respondents urged that judicial enforcement of private agreements does not amount to state action.

That the action of state courts is to be regarded as action of the State within the meaning of the Fourteenth Amendment is a proposition which has long been established by decisions of this court. That principle was given expression in the earliest cases involving the construction of the Fourteenth Amendment. Thus, in *Virginia v. River*, 100 U. S. 393 (1880) this court stated: "It is doubtless true that a State may act through different agencies, either by its legislative, its executive, or its judicial authorities; and the prohibitions of the amendment extend to all actions of the State denying equal protection of the laws, whether it be by one of these agencies or by another." Similar expressions in giving specific recognition to the fact that judicial action is to be regarded as action of the State for the purposes of the Fourteenth Amendment are to be found in numerous cases which have been more recently decided. . . . We have no doubt that there has been state action in this case in the full and complete sense of the phrase. . . . We hold that in granting judicial enforcement of the restrictive agreements in this case, the State has denied the petitioner the equal protection of the law and that, therefore, the action of the state courts cannot stand. We have noted that freedom from discrimination by the States in the enjoyment of property rights was among the basic objectives sought to be effectuated by the framers of the Fourteenth Amendment. That such discrimination has occurred in this case is clear. Judgment of Supreme Court of Missouri reversed.

TRANSFER OF TITLE TO REAL PROPERTY

The principal methods of transferring title to real property are as follows: (1) by deed, (2) by will (devise), (3) by descent, (4) by adverse possession, and (5) by operation of law.

BY DEED

At the present time the ownership of most land is acquired by purchase. The title to such property is transferred by deed. In the case of a gift of real property the title to the property is also transferred by deed.

There are two parties to a deed, (1) the grantor (seller or giver) and (2) the grantee (purchaser or recipient). While the payment of consideration is not necessary in order for a deed to be valid, it is customary to mention in a deed the exact consideration paid for the property or (in the case of a gift) to recite some nominal consideration, such as "One dollar and other valuable consideration."

There are two general types of deeds, (1) warranty deeds and (2) quitclaim deeds. In a quitclaim deed the grantor conveys to the grantee whatever title or interest he has, if any, in the property. If he has no title or interest, the grantee gets nothing, in which case he may not hold the grantor liable for damages because of his lack of title. As a rule, a purchaser of real property should not accept a quitclaim deed from the grantor. However, quitclaim deeds are useful in special situations. For example, they may be used in removing a cloud from the title to property. They are also used where a tenant in common purchases the interests of the other tenants in common of real property.

In most situations the purchaser of real property should demand a warranty deed. If a warranty deed is used, the grantor not only conveys all of his interest in and title to the property but also makes certain warranties. Of course, even in the case of a warranty deed the grantee gets only what title or interest the grantor has, but if the title is defective the grantee may hold the grantor liable on his warranties.

The following warranties are usually made by the grantor: (1) covenant of seisin; (2) covenant against encumbrances; (3) covenant for quiet enjoyment. Under his covenant of seisin the grantor warrants that he has good title to the property and the power and authority to convey it to the grantee. Under his covenant against encumbrances he warrants that the property is free from any encumbrances, such as mortgages, tax liens, mechanics' liens, judgment liens, and so on, except those enumerated in the deed, if any. Under his covenant for quiet enjoyment the grantor covenants that the grantee, his heirs, and assigns will have quiet and peaceful enjoyment of the property; and he further agrees to defend the title to the property against all who claim to have a superior title.

Care should be taken in the execution and delivery of the deed. The names of the parties should be correctly spelled and appear in proper form in the deed. The property conveyed should be accurately described. The deed should be signed by the grantor. Some states require that the instrument be signed by the grantor and acknowledged before a notary public; some require that the deed be signed, acknowledged, witnessed, and sealed. The grantee does not sign the deed.

Even though a deed has been properly executed in every detail, title does not pass to the grantee until there is a proper delivery of the deed. Manual delivery of the deed to the grantee or to his authorized agent is safest, since it permits no question as to whether proper delivery has been made. Since delivery is largely a matter of intent on the part of the grantor, whether or not delivery to a third person will constitute a valid and legal delivery of the deed depends upon the facts of the given case. If the third person to whom the deed is delivered is an escrow agent, then the delivery is conditional, and title will not pass to the grantee until all the terms of the sales contract and the escrow agreement have been met. On the other hand, if the grantor delivers the deed to some third person under such circumstances that he thereby surrenders all dominion and control over the deed, there will be a legal delivery of the deed even though the third person is to deliver the deed to the grantee at some later date. But if the grantor makes delivery of the deed to his own agent and continues to exercise dominion and control over the deed, the delivery will be ineffectual to vest title in the grantee. Or if the grantor places the deed in his safety deposit box at the bank, with a note attached directing that on his death the deed is to be delivered to the grantee, the delivery is ineffective; nor will the deed in such case be effective to convey the title to the grantee as a devise (will), since the requirements as to the proper execution of a will were not met.

In the negotiation of a real estate transaction the parties should always place the terms of their agreement in a written contract. All the terms which the parties have agreed upon orally should be inserted in the written contract; otherwise they are not binding under the Statute of Frauds. Since a few days are generally required for the examination of the abstract and for the grantee to arrange for the financing of the purchase, the parties sometimes agree to place their contract in the hands of an escrow agent until they are in a position to make final settlement. Usually the contract is placed in escrow with a bank, an attorney, or a real estate broker. If the parties are able to carry out their obligations under the contract, they usually meet with the escrow agent for final settlement. On the "settlement day" the grantor will hand to the agent a properly executed warranty deed and usually an abstract, and the grantee will make the payment agreed upon and sign any notes and mortgages required under the terms of the contract. If a lending agency (mortgagee) is involved, it will also have a representative present to look after its interests in the transaction. After the parties have performed all of their contractual obligations, the escrow agent will hand over to them the legal instruments to which they are entitled.

An abstract is merely a history of the title of the property. It has nothing to do with the passage of title, nor does it in any way guarantee title. The seller is usually required by the sales contract to "bring the abstract down to date." He employs a professional abstractor to perform this duty for him. He then gives the abstract to the purchaser so that the purchaser's attorney may satisfy himself that the seller has good title to the property. Abstracts have little or no importance where the purchaser is able to secure title insurance, since a title insurance company will not insure title until its own attorneys have determined by a careful search that the title to the property appears to be clear. If the title insurance company later proves to have been mistaken and the purchaser loses the property to some third person who has a superior title, the title insurance company is required to indemnify the purchaser.

It is important that the purchaser immediately file his deed for recording in the proper office at the court house in the county in which the property is located. By doing so he gives constructive notice to everyone that he is the new owner of the property. All third persons are charged with such notice. Therefore, if the grantor should attempt to sell (or mortgage) the same property to another person, the first grantee will be protected if he recorded his deed, even though the second grantee (or mortgagee) were an innocent purchaser for value and without notice.

Costello v. Costello et al.
136 Conn. 611, 73 A. (2d) 333 (1950)

This was an action by Elizabeth G. Costello, administratrix of the estate of James R. Costello (plaintiff) against John R. Costello et al. (defendants). Judgment for plaintiff, and defendants appealed. Affirmed.

In this action the plaintiff, as administratrix of her deceased husband's estate, sought a decree setting aside a deed to certain real estate executed by him purporting to convey an undivided two-thirds interest to their son, James R. Costello, Jr., and an undivided one-third interest to his brother John R. Costello.

On February 9, 1918, Elizabeth G. Costello was married to James R. Costello, who died on August 19, 1946, without leaving a will. On April 1, 1941, James R. Costello signed a quitclaim deed purporting, "for the consideration of love and affection received to my full satisfaction," to convey the property to his son and brother. The deed was prepared by and executed in the office of Attorney O'Brien. Shortly after James's death the attorney took the deed from a folder containing other papers relating to the affairs of the intestate which was kept in a filing cabinet in his office and showed it to James, Jr. After the attorney had communicated with the defendant John Costello the deed was recorded. The intestate in making return of his taxable property had sworn that he was the owner of the property involved in this suit. On April 24, 1941, he gave and executed a fifteen-year lease of the property.

Plaintiff contends that the deed was void for lack of proper delivery.

BROWN, C.J. One may not make a valid transfer of property where the intent is not to convey a present interest, but solely to create interests which will arise at death, except in compliance with the requirements of the Statute of Wills; and any such attempted transfer is void. The defendants could prevail in this case only upon the basis of a conditional delivery. This "is and can only be made by placing the deed in the hands of a third person to be kept by him until the happening of the event upon the happening of which the deed is to be delivered over by the third person to the grantee. . . . But it is an essential characteristic and an indispensable feature of every delivery, whether absolute or conditional, that there must be a parting with the possession of the deed, and with all power and control over it, by the grantor for the benefit of the grantee at the time of the delivery. To constitute a delivery, the grantor must part with the legal possession of the deed and of all right to retain it. The present and future dominion over the deed must pass from the grantor." *Foster v. Woodhouse,* 59 Conn. 568.

What the intestate's intent was, and whether or not he had possession or control of the deed upon or after its delivery to Attorney O'Brien, on April 1, 1941, presented questions of fact for the determination of the jury. The jury found that there was no intent on the part of the intestate to relinquish possession and control of the deed, and rendered a verdict for the plaintiff. We find no error. Judgment affirmed.

Gross v. Housner

322 Mich. 448, 34 N. W. (2d) 38 (1948)

This was a bill in equity by Robert F. Gross and wife (plaintiffs) against Paul Housner, administrator of the estate of Ben Robinson, deceased, and others (defendants). Decree for plaintiff and defendants appealed. Affirmed.

The bill of complaint was filed by the plaintiff for specific performance of an escrow agreement and for other relief.

On March 29, 1946, an oral agreement was made by the plaintiffs with the decedent Ben Robinson whereby the plaintiffs were to become the owners of the premises designated as 1220 Allen Street, Lansing, Michigan, the house and lot owned and occupied by Ben Robinson. Under the agreement the plaintiffs were to keep Mr. Robinson's house, care for him, pay certain specified bills, assume his necessary living expenses from time to time, and, upon his death, pay his funeral expenses, in return for which the plaintiffs were to receive title to the above premises together with the household goods. On March 29, 1946, the plaintiffs went into possession of the premises.

On April 12, 1946, the plaintiffs, R. F. Gross and Elaine Gross, his wife, went with Ben Robinson, a man then 80 years of age, to the office of Walter O. Estes, attorney. A quitclaim deed was drawn wherein Ben Robinson, a single man, conveyed the property to the plaintiffs. Mr. Robinson deposited the deed in the hands of W. O. Estes, attorney, as escrow agent, without reserving any right to recall or control it, but with instructions to deliver the same for record only upon his (Mr. Robinson's) death. The escrow agreement was reduced to writing and signed by the parties.

On April 16, 1946, a disagreement arose between Mr. Robinson and the plaintiffs because the plaintiffs, following doctor's orders, refused to give Mr. Robinson money to buy beer or whiskey. Mr. Robinson obtained intoxicants elsewhere, became unruly, and was finally put in jail. The plaintiffs tried to get Mr. Robinson to return home but he refused to do so. On April 20, 1946, Robinson went to the home of a grandson, Russell Post. Post not having room for Robinson in his home, Robinson returned to 1220 Allen Street on April 21, 1946. On April 22, 1946, Robinson went to the office of the escrow agent and demanded that he destroy "the papers." The agent destroyed the deed and made some notations on the escrow agreement. Robinson died on April 30, 1946. The plaintiffs filed this suit asking for specific performance of the escrow agreement.

REID, J. The trial judge found the escrow agreement valid. He further found that the destruction of the deed in no way affected the rights of the plaintiffs and that there was no evidence of any written cancellation of the rights of the plaintiffs. He also found that the written agreement was not in fact rescinded and that it is binding upon the heirs and administrators of the estate of the decedent. A careful review of all the testimony convinces us of the correctness of the above findings on the part of the trial court. The testimony is very clear that Elaine Gross did not consent to any rescission. She seems to have had an interest by the entireties under the deed.

At the time of making the agreement the decedent was 80 years of age. The plaintiffs did everything within their power to take care of him, and during the brief period of his remaining lifetime they carried out their agreement with him.

"When a deed which has been duly executed has been put into the hands of a third person to be, by him, delivered to the grantee at a future time or upon the performance of certain conditions or the happening of some event, it is said to be delivered 'in escrow' and the deed will not be effective unless the condition be performed or the event happens, and the Michigan courts have held that where a grantor makes a deed to another and deposits the deed with a third party, to be held by such third party until the grantor's death and to be delivered to the grantee named in the deed, the grantor reserving no dominion or control over the deed during his lifetime, a valid delivery is thereby made and an immediate estate is vested in the grantee, subject to a life estate in the grantor." *Cook v. Sadler*, 214 Mich. 582.

In the case at bar, the conditions set forth in the escrow agreement were either fully performed by the grantee or the grantees were prevented from making a full performance either by the actions of the grantor or by the administrator of the grantor's estate, following the grantor's death. Judgment affirmed.

BY WILL

Title to both real and personal property may be acquired by will (testamentary gift). A will may be broadly defined as a written declaration made by a person wherein he states his desires or wishes as to the distribution of his property upon his death. If his declaration (will) is in conformity with the applicable state statutes it will be valid and enforceable.

The person who makes a will, if a man, is called a *testator;* if a woman, a *testatrix.* The persons named in the will to receive property are called *beneficiaries.* A beneficiary who receives personal property is called a *legatee,* and the property which he receives is known as a *legacy.* The testator is said to *bequeath* personal property. A beneficiary who receives real property is known as a *devisee,* and the gift is called a *devise.*

To be capable of making a valid will, a person must meet the requirements specified by the applicable state statutes as to age and mental capacity. Most statutes provide that the testator must be at least 21 years of age; but some specify a lower age requirement for females than for males. Some state statutes require that the testator be at least 21 years of age to dispose of his real property by will but permit him to dispose of his personal property at an earlier age, such as 18 years. Married women, as a general rule, have full testamentary capacity. The testator must be of "sound and disposing mind" at the time he makes his will; that is, he must be mentally competent and he must have testamentary intent.

The statutes of the various states set out certain formal requirements for making a will. While these requirements vary from state to state, they are, in general, as follows: (1) a will must be in writing; (2) it must be signed (and in many jurisdictions sealed) by the testator or testatrix; (3) it must be attested by two (in some states three) witnesses; and it must be published by the testator or testatrix. A will may be written in longhand, typed, or printed. Printed form wills may be used. The statutes require that the signature of the testator be placed at the end of the will. The signature of the testator must be followed by an *attestation clause*, which states the formalities that were followed in the execution of the will and is signed by the witnesses to the will. The statutes generally require that the testator must sign in the presence of the witnesses, and that the witnesses must sign in the presence of the testator and of each other. The requirement of publication is met by the testator's announcing to the witnesses that the document which they are about to sign is his last will and testament. It is not required that the witnesses read the will or know its contents. One who is named as a beneficiary in a will should not witness the will, for if he does so he may be disqualified to take under the will. A beneficiary, however, may serve as executor of the will.

A testator may, at his discretion, revoke his will. He may destroy it or cancel it by methods usually described explicitly in the statutes. Or he may revoke it by executing a new will. While it is customary to state in a new will that all previous wills are revoked and of no effect, if the testator fails to make such a statement in the new will the courts have generally held that the execution of a new will has the legal effect of revoking all previous wills. Since the testator may revoke his will at his discretion, beneficiaries named in a will have no assurance before the death of the testator that they will receive anything. They have no "rights" under the will until the testator's death.

A testator may also change or modify his will by adding to it a *codicil*. A codicil, to be effective, must be executed with the same formalities as the will itself. The testator may not modify his will by merely crossing out parts of it or inserting names or clauses.

A number of the states recognize by statute what are called *holographic wills*. A holographic will is one *wholly* written in the handwriting of the testator and signed by him. Some states, but not all, require also that the will be dated in his hand. A holographic will need not meet the requirements of formal execution and attestation, but some of the state statutes require that the will be witnessed. It is not required that the signature of the testator appear at the end of the will, as in the case of ordinary wills.

If the testator signs his name on the instrument, and it appears that he intended it to be his signature, it will constitute a valid signature.[1]

Under narrowly restricted conditions most of the states recognize oral wills, called *nuncupative wills*. Almost all such states permit only personal property to be disposed of by oral will, and some states place a limit upon the amount of personal property that may be so disposed of. Some states recognize nuncupative wills only in the case of soldiers and sailors in active military service. The oral declaration must be made during the testator's last illness. He must declare his words to be his will and ask one or more persons to bear witness to his declaration. Usually the testimony of the witness is required to be reduced to writing within a designated period of time after the declaration.

Bryan v. Bigelow, et al.

17 Conn. 604, 60 *Atlantic Reporter*, 266 (1905)

Supreme Court of Errors of Connecticut

Appeal from Superior Court, New Haven County; Robinson, J.

Bill by William J. Bryan, as executor of the will of Philo S. Bennett, deceased, against Delia A. Bigelow, William J. Bryan, individually and as trustee, and others. A demurrer to the substituted answer of Bryan as a defendant having been sustained, and a motion by him for leave to file a cross-complaint having been denied, the case was heard, facts found, and judgment rendered that the clause in the will containing a bequest of $50,000 in trust to testator's widow was inoperative, and that the sum became a part of the residuary estate, from which defendant Bryan appeals. Affirmed.

The plaintiff is the executor of the will of Philo S. Bennett, late of New Haven, who died August 9, 1903, leaving a will dated May 22, 1900. The defendants are William J. Bryan as an individual and as a trustee under the will, Mrs. Mary Baird Bryan as trustee under the will, Grace Imogene Bennett widow of the testator, and the other residuary legatees under section 34 of the will. In his complaint the executor asks the superior court to settle the construction of the will in certain particulars, to direct the plaintiff as to his duty in the matters relating thereto, and to order the defendants to set forth their several claims, and submit them to the decision of the court.

The second, twelfth, and thirty-fourth sections of the will are as follows:

"Second. I give and bequeath to my wife Grace Imogene Bennett, the sum of seventy-five thousand dollars ($75,000) absolutely, together with three houses in Bridgeport, Conn., located at 144, 146, 148 Maple Street. Also, all paintings, pictures, furniture, jewelry, bric a brac, etc., which I possess, the

---

[1] The following states have statutes which recognize holographic wills as valid, if they are executed in compliance with such statutes: Arizona, Arkansas, Kentucky, Louisiana, Mississippi, North Carolina, Tennessee, Texas, West Virginia, Virginia, California, Idaho, Montana, Nevada, North Dakota, Oklahoma, South Dakota, Utah, and Wyoming.

same to be received by her in lieu of dower or of her statutory interest in my estate."

"Twelfth. I give and bequeath unto my said wife, Grace Imogene Bennett, the sum of fifty thousand dollars ($50,000), in trust however, for the purposes set forth in a sealed letter which will be found with the will."

"Thirty-fourth. All the rest and residue of my estate of every nature and description I give and bequeath to my wife, my sister Delia A. Bigelow, and my half-brother, George A. Cable, to be divided among them as follows:

"One-half to my said wife, and one-fourth each to my said sister and said half-brother."

The said residuary legatees allege in their answer and claim that paragraph 12 of the will is invalid, that the $50,000 named therein is disposed of by the thirty-fourth section of the will, and that the executor should be directed to pay the same to said residuary legatees, as provided in said section 34.

Mr. Bryan, as a defendant and claimant in his individual capacity, and as trustee under the trust alleged to have been created by the sealed letter referred to in section 12 of the will, alleges in his answer and claim that section 12 of the will is valid, and that the executor should pay the $50,000 named therein to Grace Imogene Bennett, in trust to pay the same to Mr. Bryan, and that Mr. Bryan is entitled to receive said sum, either as an individual or a trustee under the trust described in said sealed letter. Said answer and claim further alleges: That after the death of Mr. Bennett there was found in his box in the vault of the Merchants' Safe Deposit Company, in New York City, with the will, a sealed envelope, bearing this superscription in Mr. Bennett's handwriting: "Mrs. P. S. Bennett. To be read only by Mrs. Bennett, and by her alone, after my death. Philo S. Bennett," which envelope inclosed the following letter, in the handwriting of Mr. Bennett, made Exhibit 1 of said answer and of the finding of facts:

"New York, 5/22/1900.

"My dear Wife:

"In my will just executed I have bequeathed to you seventy-five thousand dollars (75,000) and the Bridgeport houses, and have in addition to this made you the residuary legatee of a sum which will amount to twenty-five thousand more. This will give you a larger income than you can spend while you live, and will enable you to make bountiful provision for those you desire to remember in your will. In my will you will find the following provisions:

"I give and bequeath unto my wife, Grace Imogene Bennett, the sum of fifty thousand dollars (50,000), in trust, however, for the purpose set forth in a sealed letter which will be found with this will.

"It is my desire that the fifty thousand dollars conveyed to you in trust by this provision shall be by you paid to William Jennings Bryan, of Lincoln, Nebraska, or to his heirs if I survive him. I am earnestly devoted to the political principles which Mr. Bryan advocates, and believe the welfare of the nation depends upon the triumph of those principles. As I am not as able as he to defend those principles with tongue and pen, and as his political work prevents the application of his time and talents to money making, I consider it a duty, as

I find it a pleasure, to make this provision for his financial aid, so that he may be more free to devote himself to his chosen field of labor. If for any reason he is unwilling to receive this sum for himself, it is my will that he shall distribute the said sum of fifty thousand dollars according to his judgment among educational and charitable institutions. I have sent a duplicate of this letter to Mr. Bryan, and it is my desire that no one excepting you and Mr. Bryan himself shall know of this letter and bequest. For this reason I will place the letter in a sealed envelope, and direct that it shall be opened only by you, and read by you alone. With love and kisses,

"P. S. Bennett."

—That after the death of Mr. Bennett there was found in the safe at his place of business in New York, in an envelope bearing the superscription in Mr. Bennett's handwriting, "Copy of letter in Safe Deposit Co. Vault Wool Exchange," the document made Exhibit 2 in the answer and finding, being a typewritten duplicate of said Exhibit 1, with the omission of the signature and of the last four words of said Exhibit 1. That Exhibit 2 was drawn up at the same time that the will was written, and before the will was executed. That Exhibit 1 was copied from Exhibit 2, and that said acts of drawing up, executing, and depositing the will and said Exhibits 1 and 2 were parts of one transaction.

Paragraph 12 of said claim states that, though counsel are not informed as to the fact, it is averred that Mr. Bennett, during his lifetime, informed his wife of the contents of section 12 of the will, and of his desires as to the trust therein mentioned, as expressed in Exhibit 1. Said answer also asks for a disclosure as to said alleged facts. The trial court sustained a demurrer to so much of said answer and claim as alleges said facts, upon the ground, in substance, that, in so far as they were pertinent to the questions to be considered in this proceeding, the defendants were entitled to prove them without pleading them.

Upon objection by the other claimants, the superior court denied the motion of the claimant Bryan for leave to file a cross-complaint containing the allegations of fact and request for a disclosure made in said answer.

The following are among the facts stated in the finding: Mr. Bennett hired a box vault of the Merchants' Safe Deposit Company in the Wool Exchange, in New York, which he first opened May 23, 1900, at 11:07 A.M., and it was never opened again until after his death, when it contained only the will and the sealed envelope bearing the subscription and inclosing the letter Exhibit 1, as described in the answer of Mr. Bryan, the will and envelope not being physically attached together. Mr. Bennett went to Mr. Bryan's home in Nebraska, arriving there several days before May 22, 1900, and having with him memoranda for his will, which was thereupon drawn up, as was also Exhibit 2. Both said documents, the will not having then been dated or executed, were taken away by Mr. Bennett some days before May 22, 1900. A few days after May 22, 1900, there came by mail to Mr. and Mrs. Bryan an envelope inclosing Exhibit 3, being a copy of Exhibit 1, and also a letter to Mr. and one to Mrs. Bryan, the material parts of which, called respectively Exhibits 4 and 5, are as follows:

EXHIBIT 4

"New York, 5/22/1900.

"My dear Mr. Bryan:

"I inclose a duplicate letter, which I have placed in a sealed envelope, with instructions that it shall be opened by Mrs. Bennett, and read by her when alone. I have stated therein the reasons for the provisions made for you, and I sincerely hope you will accept the sum of fifty thousand dollars for yourself. Give ten thousand dollars to your wife, and invest fifteen thousand dollars for the benefit of your three children, giving five thousand dollars to each, whenever you think it wise to turn the money over to them.

"If for any reason you decline to receive the entire sum, or any part thereof, I shall trust you to distribute the same according to your judgment among educational and charitable institutions.

"Sincerely yours,

P. S. Bennett."

EXHIBIT 5

"New York, 5/22/1900.

"Dear Mrs. Bryan:

"Inclosed you will find copy of letter left with will for Mrs. Bennett; also, letter to Mr. Bryan. It affords me a vast amount of pleasure and satisfaction to make this provision for you, Mr. Bryan, and the children. My will is deposited in one of the 'Merchants' Safe Deposit Co.' boxes, located in the 'Wool Exchange,' on West Broadway, New York City. Mr. Sloan, my partner, has a box there, in which he keeps his private papers, &c. . . .

"With much regard, I am sincerely yours,

"P. S. Bennett."

Exhibit 2 was found, after Mr. Bennett's death, in his safe at his place of business, in an envelope superscribed as stated in the answer of Mr. Bryan. Neither the will nor Exhibit 1 were ever in Mr. Sloan's safe deposit box.

Upon the trial in the superior court the claimant Mr. Bryan offered in evidence Exhibit 1, and also the other exhibits in connection therewith, including the superscriptions upon said envelopes. Among the purposes for which such evidence was offered are these, in substance: (1) To prove a declaration by the testator of the trust created by section 12 of the will; (2) to rebut any claim of a resulting trust in favor of the residuary legatees; (3) to prove the existence of Exhibit 1 at the time, and of its equivalent, Exhibit 2, prior to the time, of the execution of the will; (4) to prove the existence of and to identify the beneficiary capable of taking and entitled to take the legacy given by section 12 of the will; (5) to enable the court to properly construe section 12 of the will, and to establish the validity of the bequest made in that section. This evidence was excluded by the court.

*   *   *

HALL, J. (after stating the facts). This is an action brought by William J. Bryan as executor of the will of Philo S. Bennett to determine the construction to be placed upon a certain clause of Mr. Bennett's will upon the ground that there is such a question as to the proper construction of said clause that the executor cannot safely discharge the duties of his office without the advice and protection of a court of chancery. The questions presented by this appeal are stated in the following inquiry propounded by the executor in paragraph 9 of the complaint: "Are the bequests and trusts mentioned in section 12 of said will valid, and is said Grace Imogene Bennett, in said section named, or are the residuary legatees, entitled to receive the fifty thousand dollars therein mentioned, or is William J. Bryan entitled to receive the said sum?" The real question to be considered is whether the trust upon which the $50,000 was given to Mrs. Bennett has been lawfully created. If it has not, the money should not be paid to her, either as an individual or as a trustee. Mrs. Bennett herself makes no claim, either as an individual or as a trustee, to any interest in the money as a legatee under the twelfth clause of the will. If the trust upon which the sum is given to her by paragraph 12 is neither disclosed by the will itself nor created by the sealed letter, the gift to her as trustee becomes inoperative, and the beneficial interest in the sum named results to the residuary legatees named in section 34 of the will. *Perry on Trusts* (5th Ed.) §§ 92, 150; *Lewin on Trusts* (Am. Ed.) 1888, with notes 144; *Phelps v. Robbins*, 40 Conn. The controversy is therefore one between Mr. Bryan and an individual, and as an alleged trustee under the sealed letter Exhibit 4 upon the one hand, and the residuary legatees, of whom Mrs. Bennett is one, upon the other; and issue between them being whether a valid bequest of the $50,000 named in the sealed letter and in section 12 of the will has been made to Mrs. Bennett in trust either by force of the sealed letter itself or in the twelfth paragraph of the will, or by the sealed letter and said paragraph together.

The sealed letter is an instrument of both a dispositive and testamentary character. It directs to whom the money shall be paid by Mrs. Bennett, and it directs that it shall be paid after the death of the testator, without giving any interest in the sum named to take effect during his life. No effect can be given to this letter as a part of the will, even if the evidence offered proves that it was in existence, and known to the testator, at the time the will was executed. We held in *Bryan's Appeal*, 77 Conn. 240–247, 58 Atl. 748, that there was no such clear explicit reference in the will itself to any specific document as to incorporate the sealed letter into the will, and that such defective reference in the will could not be helped out by parol evidence. The letter cannot operate as a declaration of the trust upon which the money was bequeathed to Mrs. Bennett. Our statute of wills is not only directory, but prohibitory. *Irwin's Appeal*, 33 Conn. 128. To treat this letter as an operative declaration of trust would be, in effect, to hold that a testamentary disposition of property could be made by an instrument not executed in conformity with the statute regulating such transfers of property. Mr. Perry, in his treatise on the law of *Trust and Trustee*, vol. 1, § 92 (5th Ed.), in discussing the question of whether a parol expression of intention by a testator to create a trust, though void as a devise or bequest, may yet be good as a declaration of trust, and quoting with approval the language of *Lewin on Trusts*, says: "We may therefore safely assume as an established rule that, if the intended disposition be of a testamentary character, and not to take effect in the testator's lifetime, but ambulatory until his death, such disposition is inoperative, unless it be declared in writing in strict conformity with the statutory enactments regulating devises and bequests."

*   *   *

But it is urged that the twelfth clause of the will and the sealed letter, read together, clearly show the purposes to which the testator intended the $50,000 given to Mrs. Bennett in trust should be devoted by her, and show a valid bequest to her as trustee, and that the sealed letter and other exhibits offered in evidence should have been received for the purpose of showing such intention of the testator, and of thus enabling the court to properly construe the will. It may be conceded that such an intention of Mr. Bennett is clearly shown by these exhibits, but it does not follow that they are for that reason admissible as evidence, or that they can be considered in construing the will. While extrinsic evidence may be admitted to identify the devisee or legatee named, or the property described in a will, or to make clear the doubtful meaning of language used in a will, it is never admissible, however clearly it may indicate the testator's intention, for the purpose of showing an intention not expressed in the will itself, or for the purpose of proving a devise or bequest not contained in the will. "It is a settled principle that the construction of a will must be derived from the words of it, and not from extrinsic averment."

*   *   *

The evidence offered was not admissible upon the ground of a latent ambiguity in the language of the will. There is no latent ambiguity in the language of paragraph 12. What the testator has said in this clause of the will is clearly stated; and what he intended to say in this paragraph concerning the gift of the beneficial interest in the $50,000 and the name of the beneficiary he has evidently fully stated. We are unable to determine from the language of the will what use it was intended Mrs. Bennett should make of the sum bequeathed to her as trustee, not because the meaning of the language of paragraph 12 is doubtful or obscure, but because the language used does not state or assume to state the use which it was intended Mrs. Bennett should make of the sum so given to her in trust. In the words of the sealed letter, "It is my desire that the $50,000 conveyed to you in trust by this provision [paragraph 12 of the will] shall be by you paid to William Jennings Bryan of Lincoln, Nebraska, or to his heirs if I survive him," and not in the will, we discover the real gift which the testator intended to make. The sealed letter and Exhibits 2, 3, 4, and 5 were inadmissible for the purposes of construction and interpretation because the intended bequest described in them is not contained in the will. The gift itself fails because it is an attempted testamentary disposition of property by an instrument not executed as a will, and which we have held not to be a part of it, without disclosing in the duly executed will either the purpose of the bequest to the so-called trustee or the name of the person who was to receive the benefit of the gift.

The excluded evidence was not admissible to rebut a resulting trust to the residuary legatees. "The resulting trusts which can be rebutted by extrinsic evidence are those claimed upon a mere implication of law, not those arising on the failure of an express trust for imperfection or illegality." *Woodruff v. Marsh*, 63 Conn. 125–141, 26 Atl. 846, 852, 38 *Am. St. Rep.* 346. The cases of *Dowd v. Tucker*, 41 Conn. 197, *Buckingham v. Clark*, 61 Conn. 204, 23 Atl. 1085, and other cases in which trusts ex maleficio have been declared against persons who have obtained property by promising to apply it to certain purposes, have been cited as applicable to this proceeding. Assuming that while the $50,000 was still in the hands of the executor the superior court as a court of equity might in this proceeding, in directing to whom the money should be paid, have considered whether, if paid to Mrs. Bennett or the residuary legatees, they, or either of them, could be held to be trustees ex maleficio by reason of an express or implied promise to apply the money to the purposes named in the sealed letter, we cannot find error in the judgment of the superior court, since neither the evidence excluded nor the facts proved show any agreement, express or implied, by Mrs. Bennett or the other residuary legatees to accept the money upon the trust described in Exhibit 1, or that during the lifetime of the testator they even knew of any of the provisions of the twelfth clause of the will. Proof that Mrs. Bennett possessed such knowledge was not prevented by the rulings of the court sustaining the demurrer to Mr. Bryan's answer and denying his motion for leave to file a cross-complaint. These rulings were not upon the ground that evidence of that fact was inadmissible; and an opportunity was apparently given to the claimant Mr. Bryan during the trial of the case to offer the evidence of Mrs. Bennett, without objection, as to the facts upon which a disclosure was asked for. Further discussion of these rulings is unnecessary, since they did not prevent the claimant Mr. Bryan from proving upon the trial all the facts alleged in his answer and cross-complaint.

There is no error. The other Judges concurred.

BY DESCENT

If a person dies intestate (without leaving a will) his property goes to his heirs and next of kin under the statutes of descent and distribution. The decedent's personal property is distributed according to the statutes of the state of his residence; his real property, according to the statutes of the state or states in which his real property is located.

Estates of decedents are administered by special courts created to handle such estates. These courts are usually called probate courts, but in some states they are known by some other name, such as orphans' courts or surrogate courts. If the decedent dies intestate, administration is usually commenced by someone's filing an application or petition with the court for the appointment of an *administrator*. If the petition is granted, the court issues *letters of administration* to the person who is appointed as administrator. If the decedent dies testate he usually names or nominates someone in his will to act as *executor* of his estate. If the person named does not refuse to serve, and if the court finds no objection to his appointment, such person will be appointed as executor and will receive *letters testamentary* from the court. Executors and administrators are called personal representatives of the decedent's estate. Administrators are in almost all cases required to file a bond. Testators often specify in their wills that the named executor or executors are not required to furnish bond, and the court will respect such a wish unless it feels that a bond is necessary to protect the interests of the beneficiaries and creditors.

The personal representative is usually required, by statute, to publish a notice of his appointment and to notify creditors to file their claims against the estate. Within the time specified in the statute the personal representative must make and file an inventory of the decedent's personal property. This is followed by an appraisal of the decedent's property by appraisers appointed by the court. The personal representative may pay or refuse to pay claims against the estate, depending upon whether he considers such claims valid. He must, if necessary, file suit to recover debts and obligations owed to the estate, and make every effort to care for and preserve the assets of the estate. He must pay any necessary state and federal estate and inheritance taxes and see that necessary income tax returns are filed and the taxes paid. When all such affairs have been administered, the personal representative makes a final accounting to the court. If the court is satisfied, it will order the distribution of the remaining assets of the estate according to the terms of the will, or, if the decedent died intestate, to the heirs at law. When this distribution has been accomplished, the personal representative is discharged by the court.

If one dies without leaving any property, or if all of the property, both personal and real, is owned jointly or by the entireties, so that ownership passes automatically to another, no administration of his estate is necessary. But if the decedent owns property individually, administration is usually necessary, where there are unsatisfied creditors of the decedent, or where his estate contains real property. Creditors may force administration of the estate, and administration is necessary in order to clear the title to the real property if the property was not held by the decedent and his wife as tenants by the entireties. It is also necessary to the transference of the title to securities, automobiles, bank accounts, and the like, not owned jointly by the decedent and his wife.

In re Garrett's Estate

Appeal of Platte, Appeal of Wismiller,

Appeal of Hoover, Appeal of Marsh et al.

372 Pa. 438, 94 A. (2d) 357 (1953)

Supreme Court of Pennsylvania

Rehearing Denied Feb. 13, 1953

Proceedings in the matter of estate of decedent, wherein certain claimants appealed from the definitive decree of the Orphans' Court, Philadelphia County, No. 2552 of 1932, Charles Klein, P.J., rejecting their claims and awarding the decedent's residuary estate to certain named next of kin. The Supreme Court, Nos. 188–191, 195, 200, 208, 214–219, and 226, January term, 1952, Per Curiam, held, inter alia, that evidence sustained dismissal of the claims. Affirmed.

PER CURIAM. Henrietta E. Garrett died a resident of Philadelphia County on November 16, 1930, intestate as to her residuary estate of over $17,000,000. Nearly 26,000 claims were filed in the Court below by persons claiming the estate as next of kin. The Orphans' Court appointed a Master and Examiners who held some 2,000 hearings and took the testimony of over 1,100 witnesses. The record composed mainly of testimony and exhibits, totals 390 volumes covering over 115,000 pages. After a painstaking examination of the thousands of claims which were presented, the Master submitted to the Orphans' Court on September 18, 1950, a 900 page report which included 2,077 findings of fact and 36 conclusions of law. The Master found that the decedent, Henrietta E. Garrett, nee Schaeffer, was survived by three first cousins, Herman Adolph Kretschmar, Howard Sigismund Kretschmar and Johann Peter Christian Schaeffer I, and that these relatives were entitled, as next of kin, to her estate under the Intestate Act of June 7, 1917, *P. L.* 429, 20 *P. S.* § 1 *et seq.*

Judge Klein, who sat as Auditing Judge in the Orphans' Court, adopted all of the findings of fact and all of the conclusions of law found or made by the Master (except one which is immaterial in the determination of this appeal); his adjudication covering 369 pages was confirmed absolutely by the Orphans' Court on January 10, 1952; the schedule of distribution filed pursuant to the adjudication was approved on January 31, 1952.

On June 30, 1952, all the appeals to this Court as of the above term and numbers were consolidated for the purpose of argument and disposition. What is said hereinafter in this Opinion will apply in general to all the appeals. . . .

The Attorney General of the Commonwealth of Pennsylvania vigorously contended for 15 years that Henrietta E. Garrett died without leaving any next of kin to survive her and consequently her residuary estate escheated to the Commonwealth. Thereafter a compromise was executed which in effect recognized that the three above named persons were first cousins and next of kin of Henrietta E. Garrett. The compromise agreement was approved by the Attorney General of Pennsylvania, the Governor of Pennsylvania, the Auditor General and the Assistant Secretary of Revenue of Pennsylvania and the Attorney General of the United States.

The findings of the Master adopted by the Court satisfied everyone except 26,000 disappointed claimants. It is therefore not surprising to find, 22 years after the death of Henrietta E. Garrett, that some persons still sincerely believe that they are entitled to her estate as next of kin and cannot understand how any Court can fail to recognize their close relationship to their dear and treasured Henrietta whom they never saw or knew but of whom they have recently become so fond.

In view of all the foregoing facts, the burden of proving any claim at this late date must in fairness and justice be a heavy one for, unlike Tennyson's brook, the Garrett estate cannot go on forever.

THE MARSH CLAIMS. The Marsh claims are based upon their alleged relationship on decedent's maternal line. When their claim was listed for hearing before the Master on April 2, 1941, they requested a continuance which was refused, and their claim, like countless others under similar conditions, was marked "Passed." Claimants did nothing to prove their claim until after the Master notified them on November 15, 1949, and again on November 30, 1949, that if they wished to present a petition to reopen their claim they should do so within two weeks. This they failed to do. When their counsel wrote to the Master on November 21, 1950, requesting a hearing, the Master refused because counsel's "letter suggests no reason which would justify the granting of a rehearing of these claimants." Claimants ascribe their delay to the refusal of the Master to show them certain exhibits which they needed to complete their genealogical proofs. The Master at his first hearing on January 14, 1937, wisely issued the following notice: "Claimants must prove their claims at their own expense and in accordance with the law and practice of the Commonwealth of Pennsylvania, U. S. A. *We will not assist or advise claimants respecting proof or procedure.*"

* * *

Moreover the Auditing Judge found as a fact that the claimant and his brothers and sisters are not related in any way to the decedent. Equally important, according to their own contention, the closest relationship of any member of the Marsh family to Henrietta E. Garrett was a second cousin. Each of these findings is sufficient to bar these claims. "The law is well settled in Pennsylvania that under the Intestate Act of June 7, 1917, P. L. 429 [20 P. S. § 1 et seq.], first cousins take the entire estate to the exclusion of first-cousins-once-removed, and of second cousins."

* * *

We find no merit in any of the Marsh contentions.

THE PLATTE CLAIMS. The learned Auditing Judge after tracing the genealogy of the present appellant and of the Platte group quoted with approval from the report of the Master as follows: "The case represented by Mrs. Platte is a preposterous case, contending a woman born by the name of Louisa in Germany, stayed there until 1870, then came to this country, married

Walter Garrett and died as Henrietta E. Garrett. The proof of such an allegation is absolutely lacking." We agree that there was no legally competent evidence to support the claim of this appellant. Mrs. Platte in her brief of argument said that counsel for the successful next of kin and the Judges and the West Publishing Company knew that she and her family were the lawful heirs, but counsel for the Commonwealth and others kept this racket going because of their greed for money. This appellant seems to think that slander, libel and vitaapuration can take the place of proof. There was no evidence to substantiate these false and unjustifiable allegations; and no evidence legally sufficient to prove her claim.

THE WISMILLER CLAIM. Caroline McDonald Wismiller claims she is a first cousin of a girl named Charlotte Mooney and that Charlotte Mooney was actually Henrietta E. Garrett. The Wismiller claim is thus summarized by the learned Auditing Judge: "According to her story, Henrietta E. Garrett, the decedent, was not really Henrietta E. Garrett, nee Schaefer, but Charlotte Mooney, daughter of the claimant's uncle, Peter Lawler Patrick Mooney. She stated that her uncle married very young in Ireland, that a daughter, Charlotte, was born of this marriage, that the real Henrietta E. Schaefer died when she was a child, and that the Schaefers took Charlotte into their home, and raised her as their own child. . . .

"The claimant was unable to substantiate any of her fantastic allegations with proof of any kind and relied entirely upon the photographs of Henrietta E. Garrett which appeared in the *Saturday Evening Post* and upon statements alleged by her to have been made by a family named Young, who were [neighbors but] completely unrelated by blood or marriage to the family of the real Henrietta E. Garrett." These statements alleged by her to have been made by a family who were not proved by other evidence to be related to the family of the real Henrietta E. Garrett are inadmissible. *In re Garrett Estate*, 371 Pa. 284, 288, 89 A. (2d) 531; *In re Link's Estate* (No. 1), 319 Pa. 513, 520, 180 A. 1; *Sitler v. Gehr*, 105 Pa. 577, 596. "Pedigree is an exception, arising ex necessitate, to the hearsay rule. . . . Declarations as to pedigree are admissible if (1) the declarant is dead; (2) the declarations were made before the controversy arose or as is frequently said, 'ante litem motam'; and (3) the declarant was related to the family of which he spoke, and this relationship is proved by evidence dehors the declaration."

There is no merit in this appeal.

EVA V. HOOVER CLAIM. Mrs. Hoover's claim is based on the theory that her mother, Mrs. Mick, was not her mother at all, but that she is the daughter of a Mrs. Henrietta E. Garrett of Philadelphia. Mrs. Mick lived with her husband and several children in a small farming village in West Virginia which could be reached from the nearest railroad station by stagecoach in two days. According to Mrs. Hoover, a stranger who said her name was Henrietta E. Garrett of Philadelphia appeared at the Mick home in October 1873, accompanied by a man who was not her husband and a small baby, recently born in the hills of West Virginia. She begged Mrs. Mick to take her child who was born on September 1, 1873, and keep it in exchange for Mrs. Mick's baby who was also born on September 1, 1873 but died the night of the unexpected visit. Mrs. Mick took the baby, who is the present claimant, and raised her as her own child until she wrote her the following letter on March 1, 1912:

"March 1st, 1912

Dear Eva

i am getting worse every day i wrote you to come home but am afraid you wont get here until too late and to ease my mind i must write and tell you of a secret i have kept for years it hurts to tell you i hae always loved you as if you had been my own but you are not my child it was the first week in October 1873 a man and a woman with a baby asked to stay all Night Mr was away from home and my baby was sick so i was glad to have them stay that night my baby died with membranous croupe who said her name was Henrietta E. Garrett of Philadelphia Pa. begged me to take her child a girl born on September the 1st same day my baby was born She said her husband didnt like children any was glad that the Dr told him they would never have any and she was scarred to tell him she was with child and while on a visit to friends the baby was born and on her way home she was going to put it in an orphanage she gave me one hundred dollar and took my baby with her said the man would bury it. three years later she wrote and wanted to adopt you guess her conscience hurt her i wrote her you had died

Good bye

(Signed) Jane L. Mick

Wit by—
Samuel B. Myers
S. J. Mick"

Mrs. Mick's signature was declared to be genuine by a handwriting expert produced by claimant.

The husband of Henrietta E. Garrett, Walter Garrett, never knew he had a child because he said in his will which was dated March 3, 1890, 17 years after the exchange of babies, that he and his wife had not been blessed with any children clearly indicating that he would have liked to have had children but never had had any. Birth records and other documents conflict with the claimant's story of her birth and with several of her other contentions. Two handwriting experts produced by the Government of the United States testified that the entire letter was a forgery. A son-in-law of Samuel B. Myers, an alleged witness to the letter, testified that the signature of his father-in-law was a forgery. The Auditing Judge disbelieved the testimony of claimant and her witnesses and said her claim "still appears to be fantastic, preposterous and taxes credulity."

The aforesaid letter of March 1, 1912, and other testimony upon which Mrs. Hoover principally relied was hearsay and clearly inadmissible. See *In re Garrett Estate*, 371 Pa. 284, 89 A. (2d) 531, supra; *In re Link's Estate* (No. 1), 319 Pa. 513, 180 A. 1, supra; and *Sitler v. Gehr*, 105 Pa. 577, supra.

However, even if all her evidence were admissible, where testimony is improbable or conflicts with likely facts or circumstances or public records or where for any reason its credibility is doubtful, a jury or Judge is not compelled to accept it as true, even though it be uncontradicted. "There is nothing which is approved by the court en banc, is conclusive on the appellate courts as verity uncontradicted testimony. Credibility of witnesses is always for the finders of fact. *Nanty-Glo Borough v. American Surety Co.*, 309 Pa. 236, 163 A. 523. The disbelief of witnesses by a chancellor or . . . auditing judge which is approved by the court en banc, is conclusive on the appellate courts in the absence of proof of bias, prejudice, prejudgment, or capricious disbelief. . . . *In re Pusey's Estate*, 321 Pa. 248, 184 A. 844."

*   *   *

If testimony of the kind and character on which Mrs. Hoover or the Platte group or Mrs. Wismiller rely were to prevail, there would be little, if any, reason to keep birth, baptismal, marriage, church and other genealogical records since a next of kin who based his pedigree upon genealogical records would have little chance of ever inheriting the estate of an ancestor or near relative who died intestate.

Eva H. Hoover, although she claims to be the daughter of Henrietta E. Garrett, admits (in her brief of argument in this Court) that she "does not know if Eva V. Hoover was entitled to share in the Garrett Estate." Nevertheless, Mrs. Hoover contends, although she has no authority to support her contentions, that she was deprived of due process and of the equal protection of the laws because her claim was not treated in the same manner as other claims in the Garrett Estate, viz., she was permitted only several days before the hearing of her claim to examine decedent's personal effects and the records of testimony before the Master, but was never permitted to examine the investigation reports obtained by the Master.

Mrs. Hoover did not notify anyone of her claim until February 1946, when she alleges that she learned for the first time that the Estate of Henrietta E. Garrett was being administered in Philadelphia. On February 12, 1946, Mrs. Hoover came from her home near Pittsburgh to Philadelphia and presented to the Master and examiners the aforesaid letter from Mrs. Mick dated March 1, 1912, and later testimony to establish her claim. She was given five weeks' notice of the hearing of her claim before the Auditing Judge on May 14–19, 1951.

"The fundamental requirements of due process in a proceeding affecting property interests are (1) a notice of proceedings appropriate to the nature of the case . . . and (2) an opportunity to be heard.

. . . Due process does not require a Master or Court to investigate a claim or prepare evidence for the the claimant. It is crystal clear that Mrs. Hoover was not deprived of her constitutional right of due process.

The Master, with the approval of the Orphans' Court of Philadelphia County, notified all claimants as hereinabove set forth: "claimants must prove their claims at their own expense and in accordance with the law and practice of the Commonwealth of Pennsylvania, U. S. A. We will not assist or advise claimants respecting proof of procedure."

The successful next of kin proved their individual claims by testimony covering approximately 50 volumes and without any assistance from the Master or Examiners. Nevertheless, Mrs. Hoover states that the examiner had no right to refuse to permit her to examine certain investigation reports since he advised her "claimants were given access to data in the possession of the estate custodian only when they had satisfied the Examiner that there was some possibility of kinship with the decedent." Even if we were to interpret this statement of the examiner as sweepingly as appellant does, there was no obligation upon the Master or the Court below to assist any claimant to prove her claim and there was no abuse of discretion in refusing to show this appellant, whose story is so improbable, the investigation records which had been obtained by the Court. "The inequality . . . [prohibited by the Fourteenth Amendment to the Constitution] is only such as is actually and palpably unreasonable and arbitrary."

*   *   *

Considering the fact that there were 26,000 claimants any other ruling by the Court would have opened the door wide to claims of favoritism and fraud and would have resulted in fishing expeditions which would likely have dragged out this extraordinary estate not for 22 years, but for a century. We find no error of law, no abuse of discretion, and no denial of due process or equal protection of the laws in this claim by the Master or Examiners or the Court below.

The Master and Examiners also took the position that Mrs. Hoover's claim was barred by the Act of June 7, 1917, P. L. 429, Sec. 21, as amended by the Act of June 4, 1943, P. L. 872, 20 P. S. 134, which barred all claims of next of kin which are not presented within 7 years of the death of a decedent. It is unnecessary to discuss or decide the constitutionality of this amendment.

We have considered all of the other contentions of each appellant and find no merit in any of them.

The Decree of the Orphans' Court of Philadelphia County is affirmed in each case involved in these appeals; costs to be paid by each appellant respectively.

Walker v. Matthews

191 Miss. 489, 3 So. (2d) 280 (1941)

Supreme Court of Mississippi

Appeal from Chancery Court, Lauderdale County; A. B. Amis, Sr., Chancellor.

Suit by Mack Walker and another against Will Matthews and others for a determination of the legal heirs of George Matthews, deceased. From an unsatisfactory decree, Mack Walker and another appeal.

Reversed and remanded.

ROBERDS, J. On the night of August 19, 1940 George Matthews, a negro, some seventy years of age, died, intestate, at his home five miles northwest of Meridian in Lauderdale County, Mississippi, where he lived alone. He had some ten thousand dollars in cash, other personal property of small value, and his home, consisting of eight acres of land.

Immediately there was a scramble for his property. Mack Walker and Harriett Davis, claiming to be second cousins and heirs at law of Matthews, filed a petition in the chancery court to have determined who were his legal heirs. They made parties to this petition a number of persons claiming to be collateral heirs of decedent and also one Mattie Tate Matthews and one Fannie, or Tiney, Collins Matthews, claiming to be widows of decedent and one Will Matthews, son of Fannie Matthews, claiming to be the lawful son and heir of George Matthews.

The chancellor on the hearing limited the evidence and trial to the questions (1) whether either Mattie or Fannie was the lawful widow of decedent, and, if either, which one, and (2) if Fannie were such widow, whether her son, Will, or Pippen Cat, as he was usually called, was the legitimate child of George Matthews and entitled to inherit his estate along with his mother Fannie, for if there is a widow or a child entitled to inherit, the collateral heirs are excluded.

After an extended trial, lasting some four days, the chancellor found that Fannie was the common law wife of George Matthews and Will was his legitimate son and that they, Fannie and Will, were his only heirs at law. From that finding and decree this appeal is taken.

The questions, therefore, for decision on this appeal are (1) whether Mattie or Fannie or either is the lawful widow of George Matthews, and, if either, which, and (2) if either is his widow, whether such widow is entitled to inherit his property, and (3) whether Will is his legitimate son and entitled to share in such inheritance.

We will try to weave into the warp of the life of this Lothario the woof of his nuptial and concubinage experiences in an effort to picture the fabric of his earthly existence. He appears to have about lived to the limit of his physical and mental powers. He was a fireman on a railroad, and, like the sailor with a sweetheart in every port, it was his desire to have one at each depot along his route. As he neared the end of life's run we find him returning to the old home, and, as his engine was pulling into the terminal and its fires were burning low, sitting on his front porch, murmuring over and trying to read his Bible. That night the fires went out.

In 1898 he was a young man, living on this same farm with his mother, his father being dead. Already he was the father of an illegitimate child, and wonder of wonders, the mother of this child, who testified on the hearing, did not claim to be his common law wife. He had already served a term in the Mississippi penitentiary.

His mother died in 1899. He went away for awhile, and when he returned he brought back a girl named Lillie Mason. Just where he met her is not shown.

She was born and reared and had lived at Marion Junction, Dallas County, Alabama. He brought her either from Mobile or New Orleans, the witnesses were not sure which place he said. He said he had married her and he introduced her as his wife. He lived with her as his wife at the old home place. He held her out in the community as his wife. It is not shown whether there was a license or a marriage ceremony at any place. He would go away for short times and leave Lillie with Mr. and Mrs. Pearce, neighbors, living about 150 yards from his home. Mr. Pearce operated a store. He testified in the case. At the time of the trial he was mayor of Shuqualak, Mississippi. George told Mr. and Mrs. Pearce to take care of Lillie while he was gone and to let her have from the store what she needed and he would pay for it. This was done. Lillie worked and cooked for Mr. and Mrs. Pearce during the times George was gone and apparently some of the time when George was at home. This situation continued until 1902, when George got a job as a railroad fireman with the Southern Railway Company. His first run was from Selma, Alabama, to Rome, Georgia. Later he fired on a switch engine on the yards at Selma. Selma was a division point on the railroad. It was necessary that George live in Selma to do his railroad work. George carried Lillie to Selma in 1902 and placed her in a house "just across the railroad from the depot." Here they lived together as man and wife, holding themselves out as such, until she died in 1911. George paid all the expenses of her last illness, engaged a nurse for her and buried her at the family cemetery, "Shady Rest," at Masillon, about two miles west of Marion Junction. George and Lillie had no children. The testimony is abundant to prove all the common law elements of a common law marriage between them beginning in 1899 and continuing until the death of Lillie in 1911.

We now take up the thread of Fannie Collins. She was reared in Choctaw County, Alabama. Lauderdale County joins Clarke County, Mississippi, on the north; Choctaw County, Alabama, lies immediately to the east of Lauderdale and Clarke Counties; on the east of Choctaw County is Maringo County and on the east of Maringo is Dallas County. Therefore, Choctaw County is between Selma and Meridian. George appears to have met Fannie at Christmas 1902 and Fannie's pleadings say she and George began to live together about January, 1903. There is proof to the effect that George and Fannie then lived together for awhile at Marion Junction, which is twelve miles west of Selma. This was a junction point on the railroad; the trains operated over a "Y" to change their courses to Akron, Meridian and Mobile. Some of the train crews had a meal there; the trains remained there from ten to thirty minutes. It is claimed for Fannie that she and George lived at Marion Junction as man and wife until their son Will was born, October 16, 1903, and there is proof to that effect, although it is far from satisfactory. Fannie then claims, and there is proof to sustain the claim, that she and George went through a ceremonial licensed marriage on April 1, 1904, at the house of her grandmother, Martha Pressley, four miles west of Enterprise, Clarke County. Will was left at Martha's and Fannie and George went back to Marion Junction and continued to live there as man and wife, according to Fannie's proof, until around the first of 1905, when Fannie left George and went back to her mother's in Choctaw County. At any rate, on March 11, 1905, about eleven months after she claims to have married George, we find Fannie going through a statutory, licensed, ceremonial marriage at Butler, county site of Choctaw County, Alabama, with one George Jones, sometimes called Seale or Brewster. In this license she is designated Tiney Collins. Tiney and Jones lived together as man and wife in the neighborhood where they were married until the fall of 1911, when Fannie left Jones and went to Quitman, Clarke County, Mississippi. Some of the witnesses say she went with a man named Brown. She appears to have worked at Quitman for a short time at a hotel, when she went to Louisiana, in which state she seems to have since resided and in which she lived at the time of the trial. Tiney and Jones had at least two, and maybe, three, children. It is claimed Will, or Pippen Cat, was their child. Later, after going to Louisiana, Fannie went by the name of Munday and at the time of the trial was known as Marsh. In 1912 Jones was killed near Butler, Alabama.

We go back now and take up another thread. During the last illness of Lillie in 1911 George had procured a nurse for her whose name was Mattie Tate. She lived at Selma and was around 16 years old, about George's favorite age. Shortly after the death of Lillie and in 1912 George brought Mattie to Meridian, and there at Black's Hotel, operated by a negro, he went through a marriage ceremony with Mattie. The record is not specific whether it is claimed a license had been issued, but none is shown to have been issued, although witnesses detail the wedding ceremony. About this time George was transferred from Selma to Mobile, where he fired on a switch engine until he retired on a railroad pension around 1938. He carried Mattie to Mobile and there they lived as man and wife, the exact time not being shown, perhaps from three to five years. Anyway, during that time, whatever its duration, they lived in the same house, held themselves out as man and wife and were known to the public as man and wife.

Sometime later, apparently during the period from 1914 to 1917, the time not being definitely shown, Mattie left George and returned to her old home at Selma, where she had continued to live to the time of the trial. On April 12, 1937, she married one Josh Minter in Dallas County, Alabama, under a statutory license, the application for which, made by Minter, said it was his second and Mattie's first marriage, and gave her name as Mattie Tate. She has two living children by Minter and at the time of the trial they were living together as man and wife at Selma. George and Mattie had no children.

Mattie's departure did not seem to greatly disturb George. We find him next at Hot Springs, Arkansas, at the boarding house of one Susie Cole. He proceeded to marry the landlady's daughter, Jessie. This was a licensed, statutory marriage; it took place in Garland County, Arkansas, May 17, 1921. George, in some of his later conversations, intimated he did not marry Jessie; she married him. He said "she pulled down the shades and called the officers." Anyway, they were married and George until the day of his death recognized Jessie thereafter as his lawful wife. All of his railroad passes were issued to him and Jessie as his wife, even up to the last year of his life, although Jessie died September 13, 1927. In his application for railroad retirement pension October 29, 1937, he referred to Jessie as his wife.

Jessie did not like Mobile. She would go there about twice a year and remain with George a week or two. George did not appear to encourage these visits, because, as he said, each time she came it cost him $100. In fact, George gave evidence of his feelings towards his marriages, by saying to witnesses that his first marriage to Lillie cost him $2.50; his second to Mattie $5; and his third to Jessie $500. At this ratio George could not have married many more times. George and Jessie had no children.

So far as the record shows, this ends his matrimonial adventures, although after he came back to the old home on his retirement he did approach a lady friend of long ago with the suggestion he had plenty with which to take care of her if she cared to come and live with him. She did not accept.

We shall now undertake to unravel this tangled skein, apply the rules of law and presumptions and determine the rights of the parties.

And the first knot is that of Lillie and Fannie, and we find and hold that Lillie was the wife of George Matthews before and during the time of his relations with Fannie, and, being the husband of Lillie, he could not and never did become the legal husband of Fannie. We reach this conclusion through these processes:

1. George brought Lillie from another state. They said they were married. He introduced her as his wife and he lived with her as such. There is no other proof as to whether there was, or was not, a statutory or common law marriage in the other state. In the absence of all proof to the contrary we must presume they had legally become man and wife in the other state. Annotations, 34 *A. L. R.* 371. As stated in *Divorce and Separation in Mississippi* by Amis, p. 24, § 10, "In general, the law favors marriage and will indulge every reasonable presumption in favor of the validity thereof." *Alabama & V. Ry. Co. v. Beardsley,* 79 Miss. [417], 422, 30 So. 660 [89 *Am. St. Rep.* 660]; *Sullivan v. Knights of Pythias,* 97 Miss. 218, 52 So. 360; *McAllum v. Spinks,* 129 Miss. 237, 91 So. 694." In 38 *C. J.* p. 1325, § 100, "If a marriage in fact is established by evidence or admission, it is presumed to be regular and valid, and the burden of adducing evidence to the contrary rests on the party who attacks it, even though it involves the proving of a negative." In 35 *Am. Jur.* p. 303, § 191, it is said, "It is a fundamental maxim of our law that where man and woman are living together as husband and wife, marriage should always be presumed." A contrary rule would be dangerous to society. A man goes away to another state for a time; he returns with a woman and they announce they have married; they live together as man and wife; they hold themselves out in the community as man and wife; this situation continues for thirteen years and until the death of the woman. What shall the law presume, in the absence of proof to the contrary? That they are living in a lawful or a criminal state? As was said in *Travers v. Reinhardt,* 205 U. S. 423, 27 S. Ct. 563, 567, 51 *L. Ed.* 865, "The law has wisely provided that marriage may be proved by general reputation, cohabitation, and acknowledgment; when these exist, it will be inferred that a religious ceremony has taken place; and this proof will not be

invalidated because evidence cannot be obtained of the time, place, and manner of the celebration of the marriage. . . ."

The testimony is abundant to show all the elements of fact of a common law marriage between George and Lillie from 1899 to her death in 1911. The Chancellor stated his findings in these words: "It is also in evidence that in 1899 George, who had been away from his home west of Meridian for some months, came back home with a woman named Lillie, and that he told people that she was his wife, and lived with her as such. There is no proof they were ever ceremonially married, or that they were ever married in any way anywhere, but he told people around there that she was his wife. This woman stayed around there some time; George would go away and be gone two or three months and come back, then he would stay with her awhile and leave again. That kept up until 1902 when George went to Selma and got a job as fireman on the locomotive of the Southern Railway, when he took Lillie and installed her in a house right across from the depot in Selma, and that he continued to live with her there until she died in 1911."

We construe the evidence as establishing such facts much more strongly than did the Chancellor. It is true that common law marriages were not recognized in Mississippi from 1892 to 1906. (*Olivari v. Clark*, 175 Miss. 883, 168 So. 465), but they were recognized in Alabama during the time George and Lillie lived together in that state. *White v. Hill*, 176 Ala. 480, 58 So. 444. The lower court attached much importance to the idea that the relation being unlawful in Mississippi it is presumed to have continued in that status in Alabama. The proof disproves the presumption. The only reason the relation was unlawful in Mississippi was because the law did not recognize common law marriages, not because the elements thereof were not shown as facts. But the same facts were shown to exist after they went to Alabama and until the death of Lillie and common law marriages were there recognized. In the Travers case, supra, it was announced that where parties lived together in Virginia and the relation was unlawful because of lack of a license, then moved to Maryland where such relation was unlawful because of lack of a religious ceremony, and then moved to New Jersey, where common law marriages were lawful, that they became man and wife under the laws of New Jersey, where all the elements of fact of a common law marriage were established in New Jersey. The facts existing while they were in Virginia and Maryland were important in determining the facts after going to New Jersey. Under the proof in this record George and Lillie became common law man and wife in Alabama and under the law of comity it will be recognized here. . . .

This status existed before and when George met Fannie; therefore, Fannie could not have become his wife. This makes it unnecessary for us to decide whether the facts disclosed by this record are sufficient to constitute George and Fannie common law husband and wife had there been no legal impediment to such status. It is also unnecessary for us to say what effect her statutory licensed marriage to George Jones in March, 1905, had upon her right to inherit the property of George Matthews.

It also follows from the foregoing that Will, or Pippen Cat, is not the legitimate son of George Matthews, if, in fact, he is his son at all. The great weight of the evidence shows he is in fact the son of George Jones and not of George Matthews, but it is not necessary for us to say whether we would reverse the finding of the chancellor on that question. It, therefore, follows that Will is not an heir at law of George Matthews.

We come now to the rights of Mattie. George went through a ceremony of marriage with her in Meridian, Mississippi, in 1912. It is not clear whether it is claimed there was a license. No license is shown to have issued and the witnesses do not undertake to say whether the preacher had a license at the time of the ceremony. Apparently he did not have such license. However, the ceremony was public evidence of their intention to assume the status of man and wife. There was no impediment and common law marriages were then recognized in this state. They moved to Alabama and lived together as man and wife for some time, the exact time not being shown, but the evidence is sufficient to establish a common law marriage. However, Mattie is not entitled to inherit from George for these reasons:

After ther separation both George and Mattie went through statutory marriages, under regular licenses, and each thereafter recognized these marriages as valid and lawful, George with Jessie Cole until his death and Mattie with Josh Minter to the time of the trial, and presumably, at this time, Mattie and Josh having at the time of the trial two living children. In Mississippi, and most of the states, the fact of a subsequent marriage is of itself sufficient to raise a presumption that a former marriage has been terminated by a decree of divorce, in the absence of proof to the contrary. The presumption may be rebutted by proof but there is no proof here to rebut it. The proof could have been made, since George and Mattie, after their separation, have lived only in Mobile and Dallas Counties, Alabama, and George in Lauderdale County, Mississippi, for about a year and a half before his death. . . . The burden of showing the invalidity of a marriage solemnized in due form is upon the person attacking it.

Another question which arises is whether Mattie is now estopped to claim she is the lawful wife of George and lay claim to his property as such. She went through a statutory, licensed marriage with Josh Minter. The application for the license gave her name as Mattie Tate and stated this was her first marriage. She is now living with him as man and wife at Selma and they have two children. The cases are divided on this question. An annotation in 71 *A. L. R. subhead* IV, p. 287 shows Colorado, California, South Carolina and North Carolina imposing an estoppel; Georgia, Arkansas and Oklahoma as not imposing such bar. In the Arkansas case, *Estes v. Merrill*, 121 Ark. 361, 181 S. W. 136, however, the wife believed in good faith a divorce had been granted and involved an attack on the validity of the divorce and a claim of right of dower. This exact question has not been decided by this Court. In *Williams et al. v. Lee et al.*, 130 Miss. 481, 484, 94 So. 454, 28 *A. L. R.* 1124, this Court held that failure of the wife to either encourage or dissent to the illegitimate marriage of her husband, mere knowledge and silence, did not estop her from asserting her heirship, citing *Darrow v. Darrow*, 201 Ala. 477,

78 So. 383 to the same effect. In *Williams v. Johnston*, 148 Miss. 634, 114 So. 733, this Court held that wilful desertion of the wife by the husband and subsequent marriage to another woman and living apart from her for thirty years estopped the husband from renouncing the wife's will and inheriting a child's part of her estate. In *Joy v. Miles et al.*, 190 Miss. 255, 199 So. 771, we said: "When the proof discloses, as it does in this case, that a wife seeking to set aside an invalid divorce decree obtained by her husband had become married to another man subsequent to the rendition of such decree, it cannot be said that she comes into a court of equity with clean hands asking for affirmative relief. Moreover, even if it be true—and the chancellor found to the contrary—that she did not know of the decree at the time of her second marriage, such want of knowledge would afford less excuse for having entered into the bigamous relationship with her second husband than if she had known of the divorce proceedings, since she did know that her former husband was still alive, and that she herself had not obtained a divorce. Nor does the fact that she did not remarry until after her former husband had married another woman, following the rendition of the divorce decree in his favor, prevent his second wife from pleading such fact in defense of a suit to set aside the decree of divorce for the sole purpose of enabling the complainant in such a suit to obtain the life insurance left by the divorced husband at the time of his death, and which was payable to his widow."

The majority rule is that desertion or abandonment is generally held to be a bar to any right to share in the estate of the deceased spouse. Annotation 71 *A. L. R.*, p. 285.

We hold that under the facts of the case at bar and the applicable rules of law Mattie Tate (Minter) is estopped to assert heirship to the estate of George Matthews, deceased.

Reversed and remanded.

BY ADVERSE POSSESSION

Title to real property may be acquired by what is known as adverse possession. In order to acquire title by this method the adverse claimant's possession must be (1) hostile, i. e. without the consent of the owner and without recognition of the owner's superior claim, (2) actual, (3) open and notorious, (4) exclusive, and (5) continuous for the statutory period (twenty years in most states, but a shorter period in some). The statutes of a few states specify as an additional requirement the payment of taxes by the adverse occupant.

To meet the requirement that adverse possession must be continuous it is not necessary that one adverse claimant have possession for the entire statutory period. The courts permit the "tacking" of the periods of two or more successive adverse occupants in order to make up the statutory period, provided there is no lapse between occupancies.

Pugh v. Conway

299 N. E. (2d) 214 (1973)

Court of Appeals of Indiana

This was an action for declaratory judgment as to prescriptive easement for disputed area. . . . Prescriptive easement [granted] as to portion of disputed area and title to remainder of disputed area was quieted in defendant, and plaintiff appealed. . . . Judgment affirmed.

BUCHANAN, J. In September of 1939, Pugh purchased the east one-half of Lot 4 in Banta's Addition in Windfall, Indiana, the east line of which has a common boundary with Lots 2 and 3 of the same addition.

Late in 1939 or in 1940, Pugh, without a survey or actual knowledge of the boundary line between her Lot 4 and Lots 2 and 3, constructed an additional room onto the existing residence on Lot 4, which new construction encroached approximately 3 feet onto Lot 3.

Until 1954 Pugh and her tenants mowed and cared for a strip of ground extending approximately three feet beyond, or east of, the foundation of the encroaching room and running from north to south along the west end of Lots 2 and 3. This strip of ground is illustrated by the following drawing, and is hereinafter referred to as the Disputed Area, being that part of Lots 2 and 3 enclosed within points A, B, C and D. . . . The area enclosed between points

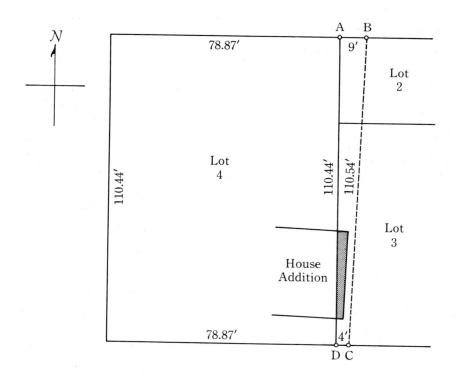

A, B, C & D = the Disputed Area. Geographically the Disputed Area is definable by the existence of a natural channel or slope running from the northern boundary of Lot 2 to the southern boundary of Lot 3.

In 1968 a contract buyer of Lot 4 from Pugh planned to install a gas line over Lot 3 in order to service the Pugh house on Lot 4 and asked permission of Lawrence to install the gas line, to which Lawrence responded: "Why, sure, it won't bother me."

Not until 1969 was it determined by survey that the addition to Pugh's house encroached on Lot 3. Lawrence testified he never denied Pugh or any of her tenants free access to that part of Lot 3 upon which Pugh's house encroached and was willing to allow the house to remain there. The issues raised by Pugh may be resolved as one question: Did the trial court properly limit Pugh's prescriptive easement to that portion of the Disputed Area upon which Pugh's house encroached?

Pugh argues that the facts in evidence showed she met the requirements of a prescriptive easement by her continued, uninterrupted, and adverse use of the entire disputed Area for more than twenty years; and that the easement ripened even though Lawrence acquiesced in the use.

Lawrence elevates acquiescence to permission and apparently contends a license was granted or that by reason of this permission Pugh's use was not adverse or inconsistent with the rights of Lawrence and so prescriptive easement could not result. Also, it is argued that Pugh's use was interrupted in 1955 by the planting of a garden in the Disputed Area and continued use thereafter by Lawrence of the entire Disputed Area so as to stop the running of the 20 year period.

. . . It is our opinion that the trial court properly limited Pugh's prescriptive easement to that portion of the Disputed Area upon which Pugh's house stood.

. . . In order to establish the existence of a prescriptive easement across the land of another, the evidence must show an actual, hostile, open, notorious, continuous, uninterrupted, and adverse use for twenty years under claim of right, or such continuous adverse use with the knowledge and acquiescence of the owner of the servient land. . . . The existence or nonexistence of a prescriptive easement is a question of fact for the trier of facts. . . . Further, each of the elements of a prescriptive easement must be established by the party asserting the prescriptive right. Failure to prove any one of such elements is fatal. . . .

Gathering together the principles enunciated above and remembering that on appeal we do not weigh the evidence or determine the credibility of witnesses, it is plain that Pugh failed to establish the existence of a prescriptive easement because there was evidence that the use was not continuous and uninterrupted for a period of twenty years. Pugh's adverse use began in 1939 or 1940 and continued uninterruptedly until 1954, at which time there was evidence that Bailey (a tenant of Lawrence) planted a garden in most of the Disputed Area which Lawrence replaced in 1955 with grass and continuously mowed and maintained thereafter.

While it is our holding that Pugh, as one seeking to establish a prescriptive easement, failed to establish that the adverse use was continuous and uninterrupted for the required twenty-year period, we express doubt whether there is a meaningful distinction between "'continuous" and "uninterrupted." Neither the Indiana cases cited above nor the dictionary definition of these two words would indicate that they are anything other than synonyms—a legal tautology handed down through the years.

Because we reach the conclusion that the trial court could have properly determined that Pugh's use was interrupted short of the twenty-year period, the character of that use and whether it was acquiesced in for a licence granted, is of no consequence. Pugh appeals from a negative judgment, having failed to prove at least one essential element of proof necessary to recovery.

The judgment of the trial court is therefore affirmed.

BY OPERATION OF LAW

Title to real property may be transferred to a purchaser by operation of law through execution and judicial sales. Such sales are usually without the consent of the owner. (1) A judgment creditor of a property owner may levy on the property of the judgment debtor and sell it in order to satisfy his judgment. (2) A mortgagee may foreclose his mortgage and have the property sold to satisfy his claim against the mortgagor. (3) Property may be sold for taxes in order to satisfy the claim of the state or municipality against the property. (4) A mechanic's lien may be foreclosed and the property sold in order to satisfy the claim of the lienor.

In the foregoing instances the purchaser receives a deed from the sheriff or other officer who made the sale. A sheriff's deed is very much like a quitclaim deed in that it does not contain covenants of warranty.

By order of the probate court an executor or administrator of an estate may sell real property belonging to the estate. In such cases an executor's or administrator's deed is given to the purchaser. Such deeds do not contain covenants of warranty.

TYPES OF CO—OWNERSHIP

If one person owns a parcel of real property he is said to have an *estate in severalty*.[1] If two or more persons own undivided interests in a given piece of property, they are *co-owners* of the property. By "undivided interests" is meant that the co-tenants do not own separate parts of the property individually, but each has an interest in the property as a whole. For example, if A and B are co-owners of a tract of land, A is not the owner of one portion of the land and B of the other portion, but each has a part interest in the entire tract. Their interests may be equal or unequal,

---

[1] If the student is puzzled by this name for ownership by one person, he should bear in mind that the original meaning of *several* was *separate*.

depending upon the circumstances and the type of co-ownership. A and B may each own a half interest; or A may have, say, a one-third interest and B a two-thirds interest in the tract as a whole.

There are five types of co-ownership in real property: (1) tenancy in common, (2) joint tenancy, (3) tenancy by the entireties, (4) community property, and (5) tenancy in partnership.[1]

TENANCY IN COMMON

Under a tenancy in common the co-owners are not required to have equal interests in the property, but they do have equal rights to the possession and enjoyment of the property (unity of possession). A tenant in common may sell his share in the property, or he may devise it to his heirs. If he dies intestate his share goes to his heirs at law. Tenancies in common may be destroyed through a partition proceeding in a court of equity.

JOINT TENANCY

Unlike a tenancy in common, for which the only "unity" required is unity of possession, a joint tenancy requires four "unities": (1) unity of interest, (2) unity of title, (3) unity of time, and (4) unity of possession. These requirements are met (1) if the joint tenants have equal shares in the property; (2) if their ownership is traceable to the same instrument; (3) if their ownership began at the same time; and (4) if they have equal rights to possession and enjoyment of the property. A joint tenancy may be created either by grant (deed) or by devise (will).

The outstanding characteristic of a joint tenancy is the *right of survivorship*. When a joint tenant dies, his interest does not pass to his heirs but goes to the surviving joint tenant or tenants. Thus, if A, B, and C are joint tenants and A dies, B and C remain joint tenants but each now owns a one-half interest in the property instead of his original one-third interest. In other words, A's undivided interest is merged in the interests of his co-owners. If B dies, C becomes the complete owner of the property. He then has an estate in severalty.

Though a joint tenant cannot, because of the right of survivorship, disturb a joint tenancy by devising his interest in the joint tenancy, he may do so by deeding it to some outside party. For example, A, B, and C are joint tenants. A may sell and convey his undivided interest to X. In such case X becomes a tenant in common in relation to B and C, but B and C continue to be joint tenants in relation to each other. If B should deed his interest to Y, then X, Y, and C would be tenants in common. Joint tenancies are also subject to partition in a court of equity.

[1] In most states the first three types are also recognized in the case of personal property.

While joint tenancies are not looked upon with favor in this country, usually they may still be created, under modern statutes, if the grantor or devisor makes it clear that it is his intention to create such a tenancy. This may be accomplished if the grantor or devisor conveys or devises "to X and Y, as joint tenants with the right of survivorship, and not as tenants in common."

TENANCY BY THE ENTIRETIES

A tenancy by the entireties is, in effect, a joint tenancy between husband and wife. In addition to the four unities required in the case of a joint tenancy, a fifth unity is required to create a tenancy by the entireties, namely, unity of person. That requirement is met if the tenants are husband and wife. The doctrine of survivorship exists in the case of a tenancy by the entireties. Consequently, upon the death of one of the joint-owners the survivor possesses the entire estate as an estate in severalty. The heirs take nothing.

A tenancy by the entireties may not be destroyed by grant (deed) or devise (will) by one of the tenants acting alone. Such a tenancy may be destroyed only by the joint action of the co-tenants. Thus, the husband and wife may sell and convey their property which they hold as tenants by the entireties, if both sign the deed. In case of divorce the parties become tenants in common. A tenancy by the entireties is not subject to execution by a judgment-creditor of one of the co-tenants. It is, however, subject to execution by a creditor who has judgment against both the husband and wife on a joint obligation.

Since, under the right of survivorship, the survivor takes the whole property, administration on such property is not necessary. Thus, the costs of administration are saved when property is held by the husband and wife as tenants by the entireties. In some states the survivor is exempt from the payment of inheritance taxes upon such property. In Maryland, for example, this exemption applies to both real and personal property held either jointly by the husband and wife or as tenants by the entireties. In some jurisdictions the surviving tenant pays an inheritance tax on half of the appraised value of the property held as joint tenancies or tenancies by the entireties.

COMMUNITY PROPERTY

The type of co-ownership of property between husband and wife which is known as community property exists in the states of Arizona, California, Idaho, Louisiana, Nevada, New Mexico, Texas, Washington, and a few others. The principles underlying this type of co-ownership had their origin in the Civil Law and were brought to the aforementioned states by the early French, Spanish, and Mexican settlers.

In the states where community property exists, all property acquired through the efforts and labor of husband or wife during their marriage becomes community property. However, any property owned by either at the time of the marriage, and any acquired by either after the marriage by gift, devise, bequest, or descent, and the income from such property, is separate property of the husband or wife. The husband generally has the management and control of community property. However, some state statutes provide that the husband may not lease (except in the case of short-term leases), convey, or encumber community land without the wife's consent.[1]

TENANCY IN PARTNERSHIP
See Chapter 39.

Short v. Milby et al.
64 A. (2d) 36 (Del.) (1949)

This was a suit by Emma Short (plaintiff) against Charles R. Milby, Amy E. Milby, and others (defendants). Decree for complainant.

On April 11, 1934, John J. Yoder and Mary A. Yoder, his wife, conveyed a tract of land to Willard M. Short, a single man, and Emma Short, his sister, a single woman. The habendum clause stated that the land bargained for and sold to the parties of the second part, "their heirs and assigns," was for their use "jointly and not as common tenants, their heirs and assigns forever." On August 14, 1946, Willard M. Short died intestate and unmarried. He left surviving him, as his only heirs at law, four sisters, including plaintiff, three brothers, and seven nephews and nieces.

On April 21, 1948, the plaintiff entered into a contract in writing, whereby she agreed to sell, and Charles R. Milby and Amy E. Milby, his wife, agreed to purchase, the said land for $6,500. The purchase price was to be paid on or before June 1, 1948, "upon the execution and delivery of a good and sufficient deed conveying the said land by a good, marketable title in fee simple, free and clear of all liens and encumbrances." Mr. and Mrs. Milby refused to comply with their contract on the ground that plaintiff did not have absolute title to the property. Plaintiff brought this bill in equity for specific performance of the contract.

HARRINGTON, C. The question is whether the Yoder deed of April 11, 1934, conveyed an estate in joint tenancy to Willard M. Short and Emma Short. When such an estate is created, the right of the survivor to take on the

1 Burby, *On Real Property*, p. 318, West Publishing Co., St. Paul, Minn., 1943.

death of the other tenant is an incident of the estate. Tiffany, *Real Property*, 5th. ed., p. 408.

Section 3734 of the revised Code of 1935 provides: "Sec. 1. Estates in Joint Tenancy. Created by Express Words: No estate in joint tenancy, in lands, tenements, or hereditaments, shall be held, or claimed, by or under any grant, devise, or conveyance made to any person, other than to executors or trustees, unless the premises therein mentioned shall be expressly granted, devised, or conveyed to such persons, to be held as joint tenants and not as tenants in common."

The language of the statute reflects the modern rule and clearly shows that joint tenancies are not favored and can only be created by clear and definite language not reasonably capable of any different construction. *Cookman v. Silliman*, 22 Del. Ch. 303, 2 A. (2d) 166.

The conveyance to Willard M. Short and Emma Short "jointly and not as common tenants, their heirs and assigns forever" clearly indicates the grantor's intent to create a joint tenancy. In *Davis v. Smith*, 4 Harr. 68, the court held that a devise to the testator's two grandsons "jointly" did not necessarily mean in joint tenancy as tenants in common would also hold an estate jointly until severance. A decree will be entered compelling the defendants to perform their contract.

REVIEW CASES

1. Deegan, a minor, made a will, leaving to Harris a sum of money and a leasehold interest in a lot. Wager was named executor. After Deegan's death Holzman contested the will, claiming that the leasehold belonged to her as Deegan's sole heir at law. She contended that the will was void because it was made when Deegan was a minor. Under the applicable statute minors were permitted to dispose of personal property but not of real property. Judgment for whom? (Holzman v. Wager, 114 Md. 322, 79 A. 205)

2. Navarre and Riddle rented a safety deposit box at a bank. In the lease agreement appeared the following: "It is hereby declared that all property of every kind, at any time heretofore or hereafter placed in said box, is the joint property of both lessees and upon the death of either passes to the survivor." Each party had a key and separate access to the box. Navarre died, and Riddle claimed the contents of the box. They were also claimed by the heirs of Navarre, who brought this suit. Judgment for whom? (Brown et al. v. Navarre et al., 64 Ariz. 262, 169 P.(2d) 85)

3. Yohn and others bought a plot of wooded land at a tax sale. It was later found that the sale had been based upon a double tax assessment and that the legal owner, Walthall, had paid the taxes on one assessment. Walthall sued Yohn and others to quiet title to the land. The defendants claimed title to the land by adverse possession, in that they had made intermittent visits to the property, had put up two signs on it, and had granted some easements to others over the property. Holding? (Walthall v. Yohn et al., 252 Ala. 262, 40 So.(2d) 705)

4. Boyd sued Slayback, administrator of the estate of Taggart, to quiet title to certain lands alleged to have been sold to Boyd by Taggart. The deeds to the property were discovered among the effects of Taggart after his death. Slayback denied that the deeds had ever been delivered. Boyd maintained that after their execution and delivery they had been left with Taggart. The judge charged the jury to the effect that since the deeds were duly executed, they were presumed in law to have been delivered. Was the judge correct in his instruction to the jury? (Boyd v. Slayback, 63 Cal. 493)

5. Lotspeich left to his widow a life estate in certain land, with remainder to his children. She later deeded the land to Dean by warranty deed, at the same time delivering to him a quitclaim deed purportedly signed by all the children of Lotspeich. Dean remained in unquestioned possession of the land for fourteen years, when the children of Lotspeich brought suit. It was shown that the quitclaim deed was a forgery. Lotspeich's widow was still alive. Dean claimed title to the land by adverse possession, the statutory period being ten years. Holding? (Lotspeich et al. v. Dean et al., 53 N. M. 488, 211 P.(2d) 979)

6. In 1870 Bauman erected a building which had a stairway extending several feet onto the sidewalk. Thereafter the building was in continuous use. In 1899 Engleman bought the property. Some years later the city gave him notice to remove the stairway within thirty days, whereupon he filed a bill to restrain the enforcement of the order. Engleman maintained that he had a prescriptive right to use the stairway. Was he right in this contention? (Engleman v. Kalamazoo, 229 Mich. 603, 201 N. W. 880)

Landlord and Tenant

25

NATURE AND CREATION OF THE RELATION

NATURE

A very large number of people are concerned with the law governing the relationship of landlord and tenant. The reason for this is not only that so many people "rent" the houses and apartments in which they live, but also that a great amount of property is "rented" for business purposes.

The relationship of landlord and tenant exists where certain real property owned by one person is in the possession of another person, with the owner's consent. For the use and enjoyment of the premises the occupant agrees to pay rent.

CREATION

The relationship of landlord and tenant is created by a contract, which is either express or implied. There are two parties to the contract, (1) the landlord, or lessor, and (2) the tenant, or lessee. The contract itself is known as a *lease*. The effect of a lease-contract is to carve out of the landlord's estate a smaller estate, known as a leasehold estate. As we saw in Chapter 24, all leasehold estates are personal property and are technically known as chattels real. A lease, therefore, is not only a contract but is in effect a conveyance or grant of a leasehold estate in real property.

The fundamental requirements for the creation of a leasehold estate are as follows:

(1) The occupation of the tenant must be subordinate to the title of the landlord. This fact is recognized by the tenant when he takes possession of the property with the consent of the landlord and when he pays rent. The tenant may not deny the landlord's title to the property.

(2) The landlord must possess a reversionary interest. This means that upon the expiration of the term set out in the lease, the tenant must return the possession of the property to the landlord.

(3) The tenant must have the exclusive right to the possession and control of the premises.

(4) Under the terms of the contract an estate must be conveyed by the landlord to the tenant.

While at early common law any leasehold estate could be created by an oral agreement between the lessor and lessee, the English Statute of Frauds (1677) required that leases which were to run for more than three years had to be in writing. While some states still follow the provisions of the English Statute of Frauds, many have modified its provisions by statute, to the extent that any lease for more than one year must be in writing to be enforceable. The time at which the one-year term begins to run is usually held to be the date on which the parties enter into the lease-contract, and not the day on which the tenancy is to begin. In some states, however, an oral contract for a tenancy not to exceed one year is valid and enforceable without regard to the date on which the agreement was made.

The study of the law governing the relationship of landlord and tenant may be simplified if it is realized that the common law principles governing the relationship have been considerably modified by statute, and that even where they continue in general force they give way to the express intentions of the parties. Hence it is doubly important for both the landlord and the tenant to study carefully the terms of the proposed lease before they sign it. It should be remembered that the common law principles were established many years ago, and if they should seem harsh and not adapted to modern economic conditions the parties should make certain that the lease contains provisions which more nearly conform to their intentions and desires. Since a lease is fundamentally a contract, the parties are privileged to place in it any terms upon which they may agree so long as such terms are not illegal. The significance of these comments will become clearer as we progress in our study of this chapter.

CLASSIFICATION

Leasehold estates are classified as follows: (1) estates for years, (2) estates from year to year, or periodic tenancies, (3) estates at will, and (4) estates at sufferance.

An *estate for years* is an estate which has been created for a definite time. For example, A (lessor) leases his house and lot to B (lessee) for a period of one year. As a result of the lease an estate or tenancy for one year is "carved out of" A's fee simple estate in the property. It is for a definite period and terminates automatically upon the expiration of the term. No notice to terminate the lease is required of either A or B.

Estates from year to year, or periodic tenancies, are created for indefinite periods. They may be from year to year, from month to month, or from week to week. For example, A rents his house to B, for no definite period, but B agrees to pay $100 a month to A as rent. This is a periodic tenancy from month to month. If it is agreeable to A and B, B might continue in possession of the property for many months, or even years, by paying A the agreed-upon rent as it falls due each month. Many people rent houses and apartments in this manner. The statutes generally provide that a thirty-day written notice, from the last rent-payment date, must be given in order to terminate the tenancy.

A *tenancy at will* is one wherein the tenant enters into possession of the lands or tenements of another, lawfully, but for no definite term or purpose. At common law a tenancy at will may be terminated at any time by either party. Some states have statutes requiring notice of intent to terminate such tenancy.

In the case of a *tenancy at sufferance* the tenant wrongfully holds over after the expiration of his term. Such a tenant comes into possession of the property rightfully, but he continues in possession wrongfully after his right to continue in possession has terminated. For example, A has a mortgage on B's house and lot. B defaults in the payment of the note and A forecloses on the mortgage. After the property is sold at the foreclosure sale, B holds over and refuses to surrender possession. He is a tenant at sufferance and is not entitled to notice to vacate the property.

COVENANTS

Leases, like deeds to real property, contain certain implied and express covenants. For example, it is implied (if not expressly stated) in every lease that the lessor covenants that the lessee shall have the right to the exclusive possession and control of the premises, that he shall have quiet enjoyment of the premises, and that the lessor has the power to demise or lease the premises to him. But at common law the landlord does not impliedly warrant the condition or suitability of the premises. It is the duty of the lessee to inspect the premises for himself to determine their suitability for his purposes. He must rely upon his own judgment in the matter. The principle of caveat emptor applies, unless it can be shown that the landlord was guilty of fraud. However, the lessor does have a duty to warn the lessee of any latent defects in the premises, if such exist and are known to him but unknown to the lessee. Failure to do so is deemed to constitute fraud. Under some state statutes these common law rules have been modified to the extent that the lessor is held impliedly to warrant that the premises are habitable and safe for occupancy. The tenant may also insist upon an express warranty covering the condition of the premises and their adaptability to his needs.

The tenant impliedly covenants that he will not commit waste and that he will return the premises at the end of the term in the same condition as he received them, less the usual wear and tear occasioned by such occupancy.

The parties to a lease generally place in the instrument a number of express covenants having to do with such matters as the right of the landlord to enter the premises for certain purposes, duty to repair the property, option to renew the lease, amount of rent to be paid, whether or not the lessee must obtain the written consent of the lessor before he may assign or sublet the premises, and so on.

In the execution of a lease both the lessor and the lessee must sign the instrument. The statutes of some states require that long-term leases be recorded, in which case it is necessary to have the lease acknowledged. Some state statutes also require that certain leases be under seal.

Lamont Building Co. v. Court
147 Ohio St. 183, 70 N. E. (2d) 447 (1946)

This was an action by the Lamont Building Company (plaintiff) against Marvin Court (defendant). Judgment for defendant, and plaintiff appealed. Reversed.

This was an action of forcible entry and detainer by the plaintiff against the defendant to obtain possession of an apartment.

On February 19, 1945, plaintiff rented to defendant, on a month-to-month basis, an apartment in an apartment house in Cleveland. At the time, defendant was advised that the occupancy was to be confined exclusively to adult persons. Defendant and his wife moved into the apartment. In the course of a few months a child was born to them, and plaintiff asked defendant to move, which he refused to do. Hence, plaintiff brought this action.

ZIMMERMAN, J. As succinctly stated in 12 *Amer. Jur.* 641, Section 149: "It is the inherent and inalienable right of every man freely to deal or refuse to deal with his fellow men. Competent persons ordinarily have the utmost liberty of contracting, and their agreements voluntarily and fairly made will be held valid and enforceable in the courts. Parties may incorporate in their agreements any provisions that are not illegal or violative of public policy."

Ordinarily, the owner of real property may surround its occupation and use by others with such reasonable restrictions as he may deem fit and proper. Here, the plaintiff was the owner of an apartment building. The defendant rented an apartment and moved into it with knowledge of the condition that its occupancy was to be solely by adults. On the first month's rent receipt given the defendant was the notation, "Specific rental rule—No pets—Adults only." In bringing a child to dwell in the apartment against the plaintiff's stipulation to the contrary, the defendant breached a material part of the agreement.

We know of no constitutional provision, statutory enactment or decision by this court denying the plaintiff the privilege of imposing a condition of the kind involved here. Nor can we conceive that such a condition may be classed as injurious to the public or in contravention of any established interest of society. . . . Notwithstanding we may be sympathetic toward the defendant and his problem of securing living accommodations for himself and family, we cannot allow that sympathy to prevail over the plaintiff's legal rights. Judgment reversed.

Hopkins v. Murphy
233 Mass. 476, 124 N. E. 252 (1919)

This was an action by Walter A. Hopkins (plaintiff) against James J. Murphy (defendant). Judgment for plaintiff, and defendant appealed. Affirmed.

This was an action to recover rent under a written lease of the upper suite in a two-family house. Defendant denied liability and contended that he was constructively evicted from the premises by reason of the presence in the suite of a large number of cockroaches. There was no evidence to show that there were any cockroaches in the leased premises until about December 1, 1915, more than two years after defendant's occupancy began; it appeared that, as soon as plaintiff was notified by defendant of their presence, he sent a man to the house to destroy them, but his efforts in that direction were not successful.

CROSBY, J. It is well settled that in a lease of real estate no covenant is implied that it should be fit for occupation; and this is true of a lease of a building for a dwelling house. *Royce v. Guggenheim*, 106 Mass. 201; *Pomeroy v. Tyler*, 9 N. Y. 514. In the absence of an express agreement between the parties or of fraudulent representations or concealment by the lessor, the lessee takes the demised premises as they exist and the rule of caveat emptor applies. *Skally v. Shute*, 132 Mass. 387. To constitute constructive eviction, it must appear that by his intentional and wrongful act the landlord has deprived the tenant of the beneficial use or enjoyment of the whole or a part of the leasehold.

The record shows that the demised premises were in a new building and had not been occupied before the defendant's tenancy began, and that no cockroaches were seen there by the defendant until more than two years thereafter. There is nothing to indicate that the plaintiff was responsible for the presence of the insects or that he failed in any duty which he owed to the defendant. His unsuccessful attempt to exterminate them could not be found to be a constructive eviction of the defendant. Judgment for plaintiff affirmed.

RIGHTS, DUTIES, AND LIABILITIES OF THE PARTIES

RIGHT TO POSSESSION

Under the common law the lessee is entitled to the exclusive possession and control of the premises during the term of the lease. This right of the lessee is something more than a mere license. The right of a licensee to come upon property is merely permissive. His license gives him no right to the possession of the premises; it merely saves him from being a trespasser. The lessee, on the other hand, has the right to exclusive possession and control as against the whole world (save one with a paramount title), including the lessor. It is true that in most states the lessor, without reserving the right, may enter the premises to determine whether waste has been or is being committed, to collect the rent, to make repairs, if he has covenanted to make repairs, and for the purpose of complying with police regulations. But the lessor has no right to enter the premises for any other purposes without the lessee's consent. If he does so he is a trespasser. In fact, he may not even place upon the premises "for rent" signs, or enter the premises for the purpose of showing prospective renters around.

If the landlord violates his implied covenant of quiet and peaceful possession and interferes with the tenant's possession, he may be held liable for constructive eviction. For such interference the tenant has certain possible remedies. In the first place, the tenant may be able to enjoin the landlord from such interference. Secondly, the tenant may have a cause of action against the landlord for damages resulting from the breach of his implied covenant of quiet possession. In the third place, the tenant may vacate the premises and refuse to pay further rent.

From the viewpoint of the landlord the foregoing common law rules seem to be harsh and undesirable. Consequently, it is quite common to find in leases some provision whereby the landlord reserves the right to enter upon the premises for certain purposes, such as to display "for rent" signs and to show prospective renters about the premises.

Brooks v. LaSalle National Bank

11 Ill. App. (3d) 791, 298 N. E. (2d) 262 (1973)

Lessee brought action for an injunction requiring defendants to restore him to possession of apartment and his personal property located therein, and defendants counterclaimed for unpaid rent and telephone charges. The . . . Court . . . granted injunction, and defendants appealed. Affirmed.

McGLOON, J. Defendants pursue this interlocutory appeal from an injunctional order of the . . . court . . . commanding them to restore plaintiff to possession of Apartment . . . and his personal property located therein.

Defendants obtained an order of the court staying the force and effect of the injunctional order pending this appeal. . . . Affirmed.

The chancellor ordered the temporary injunction on the basis of the allegations of plaintiff's verified complaint and defendants' verified answer. The allegations which arise from the pleadings are as follows: Plaintiff, Stanton Brooks, entered into a one-year lease as lessee with lessor, Blackwood Apartment Hotel, which was owned by defendant Green. . . . On February 25, 1972, plaintiff attempted to enter his apartment at the Blackwood Apartment Hotel, but the door was "plugged" in such a way that his key would not open it. At this time plaintiff had $2,855 of personal property located in the apartment. Plaintiff's demand for admittance to the premises was refused. Plaintiff's attorney telephoned defendant Kreps in order to demand a return of the premises and the personal property, but she refused. Plaintiff's attorney also sent a letter to Kreps making the same demands, but at the time plaintiff filed his complaint on March 10, 1972, he had not been allowed to re-enter the apartment nor had his personal property been returned.

In their answer, defendants allege that plaintiff was in arrears for his January, 1972, rent in the amount of $100.18 and for his February, 1972, rent in the amount of $175. Plaintiff presented defendants a check for $100.18 as payment for the January arrearages, but such check was returned for insufficient funds. Under the terms of the lease, the lessor provided a furnished apartment, linens, maid service, and telephone switchboard service. Clause 13 of the lease provided, in pertinent part:

It is expressly agreed, between the parties hereto, that if default be made in the payment above reserved or any part thereof, . . . it shall be lawful . . . to declare said term ended, to reenter said demised premises or any part thereof and the said party of the second part (lessee), or any other person or persons occupying the same to expel, remove and put out, using such force as he may deem necessary in so doing, and the said premises again to repossess and enjoy as in his first estate.

*   *   *

Defendant Kreps verbally notified the plaintiff that the check for $100.18 had been twice returned unpaid and that he owed a total of $278.28, which included overdue rent and telephone charges. She warned him that unless she received a certified check for the total amount in two days, she would terminate his tenancy. The answer further averred that the plaintiff became abusive, threatened to damage or destroy the furnishings in the apartment, and refused to pay the past-due rent.

In their answer, defendants relied on Clause 13 of the lease to justify their obtaining possession of the apartment without resorting to legal proceedings. They also asserted an innkeeper's lien on the plaintiff's personal property pursuant to *Ill. Rev. Stat.* 1971, ch. 82, par. 57. They objected to the plaintiff's seeking equitable relief, because they claim that he did not comply with the equitable maxims of "clean hands" and "a plaintiff who seeks relief from a court of equity, must himself offer to do equity."

Defendants counterclaimed for $453.28, which represented the unpaid rent for three months and telephone charges. In addition to asserting an innkeeper's lien on plaintiff's personal property, defendant claimed a right to distrain the personal property for the past-due rental pursuant to *Ill. Rev. Stat.* 1971, ch. 80, par. 16.

The granting of a temporary injunction resides in the sound discretion of the chancellor. Unless we find an abuse of discretion, we will not set aside the chancellor's order. (*Schultz v. Agenlian* (1967), 90 Ill. App. (2d) 131, 234 N. E. (2d) 345.) In deciding whether to issue a preliminary mandatory injunction, it is proper for the chancellor to balance the relative convenience and injury to the parties which would result. (*Davis v. East St. Louis and Interurban Water Co., Inc.* (1971), Ill. App., 270 N. E. (2d) 424.) In the instant case the injury and inconvenience to the plaintiff of being unknowingly and suddenly without a place to live and without his basic personal belongings is severe in comparison to the defendants having to allow the plaintiff the use of one of their apartments pending resolution of the issues on the merits. We believe the chancellor acted fairly in temporarily relegating the plaintiff and defendants to positions which would create the least injury to both parties.

For the above reasons, the order of the . . . court of . . . is affirmed.

Judgment is affirmed.

RIGHT TO USE

The legal limitations placed upon the tenant in the use of the premises are not particularly severe. So long as he uses the premises in a legal manner in which they are ordinarily employed and for which they are adapted, he is within his rights. However, he is naturally not permitted to commit waste; if he does so, he is liable for damages. And the tenant is required to use the property in a "tenantlike manner."

Leases at times contain provisions which restrict the use of the premises to certain types of businesses or lines of endeavor, or prohibit the use of the premises for certain designed purposes, e.g. the operation of a tavern, filling station, or pool hall. Where such restrictions exist in a lease, they bind the lessee.

Edwards v. Roe

68 Misc. (2d) 278, 327 N. Y. S. (2d) 307 (1971)

Landlord sought to evict tenant under section of rent, eviction and rehabilitation regulations prohibiting the use of premises for immoral or illegal purposes. Petition dismissed.

YOUNGER, J. The question for decision is whether chastity is a prerequisite to maintenance of the landlord–tenant relationship.

Respondent, an unmarried lady, lives in rent-controlled premises owned by petitioner. For reasons best left unspoken, petitioner concluded, in October, 1971, that respondent had, from time to time over the preceding several months, engaged in sexual intercourse with a certain gentleman. Acting promptly, petitioner served upon respondent a "notice of termination of tenancy" on the ground that she had used the premises for "illicit relations." Respondent declined to vacate, whereupon petitioner commenced this hold-over proceeding.

The evidence demonstrates that petitioner's conclusion as to respondent's conduct is founded in fact, with this qualification: while respondent has been unchaste, she is neither disorderly nor a prostitute.

What I must decide, then, is whether an unmarried female who, in her apartment, privately engages in sexual intercourse thereby subjects herself to eviction.

The Real Property Actions and Proceedings Law, section 711(5), authorizes removal of a tenant who uses the premises "as a bawdy-house, or house or place of assignation for lewd persons, or for purposes of prostitution, or for any illegal trade or manufacture, or other illegal business." The Advisory Committee Notes state that this is meant to cover "only illegal use . . . for commercial purposes," which, as mentioned above, is not the case here. Hence the statute is inapplicable.

Section 52(d) of the Rent, Eviction and Rehabilitation Regulations goes beyond section 711(5) of the *RPAPL* by permitting an eviction based upon use of the premises for *any* "immoral or illegal purpose," whether commercial or otherwise. Accepting *arguendo* the validity of the regulation, I note that respondent has done nothing illegal, for the law of New York does not proscribe normal sexual intercourse carried out in private between unmarried consenting adults. So much for illegality.

With respect to immorality, one should say little precisely because there is so much to say. "Values are incommensurables; and the law is full of standards that admit of no quantitative measure. . . ." *Posusta v. United States*, 285 F. (2d) 533, 535 (2d Cir. 1961) (L. Hand, J.). If the test be personal to me, I hold that, without a showing—and there is none—that she has harmed anyone, respondent has done nothing immoral. And if the test be the response of the "ordinary" or "average" man or woman, assuming that it makes sense to posit the existence of such a person, I hold that, given the ethical standards of the day, respondent has done nothing immoral.

In sum, acts of sexual intercourse between unmarried consenting adults involving neither public disorder nor prostitution do not constitute a basis for eviction under section 711(5) of the *RPAPL* or Section 52(d) of the Rent, Eviction and Rehabilitation Regulations.

Petition dismissed.

DUTY TO PAY RENT

Rent is the consideration paid by tenant to the landlord for the occupation, use, and enjoyment of the premises. Rent may be in the form of money, services, or chattels.

Under the common law, rent is due and payable at the end of the pay period. Thus, if the tenant is to pay his rent monthly, under the common law he is not required to pay until the end of the month. Or, if it is an agricultural tenancy, the tenant is required to pay at the end of the tenancy. However, this rule is often changed by the terms of the lease, by custom, or by statute.

At common law the tenant is not discharged of his duty to pay rent even though the building is damaged or destroyed; and the fact that such destruction is no fault of the tenant makes no difference. Thus, if the building which the tenant has rented is totally destroyed by fire or tornado, he is still obligated to pay the rent for the rest of the term. The courts have, however, very generally made an exception to this rule where the premises rented are an apartment or rooms in a building. The reason for this harsh common law rule is the theory that the tenant rents not only the building but the land upon which it stands, and it is held that the building is a mere incident to the demise. The land still remains to the tenant. The tenant is not, however, obligated to replace the building with another building. In many states the rule has been changed by statute, wherein the tenant is discharged of his duty to pay rent for the remainder of the term in case the building is destroyed or so greatly damaged that it cannot be used for the purposes intended by the tenant. It is also quite common to place such a provision in the lease. One who contemplates leasing certain premises as a home or for commercial purposes should be certain either that there is a statute which protects him or that a provision is inserted in the lease which will discharge him of his liability to pay rent if the building is damaged or destroyed.

In the absence of a statute or agreement so providing, the landlord does not have a lien upon the personal property of the tenant for rent which is in default. However, a number of the states have statutes which give to the landlord a lien upon the personal property of the tenant which is upon the premises covered by the lease. While such statutes are usually applicable to agricultural tenancies alone, local statutes should be consulted to determine the scope and application of such statutory liens.

Nashville, C. & St. L. Ry. v. Heikens
112 Tenn. 378, 79 S. W. 1038 (1904)

This was an action by I. H. Heikens (plaintiff) against the Nashville, C. & St. L. Ry. (defendant). Judgment for plaintiff, and defendant appealed. Reversed and remanded.

Plaintiff was the owner of a mill and equipment. He leased the property to Hubert Cherry. The mill was destroyed by fire which resulted from sparks emitted from defendant's engine. Plaintiff (landlord) filed suit against defendant to recover damages for the burning of his mill and was given a verdict and judgment for $5,000. Defendant appealed.

Defendant contended that there were two interests in the property—one the interest of the lessee, and the other the interest of the reversioner, the owner in fee of the property (landlord); that each had a right to sue for an injury to his interest, but that neither had a right to sue for an injury to the right of the other; and that in a suit by the reversioner (plaintiff) for an injury to his interest the circuit judge could not lawfully ignore the existence of the leasehold estate of Cherry, and instruct the jury to allow to the reversioner damages for the injuries inflicted upon the whole interest in the property.

NEIL, J. It is insisted by the defendant in error (plaintiff) that when the property was destroyed by fire the leasehold estate ceased, and nothing was left but the reversion, citing a number of cases. In all the foregoing cases it appeared that the property rented was a room or apartment in a building, or some part of the building, as distinguished from the whole building. In this class of cases the authorities are practically uniform in holding that the destruction of the building brings the interest of the lessee to an end. The reason given is that the lease of such a portion of a building does not carry with it any interest in the land.

The current of authority is almost without exception that, where a building is rented without any language indicating that only the building itself is leased, as distinguished from the subjacent land, both the building and the land pass under the lease, and a destruction of the building will not end the lease, but that the lease will continue to the end of the term, and the lessee is liable for the rent up to the expiration of such term.

In the present case the two interests referred to still exist and the reversioner and the tenant each have a right of action for the injury to which he was subjected by the fire. In Sutherland on Damages it is said: "The same act may be injurious to several persons having different interests—to the person having a limited estate in possession, and the person or persons having the fee subject to that possessory title. The owner of the reversionary or expectant state has no claim for damages where a wrong affects only its present enjoyment, and when it affects the value of the whole estate in possession and in expectancy he has no claim for damages except for the injury to the inheritance." Vol. 4, Sec. 1033.

Applying these principles, it is clear that the circuit judge committed error in instructing the jury that they should allow to the defendant in error (plaintiff) the whole value of the mill and equipment, taking no account of the value of the leasehold interest. This value should have been proven, and the jury should have been instructed to deduct it from the total valuation of the mill. Reversed and remanded.

DUTY TO REPAIR

Under the common law the landlord has no obligation to the tenant to make repairs to the property leased to him. In fact, the tenant owes to the landlord a duty to make such repairs as are necessary to maintain the premises in the condition in which the tenant received them. If he fails to do so he is guilty of committing waste and will be liable to the landlord for same. This rule, which no doubt is contrary to the view that is held by most persons, grew out of the common law rule that the tenant was entitled to the exclusive possession of the premises, even as against the landlord himself. In consequence of that rule it was held to be the tenant's and not the landlord's duty to make all necessary repairs during the tenancy, in order that the property might not deteriorate and decline in value. Of course, the tenant is not required to make major repairs to the premises. He is required only to make such repairs as are necessary to protect and maintain the property in the condition in which he received it.

Where the landlord operates an apartment house or a house wherein he leases rooms to a number of different persons, he is required under the common law rule to keep in repair the halls, stairways, basement, roof, elevators, and so on. The theory is that he retains dominion and control over such places and hence is required to keep them in proper repair. The tenants do not have exclusive possession and control of these parts of the building, and therefore have no duty to keep them in repair.

Certain statutory modifications of the common law rules as to repairs are found in some of the states. However, the tenant's interests will be best protected if he can succeed in having a stipulation inserted in the lease-contract to the effect that it is the landlord's responsibility to make all necessary repairs.

Siggins v. McGill et al.

72 N. J. L. 263, 62 A. 411 (1905)

This was an action by John Siggins (plaintiff) against Julia Thayer McGill and others (defendants). Judgment for plaintiff, and defendants appealed. Affirmed.

Plaintiff was a tenant of defendants, occupying an apartment in a building owned by them in Jersey City. There were several apartments in the building, and these were separately rented out by defendants to different families. The halls and stairways of the building were used in common by the several tenants. While descending one of these stairways, plaintiff stumbled and fell, sustaining personal injuries. This action was brought to recover compensation therefor from the landlords, upon the ground that plaintiff's fall was due to the bad condition of the stair covering.

Defendants contended that plaintiff knew, or ought to have known, the condition of the stair covering, and had assumed the risk; and that he was guilty of contributory negligence.

PITNEY, J. Since the building was occupied by several families, who had the use of the halls and stairways in common, there rests upon the defendants the duty of using reasonable care to keep the halls and stairways in proper condition for the common use of the tenants. In this state it is established as a general rule that the landlord is not liable for injuries sustained by a tenant or his family or guests by reason of the ruinous conditions of the premises demised; there being upon the letting of a house or lands no implied contract or condition that the premises are or shall be fit and suitable for the use of the tenants. So it was held by the Supreme Court in *Naumberg v. Young,* 44 N. J. L. 33; *Mullen v. Ranier,* 45 N. J. L. 520. But it is recognized that this rule does not apply to those portions of his property (such as passageways, stairways, and the like) that are not demised to the tenant, but are retained in the possession and control of the landlord for the common use of the tenants and those having lawful occasion to visit them; the way being used as appurtenant to the premises demised. With respect to such ways, it has been held by our Supreme Court that the landlord is under the responsibility of a general owner of real estate who holds out an invitation to others to enter upon and use his property, and is bound to see that reasonable care is exercised to have the passageways and stairways reasonably fit and safe for the uses which he has invited others to make of them.

The defense that the plaintiff knew the condition of the stair covering and assumed the risk, and further that he was guilty of contributory negligence, are untenable; they being at least disputable questions of fact for the jury's determination. Judgment for plaintiff affirmed.

RIGHT TO ASSIGN OR SUBLEASE

Under the common law the tenant has a right to assign or sublet the premises, during the term of the lease, without the consent or permission of the landlord. However, the landlord generally insists that a provision be inserted in the lease to the effect that the tenant may not assign or sublease the premises without the consent of the landlord. Such consent may be given at the time the property is sublet, or afterwards. Usually the landlord does not object to an assignment or subletting of the property if he is of the opinion that the subtenant will take proper care of the property.

There is a distinction between an assignment and a sublease. In the case of an assignment the tenant transfers to the subtenant his entire remaining interest in the lease. In the case of a sublease the tenant merely transfers to the subtenant a portion of his interest in the lease; that is, the tenant may sublet for only a portion of the term remaining, or he may sublet a portion, but not all, of the premises. In the case of a sublease the tenant has a reversionary interest in the premises; but not so in the case of an assignment.

When a tenant assigns or subleases the premises he remains liable on the lease to the landlord. He is responsible for the payment of the rent and for the carrying out of all of his other duties and obligations under the lease. This is true unless the landlord agrees to a novation, in which case the subtenant is "substituted" for the tenant, and the tenant is discharged of all his duties under the lease. For his own protection the tenant should require that the subtenant agree to indemnify him for any losses which he may suffer by reason of default or wrongful act on the part of the subtenant.

Wainwright et al. v. Bankers' Loan & Investment Co.
112 Va. 630, 72 S. E. 129 (1911)

This was an action by the Bankers' Loan & Investment Company (plaintiff) against W. H. Wainwright and another (defendants). Judgment for plaintiff, and defendants appealed. Reversed.

This was an action for rent alleged to be due under a certain lease. The lease was dated April 2, 1907. It demised the premises to defendants for the term of five years, determinable at the option of the lessees in certain contingencies before the expiration of the term. Among other provisions, the lease stipulated that the property should be used "for a hotel, billiard and pool room, and a saloon," and defendants covenanted not to use the building for any other purpose, "or to sublet said building, or any portion thereof, to be used for any other purpose without the consent" of the lessor. The lease also stipulated that in the event a license could not be obtained for the sale of liquor, or, if obtained, in the event that the right to conduct a barroom should cease, the lessees, at their option, might abrogate the contract by giving proper notice.

Defendants (Wainwright and Ayres) took possession of the property in May, 1907, and sublet the hotel portion, conducting personally the barroom as partners, until February 14, 1908, when Wainwright sold his interest to Ayres. Ayres continued the business until July 17, 1908, when he assigned one-half of his interest to Moore. Ayres and Moore then continued the business jointly until March, 1909, when Ayres assigned his interest to Moore. In April, 1909, Moore made application for a barroom license for the license year commencing May 1, 1909, but the license was denied. Thereupon Moore and Ayres on April 30, 1910, gave notice to the lessor of their election to terminate the tenancy.

Plaintiff refused to accept surrender of the property and declared that it proposed to hold the original lessees responsible for the entire rent. This action grew out of the refusal of the original lessees (defendants) to pay the rent claimed to be due and owing by the plaintiff.

WHITTLE, J. It is settled law that, in the absence of express prohibition, all leases are assignable. The general doctrine is stated in Taylor's *Landlord and Tenant*, Sec. 402, as follows: "The power of assignment is incident to the estate of every lessee, unless he has been restrained by the terms of his lease. A covenant, however, not to assign or underlet the premises, without the express permission of the landlord, . . . is frequently inserted in a lease." In Section 407, the learned author observes: "Covenants of this description (not to assign or underlet) are construed by courts of law with the utmost jealousy, to prevent the restraint from going beyond the express stipulation." So, in 2 *Minor on Real Property*, Sec. 1226, after stating the general rule that every estate and interest in lands and tenements may be assigned, it is said "that if, in leases for life or years, it is intended to restrict or bar the power of assignment, it must be done by special and precise stipulations." The author goes on to state: "Such restrictions are not favored by the law and are strictly construed."

The language employed in this instance is plain and unambiguous. The premises are to be used "for a hotel, billiard and pool room, and a saloon," and the lessees "agree not to use said building for any other purpose, or to sublet said building, or any portion thereof, to be used for any other purpose without the consent" of the lessor. The manifest intendment of this covenant is that the lessee may sublet the premises without the consent of the lessor for the purposes specified; and it was not contended in argument that the assignment to Moore was a violation of the restrictive covenant.

There was no contention that the assignment relieved the original lessees, Wainwright and Ayres, from personal liability to pay rent, and to see that all covenants imposed upon them by the contract were performed. But they did contend that the assignment to Moore was valid, and that, in certain contingencies, he had the right to give notice and terminate the tenancy. In these contentions the defendants were plainly within their right under the contract. They introduced evidence tending to show that they and their subtenants had discharged all the obligations imposed upon them by the terms of the lease, that the contingency had arisen which authorized its abrogation, and that due notice of their election to terminate the tenancy had been given. The court ought, therefore, to have held as matter of law that the various assignments of the lease were lawful; and, pertinent issues raised by the evidence should have been submitted to the determination of the jury. Judgment reversed.

RIGHT TO TRANSFER REVERSIONARY INTEREST

The reversionary interest of the landlord may be transferred, either voluntarily or by operation of law. The owner of the property and the reversionary interest may sell the property and assign the reversionary interest in the lease to the purchaser. Under such circumstances the vendee "steps into the shoes" of the vendor. The vendee has the same rights and duties under the lease, that the vendor had. The rights and obligations of the tenant remain unchanged.

After the transfer of a reversionary interest, unless it is otherwise provided, the transferee is entitled to receive from the tenant any rent that becomes due subsequent to the transfer. However, in order to protect himself in this respect, the transferee must immediately notify the tenant that he is now the landlord under the lease and that rents must be paid to him. If he fails to give such notice and the tenant, not knowing of the transfer, pays his rent to the transferor, the tenant will be discharged of his liability to the extent of the payments made.

The landlord may assign his rights to receive the payment of rent without assigning his reversionary interest. If he does so, the assignee must notify the tenant of the assignment in order to protect his rights under it.

If the landlord sells the property, the rights of the tenant under his lease are not affected. Even though he may not have recorded his lease, his occupation of the premises is held to be sufficient to put any prospective purchaser on notice that he has, or may have, some interest in the property. His occupancy should cause the prospective purchaser to inquire as to his interest. If he fails to do so and proceeds to buy the property, he takes subject to all the rights of the tenant to continue to occupy the premises until the end of his term, assuming, of course, that he complies with all his obligations under the lease.

LIABILITY OF THE LANDLORD

The liability of the landlord to the tenant and to third persons for injuries sustained while upon the premises is largely determined by two factors, (1) the degree of the landlord's control of the premises and (2) whether or not the injury was due to his negligence or breach of duty.

As we have heretofore seen, the landlord does not impliedly warrant that the premises are safe and adaptable to the use of the tenant, nor that he will keep the property in repair. Furthermore, since the tenant is entitled to exclusive possession of the premises, unless otherwise agreed, the landlord has no control over the premises. Because of these basic rules the courts hold that the landlord is not generally liable to the tenant for any injuries sustained by the tenant while on the premises. However, he is held liable if the injury sustained is due to some latent defect or dangerous condition of the premises, known to him but not to the tenant. For example, in one case the court held the landlord liable for renting an apartment to a tenant without notifying him that the previous tenant and his family had had smallpox during their tenancy. The courts also hold the landlord liable to the tenant of an apartment house for any injuries sustained by the tenant while making use of the hallways, lobbies, basements, stairways, or elevators. This is due to the theory that the landlord, not the tenant, has dominion and control over such parts of the apartment house.

It must be observed that in all such cases, in order to secure a judgment for damages against the landlord, the tenant must prove that his injury was a result of the landlord's negligence.

Similar rules of law cover the relationship of the landlord to third persons. If the landlord has not covenanted to repair the premises and has not reserved the right to re-enter the property as he wishes, he is likely not to be liable to third persons, such as the guests and licensees of the tenant, who are injured while on the premises. The tenant himself owes such persons the duty of reasonable care in keeping the premises in a safe condition, and is liable for the breach of such duty. The landlord is, of course, liable to third persons who are injured, owing to his negligence, while within any part of the premises which are under his control, such as elevators, hallways, and stairways.

Faucett v. Provident Mutual Life Insurance Co.

244 Ala. 308, 13 So. (2d) 182 (1943)

This was an action by Stella T. Faucett, as administratrix of the estate of Ella Yarworth, deceased (plaintiff) against the Provident Mutual Life Insurance Co. (defendant). Judgment for defendant, and plaintiff appealed. Reversed and remanded.

This was an action to recover damages for death by wrongful act. Plaintiff's intestate was alleged to have come to her death from injuries received from the falling of overhead plaster in the hallway of the residence occupied by her at the time of the accident.

Defendant leased the building to Arthur and Roderick Cole as a residence, under a written lease, which contained the following covenant on the part of the lessees: "not to assign this lease, nor underlease, nor let said premises or any part or interest therein without the written consent of the lessor hereon endorsed." Afterwards Arthur and Roderick Cole sublet a portion of the premises to Edward Yarworth. Yarworth and his wife, Ella Yarworth, resided there until Mrs. Yarworth's death.

Plaintiff alleged that the death of Ella Yarworth was a result of the negligence of defendant in failing to give notice to its lessees (Arthur and Roderick Cole) of the latent defect in the plastering, known to defendant, but unknown to the lessees or the sublessees. Plaintiff further alleged that defendant (lessor) waived the requirement of written consent to sublet the premises for the following reasons: (1) Arthur and Roderick Cole, at the time they signed the lease, told defendant's agents that they would probably sublet a part of the premises and no objections were made by defendant's agents; and (2) Defendant knew of the subletting of the premises to Yarworth and accepted the payment of rent from the Coles, knowing that part of the money with which they paid the rent came from Yarworth.

BOULDIN, J. The lease expressly declared no obligation on the lessor to repair, and negatived any warranty of the fitness of the property for the use for which it was leased, or liability for damages from defects in the premises. The lessor had a legal right to insert such stipulations in the lease. However, notwithstanding such right, and regardless of the fact that a lessee takes the property as it is, with no duty on the part of the lessor to repair, the lessor is under a duty to give notice of latent defects, known to him to be dangerous to occupants and which were not necessarily discoverable by the lessee. Leasing the property, putting the lessees in a position of concealed peril, without giving notice thereof, is a breach of duty and negligence which will render the lessor liable for personal injuries or death resulting from such defects. This liability extends to the lessee and those occupying the premises in his right. This includes a subtenant and his family, if the lessee is authorized to let to a subtenant. The subtenant, in such case, acquires an estate with the same incidents with regard to the safety of the premises as the tenant in chief. *Lacey v. Deaton*, 228 Ala. 368, *Smith v. Hallock*, 290 Ala. 981, 98 So. 781.

The main question in the case at bar is whether or not the attempted lease by the Coles (lessees) to Ed Yarworth was valid, since the Coles did not secure from the defendant written authority to sublet the premises. However, such consent may be given after the subletting; and the fact that such consent was given was evidenced by the knowledge, on the part of the defendant, that the premises were sublet to Ed Yarworth, and the acceptance of the rent from the Coles, knowing that part of the money paid came from Yarworth. These facts make it evident that the defendant waived the requirement of written consent to sublet the premises. Reversed and remanded.

TERMINATION OF THE RELATION

The principal ways in which leases are terminated are as follows: (1) by the expiration of the term provided for in the lease, (2) by notice, (3) by surrender, (4) by forfeiture, (5) by eviction, (6) by destruction of the premises (under certain circumstances). A lease is not terminated by the death of either party.

TERMINATION BY EXPIRATION OF TERM

In a tenancy for years, a definite termination date is specified in the lease. Such a lease automatically terminates on the specified date without the requirement of a notice by either the landlord or the tenant.

TERMINATION BY NOTICE

In a periodic tenancy, such as from year to year, or from month to month, notice is required to terminate the lease. Such a tenancy continues until one party or the other gives notice of his intention to terminate the relation. The common law requires a six-months notice to terminate a tenancy from year to year, and comparable periods for a tenancy from month to month, or from week to week. Today the matter of notices is largely covered by statute, but the state statutes vary considerably. In the case of a tenancy from month to month, it is quite generally required that a thirty-day written notice be given. While the statutes usually require that some type of notice be given in the case of a tenancy at will, no notice is required in the case of a tenancy at sufferance.

TERMINATION BY SURRENDER

Since the lease is basically a contract, the parties are privileged to surrender their rights under it upon any terms on which they are able to agree. Consequently, the tenant may surrender or give up his rights under the lease to the landlord, and, if the landlord is willing to accept, the lease is terminated.

TERMINATION BY FORFEITURE

Statutes in some of the states provide for termination by forfeiture, and leases often contain provisions which give the landlord the right of forfeiture in the event the tenant breaches some important provision of the lease, such as the payment of rent, or a restriction on the assignment of the lease. Since forfeitures are not looked upon with favor, the courts interpret such statutes and lease provisions quite strictly, keeping in mind the rights of the tenants.

TERMINATION BY EVICTION

The relation of landlord and tenant may be terminated by the eviction of the tenant, in which case the tenant is discharged of his duty to pay future rent installments. The eviction may be actual or constructive. An act on the part of the landlord may so deprive the tenant of the peaceful use and enjoyment of the premises that it constitutes constructive eviction. However, the court will not hold that there has been constructive eviction in such cases unless the tenant abandons the premises.

TERMINATION BY DESTRUCTION OF THE PREMISES

At common law the destruction of a building on the leased premises does not terminate the lease and discharge the tenant from the duty of paying his rent. However, this rule has been changed in many states by statute, and it may also be nullified by the agreement of the parties. In such cases the destruction of the subject matter of the lease results in the termination of the lease. And, of course, even under the common law the destruction of the apartment house or rooming house resulted in terminating the leases of the tenants.

REVIEW CASES

1. Luedtke sued Phillips, owner of the apartment which Luedtke rented, for injuries sustained when a wall cabinet fell on her. She contended that Phillips had permitted the cabinet to be installed in a negligent manner. Under the written lease which she had signed, she had agreed to assume all risks to person or property due to either latent or patent defects. The lease further stipulated that Phillips had no duty to repair the premises. Judgment for whom? (Luedtke v. Phillips et al., 190 Va. 207, 56 S. E.(2d) 80)

2. Carbon Fuel Co. leased a house to Gregory, stipulating that it should be occupied by Gregory's family only, but making no other limitation as to its use. Gregory sold ice cream and other articles on the premises, and Carbon Fuel Co. tried to evict him for doing so. The rent control law in force at that time stated that a landlord could not terminate a lease unless he could show substantial reason. The lower court held that there were insufficient grounds for eviction, and the company appealed. Ruling? (Carbon Fuel Co. v. Gregory, 131 W. Va. 494, 48 S. E.(2d) 338)

3. Kearines brought an action in tort against her landlord, Cullen, for personal injuries received when a defective step gave way under her. The building was a dwelling house divided into two separate units with a front door for each. One unit was rented to Kearines and the other to another family. The front doors, standing side by side, had thresholds a foot above ground level, and the step in question ran in front of the two doors and gave access to both. Cullen contended that he retained no possession or control over the step. Judgment for whom? (Kearines v. Cullen, 185 Mass. 298, 67 N. E. 243)

4. Richard Paul, Inc., a manufacturer of textiles, leased business premises from the Union Improvement Co. for a period of three years. The landlord agreed in the lease to make certain repairs but failed to do so. Richard Paul, Inc., made the repairs itself, in the amount of $565.63, and then brought suit. It asked judgment for $17,050, alleging that the Union Improvement Co. knew what use the tenant was to make of the building and that its failure to make the agreed repairs resulted in the loss of contemplated profits. What ruling? (Richard Paul, Inc. v. Union Improvement Co., 59 F. Supp. 252)

5. Leech leased an apartment from Husbands for a two-year term but moved out after a few months, claiming constructive eviction by reason of the fact that the apartment was infested with vermin, bugs, and disease germs. The issue in the ensuing action was whether there was an implied warranty that the apartment would be fit for habitation or would remain so. Judgment for whom? (Leech v. Husbands, 152 A. 729)

Secured
Transactions

26

Credit plays an extremely important part in the day-to-day process of carrying on modern business. If all business were transacted upon a cash basis, business activity would be greatly retarded and many human wants that are now fulfilled would go unsatisfied. As a result of the many security devices that are available, we are able to put to work great reservoirs of credit in our quest to satisfy human wants and raise our standard of living.

Credit is created when one man lends money to another or forgoes the payment of some obligation until some future date. Of course, even without modern credit devices a limited amount of credit would be extended upon the mere unsecured promise of the borrower to pay his obligation at a time mutually agreed upon. But one who extends credit generally requires something more than such an unsecured promise. There are a number of reasons for such a requirement. The lender may have some question as to the honesty and integrity of the borrower. Or the lender may have a feeling of uncertainty as to the ability of the borrower to carry out successfully the business plans and schemes which he has in mind. Most important, the lender wishes to obtain a lien upon, or some proprietary interest in, some of the borrower's property, or the personal credit of some third party or parties, so that if the borrower runs into financial difficulties the lender will be more likely to secure the payment of the debt. If the creditor is given a lien or some proprietary interest in the debtor's property, he will be a secured creditor and have priority over unsecured creditors of the borrower in the event of bankruptcy. For these reasons lenders usually demand some type of security for their loans.

The numerous security devices that have been developed to facilitate the extension of credit are founded either upon property or upon personal security. The borrower may have real or personal property which he can offer as security; or he may be able to obtain the personal credit of others. When real property is offered as security, the principal security devices available are (1) real property mortgages and (2) deeds of trust. Where personal property is the security, the devices generally used are (1) chattel mortgages, (2) conditional sales contracts, (3) pledge agreements, and (4) trust receipts. Where personal credit is used as a basis for extending credit, we have (1) surety contracts and (2) guaranty contracts.

Security devices founded upon real or personal property give to the obligee a lien upon, or some proprietary interest in, the property of the obligor, arising out of contract. In addition to such contractual liens there are a number of common law and statutory liens. Common law liens arise out of the relation of the parties; statutory liens are created by legislative enactment.

There are usually two legal instruments connected with a security transaction: (1) a promissory note or bond, which evidences the debt or obligation; (2) the security device, which secures the debt or obligation.

REAL PROPERTY AS SECURITY

REAL PROPERTY MORTGAGES

NATURE AND CREATION.   Real property is often used as security for the payment of a debt or for the performance of some other obligation or act. Such a security transaction is accomplished through the use of a mortgage. There are two parties to a mortgage, the *mortgagor* (debtor) and the *mortgagee* (creditor). Through the execution of the mortgage the debtor conveys an interest in his estate in real property to the creditor to secure the performance of his obligation to the creditor.

The debt or obligation of the debtor is evidenced by a note or bond. The mortgage is the security given by the debtor to the creditor to insure his faithful performance of his obligation. Hence, all such transactions involve the execution of two legal instruments, (1) a note or bond, and (2) a mortgage.

The formalities in the execution of a mortgage are governed by statute. While there is considerable variation in the statutes, they all require that a mortgage be signed by the mortgagor. They also generally require that it be either acknowledged or witnessed, and in some instances it must be under seal. Some state statutes provide that mortgages must be executed with the same formalities as are required in the execution of deeds.

TITLE THEORY AND LIEN THEORY.   There are two theories as to mortgages, the *title theory* and the *lien theory*.

The title theory of mortgages was the first to develop. The early common law courts held that the mortgagor conveyed to the mortgagee the title to the property subject to the mortgagor's right to the return of the property if he performed his obligation under the mortgage contract. The mortgage was in the form of a deed but the deed contained what was called a *defeasance clause.* The mortgage designated a day, called the "law day," when the mortgagor had to pay the debt or perform some other act required in the mortgage. If he performed on the "law day" he was entitled to a reconveyance of the property; but if he failed to do so the title to the property became absolute in the mortgagee.

In many instances the common law or title theory of mortgages proved harsh and unfair to the mortgagor. Often the security was of greater value than the debt which it secured; yet if the mortgagor was unable to pay or perform on the "law day" he lost his property. Recognizing these inequities, the equity courts began to grant certain relief to mortgagors. In the first place they took the view that the mortgagee did not acquire the legal title to the property, but only a lien upon the title as security. The mortgagor was not only entitled to the possession of the property but he also retained the legal title, subject to the mortgagee's lien upon the title. In the second place, the equity courts gave to the mortgagor what was termed an *equity of redemption,* which entitled him to "redeem" the property subsequent to the "law day." This meant that if the mortgagor defaulted in payment on the "law day," the title to the property did not automatically become absolute in the mortgagee, since the mortgagor could still pay the debt and redeem the property. However, the equity courts felt that it was unfair to the mortgagee to allow the mortgagor an indefinite time in which to "redeem." Therefore the mortgagee was granted the right to file a bill in equity asking that the mortgagor's equity of redemption be foreclosed. The courts would, in such cases, decree the foreclosure of the mortgagor's equity of redemption and designate a time within which the mortgagor had to redeem the property or else lose it. The period allowed was usually fixed at from six to twelve months.

Today the states are classified as title theory states and lien theory states, according to the theory which they have adopted. Most of them are lien theory states. But it should be observed that even in the states which still follow the title theory it has been so radically modified by statute that there is very little difference, with regard to determining the rights of the parties, between the two groups of states.

RECORDING OF MORTGAGE.   All states now have statutes which require that the mortgagee record his mortgage. Such recording is necessary in order that the mortgagee may protect his mortgage against subsequent bona fide purchasers or mortgagees of the property. **Recording of a** mortgage is constructive notice of the existence of the mortgage.

A mortgage is, of course, valid and binding as between the mortgagor and the mortgagee even though it is not recorded. But a different rule applies when an innocent third party is involved. Since the mortgagor is permitted to retain possession of the property, he is to all outward appearances the owner of the property. If he approaches some third party for a loan, the third party, finding no outstanding mortgages recorded at the court house, may innocently extend credit secured by a mortgage on the same property. If the third party records the mortgage, he will be protected as against any prior unrecorded mortgages. For his own protection the mortgagee should immediately file his mortgage for recording.

SALE OF PROPERTY BY MORTGAGOR. A mortgagor may sell and transfer his interest in the mortgaged property without first obtaining the mortgagee's consent. The reason is that such sale and transfer do not discharge the mortgagor on his note to the mortgagee nor release the mortgagee's mortgage upon the property. The purchaser from the mortgagor receives no greater rights or interests than the mortgagor (seller) had.

The purchaser (transferee) of mortgaged property may either (1) buy subject to the mortgage or (2) assume and agree to pay the mortgage. If he buys subject to the mortgage, he does not become personally liable on the note held by the mortgagee. He does not agree to pay the note under any circumstances. However, the property which he buys is still subject to the mortgage. Hence if there is a default in the payment of the note, the mortgagee may foreclose the mortgage and sell the property. If the proceeds from the sale of the property do not satisfy the note, the transferee has no further liability; the most that he can lose is his investment in the property. On the other hand, if the purchaser assumes and agrees to pay the mortgage, he becomes personally liable to pay the debt which is evidenced by the note. In the case of a default in the payment of the debt, the mortgagee may foreclose the mortgage and sell the property. If the proceeds of the sale are not sufficient to pay the debt, the mortgagee may ask for a deficiency judgment against both the mortgagor (transferor) and the purchaser (transferee). If the transferee pays the deficiency judgment, the debt is discharged. If the mortgagor pays the deficiency judgment, then he may recoup from the transferee. The mortgagor was not discharged of his liability on the debt when he transferred the property to the purchaser; rather, by the transfer the purchaser became the primary debtor and the mortgagor became the surety. Consequently, if the mortgagor is required to pay the deficiency judgment to the mortgagee he is entitled, as a surety, to reimbursement from the principal debtor, the transferee. The liability of a transferee to a mortgagee is based upon the third-party beneficiary theory. The mortgagee is a creditor beneficiary.

MORTGAGEE'S RIGHT OF TRANSFER.   The mortgagee may sell and transfer his interest in the mortgaged property. This is accomplished by the indorsement of the note and the assignment of the mortgage to the purchaser. The purchaser should immediately record the assignment of the mortgage and give notice to the mortgagor or his transferee, as the case may be.

FORECLOSURE.   The procedures which the mortgagee must follow in order to protect his interests in the event of default on the part of the mortgagor or his transferee are provided for in the statutes of the various states. While a number of forms of foreclosure are provided for, the following are the most common: (1) a suit in equity to foreclose; (2) sale of the property in conformity with a power of sale clause in the mortgage.

The most common method of foreclosure is by filing a bill in equity asking that the mortgagor's equity of redemption be foreclosed. Under strict foreclosure the mortgagee obtains absolute title to the property if the mortgagor fails to exercise his right to redeem the property. This method of foreclosure is not favored by the courts and is seldom used unless the mortgagor is insolvent or the mortgagee agrees to accept the property in full satisfaction of the mortgagor's debt to him. The courts usually decree instead a foreclosure and sale of the property. The statutory requirements as to notice and conduct of the sale must be followed. The property is sold at public auction and the mortgagee may bid at the sale. If the property does not sell for enough to satisfy the debt, the mortgagee is entitled to a deficiency judgment for the balance due. On the other hand, if the property sells for more than enough to satisfy the mortgage debt, the mortgagor, or his transferee, is entitled to the balance, unless there is a second mortgage on the property, in which case the holder of the second mortgage is entitled to the balance.

If a mortgage contains a provision that in case of default in payment of the debt the mortgagee has the power to sell the property under the terms of the mortgage, then it is not necessary to foreclose the mortgage in a court of equity. Such a provision in a mortgage in effect makes the mortgagee the agent of the mortgagor to sell the property. The power of sale clause usually includes the provision that the property may be sold at either a public or a private sale. The mortgagee is entitled to a deficiency judgment if the property does not sell for enough to satisfy his claims.

As we have seen, under modern foreclosure statutes the mortgagor is given a statutory right of redemption *after* the foreclosure and sale of the property. The period of redemption allowed the mortgagor varies from six months in some states to two years in others. If the mortgagor fails to redeem within the statutory period, the purchaser is entitled to receive a deed to the property.

Steinert v. Galasso
69 A. (2d) 841, 363 Pa. 393 (1950)

This was a suit by Helen A. Steinert (plaintiff) against Benny Galasso (defendant). Judgment for plaintiff, and defendant appealed. Affirmed.

Plaintiff was the mortgagee of a purchase-money mortgage made by Robert Wasyl, dated October 6, 1928, securing a debt payable in three years. After reducing the principal to $1,700, he conveyed the mortgaged property to defendant in 1937, subject to the balance due, defendant assuming and agreeing to pay the debt. In 1945, after expiration of the mortgage term, defendant conveyed the property to Maurice Murphy, who also assumed and agreed to pay the debt. Wasyl died in 1937; the mortgage had not been foreclosed; no proceedings to collect were taken against him; no letters testamentary or of administration have issued. We have, then, a suit by the mortgagee against the mortgagor's (Wasyl) grantee (Galasso) who had assumed a liability and had conveyed the property to another (Murphy).

In his brief, appellant-defendant stated his position as follows: "The proper procedure by a mortgagee to hold a grantee to his covenant in a deed is to have the suit brought in the name of the mortgagor (Wasyl) to the use of the mortgagee (Steinert); this can only be done by and with the consent of the mortgagor; the plaintiff has not done so. The mortgagee sues directly in her own name. By the second section of the Act of 1878, 'The right to enforce such personal liability shall not enure to any person other than the person with whom such an agreement is made.' As plaintiff mortgagee is not a person with whom the covenant in the deed from Wasyl to Galasso was made, she is directly excluded by the statute from bringing an action against Galasso to enforce the agreement, and as the statute must be strictly pursued, she cannot maintain her present suit."

LINN, J. In other words, the defendant contends that section 2 of the Act of 1878 disqualifies plaintiff-mortgagee from enforcing, in this suit, defendant's promise to pay the debt. He contends that, within the words of the statute, he "has bona fide parted with the encumbered property" and that his assumption was not a "continuing liability." This contention was properly rejected by the common pleas, whose judgment was affirmed by the Supreme Court, 163 Pa. Super. 576, 63 A. (2d) 443.

It is settled that by taking "under and subject" without more, the grantee agrees to indemnify his grantor against loss, and that a grantee who (in the words of the Act of 1878) "Shall, by an agreement in writing, have expressly assumed a personal liability" for the debt, thereby agrees to indemnify not merely against loss but against liability. *Ryzye et ux. v. Brown et ux.*, 320 Pa. 213, 181 A. 783. In taking "under and subject," the grantee assumes an obligation enforceable when (but not before) the grantor sustains loss, but in case of agreement to pay the debt, the grantor's liability to his creditor may be enforced when the debt matures and remains unpaid, without waiting until the grantor has paid.

It is also settled that, in order to avoid circuity of action, such indemnity contracts may be enforced in a single action in the name of the mortgagor (Wasyl) to the use of the mortgagee (plaintiff) against the grantee (defendant). The use-suit is a familiar procedure. The mortgagee may also bring suit in her own name as beneficiary of the contract by which defendant expressly assumed payment of the mortgage debt. *Fair Oaks Building & Loan Association v. Kahler*, 320 Pa. 245, 181 A. 779.

The defendant argues that Wasyl, the mortgagor, is dead, and as no administration has been had, there is no nominal or legal plaintiff to consent and therefore his obligation cannot be enforced although he has no defense on the merits. His suggestion must be rejected. He has no defense. His agreement to pay the debt, which was then overdue, created liability which continued until the debt was discharged; it was a continuing liability as the words were used in section 2 of the Act of 1878. It created an obligation to the mortgagee creditor beneficiary. Neither Wasyl, if living, nor his personal representative, would be heard to object to becoming the legal plaintiff in a suit-to-use because the judgment in such suit discharging the obligation was for the benefit of Wasyl or his estate. In such circumstances this court has tried the suit as if brought to-the-use. *Patton et al. v. Pittsburgh, Cincinnati & St. Louis Ry. Co.*, 96 Pa. 169.

DEEDS OF TRUST

A deed of trust or trust deed is a type of security device that is sometimes used where real property is given as security for a debt.[1] There are three parties to a deed of trust, (1) the borrower, (2) the trustee, and (3) the lender or beneficiary. The borrower (grantor) conveys the legal title to the property to the trustee (grantee) to hold in trust as security for the payment of his debt to the lender or beneficiary. If the borrower pays the debt as agreed, the debt becomes void. If, however, he defaults in the payment of the debt, the trustee may sell the property at a public sale, under the terms of the deed of trust. While the deed of trust is used extensively in a number of jurisdictions, the courts in some states have treated it as a mortgage and require foreclosure in case of default on the part of the debtor.

[1] A chattel mortgage in the form of a deed of trust is sometimes used in the case of personal property.

Corporations generally use a deed of trust instead of a mortgage as security for their bond issues.

THE LAND CONTRACT

A land contract is a type of security device that is sometimes used where real property is given as security for a debt, but as a rule is used less often than a real property mortgage or a deed of trust. The land contract is used to secure the balance of the purchase money due under a contract to purchase real estate. The purchaser takes on all the outward appearances of a record owner by taking possession, paying all taxes, and keeping the premises in repair, but receives no deed and has only the land contract to show for his equitable ownership in the property. Often the land contract is not recorded. The purchaser usually makes monthly payments as required under the land contract, and when the property is paid for in full, he receives a deed from the seller.

Should the purchaser under the land contract default in his payments, generally it is easier for the seller to regain possession than it is in the usual sale where a deed is given and recorded and a mortgage or deed of trust is put on record. But the complexity of regaining possession under the land contract will depend upon the law of the jurisdiction where the property is located. The land contract may provide that in the event of default, the payments made by the purchaser are to be considered as rent, and that the purchaser forfeits all rights under the agreement, and must vacate the premises.

PERSONAL PROPERTY AS SECURITY

UNIFORM COMMERCIAL CODE

The Uniform Commercial Code, Article 9, Secured Transactions, sets out a comprehensive scheme for the regulation of security interest in personal property and fixtures. It supersedes existing legislation dealing with such security devices as chattel mortgages, conditional sales, trust receipts, factor's liens, and assignments of accounts receivable. Consumer installment sales and consumer loans present special problems of a nature which makes special regulation of them inappropriate in a general commercial codification. Many states now regulate such loans and sales under small loan acts, retail installment selling acts, and the like. While the Code applies generally to security interests in consumer goods, it is not designed to supersede such regulatory legislation. Nor is it designed as a substitute for small loan acts or retail installment selling acts in any state which does not presently have such legislation.

Existing law recognizes a wide variety of security devices, which came into use at various times to make possible different types of secured financing. Differences between one device and another persist in formal requisites, in the secured party's rights against the debtor and third parties, in the debtor's rights against the secured party, and in filing requirements, despite the fact that today many of these differences no longer serve any useful function.

The aim of the Code is to provide a simple and unified structure within which the immense variety of present-day secured financing transactions can go forward with less cost and with greater certainty. Under the Code, the traditional distinctions among security devices, based largely on form, are not retained; the Code applies to all transactions intended to create security interests in personal property and fixtures, and the single term "security interest" substitutes for the variety of descriptive terms which has grown up at common law and statutes. This does not mean that the old forms may not be used. On the contrary, the Code makes it clear that they may be used.

The Code makes possible a radical simplification in the formal requisites for creation of a security interest. A more rational filing system replaces the present system of different files for each security device.

POLICY AND SCOPE OF SECURED TRANSACTIONS.   Sec. 9–102 states that the Code applies with certain exceptions: (1) (a) To any transaction (regardless of its form) which is intended to create a security interest in personal property or fixtures including goods, documents, instruments, general intangibles, chattel paper, accounts or contract rights; and also (b) to any sale of accounts, contract rights, or chattel paper.

(2) This subtitle applies to security interests created by contract including pledge, assignment, chattel mortgage, chattel trust, trust deed, factor's lien, equipment trust, conditional sale, trust receipt, other lien or title retention contract, and lease or consignment intended as security. This subtitle does not apply to statutory liens except as provided in Sec. 9–310.

WHEN SECURITY INTEREST ATTACHES.   Sec. 9–204 states three basic prerequisites to the existence of a security interest: agreement, value, and collateral. When these three coexist, a security interest may attach. However, the Code states that unless postponed by explicit agreement, the security interest automatically attaches when the three stated events have occurred. In many cases perfection of a security interest will depend on the additional step of filing a financing statement.

AFTER–ACQUIRED PROPERTY. Many financing transactions contemplate that the collateral will include both the debtor's existing assets and also assets thereafter acquired by him in the operation of his business. Interests in after-acquired property have never been considered as involving transfers of property for antecedent debt merely because of the after-acquired feature, nor should they be so considered. This rule is of importance principally in insolvency proceedings under the Federal Bankruptcy Act or state statutes which make certain transfers for antecedent debt voidable as preferences. The determination of when a transfer is for antecedent debt is largely left by the Bankruptcy Act to state law.

William Iselin & Co. v. Burgess & Leigh Ltd.
52 Misc. (2d) 821, 276 N. Y. S. (2d) 659 (1967)

This was an action by William Iselin & Co., Inc. (petitioner) against Burgess & Leigh Ltd. et al. (respondents). Levy is vacated and petitioner has the right to possession and sale of the inventory.

Petitioner seeks to vacate an execution levy made by the Sheriff on behalf of one of the respondents against the property and inventory of Maddock and Miller, Inc. (hereinafter called "Debtor") upon the ground that petitioner has a prior security interest and is entitled to immediate possession.

Petitioner is engaged in the business of factoring and commercial financing. The Debtor, one of petitioner's clients, is currently unable to pay its obligations as they mature. The named respondents, other than the Sheriff, are judgment creditors of the Debtor.

Petitioner entered into two written agreements with the Debtor on May 20, 1965. The first was an accounts receivable financing agreement pursuant to which the petitioner agreed to make loans and advances to the Debtor upon the security of its accounts receivable. All such advances, as well as all other obligations owed by the Debtor to petitioner, were payable on demand. The second agreement was entitled "security agreement—merchandise inventory" which provides that Debtor grants to petitioner a continuing general lien upon and a security interest in its entire merchandise inventory then existing or thereafter acquired, as security for the payment in full of all loans and advances made by petitioner in conjunction with the financing agreement. The security agreement further provides that upon the breach of that agreement or of the financing agreement, or upon the non-payment when due of any obligations owed by Debtor to petitioner, petitioner shall have the right to foreclose its lien and security interest, to take possession of the collateral without judicial process, and to sell at public or private sale.

SCHWEITZER, J. Since Debtor's place of business and its warehouse were both in New York County, the security interest created by the security agreement was perfected by due filing of a financing statement with the New York

County Clerk and the New York Department of State on May 21 and May 24, 1965, respectively, pursuant to the Uniform Commercial Code.

One of the respondents, Burgess and Leigh Ltd., obtained a judgment against the Debtor, which was entered in the New York County Clerk's office on or about September 28, 1966 and upon which execution was issued to the Sheriff on or about October 10, 1966. Pursuant to such execution, the Sheriff levied on the Debtor's fixtures and inventory on October 14 and October 21, 1966.

Thereafter, petitioner on or about November 3, 1966 made written demand for payment of the indebtedness which was due and owing by Debtor under the financing agreement and which was payable on demand, pursuant thereto. Debtor defaulted and petitioner contends that thereupon its right to possession of the collateral accrued.

The sole question before this court is whether petitioner has the exclusive right to possession and sale of the collateral, pursuant to its security agreement and the U. C. C.

The validity of the security agreement which secures both present and future advances and which covers both existing and afteracquired inventory is not controverted and accordingly petitioner's security interest attached to such inventory (U. C. C., Sec. 9–204). Petitioner's security interest was perfected by proper filing in May, 1965 (U. C. C., Sec. 9–302), and thereupon petitioner's security interest took priority over all unfiled and unperfected interests (U. C. C., Sec. 9–301), including the rights of judgment creditors who thereafter issued execution, since the liens of such creditors are perfected only by the issuance of execution, pursuant to Rule 5202 (a) C. P. L. R. On default, it would appear that petitioner became entitled to immediate possession of the collateral both by virtue of the express provisions of the security agreement and of the U. C. C., Sec. 9–503.

Thus, by both contract and statute, petitioner has established its right to take possession of the collateral, without judicial process, and it did so, as confirmed by the November 9, 1966 letter agreement between petitioner and Debtor. After the default, the Debtor lost its right of possession and sale and retained only a contingent right in the surplus, if any, after sale. Petitioner's right to sell the collateral exists both by express provisions of the security agreement and of the U. C. C., Sec. 9–504.

Accordingly, the right to possession and sale of the collateral, in the case at bar, passed from the Debtor to the petitioner at the time of default. Whether or not the Debtor had such rights at the time the levy was made, the Debtor did not have them after default, and the levy is ineffective to transfer such right. Therefore, the levy is vacated and petitioner is adjudged to have the right to possession and sale of the inventory of the Debtor.

FUTURE ADVANCES.   Sec. 9–204 of the Code provides that obligations covered by a security agreement may include future advances or other value whether or not the advances or value are given pursuant to commitment.

WHEN POSSESSION BY SECURED PARTY PERFECTS SECURITY INTERESTS WITHOUT FILING.   Sec. 9–305 of the Code states that a security interest in letters of credit and advices of credit, goods, instruments, negotiable documents, or chattel paper may be perfected by the secured party's taking possession of the collateral. If such collateral other than goods covered by a negotiable document is held by a bailee, the secured party is deemed to have possession from the time the bailee receives notification of the secured party's interest. A security interest is perfected by possession from the time possession is taken without relation back and continues only so long as possession is retained. The security interest may be otherwise perfected as provided before or after the period of possession by the secured party.

As under the common law of pledge, no filing is required by the Code to perfect a security interest where the secured party has possession of the collateral. This section permits a security interest to be perfected by transfer of possession only when the collateral is goods, instruments, documents, or chattel paper: that is to say, accounts, contract rights, and general intangibles are excluded. A security interest in accounts, contract rights, and general intangibles—property not ordinarily represented by any writing whose delivery operates to transfer the claim—may be perfected only by filing, and this rule would not be affected by the fact that a security agreement or other writing described the assignment of such collateral as a pledge.

PLACE OF FILING.   Sec. 9–401 of the Code specifies three alternative places of filing: local (in the county), with the state's Secretary of State, and filing both locally and with the Secretary of State. Thus, one must rely upon the Code and its interpretation to ascertain the proper place of filing in each state.

ERRONEOUS FILING.   Sec. 9–401(2) of the Code states that a filing which is made in good faith in an improper place, or not in all of the places required by this section, is nevertheless effective with regard to any collateral as to which the filing complied with the requirements of this subtitle and is also effective with regard to collateral covered by the financing statement against any person who has knowledge of the contents of such financing statement.

FORMAL REQUIREMENTS OF FINANCING STATEMENT.   Sec. 9–402 sets out the simple formal requisites of a financing statement under the Code. These requirements are: (1) signatures and addresses of both parties; and (2) a description of the collateral by type or item. Where the collateral is growing crops or fixtures, the financing statement must also contain a description of the land concerned. Sec. 9–110 provides that any description of personal property or real estate is sufficient whether or not it is specific if it reasonably identifies what is described.

This section adopts the system of "notice filing" which has proved successful under the Uniform Trust Receipts Act. What is required to be filed is not the security agreement itself, as under chattel mortgage and conditional sales acts, but only a simple notice which may be filed either before the security interest attaches or thereafter. The notice itself indicates merely that the secured party who has filed may have a security interest in the collateral described. Further inquiry from the parties concerned will be necessary to disclose the complete state of affairs. Sec. 9–208 provides a statutory procedure under which the secured party, at the debtor's request, may be required to make disclosure. Notice filing has proved to be of great use in financing transactions involving inventory, accounts, and chattel paper, since it obviates the necessity of refiling on each of a series of transactions in a continuing arrangement where the collateral changes from day to day. Where other types of collateral are involved, the alternative procedure of filing a signed copy of the security agreement may prove to be the simplest solution. This section departs from the requirements of many chattel mortgage statutes that the instrument filed be acknowledged or witnessed or accompanied by affidavits of good faith. Those requirements do not seem to have been successful as a deterrent to fraud; their principal effect has been to penalize good faith mortgagees who have inadvertently failed to comply with the statutory niceties. They are here abandoned in the interest of a simplified and workable filing system. The Code allows the secured party to file a financing statement signed only by himself where the filing is with reference to collateral already subject to a security interest in another jurisdiction when brought into this state, or with reference to proceeds when his security interest in the original collateral was perfected.

Howarth v. Universal C.I.T. Credit Corporation
203 F. Supp. 279 (1962)

This was an action by Walter O. Howarth et al. (plaintiffs) against Universal C.I.T. Credit Corporation (defendant). Judgment for plaintiff, trustee in part and for defendant in part.

The plaintiff, trustee in bankruptcy of Spohn Motor Company, Inc. (Spohn), brought this action to recover from the defendant, Universal C.I.T. Credit Corporation (UCIT), the value of property transferred to UCIT from Spohn within four months of filing the petition in bankruptcy.

MARSH, D.J. It seems certain that a finance company which advances money for wholesale financing of *new cars* can perfect a valid security interest therein by filing a financing statement in the offices of the Secretary of the Commonwealth and the Prothonotary of the County in which the dealer does business. U. C. C. Secs. 9–302(1), 9–401(1) (a); *Sterling Acceptance Co. v. Grimes*, 194 Pa. Super. 503, 168 A. (2d) 600 (1961); *Taylor Motor Rental, Inc. v. Associates Discount Corp.*, 196 Pa. Super, 182, 173 A. (2d) 688 (1961); cf. *Girard Trust Corn Exchange Bank v. Warren Lepley Ford, Inc.* (No. 1), 12 Pa. Dist. & Co. (2d) 351, 357 (1957). As we see it, this is because the Motor Vehicle Code of 1939 at Sec. 201(b) provides that a dealer, such as Spohn, "need not obtain certificate of title for *new* motor vehicles * * * until and before sale thereof."

Likewise, Sec. 207(c) of the Motor Vehicle Code, which was in effect at the time Spohn's used cars were sold (Act of June 29, 1937, P. L. 2329, Par. 207(c)), provided that a dealer in used cars "shall not be required to apply for a certificate of title" but shall notify the Department of the acquisition of the vehicle within ten days. Therefore, it is our opinion that a company such as UCIT engaged in wholesale financing may perfect a valid security interest in *used* cars by filing a financing statement pursuant to Secs. 9–302 (1) and 9–401 (1) (a) of the U. C. C.

In view of the similarity of Secs. 203(b) and 207(c) of the Motor Vehicle Code, we cannot perceive any good reason why a lender engaged in wholesale financing cannot perfect a valid security interest in used cars by the same method he employs to perfect a valid security interest in new cars.

Our conclusion finds support in the underlying purposes and policies of the U. C. C., enacted subsequent to these sections of the Motor Vehicle Code, which are: "(a) to simplify and modernize and develop greater precision and certainty in the rules of law governing commercial transactions; (b) to preserve flexibility in commercial transactions and to encourage continued expansion of commercial practices and mechanisms through custom, usage and agreement of the parties." Section 1–102 (2).

In addition we think it simplifies the means whereby a dealer's prospective creditors may protect themselves. A creditor who must search the records in the offices of the Secretary of the Commonwealth and the Prothonotary of the County for notice of encumbrances on new cars in a dealer's inventory at the same time will get notice of encumbrances on the used cars in his inventory. This method seems to be much more convenient and effective than if the creditor in order to protect himself should be forced to demand an inspection of the dealer's title certificate to each used car in his inventory,—a certificate which the dealer is not required to obtain under the Motor Vehicle Code.

The Agreement for Wholesale Financing provides: "Until payment in full, we [Spohn] will hold all proceeds separately and in trust for you [UCIT]." In our opinion, this agreement creates a security interest in all proceeds arising from the sale of any collateral for the entire debt owing to UCIT by Spohn.

The security interest in all proceeds was perfected by filing the Financing Statement (Ex. B), which specifies: "The following proceeds are also covered," inter alia, "cash taken in the sale * * * of the property * * *." Since there is a remainder due on the Spohn debt, we hold that UCIT is entitled to retain all the money it received from the sale of the 11 used cars.

Even if the stipulation is disregarded, we cannot agree with plaintiff-trustee's argument that the description in the Financing Statement is insufficient to perfect a security interest in these items.

U. C. C. Sec. 9–402 (1) provides: "A financing statement is sufficient if it * * * contains a statement indicating the types * * * of property covered." U. C. C. Sec. 9–110 provides: "For the purposes of this Article any description is sufficient whether or not it is specific if it reasonably identifies the thing described." We find that the security agreements and the Financing Statement reasonably identify the motor parts and accessories in Spohn's inventory, and that the description in the Financing Statement is sufficient to give notice to potential creditors. *National-Dime Bank of Shamokin v. Cleveland Brothers Equipment Co., Inc.*, 20 Pa. Dist. & Co. (2d) 511 (1959). Therefore, UCIT is entitled to retain the money received from the sale of these items.

CONTINUATION STATEMENT.   Sec. 9–403 of the Code states that a continuation statement may be filed by the secured party (i) within six months before and sixty days after a stated maturity date of five years or less, and (ii) otherwise within six months prior to the expiration of the five-year period specified in subsection (2). Any such continuation statement must be signed by the secured party, must identify the original statement by file number, and must state that the original statement is still effective. Upon timely filing of the continuation statement, the effectiveness of the original statement is continued for five years after the last date to which the filing was effective, whereupon it lapses in the same manner as provided in subsection (2) unless another continuation statement is filed prior to such lapse. Succeeding continuation statements may be filed in the same manner to continue the effectiveness of the original statement. Unless a statute on disposition of public records provides otherwise, the filing officer may remove the record of a lapsed statement from the files and destroy it.

PRIORITY OF SECURITY INTERESTS.   Sec. 9–307 of the Code provides for perfection and priority of buyers of goods and states that a buyer in ordinary course of business other than a person buying farm products from a person engaged in farming operations takes free of a security interest created by his seller even though the security interest is perfected and even though the buyer knows of its existence.

In the case of consumer goods having an original purchase price not in excess of $500 and in the case of farm equipment having an original purchase price not in excess of $500 other than fixtures, a buyer takes free of a security interest even though perfected if he buys without knowledge of the security interest, for value and for his own personal, family, or household purposes or his own farming operations unless prior to the purchase the secured party has filed a financing statement covering such goods.

Gray v. Raper
115 Ga. App. 600, 155 S. E. (2d) 670 (1967)

This was an action by Frankie I. Raper et al. (plaintiffs) against Glen Gray et al. (defendants). Judgment for plaintiffs and defendants appealed. Judgment reversed.

Frankie Ida Raper filed a money rule against the Sheriff of Whitfield County alleging that she had a judgment against one Alvin Raper on which execution had been levied by the sheriff, who had collected $180 which he refused to pay over to her. Glen and Bessie Gray intervened in the proceedings, alleging that they were the holders of a note and chattel mortgage recorded May 26, 1965, on a Ford automobile belonging to Alvin Raper, upon which Frankie Raper's fi. fa. had been levied; that the $180 held by the sheriff constituted the net proceeds of the sale of this vehicle, and that the intervenors are entitled to the money because the bill of sale to secure debt was recorded prior to the date of the judgment upon which the plaintiff in fi. fa. had the execution levied.

Proceedings on trial of money rule. The Superior Court, Whitfield County, J. T. Pope, Jr., J., rendered judgment from which intervenors appealed.

DEEN, J. Under the agreed statement of facts, appellees Gray did not perfect their security interest in the automobile because they did not file a financing statement as required by Code Ann. Sec. 109A-9-302 (1) (d) where the subject property is an automobile. They did, however, foreclose the mortgage on September 6, 1966, and place it in the hands of the sheriff for collection, but the plaintiff in fi. fa. had caused her execution to be levied on September 3, based on a May 2nd judgment. Thus, by her prior levy, Mrs. Raper was entitled to the funds unless her judgment was subordinate to the Grays' prior but unperfected security interest in the car. The rule governing priorities here is spelled out in Code Ann. Sec. 109A-9-301, where one who acquires a lien on property by levy (a "lien creditor" under subsection (3) who becomes such "without knowledge of the security interest and before it is perfected" (Subsection 1(b)) has priority over another with a prior but unperfected security interest. Given the facts above stated, Mrs. Raper was not entitled to priority over the Grays to the net proceeds in the hands of the sheriff arising from the sale of the automobile if she had acted with knowledge of the existence of the unsatisfied mortgage.

On the trial of the money rule the Grays offered Alvin Raper, plaintiff's former husband and owner of the automobile, as a witness prepared to testify that the plaintiff had actual knowledge of the mortgage held by the Grays prior to her judgment and levy. The court refused to allow the testimony because "intervenors had failed to allege such notice or knowledge" in their pleading. They did, however, allege that they were entitled to the fund because of a prior recorded chattel mortgage, and this allegation could be proved in either of two ways: by showing that they had a prior perfected security interest in the collateral (Code Ann. Sec. 109A–9–201), or by showing that the plaintiff, at the time of her judgment and levy, had actual knowledge of their interest whether perfected or not (Code Ann. Sec. 109A–9–301 (1) (b)). The one is constructive and the other actual notice. Both are relevant to the issue, which was one of priority. Had the plaintiff wished to know which route the intervenors intended to follow she might have demurred specially to the allegation and obtained further informaton, but no such information was called for. Evidence not otherwise objectionable is relevant and admissible if it tends to make the proposition at issue either more or less probable. *Todd v. German-American Ins. Co. of New York*, 2 Ga. App. 789, 59 S. E. 94; *Summit Wagon Co. v. Lowery*, 6 Ga. App. 147, 64 S. E. 489; *Tifton, T. & G. Ry. Co. v. Butler*, 4 Ga. App. 191, 60 S. E. 1087. Indubitably, in the absence of demurrer, either party in every cause should be allowed full opportunity to introduce all evidence competent and relevant to support the case alleged by him. *Spivey v. Barwick*, 157 Ga. 853 (2), 122 S. E. 594; *Nobles v. Webb*, 197 Ga. 242, 246, 29 S. E. (2d) 158, and compare *Tumlin v. Crawford*, 61 Ga. 18 (1).

The trial court erred in rejecting testimony relevant to the intervenors' claim of priority to the proceeds of the sale.

Judgment reversed.

Sec. 9–310 of the Code gives priority of certain liens arising by operation of law and states that when a person in the ordinary course of his business furnishes services or materials with respect to goods subject to a security interest, a lien upon goods in the possession of such person given by statute or rule of law for such materials or services takes priority over a perfect security interest unless the lien is statutory and the statute expressly provides otherwise.

Commerce Acceptance of Oklahoma City, Inc. v. Press

428 P. (2d) 213 (1967)
Supreme Court of Oklahoma

This was an action by Commerce Acceptance of Oklahoma City, Inc. (plaintiff) against Jerry Press (defendant). Judgment for plaintiff for possession of automobile, subject to garageman's lien, and the plaintiff appealed. Judgment affirmed.

Plaintiff held a recorded chattel mortgage on a certain automobile. Plaintiff commenced an action in replevin to recover the automobile against defendant. Defendant defended the action on the grounds that his possessory lien for towing charges, repairs and storage for the automobile had priority over plaintiff's previously perfected security interest.

The cause was submitted upon stipulation and the trial court held defendant's possessory lien had priority over plaintiff's chattel mortgage and rendered judgment for the plaintiff for possession of the automobile, subject, however, to defendant's lien. Plaintiff appealed from the order overruling its motion for a new trial.

IRWIN, Vice C.J. The issue is: When a garageman acquires a valid lien for towing, repairing and storing an automobile, and retains possession of it for the unpaid charges, does such lien have priority over a previously perfected security interest while the automobile is in the possession of the garageman?

Plaintiff perfected its security interest and defendant did the repair work and furnished the services after the effective date of the Oklahoma Uniform Commercial Code. And, it is not contended that the repair work and services performed by defendant did not protect, improve and safekeep the automobile in question.

The Uniform Commercial Code became effective on January 1, 1963; Sec. 91 was amended in 1955; Secs. 131 and 132, supra, were enacted in 1913; and the issue presented is one of first impression.

Sec. 9–310, of the Uniform Commercial Code, provides: "When a person in the ordinary course of his business furnishes services or materials with respect to goods subject to a security interest, a lien upon goods in the possession of such person given by statute or rule of law for such materials or services takes priority over a perfected security interest unless the lien is statutory and the statute expressly provides otherwise." Both parties agree that defendant had a statutory lien upon the automobile in question. Therefore, since defendant retained possession of the automobile, under the clear language of the above enactment, defendant's lien takes priority over plaintiff's perfected security interest unless the statute giving defendant his lien "expressly provides otherwise."

Sec. 9–310, of the Uniform Commercial Code, relates to the priority of liens. As previously stated, under the above provision, defendant's lien takes priority over plaintiff's perfected security interest unless the statute giving defendant his lien "expressly provides otherwise." Since defendant had a statutory lien and possession of the automobile, and the statute granting him such lien did not expressly provide that a previously perfected security interest would have priority or such lien was subject to all prior liens, under the provision of Sec. 9–310 of the Uniform Commercial Code, defendant's lien takes priority over plaintiff's perfected security interest.

Plaintiff contends that under the stipulation, defendant gained possession of the automobile for the sole purpose of repairing it and there was no stipulation that there was a contract for storage. Plaintiff argues that before any charge for storage can be had there must be a contract for such storage.

In defendant's amended answer he alleged the owner of the automobile agreed to pay him for the repairs and storage. The trial court found that defendant stored the automobile at the request of the owner. Although there was no stipulation that there was a contract for storage, in view of the record presented, we can not conclude that the trial court erred in granting a lien for storage.

Judgment affirmed.

All the Justices concur.

Sec. 9–312 (2) of the Code states the priority among conflicting security interests in the same collateral, such as in crops, where new value is given to enable the debtor to produce the crops during the production season, and given not more than three months before the crops become growing crops by planting or otherwise, takes priority over an earlier perfected security interest to the extent that such earlier interest secures obligations due more than six months before the crops become growing crops by planting or otherwise, even though the person giving new value had knowledge of the earlier security interest.

Sec. 9–312 (3) states that a purchase-money security interest in inventory collateral has priority over a conflicting security interest in the same collateral if (a) the purchase-money security interest is perfected at the time the debtor receives possession of the collateral; (b) any secured party whose security interest is known to the holder of the purchase-money security interest or who, prior to the date of the filing made by the holder of the purchase-money security interest, had filed a financing statement covering the same items or type of inventory, has received notification of the purchase-money security interest before the debtor receives possession of the collateral covered by the purchase-money security interest; and (c) such notification states that the person giving the notice has or expects to acquire a purchase-money security interest in inventory of the debtor, describing such inventory by item or type.

Sec. 9–312 (4) states that a purchase-money security interest in collateral other than inventory has priority over a conflicting security interest in the same collateral if the purchase-money security interest is perfected at the time the debtor receives possession of the collateral or within ten days thereafter.

Sec. 9–312 (5) states that in all cases not governed by other rules stated in this section (including cases of purchase-money security interests which do not qualify for the special priorities set forth in subsections (3) and (4) of the section), priority between conflicting security interests in the same collateral shall be determined as follows: (a) in the order of filing if both are perfected by filing, regardless of which security interest attached first under Sec. 9–204 (1) and whether it attached before or after filing; (b) in the order of perfection unless both are perfected by filing, regardless of which security interest attached first under Sec. 9–204 (1) and, in the case of a filed security interest, whether it attached before or after filing; and (c) in the order of attachment under Sec. 9–204 (1) so long as neither is perfected.

Sec. 9–312 (6) states that for the purpose of the priority rules of the immediately preceding subsection, a continuously perfected security interest shall be treated at all times as if perfected by filing if it was originally so perfected and it shall be treated at all times as if perfected otherwise than by filing if it was originally perfected otherwise than by filing.

McDonald v. Peoples Automobile Loan & Finance Corp.
115 Ga. App. 483, 154 S. E. (2d) 886 (1967)

This was an action by Homer McDonald (plaintiff) against Peoples Automobile Loan & Finance Corporation of Athens, Inc. (defendant). Judgment for defendant and plaintiff appealed. Judgment affirmed.

A used automobile wholesaler which had sold two automobiles on credit to automobile retailer filed claim and bond for the automobiles against retailer's financier which had, under its security agreement also covering the two automobiles, foreclosed, obtained issuance of chattel mortgage fieri facias, and caused entire inventory of retailer to be levied on. The Superior Court of Clarke County, James Barrow, J., directed a verdict by which automobiles were found subject to the levy, and wholesaler appealed.

FRANKUM, J. In the latter part of 1965 McDonald, trading as Hi Point Motors, sold to Thurmond a 1965 Oldsmobile for $2,500 and a 1965 Ford Mustang for $2,450. He held a title certificate to the Oldsmobile which had been issued to McDonald's Used Cars by the State Revenue Commissioner, and a certificate of title to the Mustang issued by the Revenue Commissioner to Julian W. and Julian E. Strickland, assigned in blank. These McDonald retained with the understanding that they would be delivered upon payment of the purchase price. However, within a week after the sales were made bills of sale were executed to Thurmond by Hi Point Motors, with the descriptions of the vehicles left blank but, as McDonald testified, with authority to fill them in.

These bills of sale, completed by filling in the descriptions of the vehicles, with motor and serial numbers, were taken by Thurmond to Peoples and used in procuring advances of $2,550 on the Oldsmobile and $2,425 on the Mustang, for which Thurmond executed collateral promissory notes in the manner above described.

At the time of making these advances Peoples did not require production of title registration certificates. The manager of Peoples testified that advances were generally made to dealers on bills of sale because of the delay incident to procuring title certificates from the Revenue Department.

In January, 1966, Peoples learned that Thurmond had sold some nine vehicles out of trust; that is to say, had sold the vehicles and failed to pay to Peoples the amounts which it had advanced against them, and had procured the retail financing for the customer at other places. Because of that Peoples accelerated all of the indebtedness owing on Thurmond's inventory, as it was authorized to do under the security agreement, and foreclosed, obtained the issuance of a chattel mortgage fi. fa. and caused the inventory to be levied on. The Oldsmobile and Mustang which Thurmond had acquired from McDonald were included in the levy, and he filed claim and bond for them.

The issue thus made came on for trial and at the conclusion of the evidence a verdict was directed by which the cars were found subject to the levy.

McDonald admits that he sold the two cars to Thurmond for specified prices, on credit—to be paid when they were resold. He admits that he executed and delivered to Thurmond bills of sale covering the vehicles, and that the transactions (including the bills of sale) were in the name of Hi Point Motors to facilitate financing by Thurmond. What he attempted to do was to create, by oral agreement (there was no written security agreement or retention of title between him and Thurmond), a security interest in the cars running from Thurmond to him.

Clearly, the transactions here are subject to the provisions of the Uniform Commercial Code, and the matter of whether they are valid and, if so, which has priority must be determined under it.

Was the security interest claimed by McDonald valid? Certainly as to third parties it is unenforceable under the Statute of Frauds as contained in Sec. 109A-9-203, since he had surrendered possession of the vehicles and had not obtained *signed* security agreement. This is an absolute requisite to the enforceability of the security interest.

The official comment to the Code states that "The formal requisites stated in this Section [Sec. 109A-9-203] are not only conditions to the enforceability of a security interest against third parties. They are in the nature of a Statute of Frauds. Unless the secured party is in possession of the collateral, his security interest, absent a writing which satisfies subsection (1, b), is not enforceable even against the debtor, and cannot be made so on the theory of equitable mortgage or the like." It is important to keep in mind that the retention of the title certificates by McDonald plays no part in the determination of whether he has a valid security interest in the vehicles running from Thurmond to him, for each provision of Article 9 (Secured Transactions) with regard to the rights, obligations and remedies applies whether title to collateral is in the secured party or in the debtor. Code Ann. Sec. 109A-9-202. Thus, whether McDonald has a valid security interest must be otherwise determined. Under Sec. 109A-9-204 a security interest cannot attach until there is an agreement, and under Sec. 109A–9–203 the agreement must be in writing unless the creditor keeps possession of the collateral.

But assuming that there was a valid agreement creating a security interest in McDonald, what of the priorities? Peoples did obtain a written agreement and did perfect its security interest by filing in accordance with the provisions of Sec. 109A–9–302. Since McDonald did not perfect his security interest by the requisite filing, he could have no more than an unperfected interest which is subordinate to that of Peoples. Sec. 109A–9–301 and 109A–9–312. "A purchase money security interest in *inventory* collateral has priority over a conflicting security interest in the same collateral *if* (a) the purchase money security interest is perfected at the time the debtor receives possession of the collateral; *and* (b) any secured party whose security interest is known to the holder of the purchase money security interest or who, prior to the date of the filing made by the holder of the purchase money security interest, had filed a financing statement covering the same items or type of inventory, has received notification of the purchase money security interest *before the debtor receives possession* of the collateral covered by the purchase money security interest; *and* (c) such notification states that the person giving the notice has or expects to acquire a purchase money security interest in inventory of the debtor, describing such inventory by item or type." Code Ann. Sec. 109A–9–312(3). (Emphasis supplied.)

It is obvious that McDonald simply could not qualify his security interest (assuming that he had a valid agreement therefor) for priority. Whatever notice of it that may have been brought to the attention of Peoples did not come before Thurmond took possession of the cars.

We must agree that the cases of *Citizens & Southern National Bank v. Capital Construction Co.*, 112 Ga. App. 189, 144 S. E. (2d) 465, *Dunford v. Columbus Auto Auction*, 114 Ga. App. 407(1), 151 S. E. (2d) 464 and *Guardian Discount Co. v. Settles*, 114 Ga. App. 418, 151 S. E. (2d) 530 are controlling here.

Nor is the proposition that Peoples did not give new value upon making the advances on these cars supported by the record. The manager of Peoples testified (and it is not disputed) that although Thurmond indorsed the checks representing the advancements and delivered them back to Peoples, he was credited with these amounts on vehicles which had been previously floor planned and which Thurmond had sold and was paying off, in accordance with the floor plan or security agreement. New money was advanced, though it was immediately used to retire other obligations owing to Peoples. Even if this be regarded as payment on a pre-existing debt it was value under the definition in Sec. 109A–1–201 (44) (b).

The verdict was properly directed.

Judgment affirmed.

PROCEEDS—SECURED PARTY'S RIGHTS ON DISPOSITION OF COLLATERAL.

Under Sec. 9–306 of the Code the secured party may state in the financing statement that proceeds are covered in addition to the collateral. Proceeds includes whatever is received when collateral or proceeds is sold, exchanged, collected, or otherwise disposed of. The term also includes the account arising when the right to payment is earned under a contract right. Money, checks, and the like are "cash proceeds." All other proceeds are "non-cash proceeds."

DEFAULT.   When a debtor is in default under a security agreement, a secured party has the rights and remedies provided in the security agreement with certain exceptions stated in Sec. 9–501 of the Code. The debtor may by agreement waive his right to any surplus proceeds from sale of collateral over and above payment of the debt, or waive his right to redemption of collateral, or waive the secured party's liability for failure to comply with the Code. Sec. 9–501 (5) states that when a secured party has reduced his claim to judgment the lien of any levy which may be made upon his collateral by virtue of any execution based upon the judgment shall relate back to the date of the perfection of the security interest in such collateral. A judicial sale, pursuant to such execution, is a foreclosure of the security interest by judicial procedure within the meaning of this section, and the secured party may purchase at the sale and thereafter hold the collateral free of any other requirements.

In Re Yale Express System, Inc.
370 F. (2d) 433 (1966)

This was an action by Fruehauf Corporation et al. (plaintiffs) against Yale Express System, Inc. (defendant). Plaintiffs' petition denied. Reversed and remanded.

The basic facts underlying the present controversy are not in dispute. At various times during the summer and fall of 1964, the Yale Express System ("Yale") purchased 50 trailers and 62 truck bodies from the Fruehauf Corporation ("Fruehauf"). The cost of these vehicles was $379,208.50. Yale agreed to make cash payments 30 days after delivery of each unit of truck bodies and 90 days delivery after each unit of trailers.

Fruehauf contends that in extending this credit it relied on information furnished in a Dun & Bradstreet report issued on June 9, 1964, with respect to Yale's financial state. That report, which rated Yale as "Aa A1," summarized the consolidated financial statement prepared by Yale's certified public accountants, Peat, Marwick, Mitchell & Company, for the year ending December 31, 1963. This statement disclosed that Yale's net income for 1963 was $1,140,665.

In February, 1965, approximately two months after delivery to the debtor of the last piece of equipment, Fruehauf was told by Yale's representatives that the financial statement for the year ending December 31, 1963 was inaccurate. Fruehauf's auditors announced that Yale's operations for 1963, originally reported as showing a profit in excess of $1,000,000, had resulted, in fact, in a net loss of $1,254,602. Upon learning of this, Fruehauf took the position that it had a right to reclaim the trailers and truck bodies it had sold to Yale on credit. Thereafter, negotiations ensued between the two parties, and eventually an agreement was entered into on March 26, 1965. In it Fruehauf waived its asserted right to reclaim the trailers and truck bodies, and allowed Yale to pay for the equipment on an installment basis over a period of 68 months. To secure these payment obligations, Yale gave Fruehauf chattel mortgage liens on the trucks and trailers. These security interests were duly filed in accordance with the provisions of the New York Uniform Commercial Code ("Code").

Two months later, on May 24, 1965, Yale filed a petition for reorganization under Chapter X of the Bankruptcy Act. On October 11, 1965, Fruehauf, claiming that Yale had failed to make 5 of the required installment payments that had become due, informed Yale's trustee that it was exercising its right under the security agreements to repossess the collateral. A formal demand was made for immediate possession, but the trustee refused to release the collateral valued at $380,000, on which less than $15,000 had been paid.

Following this refusal, Fruehauf filed its Petition for Reclamation in Yale's Chapter X proceedings. Judge Tyler there concluded that even if he assumed that Fruehauf had a valid security interest, it would not be entitled to reclaim unless it demonstrated that the trucks and trailers were not the "property of the debtor."

KAUFMAN, C.J. This appeal seeks to have us determine whether a creditor, armed with a security interest perfected under the Uniform Commercial Code, is entitled to reclaim property held by the trustee for a debtor being reorganized under Chapter X of the Bankruptcy Act. Section 9–202 declares the policy of Article 9 of the Code stating that "[e]ach provision of this Article with regard to rights, obligations and remedies applies whether title to collateral is in the secured party or in the debtor." In short, it does not matter whether the security agreement is in the form of a chattel mortgage or a conditional sales contract. In either case, the secured party has the right upon default by the debtor to take possession of the collateral (Sec. 9–503) and to sell, lease or otherwise dispose of it, applying the proceeds to the indebtedness (Sec. 9–504).

"The Uniform Commercial Code was designed to bring the body of commercial law into the contemporary world of business. * * * It would hardly be consistent with that design * * * to reestablish in new form limitations which reflect a passion for legal technicality over commercial reality. * * * The Code has eliminated the older, technical and restricted categories of security agreements. Gone are the definitional difficulties and transactional fictions of the chattel-mortgage, the conditional sale, the trust receipt. In their stead is a general set of rules for the creation of a security interest in the secured party." (*In the Matter of United Thrift Stores, Inc.*, 363 F. (2d) 11, 14 (3 Cir. 1966))

We, therefore, in keeping with the developments in the body of recent commercial law, conclude that Fruehauf's right to reclaim the trailers and truck bodies cannot hang on whether its security agreement is labeled a "conditional sales contract" or a "chattel mortgage," since the Uniform Commercial Code has abolished the technical distinctions between the various security devices. We therefore find it necessary to reverse Judge Tyler's order, and to remand the case to the district court to decide, in light of this opinion, whether Fruehauf is entitled to reclamation.

SECURED PARTY'S RIGHT TO POSSESSION AFTER DEFAULT. Sec. 9–503 (1) states that unless otherwise agreed a secured party has on default the right to take possession of the collateral. In taking possession a secured party may proceed without judicial process, if this can be done without breach of the peace, or he may proceed by action. If the security agreement so provides, the secured party may require the debtor to assemble the collateral and make it available to the secured party at a place to be designated by the secured party which is reasonably convenient to both parties. Without removal a secured party may render equipment unusable, and may dispose of collateral on the debtor's premises, under Sec. 9–504.

(2) If a secured party elects to proceed by process of law he may proceed by writ of replevin or otherwise.

Kroeger v. Ogsden
429 P. (2d) 781 (1967)
Supreme Court of Oklahoma

This was an action by Chuck Ogsden (plaintiff) against Karl Kroeger et al. (defendants). Judgment for plaintiff and defendants appealed. Judgment reversed and remanded with directions.

This appeal involves an action brought by defendant in error, hereinafter referred to as "plaintiff," for replevin and for damages, and other relief, against plaintiffs in error, hereinafter referred to as "defendants," on account of the latter's alleged conversion of plaintiff's Beechcraft Bonanza Airplane, in purporting to repossess it from him.

In return for some cash and a Cessna Airplane, plaintiff, a farmer and rancher in the Boise City area of western Oklahoma, acquired the Bonanza in September, 1962 from a Midwest City man, John Harold Wood, who had mortgaged it as security for a promissory note he executed and delivered to one Leo Overture, in July, 1961, for $6024.00. The defendant, Karl Kroeger Finance Company, acquired the note and mortgage by assignment from Overture. Plaintiff did not have actual notice of said defendants' note and mortgage until Overture defaulted in his payments thereon, and he had received a letter dated March 27, 1963, written for the Finance Company by the defendant Karl Kroeger.

Thereafter, nothing further having been paid on the above balance, one L. J. Canavan, as agent for defendants, learned by telephoning plaintiff at Boise City that the Bonanza was in a hangar at the Boise City Municipal Airport. Thereafter, the defendant Finance Company's manager, a Mr. Myrick, flew Mr. Canavan and an unnamed individual who was a pilot, to Boise City. There they took possession of the Bonanza and the pilot flew it back to Oklahoma City, where it was sold at a chattel mortgage foreclosure sale on August 10, 1964, to the defendant Karl Kroeger Finance Company for $2600.00, by application and credit on the mortgage indebtedness.

BLACKBIRD, J. Defendants argue that our statutes and decisions make it lawful for the holder of a chattel mortgage, in such a situation, to take possession of the mortgaged property if this can be done in an orderly manner and without a breach of the peace. Defendants also cite the provisions of the Uniform Commercial Code adopted in this State as Tit. 12A O. S. 1961, Sec. 9–503 and quotations from *Malone v. Darr*, 178 Okl. 443, 62 P. (2d) 1254; *First National Bank and Trust Company of Muskogee v. Winter*, 176 Okl. 400, 55 P. (2d) 1029; *Leedy v. General Motors Acceptance Corp.*, 173 Okl. 445, 48 P. (2d) 1074, and other cases.

Appellate court reports are replete with cases in which the holders of chattel mortgages, or conditional sales contracts, have, upon default in the payment of the indebtedness on the chattel covered thereby, taken possession of it, unbeknownst at that time to the obligor, without being held to have committed conversion, even when the chattel was taken from the obligor's private premises. If, before the repossession, the mortgage lien was binding upon plaintiff, as the trial court's finding that he had constructive notice of it would ordinarily indicate, we think that holding it extinguished, on the ground of conversion, under the circumstances of this case, would be (to use the words of the North Carolina Court in the Rea Case, *supra*) "a fraud on the rights of the mortgagee (in this case, his assignee) and would very much impair the value of chattel mortgages as securities." As the trial court's judgment has no express and valid basis, in the face of its error, and must therefore be reversed, it is unnecessary to discuss other assignments of error.

In accord with the foregoing, the judgment of the trial court is hereby reversed insofar as it decrees recovery by plaintiff against the defendants of the sum of $3500.00, costs, and interest, or possession of the Beech Bonanza Airplane involved, and this cause is remanded to said court free of defendants' chattel mortgage lien; with instructions to vacate said judgment, as to such recovery, and to enter a new judgment in favor of the defendants on the issues therein initially adjudicated. As to any proper issues not determined by said judgment and this opinion and reserved by the trial court for future determination, we express no opinion.

TERMINATION STATEMENT.   In accordance with Sec. 9–404 of the Code, when all outstanding obligations are paid in full, the secured party must on written demand by the debtor send the debtor a statement that he no longer claims a security interest under the financing statement, which shall be identified by a file number. If the secured party fails to send such termination statement within ten days after proper demands therefor, he shall be liable to the debtor for one hundred dollars and in addition for any loss caused to the debtor by such failure.

PERSONAL SECURITY

SURETY AND GUARANTY CONTRACTS

NATURE AND CREATION.   For convenience of classification suretyship may be regarded as a generic term applicable to those types of contracts wherein one party obligates himself to another party for the purpose of securing the performance of an obligation by a third party. The relationship created by contracts of suretyship involves three parties, (1) the principal debtor (obligor), (2) the surety or guarantor, and (3) the creditor (obligee). While a contract of suretyship may involve the performance of any legal obligation of the principal debtor to the creditor, we are here particularly interested in its application as a means of securing credit. The principal difference between this type of security transaction and the types that we have heretofore studied is in the nature of the security given by the debtor or obligor to the creditor or obligee. Instead of a lien or some other type of proprietary interest in either real or personal property, the security received by the creditor in the case of a suretyship transaction is the credit of some third person or persons. Thus, if A wishes to buy goods on credit or to negotiate a loan and B demands security, and A does not own either real or personal property which he may offer B as security, he may still be able to obtain credit if he is in a position to use the personal credit of some third party. For example, A would like to buy groceries from B, a local retail merchant, but B refuses to extend the credit because of A's poor financial standing. C, who has good credit, agrees with B that if he extends the desired credit to A and A fails to pay, C will pay. If B, upon the basis of this agreement, extends credit to A, C will be liable to B if A does not pay. Under such circumstances C has literally "loaned" his personal credit to A in order to enable A to obtain the desired credit from B.

Suretyship contracts are generally classified as (1) surety contracts and (2) guaranty contracts. Guaranty contracts are further classified as (1) absolute and (2) conditional. In a surety contract the surety is referred to as a "strict surety." This term is applied to a surety because he is a co-debtor with the principal debtor for the payment of the debt or the performance of the obligation which the principal debtor owes the creditor. The surety is an original promisor and debtor, along with the principal debtor, and is primarily liable with the principal debtor for the payment or performance. He is usually, though not always, a party to the same instrument signed by the principal debtor. In the case of a guaranty contract, on the other hand, the guarantor's liability arises out of a separate contract. A guarantor does not agree, as does a strict surety, to pay the debt or perform the obligation. He merely agrees to pay or perform *if the principal debtor fails to pay or perform*. The surety is liable "from the beginning," whereas the guarantor does not become liable until the principal debtor has defaulted. A guarantor is thus not primarily liable, like a surety, but secondarily liable. If the guaranty is *absolute*, the obligation of the guarantor to perform, once the principal debtor has defaulted, is unconditional. If the guaranty is *conditional*, the duty of the guarantor to perform does not arise upon the default of the principal debtor, but only after the creditor has exhausted all of his legal remedies against the principal debtor.

Since a surety is a primary party to the contract and therefore liable from the beginning, he is not entitled to notice of default on the part of the principal debtor, and is bound without such notice. A guarantor is entitled to notice of default, within a reasonable time after default, in order to fix his liability. Failure to give such notice discharges the guarantor from all liability.

Suretyship contracts are quite generally used in building and construction work. *Performance bonds* are often required of contractors to insure the faithful performance of building contracts. Such bonds are often broad enough to cover the payment of the wages of the employees on the project and all subcontractors and materialmen. Such provisions protect the person having the work done from mechanics' and materialmen's liens. *Bail bonds* are required of public officials, executors and administrators, and the like. While fidelity bonds, which are often required of certain types of employees, are generally looked upon as surety bonds, technically they are indemnity bonds. The agreement in a fidelity bond is not to pay if the employee does not pay, but to indemnify the employer in case of defalcation or embezzlement of funds by the employee.

DEFENSES AVAILABLE TO SURETY OR GUARANTOR.   Most defenses which the principal debtor has against the creditor are available to the surety or guarantor. However, there are certain defenses which the principal debtor has against the creditor which are personal to the debtor and are therefore not available to the surety or guarantor. For instance, the debtor may set up as a defense against the creditor his own infancy, insanity, or bank-ruptcy, and the running of the statute of limitations on the debt or obliga-tion; but these defenses are not available to the surety or guarantor. Exam-ples of defenses available to the principal debtor which may be made use of by the surety or guarantor are the following: (1) payment or perform-ance by the principal debtor; (2) tender of performance by either the principal debtor or the surety; (3) release of the principal debtor by the creditor, unless the surety consents to such release and the creditor re-serves his rights against the surety.

The surety may also have certain defenses available against the creditor in addition to those which he derives through the principal debtor. Ex-amples of such defenses are (1) his own infancy, insanity, or bankruptcy; (2) the running of the statute of limitations on his surety or guaranty con-tract; (3) nondisclosure of material facts concerning the principal debtor, known by the creditor but unknown by the surety; (4) modification of the surety contract by the creditor without the surety's consent; (5) ex-tension of the time for performance of payment, provided the extension is supported by consideration.

REMEDIES OF SURETY OR GUARANTOR.

The surety or guarantor has the following remedies, depending upon the terms of the contract and the facts of the given case: (1) reimbursement, (2) subrogation, and (3) con-tribution.

If the principal debtor defaults and the surety or guarantor is required to pay the debt or perform the obligation, he is entitled to be *reimbursed* by the principal debtor. The law implies a promise, on the part of the principal debtor, to indemnify the surety or guarantor in the event that he is required to pay the debt or perform the obligation under the con-tract.

After the surety or guarantor has paid the debt or performed the obli-gation, he is *subrogated* to any rights that the creditor has against the principal debtor. It is not uncommon, in a security transaction, for the principal debtor to pledge certain securities to the creditor as security, in addition to the contract of suretyship. In such cases, after the surety or guarantor has fully performed by discharging the principal debtor of his obligation to the creditor, the surety or guarantor is subrogated to any rights which the creditor had in the securities pledged by the principal debtor. A surety's right of subrogation is derived from equity law, and the surety has such right even though it is not provided for in the contract of suretyship.

In the event that there are two or more co-sureties or co-guarantors, the creditor is privileged to recover from any one or all of them. If the creditor recovers from one of the sureties, such surety is entitled to *contribution* from the other co-sureties. If one of the sureties is insolvent, the surety who performed the obligation is entitled to a proportionate share from the solvent surety or sureties. In other words, the loss is distributed equally among the solvent sureties. This is true unless the contract provides otherwise.

Short v. Sinai
50 Nev. 346, 259 P. 417 (1927)

This was an action by Charles Short (plaintiff) against Charles Sinai and another (defendants). Judgment for plaintiff, and defendants appealed. Affirmed.

This was an action whereby plaintiff sought to recover against Charles Sinai, as principal, and L. Devincenzi, as surety, upon an alleged undertaking of Sinai and Devincenzi to protect plaintiff against a certain partnership debt owed by him and Sinai as partners.

On or about February 15, 1922, plaintiff Short and defendant Charles Sinai were partners operating a clothing store in the city of Reno, known as "The Smart Shop." On or about the date last mentioned they dissolved the partnership, and Sinai agreed to assume certain debts owing by Short and Sinai, copartners, upon the consideration of the payment of certain debts by Short. At the time of the dissolution of the partnership, Sinai and Devincenzi entered into an agreement which read, in part, as follows: "Be it known that we, Charles Sinai and L. Devincenzi, as principal and surety respectively, are held and firmly bound unto Charles Short, in the sum of $4,500, to be paid to the said Charles Short; for which payment well and truly to be paid, we bind ourselves, our heirs, executors, and administrators, jointly and severally, firmly by these presents. . . . The condition of the above obligation is such that, if the above bounden Charles Sinai shall well and truly pay unto the following named creditors of the Smart Shop, or in any manner release the above Charles Short from any obligation of debt to the said following named creditors, then the above obligation to be void; otherwise, to remain in full force and effect." (Here followed a list of creditors and their claims.) The foregoing instrument was signed and acknowledged before a notary public by Sinai and Devincenzi.

The complaint alleged that, after making the bond, Sinai and Devincenzi paid certain of the creditors named therein but failed and refused to pay the claims of Alfred Decker & Cohen, one of the said creditors, whose claim amounted to $452.30. It further alleged that said creditor made demand upon plaintiff for payment and threatened suit, and that plaintiff, having no defense, paid the said claim. Plaintiff alleged a breach of the foregoing agreement and asked to be indemnified.

Defendant Devincenzi filed a separate answer to the complaint denying any liability. Plaintiff obtained judgment, and defendant Devincenzi appealed.

DUCKER, J. The result of this appeal, as we view it, turns upon the question of whether or not the obligation sued upon is one of guaranty or suretyship. If it is the former, the judgment must be reversed; if the latter, it must be affirmed. As has been repeatedly pointed out, an obligation of a guarantor possesses some of the elements of suretyship and because of this fact some courts have confused the two, yet there are certain well-defined lines of demarcation between the two relationships.

We know of no statement which more clearly points out the distinction between the two relationships than that given in *McMillan v. Bull's Head Bank*, 32 Ind. 11, and hence adopt it as our guide in this case. It reads: "The surety is bound with his principal as an original promisor; he is a debtor from the beginning, and must see that the debt is paid, and is held, ordinarily, to know every default of his principal, and cannot protect himself by the mere indulgence of the creditor, nor by want of notice of the default of the principal, however such indulgence or want of notice may, in fact, injure him. Being bound with the principal, his obligation to pay is equally absolute. On the other hand, the contract of a guarantor is his own separate contract; it is in the nature of a warranty by him that the thing guaranteed to be done by the principal shall be done, not merely an engagement jointly with the principal to do the thing. A guarantor not being a joint contractor with his principal, is not bound to do what the principal has contracted to do, like a surety, but only to answer for the consequences of the default of the principal. The original contract of the principal is not his contract, and he is not bound to take notice of its nonperformance, and therefore the creditor should give him notice; and it is universally held that, if the guarantor can prove that he has suffered damage by the failure to give such notice, he will be discharged to the extent of the damage thus sustained. It is not so with a surety." 2 *Williston, Contracts*, Sec. 1211; *Rouse v. Wooten*, 140 N. C. 557, 53 S. E. 430.

In the instant case Devincenzi is not bound to the creditors of Short and Sinai, but he is bound with Sinai as an original promisor to the agreement made by Sinai with Short that he (Sinai) would pay certain of the creditors of the partnership. He is a debtor from the beginning, and could not protect himself by the mere indulgence of Short, nor because of want of notice of the default of the principal, which he could have done if a mere guarantor. This being true, it is not a case of a promise to answer for the debt, default, or miscarriage of another, and hence the consideration need not be stated. Judgment affirmed.

LIENS

NATURE AND CREATION

Liens or security interests which exist in the various types of security transactions which we have thus far studied are created by the contract of the parties. If the parties involved have not contracted for and agreed to the creation of such liens or security interests, they will not be imposed upon the parties by law.

In addition to these various security devices which emanate from the agreement of the parties there are a number of liens which do not trace their origin to some contract, but arise out of the common law or by statute. In other words, under proper conditions such liens exist, not because the parties have so contracted, but because certain parties are given the benefit of such liens by law, either common or statutory.

COMMON LAW LIENS

The common law lien, as a security device, is of ancient origin. Such liens existed only in the case of personal property, none having developed in relation to realty. Common law liens were coupled with the bailment of personal property, and where such liens existed they were given to the bailee in order to secure to him the payment of his charges for services rendered to the bailor.

The principal common law liens were those given to (1) innkeepers, (2) common carriers, (3) warehousemen, and (4) artisans. The innkeeper was given a lien on the luggage and other property which the guest brought with him, in order to secure the payment of the charges for the services and accommodations furnished the guest. The common carrier was given a lien on the property transported by the carrier in the performance of his contract with the shipper. A similar lien was given to the warehouseman who stored goods under a bailment contract. The reason given by the early common law courts for giving liens to innkeepers, common carriers, and warehousemen was the fact that they were engaged in a public calling. They dealt with the public and were required to serve all alike. For that reason it was felt that they should be given a lien upon the property turned over to them or brought upon their premises, in order to secure the payment of their charges for services rendered. The early common law courts also gave to the artisan a lien for his charges for improving the value of the bailor's personal property by the application of labor and materials.

The common law lien is possessory in nature; that is, the continuance of the lien is dependent upon the bailee's retaining possession of the property. If he should voluntarily surrender possession to the bailor he loses his lien. This does not, of course, discharge the debt of the bailor to the bailee. If the bailor should wrongfully obtain possession of the property by some trick or artifice, the lien is not lost.

The right of the creditor, under his lien, extends only to the possession of the property. In other words, if the debtor fails to pay, the creditor may not advertise and sell the property unless the contract permits him to do so. He is required to sue and obtain judgment upon the contract and then levy upon and sell the property at a judicial sale.

STATUTORY LIENS

At the present time most, if not all, of the foregoing common law liens have been enacted into statutory law. In many instances their application has been extended and certain changes have been made to bring them into conformity with modern conditions. The common carrier's lien and the warehouseman's lien are provided for in the Uniform Commercial Code.

The legislatures of the various states have also enacted numerous statutes whereby new liens have been created. Such liens not only apply to certain types of transactions which involve personal property but also are extended to certain transactions which involve real property. An examination of the statutes or code of any state will reveal not only sections which cover the old common law liens but also sections which create new liens, such as mechanics' liens, materialmen's liens, liens given to garages, hospitals, jewelers, landlords, boarding houses, banks, brokers, and the like. There are also judgment liens and tax liens.

Statutory liens are too numerous, and the state statutes too much lacking in uniformity, to permit full discussion here. The student should check the statutes or code of his own state. However, the prevalence and importance of mechanics' liens justify a brief statement concerning their nature and application.

Every state has some type of statute covering mechanics' liens. It should be understood that mechanics' liens apply only to real property. The purpose of a mechanics' lien is to secure to those who apply work and material in the construction or repair of a building the payment of their charges. While the statutes are not uniform in regard to those who are covered by such liens, they usually apply to prime contractors, subcontractors, laborers, and materialmen. Some statutes are broad enough to cover draftsmen, architects, timekeepers, and other such persons who directly or indirectly have some part in the performance of the construction contract. The statutes usually limit the lien to work performed on the premises and material actually used on the job. In order for the lienor to establish or perfect his lien he must file notice of his claim in the office of the clerk of the court having jurisdiction over such matters. This notice is usually required to be filed within sixty or ninety days after performing the last work or supplying the last material to the structure being erected. Failure to comply with this requirement results in the loss of the lien. This means that the lienor may no longer look, for the satisfaction of his claim, to the person having the building erected; if he is to recover at all he must be able to do so from the party with whom he originally contracted. For example, the materialman who furnished materials to the contractor may look to the contractor alone for the satisfaction of his claim if he loses his lien by failure to file and give proper notice of his claim.

The statutes require that after the lienor has given proper notice of his claim he must file suit and obtain judgment before he may levy upon and sell the property for the purpose of satisfying his claim against the property owner.

Since the property owner runs a risk of being subject to mechanics' and materialmen's liens, he will do well to require of the contractor a performance bond. It should be broad enough in coverage to protect the property owner from all such liens.

General Motors Acceptance Corporation
v.
Colwell Diesel Service & Garage, Inc.
302 A. (2d) 595 (1973)
Supreme Judicial Court of Maine

The holder of perfected purchase money security interest in truck brought replevin action, and the truck repairer which had valid mechanics' lien counterclaimed for damages for conversion. . . . Judgment in favor of repairer on counterclaim, and holder of security interest appealed. . . . Appeal denied.

DUFRESNE, C.J. The instant appeal questions the propriety of the ruling below that Colwell Diesel Service & Garage, Inc., the appellee, hereinafter referred to as Colwell, had a valid mechanics' lien entitled to priority over the lien of General Motors Acceptance Corporation, the appellant, whose lien arose by virtue of a perfected purchase-money security interest.

By agreed statement of facts submitted to the Justice below, it appears that one James F. Rafferty purchased a 1962 International tractor truck from Bean & Conquest, Inc. under a retail instalment contract. This agreement was executed on October 16, 1968 and, on the same date, was negotiated and assigned to the appellant. It is conceded that the appellant complied with all filing requirements under the law and held a perfected security interest in the chattel paper and in the 1962 International tractor truck. In 1969 Rafferty contracted with Colwell for repairs to the truck and, pursuant to said contract, Colwell did provide labor and materials and making the repairs which were completed on April 23, 1969 and amounted, in terms of reasonable value, to the sum of four hundred and fifty-one dollars and four cents ($451.04). Although authorized to make repairs under the terms of the retail instalment contract, Rafferty did not secure the consent of the appellant prior to contracting for such repairs with Colwell.

Upon Rafferty's failure to pay the repair bill, Colwell retained possession of the truck claiming a mechanics' lien thereon. A notice of lien-claim . . . was filed. . . . Colwell brought its complaint against Rafferty to enforce its mechanics' lien. . . . Rafferty defaulted and this gave rise to a judgment in favor of Colwell against Rafferty . . . with execution, as stated in the agreed statement of facts, "issued to Defendant [Colwell] against James Rafferty for the sum of $451.04 plus costs of $14.61" on October 30, 1969. The record does not disclose that such judgment was anything more than a personal judgment. As a matter of fact, the appellant in July 1969 had recovered possession of the truck from Colwell by prosecuting its complaint in replevin, wherein the appellee denied appellant's right to possession and, by way of counterclaim, sought damages for conversion. General Motors Acceptance Corporation appeals from the trial Court's judgment in favor of Colwell on its counterclaim in the amount of $451.04 plus costs. The appeal must be denied.

It is a well-settled principle of the common law that he who by labor, skill or materials adds value to the chattel of another whether under an express or an implied agreement has a possessory lien thereon for the value of his services and materials, and may retain the chattel in his possession until the same be paid. See, *Taggard v. Buckmore*, 1856, 42 Me. 77. This right rests upon principles of natural justice and commercial necessity. . . .

The common law repairman's lien, also known as an artisan's lien, has been held to survive the enactment of our statutory mechanics' lien. In *Crosby v. Hill*, 1922, 121 Me. 432, 117 A. 585, our Court ruled that the statutory lien for repairs did not supersede or destroy the common law lien, nor did it create a new right, but merely provided a new and additional remedy.

The immediate issue before us is, whether the appellee, Colwell, had a valid common law mechanics' lien upon the truck, at the time it was deprived of the possession of it in the replevin action, which takes priority over the appellant's prior perfected security interest? Resolution of this issue, in turn, will depend upon the proper interpretation to be given to the pertinent provisions of the Uniform Commercial Code.

The language of 11 *M. R. S. A.*, § 9–310 makes it clear that the lien of the holder of a perfected security interest is subordinate to the possessory lien of one who in the ordinary course of his business furnishes services or materials with respect to goods subject to the security interest, whether the possessory lien be based upon the common law or a statute, unless the lien is statutory and the statute expressly provides otherwise.

We hold that it was the purpose of the Uniform Commercial Code as adopted in Maine to give priority to common law mechanics' liens, where the repairman retains possession of the repaired goods. There was no error below.

Appeal denied.

All Justices concurring.

REVIEW CASES

1. Hoey Motor Co., operating under the Uniform Conditional Sales Act, sold an automobile on a conditional sales contract to Hutchinson, who gave a note along with the conditional sales contract as security. The motor company assigned the note and contract to Hare & Chase, who, after default in the car payments, repossessed the car, sold it, and sought a deficiency judg-

ment for the balance due. Hutchinson contended that Hare & Chase was not entitled to a deficiency judgment, since it had elected to repossess and sell the car. Holding? (Hare & Chase, Inc. v. Hutchinson et al., 138 A. 611)

2. Fynn & Anderson contracted to sell real estate to Kenrick and another. The property was encumbered by a $5,000 mortgage held by Hill, trustee. The contract recited that in return for the deed and conveyance Kenrick et al. were to "pay the sum of $6,500, of which $100 has been paid this day, balance above mortgage is to be paid in cash upon delivery of said deed." Default was made in the mortgage installments, the property was sold for $4,500, and a deficiency judgment was sought. The question at issue was whether under the agreement Kenrick et al. assumed and agreed to pay the mortgage or simply purchased the property subject to the mortgage. Holding? (Fynn & Anderson v. Kenrick and Another, 285 Mass. 446, 189 N. E. 207)

3. Burnley purchased a soda fountain from Tuffs and gave him notes payable one each month, title to the fountain to remain in Tuffs until all the notes were paid. After Burnley had received possession of the fountain and had paid several of the notes, his store was destroyed by fire. He refused to pay the further notes as they became due, and Tuffs sued to enforce payment. Holding? (Burnley v. Tuffs, 66 Miss. 48, 5 So. 627)

4. Foster gave a collateral note, secured by a diamond ring, to Hamaker for a $300 loan. Abrahams, an attorney, bought the note from Hamaker, who delivered the note and the ring to him. When the note came due, Foster tendered payment in full, but Abrahams held the note and the ring for a debt which Foster owed him for legal services. Foster refused to pay the old debt. Has she a right to the ring upon payment of the note? (Foster v. Abrahams, Cal. Dist. Court of Appeals, 241 P. 274)

5. The contractor in charge of building a house for Brown engaged the Electric Contracting Co. to do the electrical work. The Electric Co. was not paid by the contractor and consequently filed notice of lien and brought suit against Brown. The defense was that the lien was not filed within the statutory 60-day period. The evidence showed that the work had been completed ready for use on March 10th, except that a certain type of ground clamp required by city ordinance was not then available. With the city inspector's consent, a different type of clamp was installed. On April 25th two employees of the Electric Co. returned to replace this clamp with the type required. Notice of lien was filed on June 13th. Judgment for whom? (Electric Contracting Co. v. Brown et al., 39 So. (2d) (La.) 100)

6. Through Brock's negligence his car collided with Wilson's. Brock told Wilson to take his car to Malenock's garage and have it repaired, and promised that he would pay Malenock. Malenock agreed to repair the car and collect from Brock. After the repairs had been made, Brock refused to pay, and Malenock refused to turn over the car to Wilson unless he paid for the repairs. Wilson sued Malenock for conversion, contending that Malenock had lost his common law lien by agreeing to look to Brock for payment. Was Wilson correct in his contention? (Wilson v. Malenock, 128 Pa. Sup. 544, 194 A. 508)

Sales

part V

The Contract:
Its Nature and
Formation

27

INTRODUCTION

The Law of Sales deals with the law governing the sale of personal property, as distinguished from real property. Since many of the needs and wants of mankind are satisfied through the various processes involved in the purchase and sale of goods and merchandise, and since practically everyone is involved, directly or indirectly, in some phase of the process of moving goods and merchandise from the producer to the ultimate consumer, a knowledge of the laws governing the sale of personal property is of practical importance to almost everybody.

Sales contracts have many characteristics in common with other contracts, and in our study of them we shall draw heavily upon what we have already learned about contract law. We shall discover, however, that sales contracts also possess certain special features that set them off from other contracts.

THE UNIFORM SALES ACT

In 1906 the National Conference of Commissioners on Uniform State Laws prepared what is known as the Uniform Sales Act, and recommended its adoption by the various states. In preparing the Act the Commissioners drew many ideas from the English Sale of Goods Act of 1893, which in turn codified principles that had their origin in the Law Merchant and the early common law.

The major object of the Act was not to revise or reform the Law of Sales but to make it uniform in the various jurisdictions. Actually, on most matters the law was already uniform. Where conflicts and differences existed, the Commission resolved them by agreeing upon rules which seemed likely to serve best the needs and purposes of merchants and other parties concerned.

THE UNIFORM COMMERCIAL CODE

As was explained in Chapter 2 of this book, the uniform laws dealing with commercial transactions have been revised and unified by the joint labors of the American Law Institute and the National Conference of Commissioners on Uniform State Laws. The result of their work, which has been changed, revised, and supplemented, and is presently known as the 1962 Official Edition, is called the Uniform Commercial Code (U. C. C.). Article 2 of the Code, entitled "Sales," embodies a complete reorganization and modernization of the Uniform Sales Act.

Since all jurisdictions in the United States except Louisiana have in 1968 adopted the Uniform Commercial Code, the discussion of the Law of Sales in this book is based upon the Uniform Commercial Code and comparable statutes and the court decisions interpreting those acts.[1]

SCOPE OF ARTICLE 2, SALES, OF THE UNIFORM COMMERCIAL CODE

Article 2, on Sales, of the Code applies to transactions in goods, but it does not apply to security transactions and things in action (choses in action) even though they may be unconditional contracts to sell or present sales. The coverage of the present Article 2 on Sales is much more extensive than that of the old Sales Act, extending to the various bodies of case law which have been developed both outside of and under the latter.

The arrangement of the present Article is in terms of contract for sale and the various steps of its performance. The legal consequences are stated as following directly from the contract and action taken under it without resorting to the idea of when property or title passed or was to pass as being the determining factor. The purpose is to avoid making practical issues between practical men turn upon the location of an intangible something the passing of which no man can prove by evidence, and to substitute for such abstractions proof of words and actions of a tangible character.

SALE AND CONTRACT TO SELL

The Law of Sales covers two types of contract, (1) sales and (2) contracts to sell. As defined in the Uniform Commercial Code, "a sale of goods consists in the passing of title from the seller to the buyer for a

---

[1] The text of the Uniform Commercial Code is reprinted in the Appendix.

price." [1] and a contract for sale of goods includes both a present sale of goods and a contract to sell goods at a future time.[2] It will be observed from these definitions that in the case of a *sale* the property in or title to the goods passes at once, and the contract is therefore executed; while in the case of a *contract to sell* the property in the goods is to pass at some future date, and the contract is therefore executory. This distinction often becomes important in determining which party must bear the loss where the goods are damaged, destroyed, or lost. Prior to the adoption of the U. C. C., as a general rule the risk of loss fell upon the party who owned the goods, unless the parties stipulated otherwise.

THE CONTRACT

Since sales and contracts to sell are contracts, they must meet the four essentials of contracts: mutual assent, consideration, parties with legal capacity to contract, and legal subject matter. If any one of these essentials is lacking in a given transaction, the negotiations will not produce a valid contract.

Some sales and contracts to sell must, in addition, be in writing if they are to be enforceable. In negotiating a sales contract one should always keep in mind the requirements of the Statute of Frauds, discussed in Chapter 12.

STATUTE OF FRAUDS

Sec. 2–201 of the Code states that (1) except as otherwise provided in this section a contract for the sale of goods for the price of $500 or more is not enforceable by way of action or defense unless there is some writing sufficient to indicate that a contract for sale has been made between the parties and signed by the party against whom enforcement is sought or by his authorized agent or broker. A writing is not insufficient because it omits or incorrectly states a term agreed upon, but the contract is not enforceable under this paragraph beyond the quantity of goods shown in such writing.

(2) Between merchants, if within a reasonable time a writing in confirmation of the contract and sufficient against the sender is received and the party receiving it has reason to know its contents, it satisfies the requirements of subsection (1) against such party unless written notice of objection to its contents is given within ten days after it is received.

(3) A contract which does not satisfy the requirements of subsection

1 Sec. 2–106 (1).
2 Sec. 2–106 (1).

(1) but which is valid in other respects is enforceable if the goods are to be specially manufactured for the buyer and are not suitable for sale to others in the ordinary course of the seller's business, and if the seller, before notice of repudiation is received and under circumstances which reasonably indicate that the goods are for the buyer, has made either a substantial beginning of their manufacture or commitments for their procurement; or if the party against whom enforcement is sought admits in his pleading, testimony, or otherwise in court that a contract for sale was made, but the contract is not enforceable under this provision beyond the quantity of goods admitted; or with respect to goods for which payment has been made and accepted or which have been received and accepted.

A contract for sale of goods may be made in any manner sufficient to show agreement, including conduct by both parties which recognizes the existence of such a contract. An agreement sufficient to constitute a contract for sale may be found even though the moment of its making is undetermined. Even though one or more terms are left open, a contract for sales does not fail for indefiniteness if the parties have intended to make a contract and there is a reasonably certain basis for giving an appropriate remedy.

FIRM OFFERS

An offer by a merchant to buy or sell goods in a signed writing which by its terms gives assurance that it will be held open is not revocable, for lack of consideration, during the time stated—or, if no time is stated, for a reasonable time—but in no event may such period of irrevocability exceed three months; but any such term of assurance on a form supplied by the offeree must be separately signed by the offeror.

OFFER AND ACCEPTANCE

Unless otherwise unambiguously indicated by the language or circumstances, an offer to make a contract shall be construed as inviting acceptance in any manner and by any medium reasonable in the circumstances; an order or other offer to buy goods for prompt or current shipment shall be construed as inviting acceptance either by a prompt promise to ship or by the prompt or current shipment of conforming or non-conforming goods, but such a shipment of non-conforming goods does not constitute an acceptance if the seller seasonably notifies the buyer that the shipment is offered only as an accommodation to the buyer. Where the beginning of a requested performance is reasonable mode of acceptance, an offeror who is not notified of acceptance within a reasonable time may treat the offer as having lapsed before acceptance.

ADDITIONAL TERMS IN ACCEPTANCE OR CONFIRMATION

A definite and seasonable expression of acceptance or a written confirmation which is sent within a reasonable time operates as an acceptance even though it states terms additional to or different from those offered or agreed upon, unless acceptance is expressly made conditional on assent to the additional or different terms. The additional terms are to be construed as proposals for addition to the contract. Between merchants such terms become part of the contract unless: the offer expressly limits acceptance to the terms of the offer; the terms materially alter the contract; or notification of objection to the terms has already been given or is given within a reasonable time after notice of them is received. Conduct by both parties which recognizes the existence of a contract is sufficient to establish a contract for sale although the writings of the parties do not otherwise establish a contract. In such case the terms of the particular contract consist of those terms on which the writings of the parties agree, together with any supplementary terms incorporated under any other provisions of this Act.

Newton v. Allen

220 Ga. 681, 141 S. E. (2d) 417 (1965)

Supreme Court of Georgia

This was an action by Miriam Newton Allen (plaintiff) against Jack C. Newton, Jr. (defendant). Judgment for plaintiff and defendant brought error. Affirmed.

Miriam Newton Allen filed a petition against Jack C. Newton, Jr., and W. L. Sparks in the Superior Court of Jenkins County charging the invalidity of the timber lease which they rely upon for the right to work the turpentine on her land. The instrument is as follows: "I, Mrs. Miriam N. Allen, do lease all of my workable timber for turpentine on all lands owned or controlled by me to Jack C. Newton, Jr., for a period of five years for a percentage of 30% of each and every dipping. Plus payment for cups all ready up. To include government payment of timber already cut. Signed this 6th day of January, 1964. Witness by Georgia M. Newton this 6th day of January 1964. /s/ Miriam N. Allen (L.S.) /s/ Jack C. Newton, Jr."

GRICE, J. The validity of an instrument purporting to lease timber for turpentine purposes is controlling upon this review. . . .

The petition as amended made, insofar as material here, the allegations which follow. The plaintiff, owner of certain described lands, entered into the above quoted agreement with the defendant Newton for the working of turpentine on her lands. Both defendants are using her timber thereon for turpentine purposes although she has advised them that she does not recognize the agreement as legal and binding and has demanded that they desist from further trespasses. She has offered to make restitution and to reimburse them for any expenses they have incurred in working the turpentine, but they have not responded to her offer and are continuing the trespasses and damage to her timber. The prayers included temporary and permanent injunction from going upon and using her land, accounting for gum taken and monetary damages.

To the foregoing petition, the defendants urged their general demurrer asserting that the petition did not set out a cause of action since it showed upon its face that the instrument is valid. The assignment of error here is to the overruling of such demurrer.

The plaintiff's right to the relief she seeks depends upon the validity of the purported lease agreement. As we view it, the sufficiency of the description of the land on which the timber stands is determinative of that issue.

The instrument provides that "I * * * do lease all of my workable timber for turpentine on all lands owned or controlled by me * * * for a period of five years for a percentage of 30% of each and every dipping * * *"

This writing purports to lease, for a period of five years, all of the plaintiff's timber suitable for turpentine purposes. The parties evidence no intent to pass a lesser interest so it will be presumed that they intended to convey an estate for years. *Warehouses, Inc. v. Wetherbee*, 203 Ga. 483(c) (by five Justices), 46 S. E. (2d) 894. The fact that the use is limited to turpentine purposes does not reduce the interest transferred to a mere usufruct where there is no indication that the parties so intended. *Warehouses, Inc. v. Wetherbee*, 203 Ga. 483, 490–491, 46 S. E. (2d) 894, *supra*.

This instrument, then, purported to convey an estate for years in standing timber, which is realty. *Coody v. Gress Lumber Co.*, 82 Ga. 793(1), 10 S. E. 218. Code Sec. 85–801 provides that if an estate for years "* * * is in lands, it passes as realty."

Our Code, Sec. 20–401(4), requires, in order to bind the promisor, that "Any contract for sale of lands, or any interest in, or concerning them" must be in writing. Lease contracts which convey an estate for years fall within this section. See *Baxley Hardware Co. v. Morris*, 165 Ga. 359(1), 140 S. E. 869. Such leases of standing timber must describe the land upon which the timber stands, with sufficient certainty for identification or give a key by which it may be identified. *Clarke Brothers v. Stowe*, 132 Ga. 621(3), 64 S. E. 786. See also *Blumberg v. Nathan*, 190 Ga. 64, 8 S. E. (2d) 374.

Thus, the question is whether the description "all lands owned or controlled by me" meets these requirements.

We hold that it does not. It fails to describe any particular land or to furnish any key to make certain the identification of lands owned by plaintiff. Nor does it identify in any manner the lands "controlled" by her.

We are mindful that this court has held a devise of "all of my lands" to be a sufficient description to operate as color of title by will. *Harriss v. Howard*, 126 Ga. 325, 55 S. E. 59 (one Justice absent). However, the opinion (at page 330, 55 S. E. at page 61) was at pains to state that "We recognize, of course, the difference between a will and a deed, and the great liberality allowed in making wills and passing title by them."

In *Sarmon v. Liles*, 150 Ga. 338, 103 S. E. 797, a timber lease description quite similar to the one here was adjudged by this court (one Justice dissenting) to be insufficient. The record in that case disclosed the wording there to have been "the standing cypress timber on the lands of the party of the first part."

In *Blue Ridge Apartment Company, Inc. v. Telfair Stockton & Company, Inc.*, 205 Ga. 552, 560 (one Justice dissenting), 54 S. E. (2d) 608, this court held that the descriptive language "*all* the assets, tangible and intangible, *property, real,* personal and mixed, business and good will of the company * * *" was not sufficient to pass title to land. (Emphasis ours.) In that opinion a thorough history was provided as to descriptions in conveyances in the light of the blanket "all."

We regard the above cited decisions as controlling upon the description issue here and therefore hold that the language in the instant document was insufficient to convey any interest to the defendant Newton.

There is no merit in the defendants' contention that the instrument here purported to lease or sell only the turpentine itself and thus constituted a contract for the sale of personalty under the Uniform Commercial Code (Ga. L. 1962, p. 156 et seq.; Code Ann. Title 109A). This writing purported to lease the *trees* themselves, not merely the product thereof, and therefore was a lease of realty. This court held in *Adcock v. Berry*, 194 Ga. 243 (2a, 2b), 21 S. E. (2d) 605 that Code Sec. 85–1901, declaring that all crops, matured and unmatured are personalty, and Code Sec. 85–1902, providing that the word "crops" includes crude gum from a living tree, apply only to the fruits and products of plants, trees and shrubs and do not refer to the plants, trees and shrubs themselves. The Uniform Commercial Code does not purport to change the law relating to instruments which transfer an interest in land.

The petition shows that the purported lease agreement under which the defendants claim the right to take turpentine from plaintiff's timber, is void for lack of adequate description of the land. Therefore, the plaintiff is entitled to the relief she seeks. The judgment overruling the general demurrer to the petition is

Affirmed.

Woods v. Van Wallis Trailer Sales Company

77 N. M. 121, 419 P. (2d) 964 (1966)
Supreme Court of New Mexico

An action by Ernest Woods and Thula Mae Woods (plaintiffs) against Van Wallis Trailer Sales Company (defendant). Judgment for defendant, and plaintiffs appealed. Judgment affirmed.

This is a proceeding by buyers (Woods), plaintiffs, seeking rescission of agreement to purchase a new mobile home and restitution of monies paid.

MOISE, J. Plaintiffs-appellants appeal from the trial court's refusal to grant rescission of an agreement to purchase a new mobile home, and restitution of monies paid. On September 24, 1962 the parties entered into a purchase order agreement for a new 1962 Chickasha mobile home. Defendant-appellee agreed to accept in trade appellants' New Moon trailer and grant a credit of $1,450.00. Appellants made a down payment of $1,570.65, leaving an unpaid balance of $5,714.70 to be paid over a 7-year period. After credit for the cash payment and trade-in was allowed, a chattel mortgage and note dated October 9, 1962, were executed by both appellants, calling for 84 monthly payments of $115.72, or a total of $9,720.48, including insurance, the $164.70 extra for the skylight, and finance charges.

When the mobile home in question arrived from the manufacturer it differed from the one ordered in three respects. It was a 1963 model, instead of a 1962 model; the attached expandable room was approximately one foot narrower than the one ordered; and, it had a skylight at an additional cost of $164.70.

Appellants' principal contention is to the effect that Ernest Woods, the husband, being head of the community with sole power to manage, control and dispose of the personal property of the community, never had accepted the house trailer delivered by appellee, and that accordingly they were entitled to rescind the contract.

Complaint is made that the court found that the acts of the wife were performed on behalf of the husband and were authorized by him, and that there is no evidence to support the same. Without detailing the proof as to what transpired between appellee and appellants, and who was present on each occasion, it is sufficient to point out that after the discrepancies or deficiencies in the trailer tendered to appellants were known, and they had expressed their dissatisfaction, the wife, with or without authority, withdrew the objections, whereupon the new trailer was delivered to appellants' lot in Los Lunas. A few days later the husband authorized removal by appellee of the old trailer in which they had been living and which was traded in on the new one. This was in the nature of a partial payment as provided in the purchase agreement. Also, after a washing machine had been removed from the old trailer and placed in the new one, the husband paid for installation of gas lines in the trailer to comply with the New Mexico code, although the court found that was to be done without expense to appellants.

We are impressed that the brief recounting of the facts above discloses that if proof of the wife's authority is not sufficient to support the court's finding to that effect, at least it does support the court's conclusion that the appellants, by their words and conduct, accepted the trailer. Whether this results from authority or ratification we do not consider material.

After having a reasonable opportunity to inspect and with full knowledge of the trailer's defects, the making of partial payments, performing acts of dominion, as well as acts inconsistent with any intention to rescind, amount to an acceptance or ratification. *Terry v. Humphreys*, 27 N. M. 564, 203 P. 539; Sec. 50A-2-606(1), N. M. S. A. 1953; *Park County Implement Co. v. Craig* (Wyo.

1964) 397 P. (2d) 800. There is no question that the appellants had the right, had they chosen to do so, to reject the tendered non-conforming goods. Sec. 50A–2–601, N. M. S. A. 1953. However, the burden was on appellants to make a timely and unequivocal rejection if they did not intend to accept the goods as delivered. Sec. 50A–2–602, N. M. S. A. 1953; *Hudspeth Motors, Inc. v. Wilkinson*, 238 Ark. 410, 382 S. W. (2d) 191.

Grandi v. LeSage, 74 N. M. 799, 399 P. (2d) 285, is clearly distinguishable. There the buyer accepted the goods without knowledge of the non-conformity and it was quite proper to allow revocation of acceptance under Sec. 50A–2–608, N. M. S. A. 1953.

Nor do we find merit in appellants' contention that since the retail installment contract was not completed before signing, as required by Sec. 50–15–7, N. M. S. A. 1953, the appellants have the right of rescission. Assuming, without deciding, that the provision is applicable, the right to rescind under Sec. 50–15–7(A) (3), N. M. S. A. 1953, by its own language applies only to "a buyer who has not received delivery."

Appellants further contend that the dealings between the parties were not "fair and equitable" as the trial judge concluded. They contend that the appellee attempted to collect $164.70, the price of the skylight, twice, by adding it onto the retail installment contract and also by attempting to collect it in cash. We hold that this contention has no merit.

Finding no error, the judgment appealed from is affirmed.

It is so ordered.

Associated Hardware Supply Co. v. Big Wheel Distributing Co.
355 F. (2d) 114 (1966)

This was an action by Associated Hardware Supply Co., supplier (plaintiff and appellee), to recover balance of open unpaid account for merchandise sold and delivered to Big Wheel Distributing Co. (defendant and appellant). Judgment for plaintiff and defendant appealed.

In the Federal District Court the plaintiff sued the defendant for the balance due on goods delivered on open account, and the defendant filed a counterclaim and alleged fraud.

STANLEY, C.J. This appeal raises several questions involving the Uniform Commercial Code as adopted in Pennsylvania. Two questions involving the interpretation and application of the Code were raised in the district court and argued here. The first of these concerns the Sales Article's Statute of Frauds, U. C. C. Sec. 2–201. It has been argued that the goods sold between March and June, 1964, were personalty, the price of which exceeded $500.00, and must be represented by a writing. This issue is readily resolved by either of two subsections of U. C. C. Sec. 2–201. First, it is not disputed that the goods have been received and accepted by the defendant. This being so, the transaction is clearly without the Statute of Frauds, U. C. C. Sec. 2–201 (3) (c). Even if this were not so, it is also admitted that Big Wheel received invoices for the sales in question which contained the letterhead of Associated, the quantity and price terms. Because it is clear that the parties are "merchants" within the meaning of the Code, U. C. C. Sec. 2–104 (1), and since no written objections to the invoices were sent within ten days of their receipt, the Statute of Frauds is satisfied. U. C. C. Sec. 2–201 (2).

The second and perhaps more difficult question is whether the March–June, 1964, sales or any of the sales between the parties are represented by corresponding confirmatory memoranda or other writing "intended by the parties as a final expression of their agreement." U. C. C. Sec. 2–202. Although this problem is more directly related to the defenses and counterclaims of Big Wheel insofar as whether evidence of prior oral agreements is admissible, the parol evidence rule is a substantive rule of contracts, and consequently, will be discussed here.

"Ever since the leading case of *Gianni v. R. Russell & Co., Inc.* * * * it has been well settled law in Pennsylvania that: . . . Where parties, without any fraud or mistake, have deliberately put their engagements in writing, the law declares the writing to be not only the best, but the only, evidence of their agreement:" * * * "all preliminary negotiations, conversations and verbal agreements are merged in and superseded by the subsequent written contract * * * and "unless fraud, accident, or mistake be averred, the writing constitutes the agreement between the parties, and its terms cannot be added to nor subtracted from by parol evidence."

Since the parol evidence rule, under the circumstances here, does not apply, and the counterclaim was improperly dismissed, we think the entry of summary judgment on the principal claim was untimely. After issuing an appropriate order, it may proceed to trial on the issues involving factual disputes.

The orders of the district court will be vacated and the cause remanded for disposition not inconsistent with this opinion.

E. A. Coronis Assocs. v. M. Gordon Constr. Co.
90 N. J. Super. 69, 216 A. (2d) 246 (1966)

This was an action by E. A. Coronis Associates, a corporation (plaintiff), against M. Gordon Construction Co., a corporation (defendant). Judgment for defendant, and plaintiff appealed. Reversed and remanded.

This litigation began when plaintiff brought suit on three contracts not here pertinent. Defendant admitted liability thereon, but counterclaimed for breach of a contract to supply and erect structural steel on one of its projects. Gordon is a general contractor. In anticipation of making a bid to construct two buildings at the Port of New York Authority's Elizabeth Piers it sought bids from subcontractors. Coronis designs, fabricates, supplies and erects structural steel. On April 22, 1963 it sent the following letter to Gordon:

April 22, 1963

Mr. David BenZvi
Gordon Construction Co.
Elizabeth Avenue
Linden, N. J.

Subject:
Bldgs. 131 & 132
Elizabeth Port Authority Piers
Structural Steel

Dear Mr. BenZvi:

  We regret very much that this estimate was so delayed. Be assured that the time consumed was due to routing of the plans through our regular sources of fabrication.

  We are pleased to offer:
All structural steel including steel girts and purlins
Both Buildings delivered and erected $155,413.50
All structural steel equipped with clips for wood girts & purlins
Both Buildings delivered and erected 98,937.50
NOTE:
This price is predicated on an erected price of .1175 per Lb. of steel and we would expect to adjust the price on this basis to conform to actual tonnage of steel used in the project.

  Thank you very much for this opportunity to quote.

                                Very truly yours,
                                E. A. CORONIS ASSOCIATES
                                /s/ Arthur C. Pease
                                Arthur C. Pease

Gordon contends that at some date prior to April 22 the parties reached an oral agreement and that the above letter was sent in confirmation.

  Bids were opened by the Port Authority on April 19, 1963, and Gordon's bid was the lowest. He alleges that Coronis was informed the same day. The Port Authority contract was officially awarded to Gordon on May 27, 1963 and executed about two weeks later. During this period Gordon never accepted the alleged offer of Coronis. Meanwhile, on June 1, 1963, Coronis sent a telegram, in pertinent part reading: "Due to conditions beyond our control, we must withdraw our proposal of April 22nd 1963 for structural steel Dor Buildings 131 and 132 at the Elizabeth-Port Piers at the earliest possible time we will resubmit our proposal." Two days later, on June 3, 1963, Gordon replied by telegram as follows: "Ref your tel. 6–3 and for the record be advised that we are holding you to your bid of April 22, 1963 for the structural steel of cargo bldgs 131 and 132." Coronis never performed. Gordon employed the Elizabeth Iron Works to perform the work and claims as damages the difference between Coronis' proposal of $155,413.50 and Elizabeth Iron Works' charge of $208,000.

COLLESTER, J.AD. Gordon contends that the April 22 letter was an offer and that Coronis had no right to withdraw it. Two grounds are advanced in support. First, Gordon contends that the Uniform Commercial Code firm offer section, N. J. S. 12A:2-205, N. J. S. A., precludes withdrawal and, second, it contends that withdrawal is prevented by the doctrine of promissory estoppel.

Prior to the enactment of the Uniform Commercial Code an offer not supported by consideration could be revoked at any time prior to acceptance. *American Handkerchief Corp. v. Frannat Realty Co.*, 17 N.J. 12, 109 A. (2d) 793 (1954). The drafters of the Code recognized that the common law rule was contrary to modern business practice and possessed the capability to produce unjust results. See Corbin, "The Uniform Commercial Code—Sales, Should it be Enacted," 59 *Yale L. J.* 821, 827 (1950). The response was section 2-205 (N. J. S. 12A:2-205, N. J. S. A.) which reverses the common law rule and states: "An offer by a merchant to buy or sell goods in a *signed writing which by its terms gives assurance that it will be held open* is not revocable, for lack of consideration, during the time stated or if no time is stated for a reasonable time. * * *" (Emphasis added.)

Coronis' letter contains no terms giving assurance it will be held open. We recognize that just as an offeree runs a risk in acting on an offer before accepting it, the offeror runs a risk if his offer is considered irrevocable. Cf. *James Baird Co. v. Gimbel Bros., Inc.*, 64 F. (2d) 344 (2 Cir. 1933). In their comments to section 2-205 of the Code the drafters anticipated these risks and stated: "However, despite settled courses of dealing or usages of the trade whereby firm offers are made by oral communication and relied upon without more evidence, such offers remain revocable under this Article since authentication by a writing is the essence of this section." Uniform Commercial Code (N. J. S. 12A:2-205, N. J. S. A.), comment, Par. 2.

We think it clear that plaintiff's writing does not come within the provision of section 2-205 of a "signed writing which by its terms gives assurance that it will be held open." See *Wilmington Trust Company v. Coulter*, 200 A. (2d) 441 (Del. Sup. Ct. 1964).

Having so concluded, we need not consider the question of whether the Coronis letter was an offer or whether the letter dealt with "goods." We note in this connection that Coronis quoted the price for structural steel delivered and erected.

Revised and remanded.

BILL OF SALE

A bill of sale is a written instrument whereby the vendor (seller) *transfers* to the vendee (purchaser) the title to the personal property named in the instrument. Title passes upon a valid delivery and acceptance of a properly executed bill of sale. It is therefore not used in the case of a contract to sell, where title is to pass at some future time, but in the case of a sale, where title passes at once. A bill of sale performs the same function in the sale of personal property that a deed performs in the sale of real property. In each case the instrument stands as written evidence of the intentions of the parties and of the transfer of title to property.

In the sale of personal property it is by no means always necessary to use a bill of sale; in fact, in most instances a bill of sale is not required. It is necessary only (1) where a statute requires that it be used or (2) where by the agreement of the parties a bill of sale is to be given to the vendee.

Though the statutes of a few states prescribe that a particular form be used, in most states no such requirement is made. In general all that is necessary is to set out the date of the instrument, the names of the parties, a clear description of the property sold, and the consideration. The bill of sale must always be signed by the vendor. Most, if not all, states require that the vendor's signature be acknowledged. In some states the instrument must be under seal, and in some states it must be recorded. Statutes which prescribe use of the seal and recording sometimes provide that these formalities may be waived if the delivery of the bill of sale is simultaneous with the delivery of the property sold. Because of the variation from state to state, local statutes should be checked on these points.

Hull v. Ray
80 Calif. A. 284, 251, P. 810 (1926)

This was an action by John S. Hull (plaintiff) against Carl Ray (defendant). Judgment for defendant, and plaintiff appealed. Reversed.

Plaintiff brought this suit to rescind a contract to purchase certain registered cattle. On November 13, 1922, defendant agreed, in writing, to sell plaintiff 16 head of registered cattle and 4 head of unregistered stock for the sum of $3,500. The pedigreed stock were registered with the American Jersey Cattle Club of New York, and defendant held the certificates of such registered stock in his own name. By the terms of the agreement defendant agreed to execute and deliver to plaintiff "a good and sufficient bill of sale of said cattle, together with a warranty of title." The only instruments which defendant supplied to the plaintiff, pursuant to the contract, were as follows:

"BILL OF SALE

Received of John S. Hull, payment in full for 20 head of Jerseys, bought of me on November 13, 1922.   (Signed) Carl Ray."

"TRANSFER OF OWNERSHIP

Send this paper for record to the American Jersey Cattle Club, No. 324 W. Twenty-third St., New York. (See directions on back.)

I sold to John S. Hull of Nester, Cal., the following Jersey animal, _____ (male; female). Names _____. Herd Register No. _____. Date of delivery to buyer _____.

I hereby authorize the transfer of ownership as above, to be registered on the books of the American Jersey Cattle Club.

(Signed) Carl Ray, Lankersham, Cal."

The lower court found that defendant did furnish to plaintiff "warranty of title, and certificates of record, transfer of ownership, indorsed to plaintiff, and authorizing the American Jersey Cattle Club to transfer said registered cattle into the name of plaintiff"; but that "defendant declined and refused to supply plaintiff with any other or different instrument." Upon the basis of these findings the court rendered judgment for defendant. Plaintiff appealed.

THOMPSON, J. Where findings are irreconcilably in conflict, the judgment must be reversed, for the reason that it is impossible, under such circumstances, to determine which findings controlled the court in rendering its judgment.

A bill of sale is not required to be under seal, nor couched in any peculiar form, so long as it sufficiently describes the property sold and contains language importing actual transfer of title. A bill of sale is a written agreement by which one person transfers his title to goods or chattels to another person. In *Putnam v. McDonald*, 72 Vt. 2, 47 A. 159, it was held that a signed instrument in the following language, "Terms cash. P. to M. dr one bicycle, $47.50, paid July 27, 1896," constituted a mere receipt, and was not a bill of sale. The court there said: "A bill of sale is a writing evidencing the transfer of personal property from one person to another. The nature of the writing would seem to require that it contain some statement of the fact of transfer." In *Houghton v. Carpenter*, 40 Vt. 588, it was said that a bill of sale must contain the substantial elements of a contract, and one of the defects pointed out in this writing was that it did not contain any words importing a transfer of title.

In the instant case, the defendant agreed to furnish the plaintiff with a "good and sufficient bill of sale." The document hereinbefore mentioned, termed a "bill of sale," is nothing more than an ordinary receipt for the purchase price of cattle. It does not purport to acknowledge the transfer of title to the stock. The form and language used in that document are insufficient to constitute a bill of sale.

The findings are irreconcilable, and the judgment must therefore be and is reversed.

EXISTING AND FUTURE GOODS

Sec. 2–105 of the Code defines goods as all things (including specially manufactured goods) which are movable at the time of identification to the contract for sale other than the money in which the price is to be paid, investment securities, and things in action.

The general rule is that one may not make a present sale of nonexisting goods or of goods that he does not own. Since a sale involves the immediate passage of title, one obviously cannot make a sale of goods to which he does not possess title. But one may make a contract to sell such goods, since it is possible that he may acquire title to them by the time he is required to make delivery under the terms of the contract. Goods which form the subject of a contract to sell may be either existing goods, owned or possessed by the seller, or goods to be manufactured or acquired by the seller after the making of the contract to sell. There may be a contract to sell goods, the acquisition of which by the seller depends upon a contingency which may or may not happen. Sec. 2–105 of the Code states that goods must be both existing and identified before any interest in them can pass. Goods which are not both existing and identified are "future" goods. A purported present sale of future goods or of any interest therein operates as a contract to sell. There may be a sale of a part interest in existing identified goods.

Some courts have recognized an exception to the rule that one may not sell property which does not exist or which he does not "presently own." Under the *doctrine of potential existence* these courts have held that one may sell and pass immediate title to something that does not actually exist, provided it has "potential existence" and the seller owns or controls the source from which it comes. For example, the owner of animals may sell their prospective offspring, if they are in "potential existence," or the owner or lessee of land may sell the future crop from the land, if such crop is planted.[1] Sec. 2–105 of the Code states that "goods" also includes the unborn of young animals and growing crops and other identified things attached to realty as described in the section on goods to be severed from realty (Sec. 2–107).

DESTRUCTION OF GOODS

We have already become familiar with the rule that when the subject matter of an attempted contract has been destroyed, without the knowledge of the parties, before the contract is consummated, the agreement of the parties is absolutely void. This rule applies to purported sales of identified goods and contracts to sell specific goods. Sec. 2–613 of the Code states that where the contract requires for its performance goods identified when the contract is made, and the goods suffer casualty without fault of either party before the risk of loss passes to the buyer, or in a

[1] 77 *C. J. S.*, Sales, sec. 14(b), p. 603.

proper case under a "no arrival, no sale" term (Sec. 2–324), then if the loss is total the contract is avoided; and if the loss is partial or the goods have so deteriorated as no longer to conform to the contract, the buyer may nevertheless demand inspection and at his option either treat the contract as avoided or accept the goods with due allowance from the contract price for the deterioration or the deficiency in quantity but without further right against the seller.

THE PRICE

The definitions of a sale and a contract to sell in the U. C. C. show that the consideration is the "price" agreed upon. Questions sometimes arise as to just when and how the price may be fixed. Can there be a sale or a contract to sell if the price is not designated in the contract? According to Sec. 2–305 of the U. C. C., the price may be fixed by the contract, or it may be left to be fixed in such manner as may be agreed upon (e.g. the parties may agree that the price will be the market price on a given date), or it may be determined by the course of dealing between the parties. Where the price is not fixed by one of these methods, then the buyer must pay a reasonable price. A reasonable price is generally held to be the current market price.

While the price is usually made payable in money, it may be made payable in goods, realty, or otherwise (Sec. 2–304).

Republic-Odin Appliance Corp. v. Consumers Plumbing and Heating Supply Co.
29 Pa. D. & C. (2d) 307, 45 Erie Co. Leg. J. 121 (1961)

This was an action by Republic-Odin Appliance Corporation (plaintiff) against Consumers Plumbing and Heating Supply Company (defendant). Judgment for plaintiff.

This is an action in assumpsit on an open book account for the purchase price of goods sold and delivered. From March 4, 1958, until March 19, 1959, there was a series of transactions in which plaintiff sold and delivered merchandise to the defendant on the order of Albert C. Cole, its manager. Upon the merchandise thus delivered there remains an unpaid balance of $4,507.98. There was no express agreement between the parties with respect to the prices to be charged for goods sold by plaintiff to defendant, the understanding between the parties being that prices would be charged according to current catalogue listings.

LAUB, J. Plaintiff proceeded in this case on the theory of quantum valebant, i.e., that there was an implied assumpsit in defendant to pay for goods sold and delivered to it. Since there was no set price for each item agreed upon, and no express contract other than a general understanding with respect to catalogue prices, plaintiff, if entitled to recover, can recover the reasonable value of the goods at the time of delivery: Uniform Commercial Code of April 6, 1953, P.L. 3, 12A P. S. 2–305.

There is only one question before us for disposition and that is whether the Ohio corporation (hereinafter to be referred to as "Ohio") was the purchaser of the goods in question or whether the purchaser was the Pennsylvania company (hereinafter to be referred to as "Pennsylvania"). Plaintiff's theory, upon which it depends for recovery, is that the goods were ordered and delivered by and for the sole benefit of Pennsylvania; that although Ohio was, in a sense, a guarantor of Pennsylvania's obligations, Ohio's obligation, if any, was secondary and not primary. It is plaintiff's view that it is not concerned with the bookkeeping ramifications of the two corporations, established solely for their own convenience, but that it is entitled to be compensated for the sales made by it on order by Pennsylvania's authorized manager. Defendant, on the other hand, maintains that the goods were purchased by and for Ohio and that, according to its internal workings and understanding, Pennsylvania was a mere customer of Ohio; that this plan was understood and agreed to by plaintiff, who refused to sell to Pennsylvania on its own credit but insisted upon the sales being made on Ohio's credit exclusively.

Defendant is obligated to pay to plaintiff for the goods sold and delivered to it by plaintiff which have not been paid for.

Consumers Plumbing and Heating Supply Co., an Ohio corporation, orally guaranteed the debts of defendant in the premises but such guarantee did not relieve defendant of its obligation to pay for goods which it ordered and received on its own behalf.

Plaintiff is entitled to recover in this action against defendant.

REVIEW CASES

1. A. M. Webb & Co., a New York dealer in sportswear, signed a "memorandum of agreement" with Robert P. Miller Co., operator of a mill for the manufacture of sportswear, to take the total output of the mill for five years. No price was stipulated for the goods. The manufacturer violated the agreement by selling a portion of the mill's output to others, and A. M. Webb & Co. brought suit, seeking damages and equitable relief. The question to be determined was whether the failure to stipulate the price rendered the agreement void. (A. M. Webb & Co., Inc. v. Robert P. Miller Co., 157 F.(2d) 865)

2. On April 17th, as the schooner *Florence Reed* was about to ·sail from Gloucester on a fishing voyage, John Low & Son, its owner, gave the following writing to Alfred Low & Co.: "We, John Low & Son, hereby sell, assign and set over unto Alfred Low & Co. all the halibut that may be caught by the master and crew of the schooner *Florence Reed*, on the voyage upon which she is about to proceed from the port of Gloucester to the

Grand Banks. . . ." Delivery was to be at the dock of Alfred Low & Co. on the ship's return. A price was specified, and John Low & Son received part payment. Before the ship returned, John Low & Son was adjudged bankrupt, and the ship and its cargo were handed over on arrival to the assignees in bankruptcy. Alfred Low & Co. filed an action in replevin to recover the halibut, contending that the sale of the fish to them had been effected when the above instrument was executed. Was this contention tenable? (Alfred Low & Co. v. William Pew & Another, 108 Mass. 347)

3. Jameson, a distributor of binder twine under a working agreement with a Chicago company, engaged Needham as a sales agent. Under their written agreement Needham was to be paid a commission of "3½ per cent on all sales." He procured from various dealers in Iowa a considerable number of orders, which were directed to and signed by Jameson as distributor. As it turned out, a large portion of the twine ordered was never delivered to the dealers or paid for by them. Needham sued Jameson for commissions on this undelivered twine. Was he entitled to a judgment? (Needham v. Jameson, 66 S. D. 131, 279 N. W. 536)

4. Under an oral contract with Henry J. Handelsman, Jr., Inc., Lome agreed to have manufactured and to deliver 100,000 cameras with cases. The cameras and cases were to be of specified design and size and to be marked "Photo Master Camera and Case," which would indicate that they were a line of goods sold by Henry J. Handelsman, Jr., Inc. The cameras were not delivered as agreed, and the firm sued Lome and S. E. Schulman Co., which had meanwhile become a party to the agreement. The defense was that the agreement was oral and that the amount involved exceeded the statutory minimum of $500. Judgment for whom? (Henry J. Handelsman, Jr., Inc. v. S. E. Schulman Co. et al., 319 Ill. App. 479, 48 N. E.(2d) 416)

5. On Nov. 1, 1930, McCarn, as president of Pan-American Wallpaper & Paint Co., a corporation, made a written offer to buy 200 shares of the corporation's stock at a stipulated price from Staples. Staples did not accept the offer at that time. On Feb. 10, 1931, McCarn orally renewed his offer on behalf of the corporation, and Staples orally accepted. The price of stock fell, Staples tendered the stock, and the corporation refused to accept it. Staples sued the corporation. The main defense was that the contract did not comply with the Statute of Frauds. Was this contention correct? (Staples v. Pan-American Wallpaper & Paint Co., 63 F.(2d) 701)

Risk of Loss and Transfer of Title

28

PASSING OF TITLE

The principal objective of a sale or a contract to sell goods at common law and under the Uniform Sales Act was to pass title from the seller (vendor) to the purchaser (vendee), and the exact time of the passage of title was very important in a sales transaction. The basic rule was applied that the title to the goods passed when the parties intended that it pass. Therefore, the parties could specify that the title or property would pass at whatever time they would agree upon. However, it was the exception rather than the rule for the parties to sales transactions to make explicit their intentions as to the time when title was to pass. The courts therefore developed certain rules to apply where the parties themselves failed to make their intentions clear. These rules, often referred to as presumptions, were incorporated in the Uniform Sales Act.

The Uniform Commercial Code in Article 2 regarding sales deals with the issues between seller and buyer in terms of step-by-step performance or non-performance under the contract for sale and not in terms of whether or not "title" to the goods has passed. However, the Uniform Commercial Code has laid down certain rules regarding the passage of title. Sec. 2–401 of the Code states that title to goods cannot pass under a contract for sale prior to their identification to the contract, and unless otherwise explicitly agreed the buyer acquires by their identification a special property as limited by this Act. Any retention or reservation by the seller of the title (property) in goods shipped or delivered to the buyer is limited in effect to a reservation of a security interest. Subject to these provisions and to the provisions of the Article on Secured Transactions, title to goods passes from the seller to the buyer in any manner and on any conditions explicitly agreed on by the parties. Unless otherwise explicitly agreed, title passes to the buyer at the time and place at which the seller

643

completes his performance with reference to the physical delivery of the goods, despite any reservation of a security interest and even though a document of title is to be delivered at a different time or place; and in particular and despite any reservation of a security interest by the bill of lading, if the contract requires or authorizes the seller to send the goods to the buyer but does not require him to deliver them at destination, title passes to the buyer at the time and place of shipment; but if the contract requires delivery at destination, title passes on tender there. Unless otherwise explicitly agreed where delivery is to be made without moving the goods, if the seller is to deliver the document of title, title passes at the time when and the place where he delivers such documents; or if the goods are at the time of contracting already identified and no documents are to be delivered, title passes at the time and place of contracting. A rejection or other refusal by the buyer to receive or retain the goods, whether or not justified, or a justified revocation of acceptance revests title to the goods in the seller. Such revesting occurs by operation of law and is not a "sale."

Sec. 2–403 of the Code states that a purchaser of goods acquires all title which his transferor had or had power to transfer except that a purchaser of a limited interest acquires rights only to the extent of the interest purchased. A person with voidable title has power to transfer a good title to a good faith purchaser for value. When goods have been delivered under a transaction of purchase, the purchaser has such power even though the transferor was deceived as to the identity of the purchaser, or the delivery was in exchange for a check which was later dishonored, or it was agreed that the transaction was to be a "cash sale," or the delivery was procured through fraud punishable as larcenous under the criminal law. Any entrusting of possession of goods to a merchant who deals in goods of that kind gives him power to transfer all rights of the entruster to a buyer in ordinary course of business. "Entrusting" includes any delivery and any acquiescence in retention of possession regardless of any condition expressed between the parties to the delivery or acquiescence, and regardless of whether the procurement of the entrusting or the possessor's disposition of the goods has been such as to be larcenous under the criminal law. The rights of other purchasers of goods and of lien creditors are governed by the articles on Secured Transactions, Bulk Transfers, and Documents of Title.

IDENTIFIED GOODS

Sec. 2–501 (1) of the Code provides that in the absence of explicit agreement identification of goods occurs (a) when the contract is made if it is for the sale of goods already existing and identified; (b) if the contract is for the sale of future goods other than those described in paragraph (c), when goods are shipped, marked, or otherwise designated by the seller as goods to which the contract refers; (c) when the crops are planted or otherwise become growing crops, or when the young are conceived if the contract is for the sale of unborn young to be born within twelve months after contracting, or for the sale of crops to be harvested within twelve months or the next normal harvest season after contracting, whichever is longer.

For example, A owns a television set, which he wishes to sell. He shows the set to B and offers to sell it to B for $200. B accepts the offer. If no further conditions are laid down, the title to the television set will pass immediately, since the "goods" are identified. Even if it is agreed that B is to pay the $200 in thirty days and to receive possession at that time, the title and risk pass at once, since payment and delivery are not conditions precedent to the passage of title unless the parties intend otherwise. This should become quite clear to us when we recall that many people have "charge accounts" and that they frequently receive immediate possession of the goods purchased and pay for them at some later date.

If the goods are identified but something remains to be done by the seller to put the goods into a deliverable state the risk of loss in and title to the goods does not pass until such thing is done. For example, A buys a suit from B. The suit requires alterations, which under the agreement B obligates himself to make. Title and risk of loss passing in the suit from B to A will be postponed until the alterations are made in accordance with the terms of the contract. Consequently, if the suit should be stolen or destroyed by fire before the alterations are made, the loss would fall upon B.

Identified goods are generally thought to be those goods that have been agreed upon at the time a contract or contract of sale is made, and usually marked in some manner, set aside, and appropriated to the contract. However, there is an exception in the case of fungible goods, discussed later in this chapter. Generally speaking, identification may be made in any manner "explicitly agreed to" by the parties. In view of the limited function of identification, there is no requirement in this section that the goods be in deliverable state or that all of the seller's duties with respect to the processing of the goods be completed in order that identification occur. For example, despite identification the risk of loss remains on the seller under the risk-of-loss provisions until completion of his duties as to the goods, and all of his remedies remain dependent upon his not defaulting under the contract. Undivided shares in an identified fungible bulk, such as grain in an elevator or oil in a storage tank, can be sold. The mere making of the contract with reference to an undivided share in an identified fungible bulk is enough to effect an identification if there is no explicit agreement otherwise.

Motors Ins. Corp. v. Safeco Ins. Co. et al.
412 S. W. (2d) 584 (1967)

This was an action by Safeco Insurance Company of America, James C. Grugin, and Scott Oldsmobile, Incorporated (plaintiffs) against Motors Insurance Corporation (defendant). Judgment for plaintiff, and defendant appealed. Reversed.

This was an action arising out of destruction of buyer's automobile after a final and firm trade of his old automobile had been made for the new automobile but before title papers had been processed and check for cash due had been delivered by buyer to seller, for determination whether buyer's or seller's insurer was liable.

CULLEN, Commissioner. A motion for appeal previously having been sustained, we have before us the appeal of Motors Insurance Corporation from a judgment holding it liable to the appellees Scott Oldsmobile, Incorporated, and James C. Grugin in the amount of $1277 (less certain credits) under a collision insurance policy. The policy was issued to Scott Oldsmobile covering automobiles "owned" and "held for sale" by it. Motors Insurance Corporation maintains that the automobile in question, the damages to which furnish the basis of the claim under the policy, had been sold and delivered to appellee Grugin before it was damaged (in an accident which occurred when Grugin's son was driving the car), and therefore the automobile was not "owned" or "held for sale" by Scott Oldsmobile at the time the damage occurred.

Grugin's son smashed up the car on a Friday night. Earlier in the day Grugin and Scott Oldsmobile had agreed on a "trade," and each testified that it was understood that the trade was final and firm. Grugin turned over his old car to Scott, and Scott gave Grugin unqualified and unconditional possession of the new car. All that remained was for title papers to be processed and for Grugin to return the next day with a check for the cash due on the trade. After the accident Grugin did pay the cash and the sale and title papers were fully executed and delivered.

Grugin and Scott are in full agreement that the car was "sold" to Grugin on the day of the accident. However, Grugin's personal insurer, the appellee Safeco Insurance Company, denied coverage on the ground that "ownership" had not passed to Grugin and therefore Motors Insurance Corporation, as Scott's insurer, was liable. The instant lawsuit was brought to determine which of the two companies was liable. The circuit court adjudged that the automobile was "still owned" by Scott "despite any oral negotiations."

We think the judgment is clearly erroneous. There had been a physical delivery of the automobile to Grugin as a purchaser. Under the Uniform Commercial Code, K. R. S. 355.2–401, title passed at the time and place of such delivery. Also under the Code, K. R. S. 355.2–201, it is provided that it is not necessary that a contract of sale be in writing in order to be enforceable with respect to goods "which have been received and accepted."

The fact that the title *papers* had not been delivered did not require that Scott still be considered the "owner" within the meaning of the insurance policy. See *Campbell v. State Farm Insurance Co.*, Ky., 346 S. W. (2d) 775; *Siler v. Williford*, Ky., 350 S. W. (2d) 704.

Safeco maintains that *Rash v. North British & Mercantile Ins. Co.*, Ky., 246 S. W. (2d) 990, is controlling. We think not. There the automobile was not delivered to the customer as a purchaser or with any intent to pass title; the customer simply was permitted to use the automobile temporarily, as a bailee, for the purpose of trying to find a source of funds which would put him in shape to become a purchaser.

If, as between Scott and Grugin, ownership had passed and an effective sale had been accomplished, obviously the automobile was not thereafter "owned" or "held for sale" by Scott within the meaning of the Motors Insurance policy. The policy does not undertake to determine what constitutes ownership; necessarily that must be determined by the law of sales.

The judgment is reversed as it relates to Motors Insurance Company with directions to enter judgment dismissing the claims against Motors Insurance Company.

All concur.

Undercofler v. Eastern Air Lines, Inc.
221 Ga. 824, 147 S. E. (2d) 436 (1966)
Supreme Court of Georgia

This was an action by Eastern Air Lines, Inc. (plaintiff) against Hiram K. Undercofler et al. (defendants). Judgment for plaintiff, and defendants appealed. Judgment affirmed, with direction that the restraint against the defendants' assessment of taxes on the food be deleted from the restraining orders. The facts are found in the opinion.

GRICE, J. An air carrier's petition, seeking relief against sales and use taxes on certain personal property, is for appraisal here.

The carrier contends that it is not subject to the Georgia Retailers' and Consumers' Sales and Use Tax Act (Ga. L. 1951, p. 360, as amended) for fuel and parts purchased and brought into Georgia for use, and actually used, exclusively in interstate commerce, and for food purchased in Georgia and served to passengers outside Georgia on interstate flights.

Litigation over this issue began when the carrier, Eastern Air Lines, Inc., filed in the Superior Court of Fulton County its petition which, as amended, named as defendants "Hiram K. Undercofler, who is State Revenue Commissioner of the State of Georgia, and E. J. Olmstead, who is Director of the Sales and Use Tax Unit of" that department. It sought injunction and declaratory relief against assessments for such taxes for a designated period. Two temporary orders were entered, restraining the defendants as prayed. The defendants interposed general and special demurrers to the petition.

Our conclusion that the fuel and parts involved here are excluded from the tax imposed by this Act is strengthened by well established rules of statutory construction.

We must consider the allegations of the petition in the light of the provisions of the Act relating to sales made in Georgia.

The petition alleges that plaintiff serves meals to passengers on its interstate flights, that such meals are purchased by plaintiff in Georgia ready-to-eat and put into the galleys of its aircraft just prior to departure, and that the meals are not served until the Georgia State line is passed. It alleges that no separate charge is made for the meals, but that the price of them is included in the cost of the tickets.

Plaintiff contends that its purchase of the meals from the supplier is not taxable because such purchase is for resale, and that its sale to its passengers is exempt because such sale occurs beyond the jurisdiction of this State.

We agree that plaintiff's purchase of meals from the supplier is not a taxable event. The Act does not impose a tax on the purchase of property for resale, except under limited conditions not applicable here. See Code Ann. Sec. 92-3402a, 92-3403a (d).

However, we conclude that plaintiff's sale of the meals to its passengers is a taxable event. As we view what is alleged, such sale occurs when the ticket, the cost of which includes the price of the meal, is purchased. Therefore, when the ticket is purchased in this State, the sale occurs in this State, regardless of where the aircraft is when the meal is served.

The fact that actual delivery of the meal does not occur until later does not prevent perfection of its sale at the time of purchase of the ticket. The passenger impliedly consents for delivery to be made during the flight. Under these circumstances, the sale is complete when the ticket is bought. See Code Sec. 96-107; Ga. L. 1962, pp. 156, 183 and 204, Code Ann. Sec. 109A-2-301, 109A-2-503.

The fact that the price of the meal is included in the cost of the ticket does not prohibit a tax on the meal. We must conclude from the allegations that "the price of the meal" is a known amount and hence separable from the charge made for transportation.

The Act provides that "Retail Sale" or "Sale at retail" means "A sale to a consumer or to any person for any purpose other than for resale in the form of tangible personal property * * *" (Code Ann. Sec. 92-3403a), and "* * * Every person making a sale or sales of tangible personal property at retail in this State shall be a retailer and a dealer * * * and shall be liable for a tax thereon at the rate of three per cent of such gross sale or gross sales, or the amount of taxes collected by him from his purchaser or purchasers * * * whichever is greater * * *." Code Ann. Sec. 92-3402a.

Therefore, the plaintiff is liable for tax on the meals sold to its passengers.

The taxation of plaintiff's sale of food places no burden on interstate commerce such as would offend such Constitutional provisions. It is merely a tax due to a local transaction, the sale of the meal. See *Oxford v. Blankenship*, 106 Ga. App. 546, 127 S. E. (2d) 706; *Eastern Air Transport v. South Carolina Tax Commissioner*, 285 U. S. 147, 152, 52 S. Ct. 340, 76 L. Ed. 673; 15 *Am. Jur.* (2d) 668, *Commerce*, Sec. 32.

Judgments affirmed, with direction that the restraint against the defendants' assessment of taxes on the food be deleted from the restraining orders.

UNIDENTIFIED GOODS AND FUTURE GOODS

Unidentified goods are goods that have not been specifically ascertained and appropriated to the terms of the contract, i.e. "set aside for the purchaser." For example, A, a dealer in Chevrolet cars, has twenty-five Bel Air cars on the floor of his showroom. B enters into a contract with A to buy five of these twenty-five cars. When the contract is made, the goods are not identified. Title passes to B when the five cars are collected from the group of the twenty-five on the floor and set aside as B's cars.

Section 2–105 (2) states that goods which are not both existing and identified are "future" goods. A purported present sale of future goods or of any interest therein operates as a contract to sell. For example, A, a manufacturer of men's clothing, enters into a contract with B under which he agrees to deliver five hundred suits thirty days from the date of the contract. A must either manufacture the suits or acquire them from some other manufacturer. Such goods are future goods and title and risk of loss will not pass to B until the goods are identified and appropriated to the terms of the contract.

If, under the terms of the contract, the seller agrees to deliver the goods to a carrier for the purpose of transmission to the buyer, the seller is presumed to have unconditionally appropriated the goods to the contract when he delivers them to the carrier, and the title and risk of loss passes to the buyer at that time. The same rule applies when the seller delivers the goods to a bailee for the purpose of holding them for the buyer.

The U. C. C. makes a distinction between a situation wherein the seller agrees to *deliver* the goods to the buyer and one wherein he agrees to *send* the goods to the buyer. If the contract requires or authorizes the seller to send the goods to the buyer but does not require him to deliver them at destination, title passes to the buyer at the time and place of shipment; but if the contract requires delivery at destination, title passes on tender there.[1] If the contract authorizes or requires the seller to send the

[1] U. C. C., Sec. 2–401 2 (a) and (b).

goods to the buyer, delivery of the goods to a carrier (whether named by the buyer or not) for the purpose of transmission to the buyer is deemed to be delivery of the goods to the buyer (unless, of course, a contrary intent appears), and the property in the goods passes to the buyer upon the delivery of the goods to the carrier. The seller (delivering goods) must pay the transportation charges and bear the risk of loss during transportation. The trip would be the seller's trip. The seller (sending goods) does not assume any financial liability for the transportation costs nor any legal liability in case the goods are lost, stolen, damaged, or destroyed in transit. The trip is the buyer's trip. Title passes when the goods are turned over to the carrier.

Silver v. Sloop *Silver Cloud*
259 F. Supp. 187 (1966)

This was an action by Norman Silver (plaintiff) against the Sloop *Silver Cloud*, her engines, tackle, apparel, etc. (defendant) on a motion to grant plaintiff immediate possession of the vessel, Sloop *Silver Cloud*. Judgment for defendant. Motion denied.

On May 24, 1965, defendant A. LeComte Company, Inc. entered into a contract with plaintiff whereby said defendant agreed to build a sloop for plaintiff for $27,750.00. The vessel was to be constructed in Holland according to specifications set forth in the written agreement. On October 4, 1965, a further agreement was entered into by the same parties which provided for the installation of certain extra equipment in said vessel at an additional cost of $3,309.00. The sloop was to be delivered to plaintiff in May 1966.

Clause 3 of the printed contract of May 24, 1965, provided that: Title to the vessel hereby ordered shall not pass to purchaser until the entire purchase price and any extra or additional charges have been paid in full or security acceptable to builder given therefor, and builder has delivered its bill of sale or as hereinafter provided.

The vessel had been launched in Holland and had been transported to New York, where, on May 26, 1966, defendant offered the vessel to plaintiff. Plaintiff had already paid $27,750.00 as of that date. Plaintiff examined the sloop and found it to be defective in that, among other things, a gas engine had been installed rather than a diesel engine, and the builder had failed to install a seventh bunk as per the agreement of October 4, 1965. Other extras which had not been ordered had been installed on the vessel. These extras had a value of nearly $1,000.00 according to defendant's allegation. Plaintiff does not dispute this.

TENNEY, D.J. On July 8, 1966, plaintiff instituted an action in this Court requesting a warrant of arrest of the said vessel, an award to him of possession and damages for breach of contract in the sum of $50,000.00. The sloop was arrested on that day with notice of seizure given the defendant. Upon failure of defendant to make claim to *Silver Cloud* within 10 days, plaintiff commenced this possessory or petitory action.

The Uniform Commercial Code (hereinafter cited as "U. C. C."), which was in effect in New York when the agreement in issue was made, provides at Sec. 1–105 that this law shall apply "to transactions bearing an appropriate relation to this state" unless the parties agree that the law of another state having a reasonable relation with the transaction shall apply. No contrary provision appears in this contract. Here, the contract was made in New York and payment and delivery were to be in New York. Therefore, the U. C. C. is applicable to this transaction.

Plaintiff alleges that under Sec. 2–401 (2) (b) of the U. C. C., where the contract requires delivery at destination, title passes on tender of the goods. This would be true except that the section cited prefaces this statement with the phrase "unless otherwise explicitly agreed." Clause 3 of the May 24, 1965, contract has been previously set forth in full. I hold that this clause fulfills the requirement of the U. C. C. in that an explicit statement can alter the title-passing provision. Plaintiff's argument that Clause 3 contravenes the statutory provisions of the U. C. C. is without merit. He argues that the contract clause relating to passing of title cannot contravene the provisions of the statute. Obviously, the provision does not conflict with the statute since the section specifically allows the parties to determine when title shall pass.

Plaintiff further alleges that title to future goods passes to the buyer when they are "shipped, marked, or otherwise designated by the seller as goods to which the contract refers," under U. C. C. Sec. 2–501 (1) (b). This argument is erroneous. The section states nothing as to passing of title; it only sets forth the manner in which identification of the goods to the contract will be made, thus giving the buyer a "special property" and an insurable interest in the goods. These are not the equivalent of placing title in the buyer. U. C. C. Sec. 2–401 (1) provides that title cannot pass prior to identification; it does not provide that title must pass once the goods are identified. Therefore, under these provisions, plaintiff has not established that title has passed. The motion for possession of the vessel is denied. It is so ordered.

Semple v. State Farm Mutual Automobile Insurance Co.
215 F. Supp. 645 (1963)

This was an action by Thomas Semple (plaintiff) and Don P. Brown (intervening plaintiff) against State Farm Mutual Automobile Insurance Company (defendant). Judgment for defendant.

This action was brought to recover on an automobile liability insurance policy. Warren Witmer, who owned a car, agreed after some negotiations to sell it to Semple. Some days later, late at night, when the car was standing parked at Semple's place of employment, Semple paid Witmer the balance of the purchase price. At that time Witmer turned over to Semple the keys to the car and the Pennsylvania certificate of title, bearing Witmer's signature at the appropriate place. They agreed to appear some hours later (in the daytime) before a notary public for Semple to swear to the assignment of the certificate of title. Witmer then departed, leaving the car at Semple's place of employment. Before the next day dawned, Semple drove the car and injured Brown. It is alleged that since all these facts occurred in Pennsylvania, and since the policy was delivered there, Pennsylvania law applies and that diversity arises from defendant's Illinois citizenship. The automobile liability policy issued by defendant in this case contained the following provisions: (Definitions) "Named Insured—means the individual so designated in the declarations * * *." (Warren Witmer) "Insured * * * the unqualified word 'insured' includes (1) the named insured, and also includes * * * (3) any other person while using the automobile, provided the actual use of the automobile is with the permission of the named insured. * * *" (Policy Conditions) "6. Assignment. No interest in this policy is assignable unless the company's consent is endorsed hereon." There is no endorsement of consent.

GRIM, D.J. It is clear that since Witmer did not take the affidavit to the assignment of the title certificate prior to the happening of the accident, there was a failure, in this particular at least, to comply with the formalities required by the Pennsylvania Vehicle Code with respect to the significance of the certificate of title. With respect to the significance of the certificate of title under that statute, the Pennsylvania Supreme Court said in *Majors v. Majors*, 349 Pa. 334, 338, 37 A. (2d) 528, 529 (1944): "* * * (T)he primary purpose of the act was not designed to establish the ownership or proprietorship of an automobile, but rather to register the name and address of the person having the right of possession, and to furnish persons dealing with one in possession of an automobile a means of determining whether such possession was prima facie lawful. *Braham & Company v. Steinard-Hannon Motor Co.*, 97 Pa. Super. 19, 23." The Braham case, in speaking of an earlier similar statute, said: "It is clear that the primary purpose of the Act * * * was to protect the public against the theft of automobiles and their resale by the thief, and to facilitate the recovery of stolen automobiles. It was a police measure. * * *"

It appears from these holdings that in Pennsylvania a certificate of title does not constitute more than some evidence of ownership. Witmer's failure to take the affidavit to the assignment of the certificate did not operate to prevent actual transfer of ownership of the car. The car was a chattel, and the buyer and seller took all the steps necessary under Sec. 2-401 (2) of the Uniform Commercial Code, 12A P. S. Sec. 2-401 (2), to transfer ownership of the car to the buyer, Semple. This section provides: Unless otherwise explicitly agreed, title passes to the buyer at the time and place at which the seller completes his performance with reference to the physical delivery of the goods * * *." In this case the car ("the goods") was left at Semple's place of employment at a time when Semple was at that place, and at that time Witmer turned the keys over to him. This constituted physical delivery of the goods, and under Sec. 2–401 (2) title then passed to Semple. Even though the delivery of the keys might be considered a symbolic delivery, as in livery of seisin, they placed in Semple the power to operate the car. At the time of the accident, therefore, the car was Semple's and not Witmer's. When Witmer transferred ownership to the car he also gave permission to Semple to drive it, but by parting with ownership Witmer divested himself of the power to determine who had permission to drive it. His power to give such permission was then no more than the power of any stranger to give permission. For this reason the "permission" provision of the policy could not come into operation to constitute Semple an "insured" under the policy. Judgment is entered in favor of the defendant and against the plaintiff and the intervening plaintiff. The motion of plaintiff to open the record for the taking of additional testimony is denied.

FUNGIBLE GOODS

An exception to the rule that goods must be identified before title passes is found in the case of fungible goods. Fungible goods are defined in the U. C. C. as follows: "Fungible" with respect to goods or securities means goods or securities of which any unit is, by nature or usage of trade, the equivalent of any other like unit [1]—for example, oil, flour, sugar, and small grain such as wheat, oats, or clover seed. Goods which are not fungible shall be deemed fungible to the extent that under a particular agreement or document unlike units are treated as equivalents.

In the case of the sale of fungible goods, separation of the quantity of goods sold from the mass of which the goods are a part is not a condition precedent to the passage of title to the goods purchased. An undivided share in an identified bulk of fungible goods is sufficiently identified to be sold although the quantity of the bulk is not determined. Any agreed proportion of such a bulk or any quantity thereof agreed upon by number, weight or other measure may to the extent of the seller's interest in the bulk be sold to the buyer, who then becomes an owner in common.[2]

Sec. 2–501 of the U. C. C. states that in the absence of explicit agreement, identification occurs when the contract is made if it is for the sale of goods already existing and identified. Undivided shares in an identified fungible bulk, such as grain in an elevator or oil in a storage tank, can be sold. The mere making of the contract with reference to an undivided share in an identified fungible bulk is enough to effect an identification if there is no explicit agreement otherwise. For example, A has 1,000 bushels of wheat in his granary. He sells 500 bushels to B. Title to an un-

[1] U. C. C., Sec. 1–201 (17).
[2] U. C. C., Sec. 2–105 (4).

divided one-half interest in the 1,000 bushels of wheat immediately passes to B. A and B become tenants in common of the entire mass of 1,000 bushels of wheat. At this point neither A nor B can claim full title to any particular bushel of wheat. If 500 bushels of the wheat should be destroyed by fire the loss would fall equally upon A and B. They would then be tenants in common of the remaining 500 bushels of wheat.

United States v. Amalgamated Sugar Co.
72 F. (2d) 755 (1934)

This was an action by the United States of America (plaintiff) against the Amalgamated Sugar Company (defendant). Judgment for defendant, and plaintiff appealed. Affirmed.

The Commissioner of Internal Revenue laid a deficiency income and excess profits tax of $210,810.56 for the year 1918 against defendant. Defendant manufactures, refines, and sells beet sugar at wholesale. Throughout its existence it has consistently and uniformly kept its books of accounts on the accrual basis and has made its income tax returns accordingly. Defendant manufactured 924,516 bags of sugar during its fiscal year ending February 28, 1917, and to about the middle of February it had sold and delivered 411,907 bags of it. During that month contracts were entered into for the sale of 190,374 additional bags. That left 322,235 bags on hand unsold and undelivered at the end of the fiscal year. In making its return for the fiscal year 1917, defendant reported as subject to tax the proceeds of the 411,907 bags sold and delivered and the proceeds of the 190,374 bags sold but undelivered. The tax was computed and paid accordingly. In June, 1925, the Commissioner determined that the proceeds of the sale of the 190,374 bags should have been included in the return for the fiscal year 1918, and thereupon imposed the deficiency assessment. That action rested upon the legal conclusion that the several sales were not consummated and title did not pass upon execution of the contract, in 1917, but upon delivery of the sugar, in 1918. Defendant sought a redetermination by the Board of Tax Appeals. The Board determined that the assessment was wrongfully made. Plaintiff appealed to the District Court, and the holding of the Board of Tax Appeals was affirmed. Plaintiff then appealed to this court.

BRATTON, J. The first inquiry which we enter is that of title to the 190,374 bags of sugar at the close of the fiscal year 1917. If the defendant owned it, the tax was properly imposed; if not, it was wrong. The contracts were executed and entered into during the fiscal year ending February 28, 1917, but the sugar was delivered and the purchase price paid soon after March 1st, during the ensuing fiscal year. Each of them created a present obligation of sale and purchase of a specified quantity of sugar at a definite, fixed, and determined price, and provided that shipment should be made in proportionate quantities and at intervals during the life of the contract, but that all of it should be ordered shipped as soon as possible. It is and has been the uniform custom existing in the sugar industry and in the conduct of the defendant's business for the purchaser to have sugar delivered at such places and in such quantities as his needs may require, and if not delivered within thirty days from the date of the contract, invoice is sent and payment made despite the fact that some or all of it remains in the warehouse of the seller. Oftentimes it is resold repeatedly before delivery and payment. Such a contract is regarded generally throughout the industry as an outright sale with the right of the purchaser to resell and direct immediate or deferred delivery according to his wishes, but the transaction is treated as one of sale with title presently vesting in the purchaser.

The Board found that the parties in each instance in question intended to make a sale with immediate passage of title and that such was the effect of the transaction. Is the finding supported by evidence? In the first place, each contract refers to the transaction as a sale, not an agreement to sell at a future time. This is persuasive. The defendant kept a record in the form of a memorandum purporting to show the total amount of sugar manufactured and the quantity sold. That record was posted from day to day, thereby indicating currently the amount of sugar manufactured, the amount sold, and the amount on hand subject to sale. Sugar embraced in contracts but not paid for, nor shipped, was included along with that paid for and delivered. That suggests that the defendant regarded such contracts as constituting present sales. The fact that the sugar remained in the warehouse subject to shipping instructions does not argue that title had not passed. If a broker made a sale his commission was entered on the books of the defendant and settlement currently made regardless of the time the payment of the purchase price was received or the sugar delivered. The insurance carried by the defendant contained a provision that it covered sugar sold but not delivered, again indicating that such sugar was regarded as the property of the purchaser. And the fact that the purchase price was paid thirty days after the contract was executed, whether the sugar had been delivered or not, and that a resale was often made during that time indicated that the purchaser understood he purchased the property upon execution of the contract. In fact, all the testimony was to the effect that the parties intended that title should pass concurrently with the execution of the contract.

Whether a contract is one of sale or one to sell depends very largely upon the intention of the parties. If they intend a present transfer of title, it is a contract of sale; otherwise, it is a contract to sell. As between the contracting parties, neither immediate delivery of the chattels nor payment of the purchase price is essential to effect a present sale with immediate transfer of title. *Hatch v. Oil Co.*, 100 U. S. 124, 25 L. Ed. 554.

But it is contended that the contracts were executory and that title remained in the company on February 28, 1917, because the property had not been segregated and identified in separate form. Beet sugar of a standard and uniform grade, in bags of one hundred pounds each, is fungible property. In that respect it falls within the same class as flour, grain, and oil. Title to an unseparated part or unit of a larger quantity of fungible property passes under a valid contract of sale without separation, or segregation, if that is the intention of the parties. Segregation is not essential to the validity of a sale of chattels of that kind. The owners of the respective interests are tenants in common. And that doctrine should apply, in the absence of some forbidding circumstance, although the property may be in two or more parts or parcels if it is a part of a common stock or supply. The contracts in question were to be filled with sugar manufactured by the defendant during the previous refining season and stored as a common stock in its warehouses in Utah and Idaho, for sale to its various customers. The sugar was one entity or mass although geographically separated and located in different places. The fact that it was stored in different warehouses used in the operation of the business did not render inapplicable the ordinary rules respecting the sale and passage of title to a part of fungible property without separation or segregation.

We think it is clear that title to the sugar passed eo instanti upon the execution of the contracts and that thereafter the defendant held it in bailment for the respective purchasers.

Judgment for defendant affirmed.

SALE ON APPROVAL AND SALE OR RETURN

In an effort to obtain more sales, a seller may deliver goods to the buyer on approval or on trial. In this case only the possession of the goods passes to the buyer; the title is retained by the seller. If the buyer signifies his approval or acceptance, the title then passes to him. If the buyer does not signify his approval or acceptance to the seller, but retains the goods without giving notice of rejection, title will pass to the buyer upon the expiration of the time fixed in the agreement, or, if no time has been fixed, within a reasonable time. What is a reasonable time is a question of fact in each case.

As an added inducement to buyers, a seller will sometimes sell goods to a buyer under an agreement whereby the buyer has the option of returning the goods instead of paying the purchase price. A sales transaction of this nature is known as a sale or return. The title and risk of loss to the goods passes to the buyer on delivery, but the buyer may revest the title and risk of loss in the seller by returning or tendering the goods within the time specified in the contract, or, if no time has been specified, within a reasonable time.

Unless otherwise agreed, if delivered goods may be returned by the buyer even though they conform to the contract, the transaction is a "sale on approval" if the goods are delivered primarily for use, and a "sale or return" if the goods are delivered primarily for resale. Except as provided in Sec. 2–326 (3), goods held on approval are not subject to the claims of the buyer's creditors until acceptance; goods held on sale or return are subject to such claims while in the buyer's possession. Any "or return" term of a contract for sale is to be treated as a separate contract for sale within the statute of frauds of the U. C. C. and as contradicting the sale aspect of the contract on parol or extrinsic evidence as provided in the U. C. C.

Hales v. Henry Black, Limited, Inc.
264 P. (2d) 355 (Okla.) (1953)

This was an action by Henry Black, Limited, Inc. (plaintiff) against Hales Jewelry Company (defendant). Judgment for plaintiff, and defendant appealed. Reversed and remanded.

Plaintiff brought this action to recover $870, together with interest from January 1, 1948, representing the cost of merchandise shipped to defendant. At the close of the evidence the court directed a verdict for plaintiff and entered a judgment against defendant. The only question before this court is whether or not the trial court committed error in directing a verdict for plaintiff, defendant complaining that the cause should have been submitted to the jury.

The evidence showed that plaintiff is a corporation with its principal place of business in New York City, and that in October, 1947, it mailed defendant jewelry company, in Oklahoma City, certain jewelry valued at $870, which defendant had previously ordered on open account. Defendant's evidence indicated that the goods were received by defendant and promptly repacked and delivered to the Railway Express Company for return to plaintiff. Apparently the goods were either lost in transit or misappropriated after their return to plaintiff. Through past dealings it was mutually understood between the parties that all sales would be shipped to the buyer and that if the buyer elected he might within a reasonable time notify the seller that he did not wish to keep the merchandise and could then return it without obligation to pay any money in connection with the returned shipment. When the goods involved in this lawsuit arrived they were inspected by defendant, and, according to defendant's evidence, defendant elected to return the goods. Mrs. Hales testified that she supervised the packing of a parcel containing the goods valued at $870 and also other goods valued at $3300. This package, according to Mrs. Hales, was then delivered to the Railway Express Company addressed to plaintiff in New York City, and defendant was given receipt #20–45–64 by the Railway Express Company. The receipt was received in evidence, indicating a declared value of $3300 and bearing the following notation in ink: "This shipment del'd Nov. 24, 1947. Henry Black by (illegible signature). 12 P.M." Plaintiff admitted receiving the shipment but insisted that it contained only merchandise valued at $3300 and did not include the merchandise involved in this lawsuit and valued at $870.

PER CURIAM. From the evidence it clearly appears that this transaction was not an absolute sale upon arrival of the goods in Oklahoma City, but was a sale or return transaction. Subsequent correspondence of the parties, received in evidence, shows that both parties interpreted their contract as a sale which could be voided by the purchaser upon prompt exercise of his option to return the merchandise. Subsequent conduct of the parties to a contract may be considered in arriving at their intentions. *Victory Investment Corp. v. Muskogee Electric Traction Co.*, 150 F. (2d) 889.

We have held in *Johnson v. Curlee Clothing Co.*, 112 Okla. 220, 240 P. 632, that under a sale or return contract the purchaser must bear the loss, as against the seller, if the merchandise is damaged while being returned to the seller. This is the reason that title is in the purchaser until he actually returns the goods to the seller, and the owner of personal property must bear the risk of loss or damage to the property. The carrier becomes the agent of the purchaser while the goods are being returned to the seller. However, once the goods sold under sale or return are actually returned to the seller or his agents, title again vests in the seller, and as against the purchaser, the seller must bear the risk of loss or damage. Accordingly, if the goods were lost while in transit plaintiff must prevail; but if they were delivered to the plaintiff or plaintiff's agent by the carrier and subsequently misappropriated or lost, defendant must prevail. We think defendant's direct testimony that the goods were packed in shipment #20–45–64, which plaintiff admits receiving, is sufficient to send the case to the jury. For the purposes of the motion for a directed verdict we must assume that defendant's evidence is true and that in fact shipment #20–45–64 included not only the $3300 merchandise but also, at the time of delivery to the carrier, included the $870 merchandise. There is at least strong circumstantial evidence that shipment #20–45–64 arrived at plaintiff's store intact. Plaintiff admits the package arrived and that the $3300 merchandise was removed from it. This was a sealed air express package. Plaintiff at no time claimed that shipment #20–45–64 had been tampered with. Reasonable men could have concluded from the evidence that package #20–45–64 arrived containing the same contents as at the time of shipment from Oklahoma City. There was a disputed question of fact and the trial court should have submitted the cause to the jury under appropriate instructions. The cause is reversed and remanded for a new trial.

CASH SALES

The presumption is that if a sale is made and there is no mention that the seller is agreeing to extend credit to the buyer, the sale is for cash. In such case title does not pass to the buyer until the agreed price is paid.

The Uniform Commercial Code states: "Unless otherwise agreed payment is due at the time and place at which the buyer is to receive the goods even though the place of shipment is the place of delivery." [1]

Over-the-counter sales in retail stores illustrate the situation involved in cash sales transactions.

Evans Products Company v. Jorgensen
421 P. (2d) 978 (1966)
Supreme Court of Oregon

This was an action by Evans Products Company (plaintiff) against Karl Jorgensen and Richard Jorgensen (defendants). Judgment for defendants, and plaintiff appealed. Reversed.

This is an action by lender to foreclose lien on inventory of manufacturer in possession of defendant, supplier of raw materials, and for personal judgment.

DENECKE, J. This suit involves a question of priority under the Uniform Commercial Code (U. C. C.) between a secured party with a "floating lien" and a supplier of raw materials to the debtor. O. R. S. 71.2010 (37) provides: "The retention or reservation of title by a seller of goods notwithstanding shipment or delivery to the buyer is limited in effect to a reservation of a 'security interest.'" O. R. S. 72.4010 (1) also states this proposition.

Defendants did not attempt to create nor perfect any purchase money security interest in the veneer (that was the only interest they could reserve when delivery was made) and, therefore, Evans' security interest must prevail unless another section of the U. C. C. gives priority to defendants. O. R. S. 79.2010.

"A buyer in ordinary course of business as defined in subsection (9) of O. R. S. 71.2010 * * * takes free of a security interest created by his seller even though the security interest is perfected and even though the buyer knows of its existence." O. R. S. 71.2010 (9) states a sale in the ordinary course of business does not include a transfer "in total or partial satisfaction of a money debt."

If the transfer from Coos to defendants was a sale in the ordinary course of business, defendants acquired the plywood free of Evans' security interest. The issue under both the statutes and the agreement is whether the transfer was in satisfaction of a debt.

O. R. S. 72.5070 (2) provides: "Where payment is due and demanded on the delivery to the buyer of goods or documents of title, his right as against the seller to retain or dispose of them is conditional upon his making the payment due." We will assume for the moment that the agreement between defendants and Coos called for payment upon delivery of the veneer. Comment 3 to O. R. S. 72.5070 states: "Subsection (2) deals with the effect of a conditional delivery by the seller and in such a situation makes the buyer's 'right as against

[1] U. C. C., Sec. 2-310 (a).

the seller' conditional upon payment. These words are used as words of limitation to conform with the policy set forth in the bona fide purchase sections of O. R. S. 72.1010 to 72.7250." We interpret the seller's right to have the buyer's right to the goods conditional upon payment, even after delivery, to be applicable only as between buyer and seller and not as to third persons having the status of Evans who acquire some intervening interest. *Greater Louisville Auto Auction v. Ogle Buick, Inc.*, Ky., 387 S. W. (2d) 17, 20 (1965), appears to so interpret the U. C. C. as to certain classes of intervening third persons. To interpret it to the contrary would be reverting to the pre-U. C. C. concept of a "cash sale" which was explicitly changed by the enactment of the U. C. C. Further, there is no evidence that as a matter of fact any right under O. R. S. 72.5070 (2) was exchanged, i.e., that defendants had any right to the veneer after delivery which could be exchanged.

The trial court found Coos was insolvent and we accept that finding. O. R. S. 72.7020 (2) provides for reclamation when an insolvent buyer has received goods on credit. However, the defendants did not reclaim the veneer, demand the return of the veneer, or say or do anything which could reasonably be construed as exchanging their right to reclaim the veneer for the plywood.

The only tenable interpretation of the transfer of the plywood to defendants is that it was received in satisfaction of the debt owing on the veneer. Thus, the transfer violates the terms of the security agreement and Evans' interest continues in the collateral, and this was not a sale in the ordinary course of business.

Defendants lastly contend, and the trial court made a legal conclusion, that Evans would be unjustly enriched if it were allowed to recover the plywood or its price. Defendants' chief argument is that if plaintiff prevails in this suit it will have the veneer for which defendants have not been paid or the plywood made from such veneer, as well as the plywood which is the subject of this suit, or the value thereof.

The purpose and effectiveness of the U. C. C. would be substantially impaired if interests created in compliance with U. C. C. procedures could be defeated by application of the equitable doctrine of unjust enrichment. We have held that Evans acquired a security interest in the veneer upon its delivery to Coos. It is admitted that Evans had a security interest in the plywood delivered by Coos to defendants and we have held that such security interest was not divested; therefore, under U. C. C. Evans is entitled to both the veneer and the plywood. If the defendants had refused to deliver the veneer except for cash upon delivery, not upon invoice, or if defendants had perfected a purchase money security interest in the veneer, they would have had either the cash or a prior security interest in the veneer. They did not avail themselves of the protection afforded under the U. C. C. while Evans did and, therefore, Evans is entitled to prevail.

Reversed.

SHIPPING CONTRACTS

By usage and custom, certain types of contracts have been given a special meaning in the Law of Sales. Among these special types of contracts are F. O. B., F. A. S., C. I. F., and C. & F. (C. F.) contracts.

The initials F. O. B. mean "free on board." F. O. B. contracts are of two types: (1) F. O. B. place of shipment and (2) F. O. B. place of destination. If the contract is F. O. B. place of shipment, the seller agrees to pay all expenses and stand the risk required to deliver the goods to the carrier. The buyer must pay the transportation charges of the carrier. The carrier is the buyer's agent, and the trip is the buyer's trip. Title to the goods passes to the buyer upon delivery of the goods to the carrier. As between the seller and the buyer, the risk of loss in transit falls upon the buyer, though he may of course have some recourse against the carrier in case of loss. This type of situation is in accordance with Sec. 2–319 of the U. C. C.

If the contract is F. O. B. place of destination, the seller agrees to pay the transportation charges, either to the buyer's place of business or to some other specified destination. In this case the trip is the seller's trip, and the risk of loss is on the seller, with a possibility of recoupment from the carrier in case of loss. The title does not pass until the goods are turned over by the carrier to the buyer. This is compatible with Sec. 2–319 of the U. C. C.

Sec. 2–319 (2) states that, unless otherwise agreed, the term F. A. S. "free alongside" vessel at a named port, even though used only in connection with the stated price, is a delivery term under which the seller must at his own expense and risk deliver the goods alongside the vessel in the manner usual in that port or on a dock designated and provided by the buyer, and obtain and tender a receipt for the goods in exchange for which the carrier is under a duty to issue a bill of lading. Unless otherwise agreed, the buyer must seasonably give any needed instructions for making delivery, including, when the term is F. A. S. or F. O. B., the loading berth of the vessel, and in an appropriate case its name and sailing date. The seller may treat the failure of needed instructions as a failure of co-operation. He may also at his option move the goods in any reasonable manner preparatory to delivery or shipment. Under the term F. O. B. or F. A. S. vessel, unless otherwise agreed, the buyer must make payment against tender of the required documents, and the seller may not tender or the buyer demand delivery of the goods in substitution for the documents.

The initials C. I. F. in a *C. I. F. contract* stand for "cost, insurance, and freight." Under such a contract it is provided that the buyer is to pay the seller a lump sum which includes the cost price of the goods, the transportation charges to the point of destination agreed upon, and the cost of insurance to cover the goods while in transit. This type of contract came into existence because experience showed that in certain situations—particularly in the case of foreign trade—it was much easier for the seller than for the buyer to arrange for insurance and transportation. In such situations it became customary for the seller to quote the buyer a price that covered not only the cost of the goods, but also insurance and transportation charges. If the buyer accepted the offer, the seller was required to arrange for the insurance and transportation of the goods. When he had taken care of these matters, according to the terms of the contract, and presented the required documents, i.e. bill of lading, insurance policy, and invoice, he was entitled to be paid by the buyer.

The term C. & F. or C. F. means that the price includes cost and freight to the named destination. Unless otherwise agreed, the term C. & F. or its equivalent has the same effect and imposes upon the seller the same obligations and risks as the C. I. F. term except the obligation as to insurance.

It is held, with little dissent, that in a C. I. F. contract the title to the goods passes to the buyer at the time the goods are turned over to the carrier by the seller.

The C. I. F. contract is not a destination but a shipment contract with risk of subsequent loss or damage to the goods passing to the buyer upon shipment if the seller has properly performed all his obligations with respect to the goods. Delivery to the carrier is delivery to the buyer for purposes of risk and "title." Delivery of possession of the goods is accomplished by delivery of the bill of lading, and upon tender of the required documents the buyer must pay the agreed price without awaiting the arrival of the goods, and if they have been lost or damaged after proper shipment he must seek his remedy against the carrier or insurer. The buyer has no right of inspection prior to payment or acceptance of the documents.

Continental Ore Corporation v. The United States
423 F. (2d) 1248 (1970)
United States Court of Claims

The seller of fertilizer and cement to the United States under C. & F. contracts brought actions against the United States for war risk surcharges. The Court of Claims . . . held that seller was liable for the surcharges.

Seller's motions for summary judgment denied, cross motions of United States for summary judgment granted, and petitions dismissed.

DURFEE, J. These two cases, which involve the same question of law, were consolidated for oral argument. Both sides are moving for summary judgment.

Plaintiff entered into two contracts, commonly known as C. & F. contracts, with the Commodity Credit Corporation ("C. C. C."). A C. & F. contract is one in which the seller pays cost and freight to a named destination. Commodity Export Contract OBS–AID–65–83 is the contract involved in Ct. Cl. No. 258–68. This contract was entered into by the parties in May 1965, and called for delivery of certain quantities of urea fertilizer to Vietnam. Simultaneously with the signing of this contract, plaintiff entered into a contract with a supplier in Taiwan to supply the fertilizer. Ct. Cl. No. 259–68 involves Commodity Export Contract OBS–AID–65–80, entered into in April 1965. This contract called for the delivery of cement to Vietnam; once again plaintiff entered into a contract with a Taiwan supplier to supply the cement. The contracts in each case stated that the procurements were authorized by the Agency for International Development ("A. I. D."), and that A. I. D. would transfer to C. C. C. dollars in an amount equal to the total exchange value of the material which was delivered and accepted by A. I. D. Plaintiff was to be compensated with agricultural commodities from C. C. C. inventory or reimbursement for vegetable oils it acquired from U. S. free-market stocks. The Taiwan supplier in each case shipped the goods with States Marine Lines, Inc. On or about May 28, 1965, the shipping line imposed war risk surcharges.

The Taiwan suppliers notified plaintiff that further shipments would be discontinued if the surcharges were not paid by plaintiff or C. C. C. Plaintiff thereupon requested C. C. C. to pay these surcharges, but C. C. C refused. Plaintiff then paid the $110,050.18 in surcharges assessed on the urea fertilizer shipments, and it was billed $370,950.00 on the cement shipments, which amount remains unpaid.

Plaintiff appealed the decisions by the contracting officer, which were to the effect, in both cases, that C. C. C. was not liable for war risk surcharges assessed by ocean carriers, to the Contract Disputes Board for the Commodity Credit Corporation (hereinafter "the Board"). The Board, after considering the nature of war risk surcharges, denied plaintiff's appeal. Plaintiff is now suing under Section 2 of the Wunderlich Act, 41 U. S. C. § 322 (1964), and is contending that as a matter of law, war risk surcharges imposed by the carrier are to be borne by the buyer under a C. & F. contract.

In their briefs, and during oral argument, both parties contended that the Uniform Commercial Code ("the U. C. C.") supported their respective positions. Although the application of the U. C. C. does not govern our case, it does furnish further evidence that it is the seller's responsibility for war risk surcharges. Section 2–320 deals with C. I. F. and C. & F. terms, and states as follows:

(1) The term C. I. F. means that the price includes in a lump sum the cost of the goods and the insurance and freight to the named destination. The term C. & F. or C. F. means that the price so includes cost and freight to the named destinations.

(2) Unless otherwise agreed and even though used only in connection with the stated price and destination, the term C. I. F. destination or its equivalent requires the seller at his own expense and risk to

(a) put the goods into the possession of a carrier at the port for shipment and obtain a negotiable bill or bills of lading covering the entire transportation to the named destination; and

(b) load the goods and obtain a receipt from the carrier (which may be contained in the bill of lading) showing that the freight has been paid or provided for; and

(c) obtain a policy or certificate of insurance, including any war risk insurance, of a kind and on terms then current at the port of shipment in the usual amount, in the currency of the contract, shown to cover the same goods covered by the bill of lading and providing for payment of loss to the order of the buyer or for the account of whom it may concern; but the seller may add to the price the amount of the premium for any such war risk insurance; and

(d) prepare an invoice of the goods and procure any other documents required to effect shipment or to comply with the contract; and

(e) forward and tender with commercial promptness all the documents in due form and with any endorsement necessary to perfect the buyer's rights.

(3) Unless otherwise agreed the term C. & F. or its equivalent has the same effect and imposes upon the seller the same obligations and risks as a C. I. F. term except the obligation as to insurance.

*   *   *

As can be seen, subparagraph 2(c) allows the seller in a C. I. F. contract to pass on the cost of war risk insurance to the buyer. Moreover, Comment 3 to § 2–320 states:

"The insurance stipulated by the C. I. F. term is for the buyer's benefit, to protect him against the risk of loss or damage to the goods in transit. A clause in a C. I. F. contract 'insurance—for the account of sellers' should be viewed in its ordinary mercantile meaning that the sellers must pay for the insurance and not that it is intended to run to the seller's benefit."

Thus, in a C. I. F. contract, where the seller is obligated to pay the regular insurance on the goods, the cost of war risk insurance can be passed on to the buyer. This is entirely consonant with the purpose for that insurance, i.e., that it is for the buyer's benefit. Additional guidance is furnished by a comment in Williston on Sales: "War risk insurance under this term [C. I. F.] is to be obtained by the seller at the expense and risk of the buyer." . . . Just as war risk insurance is the responsibility of the buyer, because it is for his benefit, so war risk surcharges are the responsibility of the seller, because it is a charge for carrying the goods, for which the seller is responsible. Since C. & F. contracts are identical to C. I. F. contracts except for the insurance term, war risk surcharges are borne by the seller in C. & F. contracts as well.

*   *   *

Since we have decided that plaintiff must bear the cost of the war risk surcharges, and cannot recover in the instant actions, we need not consider the argument which pertains only to Contract OBS–AID–65–80, the subject of Ct.

Cl. No. 259–68. Plaintiff contended that the war risk surcharges for which it was billed had been paid into suspense accounts in Veitnamese banks by the Vietnamese importers, to be paid over to A. I. D. if plaintiff were successful in these suits. Accordingly, plaintiff argued, there was a constructive trust for plaintiff's benefit, and the Government could make payment without any cost to itself. The Government retorted that these funds could not be converted into dollars; hence, A. I. D. would require additional funds to pay plaintiff. However, all this is immaterial, since plaintiff is responsible for the surcharges.

For the foregoing reasons, plaintiff's motions for summary judgment are denied, defendant's cross-motions for summary judgment are granted, and the petitions are dismissed.

Permalum W. & A. Mfg. Co. v. Permalum W. Mfg. Corp.
412 S. W. (2d) 863 (1967)

This was an action by Permalum Window Mfg. Corporation (plaintiff) against Permalum Window and Awning Mfg. Corporation (defendant). Judgment for the plaintiff, and defendant appealed. Judgment affirmed.

This is an action for debt brought by plaintiff, owner of raw materials, against defendant, processor, which agreed to make storm windows for owner's account. The processor counterclaimed for breach of contract.

WILLIAMS, C.J. Appellee Permalum Window Mfg. Corporation of New York (hereinafter referred to as New York) sued appellant Permalum Window and Awning Manufacturing Company of Louisville (hereinafter referred to as Louisville) for $8,541.23 due on account. Louisville counterclaimed for $564.88 overpayment and for $10,000 damages for New York's breach of contract.

In January, 1961 New York's factory was gutted by fire. They had orders that should be filled. Steinek, owner of 50 per cent of the stock, and secretary of the corporation, came to Kentucky and made an oral contract with Louisville whereby New York would furnish the raw materials and Louisville would produce storm windows to fill New York's orders. Under the arrangement, at the end of a month the cost of the raw materials was to be balanced against the cost of the finished product to determine who owed any money on the mutual account. As an incentive New York was to give Louisville a 15 per cent discount on all extrusions used in the manufacture of New York's orders. The cost of accessories was to be the base cost. Louisville was to pay common carrier charges F. O. B. New York and New York was to pay freight F. O. B. Louisville.

This business relationship continued until Louisville wrote New York that prices on the finished product must be raised in order for it to continue production. New York immediately discontinued relations for production purposes as of June 2, 1961.

New York proved its accounts by records made in the ordinary course of business and by oral testimony.

As for delivery, Louisville agreed to pay common carrier charges for shipment of raw materials from New York to Louisville. Thus Louisville was to receive the goods F. O. B. New York. New York agreed to pay charges for finished materials shipped to it. In fact, New York furnished a truck for freight purposes.

Louisville cites K. R. S. 355.2–301, the Uniform Commercial Code, on General Obligations of Parties: "The obligation of the seller is to transfer and deliver and that of the buyer is to accept and pay in accordance with the contract." However, the comment explaining this section says: "* * * In order to determine what is 'in accordance with the contract' under this Article usage of trade, course of dealing and performance, and the general background of circumstances must be given due consideration in conjunction with the lay meaning of the words used to define the scope of the conditions and duties."

The Uniform Commercial Code is more specific when it comes to delivery of F. O. B. shipments. K. R. S. 355.2–504 is the key to the contention of no delivery in this case.

"Section 2.504. SHIPMENT BY SELLER. (1) Where the seller is required or authorized to send the goods to the buyer and the contract does not require him to deliver them at a particular destination, then unless otherwise agreed he must (a) put the goods in the possession of such a carrier and make such a contract for their transportation as may be reasonable having regard to the nature of the goods and other circumstances of the case; and (b) obtain and promptly deliver or tender in due form any document necessary to enable the buyer to obtain possession of the goods or otherwise required by the agreement or by usage of trade; and (c) promptly notify the buyer of the shipment. Failure to notify the buyer under paragraph (c) or to make a proper contract under paragraph (a) is a ground for rejection only if material delay or loss ensues."

The comment following this section is pertinent. "1. The section is limited to 'shipment' contracts as contrasted with 'destination' contracts, or contracts for delivery at the place where the goods are located. The general principles embodied in this section cover the special cases of F. O. B. point of shipment contracts and C. I. F. and C. & F. contracts. Under the preceding section on manner of tender of delivery, due tender by the seller requires that he comply with the requirements of this section in appropriate cases."

Thus the parties had what is known as a shipment contract and delivery under it is not at the destination but at the point of departure. New York proved it shipped the goods and Louisville did not affirmatively plead they were not received. In our opinion New York fulfilled its duty and established a prima facie case of debt.

The final contention is that the trial court erred in refusing to submit an instruction on Louisville's alleged $10,000 damages caused by New York's delay in shipment and merchantability of materials shipped. When a counterclaim for damages is not proved, the trial court may refuse to submit an instruction on it.

Louisville counterclaimed that the raw materials it received were delayed and were of poor quality. It did not object to the quality on inspection or use of the goods. It accepted them. Objection came when the suit to collect for them was filed. Delay in objecting to the poor quality of goods is ground for estoppel in a suit for damages for unmerchantable material or material unfit for a particular purpose known to the vendor. *Cogan v. Wall*, 206 Ky. 89, 266 S. W. 884 (1924).

Furthermore, no evidence was presented to prove that the material was unmerchantable and unfit for the particular purpose.

The judgment is affirmed.

All concur.

C. O. D. SALES

Under a C. O. D. (collect on delivery) contract the seller makes the carrier his agent to collect from the buyer before the carrier may legally surrender possession of the goods to the buyer. Sec. 2–401 (2) states that unless otherwise explicitly agreed, title passes to the buyer at the time and place at which the seller completes his performance with reference to the physical delivery of the goods, despite any reservation of a security interest and even though a document of title is to be delivered at a different time or place; and in particular and despite any reservation of a security interest by the bill of lading. The seller merely reserves the right to possession as a means of securing payment of the purchase price. Such a reservation on the part of the seller is in the nature of a lien.

In a C. O. D. shipment the carrier is the agent of the seller to collect the payment and the agent of the buyer to transport the goods. The trip is the buyer's trip, and, as between the seller and the buyer, the risk of loss is on the buyer. He may insure the risk; and of course he may have recourse against the carrier in case of loss.

BILL OF LADING DRAFT ATTACHED TRANSACTIONS

It is common practice in the business world for sellers to attempt to protect themselves in transactions where the merchandise is transported from the seller to the buyer by way of a carrier. The following procedure is often used in such cases. Under the terms of the agreement the seller obtains an order bill of lading from the carrier. He usually indorses the bill of lading, attaches a draft to it, and turns them over to his bank, either for credit to his account or for collection. The bank then sends the bill of lading and draft to a bank located in the place where the buyer operates his business. The local bank then notifies the buyer that it has the bill of lading and draft and asks him to come in and accept or pay the draft.[1] Since the buyer cannot secure the merchandise from the carrier without first obtaining the bill of lading, properly indorsed, he will ordinarily pay or accept the draft, and the bank then surrenders the bill of lading to him. Such a procedure offers a great amount of protection to the seller. If the sale is a cash sale, the draft is paid by the buyer and an accounting is made by the local bank with the seller's bank. If the seller extends credit to the buyer, say for thirty, sixty, or ninety days, then the buyer will accept the draft and secure the bill of lading. Within the time specified in the draft the buyer is legally obligated to pay the draft; if he fails to do so, the seller may sue on the draft. His chance of recovering a judgment is much better than if he had sold to the buyer on "open account," because the matter of proof is much simpler in the former case than in the latter.

If the goods are lost, stolen, damaged, or destroyed in transit, the question as to when title passes becomes important. Unless a contrary intention is indicated, the title passes when the seller turns the merchandise over to the carrier. The trip is the buyer's trip and, as between the buyer and seller, the risk of loss is on the buyer. When goods are shipped, and by the bill of lading the goods are deliverable to the seller or his agent, or to the order of the seller or of his agent, the seller thereby reserves the property in the goods. But if, except for the form of the bill of lading, the property would have passed to the buyer on shipment of the goods, the seller's property in the goods shall be deemed to be only for the purpose of securing performance by the buyer of his obligations under the contract.

SALE BY ONE NOT THE OWNER

The general rule regarding the sale of personal property is that the buyer gets no better title to the goods than the seller had before the sale. This is generally true even though the purchaser is a bona fide purchaser for value and without notice of any defect in the seller's title. For example, B steals a watch from A and sells the watch to C, who has no notice that the watch was stolen. If A discovers that C has the watch, A may replevy the watch from C. C acquired only the title that B had, and B had only the "title" of a thief. The same situation would exist if B had found the watch and sold it to C, since the transaction would give C only the title of a finder.

The Law of Sales makes certain exceptions to the foregoing general rule. Where these exceptions apply, a good faith purchaser for value without notice acquires good title even against the rightful owner.

[1] If it is a cash sale the buyer must pay the draft. If he is buying on credit he accepts the draft.

(1) Sec. 2–403 (1) provides that a person with voidable title has power to transfer a good title to a good faith purchaser for value even though the person securing the voidable title acquired it by deceiving the transferor as to the identity of the purchaser, or the delivery was in exchange for a check which is later dishonored, or it was agreed that the transaction was to be a "cash sale," or the delivery was procured through fraud punishable as larcenous under the criminal law. For example, if A, an infant, sells his radio to B, A may avoid the contract and get the radio back from B; but if before he exercises this right B sells the radio to C, a good faith purchaser for value, and without notice of B's defect of title, A may not get the radio back from C.

(2) Sec. 2–403 (2) states that any entrusting of possession of goods to a merchant who deals in goods of that kind gives him power to transfer all rights of the entruster to a buyer in the ordinary course of business. Sec. 1–201 (9) states that a buyer in ordinary course of business means a person who in good faith and without knowledge that the sale to him is in violation of the ownership rights or security interest of a third party in the goods buys in ordinary course from a person in the business of selling goods of that kind but does not include a pawnbroker. "Buying" may be for cash or by exchange of other property or on secured or unsecured credit, and includes receiving goods or documents of title under a pre-existing contract for sale, but it does not include a transfer in bulk or as security for or in total or partial satisfaction of a money debt. Thus, if A takes his bicycle to B, a bicycle dealer, for repairs, and B sells it to C in the ordinary course of business, C would obtain good title to the bicycle. This is due to the fact that A entrusted his bicycle to B, a merchant, dealing in bicycles (goods), who could pass good title to C in the ordinary course of business.

(3) Sec. 2–403 (3) states that "entrusting" includes any delivery and any acquiescence in retention of possession regardless of any condition expressed between the parties to the delivery or acquiescence and regardless of whether the procurement of the entrusting or the possessor's disposition of the goods has been such as to be larcenous under the criminal law. Thus, if A sells a horse to B and agrees to keep the horse a few days until B can come for him, and if before B's arrival A sells the horse to C, C will get good title to the horse.

Charles S. Martin Distributing Company v. Banks
111 Ga. App. 538, 142 S. E. (2d) 309 (1965)

This was an action by Charles S. Martin Distributing Company, Inc. (plaintiff) against W. H. Banks (defendant). Judgment for defendant and plaintiff brought error. Affirmed.

The uncontradicted evidence adduced on the trial disclosed that the scheduled property, which consisted of furniture and appliances, had been entrusted by the plaintiff wholesaler to the defendant, a retail dealer in such goods, for retail sale under a "floor plan" arrangement; that all of the scheduled property had been sold by the defendant in the regular course of his business prior to the institution of the suit; and that the amount sued for represented the unpaid balance owed to the plaintiff by the defendant under the terms of this agreement.

JORDAN, J. In a suit in trover, the denial of any paragraph alleging facts essential to the plaintiff's recovery forms a valid, issuable defense; hence an answer containing such denial is not subject to general demurrer. *Thompson v. Reese*, 105 Ga. App. 826, 827, 125 S. E. (2d) 726. The defendant in his answer denied each paragraph of the plaintiff's petition and the trial court did not err in overruling plaintiff's motion to strike in the nature of a general demurrer.

To recover in a trover action, the plaintiff must first show that he had legal title to or the right of possession of the property in dispute at the time of the institution of the suit, *Bush v. Smith*, 77 Ga. App. 329, 330, 48 S. E. (2d) 582, *Hinchcliffe v. Pinson*, 87 Ga. App. 526, 527, 74 S. E. (2d) 497, *Jackson v. G.M.A.C.*, 103 Ga. App. 865, 120 S. E. (2d) 810; and where legal title and right of claim to the property has passed out of the plaintiff before the suit is filed, there can be no recovery by him. *Hall v. Simmons*, 125 Ga. 801(2), 54 S. E. 751; *Prater v. Painter*, 6 Ga. App. 292, 64 S. E. 1003; *Sims v. Nelson*, 31 Ga. App. 271, 272(2), 121 S. E. 863; *Georgia Cas. Co. v. McRitchie*, 45 Ga. App. 697, 702, 166 S. E. 49.

Accordingly, where as here, the undisputed evidence disclosed that legal title and right of claim to the scheduled property had passed out of the plaintiff-wholesaler and into the purchasers at retail from the defendant by operation of law prior to the filing of this suit (Code Ann. Sec. 109A–2–403 (2): "Any entrusting of possession of goods to a merchant who deals in goods of that kind gives him power to transfer all rights of the entruster to a buyer in ordinary course of business"), an action in trover was not an appropriate remedy by which the plaintiff could recover the unpaid balance owed by the defendant under the terms of the "floor plan" agreement, *Sims v. Nelson*, 31 Ga. App. 271, 272 (2), 121 S. E. 863, supra; and the trial court did not err in so ruling, as contended in the motion for new trial.

The case of *Hogg v. Simmons*, 94 Ga. App. 83, 93 S. E. (2d) 779, cited and relied upon by the plaintiff as authority for its right to sue the defendant in trover, involved the wrongful disposal of property by a conditional vendee under circumstances which did not divest the vendor of his legal title, in which event an action in trover against the vendee was appropriate, and the principles of law applied in that case are not applicable here. See, in this connection, *Georgia Cas. Co. v. McRitchie*, 45 Ga. App. 697, 702, 166 S. E. 49, supra.

The case of *National City Bank of Rome v. Adams*, 30 Ga. App. 219, 117 S. E. 285, also relied upon by the plaintiff, holds that the plaintiff's right to an accounting in a situation such as this is against the defendant retailer to whom he has entrusted his goods for sale and not against those who purchased the goods; but it is not authority for the contention that trover is an available remedy by which the plaintiff may pursue his claim against the defendant.

The trial court did not err in entering judgment for the defendant and in denying the plaintiff's motion for new trial.

Judgment affirmed.

BULK TRANSFERS LAW

A number of years ago it was not uncommon for an unscrupulous retailer to sell his entire stock of goods and abscond with the money, without paying the wholesalers and other creditors who had sold him the goods on credit. This practice became so frequent and serious that the National Association of Credit Men launched a campaign to induce the various state legislatures to adopt adequate legislation to deal with the problem. As a result, today every state in the Union has such legislation, and it is contained in the Uniform Commercial Code.

Sec. 6–102 provides that a bulk transfer is any transfer in bulk, and not in the ordinary course of the transferor's business, of a major part of the materials, supplies, merchandise, or other inventory of an enterprise. A transfer of a substantial part of the equipment of such an enterprise is a bulk transfer if it is made in connection with a bulk transfer of inventory, but not otherwise. The enterprises subject to the Code are all those whose principal business is the sale of merchandise from stock, including those who manufacture what they sell. All bulk transfers of goods are subject to the U. C. C. except those specified by the Code, some of which are: those made to give security for the performance of an obligation; general assignments for the benefit of all the creditors of the transferor, and subsequent transfers by the assignee thereunder; transfers in settlement or realization of a lien or other security interest; sales by executors, administrators, receivers, trustees in bankruptcy, or any public officer under judicial process; sales made in the course of judicial or administrative proceedings for the dissolution or reorganization of a corporation and of which notice is sent to the creditors of the corporation pursuant to order of the court or administrative agency.

Except as provided with respect to auction sales, a bulk transfer is ineffective against any creditor of the transferor unless the transferor furnishes a list of his existing creditors and the parties prepare a schedule of the property transferred sufficient to identify it; and the transferee preserves the list and schedule for six months next following the transfer and permits inspection of either or both and copying therefrom at all reasonable hours by any creditor of the transferor, or files the list and schedule in a public office specified by the state statute. The list of creditors must be signed and sworn to or affirmed by the transferor or his agent. It must contain the names and business addresses of all creditors of the transferor, with the amounts when known, and also the names of all persons who are known to the transferor to assert claims against him even though such claims are disputed. If the transferor is the obligor of an outstanding issue of bonds, debentures, or the like for which there is an indenture trustee, the list of creditors need include only the name and address of the indenture trustee and the aggregate outstanding principal amount of the issue. Responsibility for the completeness and accuracy of the list of creditors rests on the transferor, and the transfer is not rendered ineffective by errors or omissions therein unless the transferee is shown to have had knowledge. Any bulk transfer subject to the U. C. C. except one made by auction sale is ineffective against any creditor of the transferor unless at least ten days before he takes possession of the goods or pays for them, whichever happens first, the transferee gives notice of the transfer. Sec. 6–111 of the Code provides for a limitation, which states that no action under this Article shall be brought or levy made more than six months after the date on which the transferee took possession of the goods unless the transfer has been concealed. If the transfer has been concealed, actions may be brought or levies made within six months after its discovery.

It is generally held that since Bulk Transfers Laws are enacted for the purpose of protecting the creditors of the seller, failure to comply with the requirements of such acts will not void the sale as between the seller and the buyer. If there are creditors they may attach or levy upon the goods in the hands of the buyer. If the creditors take no action, or if there are no creditors, the buyer and seller are bound under the contract.

Escalle v. Mark
43 Nev. 172, 183 P. 387 (1919)

This was an action by Peter Escalle (plaintiff) against Frank Mark (defendant). Judgment for plaintiff, and defendant appealed. Affirmed.

This action was instituted by plaintiff to recover from defendant the balance of the purchase price of a one-half interest in and to a hotel and saloon business conducted by plaintiff in Reno, and a like interest in the stock, fixtures, furnishing, furniture, and appurtenances thereof.

Defendant set up as a defense the failure of plaintiff to comply with the Bulk Sales Act of the state of Nevada.

COLEMAN, C.J. The only point urged upon our consideration as a reason why the judgment and order appealed from should be reversed is that prior to the making of the sale Section 2 of the Bulk Sales Act was not complied with. That section reads: "Whenever any person shall bargain for or purchase any portion of a stock of merchandise otherwise than in the ordinary course of trade and in the regular and usual prosecution of the seller's business, or an entire stock of merchandise in bulk, for cash or on credit, and shall pay any part of the price, or execute and deliver to the vendor thereof or to his order, or to any person for his use, any promissory note or other evidence of indebtedness, for said purchase price or any part thereof, without at least five days previously thereto having demanded and received from the said vendor or his agent the statement provided for in Section 1 of this Act, and verified as there provided, and without notifying also at least five days previously thereto, personally or by registered mail, every creditor as shown upon said verified statement when said proposed sale or transfer is to be made, and the time and conditions of payment, and without paying or seeing to it that the purchase money of said property is applied to the payment of bona fide claims of the creditors of the vendor as shown upon said verified statement, share and share alike, such sale or transfer shall be fraudulent and void."

It is true that the statute says that when there is a failure to comply with Section 1 of the Act the sale shall be "fraudulent and void"; but did the Legislature mean that a sale should be absolutely "void" as between parties, regardless of the fact that no creditor was prejudiced thereby? We think not. It is a cardinal rule of statutory construction that the legislative intent controls. Let us ascertain what evil the Legislature sought to remedy by enacting the Bulk Sales Law. 12 *Ruling Case Law*, p. 525, states that the Bulk Sales Law has but one aim, namely, "to prevent a sale of goods in bulk until the creditors of the seller have been paid in full." It is common knowledge that the main purpose of the law is to protect the wholesaler. "The object of this act was, no doubt, to protect the wholesale merchants particularly against fraudulent sales by retailers; but the act by its terms protects all creditors of merchants alike." *McDaniels v. Connelly Shoe Co.*, 30 Wash. 549, 71 P. 37.

This being the purpose of the law, how can it be successfully urged, as contended by appellant (defendant), that we should hold that such a sale as here in question was absolutely void? It is true that the statute says a sale shall be void when the terms of the act are not complied with; but to our minds, when construed in the light of the purpose of the statute, it was clearly the intention of the Legislature that the sale should be voidable only. But all rules of construction aside, it seems to us that no other conclusion can be reached from a reading of the entire act itself, especially Section 4. This section provides that, if the vendor produces and delivers a written waiver of the requirements of the act as to notice to creditors, from at least a majority in number and amount of his creditors, the provisions of the act shall not apply. If it was the purpose of the Legislature in enacting the law to protect any but creditors, the section just referred to is a most remarkable one. In fact, we cannot escape the conclusion, from a consideration of this very section, that the sole purpose of the law is to protect creditors. If such was not the intention, the Legislature would never have embodied Section 4 into the Act, because it would manifestly have made the Act inconsistent in its operation.

As between the parties to the sale, the title passed to the vendee, and it remains in him until it is vacated by a creditor of the vendor upon proceedings instituted for that purpose, or until the vendee disposes of the property. Though the word "void" is used in the statute, in legal effect, it means voidable at the instance of an attaching creditor. If the vendor has no creditors there are no creditors to protect. As between the immediate parties to the contract the sale is only voidable. Judgment affirmed.

REVIEW CASES

1. In reply to an inquiry, O'Keefe wrote to Leistikow that he had 70 bushels of clean flax seed priced at $2 per bushel. Leistikow replied: "I will take the 70 bushels of flax you have on the Ops farm at $2 per bushel for seed. Kindly keep it for me and oblige." O'Keefe ordered his son, with whom the flax seed was stored as part of a larger mass, to let Leistikow have 70 bushels when he applied for it, and then sent Leistikow a bill for $140. Soon afterward Leistikow wrote O'Keefe that he had sold his farm and no longer had any need of the flax seed. O'Keefe filed suit for the contract price. The question to be determined was whether title had passed to Leistikow. (O'Keefe v. Leistikow, 14 N. D. 355, 104 N. W. 515)

2. Green delivered to Vollman a diamond valued at $18,000 to be sold subject to the following agreement: "These goods are sent for your inspection and remain the property of Henry Green and are to be returned on demand. Sale takes effect only from date of approval of your selection, and a bill of sale rendered." Vollman passed the diamond on to Cohn, who sent it to another dealer named Arnow. Arnow sold it to Wachs and Mann, innocent purchasers for value. Green was not paid for the diamond, and he sued Wachs and Mann to recover the stone or its value. Ruling? (Green v. Wachs et al., 254 N. Y. 437, 173 N. E. 575)

3. Blair ordered construction materials from McPhillips Manufacturing Co. on Oct. 26, 1936, F. O. B. job site in Alabama. An Alabama sales tax became effective on March 1, 1937. The materials were delivered after March 1, 1937. Can the state collect a sales tax on the transaction? (McPhillips Manufacturing Co. et al. v. Curry, Com'r of Revenue, et al., 2 So. (2d) 600)

4. Allen and Heim Brewery entered into a contract which provided, among other things: "Heim Brewery agrees to allow a rebate of $1.50 for each case of empty bottles returned to Heim Brewery. . . . It is mutually agreed that Allen is to pay the net price only on the bottled beer, but it is distinctly understood and agreed to by Allen that he will pay cash for all cases or bottles not returned to Heim Brewery, at the rate of $1.50 per case." Allen later went into bankruptcy. At the time he had a number of cases and empty bottles, which were claimed both by the brewery and by the trustee in bankruptcy. Was the transaction a "sale or return" or a bailment Wachs et al., 254 N. Y. 437, 173 N. E. 575)

5. Fredericks contracted to sell Hahn a certain quantity of hard wood, which was to be taken from a large pile containing both hard and soft wood and to be measured as it was removed. Before the wood had been removed, the whole pile burned. Fredericks sued for the contract price. Judgment for whom? (Hahn v. Fredericks, 30 Mich. 223, 18 A. Rep. 119)

6. Rail sued Little Falls Lumber Co. for $47.90 due on the following agreement signed by both parties: "I, Case Rail, hereby sell to the Little Falls Lumber Co. 247 logs marked 'C. R.' and scaling 61,300 feet, at $7.00 per thousand feet, to be delivered by me in the Mississippi River, the same being now banked on the Crow River, at Pillager." Payment was to be $150 down, $120 when the logs were delivered in the Mississippi River, and the rest on demand after such delivery. Before the logs were put into the river, some of them were destroyed and others much damaged by a forest fire. Did title pass before the fire? (Rail v. Little Falls Lumber Co., 47 Minn. 422, 50 N. W. 471)

Warranties

29

In order to induce a prospective buyer to purchase his goods, a seller often represents them as possessing certain desirable qualities. Such representations are sometimes mere "seller's talk" or "puffing" which the buyer is not justified in taking at face value. Under proper circumstances, however, certain representations concerning the goods will be held to be *warranties*,[1] and the seller will be bound by them.

Warranties may be either (1) express or (2) implied.

EXPRESS WARRANTIES

Sec. 2–313 of the U. C. C. states that express warranties by the seller are created as follows: Any affirmation of fact or promise made by the seller to the buyer which relates to the goods and becomes part of the basis of the bargain creates an express warranty that the goods shall conform to the affirmation or promise. Any description of the goods which is made part of the basis of the bargain creates an express warranty that the goods shall conform to the description. Any sample or model which is made part of the basis of the bargain creates an express warranty that the whole of the goods shall conform to the sample or model. It is not necessary to the creation of an express warranty that the seller use formal words such as "warrant" or "guarantee" or that he have a specific intention to make a warranty, but an affirmation merely of the value of the goods or a statement purporting to be merely the seller's opinion or commendation of

---

[1] One often hears on radio and television or reads in the newspaper that a seller "guarantees" his product as possessing certain designated qualities. What is actually meant is that he "warrants" it as possessing those qualities. Where a "guaranty" is involved, the guarantor guarantees to a creditor the payment of the debt of the debtor.

the goods does not create a warranty. Statements like "This coat is worth $200" are not considered affirmations of fact.

It will not be held to be a warranty unless it is made part of the basis of the bargain to induce the buyer to purchase the goods.

If an express warranty proves to be untrue, the seller will be liable to the buyer for breach of the warranty. The fact that the seller thought that his statement was true is no defense. Thus, in the case of *Lentz v. Omar Baking Co.*,[1] the plaintiff, a cripple, wanted to buy a gentle horse to drive. He negotiated with the defendant relative to buying such a horse. He explained to the defendant that he must have a gentle animal because of his age and physical condition. The defendant in all sincerity assured the plaintiff that the horse in question was gentle, and the plaintiff, relying upon this assurance, purchased the horse. As the plaintiff was attempting to drive him to a buggy, the horse ran away and seriously injured the plaintiff. When the plaintiff filed suit for damages, alleging a breach of an express warranty, the defendant set up as a defense his innocence or lack of knowledge of the evil propensities of the horse. But the plaintiff obtained judgment. The court said: "It is not necessary to prove the seller's knowledge of the evil propensities of the horse where there is an express warranty, in order to recover for the breach. Therefore, the common law rule of scienter is not applicable."

If the representations of the seller prove to have been false and the seller knew or should have known when he made them that they were false, and if the buyer innocently relied upon such representations in purchasing the goods, the seller is liable to the buyer in a tort action of deceit.

No warranty exists where the goods possess defects which are obvious to a casual observer or which could be disclosed by reasonable inspection. For example, A says to B, "This horse is sound in every respect." Actually the horse is blind in one eye, and such fact could have been observed by a casual inspection of the horse. In such case B could not recover from A. A purchaser is not protected against the consequences of his own gullibility when he negotiates a sales contract. But if the defects complained of are latent, i.e. difficult or impossible, under the circumstances, for the buyer to discover, even upon inspection, then the seller is bound if he has warranted the goods against such defects.

An express warranty may be either oral or in writing.

[1] 125 Nebr. 861, 252 N. W. 410 (1932).

Stone v. Farmington Aviation Corporation
253 S. W. (2d) 410, 363 Mo. 803 (1953)

This was an action by one Stone (plaintiff) against the Farmington Aviation Corporation (defendant). Judgment for plaintiff, and defendant appealed. Reversed.

On August 31, 1947, plaintiff was injured in an airplane crash at Grand Glaize Airport, south of Bagnall Dam. He had a verdict and judgment for $10,000 against defendant, and defendant appealed.

Plaintiff's sole submission was breach of an alleged express warranty.

The facts were as follows: Defendant, operator of an airport and flying school at Farmington, Missouri, rented planes to licensed pilots. One of defendant's officers and agents, Lovitt, had given plaintiff the instruction and training which enabled him to secure his private pilot's license, then requiring 20–30 flying hours. Thereafter, plaintiff had flown several of defendant's planes and had over 100 flying hours on August 31, 1947.

Several days before August 31, 1947, plaintiff told Lovitt that he was to be married on that date and wanted to rent a plane for the purpose of flying with his bride to the Grand Glaize Airport on that day. Plaintiff asked for a certain plane but was told that it would not be available. Plaintiff asked about the course to Grand Glaize Airport. Lovitt said that he need not plot a course, that plaintiff could follow a series of steel towers. Defendant agreed to rent plaintiff a plane for his honeymoon trip at $8.50 per hour flying time. On August 31st, about noon, plaintiff and his bride came to the airport. He testified: "A. When I arrived at the airport, I asked them if the plane was ready, and I believe at that time they were fueling the plane and making it ready, and it was, within a few minutes, ready, and when I got out to get in the plane, I looked the plane over from the outside. I asked him if it was ready to go and in good shape and they informed me that it was. Q. What did they say? A. They said, 'It is all ready to go; it is in good shape.' Q. Who said that? A. That was Mr. Lovitt."

Plaintiff, with his wife as passenger, flew west and while he was preparing to land at the Grand Glaize Airport, oil was suddenly sprayed over the windshield's left side. Plaintiff claimed that this interference with his vision prevented him from seeing an electric transmission line on Highway 54. The plane's wheels struck the wires, the plane "nosed" downward and crashed, and plaintiff was injured.

LOZIER, COMMISSIONER. The sole theory upon which plaintiff submitted his case was: Lovitt's representation (that the plane was "ready to go" and was "in good shape") was an express warranty that the plane "had been inspected and made ready for flying and was in good mechanical condition and fit for the trip plaintiff intended to make"; that plaintiff relied on such "warranty"; and that plaintiff's injuries were the direct and proximate result of defendant's breach of (express) warranty "in furnishing him with a plane that leaked oil."

An express warranty may be oral, need not be stated in technical words or make specific reference to a particular defect or condition covered thereby, and may be inferred from an affirmation or representation of facts; the scope of an alleged express warranty depends upon construction, in the light of all the surrounding circumstances, of the language used; and, generally, the scope and breach of an alleged warranty are for the jury. *Turner v. Central Hardware*, 353 Mo. 1182, 186 S. W. (2d) 603. However, where the uncontroverted facts do not reasonably support more than one inference, these matters are for the court. 77 C. J. S., Sales, Sec. 369, p. 1035.

We do not believe that, under the circumstances, the jury could reasonably find that Lovitt's statement was a positive affirmation or representation that no defect or condition would develop in the motor which would cause the oil to spray on the windshield. Plaintiff was a pilot with over 100 flying hours. Lovitt had been plaintiff's instructor during plaintiff's first 20–30 flying hours, those preceding the issuance of plaintiff's pilot license. Plaintiff had thereafter rented defendant's plane. When plaintiff arranged with Lovitt to rent a plane for his trip and had him check the course to Grand Glaize Airport, plaintiff asked for a particular plane. Arriving at the airport, plaintiff saw the plane he was to fly, one which he himself had flown a few days ago. He first "asked if the plane was ready, and I believe at that time they were fueling the plane and making it ready, and it was, within a few minutes, ready." Plaintiff himself made a "casual inspection of the plane's controls; surface and outside." Plaintiff then "asked them if it was ready to go and in good shape." Lovitt's reply was: "It is all ready to go; it is in good shape." Obviously the two pilots were talking about the same thing—the plane's being "ready to take off." In all probability plaintiff, in his question, was referring to the mandatory (Federal regulations) preflight inspection, an inspection with which plaintiff was undoubtedly familiar. In any event, viewed against the background of all the other circumstances, Lovitt's representation, in the same language plaintiff had used in his inquiry, cannot reasonably be construed as an express warranty that "no mechanical defects will develop on your trip which will cause oil to spray on the windshield." Furthermore, in the absence of a provision to the contrary, an express warranty applies only to defects existing at the time of the sale or bailment. The sudden oil spray did not take place until some 1½ or 2 flying hours after plaintiff left the airport at Farmington. Reversed.

Strauss v. West
216 A. (2d) 366 (1966)

This was an action by Joseph R. Strauss (plaintiff) against Richard West (defendant). Judgment for plaintiff and defendant appealed. Affirmed.

The uncontradicted evidence discloses that plaintiff was the owner of a race horse stabled at Belmont Park, a race track located in New York, when on April 27, 1962 it was purchased by defendant and at the latter's request was shipped over the road for delivery at Suffolk Downs in Massachusetts.

On the day of the sale defendant was accompanied by John D. Canzano, a professional horse trainer with twenty-three years' experience, who assisted him in negotiating the purchase. The horse was shown to them by Lawrence Gieger, a public horse trainer who was acting as agent for plaintiff.

Mr. Gieger refused to have the horse galloped for the reason that it had raced the previous day, but he assured defendant and his agent that the horse was sound. The horse was brought from the stable, walked in the presence of defendant and his trainer, and examined by the latter, who found nothing wrong with the animal.

The plaintiff's agent accepted defendant's check in the sum of $1,800 payable to plaintiff, whereupon the parties agreed title passed to defendant.

POWERS, J. This is an action of assumpsit to recover the agreed consideration for the sale of a race horse which, after delivery, the defendant rejected for an alleged breach of warranty. The case was tried to a superior court justice, sitting without a jury, and resulted in a decision for the plaintiff. It is before us on the defendant's exceptions to the decision and to an evidentiary ruling.

The defendant's trainer testified that within an hour and a half after the horse arrived, he had it saddled and mounted to observe how it galloped, and that when it started to gallop it almost fell down. After some adjustments another attempt was made but again, after a shorter gallop, the horse almost fell.

He further testified that he then examined the horse's front legs and found a bowed tendon in the left leg, and that on April 29 and April 30 he made seven or eight telephone calls to New York in an unsuccessful effort to speak to the trainer Gieger. Thereupon on May 1, 1962, defendant stopped payment on the check and on May 3, trainer Canzano shipped the horse back to New York.

The plaintiff's trainer testified that there were several possible ways by which a horse might sustain a bowed tendon and included traveling in a van for a considerable distance as one of them.

The trial justice found as a fact that the horse was sound at the time it was purchased and rendered decision for plaintiff in the sum of $1,800 with interest.

In support of his exception to the decision, defendant argues that the case is controlled by the provisions of the Uniform Commercial Code, G. L. 1956, Secs. 6A–2–313, 6A–2–513, and 6A–2–601. These sections set forth the conditions on which a warranty is established, the buyer's right to inspect and his right to reject for breach of warranty, respectively.

The question before us then is whether in making the finding of fact on which his decision is predicated, the trial justice misconceived or overlooked material evidence. We have carefully reviewed the record before us and conclude that he did not. It becomes readily apparent that the trial justice gave great weight to the testimony of plaintiff's trainer as to the condition of the horse at the time of the sale. Further, he emphasized with particularity his impression of defendant's trainer's skill and manifestly concluded that if a bowed tendon were present at the time Canzano examined the horse at Belmont Park, he would have discovered it. The defendant's exception to the decision therefore is without merit.

All of the defendant's exceptions are overruled, and the case is remitted to the superior court for entry of judgment on the decision.

WARRANTY IN SALE BY DESCRIPTION OR BY SAMPLE OR BY MODEL

Where there is a contract to sell or a sale of goods by description, there is an express warranty that the goods shall correspond with the description; and if the contract or sale is by sample as well as by description, it is not sufficient that the bulk of the goods correspond with the sample if the goods do not also correspond with the description.

In the case of a contract to sell or a sale by sample, there is an express warranty that the bulk will correspond with the sample in quality. In such a sale the buyer shall have a reasonable opportunity of comparing the bulk with the sample. The one exception to this rule is the case of a C. O. D. sale.

If the seller is a dealer in goods of the kind that is the subject of the sales transaction, there is an express warranty that the goods shall be free from any defect rendering them unmerchantable which would not be apparent on reasonable examination of the sample or model.[1]

Brown & Co. v. Standard Hide Co.

301 P. 543, 152 A. 557 (1930)

This was an action by Brown & Company (plaintiff) against the Standard Hide Company (defendant). Judgment for plaintiff, and defendant appealed. Affirmed.

Defendant, a dealer in hides, offered, on July 30, 1927, by telegram to sell to plaintiff three carloads of "first salted" selected skins at 22¢ per pound. The words used, under the custom of the trade, meant hides properly salted to prevent decay, and not those unprotected by the process mentioned, or those resalted, in either of which events "salt rust" would appear when the hides were tanned, destroying the grain of the leather manufactured. A telephone conversation followed between the parties, in which the proposed sale was discussed and a lesser price was determined on. On August 2nd defendant, in writing, tendered the number desired at 20½¢, in accordance with the conversation to which it referred, and on August 3rd plaintiff expressed its willingness to buy, agreeing to pay the sum fixed by telephone. A letter of credit was forwarded on August 4th, and drafts, sent subsequently with the bill of lading, were duly honored.

Thereafter an employee of plaintiff was sent to defendant's warehouse to inspect the goods offered, as permitted in the telegram referred to, for they were to be "selected." His investigation raised doubt that the hides were "first

[1] U. C. C., Sec. 2–313.

salted." He thereupon refused to accept them and so reported to his employer, advising him of the discovery made. The latter immediately called the chief executive of defendant company on the telephone and was advised that if any of the skins forwarded were found not to be as warranted, a reduction in price would be made. As a result, the entire 15,000 were shipped to plaintiff and paid for. They were immediately started to be put through the tanning process. When the first batch was removed, the presence of salt rust was discovered, making the finished product useless for the purpose intended. Plaintiff filed this action to recover for the loss sustained.

The defense was that there was no warranty of quality.

SADLER, J. The Sales Act declares that "Any affirmation of fact or any promise by the seller relating to the goods is an express warranty if the natural tendency of such affirmation or promise is to induce the buyer to purchase the goods, and if the buyer purchases the goods relying thereon." This section, we believe, applies to the case at bar. However, even if not an express warranty that the hides were properly "first salted," as the term was understood by the trade, the words used would impose responsibility on the seller, under Section 14, which provides that "Where there is a contract to sell or a sale of goods by description, there is an implied warranty that the goods shall correspond with the description." Under such circumstances a recovery can be had since the hides did not correspond with the description. Judgment affirmed.

WARRANTY OF TITLE

In a contract for the sale of goods, the seller warrants that the title conveyed shall be good, and its transfer rightful; and that the goods shall be delivered free from any security interest or other lien or encumbrance of which the buyer at the time of contracting has no knowledge. A warranty of title will be excluded or modified only by specific language or by circumstances which give the buyer reason to know that the person selling does not claim title in himself or that he is purporting to sell only such right or title as he or a third person may have. Unless otherwise agreed, a seller who is a merchant regularly dealing in goods of the kind warrants that the goods shall be delivered free of the rightful claim of any third person by way of infringement or the like, but a buyer who furnishes specifications to the seller must hold the seller harmless against any such claim which arises out of compliance with the specifications.[1] By these warranties the seller warrants the title to the goods to the buyer, subject, of course, to any declared charges or encumbrances, such as chattel mortgages. In case of a breach of any one of these warranties, the buyer would have a cause of action against the seller for breach of warranty. With few exceptions the seller warrants the title to the buyer in every sale or con-

---

[1] U. C. C., Sec. 2-312.

tract to sell. Among these exceptions are cases where goods are sold under judicial process, as by a sheriff under a writ of execution, or by a mortgagee in a foreclosure sale.

Frank v. McCafferty Ford Company
192 Pa. Super. 435, 161 A. (2d) 896 (1960)

This was an action by Anthony J. Frank and Margaret E. Frank (plaintiffs) against McCafferty Ford Company et al. (defendant). Judgment for plaintiffs, and defendant appealed. Judgment affirmed.

Action in assumpsit for breach of warranty of title in sale of a stolen automobile where the defendant seller joined a co-seller as an additional defendant.

In January of 1958 Broad Motors Company, warranting good title, sold a used 1957 Ford Thunderbird automobile to McCafferty Ford Company for a consideration of $2,400. In February, 1958, McCafferty Ford Company, warranting good title, sold the automobile to Anthony J. and Margaret E. Frank for a consideration of $3,056.50.

WOODSIDE, J. Broad Motors Company is appealing from a judgment entered against it for the sum it received for the sale of a stolen automobile.

In July of 1958 agents of the Federal Bureau of Investigation informed the Franks that the automobile was a stolen car. The Franks immediately notified their vendor, McCafferty Ford Company, who immediately notified its vendor, Broad Motors Company.

Later that month Allstate Insurance Company informed the Franks that it had title to the automobile, which had been stolen from its assignor. The Franks immediately notified McCafferty Ford Company, who immediately notified Broad Motors Company.

Allstate Insurance Company thereafter filed a complaint in replevin with bond against the Franks in the Court of Common Pleas of Montgomery County. The Franks immediately notified McCafferty Ford Company and requested it to appear and defend title in the action. McCafferty Ford Company immediately notified Broad Motors Company and requested it to appear and defend title in the action. Neither company appeared, and a default judgment was entered in favor of Allstate Insurance Company.

Anthony J. and Margaret E. Frank then filed a complaint in assumpsit against McCafferty Ford Company in Philadelphia Municipal Court for breach of warranty of title. McCafferty Ford Company joined Broad Motors Company as an additional defendant, pursuant to Rule 2252 (a) of the Pennsylvania Rules of Civil Procedure, 12 P. S. Appendix.

The case was tried before Judge John Robert Jones, sitting without a jury. Over the objections of both defendants, the plaintiffs introduced into evidence as an exhibit an exemplified copy of the proceedings in replevin. Decision was rendered for the plaintiff against the defendant in the amount of $3,056.50 plus interest, and for the defendant against the additional defendant in the amount of $2,400 plus interest.

The defendant filed exceptions to the findings of the trial judge; the additional defendant moved for judgment n. o. v., or in the alternative, for a new trial. The trial judge dismissed the defendant's exceptions and denied the motions for judgment n. o. v. and for a new trial.

Broad Motors Company appealed from the entry of judgment against it. McCafferty Ford Company then appealed from entry of judgment against it.

Under Section 2–312 of the Uniform Commercial Code of April 6, 1953, P. L. 3, 12A P. S., Sec. 2–312, there was in the contract of sales involved in this case a warrant by the sellers that the title conveyed was good and its transfer rightful.

Judgment affirmed.

IMPLIED WARRANTIES

HISTORY AND CLASSIFICATION

In the early development of the Law of Sales the ancient doctrine of *caveat emptor* (let the buyer beware) prevailed. It was felt that buyers should not expect to be able to believe or rely upon what the sellers told them about their goods and merchandise; they should inspect the goods and make up their own minds. If a buyer could secure an express warranty from the seller, the courts would recognize and enforce it; but implied warranties as we know them today did not exist.

While the doctrine of caveat emptor is not entirely unknown today in sales transactions, it has been greatly limited and reduced in importance; the tendency is to limit it further as time goes on. This change has been due to revolutionary changes in marketing conditions and processes during the past century, coupled with a feeling that it is socially desirable to give greater protection to buyers. In the formative days of the Law of Sales, when the full force of the doctrine of caveat emptor was applied to sales transactions, the marketing processes were relatively simple. The seller was usually the producer of the product to be sold. Buyer and seller met face to face when the contract was negotiated and the goods were available for the buyer to inspect. Thus, it was held that if the seller was not guilty of fraud there was no reason to protect the buyer against the seller. He was presumed to be just as able as the seller to protect himself. If fraud did exist, the law gave the buyer a remedy against the seller in making available to him a tort action of deceit. And if the buyer had any doubts about the merchandise, he could refuse to buy unless the seller gave him an express warranty, which the courts would recognize.

Today the processes of marketing are much more complex. Seldom do the original producer or processor and the ultimate consumer know or see each other. More often than not the buyer has no opportunity to inspect the goods before negotiating the contract. And where an opportunity to inspect or examine the merchandise exists, the buyer is often not in a position to make an adequate inspection or capable of doing so. Owing to scientific developments, many of the products purchased by people today are so complicated that only an expert can judge them; hence the buyer has to rely more and more upon the knowledge and good faith of the seller.

It finally became evident, therefore, that the doctrine of caveat emptor must be modified in order to give greater protection to buyers. This was accomplished by the courts' gradual recognition of the existence of certain *implied warranties* in sales transactions, which arise by operation of law and not as a result of any agreement between the parties or by "an affirmation of fact or promise by the seller." These implied warranties were later incorporated in the Uniform Sales Act; they are also continued in the Uniform Commercial Code.

For convenience in discussion, implied warranties may be classified as follows: (1) implied warranty of merchantability, and (2) implied warranty of fitness for a particular purpose.

Meyer v. Packard Cleveland Motor Co.
140 N. E. 118, 106 Ohio St. 328 (1922)

This was an action by the Packard Cleveland Motor Co. (plaintiff) against John D. Meyer (defendant). From a judgment for plaintiff, affirmed by the Court of Appeals, defendant appealed. Reversed and remanded.

Plaintiff brought this action against defendant on an account for $906.40, for work and repairs done on a motor truck originally purchased from plaintiff by defendant.

Defendant testified that he wanted to buy a motor truck, and that he noticed a newspaper advertisement of "rebuilt trucks," which was introduced in evidence. Among other things the advertisement stated: "Come in and buy a Rebuilt Guaranteed Packard." "A rebuilt Packard carries the same warranty as a new truck." Defendant testified that, relying upon the newspaper advertisement, he went to plaintiff's place of business and discussed the purchase of a truck. The salesman orally agreed that the trucks were warranted as advertised. Relying upon such oral statement and the newspaper advertisement, defendant purchased a truck by signing a written order or contract. The truck proved defective. He took the truck back to plaintiff, and the repairs involved in this action were made on the truck.

Plaintiff contended that the truck was in perfect running order and repair when it was sold to defendant. It further alleged that the written order or contract signed by defendant contained the following statement: "All promises, verbal understandings or agreements of any kind pertaining to this purchase, not specified herein, are hereby expressly waived."

WANAMAKER, J. The defendant's attention was first directed to this truck by the plaintiff's newspaper advertisement, which stated that "A rebuilt Packard carries the same warranty as a new truck." Thereafter the defendant signed an order to buy the truck. The defendant claims that he relied upon the representations contained in the advertisement.

It is quite clear and conclusive that the language in the written order or contract of sale, "all promises, verbal agreements or agreements of any kind pertaining to this purchase not specified herein, are hereby expressly waived," relates solely to any special contracts or arrangements expressly made by the parties outside of the general custom or usage in such sale of goods. It in no wise negatives or nullifies the things or matters set forth by the plaintiff in its general newspaper advertisements which appear in evidence in this case. Whether or not the newspaper advertisements, and the things and matters therein set forth, were relied upon by the purchaser as essentially descriptive of the truck he purchased and entered into the contract between the parties, is a question for the determination of the jury. Again, whether or not the repairs were fairly and justly referable to defects in the rebuilding of the truck by the plaintiff, is also a question for the jury.

It may be urged that this is a substantial modification of the ancient doctrine of caveat emptor, let the buyer beware. Is it not high time, however, that the doctrine should be somewhat modified; at least that it should have no higher place in the business life of a nation than the companion doctrine, "let the seller beware"? There is entirely too much disregard of law and truth in the business, social and political world of today. . . . It is time to hold men to their primary engagements to tell the truth and observe the law of common honesty and fair dealings. Honest men need not fear it; dishonest men should be kept in fear of it.

Reversed and remanded.

Fox Pools, Inc. v. Villarose et ux.

77 York Leg. Rec. 165 (1964)

This was an action by Fox Pools, Inc. (plaintiff) against John Villarose and Doris M. Villarose (defendants). Judgment for plaintiff, and defendants appealed. Judgment is opened for purposes of permitting the defendants to enter a defense to the case. The facts are found in the opinion.

BUCKINGHAM, J. Plaintiff entered a note against defendants for $315.24 by virtue of a judgment note. Defendants seek to have the judgment opened on the grounds that the note was executed by them pursuant to an oral agreement whereby plaintiff agreed to sell and defendants agreed to buy a swimming pool 24 feet in diameter. When the pool was delivered and attempted to be assembled and installed by defendants, they found it to be only 22 feet in diameter. It was, therefore, unusable since the area permanently set aside for the pool in their yard was 24 feet in diameter. The pool was defective in another respect in that parts of it were jagged and rough and would have ripped the pool liner had it been installed. Upon discovering these defects, defendants notified plantiff, who thereupon sent other parts to defendants to rectify the same. Even with the additional parts, however, the pool still did not fit, for when it was assembled again, the pool was found to be larger than 24 feet in diameter. Defendants again complained to plaintiff, who thereupon refused to do anything further for the defendants, who then refused to pay any more for the pool. Plaintiff's only defense to the allegations of defendants is that the defendants, upon receipt of the unassembled pool, signed a certificate that states, "we hereby acknowledge receipt in satisfactory condition of the materials described in our Credit Application . . ."

The depositions of the defendants were taken but plaintiff submitted none. It is quite clear from this testimony that in truth the pool did not meet the specifications of the bargain and that the defendants could in no way make use of the pool. It is further very evident that the defendants signed the certificate of satisfaction upon receipt of the pool but before they attempted to assemble it. Thus, they did not know in fact that at the time they signed the certificate that the pool was unsuitable for their purposes and was unsatisfactory. The evidence of this is overwhelming, witness the testimony of the defendants that after they signed the certificate of satisfaction, plaintiff furnished them additional equipment in an attempt to meet the defendants' requirements.

A petition to open judgment is addressed to the discretion of the court and is decided on equitable principles, *Roche vs. Rankin*, 406 Pa. 92 (1962). Moreover, failure on the part of the plaintiff to give depositions is a ground to open the judgment. *Howie vs. Lewis*, 196 Pa. 558 (1900). Clearly there was a failure of consideration in this case since the defendants were prevented from using the materials delivered solely because they were defective. Failure of consideration is a ground for opening a judgment. 7 Standard Pennsylvania Practice, Chapter 30, Sec. 77.

Moreover, there was a breach of warranty on the part of plaintiff. The Uniform Commercial Code provides that any description of goods by the seller which is made on the basis of the bargain creates an express warranty that the goods shall conform to the description. U. C. C. Sec. 2–313. In this case the plaintiff described the swimming pool sold as having a 24 foot diameter. This was made the basis of the bargain as it was a diameter specifically requested by the defendants. Since the pool delivered to the defendants did not have a diameter of 24 feet, even after corrective action was taken by the plaintiffs, this constituted a breach of an express warranty by the plaintiff.

The Code also provides that a seller who is a merchant with respect to goods of the kind sold, warrants by implication that they are merchantable. This implied warranty of merchantability means, among other things, that they are fit for the ordinary purposes for which such goods are used. U. C. C. Sec. 2–314. Since the plaintiff, Fox Pools, Inc., is a merchant, i.e. one who deals in goods of the kind (U. C. C. Sec. 2–104), with respect to swimming pools it made an implied warranty that the pool sold to the defendants would be fit for the ordinary purposes for which swimming pools were used. Since the defendants' testimony was that the pool could not be constructed so as to hold water (Deposition p. 5), this constituted a breach of an implied warranty by the plaintiff.

Breach of warranty is a ground for opening a judgment *Berwick Store Co. v. Zadyejka*, 76 Pa. Super. 461 (1921).

Defendants' petition to open judgment is granted.

Vlases v. Montgomery Ward & Company
377 F. (2d) 846 (1967)

This was an action by Paul Vlases (plaintiff) against Montgomery Ward & Company (defendant). Judgment for plaintiff, and defendant appealed. Affirmed.

This case revolves around the charge that defendant-appellant, Montgomery Ward, was liable for the breach of implied warranties in the sale of one-day-old chickens to the plaintiff-appellee, Paul Vlases. The latter came to this country from Greece when he was sixteen, and until 1954 his primary occupation was that of a coal miner. He had always raised chickens but because of his job as a miner his flocks were small, ranging from between twenty-five to one hundred chicks. In 1958 plaintiff began the construction of a two-story chicken coop large enough to house 4000 chickens and a smaller side building where he could wash, grade, and sell the eggs. Vlases worked alone on the coop, twelve hours a day, fifty-two weeks a year, until its completion in 1961. In November of 1961 plaintiff placed an order at defendant's outlet store in Brownsville, Pennsylvania for the purchase of 2000 one-day-old chicks. The chickens selected by the plaintiff from Ward's catalogue were hybrid Leghorns and were noted for their excellent egg production. On December 21, 1961 plaintiff received the chickens and placed them on the first floor of the coop, which had been equipped with new brooders, feeders, and within a short time, waterers. As a further hygienic precaution, wire and sugar cane were placed on the ground so the chickens would not come in contact with the dirt floor. For the first six months Vlases slept in the coop in order to give the chicks his undivided attention.

During the first few weeks after delivery the chickens appeared to be in good health, but by the third week plaintiff noticed that their feathers were beginning to fall off. This condition was brought to the attention of Mr. Howard Hamilton, who represented the Agway Corporation, which was supplying the plaintiff with feed on credit. In February, 1962 Mr. Hamilton took five chickens to the Bureau of Animal Industry Diagnostic Laboratory, where they were examined by Dr. Daniel Ehlers. The examination revealed signs of drug intoxication and hemorrhagic disease involving the weakening of blood vessels. Four chicks were brought to Dr. Ehlers in May, 1962 and were found to be suffering from fatigue. On August 14, 1962, Mr. Hamilton brought three chickens to the laboratory, where Dr. Ehlers' report noted that two of the chicks were affected with visceral leukosis, one with ocular leukosis, one had bumble foot, and one had been picked. Visceral and ocular leukosis are two types of avian leukosis complex or bird cancer, which disease infected plaintiff's flock, either killing the chicks or causing those remaining to be destroyed.

McLAUGHLIN, C.J. Plaintiff in this two-count suit in assumpsit charged negligence and breach of warranty with jurisdiction resting on the diversity provisions of 28 U. S. C. A. Sec. 1332. After the second day of trial the negligence claim was dropped, leaving the breach of warranty as the sole problem for the jury's consideration. A verdict was returned in favor of the plaintiff in the amount of $23,028.77. Montgomery Ward appeals from the resultant judgment.

The two implied warranties before us are the implied warranty of merchantability, 12A P. S. Sec. 2-314, and the implied warranty of fitness for a particular purpose, 12A P. S. Sec. 2-315. Both of these are designed to protect the buyer of goods from bearing the burden of loss where merchandise, though not violating a promise expressly guaranteed, does not conform to the normal commercial standards or does not meet the buyer's particular purpose, a condition upon which he had the right to rely. Were it to be assumed that the sale of 2000 chickens infected with avian leukosis transgressed the norm of acceptable goods under both warranties, appellant's position is that the action will not lie in a situation where the seller is unable to discover the defect or cure the damage if it could be ascertained. That theory does not eliminate the consequences imposed by the Code upon the seller of commercially inferior goods. It is without merit. The judgment of the District Court will be affirmed.

IMPLIED WARRANTY OF FITNESS FOR A PARTICULAR PURPOSE

The general rule is that the doctrine of caveat emptor applies to a sales transaction as far as the quality of the goods is concerned. But "where the buyer, expressly or by implication, makes known to the seller the particular purpose for which the goods are required, and it appears that the buyer relies on the seller's skill or judgment (whether he be the grower or manufacturer or not), there is an implied warranty that the goods shall be reasonably fit for such purpose." Thus, if A buys a radio from B and B does not expressly warrant the quality of the radio, and no further facts are involved than herein assumed, A buys the radio "as is." But suppose a case in which A tells B that he wants a radio that will enable him to tune in on broadcasting stations all over the world; B recommends a particular radio; and A, relying upon B's recommendation, purchases from B that particular radio. Here there would be an implied warranty that the radio is suitable for A's particular purpose.

The same rules apply to an article sold under its patent or trade name. If A goes to B's store, asks for Dr. Brown's tooth paste, and buys a tube of it, there is no implied warranty of the product's suitability or fitness for a particular purpose. But if A tells B that he wants a low-abrasive tooth paste and B suggests Dr. Brown's with the result that A purchases a tube of that brand, there would be an implied warranty of suitability. The crucial point is that A has made known his requirements to B and has relied upon B's judgment, not his own, in making the purchase.

These rules apply to retailers as well as to growers, processors, and manufacturers. They also apply alike to new and secondhand goods. At common law there was no implied warranty of suitability in the sale of secondhand goods.

In the sale of food for human consumption, there is an implied warranty that the food is fit for human consumption, and such warranty is applicable to retailers as well as to manufacturers. This has long been the rule at common law, and it has been made a part of the Uniform Commercial Code. When the rule developed, food was usually sold in bulk, and the seller was able to inspect the merchandise to determine its fitness for human consumption. In the past few decades, however, it has become increasingly the practice to place food products that are marketed through retail stores in cans and other types of packages. The retailers therefore contend that they are in no better position than the purchaser (consumer) to know whether the food is fit for human consumption, and that they should not be subject to an implied warranty of suitability. Most courts, nevertheless, hold that retailers are subject to such a warranty. They argue, for one thing, that the retailer is in a better position than the consumer to know about the reputation of manufacturers, canners, and processors of food products. Furthermore, many courts have taken the position that it is socially desirable to make available to the consumer a more convenient method of recovering damages for his injuries, by permitting him to sue the local retailer. If he recovers a judgment against the retailer, the retailer may in turn sue and obtain judgment against the manufacturer, canner, jobber, or processor from whom he purchased the food, for there is an implied warranty of suitability running between such sellers and the retailer.

The question has often arisen whether there is an implied warranty of suitability in the case of the sale of food by hotels, restaurants, cafeterias, and other types of eating places. There is a complete split of authority on this matter. It would appear from a study of the cases that a majority of the courts have held that there is no implied warranty of suitability in such cases. They have taken the position that the diner buys service and not food; it is said that there has been only an "uttering" of food, not a sale. Today, however, the courts show a growing tendency to reject this idea and to place operators of restaurants and other eating places on the same basis as retailers of food products. This is also the position of the Uniform Commercial Code, which provides in Section 2–314: "The serving for value of food or drink to be consumed either on the premises or elsewhere is a sale." The Comment covering this section states emphatically, "Cases to the contrary are rejected."

Ray v. Deas
112 Ga. App. 191, 144 S. E. (2d) 468 (1965)

This was an action by Marguerite F. Deas (plaintiff) against J. D. Ray (defendant). Judgment for plaintiff, and defendant appealed. Affirmed.

This is an action by a patron against a restauranteur for injury received when patron allegedly broke a tooth while biting into a hard, unyielding substance in a hamburger sandwich.

FRANKUM, J. "Any person who knowingly or carelessly sells to another unwholesome provisions of any kind, the defect being unknown to the purchaser, by the use of which damage results to the purchaser or his family, shall be liable in damages for such injury." Code Sec. 105–1101. It has been held, in applying the principles enunciated by this Code section, that one who negligently furnishes food or drink containing a foreign substance which causes injury or damage to the consumer thereof may be held liable therefor. *Watson v. Augusta Brewing Co.*, 124 Ga. 121, 52 S. E. 152, 1 L. R. A., N. S., 1178; *Bailey v. F. W. Woolworth, Inc.*, 106 Ga. App. 264, 126 S. E. (2d) 686. Count 1 of the petition which alleges that the plaintiff was a customer of the defendant restauranteur; that the defendant served or delivered to the plaintiff a hamburger sandwich; that the plaintiff, while in the act of consuming the sandwich, sustained an injury when she bit into a hard unyielding substance contained in the sandwich which broke one of her teeth, and thereby resulted in specified damages to her; that the defendant was negligent in failing to properly inspect the ingredients of the sandwich, and that this negligence was the proximate cause of the plaintiff's injuries and damages sued for, stated a cause of action as against the defendant's general demurrer filed thereto. In a case of this kind actual knowledge on the part of the defendant of the presence in the food of the thing or quality which results in damage to the plaintiff is not essential, provided the plaintiff alleges and proves negligence on the part of the defendant in preparing the food. In such a case as against a general demurrer, mere general averments of negligence are sufficient. *Yeo v. Pig & Whistle Sandwich Shops*, 83 Ga. App. 91, 96 (1), 62 S. E. (2d) 668. Count 1 of the petition stated a cause of action against the defendant, and the trial court did not err in overruling the general demurrer thereto.

Prior to the enactment of the Uniform Commercial Code it was the settled law in Georgia that a restaurateur who furnished unwholesome food or food containing a foreign substance or dangerous object to a customer who was injured thereby was not liable upon the theory of an implied warranty. *Yeo v. Pig & Whistle Sandwich Shops, supra*, 83 Ga. App. at page 95, 62 S. E. (2d) 668. The rule of law thus announced and applied in the Georgia courts was clearly based upon the proposition that the furnishing of food by a restaurateur for consumption on the premises did not amount to a sale, but was in fact the rendition of a service solely for the purpose of satisfying the customer's immediate desires and need to be fed. See the excellent discussion and review of authorities in *Rowe v. Louisville*, etc. R. Co., 29 Ga. App. 151, 153, 113 S. E. 823. However, the plain, unambiguous, and express language of Sec. 2-314 of the Uniform Commercial Code (Code Ann. Sec. 109A-2-314) provides: "Unless excluded or modified * * *, a warranty that the goods shall be merchantable is implied in a contract for their sale if the seller is a merchant with respect to goods of that kind. Under this section the serving for value of food or drink to be consumed either on the premises or elsewhere is a sale." The legislature has thus evidenced a manifest intention of abrogating and repealing the substantive rule of law announced by the courts in cases such as Yeo and Rowe. It follows that count 2 of the petition in this case alleging substantially the same facts as alleged in count 1 and basing the plaintiff's right to recover on a breach of an implied warranty of merchantability, stated a cause of action, and the trial court did not err in overruling the general demurrer, nor in overruling the special demurrer to paragraph 14 of count 2, attacking the allegations respecting warranty on the ground of irrelevancy and immateriality.

Judgment affirmed.

DO WARRANTIES RUN WITH THE GOODS?

The general rule is that the warranties of the seller do not "run with the goods"; that is, the warranties of a seller to a buyer do not continue to be effective and binding against the seller if the buyer should afterwards sell the goods to someone else.[1] If A sells certain goods to B under an express warranty and B then sells the goods to C, a subpurchaser, A is not liable to C in case of the breach of the warranty made by A to B. The warranty made by A to B does not "run with the goods." This rule of law is based upon the concept that when B sells to C, a new contract results, and since there is no privity of contract between A and C, A is not contractually liable to C. Of course, if the goods were not as warranted by A to B, and B made a similar warranty to C, and C recovered against B, B in turn could recover against A on A's warranty to B.

As we well know, manufacturers often warrant their products "against defects in materials and workmanship" for a designated period of time. The courts have usually held the manufacturer liable to the ultimate purchaser on such warranties. In a sense it may be said that in such cases the manufacturer agrees to waive the protection of the general rule that "warranties do not run with the goods."

An important exception to the rule that the seller's warranties do not

[1] The rule is just the opposite in the case of the sale of real property. Where real property is sold and transferred under a warranty deed, the warranties contained in the deed do "run with the title or property."

"run with the goods" is found in the case of the sale of food for human consumption. We saw in the preceding section that a consumer may recover in an action against a retailer (and, in some courts, against a restaurant owner) who has sold him food not fit for human consumption. He can also recover in an action against the manufacturer, canner, or processor who sold the food to the retailer or restaurant owner. For example, A, a canner, sells canned beans to B, a retailer, and B sells several cans to C, a consumer. While eating the beans from one of the cans, C injures his mouth on a nail which was in the beans. C could recover against A in a contract action based upon the breach of an implied warranty that the beans were fit for human consumption. A slightly different problem arises where the injury occurs to D, a member of C's family or a guest in C's home. Since B, the retailer, sold the beans to C and not to D, some courts have had difficulty in finding any contractual basis upon which to allow D to recover against either A or B. However, a number of courts have allowed D to recover, upon the broad basis of public policy. The courts so holding take the position that under our present-day complicated system of marketing, the injured consumer is entitled to this added protection. Under such circumstances it is felt that the manufacturer or processor was in a better position to prevent the injury than was the consumer who was injured.

There is a strong tendency in the direction of giving greater protection to the ultimate consumer of food, whether he be the purchaser or some member of the purchaser's family, or even a guest of the purchaser. The Uniform Commercial Code states (Sec. 2–318): "A seller's warranty whether expressed or implied extends to any natural person who is in the family or household of his buyer or who is a guest in his home if it is reasonable to expect that such person may use, consume or be affected by the goods and who is injured in person by breach of warranty. A seller may not exclude or limit the operation of this section." The Comment on this section states: "The purpose of this section is to give the buyer's family, household and guests the benefit of the same warranty which the buyer received in the contract of sale, thereby freeing any such beneficiary from any technical rule as to 'privity.'"

Yentzer v. Taylor Wine Company
414 Pa. 272 199 A. (2d) 463 (1964)
Supreme Court of Pennsylvania

This was an action by Frederick W. Yentzer (plaintiff) against Taylor Wine Company, Inc. (defendant). Judgment for defendant, and plaintiff appealed. Judgment reversed.

The facts pleaded may be summarized as follows: Plaintiff, employed as manager of a hotel, personally purchased from a state liquor store, on behalf of his employer, four bottles of champagne produced and bottled by the defendant-corporation. The wine was intended for use and consumption by guests of the hotel. While plaintiff and other employees were preparing to serve the wine, a cap from one of the bottles suddenly ejected, propelled through the air and hit plaintiff in the eye, resulting in serious injury. This suit followed, based upon an alleged breach of the following implied warranties: (1) that the goods were adequately and safely packaged; (2) that the goods were fit for the ordinary purposes for which such goods were sold.

COHEN, J. In this action in assumpsit, plaintiff appeals from the judgment of the court below sustaining preliminary objections in the nature of a demurrer and dismissing the complaint.

The lower court determined that our recent decision in *Hochgertel v. Canada Dry Corp.*, 409 Pa. 610, 187 A. (2d) 575 (1963), controlled and dismissed the complaint. We do not think that the rigid construction we placed on a seller's warranty in Hochgertel should be extended to a situation such as this.

The Uniform Commercial Code, Section 2–318, 12A P. S., Sec. 2–318 reads as follows: "A seller's warranty whether express or implied extends to any natural person who is in the family or household of his buyer or who is a guest in his home if it is reasonable to expect that such person may use, consume or be affected by the goods and who is injured in person by breach of the warranty. A seller may not exclude or limit the operation of this section."

Comment 3 to this section states: ". . . Beyond this, the section is neutral and is not intended to enlarge or restrict the developing case law on whether the seller's warranties, given to his buyer who resells, extend to other persons in the distributive chain." In Hochgertel we noted that an employee of the purchaser was not within the group to which the warranty of merchantability was specifically extended by Section 2–318 and on this basis refused to extend to such employee the benefit of the warranty.

However, we also recognized that we had abandoned the strict privity requirement in food cases and now permit in such actions the extension of the warranty of merchantability to persons within the distributive chain. While this statement in Hochgertel specifically referred to employer sub-purchasers, we did not foreclose the inclusion of the actual purchaser even though he be an employee of the party to whom title to the product passed.

"Buyer" is defined in Section 2–103 of the Code, 12A P. S., Sec. 2–103 as "a person who buys or contracts to buy." Plaintiff is clearly a buyer within this definition and he is therefore definitely in the distributive chain. Were he an employee who had not "contracted to buy" the product, Hochgertel would control. But since the plaintiff was cast in the important role of "buyer" and consummated the "contract to buy" for his employer, the fact that he is an employee does not exclude him from the benefits of the warranty and deprive him of a right of action.

Judgment reversed.

NON–WARRANTY OR DISCLAIMER

If it is not forbidden by statute, the parties may agree that the goods are sold by the vendor to the vendee without any warranties, either express or implied. And at times vendors try to limit their liabilities by placing similar disclaimers of warranties on their letterheads and sales tickets. All such agreements and provisions, however, are strictly construed by the courts, and unless they have been carefully and properly drawn they will be disregarded by the courts. For example, in *Bekkevold v. Potts et al.*[1] the contract contained this provision: "No warranties have been made in reference to said motor vehicle by the seller to the buyer unless expressly written hereon at the date of purchase." None were written thereon. The court, in holding the vendor liable, said: "We are of the opinion that the parties intended to say that no contractual warranties had been made; that the seller had not spoken or written any warranty in reference to the outfit. There was no other way by which such warranties could have been 'made.' No action of the parties was necessary to 'make' that implied warranty of suitability which the law writes into it. We must conclude that the parties did not intend to exclude the implied warranty which could easily have been done in unmistakable terms had they so chosen. Hence there was no error in receiving the evidence to prove the breach thereof."

This strictness of construction is justified by the present-day inequality in the bargaining positions of the vendor and the vendee. The vendor is usually in a much stronger bargaining position, and hence is often able to force such provisions on the vendee. The courts therefore tend to give the vendee the benefit of any legal loophole. This tendency is also reflected in the Uniform Commercial Code (Sec. 2–316): "(1) Words or conduct relevant to the creation of an express warranty and words or conduct tending to negate or limit warranty shall be construed wherever reasonable as consistent with each other; but subject to the provisions of this Article on parol or extrinsic evidence (Section 2–202) negation or limitation is inoperative to the extent that such construction is unreasonable.

"(2) Subject to subsection (3), to exclude or modify the implied warranty of merchantability or any part of it the language must mention merchantability and in case of a writing must be conspicuous, and to exclude or modify any implied warranty of fitness the exclusion must be by a writing and conspicuous. Language to exclude all implied warranties of fitness is sufficient if it states, for example, that 'There are no warranties which extend beyond the description on the face hereof.'

"(3) Notwithstanding subsection (2), (a) unless the circumstances in-

---

[1] 173 Minn. 87, 216 N. W. 790 (1929).

dicate otherwise, all implied warranties are excluded by expressions like 'as is,' 'with all faults' or other language which in common understanding calls the buyer's attention to the exclusion of warranties and makes plain that there is no implied warranty; and (b) when the buyer before entering into the contract has examined the goods or the sample or model as fully as he desired or has refused to examine the goods there is no implied warranty with regard to defects which an examination ought in the circumstances to have revealed to him; and (c) an implied warranty can also be excluded or modified by course of dealing or course of performance or usage of trade.

"(4) Remedies for breach of warranty can be limited in accordance with the provisions of this Article on liquidation or limitation of damages and on contractual modification of remedy (Sections 2–718 and 2–719)."

Difficulty may arise regarding the interpretation of conflict of warranties. Sec. 2–317 states that warranties whether express or implied shall be construed as consistent with each other and as cumulative, but if such construction is unreasonable the intention of the parties shall determine which warranty is dominant. In ascertaining that intention the following rules shall apply: Exact or technical specifications displace an inconsistent sample or model or general language of description; a sample from an existing bulk displaces inconsistent general language of description; and express warranties displace inconsistent implied warranties other than an implied warranty of fitness for a particular purpose.

Hunt v. Perkins Machinery Co.
226 N. E. (2d) 228 (1967)

This was an action by Harry E. Hunt, Jr. (plaintiff) against Perkins Machinery Company, Inc. (defendant). Judgment for plaintiff, and defendant appealed. Affirmed.

This was an action by a fisherman against a diesel engine distributor for breach of implied warranties of merchantability and of fitness for a particular purpose.

Hunt, an experienced commercial fisherman, got in touch with the defendant (Perkins), a distributor of Caterpillar Tractor Company's products. He was considering the purchase of a diesel engine for his fishing boat. In the fall of 1960, Perkins's sales manager, one Rideout, went to Hunt's house in Orleans to acquaint him with the various Caterpillar diesel engines available. At Rideout's suggestion, Hunt went to Maine to look at a boat equipped with such an engine. In January, 1961, Hunt signed a purchase order for one Caterpillar Model D330 engine with a 1.2 to 1 reduction gear (instead of one reduction gear ordinarily supplied by the manufacturer) and certain specified accessories. The written portion of the purchase order was prepared (except for the signatures) by Rideout. It was on a "pad of paper containing several copies separated by carbon paper."

Hunt did not read anything on the back of the order when he signed it. "The original and all * * * copies of the * * * [o]rder were taken by Rideout * * * for signature by an official" of Perkins. Hunt received a fully executed copy of the order by mail a few days later.

The face of the purchase order contains a statement of the property sold, acknowledgment of a $500 deposit, a statement of the balance ($4095) due, and certain miscellaneous information. In the center of the face of the order in bold face type capitals appears the statement "BOTH THIS ORDER AND ITS ACCEPTANCE ARE SUBJECT TO 'TERMS AND CONDITIONS' STATED IN THIS ORDER." On the reverse side of the order at the top in the same bold face type capitals appear the words "TERMS AND CONDITIONS." Underneath those words there are eleven numbered paragraphs. Included among the numbered paragraphs are those set out in the margin.[1]

After Hunt had received his executed copy of the order, he took his boat to Plymouth Marine (Railways Marine) to have it prepared for the new engine. Seven or eight days later Hunt by telephone learned from Rideout that there would be a delay in delivery. Rideout then told Hunt that he could tear up the contract and forget the engine if he wanted to do so. Hunt decided to go through with the purchase because his boat was already at Marine and the old engine had been removed.

The engine was delivered to Marine on March 6, 1961, and was thereafter installed in the boat by Marine. This installation work included everything that was necessary to connect the engine, with the exception of the initial starting. That was done by employees of Perkins. Marine was not connected with, nor acting for, Perkins at any time. Its work was not controlled by Perkins. It was engaged by and paid by Hunt.

After the engine was installed a series of mechanical problems arose, each of which was corrected by Perkins at no expense to Hunt other than the time involved while the repairs were being made. The engine, when running, gave off excessive quantities of heavy black smoke, which caused the boat to become dirty, inside and out, and rendered Hunt's work on the boat unpleasant. This condition persisted until the removal of the engine. At Hunt's request Perkins,

---

[1] The relevant terms and conditions are the following: "1. *Acceptance.* This order is subject to acceptance by Seller only at Seller's place of business in Massachusetts and shall become a binding contract only when a copy has been accepted in writing and * * * returned to Buyer. 2. *All Agreements.* This written order when accepted by Seller shall be the * * * exclusive statement of all terms of the agreement between the parties other than such additional agreements as may be contained in any contracts, notes or other documents specified herein. No representations of any kind have been made except as set forth in this order or in the other documents specified herein. 3. WARRANTIES. SELLER MAKES NO WARRANTIES (INCLUDING * * * ANY WARRANTIES AS TO MERCHANTABILITY OR FITNESS) EITHER EXPRESS OR IMPLIED WITH RESPECT TO THE PROPERTY UNLESS ENDORSED HEREON IN WRITING. BUYER SHALL BE LIMITED TO THE WARRANTIES OF THE RESPECTIVE MANUFACTURERS OF THE PRODUCTS SOLD. * * * 6. *Limitation of Liability.* Seller shall not be liable for any property damage or for any * * * injuries * * * suffered in connection with the operation or installation of the [p]roperty. * * *"

on several occasions and by a variety of means, attempted without success to curtail the smoking.

About July 20, 1961, the engine was removed by Hunt and put on the dock at Marine's plant. Hunt called Perkins and reported that he had removed the engine and advised Perkins to get it. The engine is still on Marine's premises.

In July, 1961, Hunt purchased a new engine from another manufacturer. This new engine has performed satisfactorily.

CUTTER, J. Hunt's evidence of damages consisted of a showing of cash payments to Marine of $761.49 for installation work and testimony that he lost $250 each day when he was prevented from fishing as a result of Perkins' work on the boat. Perkins worked on the boat on about ten different occasions between the installation of the engine and June, 1961.

The trial judge denied motions for directed verdicts in this action in two counts, count 1 for breach of an implied warranty of merchantability and count 2 for breach of an implied warranty of fitness for a particular purpose. The jury returned verdicts for $5357. Perkins brings before us exceptions to the denial of directed verdicts and to the judge's refusal to order verdicts entered for Perkins under leave reserved. There was evidence from which the facts stated above could have been found.

1. This case presents issues under the Uniform Commercial Code (see St. 1957, c. 765, Sec. 1) concerning excluding or modifying (a) the implied warranty of merchantability under G. L . c. 106, Sec. 2–314,[1] and (b) the implied warranty under c. 106, Sec. 2–315, that goods shall be fit for a particular purpose.[2] Section 2–316 (2) reads, in part: "(2) * * * [T]o exclude or modify the implied warranty of merchantability or any part of it the language must mention merchantability *and in case of a writing must be conspicuous*, and to exclude or modify any implied warranty of fitness the exclusion must be by a writing and *conspicuous*. Language to exclude all implied warranties of fitness is sufficient if it states, for example, that 'There are no warranties which extend beyond the description *on the face hereof*' " (emphasis supplied). Section 2–316 (2) must be read with Sec. 1–201 (10) which provides, in part: " 'Conspicuous': A term * * * is conspicuous when it is so written that a reasonable person against whom it is to operate *ought to have noticed it*. A printed heading in capitals (as: NONNEGOTIABLE BILL OF LADING) is conspicuous. Language in the body of a form is 'conspicuous' if it is in larger or other contrasting type or color. * * * Whether a term or clause is 'conspicuous' * * * is for decision by the court" (emphasis supplied).

[1] Section 2–314 reads: "(1) Unless excluded or modified by Section 2–316, a warranty that the goods shall be merchantable is implied in a contract for their sale if the seller is a merchant with respect to goods of that kind. * * * (2) Goods to be merchantable must at least be such as * * * (c) are fit for the ordinary purposes for which such goods are used * * *."

[2] Section 2–315 reads: "Where the seller * * * has reason to know any particular purpose for which the goods are required and that the buyer is relying on the seller's skill or judgment to select or furnish suitable goods, there is unless excluded or modified under * * * [Sec. 2–316] and implied warranty that the goods shall be fit for such purpose."

Hunt concedes that Perkins's disclaimer of warranties would have been effective if the disclaimer language in the "Terms and Conditions" (fn. 1), instead of being on the back of the contract form had been (a) on the face of the purchase order, or (b) had been referred to on the face of the order by words such as "see other side" or "as stated on the reverse hereof." The first question for decision is whether the disclaimer of the warranties on the back of this purchase order was "conspicuous." 1

Some light is shed upon the meaning of "conspicuous" in Par. 1–201 (10) by the official comment on the subsection, which says in part, "This is intended to indicate some of the methods of making a term attention-calling. But the test is whether attention can reasonably be expected to be called to it." 2 See 1957 official Text, p. 26. Most commentators discuss the issue in general terms.3

The decided cases are not controlling. In *Boeing Airplane Co. v. O'Malley*, 329 F. (2d) 585, 593 (8th Cir.), a disclaimer "merely in the same color and size of other type used for the other provisions" was treated as not conspicuous. In *Minikes v. Admiral Corp.*, 48 Misc. (2d) 1012, 1013, 266 N. Y. S. (2d) 461, 462 (Dist. Ct.), a "disclaimer * * * smaller, not larger, than the rest of the purchase order" was held not conspicuous. In *Roto-Lith, Ltd. v. F. P. Bartlett & Co.*, 297 F. (2d) 497, 498–500 (1st Cir.), effect was given to a disclaimer in type "still conspicuous" on the back of the acceptance of an order, which was referred to on the front of the order in the following terms, "All goods sold without warranties, express or implied, and subject to the terms on reverse side." See for a case disregarding a disclaimer in relatively small type on the back of a form, *Berk v. Gordon Johnson Co.*, 232 F. Supp. 682, 686–688 (E. D. Mich.).

Under Sec. 2–316(2) read with the last sentence of Sec. 1–201(10), it is a question of law for the court whether a provision is conspicuous. We are in as good a position to decide that issue as the trial judge, for a photographic copy

1 See as to the effect of a general disclaimer of implied warranties prior to the adoption of the code, *S. F. Bowser & Co. Inc. v. Independent Dye House, Inc.*, 276 Mass. 289, 296, 177 N. E. 268; *Dekofski v. Leite*, 336 Mass. 127, 129, 142 N. E. (2d) 782; *Hall v. Everett Motors, Inc.*, 340 Mass. 430, 432, 165 N. E. (2d) 107. For the distinction in pre-code cases between disclaimers or limitations of liability in contracts and those in small tickets or receipts, compare *Henderson v. Canadian Pac. Ry.*, 258 Mass. 372, 376, 155 N. E. 1, and *D'Aloisio v. Morton's Inc.*, 342 Mass. 231, 234–236, 172 N. E. (2d) 819 with *Kergald v. Armstrong Transfer Exp. Co.*, 330 Mass. 254, 255–256, 113 N. E. (2d) 53.

2 See, to similar effect, Duesenberg and King, *Sales & Bulk Transfers under the Uniform Commercial Code*, vol. 3, Sec. 7.03, esp. pp. 7–33 to 7–37. After paraphrasing the official comment, the authors go on to say, "In the case of a disclaimer of warranties, it is suggested that a contrasting size of type be used at a minimum, and, if it is at all possible, different color type should also be used. When contrasting size of type is mentioned, this would mean that the language disclaiming the warranty of merchantability should be in larger size type. The color of the type could be a darker shade of black, or perhaps a yellow or red, or some other color that would call attention to the disclaimer." This, of course, may be merely a counsel of caution.

3 See Cudahy, *Limitation of Warranty under the Uniform Commercial Code*, 47 Marquette L. Rev. 127, 137–139, 144–146; Lauer, *Sales Warranties under the Uniform Commercial Code*, 30 Mo. L. Rev. 259, 282–285; notes, 43 B. U. L. Rev. 396, 398–402, 38 Ind. L. J. 648, 670–675, 112 U. of Pa. L. Rev. 564, 583–589.

of both sides of the purchase order is before us. We decide the issue by applying the statutory test under Sec. 1–201(10) of what is conspicuous, viz. whether "a reasonable person against whom * * * [the disclaimer] is to operate ought to have noticed it."

In the opinion of a majority of the court, the provisions on the front of the purchase order did not make adequate reference to the provisions on the back of the order to draw attention to the latter. Hence the provisions on the back of the order cannot be said to be conspicuous although printed in an adequate size and style of type. The disclaimer was not effective.

Exceptions overruled.

TORT LIABILITY OF SELLER

While, as we have seen, a seller is not liable to a subpurchaser in a contract action for breach of warranty,[1] he is liable, under certain circumstances, in a tort action for negligence. Thus, the tort liability of the seller extends not only to the immediate buyer but to any subsequent buyer who may be reasonably expected to be injured if the product, upon being put to use, proves defective. The degree of care which the seller must exercise is that which a reasonable man of ordinary prudence would use under the same or similar circumstances.

Most courts have held that, in the case of a manufacturer or processor of foods and drugs, if the ultimate consumer is injured by the use of such products, there is an inference of negligence on the part of the manufacturer or processor. In such case the doctrine of res ipsa loquitur (the thing speaks for itself) is usually applied.[2] This means that, if the plaintiff (consumer) is able to prove that he purchased the product and was injured in making normal or customary use of it, he has established a prima facie case; and if the defendant (manufacturer or processor) is unable to show that he exercised reasonable care in the manufacture or preparation of the product, the plaintiff will be entitled to judgment. The doctrine of res ipsa loquitur has also been applied to other products where such products have been considered to be inherently dangerous, such as explosives and other inflammable materials.

The doctrine of res ipsa loquitur does not apply to other sellers, such as wholesalers, jobbers, or retailers.[3] Such sellers are charged with the

---

[1] Except in the case of the sale of food for human consumption.

[2] In explaining the nature of the doctrine of res ipsa loquitur, the court, in *Scott v. London & St. Katherine Docks Co.*, 3 H. & C., 596, said: "There must be reasonable evidence of negligence; but where the thing is shown to be under the management of the defendant or his servants, and the accident is such as in the ordinary course of things does not happen if those who have the management use proper care, it affords reasonable evidence, in the absence of explanation by the defendants, that the accident arose from want of care."

[3] But the doctrine is usually applied where food is sold by a restaurant, cafeteria, or other eating place.

duty of making a reasonable inspection of the goods which they sell, and of advising those who buy from them of any latent defects of which they have knowledge. If they have performed these duties, they will be held not to have been negligent, and therefore are not liable to the purchaser by way of damages.

Centineo v. Anheuser-Busch, Incorporated
276 So. (2d) 352 (1973)
Court of Appeal of Louisiana

This was an action against beer bottler seeking to recover damages for personal injuries and medical expenses incurred by plaintiff when she was cut by exploding beer bottle. . . . Judgment for plaintiff and defendant appealed. Amended and affirmed.

REGAN, J. Plaintiffs, Annette and Joseph Centineo, filed this suit against the defendant, Anheuser-Busch, Inc., endeavoring to recover $73,667.65 for personal injuries and medical expenses incurred by and on behalf of Mrs. Centineo when she was cut by fragments of flying glass which emanated from an explosion of a large bottle of Busch Bavarian beer.

Plaintiffs alleged that the bottle (1) had been delivered to the grocery store they operated by one of defendant's agents; (2) was carefully and properly handled at all times prior to the explosion after it came into their possession; and (3) exploded as Mrs. Centineo attempted to remove it from a cooler without any apparent cause.

Plaintiff then pleaded res ipsa loquitur.

Defendant answered and in effect generally denied the allegations of plaintiffs' petition. . . . In the alternative, the defendant pleaded that the contributory negligence of Mrs. Centineo in the handling of the bottle barred her recovery.

From a judgment awarding Mrs. Centineo $3,800.00 for pain and suffering, dismissing her husband's claim for medical expenses for lack of proof and assessing costs equally against plaintiffs and the defendant, the defendant has appealed.

Plaintiffs have answered the appeal requesting an increase in quantum and a reversal of that part of the decree assessing them with part of the costs.

*   *   *

Thus we turn our attention to an examination of the testimony so as to ascertain whether plaintiff has made out a prima facie case.

The record discloses that the plaintiffs were owners of a small grocery store in New Orleans. On June 28, 1969, Mrs. Centineo was serving a customer who wanted to purchase a bottle of Busch Bavarian beer. She walked to the cooler where this brand of beer was kept, slid back the lid and reached into the cooler. Just as she picked up a quart bottle she heard an explosion. Within seconds she noticed her left arm bleeding profusely. She testified emphatically that she did not knock the bottle either against another bottle or the side of the cooler and she did not know why the bottle exploded. It should be pointed out that Mrs. Centineo, during interrogation indicated that she was not sure whether or not she touched the bottle before she heard the explosion; however, when questioned closely and repeatedly on this point, she said she was fairly certain she had picked up the bottle.

She was the only eyewitness to the explosion. Her husband and daughter were both in the store when the incident occurred. They both heard the noise and saw Mrs. Centineo bleeding immediately thereafter.

Joseph Centineo testified that he found the top part of the bottle with a Busch Bavarian cap still sealing the opening. The other fragments fell into the cooler and were ultimately washed out or fell to the floor and were swept out.

* * *

The implication and the whole tenor of the record leads us to the conclusion that the beer was delivered by an Anheuser-Busch truck. That it was in fact delivered by defendant's agent is established by virtue of a question propounded by defense counsel in examining Anderson Carter, Jr., an assistant supervisor employed by the defendant, who related that his duties consisted of inspecting the incoming boxcars and the loading of trucks in the New Orleans area. The question asked was:

"Would you please tell us the procedure used from the time the incoming boxcars or trucks come into New Orleans until the time they are put on the trucks to go out to *the retail stores?*" (Emphasis added).

We are convinced that the trial court correctly invoked the doctrine of res ipsa loquitur. It was proved that Mrs. Centineo was injured by an exploding bottle, delivered by one of the defendant's agents to the store and properly handled until the moment that it exploded. The extension of the doctrine of res ipsa loquitur in bottle explosion cases to include offending instrumentalities not within the exclusive control of the defendant at the time the accident occurred was explained at length in *Johnson v. Louisiana Coca-Cola Bottling Co.* [63 So. (2d) 459, 463 La. App. (1953)] as follows:

"No citation of authority is necessary to sustain the proposition that the sole purpose of the doctrine of res ipsa loquitur is to inferentially establish negligence on the part of defendant and for it to be applicable, the instrumentality which causes the injury must be under the exclusive control of the defendant, however, the doctrine has been extended, and reasonably so, to that class of cases where the instrumentality causing the damage is in the actual possession of the plaintiff, but is considered to be in the constructive control of the defendant, because sufficient proof has been adduced revealing that it is in the same condition as when it left the defendant's possession. Obviously, the prevailing jurisprudence of this State has placed bottle explosion cases in this category."

* * *

"Under the jurisprudence, therefore, for res ipsa loquitur to apply a person injured by an exploding bottle is not required to trace the history of that particular bottle from the moment it was delivered to the retailer until it explodes. It is sufficient that the injured person prove that he himself was free from fault and that no blow or dropping by him or by some third person caused the bottle to explode . . . ; *in short, it is sufficient for him to prove only that the bottle exploded from apparently unknown cause while or after being normally handled in an ordinary retail transaction.*" (Emphasis added).

To reiterate, we are convinced that the rule of res ipsa loquitur is applicable to the fact hereof. . . .

. . . Defendant argues that the quantum is excessive. We agree. As a result of the explosion, Mrs. Centineo was cut by flying glass. The only significant laceration was on the inside of the left arm opposite the elbow. It left a two inch scar that healed with a keloid formation. The excess tissue accentuates the scar and gives it a somewhat raised appearance. Mrs Centineo complained of pain (like needles and pins) in the area and swelling of the left hand and arm. Dr. Louis Krust, her plastic surgeon, stated that the swelling was not related to the scar and the "needle and pin" sensation was possible but not probable. Her general practitioner felt the complaints of "needle and pin" pain was consistent with the injury.

Shortly after this accident, Mrs Centineo had a mastectomy performed upon her, and the swelling hand may or may not be related to this operation. However, all medical testimony established that the swelling was not caused by the laceration to the arm.

Plaintiffs insist the award is inadequate. To support this position several cases have been cited wherein much higher awards have been given for scars. But these were facial scars and, in our opinion, are not comparable because of the cosmetic damage.

* * *

For the reasons assigned, the judgment appealed from is amended to reduce the award to Mrs. Centineo from $3,800.00 to $2,000.00 and to tax expert fees against the defendant. In all other respects, the judgment appealed from is affirmed. Other than expert fees taxed against the defendant, each litigant is to pay his own court costs.

Amended and affirmed.

Lonzrick v. Republic Steel Corp.

35 Ohio Ops. (2d) 404, 218 N. E. (2d) 185 (1966)

Supreme Court of Ohio

This was an action by Lonzrick (plaintiff) against Republic Steel Corporation (defendant). Judgment for defendant in the Court of Common Pleas, and defendant appealed. The Court of Appeals reversed and remanded with instructions. Court of Appeals affirmed by Supreme Court of Ohio.

The allegations of the petition and all reasonable inferences therefrom will support the following statement of facts:

Defendant manufactured and sold certain steel roof joists. In selling those joists, defendant impliedly warranted that they were fit for the ordinary purposes for which such steel roof joists are used. (Section 1302.27, Revised Code, reads in part: "Goods to be merchantable must be at least such as * * * [3] are fit for the ordinary purposes for which such goods are used.") Those joists were defective because they were not fit for the ordinary purposes for which such joists are used. As a proximate result of being so defective, those joists came apart and fell on and injured plaintiff. At that time, plaintiff was working as a structural iron worker on the ground in an area where the joists had been installed directly overhead and was thus in a place where his presence was reasonably to be anticipated by defendant.

The Court of Appeals held that this petition states a good cause of action in tort, based upon the theory of breach of warranty.

This is a products liability case. In such a case, there are three possible causes of action which the plaintiff may pursue:

(1) An action in tort which is grounded upon negligence. Such cause of action does not require the allegation of a contractual relationship between the plaintiff and the defendant. The petition in this case does not allege negligence and does not state facts which constitute negligence.

(2) A cause of action which is based upon contract. Such a cause of action requires that there be a contractual relationship between the plaintiff and the defendant. The petition in this case does not allege a contract and it does not allege a breach of a contractual warranty. It does not allege any contractual relationship between the plaintiff and the defendant.

(3) An action in tort which is based upon the breach of a duty assumed by the manufacturer-seller of a product. This duty is assumed by the manufacturer by reason of his implicit representation of good and merchantable quality and fitness for intended use when he sells the product. This duty is breached when a defect in the product causes the collapse of the product and is the direct and proximate cause of injury to a person whose presence the defendant could reasonably anticipate. This is the cause of action which the petition in this case states.

In this action the plaintiff is required to allege and prove that there was a defect in the steel joists manufactured and sold by the defendant, that such defect existed at the time the joists were sold by the defendant, that the defect was the direct and proximate cause of plaintiff's injuries, and that the plaintiff, at the time he was injured, was in a place where his presence was reasonably to be anticipated by the defendant.

It is conceded by both parties that the plaintiff does not have an action based upon a contract because there was no contract of sale between the plaintiff and the defendant and, therefore, no contractual relation (privity) between the parties.

The position of the defendant is that the plaintiff's petition does not state a cause of action because it does not allege negligence, does not allege an express warranty and does not allege any contractual relationship between the plaintiff and the defendant.

The plaintiff concedes that this petition does not allege negligence, does not allege an express warranty and does not allege any contractual relationship between the plaintiff and the defendant. The plaintiff asserts that the petition states a cause of action in tort based upon an implied warranty.

The basic question for the court to decide is the same as the question was in *Welsh v. Ledyard*, 167 Ohio St. 57, 146 N. E. (2d) 299, in *Rogers v. Toni Home Permanent Co.*, 167 Ohio St. 244, 147 N. E. (2d) 612, 75 A. L. R. (2d) 103, and in *Inglis v. American Motors Corp.*, 3 Ohio St. (2d) 132, 209 N. E. (2d) 583. Is the plaintiff restricted to prosecuting his action for damages on the basis of negligence alone, or may he proceed in tort on the theory of breach of warranty?

This is an action in tort for breach of an implied warranty. The warranty in this case is the manufacturer's representation, implicit in the sale of the steel joists, that they were of good and merchantable quality, fit and safe for their ordinary intended use. This created a duty upon the manufacturer-seller, which duty was breached when the joists proved defective and collapsed because of the defect, injuring plaintiff.

The petition in this case states a good cause of action grounded in tort, based upon a breach of the representations which are implicit when a defendant manufactures and sells a product which, if defective, will be a dangerous instrumentality.

Judgment affirmed.

Caudle v. Bohannon Tobacco Co.

220 N. C. 105, 16 S. E. (2d) 62 (1941)

Supreme Court of North Carolina

This was an appeal from superior court, Warlick, J.

This was an action by Mrs. J. W. Caudle against the F. M. Bohannon Tobacco Company for injuries caused by a fish hook embedded in a plug of tobacco manufactured by defendant. From a judgment for plaintiff, the defendant appeals.

No error.

This is an action for actionable negligence, brought by plaintiff against the defendant alleging damage. The defendant introduced no evidence. The evidence on the part of plaintiff is to the effect that the defendant is engaged in the manufacture and sale of plug tobacco in Winston-Salem, N. C., under different brands—one of which was that of "Red, White and Blue."

E. M. Gough, a retail merchant of Surry County, N. C., testified . . . "As a merchant I have been buying from the Bohannon Tobacco Company such brands of plug chewing tobacco as Detective, Lucky Joe, Favorite and Red, White and Blue."

Gough sold to plaintiff's husband, who traded with him and usually bought the Bohannon brands—one of the brands being the "Red, White and Blue." Plaintiff's husband testified to the effect that he and his wife chewed "Red, White and Blue" tobacco and he bought a plug from Gough about the 1st day of January, 1939. "I cut it in two and gave my wife half and put the other half in my pocket. I bought it at the store of Mr. Gough. . . . I came straight on home the day I bought it. She was chewing on it something like two or three days. She started using it as quick as I gave it to her. She had no other tobacco. It was just a short plug. It had a seam in the middle of it to cut it by. It was a ten-cent piece, the best I recall. It had a seam in the middle, which made an equal division, and I gave her half and took the other. . . . I had been away from home about an hour. I started down there and saw my wife coming, bent over with her hand over her mouth. I knew something was the matter because she was well when I left home. I asked her what was the matter. (The Court limited the evidence to corroboration.) She says, 'I have got something in my mouth. I bit it off with a piece of tobacco.' I says, 'Let me see.' I looked in her mouth and saw a wire sticking through her teeth, sticking through her lower teeth into the gum. The hook part was hooked back in the gum on the lower side. I didn't try to fool with it." . . .

He further testified as to the impairment of his wife's health, which had been good before: "She was up at night for a while a whole lot, because she was suffering. She couldn't sleep and couldn't rest. That situation existed for something like four months, all the time Dr. Tillotson was tending on her. My wife weighed approximately 165 pounds on the 5th day of January, 1939. I don't know what her weight was during that four month period but she fell off considerably. I didn't have her weighed but she got mighty lean and fell off a whole lot. She couldn't eat. Ate from the corner of her mouth for a long time. She would drink milk and eat from the side of her mouth. She ate only liquids during that time and she couldn't stand anything with any salt in it. I saw inside her mouth. It was raw and sore in there. That got on the outside. It finally broke out all over her face when she was going to the hospital in Mount Airy. No dentist other than Dr. Fry treated her mouth any time lately. Dr. Hardin bridged her teeth way back, years before that. After that bridge came out, the teeth that the bridge was swung to rotted out. I saw the condition of her teeth, I could see the condition was bad, they rotted."

Plaintiff testified, in part: "My husband and I have been married for about 43 years. I am 61 years of age now. I do not now chew tobacco, but I used to chew. I think I took a chew of tobacco off the plug which is handed to me. I know I did. The fish hook handed to me is the one that was in my mouth when I bit the tobacco. That bridgework was in my mouth at one time. It was the 5th day of January, 1939 that I bit into the plug of tobacco and got the fish hook in my mouth. I reached up on the mantel board. I had the tobacco in the poke he gave it to me in. I was sitting there sewing and reached up and got the piece of tobacco, taken it out and taken a chew of tobacco. When I first bit it. I thought it was a stem I had. I bit down a little bigger. Whenever I bit the chew off, something slipped through my teeth and come into my lip. I just started off that way to get somebody to help me get it out, do something; I didn't know what. . . . I always chewed plug tobacco, manufactured tobacco. I always told him when he went to the store to get 'Red, White and Blue,' because I liked that brand better than any brand of tobacco I ever chewed. When he got the fish hook out of my mouth, he took out the chew of tobacco in my mouth. The fish hook was plumb through my teeth and sticking in my lip. . . .

W. W. Ball testified, in part: "I live in Dobson. I chew tobacco and did in 1939, during the January or February Term of Court that year. I chew different kinds but at that time I was chewing 'Red, White and Blue,' which is manufactured by the F. M. Bohannon Company. It was the same type as plaintiff's Exhibit A, a short plug pretty thick. That is the same kind I was chewing.

"Q. Mr. Ball, did you bite into a plug of this in Court about the first Court in 1939, January or February? A. I bought a dime's worth at the time.

"Q. Please tell His Honor and the jury what you found in it?

"The Court: Was it 'Red, White and Blue' tobacco? A. Yes, sir.

"The Court: Did it have a tag on it? A. Yes, sir.

"Q. What did you find in it, if anything? A. I bit in it and it didn't bite right. I taken it out of my mouth and broke out the piece where I couldn't bite and I pulled it open. I knew there was something or other in it. I thought it was a piece of wood, and it looked more like a rat's claw or foot.

"Q. Just describe what it was. A. I couldn't describe positively it was a rat's foot. The best of my opinion it was a rat's foot.

"Q. Go ahead and describe it. How long was it? A. It was short, something like a wharf rat's foot. Pretty good sized or squirrel's.

"The Court: Just describe it, whether it was hard or soft. A. It was hard and I couldn't bite it. I took it out and opened it up, the piece of tobacco, and looked at it.

"Q. How long was it? A. It wasn't very long, about as long as an ordinary rat's foot. I have killed wharf rats.

"Q. How was it shaped? A. I didn't pay so much attention to it after I saw what it looked like to me. I just throwed it down. Just like a rat's foot.

"Q. Please tell His Honor and the jury if it was sharp at one end and broader at the other.

"The Court: Just describe the object. A. It looked like there was a little more to one end of it than there was to the other."

* * *

The issues submitted to the jury and their answers thereto, were as follows:

"1. Was the plaintiff injured by the negligence of the defendant, as alleged in the complaint? Ans: Yes.

"2. What amount of damage, if any, is the plaintiff entitled to recover of the defendant? Ans: $1,200.00."

The Court below rendered judgment on the verdict. The defendant made several exceptions and assignments of error and appealed to the Supreme Court. The material ones will be considered in the opinion.

CLARKSON, J. At the close of plaintiff's evidence, the defendant made a motion for judgment as in case of nonsuit. C. S. § 567. The Court below overruled this motion and in this we can see no error.

The plaintiff's cause of action is based on the alleged negligence of the defendant in the manufacture and sale of a plug of tobacco containing a fish hook.

It is well settled in this jurisdiction that to hold the manufacturer liable, the basis of liability is negligence rather than implied warranty, although in some jurisdictions a recovery may be had under implied warranty. . . .

We think the present action is similar to *Corum v. Tobacco Co.*, 205 N. C. 213, 171 S. E. 78, and *Daniels v. Swift & Co.*, 209 N. C. 567, 183 S. E. 748. The Corum Case, supra [205 N. C. 213, 171 S. E. 79], was tried by Schenck, J., in the Superior Court and from a verdict for plaintiff an appeal was taken to this Court and there was found no error in the judgment of the lower Court. The facts: "The defendant manufacturers a brand of plug or chewing tobacco known as 'Apple Sun-cured.' It sold some of this tobacco to J. W. Smitherman, a wholesale merchant in Winston-Salem, who in turn sold it to Norman Brothers at East Bend, in Yadkin county. On June 4, 1931, the plaintiff bought a plug of it from Norman Brothers and returned to his home, which is about a mile from East Bend. He offered evidence tending to show that at 1:30 o'clock while going back to East Bend he put a part of the plug in his mouth to bite off a chew and 'jerked the tobacco,' when a fishhook which was embedded in the plug 'stuck on the inner side of his lip and came out on the outside'; that with the fishhook and the tobacco he went to a physician who removed the hook; that after its removal, the plaintiff 'prized the tobacco open' and found a mark inside 'whre the fishhook had been lying'; that on the end of the hook there was a piece of string about two inches long; that he suffered pain, was given antitoxin to prevent tetanus, had difficulty in opening and closing his mouth, and complained of stiffness in his jaw and neck." The Court, in its opinion said, at page 215 of 205 N. C., at page 80 of 171 S. E., Adams, J.: "There are many decisions to the effect that one who prepares in bottles or packages food, medicines, drugs, or beverages, and puts them on the market, is charged with the duty of exercising due care in the preparation of these commodities, and under certain circumstances may be liable in damages to the ultimate consumer. . . . In this case the plaintiff adduced evidence tending to show that the defendant is the sole manufacturer of 'Apple Sun-cured Tobacco'; that the tobacco in question was of this brand and had the appearance of having recently come from the store; that it was protected by a wrapper; that all the wrapper had not been removed at the time of the injury; that when a part of it was torn away the imprint of the fishhook and a string which had been embedded in the plug of tobacco was discovered; that some other foreign substance had been found in the same brand of tobacco within two months preceding the injury; and that the foreman of the machine room had previously had complaints that other foreign substances had been left in the manufactured product. . . . Without the necessity of invoking the maxim res ipso loquitur, the plaintiff introduced independent evidence which called for a verdict."

In *Daniels v. Swift*, supra, it was held: "Plaintiff's evidence tended to show that he was injured by particles of glass eaten by him in sausage prepared by defendant manufacturer, and that a short time prior to his injury plaintiff had found grit in similar sausage prepared by defendant, and that the deleterious substances were found inside the casings in which the sausage was stuffed. Held: The evidence was sufficient to be submitted to the jury on the issue of defendant's negligence." The above-cited cases have never been overruled, and, therefore, are the law in this case.

Upon examination of the evidence in the present case respecting the circumstances relied on by the plaintiff to show negligence, we find that the witness Ball, within two months of the time of the injury sustained by the plaintiff, while taking a chew of the same brand of tobacco manufactured by the defendant, discovered what appeared to be a rat's claw, or squirrel's foot. The appellant contends that such evidence is incompetent on the grounds of being opinion evidence from an unqualified witness. The witness, having testified that it was a foreign substance, could certainly go further and testify what it looked like. He made no minute examination of what he found, having been repulsed with the idea of having had it in his mouth. To show his disgust and repulsion at the experience, he "just throwed it down."

The charge of the Court below covered every aspect of the case and applied the law applicable to the facts. We see no merit in any of the exceptions and assignments of error made by defendant. We see no prejudicial or reversible error in the contentions of the Court below in regard to expenditures for medical and hospital bills. Defendant relied mainly on the motion to non-suit, which cannot be sustained under the authorities applicable to the facts in this case.

For the reasons given, in the judgment of the Court below we find no error.

REVIEW CASES

1. Ryan through his wife, who acted as his agent, bought a loaf of bread at the Progressive Grocery Stores. The loaf contained a pin which injured Ryan's mouth. Ryan sued Progressive Grocery Stores for breach of warranty. Holding? (Ryan v. Progressive Grocery Stores, Inc., 255 N. Y. 388, 175 N. E. 105)

2. Hoover ordered from the Utah Nursery Co. half a pound of Utah Chinese celery seed. He sowed the seed on two acres of land. The crop proved to be celeriac, a less valuable species than the one he had ordered. The bag in which the seed had been sent bore a statement that "Utah Nursery . . . gives no warranty, express or implied, as to the description, quality, or productiveness of any seeds it sells." By custom and usage, seed vendors in Utah did not give warranties. Hoover sued the Utah Nursery Co. for damages. Holding? (Hoover v. Utah Nursery Co., 79 Utah 12, 7 P.(2d) 270)

3. Flynn sued Bedell Co. for damages to her person caused by a dyed fur collar on a coat which she had bought from the company. She testified that she had no experience in dealing with fur; that, overhearing another customer complain of a fur collar that had discolored her neck, she asked the clerk what kind of fur was on the coat she was examining and whether it was dyed, and was assured that it was black fox and was not dyed. Was there an implied warranty of suitability or fitness? (Flynn v. Bedell Co. of Massachusetts, 242 Mass. 450, 136 N. E. 252)

4. G. McClelland & Son sold Espe an automobile which they had bought from Mills and which had been transferred some nine times before Mills became the owner. The car proved to have been stolen and the motor number changed. A statute forbade the possession of a car in this condition, and the sheriff took the car from Espe. She sued G. McClelland & Son to recover the price she had paid them for it. The defense was that the defects in the car were latent, that there was no implied warranty covering latent defects, and that Espe had had an equal opportunity with the dealer to detect any defects. Judgment for whom? (Espe v. G. McClelland & Son, 268 Iowa 512, 226 N. W. 130)

5. The Buick Motor Co. sold one of its cars to a retail dealer, who in turn sold it to MacPherson. While he was driving the car, one of the wheels suddenly collapsed, and he was thrown from the car and injured. The defective wheel had been purchased by the Buick Motor Co. from another manufacturer, but its defects could have been discovered by reasonable inspection at the factory. MacPherson sued the Buick Motor Co. in tort, alleging negligence. The company defended on the ground that it owed no duty of care and vigilance to anyone but the immediate purchaser. Judgment for whom? (MacPherson v. Buick Motor Co., 217 N. Y. 382, 111 N. E. 1050)

6. Tinius Olsen Testing Machine Co. manufactured especially for Wolf Co. a machine designed to determine the balance of certain rotary parts. One of the warranties on the machine was that it would indicate directly the amount of imbalance without the necessity of using charts or making mathematical calculations. This warranty was breached; and a month after the machine had been set up, Wolf Co. notified the machine company of this fact and demanded a rescission of the contract. The machine company brought suit for the amount due on the machine. Was Wolf Co. entitled to a rescission? (Tinius Olsen Testing Machine Co. v. Wolf Co., 297 Pa. 153, 146 A. 541)

Performance and
Remedies

30

PERFORMANCE

In the case of a sale or a contract to sell, it is the obligation of the seller to transfer and deliver [1] the goods and the duty of the buyer to accept and pay for the goods, in accordance with the terms of the contract. If the parties have not agreed that credit is to be extended by the seller to the buyer, it is presumed that a sale or a contract to sell is a cash transaction. This means that delivery of the goods and payment of the purchase price are concurrent conditions. The seller must be ready and willing to give possession of the goods to the buyer in exchange for the price, and the buyer in turn must be ready and willing to pay the price in exchange for possession of the goods.

Sec. 2–310 (a) of the Uniform Commercial Code states that unless otherwise agreed payment is due at the time and place at which the buyer is to receive the goods even though the place of shipment is the place of delivery.

DELIVERY

Sec. 2–307 of the Code states that unless otherwise agreed, all goods called for by a contract for sale must be tendered in a single delivery and payment is due only on such tender; but where the circumstances give either party the right to make or demand delivery in lots, the price if it can be apportioned may be demanded for each lot.

In the absence of a specified place for delivery, Sec. 2–308 of the Code provides that unless otherwise agreed the place for delivery of goods is the seller's place of business or if he has none, his residence; but in a con-

---

[1] "Delivery" in this sense means tendering possession of the goods in exchange for the purchase price.

711

tract for sale of identified goods which to the knowledge of the parties at the time of contracting are in some other place, that place is the place for their delivery; and documents of title may be delivered through customary banking channels.

MANNER OF SELLER'S TENDER OF DELIVERY

Sec. 2–503 provides that (1) tender of delivery requires that the seller put and hold conforming goods at the buyer's disposition and give the buyer any notification reasonably necessary to enable him to take delivery. The manner, time, and place for tender are determined by the agreement and the U. C. C., and in particular (a) tender must be at a reasonable hour, and if it is of goods they must be kept available for the period reasonably necessary to enable the buyer to take possession; but (b) unless otherwise agreed the buyer must furnish facilities reasonably suited to the receipt of the goods.

(2) Where the case is within the next section respecting shipment, tender requires that the seller comply with its provisions.

(3) Where the seller is required to deliver at a particular destination tender requires that he comply with subsection (1) and also in any appropriate case tender documents as described in subsections (4) and (5) of this section.

(4) Where goods are in the possession of a bailee and are to be delivered without being moved, (a) tender requires that the seller either tender a negotiable document of title covering such goods or procure acknowledgment by the bailee of the buyer's right to possession of the goods; but (b) tender to the buyer of a non-negotiable document of title or of a written direction to the bailee to deliver is sufficient tender unless the buyer seasonably objects, and receipt by the bailee of notification of the buyer's rights fixes those rights as against the bailee and all third persons; but risk of loss of the goods and of any failure by the bailee to honor the non-negotiable document of title or to obey the direction remains on the seller until the buyer has had a reasonable time to present the document or direction, and a refusal by the bailee to honor the document or to obey the direction defeats the tender.

(5) Where the contract requires the seller to deliver documents, (a) he must tender all such documents in correct form, except as provided in this Article with respect to bills of lading in a set and (b) tender through customary banking channels is sufficient and dishonor of a draft accompanying the documents constitutes non-acceptance or rejection.

Sec. 2–504 of the Code states that where the seller is required or authorized to send the goods to the buyer and the contract does not require him to deliver them at a particular destination, then unless otherwise agreed he must put the goods in the possession of such a carrier and make such a contract for their transportation as may be reasonable having regard to the nature of the goods and other circumstances of the case; and obtain and promptly deliver or tender in due form any document necessary to enable the buyer to obtain possession of the goods or otherwise required by the agreement or by usage of trade; and promptly notify the buyer of the shipment. Failure to promptly notify the buyer of the shipment of the goods or failure to put the goods in the possession of the carrier and make a contract for their transportation is a ground for rejection only if material delay or loss ensues.

Sec. 2–505 provides that a seller may retain a security interest in the goods shipped where the seller has identified goods to the contract by or before shipment: his procurement of a negotiable bill of lading to his own order or otherwise reserves in him a security interest in the goods. His procurement of the bill to the order of a financing agency or of the buyer indicates in addition only the seller's expectation of transferring that interest to the person named: a non-negotiable bill of lading to himself or his nominee reserves possession of the goods as security, but except in a case of conditional delivery a non-negotiable bill of lading naming the buyer as consignee reserves no security interest even though the seller retains possession of the bill of lading. When shipment by the seller with reservation of a security interest is in violation of the contract for sale, it constitutes an improper contract for transportation within the preceding section but impairs neither the rights given to the buyer by shipment and identification of the goods to the contract nor the seller's powers as a holder of a negotiable document.

Sec. 2–507 of the Code states that tender of delivery is a condition to the buyer's duty to accept the goods and, unless otherwise agreed, to his duty to pay for them. Tender entitles the seller to acceptance of the goods and to payment according to the contract. Where payment is due and demanded on the delivery to the buyer of goods or documents of title, his right as against the seller to retain or dispose of them is conditional upon his making the payment due.

Sec. 2–508 states that where any tender or delivery by the seller is rejected because non-conforming and the time for performance has not yet expired, the seller may seasonably notify the buyer of his intention to cure and may then within the contract time make a conforming delivery. Where the buyer rejects a non-conforming tender which the seller had reasonable grounds to believe would be acceptable with or without money allowance, the seller may, if he seasonably notifies the buyer, have a further reasonable time to substitute a conforming tender.

ACCEPTANCE

A buyer is held to have accepted the goods if they are tendered to him and he intimates to the seller that he has accepted them, or if the goods have been delivered to him and he performs some act in relation to them which is inconsistent with the ownership of the seller (for example, if he sells a part or all of them to some third party), or if, after the lapse of a reasonable time, he retains the goods without intimating to the seller that he has rejected them. Sec. 2–606 (2) states that acceptance of a part of any commercial unit is acceptance of that entire unit.

As a general rule, the buyer is not deemed to have accepted the goods until he has had a reasonable opportunity to inspect or examine them to ascertain whether they conform to the terms of the contract. Opportunity to inspect is held to be a condition precedent to the buyer's obligation to pay the purchase price. He may, however, contract to pay before inspection. A familiar example of this situation is a C. O. D. sale, where as a rule the buyer must accept delivery of the goods and pay for them before he may inspect them. This same rule applies when goods are shipped to the buyer under an order bill of lading with draft attached, which the buyer is required to pay or accept before he can secure the bill of lading and thus obtain possession of the goods.

Acceptance of the goods by the buyer does not bar an action for damages against the seller for breach of any promise or warranty in the contract, provided the buyer gives notice to the seller of such breach within a reasonable time after the buyer knows, or ought to know, of it.

Sec. 2–607 of the Code states that the buyer must pay at the contract rate for any goods accepted. Where the goods have been accepted by the buyer, and there is a claim for infringement or breach of warranty and the buyer is sued as a result of such infringement or breach of warranty, he must notify the seller within a reasonable time after he receives notice of the litigation or be barred from any remedy against the seller for liability established by the litigation.

Unless the parties have agreed otherwise, a buyer need not return goods that have been wrongly delivered. It is sufficient if he notifies the seller that he refuses to accept them. It is the seller's responsibility to arrange to have the goods returned to him.

If the seller is ready and willing to deliver the goods and requests the buyer to take delivery, and the buyer does not accept delivery within a reasonable time after such request is made, he is liable to the seller for any loss occasioned by his neglect or refusal to take delivery. He is also liable for a reasonable charge for the care and custody of the goods.

Julian C. Cohen Salv. Corp. v. Eastern Elec. Sales Co.
205 Pa. Super. 26, 206 A. (2d) 331 (1965)

This is an action by Julian C. Cohen Salvage Corporation (plaintiff) against Eastern Electric Sales Company (defendant). Judgment for plaintiff, and defendant appealed. Affirmed.

The undisputed facts are as follows:

In the later part of June, 1963, plaintiff, located in Bladensburg, Maryland, and defendant, located in Philadelphia, both acting by a duly authorized agent, had a telephone conversation in which plaintiff advised defendant that it had a quantity of electric cable for sale. Arrangements were made for defendant to send one of its employees to Bladensburg, Maryland to examine the cable. After this employee examined the cable and returned to Philadelphia, another oral conversation transpired as a result of which plaintiff shipped the cable, weighing 36,440 pounds, to defendant in Philadelphia. The cable was run off plaintiff's reels to defendant's reels, and was taken by defendant's employees and placed in defendant's warehouse, where it still remains.

PER CURIAM. The plaintiff brought this action in assumpsit for the cable allegedly sold and delivered. The defendant's position at trial was two-fold: (1) there was no contract between the parties, and (2) even if there was a contract it is unenforceable because of the statute of frauds.

Defendant's reliance on the Statute of Frauds to vitiate this contract is misplaced. Section 2–201 (1) of the Uniform Commercial Code (12A P. S., Sec. 2–201 (1) provides that a contract for the sale of goods in excess of $500 is not enforceable "Unless there is some writing sufficient to indicate that a contract for sale has been made between the parties and signed by the party against whom enforcement is sought, or by his authorized agent or broker."

In this case plaintiff introduced into evidence a written sales order which contained plaintiff's name, the notation, "SOLD TO: Eastern Electric," the date, the name of the shipper, the quantity and description of the goods, and the weight of the goods, as well as the notation, "Your Order Number," and "Our Sales Number." This form was admittedly signed by an authorized agent of the defendant's company. This writing was sufficient to satisfy the requirements of the Statute of Frauds. "All that is required is that the writing afford a basis that the offered oral evidence rests on a real transaction." Uniform Commercial Code, No. 1, to Sec. 201.

See also *Harry Rubin & Sons, Inc. v. Consolidated Pipe Co. of America, Inc.*, 396 Pa. 506, 153 A. (2d) 472 (1959). As stated in that case, at page 512, 153 A. (2d) at page 476. "Its object is the elimination of certain formalistic requirements adherence to which often resulted in injustice, rather than the prevention of fraud." This writing clearly afforded a basis for believing that the oral evidence rests on a real transaction. The fact that price was omitted (and it was the only relevant term omitted) is not fatal since "A writing is not insufficient because it omits * * * a term agreed upon. * * *" 12A P. S., Sec. 2–201 (1). See also, Pennsylvania Bar Association Notes to this section.

There is another reason why the Statute of Frauds does not preclude a verdict for plaintiff in this case. Sec. 2–201 (3) (c) of the Code (12A P. S., Sec. 2–201 (3) (c)) provides: "A contract which does not satisfy the requirements of subsection (1) but which is valid in other respects is enforceable with respect to goods which have been received and accepted." That the cable was received there can be no doubt. After it was received by defendant it was run from one reel to another by several of the defendant's employees who admitted they inspected it at that time. It was then tagged and placed in the defendant's warehouse, where it remains.

In order to avoid the conclusion that defendant had accepted the cable, defendant offered testimony that it had notified plaintiff of its rejection shortly after the cable was received. However, there was no written notice of rejection. Moreover, the testimony that defendant notified plaintiff of the rejection of these goods is not credible, particularly in view of the fact that defendant still has the cable in its possession and has never offered to return it or attempted to return it to the plaintiff.

Therefore, in view of its failure to act with respect to the cable it is clear that the defendant accepted the goods in question and a valid and enforceable contract exists between the parties. Sec. 2–606 (1) (b) and Sec. 2–602 of the Uniform Commercial Code. (12A P. S., Sec. 2–606 (1) (b) and 12A P. S., Sec. 2–602.)

There is due and owing the plaintiff the sum of $7,200.11, including interest to the date of the verdict, for goods sold and delivered under the terms of the contract and the court entered a verdict for this amount.

Accordingly, and for the foregoing reasons, defendant's exceptions to the findings and verdict of the Trial Judge are dismissed.

Marbelite Company v. City of Philadelphia
208 Pa. Super. 256, 222 A. (2d) 443 (1966)

This is an action by The Marbelite Company, Inc. (plaintiff) against The City of Philadelphia (defendant). Judgment for plaintiff and defendant appealed. Affirmed.

Plaintiff filed an action in assumpsit seeking to recover the contract price of certain traffic signal equipment purchased by the City. This equipment was delivered to defendant in June and July of 1962, and is being used by the City of Philadelphia. Said defendant by way of New Matter in its answer contends that the equipment did not meet specifications and was not accepted by it. It further asserts that plaintiff at the time it was issued the purchase orders had on its payroll certain of defendant's employees who improperly permitted plaintiff to obtain bids, and that the orders were obtained as a result of rigged bidding. Finally, defendant states that plaintiff failed to exhaust its administrative remedies in accordance with the Philadelphia Home Rule Charter.

Plaintiff's reply denies that the employment by it of city employees as consultants was unlawful. It pleads that it properly and lawfully submitted its bids and received its orders in strict compliance with the Home Rule Charter and all other applicable provisions of the law. Moreover, it denied that any of the materials was faulty or failed to meet specifications in any manner. It was on this state of the record that plaintiff filed a motion for judgment on the pleadings.

PER CURIAM. In analyzing the pleadings under the applicable statutes and principles of law, we believe that as a matter of law the defendant accepted the traffic signal equipment. Sec. 2–606 of the Uniform Commercial Code 12A P. S., Supp. p. 66, defines "acceptance" as follows: "(1) Acceptance of goods occurs when the buyer * * * (c) does any act inconsistent with the seller's ownership; * * *"

Defendant City in its answer or New Matter does not deny that it is using the equipment. Nor does it state the manner, if any, that it was damaged or harmed by the alleged failure to comply with certain specifications, or the manner in which the purchase orders were issued or the bids obtained.

We believe the use of the equipment by defendant is patently inconsistent with the seller's ownership and, therefore, constitutes acceptance under the Uniform Commercial Code: *Lang v. Fleet*, 22 Pa. Dist. & Co. R. (2d) 361, affirmed per curiam *F. W. Lang Co. v. Fleet*, 193 Pa. Super. 365, 165 A. (2d) 258.

Since we have determined that defendant accepted the equipment he is obligated to pay the contract price therefor. Payment would not in any manner preclude defendant from seeking such affirmative relief as may exist for the alleged failure of the equipment to comply with specifications.

The City had ample time to inspect, examine and test the equipment to determine whether the goods were of the quality warranted. Despite this it has never offered to return the traffic signal equipment, or to claim monetary damages in any amount. Its position appears to be that even though it has used the equipment for a long period of time and has suffered no harm, it is not obligated to pay any sum to plaintiff.

In view of the foregoing, we have heretofore entered judgment on the pleadings in favor of plaintiff, The Marbelite Company, Inc., and against defendant, City of Philadelphia.

UNPAID SELLER'S RIGHTS AGAINST THE GOODS

Where the buyer has not yet taken legal possession of the goods, the unpaid seller may be entitled, under carefully defined circumstances, to protect his interests by exercising certain rights against the goods.

SELLER'S REMEDIES ON DISCOVERY OF BUYER'S INSOLVENCY

Sec. 2–702 states that where the seller discovers the buyer to be insolvent he may refuse delivery except for cash including payment for all goods theretofore delivered under the contract, and stop delivery. Where the seller discovers that the buyer has received goods on credit while insolvent he may reclaim the goods upon demand made within ten days after the receipt, but if misrepresentation of solvency has been made to the particular seller in writing within three months before delivery, the ten-day limitation does not apply. Except as provided in this subsection the seller may not base a right to reclaim goods on the buyer's fraudulent or innocent misrepresentation of solvency or of intent to pay. The seller's right to reclaim goods is subject to the rights of a buyer in ordinary course or other good faith purchaser or lien creditor. Successful reclamation of goods excludes all other remedies with respect to them.

RIGHTS OF STOPPAGE IN TRANSIT

If the buyer is or becomes insolvent, the unpaid seller, if he has parted with possession of the goods, may retake possession of them at any time while they are still in transit, whereupon his rights with respect to them become the same as if he had never parted with their possession. If he has delivered part of the goods to the buyer, he usually has a right of stoppage in transit against the remainder.

Goods are deemed to be in transit from the time when they are delivered to the carrier for transmission to the buyer until the buyer or his agent takes delivery of them (either at their destination or before), or until the carrier, after their arrival at their appointed destination, acknowledges to the buyer or his agent that it holds the goods on his behalf. Moreover, they are deemed to be in transit if the buyer rejects delivery of them and they are still in the carrier's possession, even though the seller refuses to take them back by accepting possession of them. But if the carrier wrongfully refuses to deliver the goods to the buyer or his agent, the goods are held to be no longer in transit.

The unpaid seller may exercise his right of stoppage in transit in either of two ways: (1) he may obtain actual possession of the goods, or (2) he may give notice of his claim to the carrier. In the latter case, the carrier must use reasonable diligence to prevent delivery of the goods to the buyer. If it succeeds in thus carrying out the seller's stop order, it then owes the seller a duty to redeliver the goods to him, at his expense. However, if the goods have been shipped under an order bill of lading the carrier is not obligated to redeliver the goods to the seller unless the order bill of lading is surrendered to it for cancellation. The reason for this rule is that the seller may have sold and transferred the bill of lading to some third person, and if the third person is a bona fide purchaser for value he alone is entitled to obtain possession of the goods (U. C. C., Sec. 2–705).

Kasden v. New York, N. H. & H. R. Co.
104 Conn. 479, 133 A. 573 (1926)

This was an action of replevin by Harris Kasden and others (plaintiffs) against the New York, New Haven & Hartford Railroad Company (defendant). Louis H. Resnick and another, doing business as the American Steel & Iron Company, were cited in as defendants, and from judgment for them for $3,988 in damages, on their counterclaim, plaintiffs appealed. No error.

Plaintiffs claimed ownership and possession of 40,000 pounds of brass borings contained in a freight car in the possession of defendant railroad and located in the freight yard at Bridgeport.

On September 9, 1924, defendant American Steel & Iron Company shipped the carload of borings from Billerica, Mass. to themselves at Bridgeport, Conn., and the carrier, the Boston & Maine Railroad Company, issued to this defendant a straight bill of lading, naming it as both consignor and consignee, and plainly marked "non-negotiable." On September 13th defendant arranged, by telephone, to sell the metal to the Bridgeport Iron & Steel Co., and placed the following indorsement on the bill of lading: "Deliver to Bridgeport Iron & Metal Company or order, the American Steel & Iron Company, by Louis H. Resnick," and forwarded it to the Bridgeport Company. On Sunday, September 14th, defendant learned that the Bridgeport Company was insolvent, and on Monday morning notified agents of the New York, New Haven & Hartford Railroad Co., in whose possession, as connecting carrier, the car then was, that the car was not to be delivered to anyone but defendant. At the time the stop order was given, no demand had been made by or for the Bridgeport Company for delivery of the car. On September 15th, but subsequent to the receipt by the railroad company of the stop order, plaintiffs, who were engaged in the metal business in New Haven, purchased the carload of borings from the Bridgeport Company, paid $2,775 toward the purchase price, and received the bill of lading with the added indorsement, "Bridgeport Iron & Steel Co., Edward Goldberg, Treasurer." Thereafter, on the same day, plaintiffs presented the bill of lading to the railroad company and demanded the shipment, but the railroad company, because of receipt of the stop order, refused delivery. It did not appear that plaintiffs, at the time of their purchase of the shipment from the Bridgeport Iron & Steel Co., knew that the latter was insolvent or that delivery of the goods had been stopped by defendant.

HINMAN, J. The reasons of appeal present the propositions that the indorsement of the bill of lading by the defendant American Steel & Iron Co., in the form above stated, rendered the same negotiable; that the defendant, by such indorsement, is estopped from denying that the bill was negotiable; and that the defendant had no right of stoppage in transitu as against the plaintiffs, as purchasers in good faith.

The Act of Congress of August 29, 1916, relating to bills of lading, provides, in Section 1, that "Bills of lading issued by any common carrier for the transportation of goods . . . from a place in one state to a place in another state . . . shall be governed by this act." In Sec. 2 a "straight bill" is defined as one "in which it is stated that the goods are consigned or destined to a specified person," and in Sec. 6 it is provided that "a straight bill shall have placed plainly upon its face by the carrier issuing it 'nonnegotiable' or 'not negotiable.'" The trial court found that the present bill of lading was a straight bill, and plainly marked nonnegotiable. Section 29 provides: "A bill may be transferred by the holder by delivery, accompanied with an agreement, express or implied, to transfer the title to the bill or to the goods represented thereby. A straight bill cannot be negotiated free from existing equities, and the indorsement of such a bill gives the transferee no additional rights."

The very evident intention and accomplishment of the act is to make straight bills nonnegotiable, and if the form of indorsement by the Bridgeport Co. might, standing by itself, be regarded as an attempt to convert the bill into an order bill, such would be an alteration after issue, without authority from the carrier, and void under Section 13 as well as futile under Section 29. It is clear, then, that the form of the indorsement worked no change in the nature or effect of the bill, that it continued to be nonnegotiable, and both as to the original and subsequent transferees it is to be treated as subject to such limitations as are imposed by law upon such bills.

As between the defendant American Steel & Iron Co. as the sellers and the Bridgeport Iron & Metal Company as the original buyer and transferee, the rights and remedies of an unpaid seller, including the right of stoppage in transitu in case of the buyer's insolvency, manifestly would obtain.

The sale of the goods by the buyer while they are in transit does not deprive the seller of his right to stop the goods. Unless a negotiable document of title is negotiated for value or the seller has consented to the subsale, the right of stoppage in transitu still remains. Since the bill of lading here was not a "negotiable document of title," this established principle of law of sales would seem to be, of itself, sufficient to sustain the defendants' right of stoppage in transitu as against these plaintiffs as well as against the original buyer.

Under provisions of state bills of lading statutes which are similar to Section 29 of the federal act, it is held that indorsement of a nonnegotiable bill of lading is ineffectual to confer any additional right, and the transferee obtains only such interest as the transferor had.

The trial court was correct in concluding that the nonnegotiable bill of lading issued to the defendant American Steel & Iron Co. remained such notwithstanding the indorsement of it; that the plaintiffs were chargeable with knowledge of the nature of the bill and the title they obtained thereby; and that the defendant retained the right to stop the goods in transitu and effectively exercised that right, and hence was entitled to recover their agreed value. There was no error.

REMEDIES FOR BREACH OF THE CONTRACT

SELLER'S REMEDIES

The following remedies are available to the seller for breach of contract: (1) an action for the purchase price, or (2) an action for damages for non-acceptance of the goods, or (3) a right to resell.

ACTION FOR PURCHASE PRICE. Sec. 2–709 of the Code states that when the buyer fails to pay the price as it becomes due, the seller may recover, together with any incidental damages, the price of goods accepted or of conforming goods lost or damaged within a commercially reasonable time after risk of their loss has passed to the buyer; and of goods identified to the contract if the seller is unable after reasonable effort to resell them at a reasonable price or the circumstances reasonably indicate that such effort will be unavailing. Where the seller sues for the price, he must hold for the buyer any goods which have been identified to the contract and are still in his control except that if resale becomes possible, he may resell them at any time prior to the collection of the judgment. The net proceeds of any such resale must be credited to the buyer and payment of the judgment entitles him to any goods not resold. After the buyer has wrongfully rejected or revoked acceptance of the goods or has failed to make a payment due or has repudiated the contract, a seller who is held not entitled to the price shall nevertheless be awarded damages for non-acceptance.

ACTION FOR DAMAGES FOR NON–ACCEPTANCE OF THE GOODS. If the buyer wrongfully neglects or refuses to accept and pay for the goods, the seller may maintain an action against him for damages for non-acceptance. In this case the seller does not ask for a judgment for the full contract price but merely asks for a judgment for the damages suffered by him as a result of the buyer's refusal or failure to carry out his part of the contract.

The general rule as to the measure of damages is that the seller is entitled to the amount of the estimated loss directly and naturally resulting, in the ordinary course of events, from the buyer's breach of the contract. Sec. 2–708 of the Code provides that the measure of damages for non-acceptance or repudiation by the buyer is the difference between the market price at the time and place for tender and the unpaid contract price together with any incidental damages, but less expenses saved in consequence of the buyer's breach. If the measure of damages provided above is inadequate to put the seller in as good a position as performance would have done, then the measure of damages is the profit (including reasonable overhead) which the seller would have made from full performance by the buyer, together with any incidental damages with due allowance for costs reasonably incurred and with due credit for payments or proceeds of resale. If special circumstances are shown to exist, they will be taken into consideration in assessing the damages.

RESALE OF THE GOODS.   In the event of a breach by the purchaser of the contract to sell goods, the seller may resell the goods concerned or the undelivered balance thereof. Where the resale is made in good faith and in a commercially reasonable manner the seller may recover the difference between the resale price and the contract price together with any incidental damages, less expenses saved in consequence of the buyer's breach. Except as otherwise provided in the U. C. C. or unless otherwise agreed, resale may be at public or private sale. The aggrieved seller may identify and treat as the subject of resale goods which have demonstrably been intended for the particular contract even though those goods are unfinished. Where the goods are unfinished an aggrieved seller may in the exercise of reasonable commercial judgment for the purposes of avoiding loss and of effective realization either complete the manufacture and wholly identify the goods to the contract or cease manufacture and resell for scrap or salvage value or proceed in any other reasonable manner (see Sec. 2–704).

L. W. Foster Sportswear Co. v. Goldblatt Bros., Inc.
356 F. (2d) 906 (1966)

This is an action by L. W. Foster Sportswear Co., Inc. (plaintiff) against Goldblatt Brothers, Inc. (defendant). Judgment for defendant notwithstanding the verdict, and plaintiff appealed. Affirmed in part, reversed in part, and remanded.

This is a diversity action for recovery, under Count I, of a "balance due" on goods Foster, a Philadelphia clothing manufacturer, sold and delivered to Goldblatt of Chicago; and, under Count II, for damages for Goldblatt's alleged breach of contracts. The jury returned a verdict for Foster on Count I for $76,246.56; and a separate verdict for $20,830.26 in its favor on Count II. Judgment was entered on these verdicts. The district court ultimately granted Goldblatt's motion for judgment notwithstanding the verdict on Count I, entering judgment for Foster for $14,840.78, the amount defendant admitted was due plaintiff, plus interest; and denied Goldblatt's motion for judgment notwithstanding the verdict or a new trial on Count II, and Foster's motion to amend the original judgments on both counts to include 5 per cent statutory interest. Foster has appealed and Goldblatt has cross-appealed.

KILEY, C.J. We think the question of fact whether there were oral agreements authorizing the charging of the various debits was properly submitted to the jury. The jury could have decided, as it presumably did decide, that the evidence preponderated in favor of Foster. Thus there is no basis for sustaining the defense of accord and satisfaction on the theory of express agreement.

The district court instructed the jury that the measure of damages under Count II "is the difference between the agreed price and the market value of the goods in Chicago, Illinois, at the time the goods would have been delivered [if a delivery date was specified] * * * or at the time when defendant refused * * * to issue delivery instructions [if no delivery date was specified]. * * *" This was correct.[1] The record supports the instruction. We think Foster's theory of damages was proven and the instruction not erroneous.

The judgment notwithstanding the verdict on Count I is reversed. The judgment on Count II is affirmed. The cause is remanded with directions to reinstate the judgment entered on the verdict on Count I, and to amend the judgments on both counts to include an allowance of statutory interest at five (5) per cent per annum from June 27, 1959 to the date of the entry of the judgments.

Affirmed in part, reversed in part, and remanded.

BUYER'S REMEDIES

Under proper circumstances, one or another of the following remedies may be available to the buyer: (1) an action for non-conformity or defective goods, or (2) an action for damages for non-delivery, or (3) a suit for specific performance.

ACTION FOR NON–CONFORMITY OR DEFECTIVE GOODS. Sec. 2–714 of the Code permits the buyer to recover damages for non-conformity or defective goods. The Code states that where the buyer has accepted goods and has given notification to the seller regarding the defects or non-conformity, he may recover as damages the loss resulting in the ordinary course of events from the seller's breach as determined in any manner which is reasonable.

ACTION FOR FAILING TO DELIVER THE GOODS. If the property in the goods has not passed to the buyer, and the seller wrongfully neglects or refuses to deliver the goods, the buyer may maintain an action against the seller for damages for non-delivery. Since the goods do not belong to the buyer, he may sue only for the damages resulting from the breach

---

[1] This familiar measure of damages for non-acceptance is recognized both under the old sales law, see Ill. Rev. Stat. ch. 121½, Sec. 64(3) (1959 ed.), and the new Commercial Code, Ill. Rev. Stat. ch. 26, Sec. 2–708 (1965 ed.).

of the contract. The damages are measured by the loss directly and naturally resulting to the buyer, in the ordinary course of events, from the seller's breach of the contract. Where there is an available market for the goods, the measure of damages, in the absence of special circumstances, is the difference between the contract price and the market or current price of the goods at the time the buyer learned of the breach and the contract price together with any incidental and consequential damages, but less expenses saved in consequence of the seller's breach. Market price is to be determined as of the place for tender or, in cases of rejection after arrival or revocation of acceptance, as of the place of arrival.

SUIT FOR SPECIFIC PERFORMANCE. The general rule is that neither party to a contract to sell or a sale of personal property is entitled to a decree of specific performance in equity. However, there are exceptions to this general rule. If the goods are highly unusual or unique in nature, or if they are very difficult or impossible to obtain in the open market or from some other source, so that money damages are a markedly inadequate remedy, a court of equity may decree specific performance of the contract.[1]

Sec. 2–716 of the Code states that specific performance may be decreed where the goods are unique or in other proper circumstances. The decree for specific performance may include such terms and conditions as to payment of the price, damages, or other relief as the court may deem just. The buyer has a right to replevin for goods identified to the contract if after reasonable effort he is unable to effect cover for such goods, or if the circumstances reasonably indicate that such effort will be unavailing, or if the goods have been shipped under reservation and satisfaction of the security interest in them has been made or tendered.

McCormick Dray Line, Inc. v. Lovell
6 Lycoming 55, 13 Pa. D. & C. (2d) 464 (1957)

This is an action by McCormick Dray Line, Inc. (plaintiff) against John E. Lovell and Eudora F. Lovell (defendants). Judgment for plaintiff and defendants appealed. Judgment affirmed.

The complaint in this case was filed to compel defendants to specifically perform a contract for the sale of defendants' trucking business, its good will, a piece of real estate, and transfer of I. C. C. and P. U. C. certificates as owned by defendants.

GREEVY, J. The present contract calls for the transfer of I. C. C. and P. U. C. certificates of public convenience and for the sale of a going business and its

---

[1] In accordance with the doctrine of mutual remedies (see p. 314 above) this remedy is available under proper circumstances to both buyers and sellers.

good will. The actual damages of a vendor's failure to comply with such an agreement are impossible of precise calculation so that there is no adequate remedy at law. With respect to the remedy of specific performance the Uniform Commercial Code provides (12A P. S., Sec. 2–716): "(1) Specific performance may be decreed where the goods are unique or in other proper circumstances."

The I. C. C. and P. U. C. rights are unique and therefore proper subject of a decree of specific performance. "A decree for specific performance is not a matter of right but a matter of grace, and will not be granted unless plaintiff is clearly entitled thereto, and there is no adequate remedy at law, and the Chancellor believes that justice requires it": *Mrahunec v. Fausti*, 385 Pa. 64, 68.

"While it is sometimes stated that specific performance is not a matter of right but one of grace, it is established law that the discretion of the Chancellor in any given case must be exercised in accordance with accepted judicial principles. Where a contract is adjudicated to be one which does not offend against conscience, fairness and equity, the right to specific performance becomes one of right, and not merely of grace": *DiPompeo v. Preston*, 385 Pa. 512, 519.

In our opinion, filed May 24, 1957, we stated that specific performance may be decreed where the goods are unique and that Interstate Commerce Commission and Public Utility Commission rights are unique.

The test of uniqueness must be made in terms of the total situation which characterizes the contract and here, because specific performance attaches to a material portion of the subject matter of the contract, specific performance will be allowed to the entire contract. We find that plaintiff is ready, willing, desirous, prompt, eager and able to carry out the terms of the contract.

This is clearly a case for relief by specific performance and inasmuch as the contract involves accounting and adjustment between the parties and contains a warranty upon the part of defendant, John E. Lovell, it will be necessary for the court to retain jurisdiction in order to see that the contract is carried out according to its terms.

Because real estate is part of the subject matter of the contract between the parties and because of the uniqueness of the certificates of public convenience issued to defendant, John E. Lovell, by the Pennsylvania Public Utility Commission and the Interstate Commerce Commission, set forth in exhibit "A" of plaintiff's exhibit no. 1, attached to the complaint, plaintiff is entitled to specific performance upon defendants' part of the contract for the sale of defendant's, John E. Lovell's, trucking business.

MISCELLANEOUS PROVISIONS

PROOF OF MARKET PRICE

Sec. 2–723 of the Code states that if an action based on anticipatory repudiation comes to trial before the time for performance with respect to some or all of the goods, any damages based on market price shall be determined according to the price of such goods prevailing at the time when the aggrieved party learned of the repudiation. If evidence of a price prevailing at the times or places described in this article is not readily available, the price prevailing within any reasonable time before or after the time described or at any other place which in commercial judgment or under usage of trade would serve as a reasonable substitute for the one described may be used, making any proper allowance for the cost of transporting the goods to or from such other place. Evidence of a relevant price prevailing at a time or place other than the one described in this article offered by one party is not admissible unless and until he has given the other party such notice as the court finds sufficient to prevent unfair surprise.

LIQUIDATION OR LIMITATION OF DAMAGES

Sec. 2–718 of the Code states: (1) Damages for breach by either party may be liquidated in the agreement but only at an amount which is reasonable in the light of the anticipated or actual harm caused by the breach, the difficulties of proof of loss, and the inconvenience or nonfeasibility of otherwise obtaining an adequate remedy. A term fixing unreasonably large liquidated damages is void as a penalty.

(2) Where the seller justifiably withholds delivery of goods because of the buyer's breach, the buyer is entitled to restitution of any amount by which the sum of his payment exceeds (a) the amount to which the seller is entitled by virtue of terms liquidating the seller's damages in accordance with subsection (1), or (b) in the absence of such terms, 20 per cent of the value of the total performance for which the buyer is obligated under the contract or $500, whichever is smaller.

(3) The buyer's right to restitution under subsection (2) is subject to offset to the extent that the seller establishes (a) a right to recover damages under the provisions of this article other than subsection (1), and (b) the amount or value of any benefits received by the buyer directly or indirectly by reason of the contract.

(4) Where a seller has received payment in goods, their reasonable value or the proceeds of their resale shall be treated as payments for the purposes of subsection (2); but if the seller has notice of the buyer's breach before reselling goods received in part performance, his resale is subject to the conditions laid down in this article on resale by an aggrieved seller (Sec. 2–706).

STATUTE OF LIMITATION IN CONTRACTS FOR SALE

Sec. 2–725 of the Code provides: "(1) An action for breach of any contract for sale must be commenced within four years after the cause of action has accrued. By the original agreement the parties may reduce the period of limitation to not less than one year but may not extend it.

(2) A cause of action accrues when the breach occurs, regardless of the aggrieved party's lack of knowledge of the breach. A breach of warranty occurs when tender of delivery is made, except that where a warranty explicitly extends to future performance of the goods and discovery of the breach must await the time of such performance, the cause of action accrues when the breach is or should have been discovered.

"(3) Where an action commenced within the time limited by subsection (1) is so terminated as to leave available a remedy by another action for the same breach such other action may be commenced after the expiration of the time limited and within six months after the termination of the first action unless the termination resulted from voluntary discontinuance or from dismissal for failure or neglect to prosecute.

"(4) This section does not alter the law on tolling of the statute of limitations nor does it apply to causes of action which have accrued before this Act becomes effective."

REVIEW CASES

1. Moloney agreed to sell all the stock of the Ottawa Gaslight and Coke Co., which was not obtainable on the open market, to Cressler, who agreed to buy. Later Cressler changed his mind and refused to accept the stock. Moloney brought suit for specific performance. Judgment for whom? (Moloney v. Cressler, 236 F. 636)

2. Warren contracted to buy from Burrows & Kenyon certain quantities of lumber, a specified amount to be "merchantable long-leaf yellow pine, rough," and the rest of another variety. When the lumber arrived, there was too much of the first variety and too little of the second. Warren refused to accept the lumber, and Burrows & Kenyon sued. Ruling? (Burrows & Kenyon, Inc. v. Warren, 9 F.(2d) 1)

3. Ogden sold a quantity of apples under a credit arrangement to Sternick, who took an option to leave the apples in cold storage with Ogden until May 1st. Before the option time had expired, Ogden noticed signs of deterioration in the apples and urged Sternick to take them and pay for them, but Sternick refused. Ogden resold the apples to other parties and sued Sternick for the deficiency balance due on the contract price. Holding? (Ogden v. Sternick, 10 N. J. S. 194, 76 A.(2d) 909)

4. Leopold ordered a quantity of weighing scales from Rock-Ola Manufacturing Corp. on agreed terms, $1,500 cash and balance on credit. Leopold sent a check for $1,500 to Rock-Ola Corp. The check was returned marked "not sufficient funds"; however, it was eventually paid. Rock-Ola Corp. investigated Leopold, found that he was insolvent, and refused to carry out the contract unless paid in full in cash. Leopold refused, and his pay-

ment was returned to him. He bought the scales elsewhere and then filed this suit in damages. Holding? (Rock-Ola Manufacturing Corp. v. Leopold, 98 F.(2d) 196, 117 A. L. R. 1101)

5. Farrell agreed to sell and a customer agreed to buy a safe on credit. It was shipped by rail over the route of Richmond & D. R. Co. Before the safe reached the customer, Farrell learned that the customer was insolvent, and he had the safe stopped in transit. The railroad claimed the safe for a debt owed to it by the said customer of Farrell, and Farrell also claimed the safe. Who gets the safe? (Farrell v. Richmond & D. R. Co., 102 N. C. 390, 9 S. E. 302)

Commercial
Paper

part VI

Introduction

31

Negotiable instruments perform an exceedingly important function in modern economic life. They are constantly made use of in the business world, and practically everyone has occasion to use them in one form or another. It has been estimated that 90 per cent of our business is done on credit; and the extension of credit on this scale would be impossible without the use of negotiable instruments. They are therefore an indispensable part of our business life. The law relating to them is technical and somewhat difficult, yet their use is so widespread, and ignorance of their nature may be so costly, that everyone should make a special effort to acquire an understanding of them.

Before the creation of money as a medium of exchange, the little business that was transacted was carried on through bartering. The barter system was cumbersome and retarded the development of business and trade. For that reason money was devised as a medium of exchange. In order that it might serve this purpose, money has been endowed with certain legal characteristics so that the transferee may always be sure of acquiring good title to it whether his transferor had such title or not. If A purchases something from B and pays B with a $10 bill, B will get good title to the bill even though A stole it or found it, provided that B does not know that the bill was stolen or found. If this were not the law, money could not serve its true purpose of facilitating commerce and business. Money would lose much of its utility as a medium of exchange if the transferee were required to ascertain, at his peril, the title of the transferor. With few exceptions, the law is different in the sale of chattels. If A sells a watch to B, even though B is an innocent purchaser for value and without notice of any defects in A's title, B acquires only the title, if any, that A possessed. Consequently, if A were a thief or a finder, B would not acquire good title against the rightful owner of the watch. If X were the owner and B refused to surrender possession of the watch to him, X could either replevy the watch or recover damages for the conversion of the watch in an action of trover.

In this respect negotiable instruments stand somewhere between money and chattels. The transferee of a negotiable instrument is given less protection than the transferee of money, but he is given much more protection than the purchaser or transferee of tangible personal property. Though negotiable instruments lack the complete and full negotiability of money, they possess characteristics which enable them to do much of the work of money in serving as a medium of exchange and which account for their widespread use as credit instruments. The legal attributes which make these functions possible are discussed in the following chapters.

ORIGIN AND DEVELOPMENT

Negotiable instruments are not of recent origin; some authorities trace their use back as far as the Egyptian and Babylonian empires. They were known to the Romans and to the traders of the Mediterranean world during the Dark Ages. Our modern negotiable instruments trace their beginning back to the merchants and traders of the Middle Ages, and our present-day law of negotiable instruments has its roots in the law merchant, which embodied the usages and customs of those medieval businessmen. In the course of time the law merchant was absorbed into the common law.

The bill of exchange was the first type of negotiable instrument devised and used by the merchants. It sprang from practical necessity. As the merchants traveled about from one international fair to another, carrying with them gold and silver to pay for the things they purchased, they were constantly in danger of theft and loss. To circumvent this danger they established the custom of depositing their gold and silver, first with the goldsmiths and silversmiths, and later with the bankers, and accepting in return a piece of paper or memorandum evidencing the transaction. The practice of "drawing" upon these accounts, in the payment of purchases, by ordering the holder of the funds to pay specified sums to designated payees (sellers) finally resulted in the bill of exchange. Thus it became possible to make purchases and to transfer credit from the buyer to the seller without actually carrying gold and silver about. The promissory note was devised during the latter part of the sixteenth century and was finally made negotiable by an act of Parliament early in the eighteenth century. Checks had their advent soon after promissory notes came into use.

In this country the courts of the colonies and of the early states were greatly influenced by the law merchant and the decisions handed down by the courts of England. The decisions of the various courts were not always uniform, but during the early history of the nation this mattered little. Transportation and communication were difficult, and there was little trade and commerce between the various states. But as new states were added and trade and commerce developed on a larger scale, lack of uniformity in the law of the various states in regard to negotiable instruments became an increasingly serious handicap. This was especially felt after the Civil War, when the frontier was pushed on to the Pacific, many new states were admitted to the Union, better means of transportation and communication developed, and merchants began to operate upon the basis of a national market. Demands grew for greater uniformity in the law of "bills and notes" or "commercial paper," particularly after 1882, when the British codified their law of negotiable instruments. Finally in 1894, through the efforts of the American Bar Association and the American Bankers Association, a Committee on Commercial Law was appointed to prepare a model act covering negotiable instruments. By 1896 a draft was ready, and the various state legislatures were urged to adopt the model act. The following year nine states enacted the act, which was called the Uniform Negotiable Instruments Law, and by 1924 it had been adopted, in some instances with minor modifications, by every state in the Union, together with the District of Columbia, Hawaii, and Alaska.

The N. I. L., as it is generally referred to, did much to bring about uniformity in the law of negotiable instruments in this country. The drafters of the act did not attempt to reform the law of negotiable instruments but to make it uniform. In most respects there were no conflicts in the law in the various states; only where there was a "split in authority" on some point of law did the drafters have to make a choice. Since the preparation and adoption of the N. I. L., new banking and business practices have developed; moreover, decisions of the various state courts on some matters covered by the N. I. L. exhibit inconsistencies, and in certain areas considerable uncertainty exists in the law. For these reasons the National Conference of Commissioners on Uniform State Law and the American Law Institute, which drafted the Uniform Commercial Code in 1950, undertook a complete overhaul and modernization of the law pertaining to negotiable instruments. This revision appears as Article 3 of the Code, under the title "Commercial Paper."

UNIFORM COMMERCIAL CODE

Since all states except Louisiana have adopted the Uniform Commercial Code, the following discussion is based upon its provisions.

TYPES OF COMMERCIAL PAPER

There are two basic types of commercial paper: drafts or bills of exchange and checks, which are orders to pay; and promissory notes and certificates of deposit, which are promises to pay. The Uniform Commercial Code lists them separately as follows: (1) drafts (bills of exchange), (2) promissory notes, (3) checks, and (4) certificates of deposit.

DRAFT (BILL OF EXCHANGE)

A draft or bill of exchange is defined as an unconditional order in writing addressed by one person to another, signed by the person giving the order, requiring the person to whom it is addressed to pay on demand or at some definite time a sum certain in money to order or to bearer.

$500.00   January 2, 1975

Thirty days after date-----------------------Pay to

the order of James Brown -------------------------

Five Hundred and no/100--------------------Dollars

Value received and charged the same to the account of

To: Ronald Parks
       College Park, Maryland   *George Dokes*

DRAFT (BILL OF EXCHANGE)

It should be carefully noted that a draft or bill of exchange is an order to pay money. Three original parties are involved: (1) the *drawer*, who gives the order; (2) the *drawee*, to whom the order is given; and (3) the *payee*, who is to receive the money. If the drawee accepts the order and agrees to pay, he becomes the *acceptor*. Actually, the money is payable to the payee or his order, or to bearer. Consequently, the payee may, if he wishes, transfer his rights under the instrument to someone else. If he does so by indorsement and delivery, he is called the *indorser* (or *transferor*), and the party to whom he transfers the instrument is called the *indorsee* (or *transferee*).

PROMISSORY NOTE

A promissory note is defined as an unconditional promise in writing made by one person to another signed by the maker engaging to pay on demand, or by a definite time, a sum certain in money to order or bearer.

$500.00   January 2, 1975

Ninety (90) days after date I promise to pay to the

order of James Brown----------------------------------

Five Hundred and no/100----------------------- Dollars

Value Received.

No. 567   Due 4-2-69   *George Dokes*

PROMISSORY NOTE

It should be observed that a negotiable promissory note is a *promise* to pay money. There are two original parties to a note: (1) the *maker*, who promises to pay the money, and (2) the *payee*, to whom the maker promises to pay the money. As in the case of a bill of exchange, the money is payable to a named payee or his order, or to bearer. If the payee transfers his rights under the instrument to someone else by indorsing and delivering the instrument, he is known as an *indorser* (or *transferor*), and the party to whom he transfers the instrument is known as the *indorsee* (or *transferee*).

January 2, 1975   No. 178

COLLEGE PARK STATE BANK
College Park, Maryland

Pay to the
    Order of James Brown----------------------$500.00

Five Hundred and no/100----------------------Dollars

For: One Motor Scooter #603   *George Dokes*

CHECK

CHECK

A check is defined as a draft (bill of exchange) drawn on a bank payable on demand. A check is nothing more than a special type of bill of exchange.

There are various types of bills of exchange or drafts, based primarily upon the use to which they are put. Aside from checks, the most common types are: (1) bank drafts, (2) bank acceptances, and (3) trade acceptances.

BANK DRAFT

Basically, a bank draft is a check drawn by one bank on another bank. Personal checks, as everyone knows, are not always acceptable as payment for goods or services. Unless A is well known to B, B may hesitate to accept A's check, because he is not certain of A's credit. But if A has a bank draft in which he is named as payee, B will probably accept the draft, for he has faith in the credit of the drawer and drawee named in the draft. Since bank drafts provide a safe and satisfactory method of transferring funds, banks provide such facilities to their customers. For instance, the X bank will keep a sizable amount of money on deposit with the Y bank (usually a well-known bank in some large city). If A is required to make a payment to B and B is unwilling to accept in payment A's personal check, A can go to the X bank and purchase a bank draft to remit to B. What actually happens is that the X bank writes a check (it is, of course, called a draft) against its account in the Y bank and gives it to A. A pays the X bank the amount of the check plus a small amount for the service, known as exchange. The X bank is the drawer of the draft, the Y bank is the drawee; the payee may be named as either A or B, as A prefers. If A is named as payee, he will have to indorse the draft before giving or sending it to B.

BANKER'S ACCEPTANCE

This type of bill of exchange is used in financing the purchase and sale of goods and commodities. The buyer arranges ahead of time for his bank to accept a draft (banker's acceptance) drawn upon it by the seller. The buyer is usually required to give his bank a promissory note covering the amount of the acceptance and to secure the note with sufficient collateral. Since a banker's acceptance has behind it the credit of the bank, it is readily discountable.

CERTIFICATE OF DEPOSIT

This form of bill of exchange is an acknowledgment by a bank of receipt of money with an engagement to repay it.

```
CERTIFICATE OF DEPOSIT

No. 674                                    January 2, 1975

              COLLEGE PARK STATE BANK
              College Park, Maryland            $500.00


James Brown  has deposited in this bank
Five Hundred and no/100--------------------- Dollars
Payable to James Brown  or order twelve (12) months
after date on return of this certificate properly indorsed with in-
terest at the rate of five (5) per cent per annum if allowed to
remain twelve (12) months.
No interest after twelve (12) months.      George Dokes
                                             President
```

CERTIFICATE OF DEPOSIT

A bank issues a certificate of deposit to borrow money usually for a
year or less, and no interest is earned unless the money is left on deposit
for a time specified in the instrument. To be negotiable, as any other negotiable instrument, it must be in writing, signed by the maker, contain
an unconditional promise to pay a sum certain in money, payable on demand or at a definite time, and be payable to order or bearer.

TRADE ACCEPTANCE

Another type of bill of exchange used by buyers and sellers of goods is
a draft drawn by the seller upon the buyer, who agrees ahead of time to
accept the draft for the amount of the goods purchased.

For example, A, a wholesaler in Baltimore, sells certain merchandise to
B, a retailer in Cumberland, Maryland. It is agreed that B shall have sixty
days in which to pay the obligation. B further agrees to accept a sixty-day
time draft drawn upon him by A for the full amount of the obligation. A
ships the merchandise via the B. & O. Railroad and receives an order bill
of lading. A prepares a draft (trade acceptance) for the amount due, attaches it to the bill of lading, and turns the instruments over to his bank,
which forwards them to a bank in Cumberland. The Cumberland bank
notifies B that his draft has arrived and asks him to come to the bank and
accept the draft. When B accepts the draft he is given the bill of lading
so that he may claim the merchandise from the railroad. Upon the expira-

No. 547 $500.00

                                        January 2, 1975

    On March 2, 1975, pay to the

Order of Ourselves------------------------------------

Five Hundred and no/100--------------------- Dollars

    This obligation of the acceptor hereof arises out of the purchase
of goods from the drawer. The acceptor may make this acceptance
payable at any bank, banker, or trust company in the United States
which he may designate.

To: James Brown (Drawee)
        100 Elm Street   *George Dokes*
        Dallas, Texas   *Robert Starnes*
Due: March 2, 1975   (Sellers–Drawers)

TRADE ACCEPTANCE

tion of sixty days the draft is presented to B and demand for payment is
made. The use of the trade acceptance in financing such transactions is
far superior to the open account. While a buyer may readily dispute the
amount of an open account, he may not dispute the amount of the debt
where a trade acceptance is used, since by accepting the draft he admits
the amount of the debt.

Bills of exchange may be either inland (or domestic) or foreign. An inland bill of exchange is a bill which is, or on its face purports to be, both
drawn and payable within the United States. A foreign bill of exchange
on its face appears to be drawn or payable outside of the states and territories of the United States and the District of Columbia (Section 3–501
(3), U. C. C.). Unless evidence to the contrary appears on the face of the
bill, the holder may treat it as an inland bill.

Negotiable promissory notes are usually classified on the basis of the
type of security given to secure the note. A *collateral note* is secured by
collateral which has been pledged, as represented by the pledge agreement. A *chattel mortgage note* is secured by a chattel mortgage. A *title-
retention note*, used where goods are sold under a conditional sales contract, is secured by the seller's retention of the title to the goods. A *judgment note* is not distinguished from other kinds of notes by the type of
security given but by a special provision in the note itself, which, in effect,
gives the payee the authority to take or confess judgment against the
maker without formal trial. In other words, if the maker defaults in the

payment of the note, the payee may file suit on the note and, without securing service on the maker, confess judgment against the maker when the case comes up for trial. Such a provision constitutes the payee the agent of the maker to confess judgment against him. Judgment notes are not valid in all states.

DIFFERENCE BETWEEN ASSIGNMENT AND NEGOTIATION

It is important at this point to distinguish between assignment and negotiation. The term *transfer* is a more general term which includes both assignment and negotiation. If a simple contract or a non-negotiable instrument is transferred, it is *assigned*. If a negotiable instrument is transferred, it is *negotiated*.

An important difference exists between the transfer of an instrument by assignment and the transfer of an instrument by negotiation. As we saw in an earlier chapter, an assignee of rights under a simple contract "steps into the shoes" of the assignor. Hence any defense which the obligor (the other party to the original contract) could set up against the obligee (assignor) he can set up against the assignee. For example, A sells B certain merchandise under a contract which contains an express warranty. A assigns his claim to payment to C. The warranty is breached, and B refuses to pay C, who thereupon files suit against B. B could set up the breach of the express warranty as a defense against C just as he could have set it up against A if there had been no assignment. In fact, any defense which B would have had against A he could set up against C.

The situation is different where a negotiable instrument is negotiated by the payee to some outside party. In that case the indorsee does not "step into the shoes" of the indorser. For example, A is the maker of a negotiable promissory note and B is the payee. If B sells and negotiates the note to C, an innocent purchaser for value without notice, most defenses which A could have set up against B if B had kept the note are "cut off" as against C. In other words, in most types of cases an indorsee is in a better position than his indorser. Actually, what takes place is that all *personal defenses* which A might have against B will be cut off if the instrument is negotiated to C, provided C is a holder in due course; [1] only *real defenses*, if any, may be set up against C. The difference between personal and real defenses is explained in detail in Chapter 34. It is desirable at this point, however, to give a few examples of each type of defense. Examples of personal defenses are lack or failure of consideration, breach of warranty, and payment. Examples of real defenses are forgery, infancy, and insanity.

---

[1] The requirements for a holder in due course are discussed in Chapter 34.

Requirements of
Negotiability

32

The existence of a debt, the obligation to pay it, and the right to receive payment may be evidenced either by a simple contract in writing or by a negotiable instrument. For example, A may sell and deliver to B certain merchandise under a written contract whereby B agrees to pay A $5,000 thirty days from date. The debt of B to A is evidenced by a simple contract in writing. The contract likewise evidences A's right to receive payment of the $5,000. If A should transfer his right or claim against B to C, the transfer would be accomplished by an assignment. But suppose that A delivers the merchandise to B and B gives A a negotiable promissory note for $5,000 payable in thirty days. Now B's obligation and A's right to receive the money are evidenced by a negotiable instrument. If A should transfer his right or claim against B to C, he would do so by negotiation.

The essential difference between the two instruments is a difference of *form*. To attain the status of a negotiable instrument, an instrument evidencing an obligation to pay a debt must meet certain formal requirements. If it meets them, it is ipso facto a negotiable instrument. If it fails to meet any one or more of them, it is not a negotiable instrument. In other words, if an instrument is negotiable, it is negotiable because of its form.

The requirements for a negotiable instrument are set forth in Sec. 3–104 of the U. C. C. as follows:

(1) Any writing to be a negotiable instrument within this article must
(a) be signed by the maker or drawer;
(b) contain an unconditional promise or order to pay a sum certain in money and no other promise, order, obligation, or power given by the maker or drawer except as authorized by this article;

(c) be payable on demand or at a definite time; and

(d) be payable to order or to bearer.

As between the immediate parties to the instrument, the obligor may set up against the holder any defense or defenses he may have, whether real or personal. This is the case both where the instrument is negotiable and where it is non-negotiable. And if the instrument is non-negotiable and the holder transfers (assigns) it to a third party, the obligor may set up both real and personal defenses against him. But if the instrument is negotiable and is transferred (negotiated) to a third party who is a holder in due course, the personal defenses of the obligor are cut off as against the third party (transferee). Hence, where an instrument has been transferred to one who qualifies as a holder in due course, and the obligor has some personal defense which he would like to set up against the transferee (plaintiff), the obligor must first be able to show that the instrument sued upon is non-negotiable. If he cannot do so, his defense is cut off. Many of the following cases illustrate this point.

The fact that an instrument is negotiable does not insure that it is valid or enforceable. An instrument that meets all the formal requirements and is therefore negotiable may be invalid and unenforceable because it does not meet the four essentials of a contract. For example, A fraudulently secures B's signature to a promissory note naming A as payee by telling him that the instrument is a petition which he wants B to sign. Even though the note meets all the formal requirements for a negotiable instrument, still it is invalid and unenforceable. To take another example, A, an infant, buys $500 worth of merchandise from B and signs a promissory note, in which he promises to pay the $500 six months from date. Since infancy is a real defense, A may set up the defense against B or any subsequent transferee. The note may meet all the formal requirements set out in Sec. 3–104 of the U. C. C., yet it would be uncollectible as against A, the infant.

As between the original parties to the instrument, consideration is required. If A (maker) gives B (payee) a note for $100, B cannot collect the note from A unless he has given A consideration for the note; if he has not done so, and if he sues A on the note, A may set up as a defense the lack of consideration. However, B does not have to allege and prove consideration; rather A must set up lack of consideration as a defense. Sec. 3–303 of the U. C. C. provides that a holder takes the instrument for value (a) to the extent that the agreed consideration has been performed or that he acquires a security interest in or a lien on the instrument otherwise than by legal process; or (b) when he takes the instrument in payment of or as security for an antecedent claim against any person whether or not the claim is due; or (c) when he gives a negotiable instrument for it or makes an irrevocable commitment to a third person.

Sec. 3–408 of the U. C. C. states, "want or failure of consideration is a defense as against any person not having the rights of a holder in due course (Sec. 3–305)." The U. C. C. expressly provides that a negotiable instrument must contain certain elements to be negotiable. For example, it is required to be "payable to order or bearer," the maker or drawer need not use the word "order" or the word "bearer" so long as he uses language which clearly indicates his intention to satisfy this requirement. However, as a matter of business expediency it is well to use the exact words set out in the act, so that no question may rise as to the intentions of the parties.

IN WRITING AND SIGNED

As we have seen, Sec. 3–104 of the U. C. C. provides that any writing in order to be a negotiable instrument must be signed by the maker or drawer. This section is couched in general terms and does not specify any particular method of writing or manner of signing the instrument. The application of these general rules in specific cases is left to the courts.

The courts have held that the instrument may be written upon any substance that is capable of receiving the writing, so long as the instrument possesses the quality of durability. Paper is, of course, the material universally used; but there is no *legal* objection to the use of other durable materials, such as wood, metal, or stone.

While it is the practice to use printed blank forms, the instrument may perfectly well be typed or handwritten.

The courts have held that the signature may be handwritten with pen or pencil, printed, typed, or affixed by means of a rubber stamp, so long as it is clear that the signer of the instrument adopted it as his signature and intended it as such. On the same condition an assumed name, or an "X" or other mark, will serve. The principal difficulty in such cases is the matter of proof. The signature of a party may be affixed by a duly authorized agent; the form to be used in such a case has been discussed in Chapter 20.

By common practice the signature of the maker or drawer usually appears in the lower right-hand corner of the instrument, but this is not required by the U. C. C. The signer may affix his signature wherever he likes, provided he makes clear the capacity in which he intended to sign.

It is not required that a negotiable instrument be dated, or that the place where it was drawn or the place where it is payable be indicated.[1]

[1] U. C. C., Sec. 3–114.

Leahy v. McManus

237 Md. 450, 206 A. (2d) 688 (1965)

This was an action by Emily Maury D. Leahy, executrix of the estate of Arthur Hamilton Leahy (plaintiff) against Charles E. McManus, Jr. and Multi-Krome Color Process, Inc. (defendants). Judgment for defendant, McManus, and against defendant Multi-Krome Color Process, Inc., and plaintiff appealed. Judgment affirmed.

This appeal is from a judgment absolving the individual appellee from personal liability on a note of the corporate appellee, on the ground that the former signed in a representative capacity.

The note, dated April 15, 1957, reads: "—Four months after date we promise to pay to order of A. Hamilton Leahy—One Thousand and no/100—Dollars Payable at ——. Without defalcation, value received, with interest." There follows authority to confess judgment. The note bears the stamped name of Multi-Krome Color Process, Inc. (the corporation); immediately below are the signatures and seals of the individual appellee, C. E. McManus, Jr. (McManus) and C. E. Delauney (Delauney), without designation of any representative capacity. A. Hamilton Leahy (Leahy), the payee of the note, died on October 10, 1962, and suit on the note was brought in the Circuit Court for Baltimore County by his executrix, the appellant herein. Judgment by confession was entered against both the corporation and McManus; McManus filed a motion to vacate the judgment, stating under oath that he had signed the note solely as an officer of the corporation; testimony was taken on the motion, and Judge Turnbull vacated the judgment against McManus, setting the case to be heard on the merits.

OPPENHEIMER, J. At the conclusion of the testimony, the lower court held that there was a *prima facie* case against McManus, but found that, on the evidence, Leahy knew that McManus and Delauney, were signing in representative capacities and accepted the note as the obligation of the corporation alone. The court's verdict was for McManus; the judgment against the corporation remained undisturbed.

The appellant's principal contention is that the lower court erred in finding that McManus signed the note only in a representative capacity. It is clear, as the appellant contends, that an endorsement can be written anywhere on the instrument; that a person may endorse a negotiable instrument in a representative capacity in such terms as to negative personal liability; and that, in the absence of such express negation, the endorser is liable to a holder for value. Code (1957) Art. 13, Sections 52, 65, 87. It has been held that ordinarily a corporation may validly sign an instrument by stamp. *Farmington State Bank v. Delaney*, 167 Minn. 394, 209 N. W. 311, 46 A. L. R. 1495 (1926); *Metropolitan Discount Co. v. Davis*, 69 Okl. 111, 170 P. 707, 7 A. L. R. 670 (1918). See generally, Annot. 46 A. L. R. 1498 (1927). Even though no holder for value is here involved, absent permissible evidence that McManus signed only in a representative capacity, he would be liable as a maker or an endorser.

As between the parties, in this State, while a person who signed a note made by a corporation is *prima facie* liable to the payee, if there is conflict in the evidence relative to the circumstances, the individual who signed that note is not liable if he affirmatively shows an understanding between him and the payee that there was to be no personal liability. *Belmont Dairy Co. v. Thrasher*, 124 Md. 320, 92 A. 766 (1914). While the Uniform Commercial Code was not in effect at the time of the transaction here involved, the Code embodies this principle. Code (1957) Art. 95B, Sections 3–402, 3–403.

In this case, there was ample evidence of ambiguity in the evidence as to the circumstances under which the note was executed. While there was no testimony of conversations between Leahy and McManus, the relationship of Leahy to the company, the fact that Delauney, who also signed the note, was one of the officers whose signature was required to bind the corporation, and Leahy's failure to attempt to hold McManus personally liable for over four years, were factors supporting McManus' contention of an understanding with Leahy that he, McManus, signed only in a representative capacity. We have considered all the evidence and do not find the judgment of the lower court was clearly erroneous. Maryland Rule 886 a.

The appellant argues that the testimony of McManus as to the capacity in which he signed the note should not have been admitted under the Dead Man's Statute, Code (1957) Art. 35, Section 3. However, this testimony was adduced only on cross-examination; an adverse party who is cross-examined as to a transaction with a decedent has been "called to testify by the opposite party" and therefore his answers are admissible under the express exception to the prohibitions of the statute. *Cooper v. Davis*, 226 Md. 371, 375, 174 A. (2d) 144 (1961) and cases therein cited.

Judgment affirmed; costs to be paid by appellant.

AN UNCONDITIONAL PROMISE OR ORDER TO PAY A SUM CERTAIN IN MONEY

Sec. 3–104 of the U. C. C. requires that an instrument, in order to be negotiable, "must contain an unconditional promise or order to pay a sum certain in money." Upon analysis it will be seen that this provision contains several separate requirements, which will be discussed in order.

UNCONDITIONAL PROMISE OR ORDER TO PAY

First of all, if an instrument purports to be a promissory note it must contain a *promise to pay*, and if it purports to be a bill of exchange or draft it must contain an *order to pay*. The U. C. C. does not require that the specific word "promise" or "order" be used in the instrument, but if it is not used, then the language that is used must convey an equivalent meaning.

For example, a mere acknowledgment of a debt, such as an I. O. U., is not equivalent to a promise to pay the debt. Similarly, a mere request or an authorization to pay is not equivalent to an order to pay.

Sec. 3–104 (b) makes it clear that the promise or order to pay must be *unconditional*. Sec. 3–109 (2) provides that an instrument payable upon a contingency is not negotiable, and the happening of the event does not cure the defect.

A promise or order to pay out of a particular fund is not unconditional. The theory behind this rule is that the general credit of the party primarily liable (the maker of a promissory note, or the acceptor of a bill of exchange) must be back of the instrument, and this is held not to be the case if the instrument is payable only out of a particular fund. But the mere indication of a particular fund out of which reimbursement is to be made, or of a particular account which is to be debited, does not make the instrument conditional. Nor does a notation indicating the transaction which gave rise to its existence; for example, "Payment of house rent for January, 1955," or "Payment in full of my account." These are treated as mere memoranda and do not affect the negotiability of the instrument.[1]

If the instrument is secured by a mortgage and bears on its face the statement that it is secured by a certain mortgage, recorded in the Office of the Recorder of Deeds, the instrument is negotiable. But if the statement is to the effect that the instrument is secured by a mortgage and is "subject to its terms and conditions," the instrument is not negotiable, and in the hands of a holder in due course is subject to both real and personal defenses.[2] It has been held that a statement "as per contract" does not affect the negotiability of the instrument, but that a statement that the payment of the instrument is "subject to the terms of the contract" destroys the negotiability of the instrument.

SUM CERTAIN

The sum payable at maturity must be certain, and must be determinable by reference to the instrument itself. If it is necessary to go outside the instrument in order to determine the amount due at maturity, the sum payable is not a "sum certain." For example, a note which provided for "the payment of all taxes levied against the property" was held not to be for a sum certain. But Sec. 3–106 of the U. C. C. provides that (1) The sum payable is a sum certain even though it is to be paid (a) with stated interest or by stated installments; or (b) with stated different rates of interest before and after default or a specified date; or (c) with a stated discount or addition if paid before or after the date fixed for payment; or

[1] U. C. C., Sec. 3–105.
[2] *Musto v. Grosjean et al.*, 208 Cal. 453, 281 Pac. 1022.

(d) with exchange or less exchange, whether at a fixed rate or at the current rate; or (e) with costs of collection or an attorney's fee or both upon default.

IN MONEY

Sec. 1–201 (24) of the Code states that "Money means a medium of exchange authorized or adopted by a domestic or foreign government as part of its currency." The promise or order to pay must be a promise or order to pay in *money;* no other form of payment will serve. This requirement is, in fact, the thing that largely distinguishes negotiable instruments from somewhat similar instruments, such as order bills of lading, order warehouse receipts, and corporate stocks. These types of instruments are said to be quasi-negotiable. They have most of the attributes of negotiability possessed by promissory notes and bills of exchange, but none of them contains a promise to pay a sum certain *in money*. Under such contracts the parties agree to do something other than pay money.

The negotiable character of an instrument otherwise negotiable is not affected by a provision which gives the holder an election to require something to be done in lieu of payment of money. For example, if A makes a promissory note in the amount of $1,000 payable to B or order, and the instrument contains a provision that it may be paid either in money or in wheat, at the option of the *holder* (who would be B or a subsequent transferee), the instrument would be negotiable. The reason for this is that such a provision does not limit in any way the holder's right to be paid in money if he so elects. Of course the act does not grant a similar option to the *maker* of a promissory note or the *acceptor* of a draft, for such a grant would clearly be incompatible with the holder's right to be paid in money.

An instrument containing an order or promise to do any act *in addition to* the payment of money is non-negotiable. But the negotiable status of an instrument is not affected by a provision authorizing the sale of collateral securities in case the instrument is not paid at maturity, or authorizing a confession of judgment under the same condition, or waiving the benefit of any law intended for the advantage or protection of the obligor.[1]

The U. C. C. provides that the validity and negotiable character of an instrument are not affected by the fact that it "designates a particular kind of current money in which payment is to be made." The intent of this provision was to resolve a conflict that existed in the decisions over the question whether an instrument which was expressed to be "payable in currency" or "payable in current funds" was "payable in money," and therefore negotiable. While the conflict was not completely settled by the

[1] U. C. C., Sec. 3–112.

incorporation of this provision in the U. C. C., it would appear that the overwhelming view of the courts today is to the effect that such instruments are negotiable.[1]

The courts are agreed that if the sum stated to be payable is payable in the legal tender of the country in which it is made payable, it is "payable in money." Thus, an instrument drawn in London and payable in New York in American money would be "payable in money." But what if it is made payable in New York in English pounds? While the earlier cases seem to hold that such an instrument would not be "payable in money," the more recent cases take the opposite view. The U. C. C. provides and the majority rule is that such instruments are negotiable.[2]

Merson v. Sun Insurance Company of New York
44 Misc. (2d) 131, 253 N. Y. S. (2d) 51 (1964)

This was an action by Erwin Merson (plaintiff) against Sun Insurance Company of New York (defendant). Judgment for plaintiff.

The defendant and drawer issued to the payee a bill of exchange by mistake. The payee endorsed the instrument to the plaintiff, who took it without notice of any defects and qualified as a holder in due course. The drawee bank did not accept the draft, and the plaintiff sued the defendant drawer to collect on the obligation.

GREENFIELD, J. The draft issued by the insurance company in this case was a fully negotiable bill of exchange (Negotiable Instruments Law, Pars. 20, 210). The words "upon acceptance" meant acceptance by the drawee bank (Negotiable Instruments Law, Par. 220). These words did not render the instrument conditional, since presentment for acceptance may be required for any check or bill of exchange (Negotiable Instruments Law, Par. 240; cf. Uniform Commercial Code, Secs. 3–410(2). A trade acceptance has always been deemed a negotiable instrument (*Citizens' Trust Co. of Utica v. R. Prescott & Son, Inc.,* 221 App. Div. 420, 422, 223 N. Y. S. 184, 187; *Atterbury v. Bank of Washington Heights,* 241 N. Y. 231, 239, 149 N. E. 841, 844; *Mintz v. Kerry,* 7 Misc. (2d) 76, 160 N. Y. S. (2d) 271; 11 American Jurisprudence (2d), Secs. 15, 146), a banker's acceptance even more so. Non-acceptance may be signified by the drawee bank either because it does not have sufficient funds of the drawer, or

[1] U. C. C., Sec. 3–107, provides that "(1) An instrument is payable in money if the medium of exchange in which it is payable is money at the time the instrument is made. An instrument payable in 'currency' or 'current funds' is payable in money."

[2] U. C. C., Sec. 3–107 (2): "A promise or order to pay a sum stated in a foreign currency is for a sum certain in money and, unless a different medium of payment is specified in the instrument, may be satisfied by payment of that number of dollars which the stated foreign currency will purchase at the buying sight rate for that currency on the day on which the instrument is payable, or, if payable on demand, on the day of demand. If such an instrument specifies a foreign currency as the medium of payment the instrument is payable in that currency."

because the drawer has instructed it not to pay—exactly as in the case of a negotiable check or note.

Plaintiff, to whom the instrument was endorsed by the payee, took without notice of any defect, and is a holder in due course. The drawee bank did not irrevocably accept the draft by notification or delivery, despite its tentative approval of it (*Philadelphia First National Bank v. National Park Bank*, 181 App. Div. 103, 168 N. Y. S. 422); hence the holder's right of recourse accrued against defendant, as the drawer (Negotiable Instruments Law, Sec. 248). The defense of mistake in issuing the instrument is of no avail against plaintiff.

D'Andrea v. Feinberg
45 Misc. (2d) 270, 256 N. Y. S. (2d) 504 (1965)

This was an action by Vincent P. D'Andrea and V. David Levitt (plaintiffs) against Samuel Feinberg and Sain Builders, Inc. (defendants). Judgment for defendant and plaintiff appealed. Judgment reversed, and summary judgment awarded to plaintiff.

The plaintiffs as holders in due course of a promissory note in the face amount of $4,000 have moved for summary judgment. The maker of the note is Sain Builders, Inc. and the note is executed on behalf of the maker by Samuel Feinberg as president. The note is endorsed by Samuel Feinberg in his capacity as president of the corporation and individually. The action was commenced against the corporation and against Samuel Feinberg individually.

DILLON, J. The note was duly presented for payment, was dishonored and protested. The corporate defendant is involved in bankruptcy proceedings in the Federal District Court and in connection therewith an order has been signed staying all actions against it until a final decree has been entered in the bankruptcy proceedings. Accordingly, the motion for summary judgment as against the corporation is denied.

On behalf of the individual defendant, it is urged that plaintiffs are not holders in due course because at the time they acquired the note they were aware of the existence of a contract between the corporate defendant and the payee of the note. This fact cannot be disputed because the note itself has endorsed thereon, in the lower left hand corner the legend "as per contract." It is argued that the endorser should not be held liable on the note until such time as the primary obligation between the maker and the payee has been resolved. The court is thus faced with two questions: (1) whether the note is a negotiable instrument; and (2) whether the plaintiffs are holders in due course.

The note meets all the requirements of Section 3–104 of the U. C. C. with the possible exception that it does not contain an unconditional promise because of the legend "as per contract." Section 3–105 (1) (c) expressly states that an unconditional promise "is not made conditional by the fact that the instrument * * * (c) refers to or states that it arises out of a separate agreement or refers to a separate agreement for rights as to prepayment or acceleration."

The official comment on the above quoted provision (*McKinney's Book* 62½, Part 2, page 27) is that it was "intended to resolve a conflict, and to reject cases in which a reference to a separate agreement was held to mean that payment of the instrument must be limited in accordance with the terms of the agreement, and hence was conditioned by it." The court is satisfied that the legend "as per contract" does not affect the negotiability of an instrument as would a statement that the instrument "is subject to or governed by any other agreement" (Uniform Commercial Code, Sec. 3–105 (2) (a); *Enoch v. Brandon*, 249 N. Y. 263, 164 N. E. 45).

The court determines that the note being sued upon is a negotiable instrument and that the plaintiffs are holders in due course. Since a cause of action against "an indorser of any instrument accrues upon demand following dishonor of the instrument," (Uniform Commercial Code, Sec. 3–122 (3)) it is clear that the plaintiffs need not first recover judgment against the maker as the individual defendant urges.

Accordingly, the action is severed and plaintiffs are awarded summary judgment as prayed for against the individual defendant.

PAYMENT ON DEMAND OR AT A DEFINITE TIME

Negotiable instruments could hardly serve as a useful substitute for money if they were not required to specify as a time of payment a time that is certain to arrive.

PAYABLE ON DEMAND

Sec. 3–108 of the U. C. C. provides that instruments payable on demand include those payable at sight or on presentation [1] and those in which no time for payment is stated.

In the case of a demand instrument, not only may the holder demand payment at any time, but the party who is required to pay the instrument may make payment at any time he chooses before the holder demands it. The courts have held that the time of payment in such types of instruments is not uncertain since the time of payment is immediately, subject to the option of the obligor not to tender payment immediately (unless it is demanded) and the option of the holder not to demand payment immediately.

PAYABLE AT A FIXED TIME

No difficulty arises as to the time of payment if the instrument specifies a definite due date. Thus, if the instrument specifies that it is payable on July 1, 1975, the time of payment is definite and fixed.

---

[1] The term "on demand" is usually used in the case of promissory notes, while "at sight" and "on presentation" are used in the case of bills of exchange.

PAYABLE AT A DEFINITE TIME

The time specified for payment need not be a fixed time, but it must be a time that is certain to arrive. Sec. 3–109 of the U. C. C. states that (1) An instrument is payable at a definite time if by its terms it is payable (a) On or before a stated date or at a fixed period after a stated date; or (b) at a fixed period after sight; or (c) at a definite time subject to any acceleration; or (d) at a definite time subject to extension at the option of the holder, or to extension to a further definite time at the option of the maker or acceptor or automatically upon or after a specified act or event.

(2) An instrument which by its terms is otherwise payable only upon an act or event uncertain as to time of occurrence is not payable at a definite time even though the act or event has occurred. Thus an instrument may specify that it is payable "30 days after date," or "30 days after sight," or "on or before May 1, 1975." But as we have already seen, an instrument payable upon a *contingency* is not negotiable, and the happening of the event does not cure the defect. An instrument made payable "when I reach the age of 25" is payable upon a contingency and is, therefore, not negotiable, nor does it become negotiable when the maker or drawer becomes 25. The same would be true of an instrument made payable "30 days after my return from a trip around the world," or "upon the arrival of the Queen Mary at the port of New York." In such cases the time is not "definite" since the contingency specified may never happen.

It is not uncommon for the parties to place in an instrument an *acceleration clause*. Such a clause has the effect of moving forward the date of payment of the instrument. The clause may provide that the acceleration is to occur automatically upon the happening of a specified act or event, or that it is to be at the election of either the holder of the instrument or the party primarily liable to pay the instrument (maker or acceptor).

It is sometimes of considerable convenience to the obligor or debtor if he is privileged to pay the instrument prior to the date specified in the instrument. If he can do so he can discharge the debt and stop the running of the interest. This may be accomplished by incorporating in the instrument a provision (acceleration clause) to the effect that it is payable "on or before" a designated date, say, April 13, 1975. The instrument would be held to be payable at a definite time, for it would be payable in any event on April 13, 1975. In financing the purchase of a house it is often provided that the note is payable on a certain date but that the maker is privileged to pay the balance due or any part of it at any time or at some specified time, such as an interest-paying date. Sometimes such provisions place a minimum upon the amount that may be paid as part payment. Such an acceleration clause does not prevent an instrument, otherwise negotiable, from being negotiable.

A study of the cases reveals a rather wide variety of clauses which provide for the acceleration of the time of payment of the instrument at the option of the holder. The courts have held that some of these clauses do not affect the negotiability of the instrument, but with respect to others there is a lack of unanimity among the courts.

An installment note frequently contains an acceleration clause providing that in case of default in the payment of an installment, or of interest, the holder may, at his election, demand immediate payment of the balance due on the note. The courts quite generally hold that such an acceleration clause does not affect the negotiability of the note.

Most courts, but not all, hold that an instrument is not negotiable if it provides for the acceleration of the payment date at the option of the holder if the maker fails to furnish additional collateral, on demand of the holder, to make up for the depreciation of the security originally pledged by the maker. The courts taking this view hold that such a provision not only makes the time of payment uncertain but also requires the maker to do something in addition to the payment of money, namely, furnish additional security.

An overwhelming majority of the courts holds that an instrument is negotiable even though it is payable on a fixed date and contains an acceleration clause which permits the holder to demand immediate payment of the instrument if he deems himself insecure. Such a provision in a demand instrument does not affect the rights of the parties, since the holder of a demand instrument may in any case demand payment at any time.

Sometimes an instrument contains an acceleration clause which provides that the maturity date may be hastened by the holder, at his election, upon the happening of certain designated events, which, however, are wholly under the control of the obligor. For example, it may be provided that the holder may, at his election, demand immediate payment of the instrument if the obligor mortgages the property, fails to pay the taxes, becomes bankrupt, or removes the property from the county. Since the obligor has control over the events designated, it is he and not the holder who actually determines whether the maturity date may be hastened. For this reason, most courts hold that such a provision does not affect the negotiability of the instrument.[1]

[1] U. C. C., Sec. 3-109, provides that "(1) An instrument is payable at a definite time if by its terms it is payable . . . (c) at a definite time subject to any acceleration." In the comment it is said that "Subsection 1 (c) is intended to mean that the certainty of time of payment or the negotiability of the instrument is not affected by *any* acceleration clause, whether acceleration be at the option of the maker or the holder, or automatic upon the occurrence of some event, and whether it is conditional or unrestricted."

Master Homecraft Company v. Zimmerman
208 Pa. Super. 401, 222 A. (2d) 440 (1966)

This was an action by Master Homecraft Company (plaintiff) against Edward T. Zimmerman et al. (defendants). Judgment for plaintiff, and defendants appealed. Reversed without prejudice and remanded with direction to allow filing of petition to open the judgment.

The appellant company contracted to remodel the appellees' home. In connection with this work, the appellees on August 4, 1964, executed a judgment note in the principal amount of $9,747. On the same date, at the direction of Edward Berg, partner of appellant company, the Prothonotary entered a judgment against appellees in the principal amount of the note.

On September 17, 1964, execution was issued by appellant upon the judgment and appellees' funds on deposit with the First National Bank of Export were attached on a writ naming the bank as garnishee. Following the allowance of a rule and the filing of an answer, the Court of Common Pleas of Westmoreland County ordered the judgment stricken on the grounds that it was impossible to determine from the face of the note the amount due or the date of maturity. Appellant entered its appeal and secured the issuance of a supersedeas.

SPAULDING, J. This appeal is from an order of the Court of Common Pleas of Westmoreland County making absolute a rule to strike off a judgment entered in favor of the Master Homecraft Company, appellant, on a judgment note executed by Edward T. and Alice Zimmerman, appellees.

The note in question reads in part:

$9,747.00   No. . . . .
(Total Amount of Note)   Pittsburgh, Pa. 8/4/64

For value received, I/we or either of us promise to pay to the order of MASTER HOMECRAFT COMPANY, the sum of Nine Thousand Seven Hundred Forty-seven Dollars in . . . . monthly installments of $. . . . . each, beginning on the   day of . . . . , 19. . ., and continuing on the same day of each and every month thereafter until the full amount thereof is paid. * * *

The note is not rendered defective because the blanks for alleged installment payments appear unused. On its face the note designates a principal sum of $9,747. The failure to fill in the monthly installment blanks does not indicate that no principal sum was intended.

The Uniform Commercial Code provides: "Instruments payable on demand include those payable at sight or on presentation and those in which no time for payment is stated." April 6, 1953, P. L. 3, 12A P. S., Sec. 3–108. (Emphasis added.) Under this section, the note in question is a demand note, due and payable immediately.

Reversed without prejudice and remanded with direction to allow filing of petition to open the judgment.

Federal Factors, Inc. v. Wellbanke

406 S. W. (2d) 712 (1966)

This was an action by Federal Factors, Inc. (plaintiff) against Joe Wellbanke (defendant). Judgment for defendant, and plaintiff appealed. Judgment reversed.

This was an action by holder on trade acceptances. One acceptor asserted that the instruments were not negotiable and that he was entitled to interpose defense of certain breaches of contract by the drawer. The Circuit Court, Faulkner County, Russell C. Roberts, J., sustained acceptor's contention, and holder appealed.

SMITH, J. The appellant, claiming to be a holder in due course, brought this action to enforce three instruments entitled Trade Acceptances, executed by the appellee Wellbanke and by Richard J. Martin. Wellbanke contended that the instruments were not negotiable and that he was therefore entitled to interpose in his defense certain breaches of contract on the part of the drawer, Chemical Products, Inc. The trial court, sitting without a jury, sustained Wellbanke's contentions. Negotiability is now the main issue.

In October 1962 Wellbanke and Martin signed a contract by which they became exclusive local dealers for Chemical Products. In the contract they agreed to purchase a quantity of merchandise, which was to be shipped to them for resale. At the trial Wellbanke testified that Chemical Products violated certain oral assurances that its agent had given, such as a promise to prepay the freight on the shipment and a promise not to transfer or assign the Trade Acceptances to anyone else.

The three instruments, evidencing the unpaid purchase price, were alike except for serial numbers and dates of maturity. Apart from inessential matters such as the drawer's telephone number, the instruments were in this form:

Chemical Products Incorporated
Salt Lake City, Utah

No. 687   October 5, 1962.
On November 10, 1962 Pay to the order of Chemical Products, Inc. Two Thousand Four Hundred Thirty-two and no/100 Dollars ($2,432.00).
The transaction which gives rise to this instrument is the purchase of goods by the acceptor from the drawer.

Chemical Products, Inc.
By Bob Chron

Accepted at Conway, Ark. on Oct. 5, 1962.
Payable at First National Bank
Bank Location Conway, Ark.
Buyer's Signature Joe Wellbanke
    & Richard J. Martin

Neither the trial court nor the appellee's attorney has suggested any reason for holding the instruments to be nonnegotiable. To the contrary, they contain all the elements of negotiability specified by the Uniform Commercial Code. Ark. Stat. Ann., Secs. 85-3-104 (Add. 1961). The mere reference to the transaction giving rise to the instruments does not affect negotiability. *Trice v. People's Loan & Inv. Co.*, 173 Ark. 1160, 293 S. W. 1037 (1927); Ark. Stat. Ann., Secs. 85-3-119. In view of the undisputed proof that the plaintiff was a holder in due course it took the instruments free from the defenses relied upon by Wellbanke. Section 85-3-305.

Upon remand it is possible, although unlikely, that one other matter may arise. The appellant insists that the appellee's failure to answer requests for admissions of fact within ten days, as requested, had the effect of admitting the truth of the requests. Counsel for the appellee states in his brief that he was given an extension of time for answering the requests. No such extension, however, appears in the record. Unless the asserted extension is proved the requests must be taken to have been admitted. Ark. Stat. Ann., Sec. 28-358; see *White River Limestone Products Co. v. Missouri-Pac. R. R.*, 228 Ark. 697, 310 S. W. (2d) 3 (1958). In all probability, however, the negotiability of the Trade Acceptances makes this matter immaterial.

Reversed.

PAYABLE TO ORDER OR TO BEARER

Sec. 3-104 of the U. C. C. provides that an instrument to be negotiable "must be payable to order or to bearer." The words "order" and "bearer" are often referred to in the cases as "words of negotiability." While these exact words are not required to be used, it is necessary to use words of similar import.

Under Sec. 3-110, an instrument is payable to order when by its terms it is payable to the order or assigns of any person therein specified with reasonable certainty, or to him or his order, or when it is conspicuously designated on its face as "exchange" or the like and names a payee. In either case the specified payee must be "named or otherwise indicated with reasonable certainty." Such payee may be the maker or drawer, or the drawee, or one who is neither maker, drawer, nor drawee. The instrument may be made payable to the order of two or more payees jointly (e.g. "to the order of A and B") or to one or some of several payees (e.g. "to the order of A or B"). Or it may be made payable to the order of an estate, trust, or fund, an office, or officer, a partnership or unincorporated association.

Sec. 3-111 provides that an instrument is payable to bearer when by its terms it is payable to (a) Bearer or the order of bearer; or (b) A specified person or bearer; or (c) "Cash" or the order of "cash," or any other indication which does not purport to designate a specific payee.

Zander v. New York Security & Trust Co.

39 Misc. 98 (1902)

This was an action by Caroline Zander (plaintiff) against the New York Security & Trust Company (defendant). Judgment for plaintiff, and defendant appealed. Affirmed.

This was an action to compel issue of a new certificate of deposit for one lost. It was alleged by plaintiff, and admitted by demurrer, that on or about July 11, 1901, plaintiff deposited with defendant the sum of $500 and received therefor the following certificate or receipt:

"The New York Security & Trust Company, New York, July 11, 1901, has received from Caroline Zander the sum of $500 of current funds, upon which the said company agrees to allow interest at the annual rate of 3 percent, from this date, and on five days' notice will repay, in current funds, the like amount with interest, to the said Caroline Zander or her assigns, on return of this certificate, which is assignable only on the books of the company."

Plaintiff always remained the owner of the certificate; she never assigned it or any part of it. Before September 9, 1901, she lost or inadvertently destroyed the certificate. She therefore demanded that defendant issue a new certificate, which defendant refused to do. Plaintiff filed this action, and defendant demurred to her petition. The demurrer was interposed for the purpose of enabling defendant to insist that plaintiff should be required to give the security specified by statute.

SCOTT, J. Sec. 17 of the statute refers to lost *negotiable paper*, and the question which presents itself is, therefore, whether or not the certificate of deposit given by the defendant is negotiable.

Sec. 20 of Chapter 612, known as the Negotiable Instruments Law, declares that an instrument to be negotiable "must be payable to order or to bearer." The receipt or certificate in the present case is not negotiable. The money represented by it is not payable "to order or bearer," but "to the plaintiff or her assigns." It is, therefore, what is known to the law as a non-negotiable instrument. In an action upon lost or destroyed instruments of this description, it is not necessary that the plaintiff should give or tender indemnity. *Wright v. Wright*, 54 N. Y. 437. The demurrer must be overruled.

DRAWEE MUST BE INDICATED
WITH REASONABLE CERTAINTY

Where the instrument is addressed to a drawee he must be named or otherwise indicated therein with reasonable certainty. For example, a check which failed to name the bank on which it was drawn would be non-negotiable for want of a drawee.

RULES OF CONSTRUCTION

Sec. 3–118 of the U. C. C. provides certain rules of construction to be applied where the language of an instrument is ambiguous or where there are certain omissions in the instrument. These rules are as follows: (a) Where there is doubt whether the instrument is a draft or a note, the holder may treat it as either. A draft drawn on the drawer is as effective as a note. (b) Handwritten terms control typewritten and printed terms, and typewritten terms control printed terms. (c) Words control figures except that if the words are ambiguous, figures control. (d) Unless otherwise specified, a provision for interest means interest at the judgment rate at the place of payment from the date of the instrument, or if it is undated from the date of issue. (e) Unless the instrument otherwise specifies, two or more persons who sign as maker, acceptor or drawer, or indorser and as a part of the same transaction are jointly and severally liable even though the instrument contains such words as "I promise to pay." (f) Unless otherwise specified, consent to extension authorizes a single extension for not longer than the original period. A consent to extension, expressed in the instrument, is binding on secondary parties and accommodation makers. A holder may not exercise his option to extend an instrument over the objection of a maker or acceptor or other party who in accordance with Sec. 3–604 tenders full payment when the instrument is due.

Guthrie v. National Homes Corporation

394 S. W. (2d) 494 (1965)

Supreme Court of Texas

This was an action by National Homes Corporation (plaintiff) against N. E. Guthrie, Jr. and John D. Crow (defendants). Judgment for plaintiff and defendant Guthrie alone appealed. Judgment reformed.

National Homes Corporation sued N. E. Guthrie, Jr. and John D. Crow and recovered judgment upon a jury verdict against both for $780.00, owing upon what it alleged was a negotiable promissory note. The Court of Civil Appeals affirmed. 387 S. W. (2d) 158. Guthrie alone has appealed and he has done so without bringing forward a statement of facts. He urges that he is not liable on a negotiable instrument on which his name nowhere appears, and also that the note contains a variance between the figures and the unambiguous written words that state the amount payable, in which case the courts below should have given controlling effect to the written words.

POPE, J. It is our opinion that the instrument sued upon was not a negotiable instrument, and Guthrie is bound by the jury finding that he ratified it. We sustain Guthrie's contention that the unambiguous written words control the figures.

The instrument sued upon is as follows:

"$5780.00   Electra   Texas   ⅜   1962
"Ninety (90) Days after date for Value Received I Promise To Pay to the Order of NATIONAL HOMES CORPORATION Five Thousand Eighty and 00/100 Dollars at Earl Avenue at Wallace, Lafayette, Indiana
It is hereby understood that $1000. overpayments will be made on future house deliveries until this obligation is paid.
With Interest at 6.5% per annum after date. All parties to this note, including endorsers and guarantors thereof, hereby waive presentment and demand for payment, protest, and notice of dishonor.
No. ——————— Due ——————— /s/ John D. Crow, Crow Construction Co."

The instrument is non-negotiable. These words were written in longhand on the face of the note, "It is hereby understood that $1000. (sic) overpayments will be made on future house deliveries until this obligation is paid." *Goldman v. Blum and Heidenheimer Bros.*, 58 Tex. 630 (1883) says: "* * * though the agreement or written instrument may have to some extent the form of a promissory note, and may use in its body the conventional terms that ordinarily invest such instruments with the character of negotiability, but if, by a stipulation in the body of the instrument, these elements which give it negotiability are limited and qualified, the negotiability of the instrument is destroyed * * *." See also, *Martin v. Shumatte & Matthews*, 62 Tex. 188 (1884). The additional terms written into the note burden it with the conditions of an extrinsic agreement and render it non-negotiable. *Lane Co. v. Crum*, Tex. Com. App., 291 S. W. 1084 (1927); *Texas Land & Cattle Co. v. Carroll & Iler*, 63 Tex. 48 (1885).

When there is a variance between unambiguous written words and figures the written words control, and the trial court erred in giving judgment based upon the figures. The amount payable was therefore "Five Thousand Eighty and 00/100 * * * Dollars" and according to the jury $5,000 has been paid. National Homes Corporation should have judgment for only eighty dollars.

The judgments of the trial court and the Court of Civil Appeals are accordingly reformed so that National Homes Corporation shall have judgment for the sum of eighty dollars. Costs are adjudged against the National Homes Corporation.

REVIEW CASES

1. Gay brought his action on the following instrument: "Marlboro, Sept. 23, 1881. I. O. U. E. A. Gay the sum of seventeen dollars 50/100, for value received. (signed) John R. Rooke." Is the foregoing instrument negotiable? (Gay v. Rooke, 151 Mass. 115, 23 N. E. 835)

2. Haggard brought suit against Mutual Oil & Refining Co. on the following check: "Winchester Bank, Winchester, Ky. Pay to Arco Refinery Construction Co. twenty-five hundred and no/100 dollars for a/c constructing refinery, switch, and loading racks, Win. Ky. (signed) Mutual Oil & Refining Co., by C. L. Ball, Pres." Is the check a negotiable instrument? (Haggard v. Mutual Oil & Refining Co., 204 Ky. 209, 263 S. W. 745)

3. White, indorsee of several promissory notes, brought action on the notes against the maker, Hatcher. The notes, which had been given in the purchase of an automobile, were payable on different dates, but all contained this provision: "In default of payment on any of the said notes, the whole shall become due and payable." Hatcher contended that this provision made the notes non-negotiable and that he was therefore entitled to set up his personal defense of failure of consideration. Judgment for whom? (White v. Hatcher et al., 135 Tenn. 609, 188 S. W. 61)

4. The First National Bank of Montgomery sued the Town of Luverne on a note acquired from a third party, in due course for value and before maturity. The note contained a stipulation that the maker "has the option and right to pay this note in its improvement bonds." Could the town set up its personal defense of payment? (First National Bank of Montgomery v. Town of Luverne, 235 Ala. 696, 180, So. 283)

5. McCowat was the holder of a note which Ryrie had obtained by fraud from Robert and Margaret Saltmarsh. The note contained the following provision: "I promise to pay . . . the taxes assessed in the state of Washington upon the mortgage given to secure this note and the debt thereby secured, or upon this note or any part thereof. . . ." Were the Saltmarshes entitled to set up against McCowat their personal defense of fraud? (Collidge & McClaine v. Saltmarsh et al., 96 Wash. 541, 165 P. 508)

6. A. D. Gibbs executed and delivered to his son, B. C. Gibbs, a promissory note for $5,000, to be paid out of A. D. Gibbs' estate four months after his death to B. C. Gibbs, or order, "for labor." A. D. Gibbs died intestate on April 11, 1934, and B. C. Gibbs was appointed administrator. On June 28, 1934, he sold the note to Murrell for a valuable consideration; but when the note matured he refused, as administrator, to pay it, and Murrell brought suit on the instrument. The defense was that no consideration had been given by the payee-indorser and that the instrument was non-negotiable because it was not payable on demand or at a fixed or determinable future time. Ruling? (Murrell v. Gibbs' Administrator et al., 275 Ky. 124, 120 S. W.(2d) 1018)

7. A trade acceptance drawn on the Gem State Oil & Produce Co. was accepted by the company and was later transferred by the payee to McCornick & Co., Bankers, who sued the acceptor on the instrument. On the margin of the instrument appeared the following: "The obligation of the acceptor of this bill arises out of the purchase of goods from the drawer. In the event the acceptor suspends payment, gives a chattel mortgage, suffers a fire loss, disposes of his business, or fails to meet at maturity any prior trade acceptance, this trade acceptance, at the option of the holder, shall immediately become due and payable." The defendant company con-

tended that the instrument was non-negotiable and that it could therefore set up its personal defense of payment. Judgment for whom? (McCornick & Co., Bankers v. Gem State Oil & Produce Co., 38 Idaho 470, 222 P. 286)

8. Hannah Segal received a promissory note in the amount of $1,100 from A. Segal. His signature was in the upper left-hand corner of the note, and in respect to the other written matter it was upside down. After A. Segal's death his administrator refused to pay the note for the reason that the signature was in the wrong place on the note. Holding? (Zimmerman v. Segal et al., 288 Ky. 33, 155 S. W.(2d) 20)

Negotiation

33

A negotiable instrument is transferred from one party to another by what is known as *negotiation*. Negotiation has the effect of conveying the title to the instrument from the transferor to the transferee or holder. Sec. 3–202 of the U. C. C. states: "Negotiation is the transfer of an instrument in such form that the transferee becomes a holder." A holder is defined in Sec. 1–201 (20) as a person who is in possession of a document of title or an instrument or an investment security drawn, issued, or indorsed to him or to his order or to bearer or in blank. Strictly speaking, these definitions would permit the term "negotiation" to include the original transfer of the instrument to the payee, as well as transfers by the payee and subsequent transferors. In practice, however, the term "issue" is usually applied to the first delivery of the instrument to the payee. In accordance with this distinction, it may be said that the first holder acquires title by issuance, and subsequent holders by negotiation.

The requirements for negotiation of an instrument depend upon whether it is payable to order or payable to bearer. The negotiation of an order instrument requires (1) the indorsement of the holder and (2) delivery. The negotiation of a bearer instrument requires delivery alone.

INDORSEMENT

GENERAL REQUIREMENTS

The U. C. C., Sec. 3–202 (2) specifies an indorsement must be written by or on behalf of the holder and on the instrument or on a paper so firmly affixed thereto as to become a part thereof (called an allonge). Indorsements are customarily placed on the back of the instrument, though the statute does not so require. No method of affixing an indorsement is prescribed; any method that meets the approval of the courts may therefore be used. Most commonly an indorser indorses in his own handwriting in ink or pencil; but an indorsement may be typed on the instrument or affixed by means of a rubber stamp.

Where the name of a payee or indorsee is wrongly designated or misspelled, he may indorse the instrument in the same form, adding, if he thinks fit, his proper signature.[1]

If an instrument is made payable to the order of two or more payees or indorsees jointly, e.g. "to the order of A and B," the instrument may be negotiated only by the indorsement of *all* such joint obligees, unless they are partners, or unless one has authority to indorse for the other or others.[2] On the other hand, if the instrument is made payable to the order of *one* of two or more payees or indorsees, e.g. "To the order of A or B," it may be negotiated by the indorsement of any one of the named payees or indorsees. If the instrument is made payable "to the order of A and/or B," it is interpreted as payable in the alternative, and hence may be negotiated or paid by the indorsement of any one of the payees named.

The indorsement must be an indorsement of the entire instrument. An indorsement which purports to transfer to the indorsee only a part of the amount payable, or to transfer the instrument to two or more indorsees severally, does not operate as a negotiation of the instrument. However, a partially paid instrument may be indorsed as to the residue.[3]

Under Sec. 3–207 of the U. C. C. the indorsement of an instrument by an infant "is effective." However, the infant incurs no liability by his indorsement; if he is sued on it, he may set up his infancy as a real defense.[4] There is a split in authority as to whether an infant may repudiate his indorsement and get the instrument back from a subsequent holder.[5]

The indorsement of a negotiable instrument (together with delivery) has two distinct results. First, it passes title to the instrument. Secondly, it places the credit of the indorser behind the instrument, as regards all subsequent transferees or holders.[6] The type of indorsement placed on the instrument determines the extent of the indorser's liability.

A forged indorsement is entirely inoperative. Hence on an order instrument it passes no title to the instrument.

[1] Sec. 3–203.
[2] Sec. 3–202 (3).
[3] Sec. 3–202 (3).
[4] Sec. 3–207 extends the same rule to a corporation that indorses an instrument without legal capacity to do so or to "any other person without capacity"; this would of course include the same persons.
[5] U. C. C., Sec. 3–207, provides that he may do so except against a holder in due course.
[6] This is true not only of order instruments but also of bearer instruments, when indorsed, even though the latter do not require indorsement for negotiation (Sec. 3–417).

Cooper v. Albuquerque National Bank

75 N. M. 295, 404 P. (2d) 125 (1965)

Supreme Court of New Mexico

This was an action by Charles A. Cooper, et al. (plaintiffs) against Albuquerque National Bank (defendant). Judgment for plaintiffs and defendant appealed. Reversed.

Appellees filed suit alleging that from October 14, 1953, to March 15, 1958, certain checks drawn in favor of appellees in the total amount of $119,551.35 were paid by appellant Bank on forged, unauthorized, unlawful, fraudulent, or irregular endorsements; that appellees had no knowledge thereof until October 28, 1958, but that appellant knew or should have known thereof prior to said date.

CHAVEZ, J. Appellant's answer denied both the alleged amount of such checks and that the endorsements on such checks were forged, unauthorized, unlawful, fraudulent, or irregular. Appellant also denied that it had knowledge of any such checks having been wrongfully endorsed and that appellees didn't have knowledge thereof. As a separate and alternative defense, appellant alleged that appellants were estopped from maintaining the action because the conduct of appellees and their predecessors was the proximate cause of their loss, that appellees' loss resulted proximately from their own negligence, that appellees' loss resulted solely and proximately from the breach by appellees or their predecessors of their fiduciary duties as Trustees of the New Mexico Pipe Trades Welfare Trust Fund; and that appellees were guilty of laches. Appellant further alleged, as an alternative defense, that it had no knowledge of any breach of fiduciary obligation to appellees by any fiduciary of appellees, and that it had no duty to make inquiry in that regard.

Brady on Bank Checks, 2d Ed., Par. 48, Form of indorsement, p. 73, states: "* * * a rubber stamp indorsement is valid and sufficient to transfer title to the instrument indorsed, when made by one having authority, * * *."

Appellees contend that appellant had actual notice of Peke's breach of his authority because of the signature cards signed for the Trust Fund. In view of our holding that Peke had authority to make the deposits, regardless of the signature cards, and there being no further allegations or evidence of any knowledge on the part of appellant which would amount to bad faith, it follows that appellant was not put upon inquiry as to the amount Peke was authorized to deposit, and we hold that appellant is not responsible for the amount deposited by Peke which exceeded what he was authorized to deposit. Compare *Transport Trucking Company v. First National Bank*, 61 N. M. 320, 300 P. (2d) 476.

The judgment of the district court is reversed and remanded with direction to set aside the judgment heretofore entered and enter a judgment dismissing appellees' complaint. It is so ordered.

Voris v. Schoonover et al.

91 Kan. 530, 135 P. 607 (1914)

This was an action by Ezra C. Voris (plaintiff) against Frank Schoonover and H. J. Oldham (defendants). Judgment for plaintiff, and defendants appealed. Affirmed.

BENSON, J. The question to decide is whether the indorsement of the promissory note, which is the subject of this action, is sufficient to constitute the plaintiff a holder in due course, as defined in the Negotiable Instruments Law.

The promissory note in question recites a promise "to pay to the order of Law W. Cochran or R. F. Dygert." It is agreed that the note was indorsed before maturity by Cochran, while he had it in his possession; that he delivered it to the plaintiff for value, who took it without notice or knowledge of any infirmity or defect in title, and without any bad faith. It is also agreed that if the indorsement of Cochran was sufficient without the indorsement of Dygert, the defendants have no defense.

Sec. 15 provides: "The instrument is payable to order where it is drawn payable to the order of a specified person or to him or his order. It may be drawn payable to order of : (4) two or more payees jointly; or (5) one or some of several payees." It will be observed that subdivision 4 refers to joint payees, while subdivision 5 refers to one or some of several payees. This instrument falls under this last subdivision. Section 48 of the same law declares that "where an instrument is payable to the order of two or more payees or indorsees who are not partners, all must indorse, unless the one indorsing has authority to indorse for the others." Construing this section with the subdivision 4 of section 15, a note payable "to A and B" must, if the payees are not partners, be indorsed by both, but if payable "to A or B," the order to pay is complete on the indorsement of either.

Where a note is made payable "to A or B," the indorsement of either constitutes the order, and is sufficient. The district court so held; and the judgment is affirmed.

KINDS OF INDORSEMENTS

The U. C. C. states that an indorsement may be either special or in blank; and it may also be either restrictive or qualified.

BLANK INDORSEMENT. A blank indorsement is one which does not specify an indorsee. For example, John Doe may indorse in blank an instrument drawn to his order by simply writing or stamping his name "John Doe" on the back of the instrument. The effect of placing a blank indorsement on an order instrument is to make it payable to bearer and negotiable by delivery alone. Blank indorsement is therefore dangerous, since a thief or finder can pass good title to the instrument. To protect transferees against this danger, Sec. 3-204 (3) of the U. C. C. provides: "The holder may convert a blank indorsement into a special indorsement by writing over the signature of the indorser in blank any contract consistent with the character of the indorsement." Thus the transferee may write above the blank indorsement the words "Pay to the order of" plus his own name.

SPECIAL INDORSEMENT.   As defined in Sec. 3-204 of the U. C. C., "A special indorsement specifies a person to whom or to whose order it makes the instrument payable. Any instrument specially indorsed becomes payable to the order of the special indorsee and may be further negotiated only by his indorsement." Thus, if John Doe, the holder of an order instrument, wishes to negotiate it to Richard Roe by placing on it a special indorsement, he may do so by indorsing it in either of the following ways:

> (1) *Pay to the order of Richard Roe*
> [or *Pay to Richard Roe or order*]
> *John Doe*
> (2) *Pay to Richard Roe*
> *John Doe*

In the past courts have been unable to agree upon whether the following is a valid special indorsement or merely an assignment of the instrument: "I hereby assign the within instrument to John Doe" (or some similar words). The word "assign" is of course the root of the difficulty. The majority of the courts today and the U. C. C. hold such indorsements to be valid special indorsements, treating the word "assign" as surplusage.[1]

A special indorsement placed upon an instrument which was, in its origin, a bearer instrument is changed into an order instrument.

But what of an instrument which began as an order instrument but which has been indorsed in blank and has thus been converted into a bearer instrument? We have already seen that such an instrument may be further negotiated by delivery alone; but let us assume that the transferee places a special indorsement on the instrument following the blank indorsement. Does the instrument remain a bearer instrument, or is it reconverted into an order instrument? Upon this point the courts do not agree. Some courts, applying the adage "Once a bearer instrument, always a bearer instrument," hold that the instrument remains a bearer instru-

---

[1] U. C. C., Sec. 3-202, "(4) Words of assignment, condition, waiver, guaranty, limitation or disclaimer of liability and the like accompanying an indorsement do not affect its character as an indorsement." COMMENT: "Subsection (4) is intended to reject decisions holding that the addition of such words as 'I hereby assign all my rights, title and interest in the within note' prevents the signature from operating as an indorsement."

ment despite the addition of a special indorsement. Other courts hold that the effect of the special indorsement is to return the instrument to its original status as an order instrument. This is the majority view. Sec. 3–204 of the U. C. C. provides: "(1) A special indorsement specifies the person to whom or to whose order it makes the instrument payable. *Any* instrument specially indorsed becomes payable to the order of the special indorsee and may be further negotiated only by his indorsement. (2) An indorsement in blank specifies no particular indorsee, and may consist of a mere signature. An instrument *payable to order* and *indorsed in blank* *becomes payable to bearer* and may be negotiated by delivery alone *until* *specially indorsed* . . ." COMMENT: "The principle here adopted is that the special.indorsee, as the owner even of a bearer instrument, has the right to direct the payment and to require the indorsement of his indorsee as evidence of the satisfaction of his own obligation. The special indorser may of course make it payable to bearer again by himself indorsing in blank." Effect of section: (1) an order instrument, when indorsed in blank, becomes a bearer instrument; but if this blank indorsement is followed by a special indorsement, the instrument reverts to an order instrument; (2) a bearer instrument, when indorsed specially, requires the indorsement of the indorsee before it may be further negotiated.

RESTRICTIVE INDORSEMENT. Sec. 3–205 of the U. C. C. states that an indorsement is restrictive which either (a) is conditional; or (b) purports to prohibit further transfer of the instrument; or (c) includes the words "for collection," "for deposit," "pay any bank," or like terms signifying a purpose of deposit or collection; or (d) otherwise states that it is for the benefit or use of the indorser or of another person.

Sec. 3–206 of the Code states that (1) No restrictive indorsement prevents further transfer or negotiation of the instrument.

(2) An intermediary bank, or a payor bank which is not the depositary bank is neither given notice nor otherwise affected by a restrictive indorsement of any person except the bank's immediate transferor or the person presenting for payment.

(3) Except for an intermediary bank, any transferee under an indorsement which is conditional or includes the words "for collection," "for deposit," "pay any bank," or like terms (subparagraphs (a) and (c) of Sec. 3–205) must pay or apply any value given by him for or on the security of the instrument consistently with the indorsement and to the extent that he does so he becomes a holder for value. In addition such transferee is a holder in due course if he otherwise complies with the requirements of Sec. 3–302 on what constitutes a holder in due course.

(4) The first taker under an indorsement for the benefit of the indorser

or another person (subparagraph (d) of Sec. 3–205) must pay or apply any value given by him for or on the security of the instrument consistently with the indorsement and to the extent that he does so he becomes a holder for value. In addition such taker is a holder in due course if he otherwise complies with the requirements of Sec. 3–302 on what constitutes a holder in due course. A later holder for value is neither given notice nor otherwise affected by such restrictive indorsement unless he has knowledge that a fiduciary or other person has negotiated the instrument in any transaction for his own benefit or otherwise in breach of duty (subsection (2) of Sec. 3–304).

The U. C. C. makes drastic changes in the case of restrictive indorsements. In effect, they are converted into conditional indorsements. An indorsement reading Pay A only, or any other indorsement purporting to prohibit further transfer, is without effect for that purpose. A subsequent indorsee still becomes a holder. The indorsement is to be construed as if it is to be treated like any other conditional indorsement. The following is a conditional indorsement:

Pay to the order of Richard Roe upon delivery of one Ford truck # 17,568 on June 1, 1975.

JOHN DOE

QUALIFIED INDORSEMENT.   Sec. 3–202 of the U. C. C. recognizes a qualified indorsement may be made by adding to the indorser's signature the words "without recourse," or any words of similar import. Such an indorsement does not impair the negotiable character of the instrument.

The following illustrate the form of a qualified indorsement:

(1) *Without recourse*
    John Doe
(2) *Pay to the order of Richard Roe*
    Without recourse
    John Doe

The effect of such an indorsement is to relieve the indorser of his conditional liability to pay the instrument if the party primarily liable to pay the instrument does not pay it. However, a qualified indorser still remains liable on certain implied warranties. The nature of this liability is discussed in Chapter 35.

Held v. Moore

59 Lanc. Rev. 111 (1964)

This was an action by Lawrence Held (plaintiff) against Herbert U. Moore and Lois Moore (defendants). Motion for summary judgment granted to plaintiff.

On August 12, 1960 Herbert U. Moore executed and delivered to the plaintiff a promissory note in the principal sum of $15,000.00 with interest at 6%. The note was payable on the same day at Brooklyn, New York. At the time of the execution and delivery of said note, the defendant, Lois Moore, signed her name on the back thereof under the following indorsement: "For value received the undersigned and each of them hereby forever waives presentment, demand, protest, notice of protest and notice of dishonor of the within note and the undersigned and each of them guarantees the payment of said note at maturity and consents without notice to any and all extension of time or terms of payment made by holder of said note."

The complaint further alleges that the note was presented to Herbert U. Moore for payment but payment was refused. On July 18, 1963 the note was presented to Lois Moore for payment but she also refused payment. The defendant in her answer admitted the execution of the note but denies that she knew in what capacity she signed the note or the reason for her signing. The defendant further denies that the note was presented to her for payment on July 18, 1963, or at any other time but admits that she has not paid the note.

JOHNSTONE, J. The plaintiff seeks to recover the sum of Fifteen Thousand (15,000.00) Dollars, together with interest, on a promissory note given him by Herbert U. Moore and indorsed by Lois Moore. Judgment has been entered against Herbert U. Moore for failure to file an answer to the plaintiff's complaint. The other defendant has filed an answer and the plaintiff has filed a motion for judgment on the pleadings against her.

In considering the plaintiff's motion for judgment on the pleadings, we will accept as true all allegations of the defendant's answer in denial of the plaintiff's allegations in his complaint: *Cary v. Lower Merion School Dist.*, 362 Pa. 310. Judgment will only be granted if the case is clear and if there are no issues of fact: *Waldman et al. v. Shoemaker*, 367 Pa. 587.

The defendant's answer sets up none of the common defenses to an action of this kind, such as payment, release, failure of consideration, fraud, illegality, duress, or the statute of limitations. She in effect says, I signed the note but I don't know why or in what capacity I signed it. Does this constitute a good defense or is it a valid reason for not entering judgment on the pleadings? We think not. The Uniform Commercial Code provides in Sec. 3–414 that in the absence of a qualified indorsement, the indorser engages upon dishonor and any necessary notice of dishonor and protest to pay the instrument according to its tenor at the time of his indorsement. The defendant specifically guaranteed payment of the note at maturity by the indorsement on the back of the note. This makes her liable to the payee (plaintiff) of the note if payment was not made by the maker: *Shaffstall v. McDaniel*, 152 Pa. 598., Sec. 3–416 of the Code provides, (1) "Payment guaranteed" or equivalent words added to a signature means that the signer engages that if the instrument is not paid when due he will pay it according to its tenor without resort by the holder to any other party.

While the defendant alleges that she did not know the effect of her signature on the note, her signature was voluntarily made and she must be held responsible for the legal effect of her act. Under Section 3–416 of the Code such an indorser who guarantees payment waives not only presentment, notice of dishonor and protest, but also all demand upon the maker. The indorsement on the note in question specifically contains the same provisions as the Code.

The averments by the defendant in her answer that proof is required of presentment and notice of dishonor and that no demand for payment was made on her are immaterial since by her indorsement, she waived all such prerequisites to suit on the note. Even before the Uniform Commercial Code it was possible to waive the requirements of presentment and demand: *Helfrich v. Snyder*, 269 Pa. 527. It is clear beyond any doubt, in our opinion, that the defendant has not stated a valid defense to the plaintiff's complaint and that there are no disputed questions of fact to be determined by a jury.

And now, January 10, 1964, for the reasons stated herein, judgment on the pleadings is hereby entered in favor of the plaintiff, Lawrence Held, and against the defendant, Lois Moore, in the sum of $15,000.00, together with interest at the rate of 6 percent per annum from August 12, 1960 to this date.

National Bondholders Corp. v. Cheeseman et al.
8 S. E. (2d) 391, 190 Ga. 166 (1940)

This was a suit by the National Bondholders Corporation (plaintiff) against Mrs. Trux L. Cheeseman and others (defendants). Defendant Cheeseman demurred. Demurrer was sustained, and plaintiff appealed. Reversed.

Plaintiff brought suit against O. R. Muse and Mrs. Trux L. Cheeseman. It was alleged that defendant Muse executed and delivered six promissory notes in favor of the Mortgage Guarantee Company of America, dated December 1, 1930, aggregating $3,500 principal; and that he executed and delivered a mortgage in favor of the Mortgage Guarantee Company of America to secure the notes, the mortgage conveying certain described land in De Kalb County, Georgia. The petition further stated that after the execution of the notes and mortgage, defendant Muse conveyed by warranty deed the land described in the mortgage to Mrs. Trux L. Cheeseman, this deed containing a clause providing that as a part of the consideration the purchaser assumed and agreed to pay a first mortgage for $3,416.51 with interest, due the Mortgage Guarantee Company of America and that defendant Cheeseman accepted the deed and entered into possession of the land thereunder. There was a default in the payment of the notes, and the mortgage was foreclosed on February 5, 1935, and sold to John E. Lee. After crediting the net proceeds from the sale there remained a balance due and unpaid of $2,768.21. It was for this sum that plaintiff filed this action against Muse and Mrs. Cheeseman. The petition also alleged that plaintiff was the owner and holder of the note sued on. Mrs. Cheeseman filed a demurrer, in which she attacked plaintiff's petition on the ground that it was not alleged whether or not the notes sued on were indorsed to plaintiff for value, before maturity, or that they were indorsed or transferred to plaintiff in due course. The demurrer was sustained and the action was dismissed. Plaintiff appealed.

DUCKWORTH, J. The demurrer contains no valid attack upon the petition. The petition conforms to all legal requirements with reference to showing the plaintiff's right to sue on the note, when it sets forth a copy of the note, showing indorsement in blank by the payee and the amount due thereon, and alleges that the plaintiff is the owner and holder thereof. These facts make a prima facie case of a "holder in due course." Code, Sec. 14–509. When the Mortgage Guarantee Company of America, the payee, signed its name on the back of the note sued on, that, without more, constituted an indorsement in blank. With this, the only indorsement in blank appearing on the note, the note is payable to "bearer." And it may be negotiated by delivery alone. Sec. 14–405. Plaintiff did not have to allege and prove that when the note was transferred to it (National Bondholders Corp.) the note was indorsed by its transferor (Mortgage Guarantee Company of America). The note could be negotiated by delivery, without indorsement. Therefore, it was error to sustain the demurrer and dismiss the action.

James Talcott, Inc. v. Fred Ratowsky Associates, Inc.
84 Dauph. 258 (1965)

This was an action by James Talcott, Inc. (plaintiff) against Fred Ratowsky Associates, Inc. (defendant). Judgment for plaintiff.

On September 8, 1959, Sayve Corporation of America (hereinafter referred to as Sayve) sold a coin-operated laundry, including building, to M. G. B. Corporation (hereinafter referred to as M. G. B.). Part of the consideration was an installment judgment note and an installment sales contract. Ratowsky is the payee on the note and designated as the seller on the sales contract. It appears that arrangements had been made by Sayve with Talcott to purchase the note. However, Talcott "required an additional signature together with those of M. G. B. Corporation and its principals before . . . Talcott . . . would consent to purchase the note." Ratowsky had sold no equipment in conjunction with the transaction nor did any money pass through his hands. On the same day, to wit, September 8, 1959, Ratowsky, at the request of Sayve, endorsed the note "pay to the order of James Talcott, Inc., 225 Fourth Avenue, New York, New York." On the same day Ratowsky delivered the note to

Sayve that it might be delivered to Talcott. Before Sayve delivered the note to Talcott on October 8, 1959, the note was altered without Talcott's knowledge in that the name of the payee on the endorsement of the note was changed from Talcott to Sayve Corporation. There was attached to the note a separate instrument upon which Sayve was the unconditional endorser with recourse. The same was clipped to the note. Sayve "agreed that it would completely indemnify and save . . . Ratowsky . . . harmless from any loss in connection with the endorsement." Talcott relied on all the endorsements appearing on the note in extending credit thereon. M. G. B. defaulted on the note on July 1, 1961. On May 27, 1962 Talcott returned the note to Sayve, who endorsed the note "pay to the order of James Talcott, Inc. with recourse." On March 13, 1963 the laundry was damaged by fire and the insurance carrier paid Talcott $5,000 and on April 29, 1963 M. G. B. paid $2,000 to Talcott. There is presently due and owing on the note the sum of $13,272.20.

SHELLEY, J. This matter comes before us on a case stated basis. The parties, under the provisions of the Act of April 22, 1874, P. L. 109, 12 P. S. 688 et seq., have entered into a stipulation for the trial of this case without a jury. The parties have also stipulated the facts.

In conjunction with the sale an installment sales contract was executed and transferred by the various parties at approximately the same time, in the same manner, under the same circumstances and with the same alteration as took place in the transfer of the note.

Attached to the amended complaint as Exhibit "A" was the note referred to above and "clipped" to it was a paper which the plaintiff contends was an "allonge."

An "allonge" is a piece of paper annexed to a bill of exchange or promissory note on which to write endorsements for which there is no room on the instrument itself.

The defendant contends that the attached paper was not an "allonge."

The answer to the question must be found in an interpretation of the Uniform Commercial Code (hereinafter referred to as U. C. C.) which provides that "an indorsement must be written by or on behalf of the holder and on the instrument or on a paper so firmly affixed thereto as to become a part thereof," as applied to the circumstances of this case.

The Negotiable Instruments Act provided that "the indorsement must be written on the instrument itself or upon a paper attached thereto . . ." A comparison of the provisions of the two acts indicates that the legislature intended by the provision of the Uniform Commercial Code to sanction the use of the "allonge" but added the additional provision that the "allonge" be not merely attached to the instrument but required that it be *firmly affixed* to the note. There is no doubt that the reason for this added requirement was that it was not intended to establish the loose and undesirable practice of making regular endorsements of commercial paper by a writing on the back of any other paper or document to which it might have been temporarily attached, as by pinning, especially when there is ample space for the endorsement on the back of the instrument itself.

As we understand the word "clip," it means to "clasp" or "fasten with a clip," which usually denotes a temporary method of attachment and is not nearly as secure as the method of stapling or riveting or the use of an adhesive preparation, such as glue, mucilage or paste.

An examination of the note indicates that there was sufficient space on the back of the note for a second endorsement; in fact one was eventually placed thereon after default by the maker. It is also noted that only the note was attached to the original complaint without any additional paper. Reference to an alleged "allonge" first appeared in the amended complaint. This would indicate that as a matter of law any arrangement which is so flexible could not possibly meet the requirements of the Uniform Commercial Code. The plaintiff itself, by its own acts, has indicated its doubt in the efficacy of the endorsement which appeared on the alleged "allonge" by having the endorsement re-executed by Sayve.

We, accordingly, conclude that the paper attached to the note was not an "allonge."

Section 3–415 (1) of the U. C. C. provides: "An accommodation party is one who signs the instrument in any capacity as surety for another party to it." The stipulation avers facts from which we must conclude that Ratowsky was an accommodation party.

The U. C. C. defines a holder as "a person who is in possession of . . . an instrument . . . issued or indorsed to him or to his order . . ." Because the paper attached to the note was not an "allonge," it is clear that on October 8, 1959, plaintiff was not in possession of an instrument endorsed to it or to its order and, therefore, was not a holder.

However, in Section 3–415 (2), 12A P. S. 3–415 (2) U. C. C. defines the contract of an accommodation party.

We agree with the plaintiff's interpretation of Section 3–415 (2). The word "holder" has been given a precise definition by the framers of the U. C. C. The importance of a person acquiring the status of a "holder" is evident from Section 3–202 in that a person becomes a "holder" only through negotiation and that only a "holder" may make an endorsement. Furthermore, the entire Part 3 of Article 3 of the U. C. C. deals with the rights of a person who qualifies as a "holder."

But even more significant is Part 4 of Article 3 which deals with the liability of parties. Thus, Section 3–413 (2) imposes a duty on the drawer to pay *either* the "holder" *or* any endorser who has "taken" up the instrument. Similarly, Section 3–414 (1) provides that an endorser must pay *either* the "holder" *or* any subsequent endorser who has "taken" up the instrument. The absence of the word "holder" in the very next section, i.e. 3–415 (2), supra, leads us to only one conclusion. The legislature must have intended that the accommodation party is liable to a person who has "taken" the instrument for value before it was due, even though that person is not a "holder."

Accordingly, we conclude that the defendant is liable to the plaintiff in the sum claimed to be due on the note, to wit, $13,272.20, with interest.

DELIVERY

Whether a negotiable instrument is an order instrument, requiring indorsement for negotiation, or a bearer instrument, not requiring indorsement, its negotiation requires delivery. Delivery is a condition precedent to the liability of all parties to the instrument and to the transfer of rights under the instrument. Sec. 1–201 (14) of the U. C. C. defines "delivery" as voluntary transfer of possession. Every contract on a negotiable instrument is incomplete and revocable until delivery of the instrument for the purpose of giving effect thereto. As between immediate parties, and as regards a remote party other than a holder in due course, the delivery, in order to be effectual, must be made either by or under the authority of the party making, drawing, accepting or indorsing, as the case may be; and in such case the delivery may be shown to have been conditional, or for a special purpose only, and not for the purpose of transferring the property in the instrument. But where the instrument is in the hands of a holder in due course, a valid delivery thereof by all parties prior to him so as to make them liable to him is conclusively presumed. And where the instrument is no longer in the possession of a party whose signature appears thereon, a valid and intentional delivery by him is presumed until the contrary is proved.

In re Martens' Estate
226 Iowa 162, 283 N. W. 885 (1939)

Mabel Martens Bonk filed a claim, based on a note for $1,500, against the estate of her mother. The claim was denied by the administrator, and a petition was filed in the circuit court to secure the allowance thereof. Her claim in the circuit court was denied and she appealed. Affirmed.

At the trial appellant testified that she was the daughter of the deceased. She identified Exhibit A as a note in the handwriting of her mother, dated March 1, 1930, promising to pay her $1,500 on December 1, 1930, and signed by the decedent. On the back of the note was the endorsement: "This money is coming to her for teaching $1,000 and $500 is what the rest got also. Mother."

The decedent died January 2, 1936. The administrator qualified on March 1, 1936. Appellant testified that, about March 11, 1936, in examining the contents of her mother's safe, she discovered an envelope on which, in her mother's handwriting, was the notation: "Please give this to S. Fisher in case of death. Mabel Martens from Mother"; she delivered the envelope to said Simon Fisher at his law office shortly after she discovered it; Fisher opened the envelope, which was sealed, in her presence and in the presence of the administrator; the note, Exhibit A, was found in the envelope; her mother had told her that, in case of death, there was a letter for her, but she knew nothing of any note; she found the envelope after the administrator had made an examination of the contents of the safe and not discovered it; she had loaned her parents $1,000 from time to time out of money earned teaching school; her brothers and sisters each had received $500 when they were married; she married subsequent to March 1, 1930, and did not receive her $500.

MILER, J. Apparently the trial court held that the claim should be denied because the record failed to establish legal delivery of the note, which formed the basis of appellant's claim. We hold that there was no error in this decision.

Section 9476 of the Code provides that every contract on a negotiable instrument is incomplete and revocable until delivery of the instrument for the purpose of giving effect thereto.

Obviously, the note here sued upon could not be made the basis of a valid claim against the estate unless there was a legal delivery of the same, during the lifetime of the decedent. Our decisions, relative to analogous situations, are reviewed in the recent case of *Orris v. Whipple*, 280 N. W. 615, wherein we state: "All there is to show delivery in this case is that the deed was prepared and executed by Miss Aken; that she told others that she wanted the plaintiffs to have the property, and that she had prepared papers so providing. She put the deeds in her safety deposit box and retained the key. We do not think these admitted facts show a legal delivery of the deeds in question."

The position taken by this court in the Orris case is controlling here. Our statement of the facts herein is more favorable to appellant than the record warrants. However, the decisive factor is that, even when we so consider the evidence, the record fails to establish delivery of appellant's note during the lifetime of the deceased. As above pointed out, the trial court's decision on the issue of delivery was right. The judgment entered pursuant thereto must be, and it is, affirmed.

REVIEW CASES

1. Burdick and Ewing gave a negotiable promissory note to Wheeler for a plot of land. Wheeler wrote on the back of the note these words: "I hereby assign this note over to E. H. Farnsworth this November 1, 1910. (signed) J. A. Wheeler," and delivered it to Farnsworth. The note was not paid when due, and Farnsworth brought suit against Burdick and Ewing. They contended that the note had been assigned to Farnsworth and not negotiated to him, and set up their personal defense of failure of consideration. Judgment for whom? (Farnsworth v. Burdick et al., 94 Kan. 749, 147 P. 863)

2. Blackman was a soliciting agent of the Royal Mutual Life Insurance Co. He sold insurance to Spies, who signed and delivered to him a note for

$268, payable in thirty days to the order of the Royal Mutual Life Insurance Co. or Blackman. The Union Bank of Bridgewater bought the note from Blackman, who indorsed it and delivered it to the bank. The note contained this provision: "In case of the death of the insured before this note falls due, the above amount with interest shall be deducted from the amount of the policy." Spies refused to pay the note when it fell due, and the bank sued him. The defenses were: (1) the aforementioned clause prevented the note from being a negotiable instrument, and the defendant could therefore set up his personal defense of fraud; (2) the bank was not the owner of the note, since only one of the payees had indorsed it. Ruling? (Union Bank of Bridgewater v. Spies, 151 Iowa 178, 120 N. W. 928)

3. Robert Porter had in his possession for safekeeping a promissory note payable to the order of his brother Jabez. The note, made by Brown and another, was for $1,000 and had been given to Jabez for a loan made to Brown. Jabez died without indorsing the note. Sometime later Robert agreed with Wood to the effect that if Wood would collect the note, he could have the interest due on it. Wood sold the note to Mills for $1,000. Mills sued Robert Porter for failure of title to the note. Did the lack of indorsement affect Mills' right to recover? (Mills v. Porter, 5 Thompson and Cook, Supreme Court Reports New York 63)

4. Baroch, secretary to the Greater Montana Oil Co., agreed during a board meeting to lend the corporation $4,600 and to take a promissory note in return. The note was to be signed for the corporation by the president and by himself as secretary. A further stipulation was that Baroch was to have all sixteen of the original stockholders sign the note. Baroch had only six stockholders sign the note, which he kept in his possession. He later sued the corporation on the note. The question for determination was whether there could be a delivery of the note until all the stockholders had signed it. (Baroch v. Greater Montana Oil Co., 70 Mont. 93, 225 P. 800)

5. B. S. Davis and others executed and delivered a promissory note, payable to Vincent Mercantile Co. or bearer. The note was transferred by delivery to E. E. Florey and T. C. Florey without being indorsed. The Floreys later brought an action to recover on the note from the makers. The defense was that the instrument had not been negotiated to the plaintiffs. Holding? (Davis v. Florey, 16 Ala. A. 264, 77 So. 413)

Holder in
Due Course

34

REQUIREMENTS OF A HOLDER IN DUE COURSE

The U. C. C. makes a distinction between a *holder* and a *holder in due course*. As we have already seen, Sec. 1–201 (20) states that "Holder" means a person who is in possession of a document of title or an instrument or an investment security drawn, issued, or indorsed to him or to his order or to bearer or in blank.

Sec. 3–302 states: (1) "A holder in due course is a holder who takes the instrument (a) for value; and (b) in good faith; and (c) without notice that it is overdue or has been dishonored or of any defense against or claim to it on the part of any person."

Sec. 3–302 of the U. C. C. provides that a holder, in order to be a holder in due course, must take the instrument for value and in good faith.

TAKEN FOR VALUE

Sec. 1–201 (44) defines "value" as follows: "Value." Except as otherwise provided with respect to negotiable instruments and bank collections (Sections 3–303, 4–208 and 4–209) a person gives "value" for rights if he acquires them (a) in return for a binding commitment to extend credit or for the extension of immediately available credit whether or not drawn upon and whether or not a charge-back is provided for in the event of difficulties in collection; or (b) as security for or in total or partial satisfaction of a pre-existing claim; or (c) by accepting delivery pursuant to a pre-existing contract for purchase; or (d) generally, in return for any consideration sufficient to support a simple contract."

Sec. 3–303 states that "A holder takes the instrument for value (a) to the extent that the agreed consideration has been performed or that he acquires a security interest in or a lien on the instrument otherwise than by

775

legal process; or (b) when he takes the instrument in payment of or as security for an antecedent claim against any person whether or not the claim is due; or (c) when he gives a negotiable instrument for it or makes an irrevocable commitment to a third person."

Thus, if a purchaser has paid nothing but has merely agreed to pay at a later date, and if before he has made such payment it is discovered that the title of the transferor is defective or the party primarily liable has a valid defense, the transferee has not paid value, and is therefore not a holder in due course. If the transferee has paid a part of the promised consideration prior to acquiring such knowledge, he is a holder in due course only to the extent of his payment; and no subsequent payments by him to the transferor would alter his status.

Sec. 4–209 of the U. C. C. provides: "For purposes of determining its status as a holder in due course, the bank has given value to the extent that it has a security interest in an item provided that the bank otherwise complies with the requirements of Section 3–302 on what constitutes a holder in due course."

A bank is held not to have paid value for a note that it has discounted for a customer merely by crediting his account with same. Not until the bank has honored and paid checks drawn by the depositor against the account to the full amount thus credited is the bank held to have given value and hence to be a holder in due course. In determining whether a bank has given value in such cases, most courts apply the rule that "the first money in is the first money out," i.e. that the first debits are charged to the first credits. An example will make this clear. At the opening of business on June 1, A has a credit balance of $5,000 at his bank. At 10 A.M. he discounts a note for $2,000 with the bank, which credits his account with that amount. During the day the bank honors and pays A's checks for $4,000, so that at the end of the day he has a credit balance of $3,000. Though the bank has honored and paid A's checks for more than the amount of the note, an overwhelming majority of the courts would hold that it has not paid value for the note. The reason is that the $4,000 was debited against "the first money in," the $5,000 credited to A when the bank opened for business. Let us suppose, however, that the checks paid amounted to $10,000 instead of $4,000, and that in addition to discounting the note in the morning, A deposits $6,000 to his account during the afternoon. Again he ends the day with a credit balance of $3,000, but in this case the bank will be held to have paid value for the note, since in honoring A's checks it first drew against his credit of $5,000, then his credit of $2,000, and finally his credit of $6,000.

If a negotiable instrument is given as security for a loan, the lender has given value for the security to the extent of the amount of the loan. Thus, if A borrows $500 from the B bank and pledges a promissory note for

$800, which he holds against C, the bank will be a holder (of the pledged note) for value to the extent of $500 (Sec. 3–303 (a)).

While an antecedent or pre-existing debt is past consideration and would not constitute a valid consideration under contract law, it is stated to be "value" under Sec. 1–201 (44) (b). Thus, if A owes B $100 on an open account, and A and B agree that A shall give B a note for $100 and discharge the open account, the pre-existing debt (open account) would constitute sufficient consideration (value) for the note. The same result would follow if A held a note against X and negotiated it to B in payment of his account with B.

Pazol v. Citizens National Bank of Sandy Springs
110 Ga. App. 319, 138 S. T. (2d) 442 (1964)

This was an action by Citizens National Bank of Sandy Springs (plaintiff) against Sidney Pazol (defendant). Defendant's demurrer overruled and defendant appealed. Affirmed.

The Citizens Bank of Sandy Springs sued Sidney Pazol to recover $49,600, the amount of a check drawn on the Fulton National Bank of Atlanta by the defendant and payable to Edison & Seiden Construction & Development Company, Inc. The petition alleged that the check was dated January 4, 1964, and was executed and delivered to the payee on or about that date; the copy of the check, attached as an exhibit to the petition, bore the date "January 4, 1963"; that on or about January 9, 1964, the payee caused the check to be indorsed and deposited in its checking account with the plaintiff bank; that the plaintiff credited the payee-depositor's account with the amount of the check upon its deposit and on that day and the following day, prior to having any notice of dishonor of the check, permitted the payee-depositor to withdraw the full amount of the check; that the plaintiff duly presented the check for collection to the payor bank, but that the check was dishonored by the payor pursuant to the defendant's stop payment order and was returned to the plaintiff on or about January 13, 1964; that the plaintiff had taken the check in good faith, before it was overdue or had been dishonored and without notice of any defense against or claim to it on the part of any person; that the defendant had failed and refused to pay the plaintiff the amount of the check on demand.

FELTON, C.J. The court overruled the defendant's general demurrer to the petition, to which judgment he excepts.

The plaintiff was a holder in due course as defined by Code Ann. Sec. 109A–3–302 (1), which requires that the holder take the instrument "(a) for value; and (b) in good faith; and (c) without notice that it is overdue or has been dishonored or of any defense against or claim to it on the part of any person." Regarding requirement (a), Code Sec. 109A–4–209 provides as follows: "For purposes of determining its status as a holder in due course, the bank has given value *to the extent that it has a security interest in an item* provided that the bank otherwise complies with the requirements of 109A–3–302 on what constitutes a holder in due course." (Emphasis supplied.) Code Ann. Sec. 109A–4–208 (1) provides that "[a] bank has a security interest in an item * * * (a) in case of an item deposited in an account to the extent to which credit given for the item has been withdrawn or applied." Code Ann. Sec. 109A–3–303 also provides that a holder takes an instrument for value to the extent that he acquires a security interest in the instrument. Code Ann. Sec. 109A–3–205 defines a restrictive indorsement as one which "(c) includes the words 'for collection,' 'for deposit,' 'pay any bank,' or *like terms signifying a purpose of deposit or collection*." (Emphasis supplied.) Code Ann. Sec. 109A–3–206 (3) provides that the transferee of an instrument with such an indorsement" * * * must pay or apply any value given by him for or on the security of the instrument consistently with the indorsement and to the extent that he does so he becomes a *holder for value*. In addition such transferee is a *holder in due course* if he otherwise complies with the requirements of 109A–3–302 on what constitutes a holder in due course." (Emphasis supplied.) By causing the check to be indorsed "for deposit," as alleged, the payee signified its purpose of deposit and the plaintiff bank, by applying the value given consistently with this indorsement by crediting the payee-depositor's account with the amount of the check, became a holder for value.

Regarding requirement (b) of a holder in due course (Code Ann. Sec. 109A–3–302 (1), there is nothing on the face of the petition to indicate a lack of good faith on the part of the plaintiff in accepting the check. Good faith is presumed until questioned by appropriate pleadings.

The liability of the drawer to pay the amount of his dishonored check is established by Code Ann. Sec. 109A–3–413 (2): "The drawer engages that upon dishonor of the draft and any necessary notice of dishonor or protest he will pay the amount of the draft to the holder or to any indorser who takes it up. * * *" Under Code Ann. Sec. 109A–3–511 (2), notice or protest is entirely excused when "(b) such party has himself dishonored the instrument or has countermanded payment or otherwise has no reason to expect or right to require that the instrument be accepted or paid."

The fact that the presumption of the plaintiff-depositary bank's agency of the payee-depositor for collection purposes continued even after the credit given the depositor had been withdrawn, does not negative the right of the bank to bring an action in its own name against the defendant-drawer. As indicated hereinabove, a holder may enforce payment of an instrument in its own name whether or not it is an owner of it. Code Ann. Sec. 109A–3–301.

The net result in the present case is that the plaintiff bank continued to be the payee-depositor's agent for collection even after the credit was withdrawn and, had the plaintiff bank been able to obtain a final settlement for the check, the settlement made with the depositor would have become final and the agency status terminated; however, since the plaintiff bank was unable to obtain a settlement, either final or provisional, from the payor bank by reason of the stop payment order of the defendant-drawer, the plaintiff bank became a holder in due course (all the requirements of Code Ann. Sec. 109A-3-302 having been met) with a security interest in the item which enabled it to enforce payment against the drawer, with the right of charge-back (Code Ann. Sec. 109A-4-212) against its depositor's account in the event that a judgment cannot be obtained against the drawer.

2. Regarding requirement (c) of a holder in due course, the fact that the copy of the check attached as an exhibit to the petition bears a date more than one year prior to the time the instrument was alleged to have been transferred to the plaintiff bank does not subject the petition to a general demurrer on the ground that the petition shows that the bank had notice that the check was overdue. While it is true that "[w]here the instrument or any signature thereon is dated, the date is presumed to be correct," Code Ann. Sec. 109A-3-114 (3) (Ga. L. 1962, pp. 156, 244), this presumption is not conclusive, and may be overcome by parol evidence that it was in fact made on another date. *Mutual Fertilizer Co. v. Henderson*, 18 Ga. App. 495 (1), 89 S. E. 602; this evidence not being inadmissible as seeking to vary the contents of the instrument. *Waynesboro Planing Mill v. Perkins Mfg. Co.*, 35 Ga. App. 767 (5), 134 S. E. 831; *Wiggins v. First Mutual Bldg. & Loan Assn.*, 179 Ga. 618, 176 S. E. 636. It is alleged that the plaintiff gave credit for the check prior to receiving any knowledge or notice of its having been dishonored and without notice of any defense against or claim to it on the part of any person. This allegation is sufficient as against a general demurrer to allege compliance with requirement (c) of a holder in due course. The petition therefore alleges the plaintiff to be a holder in due course, with the rights incident thereto as set out in Code Ann. Sec. 109A-3-305.

The court did not err in its judgment overruling the general demurrer to the petition.

Judgment affirmed.

TAKEN IN GOOD FAITH

Sec. 1-201 (19) of the U. C. C. states that "good faith" means honesty in fact in the conduct or transaction concerned.

The "good faith" clause does not require that the holder make an extensive investigation of the instrument before he takes it, but as a rule it requires him to look into any suspicious or unusual circumstances that may exist. In determining whether a holder has acted in good faith, his previous business experience is taken into consideration. Circumstances which a banker or an experienced businessman could not ignore without arousing suspicion that he was guilty of collusion might pass unnoticed by a person not accustomed to dealing with negotiable instruments. Carelessness, ignorance, or stupidity is not equivalent to bad faith.

The fact that a negotiable instrument has been purchased at a considerable discount does not necessarily indicate bad faith on the purchaser's part, though under some circumstances it may be held to do so. If the instrument was taken in good faith, the fact that it was purchased at a discount would not prevent the purchaser from recovering the full amount due on the instrument at its maturity.

Finance Company of America v. Wilson
115 Ga. App. 280, 154 S. E. (2d) 459 (1967)

This was an action by the Finance Company of America (plaintiff) against Elbert F. Wilson (defendant). Plaintiff's motion for summary judgment was denied, and plaintiff appealed. Reversed.

On motion for summary judgment in this case the plaintiff brought suit against the defendant Wilson for the unpaid balance on a promissory note regular on its face, signed by Wilson and made payable to the Citizens Bank, endorsed by the bank to Stockbridge Investment Corporation and by the latter to the plaintiff, the uncontroverted affidavit attached to the motion for summary judgment showing the endorsements to have been by authorized personnel, before maturity of the instrument, for value and without notice of a defense.

DEEN, J. Under the Uniform Commercial Code a holder takes commercial paper for value to the extent that he acquires a security interest therein (Code Ann. Sec. 109A–3–303 (a)) or takes it as security for an antecedent claim; and is a holder in due course where he takes the paper for value, in good faith, and without notice that it is overdue, has been dishonored, or is subject to the claim or defense of another person (Code Ann. Sec. 109A–3–302 (1)).

The defendant contends that the trial court properly denied the motion for summary judgment on the sole ground that the plaintiff, who held this and other commercial paper as collateral for a loan to Stockbridge Investment Corporation in the amount of $6,766.32 and antecedent loans of over $300,000 proceeded, after default by Stockbridge in its own obligations, to advertise and sell this and other notes at a judicial sale at which it repurchased them in its own name. Defendant relies on Code Ann. Sec. 109A–3–302 (3): "A holder does not become a holder in due course of an instrument: (a) by purchase of it at judicial sale or by taking it under legal process." Defendant, however, ignores Code Ann. Sec. 109A–3–201 which provides that the transferee of an instrument takes all rights of the transferror unless he has been a party to fraud or illegality affecting the instrument. It is specifically provided that a prior holder with notice of a defense or claim cannot improve his position by taking from a later holder in due course. The status of one against whom a defense might have been urged in his prior capacity will not improve by interposing such a holder, but in the same vein one with the rights of a holder in due course, and who has not otherwise lost such rights, does not diminish his status by purchasing at a judicial sale although he may not *by virtue of such purchase alone* become a due course holder. That the Code has in this respect adhered to existing law see former Code Sec. 14–508; *Veal v. Jenkins*, 58 Ga. App. 4 (3), 197 S. E. 328; Code Sec..39–1303.

The trial court erred in denying the motion for summary judgment.

Judgment reversed.

WITHOUT NOTICE THAT IT IS OVERDUE OR HAS BEEN DISHONORED

The general rule is that if one purchases an instrument after maturity, he is not a holder in due course. The courts take the position that if a negotiable instrument is still in circulation after it is due, one should be suspicious of it. Such fact has the legal effect of putting one on notice that something is probably wrong with the instrument, for otherwise it would have been paid when due.

An instrument payable on a fixed date matures on that date, and if it is purchased after that date it is clearly purchased after it is overdue. More difficulty rises where the instrument is payable on demand. Such an instrument becomes overdue within a reasonable time after its issue. In determining what is a reasonable time or an unreasonable time, regard must be had to the nature of the instrument, the usage of trade or business (if any) with respect to such instruments, and the facts of the particular case.

Since checks are customarily issued for immediate use, a reasonable time is a relatively short period, by the U. C. C. presumed to be thirty days. We find, from a study of the cases, that the time ranges from a day or so to as many as twenty-four days.[1] A reasonable time is a longer time in the case of demand notes and sight drafts, even though such instruments are payable "at sight" or "on presentation." The reason for this distinction is that demand notes and sight drafts, unlike checks, are widely used in trade or business as credit instruments. This is particularly true of demand notes, which usually bear a specified rate of interest, indicating that the parties do not intend immediate payment. In certain cases the courts have held that such notes were not overdue when they had been in circulation for several months or even for several years. In one case it was held that a demand note was not overdue even though it was purchased six years after its issue. That particular note was an installment note and bore interest, and the maker had rather consistently made his installment and interest payments.[2] Under different circumstances courts have held that demand notes were overdue within a much shorter time.

[1] *Anderson v. Elem*, 111 Kans. 713, 208 P. 573 (1922). Here a check was in circulation for twenty-four days and the court held that it was not overdue.

[2] *Louisiana Mortgage Corporation, Inc. v. Pickens et al.*, La. App. Ct. of Appeals, 182 So. 385 (1938).

By the Code a holder is not a holder in due course if he purchased the instrument knowing that it had previously been dishonored, i.e. that the party primarily liable had refused to accept or to pay the instrument when it was presented. Dishonor is explained in detail in Chapter 36.

Sec. 3–304 (3) states that a purchaser has notice that an instrument is overdue if he has reason to know (a) that any part of the principal amount is overdue or that there is an uncured default in payment of another instrument of the same series; or (b) that acceleration of the instrument has been made; or (c) that he is taking a demand instrument after demand has been made or more than a reasonable length of time after its issue. A reasonable time for a check drawn and payable within the states and territories of the United States and the District of Columbia is presumed to be thirty days. Sec. 1–201 (31) states that "Presumption" or "presumed" means that the trier of fact must find the existence of the fact presumed unless and until evidence is introduced which would support a finding of its non-existence.

WITHOUT NOTICE OF ANY DEFENSE OR CLAIM TO IT ON THE PART OF ANY PERSON

In order for a holder to qualify as a holder in due course, the instrument must be complete as to form, and must be free from any irregularities that would put the purchaser on notice that something may be wrong with it.

By Sec. 3–302 (c) of the U. C. C. a holder of an instrument is not a holder in due course if he takes the instrument when he has notice of any defense against or claim to it on the part of any person. Under Sec. 1–201 (25) a person has notice of a fact when (a) he has actual knowledge of it; or (b) he has received a notice or notification of it; or (c) from all the facts and circumstances known to him at the time in question he has reason to know that it exists. A person "knows" or has "knowledge" of a fact when he has actual knowledge of it. "Discover" or "learn" or a .word or phrase of similar import refers to knowledge rather than to reason to know. The time and circumstances under which a notice or notification may cease to be effective are not determined by the Code.

Sec. 3–304 provides (1) The purchaser has notice of a claim or defense if (a) the instrument is so incomplete, bears such visible evidence of forgery or alteration, or is otherwise so irregular as to call into question its validity, terms or ownership or to create an ambiguity as to the party to pay; or (b) the purchaser has notice that the obligation of any party is voidable in whole or in part, or that all parties have been discharged.

(2) The purchaser has notice of a claim against the instrument when he has knowledge that a fiduciary has negotiated the instrument in payment

of or as security for his own debt or in any transaction for his own benefit or otherwise in breach of duty.

One should be wary about taking an instrument that contains unfilled blanks. The courts hold that such fact should put a would-be purchaser on notice that something may be wrong with the instrument; and if the court considers the particular omission material, it will hold that the holder is not a holder in due course.

The following are examples of instruments which the courts have held to be not complete on their face, because of omissions or unfilled blanks:

(1) "On or before four _____ after date."

(2) "_____ after date."

(3) "I promise to pay to the order of _____."
Here the name of the payee was omitted.

(4) "To _____. Accepted January 1, 1975."
Here the name of the drawee was omitted. The instrument was accepted by the intended drawee, but the court nevertheless held that the instrument was not "complete on its face."

The following are examples of instruments which the courts have held to be complete in spite of omissions or unfilled blanks:

(1) "_____ promise to pay to the order of John Doe." The omission of the pronoun "I" or "we" is held not to be a material omission.

(2) "For value received, with interest at _____ per cent per annum." In such a case the courts hold that the legal rate applies.

(3) An instrument in which the amount payable is expressed in words but the space provided for expressing it in figures is left blank.

Despite the foregoing general rule, the U. C. C. recognizes that an incomplete instrument when completed in accordance with the authority given is effective as completed (Sec. 3–115). In order, however, that any such instrument when completed may be enforced against any person who became a party thereto prior to its completion, it must be filled up strictly in accordance with the authority given and within a reasonable time. But if any such instrument, after completion, is negotiated to a holder in due course, it is valid and effectual for all purposes in his hands, and he may enforce it as if it had been filled up strictly in accordance with the authority given and within a reasonable time. Suppose that A signs a note and gives it to B, but neglects to fill in the amount payable. If B fills in the amount payable and negotiates the bill to C, a holder in due course, C may enforce the bill against A even though B did not fill in the blank "strictly in accordance with the authority given" by A to B. Of course, if C knew that B had exceeded his authority in filling in the blanks,

C would not be an innocent purchaser of the instrument and could not qualify as a holder in due course under Sec. 3–302 of the U. C. C.

Under Sec. 3–304, the instrument must not give notice to purchaser of claim or defense. Such irregularities as erasures, alterations, or obvious insertions on the face of the instrument should put the purchaser on his guard, for they may prevent him from becoming a holder in due course. The courts have held instruments "irregular" in the following instances: (1) where the instrument was stamped "paid"; (2) where the word "canceled" was written across the face of the instrument; (3) where a usurious rate of interest was charged and such fact was apparent on the face of the instrument.

Sec. 3–304 of the U. C. C. provides that knowledge of the following facts does not of itself give the purchaser notice of a defense or claim (a) that the instrument is antedated or postdated; (b) that it was issued or negotiated in return for an executory promise or accompanied by a separate agreement, unless the purchaser has notice that a defense or claim has arisen from the terms thereof; (c) that any party has signed for accommodation; (d) that an incomplete instrument has been completed, unless the purchaser has notice of any improper completion; (e) that any person negotiating the instrument is or was a fiduciary, (f) that there has been default in payment of interest on the instrument or in payment of any other instrument, except one of the same series. (5) The filing or recording of a document does not of itself constitute notice within the provisions of this Article to a person who would otherwise be a holder in due course.

(6) To be effective, notice must be received at such time and in such manner as to give a reasonable opportunity to act on it. The courts have held that the fact that an instrument has been post-dated or antedated does not make it "irregular." They have also held that an instrument is not made "irregular" by the fact that the body of the instrument and the signature are not in the same handwriting. The holder must have such knowledge at the time when he purchases the instrument; if he finds it out later it will not prevent him from being a holder in due course.

The title of the person who negotiates the instrument is said to be defective when he obtained the instrument, or any signature to it, by fraud, duress, or other unlawful means, or for an illegal consideration, or when he negotiates it in breach of faith, or under such circumstances as amount to a fraud. Sec. 3–115 provides that "(1) When a paper whose contents at the time of signing show that it is intended to become an instrument is signed while still incomplete in any necessary respect it cannot be enforced until completed, but when it is completed in accordance with authority given it is effective as completed."

National Currency Exchange, Inc. #3 v. Perkins

52 Ill. App. (2d) 215, 201 N. E. (2d) 668 (1964)

This was an action by National Currency Exchange, Inc. (plaintiff) against Herbert J. Perkins (defendant). Judgment for plaintiff and defendant appealed. Affirmed.

This is an action on a check drawn May 14, 1960 and dated May 16, 1960. Prior to the due date of the check, on May 14, the payee, John Stauropoulos, endorsed and cashed the check at plaintiff's currency exchange. The drawer, defendant Perkins, instructed drawee bank, Commercial National Bank of Chicago, to stop payment on the check on May 16. The plaintiff presented the check to the drawee bank for payment but it was dishonored. Plaintiff secured a default judgment against Stauropoulos, the payee therein, which judgment remains unsatisfied. Consequently, plaintiff brought the instant action against the defendant, the drawer thereof. The trial court found against defendant, and entered judgment on the instrument.

The facts are uncontroverted. The defendant, Perkins, is engaged primarily in the distribution of amusement machines. On May 14 he was contacted by a customer and restaurant owner, John Stauropoulos, who informed defendant of his intention to open a second restaurant. In return for permitting defendant to install an amusement machine in his proposed restaurant, Stauropoulos asked defendant to lend him $450.00.

Desiring to obtain this business, defendant issued the check, postdating it for the purpose of investigating Stauropoulos' reputation and background. Upon discovering that Stauropoulos was insolvent and about to close his one restaurant, and that he had no intention of opening a second one, defendant, at the opening of business Monday morning, May 16, instructed his bank to stop payment on the check.

KLUCZYNSKI, J. The sole question presented to this court, which is one of first, and perhaps last, impression in this State is whether one who purchases for value and in good faith a postdated check before its maturity or due date is a holder in due course and does not take the check subject to whatever defenses are available as between the original parties.

Plaintiff deposited the check in its account at the Exchange National Bank, but it was returned with the notation that payment had been stopped on May 16.

The weight of authority is that the mere fact that a postdated check is negotiated prior to the date it bears, does not prevent the transferee from becoming a holder in due course.

The question posed by this appeal is not one dealt with by any specific provision of the N. I. L. and the instant decision is, perhaps, best rendered by weighing the policy consideration attendant to the problem presented. Though inapplicable to the instant case because the situation arose prior to the effective date of the Uniform Commercial Code (Chap. 26, et seq. Ill. Rev. Stat. (1963)), Sec. 3–304 (4) (a) thereof addresses itself to the question before us. That section reads: "(4) Knowledge of the following facts does not of itself give the purchaser notice of a defense or claim (a) that the instrument is antedated or postdated."

It is a purchaser who knows at the time of the purchase of an asserted defense, or of facts or circumstances which may create a defense who is precluded from being a holder in due course, and then on the theory of "bad faith." The rule announced here not only favors negotiability but is consistent with sound commercial practice and experience, as evidenced by the relevant provisions quoted above from the recently enacted Uniform Commercial Code, now the law in Illinois. Therefore, the judgment of the lower court finding plaintiff to be a holder in due course and entitled to recover on the instrument is affirmed.

Affirmed.

United Securities Corporation v. Bruton
213 A. (2d) 892 (1965)

This was an action by United Securities Corporation (plaintiff) against Cora E. Bruton (defendant). Judgment for defendant and plaintiff appealed. Judgment affirmed.

Appellee Cora E. Bruton purchased two wigs from The Wig Shoppe, Inc. and in payment therefor gave her promissory note for $322.98. Two weeks later she returned one of the wigs to The Wig Shoppe, and complained of defects in its workmanship. After paying approximately one-half of the note she refused to make further payments.

HOOD, C. J. This action was brought by United Securities Corporation, to whom The Wig Shoppe had sold the note two days after its execution, for the balance of the note.

The trial court found that United Securities was not a holder in due course, and gave judgment for appellee.

On this appeal United Securities asserts that it relies upon Title 28, Section 409, of the District of Columbia Code, 1961 ed., which provides that: "Every holder is deemed prima facie to be a holder in due course * * *," and claims it was denied the benefit of the statutory presumption.

Appellant overlooks the fact that Title 28, Section 409, of the 1961 Code has been superseded by D. C. Code 1961, Sec. 28:3–307 (Supp. IV, 1965), a part of the Uniform Commercial Code, effective in this jurisdiction since January 1, 1965. Section 28:3–307 (3) provides: "After it is shown that a defense exists a person claiming the rights of a holder in due course has the burden of establishing that he or some person under whom he claims is in all respects a holder in due course."

Although the entire transaction occurred prior to the effective date of the

Uniform Commercial Code, the trial occurred after the effective date, and the burden of proof, a procedural matter, was controlled by the law existing at date of trial. There is no vested right in a rule of evidence, and a statute relating solely to procedural law, such as burden of proof and rules of evidence, applies to all proceedings after its effective date even though the transaction occurred prior to its enactment. Procedural statutes are the exception to the general rule against retroactive application, if indeed the application can be considered retroactive. The savings clause of the Act under consideration preserves the "rights, duties and interests" of the parties to transactions entered into prior to its effective date, but we do not construe this as an intention by Congress that procedural changes made by a statute should not apply in court proceedings for the enforcement of such rights, duties and interests.

In the case before us a defense of defective workmanship in the article sold was shown. Appellant made no attempt to meet the merits of that defense, but sought to avoid the defense by its claim of being a holder in due course. Under present law the burden was on appellant to prove that it was "in all respects a holder in due course." The only evidence offered by appellant to establish its status as a holder in due course was that it "purchased" the note on the date shown on the endorsement. It offered no evidence of the price paid and no explanation why the note was payable at its office, or why the note was purchased so promptly after its execution, or what was the relationship between it and the payee. Under these circumstances the court could, as it did, find that appellant had failed to sustain its burden of proving it was a holder in due course.

Affirmed.

MAY A PAYEE BE A HOLDER IN DUE COURSE?

The general rule is that a payee cannot qualify as a holder in due course. In most transactions the payee deals directly with the maker or drawer, and therefore has knowledge of any defense which might be available to the maker or drawer. A few courts have held that under no circumstances may a payee be a holder in due course. It is their contention that one cannot be a holder in due course, unless the instrument has been "negotiated" to him from another holder, and that this is not the situation in the case of a payee, since he is the first holder, and the instrument has been "issued" and not "negotiated" to him.

However, under the U. C. C., Sec. 3–302, a payee may be a holder in due course. COMMENT: "Subsection (2) is intended to settle the long continued conflict over the status of the payee as a holder in due course. The conflict has turned very largely upon the word "negotiated" in the original Section 52 (4), which is now eliminated. The position here taken is that the payee may become a holder in due course to the same extent and under the same circumstances as any other holder. This is true whether he takes the instrument by purchase from a third person or directly from the obligor." The situations involved are those where the payee deals with the maker not directly but through a third person, such as an agent. For example, A wishes to purchase certain merchandise from B. He does not know what the merchandise will cost, so he makes out a check, complete and regular in every respect except that he does not fill in the amount. He gives the check to his agent C and directs him to go to B's place of business, purchase the merchandise, fill in the correct amount and give the check to B, and bring the merchandise back with him. But C fills in the check for a larger amount, and B in good faith pays him the difference in money, which C appropriates to his own use. Most courts would hold that B was a holder in due course of the check, especially if it could be shown that A was negligent or imprudent in his choice of C as an agent.

Crest Finance Co. v. First State Bank of Westmont
37 Ill. (2d) 243, 226 N. E. (2d) 369 (1967)

This was an action by Crest Finance Company, Inc., et al. (plaintiffs) against First State Bank of Westmont, et al. (defendants). Judgment for defendants and plaintiffs appealed. Reversed and remanded.

The Finance company brought action against the bank for declaration that the company was entitled to possession of certain commercial paper, to enjoin the bank from disposing of or encumbering the paper, and praying for its return. Thereafter the Federal Deposit Insurance Corporation, which was appointed receiver for the bank, was granted leave to intervene and to make the owner of the company's stock, who sold the stock, a third-party defendant. The Circuit Court, Cook County, John J. Lupe, J., entered a decree adverse to the company and the seller of the stock, and they appealed. The Appellate Court for the First District, 66 Ill. App. (2d) 364, 214 N. E. (2d) 526, reversed and remanded.

HOUSE, J. The effect of Article 3 of the Code (Ill. Rev. Stat. 1965, Chap. 26, Sec. 3-101 et seq.) must be considered. Section 3-302 (1) reads: "A holder in due course is a holder who takes the instrument (a) for value; and (b) in good faith; and (c) without notice that it is overdue or has been dishonored or of any defense against or claim to it on the part of any person." Section 3-302 (2) states: "A payee may be a holder in due course." Section 3-303 provides: "A holder takes the instrument for value (a) to the extent that the agreed consideration has been performed or that he acquires a security interest in or a lien on the instrument otherwise than by legal process; or (b) when he takes the instrument in payment of or as security for an antecedent claim against any person whether or not the claim is due; or (c) when he gives a negotiable instrument for it or makes an irrevocable commitment to a third person."

The cashier's checks delivered to Niederberger [payee], one signed by an assistant cashier and the other two signed by Willard, the cashier of Westmont, were negotiable instruments. If Niederberger became a holder in due course, the drawer bank (Westmont) could not recover from the paying banks nor from Niederberger. There is no evidence to substantiate lack of good faith on Niederberger's part or that he had any notice of any infirmities in the drawing or delivery of the checks at the time of delivery, so that provisions (b) and (c) of Section 3–302 (1) were complied with. (Subsequent knowledge does not impair holder-in-due-course status; Sec. 3–304 (6); see Comment 12, Sec. 3–304 of the Code; cf. *Drumm Construction Co. v. Forbes*, 305 Ill. 303, 137 N. E. 225, 26 A. L. R. 764.) This leaves only the question of whether Niederberger gave "value" for the three checks to determine his holder-in-due-course status.

The receiver asserts that placing the stock in escrow was an executory contract and that the agreed consideration (delivery of the stock) had not been performed in accordance with Section 3–303 (a) of the Code so that Niederberger had not parted with "value" for the checks. This ignores the "irrevocable commitment" language in Section 3–303 (c) which, according to Comment 6 is new but recognizes an exception to the rule that an executory promise is not value. "Irrevocable commitment" in Section 3–303 (c) cannot be read to mean complete performance, otherwise it would be surplusage because the situation would have been covered by Section 3–303 (a). Here, Niederberger made an actual, physical delivery of the certificates evidencing ownership of the stock to the escrow agent without anything further to be done on his part except notify the escrowee when he had been relieved of his bank guarantees. Thus the transfer was irrevocable. The only remaining act to complete delivery was solely within the power of the buyer; that is, to either substitute his name on the guaranteed paper or pay the obligations. The failure to endorse was unimportant since assignment was legally enforcible under the terms of the agreement. In our opinion, delivery to the escrow agent and the agreement to execute all documents necessary to consummate the sale constituted an "irrevocable commitment" within the meaning of Section 3–303 (c), comparable to an unrestricted letter of credit used as an illustration in Comment 6 heretofore referred to.

The fact that Brock (or his principal) was a beneficiary of the escrow agreement does not, in our view, affect the irrevocable character of the escrow commitment made by Niederberger, nor render it a commitment of a type not covered by Section 3–303 (c). For example, had the Crest stock increased in value, the receiver, upon fulfillment of the escrow condition, might·by appropriate proceedings, obtain Brock's interest in the Crest shares, demand delivery of the certificate by the escrowee, and demand completion of the transfer by the escrowee. Niederberger and the escrowee would have had no defense to this demand.

Judgment of Appellate Court affirmed in part and reversed in part and cause remanded to the Circuit Court for further proceedings.

A HOLDER THROUGH A HOLDER IN DUE COURSE

The general rule is that if the holder of a negotiable instrument is not a holder in due course, the instrument is subject to the same defenses to which it would be subject if it were not a negotiable instrument. However, an important exception is made in the case of a holder who is not himself a holder in due course but derives his title through a holder in due course. Sec. 3–201 of the U. C. C. provides: "(1) Transfer of an instrument vests in the transferee such rights as the transferor has therein, except that a transferee who has himself been a party to any fraud or illegality affecting the instrument or who as a prior holder had notice of a defense or claim against it cannot improve his position by taking from a later holder in due course." In such case the transferee "steps into the shoes" of his transferor, and takes free from any personal defenses which the party primarily liable may possess, even though he knows of such defenses when he takes the instrument.

The reason for giving the holder through a holder in due course such a preferred position is not to favor the holder himself but to make the instrument more valuable to the holder in due course by safeguarding its marketability. If this rule of law did not exist, a holder in due course might be deprived of his market for the instrument if the party primarily liable intimated that he had some personal defense to the instrument. As some courts have said, a holder in due course is entitled to have the whole world for his market.

Wheeler v. Wallace
167 S. W. (2d) 1043 (Tex.) (1943)

This was an action by Edward R. Wallace (plaintiff) against Stella Wheeler (defendant). Judgment for plaintiff, and defendant appealed. Reversed and remanded.

Plaintiff filed this action against defendant to recover upon a promissory note. Plaintiff claimed to hold through a holder in due course. Defendant denied these claims. The cause was submitted to a jury, which found that the note was without consideration and that plaintiff and John E. Hill, president of the Amarillo Investment Co., each knew before purchasing the note that it was without consideration. No issue was submitted as to whether the note was transferred before its maturity, but the testimony was conclusive that each of such transfers occurred prior to the maturity of the note. Plaintiff filed a motion for judgment non obstante veredicto, which motion was granted and judgment rendered in favor of plaintiff for his debt and for foreclosure of his attachment lien. Defendant appealed.

FOLLEY, J. The appellant asserts, first, that the testimony did not warrant the judgment non obstante veredicto. With this contention we cannot agree. The testimony conclusively shows that the Amarillo Investment Company was a purchaser for value before maturity and without notice of any infirmities in the instrument. The plaintiff derived his title through this holder in due course and he was not party to any fraud or irregularity affecting the instrument. A holder who derives his title through a holder in due course, and who is not himself a party to any fraud or illegality affecting the instrument, has all the rights of such former holder in respect of all parties prior to the latter. In 6 *Tex. Jur.* 705, Sec. 91, with reference to this provision of the statute, it is said: "In the application of this rule it is immaterial that the transferee did or did not pay value, or that he purchased the paper after the date of its maturity, or that he had notice of existing equities at the time of the transfer."

[NOTE: The judgment was reversed and remanded on grounds other than those contained in this abstract of the case.]

DEFENSES

There are two classes or groups of defenses, (1) real and (2) personal. A holder in due course is subject to real defenses but not to personal defenses. A holder who is not a holder in due course is subject to both groups of defenses. He therefore stands essentially in the same position as an assignee of a simple contract.

The U. C. C. brings together real and personal defenses in Sections 3–305 and 3–306. Most of the real and personal defenses have their origin in the decisions of the various state and appellate courts.

In the following discussion it will be observed that certain defenses may be either real or personal, depending upon the circumstances involved.

REAL DEFENSES

Sec. 3–305 of the U. C. C. states that to the extent that a holder is a holder in due course he takes the instrument free from (1) all claims to it on the part of any person, and (2) all defenses of any party to the instrument with whom the holder has not dealt except (a) infancy, to the extent that it is a defense to a simple contract; and (b) such other incapacity, or duress, or illegality of the transaction, as renders the obligation of the party a nullity; and (c) such misrepresentation as has induced the party to sign the instrument with neither knowledge nor reasonable opportunity to obtain knowledge of its character or its essential terms; and (d) discharge in insolvency proceedings; and (e) any other discharge of which the holder has notice when he takes the instrument.

Real defenses are those defenses that may be set up against any holder, including a holder in due course. In general it may be said that a real defense arises:

(1) Where the instrument never became a valid and enforceable contract because of some defect in its inception or execution, or because of the incapacity of the party who executed it; for example, where the signature of the maker or drawer was forged, or where the maker or drawer was an infant when he executed the instrument.

(2) Where the transferee (holder) never acquired a valid title to the instrument; for example, where the transferor's signature was forged.

(3) Where the courts hold that upon grounds of public policy such contract should not be enforced; for example, where a negotiable instrument growing out of an illegal act or transaction is made void by statute.

The following are the most usual types of real defenses: forgery; fraud in the inception or execution; infancy; insanity; material alteration; intoxication, if of an extreme nature; duress, if of an extreme nature; illegality, if the instrument has been made void by statute, and discharge in insolvency proceedings.

FORGERY. A forged signature, whether that of maker or drawer or that of indorser, is wholly inoperative. Hence forgery is a real defense against any holder, except where the forgery was a result of negligence on the part of the party against whom it is sought to enforce the instrument.[1]

FRAUD IN THE INCEPTION OR EXECUTION. In the case of fraud in the inception or execution of an instrument the payee secures the signature of the maker or drawer by causing him to believe that he is signing some other type of instrument or paper. Under such circumstances it is not the intention of the maker to become a party to a negotiable instrument. The payee may have told the maker that he was signing an ordinary contract, or some sort of petition, or even an autograph album. In such cases the courts hold that if the maker has been guilty of negligence he is estopped from setting up the defense of fraud in the inception against a holder in due course.

INFANCY. Under contract law a contract is voidable as to an infant. Similarly, under the Uniform Commercial Code, Sec. 3–305 (2) (a) an infant may set up his infancy as a defense to the extent that it is a defense to a simple contract.

INSANITY. Insanity may usually be set up as a real defense against any holder. This is clearly the case where a person has been judicially de-

[1] U. C. C., Secs. 3–404 and 3–406.

clared insane. And most courts hold that insanity is a real defense against any holder who knew of the insanity, even though the signer of the instrument had not been judicially declared insane. Some courts have held that if the holder did not know that the signer was insane and the signer had not been judicially declared insane, the defense of insanity may not be set up against a holder in due course.

MATERIAL ALTERATION. If a negotiable instrument is materially altered without the assent of all parties liable on the instrument, such alteration has the effect of avoiding the instrument, except as against the party who made, authorized, or assented to the alteration and subsequent indorsers.

Sec. 3–407 states that "(1) Any alteration of an instrument is material which changes the contract of any party thereto in any respect, including any such change in (a) the number or relations of the parties; or (b) an incomplete instrument, by completing it otherwise than as authorized; or (c) the writing as signed, by adding to it or by removing any part of it."

However, if an instrument which has been materially altered is negotiated to a holder in due course who was not a party to the alteration, he may enforce payment of the instrument according to its original tenor. Thus, if the instrument was originally drawn for $100 and it was altered and raised to $150, a holder in due course could enforce payment of the instrument against the maker for the original amount of $100.

Sec. 3–407 states that "(2) As against any person other than a subsequent holder in due course (a) alteration by the holder which is both fraudulent and material discharges any party whose contract is thereby changed unless that party assents or is precluded from asserting the defense; (b) no other alteration discharges any party and the instrument may be enforced according to its original tenor, or as to incomplete instruments according to the authority given.

"(3) A subsequent holder in due course may in all cases enforce the instrument according to its original tenor, and when an incomplete instrument has been completed, he may enforce it as completed."

DISCHARGE IN INSOLVENCY PROCEEDINGS. Sec. 3–305 provides that a discharge in insolvency proceedings is a real defense and consequently is good against a holder in due course. Based upon this section, a person who has been discharged in bankruptcy or in an insolvency proceeding on a $50,000.00 note in the hands of a holder in due course has a complete defense.

Unadilla National Bank v. McQueer
27 A. D. (2d) 778, 277 N. Y. S. (2d) 221 (1967)

This was an action by Unadilla National Bank (plaintiff) against H. J. Mc-Queer and Johnson's Garage, Inc. (defendants). Judgment for plaintiff and defendants appealed. Judgment and order reversed.

On March 17, 1966 McQueer purchased a truck and milk cooling tank from the defendant Johnson's Garage, Inc., for the sum of $10,698. He signed a note for this amount on one of plaintiff's printed forms supplied by the garage. Rex Hinman, general manager of Johnson's Garage, wrote in the terms of payment in his own hand before McQueer signed. Johnson's Garage, Inc., was the payee and there was a reference to the sale between Johnson's Garage and McQueer typed on the note. Affidavits supplied by McQueer, Hinman and one Lyle Bright, who was present at the transaction, state that the note was drawn to become due in five days from date which would have been on March 22, 1966. The note, as yet unpaid, was on March 28, 1966 negotiated by the payee to plaintiff bank, which paid the face amount over to the payee, and the check was deposited in the Johnson's Garage account in an Oneonta bank. Plaintiff's employees assert in their affidavits that the note was received, accepted and posted in the regular course of business and that when it was received it was payable 45 days from date; that the bank had a policy of not accepting overdue notes; and that no one at the bank, at least not anyone who had handled the note, inserted the figure 4 before the figure 5.

McQueer on April 1, 1966, allegedly unaware that Johnson's Garage had negotiated the note to plaintiff, paid to the garage the $10,698 for the equipment which he had purchased by personal check. This was also taken and deposited by Johnson's Garage in its account at the Oneonta bank. In his affidavit McQueer states that he demanded the return of the note at the time of his payment but that Mr. Johnson said it was locked up in the garage vault and would be returned to him by mail. Despite McQueer's calls the note was never re-returned—it having been negotiated to the plaintiff three days previously. On May 1, 1966, the due date of the note based on 45 days, the bank demanded payment by the maker, McQueer, and upon his refusal this action was commenced.

AULISI, J. Defendant H. J. McQueer appeals from an order and judgment granting summary judgment to plaintiff in this action brought to collect on a note made by appellant and negotiated to plaintiff.

On the record before us, we are constrained to disagree with the Special Term that plaintiff was entitled to summary judgment. The basis of its decision was that even if there had been a material alteration of the instrument it was not so manifest as to excite suspicion and the instrument being complete and regular on its face it was accepted by the bank without notice of any material alteration and all other requisites having been met, the bank was a holder in due course.

Upon the facts presented by defendant, we must assume that there was an alteration on the note from 5 to 45 days somewhere along the line. If the alteration was effected before the transfer to plaintiff, the bank might still be deemed a holder in due course. A holder in due course is one who takes an instrument, "without notice that it is overdue or has been dishonored or of any defense against or claim to it on the part of any person" (Uniform Commercial Code, Sec. 3–302, subd. (1)). Where, as here, there is an altered instrument, the statute provides as follows: "A subsequent holder in due course may in all cases enforce the instrument according to its original tenor, and when an incomplete instrument has been completed, he may enforce it as completed" (Uniform Commercial Code, Sec. 3–407, subd. (3); see also Sec. 3–304, subd. (1) [a].) So in this case, where the note was overdue as originally drafted, the bank may claim status as a holder in due course and enforce the note if the note came to it in such condition that alteration was not noticeable.

Special Term assumed that the bank took the note after the alteration was made. We can not accept this assumption as a fact beyond dispute. All the persons who have executed affidavits here deny any knowledge of the alteration, but the crucial question still remains—who made the alteration. When there are defenses such as payment or that the paper is overdue, the burden is upon the party claiming the rights of a holder in due course to prove his status as such (Uniform Commercial Code, Sec. 3–307, subd. (3)). We do not think the burden has been met where there remains, among others, the question as to the identity of the one who made the alteration. If it was not accomplished prior to the bank's acceptance then, as to the bank's reduced status as a mere holder, questions remain as to knowledge and authority surrounding the alteration. We, therefore, are not now ready to accept the bank's contention that even as a mere holder it would have a right to payment from McQueer because the latter made payment negligently to a party who was not a holder of the note (see *Third National Bank of Buffalo v. Bowman-Spring*, 50 App. Div. 66, 63 N. Y. S. 410; *Industrial Bank of Commerce v. Hayse*, 191 Misc. 658, 77 N. Y. S. (2d) 605; *Mundet Cork Corp. v. Grupp*, 154 Misc. 798, 278 N. Y. S. 231; 42 N. Y. Jur., *Negotiable Instruments*, Sec. 582; 11 Am. Jur. (2d), *Bills and Notes*, Sec. 989; Anno: *Commercial Paper-Transferee-Defenses*, 44 A. L. R. (2d) 172–183). At any rate, whatever factual questions may arise it is our view that the bank must prove to the satisfaction of a trier of the facts that it took the note in its altered form in good faith before judgment may be entered in its favor as a holder in due course. We also leave open for trial the question whether the alteration was noticeable or not.

Judgment and order reversed, on the law and the facts, and motion denied, with costs to appellant.

First National Bank of Philadelphia v. Anderson et al.
5 Bucks Co. L. Rep. 287 (1956)

This was an action by Alfred B. Anderson, Ella Anderson, and Amy Darrah (defendants) against The First National Bank of Philadelphia (plaintiff) petitioning to open a judgment on a note taken by the bank. Petition denied.

The depositions reveal that the judgment note was executed on July 14, 1954 and appeared on the same sheet of paper as the contract. The petitioners affixed their signatures to both parts of the document. According to the petitioners' testimony, the contract, providing for the installation of twelve jalousie windows, was to be in the amount of $744.00, with monthly payments of approximately $20.00 each. It was the further contention of the petitioners that the judgment note was signed in blank and that the writing, including the figures now appearing on the judgment note, were not present at the time of execution and that their approval of the work done was to be given before any payments became due on the contract. On August 10, 1954 the Atlantic Storm Window Co. began the installation of the windows, but it is the petitioners' version that the work was improperly done and that the windows as installed were not as represented to be at the time the contract was signed.

BIESTER, P.J. This matter is before us on the petition of the above defendants to open the judgment referred to in the caption, the depositions taken in support therof and the answer filed in response thereto.

Our first inquiry must be of determination of the question of whether, under the facts revealed by the record before us, the plaintiff is a holder in due course.

Section 3–302 of the Uniform Commercial Code, the provisions of which govern the proceeding before us, states that "(1) A holder in due course is a holder who takes the instrument (a) for value; and (b) in good faith including observance of the reasonable commercial standards of any business in which the holder may be engaged; and (c) without notice that it is overdue or has been dishonored or of any defense against or claim to it on the part of any person."

It is our understanding that as to these provisions, the defendants contend that the bank was not a holder in due course in that it did not take the instrument in good faith, on the theory that it became incumbent upon the plaintiff to communicate with the payee and/or the makers of the note to determine whether the work had been satisfactorily completed before accepting the note. We find no merit in this contention.

In the instant case the three defendants all sat at the same table and each in turn signed the instrument at the places indicated by the agent of the Atlantic Storm Window Co. We have carefully read the testimony as to the circumstances under which the instruments were signed and find no possible excuse for the failure either to read the instrument, to have it read, or to seek information from others present regarding it. It is true that Alfred Anderson, one of the defendants, has but little formal education, but he is clearly not illiterate. As to Ella Anderson, she said that some of the print was too fine for her to read. The third defendant, Amy Darrah, was evidently relied upon by the other petitioners in transactions of this kind and is a bookkeeping clerk in the revenue accounting department of the Bell Telephone Company. There is no suggestion that the other parties asked her to read the contract and explain it to them and her only excuse for not reading it was that Mr. Jacobs, payee's agent, was talking and because of this talking she had no real chance to examine the documents.

The difficulty with defendants' position is that all the acts of infirmity alleged in the petition to open the judgment existed between the immediate parties to the note and not between the parties and the plaintiff as a holder in due course, and as there is no allegation that plaintiff had notice of any infirmities at the time it was negotiated to it, the defendants cannot avail themselves of such alleged infirmities as against the plaintiff as a holder in due course.

And now, to wit, February 17, 1956, the petition to open the judgment is refused and the rule granted thereon discharged at the cost of the petitioners.

PERSONAL DEFENSES

Personal defenses are those types of defenses that are cut off when the instrument is negotiated to a holder in due course, or when the holder takes through a holder in due course. Personal defenses may be set up in the following situations: (1) between the immediate or original parties to the instrument, i.e. by the maker against the payee; (2) against the holder, even though he is a holder in due course, if the instrument is not negotiable; and (3) against the holder if he is not a holder in due course.

In general, personal defenses are those that involve defects in the title of prior parties, or those that are available only to prior parties among themselves, e.g. failure of consideration, breach of warranty, or payment.

The following are the most usual types of personal defenses: failure or lack of consideration, fraud in the inducement, illegality, duress, undue influence, insanity, intoxication, non-delivery of a completed instrument, payment, set-off or counterclaim, breach of warranty, and non-delivery of an incomplete instrument (U. C. C., Secs. 3–306 and 3–408).

FAILURE OR LACK OF CONSIDERATION. As between the immediate or original parties to a negotiable instrument, the instrument must meet the essential requirements of a simple contract in order to be enforceable. One of these requirements is consideration. Thus, if the instrument lacks the requirement of consideration the payee may not enforce the instrument against the other party. If A signs a note for $100, with B named as payee, and B gives A no consideration for his promise contained in the note, B could not enforce the payment of the note against A when the note matured. However, if B should negotiate the note to C, a holder in due course, C could enforce the note against A. Of course, as we have already seen, one who is a holder in due course must have "paid value," i.e. given consideration.

FRAUD IN THE INDUCEMENT.   While fraud in the inception is a real defense, fraud in the inducement is a personal defense. In the former, as we have seen, the signer is deliberately deceived as to the nature of the instrument he is signing. In the latter, the signer of the instrument knows the nature of the instrument but is induced to sign it through misrepresentation and fraud. For example. A induces B to buy certain corporate stock by fraudulently misrepresenting the stock to B. B gives A a note for the stock and agrees to pay the note in thirty days. Before the time arrives to pay the note, B discovers A's fraud. B could set up this fact as a defense if A should sue him to recover on the note. However, if B had negotiated the note to C, a holder in due course, C could recover from B.

ILLEGALITY.   Illegality may be either a real or a personal defense, depending upon the facts of the case. Usually it is a personal defense. However, if a statute expressly or by implication makes void any negotiable instrument arising out of a particular kind of illegal act or transaction, then such illegality is held to be a real defense. Some of the states have such statutes which are applicable to wagering contracts and to contracts wherein usurious rates of interest are charged. For example, assume that a certain state statute makes it illegal to engage in gambling or betting, but does not state that any negotiable instrument given in payment of such debt is void. A and B engage in a gambling transaction. A loses, and in payment of his debt he gives B a check. If A stopped payment on the check and B brought suit. A could set up the defense of illegality against B; but if B instead negotiated A's check to C, a holder in due course, C could recover on the check against A, since under the assumed facts illegality was only a personal defense. But if the statute made void any negotiable instrument given in the payment of a gambling debt, then the illegality would constitute a real defense, and could be set up by A against any holder. As the court stated in *Whitaker v. Smith*, 255 Ky, 339, 73 S. W. (2d) 1105 (1934): "Sometimes certain kinds of contracts are declared by statute to be absolutely void and when so declared the defense of this kind of illegality is real and is available against a holder in due course. The almost universal rule regarding such contracts is that they are void and may not be enforced, not only as between the original parties thereto, but likewise are they prohibited from enforcement by one who may become the holder of them in due course, and this is upon the ground that being void they never had any obligatory force and are no more binding upon the maker than if he had never executed them. The theory upon which that conclusion is reached is that the legislature, in so providing, did so in furtherance of what it conceived to be a wholesome public policy."

DURESS.   Duress is usually a personal defense. However, if it is of an extreme nature, e.g. where one is forced to sign a negotiable instrument at the point of a gun, it is a real defense.

UNDUE INFLUENCE.   Undue influence is held to be a personal defense.

INSANITY.   See Real Defenses.

INTOXICATION.   Usually intoxication is only a personal defense. However, if the signer was so intoxicated when he signed the instrument that he was incapable of understanding the nature of his act, such intoxication *may* constitute a real defense. But since his incapacity is self-imposed, strong evidence is usually required to make the defense available against a holder in due course. Whether or not the signer repudiated his act within a reasonable time after regaining his sobriety is taken into consideration in such cases.

NON–DELIVERY OF A COMPLETED INSTRUMENT.   Lack of delivery of a completed instrument is a personal defense. Sec. 1–201 (14) states that delivery with respect to instruments, documents of title, chattel paper, or securities means voluntary transfer of possession. But where the instrument is in the hands of a holder in due course, a valid delivery thereof by all parties prior to him so as to make them liable to him is conclusively presumed." Thus, if the instrument is complete but before delivery it is lost or stolen and negotiated to a holder in due course, the non-delivery of the instrument by the maker or drawer may not be set up against the holder in due course. This situation would arise only in the case of a bearer instrument or of an order instrument which had been indorsed in blank, thereby making possible further negotiation of the instrument by delivery alone. If the instrument were an order instrument, requiring indorsement before it could be further negotiated, the thief or finder would have to forge the indorsement in order to transfer the instrument, and such forgery could of course be set up as a real defense against any holder.

PAYMENT.   Payment of a negotiable instrument *before maturity* by the party primarily liable is only a personal defense. However, payment of the instrument *at or after maturity* discharges it. It is obvious that one who pays a negotiable instrument before it is due should insist upon having the note canceled or marked "paid" and surrendered to him at the time of payment.

SET–OFF AND COUNTERCLAIM.   Set-offs and counterclaims which the maker may have against the original payee of the instrument are personal defenses and may not be set up against a holder in due course. They are examples of defenses that are available to prior parties among themselves.

BREACH OF WARRANTY.   Breach of warranty is a personal defense. For example, A buys from B certain merchandise which B has expressly warranted as possessing certain characteristics. A gives in payment his promissory note. The goods are not as warranted. A could set up breach of warranty as a defense against B, but not against a holder in due course to whom B had negotiated the note.

NON–DELIVERY OF AN INCOMPLETE INSTRUMENT.   Under Sec. 3–115 and Sec. 3–407 of the U. C. C. is stated that where an incomplete instrument has not been delivered it will, if completed and negotiated, without authority, be a valid contract in the hands of a holder in due course, and only a personal defense. This is based upon the fact that such an instrument when signed, can be held to be evidence of a contract. If the signed but incomplete instrument got into the hands of a thief or finder, a holder in due course could recover from the signer based upon the fact that the person signing made it possible for the instrument to fall into the hands of the holder in due course. The person signing the incomplete instrument is presumed to be more at fault than the holder in due course.

Mansion Carpets, Inc. v. Marinoff
24 A. D. (2d) 947, 265 N. Y. S. (2d) 298 (1965)

This was an action by Mansion Carpets, Inc. (plaintiff) against Irving and Roslyn Marinoff (defendants). Judgment for plaintiff and defendants appealed. Judgment reversed and new trial granted.

Plaintiff sued to recover upon a check issued by defendants for carpeting and floor tile installed by plaintiff in defendants' residence. Defendants counterclaimed for breach of warranty based on work not encompassed by the check.

PER CURIAM. Determination of the Appellate Term and judgment entered May 12, 1964 in the Civil Court, New York County, in favor of plaintiff after a jury trial, unanimously reversed on the law and the facts, and a new trial granted, without costs or disbursements. At the time of trial, plaintiff's claim on the check had been reduced to $415 by payment made after suit was begun. In defense, defendants offered proof of failure of consideration. The jury found for plaintiff on the $415 claim and awarded defendants $200 on their counterclaim. There must be a new trial because of the reversible error committed in instructing the jury that the check represented an unconditional promise to pay and was not subject to any defenses arising from claimed breaches of the contract pursuant to which payment was made by check. The requirement of the Uniform Commercial Code, Sec. 3–104 (1) (b) that a check contain an unconditional promise to pay applies only to the matter of the form of a negotiable instrument. As between the original parties payment by check is conditional (U. C. C., Sec. 2–511); and if the instrument is dishonored, action may be maintained on either the instrument or the obligation (U C. C., Sec. 3–802) (1) (b). Want or failure of consideration is a defense as against any person not having the rights of a holder in due course (U. C. C., Sec. 3–408). Although U. C. C., Sec. 3–302 (2) states a payee may be a holder in due course, it is obvious that plaintiff herein does not fall within the category of the type of payee contemplated by that Section. Thus, the jury should have been permitted to consider defenses to the check based upon the original transaction. It would, however, be appropriate for defendants to amend their answer to plead failure of consideration as a defense. Moreover, the jury was apparently confused by the charge, for it originally returned to announce a verdict for defendants on plaintiff's cause of action and for defendants on their counterclaim in the sum of $100. Only after the Trial Judge reiterated his direction that plaintiff was entitled to a verdict on the cause of action based on the check and sent the jury back for further deliberation, did the jury return with the verdict appealed from. In view of our conclusion as to the prejudicial effect of the erroneous charge, we are of the opinion that the interests of justice dictate a new trial as to defendants' counterclaims as well. Submission of the case on an erroneous theory may well have influenced the jury in its deliberations on the entire case.

Matthews v. Aluminum Acceptance Corporation
1 Mich. App. 570, 137 N. W. (2d) 280 (1965)

This was an action by Robert L. Matthews and Katherine Matthews (plaintiffs) against Aluminum Acceptance Corporation (defendant). Case remanded for amendment of judgment.

In April of 1962, plaintiffs Robert and Katherine Matthews were approached by representatives of All-Style Builders, aluminum siding applicators. They allege that All-Style indicated that their modest home had been chosen as a demonstration site for aluminum siding for that area. New siding was to be applied over the tar paper on their home, and in addition they were to be given a loan of $650 in cash to fix their tractor and the total price for this was to be $3,250. Further, they were to receive $100 to apply against their contract for each potential customer which All-Style brought to view their newly sided house.

To the Matthews, the alleged inducements were sufficiently alluring that they signed up for the package. The siding was applied, they were given $650, but to time of trial, no one had ever shown up to view the siding as a potential customer.

When the smoke cleared, so to speak, the Matthews learned that the instrument they had signed included a promissory note and mortgage calling for 84 equal monthly installments at the rate of $61.04 per month for a grand total of $5,127.36, not the $3,250 they had anticipated, and the instruments had been assigned to defendant Aluminum Acceptance Corporation, a firm specializing in financing siding application.

FITZGERALD, J. The matter was tried without a jury in March of 1964 and the finding of the trial court was that the mortgage was obtained by constructive forgery, that Aluminum Acceptance was not a holder in due course, and that the note in excess of $3,250 was usurious. Judgment entered canceling the mortgage and giving defendant judgment on its counterclaim in the sum of $3,250. Aluminum Acceptance Corporation appeals this judgment.

We come to the question of whether plaintiffs' proofs establish constructive forgery or fraud.

The court, in its opinion states, "This Court is convinced that the plaintiffs did not intend to execute a mortgage. They testified that at no time was there any discussion about the mortgage or that they were encumbering their premises with a lien. There was no testimony in opposition to this."

The rule in Michigan is stated in *Horvath v. National Mortgage Company* (1927), 238 Mich. 354, 213 N. W. 202, 56 A. L. R. 578, which holds that a signature deceptively procured is in law a forgery and those who subsequently acquire interest under the forged instrument are in no better position than if they had purchased with notice.

That the instruments may have been executed in blank has little probative value in the broad consideration of this case. Indeed, there is little question but that a note executed in blank gives the payee authority to fill it in *if he follows the agreed upon terms*. M. L. P. *Alteration of Instruments*, Sec. 5. If this is applied to the testimony before us, it would have permitted the payee to fill in the note in the amount of $3,250, which the plaintiffs admit they believed they were to pay.

The original agreement with All-Style had the following terms: "Contract price $3250.00. Down Payment $........ Cash on or before completion $........ Balance of $3250.00, plus finance charges payable in 84 equal monthly installments at the rate of $61.04 monthly, the first installment due sixty days after date of contractor's designated completion of said work."

It is noted that the price stated is called the "contract price" and is the sum that the Matthews agreed to pay. Yet they find themselves owing $5,127.36.

The case of *Bird Finance Corporation v. Lamerson* (1942), 303 Mich. 422, 6 N. W. (2d) 732, reaffirmed by *Gramatan National Bank & Trust Co. v. De-Graff* (1965), 374 Mich. 148, 132 N. W. (2d) 148, holds that the type of transaction as we have in the case at bar is usurious. See also *Hillman's v. Em 'N Al's* (1956), 345 Mich. 644, 77 N. W. (2d) 96.

The agreement gave defendant notice of the agreed contract price of $3,250 while the note and mortgage stated the sum of $5,127.36. Such a disparity furnishes ample notice of the infirmity of the instrument and that it was usurious, rendering it impossible for defendant to be a holder in due course and to avail itself of such defenses as a holder in due course might have.

Concluding his opinion, the trial judge ruled that the plaintiffs agreed to pay $3,250 which included the siding job and the advance of $650 in cash.

We feel that the trial court's finding and conclusions are amply upheld by the record and by law.

Case remanded for amendment of judgment in conformance with the foregoing. Costs to appellee.

REVIEW CASES

1. Franklin National Bank (indorsee) sued Roberts Bros. (maker) on a promissory note containing an unfilled blank for interest rate. Can Roberts Bros. set up a personal defense, on the ground that the instrument was incomplete and that the bank was therefore not a holder in due course? (Franklin National Bank v. Roberts Bros. Co., 168 N. C. 473, 84 S. E. 706)

2. Stefano employed Huntress, a lawyer, to represent him in a case, and gave him a note in payment. When the case came up, Huntress failed to perform. Later Heideman told Stefano that he was considering buying the note, and Stefano told him the circumstances and advised him against buying the instrument. Heideman nevertheless bought it from Huntress. When the note came due, Stefano refused to pay it, and Heideman brought suit to collect from him. Judgment for whom? (Heideman v. Stefano, 291 S. W. (Tex.) 265)

3. O'Hara and wife had a construction company make some improvements in their house, which were to be paid for in monthly payments, and gave the company their note, insured by the Federal Housing Authority. A holder in due course bought the note from the company. The company did not complete the work, and the payments were not met on the note. The Federal Housing Authority paid the note and then sued O'Hara and wife on the note. The defense was that the F. H. A. was not a holder in due course, since it took the note with knowledge of all the facts, and that the note was made on Sunday instead of Friday as stated on the note. Ruling? (United States of America v. O'Hara et ux., 46 F. Supp. 780)

4. Stricker purchased a road bond in due course and for value from a reputable dealer. The bond was payable to bearer, and was negotiable. By state statute such road bonds could be used in paying taxes. Stricker offered the bond in payment of taxes, but it was refused because of a rumor that the bond had been stolen. Stricker sued the county, and evidence showed that in fact the bond had been stolen. Holding? (Stricker v. Buncombe County, 205 N. C. 53, 172 S. E. 188)

5. Weber sued Hirsch, the maker of a demand note, for the value of the note. The payee, who was in business with Hirsch, had negotiated the note to Weber, his brother-in-law, three months and six days after it was made. The defense was that Weber was not a holder in due course because of an

unreasonable delay in negotiating the note. Ruling? (Weber v. Hirsch et al., 163 N. Y. S. 1086)

6. Rock consulted Rea, a traveling quack doctor, and was told that he had cancer. Rea agreed to cure him for $250, and Rock gave Rea a note for that amount, payable to his order. Rea treated Rock and promised to send him more medicine, but the medicine arrived C. O. D., and Rock refused to accept it. Rock then consulted a local doctor, who cured his symptoms in a week. Rea sold the note to Walters, who sued Rock on the instrument. Rock contended that Walters was not a holder in due course and that he could therefore set up against Walters his personal defense of fraud in the inducement. The evidence showed that Walters was accustomed to buy notes from Rea and that he had had "some trouble" in collecting a number of them because the parties "did not want to pay them." Ruling? Walters v. Rock, 115 N. W. 511)

Liability of
Parties

35

The liability of a party to pay a negotiable instrument is either primary or secondary. The person primarily liable on an instrument is the person who by the terms of the instrument is absolutely required to pay the same. All other parties are secondarily liable.

The following parties are primarily liable: (1) makers of promissory notes and certificates of deposit; (2) acceptors of bills of exchange (drafts and checks).

The following parties are secondarily liable: (1) drawers of bills of exchange; (2) indorsers of promissory notes, certificates of deposit, and bills of exchange.

LIABILITY OF PARTIES PRIMARILY LIABLE

LIABILITY OF MAKER

The maker of a promissory note by making it contracts unconditionally to pay the note according to its terms. It is therefore not necessary for the holder, in order to fix the maker's liability, to make demand upon him on the due date to pay the note. The maker is liable upon the note until action is barred by the statute of limitations. However, failure to give notice to the maker on the due date does stop the running of interest subsequent to that date.

In addition to contracting unconditionally to pay the note when it matures, the maker "admits the existence of the payee and his then capacity to indorse." [1] Because of these admissions the maker, when sued on the instrument, may not set up as a defense that the payee is a fictitious person, or that he (or it) does not possess capacity to indorse—for example, because the payee is an infant, or insane, or an unincorporated association, or an unlicensed foreign corporation.

[1] U. C. C., Sec. 3-413.

It should be noted that the maker does not admit the genuineness of the payee's signature. Hence he may set up as a defense the forgery of the payee's signature.

LIABILITY OF DRAWEE–ACCEPTOR

The drawee of a bill of exchange (draft or check) is not liable to the named payee unless he accepts the instrument. The mere act of A in drawing a bill of exchange on B and ordering B to pay C does not create any liability on the part of B, either as to C or as to A. Sec. 3–409 of the U. C. C. states that "(1) A check or other draft does not of itself operate as an assignment of any funds in the hands of the drawee available for its payment, and the drawee is not liable on the instrument until he accepts it." Of course, if B had previously contracted with A to accept and pay such bill to C, and later refused to accept or pay it (as the case may be), he would be liable to A on the original contract.

If the drawee accepts the bill,[1] he is thereafter known as an *acceptor*, and as such he is primarily liable. By accepting the bill he contracts unconditionally to pay it according to its tenor. Since he is unconditionally liable, the holder need not present the bill to him for payment when it is due in order to fix his liability.

In addition to assuming this liability, an acceptor by accepting the instrument admits as against all subsequent parties including the drawee the existence of the payee and his then capacity to indorse. Because of his admissions with respect to the payee, he may not set up such defenses as the following: that the payee was a fictitious person, or that the payee lacked the capacity to indorse the instrument because he (or it) was an infant, an insane person, an unincorporated association, or an unlicensed foreign corporation. The acceptor does not admit the genuineness of the payee's signature; hence he may set up as a defense the fact that the payee's signature was forged.

Whitten v. Kroeger et al.
183 Okla. 327, 82 P. (2d) 668 (1938)

This was an action by A. W. Whitten (plaintiff) against H. A. Kroeger and J. C. Walton (defendants). Judgment for defendants, and plaintiff appealed. Reversed.

Defendant Kroeger executed to defendant Walton a promissory note, in the amount of $1,200, maturing July 1, 1930. For a valuable consideration Walton indorsed the note to plaintiff Whitten. Before the maturity of the note Whitten indorsed it to Cabiness-Swan Investment Co. When the note became due

[1] The procedure is described in the next chapter.

and the maker Kroeger failed and refused to pay same, the Cabiness-Swan Investment Co. sued Kroeger, Walton, and Whitten and obtained judgment against all of them. On September 1, 1931, and January 7, 1932, respectively, Whitten paid to the Cabiness-Swan Investment Co. the sums of $183.14 and $63.95, in partial satisfaction of the judgment. Walton and Kroeger thereafter paid the balance of the judgment. Whitten filed this action against Walton and Kroeger to recover the amount he had paid in the Cabiness-Swan Investment Co. judgment. The lower court gave judgment to defendants, and plaintiff appealed.

GIBSON, J. We agree with the plaintiff that as between the parties to this action the defendant Kroeger, as the maker of the note, was primarily liable thereon; and that the defendant Walton and the plaintiff were secondarily liable in the order of their indorsements. The plaintiff, as one secondarily liable, by paying a portion of the judgment, obtained against all three parties, was remitted to his former rights as regards the prior parties, Kroeger and Walton. Kroeger is liable to the plaintiff Whitten as maker and Walton is liable to the plaintiff Whitten as indorser of the note. Judgment reversed.

Ervin v. Dauphin Deposit Trust Company
38 D. & C. (2d) 473 (1965)

This was an action by Carl E. Ervin (plaintiff) against Dauphin Deposit Trust Co. (defendant). Judgment for the plaintiff.

The complaint in assumpsit avers, in substance, in count no. 1, that the trust company accepted certain checks made payable to plaintiff for his professional services, but on which plaintiff's name was forged, collected the amounts of the checks from the various drawee banks, and paid over the amounts of the checks to a person or persons other than plaintiff. It is further averred that these checks had been "intercepted" or "removed from Plaintiff's possession by a person or persons other than Plaintiff who forged the name of the payee as an endorsement on said checks."

In count no. 2, it is averred that on other checks similarly payable, intercepted or removed, and forged, but which had been drawn on defendant, the trust company accepted them and "collected the amount of . . . [such checks] by debiting the accounts of their depositors without crediting the account of the Plaintiff."

HERMAN, J. Defendant, Dauphin Deposit Trust Company, has filed preliminary objections to the complaint of plaintiff, Carl E. Ervin, a physician of the City of Harrisburg.

The question raised by the demurrer may be fairly stated to be: Is defendant bank liable, in this action of assumpsit, for money had and received when it cashed checks payable to plaintiff-payee, whether drawn on it or on some other bank or banks, when the payee's signature was forged? We think the question must be answered in the affirmative.

In 1954, the Uniform Commercial Code became effective in Pennsylvania. The Act of April 6, 1953, P. L. 3, as amended, 12A P. S., Sec. 1-101, et seq., and Section 3-404, 12A P. S., Sec. 3-404, thereof provided:

'(1) Any unauthorized signature is wholly inoperative as that of the person whose name is signed unless he ratifies it or is precluded from denying it; but it operates as the signature of the unauthorized signer in favor of any person who in good faith pays the instrument or takes it for value."

"The rule is established by the great weight of authority that in the absence of negligence, laches, or estoppel, a payee or other check owner is entitled to recover against a collecting bank or any person, firm, or corporation cashing a check bearing a forged or unauthorized indorsement of the payee or other check owner, and procuring payment thereof from the drawee of the check."

And, further, that: "The reasoning on which these cases proceed can perhaps be summed up in the statement that one who cashes a check on a forged or unauthorized indorsement does so at his peril."

It is there further pointed out that: "This recovery is not now regarded as resting upon the theory that the payment by the bank upon a forged or unauthorized indorsement and charging it against the drawer's account constitutes an acceptance of the check rendering the drawee liable thereon, but rather, recovery has been allowed in an action of conversion by the true payee or owner of the check. . . ."

And now, December 6, 1965, the preliminary objections to the complaint are severally overruled, and defendant shall have the right to plead over within 20 days from the date of this order.

Deen et al. v. De Soto National Bank of Arcadia
122 So. 105, 97 Fla. 862 (1929)

This was a suit by J. E. Deen and another, copartners doing business under the firm name of Deen & Yarborough (plaintiffs) against the De Soto National Bank of Arcadia (defendant). Judgment for defendant, and plaintiffs appealed. Affirmed.

Deen & Yarborough were copartners doing a contracting business. They procured a contract to perform certain work for the city of Winter Haven. They sublet a part of the contract to Jelks Taylor. While Taylor was performing his contract he became indebted to the De Soto National Bank of Arcadia in the sum of $2,500, for which the bank held his note. The note became due and Taylor gave the bank an order on Deen and Yarborough for $2,500, with interest thereon at the rate of 8% per annum from the 13th day of February, 1927. The bank presented the order to Deen & Yarborough for acceptance, and the order was accepted. At the maturity of the order Deen & Yarborough refused to pay it, and thereupon the bank brought suit against Deen & Yarborough. The defense set up by Deen & Yarborough was that they were mistaken as to the status of the account between themselves and Taylor at the time the acceptance was made; that from an investigation which they had made at the time they were led to believe, and they did believe, that they owed Taylor $3,000, but they later found that they did not owe him anything. They also alleged that there was no consideration for the acceptance. They thereupon filed a bill in chancery to rescind and cancel the acceptance and to enjoin the further progress of the civil action until final adjudication of the rights of the parties in the suit for rescission (the present suit). Complainants contended that they were entitled to rescission because of the mistake as to the amount of the indebtedness due from complainants to Taylor at the time the acceptance was made. There was a demurrer to the bill, and the demurrer was sustained. Complainants appealed.

BUFORD, J. In this case Taylor, by his written order, directed Deen & Yarborough to pay to the order of the De Soto National Bank of Arcadia a certain sum of money. The bank presented the order to Deen & Yarborough and Deen & Yarborough unconditionally accepted the order and agreed to pay the same. The defense interposed is not available in a suit of this kind.

In 3 R. C. L., p. 1143, the writer says: "The legal meaning of an acceptance is that the acceptor engages to pay the instrument according to the tenor of his acceptance. In other words, it is a promise to pay. The contract of the acceptor, by his acceptance, is that he will pay the bill, upon due presentation thereof, at its maturity, or its becoming due. The drawee enters into no contract relations with the payee in respect to it until it is presented to him, nor then unless he does so by acceptance. If he accepts, he undertakes to pay according to the terms of the bill or of the acceptance; but up to the time of that act the payee looks exclusively to the drawer for his protection. However, if the drawee refuses to accept when he has funds for the purpose, he becomes liable to the drawer for the wrong done to his credit. The drawee by acceptance becomes liable to the payee or his indorsee, and also to the drawer himself. But the drawer and acceptor are the immediate parties to the consideration, and if the acceptance be without consideration, the drawer cannot recover of the acceptor. The payee holds a different relation; he is a stranger to the transaction between the drawer and acceptor, and is, therefore, in a legal sense a remote party. In a suit by him against the acceptor, the question as to the consideration between the drawer and acceptor cannot be inquired into. The payee or holder gives value to the drawer, and if he is ignorant of the equities between the drawer and acceptor, he is in the position of a bona fide indorsee. Hence, it is no defense to a suit against the acceptor of a draft which has been discounted, and upon which money has been advanced by the plaintiff, that the draft was accepted for the accommodation of the drawer. The fact that an accommodation indorser who has been compelled to pay a bill of exchange knew at the time of the indorsement that the acceptance of the bill was for accommodation will not prevent his recovery thereon against the accommodation acceptor."

And on page 1312 of the same volume it is said: "As a general proposition, an acceptance can be discharged only by payment, or a release, except in cases where to enforce the payment by the acceptor would be in violation of the agreement of the parties at the time of the acceptance. The contract of acceptance between the acceptor and the payee cannot be abrogated by the acceptor paying the drawer of the bill all he owed him. In a suit against the acceptor, he will not be permitted to insist that there was no consideration for acceptance. . . ."

A like statement of the law in this regard will be found in Bigelow on Bills, Notes, and Checks (3rd ed.), p. 125 et seq.

So it appears that there was no error in the order appealed from and the same should be affirmed and it is so ordered.

LIABILITY OF PARTIES SECONDARILY LIABLE

LIABILITY OF DRAWER

The liability of the drawer of a bill of exchange to pay the instrument is secondary and arises out of contract. When he draws the instrument he agrees to become liable on the instrument only under definitely specified conditions. These conditions are set out in Sec. 3–413 of the U. C. C., which states, in part, that the drawer "engages that upon dishonor of the draft and any necessary notice of dishonor or protest he will pay the amount of the draft to the holder or to any indorser who takes it up." In other words, the conditions are as follows: (1) the bill must be duly presented for acceptance or payment, or both (if the nature of the instrument requires both); (2) if the bill is dishonored, the necessary proceedings on dishonor must be taken; such proceedings include giving the drawer notice of dishonor.[1] If these conditions are fulfilled, the drawer agrees to pay the instrument; otherwise he never becomes liable on the instrument. It should be noted further that Sec. 3–413 (2) specifically empowers the drawer to insert in the instrument an express stipulation denying or limiting his own liability to the holder by drawing without recourse.

Sec. 3–413 (3) also provides that "The drawer by drawing the instrument admits the existence of the payee and his then capacity to indorse." Because of these admissions he may not set up as defense the non-existence of the payee or his incapacity to indorse. The drawer does not admit the genuineness of the payee's signature; therefore if the payee's indorsement has been forged he may set up the forgery as a defense.

---

[1] Presentment, notice of dishonor, etc. are discussed in Chapter 36.

Minner v. Childs

116 Ga. App. 272, 157 S. E. (2d) 50 (1967)

This was an action by Betty Minner (plaintiff) against Brown Childs (defendant). Judgment for the plaintiff and defendant appealed. Judgment reversed.

This is a suit involving an attachment seeking collection of a check which had proved worthless. The Superior Court, Bulloch County, Walton Usher, J., entered a judgment overruling defendant's motion to dismiss declaration and attachment, and defendant appealed.

The amended declaration in attachment alleges that plaintiff is a *real estate broker*, that one Cowart, owner of described real estate, *listed the same for sale* with her , that she, as agent for Cowart, agreed with the defendant *to sell the Cowart property* under stated conditions, including a payment of $700 representing the sum of Cowart's equity in the property and *plaintiff's sales commission*, and that pursuant to such agreement the defendant executed a promissory note to Cowart for $200 and a check to the plaintiff for $500. The check proved worthless, and plaintiff thereupon levied the attachment seeking collection of this amount.

DEEN, J. Construing these allegations strictly against the pleader, an inference is demanded that the $500 debt represented by the worthless check for the recovery of which the attachment was levied represented commissions due the plaintiff as real estate commissions, and that it constituted a claim for commissions for business done as a real estate broker. A petition seeking such commissions which fails to allege that the plaintiff has a license to do business in Georgia as a real estate broker is subject to general demurrer, and the third ground of the defendant's motion to dismiss the declaration in attachment as amended should have been sustained. *Moody v. Foster*, 74 Ga. App. 829 (3), 41 S. E. (2d) 560; *Mayo v. Lynes*, 80 Ga. App. 4, 55 S. E. (2d) 174.

Under Code Sec. 20-1004 a check or other draft is not an assignment of funds; it constitutes evidence of indebtedness and is not payment until it is paid unless the agreement is to the contrary. *Wilbanks v. James Talcott, Inc.*, 106 Ga. App. 770, 774, 128 S. E. (2d) 333. Former Code Sec. 14-301 specifically stated that prima facie all negotiable instruments carry a presumption of valuable consideration, and it followed from this that a suit on a check need not allege the consideration. *Gainesville News v. Harrison*, 58 Ga. App. 744, 199 S. E. 559. The present Code Ann. Sec. 109A-3-305, like former Code Sec. 14-305 categorizes want or failure of consideration as a defense. Under Code Ann. Sec. 109A-3-122 a cause of action accrues against the drawer of a draft upon demand (including notice of dishonor) following nonpayment. As to notice of dishonor, see Code Ann. Sec. 109A-3-508. Thus, under the Commercial Code as formerly, one may bring an action upon the debt evidenced by commercial paper in the form of suing directly on an instrument which imports its own consideration without setting forth the facts creating the obligation evidenced by the paper. The obligee, however, still has only one cause of action for the amount owing him, and the filing of an action based directly on the check will not inhibit him from pleading and proving the facts, including the consideration for which the check was given, and the addition of such facts to the declaration will not constitute a new cause of action.

In this case the plaintiff first alleged that the defendant was indebted to her in the sum of $500 by reason of her tender of a check in this amount which was returned by the drawee bank marked "No Account." By amendment she set out facts showing that the defendant owed a third party money representing the purchase price of real estate, that part of this sum was owing by the third party to plaintiff as real estate commissions connected with this sale and that pursuant to the provisions of the contract of sale the defendant made a check for $500 of this sum directly to the plaintiff. Such facts go only to establishing the indebtedness which constituted the consideration for the check, and do not set forth a new cause of action. The objection to the allowance of the amendment on this ground was properly overruled.

Judgment reversed.

LIABILITY OF INDORSERS

When a party indorses a negotiable instrument and negotiates it, he not only passes title to it but he assumes certain liabilities. The nature of his liabilities depends upon the type of indorsement which he places upon the instrument. If he places either a blank or a special indorsement on the instrument he is said to be an *unqualified indorser*. If he places a qualified indorsement on the instrument he is a *qualified indorser*.[1] A qualified indorsement is made by adding the words "without recourse," or words of similar import, to either a blank or a special indorsement.

Sec. 3–417 of the Code states that (2) Any person who transfers an instrument and receives consideration warrants to his transferee and if the transfer is by indorsement to any subsequent holder who takes the instrument in good faith that (a) he has a good title to the instrument or is authorized to obtain payment or acceptance on behalf of one who has a good title and the transfer is otherwise rightful; and (b) all signatures are genuine or authorized; and (c) the instrument has not been materially altered; and (d) no defense of any party is good against him; and (e) he has no knowledge of any insolvency proceeding instituted with respect to the maker or acceptor or the drawer of an unaccepted instrument.

(3) By transferring "without recourse" the transferor limits the obligation stated in subsection (2) (d) to a warranty that he has no knowledge of such a defense.

(4) A selling agent or broker who does not disclose the fact that he is

[1] The effect of the restrictive indorsement has been discussed in Chapter 33.

acting only as such gives the warranties provided in this section, but if he makes such disclosure he warrants only his good faith and authority.

It will be seen that a qualified indorser does not contract or agree to pay the instrument if the party primarily liable on the instrument does not pay it. In fact, the very purpose of placing a qualified indorsement ("without recourse") on the instrument is to escape this liability. It is clear, however, that the qualified indorser is not absolved of all liability, as many laymen think. He is liable on the implied warranties set out above.

In general, it may be said that the effect of the warranties made by the qualified indorser is to prevent him from setting up against a subsequent holder the real and personal defenses which we have heretofore studied. In effect the qualified indorser warrants to subsequent holders that all parties prior to him are free from both real and personal defenses. By his warranties he warrants that the signature of the maker or acceptor is genuine, that the party who signed, if not the maker or acceptor, had authority to sign, and that the instrument when issued was complete and properly put into circulation. Consequently, if the maker's or indorser's signature was forged or unauthorized, or if the instrument, while it was incomplete, was stolen and placed in circulation by a thief, the qualified indorser could not avail himself of such defenses, even though each of them is a real defense. The same is true in the case of such personal defenses as lack of consideration, fraud in the inducement, and breach of warranty. As a result of his warranty of title he may not set up as a defense such defenses as forgery of the payee's signature or the incapacity of the payee because of infancy or insanity. Since the indorser in his warranty warrants "That all prior parties had capacity to contract," he may not set up the incapacity of any prior parties as a defense. But since he warrants that he has no knowledge of any defense good against him, if it is proved that he had such knowledge he will be liable on the instrument. Thus, if the indorser had knowledge of the insolvency of the maker or of the existence of usurious interest, when he indorsed and negotiated the instrument, he would be liable. However, if he had no such knowledge, the fact that the instrument was actually invalid would not make him liable.

A holder who negotiates a negotiable instrument by delivery alone incurs the same liability as a qualified indorser, with one important exception. The qualified indorser is liable on his warranties not only to his immediate transferee but to all subsequent transferees. Where the negotiation is by delivery alone, the warranties extend in favor of no holder other than the immediate transferee.

Sec. 3-417 of the Code states that (1) Any person who obtains payment or acceptance and any prior transferor warrants to a person who in good faith pays or accepts that (a) he has a good title to the instrument or is authorized to obtain payment or acceptance on behalf of one who has a good title; and (b) he has no knowledge that the signature of the maker or drawer is unauthorized, except that this warranty is not given by a holder in due course acting in good faith (i) to a maker with respect to the maker's own signature; or (ii) to a drawer with respect to the drawer's own signature, whether or not the drawer is also the drawee; or (iii) to an acceptor of a draft if the holder in due course took the draft after the acceptance or obtained the acceptance without knowledge that the drawer's signature was unauthorized; and (c) the instrument has not been materially altered, except that this warranty is not given by a holder in due course acting in good faith (i) to the maker of a note; or (ii) to the drawer of a draft whether or not the drawer is also the drawee; or (iii) to the acceptor of a draft with respect to an alteration made prior to the acceptance if the holder in due course took the draft after the acceptance, even though the acceptance provided "payable as originally drawn" or equivalent terms; or (iv) to the acceptor of a draft with respect to an alteration made after the acceptance.

The unqualified indorser's liability thus falls into two parts: he is bound upon the said warranties here set forth, and he is contractually bound to pay the instrument if the party primarily liable does not pay. His liability on his warranties is unconditional. His liability under his contract to pay the instrument if the party primarily liable does not pay is conditioned upon the proper presentment of the instrument for acceptance or payment, and, in case of dishonor, receipt of a notice of dishonor. Failure in these respects will discharge the indorser from his conditional liability to pay the instrument, but not from his unconditional liability on his warranties.

It is clear that an indorser who places a qualified instead of an unqualified indorsement on a negotiable instrument gains two important advantages. In the first place, he is not bound contractually to pay the instrument if the party primarily liable does not pay it. In the second place, he gains something in regard to the warranties imposed. While the qualified indorser warrants, in Sec. 3–417 (3) that he has no knowledge of any defense good against him, all other indorsers (the unqualified indorsers) warrant in Sec. 3–417 (2) (d) that no defense of any party is good against them. Thus an unqualified indorser is bound if there is any defense good against him, even though he had no previous knowledge of such fact, while the qualified indorser would be liable only if he has such knowledge.

Commercial Credit Co. v. Blanks Motor Co.

174 Ark. 274, 294 S. W. 999 (1927)

This was an action by the Commercial Credit Company (plaintiff) against the Blanks Motor Company (defendant). Judgment for defendant, and plaintiff appealed. Reversed, and judgment rendered for plaintiff.

Plaintiff was engaged in the business of buying notes from automobile dealers given in payment of second-hand cars. Defendant sold a second-hand car to Oren Curtis, who was a minor only 19 years old, for the sum of $496.15. Of this amount $148.85 was paid in cash. The balance of $347.30 was evidenced by the note of Curtis to the order of defendant, and was payable monthly at the rate of $28.95 per month. Defendant indorsed the note "without recourse" and sold it to plaintiff. Defendant's agent who sold the car to Curtis knew, at the time of the sale, that Curtis was a minor; yet the contract of sale which Curtis signed stated his age to be 21. Plaintiff did not know when it bought the note that Curtis was a minor, and was not so advised until after Curtis had declined to complete the payments on the note.

When plaintiff filed suit against defendant for the balance due on the note, defendant set up as a defense its qualified indorsement "without recourse."

SMITH, J. As Curtis was a minor, the contract and note for the purchase price of the automobile were void and unenforceable against him. But appellant was an innocent purchaser for value of the note. The express and affirmative representation had been made in the contract of sale, to which the note was attached, that Curtis was 21 years of age, and there is no contention that appellant was advised to the contrary until Curtis defaulted in his payments.

The note was indorsed "without recourse" by appellee, and negotiated with this indorsement by delivery to appellant, and, this being true, section 7831 (N. I. L., Sec. 65) fixes the rights and obligations of the parties thereto. This section reads, in part, as follows:

"Every person negotiating an instrument by delivery or by a qualified indorsement, warrants:
(1) That the instrument is genuine and in all respects what it purports to be;
(2) That he has a good title to it;
(3) That all prior parties had capacity to contract;
(4) That he has no knowledge of any fact which would impair the validity of the instrument or render it valueless."

There was nothing in the refusal of appellee (by its qualified indorsement) to guarantee the payment of the note which operated to prevent this section of the statute from applying to the transaction between the parties. One who negotiates a note by delivery, or by a qualified indorsement, warrants that the maker has the capacity to contract. Appellee did this because the Negotiable

Instruments Law so provides, and the parties are conclusively presumed to have contracted with reference to this law, although neither of them may have known anything about the statute. There was no contract that the statute should not apply. Appellee did refuse to assume any responsibility for the payment of the note (by its qualified indorsement), but this is a very different matter from refusing to warrant that the maker of the note had the capacity to make it.

Appellant took title to the note by delivery under a qualified indorsement, and the law imputed into the transaction the warranty that the maker of the note had the capacity to make it, and the refusal of appellee to guarantee its payment was insufficient to discharge it from a liability to which its refusal did not relate.

Judgment is reversed and rendered against appellee (defendant) for the unpaid balance due on the note.

Persson v. McCormick
412 P. (2d) 619 (1966)

This was an action by Max D. McCormick (plaintiff) against Frank D. Persson, J. M. Peters, Pauline Peters, and Lillian Taylor (defendants). Judgment for plaintiff and defendants appealed. Affirmed.

Plaintiff's petition alleged that on July 3, 1962, defendant executed a promissory note payable to the order of J. M. Peters and Pauline Peters in the amount of $2,000.00 with interest at five per cent per annum, payable in monthly installments of $100.00 each commencing January 3, 1963, and continuing until paid; that thereafter and before maturity, J. M. Peters and Pauline Peters, for a good and valuable consideration, endorsed and delivered this note to Lillian Taylor, who thereafter and before maturity, for a good and valuable consideration, endorsed and delivered such note to plaintiff, who "is now the lawful owner and holder of said note"; that the note provided if any installment becomes delinquent for 15 days, the entire unpaid balance should become due and payable at the option of the holder; that the conditions of the note had been broken in that on the 3rd day of the months of February and March, 1963, defendant Persson refused to make payments as agreed. By reason of such default plaintiff asked judgment against the defendants, and each of them, for $1,900.00, the unpaid balance due and owing on the note, together with interest and attorney fees, all as provided in the note.

J. M. Peters, Pauline Peters and Lillian Taylor did not plead to nor answer the petition. Defendant filed an answer and two amended answers. The amended answer, upon which the case was heard, consisted of general denial, and specifically alleged defendant's signature was obtained by faud, and that plaintiff had knowledge prior to purchase of the note that there was a "controversy regarding the amount due on said note."

The plaintiff's reply to the amended answer contained a general denial, and specially denied knowledge of fault or defect in said note.

BERRY, J. The case was tried before a jury. Plaintiff, in his own behalf, testified he purchased the note from Lillian Taylor on January 9, 1963, for the sum of $1,650.00; that there was a balance due on the note in the amount of $1,900.00, plus interest from February, 1963. Upon plaintiff identifying the note it was admitted into evidence and plaintiff rested. Defendant's demurrer to the evidence was overruled and defendant elected to stand on his demurrer. The jury was discharged and default judgment was entered against J. M. Peters, Pauline Peters and Lillian Taylor. Judgment was also entered for the plaintiff against defendant as prayed for in the petition.

Defendant asserts only one proposition for reversal of the lower court's ruling, which is that the trial court erred "in finding that the plaintiff was in fact under the law, a holder in due course." The decisive question presented by this appeal involves the correctness of the trial court's action in overruling defendant's demurrer to plaintiff's evidence.

48 O. S. 1961, Sec. 129, provided in part: "Every holder is deemed prima facie to be a holder in due course; but when it is shown that the title of any person who has negotiated the instrument is defective, the burden is on the holder to prove that he or some person under whom he claims acquired the title as a holder in due course."

On July 21, 1961, the Oklahoma Uniform Commercial Code, 12A O. S. 1961 Sec. 1–101 et seq., was approved to become effective at midnight on December 31, 1962, 12A O. S. 1961 Sec. 3–307 repealed 48 O. S. 1961 Sec. 129, Section 3–307 (1), *supra*, provides in part: "Unless specifically denied in the pleadings each signature on an instrument is admitted." In the pleadings defendant admits having signed the note.

The statute, Section 3–307 (2), further provides: "When signatures are admitted or established, production of the instrument entitles a holder to recover on it unless the defendant establishes a defense."

This latter subsection of Section 3–307 is a rewording of the above quoted clause of former 48 O. S. 1961 Sec. 129. It is more direct and explicit. The production of the note entitles the holder to recover unless a defense is established. The term "recover on it" makes it quite clear that the holder or plaintiff is entitled to the full amount sued for, without proof of the amount or of nonpayment, unless the defendant pleads and proves some defense thereto.

It is an established rule that in a suit upon a promissory note, when the defendant by answer admits the execution of the note and pleads an affirmative defense to the plaintiff's right of recovery (as the defendant did here), the burden rests upon defendant to establish the allegations of the answer by a preponderance of the evidence. *Young v. Garrett*, 187 Okl. 595, 105 P. (2d) 257; *Fisher v. Millspaugh et al.*, 192 Okl. 127, 134 P. (2d) 579; *Rennie v. J. I. Case Threshing Machine Co.*, 94 Okl. 26, 220 P. 626; *Price v. Latimer County National Bank of Wilburton*, 119 Okl. 198, 249 P. 305; *Anderson v. Scanlon*, 174 Okl. 419, 50 P. (2d) 615. See also, *James Talcott, Inc. v. Finley*, Okl., 389 P. (2d) 988.

In this case defendant, having admitted the signing of the note, offered no evidence either to establish a defense to plaintiff's right of recovery, or that plaintiff was not a holder in due course. The question as to whether plaintiff was a holder in due course would not arise until defendant established a defense to the note sued upon.

Defendant urges that plaintiff "had notice that the note was on its face overdue so that he was not a holder in due course." After a careful examination of the exhibit of the note, we find no evidence that imparts substance to defendant's argument.

We therefore hold that the trial court was correct in overruling defendant's demurrer and entering judgment for plaintiff. The judgment of the trial court is affirmed.

LIABILITY OF ACCOMMODATION PARTIES

A person's financial position may be so weak that lenders and creditors do not feel justified in lending money or extending credit to him upon his unsecured personal note alone. If he is unable to pledge collateral security or tender a mortgage of some kind, he may still obtain the desired loan or credit if he can find a friend or business associate whose credit standing is satisfactory and who is willing to "lend his name" or credit to the instrument by becoming a party to it. If a note is used, the accommodation party may sign the instrument either as a maker or an indorser. If a bill of exchange is used, the accommodation party may sign the instrument either as a drawer, an acceptor, or an indorser. It is not necessary that the accommodation party receive consideration for becoming a party to the instrument, nor will the fact that the holder of the instrument knows that the accommodation party has not received consideration discharge the accommodation party from liability upon the instrument. Sec. 3–415 (1) of the U. C. C. defines an accommodation party as "one who signs an instrument in any capacity for the purpose of lending his name to another party to it." COMMENT: "The essential characteristic is that the accommodation party is a surety, and not that he has signed gratuitously. He may be a paid surety, or receive other compensations from the party accommodated." Such a person is liable on the instrument to a holder if taken for value before overdue, notwithstanding such holder at the time of taking the instrument knew him to be only an accommodation party.

An accommodation party is not liable to the party accommodated. Sec. 3–415 (5) states that "an accommodation party is not liable to the party accommodated, and if he pays the instrument has a right of recourse on the instrument against such party." If the accommodation party is the drawer of the instrument or an indorser thereof, and consequently secondarily liable, he is entitled to receive notice of dishonor, if the instrument is dishonored by the party primarily liable. If he pays the instrument, he has the right to recover from the accommodated party the amount he has paid.

Simson v. Bilderbeck, Inc.

76 N. M. 667, 417 P. (2d) 803 (1966)

This is an action by George Simson (plaintiff) against Bilderbeck, Inc., et al. (defendants). Judgment for plaintiff, and defendants appealed. Judgment affirmed.

In obtaining a bank loan, Bilderbeck, Inc. executed a promissory note and secured the note with a mortgage on the real property involved. In addition, plaintiff signed the note. Because of financial difficulties of Bilderbeck, Inc., and before the note was due, the bank called upon plaintiff to pay the note. Receiving payment from plaintiff, the bank assigned the note and real estate mortgage to plaintiff.

Bilderbeck, Inc. failed to pay the debt in accordance with its terms. Plaintiff sued on the note and asked that the mortgage be foreclosed. The trial court rendered judgment against Bilderbeck, Inc., and ordered the mortgage foreclosed.

The fifteen appellants were defendants in plaintiff's suit against Bilderbeck, Inc. Each of them provided labor upon or furnished materials for incorporation in the improvements constructed upon the mortgaged real estate. The trial court found that the improvements were made subsequent to the filing of the mortgage and that each of the appellants was chargeable with notice of the note and mortgage. The trial court also found that the lien of the mortgage was prior to and superior to the lien claims of the mechanics and materialmen. Appellants do not attack the priority of the mortgage lien before the note and mortgage were assigned to plaintiff.

The trial court found that plaintiff signed the note as an accommodation maker.

WOOD, J. This appeal involves priority of liens and the subrogation rights of an assignee of a note secured by real estate mortgage.

Appellants assert that in his capacity as accommodation maker plaintiff is primarily liable on the note, relying on *First Sav. Bank & Trust Co. v. Flournoy*, 24 N. M. 256, 171 P. 793. Being primarily liable, they contend that when he paid the note he paid his own obligation. They contend that this payment discharged the note and extinguished the lien of the mortgage, and thus plaintiff did not become subrogated to the prior rights of the bank. They rely on *Spire v. Spire*, 104 Kan. 501, 180 P. 209, and *Merchants' Bank & Trust Co. v. Bushnell*, 142 Tenn. 275, 218 S. W. 709. The Merchants' Bank case is distinguishable on its facts. The Spire case supports appellants' contention, but is not applicable because of the New Mexico statutes.

Section 50A-3-415 (1), N. M. S. A. 1953, states: "An accommodation party is one who signs the instrument in any capacity for the purpose of lending his name to another party to it." Section 50A-3-415 (5), N. M. S. A. 1953, provides: "An accommodation party is not liable to the party accommodated, and *if he pays the instrument has a right of recourse on the instrument against such party*" (our emphasis).

Section 50A-3-603 (2), N. M. S. A. 1953, reads: "Payment or satisfaction may be made with the consent of the holder by any person including a stranger to the instrument. Surrender of the instrument to such a person gives him the rights of a transferee (Section 3-201 [50A-3-201])." Section 50A-3-201 (1), N. M. S. A. 1953, provides: "Transfer of an instrument vests in the transferee such rights as the transferor has therein, except that a transferee who has himself been a party to any fraud or illegality affecting the instrument or who as a prior holder had notice of a defense or claim against it cannot improve his position by taking from a later holder in due course."

When plaintiff paid the note, under Sec. 50A-3-415 (5), N. M. S. A. 1953, he had a right of recourse against Bilderbeck, Inc. on the note. Under Sec. 50A-3-603 (2), N. M. S. A. 1953, plaintiff could pay the note and obtain the rights of a transferee upon surrender of the note to him. Under Sec. 50A-3-201 (1), N. M. S. A. 1953, plaintiff had the rights of the transferor bank, there being no issue as to fraud or illegality on the part of plaintiff or that plaintiff was a prior holder. Thus, as to the note, plaintiff succeeded to the bank's rights and could sue Bilderbeck, Inc. on the note. By the terms of our statutes, the note was not discharged when paid by plaintiff, the accommodation maker.

Concerning Sec. 50A-3-415, N. M. S. A. 1953, the following appears in the comment to Uniform Commercial Code, Sec. 3-415: "1. Subsection (1) recognizes that an accommodation party is always a surety (which includes a guarantor), and it is his only distinguishing feature. He differs from other sureties only in that his liability is on the instrument and he is a surety for another party to it. His obligation is therefore determined by the capacity in which he signs. * * *

"5. * * * Under ordinary principles of suretyship the accommodation party who pays is subrogated to the rights of the holder paid, and should have his recourse on the instrument."

Thus, in answer to appellants' contention, as between plaintiff and Bilderbeck, Inc., plaintiff was not principally liable. As between those two parties, when plaintiff paid the note to the bank he was subrogated to the bank's rights against Bilderbeck, Inc.

Both the note and mortgage were assigned to plaintiff. Having a right under the statute to enforce the note, he could foreclose the mortgage.

The judgment is affirmed. It is so ordered.

Niebergall v. A. B. A. Contracting & Supply Co.
24 A. D. (2d) 799, 263 N. Y. S. (2d) 589 (1965)

This was an action by the A. B. A. Contracting and Supply Company, Inc. et al. (plaintiffs) against Grover Niebergall et al. (defendants). Judgment for defendants and plaintiffs appealed. Judgment affirmed.

Action against prior indorser of a note which subsequent indorser redeemed during his lifetime. The Supreme Court, Columbia County, found for defendants, and plaintiff appealed. The Supreme Court, Appellate Division, Reynolds, J., held that evidence supported findings that indorser of note signed solely as an accommodation to a subsequent indorser to facilitate latter's securing bank acceptance of the loan, and that it was understood between them that prior indorser would not be liable to subsequent indorser in case of default.

REYNOLDS, J. Appeal from a judgment of the Supreme Court, Columbia County, dismissing appellants' complaint after trial.

Appellants seek to recover $10,000 from the respondent Merle, a prior indorser of a note which the decedent Harvey K. Niebergall, a subsequent indorser, redeemed during his lifetime. While "indorsers are *prima facie* liable in the order in which they indorse; * * * evidence is admissible to show that as between or among themselves they have agreed otherwise." (Negotiable Instruments Law, Par. 118, see also, U. C. C., Sec. 3–414 [2].) The trial court has found that there was here sufficient evidence to establish that Merle signed solely as an accommodation to Niebergall to facilitate his securing bank acceptance of the loan and that it was understood between them that Merle would not be liable to Niebergall in case of default. We concur in this determination and also the finding of the court below that since there was no evidence to the contrary such intent was carried forward to renewals of the note (*Callery v. Lyons*, 292 N. Y. 15, 53 N. E. (2d) 376).

Judgment affirmed, with costs.

ORDER IN WHICH PARTIES ARE LIABLE

Sec. 3–414 (2) of the U. C. C. provides that "unless they otherwise agree indorsers are liable to one another in the order in which they indorse, which is presumed to be the order in which their signatures appear on the instrument." Joint payees or joint indorsees who indorse are deemed to indorse jointly and severally (Sec. 3–118 (e)).

In case the party primarily liable dishonors the instrument and proper notice of dishonor is given to all parties secondarily liable, the holder is permitted, in most jurisdictions, to join in the same suit all primary and secondary parties. If the holder secures judgment against all the parties and satisfies his judgment against the party primarily liable, the judgment is satisfied and the secondary parties have no further liability on the judgment. However, if the judgment is paid by an indorser he is entitled to recoup either from the party primarily liable or from a prior indorser. If he recoups from a prior indorser, such indorser may recover his loss from the primary party or from an indorser prior to him, if there be any such indorser or indorsers.[1]

[1] See *Whitten v. Kroeger et al.* in Chapter 35 for a case in point.

REVIEW CASES

1. Woods and others made a promissory note payable to the order of Lowell-Woodward Hardware Co., which purported to be a corporation. The company later sued on the note, and the makers defended on the ground that the payee was not in fact a corporation. Holding? (Lowell-Woodward Hardware Co. v. Woods, 104 Kan. 729, 180 P. 734)

2. A check payable to the order of Albert E. Jordan was stolen. The thief forged Jordan's signature and deposited the check to his account in the Main Street Bank, which in turn indorsed the check to the Planters' National Bank of Richmond. When the forgery was discovered, the Planters' National Bank brought an action to recover from the Main Street Bank. Judgment for whom? (Main Street Bank v. Planters' National Bank of Richmond, 116 Va. 137, 81 S. E. 24)

3. The Federal Fidelity Co. received a note which bore the forged signature of Hoodepyl, and indorsed it "without recourse" to the Royal Mortgage & Finance Co. It was later sued on the note by the Royal Mortgage & Finance Co. Did the qualified indorsement protect the Federal Fidelity Co.? (Federal Fidelity Co. v. Royal Mortgage & Finance Co., 252 Ky. 716, 68 S. W.(2d) 25)

4. Rodgers applied to the Bank of Booneville for a $5,000 loan. He had the reputation in the community of being a man of considerable means, and a statement of his financial condition which he presented at the bank's request indicated that his net worth was $160,000. The bank extended the loan and took Rodgers' note for $5,000. The note was later indorsed "without recourse" and delivered for value to the Bank of Otterville. Actually, Rodgers had misrepresented his financial condition, and when the note became due he was unable to pay it. The Bank of Otterville sued the Bank of Booneville on the note. Holding? (Bank of Otterville v. Bank of Booneville, 16 S. W.(2d) (Mo.) 702)

5. Cowan signed a promissory note as maker and gave it to Hudson for a debt owed him. Without Cowan's consent Hudson induced Cowan's father to sign the note so that he could negotiate it more easily when he presented it to the bank. Hudson gave no consideration to Cowan's father. Hudson never presented the note to the bank but held it until maturity and thereafter sued Cowan and his father on the note. Was Cowan's father liable on the note? (Cowan v. Hudson, 105 Miss. 507, 62 So. 275)

6. Jones drew a check on the People's Bank & Trust Co., payable to the order of E. P. Fick, who negotiated it to Nellie Fick. Without presenting the check to the bank for payment, she demanded payment of it by Jones, and upon Jones' refusal she sued him to recover on the instrument. Judgment for whom? (Fick v. Jones, 185 Wash. 365, 55 P.(2d) 334)

Presentment,
Notice of Dishonor,
and Discharge

36

We learned in the preceding chapter that the party primarily liable to pay a negotiable instrument (the maker of a promissory note, or the acceptor of a bill of exchange) is unconditionally liable; and that consequently presentment of the instrument to him when it matures is not necessary to fix his liability. Such liability is already fixed under the contract, and it remains so until it is outlawed by the running of the statute of limitations. We saw further that the situation is very different in the case of secondary parties (indorsers of notes, and drawers and indorsers of bills of exchange). The liability of such secondary parties to pay the instrument, if the party primarily liable fails to pay, is conditional upon the happening of two events: (1) the instrument must be properly presented for acceptance or payment, or, where necessary, for both; (2) the instrument having been dishonored, notice of dishonor must be given (or, in the case of a foreign bill, the bill must be protested and notice of protest given). These two procedures are necessary to fix the liability of the secondary parties, unless a provision has been placed in the instrument *waiving* presentment, notice of dishonor, and protest. If such a provision is contained in a negotiable instrument the secondary parties become unconditionally liable to pay the instrument (if the party primarily liable does not pay) immediately upon affixing their signatures to the instrument. But in the absence of such a provision, failure on the part of the holder to carry out the prescribed procedures in every required respect will release the secondary parties from their contractual liability to pay the instrument.

The first part of the present chapter discusses the nature of these two required procedures. The second part treats of the acts which will discharge a negotiable instrument, and the acts which will discharge the primary and secondary parties to the instrument.

823

PRESENTMENT FOR PAYMENT

ACCEPTANCE

Sec. 3–503 of the U. C. C. states that (1) Unless a different time is expressed in the instrument the time for any presentment is determined as follows: (a) where an instrument is payable at or a fixed period after a stated date, any presentment for acceptance must be made on or before the date it is payable; (b) where an instrument is payable after sight, it must either be presented for acceptance or negotiated within a reasonable time after date or issue, whichever is later; (c) where an instrument shows the date on which it is payable, presentment for payment is due on that date; (d) where an instrument is accelerated, presentment for payment is due within a reasonable time after the acceleration; (e) with respect to the liability of any secondary party, presentment for acceptance or payment of any other instrument is due within a reasonable time after such party becomes liable thereon.

(2) A reasonable time for presentment is determined by the nature of the instrument, any usage of banking or trade, and the facts of the particular case. In the case of an uncertified check which is drawn and payable within the United States and which is not a draft drawn by a bank, the following are presumed to be reasonable periods within which to present for payment or to initiate bank collection: (a) with respect to the liability of the drawer, thirty days after date or issue, whichever is later; and (b) with respect to the liability of an indorser, seven days after his indorsement.

(3) Where any presentment is due on a day which is not a full business day for either the person making presentment or the party to pay or accept, presentment is due on the next following day which is a full business day for both parties.

(4) Presentment to be sufficient must be made at a reasonable hour, and if at a bank during its banking day.

Sec. 3–504 of the Code states that (1) Presentment is a demand for acceptance or payment made upon the maker, acceptor, drawee, or other payor by or on behalf of the holder.

(2) Presentment may be made (a) by mail, in which event the time of presentment is determined by the time of receipt of the mail; or (b) through a clearing house; or (c) at the place of acceptance or payment specified in the instrument, or if there be none, at the place of business or residence of the party to accept or pay. If neither the party to accept or pay nor any one authorized to act for him is present or accessible at such place, presentment is excused.

(3) It may be made (a) to any one of two or more makers, acceptors,

drawees, or other payors; or (b) to any person who has authority to make or refuse the acceptance or payment.

(4) A draft accepted or a note made payable at a bank in the United States must be presented at such bank.

(5) In the cases described in Sec. 4–210 presentment may be made in the manner and with the result stated in that section.

Presentment for payment is excused or dispensed with under certain circumstances.

Sec. 3–511 of the U. C. C. states that delay in presentment, protest, or notice of dishonor is excused when the party is without notice that it is due or when the delay is caused by circumstances beyond his control and he exercises reasonable diligence after the cause of the delay ceases to operate. Presentment or notice or protest, as the case may be, is entirely excused when the party to be charged has waived it expressly or by implication either before or after it is due; or such party has himself dishonored the instrument or has countermanded payment or otherwise has no reason to expect the right to require that the instrument be accepted or paid; or by reasonable diligence the presentment or protest cannot be made or the notice given. Presentment is also entirely excused when the maker, acceptor, or drawee of any instrument except a documentary draft is dead or in insolvency proceedings instituted after the issue of the instrument; or acceptance or payment is refused but not for want of proper presentment. Where a draft has been dishonored by non-acceptance a later presentment for payment and any notice of dishonor and protest for non-payment are excused unless in the meantime the instrument has been accepted. A waiver of protest is also a waiver of presentment and of notice of dishonor, even though protest is not required. Where a waiver of presentment or notice of protest is embodied in the instrument itself it is binding upon all parties; but where it is written above the signature of an indorser it binds him only.

Lustbader v. Lustbader
48 Misc. (2d) 133, 264 N. Y. S. (2d) 307 (1965)

This was an action by Morris S. Lustbader (plaintiff) against Sol Lustbader (defendant). Complaint dismissed.

This is an action upon a promissory note dated July 17, 1960 payable on demand and made by a corporation to one of its officers and endorsed by defendant, another officer, as an accommodation endorser. Defendant testified that in 1962 or early 1963 he "just stopping coming in" and left the corporation. Plaintiff testified that on July 11, 1963 the note was assigned to him by the payee; that by October 1963 the corporation was not operating and was insolvent;

and that in October 1963 he had a conversation with defendant, told him he wanted the note paid, and that defendant said he couldn't pay.

GELLER, J. The complaint alleges presentment of the note to the maker and due notice to defendant of presentment and non-payment, which are denied in defendant's answer. The only evidence at the trial on the subject has been set forth. It is obvious that plaintiff is relying on a theory of implied waiver and not upon the pleaded allegations. While the facts constituting waiver should have been pleaded (*Bird v. Kay*, 40 App. Div. 533, 58 N. Y. S. 170), defendant did not urge surprise but rather that plaintiff was not entitled to recover on the evidence presented.

Plaintiff's first contention with respect to waiver is based on Sec. 186 of the Negotiable Instruments Law that notice of dishonor is not required to be given to an indorser "2. Where the indorser is the person to whom the instrument is presented for payment." That provision, however, is confined to a special situation where an apparent indorser is in fact the principal debtor (see, e.g., *Witherow v. Slayback*, 158 N. Y. 649, 659, 53 N. E. 681, 683).

Plaintiff's main reliance as to waiver is that it should be implied from the fact that defendant as an officer of the corporate maker knew that it was insolvent and out of business and, therefore, knew that it would have been useless to make presentment to the corporation.

Here, of course, the evidence is that defendant left the corporation while it was still functioning, albeit in greatly reduced circumstances, so that such knowledge on his part cannot be conclusively presumed. Moreover, it has been definitely settled that the facts upon which plaintiff relies do not constitute a waiver of the statutory requirements (*Goldstein v. Brastone Corporation*, 254 App. Div. 288, 4 N. Y. S. (2d) 909, affd, 279 N. Y. 775, 18 N. E. (2d) 862).

The mere insolvency of the maker of an instrument and the knowledge thereof by the indorser furnishes no excuse for failure to present it and give notice of dishonor to the indorser. It was formerly held that, where the indorser, an officer of the corporate maker, by his affirmative act and signed assent caused it to be adjudged a bankrupt prior to maturity of the note, presentment and notice of dishonor were excused (*O'Bannon Co. v. Curran*, 129 App. Div. 90, 113 N. Y. S. 359). It should be noted in this connection that, effective September 27, 1964, Uniform Commercial Code, Sec. 3–511(3) provides that presentment is excused when the maker is in insolvency proceedings instituted after the issue of the instrument. Here there is merely a claim of insolvency and alleged knowledge thereof by defendant as an officer of the corporate maker.

In *Goldstein v. Brastone Corporation*, supra, the court said (254 App. Div. p. 290, 4 N. Y. S. (2d) p. 911): "The law treats him as it would a stranger." Pointing out the need in commercial transactions for uniformity of prescribed rules of liability, the court concluded (p. 291, 4 N. Y. S. (2d) p. 912): "It may seem a drastic rule to require notice of dishonor under such circumstances; but by long custom and by statute the rules of liability and non-liability have been determined. If exceptions are made to fit particular circumstances, then the purposeful ridigity of the law is frittered away."

The complaint must accordingly be dismissed. However, the dismissal is without prejudice, in order to permit plaintiff, if so advised, to make due presentment of this demand note, give notice of dishonor and sue thereon within the applicable period of limitation, with all defenses available to defendant, including the defense that presentment was not made within a reasonable time (see N. I. L., Sec. 131; U. C. C., Sec. 3–503 (1) (e)), a question to be determined by the nature of the instrument, any usage of business and the facts of the particular case.

Georgia Bank & Trust Company v. Hadarits
111 Ga. App. 195, 141 S. E. (2d) 172 (1965)

This was an action by Louisa D. Hadarits et al. (plaintiffs) against Georgia Bank & Trust Company (defendant). Plaintiffs' motion for summary judgment granted and defendant appealed. Judgment affirmed.

There was evidence before the court that one Jackson on May 4, 1963, drew a check for $4,335 on his account in the defendant bank payable to the plaintiff. The plaintiff presented this check to the bank on June 26, 1963, and was informed that there were insufficient funds on deposit in the drawer's account to pay the check. At the plaintiff's request a collection and exchange teller at the bank gave the plaintiff a receipt dated June 26, 1963, showing the check was "Received for collection for account of Middle Georgia Lumber Co."

Affidavits of officers of the bank and of Family Federal Savings & Loan Association, which was at the time in process of foreclosing its mortgage on Jackson's house, state that on June 25 Jackson went to Family Federal's office with a check payable to him for $5,000, and Family Federal ascertained by telephoning the First National Bank & Trust Company, the drawee, that the check was good, and Jackson proposed to deposit the check in his account in the defendant bank and to give Family Federal two checks totaling over $1,000 upon loans payable to them. An officer of Family Federal then telephoned an officer of the defendant bank and informed him of this arrangement, and the bank officer stated that the bank would pay Jackson's two checks to Family Federal provided the $5,000 check to be deposited by Jackson was paid. (At this time the balance in Jackson's account in the defendant bank was about $300.) Family Federal thereupon agreed to stop its foreclosure proceedings.

Later the same day Jackson deposited his $5,000 check and another check for $236.40 drawn on the Trust Company of Georgia to his account in the defendant bank. The drawee bank accepted the $5,000 check the same day. Upon instruction of an officer of the defendant bank with respect to a deposit of approximately $5,000 that had been made that day by Jackson, the bookkeeper wrote "Hold" on the stub of the ledger, which indicated that no checks should be paid from that deposit without authority from an officer of the bank.

The teller holding the plaintiff's check for collection inquired of the bank's bookkeeping department on the mornings of June 27, June 28, and July 1, and was told that the check was not good, and on July 2, on information from the bookkeeping department she stamped the check "Account closed" and returned it unpaid to the plaintiff.

The evidence rather imports an attempt by Family Federal to have the bank accept Jackson's checks payable to it by means of a telephone conversation. This could not be effective because the law requires that the acceptance of a check be in writing. *McMillan v. Citizens & Southern National Bank*, 37 Ga. App. 813, 142 S. E. 194; Ga. Code Sec. 14–1101 (cf. Georgia Uniform Commercial Code, effective January 1, 1964, Sec. 109A–3–410, 109A–3–104); *1 Paton's Digest* 10, Sec. 5; 10 Am. Jur. (2d) 550, Sec. 579; 9 *C.J.S. Banks and Banking*, Sec. 371, p. 788.

Under the Negotiable Instruments Law, Ga. Code, Sec. 14–1707, repealed Ga. L. 1962, pp. 156, 427 (cf. Ga. Uniform Commercial Code, Sec. 109A–3–409. Ga. L. 1962, pp. 156, 260) the holder or payee of a check which has not been accepted or certified has no right of action against the drawee bank based upon its failure or refusal to honor the check, even though at the time the check was presented for payment, the bank had sufficient funds of the drawer on deposit to pay it. *Jackson v. Fulton National Bank*, 46. Ga. App. 253, 167 S. E. 344; 10 Am. Jur. (2d) 538, Sec. 568; 9 *C.J.S. Banks and Banking*, Sec. 342a, p. 687.

HALL, J. The rule is different where a check has been accepted by the drawee for collection for the reason that the bank is the collecting agent of the holder. *II Paton's Digest* 1306, Sec. 17:1. Once the bank undertakes this agency, it is required to use ordinary or reasonable diligence and care in making the collection. See Code Sec. 13–2035, repealed by Uniform Commercial Code, Ga. L. 1962, pp. 156, 427 (cf. Georgia Uniform Commercial Code, Sec. 109A–4–101 et seq.); 9 *C.J.S. Banks and Banking*, Sec. 235, p. 491. And if, from its failure to do so, loss results to its customer, it is liable to him in damages. *Bailie v. Augusta Savings Bank*, 95 Ga. 277, 283, 285, 21 S. E. 717; *Planters Bank of Americus v. Albert Pick & Co.* 38 Ga. App. 95, 96, 143 S. E. 441; 10 Am. Jur. (2d) 672, Sec. 701; *II Paton's Digest* 1314–1315, Sec. 17:11.

We will assume arguendo, but do not decide, that under the terms of the note in the present case the bank's rights in all existing and future deposits of the maker vested on the dates of the note and each deposit made thereafter. The evidence shows nevertheless that the bank treated the account as the depositor's property on June 27 and June 28 by paying checks that it was under no duty, to their holders, to pay. In doing so the bank necessarily relinquished its present right to hold the account, at a time when it held the plaintiff's check for collection and owed the plaintiff the duty of a collection agent.

Though the bank may have had a right under the assignment to apply the account to payment of its note, when the bank after it took the plaintiff's check for collection relinquished this right, the account became accessible and it then had in it sufficient funds from which to collect the plaintiff's check and the bank violated its duty to the plaintiff to exercise reasonable diligence in collection when, for reasons of its own as stated in its officer's affidavit, it paid on presentation checks it was not obligated to pay but failed to collect the plaintiff's check then held for collection. Accord *Paige v. Springfield National Bank*, 12 Ohio App. 196; 5A Michie, *Banks and Banking*, 532, Sec. 220; ll *Paton's Digest* 1314, Sec. 17:11.

Judgment affirmed.

DISHONOR

WHAT CONSTITUTES DISHONOR

An instrument is dishonored by non-payment (1) when it is duly presented for payment and payment is refused or cannot be obtained or (2) when presentment is excused and the instrument is overdue and unpaid. When an instrument is dishonored by non-payment and notice of dishonor is given, an immediate right of recourse to all parties secondarily liable on the instrument accrues to the holder. Every negotiable instrument is payable at the time fixed in the instrument without grace.

A bill is dishonored by non-acceptance (1) when it is duly presented for acceptance and acceptance is refused or cannot be obtained, or (2) when presentment is excused and the bill is not accepted. If a bill is duly presented for acceptance and the drawee does not accept it, the person presenting the bill must treat it as dishonored by non-acceptance or he loses the right of recourse against the drawer and indorsers. And, if a bill is dishonored by non-acceptance, an immediate right of recourse against the drawer and indorsers accrues to the holder and presentment for payment is not necessary (Sec. 3–507, U. C. C.).

NOTICE OF DISHONOR

If an instrument is dishonored either by non-acceptance or by non-payment, notice of dishonor must be given to the parties secondarily liable, in order to fix their conditional liability on their contracts to pay the instrument if the party primarily liable does not pay. Any drawer or indorser to whom such notice is not given is discharged, unless he has waived notice.[1]

Sec. 3–508 (1) provides that notice of dishonor may be given to any person who may be liable on the instrument by or on behalf of the holder or any party who has himself received notice, or any other party who can be compelled to pay the instrument. In addition an agent or bank in whose hands the instrument is dishonored may give notice to his principal or customer or to another agent or bank from which the instrument was received.

---

[1] If a waiver clause has been embodied in the instrument itself, it is binding on all secondary parties; if it is written above the signature of an indorser, it binds him only.

(2) Any necessary notice must be given by a bank before its midnight deadline and by any other person before midnight of the third business day after dishonor or receipt of notice of dishonor.

(3) Notice may be given in any reasonable manner. It may be oral or written, and in any terms which identify the instrument and state that it has been dishonored. A misdescription which does not mislead the party notified does not vitiate the notice. Sending the instrument bearing a stamp, ticket, or writing stating that acceptance or payment has been refused, or sending a notice or debit with respect to the instrument is sufficient.

(4) Written notice is given when sent even though it is not received.

(5) Notice to one partner is notice to each although the firm has been dissolved.

(6) When any party is in insolvency proceedings instituted after the issue of the instrument notice may be given either to the party or to the representative of his estate.

(7) When any party is dead or incompetent, notice may be sent to his last known address or given to his personal representative.

(8) Notice operates for the benefit of all parties who have rights on the instrument against the party notified.

Goldstein v. Brastone Corporation et al.
254 App. Div. 288 N. Y. S. (2d) 909 (1938)

This was an action by Nathaniel L. Goldstein, as permanent receiver of the Equitable Merchants Association, Inc. (plaintiff) against Brastone Corporation, Hans Brassler, and Louis Bartelstone (defendants). Judgment for plaintiff, and defendants appealed. Judgment reversed and complaint dismissed.

On August 13, 1931, defendant corporation executed and delivered to Alson & Baker its note for $5,000, payable four months after date at the First National Bank, Farmingdale, New York. The note was signed by the individual defendants as the president and vice-president of the corporation, and it was also indorsed by them.

It is not disputed that the note came into the hands of the corporation of which plaintiff is the receiver and that it was a holder in due course; nor is it disputed that the note was not presented for payment on the date on which it fell due and that no notice of its dishonor was ever given to the indorsers.

Although the note became due on December 13, 1931, this action to recover thereon from the maker and indorsers was not commenced until October 20, 1936.

The question presented is whether the indorsers became liable.

DAVIS, J. The primary principles of liability are well settled. Indorsers are secondarily or conditionally liable for the payment of notes. N. I. L., Sec. 3.

Here the defendants were accommodation and irregular indorsers, for they were neither makers nor payees. In order to fix their liability, presentment for payment was necessary, except under circumstances not present here (Sec. 130, 131, 140), unless such presentment is waived (Sec. 142). Likewise, notice of dishonor must be given to the indorsers, unless waived (Sec. 160, 180). *Lackport Exchange Trust Co. v. Hyde,* 274 N. Y. 1, 8 N. E. (2d) 38.

It matters not that the indorser is an officer of the corporation and may thereby have knowledge of the date on which the note falls due. The law treats him as it would a stranger; and this is practically the rule in all jurisdictions. The officers simply lend their individual credit to the corporation, and the fact that the corporation is known to be insolvent or bankrupt furnishes no excuse for failure to give such notice. Mere knowledge of the dishonor is held not equivalent to the notice, which must come from the one who is entitled to look to the party for payment and must inform him that the note has been duly presented for payment, that it has been dishonored, and that the holder looks to him for payment. *Bovay v. Fuller,* 63 F. (2d) 280.

PROTEST

If a bill appears on its face to be a foreign bill, that is, one drawn or payable outside of the states and territories of the United States and the District of Columbia, it must be protested for non-acceptance or non-payment, as the case may be, in order to hold parties secondarily liable. Protest is not required in the case of domestic or inland bills; however, they may be, and often are, protested.

Sec. 3–509 of the U. C. C. provides: (1) A protest is a certificate of dishonor made under the hand and seal of a United States consul or vice consul or a notary public or other person authorized to certify dishonor by the law of the place where dishonor occurs. It may be made upon information satisfactory to such person.

(2) The protest must identify the instrument and certify either that due presentment has been made or the reason why it is excused and that the instrument has been dishonored by non-acceptance or non-payment.

(3) The protest may also certify that notice of dishonor has been given to all parties or to specified parties.

(4) Subject to subsection (5) any necessary protest is due by the time that notice of dishonor is due.

(5) If, before protest is due, an instrument has been noted for protest by the officer to make protest, the protest may be made at any time thereafter as of the date of the noting. Delay in protesting a bill is excused if caused by circumstances beyond the control of the holder and not imputable to his default, misconduct, or negligence, but when the cause of delay ceases to operate, the bill must be protested with reasonable dili-

gence. Protest is entirely dispensed with by any circumstances which would dispense with notice of dishonor.

Protest must be made at the place where the bill is dishonored, except that where a bill drawn payable at the place of business or residence of some person other than the drawee has been dishonored by non-acceptance, it must be protested for non-payment at the place where it is expressed to be payable, and no further presentment for payment to, or demand on, the drawee is necessary.

DISCHARGE

Negotiable instruments are usually discharged by payment by the maker or acceptor; or, if the principal debtor is an accommodation party, by payment by him. Negotiable instruments may also be discharged by their intentional cancellation by the holder. Cancellation which is made unintentionally, or under a mistake, or without the authority of the holder, is inoperative; but where an instrument or any signature on it appears to have been canceled, the burden of proof lies on the party who alleges that the cancellation was made unintentionally, or under a mistake, or without authority. Any act which will discharge a simple contract for the payment of money will discharge a negotiable instrument, e.g. the running of the statute of limitations. Finally, if the principal debtor (the maker of a promissory note, or the acceptor of a bill of exchange) becomes the holder of the instrument at or after maturity in his own right, the instrument is discharged.

Discharge of the instrument by any of the means just mentioned will of course discharge any party who is secondarily liable on the instrument. In addition, such a party will also be discharged by the following acts: (1) by the intentional cancellation of his signature by the holder; (2) by the discharge of a prior party; (3) by a valid tender of payment by a prior party; (4) by a release of the principal debtor, unless the holder's right of recourse against the party secondarily liable is expressly reserved; and (5) by any agreement binding upon the holder to extend the time of payment, or to postpone the holder's right to enforce the instrument, unless made with the assent of the party secondarily liable, or unless the right of recourse against such party is expressly reserved.

The holder may expressly renounce his rights against any party to the instrument before, at, or after its maturity. Any absolute or unconditional renunciation of his rights against the principal debtor made at or after the maturity of the instrument discharges the instrument. To be operative, a renunciation must be in writing, unless the instrument is delivered to the party primarily liable on the instrument.

If a negotiable instrument is materially altered without the assent of all the parties to the instrument, it is avoided, except as against a party who has himself made, authorized, or assented to the alteration, and subsequent indorsers. As we have already seen, however, if an instrument which has been materially altered is in the hands of a holder in due course, not a party to the alteration, he may enforce payment of the instrument according to its original tenor.

Payment of the instrument by a party secondarily liable does not discharge the instrument. The party making such payment is remitted to his former rights as regards all prior parties (Sec. 3–601 of the U. C. C.).

Reagan v. National Bank of Commerce of San Antonio
418 S. W. (2d) 593 (1967)

This was an action by the National Bank of Commerce of San Antonio, executor of the estate of William B. Lupe, deceased (plaintiff) against Rocky Reagan, Jr. (defendant). Judgment for the plaintiff, and defendant appealed. Judgment reversed and rendered.

The following facts are undisputed or stipulated: (1) The note in question was executed by defendant and delivered to the payee, William B. Lupe, who died on September 23, 1964. (2) The note, which bore no evidence of payment on its face, was in the possession of Lupe at the time of his death and came into the possession of plaintiff in its capacity as the duly qualified and acting independent executor of Lupe's estate.

All of the trial court's findings of fact are supported by the testimony of Edwin S. Brown who, at all relevant times, was a business associate of Lupe and had custody of Lupe's business records. He testified that as part of the consideration for defendant's surrender of possession of the land, and the payment by defendant of $6,000.00, Lupe agreed that he would not bring suit on the note and would make no effort to collect the note. He further stated that defendant surrendered possession of the land and paid the agreed rental for his continuing possession of the feeding area, which constituted only a small portion of the 900 acres, until May, 1963.

CADENA, J. Defendant, Rocky Reagan, Jr., appeals from a judgment rendered after a nonjury trial against him and in favor of plaintiff, National Bank of Commerce of San Antonio, Independent Executor of the Estate of William B. Lupe, Deceased, on a promissory note in the sum of $25,000.00, dated December 30, 1960, and payable on March 15, 1962.

Section 122 of the Negotiable Instruments Act (Article 5939, Sec. 122, *Vernon's Ann. Civ. St.*) provides that a renunciation by the holder of a negotiable instrument of his rights against any person liable thereon must be in writing, unless possession of the instrument is surrendered. However, Sec. 119 of the same statute expressly recites that a negotiable instrument is discharged "* * *

4, By any * * * act which will discharge a simple contract for the payment of money . . ." (U. C. C., Sec. 3–601 (2)).

A discharge of the indebtedness under Par. 4 of Sec. 119 may take place even in the absence of a written release or delivery of the instrument to the primary obligor. *Pugh v. Turner*, 145 Tex. 292, 197 S. W. (2d) 822, 172 A. L. R. 707 (1946). Here, the trial court found that Lupe, induced in part by the knowledge that defendant had no available means with which to pay the indebtedness, agreed to accept, and did accept, defendant's surrender of possession of the leased land, and the payment by defendant of $6,300.00, as satisfaction of the debt evidenced by the note. If defendant was in possession of the land as a tenant, he was under no obligation to surrender possession of any part thereof to Lupe. It is true, as plaintiff points out, that the evidence relating to the terms of the lease was rather vague, but the evidence clearly establishes that defendant and Lupe negotiated on the assumption that defendant was entitled to remain in possession of the land. Because of the surrender of possession by defendant, Lupe was able to lease the land to a third party, who raised a crop thereon in the year 1963.

It appears, then, that Lupe did receive valuable consideration for his agreement. In consideration of Lupe's agreement, defendant agreed to, and did, take action which he was under no obligation to take. The agreement by Lupe to accept the new obligations assumed by defendant as a discharge of defendant's obligations under the note operated as a discharge of the instrument under Sec. 119, Art. 5939. *Hall v. Wichita State Bank & Trust Co.*, 254 S. W. 1036 (Tex. Civ. App., 1923, writ ref'd.)

The judgment of the trial court is reversed and judgment is here rendered that plaintiff take nothing.

London Leasing Corporation v. Interfina, Inc.

53 Misc. (2d) 657, 279 N. Y. S. (2d) 209 (1967)

This was an action by London Leasing Corporation (plaintiff) against Interfina, Inc. and Fredric J. Evans (defendants). Motion for summary judgment granted.

This is a motion for summary judgment against defendants Interfina, Inc. and its president, Fredric J. Evans. On May 3, 1966 Interfina made and delivered to plaintiff a promissory note in the sum of $52,000, signed by Fredric J. Evans, as president of Interfina, and also personally endorsed by Fredric J. Evans. The note was not paid on its due date, August 2, 1966, and thereafter, on August 3, 15, and 19, Interfina, by its president, entered into letter agreements with the plaintiff extending the time for payment of the note. Fredric J. Evans signed the agreements, but only in his corporate capacity.

CRAWFORD, J. The fundamental question presented on this motion is whether a corporate officer (president) who makes a note on behalf of his corporation and, also, personally endorses that note is discharged from *per-*

sonal liability on the note by an agreement between the payee and the corporate maker, by its said president, which extends the corporate maker's time to pay the note.

The sum of $19,500 is due on the note and as against defendant Interfina there is no question that summary judgment should be granted.

In opposition to the motion as against him, defendant Evans contends that the extension agreements, which were not signed by him in his personal capacity, as a matter of law discharged him from personal liability on the note because he did not personally consent to the extension.

Section 3–606 of the Uniform Commercial Code provides: "*Sec. 3–606. Impairment of Recourse or of Collateral.* (1) The holder discharges any party to the instrument to the extent that without *such party's consent* the holder (a) without express reservation of rights releases or agrees not to sue any person against whom the party has to the knowledge of the holder a right of recourse or agrees to suspend the right to enforce against such person the instrument or collateral or otherwise discharges such person * * *" (emphasis supplied).

The code does not explicitly define the meaning of the term "consent." However, the official comment to section 3–606 (*McKinney's Cons. Laws of N. Y.*, Book 62½, Uniform Commercial Code) states: "2. Consent may be given in advance, and is commonly incorporated in the instrument; or it may be given afterward. It requires no consideration, and operates as a waiver of the consenting party's right to claim his own discharge."

In the absence of a clear code definition of "consent," this court is guided by the statement in *Stearns Law of Suretyship* (5th Ed., Sec. 6.13): "Parties to a contract may always alter it by mutual agreement and this is as true of suretyship contract as others. Accordingly, if the creditor and principal modify their contract, and the surety consents thereto, he will not be discharged. Such consent need not be expressly given, *but may be implied from the surrounding circumstances or from his conduct*" (emphasis supplied).

The application of this principle to the present question mandates a holding that defendant Evans consented to the extension. As a matter of fact he applied for, negotiated, signed in his corporate capacity and received the agreements extending the time for payment. While mere knowledge or acquiescence is not, in and of itself, sufficient to prevent discharge, the defendant's conduct here far exceeded these limits and under the special circumstances here presented, constituted consent.

Accordingly, the motion for summary judgment in the sum of $19,500 is granted as against both defendants.

REVIEW CASES

1. Doran was about to ship a carload of cattle. Friddle was ready to attach them, but he refrained from doing so because the cashier of the Bank of Magazine orally agreed to accept and pay checks drawn on the bank in Friddle's favor by Doran. Later the drawee bank refused to honor and pay

the checks. Friddle sued the bank. Ruling? (Bank of Magazine v. Friddle, 179 Ark. 53, 14 S. W.(2d) 238)

2. Jonesboro Rice Milling Co. drew a draft in favor of itself on McGill Bros., who accepted it. Bovay, president of Jonesboro Rice Milling Co., indorsed the draft, and it was discounted to Fuller Bros. On the day the draft was due it was presented to McGill Bros. but was not paid. The sole question is whether the following letter gives Bovay sufficient notice to hold him personally as an indorser: "Jonesboro Rice Milling Co., Jonesboro, Ark., Attention: Mr. Bovay. Gentleman: We just returned from Stuttgart, and the People's National Bank tells us McGill Bros. will be unable to pay the $3,480 draft of yours we hold for a few days but thinks they will be able to take it up soon. What shall we do about it? Yours truly, Fuller Bros., per J. L. W." (Bovay et al. v. Fuller et al., 63 F.(2d) 281)

3. Marshall gave to Columbia Grocery Co. a series of notes in payment of a bill he owed to it. Sometime after the notes were executed, the grocery company inserted in each note by typewriter a clause providing that if one note should be in default, the rest were to fall due immediately. The grocery company later sued Marshall. Did the alteration make the notes void? Did it prevent recovery on the original account? (Columbia Grocery Co. v. Marshall, 131 Tenn. 270, 174 S. W. 1108)

4. Burroughs, the payee of a check drawn on the First National Bank of Shreveport, wired the bank: "Is check of E. O. Shad Harper for $220 good?" The bank replied: "We have funds to pay check E. O. Shad Harper for $220." Burroughs presented the check and the telegrams to the Night & Day Bank of St. Louis, which wired the Shreveport bank: "Confirm your wire of today to W. J. Burroughs that you will honor check E. O. Shad Harper." The Shreveport bank replied: "This confirms our telegram to W. J. Burroughs that we have funds to pay draft E. O. Shad Harper for $220." The St. Louis bank cashed the check for Burroughs, but was later refused payment by the Shreveport bank. It thereupon brought suit, contending that the two telegrams sent by the Shreveport bank amounted to an acceptance of the check or a promise to pay it on presentation. Ruling? (Night & Day Bank of St. Louis v. First National Bank of Shreveport, 150 La. 954, 91 So. 405)

5. Bibee Grocery Co. sued Myers to recover on a note which he had signed as accommodation indorser. The question to be determined was whether the following letter was sufficient notice of dishonor: "A note for $669.08, given us by Yeager & Myers on May 28, 1924, was due today, and, as you are indorser on this note, we are writing to advise you that the same is due and to advise you of your liability for the payment of the same, in lieu of having the same protested. We will ask that you gentlemen please arrange to let us have payment of this note at once, as the same cannot be renewed." (Myers v. Bibee Grocery Co., 148 Va. 282, 138 S. E. 570)

6. Eassy drew a check payable to Mavidone, who negotiated it for value to Manos. Eassy stopped payment on the check. Without presenting the instrument to the bank for payment, Manos brought an action against Eassy to recover on the instrument. Judgment for whom? (Manos v. Eassy, 124 S. C. 154, 117 S. E. 222)

Checks

37

A check, as defined in Sec. 3–104 of the U. C. C., is " A draft drawn on a bank payable on demand." We have already considered the general law applicable to bills of exchange payable on demand, and much of this applies to checks. A few sections of the U. C. C., however, are applicable solely to checks. Because of this fact, and because of certain peculiar practices which have grown up in the use of checks, it is desirable to devote this chapter exclusively to their consideration.

As we shall see, the rules applicable to checks alone concern principally two matters: (1) the time within which a check must be presented in order to hold the drawer liable and (2) the certification of checks.

RELATIONSHIP BETWEEN DRAWER AND DRAWEE BANK

CREDITOR–DEBTOR AND PRINCIPAL–AGENT RELATIONSHIP

The relationship between the depositor and his bank is both (1) that of creditor and debtor and (2) that of principal and agent. The depositor is the creditor and principal; the bank is the debtor and agent. This relationship is contractual and grows out of the express or implied promises of the respective parties. Under the contract the bank agrees to honor and pay checks drawn by the depositor against his account with the bank so long as he has sufficient funds in his account to pay the checks, and so long as the checks are properly presented.

If the bank refuses to pay a check drawn by a depositor who has sufficient funds out of which such check could have been paid, with few exceptions [1] the bank will be liable to the drawer (depositor) for damages. By its refusal to pay the check the bank has breached its contract

[1] Right of set-off, attachment, etc.

with the depositor. The measure of damages suffered by the depositor through the bank failing to use ordinary care is the extent of the injury actually proved. However, where there is bad faith, it includes other damages, if any, suffered by the party as a proximate consequence. (Sec. 4–103 (5).) [1]

STOP PAYMENT ORDER

Since a bank is the agent of its depositor in honoring and paying his checks, a depositor who issues a check and then wishes for some reason not to have the bank honor and pay it may direct the bank not to pay the check when it is presented by the holder. The fact that the drawer of a check may legally stop payment of it proves upon occasion to be an effective means of protecting his interests. Suppose that A sells a used car to B, and B pays A by check. B discovers that the car is not as warranted by A, so he immediately issues a stop payment order to the drawee bank. If the bank receives the order before it has paid or certified the check, it is legally bound to dishonor the check when presented for payment; if it fails to do so, it will be liable to the depositor (B). However, if the drawee bank has already paid the check, or certified it at the request of the payee or a subsequent holder, before it receives the stop payment order, it is not liable to the drawer (B).

In the foregoing example, if the payee A, after presenting the check and being refused payment, brings an action against B, B may set up his personal defense of breach of warranty. However, if A has negotiated the check to a holder in due course, and the latter sues B, B's personal defense of breach of warranty would be cut off. This means that the holder in due course would be able to recover judgment against B on the check. B, in turn, would have a cause of action against A on the original contract for breach of warranty.

If the deposit contract between the depositor and the bank does not specify how stop payment orders are to be given, such orders may be oral, in writing, over the telephone, or in any other form which conveys to the

---

[1] U. C. C., Sec. 4–402: "A payor bank is liable to its customer for damages proximately caused by the wrongful dishonor of an item. When the dishonor occurs through mistake, liability is limited to actual damages proved. If so proximately caused and proved, damages may include damages for an arrest or prosecution of the customer or other consequential damages. Whether any consequential damages are proximately caused by the wrongful dishonor is a question of fact to be determined in each case." COMMENT: "This section rejects decisions which have held that where the dishonored item has been drawn by a merchant, trader or fiduciary he is defamed in his business, trade or profession by a reflection on his credit and hence that substantial damages may be awarded on the basis of defamation 'per se' without proof that damage has occurred. The merchant, trader and fiduciary are placed on the same footing as any other drawer and in all cases of dishonor by mistake damages recoverable are limited to those actually proved."

bank definite instructions not to pay the check. Banks prefer that such orders be in writing, and for that reason they usually stipulate in their contract with the depositor, when he first establishes his account with the bank, that such orders must be in writing. At times such a stipulation is found in the "depositors' contract" printed on the back of his deposit slip; or it may be found in the "rules and regulations" of the bank, by which the depositor, under his contract, has agreed to be bound. The U. C. C. has a provision covering this situation.[1]

The courts hold that the drawee bank is liable to the depositor if it pays a check after receiving a stop payment order. The banks attempt to reduce this broad liability by requiring that the depositor sign a written stop payment order and by inserting in the order some such restrictive provision as the following: "Should you (bank) pay this check through inadvertency, or oversight, it is expressly understood that you will in no way be held responsible." It appears that a large majority of the courts hold such provisions invalid and unenforceable.[2]

Garden Check Cash. Serv., Inc. v. First Nat. City Bank
25 A. D. (2d) 137, 267 N. Y. S. (2d) 698 (1966)

This was an action by the Garden Check Cashing Service, Inc. (plaintiff) against the First National City Bank (defendant). Judgment for defendant and plaintiff appealed. Upon appeal, the Supreme Court reversed and granted judgment for plaintiff. Upon leave to appeal, the Supreme Court reversed and judgment of the Civil Court was reinstated. The facts are found in the court's opinion.

BARSTOW, J. This action was brought to recover on a written instrument, more fully hereinafter described. Following trial in Civil Court judgment was rendered for defendant (38 Misc. (2d) 623, 238 N. Y. S. (2d) 751). Upon ap-

[1] Sec. 4-403 of the U. C. C. provides: "(2) An oral order is binding upon the bank only for fourteen calendar days unless confirmed in writing within that period. A written order is effective for only six months unless renewed in writing." COMMENT: "There is no right to stop payment after certification of a check or other acceptance of a draft, and this is true no matter who procures the certification. Normally a direction to stop payment is first given by telephone."

[2] The U. C. C. follows the majority view to the effect that such a restriction provision is inoperative. The bank is required to exercise "reasonable care," and may not relieve itself of that responsibility. Sec. 4-103 provides: "The effect of the provisions of this Article may be varied by agreement except that no agreement can disclaim a bank's responsibility for its own lack of good faith or failure to exercise ordinary care or can limit the measure of damages for such lack or failure; but the parties may by agreement determine the standards by which such responsibility is to be measured if such standards are not manifestly unreasonable." COMMENT: "The position taken by this section is that stopping payment is a service which depositors expect and are entitled to receive from banks notwithstanding its difficulty, inconvenience and expense. The inevitable occasional losses through failure to stop should be borne by the banks as a cost of the business of banking."

peal Appellate Term reversed and granted judgment for plaintiff. The issues presented being novel, as is also the instrument, and the lower courts, both in this case and others, having reached diverse results (*Rose Check Cashing Service, Inc. v. Chemical Bank New York Trust Co.*, 43 Misc. (2d) 679, 252 N. Y. S. (2d) 100, affg. 40 Misc. (2d) 995, 244 N. Y. S. (2d) 474; *Garden Check Cashing Service, Inc. v. Chase Manhattan Bank*, 46 Misc. (2d) 163, 258 N. Y. S. (2d) 918) we granted leave to appeal (24 A. D. (2d) 734).

The proof is that any person, whether a customer or not, may purchase from defendant for twenty cents a check up to the amount of $250. The instrument when issued bears the name of defendant, an identification number and the amount is machine-imbedded thereon. There is a line thereon for the date, another line prefixed by the words "Pay to the order of" and at the bottom two further lines prefixed by the words "signature" and "address" respectively. All of these four lines are blank when the instrument is delivered to the purchaser. In the upper right and left hand corners of the instrument in comparatively small type appear the words "Personal Money Order." In the upper center underneath defendant's name appear in somewhat larger type the words "Register Check." The purchaser receives with the instrument another writing bearing the same number as the first instrument. At the top are printed the words "Customer's Record Copy of Register Check-Personal Money Order Drawn On First National City Bank." There are blank lines for the date and name of the payee. At the bottom thereof it is stated that the check is sold upon two conditions: (1) that the purchaser sign his name and address after filling in a date and the name of a payee and (2) that no request for a refund or to stop payment be made to the bank unless "this Record" is submitted therewith.

On April 13, 1962 one Higgins purchased from defendant a check in the amount of $130.37. On the same date he reported to the bank that the check had been lost and requested that payment be stopped. The name of a payee, according to Higgins, had not been filled in. Defendant stopped payment and five days later delivered to Higgins a cashier's check for the amount of $130.37.

It further appears that on April 13 one Walker presented the check in its blank form to plaintiff. Upon furnishing identification satisfactory to plaintiff, Walker inserted his name as payee, signed the check with his name and received the proceeds thereof less plaintiff's fee. Following deposit the check was returned to plaintiff by defendant with the notation that payment had been stopped.

The issue presented is, whether, as plaintiff contends, the instrument is "akin to a cashier's check or a traveler's check" upon which defendant is primarily liable from the moment of issue with no right to stop payment thereon. Or, on the other hand, as defendant submits, is the instrument an unconditional order in writing addressed by the owner-drawer to the bank, requiring the latter to pay on demand the stated sum to order or to bearer with the ensuing right to the purchaser to stop payment?

"A check, strictly speaking, is a negotiable instrument, i.e., a bill of exchange drawn on a bank payable on demand" (*Irving Trust Co. v. Leff*, 253 N. Y. 359,

362, 171 N. E. 569, 571). A bill of exchange is an unconditional order in writing addressed by one person to another, signed by the person giving it, requiring the person to whom it is addressed to pay on demand a sum certain to order or to bearer (Negotiable Instruments Law, Sec. 210; Uniform Commercial Code, Sec. 3–104 (2) (a)). Such a bill becomes a check when drawn on a bank payable on demand (Negotiable Instruments Law, Sec. 321; Uniform Commercial Code, Sec. 3–104 (2) (b)).

"A cashier's check issued by a bank, however, is not an ordinary draft. The latter is a bill of exchange payable on demand. It is an order upon a third party purporting to be drawn upon a deposit of funds. * * * A cashier's check is of a very different character. It is the primary obligation of the bank which issues it * * * and constitutes its written promise to pay upon demand * * *. It has been said that a cashier's check is a bill of exchange drawn by a bank upon itself, accepted in advance by the very act of issuance" (*Matter of Bank of United States*, 243 App. Div. 287, 291, 277 N. Y. S. 96, 100).

If it could be found that the instrument before us was in substance a cashier's check drawn by defendant upon itself it would be of necessity a non-negotiable instrument. To be negotiable an instrument must be signed by the drawer (Negotiable Instruments Law, Sec. 20; Uniform Commercial Code, Sec. 3–104 (1) (a)). Cf. *Bobrick v. Second National Bank*, 175 App. Div. 550, 552, 162 N. Y. S. 147, 148, 149, affd. 224 N. Y. 637, 121 N. E. 856. Here, no officer of defendant signed the instrument and there was no place thereon for such a signature.

Similarly, the contention is advanced that the instrument herein is in the nature of a traveler's check. An examination of the form of the latter (Modern Legal Forms, Sec. 1393) reveals the dissimilarity. Such a check requires, as does the cashier's check, the signature of the issuer thereof (cf. *Sullivan v. Knauth*, 220 N. Y. 216, 222, 115 N. E. 460, 461, L. R. A. 1917F, 554).

It is unnecessary to determine what the impact would be upon plaintiff's cause of action against defendant if it should be determined that the instrument was non-negotiable (cf. *Non-negotiable Instruments*, 11 Syracuse L. R., 13–26; Uniform Commercial Code, Sec. 3–805). Any attempt to analogize the instrument herein with a cashier's or traveler's check fails.

The relationship between defendant and the purchaser of the check is reasonably clear. The latter deposited with defendant a sum of money and received therefor a writing in which defendant plainly appeared as drawee. The novel feature of the instrument was that the prospective names of drawer and payee were blank. Defendant was not primarily liable thereon (Negotiable Instrument Law, Secs. 20, 37; Uniform Commercial Code, Sec. 3–104 (1) (a), 3–401 (1)) and such liability did not arise until there was certification or acceptance of the instrument (Negotiable Instrument Law, Secs. 220, 325; Uniform Commercial Code, Secs. 3–409 (1); 3–410; 3–411). See generally 41 N. Y. Jur., *Negotiable Instruments*, Secs. 374–375.

We see small difference between the present transaction and one where a person deposits with a bank a sum of money and receives a quantity of blank checks. The obvious difference is that here a single deposit was made and a single blank check received with the amount of the deposit inserted therein. Thereafter the procedure followed the normal and customary pattern—the purchaser filled in the name of a payee, signed his name and address and delivered the instrument. Thereupon it became a negotiable instrument subject to all the rights and provisions of the then Negotiable Instruments Law. Defendant for its own purposes may have coined the words "Personal Money Order" and "Register Check" appearing on the instrument but these words in no way altered the applicable legal principles. The purchaser under his contract with defendant was the sole person who might draw on the fund and he had the clear right to stop payment prior to acceptance by the bank (*American Defense Society v. Sherman National Bank of New York*, 225 N. Y. 506, 122 N. E. 695)—a right since accorded a bank's customer by statute (Uniform Commercial Code, Sec. 4–403). This conclusion is fortified by decisions in another jurisdiction where, unlike this case, a legal "bank money order" signed by an officer of the issuing bank was held to be the equivalent of a cashier's check. (*State ex rel. Babcock v. Perkins*, 165 Ohio St. 185, 134 N. E. (2d) 839; *Cross v. Exchange Bank Co.*, 110 Ohio App. 219, 168 N. E. (2d) 910).

We attach no legal significance, so far as plaintiff's right to recover is concerned, to the customer's record copy of the transaction which provided, among other things, that such must be submitted with a request to stop payment. The proof seems to be that this copy was delivered to plaintiff by the person who cashed the check.

The general principle is well established "that notwithstanding the agreement which bankers make with their customers, to pay their checks to the amount standing to their credit, a check-holder can take no benefit from this agreement, and that a check does not operate as a transfer, or assignment of any part of the debt, or create a lien at law or in equity upon the deposit" (*Aetna National Bank v. Fourth National Bank*, 46 N. Y. 82, 87). The drawee enters into no contract relations with the holder unless and until the instrument is accepted (11 Am. Jur. (2d), *Bills and Notes*, Sec. 593; *Henderson v. Lincoln Rochester Trust Co.*, 303 N. Y. 27, 31, 100 N. E. (2d) 117, 119; Negotiable Instruments Law, Secs. 325, 220; Uniform Commercial Code, Secs. 3–409, 3–410, 3–411).

We conclude that Higgins, the purchaser of the instrument, effectively stopped payment thereon prior to its presentation to defendant by plaintiff. It follows that no cause of action has been established against defendant.

The judgment and order of Appellate Term should be reversed on the law and on the facts and the judgment of Civil Court reinstated, without costs and without disbursements.

Determination of the Appellate Term unanimously reversed, on the law and on the facts, without costs and without disbursements, and the judgment of the Civil Court reinstated.

All concur.

Marine Midland Trust Company of Rochester v. Blackburn

50 Misc. (2d) 954, 271 N. Y. S. (2d) 388 (1966)

This is an action by Marine Midland Trust Company (plaintiff) against Walter P. Blackburn (defendant). Motion for summary judgment granted, and defendant appealed. Affirmed.

The plaintiff has moved for summary judgment in its action on a check made by defendant to one Vanella in payment for a used automobile. It appears that Vanella deposited the check with the plaintiff bank and received credit and cash therefor. Defendant ascertained that Vanella had misrepresented to him that the automobile was free of liens, and so defendant stopped payment upon the check. The plaintiff secured partial repayment from Vanella of the money it advanced on the check, and brings this action to collect the balance from the defendant as drawer of the check.

WITMER, J. The defendant raises the defense of Vanella's fraud; and contends that even a holder in due course of the check, as plaintiff concededly is, takes it subject to fraud in the transaction giving rise to issuance of the check; and he relies upon Uniform Commercial Code, Sec. 3-305 (2) (c). This section provides in pertinent part as follows: "To the extent that a holder is a holder in due course he takes the instrument free from * * * (2) all defenses of any party to the instrument with whom the holder has not dealt except (c) such misrepresentation as has induced the party to sign the instrument with neither knowledge nor reasonable opportunity to obtain knowledge of its character or its essential terms."

Neither counsel nor I have found any reported case in New York involving this question arising since the effective date of the U. C. C., September 27, 1964. The quoted section does not appear, however, to have changed the law in New York with respect to the question at bar. The comment under this section in McKinney's (Book 62½, *Consolidated Laws of New York*, Part 2, Sec. 3-305, Item 7, p. 187) indicates that the section is designed to accord with the great majority of decisions under the prior law to the effect that only fraud as to the nature of the instrument itself signed by the defendant is a defense to an action by a holder in due course. (See *Gordon Supply Co., Inc. v. South Sea Apts., Inc.*, 23 A. D. (2d) 666, 257 N. Y. S. (2d) 237; *Ram Industrial v. Van De Maele*, 20 A. D. (2d) 783, 248 N. Y. S. (2d) 176; *Meadow Brook Nat. Bank v. Rogers*, 44 Misc. (2d) 250, 253 N. Y. S. (2d) 501; and *Merson v. Sun Insurance Co.*, 44 Misc. (2d) 131, 253 N. Y. S. (2d) 51.) It appears that the new section was designed to codify the prior case law in this respect; and that construction of it is adopted by the court.

The defense, therefore, is insufficient in law, and plaintiff's motion for summary judgment is granted.

DUTY OF DRAWER TO INSPECT CANCELED CHECKS

The general rule is that a drawer (depositor) has the duty to examine the statement and canceled checks returned to him by his bank, within a reasonable time after he has received them. If upon such examination he discovers any forgeries, alterations, or discrepancies in the amounts payable, he has the further duty to inform the bank promptly.[1]

Thompson Maple Products v. Citizens National Bank
211 Pa. Super. 42, 234 A. (2d) 32 (1967)

This was an action by Thompson Maple Products, Inc. (plaintiff) against The Citizens National Bank of Corry (defendant). Judgment for plaintiff in part and judgment for defendant in part. Plaintiff appealed. Judgment affirmed.

In this assumpsit action, the plaintiff, Thompson Maple Products, Inc., seeks to recover more than $100,000 paid out on a series of its checks by defendant bank, as drawee. The payee's signature on each of the checks was forged by one Emery Albers, who then cashed the checks or deposited them to his account with the defendant.

The plaintiff is a small, closely-held corporation, principally engaged in the manufacture of bowling pin "blanks" from maple logs. Some knowledge of its operations from 1959 to 1962 is essential to an understanding of this litigation.

The plaintiff purchased logs from timber owners in the vicinity of its mill. Since these timber owners rarely had facilities for hauling logs, such transportation was furnished by a few local truckers, including Emery Albers.

---

[1] U. C. C., Sec. 4–406 provides: "(1) When a bank sends to its customer a statement of account accompanied by items paid in good faith in support of the debit entries or holds the statement and items pursuant to a request or instructions of its customer or otherwise in a reasonable manner makes the statement and items available to the customer, the customer must exercise reasonable care and promptness to examine the statement and items to discover his unauthorized signature or any alteration on an item and must notify the bank promptly after discovery thereof.

"(2) If the bank establishes that the customer failed with respect to an item to comply with the duties imposed on the customer by subsection (1) the customer is precluded from asserting against the bank (a) his unauthorized signature or any alteration on the item if the bank also establishes that it suffered a loss by reason of such failure; and (b) an unauthorized signature or alteration by the same wrong-doer on any other item paid in good faith by the bank after the first item and statement was available to the customer for a reasonable period not exceeding fourteen calendar days and before the bank receives notification from the customer of any such unauthorized signature or alteration.

"(3) The preclusion under subsection (2) does not apply if the customer establishes lack of ordinary care on the part of the bank in paying the item(s).

"(4) Without regard to care or lack of care of either the customer or the bank a customer who does not within one year from the time the statement and items are made available to the customer (subsection (1)) discover and report his unauthorized signature or any alteration on the face or back of the item or does not within three years from that time discover and report any unauthorized indorsement is precluded from asserting against the bank such unauthorized signature or indorsement or such alteration.

"(5) If under this section a payor bank has a valid defense against a claim of a customer upon or resulting from payment of an item and waives or fails upon request to assert the defense the bank may not assert against any collecting bank or other prior party presenting or transferring the item a claim based upon the unauthorized signature or alteration giving rise to the customer's claim."

HOFFMAN, J. The case was tried to the court below sitting without a jury. That court entered judgment in favor of the plaintiff in the amount of $1258.51, the face amount of three checks which the defendant had paid without any endorsement whatever. It dismissed the remainder of the claim, and this appeal followed.

Sometime prior to February, 1959, Emery Albers conceived the scheme which led to the forgeries at issue here. Albers was an independent log hauler who for many years had transported logs to the company mill. For a brief period in 1952, he had been employed by the plaintiff, and he was a trusted friend of the Thompson family. After procuring blank sets of scaling slips, Albers filled them in to show substantial, wholly fictitious deliveries of logs, together with the names of local timber owners as suppliers. He then delivered the slips to the company bookkeeper, who prepared checks payable to the purported owners. Finally, he volunteered to deliver the checks to the owners. The bookkeeper customarily entrusted the checks to him for that purpose.

Albers then forged the payee's signature and either cashed the checks or deposited them to his account at the defendant bank, where he was well known. Although he pursued this scheme for an undetermined period of time, only checks paid out over a three-year period prior to this litigation are here in controversy. See Uniform Commercial Code, Act of April 6, 1953, P. L. 3, as amended, Sec. 4–406, 12A P. S., Sec. 4–406.

In 1963, when the forgeries were uncovered, Albers confessed and was imprisoned. The plaintiff then instituted this suit against the drawee bank, asserting that the bank had breached its contract of deposit by paying the checks over forged endorsements. See U. C. C., Sec. 3–404, 12A P. S., Sec. 3–404.

Both parties agree that, as between the payor bank and its customer, ordinarily the bank must bear the loss occasioned by the forgery of a payee's endorsement. *Philadelphia Title Insurance Company v. Fidelity-Philadelphia Trust Company*, 419 Pa. 78, 212 A. (2d) 222 (1965); U. C. C., Sec. 3–404, 12A P. S., Sec. 3–404.

The trial court concluded, however, that the plaintiff-drawer, by virtue of its conduct, could not avail itself of that rule, citing Sec. 3–406 of the Code: "Any person who by his negligence substantially contributes to * * * the making of an unauthorized signature is precluded from asserting the * * * lack of authority against * * * a drawee or other payor who pays the instrument in good faith and in accordance with the reasonable commercial standards of the drawee's or payor's business." 12A P. S., Sec. 3–406.

Had the legislature intended simply to continue the strict estoppel doctrine of the pre-Code cases, it could have employed the term "precluded," without qualification, as in Sec. 23 of the old Negotiable Instruments Law, 56 P. S., Sec. 28 (repealed). However, it chose to modify that doctrine in Sec. 3–406, by specifying that negligence which *"substantially contributes to * * * the making of an unauthorized signature * * *"* will preclude the drawer from asserting a forgery [emphasis supplied]. The Code has thus abandoned the language of the older cases (negligence which "directly and proximately affects the conduct of the bank in passing the forgery") and shortened the chain of causation which the defendant bank must establish. "[N]o attempt is made," according to the Official Comment to Sec. 3–406, "to specify what is negligence, and the question is one for the court or jury on the facts of the particular case."

In the instant case, the trial court could readily have concluded that plaintiff's business affairs were conducted in so negligent a fashion as to have "substantially contributed" to the Albers forgeries, within the meaning of Sec. 3–406.

Finally, the plaintiff argues that the defendant bank cannot rely on Sec. 3–406 because it did not pay the checks in accordance with "reasonable commercial standards" as required by that section. All the checks were regular on their face and bore the purported endorsement of the named payee. It is asserted, however, that the defendant bank was required, as a matter of law, to obtain the second endorsement of Albers before accepting the checks for deposit to his account.

The short answer to that contention is that the trial court did not find, nor does the record show, that obtaining such a second endorsement is a reasonable, or even a general, commercial practice, where the depositor is well-known to the bank and where his identity can later be ascertained from code markings on the check itself.

Furthermore, under the Code, the bank did not have an unqualified right to a second endorsement. A check endorsed in blank is bearer paper. It is negotiable by delivery alone, without further endorsement. See U. C. C., Sec. 3–201, 3–204, 12A P. S., Sec. 3–201, 3–204.

To the extent that banks do obtain such endorsements, they apparently do so for their own protection, over and above that provided by the warranties arising on presentment and transfer. Cf. U. C. C., Sec. 3–414, 12A P. S., Sec. 3–414 (Contract of Indorser), with U. C. C., Sec. 3–417, 12A P. S., Sec. 3–417 (Warranties).

Judgment affirmed.

BANK'S RIGHT OF SET–OFF

Under certain conditions a bank has a right of set-off against the depositor's checking account. If the depositor has borrowed money from the bank, or is indebted to the bank in some other way, and fails or refuses to pay the debt when it is due, the bank may set off the depositor's checking account against the debt. But the bank has no such right (1) if the debt is not yet due and the depositor is solvent, or (2) if the deposit is applicable to some other purpose, or (3) if there is an express agreement to the effect that the bank may not set off the depositor's account against his debt to the bank.

State Bank of Siloam Springs v. Marshall

163 Ark. 566, 260 S. W. 431 (1924)

This was an action by Charlotte Marshall (plaintiff) against the State Bank of Siloam Springs (defendant). Judgment for plaintiff, and defendant appealed. Reversed and remanded.

Plaintiff was engaged in operating a rooming and boarding house. On November 19, 1921, she had on deposit, subject to check, in the defendant bank the sum of $245.27. During the month of November, 1921, she drew four checks against this account, amounting to a total of $70.25. Each of these checks was returned marked "No funds," and the bank refused payment on the checks because it had applied the amount on deposit to plaintiff's credit in payment of a debt due in the future from her to the bank. Plaintiff therefore brought this action for damages. It appeared that plaintiff was not insolvent at the time the checks were dishonored.

The jury returned a verdict for plaintiff in the sum of $250, and the court entered judgment for plaintiff for that amount. Defendant appealed.

HART, J. At the time the plaintiff drew the checks in question on the defendant bank she had on deposit a sum subject to her check which was greater than the amount of the four checks drawn by her upon which the bank refused payment. The ground upon which the bank dishonored the checks was that it had applied the deposit of the plaintiff towards the payment of a debt which she owed the bank, which was not then due. It was also shown by the plaintiff that she was not at the time insolvent, and that the bank had no lien on her deposits. The general rule is that a bank is bound to honor checks drawn on it by a depositor, if it has sufficient funds belonging to the depositor when the check is presented, and the funds are not subject to any lien or claim; and for its refusal or neglect to do so it is liable in an action by the depositor.

In *McFall v. First National Bank*, 138 Ark. 370, 211 S. W. 919, this court held that, in case a bank wrongfully dishonors, through mistake or otherwise, a merchant or trader's check, injury to his credit may be inferred from the fact that he is a merchant or trader, and substantial damages may be awarded upon proof of that fact without anything more. The refusal to pay the check injures the credit of the merchant or trader, and because this element of damages is difficult to prove and estimate, temperate damages are allowed. They are more than nominal damages, and are such as would be a reasonable compensation for the injury to the credit of the merchant or trader.

Subsequent to the rendition of this decision the Legislature passed an act, which reads, in part: "A depositor, whether a merchant or trader or otherwise, may recover from any bank doing business in this state for or on account of its wrongful dishonor of his check only upon allegation and proof of such special damages as have approximately resulted to him therefrom."

The evident purpose of the section quoted was to change the rule announced in the decision referred to, and to require depositors in all cases to prove the amount of damages they have suffered by reason of the bank's refusing to pay their checks before they can recover more than nominal damages. In short, merchants and traders must prove actual loss to their credit before they can recover damages from a bank for refusing to pay their checks.

In the instant case the court limited the right of the plaintiff to recover against the defendant to compensation for damages to her credit. In this connection it may be stated that the plaintiff was not a merchant or trader and did not suffer any damage to her credit. Under the circumstances, the plaintiff was entitled to recover only nominal damages under the proof made. At most the plaintiff only showed that her checks were dishonored by the bank and that she suffered some inconvenience thereby. It is not shown that she suffered any loss of patronage to her rooming and boarding house, or that she was prevented from supplying her guests with food or other articles necessary for their use and comfort. Reversed and remanded.

STALE CHECKS

The expression "stale check" refers to a check which has been issued by the drawer and which has been held by the holder for a considerable time before presentation to the bank for payment. The bank cannot safely pay a "stale check," for if it does it may be held to be guilty of negligence. Caution requires that the bank secure confirmation from the drawer before cashing the check. But just when does a check become "stale"? Sec. 4–404 provides that "a bank is under no obligation to a customer having a checking account to pay a check, other than a certified check, which is presented more than six months after its date, but it may charge its customer's account for a payment made thereafter in good faith." COMMENT: "This section incorporates a type of statute adopted in 26 jurisdictions. The time limit is set at six months because banking and commercial practice regards a check outstanding for longer than that period as stale, and a bank will normally not pay such a check without consulting the depositor."

PAYMENT OF CHECKS AFTER DRAWER'S DEATH

We learned in our study of Agency Law that the general rule is to the effect that the death of the principal immediately terminates the authority of the agent to act for his principal. This rule is somewhat modified in the case of a depositor and his bank. If the depositor (principal) issues a check and dies before the check is presented to the bank (agent) for payment, and if the bank, not knowing of the death of the drawer, pays the check, the bank may debit the account of the drawer. However, if the bank knows of the death of the drawer when it pays or certifies the check, the bank may not be liable to the drawer's estate.[1]

In re Estate of Peter J. Greene
47 Misc. (2d) 140, 261 N. Y. S. (2d) 977 (1965)

This was an action by one Hoffman, claimant, against the estate of the decedent, Peter J. Greene, asserting priority of his claim on a check in the amount of $3,500. Priority denied, and he appealed. Affirmed.

COX, S. This decedent died on January 1, 1959 and the administrators of his estate now are accounting. Their account lists claims of the United States Treasury Department for additional income taxes, plus penalties and interest, for the years 1952, 1954, 1955, 1956 and 1958 amounting to $137,632.78 and gift taxes, plus penalties and interest, for the years 1954, 1955 and 1958 amounting to $9,177.94. An assessment was made by the Collector of Internal Revenue on July 20, 1962 and a final proof of claim, supplementing earlier claims, was served on the administrators in January 1963. The administrators have allowed but have not paid the claims in the total of $146,810.72. The account further states that the Treasury Department has asserted a proposed deficiency for income tax liability amounting to $301,617.73.

On December 15, 1958 the claimant Hoffman drew his company check to the order of the decedent in the amount of $3,500. This check was deposited in a bank to the decedent's credit. On January 2, 1959, the day following the decedent's death, Hoffman obtained the certification of a check in the amount of $3,500, dated December 31, 1958, drawn to the order of Hoffman's company and signed by the decedent. Thereafter, this check was deposited to the credit of Hoffman's company. Facts as to the manner in which this check came into Hoffman's possession have not been presented. Concededly the signature on the check is the decedent's and the other writing on the check is Hoffman's. The claimant's possession of the check permits the inference that it was delivered for consideration (*Matter of Kolben*, 203 Misc. 1012, 120 N. Y. S. (2d) 812). While the death of the maker did not terminate his liability upon the instrument it did operate to revoke the authority of the payee to collect from the drawee (*Matter of Kolben*, supra; *Mater of Bakri*, supra, 109 N. Y. S.

---

[1] U. C. C., Sec. 4–405: "(1) A payor or collecting bank's authority to accept, pay or collect an item or to account for proceeds of its collection if otherwise effective is not rendered ineffective by incompetence of a customer of either bank existing at the time the item is issued or its collection is undertaken if the bank does·not know of an adjudication of incompetence. Neither death nor incompetence of a customer revokes such authority to accept, pay, collect or account until the bank knows of the fact of death or of an adjudication of incompetence and has reasonable opportunity to act on it. (2) Even with knowledge a bank may for ten days after the date of death pay or certify checks drawn on or prior to that date unless ordered to stop payment by a person claiming an interest in the account."

(2d) 654; cf. Uniform Commercial Code, Sec. 4–405, effective September 27, 1964).

The contention that on December 15, 1958 Hoffman made a loan to the decedent secured by collateral has not been established by credible evidence. This claimant is a general creditor of the estate for the principal amount of $3,500 represented by the check of December 31, 1958, and for unpaid telephone bills. The amount chargeable to the estate upon the latter item is found to be $437.48.

NATURE OF LIABILITY OF DRAWER OF A CHECK

The U. C. C. provides that an uncertified check which is drawn and payable within the states and territories of the United States and the District of Columbia must be presented for payment within a reasonable time (presumed to be thirty days after date or issue, whichever is later) or the drawer will be discharged from liability thereon *to the extent of the loss caused by the delay* (italics ours) (see 3–501 (c), 3–502 (1) (b), and 3–503 (c)).[1]

The drawer of a check is in a different position from the drawer of an ordinary bill of exchange. This difference is one of the two major differences between the law relative to checks and the law relative to ordinary bills of exchange. In our study of bills of exchange we saw that the drawer of a bill of exchange was secondarily and conditionally liable to pay the instrument if the party primarily liable did not pay, provided the holder made proper presentment and gave proper notice of dishonor to the drawer. But the drawer of a check is absolutely liable on the instrument for the running of the statute of limitations, even though the holder fails to present the check to the drawee bank and, in case of dishonor, fails to give the drawer notice of dishonor. There is, however, one exception to this statement, as Sec. 3–502 (1) (b) makes clear. If the holder of the check should fail to make presentment for payment within a reasonable time, and such failure should result in loss to the drawer, then the drawer is discharged from liability to the extent of the loss caused by the delay in making proper presentment for payment. The usual cause for such loss is the failure of the drawee bank. For example, A gives B a check

---

[1] Sec. 3–501 (c) of the U. C. C. provides that in the case of any drawer, the acceptor of a draft payable at a bank or the maker of a note payable at a bank, presentment for payment is necessary, but failure to make presentment discharges such drawer, acceptor or maker only as stated in Section 3–502 (1) (b). Sec. 3–502 (1) (b) provides that any drawer or the acceptor of a draft payable at a bank or the maker of a note payable at a bank who because the drawee or payor bank becomes insolvent during the delay is deprived of funds maintained with the drawee or payor bank is discharged in respect of such funds, but such drawer, acceptor or maker is not otherwise discharged.

drawn on his bank. B does not present the check for payment within a reasonable time. The bank fails, and in the process of liquidation the depositors are paid 50¢ on the dollar. A would be discharged from liability to B to the extent of his loss, namely, 50 per cent of the check.

It should not be overlooked that the holder of a check must be vigilant and make proper presentment for payment if he wishes to fix the conditional liability of prior indorsers. If he fails to do so, they will be released, just as in the case of an ordinary bill of exchange. For example, C, the payee of a check, negotiates the check to D. In order to fix the conditional liability of C, D would have to make proper presentment and, in case of dishonor, give proper notice of dishonor to C.

Citizens Nat. Bank of Englewood v. Fort Lee S. & L. Ass'n
89 N. J. Super. 43, 213 A. (2d) 315 (1965)

This was an action by Citizens National Bank of Englewood (plaintiff) against Fort Lee Savings and Loan Association et al. (defendants). Judgment for plaintiff and defendants appealed. Judgment affirmed.

On August 27, 1963, George P. Winter agreed to sell a house in Fort Lee, New Jersey to defendant Jean Amoroso and her husband. On the same day Amoroso requested her bank, Fort Lee Savings and Loan Association (Fort Lee Savings), to issue the bank's check to her order for $3,100 to be used as a deposit on the contract for sale. Fort Lee Savings complied by drawing the check against its account with the Fort Lee Trust Company. Later that day Amoroso indorsed and delivered the check to Winter, and he deposited the check in his account at the plaintiff bank. At that time he had a balance of $225.33. After the $3,100 check was deposited the bank cashed a $1,000 check for him against his account. In addition, on August 27 or August 28, the bank cleared and charged Winter's account with four other checks totaling $291.76.

The next day Amoroso discovered that Winter had previously sold the property to a third party by agreement which had been recorded in the Bergen County Clerk's Office. Amoroso immediately asked Winter to return her money. She claims that he admitted the fraud and agreed to return the deposit. But when Mrs. Amoroso and her husband reached Winter's office they learned that he had attempted suicide. He died shortly thereafter.

Upon making this discovery, in the afternoon of August 28, the Amorosos went to Fort Lee Savings to advise it of the fraud and request it to stop payment on the check. The bank issued a written stop payment order which was received by the Fort Lee Trust Company, the drawee, on the following day, August 29. In the meantime the $3,100 check was sent by plaintiff through the Bergen County Clearing House to the Fort Lee Trust Company. By then the stop payment order had been received. Notice of nonpayment was thereafter transmitted to plaintiff.

Plaintiff contends that, under the Uniform Commercial Code, N. J. S. 12A:1–101 et seq., N. J. S. A., it is a holder in due course to the extent of the advances made on Winter's account and is entitled to recover these moneys from the drawer and payee-indorser of the check.

BOTTER, J. S. C. The central issue is whether plaintiff bank is a holder in due course, since a holder in due course will prevail against those liable on the instrument in the absence of a real defense. Of course, it must first be determined that plaintiff is a "holder" if plaintiff is to be declared a holder in due course. Amoroso contends that plaintiff bank does not own the check because it is only an agent of its depositor Winter for collection purposes and, consequently, plaintiff is not a "holder." Under the Uniform Commercial Code, the definition of "holder" includes a person who is in possession of an instrument indorsed to his order or in blank. N. J. S. 12A:1–201(20), N. J. S. A. It is clear that the bank is a holder of the check notwithstanding that it may have taken the check solely for collection and with the right to charge back against the depositor's account in the event the check is later dishonored. *Pazol v. Citizens Nat'l Bank of Sandy Springs, supra;* accord, *Citizens Bank of Booneville v. Nat'l Bank of Commerce,* 334 F. (2d) 257 (10 Cir. 1964).

To be a holder in due course one must take a negotiable instrument for value, in good faith and without notice of any defect or defense. N. J. S. 12A:3–302 (1), N. J. S. A.

This result is continued by provisions of the Uniform Commercial Code which give plaintiff a security interest in the check and the monies represented by the check to the extent that credit given for the check has been withdrawn or applied. N. J. S. 12A:4–208 and 209, N. J. S. A. See also N. J. S. 12A:4–201, N. J. S. A. and U. C. C., Comment 5 thereunder.

N. J. S. A. 12A:4–208, N. J. S. A., provides in part as follows: "(1) A bank has a security interest in an item and any accompanying documents or the proceeds of either (a) in case of an item deposited in an account to the extent to which credit given for the item has been withdrawn or applied; (b) in case of an item for which it has given credit available for withdrawal as of right, to the extent of the credit given whether or not the credit is drawn upon and whether or not there is a right of charge-back; or (c) if it makes an advance on or against the item."

N. J. S. 12A:4–209, N. J. S. A., is as follows: "For purposes of determining its status as a holder in due course, the bank has given value to the extent that it has a security interest in an item provided that the bank otherwise complies with the requirements of 12A:3–302 on what constitutes a holder in due course."

The New Jersey Study Comment under N. J. S. 12A:4–209, N. J. S. A., includes the following: "Because the bank is a holder of the item in most cases, it is possible for it to be a holder in due course if it otherwise qualifies by its good faith taking, prior to maturity, for value." See U. C. C., Sec. 3–302.

It would hinder commercial transactions if depositary banks refused to permit withdrawal prior to clearance of checks. Apparently banking practice is to the contrary. It is clear that the Uniform Commercial Code was intended to permit the continuation of this practice and to protect banks who have given credit on deposited items prior to notice of a stop payment order or other notice of dishonor. N. J. S. 12A:4–208 and 209, N. J. S. A. Amoroso attempts to raise the fraud perpetrated by Winter against Amoroso as a defense to plaintiff's claim. Plaintiff's status as a holder in due course insulates it from all personal defenses of any party to the instrument with whom it has not dealt, although real defenses may still be asserted. N. J. S. 12A:3–305, N. J. S. A. The defense raised here is fraud in inducing Amoroso to enter into the contract. There is no suggestion that either defendant signed the check without knowledge of "its character or its essential terms." N. J. S. 12A:3–305 (2) (c), N. J. S. A. Therefore the fraud is a personal defense available only against Winter and cannot be asserted against plaintiff.

Accordingly both Fort Lee Savings as drawer and Amoroso as indorser of the check are liable to plaintiff. N. J. S. 12A:3–413 (2) and 12A:3–414 (1), N. J. S. A., defining the liability of a drawer and indorser of a negotiable instrument to a holder in due course.

The motion for summary judgment will be granted in the sum of $1,066.43, plus interest.

RELATIONSHIP BETWEEN DRAWEE BANK AND HOLDER

Sec. 3–409 of the U. C. C. states that a check or other draft does not of itself operate as an assignment of any funds in the hands of the drawee available for its payment, and the drawee is not liable on the instrument until he accepts it. Under the terms of this section the drawee bank is not liable to the holder of a check unless the bank accepts, that is, certifies, the check. Thus, if a bank refuses to honor and pay a check, even though the drawer has sufficient money in the bank with which to pay the check and has not issued a stop payment order to the bank, the bank is not liable to the payee or subsequent holder of the check. No privity of contract exists between the drawee bank and the holder of a check drawn upon that bank.

CERTIFICATION OF CHECKS

In the case of an ordinary time bill of exchange, if the drawee agrees to pay the bill it is said that he "accepts" it; and when he accepts the bill he becomes primarily liable to pay it. Banks do not "accept" checks drawn upon them. However, they may "certify" checks; and when they do, such certification is acceptance.[1]

Until the bank certifies a check it is not liable to the holder of the in-

[1] U. C. C., 3–411 (1).

strument. But if it certifies the check, it becomes primarily liable on it.

A bank may certify a check at the request of the drawer, or of the payee, or of a subsequent holder. If the check is certified at the request of the drawer, the bank becomes primarily liable and the drawer secondarily liable. If the check is certified at the request of the payee, the bank becomes primarily liable and the drawer is discharged. If the check is certified at the request of a subsequent holder, the bank becomes primarily liable and the drawer and all prior indorsers are discharged from liability.[1] Here we find the second major difference between the law regarding ordinary bills of exchange and that regarding checks. If an ordinary bill of exchange is presented by the holder to the drawee for acceptance and the drawee accepts, the drawer is not discharged but becomes secondarily liable. But if a check is certified at the request of the payee or subsequent holder, the drawer is discharged. The reason is that when the check is certified, the account of the drawer is debited and a special account, usually called the "certified check account," is credited. So far as the drawer is concerned, the effect is precisely the same as if the check had been paid.

The certification must be in writing. A check is certified when the proper official of the bank writes or stamps on the check the word "certified" or some other word having similar meaning, the name of the bank, the signature and title of the certifying officer, and the date the check was certified.

The drawee bank may refuse certification at the request of the holder. Such refusal is not held to be a dishonor of the check. This is due to the fact that the drawee bank is not legally obligated to the holder either to pay or to certify the check.

Linsky v. United States
6 F. (2d) 869 (1925)

This was an action by the United States (plaintiff) against Morris Linsky (defendant). Judgment for plaintiff, and defendant appealed. Reversed.

Defendant gave an order for merchandise and a check for its price to the Board of Survey of the United States government on February 8, 1921. On February 10, 1921, the Board of Survey caused the check to be certified by the Tremont Trust Company, upon which the check was drawn. On February 15, 1921, the goods for which the check was drawn were delivered, and on February 17, 1921, the Tremont Trust Company was closed at the end of that business day by order of the bank commissioner of the Commonwealth of

---

[1] Sec. 3–411 of the U. C. C. states that (1) Certification of a check is acceptance. Where a holder procures certification the drawer and all prior indorsers are discharged. (2) Unless otherwise agreed, a bank has no obligation to certify a check. (3) A bank may certify a check before returning it for lack of proper indorsement. If it does so, the drawer is discharged.

Massachusetts. Plaintiff deposited the check in the Federal Reserve Bank at Boston on the same day that the Tremont Trust Company was closed, and the following day the check was returned because of its closing. Defendant at all times had sufficient funds deposited in the drawee bank to cover this check, and upon certification the bank had deducted and charged defendant's account with the amount of the check. The check has always been retained by plaintiff.

JOHNSON, J. Under the General Law of Massachusetts, c. 107, sec. 210, 211, if the holder of a check procures it to be certified, the drawer and all indorsers are discharged from liability thereon.

In *Minot v. Russ*, 156 Mass. 458, 31 N. E. 489, it was held that if the drawer of a check gets it certified for his own benefit and then delivers it to the payee, he is not discharged; but if the payee, for his own benefit, gets it certified, instead of getting it paid, then the drawer is discharged. All the decided cases are to the same effect. See *R. C. L.* p. 525; *Times Square Auto Co. v. Rutherford National Bank*, 77 N. J. Law 649; *First National Bank v. Whitman*, 94 U. S., 343, 24 L. Ed. 229.

Upon the record before us, there is nothing to take this case out of the operation of the law stated by the authorities. The certification of the check by the drawee bank, the Tremont Trust Co., at the request of the payee, charging the same to the account of the drawer (defendant) and retaining the funds, was equivalent to a redeposit of them by the payee. Judgment reversed.

FORGED OR ALTERED CHECKS

A bank is required to know the signature of its depositors. To this end, every depositor, upon opening an account at the bank, is required to sign a signature card in the way he expects to sign his checks. If the drawee bank thereafter honors and pays a check upon which the signature of a depositor has been forged, the bank must suffer the loss. It may not debit the account of the depositor with the amount of the check. By paying the check the bank, in effect, admits the existence of the drawer, his capacity and authority to draw the check, and the genuineness of his signature. The bank would, of course, have recourse against the forger if he could be located. However, it may not recover from the holder or previous indorsers.

The bank is not required to know the signatures of indorsers, nor does it, by paying a check, admit the genuineness of the signatures of indorsers. However, the bank contracts to honor and pay the checks of the depositor when they are "properly presented." A check with a forged indorsement is not "properly presented," and if the bank pays the check it may not charge the account of the depositor with the amount of the check. A forged indorsement does not pass title to the check. The drawer still owes the rightful owner of the check. However, since the bank does not admit the genuineness of the indorsements placed on a check, and since indorsers warrant that they have good title to the check, thus in effect warranting that no prior indorsement has been forged, the bank is entitled to reimbursement from indorsers subsequent to the forged indorsement.

If the drawee bank pays a check which has been altered so that the amount payable is increased, the bank may usually debit the account of the drawer with the original amount only. However, if the drawer, in making out the check, was negligent in not filling up the spaces properly, and if such negligence made alteration of the check possible and not obvious, the bank is not liable for the increased amount of the check.

Davis v. Commonwealth

399 S. W. (2nd) 711 (1966)

Raymond T. Davis (defendant) was convicted by the Commonwealth of Kentucky on a criminal charge of uttering a forged instrument in writing, and he appealed. Judgment affirmed.

In 1960, the appellant and Mr. and Mrs. Stark jointly formed a business corporation which was primarily financed by various bank loans. From time to time they would jointly execute promissory notes and obtain these bank loans by pledging Mr. Stark's securities as collateral.

In March of 1962, after some discussion, the Citizens Bank advised the appellant that they would consolidate these preexisting loans at various banks into one loan. For this purpose the Citizens Bank furnished the appellant with a blank promissory note form upon which the signatures of the Starks, as well as the appellant and his wife, were to be affixed. Subsequently, the appellant delivered the same note form to Citizens, completely blank, except for the signatures of the appellant, his wife, and Mr. and Mrs. Stark.

It is the signatures of Mr. and Mrs. Stark on this note to Citizens which are alleged to be forgeries and which are the subject matter of the indictment. Later, the blanks in the note were filled in by a Citizens bank official resulting in its completion as it appears in the indictment. As a result of this transaction between Citizens and the appellant, the other banks were paid in full and the various notes executed by the appellant and Mr. and Mrs. Stark at the other banks were cancelled.

HILL, J. This is an appeal from the Jefferson Circuit Court wherein the appellant, Raymond T. Davis, was sentenced to two years' confinement in the penitentiary for the offense of uttering a forged instrument in writing, as denounced by K. R. S. 434.130. More specifically, the appellant presented a promissory note to the Citizens Fidelity Bank and Trust Company in Louisville, Kentucky, (hereinafter referred to as Citizens) bearing the allegedly forged signatures of W. Ray Stark and Emma L. Stark, his wife.

The first important issue raised in this case is whether the note uttered by the appellant to Citizens Bank had legal efficacy and, therefore, the proper subject of forgery. The appellant contends that the answer to this question should be "No" since the note was not filled in with the particulars as to the date and amount. It is true that a writing must be of apparent legal efficacy or the foundation of a legal liability to be the subject of forgery. *Colson v. Com.*, 110 Ky. 233, 61 S. W. 46 (1901); *Com. v. Cochran*, 143 Ky. 807, 137 S. W. 521 (1911); *Carter v. Com.*, 311 Ky. 252, 223 S. W. (2d) 900 (1949).

However, it is pointed out in the evidence that the appellant authorized the Citizens bank official to fill in the blanks when the amount of indebtedness was ascertained. The Uniform Commercial Code [K. R. S. 355.3–115 (1)], in stating that an incomplete instrument has legal efficacy after it is completed in accordance with the authority given, provides as follows: "When a paper whose contents at the time of signing show that it is intended to become an instrument is signed while still incomplete in any necessary respect it cannot be enforced until completed, but when it is completed in accordance with authority given it is effective as completed."

In other words, the legal effect of giving an incomplete promissory note to another with the authorization to fill in the blanks is the same as delivering a complete instrument. It is the opinion of this Court that there is no merit in appellant's contention that the instrument in question was without legal efficacy and, therefore, not the proper subject of forgery.

Judgment affirmed.

REVIEW CASES

1. Dean bought a car from Cannon, giving him in payment a check drawn on the South Dorchester Bank of the Eastern Shore Trust Co. Cannon cashed the check at the Cambridge Bank of the Eastern Shore Trust Co. When the check was presented to the drawee, payment was refused on the ground that Dean had stopped payment. The Eastern Shore Trust Co. demanded of Dean that he pay the check, and upon his refusal brought suit. Holding? (Dean v. Eastern Shore Trust Co., 159 Md. 213, 150 A. 797)

2. Goukler gave his personal check to the payee for liquor, the sale of which was illegal. The payee indorsed the check to the Eastern Tire Co., buying tires with part of the money and receiving the rest in cash. Goukler stopped payment on the check and, when the tire company sued, set up illegality as a defense. Holding? (Eastern Tire Co. v. Goukler, 7 N. J. Misc. 626, 146 A. 690)

3. A check drawn in favor of the Railway Express Agency was paid by the Bank of Philadelphia under the mistaken belief that the signature of its depositor as drawer was genuine. Upon discovery of the forgery of the drawer's signature, the bank reimbursed its depositor's account and then sued the Railway Express Agency to recoup its loss. Holding? (Railway Express Agency v. Bank of Philadelphia, 168 Miss. 279, 150 So. 525)

4. The Farmers' State Bank of Brookport sent a cashier's check to Nelley, but before reaching him it was stolen by an impostor who indorsed it, presented it to the Farmers' Bank & Trust Co., took $140.85 in cash, and deposited the balance of $400. The Farmers' Bank & Trust Co. indorsed the check: "Pay to the order of any bank, banker, or trust company, all prior indorsements guaranteed." The check was then transmitted to the Brookport bank, which discovered the forgery. The Farmers' Bank & Trust Co. gave the Brookport bank the $400 on deposit but refused to pay the additional $140.85, and the Brookport bank brought suit. Judgment for whom? (Farmers' Bank & Trust Co. v. Farmers' State Bank of Brookport, 148 Ark. 599, 231 S. W. 7)

5. Parrilli, a depositor at the Banca P. Caponigri, drew a check on that bank and delivered it to the payee, Bacigalupo, on Friday, Jan. 10th. The next day Bacigalupo presented the check at the bank for payment. He was told by the cashier that Caponigri was not in, that "he made a kind of deposit this morning and we are kind of short of funds," and that Bacigalupo could "come back Monday evening and we will cash the check." Bacigalupo gave no notice of these facts to Parrilli. He returned on Monday and demanded payment, whereupon he was informed that the bank had no money and could not pay the check. Bacigalupo sued Parrilli to recover the amount of the check. Judgment for whom? (Bacigalupo v. Parrilli, 112 N. Y. S. 1040)

6. On Thursday Russ drew a check on the Maverick National Bank, had it certified by the bank, and delivered it to the payee, Minot, for valuable consideration. On Saturday Hornblower and another drew a check on the same bank and delivered it to the payees, Head and others, for valuable consideration. The payees took the check to the drawee bank, had it certified, and then deposited it to their account with the Hamilton National Bank. On Sunday the Maverick National Bank was placed under the charge of a national bank examiner, and on Monday both checks were presented for payment, payment was refused, and notice of non-payment was duly given to both drawers. The drawers were sued by their respective payees. Judgment for whom? (Minot v. Russ and Head et al. v. Hornblower and Another, 156 Mass. 461, 31 N. E. 489)

Partnerships

part **VII**

Nature and Creation of Partnerships

38

HISTORICAL BACKGROUND

Man's first excursion into the field of business was by way of the single or sole proprietorship. The proprietor owned outright his own business and managed it as he saw fit. If he needed extra capital, he would borrow it, thereby creating the relationship of debtor and creditor. If he was unable to do all the work himself, he would hire the services of others, thus creating the relationship of master and servant or of principal and agent. If he needed the use of real or personal property and did not see fit to purchase it, he could rent or lease such property, and in doing so he established the relationship of landlord and tenant and of bailor and bailee. Under a single proprietorship the liability of the proprietor was unlimited. If he was successful in the operation of his business, the profits were all his; but if he was unsuccessful, the entire burden fell upon him. The single or sole proprietorship, as a method of carrying on business, has changed little over the years.

As time progressed, single proprietors began to combine their capital, skill, labor, and managerial ability in the operation of their business undertakings. In many instances this method of conducting business proved to have certain advantages over the sole proprietorship. Out of this association developed a relationship known as the partnership. The partnership extends back at least to the days of the Romans, and in the Middle Ages the merchants made it their chief means of carrying on business. The many rules and principles that developed for conducting business by means of the partnership became an important part of the law merchant, which, as we have seen earlier, was administered by special courts set up to handle disputes that might arise between the merchants in their day-today transactions. In succeeding centuries the common law courts gradually took over this jurisdiction, and eventually the courts of equity also had a large share in shaping rules relating to partnerships. Thus the principles that now govern this type of business enterprise have been influenced by the Roman law, the law merchant, the common law courts, and the courts of equity.

It is not surprising, in view of this long history, that partnership law as it existed when English colonists brought it to America was characterized by many inconsistencies and uncertainties. This unsettled state had begun when the common law courts commenced their jurisdiction over mercantile disputes. The common law judges were unfamiliar with the usages and customs of merchants, and their often inflexible attempts to force the affairs of the business partnership into the mold of the "land law" in which they were expert brought partnership law into a somewhat confused state. It was largely because of this situation that the courts of equity assumed jurisdiction upon occasion. In this country the uncertainty that characterized partnership law during the colonial period was heightened after the founding of the Republic by the lack of uniformity in the court decisions and statutes of the ever-increasing number of states; and as time went on the difficulties were compounded by the constant growth of interstate business. When, in response to urgent demands, the Uniform Partnership Act was drafted and recommended to the various states in 1914, its sponsors said in an accompanying Explanatory Note: "There is probably no other subject connected with our business law in which a greater number of instances can be found where, in matters of almost daily occurrence, the law is so uncertain. This uncertainty is due, not only to conflict between the decisions of different states, but more to the general lack of consistency in legal theory. In several of the sections . . . there exists an almost hopeless confusion of theory and practice, making the actual administration of the law difficult and often inequitable."

At the basis of this confusion there lies a conflict of long standing as to the theoretical nature of a partnership. Businessmen today, like the merchants of the Middle Ages, are inclined to view the partnership as a distinct legal entity, separate and apart from its members. This is clearly evident in the way the books and accounts of the firm are kept. This concept of the partnership as a separate legal entity is called the *mercantile* or *entity theory*. On the other hand, the early common law courts took the position that a partnership was not a separate legal entity but merely an association of persons. The partnership as such could not sue or be sued in the name of the partnership, and the property or "common fund" was not owned by the partnership but by the partners. This concept is sometimes referred to as the *common law theory*. The Uniform Partnership Act does not completely resolve this problem. The Act does adopt, as an over-all rule, the common law theory that a partnership is not a separate legal entity but merely an association of individuals. However, certain sections of the Act, as a practical necessity, recognize the partnership as a separate legal entity. For example, Sec. 8 (3) provides that "Any estate in real property may be acquired in the partnership name. Title so acquired can be conveyed only in the partnership name." Likewise, in dealing with the dissolution and liquidation of a partnership and the marshaling of assets, Sec. 41 recognizes a distinction between "partnership creditors" and "individual creditors," and between "partnership assets" and "individual assets."

The formation of the partnership today is not as important as it has been in the past due in great part to the increasing use of the corporation as a means of business organization.

Reed v. Industrial Accident Commission
10 Cal. (2d) 191, 73 P. (2d) 1212 (1937)

This was an action by George Reed (plaintiff) against the Industrial Accident Commission (defendant). Judgment for defendant, and plaintiff appealed. Reversed and remanded.

This was a petition to review an award of the Industrial Accident Commission.

On March 11, 1935, W. B. Mellott, a building contractor, obtained a policy of workmen's compensation insurance from Hartford Accident and Indemnity Company for a period of one year. The insured was designated therein as "W. B. Mellott, Individual." Thereafter Mellott became associated with Irwin G. Gordon, another contractor, and they conducted the building contract business as "W. B. Mellott and Irwin G. Gordon, doing business as Gordon and Mellott." The policy remained unchanged. The record does not disclose whether the insurance company had knowledge of the association.

On March 5, 1936, while the policy was in force, George Reed, an employee, sustained a compensable injury and filed his application with the Commission. The Commission first decided that the insurance company was liable, but on rehearing reversed itself and gave its award against the employers alone. The employee and employers petitioned, seeking to hold the insurance company liable.

LANGDON, J. The position of the respondent is, in brief, that the policy insured W. B. Mellott, an individual, and not the partnership of Gordon and Mellott; that Reed was employed by the firm of Gordon and Mellott, and not by W. B. Mellott; and that consequently the policy did not cover the injury, because Reed's employer, the partnership, was not insured. This position is unsound on principle and contrary to prior decisions in this state.

The underlying fallacy in respondent's argument is the assumption that the partnership is a distinct unit, separate from the members thereof. Occasional suggestions of this "entity" theory of partnership are found in statutes or decisions, but apart from exceptional situations, a partnership is not considered an entity, but an association of individuals.

In consonance with this view, an employee of a partnership is an employee of each of the partners, and no individual partner may escape liability to such employee on the ground that only the partnership and not the individuals composing it can be held. It is immaterial whether the liability of the partners in their situation is joint and several, or joint, for even in the case of joint liability, a several judgment may be had against an individual partner by proper joinder and pleading. The result is that W. B. Mellott, a partner in the firm of Gordon and Mellott, was an employer of petitioner Reed, and was undoubtedly liable to Reed for workmen's compensation. Since W. B. Mellott procured insurance with respondent company to cover such liability and paid the required premium therefor, the company must perform its obligation by paying the award.

In the *First Nat. T. & S. Bank v. Industrial Accident Commission*, 213 Cal. 322, 331 P. (2d) 347, Charles Hascall and Powell carried on a business as co-partners under the firm name of "Hascall & Powell," and procured workmen's compensation insurance covering the employees of the business. Then Hascall bought Powell's interest and continued to conduct the business under the same name. The insurance carrier resisted liability for a compensable injury on the ground that it had insured a particular entity, the partnership. Describing this point as a "mere technical one," we held that it was not a good defense for the reason, among others, that a partnership was not a legal entity.

The award is annulled and the proceeding remanded to the commission for an award in consonance with the foregoing opinion.

PARTNERSHIP DISTINGUISHED FROM OTHER FORMS OF BUSINESS ORGANIZATION

PARTNERSHIP AND CORPORATION

The salient characteristics of the partnership may be made clear by describing briefly the major difference between it and its chief rival in our modern economy, the corporation. (1) A partnership arises simply out of contract; the approval of the state is not necessary. The creation of a corporation requires the consent of the state. (2) A partnership, under the common law theory, is not a separate legal entity but merely an association of individuals. A corporation is a distinct legal entity, separate and apart from the persons who are its members. (3) A partnership is dissolved by the death, incapacity, bankruptcy, or withdrawal of a partner, or by a partner's transfer of his share in the business. The existence of a corporation is not affected by the death of a stockholder or by the transfer of a stockholder's interest. (4) Partners have the right (subject to agreement among themselves to some other effect) to participate directly in the control and management of the business. Though stockholders have ultimate control over corporate policies, authority to manage the day-by-day affairs and transactions of the corporation is in the hands of elective officers. (5) A partner while acting in the partnership business is the agent of all the other partners and (where the mercantile or entity theory controls) of the partnership. The ownership of stock in a corporation does not make the stockholder the agent of the corporation. (6) The liability of partners is unlimited; that is, they are liable out of their personal estates for partnership obligations. The liability of the stockholders of a corporation is limited to the amount of their investment.

It is clear from the foregoing enumeration that the partnership has some advantages and some disadvantages in comparison with the corporation. Its chief disadvantages are the uncertainty of its duration, the inability of its members to transfer their interest without dissolving the partnership, and the unlimited liability of the partners. One of its great advantages is the ease with which it may be created, in contrast to the time, effort, and expense involved in forming a corporation. Certain other advantages are connected with the fact that it is not a separate legal entity, like the corporation. It is freer from governmental supervision and regulation, it is subject to fewer reports and fewer taxes, and it may carry on business in other states as freely as an individual may, instead of having to be licensed as the corporation does.

JOINT-STOCK COMPANY

The joint-stock company represents historically the transition between the partnership and the business corporation. It was devised to eliminate a feature of the partnership which was one of its principal disadvantages in the eyes of potential investors: namely, the inability of a partner to sell his interest without dissolving the partnership. This weakness was remedied by dividing the capital of the organization into shares which could be transferred by a holder to a new investor without disturbing the existence of the company. The practice of delegating to elective officers the authority to manage the affairs of the business also arose in the joint-stock company. The liability of the members remained unlimited. Though the joint-stock company was once used extensively, it has been almost completely superseded by the corporation, which took over the feature of transferable shares and combined it with the further advantage of limited liability.

BUSINESS OR MASSACHUSETTS TRUST

The business trust secures limited liability for its capital contributors without the necessity of incorporation, by excluding them entirely from control of the business. It is an adaptation of the old common law trust to the operation of a business enterprise. Title to the contributed property is vested in a trustee or a board of trustees who operate the business for the benefit of the contributors. The contributors are known as beneficiaries or cestui que trust, and they possess the equitable or beneficial interest in the property. Such interest is evidenced by trust certificates, which they receive in exchange for conveyance of the property to the trustees.

A business trust is created by the drafting and signing of a declaration of trust, which must be prepared with great care if it is to achieve its major objective of limiting the liability of the certificate holders or beneficiaries to the amount of their investment. If it is not drafted properly, the court may hold that the association is nothing more than a general partnership, in which case the members will have unlimited liability. The primary test is the degree of control lodged in the trustees. If the certificate holders have no control over the actions of the trustees and the management of the business, it will be held that a business trust has been created. On the other hand, if the certificate holders reserve the right to control the actions of the trustees, the court will undoubtedly hold that the association is a partnership. To ensure that a business trust and not a partnership is created, the declaration of trust should provide that the board of trustees shall fill all vacancies on the board and elect their own successors.

DETERMINATION OF THE EXISTENCE OF A PARTNERSHIP

Sec. 6 of the Uniform Partnership Act defines a partnership as "an association of two or more persons to carry on as co-owners a business for profit." Such a relationship must come about as the result of a contract, express or implied, voluntarily arrived at by parties having the intent to create a partnership. It should be understood, however, that "intent" in this connection means what the courts call *legal intent*, as distinguished from subjective or expressed intent. This means that the parties must have an intent to associate themselves in a business relationship which has the essential characteristics and elements of a partnership. If the particular association that they contemplate is of a different sort, their agreement will not create a partnership, even though they apply that name to it. To illustrate, suppose that A and B draw up and execute an agreement to associate themselves in what they term "a non-profit partnership" for some charitable or educational purpose. Their expressed intent in this agreement is to form a partnership, but they have no such legal intent, for the description clearly shows that they do not have an intent to form an association "to carry on as co-owners a business *for profit*." Their association will therefore not be a partnership, for the law will not force them into a partnership relation against their will. It must arise out of their voluntary and intentional agreement, not by operation of law. By the same criterion of legal intent, if A and B agree to associate themselves in the operation of a business and the terms of their agreement incorporate all the conditions that give rise to a partnership, the fact that they do not apply that name to it, either in their express agreement or in their own minds, will not interfere with the creation of a partnership. Since they have agreed to all the elements that are essential to the creation of a partnership, they are held to have agreed to the creation of a partnership.

Because of this distinction between subjective and legal intent it frequently becomes necessary for the court to determine whether a given relationship between two or more individuals is a partnership. If the agreement has been reduced to writing, the written instrument will form the basis of such determination. If the agreement was oral or implied, the court will give consideration to the words and acts of the parties as evidence of their intent. In either case, the object of the court is to ascertain whether the agreement created between the parties an association "to carry on as co-owners a business for profit."

The courts make a distinction between "carrying on a business" and carrying out some single project or transaction, even though its performance may take some time. For example, if A and B associate themselves in a joint undertaking to find purchasers for a certain apartment house and agree to divide the commission, the court would hold, aside from any other consideration, that they are not partners. Furthermore, not every business that yields a profit will satisfy the requirement of the definition. Its terms are interpreted to mean carrying on a business for the primary purpose of earning a financial reward or livelihood for the co-owners. A, B, and C may jointly operate a shop which regularly yields a profit, but if by their agreement all profits are to be turned over to a home for crippled children, their association is not a partnership.

An intention to share profits and losses [1] is essential to the formation of a partnership. Hence, if the evidence shows that under the agreement a party was to be excluded from sharing in the profits of the business, he will be held not to be a partner. But an agreement to share profits is not

---

[1] The Uniform Partnership Act says nothing about sharing losses; but if the parties agree to share the profits without mentioning losses, the courts will imply that they have agreed to share the losses.

in itself conclusive evidence of the existence of a partnership. Sec. 7 (4) of the Uniform Partnership Act states that the receipt by a person of a share of the profits of a business is in itself only prima facie evidence that he is a partner. Moreover, the facts will be scrutinized to ascertain whether money paid out of the firm's profits was simply a salary for services to the business or payment for some other reason. Sec. 7 (4) provides that no inference as to the existence of a partnership can be drawn "if such profits were received in payment: (a) as a debt by installment or otherwise, (b) as wages of an employee or rent to a landlord, (c) as an annuity to a widow or representative of a deceased partner, (d) as interest on a loan, though the amount of payment vary with the profits of the business, (e) as the consideration for the sale of the good-will of a business or other property by installments or otherwise." Sec. 7 (3) provides that the sharing of gross returns does not of itself establish a partnership. But if the sharing of the profits of the business is coupled with other essentials, the combination is conclusive.

The fact that a person has a voice in the management and control of the business is given consideration, but in itself it is of course not conclusive. One who is not a partner may under various circumstances be given such a privilege. But where other essential elements are present, its presence or absence may be decisive, as we have already seen in our consideration of the business trust. Where a party, under a given agreement, is to have both a share of the profits and a voice in the management, he is probably a partner.

Partners are usually co-owners of specific property used in the partnership business, though lack of such co-ownership is not fatal to the existence of a partnership. Sec. 7 (2) provides, however, that co-ownership of property "does not of itself establish a partnership, whether such co-owners do or do not share any profits made by the use of the property." It is possible for A and B to be co-owners of a building and to carry on a business in it without being co-owners of the business. But the fact of co-ownership would have much weight in the court's determination.

Sec. 7 (1) states: "Except as provided by section 16, persons who are not partners as to each other are not partners as to third persons." By the provisions of Sec. 16 one who is not actually a partner may be what is known as a *partner by estoppel*, under the following conditions: "(1) When a person, by words spoken or written or by conduct, represents himself, or consents to another representing him to any one, as a partner in an existing partnership or with one or more persons not actual partners, he is liable to any such person to whom such representation has been made, who has, on the faith of such representation, given credit to the actual or apparent partnership, and if he has made such representation or consented to its being made in a public manner he is liable to such person, whether the representation has or has not been made or communicated to such person so giving credit by or with the knowledge of the apparent partner making the representation or consenting to its being made. (a) When a partnership liability results, he is liable as though he were an actual member of the partnership. . . ." If such person consents to be held out as a partner, or holds himself out as a partner, he is estopped from denying that he is a partner if a third party, relying upon such holding out, is damaged. There is a split in authority as to whether a person who knows that he is being falsely held out as a partner but has not given his consent to such holding out is required to take affirmative steps to deny that he is a partner.

Peterson v. Eppler et al.
67 N. Y. S. (2d) 498 (1946)

This was an action by Howard L. Peterson (plaintiff) against William E. Eppler and others (defendants). On motion of defendants complaint was dismissed. Plaintiff appealed. Affirmed.

Plaintiff, in his complaint, alleged the existence of a partnership between himself and defendants, and asked for an accounting and winding up of the alleged partnership.

Defendants denied that a partnership existed between plaintiff and defendants.

BOTEIN, J. Although the agreement upon which the plaintiff bases his action for an accounting of the alleged partnership between himself and the defendants states that the plaintiff was to be a "junior partner," it expressly provides for a fixed monthly payment "as salary" in addition to a fixed percentage of the net profits derived by the firm from its accountancy practice. In addition the agreement definitely stipulates that the plaintiff was to have no other financial interest in the firm or its property or profits and that he was to have no right or authority to participate in the management and conduct of the firm's affairs except as the "capital partners" might authorize from time to time.

The Partnership Law defines a partnership as "an association of two or more persons to carry on as co-owners a business for profit." Sec. 10. It is clear from the express provisions of the contract between the parties that the plaintiff was not to be a co-owner of the business. He was limited to a salary and a share of the profits from certain business and was not even entitled to share in the profits of all the business or income of the firm. Section 40 of the Partnership Law provides that "all partners have equal rights in the management and conduct of the partnership business." The agreement, however, excluded the plaintiff from any such right. It is also to be noted, although it may not be determinative, that there is no provision for the plaintiff's sharing in the losses of the firm. In the light of the foregoing the court is constrained to hold that the plaintiff was only an employee of the firm, entitled to receive a fixed salary and a specified percentage of the net profits from some of its business. Although the fact that parties to an agreement may refer to their relationship as one of partnership is a circumstance entitled to great weight, it is by no means conclusive. The parties cannot by using the word "partnership" create such a relationship when the contract between them clearly provides that there was to be no community of interest in the business as such and no right to participate in the management of the business. *Burdick on Partnership*, 3rd Ed. pages 18, 19; *Gilmore on Partnership*, pages 8 to 10; *Smith v. Grove*, 47 Cal. App. (2d) 456, 118 P. (2d) 324.

It follows that the plaintiff is not entitled to an accounting in equity from the defendants and that his remedy, if any, is in an action at law. The motion to dismiss is granted with leave to serve an amended complaint on the law side of the court.

Walker, Mosby & Calvert, Inc. v. Burgess
153 Va. 779, 151 S. E. 165 (1930)

This was an action by C. L. Burgess (plaintiff) against Walker, Mosby & Calvert, Inc. (defendant), to recover the sum of $2,255. Judgment for plaintiff, and defendant appealed. Reversed and remanded.

On September 30, 1925, defendant entered into a written contract with one J. W. Senseney, as follows: "That the parties of the first part [Walker, Mosby & Calvert, Inc.] hereby agree to furnish three lots for the sum of $2,300, and further agree to furnish the cash capital to be used in erecting three dwellings on said lots. The said party of the second part [Senseney] hereby agrees to furnish all material and labor and erect and complete said three dwellings at actual cost, and guarantees that the said three dwellings shall not cost more than $10,500. . . . It is mutually agreed between the parties that the said three houses shall be sold by either party to this agreement, and that the party making the sale shall have the usual commission for making each sale. The entire cost of the said property, including cost of financing and cost of commission on sales, shall be accurately kept and when all three buildings have been sold the net profits or losses shall be divided equally between the parties of this agreement. . . ."

Senseney subsequently entered into a contract with plaintiff, under which plaintiff was to furnish the labor and materials for the plumbing and heating installations in the said three dwelling houses, at the price of $2,255. At the time this contract was entered into, Senseney told plaintiff of his contract with defendant and exhibited it to him. Plaintiff performed his part of the contract, but Senseney absconded from the city and was later adjudicated an involuntary bankrupt. Plaintiff therefore brought this action against defendant, alleging a partnership between it and Senseney.

Defendant denied that such a partnership existed.

CAMPBELL, J. The plaintiff bases his right of recovery on the existence of a partnership between the defendant and J. W. Senseney. There being no ambiguity in the written instrument which calls for the introduction of parol evidence to explain the existence or nonexistence of a partnership relationship, it must be determined by the terms of the instrument relied upon, construed in the light of Section 4359 of the Code of Virginia, 1924. In clause 6 of that section we read: "A partnership is an association of two or more persons to carry on as co-owners a business for profit." An examination of the agreement involved fails to disclose any language which clearly indicates that the defendant and Senseney are associates in business. The language employed does, however, indicate that the defendant entered into a contract with Senseney for the construction of certain houses which Senseney guaranteed should not exceed in cost the sum of $10,500; that Senseney was to erect and complete the buildings, that is, perform a "turn-key" job. There is no language in the agreement descriptive of the business to be "carried on."

There is no contention that the defendant ever intended a conveyance of real estate owned by it. All that defendant agreed to do according to the contract was to put up the lots and furnish the capital for the erection of the houses; all that Senseney agreed to do was to erect the houses. For the performance of his part of the contract Senseney was to be paid, after a sale of the property, 50 per cent of the profits. While in some jurisdictions it was formerly held that the sharing of profits was a conclusive test of partnership, this holding has never prevailed in this state, as is evidenced both by decision and statute.

In *Commonwealth v. Southeastern Iron Corp.*, 142 Va. 107, 128 S. E. 528, Chief Justice Prentiss said: "That it is now settled in this country that the sharing of profits and losses is not a conclusive test of partnership can be easily shown by text-writers, the precedents and statutes."

It is also to be observed that the agreement does not contemplate the "carrying on of a business for profit," but only contemplates the doing of a single act. "Carrying on" a business is a well-defined term, and means the conduct of a business for a sustained period of time for the purpose of livelihood or profit, and not merely the carrying on of some single transaction. *Cooper Mfg. Co. v. Ferguson*, 113 U. S. 725, 5 S. Ct. 739.

Another essential element of a partnership which is lacking in the agreement relied upon is the element of "co-ownership." There is no language which indicates that the parties were co-owners of the property. As we construe the agreement Senseney was in no sense a co-owner of the property, but simply an independent contractor, who by agreement was to receive remuneration out of any profits derived from the sale of the property. Reversed.

Standard Oil Co. of New York v. Henderson

265 Mass. 322, 163 N. E. 743 (1928)

This was an action by the Standard Oil Co. (plaintiff) against Thomas Henderson, Sr. (defendant). Judgment for defendant, and plaintiff appealed. Affirmed.

Plaintiff brought this action against defendant for goods sold and delivered.

On or about November 13, 1924, one Thomas Henderson, Jr., opened a gasoline station at 660 Brock Avenue, New Bedford, and put on the window of the station the words "Henderson & Son." This was the only name which appeared on the premises. On November 13, 1924, plaintiff and Thomas Henderson, Jr., executed an "equipment loan agreement" for the installation of a tank, pump, and accessories for the gasoline station. The agreement recited that it was made between the Standard Oil Company of New York and Henderson & Son, of 660 Brock Avenue, New Bedford, and it was signed: "Standard Oil Company of New York, by J. E. Winter, Henderson & Son, by Thomas Henderson, Jr." The business was conducted by Thomas Henderson, Jr., the son of defendant, who was a loom fixer employed in one of the local mills. Thomas Henderson, Jr., at the time the action was commenced and at the time of the trial, was in the state of California.

On the evidence the trial judge found that plaintiff sold and delivered the items referred to in plaintiff's declaration; that they were charged to Henderson & Son; and that the delivery slips were signed by Thomas Henderson, Jr. Plaintiff's evidence did not show that defendant was a partner in fact.

PIERCE, J. For the purposes of this case we assume the defendant was not a partner of Thomas Henderson, Jr. The record contains no direct evidence that the defendant had knowledge or notice that he was held out as a partner in the business of his son, and no circumstantial evidence to warrant a finding of such knowledge and notice, other than can logically be deduced from the evidence that he "walked past the gasoline station almost every day; that he saw the name 'Henderson & Son'" on the window of the premises, and knew that the business was conducted under the name; that he made no inquiries as to whether any credit was being extended by the plaintiff or any person or concern, relying on the fact that his name was used in connection with the business, and he did not tell anyone that he was not connected with the business or ask his son to remove his name. Other than above stated, there is no evidence reported to warrant an inference that the defendant consented to the use of the sign "Henderson & Son" on the window of the station.

On the evidence the issues which were presented at the trial were: (1) As matter of fact did the defendant consent to his being held out as a partner in a public manner? and (2) Did the plaintiff give credit to the apparent partnership on the faith that there was a partnership and that the defendant was a member of it?

The first request of the plaintiff was denied rightly. The evidence presented an issue of fact, and did not warrant the requested ruling of law that the defendant was a partner by estoppel in the business carried on under the style of "Henderson & Son." The third request was also denied rightly. There is no evidence reported to warrant a finding that the plaintiff gave credit to the apparent partnership on the faith that the defendant was a partner in the partnership. The fourth request was properly denied. The second request, which was given, read: "If the defendant permitted himself to be held out as a partner in the gasoline and oil business conducted at 660 Brock Avenue, New Bedford, he is liable to the plaintiff as a partner whether actually a partner or not." This request did not require that the judge should have entered judgment for the plaintiff; there remained open the issue whether the defendant consented to the holding out and whether the plaintiff gave the credit on the faith of the membership of the defendant.

The fifth request of the defendant—"The plaintiff cannot recover on the ground that the defendant Thomas Henderson, Sr., is liable as a partner for estoppel unless he proved by a fair preponderance of the evidence: (a) that Thomas Henderson, Sr., held himself out as a partner; (b) that such holding out was by Thomas Henderson, Sr., or his authority; (c) that the plaintiff had knowledge of such holding out; (d) that the plaintiff acted on the strength of such holding out to his prejudice"—correctly stated the law applicable to the evidence before the court. We find no error. The entry must be: "Order of appellate division dismissing report affirmed. So ordered.

CREATION OF PARTNERSHIPS

PARTNERSHIP AGREEMENT

The partnership relationship is created by a contract, either express or implied. As a general rule it may be either oral or written. However, if according to the partnership agreement the contract cannot be completed within one year, to be enforceable it must be in writing under Section 4 (5) of the Statute of Frauds. If the parties orally agree to form a partnership for a period exceeding one year, and proceed to organize and carry on business, it will be a *partnership at will,* and any partner may withdraw from it without being subject to damages for breach of the contract. It is the exercise of good business judgment to place every partnership agreement in writing.

Where the terms of the agreement are reduced to writing, the writing is usually called the *partnership agreement* or the *articles of copartnership.* No particular form is required for such a writing. It will generally set forth the following information and provisions: date and place of the agreement; names and addresses of the partners; name of the firm; nature of the business to be carried on; length of time the partnership is to exist; place where the business is to be conducted; capital investment of each partner; manner in which the business is to be managed; manner in which books and records are to be kept; limitations, if any, upon the authority of the partners to bind the firm; amount of wages or drawing account of each partner; provision for withdrawal of partners; provision for dissolution and winding up of the business; provision for continuing the business after the death of one or more of the partners; signatures of parties and witnesses. Many other special provisions may be included, relating to such matters as advances by partners to the firm, signing of surety and guaranty contracts, taking inventory, life insurance of partners for the benefit of the firm, banking arrangements, and so on.

Any provision in the partnership agreement limiting the liability or authority of a partner or partners will bind the partners inter se but will not bind innocent third parties who do not know of such limitations.

WHO MAY BE PARTNERS

Any person competent to contract may become a partner. In this respect contract law applies. Sec. 2 of the Uniform Partnership Act provides that in this context " 'Person' includes individuals, partnerships, corporations, and other associations."

INFANTS.   An infant may be a partner, but since his agreement is voidable he may withdraw from the partnership without being liable for damages for breach of the partnership contract. However, when he acts as an agent of the other partners or of the partnership, his actions bind the partners or the partnership, if he has acted within the scope of the partnership business. If an infant partner avoids the contract of partnership and withdraws, and the partnership is solvent, he is entitled to receive his interest in the partnership. If the firm is insolvent, most courts hold that his capital contribution is subject to the claim of the firm's creditors. The most that he could lose, however, would be his interest in the firm, since his individual estate is not subject to the payment of the firm's obligations.

MARRIED WOMEN.   At common law a married woman had no contractual capacity, and hence could not become a member of a partnership. However, such contractual disability of married women has been either partly or completely removed by statute in the various states. Under the statutes and court decisions of most of the states a married woman may contract to become a member of a partnership. However, in a few states a married woman is denied the right to enter into a partnership agreement with her husband. Such prohibition is said to be based upon "sound public policy."

INSANE PERSONS.   The principles of contract law apply in the case of insane persons. Usually the contract is voidable, but the contract of one who has been judicially adjudged insane is absolutely void.

CORPORATIONS. So far as the Uniform Partnership Act is concerned, a corporation may become a member of a partnership. However, under the corporation statutes of most states corporations are not permitted to become members of partnerships, and in the other states a corporation has such capacity only when granted by the articles of incorporation.

PARTNERSHIPS. Under Sec. 2 of the Uniform Partnership Act it is permissible for a partnership to become a member of another partnership.

ALIENS. While an alien may become a member of a partnership, an enemy alien may not.

Smith v. Butt & Hardin
281 Ky. 127, 135 S. W. (2d) 67 (1940)

This was an action by Butt & Hardin, a partnership (plaintiff) against Stella Roberson Smith (defendant). Judgment for plaintiff, and defendant appealed. Affirmed.

By verdict of the jury and judgment in conformity therewith, plaintiff recovered judgment against defendant for the sum of $2,624.71 on an account for goods, wares, etc. sold to Smith Cafe, it being alleged that defendant was a partner of her deceased husband, Albert Smith, in the business operated under the trade name of Smith Cafe when the goods, wares, etc. were furnished.

Defendant answered in effect that no partnership existed between herself and husband, that she made no promise to pay the alleged debt or any portion of it, and that if any promise to pay was made, it was made by her husband. Defendant further contended that a married woman is prohibited by law from forming a partnership and therefore defendant's demurrer to the petition should have been sustained.

CREAL, J. Section 2128, Ky. Statutes, is to the effect that a married woman may take, acquire, and hold real and personal property by gift, purchase, etc., and may sell it, dispose of her personal property, make contracts, sue and be sued as a single woman. The only exception made to her right to acquire, hold, control, and dispose of her estate is that "she may not make any executory contract to sell or convey or mortgage her real estate unless her husband joins in such contract." Clearly, it was the legislative purpose and intent in enacting those sections to remove all restrictions from the wife with respect to owning, holding, controlling and disposing of her property and engaging in business activities the same as if she were an unmarried woman, the only exception or restraint being that with respect to her becoming bound as surety for another or making executory contracts to mortgage or convey her real estate as above indicated.

Since the enactment of the statute above referred to, this court has in a number of cases and without exception recognized the capacity and right of a married woman to enter into a partnership with her husband, and held that as such she is liable for the partnership obligations.

It is maintained by appellant that the verdict of the jury was flagrantly against the evidence but appellees testified positively that appellant told them she was a partner of her husband, owned property and that they would not lose anything by extending credit to the firm. Others testified to similar statements; and there is much evidence as to her acts and conduct with respect to the business, tending to indicate that she was a partner. At most, it comes down to a question of the credibility of the witnesses and that was a question for the jury. Judgment affirmed.

CLASSES OF PARTNERSHIPS

Partnerships may be either (1) general or (2) special, and they may be either (1) trading or (2) non-trading.

A *general partnership* is one which has been organized to carry on some type of business over a period of years. This is the type commonly encountered in the retail and wholesale fields. A *special partnership* is usually one that is created to undertake a single large transaction or piece of business. For example, A and B may form a partnership to buy a particular tract of land for the purpose of improving it, laying it out in lots, and selling them. Upon the accomplishment of the undertaking the partnership is to end. Special partnerships are sometimes known as *joint ventures* or *joint adventures*. The principal difference between them and general partnerships is that the apparent authority of a special partner is less extensive than that of a general partner.[1]

A *trading partnership* is a partnership engaged in the buying, selling, or manufacturing of goods and merchandise. Most partnerships are of this type. A *non-trading partnership* is usually one that is engaged in the "selling" or rendering of services, such as a firm of lawyers, doctors, dentists, accountants, or brokers. The chief difference between them is that partners in a non-trading partnership have less apparent authority to bind the partnership than do partners in a trading partnership, since the type of business they are conducting does not normally require such broad powers to borrow money and obligate the firm's property.

CLASSES OF PARTNERS

A *general partner* is the usual type of partner found in most partnerships. He is active in the conduct of the firm's business and he is known to the public generally as a partner. He has the rights, powers, and liabilities of the other members of the partnership, unless otherwise agreed under the articles of copartnership.

[1] The authority of partners is discussed in Chapter 41.

A *silent partner* is one who is known to the public as a member of the partnership but who takes no active part in the operation of the partnership business.

A *secret partner* is one who takes an active part in the management and control of the partnership business but who keeps his membership in the firm a secret to the public.

A *dormant partner* is both "silent" and "secret." He takes no active part in the affairs of the firm and he keeps his relationship with the firm a secret to the public.

A *nominal partner* is a partner by estoppel. As we have already seen, he is actually not a partner at all, but for certain reasons he is estopped from denying that he is a partner.

The liability of all the foregoing types of partners is unlimited. The nature of a *limited partner* is described in the final section of this chapter.

FIRM NAME

Unless required to do so by some special statute, a partnership need not adopt a firm name, but in most cases a partnership does adopt a firm name under which to conduct its business. In choosing its firm name a partnership has wide latitude. Frequently the name contains the names of the partners, or the name of one or more of the partners and the words "and Company." A fictitious name may be chosen instead, but some states require that such a trade name be registered in some designated public office, such as that of the County Clerk.

LIMITED PARTNERSHIPS

The limited partnership is a modification of the general partnership. The principles underlying the present-day limited partnership were well understood by the merchants of the Middle Ages and recognized by the civil law, but they were not countenanced by the common law judges, and consequently limited partnerships could not be created under the common law. In 1822, however, the state of New York enacted a limited partnership act, and many other states soon followed suit. In 1916 the National Conference of Commissioners finished drafting the Uniform Limited Partnership Act, and it has since been adopted by the following jurisdictions: Alaska, Arizona, California, Colorado, Florida, Hawaii, Idaho, Illinois, Indiana, Iowa, Maryland, Massachusetts, Michigan, Minnesota, Missouri, Montana, Nebraska, Nevada, New Hampshire, New Jersey, New Mexico, New York, North Carolina, Oklahoma, Pennsylvania, Rhode Island, South Dakota, Tennessee, Utah, Vermont, Virginia, Washington, and Wisconsin.

The purpose of a limited partnership is to permit one or more partners to make capital contributions without assuming unlimited liability. Every limited partnership must have at least one general partner, whose rights, powers, and liabilities are the same as in the usual partnership; in addition it has one or more *limited partners*, who take no part in the control or management of the partnership and whose liability is limited to the amount of their capital contribution. If a limited partner takes part in the control of the business, he becomes liable as a general partner. However, he has the same rights as a general partner to inspect the partnership books, to receive information about partnership affairs, and to have dissolution and winding up by decree of court. In addition he has the right to receive a share of the profits or other compensation by way of income as provided for in the partnership certificate.

In the formation of a limited partnership the partners must prepare and execute a certificate and file it in the office of a designated county official, such as the Recorder of Deeds. The certificate must set forth, among other things, the name and the purpose of the partnership, the term for which it is to exist, the name and address of each member and an indication of whether he is a general or a limited partner, the amount of cash and a description of and the agreed value of the other property contributed by each limited partner, and the share of the profits or the other compensation by way of income which each limited partner is to receive by reason of his contribution.

REVIEW CASES

1. In September, 1905, Bedingfield, Daniel, and Clance went into business together as the Bedingfield Mercantile Co. They decided to incorporate as soon as possible, and agreed that until they could get their charter they would do business as a corporation, not a partnership. In November Clance ordered goods from Meinhard, Schual & Co., assuring them that although he had no property himself, his two associates were men of means, and that they intended to incorporate in the near future. The goods were shipped on Nov. 25th. In February, 1906, a charter was granted authorizing the incorporation of the Bedingfield Mercantile Co. The goods were not paid for, and Meinhard, Schual & Co. brought an action against Bedingfield, Daniel, and Clance as copartners. They denied the existence of a partnership, and contended that the business was being operated as a corporation and that they were therefore not personally liable on the account. Holding? (Meinhard, Schual & Co. v. Bedingfield Mercantile Co. et al., 4 Ga. App. 176, 61 S. E. 34)

2. Beebe sued to recover rent due on premises occupied by F. L. Main & Co., a partnership. The question to be determined is whether Allison was a member of the partnership in addition to Main, Collins, and Dennison,

and hence liable with them on the rent. Allison had signed an agreement with Main, who acted as general manager of the partnership, purporting to make Allison a member of the partnership, and had thereafter occupied a desk in the firm's offices. Holding? (Beebe v. Allison, 112 Wash. 145, 192 P. 17)

3. Weir, an infant, and Linthicum signed a partnership agreement to operate a grocery store. Later Linthicum filed suit to dissolve the partnership on the ground that Weir had committed fraud upon him. Weir set up the defense of infancy. Linthicum replied that Weir had misrepresented his age and that he (Linthicum) did not know when he filed suit that Weir was an infant. Was Linthicum entitled to a decree of dissolution? Was Weir personally liable on the firm's obligations? (Linthicum v. Bush, next friend of Richard H. Weir, 39 Md. 344)

4. Marousis, who secured on credit a shoeshine parlor and equipment, agreed with Coens, who was to be the manager of the business, that neither would take any compensation out of the proceeds, except room and board, until the business was paid for, and that each would then have a half interest in the business. When the business was paid for, Coens demanded that Marousis recognize him as a full partner, and Marousis refused. Had a partnership been formed? What were Coens' rights? (Coens v. Marousis, 275 Pa. 478, 119 A. 549)

5. Gordon and Marburger entered into a partnership agreement to raise and sell potatoes. Gordon was to furnish the money and Marburger was to provide the necessary management. Marburger raised and harvested the potatoes; he sold some of them and put the rest in a warehouse. Gordon meanwhile provided the necessary money. Marburger borrowed $300 from Aumiller, giving him a chattel mortgage and warehouse receipts on the potatoes as security. Aumiller knew the details of the partnership agreement. Marburger refused to divide the money from the potato crop with Gordon, and Gordon filed a suit praying for an accounting against Marburger and denying the lien of Aumiller. It was agreed at the trial that the partnership was a non-trading concern. Holding? (Gordon v. Marburger, 109 Wash. 496, 187 P. 354)

6. Borum left his widow a life estate in a house and lot, with remainder to his four children. The widow died, and the four children lived on the property, agreeing to share equally all costs of the premises. One of the children spent $1,200 more than the others on the premises, and afterward brought suit to have a receiver appointed and the property sold in order to recover the $1,200. The main question was whether there was a partnership existing between the parties. (Borum v. Deese, 196 Ga. 292, 26 S. E.(2d) 538)

Partnership
Property

39

WHAT CONSTITUTES PARTNERSHIP PROPERTY

When a partnership is formed, the partners usually contribute certain property to it. If the partnership business is operated successfully, the profits will not all be paid out to the partners as profits; instead, a portion of the earnings will usually be "plowed back" into the business. Such subsequently acquired property also constitutes a part of the partnership property. The good will of the firm is likewise a firm asset and a part of the partnership property. Sec. 8 of the Uniform Partnership Act states: "(1) All property originally brought into the partnership stock or subsequently acquired by purchase or otherwise, on account of the partnership, is partnership property. (2) Unless the contrary intention appears, property acquired with the partnership funds is partnership property."

It is sometimes difficult to determine whether the property with which the firm transacts its business is firm property, or the property of individual members of the firm, or property which the partners own jointly or as tenants in common and permit the partnership to use. Such difficulty can usually be avoided by arriving at a definite understanding in regard to the ownership of the property that is turned over to the partnership, and by clearly stating the understanding in the partnership agreement. But when such precautions are not taken and it becomes necessary to determine who owns specific property, the intentions of the parties, as evidenced by their acts and declarations, will be controlling. With respect to this problem the court, in *Klingstein v. Rockingham National Bank of Harrisonburg et al.*,[1] made the following statement: "Where the title to real estate is held by partners individually, the presumption is that the partners hold the property as tenants in common. But this presumption may be rebutted in equity. And whether the land, in fact, belongs to the

[1] 165 Va. 275, 182 S. E. 115 (1935).

880

partnership or to the individuals composing it, depends upon the intention of the parties. Among the circumstances (in addition to an express agreement) which may show the intention of the parties are: (1) the acts and declarations of the parties; (2) the acquisition of the property for partnership purposes; (3) its use by the partnership; (4) the payment for improvements thereon out of firm assets; and (5) the payment of taxes and insurance thereon by the partnership."

Both at common law and under the Uniform Partnership Act, a partnership may hold title to personal property. Under the common law, however, a partnership could not hold title to real property. The common law courts took the position that real property had to be held in the name of either a natural person or an artificial person, such as a corporation, and they did not recognize a partnership as a separate legal entity. Hence, where the common law rule prevails, title to the real property acquired by a partnership has to be taken in the name of one or all of the partners. If it is taken in the name of one of the partners, the partner holds the property in trust for his copartners. Under the Uniform Partnership Act, however, a partnership may hold title to real property in the partnership name. Section 8 (3) of the Act provides that "Any estate in real property may be acquired in the partnership name. Title so acquired can be conveyed only in the partnership name." It will be observed that the first sentence of this section is permissive, not mandatory; if the partners prefer, partnership property may be held in the names of the individual partners.

Miller v. Miller
370 Pa. 520, 88 A. (2d) 784 (1952)

This was a bill in equity by Michael Miller (plaintiff) against Edward Miller (defendant). Decree for plaintiff, and defendant appealed. Affirmed.

Michael and Edward Miller are brothers. Prior to 1949 they owned separate businesses, Edward's being in Brooklyn, N. Y., and Michael's in Allentown, Pa. After preliminary discussions extending over several months, the brothers came to an oral agreement in May, 1949, that they would pool their resources, merge their assets, and transact their separate enterprises as one business. To this end they selected a property in Slatington, Pa., which was to be the seat of the united venture. Michael paid $500 as a down payment, and Edward executed a bond and mortgage for the balance of the purchase price, which was $15,500. The new business was to operate under the name of Relco Oil & Chemical Co. By July, 1949, Edward had moved all his business assets from Brooklyn to Slatington, and by December of that year Michael's equipment, merchandise, and raw material were an integral part of the establishment at the new place. In June, 1949, both brothers visited the National Bank of Slatington, where Edward deposited $500 in his name, trading as the Relco Oil & Chemical Company.

It was understood from the time the brothers agreed to operate together that formal articles of copartnership would be drawn up. This was never done, although the brothers conducted the business as an undivided operation.

Differences arose between the two brothers as to the conduct of the firm, and Edward left it in June, 1950, withdrawing all its funds ($6,931.20) from the Slatington National Bank. Michael then filed this bill in equity praying that he and his brother Edward be declared partners and joint owners of the real estate at Slatington, and that Edward be compelled to furnish Michael a complete accounting of all business transactions engaged in by the Relco Oil & Chemical Co.

The court of common pleas, sitting as a court of equity, entered a decree granting the prayers of plaintiff, and defendant appealed to this court.

MUSMANNO, J. There can be no question whatsoever that the relationship between Michael and Edward Miller in the handling of the business at Slatington was a partnership in every phase of the law covering such a relationship. As succinctly stated by Justice Hughes, in the case of *Mattei v. Masci*, 351 Pa. 93, 40 A. (2d) 265: "Written articles of agreement are not necessary to prove a partnership, for such a relationship can exist under a verbal agreement." Further, that "the existence of a partnership may be implied from the circumstances."

The Chancellor also properly held under the evidence that the building in which the partnership business was conducted constituted a partnership asset, though title thereto was recorded in the name of Edward Miller alone. The costs, repairs, taxes, interest, and insurance on the real property were all paid from the profits of the business and not by Edward Miller alone; and, as the Chancellor observed, it is logical to assume that the parties contemplated that the principal of the mortgage would also be paid from the proceeds of the business. The defendant's execution of the mortgage for $15,000 is not, therefore, to be compared to the plaintiff's cash outlay of $500 for the down payment. The more reasonable conclusion is that the plaintiff's contribution to the real estate was to be matched by defendant's contribution to the bank account, and that the division of the profits would thenceforth establish the parties on an equal basis. Since the property was purchased with partnership funds, the fact that the record title thereto is in the name of one partner alone does not affect its status as partnership property.

We affirm, as being supported in every detail, the findings of fact and the conclusions of the law of the Chancellor and affirm the decree.

Azevedo et al. v. Sequeria et al.
132 Cal. App. 439, 22 P. (2d) 745 (1933)

This was an action by A. J. Azevedo and others (plaintiffs) against M. E. Sequeria and others (defendants). Judgment for defendants, and plaintiffs appealed. Judgment affirmed.

In 1914 a partnership was organized in the name of A. J. Azevedo & Co., consisting of seven members, including plaintiffs and defendants in this suit. There were no written articles of copartnership. A. J. Azevedo testified that he purchased with partnership funds six shares of the capital stock of the Gustine Creamery, Inc. "for the company." He afterwards purchased an additional share of the stock. Without the knowledge of defendants these shares were issued in the name of A. J. Azevedo & Co. Mr. Azevedo testified that about a year later the partnership "split up." Another dairy partnership was organized by plaintiffs, including members other than defendants. Mr. Azevedo claimed that he and his brother purchased the creamery stock as their individual property subsequent to the reorganization of the dairy partnership.

Defendants contended that when the creamery stock was purchased it was the intention of the members of the partnership that each partner would own individually one share of the stock.

Plaintiff brought this suit to quiet title to the shares of stock.

Mr. Sequeria testified that seven shares of the creamery stock were purchased so that each of the original seven partners might separately own one share. He said that the original seven partners had a conversation about the shares of stock when an accounting of the business was had at the time of the reorganization of the partnership. He testified: "Antone Azevedo said that they (the Gustine Creamery) were selling stocks in the creamery at Gustine . . . and (asked) if we wanted to buy some, and all of us said yes. . . . And afterwards he bought it, $300 worth of shares, six shares. . . . We had seven partners in that business and we all agreed to buy one more share so that each of us would have a share. . . . At that time I didn't know whether he bought it in the name of the company or for each one individually . . . but I know now that the shares were all in the name of A. J. Azevedo & Co." Azevedo was the manager of the dairy business. There was evidence to indicate that he acted as the agent for the respective members of the partnership in the purchase of the stock, and that the purchase price of the stock was originally taken from the proceeds of the business and subsequently charged to each in the final accounting.

THOMPSON, J. This evidence is sufficient to support the finding of the court to the effect that the original stock was purchased by A. J. Azevedo as the agent of each individual member of the original partnership for their private ownership, and that he wrongfully procured the issuing of the stock in the name of the partnership; that each member owned one share of the stock which earned by means of stock dividends two additional shares, and that the defendants Sequeria, Avila, and Pereira are the owners of three shares each of said stock. The judgment is therefore amply supported by the evidence.

It is true that, "unless the contrary intention appears, property acquired with partnership funds is partnership property." Sec. 2402, Civil Code (Uniform Partnership Act, Sec. 8 (2)). Almost any kind of property may be acquired and owned as partnership property. The intention with which the property is acquired and used will usually determine the question as to whether it is partnership or individual property. The intention of the parties with respect to the ownership of property acquired at the time of the organization of the partnership or subsequently may be determined by the acts or oral declarations of the parties. In the absence of evidence to the contrary, it will be presumed from the fact that if the stock is purchased in the name of the partnership and with its funds that it belongs to the partnership, and that the interest of each member therein extends jointly and not separately to the whole thereof. 20 *R. C. L.* 870, Sec. 81. But it is not unusual that real or personal property may be acquired and used for the benefit of the partnership and still be owned individually by one or more of the partners. Indeed, in the present case the plaintiffs are contending that the very stock which is involved in this suit is their individual property and not that of the partnership to which they succeeded in association with other members. From the fact that this stock was purchased from the funds of the partnership business in the name of the firm, there is a presumption that it belongs to the partnership. But that presumption has been dispelled by substantial evidence that it was the intention of the parties that the creamery stock was to be purchased and owned individually by the respective partners in equal shares. The fact that one additional share was subsequently purchased so that each of the seven members might own a share is a strong circumstance supporting the finding of the court that it was the intention of the partners that the stock should become their individual property. This was agreed to by all the partners according to Sequeria, at the settlement of their interests after the original partnership was dissolved. Judgment affirmed.

PARTNER'S RIGHTS IN SPECIFIC PARTNERSHIP PROPERTY

When the early common law courts assumed jurisdiction over partnerships, probably the most difficult problem with which they had to deal was the determination of the rights and interests of the partners in partnership property. Since they held that a partnership was not a legal entity, separate and distinct from its members, it was clear to them that the property of the firm could not belong to the partnership as such, but must belong to the partners as co-owners. But there were two different types of co-ownership which had been developed under the "land law" of the common law courts, namely, joint tenancy and tenancy in common, each with its separate characteristics.[1] Did partners hold the partnership property as joint tenants or as tenants in common? On this question the common law judges could not agree, though most of them took the position that partners were tenants in common. The merchants themselves

[1] See section entitled Joint Tenancy in Chapter 24 of this text.

took an entirely different view. Believing that a partnership was a separate legal entity, they logically held that partnership property belonged to the partnership. This conflict of opinions produced untold confusion in the law of partnership as it related to the ownership of partnership property.

The Uniform Partnership Act follows in the main the common law theory that a partnership is not a separate legal entity, but it embodies the mercantile theory as to the ownership of partnership property. Consequently, under the Act the ownership of the firm's property is held to be vested in the partnership itself. The rights of the partners in specific partnership property are neither those of joint tenancy nor those of tenancy in common, but those of a new type of co-ownership called *tenancy in partnership*. Sec. 25, which created this new tenancy, lists its incidents as follows:

(a) A partner, subject to the provisions of this act and to any agreement between the partners, has an equal right with his partners to possess specific partnership property for partnership purposes; but he has no right to possess such property for any other purpose without the consent of his partners.

(b) A partner's right in specific partnership property is not assignable except in connection with the assignment of the rights of all partners in the same property.

(c) A partner's right in specific partnership property is not subject to attachment or execution, except on a claim against the partnership. When partnership property is attached for a partnership debt the partners, or any of them, or the representatives of a deceased partner, cannot claim any right under the homestead or exemption laws.

(d) On the death of a partner his right in specific partnership property vests in the surviving partner or partners, except where the deceased was the last surviving partner, when his right in such property vests in his legal representative. Such surviving partner or partners, or the legal representative of the last surviving partner, has no right to possess the partnership property for any but a partnership purpose.

(e) A partner's right in specific partnership property is not subject to dower, curtesy, or allowances to widows, heirs, or next of kin.

The final provision (e) represents an important departure from the common law. Under the common law, following the principles of probate law, the title to specific partnership personal property held by the partnership passes, on the death of a partner, to the surviving partners for the purpose of paying partnership debts and winding up the partnership business; but the title to the real property of the partnership descends to the deceased partner's heirs and is subject to dower and curtesy rights. However, the surviving partners have a prior right to have the real property of the firm applied to the payment of the firm's debts. Consequently, under what is known as the *doctrine of equitable conversion* the firm's real property is treated as personal property for the purpose of discharging firm debts. Surviving partners may therefore sell any or all of the firm's real property in order to discharge firm debts; and this may be done without the consent of the surviving spouse, since dower and curtesy rights in the firm's real property do not come into being until all firm debts have been paid. If any real property then remains, it resumes the attributes of real property and descends to the heirs, subject to dower and curtesy rights. Under Sec. 25 (e) this distinction between real and personal property no longer operates.

The rights of judgment creditors in the partnership property and the rights of creditors in partnership property after dissolution are discussed in later chapters.

Woodward-Holmes Co. v. Nudd
55 Minn. 236, 59 N. W. 1010 (1894)

This was an action by the Woodward-Holmes Company (plaintiff) against William and Laura N. Nudd (defendants). Judgment was directed in favor of Laura N. Nudd, and plaintiff appealed. Reversed.

The real property which is the subject of this action was formerly the property of a manufacturing copartnership composed of defendant's husband and one Holmes. It was purchased, paid for, and used by the firm as a site for its manufacturing plant. The title to the property was taken in the individual names of the partners.

In an action brought by one partner against his copartner to dissolve the partnership and wind up its affairs, the property was ordered sold as one parcel, the proceeds to be applied in payment of the firm debts, and the surplus, if any, divided between the partners according to their respective interests. At the sale the property was sold to plaintiff's grantor for an amount somewhat in excess of the sum required to pay the debts of the firm, and the surplus was distributed between the partners, no part of it being paid to defendant, the widow of the deceased partner. Defendant was not made a party to the action and never joined in any conveyance of the property. Defendant in the present action, as the wife of one of the partners, claimed an inchoate interest in an undivided half of the premises. This action was brought to determine this adverse claim.

MITCHELL, J. It is well known that the English doctrine was that partnership real estate is considered as personal property for all purposes. The doctrine of the American courts on the subject is more restricted. Some of the earlier decisions in New York and Massachusetts went almost to the length of entirely subverting the equity doctrine prevalent in England; but, as remarked by Chancellor Kent, the other American decisions are not inconsistent with the more correct and improved view of the English law. It is now held with practical unanimity by the American courts that, if partnership capital be invested in land for the benefit of the company, all the incidents attached to it which belong to any other stock, so far as consistent with the statute of frauds and the technical rules of conveyancing, will be treated as personal estate until it has performed all its functions to the partnership, and thereby ceases to be any longer partnership property, and until then it is not subject to either dower or inheritance, but that after all the purposes of the partnership have been thus accomplished, whatever land remains in specie will be regarded as real estate.

The question is, at what precise moment is it reconverted into real estate, or, to speak more accurately, does it resume all the attributes and incidents of real property? We think the answer is, the moment the partnership is terminated and wound up by judgment or agreement, and it is determined that it no longer forms a part of the partnership stock, and is not required for its purposes. When a partnership is dissolved, and its affairs wound up and completely ended, and any land remains in specie, unconverted, this must be deemed a determination that it is no longer a part of the copartnership stock, and an election to hold it thereafter, individually, as real estate.

During the continuance of the partnership the partners can convey or mortgage it, in the course of their business, whenever they see fit, without their wives joining in the conveyance or mortgage, and the wives would have no dower or other interest in it. This is one of the very objects of treating partnership real estate as personal property; for otherwise the business of the firm might be stopped, and the partners unable to realize on the assets of the firm, by reason of the wife of one of them refusing to join in the conveyance or mortgage. They have the same power of disposition over it for the purposes of a dissolution of the partnership, the payment of its debts and the distribution or division of the capital among themselves; for until that is done the property has not fulfilled its functions as personalty, or ceased to be partnership property. . . . As the defendant was not a party to the former action, she is, of course, not estopped by it, nor is it evidence against her of anything except of the fact of its own rendition. But the material fact remains that in the process of dissolution of the firm, and the winding up of its affairs, in an action for that purpose, the land was sold and converted into money, and the money distributed among the creditors and partners according to law. Upon these facts, under the rules already announced, the land in the hands of the purchaser is not subject to any inchoate interest of the wives of the partners.

The court below seems to have laid special stress upon the fact that it was not made to appear on the trial that it was necessary to have sold all this property to pay the debts of the firm, but this is immaterial, either under the view of the law which we have taken, or under the view of counsel. In fact, we understood counsel to frankly concede this on the argument. Upon the facts found, judgment ought to have been ordered in favor of the plaintiff, adjudging that defendant has no interest, inchoate or otherwise, in the land. Judgment reversed.

OTHER PROPERTY RIGHTS OF A PARTNER

Sec. 24 of the Uniform Partnership Act enumerates, in addition to the right in specific partnership property which we have just been discussing, two other property rights of a partner: his interest in the partnership and his right to participate in the management. Sec. 26 defines a partner's interest in the partnership as "his share of the profits and surplus" and states that "the same is personal property."

Various aspects of these two property rights are discussed in later chapters. It is convenient here, however, to point out that, although a partner cannot assign his right in specific partnership property except in connection with the assignment of rights of all the partners in the same property,[1] he may assign his interest in the partnership. Such an assignment gives the assignee no right to participate in the management, inspect the books, or demand information about partnership affairs; it merely entitles him to receive the profits which would otherwise go to his assignor, and, in the event of the dissolution of the partnership, his assignor's interest.[2]

REVIEW CASES

1. The Davis Packing Co. was awarded a judgment against Myles individually, and had the sheriff levy upon ten cows owned by R. A. Myles & Co., a partnership of which Myles was a member. The cows were sold and the money was applied toward the judgment. R. A. Myles & Co. sued for the wrongful taking of the cattle. Holding? (R. A. Myles & Co. v. A. D. Davis Packing Co., 17 Ala. App. 85, 81 So. 863)

2. Louis Amy owned a seat on the New York Stock Exchange. He and his brother Ernest went into partnership, engaging in the banking and brokerage business under the name of H. Amy & Co. They agreed that they would share profits and losses equally and that Louis would receive $3,600 a year for the use of the seat. The partnership and the individual partners became bankrupt, and the bankruptcy court sold the seat. For purposes of distribution of assets, was the stock exchange seat to be considered as partnership property? (In re Amy, 21 F.(2d) 301)

3. Arkansas Machinery & Supply Co., a partnership, sold certain machinery to Miller, receiving in payment a note secured by a chattel mortgage on the machinery. Miller was already indebted to Hendren for other machinery, which was sold without Hendren's consent and replaced by the mortgaged machinery. Hendren took possession of the mortgaged machinery, and Wing, representative of the Arkansas Machinery & Supply Co., brought an action in replevin to retake possession of it. Hendren, as a defense, claimed that the mortgage was void because it did not name a natural or

[1] Sec. 25 (2) (b).
[2] Sec. 27.

artificial person as mortgagee. Ruling? (Hendren et al. v. Wing et al., 60 Ark. 561, 31 S. W. 149)

4. Cohen, partner of Goldberger & Cohen, assigned a commission due the partnership to pay a personal debt owed by him to Morgenthaler. Shortly thereafter Cohen became insolvent. The partnership maintained that the commission was partnership property and brought an action for an accounting. Morgenthaler claimed that he was entitled to the commission because he did not know that the partnership existed or that the commission was partnership property. Judgment for whom? (Morgenthaler v. Cohen et al., 103 Ohio St. 328, 132 N. E. 730)

5. Newton, Emmons, and Miller each acquired a one-third interest in a certain parcel of land. They then formed a partnership to carry on the business of milling and buying and selling grain. The business was conducted in a mill on the said land. The books of the firm contained no entries to show that the land was treated as firm property, but the firm gave its notes to pay for repairs to the mill and for placing new machinery in the mill. The Robinson Bank, a creditor of the firm, contended that for purposes of settling creditors' claims the property should be considered partnership property. Was the bank correct in its contention? (Robinson Bank v. Miller et al., 153 Ill. 244, 38 N. E. 1078)

Relation of
Partners
between
Themselves

40

It should always be kept in mind that parties who contemplate forming a partnership have it within their power to determine and establish the respective rights and duties of the partners to one another. This important privilege grows out of the fact that the partnership relation results from a contract among the parties, and that they may therefore work out the details as they wish, provided their agreement is within the confines of contract law. Prospective partners should therefore consider carefully what relationship they want to establish among themselves and make sure that the terms of their agreement actually represent their wishes in the matter. Moreover, in order to avoid later wrangling as to what their understanding was, they should reduce their agreement to writing, even in cases where writing is not required by the Statute of Frauds.

In the absence of special agreements, the rights and duties of the partners will be determined by the rules of partnership law. These rules, as they apply to a number of important relationships of the partners, are discussed in the following sections of this chapter.

RIGHTS OF PARTNERS

RIGHT TO PARTICIPATE IN MANAGEMENT

In the absence of a contrary agreement, all partners have equal rights in the management and conduct of the partnership business, even though they have not contributed equal amounts to the capital of the partnership and do not have equal interests in the profits and surplus of the business. In this regard the position of the partner differs from that of the stockholder of a corporation. However, the partners may expressly agree to delegate to one or more of the partners complete control over the business, or over some portion or segment of the business; and in some instances such delegation of authority, though not expressly given, may be implied from the acts of the parties. Such an agreement is binding upon the partners inter se, but it is not binding upon third parties unless they have notice or knowledge of such delegation of authority.

In the absence of an agreement to the contrary, a *majority* of the partners have the authority to make decisions and control the day-to-day policies of the partnership. But certain acts of the partnership require the *unanimous* approval of the partners. Unanimous consent is required for the admission of a new partner, or for any act that is in contravention of any agreement between the partners. And Section 9 (3) of the Uniform Partnership Act states specifically that "Unless authorized by the other partners or unless they have abandoned the business, one or more but less than all the partners have no authority to: (a) assign the partnership property in trust for creditors or on the assignee's promise to pay the debts of the partnership; (b) dispose of the good-will of the business; (c) do any other act which would make it impossible to carry on the ordinary business of a partnership; (d) confess a judgment; (e) submit a partnership claim or liability to arbitration or reference."

Difficulty may sometimes arise in the application of the "majority rule" where the partnership is composed of an even number of partners. If half the partners favor a particular act or policy and the other half oppose it, a deadlock results. The Uniform Partnership Act makes no provision for breaking such deadlocks. Consequently, unless the articles of copartnership contain a provision for handling situations of this kind, a stalemate will exist. At times such a deadlock has led to the dissolution of the partnership.

While the courts recognize and enforce the majority rule for conducting the ordinary affairs of a partnership, they do require that the majority act in good faith. The courts will not permit the majority to adopt a course of dealing that will lead to the exploitation of the minority. It is sound policy for those partners who constitute the majority to consult with the minority partners and permit them to argue their point of view. Such action on the part of the majority is strong evidence of good faith.

Markle et al. v. Wilbur et al.
200 Pa. 457, 50 A. 204 (1900)

This was a suit by George B. Markle and others (plaintiffs) against E. P. Wilbur and others (defendants). Decree for plaintiffs, and defendants appealed. Reversed.

The bill set forth that on December 30, 1889, plaintiffs entered into partnership with John Markle, William Lilly, E. P. Wilbur, and Ida Markle for the purpose of mining coal upon lands held by the firm under lease from the Union Improvement Company. Plaintiffs further alleged, among other things, (1) that it was agreed at the execution of the articles of partnership that John Markle would not act as manager unless his management should be satisfactory to all interests, but against protests he continued to do so, his management being unsatisfactory; (2) that John Markle was guilty of gross mismanagement; (3) that John Markle secretly employed one Smith and paid him a salary of $10,000 a year; (4) that John Markle was guilty of gross mismanagement in building the "Jeddo Tunnel"; and (5) that John Markle built for himself a house for $16,000 at the expense of the partnership. Plaintiffs asked for a dissolution of the partnership, the appointment of a receiver, and an accounting.

Defendants contended that all actions taken were reasonable and had the support of the majority of the partners.

The lower court held for plaintiffs, and defendants appealed.

DEAN, J. We may say at the outset that we fail to find any evidence of dishonesty, bad faith, conspiracy, or overreaching by defendants, or any one of them. There may have been mistakes of judgment in planning and conducting the business, but there was no unfairness or dishonesty. The plaintiffs, if they get such relief as they ask, must get it because of gross mismanagement of the partnership business, or because of wholly unauthorized acts in conducting the business. We do not understand that the court below found as a fact that defendants in any instance acted in bad faith toward their copartners, but it does find that they expended the partnership money extravagantly in improvements and salaries, against the protest of the minority. We cannot agree that the defendants acted without authority. In any view of the evidence, the management, good or bad, was expressly authorized or subsequently ratified by a very large majority of the partners in number and value.

Who determines whether the particular act complained of is necessary for the successful carrying on of a partnership? If, on a mere complaint and non-assent of the minority, there is no power in the majority, then the minority, in effect, carries on the partnership. If it is determined by the court on conflicting evidence, then the court carries it on. This is not the law. The rule laid down in Story, *Partnership*, Sec. 123, is stated thus: "But another question may arise, and that is whether, in case of partnership, the majority is to govern in case of a diversity of opinion between the partners as to the partnership business and the conduct thereof, or whether one partner can, by his dissent, arrest the partnership business, or suspend the ordinary powers and authority of the other partners in relation thereto against the will of the majority, where there is no stipulation in the partnership articles to control or vary the result (for, if there be any stipulation, that ought to govern). The general rule would seem to be that each partner has an equal voice, however unequal the shares of the respective parties may be; and the majority, acting fairly and bona fide, have the right and authority to conduct the partnership business within the true scope thereof, and dispose of the partnership property, notwithstanding the dissent of the minority." In *Clarke v. Railroad Co.*, 136 Pa. 408, 20 A. 562, it is stated: "This leads us to consider the manner in which the business of a firm must be conducted. The firm must have its origin in the mutual confidence reposed by the persons who comprise it in each other's skill, integrity, and capacity. Its members are bound by the nature of their compact to the exercise of good faith towards each other and the common enterprise for which they have united. Differences of opinion about questions of administration are to be anticipated. . . . It was the rule at common law that the contracts of partnership must be governed, like other agreements, by the principles of natural law and justice. It has accordingly been held that, where a firm consists of more than two persons, the majority, acting fairly and in good faith, may direct the conduct of its affairs as long as they keep within the purpose and scope of the partnership. In such case the minority must yield, so long as the majority do not transcend or pervert the powers with which the firm has been invested. If the number of partners should in any given case be an even number, and they should be evenly divided in opinion, with no provision for such a contingency in their articles, then it may be that, as to that subject, the power of the firm to act is suspended so long as the even division continues, and, if the subject be one upon which action is essential to the purposes of the partnership, such disagreement might work a dissolution by rendering the further prosecution of the common enterprise impossible. The same consequences could not flow, however, from the dissent of a minority because, within the purpose of the partnership and for the promotion of its interest, the majority have the right to control."

The facts of the case do not indicate that the defendants exceeded their authority. Judgment reversed.

RIGHT TO SHARE IN PROFITS AND SURPLUS

In the absence of an agreement to the contrary, partners are entitled to share equally in the profits and surplus of the business. This is the rule both at common law and under the Uniform Partnership Act. This rule applies even though the partners have contributed unequal amounts of capital or of services. If the firm sustains losses, the partners, in the absence of contrary agreement, share the losses equally.

If the partners provide in the partnership agreement for an unequal sharing of profits but fail to specify how losses shall be shared, they share losses in the same proportion as profits.

Williams v. Pedersen
47 Wash. 472, 92 P. 287 (1907)

This was an action by Clarence E. Williams (plaintiff) against Elbert Pedersen (defendant). Judgment for plaintiff, and defendant appealed. Affirmed.

This was an action between partners for an accounting, settlement, and dissolution. The partners conducted a logging business. The partnership at first consisted of Williams, Pedersen, and Hansen. After the firm business had continued a few weeks, Hansen dropped out, and Williams and Pedersen continued operations as a firm. The court found that they cut 330,800 feet, board measure, of sawlogs, and that each was entitled to receive one half of the net proceeds from the logs. Pedersen was to receive one dollar per thousand stumpage for the logs cut. The logs were sold to the Day Lumber Company, and Pedersen collected the proceeds of the sale, with the exception of $140 collected by Williams. The court found that Williams had also received in other ways the further sum of $107.50, making in all $247.50 received by him. After allowing Pedersen for stumpage, and expenses, the court found that there was a balance in his hands of $540.68 belonging to Williams. Judgment was entered in favor of Williams against Pedersen for the sum of $540.68 and for the dissolution of the partnership. Pedersen appealed.

As a defense defendant claimed that plaintiff was away much of the time while the logs were being cut and that plaintiff was not entitled to share in the logs cut while he was away.

HADLEY, C.J. The evidence sharply conflicts as to the amount of time the plaintiff was absent in person. His testimony was to the effect that he was there practically all the time and that when he was away his brother worked in his place. Nothing in the record indicates that the court should not have accepted the plaintiff's testimony as true, and, if true, he reasonably did his share of the work, or caused it to be done. The partnership had not been dissolved and its work discontinued, even under the defendant's theory, at such times as the plaintiff was absent and assisted therein. The defendant seems to adopt the theory that the partnership work was so intermittently done that it ceased when the plaintiff was away and that the defendant then cut logs at the same place on his own account and not that of the partnership. We think the evidence does not justify the defendant's position. The partnership undertook to cut the timber and there had been no agreed cessation of its work as such. The partnership operations, therefore, continued although the plaintiff was for a time away from the work. Even if it be true that the defendant did the greater amount of work about the firm's business, still no agreement between the partners is shown that one was to receive a greater share of the partnership earnings for his services by reason of the absence of the other. In the absence of such an agreement one partner is not entitled to recover from the other by reason of inequality of services.

There are instances where the course of dealing of the partners is such, and also where the services rendered are of such an extraordinary character, that the law implies a contract to pay one partner for extra services, but such facts are not established by the evidence here. The findings are sustained by the evidence in the record and we see no reason for disturbing them. Judgment affirmed.

RIGHT TO COMPENSATION

Unless there is agreement to the contrary, a partner is not entitled to a salary for his services. It is presumed that the partners will be compensated for their services through the receipt of profits derived from the operation of the business. Sec. 18 (f) of the Uniform Partnership Act provides: "No partner is entitled to remuneration for acting in the partnership business, except that a surviving partner is entitled to reasonable compensation for his services in winding up the partnership affairs." Before the adoption of the Uniform Act there was a split in authority as to whether a liquidating partner is entitled to compensation, and some states that have not adopted the Act still hold that he is not.

Even though a partner has rendered some extraordinary service he is usually held not to be entitled to additional compensation, unless the partnership agreement or some special agreement allows him payment for such services. The courts have generally held that if one partner becomes seriously ill and the other partners carry on with the business, such partners are not entitled to be paid for their extra services.

Some courts, in case of liquidation, have permitted a partner to claim an allowance as against his partner where the partner had failed or refused to perform the services required of him under the partnership agreement.

Lindsey v. Stranahan
129 Pa. 635, 18 A. 524 (1889)

This was a suit by J. K. Lindsey (plaintiff) against J. A. Stranahan (defendant). Decree for defendant, and plaintiff appealed. Affirmed.

This suit was to settle the copartnership business existing under the firm name of J. K. Lindsey & Co.

PER CURIAM. There is but a single question in this case: Is J. K. Lindsey, the plaintiff, entitled to compensation for his services as a partner? It is conceded that there was no express contract that he should be paid for such services and there is no principle better settled than that the law will not imply a contract in such cases. The reason is that the partner is but attending to his own affairs. This rule is inexorable; as much so as that between parent and child. Were it otherwise, we might have a contract between the partners upon the settlement of every partnership account as to the value of their respective services. It is true this principle may work hardship in particular cases—almost every general rule does; but that is a weak argument against the soundness of the rule. When the copartnership agreement contemplates that one partner shall manage the business or do more than his share of the work, it is easy to provide for this compensation in the agreement itself; and if no such stipulation is then made, as before said, the law will not imply one. *Beatty v. Wray*, 19 Pa. St. 516, *Brown's Appeal*, 89 Pa. St. 139. Affirmed.

RIGHT TO INSPECT BOOKS AND RECORDS

Unless the partners have otherwise agreed, they have an equal right to inspect and copy the books and records of the partnership. The partnership records must be kept at the principal place of business of the partnership, and must be accessible to the partners at all times.

Katz v. Brewington
71 Md. 79, 20 A. 139 (1889)

This was a suit by Charles Brewington (plaintiff) against Louis Katz (defendant). Judgment for plaintiff, and defendant appealed. Affirmed.

Charles Brewington filed a bill of complaint against Louis Katz, alleging that in May, 1887, they had entered into a copartnership under the name of L. Katz & Co., and that the business had been carried on under the firm name until the filing of the bill. It was further charged that the books of the firm were in the possession and control of Louis Katz, who refused to permit complainant to have access to the same, and that Katz had sole control and possession of the goods of the firm, and was disposing of the same in fraud of complainant; that complainant no longer felt safe with the books and assets of said firm in the possession of Katz, and desired that the said copartnership should be wound up under the order and direction of the court; that Katz absolutely excluded complainant from all control of the business; and refused to give him any information in regard to the business of the firm, having carried the books of the firm away from the place of business of the firm, and refused to discuss the place where the books were deposited.

The lower court ordered an injunction and set down for hearing the application for a receivership. Defendant appealed.

BRYAN, J. The agreement of partnership required Katz to furnish all the capital, and the profits were to be equally divided after payment of debts and expenses. It was not alleged by the complainant that any profits had been made or that there were any debts due by the partnership. It was, however, alleged that the defendant had excluded him from all control of the business of the firm and had refused to give him any information respecting it, and had carried away the books from the place of business, and had refused to disclose the place in which they were. Each partner has an equal right to take part in the management of the business of the firm. Although one of them may have an interest only in the profits and not in the capital, yet his rights are involved in the proper conduct of the affairs of the firm so that profits may be made. So each partner has an equal right to information about the partnership affairs and to free access to its books. The complainant has a right to learn from the books whether there were profits and whether there were debts. If he were denied this information, as charged in his bill of complaint, a sufficient reason appears for not alleging that profits had been earned and that debt existed.

Order must be affirmed.

RIGHT TO REPAYMENT OF CONTRIBUTIONS

In addition to their original capital contributions, partners sometimes make advances or contributions to the assets of the firm. In a sense these are loans to the partnership. The courts have always held that a partner is entitled to a return of his advance or contribution to the firm assets after the firm liabilities have been satisfied, and the Uniform Partnership Act contains a provision to this same effect (Sec. 18 (a)). If there are not sufficient firm assets available to repay the advance, the partner who made it is entitled to a ratable contribution from the other partners.

Before the adoption of the Uniform Partnership Act the courts were not in agreement as to whether the partner who made the advance was entitled to interest. The majority of the courts held that he was not entitled to interest unless it was agreed when the advance was made that he should receive interest. However, Sec. 18 (c) of the Uniform Partnership Act provides that he shall be paid interest from the date when the advance was made.

RIGHT TO BE INDEMNIFIED

A partner is entitled to be indemnified if he pays firm debts or obligations out of his personal estate. For example, if the liquid assets of the firm are inadequate to pay a firm note when it becomes due and one of the partners pays the note out of his own funds, he is entitled to be indemnified. The same would apply in the case of the payment of insurance, taxes, or any other valid obligation of the firm. However, a partner is not aways entitled to reimbursement. For instance, if while acting within the scope of the partnership business he should negligently operate the firm's truck and injure X, and should pay X for his injuries, he would not be entitled to be indemnified by the partnership. Indeed, if X sued the partnership and obtained judgment, and the firm paid the judgment, the firm would be entitled to indemnification from the negligent partner. Sec. 18 (b) of the Uniform Partnership Act provides that "The partnership must indemnify every partner in respect of payments made and personal liabilities reasonably incurred by him in the ordinary and proper conduct of its business, for the preservation of its business or property."

A partner who pays a legitimate firm obligation out of his own personal estate is entitled to interest from the date of the payment.

RIGHT TO AN ACCOUNTING

A partner is always entitled to an accounting upon the dissolution of the partnership. If the parties find themselves unable to adjust their accounts and wind up the partnership business in an amicable fashion, a partner may file a bill in equity, asking for an accounting. An accounting may not be obtained at law.

The right to an accounting at other times may of course be established by special agreement. In addition, the Uniform Partnership Act provides that such right accrues if a partner is wrongfully excluded by his co-partner from the partnership business or from possession of its property, or "whenever other circumstances render it just and reasonable." [1] The right to an accounting arises also under the provisions of Sec. 21 of the Act, which reads as follows: "(1) Every partner must account to the partnership for any benefit, and hold as trustee for it any profits derived by him without the consent of the other partners from any transaction connected with the formation, conduct, or liquidation of the partnership or from any use by him of its property. (2) This section applies also to the representatives of a deceased partner engaged in the liquidation of the affairs of the partnership as the personal representatives of the last surviving partner."

DUTIES OF PARTNERS

DUTY TO EXERCISE GOOD FAITH

The relationship between partners is a highly personal one. Each partner is the agent of the other partners and may bind them while acting within the scope of the partnership business. Each partner has unlimited liability, and, as we shall soon see, one partner may not sue another partner in an action at law. The successful operation of a partnership requires the highest degree of good faith among the partners. For these reasons the courts hold that the relationship existing between partners is fiduciary in nature; that is, the relationship is one of trust and confidence.

Because of this fiduciary relationship a partner is not permitted to make a personal or secret profit at the expense of the other partners. If he does so and it is discovered, he may be made to account to the other partners. He may not conduct a competing business without the consent of the other partners. Neither may he sell his own property to the firm, nor buy goods from the firm, unless he first obtains the consent of the other partners. He must always place the interest and well-being of the partnership above that of his own. Thus, if his personal interest and that of the partnership should conflict, it is his duty to favor the interest of the partnership over his personal interest.

Alexander v. Sims et al.
220 Ark. 643, 249 S. W. (2d) 832 (1952)

This was a suit by I. T. Sims, executor of the estate of his daughter, Marguerite E. Sims, deceased (plaintiff) against Helen S. Alexander (defendant). Decree for plaintiff, and defendant appealed. Decree affirmed.

[1] Sec. 22 (a), (d).

Defendant and Marguerite Sims, were copartners, engaged in the retail jewelry business under the firm name of Sims & Alexander. The partnership began in 1942 and continued with financial success until terminated by Miss Sims' death, which occurred on April 10, 1950. The executor of her estate brought this suit to have Miss Sims' interest in the partnership determined in the partnership assets. Mrs. Alexander claimed that all of Miss Sims' interest in the partnership passed to her under the terms of a written agreement, executed October 14, 1949.

The facts showed that on September 16, 1949, Miss Sims, aged 48, entered a hospital for diagnosis and treatment, and underwent surgery on September 23rd. On the same day the attending physician informed Miss Sims' mother and Mrs. Alexander that Miss Sims had cancer in an advanced stage and would live only a short time. The physician did not inform Miss Sims of her condition until she made direct inquiry on October 15, 1949.

On October 14th, while Miss Sims was still in the hospital, and before she learned of her malignancy, Mrs. Alexander had an attorney prepare the agreement on which she relied in this suit. On the same day she took the agreement to the hospital, and she and Miss Sims signed and acknowledged it, Mrs. Alexander retaining both copies. This agreement provided inter alia "that in the event of the decease of either of the partners, all of the partnership assets shall *ipso facto* immediately become the sole and exclusive property of the surviving partner. . . ."

The next day Miss Sims for the first time made explicit inquiry of her physician as to her condition, and the physician frankly informed her of its seriousness. On February 14, 1950, Miss Sims executed her will, in which she devised and bequeathed her entire estate, including her interest in the partnership, to her parents. She died on April 10, 1950. Her father was named as executor of her estate, and is the plaintiff in this suit.

The Chancery Court refused to give effect to the agreement, and held that Miss Sims' interest in the partnership was the property of her estate. From that decree, Mrs. Alexander appealed.

McFADDIN, J. The decision in this case turns on the agreement, dated October 14, 1949, and relied upon by Mrs. Alexander. Absent any question of consideration, testamentary nature, or fraud on the part of a partner or his creditors, spouse, heirs, etc., some courts have upheld a partnership agreement in which each partner agrees that the survivor will receive all of the assets of the partnership, but such an agreement is always subject to the closest scrutiny to see if the utmost good faith was observed.

We come to the conclusion that on October 14, 1949, Mrs. Alexander obtained the execution of the written agreement, when her partner, Miss Sims, was ignorant of impending death, and when Mrs. Alexander, knowing such fact, did not divulge it to Miss Sims. Under such circumstances, we think that Mrs. Alexander failed to observe and obey the rule which requires partners to exercise the utmost good faith in their dealings with each other. In

Drummond v. Batson, 162 Ark. 407, 258 S. W. 616, Mr. Justice Hart said: "Partners are bound to conduct themselves with good faith towards each other. . . ." The Uniform Partnership Act recognizes this rule.

In Gilmore on "Partnership" the rule is stated on page 374: "Partnership is a relation of trust and confidence, and partners must observe the utmost good faith towards each other in all of their transactions, from the time they begin negotiations with each other, to the complete settlement of the partnership affairs." In 40 *Am. Jur.*, 217 et seq., the holdings from cases generally are summarized: "The relationship of partners is fiduciary and imposes upon them the obligation of the utmost good faith and integrity in their dealings with one another with respect to partnership affairs. The partners may not deceive one another by concealment of material facts. . . . The general rule that the utmost good faith is required of partners in their relationship with each other, and that, since each is the confidential agent of the other, each has a right to know all that the other knows and each is required to make full disclosure of all material facts within his knowledge in any way relating to partnership affairs, is held almost universally to apply in the case of a sale by one partner to another of his interest in the partnership." In the case at bar the effect of the agreement which Mrs. Alexander caused to be prepared and signed by Miss Sims, was the same as a sale of Miss Sims' interest in the partnership. Mrs. Alexander knew that Miss Sims had only a short time to live, and that the effect of the instrument was for Miss Sims to give all her interest in the partnership to Mrs. Alexander. Yet Mrs. Alexander, knowing all these facts, did not disclose them to Miss Sims when the agreement was signed, and Miss Sims did not learn of her serious condition and impending death until the next day. We hold that under the circumstances the agreement was susceptible of being set aside. That Miss Sims did renounce the agreement is thoroughly shown by her will, in which she bequeathed her interest in the partnership to her parents. The validity of the will is not attacked by Mrs. Alexander. Decree of the Chancery Court is affirmed.

DUTY TO DEVOTE TIME TO THE BUSINESS

If the partnership agreement does not provide otherwise, a partner is required to devote his entire time and attention to the partnership business. Therefore, if it is the intention of the partners that one of the partners is to devote none of his time to the partnership business (as in the case of a silent partner or a dormant partner), or only a portion of his time to such business, care should be taken to make such provision in the articles of partnership.

DUTY TO USE REASONABLE CARE AND SKILL

A partner is required to use reasonable care and skill. He is not liable for an honest mistake or an error of judgment, but he is liable if his carelessness amounts to gross negligence. One partner should consult with the other partner or partners concerning a given transaction, particularly where the transaction concerns matter within the peculiar knowledge of the other or others. Failure to do so is evidence of negligence and may result in liability to the partner.

Hurter et al. v. Larrabee et al.
22 Mass. 218, 112 N. E. 613 (1916)

This was an action by John C. Hurter and another (plaintiffs) against Charles M. Larrabee and others (defendants). Judgment for defendants, and plaintiffs appealed. Affirmed.

This was a bill for accounting by two retiring members of a partnership against three remaining partners. The firm carried on a wholesale dry goods business. The articles of copartnership provided, among other matters, that upon the termination of the partnership two or more of the general partners having a majority interest therein might continue the business under the firm name, and in that event should "pay to the retiring general partners for their interest in said business the amount standing to the credit of each of the retiring general partners on the books of the firm January 1, 1913, after the stocktaking of that date and after the interest and profit has been placed to each general partner's credit." The three defendants elected to continue the business, and the two plaintiffs to retire. Disagreement as to how much should be paid to plaintiffs caused this suit. The case was referred to a master, and exceptions to the master's report presented the questions to be decided. Plaintiffs' first exception was the refusal of the master to make a finding upon the negligence of defendant Brady in supervising the accounting department of the firm.

RUGG, C.J. The bookkeeping and accounting was done on a rather complicated system and was found to be full of mistakes and errors, resulting apparently from lack of care and diligence. All the partners, including Brady, believed the business to have been prosperous and were deceived as to its real condition until it was revealed by the report of an expert accountant. The master refused to make a finding as to the negligence of Brady because, although there was some evidence to show that he ought to have known that the books were badly kept and exhibited defects and errors, there were other facts which made that question irrelevant. The relation of Larrabee and Chandler, the other defendants, is the same as that of the plaintiffs to the books. They ought not to be made to pay to the plaintiffs for Brady's negligence. . . . Negligence of one partner had no bearing on this issue. The basis of the accounting fixed by the agreement is the share of each partner, after interest and profit of each is found, as shown by the books. There is no general principle of partnership which renders one partner liable to his copartners for his honest mistakes. So far as losses result to a firm from errors of judgment of one partner not amounting to fraud, bad faith, or reckless disregard of his obligations, they must be borne by the partnership. Each partner owes to the firm the duty of faithful service according to the best of his ability. But, in the absence of special agreement, no partner guarantees his own capacity. Where one assumes the duty of keeping the books, reasonable presumptions are made against him when he disputes their accuracy. But when there is good faith throughout, he is not estopped to show the truth about the books even though he may have been inefficient. *Leon v. Gardner*, 104 Iowa 176, 73 N. W. 591. Decree affirmed.

DUTY TO PROVIDE INFORMATION

A partner has a duty to provide to the other partners full information about the operations of the partnership business. Sec. 20 of the Uniform Partnership Act states: "Partners shall render on demand true and full information of all things affecting the partnership to any partner or the legal representative of any deceased partner or partner under legal disability." It is a violation of the partnership relation for one partner to withhold such information wrongfully from the other partners or to exclude them from the books and records of the firm.

When a partner is dealing on behalf of the firm with an outside party, any relevant knowledge that he acquires is imputed to the firm, and any notice that he receives relative to partnership affairs operates as notice to the firm. He therefore has a correlative duty to inform the other partners of such matters.

DUTY TO COMPLY WITH PARTNERSHIP AGREEMENT

Since a partnership agreement is a contract, the partners are bound inter se by its provisions. They are bound not only by the provisions of the agreement that endow them with unusual powers and authority, but also by any restrictions placed upon them in the exercise of the ordinary and usual powers and authority of partners.

SUITS BETWEEN PARTNERS

ACTIONS AT LAW

One partner may not maintain an action at law against another partner if the action involves partnership matters. Nor may such an action at law be brought by a partner against the partnership, or by the partnership against a partner. The principal reason given for not permitting such actions at law is the feeling on the part of the common law courts that they are not equipped to handle such matters. In order to determine whether one partner is obligated to another partner, or whether the partnership is obligated to a partner, an accounting is necessary, and the common law courts do not feel that the procedures which have been established to handle law actions are adequate to deal with matters involving an accounting of the partnership business.

Certain exceptions are recognized to the foregoing rules. (1) After a partnership agreement has been entered into but before the business is a going concern, if one of the partners fails or refuses to make his capital contribution, as agreed, action may be brought against him in a court of law for breach of the partnership agreement. This does not involve a partnership accounting. (2) After a partnership has been terminated and an accounting has been had, an action may be brought at law to recover the final balance determined to be due by one partner to another.

It should be understood that the partnership relation does not bar one partner from bringing against another partner any action at law which does not involve partnership matters.

SUITS IN EQUITY

The equity court is the proper tribunal in which to settle all controversies growing out of the partnership relationship. It is to the equity court that partners may go for an accounting and winding up of the partnership business. Moreover, under certain circumstances a partner may secure an injunction against another partner in a court of equity. For example, one partner may restrain another partner from taking or disposing of partnership assets, or from breaching some duty arising out of the partnership agreement. While an equity court may, under proper circumstances, grant specific performance of a duty arising out of the partnership agreement, it will never grant specific performance of the partnership agreement itself. This is because of the highly personal nature of the partnership relation. As we shall see in more detail in Chapter 42, a partner always has the *power*, though he may not have the *right*, to terminate the partnership and demand an accounting and a winding up of the partnership. In such a suit the court would allow the other partner any damages it thought him entitled to for the breach of the partnership agreement.

Jones et al. v. Cade
94 So. 255, 19 Ala. App. 27 (1922)

This was an action by J. M. Cade (plaintiff) against R. D. Jones and others (defendants). Judgment for plaintiff, and defendants appealed. Reversed and remanded.

Defendants, together with plaintiff, were members of a partnership doing business under the name of Eufaula Cash Store. Signing the name of the partnership and his name as president, plaintiff executed and delivered to the Bank of Eufaula a note for $491.56, the amount of the note being for money loaned by the bank to the partnership, which went into the partnership business. Before the money was loaned, defendants signed their names on the back of the note. On non-payment of the note suit was brought against the Eufaula Cash Store and plaintiff, and judgment recovered against both, after plaintiff had filed a plea that the note was not signed by him as an individual, but as president of the partnership. Execution being afterwards issued, the amount of the judgment was paid by plaintiff, who then brought this action claiming by contribution of defendants their proportionate part of the judgment rendered against plaintiff, since they were co-makers and co-obligor of said note.

MERRITT, J. Under the law applied to the undisputed facts in the case the appellee cannot recover in a court of law.

The beginning, execution, and completion of the whole transaction, whereby the note was given, was for a loan of money to the partnership, which money went into and was used for partnership purposes. This being confessedly so, a suit cannot be maintained at law between partners as such, by reason of the partnership relation. There is no rule forbidding suits at law between partners individually, but prior to a settlement of partnership business one partner cannot maintain an action at law against his copartner with reference to partnership affairs. *Bumpass v. Webb*, 1 Stew. 18, 18 Am. Rep. 34. The reason for this rule is that it is ordinarily impossible to determine whether the defendant partner is indebted to the plaintiff partner or not until the partnership accounts are settled and the true standing of the partnership ascertained; and the process and remedies afforded by a court of law are not usually adequate or appropriate to the investigation of claims requiring such an accounting. Mechem, *Partnership*, Sec. 133. Even after dissolution there is no right to sue until there has been a settlement.

In Story on Partnership, p. 364, after stating many reasons why at law a partner cannot maintain a suit against the other partners for money paid, or advanced, or contributed, or liabilities incurred, on account of the partnership, the writer then says: "But a reason, far more satisfactory, because it is in no shape founded upon technical principles, is, that until all the partnership concerns are ascertained and adjusted, it is impossible to know whether a particular partner be a debtor or a creditor of the firm; for although he may have advanced large sums of money on account thereof, he may be indebted to the firm in a much larger amount. . . . If one partner could recover against the other partners the whole amount paid by him on account of the partnership, they would immediately have a cross action against him for the whole amount, or his share thereof; and if he could only recover their shares thereof, then, in order to ascertain those shares, a full account of all the partnership concerns must be taken, and the partnership itself wound up."

In equity the partner forced to pay firm debts has his right of accounting and contribution from his copartners. *Webb v. Butler*, 192 Ala. 294, 68 So. 389. Reversed and remanded.

REVIEW CASES

1. Wisner and Field were partners. Their partnership agreement made no provision for the payment of a salary to either partner. After they had been in business for some time, Wisner claimed a commission on certain sales of land which he had consummated in carrying out the business of the firm. Was he entitled to the commission? (Wisner v. Field, 11 N. D. 257, 91 N. W. 67)

2. Kaufer and Rothman were partners and dealers in furs. In Rothman's absence Kaufer appropriated most of the furs in stock and sold them for less than their value. Rothman brought suit asking for an accounting. The question at issue was whether Kaufer was liable for the real value of the furs or the lower price at which he had sold them. Holding? (Kaufer v. Rothman, 78 N. J. Eq. 467, 131 A. 581)

3. Johnson, Fogg, and Vanderslice were partners operating a sawmill under the firm name of Wm. Johnson & Co. Dutton, a storekeeper, had extended credit to the firm. Johnson, who felt that the firm should not obligate itself further, instructed Dutton not to extend more credit to the firm and stated that he would not be responsible for any further obligations incurred at the store by the firm. However, at the request of the other two partners Dutton extended further credit, and took notes signed by Fogg for the partnership. Dutton's administrator later sued the partnership on the notes, and Johnson offered in defense his notice to Dutton. Holding? (Johnson & Co. v. Dutton's Administrator, 27 Ala. 245)

4. Mitchell and Reed were partners in the hotel business, leasing the building in which they operated. The partnership agreement stipulated that the partnership was to come to an end at the expiration of the hotel lease. Mitchell and Reed had a very profitable business and expended large sums improving the property. Two years before the lease expired, Reed secretly procured for himself a renewal of the lease, to begin at the termination of the partnership lease. When the partnership lease expired, Mitchell brought suit claiming the lease to be partnership property. Holding? (Mitchell v. Reed, 61 N. Y. 123)

5. Yorks and Tozer were partners in the purchase of a tract of land, which was taken in the name of Yorks. It was agreed that Yorks was to advance the purchase price and pay the taxes, that Tozer was to sell the land, and that after Yorks had been reimbursed with interest, the balance of the proceeds of the sale was to be divided equally between the two. The land was purchased for $450. Thereafter Yorks negotiated the sale of the land for $1560 without Tozer's knowledge. It appeared from the abstract of title that Yorks did not have good title to the land, and he paid the original patentee $525 for a conveyance of the title to himself. He then claimed that this expense should be divided between himself and Tozer. Tozer denied this, on the ground that if Yorks had consulted him he could have informed Yorks that the abstract was incorrect. Judgment for whom? (Yorks v. Tozer, 59 Minn. 78, 60 N. W. 846)

Relation of
Partners to
Third Persons

41

AUTHORITY OF PARTNERS

In dealings with third parties, the authority of a partner to bind the partnership and the other partners rests upon the fact that a partner is the agent of the partnership and of the other partners while he is acting within the scope of the partnership business. In effect, each partner is both an agent and a principal. He acts as an agent of the other partners when he acts upon their behalf, and he occupies the position of a principal when his partner acts upon his behalf. In other words, a mutual agency relationship exists among partners.

The authority of a partner to bind the partnership on contracts with third parties may be either express or implied. Any express authority which he possesses arises from specific delegations of power in the partnership agreement or subsequent agreements among the partners. Such arrangements bind the partners inter se and also third parties who have notice of them. A partner's implied authority is determined by certain general rules which are discussed in the following paragraphs.

EXTENT OF A PARTNER'S IMPLIED AUTHORITY

The extent of a partner's implied authority to bind the partnership and the other partners depends primarily upon the nature of the business which the partnership is carrying on—whether it is a trading or a nontrading partnership, whether particular customs or usages have become established in it, what types of transactions constitute its day-to-day operations. In general, it may be said that, so far as relates to third parties who have no notice of partnership agreements to a different effect, a partner has implied power to perform any act which is essential to the normal operation of the type of business in which the partnership is engaged, or, as Sec. 9 (1) of the Uniform Partnership Act puts it, any act "for apparently carrying on in the usual way the business of the partnership of which he is a member." Conversely, Sec. 9 (2) provides that "An act of a partner which is not apparently for the carrying on of the business of the partnership in the usual way does not bind the partnership, unless authorized by the other partners."

AUTHORITY TO BUY AND SELL PERSONAL PROPERTY. A partner in a trading partnership has implied authority to buy and sell goods and merchandise of the sort in which the firm regularly deals. Even though as between the partners themselves the partner has no such authority, the partnership will be bound on such a contract as to a third party who was unaware of the limitation of the partner's authority. The fact that the partner may appropriate some of the goods to his own use will not discharge the firm of its liability.

A partner who has implied authority to sell the goods of the firm in the regular course of business has also implied authority to give the usual warranties as to title, quality, and suitability.

AUTHORITY TO BORROW MONEY. Since a partner in a trading partnership has implied authority to buy goods in the regular course of business, and since it is often necessary or desirable to borrow money to finance the purchase of goods which the firm is engaged in selling, a partner in a trading partnership has implied authority to borrow money and pledge the credit of the firm for partnership purposes. Even though the partner who borrows the money and pledges the firm's credit should appropriate the money or property to his own use, the firm will still be liable on the debt, assuming that the amount of the loan was reasonable in amount and that the creditor acted in good faith.

Since a non-trading partnership is engaged in selling services, not goods and merchandise, a partner in a non-trading partnership does not have implied authority to borrow money and pledge the firm's credit.

Since the law implies that a partner in a trading partnership has authority to borrow money and pledge the firm's credit, it further implies that he has authority to secure the debt by pledging or giving a mortgage on the firm property.

AUTHORITY TO USE NEGOTIABLE INSTRUMENTS. A partner in a trading partnership has implied authority to give a promissory note or bill of exchange in the firm's name for money loaned or goods sold to the firm. If the credit was extended in good faith, the firm would be liable on the note or bill of exchange even though the partner used the money or goods himself. The unfaithful partner would of course, be liable to the other partners, or to the partnership, if the partnership is treated as a separate legal entity.

A partner has no implied authority to make the firm an accommodation party to a negotiable instrument. In rare cases a partnership has been held liable as an accommodation party where the act which made it an accommodation party was in furtherance of the partnership business.

AUTHORITY TO MAKE COLLECTIONS AND PAYMENTS. A partner has implied authority to collect the debts and obligations owed to the firm, and to pay bona fide debts of the firm. He also has implied authority to compromise and settle disputed claims and to issue receipts for the payment of debts owed to the firm. It goes without saying that a partner has no implied authority to pay his own personal debts out of the funds of the partnership; however, if he does so and if his creditor acted in good faith, the partnership may not require a return of the money from the creditor.

AUTHORITY TO HIRE AND FIRE PERSONNEL. A partner has implied authority to engage such employees and agents as are reasonably necessary to carry on the firm's business. Hence, any employee or agent who is thus employed by a partner may hold the partnership liable on the employment contract. Of course, there must be no collusion between the partner and the employee or agent or the partnership will not be bound.

A partner likewise has authority to discharge an employee or agent. Hiring and firing of firm personnel do not require unanimous consent of the partners, or even majority consent.

AUTHORITY TO INSURE. A partner has implied authority to insure firm property and to settle with the insurance company for losses covered by the policy. He also has implied authority to cancel an insurance policy.

AUTHORITY TO BIND FIRM BY A GUARANTY OR SURETY CONTRACT. As a general rule, a partner has no implied authority to bind the firm on a guaranty or surety contract. Some courts have held the firm liable on a guaranty or surety contract, agreed to by a single partner, when it was determined that the contract was in furtherance of the purposes and objectives of the partnership.

Delta Asbestos Co. v. Sanders
259 Mich. 317, 243 N. W. 16 (1932)

This was an action by Delta Asbestos Company, Inc. (plaintiff) against Dora H. Sanders and Harry R. Wells, each individually and as doing business as Security Storage and Transfer Company (defendants). Judgment for defendants, and plaintiff appealed. Affirmed.

Defendants Wells and Sanders were brother and sister and conducted a storage and trucking business under the name of Security Storage and Transfer Company, with Wells as active and managing partner. Wells, in the name of the company, signed an order for a liquid roofing product, sold by plaintiff, and the product was billed to and received by the company. This suit was brought to recover the contract price of the product. It was tried without a jury, and defendants had judgment.

WEST, J. The court below found that the matter was outside the scope of the company, and defendant Sanders, not having authorized or ratified the transaction, was not liable.

The name "Security Storage and Transfer Company" plainly indicates the scope of the business carried on. Storage in a warehouse and carriage by trucks was, and for many years had been, the sole business of the company. Defendant Wells could not depart from the scope of the partnership without authorization and bind his copartner by a wholly foreign contract. It must have been manifest to the plaintiff's agent that the purchase was not one apparently for carrying on the business of the partnership in the usual way, unless it was to make deliveries of orders procured by the plaintiff.

We find no assent by defendant Sanders, no act of ratification by her, and no evidence justifying the application of the doctrine of estoppel. As soon as defendant Sanders discovered the transaction she repudiated it and refused to be bound thereby and so notified plaintiff.

[NOTE: Wells had judgment on grounds not here included.]

Boise Payette Lumber Co. v. Sarret et al.
38 Ida. 278, 221 P. 130 (1923)

This was an action by the Boise Payette Lumber Company (plaintiff) against Jules Sarret and another, doing business as a copartnership under the firm name and style of Sarret & Stevens (defendants). Judgment for plaintiff, and defendants appealed. Affirmed.

During the years 1919 and 1920 certain goods, wares, and merchandise, consisting of lumber, fence posts, barbed wire, nails, corrugated iron, paint, coal, etc. were sold and delivered by plaintiff to the firm of Sarret & Stevens, a copartnership engaged in the business of raising and selling sheep. The purchases were made by Sarret in the name of the copartnership. It does not appear that defendant Stevens was informed that the purchases had been made until some time thereafter, when plaintiff presented him with a statement and requested payment. Defendant Stevens refused to pay for the merchandise, whereupon plaintiff instituted this action.

Stevens contended that Sarret had no authority to purchase the merchandise enumerated.

LEE, J. The evidence showed that Sarret went to the plaintiff's place of business and told its local manager that he wanted to purchase some materials for Sarret & Stevens; that they were in partnership in the sheep business; and that they needed the materials for building sheds, fences, etc., on a ranch operated by the partnership. Plaintiff thereupon sold and delivered the materials. At the time the first purchase was made Sarret also stated to the plaintiff's local manager that he had talked with the defendant Stevens about paying for the materials.

The defendant Stevens contends that the partnership was limited to the sheep business; that Sarret could not bind him by any contract not relating to that particular business; and that the plaintiff was deemed to have knowledge of the limited nature of the partnership business and the fact that its operations were restricted to the single business of raising and selling sheep. It is fundamental that, when one deals with a member of a partnership in a matter not within the scope of the business conducted by the partnership, he will be held to have dealt with such partner purely in his capacity as a private individual, even though the partner deals under the firm name. It is important, therefore, to determine whether the subject matter of the contract of sale related to the business of raising, buying, and selling sheep, the nature of the partnership admitted by defendant Stevens; i.e., whether the contract was within the scope of the business being conducted by the partnership. Whether the materials purchased were such as are ordinarily used in the sheep business was, under the pleadings in this case, a question of fact for the jury.

The witness who testified in this connection said that he had, for the past 15 years, sold merchandise to people engaged in the business of raising and selling sheep, and was familiar with the nature and character of the articles purchased by such people for use in their business. The burden was on the plaintiff to prove that the purchases made by Sarret were made within the scope and course of the particular business which the defendant Stevens admitted was conducted by the partnership, and to do this we see no reason why it was not proper to prove that sheepmen generally purchase and use such materials in carrying on their business. "In order to determine the apparent scope of the authority of a partner, recourse may frequently be had to past transactions indicating a custom or course of dealing to the firm in question or to the general custom of parties and firms similarly situated." 20 *R. C. L.* 885.

It appearing, therefore, that the materials were such as are ordinarily purchased by men engaged in the business in which the defendant Stevens admitted the partnership was engaged, the partnership was liable for the purchase price of such materials. Burdick on Partnership, 185; *McPherson v. Bristol*, 122 Mich. 354, 81 N. W. 254. Judgment affirmed.

LIMITATIONS ON AUTHORITY

The normal or usual authority which the partners have to represent and bind the firm may be, and often is, limited by the partnership agreement or by some subsequent agreement of the partners. For example, in a firm composed of A, B, and C, the authority of all three partners may be limited by a provision that no partner may pledge the credit of the firm without the consent of the other two; or the authority of A and B may be limited by a provision that only C may draw checks on the partnership bank account. Or the limitation may apply to a single transaction. For example, A wishes to enter into a contract with D, but B and C decide against it, and A is thus deprived of authority to bind the firm on this particular contract. All such limitations bind the partners among themselves, but they do not bind third parties who have no notice or knowledge of them. Such parties have a right to assume that the partners have the normal authority vested in general partners by law. Hence if A, in direct violation of the majority agreement, contracts with D, who has no knowledge of A's limitation of authority and who acts in good faith, the partnership is bound. On the other hand, third parties who know of such limitations are bound by them.

We have already seen that in partnerships composed of an even number of partners a deadlock may arise where a majority vote is necessary to decide some matter but the partners are evenly divided for and against the measure. When such a deadlock concerns the assumption of contractual obligations with a third party, the practical effect is a victory for the opponents of the measure, since by notifying the third party of their dissent they can prevent the proponents from binding the firm on the contract. To illustrate, A and B are partners. A wishes to enter into a contract with C, but B does not wish to do so. If B does not notify C of his dissent and A contracts with C, both partners are bound. But if B notifies C of his dissent, thus making him aware that the necessary majority approval is not forthcoming, and if A and C nevertheless enter into the contract, then neither the partnership nor B will be bound.

Another type of limitation is placed upon the authority of a partner by Sec. 9 (3) of the Uniform Partnership Act, which lists certain acts which "one or more but less than all the partners" have no authority to perform, unless authorized by the other partners. As we saw in an earlier chapter, this section provides in effect that unanimous consent of the partners is required to make an assignment of partnership property for the benefit of creditors, to dispose of the good will of the firm, or to do any other act incompatible with carrying on the ordinary business of the partnership, and also to confess a judgment or submit a partnership claim or liability to arbitration.

Picone v. Commercial Paste Company
215 Miss. 114, 60 S. (2d) 590 (1952)

This was an action by Commercial Paste Company (plaintiff) against Mrs. Francis Picone and another (defendants). Judgment for plaintiff, and Mrs. Picone appealed. Affirmed.

On or shortly before June 1, 1948, Mrs. Picone and Martin Cox formed a commercial partnership to buy, sell, and install floor coverings. The place of business was to be at Gulfport, Mississippi, and the name adopted by the partnership was Gulfport Linoleum Mart. That agreement was verbal. The date of the privilege license was June 1, 1948. On June 4, 1948, Cox, in the name of the firm, "By Martin Cox," signed a written order for floor covering to be shipped by plaintiff to the firm at its address in Gulfport. The order was sent to plaintiff at Columbus, Ohio.

On June 18, 1948, the partners executed written articles of copartnership containing the following clause: "Neither of the partners is to become surety, drawer, acceptor, or endorser, in any case whatever, except in and for effecting the partnership, without the consent of his copartner, and neither of the partners shall have the right to buy or contract for or on account of the partnership without the consent of his copartner; that is, both of said partners shall act conjointly and be consulted and agree on each transaction affecting the business of the partnership. This agreement is to be binding on the partners and the public generally, and for such purpose these articles of copartnership shall be recorded in the office of the Chancery clerk of Harrison County, Mississippi." The articles were so recorded on June 23, 1948.

On June 28, 1948, plaintiff shipped by truck from Columbus to Gulfport Linoleum Mart at its place of business in Gulfport the merchandise Cox had ordered. Plaintiff mailed invoice of, and later sent a number of communications about, this merchandise to the firm name at Gulfport. No payment was made on account. Finally, on October 25, 1948, Mrs. Picone wrote plaintiff a letter in which she admitted that she and Martin Cox were partners in the firm. She explained that Cox also owned and operated the Mobile Floor Covering Co. in Mobile, Alabama. Mrs. Picone further stated in her letter: "It seems that Mr. Cox placed an order with your salesman for some merchandise, which was shipped to this store. I had no knowledge of such an order, and we did not need the merchandise. I immediately got in touch with Mr. Cox in Mobile and asked him about it, and he told me that the shipment was intended for the Mobile store, so I had the merchandise transferred to Mobile."

Plaintiff obtained judgment in the County Court. This was affirmed by the Circuit Court and Mrs. Picone appealed to this court. Cox did not appeal.

ROBERDS, J. Mrs. Picone testified she did not give her assent to this order and did not know about it at the time given. She, therefore, says the quoted provision of the articles of copartnership relieves her of any liability. In support of her contention she relies upon the rule that a partnership may be limited and if those dealing with it have notice of the limitation, then the partners are not liable for acts beyond such limitations. Of course, that rule is well established. 68 *C. J. S.*, Partnership, sec. 143, p. 578; 40 *Am. Jur.*, p. 230, sec. 142. However, it has no application to the facts of this case. It is not contended plaintiff had any actual notice of limitation of the powers of the partners. It is said the written agreement was recorded and this gave constructive notice to plaintiff. But the written order to plaintiff by Cox was given June 4th, before the written agreement was made between the parties. Cox then had full power to bind the partnership within the scope of the partnership business—at least, as to plaintiff, he apparently had such power. If he did not as a fact have that power, plaintiff had no notice of the limitation. The fact that a written agreement was later made between the parties and recorded some nineteen days after the order was given could not reach back and nullify the power and authority possessed by the partners on June 4th.

The letter of Mrs. Picone of October 25th did not change or alter the rights of the parties. In that letter she admitted she was a partner with Cox in the business at Gulfport. Her reason for not paying the bill was not that she did not give her consent to the purchase but that Cox said it was intended for Cox' store at Mobile and he had returned the merchandise. The written order directed the plaintiff to ship the goods to the partnership at Gulfport, and the plaintiff refused to accept return of the merchandise. The rights of the seller must be determined by the circumstances confronting it at the time of the sale. Judgment affirmed.

LIABILITIES OF PARTNERS

CONTRACT LIABILITY

The basic rule is that all the partners are liable on partnership contracts. Under the common law their liability is *joint*, and not *joint and several*. This means that the partners are obligated on a group promise, and not on the individual promise of each partner. In other words, it is held that a partner does not agree to become individually bound, but agrees only to be bound collectively or jointly with all the other partners. Therefore it is necessary for the third-party plaintiff to sue all the partners, get service on all of them, and bring them all into court. For example, if X wishes to sue the Y partnership (composed of three partners, A, B, and C) on a firm obligation, he must file suit against all three partners. If he files suit against only A, A may plead the non-joinder of B and C. If he sues all three partners but gets service on only A and B, they may bar further proceedings by filing a plea in abatement. If they do not do so, however, X may take judgment against them, in which case his claim against the partnership is merged in the judgment, and he may not later sue C and take judgment against him. Mr. Justice Field, in the well-known case of *Mason v. Elred*,[1] commented as follows on the nature of the liability of partners on firm contracts: "Copartnerships are formed for joint purposes. The members undertake joint enterprises, they assume joint risks, and they incur in all cases joint liabilities. In all copartnership transactions this common risk and liability exists. Therefore it is that, in

[1] 73 U. S. 231 (1867).

suits upon these transactions, all the copartners must be brought in, except when there is some ground of personal release from liability, as infancy or a discharge in bankruptcy; and if not brought in, the omission may be pleaded in abatement. . . . A judgment against one upon a joint contract of several persons bars an action against the other. When the contract is joint, and one not joint and several, the entire cause of action is merged in the judgment. The joint liability of the parties not sued with those against whom the judgment is recovered being extinguished, their entire liability is gone. They cannot be sued separately, for they have incurred no several obligation; they cannot be sued jointly with the others, because judgment has been already recovered against the latter, who would otherwise be subjected to two suits for the same cause."

The common law rule as to the nature of the partners' liability for partnership obligations was not changed by the Uniform Partnership Act. But in some states it has been modified by the enactment of statutes which are sometimes referred to as *joint debtor statutes*. The general effect of such statutes is to make the position of the creditor more favorable as against the individual partners. As a rule they permit the firm creditor to proceed to take judgment against those partners upon whom he has been able to get service, and do not permit a filing of a plea in abatement. After judgment has been taken against the partners who were served, the judgment may be satisfied out of the firm property or out of the individual property of the partners against whom the plaintiff took judgment. The plaintiff may not, however, satisfy his judgment out of the separate property of the partner upon whom he did not get service and against whom he did not obtain judgment. If the plaintiff got service on all the partners and obtained judgment against all of them, he may satisfy the judgment out of partnership assets or out of the assets of the individual partners.

Heaton v. Schaeffer
340 Okla. 631, 126 P. 797 (1912)

This was an action by Henry Schaeffer (plaintiff) against C. H. Beach and W. C. Heaton, as partners (defendants). Judgment against W. C. Heaton individually, and he brought error. Reversed and remanded.

This suit was brought to recover the price of some whiskies and other saloon supplies. No service was obtained on Beach. There was a verdict and judgment against Heaton individually, and he brought error. It was his position that the judgment should have been taken against both himself and Beach. He relied on sections 5008 and 5619, Comp. Laws. Section 5008 provides that: "Every general partner is liable to third persons for all the obligations of the partnership, jointly with his copartners." Section 5619 provides that: "Where the action is against two or more defendants, and one or more shall have been served, but not all of them, the plaintiff may proceed as follows: First, if the action be against defendants jointly indebted upon contract, he may proceed against the defendants served unless the court may otherwise direct; and if he recovers judgment, it may be entered against all the defendants thus jointly indebted, so far only as that it may be enforced against the joint property of all, and the separate property of the defendants served."

RASSER, C. It is reluctantly concluded that defendant's contention is correct. The common law doctrine as to partnership obligations survives in this state, except so far as it has been modified by Section 5619, quoted above. That section enables a creditor to obtain judgment against joint obligors by service against only one, so far as the judgment affects joint property, thus changing the rule at common law that all joint obligors must be summoned, but prevents the judgment from being enforced against the individual property of the obligors not served. The statute does not permit an individual judgment to be rendered in a suit against a partnership. The theory is that, the debt being a joint one, the judgment must be joint.

In *Peabody v. Oleson*, 15 Colo. App. 346, 62 P. 234, in passing upon a similar statute, the court said: "The above section only provides a method of suing a partnership in addition to the remedy then existing. It made the service of summons upon one partner sufficient to bring the partnership into court and bind its property by the judgment. In such case no personal judgment could be obtained against the partners not served; and, as to them, the judgment rendered could bind only their interests in the partnership property. The judgment should be against the partnership, and in a proper manner the individual property of the member or members served might be reached for the purpose of satisfying it."

Many states have by statute made all contracts which were joint at common law both joint and several, and under such statutes an individual judgment can be rendered against one partner on a partnership debt. Our statute with reference to partnership debts makes them the joint debt of the partners. Reversed and remanded.

TORT LIABILITY

The liability of partners for tort is joint and several. The effect of this rule is that if one of the partners commits a tort while acting within the scope of the partnership business, all of the other partners are collectively and individually liable to the injured party. It is not necessary that the injured party sue all of the partners jointly, as in the case of firm contracts; he may proceed against any or all of them. The principles of agency law are applicable to this situation.

The tort liability of partners is the same both at common law and under the Uniform Partnership Act. Sec. 13 of the Act provides that the partnership is liable for any loss or injury caused to a third person by a tortious act performed by a partner acting in the partnership business, and Sec. 15 (a) provides that such liability is both joint and several.

CRIMINAL LIABILITY

At common law one partner is not liable for the criminal act of another partner unless he either participates in the act or authorizes it. This rule applies both to felonies and to misdemeanors.

Some special criminal statutes do have the effect of making a partner liable for violations of the statutes committed by his partner while acting in behalf of the partnership. Some of the statutes place the liability upon the firm itself. Such statutes would perhaps better be referred to as "quasi-criminal" statutes. Usually they have to do with such matters as securing a license before selling certain products or offering certain services, or obtaining authority from a designated official before performing some act. Violation of such a statute is usually punishable by the levying of a fine.

LIABILITY OF INCOMING PARTNERS

If A and B are carrying on a business as partners and agree to admit C as a new partner, the legal effect of the admission of C is to dissolve the old partnership of A and B and to create a new partnership of A, B, and C. If the firm of A and B had a creditor X, is C liable in any way to X? Unless C, in his partnership agreement with A and B, agreed to become responsible for the debts of the old partnership, C would not be *severally* obligated to X; that is, he would not be liable to X out of his own personal estate. But any contribution that C made to the new firm of A, B, and C would be available for the payment of X's claim. If C agreed with A and B that he would assume liability for the debts of the old firm of A and B, the contract would be valid and enforceable by A and B as against C. Moreover, X could enforce the agreement against C provided it could be shown that the agreement was for the benefit of X. Although there is no privity of contract as between C and X, and X has paid C no consideration for C's promise, most courts would permit X to hold C liable on his promise upon a third-party beneficiary theory. In such case X is a creditor beneficiary.[1]

Stephens v. Neely
161 Ark. 114, 255 S. W. 562 (1923)

This was a suit by H. G. Stephens and G. H. Friberg, as executors of the estate of Helena Hanks, deceased (plaintiffs) against M. Neely and Jack Mc-

[1] See section entitled Third-Party Beneficiaries in Chapter 13 of this text.

Donald (defendants). Judgment for plaintiffs against Jack McDonald, but in favor of M. Neely, and plaintiffs appealed. Affirmed.

Plaintiffs brought this suit against Jack McDonald and M. Neely, alleging that they were partners under the firm name of McDonald Bros. and seeking to recover upon a promissory note for $10,000, dated March 27, 1914, and payable to the order of Mrs. Helena Hanks, and signed by McDonald Bros.

It was proved that this note was given as a renewal of a similar note for the same amount executed in 1910, payable to the same person and signed by McDonald Bros.

According to the evidence adduced in behalf of plaintiffs, a firm composed of W. D. Reeves, Dan McDonald, and Jack McDonald was organized in 1889, to operate a sawmill in eastern Arkansas. The business prospered and continued until 1893, when W. D. Reeves withdrew from the firm. In 1905 Dan McDonald died. His widow continued in the business and it was run in the partnership name until some time in March, 1914, when Mrs. McDonald sold out her interest in the business to Jack McDonald and M. Neely. The note in this suit was given for money borrowed by the firm in 1910, and was a renewal note (renewed March 27, 1914).

HART, J. Jack McDonald made no defense to the action against him on the note by the plaintiffs. It seems that the main purpose of the action was to charge M. Neely as a partner with Jack McDonald on the renewal note which the firm of McDonald Bros. had executed to Mrs. Helena Hanks in the sum of $10,000 on March 27, 1914.

The plaintiffs insist that the court erred in giving the following instruction: "If you find from the evidence that Neely was not a partner when the note was executed, but that he after became a partner, and, by special promise or agreement, assumed liability for the debt evidenced by the note, then the court charges you as a matter of law that he is liable only on such special promise or agreement." We cannot agree with counsel for the plaintiffs in this contention. There is no presumption that an incoming partner of an existing partnership assumes liability for the previous debts of the concern. He is not bound for such debts unless he makes himself so by express agreement or by such conduct as will raise the presumption of a special promise. *Ringo v. Wing*, 49 Ark. 457, 5 S. W. 787. The promissory note signed by McDonald Bros. is the basis of this action. The law of partnership is but a branch of the law of principal and agent. The ground of liability of one partner for the acts of the other is that of implied agency within the scope of the partnership. The credit of a new member of a firm does not enter into the consideration of the creditors of the old firm, and it would be manifestly unjust to hold the new partner liable unless he, by an express or implied agreement, assumed the debts of the old firm. Hence, if Neely is personally liable at all in the present case, it is upon an express or implied agreement to pay the debts of the old firm. If his liability depends upon making such an agreement, he has the right to plead the statute of limitations in regard thereto, and his plea of the statute in bar of his liability could not be defeated by showing that his partner had made a payment on the old indebtedness since the time it is claimed he became liable therefor. In such cases it will be presumed that the partner made the payment in discharge of his own obligation, and the burden of proof would still be upon the creditor to show that the incoming partner has assumed the debts of the old firm. Hence this assignment of error is not well taken.

Judgment affirmed.

CREDITORS' RIGHTS

FIRM CREDITORS

A firm creditor may bring action against the partnership and reduce his claim to a judgment. In the satisfaction of his judgment the creditor may levy upon the assets of the partnership and sell them, as provided by statute. Since the separate property of the individual partners is also subject to the payment of firm debts, the judgment creditor of the firm may also levy upon and sell the separate property of the partners, in satisfaction of his judgment against the firm. Unless required by statute to do so, the judgment creditor of the firm is not required first to proceed against the firm assets before levying upon the assets of the individual partners.

INDIVIDUAL CREDITORS

We are familiar with the fact that a judgment creditor may levy upon the personal assets of the debtor and sell them in order to pay his judgment. But suppose that the debtor is a member of a partnership and that his assets, aside from his interest in the partnership, are insufficient to satisfy the judgment. May the judgment creditor levy upon and sell enough of the property of the partnership to satisfy his judgment?

The difficulty has always been to find some way of reaching the debtor partner's interest. A partner's property rights, aside from his right to participate in the management, which an outsider cannot invade, consist of (1) his rights in specific partnership property and (2) his interest in the partnership, i.e. his share of the profits and surplus.[1] As to the first of these, we have already seen that a partner does not own separately any part of specific partnership property. He has only a right together with his partners to possess it for partnership purposes and to have it applied, upon dissolution of the partnership, to discharge the liabilities of the partnership and the partners. Consequently, if the individual judgment creditor were to have the sheriff levy upon any of the specific partnership property, the other partners would have a right to complain that the levy is invalid since neither they nor the partnership owes the individual judgment creditor anything.

[1] Uniform Partnership Act, Secs. 24, 26.

Because of this difficulty, some courts refused any relief to an individual judgment creditor. Many of the courts, however, permitted him to levy upon and sell the debtor partner's interest in the partnership. But this "solution" of the problem was far from satisfactory. The only way in which the purchaser of such an interest at an execution sale could liquidate his interest was to ask a court of equity for an accounting and liquidation of the partnership, and such a procedure usually proved unsatisfactory to all parties concerned.

The Uniform Partnership Act sets up a more practicable method of permitting the individual judgment creditor to satisfy his judgment out of the debtor partner's interest in the firm. Sec. 28 of the Act provides that the court "may charge the interest of the debtor partner with payment of the unsatisfied amount of such judgment debt with interest thereon; and may then or later appoint a receiver of his share of the profits, and of any other money due or to fall due to him in respect of the partnership, and make all other orders, directions, accounts, and inquiries which the debtor partner might have made, or which the circumstances of the case may require."

REVIEW CASES

1. Wolff sued Madden and Green on an acceptance of Midland Lumber Co., a partnership which had been composed of Madden and Brown at the time when the acceptance was executed. Green contended that he was not liable on the acceptance since he became a member of the partnership after its execution. Was Green liable? (Wolff v. Madden et al., 6 Wash. 514, 33 P. 975)

2. Teague, while riding a bicycle, was struck by a truck which Martin and Clark owned as copartners. Clark was driving the truck at the time of the accident. Martin set up as a defense that his partner Clark was not on firm business but was using the truck on his personal account. If the evidence showed that this was true, would Martin be liable? (Teague v. Martin et al., 228 Mass. 458, 117 N. E. 844)

3. Snively sued Matheson and Dickson, copartners, to foreclose a chattel mortgage on a grading outfit, given to secure a promissory note signed by Matheson. The partnership was engaged in the contracting business. Dickson denied that Matheson had authority to bind the firm by executing the note and mortgage, since the partnership was a non-trading partnership. The articles of copartnership provided that neither partner could incur any such liability without the consent of the other. Judgment for whom? (Snively v. Matheson et al., 12 Wash. 88)

4. John Farson, Sr., and John Farson were partners in the name of Farson, Son & Co., carrying on a business of buying and selling bonds and other securities. A salesman of the firm sold to the First National Bank of Ann Arbor five bonds which were owned by the partnership. The principal

and interest of the bonds were guaranteed in writing and signed by John Farson, Sr. The bonds were not paid at maturity, and the partners refused to indemnify the bank, which brought an action on the guaranty contract. The partnership denied liability, contending that John Farson, Sr., had exceeded his authority. Holding? (First National Bank of Ann Arbor v. Farson et al., 226 N. Y. 218, 123 N. E. 490)

5. E. A. Kline, David Kline, and Morris Kline were partners doing business under the firm name Kline, on premises which they leased from Lawer for a five-year term at $177.50 per month. A renewal lease for a second five-year period was executed and was signed in the firm name by David Kline. This lease called for a monthly rental of $177.50 for the first two years and $190 during the remainder of the term. A dispute later rose over the increased rental, and the result was an action for rent brought by Lawer against the partnership. The defendants claimed that David Kline had no authority to execute the lease in question. Judgment for whom? (Lawer v. Kline, 39 Wyo. 285, 270 P. 1077)

Dissolution and Winding Up of Partnerships

42

A partnership relation, as we have seen, is established by a contract among the partners whereby they associate themselves together "for the purpose of carrying on a business for profit." If one or more of the partners cease to be associated with the others in carrying on the business, the relationship produced by the contract agreement is clearly destroyed. The legal effect of the changed relationship is the *dissolution* of the partnership.

The dissolution of a partnership is not necessarily followed by a discontinuance of the business which the partnership has been carrying on. It is common for a partnership to be dissolved and a new one immediately organized to take its place with no interruption to the business. In many cases, however, the dissolution entails the discontinuance of the business. In such cases the dissolution is followed by the *winding up* of the business of the partnership. This winding up is the process of liquidating the assets of the firm, paying firm debts, and distributing the capital and profits, if any, to the partners. Only when the winding up has been fully accomplished is the legal existence of the partnership *terminated*.

The distinctions between dissolution, winding up, and termination are explicitly made in the Uniform Partnership Act. Sec. 29 defines dissolution as "the change in the relation of the partners caused by any partner ceasing to be associated in the carrying on as distinguished from the winding up of the business." Sec. 30 states: "On dissolution the partnership is not terminated, but continues until the winding up of partnership affairs is complete."

CAUSES OF DISSOLUTION

A partnership may be dissolved (1) by the act of one or more of the partners, (2) by operation of law, or (3) by decree of the court.

DISSOLUTION BY ACT OF THE PARTNERS

A partnership may be dissolved by the act of the partners in the following ways: (1) by the expiration of a fixed time or the accomplishment of a particular undertaking; (2) by the agreement of all the partners; (3) by the express will of one or more of the partners; (4) by the expulsion of one or more of the partners.

If the original partnership agreement provides that the partnership is to continue for a fixed period, the partnership will be automatically dissolved upon the expiration of that period. Likewise, if the partnership agreement provides that the partnership is organized to accomplish a particular undertaking, the partnership will dissolve when such undertaking has been accomplished.

Even though a partnership has been organized for a definite term or for the accomplishment of a definite purpose, it may be dissolved by the mutual agreement of all the partners at any time prior to the time designated in the partnership agreement. In this respect it is like any other contract. Consideration is found in the mutual promises of the partners.

If a partnership is formed without designation of a fixed term or of a specific undertaking to be accomplished, any one or more of the partners may dissolve the partnership without being liable to the other partners for breach of the partnership agreement. Such a partnership is a partnership at will.

If the partnership has been formed for a definite time or for the accomplishment of a specific undertaking, a partner does not have the *right* to dissolve it earlier, but he has the *power* to do so. Since the relationship between partners is of such a personal nature, courts of equity will not decree specific performance of partnership agreements. As the court said, in the case of *McCollum v. McCollum*,[1] "Under the law a partnership calling for the personal services of the partners can always be dissolved, even though it constitutes a breach of contract. The right to dissolve may not exist but the power to dissolve always exists." However, a partner is liable to the other partners if he thus wrongfully terminates the partnership relationship.

The Uniform Partnership Act provides that dissolution may be brought about without violating the partnership agreement "by the expulsion of

[1] 67 S. W. (2d) 1055 (1934).

any partner from the business bona fide in accordance with such a power conferred by the agreement between the partners." [1]

Solomon and Others v. Hollander and Another
55 Mich. 256, 21 N. W. 336 (1884)

This was an action by Solomon and others (plaintiffs) against Hollander and another (defendants). Judgment for defendants, and plaintiffs appealed. Reversed and new trial ordered.

Plaintiffs, dealers in jewelry, sought to charge Hollander and Kirkwood as partners upon a promissory note for $791.92, bearing date of November 9, 1882, and signed "Hollander & Kirkwood." The note was given by Hollander, but Kirkwood denied that any partnership existed between defendants at the date of the note.

The evidence tended to show that on July 6, 1882, Hollander and Kirkwood entered into a written agreement for a partnership for one year from August 1, 1882, in the business of buying and selling jewelry, clocks, watches, etc. at Ishpeming, Michigan. Business was begun under this agreement, and continued until the latter part of October, 1882, when Kirkwood, becoming dissatisfied, locked up the goods and excluded Hollander altogether from the business. He also caused notice to be given to all persons with whom the firm had had dealings that the partnership was dissolved, and had the following inserted in the local column of the paper published at Ishpeming: "The co-partnership heretofore existing between Mr. C. H. Kirkwood and one Hollander, as jewelers, has ceased to exist; Mr. Kirkwood having purchased the interest of the latter." This was not signed by anyone. A few days later Hollander went to Chicago, and there, on November 9, 1882, he bought from plaintiffs, in the name of Hollander & Kirkwood, goods in their line amounting to $791.92, and gave to plaintiffs therefor the promissory note now in suit. When the purchase was completed, Hollander took away the goods in his satchel. Plaintiffs had before had no dealings with Hollander & Kirkwood, but they had heard there was such a firm, and were not aware of its dissolution. They claimed to have made the sale in good faith and in the belief that the firm was still in existence. On the other hand, Kirkwood claimed that Hollander and plaintiffs had conspired together to defraud him by a pretended sale to the firm of goods which plaintiffs knew Hollander intended to appropriate exclusively to himself.

The trial judge instructed the jury as follows: That Kirkwood, notwithstanding the written agreement, had a right to withdraw from the partnership at any time, leaving matters between him and Hollander to be adjusted between them amicably or in the courts; and for the purposes of this case it made no difference whether Kirkwood was right or wrong in bringing the partnership to an end. If wrong, he might be liable to Hollander in damages

[1] Sec. 31 (1) (d).

for the breach of his contract. Also, that when partners are dissatisfied, or they cannot get along together, and one partner withdraws, the partnership is then at an end as to the public and parties with whom the partnership deals, and neither partner can make contracts in the future to bind the partnership, provided the retiring partner gives the proper notice. Also, that if they should find from the evidence that there was trouble between Hollander and Kirkwood prior to the sale of the goods and the giving of the note, that Kirkwood informed Hollander in substance that he would have no more dealings with him as partner, that he took possession of all of the goods and locked them up, and from that time they ceased to do business, then the partnership was dissolved. Further, that whether sufficient notice had been given of the dissolution was a question for the jury.

There was a verdict and judgment for defendants, and plaintiffs appealed.

COOLEY, C.J. We think the judge committed no error in his instructions respecting the dissolution of the partnership. The rule on this subject is thus stated in an early New York case: The right of a partner to dissolve, it is said, "is a right inseparably incident to every partnership. There can be no such thing as an indissoluble partnership. Every partner has an indefeasible right to dissolve the partnership as to all future contracts by publishing his own volition to that effect; and after such publication the other members of the firm have no capacity to bind him by any contract. Even where partners covenant with each other that the partnership shall continue seven years, either partner may dissolve it the next day, proclaiming his determination for that purpose; the only consequence being that he thereby subjects himself to a claim for damages for a breach of his covenant. The power given by one partner to another to make joint contracts for them both is not only a revocable power, but a man can do no act to divest himself of the capacity to revoke it." *Skinner v. Dayton*, 19 Johns. (N. Y.) 513.

The instruction respecting notice was also correct. No court can determine for all cases what shall be sufficient notice and what shall not be. The question must necessarily be one of fact. But we think the judge erred in receiving evidence of Hollander's admissions or declarations tending to show fraudulent collusion between him and the plaintiff. For this error there must be a new trial.

DISSOLUTION BY OPERATION OF LAW

A partnership is dissolved by operation of law (1) by any event which makes the business of the partnership unlawful, or (2) by the death of a partner, or (3) by the bankruptcy of any partner or the partnership. When dissolution takes place by operation of law, notice to creditors and others is not necessary.

If the business carried on by the partnership was legal when the partnership was formed but becomes illegal by the enactment of certain legislation, the partnership is dissolved by operation of law. For example, the adoption of the Eighteenth Amendment and the enactment of the Volstead Act resulted in the dissolution of many partnerships.

The personal relation between partners is such that the death of a partner dissolves the partnership by operation of law. But if the partnership agreement contains a provision that the partnership is not to terminate in the event of the death of one of the partners but is to be continued by the estate of the deceased partner, or by some designated relative, the provision will be binding. Under such a provision the partnership is dissolved by operation of law, but a new partnership is immediately created which continues the business of the original partnership.

The bankruptcy of a partner or of the partnership dissolves the partnership by operation of law.

DISSOLUTION BY COURT DECREE

Under certain circumstances a court of equity may dissolve a partnership, appoint a receiver, and order an accounting and winding up of the partnership affairs. Among the causes which will justify a court of equity in decreeing the dissolution of a partnership are (1) insanity, (2) incapacity, (3) misconduct, and (4) failing condition of the business.

If a partner is adjudged insane by a court of law, such adjudication in itself does not automatically dissolve the partnership, but it will form the basis for dissolution by court decree. Proof that a partner is of unsound mind is usually sufficient to obtain a dissolution of a partnership, even though the partner has not been judicially declared insane.

Incapacity so serious that it prevents a partner from carrying out his part of the partnership agreement will usually be held to be sufficient grounds for decreeing the dissolution of the partnership. This is true unless the incapacity appears to be only temporary in nature.

A court of equity will usually decree a dissolution of the partnership upon a showing that one of the partners has been guilty of willful and persistent misconduct. Such misconduct may take many different forms. The partner may be dishonest, he may be a habitual drunkard, he may absent himself from the place of business and refuse to do his part of the work, or he may willfully breach some specific provision of the partnership agreement. For these acts and omissions, as well as many others, courts of equity will usually grant relief to the innocent partner or partners by decreeing the dissolution of the partnership. The court will also allow damages against the erring partner.

If the business is in such failing condition that it seems clearly incapable of regaining its financial stability and rendering a profit to the members of the partnership, the equity court will, upon petition and a proper showing, decree the dissolution of the partnership.[1]

[1] Uniform Partnership Act, Sec. 32.

Creel v. Creel

73 F. (2d) 107 (1934)

This was a suit by Robert T. Creel (plaintiff) against Edwin J. Creel (defendant). From an order appointing a receiver, defendant appealed. Affirmed.

It was alleged in the bill of complaint that plaintiff and defendant were brothers, and became equal partners in an automobile sales and service business; that defendant was interested in the inventive arts and was frequently absent from the business when engaged in affairs relating to his inventions; that by reason of overwork, disappointments, and threatened litigation concerning his inventions from the year 1926 to 1933, defendant became highly overwrought and nervous, and as a result grew exacting and arbitrary in his conduct relating to the business and frequently threatened to wreck and disrupt it; that in order to pacify defendant an agreement was made between the partners whereby defendant was permitted to absent himself from the conduct of the business for a period of two years, which agreement was further extended for one year, expiring January 1, 1933, and that during that time defendant withdrew money from the firm in excess of plaintiff; that upon the expiration of the agreement defendant continued to absent himself from the business, and had not returned thereto, nor cooperated with plaintiff in the conduct thereof, but was hostile and defiant toward plaintiff and neglected his obligations as a partner; and that during the period while the agreement was in force, although frequently requested by plaintiff to notify the firm's bookkeeper in respect to amounts withdrawn by defendant, defendant refused to do so, and plaintiff was without information at any time during the period as to the precise time and amount of defendant's withdrawals, and consequently of the firm's bank balance. The bill prayed for the appointment of a receiver and for the dissolution of the partnership. A receiver was appointed and defendant appealed.

MARTIN, C.J. We think that the action of the trial justice in appointing a receiver for the partnership was not erroneous. The record, fairly considered, discloses that there are such irreconcilable disagreements and dissensions between the partners in regard to the conduct of their affairs as to endanger the partnership goodwill and property. In such case the court is justified in appointing a receiver for the preservation of the assets and the liquidation of the partnership's affairs. 23 *R. C. L.* 30.

In *Jones v. Jones*, 229 Ky. 41, 16 S. W. (2d) 504, a receiver was appointed for a farm partnership conducted by two brothers. In upholding the validity of an order appointing the receiver prior to the hearing on dissolution, the court said: "The relationship existing between the partners is so strained and bitter that it is impossible to even hope for the slightest cooperation between them. There is absolutely nothing to do but to appoint a receiver to take charge of the partnership property pending a final settlement of the partnership affairs."

In *Reed v. Beals*, 77 Fla. 801, 82 So. 234, the court said: "From the examination which we have made of the authorities on this subject, we think the law may be considered as settled, that whenever the intervention of a court of equity becomes necessary, in consequence of dissensions or disagreements between the partners, to effect a settlement and closing of the partnership concerns, upon bill filed by any of the partners, showing either a breach of duty on the part of the other partners, or a violation of the agreement of partnership, a receiver will be appointed as a matter of course."

The order of the court appointing the receiver is affirmed with costs.

EFFECT OF DISSOLUTION

ON AUTHORITY OF PARTNERS

Upon the dissolution of the partnership the partners cease to be the general agents of one another with authority to bind the partnership and the other partners with respect to matters within the scope of the partnership business. After dissolution the partners have only the authority that is necessary to wind up the affairs of the partnership. The liquidating partners have no authority to continue the operation of the business in the usual way or to enter into new transactions. For example, they may sell and liquidate the stock of merchandise on hand, but as a rule they have no authority to order new merchandise or to pledge the credit of the partnership for it.

It is important to observe, however, that persons who have dealt with the firm and who have extended credit to it in the past have a right to presume that it is still a going concern unless they have knowledge or notice that it has been dissolved. For this reason it becomes imperative that proper *notice* of dissolution of the firm be given, in order to make certain that the firm will not be bound upon some contract negotiated by a member of the firm with a third party who has no knowledge of the dissolution of the firm. A third party is entitled to *actual notice* of dissolution if he has in the past extended credit to the firm. To other parties the firm must give *constructive notice* by placing in a newspaper an advertisement to the effect that the partnership has been dissolved. Notice is not required when dissolution takes place by operation of law or by decree of the court.

In a case where a partner withdraws or retires from the partnership but the business continues to operate under a reorganized partnership, the retiring partner must give actual notice to third persons who have extended credit to the firm prior to his retirement, and constructive notice to everyone else; otherwise he may be liable to third parties who extend credit to the firm in the belief that he is still a member of the firm.

ON PARTNER'S EXISTING LIABILITY

The dissolution of the partnership does not of itself discharge the existing liability of any partner.[1] Moreover, a partner who retires or withdraws from a partnership is not released from his liability to the creditors of the old partnership even where the other partners agree to assume all partnership debts and absolve him from any liability upon partnership debts and contracts. It is evident that his partners have no legal authority or capacity to "contract away" the rights of the creditors of the firm against the retiring partner. The only way in which the retiring partner may gain a release from the partnership debts is to secure from the firm creditors themselves such a release. To bind them to such a promise would require some new consideration. Of course, if the creditors should agree to substitute the remaining members of the partnership for the retiring partner and hence to release him from his liability, a novation might take place, in which case the retiring partner would be discharged of his liabilities.

Security State Bank of Benson v. Nelson
171 Minn. 332, 214 N. W. 51 (1927)

This was an action by the Security State Bank of Benson (plaintiff) against A. E. Nelson. Judgment for plaintiff, and defendant appealed. Affirmed.

On February 1, 1922, seven persons, defendant being one, signed an agreement forming a "joint partnership to do business under the name of Cash Sales Company." The declared purpose was to buy the stock of the Benson Mercantile Company and close it out. Each person was to pay in $500 and be an equal partner. It was stated in the agreement that Hagen, one of the partners, should be manager, also that the first available money should be paid on a note given to plaintiff for $5,000 to help pay for the same. This note was renewed January 4, 1923, and some payments were made thereon. Another note for $4,000 was given June 13, 1923, for money loaned by plaintiff to the partnership and used in its business. Part payments were made on this note also. The defense was, in substance, that defendant sold his share in the partnership to Hagen in April, 1922; also that the partnership did not confine the business to selling out the stock bought, but replenished the same and so continued to do business. There was no claim that the money loaned by plaintiff went to the use of anyone else than the partnership; nor that any notice was ever given to plaintiff that defendant had transferred his interest therein. All the partners except Hagen testified to not being informed of defendant's deal with Hagen until April, 1923.

HOLT, J. It being established by a written agreement executed by the defendant that a partnership was formed of which he became a member, and

[1] Uniform Partnership Act, Sec. 36.

that the plaintiff received the notes of the partnership for money loaned the firm, it follows that all the partners are liable on such notes, since neither actual nor constructive notice was had by the plaintiff of any change in the partnership. This is so elementary that we refrain from a discussion or citation of authorities. There is no evidence that the plaintiff was ever notified of any supposed limitation to the scope of the partnership business. The natural inference would be that the buyer of a mercantile stock in a place like Benson would continue the business theretofore carried on there. Nor can there be any defense in the fact that, when the loans were obtained from the plaintiff, it was not willing to have the defendant as an indorser or guarantor on the partnership notes, since it already had defendant's obligations to the full extent permitted by law. Concede that a change in the personnel of a partnership dissolves it, neither section 7412, G. S. 1923 (section 29 of the Uniform Partnership Act), nor any other provision in that act, furnishes a defense to these notes. On the contrary, (I) of subdivision (b) of (1), Sec. 7418, G. S. 1923 (section 35 of the Act) clearly entitles the plaintiff to recover as one who "had extended credit to the partnership prior to dissolution and had no knowledge or notice of the dissolution." Judgment affirmed.

WINDING UP

RIGHT TO WIND UP PARTNERSHIP AFFAIRS

Sec. 37 of the Uniform Partnership Act states: "Unless otherwise agreed the partners who have not wrongfully dissolved the partnership or the legal representative of the last surviving partner, not bankrupt, has the right to wind up the partnership affairs; provided, however, that any partner, his legal representative or his assignee, upon cause shown, may obtain winding up by the court." In the latter case the court may appoint a receiver to wind up the business. If a partner retires, dies, or becomes bankrupt, the remaining partner or partners may wind up the firm's affairs.

Without an agreement to the contrary, the partners who are entitled to wind up the partnership should not continue to operate the business; if they do so, they may be compelled in a court of equity to wind up the business. The Uniform Partnership Act provides that when a partnership is dissolved by the retirement or death of a partner, and the remaining partners, without agreement with him or his representative and without settling accounts with him or his representative, continue operating the business, "he or his legal representative as against such persons or partnership may have the value of his interest at the date of dissolution ascertained, and shall receive as an ordinary creditor an amount equal to the value of his interest in the dissolved partnership with interest, or, at his option or at the option of his legal representative, in lieu of interest, the profits attributable to the use of his right in the property of the dissolved partnership. . . ." [1] The option here provided is of course advantageous to the retired partner or to the estate of the deceased partner, for if the remaining partners have run the business at a loss, the first alternative will permit the retired partner or the deceased partner's representative to escape such loss, but if at a profit, the second alternative will permit him to share in the profit. This is an equitable arrangement, since the remaining partner or partners had no right to continue the operation of the business after the dissolution of the partnership without settling accounts with the retired partner or the deceased partner's estate.

Froess v. Froess
284 Pa. 369, 131 A. 276 (1925)

This was an action by Sarah L. Froess, administratrix of the estate of Philip J. Froess, deceased (plaintiff) against Jacob Froess (defendant) for an accounting. From the decree of the lower court both parties appealed. Decree for plaintiff modified and affirmed.

Philip and Jacob Froess were equal partners, engaged in the sale of pianos and other musical instruments, and had been so jointly interested for many years. Philip died on January 29, 1920, and Jacob continued the business as survivor for some time thereafter. Letters of administration upon the estate of the decedent were granted to the widow, and negotiations looking to the payment of her husband's share of the assets, based on a valuation of the partnership property made immediately after his death, followed, but no satisfactory arrangement as to payment could be agreed on. No consent to the continuance of the firm business was given, but the same was managed by Jacob, who took exclusive possession of the assets. The firm's affairs were not settled within a reasonable time, and a bill was filed on August 3, 1921, asking for the appointment of a receiver, an accounting by the liquidating partner, and a decree that the share found due be paid to plaintiff. After an answer and hearing, a decree was entered on October 26, 1921, granting the relief prayed for. In the following May a statement was rendered, to which some 2,500 exceptions were filed. During the pendency of the hearing notice was given of the purpose of the administratrix to demand her husband's share of the assets, with interest on the value thereof from the time of dissolution, rather than a share of any profits, and subsequently a formal election to so claim was filed in writing.

The bill for an accounting averred the amount to be $103,820.17, of which one-half belonged to each partner, and this was admitted to be correct by the answer of the defendant, but on November 9, 1923, an amendment to the latter was allowed, averring the net assets to be $90,577.71. The evidence showed an audit of the accounts by Hickey, dated one day after the death of Philip, which furnished the figures set forth in the bill. The figure of $90,577.71 was

---

[1] Sec. 42.

later established by one Brown, accountant for defendant. The second calculation was adopted by the court. This finding of fact by the court was assigned as error, as was the final decree based thereon.

SADLER, J. Admittedly, the partnership was dissolved by the death of the copartner. After the death it became the duty of the survivor to settle the partnership affairs, and all authority on his part ceased, except such as was necessary for the winding up of the business, or completing transactions then begun, but not yet finished. Uniform Partnership Act, Sec. 33.

The interest of the decedent is fixed by a valuation as of the time of the dissolution, and all members of the firm are entitled to a part of the surplus of assets over the amount necessary to pay the creditors of the firm. Partnership Act, Secs. 38, 40; also Secs. 18, 25.

"The plain duty of the surviving partner is to collect the assets of the partnership, receive and receipt for payments, pay and settle partnership debts, settle and wind up the partnership business and distribute the net surplus among the parties entitled to it." *Herron v. Wampler*, 194 Pa. 277, 45 A. 81.

The determination of the right of the deceased partner, where there has been no agreement to continue the business or dispose of the estate's interest for a fixed sum—facts found by the court in the present case—may be controlled by an election of the personal representative of the decedent to take a share of the assets and profits which have been gained by the use of the property prior to actual settlement. *Maloney's Estate*, 233 Pa. 614 82 A. 958. Or, in lieu of the latter, interest may be demanded on the value of the property, estimated as of the date of dissolution.

"The legal rule is fixed on this subject. If the survivors of a partnership carry on the concern, and enter into new transactions with the partnership funds, they do so at their peril, and the representatives of the deceased may elect to call on them for the capital, with a share of the profits, or with interest. If no profits are made, or even if a loss is incurred, they must be charged with interest on the funds they use, and the whole loss will be theirs." *Brown's Appeal*, 89 Pa. 139.

Following the recognized rule, the right to so choose was expressly provided in the Uniform Partnership Act, Sec. 42. The plaintiff is, therefore, entitled to a decree to the effect that she is entitled to elect to take one-half of the estate as of the date of the dissolution of the partnership, together with interest.

DISTRIBUTION OF ASSETS

WHERE PARTNERSHIP IS SOLVENT.   Usually, no serious difficulties arise in the distribution of the firm assets where the partnership is solvent. After the payment of the firm creditors the remaining firm assets are distributed in the following order: (1) the partners who have made advances or contributions to the firm are reimbursed; (2) the capital contributions of the partners are returned to them; (3) any balance is distributed to the partners as profits. The partners share equally in such profits, unless they have otherwise agreed.

WHERE PARTNERSHIP IS INSOLVENT BUT ALL PARTNERS ARE SOLVENT. If the partnership is insolvent and unable to pay the firm creditors in full, but all the partners are solvent, the partners must contribute to satisfy such liabilities. Unless the partners have agreed otherwise, they share equally in the losses, regardless of their capital contributions to the firm assets.

WHERE PARTNERSHIP AND ONE OR MORE PARTNERS ARE INSOLVENT. The distribution of assets and the sharing of losses raise greater problems where the partnership is insolvent and one or more of the partners are insolvent. Such a situation involves not only the assets and creditors of the firm but also the assets and creditors of the individual partners. In such cases the equity courts have long applied the doctrine of the *marshaling of assets*, and this doctrine has been incorporated in both the Uniform Partnership Act and the National Bankruptcy Act. The rules governing the marshaling of assets may be briefly stated as follows:

1. The partnership creditors have first claim to the partnership assets, and the separate creditors of each partner have first claim to the personal assets of that partner.

2. If the creditors of an individual partner cannot satisfy their claims out of the assets of that partner, they have no claim against the individual assets of the other partners; but if any partnership assets remain after all partnership creditors have been paid, then the unsatisfied creditors of the individual partners are entitled to claim payment on a pro rata basis out of the remaining partnership assets.

3. If the partnership creditors cannot satisfy their claims out of the partnership assets, and if not all the partners are insolvent, the partnership creditors are legally entitled to satisfy the balance of their claims out of the individual assets of the solvent partner or partners *after* the claims of the separate creditors of the solvent partner or partners have been satisfied in full.

REVIEW CASES

1. The Marquette Cloak & Suit Co. sued the partnership of Netter & Meyer on account for merchandise sold and delivered in 1931 and 1932. The partnership had dealt in the past with the suit company, and the business was known as a partnership. Meyer denied liability on the account sued upon, on the ground that she had withdrawn from the partnership in 1930. She gave no notice of her withdrawal to the Marquette Cloak & Suit Co. Holding? (Marquette Cloak & Suit Co. v. Netter & Meyer et al., 151 So. 820)

2. Borelli and Vitelli were partners until Borelli's death in 1937. Without formal dissolution Vitelli set aside a sum of money as a liability on the books as Borelli's interest in the partnership. No consent was granted to continue operating the partnership, but Vitelli did so until his death in 1941. In 1945 Borelli's widow, who was the sole beneficiary under his will, came to the United States, and in 1949 she made a formal claim for the sum set aside as Borelli's interest. The defense was the ten-year statute of limitations. Judgment for whom? (In re Vitelli's Estate, 92 N. Y. S.(2d) 322)

3. B. Callender & Co., a partnership, executed a note to Eustis. Hall, one of the partners, thereafter withdrew from the firm, which was immediately reorganized without interruption of business. Notice of the dissolution was printed in the newspaper, but no personal notice was given to Eustis. Hall was shortly afterward adjudicated a bankrupt. B. Callender & Co. later executed to Eustis a new note in renewal of the former one. The note was not paid, and Eustis brought suit, joining Hall with the new partners on the ground that he (Eustis) had not received legal notice of the dissolution of the old firm. Was Hall liable on the note? (Eustis v. Bolles et al., 146 Mass. 413, 16 N. E. 286)

4. Finkelstein Bros., a partnership, and the individual partners thereof were adjudged bankrupts in an involuntary proceeding. The partnership assets were insufficient to yield any surplus after payment of partnership debts. The Collector of Internal Revenue filed claim for an income tax assessed against Abraham Finkelstein, one of the partners, on income derived from the business of the partnership. Abraham Finkelstein had no personal assets. The Collector claimed that the tax against him should be paid out of the partnership assets prior to the partnership debts. The referee denied this claim. Ruling? (United States et al. v. Kaufman et al., 267 U. S. 408, 45 S. Ct. 322)

5. Bayer Bros., a partnership, bought and sold cotton goods and invested money in 160 shares of the capital stock of the Montville Finishing Corp. Differences arose between the partners, and on June 11, 1919, one of the partners gave notice that he would no longer continue in the partnership. Thereafter the partnership business ceased. On Aug. 13, 1919, the partner who became the defendant in this case purchased 76 shares of stock in the Montville Finishing Corp., without the knowledge of the other partners. On Oct. 22, 1919, all the partners signed an agreement formally dissolving the partnership and dividing the assets. Thereafter the other partners learned of the purchase of the stock and filed a suit in equity to have the shares declared for the benefit of all the partners. The defense showed that the other partners had earlier attempted to purchase the stock and had failed to do so. The further defense was that the partnership had terminated on June 11, 1919. Holding? (Bayer v. Bayer, 214 N. Y. S. 322)

Corporations

part **VIII**

Nature and
Classification of
Corporations

43

Since most large business enterprises and a large majority of the smaller ones are incorporated, and the formation of business corporations is at an accelerated rate, a knowledge of corporation law is obviously valuable to the person planning a business career.

Corporation law should not be thought of as an area of the law entirely distinct from the other great areas which we have studied. Most laymen seem to have this misapprehension. It is true that corporation law is concerned with a type of legal relationship between persons which is found nowhere else in the law. But to a very large extent the study of corporation law is the study of the application of the other great areas of the law to the form of business organization known as the business corporation. The corporation itself comes into being as the result of a contract or, upon occasion, a series of contracts. After it has been organized it is constantly engaged in the making and performance of contracts, involving many types of transactions—the buying and selling of real and personal property, the employment of personnel, the execution of leases, deeds, mortgages, the borrowing of money, the extension of credit, the execution and negotiation of negotiable instruments, and the like. In all these transactions the basic rules of contract law apply. Moreover, the corporation is liable under certain circumstances for the torts of its agents and employees, so that tort law is also involved in the study of corporation law. In this section we shall therefore be constantly encountering principles and rules of law which are already familiar to us.

HISTORICAL BACKGROUND

We saw earlier that the basic principles underlying our modern law of partnerships were worked out by the merchants of the Middle Ages and incorporated in the law merchant. But the basic principles of the modern business corporation trace back to the Roman law. The attribute which, more than anything else, differentiates the corporation from other types of business organization is the concept that it is a distinct legal being, separate and apart from the persons who compose it. It was the Roman lawyers and jurists who devised this principle of treating an association or aggregation of individuals as separate and distinct from the constituent members. The principle was never lost sight of during the Middle Ages and has passed intact to the modern business world.

In Rome the "corporate concept" was used principally for governmental purposes. Whether it was ever extended to the conduct of private business is not clear from the available records. In England it was first utilized for governmental and ecclesiastical bodies. The king, sensing the possibilities of stricter control and additional revenue, early claimed exclusive authority to grant "franchises" to groups who wished to become incorporated, and as a result the granting of franchises and liberties became a royal prerogative. But it was not until around 1600 that the corporate principle began to be applied to commercial enterprises.

It was the economic demands and challenges of the great period of exploration and colonization that produced this change. Vast trading corporations were created, not only in England but in some of the Continental countries, such as France and the Netherlands. We all know something from our history courses about the East India Company (1600), the Plymouth Company (1606), and the Hudson Bay Company (1670). These great trading companies resulted from necessity. The economic exploitation and development of the vast colonial areas which the English were establishing for themselves all over the world could not be accomplished through the use of the single proprietorship and the partnership. The economic risks were too great. The liability of the single proprietor and the partner was unlimited. Furthermore, neither type of business enterprise was adapted to the accumulation of sufficient capital for such vast undertakings. Some other type of business organization was necessary. It was at this point that the "corporation," which had for so long been used for governmental and ecclesiastical purposes, was adapted to the needs of business. The king granted franchises or charters to his courtiers and to others who had financial means. By such charters the shareholders in these vast corporations were in effect given privileges. Not only were they granted extraordinary opportunities for the economic exploitation and development of certain areas in England's rapidly growing empire, but they were also given certain governmental authority to "rule," in the name of the king, the areas over which they were granted monopolies. The corporation was held to be a separate legal entity, distinct and apart from the shareholders. The liability of the shareholders for the corporation's debts became limited to their investment in the corporation. Shares could be bought and sold without dissolving the corporation. As a result a type of business organization was devised which fairly well met the exigencies of the situation.

In this country, during the Colonial Period, the application of the "corporate concept" to business enterprises failed to develop. Not only was there little need for its use, since business was local and not extensive, but the colonists viewed the great trading corporations with disfavor as monopolies, the purveyors of special privileges, and generally undemocratic. It was only slowly that this attitude began to break down. Following the Revolutionary War the right to grant charters was vested in the state legislatures. At first any group of individuals who wanted a charter under which they could conduct a business had to secure from the state legislature a special statute granting them the privilege of operating as a corporation. This procedure proved to have decided drawbacks. If the group seeking a charter did not belong to the political party then in control of the state legislature, they found it practically impossible to obtain a charter. On the other hand, if the group had the favor of the controlling party in the state legislature, they would not only secure a charter but might also obtain some special privileges for the group. This situation often led to bribery, fraud, and political corruption of all sorts. These things became known to the people and were obnoxious to them. As a result, an entirely new system of granting charters to corporations was devised. In 1811 the state of New York enacted a general incorporation statute. This statute set out certain broad requirements which had to be met in order to secure a charter. If the group seeking a charter could qualify they were automatically entitled to a charter, regardless of their political affiliations. The charters, under the act, were granted by the Secretary of State and not by the state legislature. Soon other states followed the lead of New York and enacted similar general corporation statutes. The new procedure proved popular, since the granting of a charter was no longer a special privilege to men of wealth and political influence. Today this system of granting charters prevails in all our states, the District of Columbia, and the territories. The various state constitutions now provide that charters to business corporations must be granted under the general business corporation statute, and deny the state legislatures the authority to incorporate a business enterprise by special statute.

The foregoing brief historical account of the growth and development of the modern business corporation makes it evident that the corporation did not suddenly "spring into being." It might also be added that present-day corporation law is still dynamic and growing. The business corporation is constantly adjusting itself to economic changes and business developments. This is made evident by an examination of the new corporation codes that have been enacted by some of the states during the past decade or so.

LEGAL ENTITY OF A CORPORATION

THE CORPORATION AS A PERSON

A corporation has legal existence distinct and apart from that of its members or shareholders. It is an intangible, artificial person, and as such it has many of the legal rights of a natural person. It has a corporate name; and it may contract in its own name, hold, buy, and sell property in its own name, and sue and be sued in its own name. It is held to be a person under the provision of the Fourteenth Amendment of the federal Constitution that no state shall "deprive any person of life, liberty, or property, without due process of law; nor deny to any person within its jurisdiction the equal protection of the laws." It is also held to be a person under the provision of the Fifth Amendment which denies the federal government the right to take the life, liberty, or property of a person "without due process of law," or to take private property for public use without just compensation.

Since a corporation is a legal being separate from its members, its existence is independent of theirs. It is not terminated by the death of a member, as a partnership is, nor is it affected by the transfer of a member's interest to an outsider. It may, indeed, and often is, endowed by its charter with perpetual existence, though it may also be created for a definite period of time. Its other "personal" traits—its purposes, its powers, and its authority—are similarly independent of those of its members. They are determined at the time of its creation as a "person," by the terms of its charter and the statute under which it received its charter.

These attributes of a corporation are strikingly brought out in the well-known definition given by Chief Justice Marshall in the famous case of *Dartmouth College v. Woodward*[1] in 1803: "A corporation is an artificial being, invisible, intangible, and existing only in contemplation of law. Being the mere creature of law, it possesses only those properties which the charter of its creation confers upon it, either expressly, or as incidental to its very existence. These are such as are supposed best calculated to effect the object for which it was created. Among the most important are immortality, and, if the expression may be allowed, individuality; properties by which a perpetual succession of many persons are considered as the same, and may act as a single individual. They enable a

---

[1] 4 Wheat. (U. S.) 518, 636, 4 L. Ed. 629.

corporation to manage its own affairs, and to hold property without the perplexing intricacies, the hazardous and endless necessity, of perpetual conveyances for the purpose of transmitting it from hand to hand. It is chiefly for the purpose of clothing bodies of men in succession with these qualities and capacities that corporations were invented, and are in use. By these means, a perpetual succession of individuals are capable of acting for the promotion of the particular object, like one immortal being."

People's Pleasure Park Co., Inc. et al. v. Rohleder
109 Va. 439, 61 S. E. 794 (1908)

This was an action by one Rohleder (plaintiff) against the People's Pleasure Park Company, Inc. and others (defendants), to enforce covenants contained in a deed, and to cancel a deed and enjoin defendants from making a certain disposition of property. The injunction was granted, and defendants appealed. Decree set aside and bill dismissed.

The purposes of plaintiff's bill were to annul a conveyance of certain lands known as Fulton Park to defendant People's Pleasure Park Company, Inc. from codefendants Ida N. Butts and D. G. Fulton, and perpetually to enjoin and restrain defendants from selling or otherwise disposing of the said property, or any part thereof, to colored persons for any purpose whatsoever, or to any person for the purpose of using the same as a public park or place of amusement for colored persons.

When the property, known as Fulton Park, was first platted and sold, the deeds contained the following covenant: "The title to this land never to vest in a person or persons of African descent." The People's Pleasure Park Company was a corporation composed exclusively of Negroes.

CALDWELL, J. It will be observed that appellee rests her right to the relief she seeks upon the ground that the "covenant, condition, or stipulation" mentioned is a covenant real running with the land, made for the protection of each and every person who became the owner of a lot in Fulton Park. Her contention is that because of such covenant the title to the lot or lots conveyed should never vest in "a person or persons of African descent" or "colored persons."

Such a conveyance contemplated, by no rule of construction, vests the title to the property conveyed in "a person or persons of African descent." The conveyance was to the corporation, the People's Pleasure Park Company. "A corporation is an artificial person, like the state. It has a distinct existence—an existence separate from that of its stockholders and directors." 1 *Cook on Corporations*, Sec. 1.

Professor Rudolph Sohm, in his *Institutes of Roman Law*, pp. 104–6, says: "In Roman law the property of the corporation is the sole property of the collective whole; and the debts of a corporation are the sole debts of the collective whole." Chief Justice Marshall, in the *Dartmouth College Case*, 4 Wheat.

(U. S.) 518, defined a corporation as "an artificial being, invisible, intangible, and existing only in contemplation of law." Further recognizing the corporation as a legal entity distinct from the persons composing it, the opinion of the court in *People v. Fulton*, 11 N. Y. 94, may be cited. The court, in that case, said: "Incorporated religious societies are aggregate corporations, and whatever property they acquire, whether it be real or personal, is vested in interest in the body corporate; and while the officers have it under their control or dominion, whatever possession they have is the possession of the artificial person whose agent they are. . . ."

For the above reasons, we are of the opinion that the decree complained of is erroneous, and it will be set aside and annulled, the demurrer of appellants to the bill sustained, and the bill dismissed with costs to the appellees.

THE CORPORATION NOT A CITIZEN

Though a corporation, as we have just seen, is held to be a "person" under certain provisions of the federal Constitution, it is not given the status of a "citizen" under Article IV, Section II, which provides in part that "The citizens of each state shall be entitled to all the privileges and immunities of citizens of the several states." Nor is it given the status of a "citizen" under that portion of the Fourteenth Amendment which provides: "No state shall make or enforce any law which shall abridge the privileges or immunities of citizens of the United States." Hence, while a natural person is privileged to go into any state in the Union and carry on business within the state on the very same terms and conditions as the state's own citizens, a corporation has no such right. As we shall see in more detail in Chapter 49, a corporation is a *foreign corporation* in any state in which it was not incorporated, and must secure a license before it may carry on intrastate business there.

St. Louis & S. F. R. Co. v. State
120 Ark. 182, 179 S. W. 342 (1915)

This was an action by the State (plaintiff) against the St. Louis & S. F. R. Co. (defendant). Defendant was convicted and fined for failure to obey an order of the Railroad Commission, and appealed. Reversed.

An information was filed before a justice of the peace of Washington County, in which it was charged that defendant had failed and refused to comply with an order of the Railroad Commission of Arkansas requiring it to establish and maintain a joint interchange track at Fayetteville with the Kansas City & Memphis Railroad Company, and to do switching thereon. Judgment was rendered by default in the justice court, and an appeal was prosecuted to the circuit court, in which court a demurrer and an answer were filed. Defendant offered as a defense that the order of the Railroad Commission was void for the reason that no petition for such order, signed by 15 bona fide citizens residing within the territory affected by the petition, was ever filed.

SMITH, J. It is conceded by counsel for the State that, although there are 18 names signed to the petition, all these signers are corporations and copartnerships, except one; but it is argued that the provisions of the statute in regard to the number of signers is directory, and that the statute was substantially complied with when 15 names of individuals, corporations, and copartnerships were signed to the petition. Section 1 of the Act of 1907, under which the Railroad Commission proceeded in making the order in question, provides that the Commission shall be empowered to hear and consider all petitions for train service, depots, spurs, side tracks, etc., provided said petitions shall be signed by at least 15 bona fide citizens residing in the territory sought to be affected by said petitioners.

It has been many times decided that a corporation is not a citizen, within the meaning of the equal privileges and immunities clause of the federal Constitution; and this court has decided that Section 18, Article 2, of the constitution of this state, containing the same provisions as those of the federal Constitution, does not apply to corporations. And while it is held that corporations are persons within the meaning of the Fourteenth Amendment to the federal Constitution, which provides that no state shall deprive any person of life, liberty, or property without due process of law, nor deny to any person within its jurisdiction the equal protection of the law, it has been as often decided that corporations are not included in that portion of the same amendment which provides that "no state shall make or enforce any law which shall abridge the privileges or immunities of citizens of the United States."

The use of the qualifying words "bona fide" is significant. Evidently the Legislature did not intend to burden the Railroad Commission with the consideration of petitions for the things authorized to be petitioned for unless at least 15 bona fide citizens residing in the locality to be affected were sufficiently interested to petition therefor. . . . The Legislature having made no provision by which the assent of a corporation might be evidenced, but, upon the contrary, having used language which in its ordinary acceptation would refer only to individuals, we have concluded that the petition was not signed as required by law, and that the Railroad Commission was therefore without jurisdiction to make the order upon which this prosecution is based, and the case will therefore be reversed and dismissed.

DISREGARDING THE CORPORATE ENTITY

While the courts normally recognize the separate legal entity of corporations, they will, when necessary to reach a just and equitable result, disregard the legal fiction that the corporation possesses a separate legal personality and "pierce the corporate entity." This has been done by the courts in the following situations: (1) in cases where the stockholders have organized and made use of the corporate device as a cloak for fraud or illegality; (2) in the case of a subsidiary corporation. In instances of the first type, while normally the liability of a stockholder is limited to his investment in the business, if he participates in fraud or knowingly commits some illegal act, with the result that some third party suffers damages, the court will disregard the corporate entity and hold the stockholders liable. In the second case, while there is no legal objection if a corporation causes a subsidiary corporation to be formed, the parent corporation may be liable for the acts or obligations of the subsidiary if the parent corporation uses the subsidiary to carry out some fraudulent or illegal act.

In re Belt-Modes, Inc.
88 Fed. Supp. 141 (1950)

This was a proceeding in the matter of Belt-Modes, Inc., bankrupt, brought by the trustee to review an order of the referee allowing wage claims of the employees of Danin, Inc. The petition was sustained and the order of the referee was reversed and the wage claims were disallowed.

Prior to 1946, Belt-Modes, Inc. manufactured ladies' belts. In the early part of 1946 it began to or desired to manufacture children's and ladies' handbags. To make belts it had to sign a contract with the Beltmakers' Union, and to make pocketbooks a contract had to be signed with the Pocketbook Workers' Union.

Rather than combine both operations, on January 22, 1946, Daniel Rubin, the principal stockholder of Belt-Modes, Inc., organized a new corporation, Danin, Inc., for the purpose of manufacturing pocketbooks, and Belt-Modes, Inc. continued to make belts. This was done, it was alleged, to prevent jurisdictional disputes between the aforementioned unions.

Danin, Inc. was a separate entity. It rented its own premises, hired its own help, owned the fixtures, machinery, and equipment, had its own complete set of books and records, stationery, bank account, issued its own checks, paid its own taxes, issued financial statements, purchased insurance for itself, and participated in other normal business procedures.

The transactions between the two corporations followed the usual pattern found in a jobber-contractor relationship. At the end of every month Danin, Inc. rendered a bill to Belt-Modes, Inc. This bill was entered on the Danin, Inc. books as a debit to accounts receivable and a credit to sales, and was entered on the Belt-Modes, Inc. books by a debit to "purchases-contractors, labor and materials" and a credit to contractors payable. Danin, Inc. was only one of several contractors with whom Belt-Modes had business negotiations. All of the payrolls of Danin, Inc. were paid out of its own bank account.

On or about the middle of 1947, Danin, Inc. moved into the same premises occupied by Belt-Modes, Inc., but continued to operate separately as it had previously done until Belt-Modes, Inc. was adjudicated a bankrupt. Danin, Inc. apparently is still in existence and is not involved in this bankruptcy proceeding.

In spite of the fact that claimants herein were the employees of Danin, Inc., they filed wage claims against the estate of the bankrupt. The trustee objected to such claims on the grounds that the bankrupt was in no way obligated to said claimants, in that claimants were never employed by the bankrupt and never rendered any work, labor, or services for the bankrupt. The referee overruled these objections and allowed these claims on the ground that the said employees were actually the employees of the bankrupt. The trustee brought this appeal.

KAUFMAN, D.J. The "corporate veil" may be pierced in cases where the corporation concerned in the suit is a front or mere conduit for carrying on the business of a parent corporation, but even here the test is whether the purpose of using the subsidiary corporation as a cloak was to commit a fraud or illegal purpose. *Jenkins v. Moyse,* 254 N. Y. 319, 172 N. E. 521. The New York courts are very reluctant to disregard the corporate entity. The law in New York has been set forth in two recent decisions whose fact situations are relevant to the present case. In *Oceanic Insul-Lite Corp. v. Sullivan Dry Dock & Repair Corp.,* 191 Misc. 354, 77 N. Y. S. (2d) 489, Justice Froessel stated that the "corporate entity will not ordinarily be disregarded, except where the corporate form has been used as an instrument of wrong and injustice." In that case the court further stated: "What we have here is simply the creation of two corporations by the same interests for the purpose of keeping separate and apart different operations in connection with the repair of ships, and there is no proof that the corporate form was used as a cloak or cover for *fraud or illegality.*"

On the basis of the decided case, the findings of the referee, even if accepted, would not justify the referee's conclusion under the New York law, and the allowance of the claims of the employees of Danin, Inc. would not be justified. The conclusion of the referee is clearly erroneous. There seems to be no question about the fact that Danin, Inc. and Belt-Modes, Inc. were two separate corporations which were organized at different times for two separate and distinct purposes. It is admitted that no fraud or illegality was perpetrated on the claimants in this case, but that the corporate set-up was used specifically to prevent labor jurisdictional disputes. If these claims were to be allowed, an injustice would be done to the creditors of the bankrupt who extended credit to the bankrupt and had no way of knowing of the existence of these claimants as creditors. It is the decision of this court that the petition to review be sustained and the order of the referee be reversed and the wage claims of the employees of Danin, Inc. be disallowed.

CLASSIFICATION OF CORPORATIONS

Corporations are most commonly classified as follows: (1) public corporations, (2) quasi-public or public service corporations, and (3) private corporations. Private corporations are further subdivided into (a) stock corporations and (b) non-stock corporations.

A second classification, into (1) de jure and (2) de facto corporations, is discussed in Chapter 44.

PUBLIC CORPORATIONS

Public corporations are corporations formed by the state or federal government for governmental purposes or to carry out governmental functions. Incorporated towns and cities are examples of public corporations created by the state government. The Tennessee Valley Authority and the Federal Deposit Insurance Corporation are examples of federal public corporations.

QUASI-PUBLIC CORPORATIONS

A quasi-public corporation is, in reality, a private corporation, but it differs from the usual private corporation in that it is chartered to perform some special function in which the general public has a vital interest. Examples of such corporations are railroads, street railways, bus lines, freight lines, telephone companies, telegraph companies, water companies, gas companies, and electric power companies. From an economic standpoint these types of business enterprises are natural monopolies. Experience has shown that it is best for the state to recognize this fact by granting to such corporations a monopoly in a given area or field, at the same time reserving the right to regulate their activities very carefully in order to protect the public. For such regulatory purpose each state has established a commission, known usually as the Public Service Commission. Before a public service corporation may be chartered it must secure from the Commission a certificate of convenience and necessity. The Commission has authority to regulate such matters as the issuance of stocks and bonds and the payment of dividends. Public service corporations are often given the power of eminent domain by the state that creates them.

PRIVATE CORPORATIONS

A private corporation is organized by private individuals for private ends. It may be either a stock corporation or a non-stock corporation.

A stock corporation is organized for the purpose of producing a profit for its members. Membership in such a corporation is acquired through the purchase and ownership of stock. This is the type of corporation which we shall study in the present section on Corporations.

A non-stock corporation, often called a non-profit corporation, is organized for some purpose other than earning a pecuniary profit for its members, generally for some charitable, religious, educational, or scientific purpose. The following are at times organized as non-stock corporations: churches, colleges, universities, fraternities, libraries, hospitals, trade unions, trade associations, foundations for the promotion of scientific research, charitable undertakings, and the like. Since non-stock corporations issue no stock to their members, membership is acquired and determined by the rules and regulations set up by the corporation itself. In most states a charter for a non-stock corporation is obtained by approximately the same procedures as those required in the case of a stock corporation; however, the statutes of some states set out a different procedure for incorporating non-stock corporations.

CONTRACTUAL RELATIONSHIPS OF A CORPORATION

BETWEEN THE CORPORATION AND THE STATE

It is now firmly established by judicial decision that the charter which the corporation receives from the state represents a contract between the state and the corporation. Hence its charter has the same protection as its other contracts under the limitations placed upon the states by the federal Constitution in the provision of the Fourteenth Amendment that the state may not "take the life, liberty or property of a person without due process of law" and the provision in Article I, Section X, that no state shall pass any law "impairing the obligation of contracts."

The constitutional protection given to a corporation as against the state does not prevent the state from taxing the corporation, regulating its activities under the general police powers of the state, and taking its property under the power of eminent domain, if the property is needed for a public purpose and the corporation is justly compensated.

BETWEEN THE CORPORATION AND THE STOCKHOLDERS

A contractual relationship exists between the corporation and the stockholders. The terms of such contracts are not found in a single instrument but are found in the charter or articles of incorporation, the bylaws of the corporation, and the statute under which the corporation was organized.

BETWEEN THE STATE AND THE STOCKHOLDERS

There is, in effect, a contract between the state and the stockholders of a corporation to the effect that the corporation will grant and protect the rights of the stockholders under the corporate charter.

UNIFORM BUSINESS CORPORATION ACT

In 1928 the National Conference of Commissioners on Uniform State Laws approved the Uniform Business Corporation Act. Its intent was to make corporation law more uniform throughout the United States and its territories. Since that date, many states have adopted it.

Promotion, Creation, and Organization of Corporations

44

In order to launch a corporation as a going concern, three distinct steps must be taken. The first step involves the promotion of the proposed concern. One or more persons conceive the idea of creating a corporation, interest others in the idea, and work out detailed plans. The second step is to bring the corporation into being by obtaining the permission of the state to incorporate. This is done by submitting articles of incorporation to the proper official and securing his approval of them. When this is accomplished, in a technical legal sense a new "artificial" person is "born." But before the corporation can begin to carry out the purpose for which it was created it must set up an internal organization by choosing directors, adopting bylaws, electing officers, and so on. Such organization constitutes the third step.

The present chapter describes the legal problems involved in these three steps.

PROMOTION

WHO IS A PROMOTER

A corporation has its origin when someone conceives the idea that it would be desirable and feasible to bring about such a corporation. The idea may be to create an entirely new business enterprise, or to incorporate an already established business, such as a single proprietorship or a partnership, or even to merge presently existing corporations into a new corporation. In any one of these three situations it is necessary that certain acts be performed before the state will consent to the creation of the projected corporation. Those who perform these acts are known as promoters.

To be a promoter of a corporation one must actively engage in the task of bringing the corporation into being. Let us suppose that A and B have in mind the incorporation of a business enterprise and do all the work necessary to obtain a charter, and that C merely helps them to obtain a charter by signing the articles of incorporation. While A and B would definitely be held to be promoters, in all probability C would not be classed as a promoter. His status would be that of an incorporator. A somewhat similar situation was involved in the case of *Wheeler & Motter Mercantile Co. v. Lamberton et al.*[1] In that case the court said: "The authority or agency granted to the co-signers [of the articles of incorporation] is limited to the performance of the acts necessary to perfect the organization of the corporation. Nor does the fact that one signs and verifies the articles of incorporation and subscribes for capital stock in a proposed corporation make him a promoter thereof, within the legal significance of that equivocal and ambiguous term in cases of this character."

The work of a promoter involves many things. He usually forms the idea of organizing a corporation, develops the plans, prepares a prospectus, and possibly enters into certain pre-incorporation contracts and takes stock subscriptions. He will also no doubt assist in securing the charter by preparing and signing the articles of incorporation. Often, especially in the promotion of a large corporation, much of the promotion work is handled by professional promoters. Where this is not the case, the promoter, if he is not himself an attorney, may secure the assistance of an attorney in obtaining the charter.

Those who are promoting a projected corporation and who expect to have a part in it upon its creation and organization will have some agreement or understanding among themselves as to their rights and liabilities. Often such agreements are not reduced to writing. It is advisable, however, that the agreement to form a corporation be put in writing and be signed by all parties concerned. If such a written agreement is executed, the rights and liabilities of the parties will be governed by the rules of ordinary contract law.

PROMOTER'S LIABILITY ON PRE-INCORPORATION CONTRACTS

In the promotion of a corporation a promoter may find it desirable or necessary to enter into certain contracts. For instance, the promoter may lease a building, engage the services of attorneys, engineers, accountants, and other persons, or sign an option contract to purchase certain property. The general rule is that the promoter is personally liable on all such pre-

[1] 8 F. (2d) 957 (1925).

incorporation contracts. It is possible, however, for such contracts to be so drawn that the promoter either (1) is at no time personally liable on the contract, or (2) is personally liable on the contract until it is adopted by the corporation, at which time he will be discharged of his liability. In the first type of case it must clearly appear that the promoter does not contract with an intention of becoming personally liable and that this is understood and agreed to by the other party to the contract. Under such circumstances, the other party to the contract assumes the risk that the projected corporation may never be created, in which case he may not look to the promoter for performance. In the second type of case, if the corporation never comes into being, or if, having come into being, it fails or refuses to adopt the contract, the promoter remains liable on the contract; but if the corporation is created and adopts the contract the promoter is discharged of all personal liability on the contract. The effect of this second type of contract is to create a novation, wherein the corporation is substituted for the promoter.

In the absence of such a protective provision in the pre-incorporation contract, the promoter is not discharged of his personal liability by subsequent adoption of the contract by the corporation. In such cases both the promoter and the corporation are liable on the contract.

CORPORATION'S LIABILITY ON PROMOTER'S CONTRACTS

If there is no statutory provision to the contrary, a corporation is not liable upon the pre-incorporation contracts of its promoter. This is true even though the contracts of the promoter are entered into for the benefit of the corporation. However, the corporation after it comes into existence may adopt such contracts,[1] in which case it becomes liable upon them. A corporation may not *ratify* its promoter's pre-incorporation contracts. The reason for this distinction arises out of the law of agency. As we saw in our study of agency law, a principal may not ratify the contract of an agent unless the principal was in existence at the time the contract was entered into.

The corporation may adopt the promoter's pre-incorporation contracts expressly by formal resolution of its board of directors, or it may adopt them impliedly by *knowingly* accepting the benefits of such contracts. The rights of all parties concerned are determined as of the date of adoption and not the date when the contract was made.

A corporation is not liable for the torts of its promoter committed prior to its incorporation. The promoter is, of course, personally liable for such torts.

---

[1] Provided they are not ultra vires, i.e. beyond the authority of the corporation to make.

CORPORATION'S LIABILITY FOR EXPENSES AND SERVICES OF PROMOTER

The general rule is that a corporation is not liable to its promoter for services rendered or expenses incurred by him in the promotion, creation, and organization of the corporation, unless the articles of incorporation provide for such payment or a statute of the state of incorporation requires it. Of course, as a practical matter the promoter expects to be compensated for his work and reimbursed for his expenses in bringing about the creation of the corporation. There is usually some "understanding" between the promoter and the other persons who take part in the creation of the corporation that he is to be compensated and reimbursed. It is sometimes agreed that he will be compensated by a cash payment, or by the issuance of stock in the newly created corporation. It may also be agreed that he will become an officer of the corporation or a member of the board of directors. From what we have thus far learned about corporation law, it is obvious that the corporation, when it comes into being, will not be bound by any such pre-incorporation contracts or "understandings." However, the courts of a large majority of the states hold that if the corporation, by the adoption of a resolution by its board of directors, agrees to compensate the promoter for his services and reimburse him for any financial outlays, the corporation will be bound. A few courts have gone even farther and have held that since the corporation has accepted the benefits of the promoter's work and expenditures, a promise to compensate and reimburse him may be implied.

PROMOTER'S RELATION TO THE CORPORATION

The relation of a promoter to the corporation which he is promoting is in many respects unusual. He cannot be said to be its agent, since the corporation is not yet in existence. Yet, if the business enterprise which he is promoting eventually becomes a reality, his acts prior to incorporation will vitally affect the corporation and its stockholders. At times opportunities present themselves to the promoter to benefit personally, at the expense and to the detriment of the corporation. Because of this fact, the courts have held that a fiduciary relationship exists between the promoter and the corporation when it does come into existence, and that the promoter must therefore exercise the highest degree of loyalty and good faith in respect to the projected corporation. This fiduciary relationship extends to the original stockholders but not to future stockholders.

In view of this fiduciary relationship, the promoter is not permitted to make any secret profits from the undertaking. If he does so and is discovered, he may be compelled to disgorge. He is permitted to sell any property which he personally owns to the corporation, provided the transaction is completely open and aboveboard and the promoter does not conceal or misrepresent any material facts relating to it. If the sale by the promoter of his property to the corporation is consummated after the directors have been fully informed of the nature and terms of the agreement and have entered into the contract on behalf of the corporation, the contract will be valid.

McArthur v. Times Printing Company
48 Minn. 319, 51 N. W. 216 (1892)

This was an action by McArthur (plaintiff) against the Times Printing Co. (defendant). Judgment for plaintiff, and defendant appealed. Affirmed.

The complaint alleged that about October 1, 1889, defendant contracted with plaintiff for his services as advertising solicitor for one year, and that in April, 1890, it discharged him, in violation of the contract.

In September, 1889, one C. A. Nimocks and others were engaged as promoters in procuring the organization of defendant company to publish a newspaper. On September 12, 1889, Nimocks, as promoter, made a contract with plaintiff, on behalf of the contemplated corporation, for his services as advertising solicitor for the period of one year from and after October 1st, the date at which it was expected that the corporation would be organized. The corporation was not, in fact, organized until October 16th, but the publication of the paper was commenced by the promoters October 1st, at which date plaintiff, in pursuance of his arrangement with Nimocks, entered upon the discharge of his duties as advertising solicitor for the paper. After the organization of the corporation he continued in its employment until discharged in the following April. Defendant's board of directors never took any formal action with reference to the contract made in its behalf by Nimocks, but all the stockholders, directors, and officers of the corporation knew of this contract at the time of its organization and none of them objected to or repudiated it. On the contrary, they retained plaintiff in the employment of the corporation without any other or new contract as to his services.

MITCHELL, J. This court, in accordance with sound reason, as well as with the weight of authority, has held that, while a corporation is not bound by engagements made on its behalf by its promoters before its organization, it may, after its organization, make such engagements its own contracts. And this it may do precisely as it might make similar original contracts; formal action of its board of directors being necessary only where it would be necessary in the case of similar original contracts. It is not requisite that such adoption or acceptance be express, but it may be inferred from acts or acquiescence on the part of the corporation, or its authorized agents, as any similar original contract might be shown. *Battelle v. Pavement Co.*, 37 Minn. 89, 33 N. W. 327.

The defendant claims that the contract was void under the statute of frauds, because, "by its terms, not to be performed within one year from the making thereof," which counsel assumes to be September 12th—the date of the agreement between plaintiff and the promoter. This proceeds upon the erroneous theory that the act of the corporation, in such cases, is a ratification, which relates back to the date of the contract with the promoter, under the familiar maxim that "a subsequent ratification has a retroactive effect, and is equivalent to a prior command." But the liability of the corporation, under such circumstances, does not rest upon any principle of the law of agency, but upon the immediate and voluntary act of the corporation. Although the acts of a corporation with reference to the contracts made by promoters in its behalf before its organization are frequently loosely termed "ratification," yet a "ratification," properly so called, implies an existing person, on whose behalf the contract might have been made at the time. There cannot, in law, be a ratification of a contract which could not have been made binding on the ratifier at the time it was made because the ratifier was not then in existence. What is called "adoption," in such cases, is, in legal effect, the making of the contract binding as of the date of the adoption, and not as of some former date. The contract in this case was, therefore, not within the statute of frauds. Affirmed.

Knox et al. v. First Security Bank of Utah et al.
196 F. (2d) 112 (1952)

This was an action of De Witt Knox and another (plaintiffs) against the First Security Bank of Utah, executor of the estate of A. C. Milner, deceased, and the Milner Corporation (defendants). Judgment for defendants, and plaintiffs appealed. Judgment dismissing the action against the Milner Corporation reversed, and judgment dismissing the action against the bank, as executor of the estate of A. C. Milner, deceased, affirmed.

This was an action to recover for breach of contract. Plaintiffs alleged that in March, 1909, A. C. Milner, for value received, executed and delivered a written undertaking to Frank Knox; that, as provided in that agreement, the mining property therein referred to was conveyed to defendant Milner Corporation; and that in November, 1924, Milner, then president of the Milner Corporation, made a new agreement and undertaking on behalf of himself and the Milner Corporation to perform the original undertaking. It was further alleged that in December, 1947, the Milner Corporation entered into a longterm lease in which it leased to Columbia Iron Mining Corporation a portion of the property; that ever since that date the Milner Corporation had been and then was able to pay the $25,000 referred to in the undertakings of 1909 and 1924 from royalties and other payments under the lease, but that no part of it had been paid. A judgment for $25,000, with interest, was prayed for against both defendants.

The undertaking from Milner to Frank Knox recited that Stanley B. Milner at the time of his death was the owner of interests in certain iron property; that the estate was about to be closed and the assets thereof distributed; and that a corporation would in the immediate future be organized to be known as the Milner Corporation, to which the iron property should be deeded. The instrument then provided that Milner, for value received, would immediately cause the corporation to be organized, and would cause to be conveyed immediately to it the interests of Stanley B. Milner's estate in the iron property; and that immediately upon the organization of the corporation he would cause it to execute to Frank Knox its obligation and agreement to pay him the sum of $25,000 from the first net proceeds or profits derived by the corporation from the sale of the property or the proceeds thereof. The alleged new agreement on behalf of Milner and the Milner Corporation was in the form of a letter written on the letterhead of the corporation, addressed to plaintiff De Witt Knox, and signed by Milner. This letter stated in part: "We have a copy of the undertaking with your father relative to $25,000 to be paid from the sale or profits therefrom of iron property. Just how soon we will reach the stage when we will begin to liquidate the $25,000 agreement with your father is dependent upon the volume of business we do. You may rest assured, however, that we are keeping the agreement with your father in mind, and that it will be reached at the proper time." The $25,000 having never been paid to the plaintiffs, this action was filed.

BRATTON, C.J. The first contention urged by the plaintiff is that the complaint stated a cause of action against the defendant Milner Corporation, and that the court erred in dismissing the action against that defendant. It is argued in support of this contention that the original undertaking entered into in 1909 was a promoter's contract; that it was accepted and adopted by the defendant Milner Corporation; and that therefore such defendant is liable. It is well settled law in Utah that promoters or those contemplating the organization of a corporation do not have power to enter into a contract with binding effect upon the corporation after it is organized. They lack that power, either as agents or otherwise. But promoters or those contemplating the formation of a corporation may make a contract in furtherance of the corporation and for its benefit; and if the corporation after it comes into existence accepts or adopts the contract, it thereupon becomes the contract of the corporation and may be enforced against it. *Wall v. Niagara Mining & Smelting Co.*, 20 Utah 474, 59 P. 399. Under the law of Utah, a contract made by and with promoters which is intended to inure to the benefit of a corporation about to be organized is to be regarded as an open offer which the corporation may after its formation accept or adopt, as it chooses. And if it does, in the exercise of its own judgment, accept or adopt the contract and retain the benefit of it, it cannot reject liability under it. In the absence of acceptance or adoption of a contract of that kind, the corporation is not liable. But it is not necessary that acceptance or adoption of a contract of that kind be by express action of the corporation entered in the minutes of the directors, or that it be effectuated in any other like formal manner. It may be inferred from acts, conduct, and acquiescence.

The original undertaking was an agreement in the nature of a promoter's contract. And from what has been said it is manifest that defendant Milner Corporation is not bound by it to make payment of the $25,000 unless it was accepted or adopted in an effective manner.

The facts, as disclosed by the evidence, make it clear that the Milner Corporation adopted the contract involved in this action. The property involved was transferred to and accepted by the corporation and it received the royalties paid to it by the Columbia Iron Mining Company. Furthermore, acceptance is clearly indicated as a result of Milner's letter written to the plaintiff Knox, in November, 1924. As the president of the Milner Corporation his act bound the corporation.

The further contention of plaintiffs is that the complaint states a cause of action against the defendant bank, as executor of the estate of A. C. Milner, and that therefore the court erred in dismissing the action as against that defendant. The argument is that the original contract disclosed on its face an intention on the part of Milner to become personally liable. It is said that he obligated himself to cause the formation of the corporation, to cause the property to be conveyed to the corporation, to cause the corporation to execute an agreement to pay the father of plaintiffs $25,000 out of the proceeds derived from the property, and to instigate and supervise payment from that source. The agreement did in clear terms obligate Milner to cause the corporation to be formed, to cause the property to be conveyed to the corporation, and to cause the corporation to execute the obligation to the father of the plaintiffs. But it failed to disclose any personal obligation on the part of Milner to pay any amount. Therefore, Milner did not bear any personal liability to pay the $25,000 under either the agreement of 1909 or that of 1924.

CREATION

WHERE TO INCORPORATE

If the principal business of the corporation is to be carried on in a single state, it is generally agreed that the corporation should be incorporated in that state. However, the circumstances of a particular case may justify a variation of this generally recognized rule of procedure. The corporation law of the various states is largely statutory, and considerable variation exists from state to state. The corporation statutes of some states are considered much more liberal and desirable than those of other states.[1] Consequently, persons contemplating the incorporation of a business enterprise which is to be carried on in a state where the law is notoriously unfavorable might find it desirable to secure their charter in one of the more liberal states. If they decide to do so, it will be necessary for them, after securing their charter in another state, to obtain a license from the state in which they propose to carry on their business.

[1] Among the more "liberal" states are Delaware, Maryland, New York, Illinois, Massachusetts, Maine, and Virginia.

If the contemplated corporation will carry on business in several states, then the promoters should study carefully the advantages and disadvantages of incorporating in those states. It will be necessary for them to decide whether to incorporate in one state and qualify to operate as a foreign corporation in the other states, or to incorporate in several or all of the states in which they wish to do business.

The following are some important questions to consider in determining the relative liberality of a state's incorporation statute: How high are the organization fees? To what taxes are corporations subject? When is stock fully paid and non-assessable? May no-par value stock be issued? May par value stock be issued for less than par? Must stock qualify under the state Blue Sky Law before it may be sold? May directors' and stockholders' meetings be held outside the state? May the directors be authorized to adopt, amend, and repeal the bylaws? Under what circumstances must the directors secure the stockholders' assent to their acts? May directors delegate some or all of their authority to an executive committee?

SECURING THE CHARTER

After a decision has been reached on the state or states of incorporation, the next step is to secure a charter, or, more accurately, to obtain approval of articles of incorporation.[1] This is accomplished by preparing, executing, and filing the proposed articles of incorporation with the proper state administrative agency or official, usually the Secretary of State. Those who sign, execute, and submit the articles of incorporation are called *incorporators*.

If the articles are in proper order a certificate of incorporation or some other evidence of approval will be issued by the Secretary of State to the incorporators. If the articles are deemed not to be in conformity with the statutes of the state the Secretary of State will refuse to approve them, in which case, if the incorporators are of the opinion that the Secretary is in error, they may test his decision by bringing a mandamus proceeding. If the charter is granted it will be filed or recorded in the permanent records of the office of the Secretary of State. It must also be filed in some designated office of the county in which the principal office of the corporation is to be located. This is usually the office of the Recorder of Deeds or the office of the clerk of the Circuit or District Court. In some states it is incumbent upon the incorporators to see that the articles are

[1] "Charter," though commonly used interchangeably with "articles of incorporation," is a survival from the early days when corporations were created by the issuance of charters which endowed them with certain franchises and privileges. Under modern corporation statutes the state's consent to the creation of a corporation comes through the filing and approval of articles of incorporation.

recorded in the local county office; in other states this detail is taken care of by the office of the Secretary of State.

The incorporators may be the promoters of the corporation; they may be some or all of the promoters plus other persons who agree to become incorporators; or they may not include the promoters at all. Most of the state statutes require that there be at least three incorporators. It is sometimes provided that a certain number of the incorporators—for example, a majority or two thirds of them—must be citizens of the United States. Some states also require that at least one of the incorporators be a resident of the state of incorporation. To be an incorporator one must be a natural person with full capacity to contract. Thus an infant may not be an incorporator, nor may a corporation.

PROVISIONS OF ARTICLES OF INCORPORATION

GENERAL CONTENT. While there is some variation, from state to state, as to the content of the articles of incorporation, provisions covering the following matters are generally required:

(1) The name of the corporation.

(2) The purpose or purposes for which the corporation is formed.

(3) The post office address of the principal office of the corporation in the state.

(4) The total number of shares of stock of all classes which the corporation has authority to issue; the number and par value of the shares of stock of each class, or a statement that such shares are without par value. If the shares are divided into classes, a description of each class with the preferences, conversion and other rights, voting powers, restrictions, limitations as to dividends, and qualifications of each class.

(5) The restrictions, if any, imposed upon the transferability of shares of any class.

(6) The number of directors, which shall not be less than a designated number (usually three). If the statute so requires, the names of those who will serve as members of the board of directors for the first year.

(7) Name of resident agent. Not all states require that domestic corporations designate a resident agent or agents. In some states a resident agent may be a corporate resident agent.

(8) In some states, the names and addresses of the incorporators. It is sometimes required that it be stated that such incorporators are of "full age" or are "at least twenty-one years of age." If the statute requires incorporators to subscribe for stock, then it is usually required that the articles state the number of shares subscribed for by each incorporator.

(9) The amount of subscribed and paid-in capital stock with which the corporation will commence business. Some statutes require that a certain percentage (usually 10 per cent) of the authorized capital stock be subscribed and paid in before the corporation may commence business.

(10) Any provision not inconsistent with law which may be desired for the purpose of defining, limiting, and regulating the powers of the corporation and of the directors, and of stockholders or of any class of stockholders, and the holding of any bonds, notes, or other securities which the corporation may issue. This provision is in the nature of an omnibus provision. For example, it may be provided that the directors may adopt, amend, and repeal the bylaws; or a limitation may be placed upon the amount of the indebtedness which the corporation may incur.

CORPORATE NAME. Every corporation must adopt a name. Corporations hold property and sue and are sued under their corporate names. Before drafting and filing the articles the incorporators should inquire of the Secretary of State whether they may use the name they have chosen, for certain limitations exist. A name may not be adopted and used if it is already being used by a domestic corporation or by a foreign corporation licensed to do business within the state of incorporation. The same prohibition applies to a name so nearly like the name of some other corporation operating within the state that its use would tend to deceive or mislead the public and deprive the other corporation of some of its good will. The statutes also require that the name be such as to make clear to the public that the business is a corporation and not some other type of business enterprise, such as a partnership. It is generally required that the name contain the word "corporation," "incorporated," or "limited," or end with the abbreviation of one of these words. Some statutes provide that the name of the corporation may end with the word "company" if such word is not immediately preceded by the word "and" or some symbol therefor. It is also generally required that the name shall not contain any word or phrase which indicates or implies that the corporation is organized for any purpose other than one or more of the purposes contained in its charter.

Some state statutes provide that incorporators may reserve for a period of thirty days the exclusive right to adopt a certain name, by applying to the Secretary of State and paying a specified fee (usually $2.00). This privilege is for the purpose of protecting their right to the name during the period before they file their articles of incorporation.

DOMICILE. Every corporation incorporated under a state statute has its domicile or home in the state in which it received its charter. It has no legal existence outside the state which created it. The domicile within the state is where the principal or home office of the corporation is located. This is true even though all the business of the corporation is carried on in another state. For example, if three persons, residents of Nebraska, wished to organize a corporation and carry on business in Nebraska, and they obtain a Delaware charter and then are licensed by Nebraska as a foreign corporation, to do intrastate business in Nebraska, the domicile or home of the corporation would be in Delaware.

PURPOSE CLAUSE.   Under modern corporation statutes a corporation may be organized to carry on almost any kind of business so long as it is not illegal. The authority granted in this respect is very broad. Generally, any limitations placed upon the purposes and objectives of a corporation are imposed by the incorporators themselves when they draft the "purpose clause." Once that clause has been adopted as a part of the articles of incorporation, the corporation may not legally exceed the authority granted therein, except by amending the articles of incorporation. For that reason great care should be exercised in drafting the purpose clause.

DURATION.   The articles of incorporation may provide that the corporation is created for some definite period, at the end of which time it will terminate. If no such provision appears in the articles, then its existence is unlimited or "perpetual." However, as is explained in Chapter 50, this does not mean that the corporation may not be dissolved and its legal existence terminated.

Corning Glass Works v. Corning Cut Glass Co. et al.
197 N. Y. 173, 90 N. E. 449 (1910)

This was a suit by the Corning Glass Works (plaintiff) against the Corning Cut Glass Company and others (defendants). Judgment for defendants, and plaintiff appealed. Affirmed.

This action was brought by plaintiff to obtain an injunction which should permanently restrain defendants from doing business under the name of the "Corning Cut Glass Company," and to recover the damages sustained.

Plaintiff had been incorporated in 1875 for the purpose of manufacturing glass and glassware at Corning, New York. Its manufactures consisted in lantern globes, chimneys, tubing, bulbs, and other articles made of glass, including "blanks" furnished to glass cutters for cutting or engraving. Plaintiff had never engaged in the cutting of glass. Some years after plaintiff had established itself, defendant Corning Cut Glass Company was incorporated for the purpose of "buying, manufacturing, selling, and dealing in cut and other kinds of glass." It located its works in the town of Corning to gain the advantage of the reputation enjoyed by this city as a center of cut glass manufacture; and the adoption of its corporate name was with similar intention. The cut glass manufactured by defendant did not come into direct competition with that manufactured by plaintiff.

GRAY, J. I think that the case has been correctly decided, and that its facts do not afford support for the charge that the defendant has brought itself within the inhibition, either of the rule established by the decisions, or of our statutory provision, which forbids the adoption, in a certificate of incorporation, of the "same name as a corporation authorized to do business under the laws of this state, or a name so nearly resembling it as to be calculated to deceive."

The claim of the plaintiff to equitable relief by way of the injunction demanded is placed upon this ground: that the similarity between the names "is liable to produce confusion of business, and to mislead those transacting business with either corporation," and "to create unfair trade." It is argued that the defendant should be restrained from using the word "Corning" as part of its corporate name, and that its adoption was "the invasion of a legal right, which entitles the plaintiff to the injunction, without regard to the question of intent, or damage." The difficulty with the plaintiff's case is that it has been unable to show that its business is interfered with by any competition on the part of the defendant. Of course, the defendant would have no right to establish itself as a rival manufacturer, and, by imitation of name, to mislead the public into buying its manufactures, under the impression that they were buying those of the plaintiff. But that is not this case; for not only is there lacking the element of identity in the business carried on, but the defendant's name, clearly enough, distinguished the kind of article it would offer to the trade. The evidence shows that the manufacture of cut glass is a distinct business, in which the plaintiff had not been, and was not, engaged. Between the two concerns there has been no competition, nor rivalry, because each produces a distinct class of ware. So far as the plaintiff claims any exclusive right to the use of the name of the city in its title, it is only necessary to say that it could acquire no property in it which would entitle it to debar other manufacturers located there from using it, provided it is not used in the same verbal connection, or in such wise as to leave the business indistinguishable. The name "Corning" identifies no particular business, but, at most, would suggest to the mind a great center of the glass industry. The provision of our statute in prohibiting the adoption of a name nearly resembling that of an existing corporation, and the rule of law underlying the intervention by courts to restrain the simulation by one corporation of the name of a prior corporation, find their application when it is plain that the business of the prior corporation would, or might, be obtained, and thus the perpetration of fraud be made possible. *Charles S. Higgins Co. v. Higgins Soap Co.*, 144 N. Y. 462, 39 N. E. 490. Judgment affirmed.

WHEN CORPORATION COMES INTO BEING

Under the statutes of a few states the creation of the corporation is delayed until the holding of the organization meeting or meetings. However, the better view, followed by the statutes of most states, is that the corporation comes into existence as soon as the articles are approved by the Secretary of State. A careful analysis of the statutes and cases discloses a clear distinction between the creation of a corporation and its organization. Creation brings into being a distinct legal entity and gives it permission to organize itself into a going concern. Organization sets up the necessary "machinery" by means of which the new corporation will be able to begin to carry on business.

AMENDING THE CHARTER

The corporation statutes of all the states make provision for amending corporate charters. Most of these statutes are liberal both as to the types of amendments that may be made and the procedure that must be followed in their adoption. It may be broadly stated that any amendment may be adopted if it contains only such provisions as might have been lawfully contained in the original charter or articles of incorporation. Within the confines of this general rule the articles may be amended in any respect desired by the corporation.

The statutes set up the procedure to be followed in amending corporate charters. Usually the board of directors adopts a resolution declaring that the proposed amendment as set forth in the resolution is desirable, and the proposed amendment is then presented to the stockholders at their annual meeting or at a special meeting. To be adopted, it must receive the approval of the holders of at least two thirds, or in some states three fourths, of the voting stock. Some statutes require unanimous approval of certain types of proposed amendments.

DE JURE AND DE FACTO CORPORATIONS

When the incorporators substantially meet all the mandatory requirements under the statute of the state in which they wish to incorporate, a *de jure corporation,* i.e. a corporation as a matter of law, is created. But it sometimes happens that the incorporators attempt in good faith to create a corporation under an existing statute, receive a charter, and proceed to conduct business under the charter, not knowing that they have failed in some respect to comply with the mandatory requirements of the statute. Under such circumstances it is clear that a de jure corporation has not been created. What, then, is the legal status of the incorporators and the purported corporation?

The courts, in most of the states, apply the doctrine of de facto corporation to such situations. In other words, if the incorporators have failed to create a de jure corporation the courts will hold that they have created a *de facto corporation,* i.e. a corporation as a matter of fact, if the facts show that they have met the requirements of a de facto corporation. These requirements are as follows: (1) there must have been a valid statute in existence under which such a corporation could have been incorporated; (2) there must have been a good faith attempt by the incorporators to comply with the requirements of the statute; (3) there must have been what is generally called "user"; that is, the corporation must have been organized under the charter, business must have been conducted, and corporate powers must have been exercised. If the incorporators have failed in any respect to meet these three requirements, the court will hold that a corporation was not created and that the incorporators are liable as partners.

The Uniform Business Corporation Act recognizes the de facto doctrine.[1]

A de facto corporation has all of the rights, privileges and responsibilities of a de jure corporation. Its position, in relation to third parties, is the same as that of a de jure corporation. This means that in private litigation the other party to the suit may not collaterally attack the legal existence of the corporation by attempting to establish that a corporation was never legally created. Nor may the corporation, if it is to its advantage to do so, attack its own legal existence by setting up as a defense that it was not legally created. Only the state may attack the legal existence of a corporation and then only by a direct attack. When this is done the Attorney General directly attacks the corporation in a quo warranto proceeding. It is a direct attack because the only purpose of the proceeding is to compel the corporation to prove its legal existence. The state may not collaterally attack the legal existence of a corporation. For example, if a corporation should bring an action against the state for an alleged breach of contract, for a tax refund, or for some other purpose, the state may not set up collaterally the defense that the corporation failed to obtain a charter and therefore has no legal existence.

The explanation given for the rule that third parties may not collaterally attack the legal existence of a corporation is well stated by the court in the case of *Thies v. Weible et al.*,[2] as follows: "The reason a collateral attack by a third person will not avail against a corporation de facto, is that, if the rights and franchises have been usurped, they are the rights and franchises of the state; and it alone can challenge the validity of the franchises. Until such interposition, the public may treat those in possession and exercising corporate power under color of law as doing so rightfully. The rule is in the interest of the public and is essential to the safety of business transactions with corporations. It would produce disorder

---

[1] Sec. 9.
[2] 126 Neb. 720, 254 N. W. 420 (1934).

and confusion, embarrass and endanger the rights and interests of all dealing with the association, if the legality of its existence could be drawn
into question in every suit in which it is a party or in which rights were
involved, springing out of its corporate existence."

Finnegan v. The Knights of Labor Building Association et al.
52 Minn. 239, 53 N. W. 1150 (1893)

This was an action by Andrew F. Finnegan (plaintiff) against the Knights
of Labor Building Association, Frederick D. Hoerenberg, et al. (defendants).
Judgment for defendants, and plaintiff appealed. Affirmed.

Eight persons signed, acknowledged, and caused to be filed and recorded in
the office of the city clerk of Minneapolis, articles assuming and purporting
to form, under Law 1870, c. 29, a corporation, for the purpose, as specified in
them, of "buying, owning, improving, selling, and leasing of lands, tenements,
hereditaments, real, personal, and mixed estates, and property, including the
construction and leasing of a building in the city of Minneapolis, Minnesota, as
a hall to aid and carry out the general purposes of the organization known as
the 'Knights of Labor.'" The association received subscriptions to its capital
stock, elected directors, adopted bylaws, bought a lot, erected a building on
it, and, when completed, rented different parts of it to different parties. Plaintiff furnished plumbing for the building during its construction, amounting
to $599.50, for which he brought this action against several subscribers to the
stock, as copartners doing business under the firm name of the "Knights of
Labor Building Association." The theory upon which the action was brought
was that, the association having failed to become a corporation, it was in law
a partnership and the members were liable as partners for the debt incurred
by it.

GILFILLAN, C.J. It is claimed that the association was not a corporation
because, first, the act under which it attempted to become incorporated, to
wit, Laws 1870, c. 29, is void, because its subject is not properly expressed in
the title; second, the act does not authorize the formation of corporations for
the purpose or to transact the business stated in the articles; third, the place
where the business was to be carried on was not distinctly stated in the articles,
and they had, perhaps, some other minor defects.

It is unnecessary to consider whether this was a de jure corporation so that
it could defend against a quo warranto in behalf of the state; for, although an
association may not be able to justify itself when called on by the state to show
by what authority it assumes to be, and act as, a corporation, it may be so far
a corporation that, for reasons of public policy, no one but the state will be
permitted to call in question the lawfulness of its organization. Such is what
is termed a corporation de facto; that is, a corporation from the fact of its
acting as such, though not in law or of right a corporation. What is essential
to constitute a body of men a de facto corporation is stated by Selden, J., in

Methodist Etc. Church v. Pickett, 19 **N. Y.** 482, as "(1) the existence of a law under which a corporation with the powers assumed might lawfully be created; and (2) a user by the party to the suit of the rights claimed to be conferred by such charter or law." Since this statement leaves out of account any attempt to organize under the charter or law, we think it is defective. The definition in Taylor on Private Corporations, p. 145, is more nearly accurate: "When a body of men are acting as a corporation, under color of apparent organization, in pursuance of some charter or enabling act, their authority to act as a corporation cannot be questioned collaterally."

A substantial compliance with the mandatory requirements of the statute will make a corporation de jure. But there must be an apparent attempt to perfect an organization under the law. There being such apparent attempt to perfect an organization, the failure as to some substantial requirement will prevent the body being a corporation de jure; but, if there be user pursuant to such attempted organization, it will not prevent it being a corporation de facto.

Only the state may attack the legal existence of a corporation, and then only in a direct attack. In the case at bar the foundation for a de facto corporation having been established the existence of the corporation may not be attacked by the plaintiff. Judgment affirmed.

ORGANIZATION

ORGANIZATION MEETINGS

After the Secretary of State has approved the articles of incorporation the corporation is in existence, but before it can carry out the purposes for which it was created it must be endowed with a form or "organization." Many important decisions and steps must be taken to set up this framework. Directors and officers must be chosen. Bylaws must be drawn up and adopted. The form of the seal must be adopted and a seal obtained. The form of the stock certificate must be agreed upon. And many other things must be done before the corporation is ready to carry on business.

The corporation is "organized" by an organization meeting or meetings. The procedure varies from state to state; it will also vary somewhat within a given jurisdiction, depending upon the provisions of the articles of incorporation.

The statutes of some states require that the members of the first board of directors be named in the articles; they may further permit the articles to give to the board of directors authority to adopt the bylaws. If such authority has been given to named directors under the articles of a given corporation, it is usually not necessary to hold a meeting of the stockholders for the purpose of organizing the corporation; the only organization meeting that need be held is the meeting of the board of directors. But if such authority has not been given, or if under the statutes it is incumbent upon the stockholders to elect the first board of directors and adopt the bylaws, then a stockholders' meeting will be held to perform these functions, and afterward (usually immediately afterward) the directors will hold a meeting to complete the organization. The local statutes and the provisions of the articles of incorporation should always be consulted.

Plans for the organization meeting or meetings should be made as soon as the articles have been approved by the Secretary of State. It is advisable to send out written notices of the time and place of the meeting or meetings, but if the stockholders and directors are notified verbally and attend the meeting, and if each signs a waiver of notice, the meetings will be validly held. In all but a few states the incorporators will have finished their work when they have issued notices for the organization meeting or meetings, and will cease to exist as incorporators. Of course they may, and often do, "reappear" as stockholders, directors, and officers.

The various statutes do not agree as to what persons are entitled to attend the stockholders' organization meeting, in case such a meeting must be held. In some states only those who signed the articles are entitled to attend; in other states all those who have subscribed for stock may attend and vote.

Where no stockholders' meeting is held, the first business on the agenda at the directors' meeting will doubtless be the adoption of bylaws. In any event the directors will complete the organization of the corporation by acting upon the following matters, among others:

(1) Election of officers

(2) Adoption of a seal

(3) Adoption of the form of the stock certificates

(4) Acceptance of stock subscriptions and authorization of issuance of the stock

(5) Authorization of the payment of organization fees

(6) Adoption of promoter's pre-incorporation contracts

(7) Authorization of the payment of the promoter for his services and expenses

(8) Selection of a bank of deposit for the corporation

(9) Adoption of a resolution providing for the method of drawing and indorsing checks

(10) Adoption of a resolution authorizing and directing the officers of the corporation to take the necessary steps to qualify the stock for sale under any applicable Blue Sky Laws and the Securities & Exchange Commission

(11) If stock is to be offered for sale in another jurisdiction, adoption of a resolution directing the officers to take the necessary steps to obtain authority to make such sales

(12) If the corporation contemplates doing intrastate business in another state, adoption of a resolution authorizing the officers to obtain a license for such business

When all these and other necessary matters have been acted upon, the corporation is said to be organized. It is now ready to carry on business under the powers and authority given it by the state constitution, state statutes, articles of incorporation, and bylaws.

BYLAWS

The corporation statutes of a state are applicable alike to all corporations organized under it. The articles of incorporation of a corporation apply only to that particular corporation and provide for its framework. The bylaws complete the corporate structure. More particularly, the bylaws have to do with the internal government of the corporation. They must be in conformity with the state constitution, statutes, and articles of incorporation; otherwise they are void. They are binding upon the directors, stockholders, and officers of the corporation but are not binding upon third parties unless they have knowledge or notice of their content.

At common law the authority to adopt, amend, and repeal bylaws rests in the stockholders of the corporation. However, the statutes of most states provide that such authority may be delegated to the board of directors by placing a provision to that effect in the articles of incorporation. Some states safeguard the stockholders by providing that where the bylaws are adopted by the board of directors they are subject to repeal by the stockholders.

Bylaws usually contain provisions covering the following matters:

(1) Stockholders: annual meeting (time and place, notice, business, quorum, proxies, voting rights); special meetings (why and how called, time and place, notice, proxies, voting rights)

(2) Directors: numbers; election; terms; regular meetings (time and place, notice, quorum); special meetings (time and place, notice, quorum, purposes); removal; filling of vacancies

(3) Officers: creation of certain offices; powers and duties; compensation; removal; filling of vacancies

(4) Committees: creation of certain committees; authority

(5) Stock: issuance of stock certificates to stockholders; procedure for transfer of stock; closing of books against transfer of stock

(6) Dividends: authority of directors to declare and pay dividends; funds out of which dividends may be paid; what stockholders are entitled to dividends

(7) Books and records: kinds to be kept

(8) Amendments: amendment, alteration, and repeal of bylaws

REVIEW CASES

1. A quo warranto action was brought by the state against Ford and others to determine whether a corporation called the Washer Maid Co. had ever been brought into existence. It was charged that no corporation had been created, since the incorporators, when they signed their names to the articles of incorporation, did not sign under seal as required by the statute. Judgment for whom? (People v. Ford, 294 Ill. 319, 128 N. E. 479)

2. The Chicago Real Estate Show Corp. placed advertising with the Inter-Ocean Newspaper Co. Thereafter it became insolvent and was unable to pay the obligation. The newspaper company brought suit to hold the stockholders liable, on the theory that the purported corporation was non-existent because the prescribed certificate of organization had never been filed in the office of the recorder of deeds. Holding? (Inter-Ocean Newspaper Co. v. Robinson et al., 296 Ill. 92, 129 N. E. 523)

3. Battelle purchased certain real and personal property from Canney, who took a note and mortgage for the balance due. Shortly thereafter Battelle, Lamson, and Teak formed a corporation, the Northwest Concrete Pavement Co., they being the only stockholders. It was agreed in advance by the three that Battelle would turn over the property to the corporation and that in return he would receive a third of the stock and the corporation would assume and pay the note. After the firm was incorporated, the property was conveyed to it and was used for its benefit. The corporation did not pay the note, and Battelle was forced to pay it. He brought action for breach of contract against the corporation. Ruling? (Battelle v. Northwest Concrete Pavement Co., 37 Minn. 89, 33 N. W. 327)

4. Hogan and Lloyd were the incorporators of Holbrook Microfilming Service, a Delaware corporation incorporated in November, 1942. Shortly afterward Hogan and Lloyd got an option for the purchase of a New York company whose business they expected to continue under the new corporation, and they contracted with Kenyon to become president of the company. On April 16th Kenyon gave up his position in another company, and for two months he was steadily engaged in various kinds of work for the new corporation. Thereafter he sued the corporation to recover salary alleged due under his contract, on the theory that Hogan and Lloyd, as incorporators, had power to commit the corporation, without regard to ratification by the directors. Judgment for whom? (Kenyon v. Holbrook Microfilming Service, 155 F.(2d) 913)

5. Higgins sold to the Chas. S. Higgins Co., a corporation, a soap business for $810,000, reserving the right to stay in the same business. The soap manufactured by the corporation was often called Higgins' soap, and the corporation was often referred to as the Higgins Soap Co. Soon after the sale of the business Higgins and others organized a corporation called the Higgins Soap Co. Within a period of four months the new corporation received twenty-eight letters meant for the old corporation. The Chas. S. Higgins Co. asked the court for an injunction restraining the new company from using the name of Higgins Soap Co. Holding? (Chas. S. Higgins Co. v. Higgins Soap Co., 144 N. Y. 462, 39 N. E. 490)

Powers and Liabilities of Corporations

45

POWERS

While a natural person has the inherent power to do any and all things not prohibited by law, corporations, being merely the creatures of the state, possess only the powers and authority granted to them by the state.[1] The sources of such authority are found in the common law, the general corporation statutes, and the articles of incorporation. The powers of corporations may be classified as (1) express, (2) implied, and (3) incidental or general.

An act which exceeds the powers of a corporation is called an *ultra vires act* (literally, "beyond the powers").

EXPRESS POWERS

The express powers of a particular corporation are contained in its articles of incorporation. Many, but not all, of the express powers are enumerated in the "purpose clause" of the articles. The articles, among other things, set forth the purposes and objectives of the corporation, the nature of the business to be carried on by it, and the nature of its capital structure.

The authority of a state legislature to confer express powers upon the corporations it creates is very broad. In fact, such authority is limited only by any applicable provisions contained in the federal and state constitutions.

Since the express powers of a corporation are those powers given a particular corporation by its articles of incorporation, it follows that the ex-

[1] Sometimes corporations are incorporated by Congress, in which case their powers are derived from the statutes which create them.

press powers of all corporations are not the same. For example, one corporation may be incorporated to carry on a small, local retail business and may be authorized to issue only one class of stock; whereas another corporation may be incorporated to manufacture automobiles and may be authorized to issue more than one class of stock.

IMPLIED POWERS

The implied powers of a corporation are those powers which are necessary, appropriate, convenient, and proper to carrying out or putting into effect its express powers. Just as the doctrine of implied powers developed in the field of constitutional law when the courts endeavored, in the early days of the Republic, to determine the scope of the powers granted the federal government by the Constitution, so has the doctrine of implied powers developed in the field of corporation law. It has been the tendency, in corporation law as in constitutional law, for the courts to apply a broad or "liberal" interpretation of the express powers granted, with the result that the modern business corporation has been given a greater freedom of action.

In a given case where it is clear that the corporation does not have the express power to perform a certain act or enter into a particular contract, whether it has the implied power to do so is largely a matter of the interpretation which the court is willing to place upon the express grant of power, coupled with the facts and circumstances of the particular case. If the act or contract tends to accomplish the legitimate business for which the corporation was created, the court will hold that such power is implied. If it is not consonant with the purposes for which the corporation was formed, the court will hold that such power may not be implied.

State v. San Antonio Public Service Co.
69 S. W. (2d) 39 (1934)

This was an action by the State of Texas (plaintiff) against the San Antonio Public Service Company (defendant), to review a judgment of the Court of Civil Appeals, affirming in part and reversing in part a judgment of the District Court. The State appealed. Judgment of the Court of Civil Appeals affirmed. (NOTE: Only that portion of the case that deals with implied powers is presented in this abstract.)

The State of Texas instituted this proceeding seeking to perpetually enjoin defendant from doing certain acts alleged to be in violation of law and ultra vires of its corporate powers. The State alleged that defendant was incorporated under article 1121 of the statute "for the purpose of constructing, acquiring, maintaining, and operating lines of electric motor railway," and "for the manufacture, supplying, and selling of electricity and gas for light, heat, and power to the public and to municipalities"; and that in violation of article 1349, R. S. 1925, inhibiting a corporation from employing "its stock, means, assets, or other property, directly or indirectly for any purpose whatever other than to accomplish the legitimate business of its creation, or those purposes otherwise permitted by law," and as ultra vires of its corporate powers, defendant was employing its means and assets: (1) in the purchase for sale and the sale of all kinds and character of electric and gas appliances, maintaining a department, salesroom, and salesmen therefor, and employing in excess of $150,000 of its means and assets for such purposes.

Defendant answered, in substance: (1) that as a part of its business of manufacturing, supplying, and selling electricity and gas to the public and as incident thereto, it sold electric and gas appliances to its customers for the purpose of increasing its business and to accomplish the legitimate business of its creation.

The trial court perpetually enjoined defendant from purchasing and selling electric and gas appliances, and defendant appealed to the Court of Civil Appeals. The Court of Civil Appeals dissolved the injunction, and the State appealed.

BLAIR, J. We have reached the conclusion that under the facts and rules of law applicable, defendant had the right to engage in the purchase for sale and the sale of gas and electric appliances in connection with and as being incident to its principal business of manufacturing, supplying, and selling gas and electricity to the public for heating, lighting, and power purposes.

It is manifest that article 1349 authorizes a corporation to do whatever may "accomplish the legitimate business of its creation, or those purposes otherwise permitted by law." The statute does not necessarily add to or take from the general rule of implied powers of a corporation, but rather restates the rule by other appropriate language. That is, the rule of implied powers would authorize defendant to do those things which are incident to and reasonably necessary to the carrying out of the powers expressly granted. No distinction can be made between this rule and the provisions of the statute authorizing a corporation to do whatever may "accomplish the legitimate business of its creation." Implied powers of a corporation are necessarily "those purposes otherwise permitted by law"; and we are clear in the view that the evidence detailed shows that the sale of gas and electric appliances tends directly to increase the use and consumption by the public of gas and electricity, and therefore tends directly "to accomplish the legitimate business" of defendant, to wit, the manufacturing, supplying, and selling of gas and electricity to the public.

It is agreed in this case that the power to sell gas and electric appliances to its customers using gas and electricity for lighting, heating, and power purposes is not expressly granted by the charter of the defendant, or by specific statute; but that if defendant has such power, it is by implication, as being incident to and as reasonably necessary to accomplish the legitimate business of its creation. The implied powers of a corporation, such as are necessary to effectuate or carry out the powers expressly granted, or to accomplish the legitimate business of its creation, are not limited to such as are indispensable for those purposes, but comprise all that are necessary in the sense of appropriate and suitable, including the right of reasonable choice of means to be employed. The question presented is one of mixed law and fact.

As was stated in the case of *Malone v. Lancaster Gas Light & Fuel Co.,* 182 Pa. 309, 37 A. 932: "It would be of no use to manufacture gas if there were no customers to buy, and hence the company may fairly supply, not only the gas itself, but, incidentally, such appliances and conveniences as will induce new customers to use gas, or old ones to use more. This is a legitimate mode of extending the company's business, in direct furtherance of its charter objects."

Judgment of the Court of Civil Appeals dissolving the injunction affirmed.

INCIDENTAL OR GENERAL POWERS

What are often referred to by the courts as the *incidental powers* of corporations had their origin in the common law and not in some statutory enactment. As we have heretofore seen, the first corporations in this country received their charters from the state legislatures. The experience that the people had had with the vast trading corporations led them to believe that corporations were monopolistic and undemocratic, and that the powers granted them should be severely circumscribed. For this reason the state legislatures, in granting charters to corporations, tended to limit their powers sharply. The express powers granted were often inadequate to permit corporations to function properly. To remedy this situation the courts began to imply that corporations, by the very fact of their creation, possessed certain powers, since without these powers they could not function as corporations. Such powers were thought to be *incident* to corporate existence, and hence were often termed incidental powers.[1]

Among the incidental powers recognized by the courts are the following: the power to have perpetual succession for the period designated in the charter; the power to have a corporate name, and to contract and to sue and be sued in that name; the power to have a common seal; the power to make bylaws for the internal government of the corporation; the power to appoint directors, officers, and agents. Except as limited by its charter, a corporation has incidental power to purchase, hold, convey, mortgage,

---

[1] On occasion the courts have also referred to these powers as "implied powers." This name is logical enough, since the powers were implied from the nature of corporations in general. But the student of corporation law should distinguish carefully between those powers which are implied from the express powers granted to a particular corporation (and which therefore vary from corporation to corporation) and those which are implied because they are thought to be essential to the existence of any corporation (and which are therefore the same for all corporations). To avoid confusion, this chapter uses the designation "implied powers" for the former group and "incidental powers" for the latter.

and pledge real and personal property, to borrow money, to issue bonds, and to make, draw, accept, and indorse negotiable instruments, always provided such powers are used to carry out the purposes for which the corporation was created.

The courts take the position that a corporation does not have incidental power to lend its credit to others by serving as a surety or guarantor, or as an accommodation party. The explanation for this rule is that such an act would not usually tend to carry out the purposes and objectives for which the corporation was created. However, the courts have recognized the existence of such incidental power in a few cases where the act of serving as a surety or guarantor did promote the objectives of the corporation involved.

While the courts of a few states have taken a contrary position, the great majority of the jurisdictions in this country hold that, in the absence of express charter restrictions, a business corporation has incidental power to purchase its own stock, provided such purchase is made in good faith and does not impair the rights of creditors and stockholders. The courts generally require that such purchase be made only out of surplus profits.[1] The acquisition of the stock of other corporations has been held not to be an incident of corporate existence. However, authority to acquire the stock of another corporation is often granted where such acquisition is in furtherance of corporate objectives.

A corporation is held not to possess the incidental authority to become a member of a partnership. Under the statutes of a few states authority to do so may be granted in the articles of incorporation of a given corporation.

Most of the general corporation statutes today enumerate explicitly the powers that are possessed alike by all corporations created under those statutes. In the statutes themselves these powers are often referred to as *general powers;* elsewhere the name *statutory powers* is often applied to them. The general or statutory powers usually include all the foregoing incidental powers and others besides.

Doty v. American Telephone & Telegraph Co.
123 Tenn. 329, 130 S. W. 1053 (1919)

This was an action of ejectment by D. M. Doty (plaintiff) against the American Telephone & Telegraph Co. (defendant). Judgment for defendant, and plaintiff appealed. Affirmed.

---

[1] Stock reacquired by a corporation either by purchase or by gift is known as *treasury stock.* If the stock is not canceled it is treated as outstanding and may be resold by the corporation at any price it will bring. While such stock is held by the corporation as treasury stock it cannot be voted by the corporation, nor is it subject to the payment of dividends.

This action of ejectment was brought by plaintiff to recover from the American Telephone & Telegraph Co., a New York corporation, certain land taken by the American Telephone & Telegraph Co., a Tennessee corporation, and afterwards conveyed by the Tennessee company to the New York company, a portion of which land it was alleged the latter company unlawfully held and detained; the reference being to that portion of the land occupied by the poles, wires, cross-arms, etc., of defendant company.

It was the contention of plaintiff that under the provisions of the Act of 1883, a telephone company can be chartered only for the purpose of manufacturing electricity for telephoning purposes, and that the Act confers no power to construct lines, operate exchanges, or to do other things of like character incidental to the telephone business.

Defendant had judgment and plaintiff appealed.

GREEN, J. The Act of 1883 undoubtedly and in express terms authorized the incorporation of telephone companies and telephone and power companies. Is it reasonable to suppose that, after providing for the creation of telephone companies, it was the intention of the Legislature to restrict their powers to such an insignificant detail of the business as the manufacture of the necessary electricity? The electricity for telephone purposes is made by small batteries, not in power houses, and it requires but little of their equipment and a trivia of their attention and activities for telephone companies to manufacture all needed electricity.

The general rule undoubtedly is that the powers of a corporation are only such as its charter confers, and that, when the charter undertakes to enumerate the powers thereby given to the corporation, it is to be construed as withholding from it other powers not mentioned. This rule is usually qualified, however, by the statement that the failure to enumerate them in the charter does not deprive a corporation of such incidental powers as are reasonably necessary to accomplish the purposes for which it was organized.

Certainly, when a corporation is created for a particular purpose, by implication it is vested with such powers as are absolutely necessary for it to effect the purposes of its creation. It is not necessary that any powers at all be expressed in the charter in order to endow it with many rights. The mere creation of a corporation carries with it certain powers, which are regarded as incidents of corporate existence.

It was long since held in this state that, while "a corporation is the creature of the charter that institutes and gives it being, yet it is equally true that some things by common law are incident to a corporation, which it may do without any express provision in the charter of incorporation, as to sue and be sued, purchase and sell, make bylaws, and have a common seal. *Jonesboro v. McKee*, 2 Yerg. 167, 170.

In addition to those general powers, imputed to all corporations, whether expressly conferred or not, there are other implied powers, peculiar to each corporation, and dependent on the nature of the particular corporation. As said by this court in an early case: "The creation of a corporation for a specific purpose implies a power to use the necessary and usual means to effectuate that purpose." *Union Bank v. Jacobs*, 6 Humph. 515. This case has since been followed in Tennessee by many others, holding that, regardless of their enumeration in the charter, corporations had such implied powers as were necessary for them to accomplish the objects for which they were created. The rule, otherwise stated, is that a corporation has such implied powers as are necessarily implied from those granted.

When the Legislature, therefore, authorized the incorporation of telephone companies, the intention was that such companies should engage in the telephone business. They were authorized for the specific purpose of carrying on the telephone business. That being true, the power was given to such corporations by implication to effectuate that purpose. The usual and necessary means being the erecting of poles, the stringing of wires, the operating of exchanges, etc., the power to do such things was properly implied in telephone companies organized under the Act of 1883. The power to conduct a telephone business being granted, these others seem clearly and necessarily implied. That which is fairly implied is as much granted as that which is expressed.

Judgment affirmed.

Brinson v. Mill Supply Co., Inc.

219 N. C. 498, 14 S. E. (2d) 505 (1941)

This was an action by W. T. Brinson, in behalf of himself and all other stockholders and creditors of the Mill Supply Co. (plaintiff) against the Mill Supply Co., Inc. (defendant), for the appointment of a receiver and the liquidation of the company. E. F. Smallwood was appointed receiver, and Laura H. Harvey, executrix of the estate of Mrs. Harriet L. Hyman, filed a claim. The claim was rejected, and claimant appealed. Affirmed.

On March 14, 1931, Albert F. Patterson borrowed from Harriet L. Hyman the sum of $5,000, evidenced by his note. Fifty shares of the Mill Supply Company were deposited with the payee as collateral security. The payment of the note was also guaranteed by the Mill Supply Company by a separate contract. This guaranty contract was executed by A. F. Patterson, president, and the secretary of the defendant corporation. This action was authorized by a resolution adopted by the executive committee of the corporation.

The receiver contended that the corporation was not bound by the guaranty contract because the contract was ultra vires and beyond the authority of the corporation to make.

BARNHILL, J. Was the act of the officers of the defendant corporation, in authorizing and executing the contract of guaranty, ultra vires as contended by the receiver? The court below so concluded. In this conclusion we concur.

For a contract executed by the officer of a corporation to be binding on the corporation it must appear that (1) it was incidental to the business of the corporation; or (2) it was expressly authorized; and (3) it was properly executed.

The charter of the defendant corporation, among other things, vested it with general authority to acquire, own, mortgage, sell and otherwise deal in real estate, chattels, and chattels real without limit as to amount; to deal in mortgages, notes, shares of capital stock, and other securities; and "to do all and everything necessary, suitable, convenient, or proper for the accomplish‑ ment of any of the purposes, or the attainment of any one or more of the objects, herein enumerated, or incident to the power herein named, or which shall at any time appear conducive or expedient for the protection or benefit of the corporation, either as holder of or interest in, any property, or other‑ wise." The powers thus granted do not expressly authorize the corporation to issue accommodation paper or to guarantee the obligations of a third party.

The contract of guaranty was no part of a transaction in which the corpora‑ tion was borrowing or raising money for the purposes of its incorporation. It was clearly and exclusively an act in aid and for the accommodation of its president as an individual. From it the corporation received no benefit. Hence, it appears that the undertaking of the corporation was not directly "necessary, suitable, convenient, or proper for the accomplishment of" either of these or of any other purpose authorized by the charter.

Was the contract of guaranty incidental to or in furtherance of the powers expressly granted? If not, it was ultra vires and unenforceable. Ordinarily, the power to endorse or guarantee the payment of negotiable instruments for the benefit of a third party is not within the implied powers conferred upon a private business corporation. The general rule is that no corporation has the power, by any form of contract or endorsement, to become a guarantor or surety or otherwise lend its credit to another person or corporation. 19 *C. J. S.*, Corporations, p. 917, Sec. 1230; 7 *Fletcher on Corps.* 647; 7 *R. C. L.* 675. In the absence of express statutory authorization, a corporation has no implied power to lend its credit to another by issuing or endorsing bills or notes for his accommodation, where the transaction is not related to the busi‑ ness activity authorized by its charter as a necessary or usual incident thereto. It has no authority to use its credit for the benefit of a stockholder or officer. *Hunter v. Garanflo*, 246 Mo. 131, 151 S. W. 741.

The contract was executed for the benefit of an individual. No part of the consideration moved to the defendant corporation. It was not either expressly or impliedly authorized by its charter to enter into contracts for the accom‑ modation of a third party. To permit the payment of the claim would clearly result in an invasion of the assets of the defendant corporation in the hands of the receiver as a trust fund for the payment of legitimate creditors. Judg‑ ment affirmed.

ULTRA VIRES ACTS

EFFECT OF ULTRA VIRES CONTRACTS. Considerable inconsistency exists in the court decisions as to the effect of ultra vires contracts, but the follow‑ ing generalizations can be made from a study of the cases.

(1) Where the contract is fully executed, the court will not interfere

and will refuse to grant relief to either party. It will leave the parties where it finds them.

(2) Where the contract is wholly executory, the contract is not enforceable by either party. If one party sues the other, alleging a breach of the contract, the defense of ultra vires is available to the party being sued.

(3) Where the contract is fully executed by only one of the parties, the courts do not agree as to the legal effect of the contract. The position taken by the U. S. Supreme Court and a few state courts is that such a contract is absolutely void and unenforceable and hence no action can be brought *on the contract;* but if the person who has performed has given something of value, he is entitled to recover it or its reasonable value in *quasi-contract*. The view taken by the majority of the state courts is that the party who has performed his part of the contract may sue on the contract itself for damages for its breach. According to this view the party who has defaulted in performance is estopped from setting up as a defense that the contract is ultra vires.

WHO MAY OBJECT TO THE COMMISSION OF AN ULTRA VIRES ACT. Objection to the commission of an ultra vires act may usually be made by the state and by the stockholders, and upon occasion by the creditors of the corporation. The charter of a corporation is in effect a contract between the corporation and the state of incorporation and between the corporation and its stockholders, and it is held that, in effect, the corporation agrees not to go beyond the powers granted in the charter. If it breaches its contract by usurping additional powers, the state may proceed against the corporation. If the usurpation of power is extreme the state may file a quo warranto proceeding against the corporation and demand that its charter be forfeited. In less serious infractions of corporate power the state may file a suit in equity asking that the corporation be enjoined from committing the ultra vires act. The stockholders, too, may usually enjoin the corporation from entering into or performing a contemplated ultra vires act or contract. The courts have also permitted the creditors of a corporation to enjoin the corporation from committing an ultra vires act where the commission of such act would imperil the security of the creditors.

Temple Lumber Co. v. Miller
169 S. W. (2d) 256 (Tex.) (1943)

This was an action by A. A. Miller (plaintiff) against the Temple Lumber Company (defendant). Judgment for plaintiff, and defendant appealed. Affirmed.

Plaintiff sued defendant Temple Lumber Company, a corporation, for damages growing out of an alleged contract by which defendant contracted to construct a dwelling house for plaintiff in Denton, Texas.

The facts, as found by the trial court, were as follows: Plaintiff and defendant entered into a contract, part in writing and part oral, by which defendant was to furnish all material and labor in the construction of a house for plaintiff according to a set of plans and specifications for the sum of $3072. It was specified that changes could be agreed upon; if the cost was reduced as a result, plaintiff was to have the benefit; if increased, he should pay. Defendant's charter set out the purposes of the corporation as that of "manufacturing lumber and the purchase and sale of material used in such business and doing all things necessary and incident to such lumber business." At the time of the controversy J. E. Graham was an employee of defendant at its place of business. Plaintiff and Graham were friends of long standing and all the negotiations were between them. From the beginning Graham represented to plaintiff that defendant was back of the contract and that it was to be between plaintiff and defendant. Graham was at all times in charge of the construction and was defendant's general agent while in charge of the job. He signed the plans and specifications as follows: "O. K. Guaranteed as to performance. Temple Lumber Company, by J. E. Graham, agent." His acts in this respect were those of defendant. After the contract sued on was consummated, defendant, acting through Graham, procured one Tunniccliff to do and superintend the construction of the house. Tunniccliff was the agent of defendant; plaintiff had never had any dealings with him and never knew him until he began work. When it was reported to plaintiff that the house was completed, he made a check payable to Tunniccliff for $1072 and gave it to Graham, who indorsed it and passed it to the credit of defendant. Plaintiff borrowed $2,000 and paid it to Graham, and defendant received the proceeds. The facts found by the trial court include the findings that there were defective materials and workmanship which would require $800 to correct, and that on account of changes made in the plans, plaintiff still owed defendant $180.56. The trial court held for plaintiff, and defendant appealed.

Defendant contended, first, that Graham exceeded his authority in entering into the contract and hence defendant was not liable, and, second, that defendant was not liable since the acts contracted for were ultra vires and beyond the powers of the corporation to perform.

SPEER, J. It appears that the early English cases, as well as some by federal courts, and even the early cases decided by our state courts, are not in complete harmony with respect to the extent a corporation may go to bind itself. But the trend seems to be that even though the charter provisions do not, in so many words, authorize an act, the corporation may bind itself to do many things, when they are not against public policy and are not forbidden by law. There is a clear distinction between acts which are void because of legal inhibitions, and those which are not prohibited but are those which are not enumerated in the purpose clause of the charter. In the latter class are to be found instances which include acts which are appropriate, convenient, and suitable in carrying out the purposes for which the charter was expressly granted. *State v. San Antonio Public Service Co.*, 69 S. W. (2d) 38.

To our minds, the contract involved here was one not prohibited by law nor by any principle of public policy. We think that if the act is not prohibited by law or public policy, and it inures to the direct benefit of the corporation, and is *executed*, it is not, strictly speaking, ultra vires, and this is apparently the view taken by the trial court. Judgment affirmed.

LIABILITIES

CONTRACT LIABILITY

Since a corporation is an artificial person and possesses no physical existence of its own, all its contracts must be negotiated by its legally constituted agents. It may therefore be stated as a fundamental rule of law that a corporation is bound by such contracts if they have been entered into by a legally authorized agent, acting within the scope of his authority and on behalf of the corporation.

The general principles of contract law and agency law are applicable to contracts entered into by business corporations.

UNIFORM COMMERCIAL CODE

Article 8, Investment Security, of the Code places liability and responsibility on the part of a corporation issuing investment securities. Should a corporation overissue securities, Sec. 8–104 of the Code provides that the person entitled to the issue may compel the issuer to replace the overissue by purchase of such security in the market and delivering it to him. If a security is not available for purchase, the person entitled to the issue may recover from the issuer the price he or the last purchaser for value paid for it with interest from date of his demand. Sec. 8–104 (2) states that "overissue" means the issue of securities in excess of the amount which the issuer has corporate power to issue. Sec. 8–202 (1) imposes on a purchaser for value without notice the terms stated on the security and those made a part of it by reference to the extent that the terms referred to do not conflict with the stated terms.

Sec. 8–205 of the Code provides that "An unauthorized signature placed on a security prior to or in the course of issue is ineffective except that the signature is effective in favor of a purchaser for value and without notice of the lack of authority if the signing has been done by (a) an authenticating trustee, registrar, transfer agent or other person entrusted by the issuer with the signing of the security or of similar securities or their immediate preparation for signing; or (b) an employee of the issuer or of any of the foregoing entrusted with responsible handling of the security."

Sec. 8–202 (3) provides: "Except as otherwise provided in the case of certain unauthorized signatures on issue (Section 8–205), lack of genuineness of a security is a complete defense."

TORT LIABILITY

Corporations are liable for the torts of their officers, agents, and employees committed while acting within the scope and course of their employment. In accordance with the doctrine of respondeat superior, the acts of the agent are imputed to the principal. In other words, the liability of a corporate principal or employer for the torts of its officers, agents, and employees is essentially the same as that of a natural principal or employer. Furthermore, it is no defense to the corporation that its officer, agent, or employee was engaging in an ultra vires act or transaction at the time the tort was committed.

Examples of torts for which corporations have been held liable are negligence, assault and battery, false imprisonment, conspiracy, trespass, and nuisance.

Chamberlain v. Southern California Edison Co.
167 Cal. 500, 140 P. 25 (1914)

This was an action by Caleb Chamberlain (plaintiff) against the Southern California Edison Co. (defendant). Judgment for plaintiff, and defendant appealed. Affirmed.

The Southern California Edison Co., a corporation, was engaged in the business of manufacturing and distributing electricity for light, heat, and power. One of its employees, J. A. Lighthipe, owned an automobile which was in need of repairs. The general storekeeper of the corporation was W. T. Sterling, and J. R. Rosso was driver of one of the company's trucks in distributing supplies. Rosso was under Sterling's direction but was subject to orders also from the president, the general manager, and the assistant general manager. Sterling ordered Rosso to go to Lighthipe's residence with the company's truck, of which Rosso was the driver, and to bring Lighthipe's automobile to the shop which the corporation maintained for the repair of its own motor vehicles. The order was obeyed and while Rosso was towing Lighthipe's automobile, plaintiff was injured through Rosso's carelessness and negligence. It was shown that Lighthipe's car was repaired at the company's shop, that a bill was rendered by the company and paid by Lighthipe, and that the charges so made and paid amounted to the actual cost to the company of material and labor.

Chamberlain filed suit against defendant corporation for damages for injuries sustained and obtained judgment. Defendant corporation appealed.

MELVIN, J. The sole attack of the appellant is upon that part of the findings which declares that the truck was in charge of a servant of the defendant corporation at the time of the infliction of the injuries upon the plaintiff. In this behalf the assistant general manager of the corporation testified that he had not instructed Sterling to send for Lighthipe's car. It was not denied, however, that Sterling did give the orders to Rosso, and there was no proof that someone higher in authority than the assistant general manager did not order the work to be done. The defendant's articles of incorporation were introduced into evidence and attention was called to the fact that the repairing of automobiles is not one of the purposes for which it was organized.

The contention of appellant is that Rosso was not engaged in his master's business at the time of the accident, and that the repairing of Lighthipe's automobile was ultra vires.

The defense of ultra vires is untenable. If the defendant was a natural person and he should instruct his servant to bring an automobile to his place of business there would be no doubt of his liability for a tort such as this occurring during the time when his command was in process of execution. He could not justly defend upon the theory that he was a banker and not a blacksmith. It would make no difference if he intended to use the automobile, after repairing it, in transporting firearms across the Mexican border.

Upon a like principle the defendant corporation may not escape liability for the torts of its servants, acting under orders, upon the theory that it is not authorized to make repairs upon the instrumentality that caused the damages. To hold otherwise would be to give an artificial person an immunity not enjoyed by a natural one. A corporation acts through its officers and servants. When the plaintiff establishes the fact that the driver was acting as a servant of defendant and under orders from an officer of the corporation, who was authorized to direct him in his work, a prima facie case was established in favor of the plaintiff. The rule is that actions like the one at bar being founded not upon contract but upon tort, the defense of ultra vires is not available. Under the rule of respondeat superior a corporation is civilly liable for torts committed by its servant or agent while acting within the scope of his employment, although the corporation neither authorized the doing of the particular act nor ratified it after it was done. In the case at bar the servant acted by authority and the principal ratified the act by repairing, for a consideration, the automobile which he had taken into his shop. . . . The towing of the automobile was the natural result of the order which Rosso received from his superior. The evidence abundantly sustains the finding which is attacked. The judgment is accordingly affirmed.

CRIMINAL LIABILITY

While some of the earlier courts were of the opinion that a corporation could not be held liable for the criminal acts of its officers, agents, and employees, the overwhelming weight of authority today is to the effect that a corporation may generally be held responsible for such crimes. This is true for both common law and statutory crimes. However, the criminal liability of a corporate principal is not as extensive as that of an individual principal. The courts are almost unanimous in holding that a corporation may not be held liable for any crime which has as one of its elements the requirement of criminal intent. For example, a corporation cannot be held criminally liable for such crimes as murder, bigamy, or treason. The courts refuse to impute the criminal intent of the corporation's agent or employee to the corporation. However, many statutory crimes do not require proof of criminal intent but provide that the act of violating the statute in itself constitutes the crime. The crime may arise out of either nonfeasance or misfeasance. For example, a number of federal and state statutes, such as the workmen's compensation laws, the Social Security Act, the anti-trust laws, certain tax laws, and the Securities Acts of 1933 and 1934 require corporations to perform certain acts, and make unlawful the failure to do so. To illustrate, the Sherman Anti-Trust Law of 1890 provides, in part, as follows: "Every contract, combination in the form of a trust or otherwise, or conspiracy, in restraint of trade or commerce among the several states, or with foreign nations, is hereby declared to be illegal. Every person who shall make any such contract or engage in any such combination or conspiracy shall be guilty of a misdemeanor, and, on conviction thereof, shall be punished by a fine not exceeding five thousand dollars, or by imprisonment not exceeding one year, or both said punishments, in the discretion of the court." The term "person" includes both natural and artificial persons.

A corporation cannot be punished by imprisonment, but it may be punished by the imposition of a fine. Thus, if the penalty for violating a criminal statute is "either a fine or imprisonment or both," and if corporations are covered by the statute, the courts find no difficulty in holding that corporations are subject to the terms of the statute.

Corporations as well as individuals are held liable for contempt of court.

REVIEW CASES

1. Jemison et al., commission merchants and members of the New York Cotton Exchange, sued the Citizens' Savings Bank of Jefferson to recover commissions and sums expended on the purchase and sale of cotton futures. The defense was that the bank, as a savings bank and trust corporation, had no power to deal in speculative contracts, and that the plaintiffs were chargeable with knowledge that the bank's agent had no authority to bind it on such contracts. Judgment for whom? (Jemison et al. v. Citizens' Savings Bank of Jefferson, 122 N. Y. 135, 25 N. E. 264)

2. The Goldstein Co., a corporation engaged in the business of selling theatrical costumes, had a contract pending with the Continental Co. for the sale of a large quantity of costumes to be used in a film which the Continental Co. intended to produce. The production was threatened by the

refusal of the Woods Lumber Co. to extend further credit to the Continental Co. The Goldstein Co. guaranteed the payment of all obligations which the producing company might contract with the lumber company, and the latter supplied the producing company with building materials and merchandise. The producing company did not pay the lumber company, and the latter sued the Goldstein Co. While the action was pending, the Goldstein Co. was adjudged a bankrupt, and Moore, the trustee in bankruptcy, was substituted as defendant. The defense was that the agent of the company had no authority to bind the corporation on a guaranty contract. Judgment for whom? (Woods Lumber Co. v. Moore, 183 Cal. 497, 191 P. 905)

3. Cole was a stockholder and a director of the Cole Realty Co., a corporation. He strongly opposed certain policies which the other directors favored. It was finally agreed that he would withdraw from the corporation and that the corporation would buy his stock at a stipulated price. The corporation later refused to pay for the stock, and Cole filed a bill in equity for specific performance. The defense was that the corporation had no authority to buy its own stock. Holding? (Cole v. Cole Realty Co., 169 Mich. 347, 135 N. W. 329)

4. Dwyer was a passenger on a street car of the St. Louis Transit Co., a corporation. The conductor accused him of not paying his fare, which Dwyer had actually paid. The conductor had a policeman arrest Dwyer, who was tried and acquitted. Dwyer sued the corporation for malicious prosecution. The defense was that the conductor had no authority to have Dwyer arrested, and that he had acted to gratify his individual malice. Judgment for whom? (Dwyer v. St. Louis Transit Co., 108 Mo. App. 152, 83 S. W. 303)

5. Employees of the Rochester Railway & Light Co., a corporation, negligently installed certain fixtures, with the result that gas escaped and a person was killed. The state prosecuted the corporation, charging manslaughter in the second degree. Holding? (People v. Rochester Railway & Light Co., 195 N. Y. 102, 88 N. E. 22)

6. The Provident Stores Corp. was organized for the purpose of operating a chain of retail stores. The stock of the company was limited to 6,000 shares, of which Cranwell held 5,998. Cranwell met Fannie Tanner, aged 81, who owned 140 shares of National Biscuit Co. Stock. Cranwell contracted with her in the name of the corporation to pay her $55 per month for the loan of the stock so that he could use it as security to get a loan. The corporation paid the $55 per month for a time, and then became insolvent. Cranwell had sold the stock for his private gain. Fannie Tanner sued the corporation for the value of the stock. The receiver contended that the transaction with her was ultra vires. Holding? (Provident Stores' Receiver v. Tanner, 226 Ky. 365, 10 S. W.(2d) 1077)

Financing of Corporations

46

Corporations are financed through one or both of the following general methods: (1) the sale of their stocks; (2) borrowing. Whether one or both methods are used by a given corporation is largely a matter of financial judgment; there are very few legal restrictions or requirements to affect the choice. Corporations have a rather free hand in determining their capital structures.

UNIFORM COMMERCIAL CODE

The Uniform Commercial Code, Article 8, governs the transfer and issuance of investment securities. Investment securities by the Code definition are very comprehensive, covering every kind of security issued by a corporation. "Article 8, Investment Securities, is neither a Blue Sky Law nor a corporation code. It may be likened rather to a negotiable instruments law dealing with securities.

"It deals with bearer bonds, formerly covered by the Uniform Negotiable Instruments Law, and with registered bonds, not previously covered by any Uniform Law. It also covers certificates of stock, formerly provided for by the Uniform Stock Transfer Act, and additional types of investment paper not now covered by any Uniform Act."

FINANCING THROUGH SALE OF STOCKS

NATURE OF STOCK

In securing a charter for a corporation the incorporators decide upon the amount and kinds of capital stock which they would like authority from the state to issue. This amount is explicitly set down in the articles of incorporation. While some state statutes place a minimum limit upon the amount a corporation may be authorized to issue, few if any statutes at the present time specify a maximum.

The amount of capital stock which a corporation is authorized to have is known as *authorized capital stock*. Often a corporation does not sell and issue all of its authorized capital stock in the early stages of its organization and development. In such case that part of the stock that has been sold and issued is known as *issued and outstanding stock*, and the part that has not yet been sold and issued is known as *unissued stock*. Unissued stock, though it is available to be sold and issued, does not constitute an asset of the corporation.

Corporation statutes generally provide that stock may be issued for cash, property, labor, or services. If the stock is issued for labor and services it must be issued for past and not for future labor and services.

One who purchases stock of a corporation is a *stockholder*. By such purchase he becomes the owner of a designated number of *shares* of the capital stock of the corporation. In other words, the purchase of stock gives to the stockholder a fractional but undivided interest in the corporation. But such purchase does not have the effect of giving the stockholder an interest in the assets of the corporation. These belong to the corporation and not to the stockholders. The ownership of stock in a corporation carries with it certain rights, as, for example, (1) the right to participate to a limited degree in the management and control of the corporation, (2) the right to share in the profits of the corporation through the receipt of dividends, and (3) the right to participate in the distribution of the remaining assets upon dissolution.

A share of stock is intangible personal property—a chose in action.

UNIFORM COMMERCIAL CODE

Since the adoption of the U. C. C., a contract for the sale of stock is governed by the Statute of Frauds, Sec. 8–319 (see Appendix).

Upon the death of the stockholder the stock, like other personal property, passes to the decedent's personal representative and is available for the payment of the debts of the estate. Under the provisions of the statutes of most states stocks are made subject to execution and attachment by judgment creditors. This is not the case at common law. A share of stock constitutes a contract between the corporation and the stockholder. The rights of the stockholder are determined by the terms of that contract.

While the proprietary interest of a stockholder in a corporation is not dependent upon the receipt of a *certificate of stock*, at the present time corporations issue to their stockholders certificates of stock as evidence of such ownership. The certificate is not the stock itself but merely the evidence of ownership of a share or part of the capital stock. The certificate will designate the stockholder as the owner of a certain number of shares, specify the type of stock, and state other terms of the contract between the corporation and the stockholder.

CLASSES OF STOCK

The articles of incorporation set forth the classes or types of stock the corporation may issue, and the amount of each class of stock it may issue. These matters are, of course, determined by the incorporators themselves when they draw up and submit their articles of incorporation for approval by the proper state authority. But after the articles of incorporation have been filed and approved, the issuance of stock beyond the amount stated in the articles, or of a class not authorized by the articles, may not be made without amending the articles.

There are two basic classes of stock, (1) common stock and (2) preferred stock. Most corporation statutes today provide that both common and preferred stock may be either par value stock or no-par value stock.

Small corporations usually issue only common stock, but large corporations are generally authorized to issue both classes of stock.

COMMON STOCK. Common stock is the ordinary stock of a corporation. It possesses neither special privileges nor priorities over any other kind of stock. Sometimes large corporations issue two or more classes of common stock, such as common A and common B stock. When this is done the object is to concentrate the control of the corporation in the hands of the holders of one of these special classes of common stock. For example, the entire voting power may be placed in the holders of common A stock.

Where a single class of common stock constitutes all the stock of a corporation, the holders of the stock possess one vote for each share of stock they own. This means that each stockholder has a voice in the management of the corporation proportionate to the number of shares he owns. He is likewise entitled to receive his proportionate share of the earnings of the corporation by way of dividends, and to participate in the same proportion in the distribution of the net assets of the corporation upon dissolution.

PREFERRED STOCK. If a corporation issues preferred stock, under the terms of the contract between the corporation and the preferred stockholder the stockholder is entitled to certain specified preferences, priorities, and rights over the common stockholders. Where a corporation issues preferred stock it usually does so because it is unable to raise all the funds it needs by the sale of common stock, and hence must offer additional inducements to prospective investors. The two most common inducements offered are (1) preference in the payment of dividends and (2) preference in the distribution of the assets of the corporation in case of dissolution and liquidation. Where the stockholder is preferred in the payment of dividends it is usually provided that the stockholder will be paid a specified dividend, for example, one of 6 per cent, before any dividend is paid to the holders of common stock. It should be noted that this does not mean that an owner of preferred stock is certain of receiving the specified dividend, or any dividend. A corporation cannot pay a dividend to any stockholder, even a preferred stockholder, unless a fund exists out of which such a dividend may be legally paid.

A preferred stockholder is entitled to vote unless this right is withheld from him under the provisions of the articles of incorporation. The articles of incorporation do generally deny preferred stockholders the privilege of voting. But they sometimes provide that if the corporation should default in the payment of dividends to preferred stockholders, such stockholders automatically acquire the right to vote.

The contract with preferred stockholders sometimes provides that upon the expiration of a designated time the corporation may, at its option, *redeem* the preferred stock, at a fixed price (usually a little above par). Such a provision may prove a definite advantage to the corporation in the event of changed economic conditions under which the corporation might retire its preferred stock, remove a rather fixed item in its budget, and finance its operations through the sale of additional common stock. The corporation may, if it wishes, set up a sinking fund for the purpose of redeeming its preferred stock.

Sometimes the contract with preferred stockholders provides that the preferred stock may be *converted* into common stock, upon some predetermined basis, at the option of the holders of the preferred stock. This might prove advantageous to preferred stockholders if the corporation became especially successful in its operations and the returns on the common stock exceeded those on the preferred stock.

Preferred stock may be either *cumulative* or *non-cumulative* as to dividends. Where it is cumulative, if the corporation fails to pay the full dividend, as agreed, during a given year, the deficit must be made up in a subsequent year or years before any dividend may be paid to the holders of common stock. The dividend carries over from year to year. For example, the X Corporation has issued 6 per cent cumulative preferred stock. In 1959 it pays only 3 per cent on preferred stock, and of course nothing on common stock. Before the corporation can legally pay anything to common stockholders in 1960, it must pay 9 per cent (3 per cent arrearage and 6 per cent current dividend) to the preferred stockholders, in addition to any arrearage for years prior to 1959.

If the preferred stock is non-cumulative, the general rule is that when the corporation, during the current year, has failed to earn sufficient profits out of which dividends may be legally paid, the dividends do not accumulate but are lost to the holders of the preferred stock. But what if the corporation, during the current year, has sufficient earnings to pay dividends, but the directors decide for some reason not to pay the dividends? While the holdings of the courts are not uniform concerning this matter, many courts have taken the position that the dividends accumulate and must be paid to the preferred stockholders out of net profits in subsequent years. Where courts take this position, common stockholders may not be paid dividends until the arrearage is cleared up for the preferred stockholders.

The articles of incorporation usually specify whether the stock is cumulative or non-cumulative. Where they do not do so, most courts, though not all, hold that the stock is cumulative.

Preferred stock may be either *participating* or *non-participating* as to dividends. If the stock is participating, after the preferred stockholders have been paid their designated percentage dividend and the common stockholders have been paid the same percentage on their stock, then the preferred stockholders participate with the common stockholders in any further amount paid out as dividends. If the stock is non-participating, the preferred stockholders are never entitled to any dividend in excess of their designated percentage. It is evident that in the latter case the common stockholders may in any given year fare better than the preferred stockholders.

While the courts are not in full accord, the overwhelming majority of the courts hold that preferred stock is non-participating unless it is made participating by the terms of the articles of incorporation.

Stone v. United States Envelope Co.
119 Me. 394, 111 A. 536 (1920)

This was a bill in equity for an injunction brought by Carrie M. Stone (plaintiff) against the United States Envelope Co. (defendant). Decree for plaintiff. On appeal the decree was affirmed.

The part of the bylaws of the United States Envelope Co. material to the present case is as follows:

"ARTICLE XVI. CAPITAL

The shares of this corporation shall be divided as follows, viz., 10,000 common shares, 40,000 preferred shares.

The preferred shares shall be entitled to cumulative dividends payable semi-annually out of the net earnings of the corporation, at the rate of 7 per cent per annum, before any dividends are declared or paid on the common shares, and in case of non-payment in full of any such semi-annual dividends, the portions unpaid shall be paid out of subsequent net earnings prior to the claims of the common shares, but without interest on deferred payments, and the preferred shares shall have preference over the common shares in any distribution of the assets of the corporation in liquidation."

The bylaws also gave to the common and preferred stockholders equal voting power share for share and provided that "any shares of stock not subscribed for at the first meeting may be issued by the Board of Directors."

All the stock was issued and sold for cash at par except 2500 shares of common stock. A vote was passed to issue this stock and to offer it to stockholders both common and preferred, in proportion to their holdings, at $150 per share, a price which the case showed to be materially below its value.

In this suit plaintiff, holding 1000 shares of the common stock, asked that defendant be enjoined from carrying this vote into effect on the ground that to give the preferred shareholders a preemptive right to purchase common stock at less than its value was in effect to pay them a dividend in addition to the 7 per cent which was provided for in the bylaws and which they had received. Defendants contended that the preferred stockholders, notwithstanding that they had received their preferential dividends, were entitled to share in the surplus equity with the holders of the common stock.

DEASY, J. The respective rights of holders of common and preferred stock are fixed by contract. The contract is commonly contained in the corporate bylaws. Within wide limitations any preferential rights provided for in the bylaws will be given effect to by courts.

The question at issue in this case relates to the extent and limits of the rights that prima facie belong to preferred stock as such, i.e. rights and limitations that, in the absence of express provisions, are implied.

The plaintiff contends that where a say 7 per cent preferred stockholding is created with no stipulation in reference to participation in surplus, the preferred stockholder is entitled to 7 per cent, and that all the rest of the profits available for distribution belong to the holders of common stock; on the other hand, the defendant says that after payment of the 7 per cent dividend and perhaps an equal dividend upon the common stock, the balance of profits to be distributed must go to all the stockholders both common and preferred in proportion to their holdings and without discrimination.

Both parties present authorities sustaining their respective contentions. There are two opposing theories each of which has judicial support. One theory is that the preferred stockholder presumptively yields nothing in compensation for the benefits which he receives; that he has and holds all the rights of the common shareholder and in addition has his preferential rights. Upon this theory the defendants rely, and in support of it cite a number of cases, including *Englander v. Osborne*, 261 Pa. 366, 104 A. 614. The other theory, which we believe to be better and supported by the weight of authority, is that, in receiving the greater security of his preferential rights, the preferred stockholder impliedly agrees to accept such rights in lieu of equal participation.

The parties by a contract embodied in the bylaws have provided for the preferred stockholders a 7 per cent preferential dividend, and in case of liquidation 100 per cent. This excludes other participation.

Independent reasoning as well as what we deem to be the preponderance of authority sustains the plaintiff's position. . . . We put the decision upon the ground that where nothing to the contrary appears, the creation of preferred stock prima facie implies that the preferential rights of the stockholder are given in lieu of and to the exclusion of the equality in participation which would otherwise exist. Bill sustained.

ACQUIRING MEMBERSHIP IN A CORPORATION

Membership in a corporation may be acquired (1) by subscribing for stock prior to the creation of the corporation, (2) by subscribing for or purchasing stock from the corporation after its creation and organization, and (3) by purchasing stock of the corporation from another stockholder.

PRE–INCORPORATION SUBSCRIPTIONS. One method of acquiring membership in a corporation is to sign a *stock subscription agreement* prior to incorporation. Promoters and incorporators of corporations commonly solicit such subscriptions from their business acquaintances. If the corporation is ultimately formed, it may, through its board of directors, accept these subscriptions. Such an acceptance results in a contract and makes the subscriber a member of the corporation. In fact, some courts have held that the act of acquiring the charter and organizing the corporation is tantamount to acceptance of the subscriptions, in which case the subscribers become stockholders without the necessity of formal acceptance by the directors. The Uniform Business Corporation Act has a provision to this effect.

A considerable diversity of opinion exists in the court decisions as to the nature or legal effect of a pre-incorporation subscription. While a few courts have held that a subscriber is bound by his subscription and that it is irrevocable, most courts have taken the position that a pre-incorporation subscription is nothing more than a continuing offer and may be revoked by the subscriber prior to the creation of the corporation and acceptance of the offer. Their reason for holding that the act of signing a subscription agreement does not result in a legally binding contract is the fact that the corporation has not yet come into existence and hence there is no second party for the subscriber to contract with. It is also stated that there is no consideration given by the corporation to the subscriber for his promise to take stock in the contemplated corporation. The few states which have held that a pre-incorporation subscription is a contract find consideration in the mutual promises of the subscribers. However, since such consideration does not run between the corporation and the individual subscriber, it is difficult to find consideration in the mutual promises of the subscribers sufficient to bind the subscriber to the corporation before it has come into being.

The majority holding has given rise to a multiplicity of risks and uncertainties for promoters and incorporators, and at times results in unreasonable hardship to them. For this reason a few of the states have adopted statutes which, in effect, make pre-incorporation subscriptions irrevocable for some specified length of time. This same idea is incorporated in the Uniform Business Corporation Act, which provides that such a subscription shall be irrevocable for a period of one year.

SUBSCRIPTION AFTER INCORPORATION. After the corporation has been formed, the general rules of contract law are applicable to stock subscriptions. The offeror may be either the subscriber or the corporation. In other words, the corporation may offer to sell the stock to the subscriber, or the subscriber may offer to buy the stock from the corporation. In either situation a contract results when the offeree accepts the offer.

PURCHASE OF STOCK FROM A STOCKHOLDER. The third method—and the commonest—of acquiring membership in a corporation is by purchasing stock from a stockholder of the corporation. Every day millions of shares of stock are purchased and sold on the stock exchanges and in over-the-counter transactions. Likewise, shares of stock may be purchased and sold by the parties dealing directly with each other, without the aid of such outside agencies as stock exchanges and brokers.

Two steps must be taken in order to transfer title to the stock from the seller to the buyer. First, the seller (transferor) must deliver the certificate of stock to the buyer (transferee); the seller may indorse the certificate in blank or specially, or, if the parties prefer, the seller may make the assignment on a separate instrument. This second method of transfer is often used where the stock is being pledged as security for a loan. Second, the buyer must surrender the certificate of stock to the corporation for cancellation and the issuance of a new certificate in the name of the buyer.

Under the common law, stock certificates were held not to be negotiable instruments. Consequently, if a stock certificate indorsed in blank was lost or stolen and the finder or thief transferred it to a bona fide purchaser for value, the purchaser was held not to receive title to the certificate. In other words, the owner was protected as against the innocent purchaser for value. However, the common law rule has been changed by the Uniform Commercial Code.

UNIFORM COMMERCIAL CODE

Under the Code, stock certificates are endowed with the characteristics of negotiable instruments and are made negotiable by Article 8, Investment Securities. This means that in the illustration just given, title to the certificate passes to the innocent purchaser for value. However, if the owner's signature is forged and the certificate is then sold and transferred to a bona fide purchaser, the purchaser does not receive title as against the owner.

The bylaws usually provide that the transfer of stock can be made only on the books of the corporation. A statement to this effect is often printed on the face of the certificate. This provision is held to be merely for the protection and convenience of the corporation, enabling it to know at all times what persons are entitled to the rights of stockholders. Consequently, as between the transferor and the transferee, title to the certificate passes to the transferee upon indorsement and delivery. The transferee is the equitable owner of the stock, and, in the case of a stockholders' meeting before the stock is transferred on the books of the corporation, the transferee may demand from the transferor a proxy to vote the stock at the meeting.

The general rule is that, in the absence of restrictions imposed by statute, by the articles of incorporation or the bylaws, or by contract, a stockholder may transfer his stock to anyone he chooses. The transferability of the shares of stock in a corporation is one of the outstanding characteristics of a corporation and one of the major advantages of a corporation over a partnership. Consequently, the courts generally oppose the placing of unreasonable restrictions upon the alienation or transfer of corporate stocks. However, if the restrictions imposed by the articles of incorporation, by the bylaws, or by contract are not deemed unreasonable by the courts, they will be held to be valid. For example, restrictions designed to protect the corporation against fraudulent transfers will be upheld. An agreement by the stockholders that they will not sell and transfer their shares without first giving the corporation the option of purchasing their stock is generally held not to be unreasonable. However, a provision that a stockholder may not transfer his stock without the consent of the corporation or the consent of all the other stockholders is held to be unreasonable and, therefore, unenforceable.

Hudson Real Estate Co. v. Tower et al.
156 Mass. 82, 30 N. E. 465 (1892)

This was an action by the Hudson Real Estate Company (plaintiff) against Herman C. Tower et al. (defendants). Judgment for plaintiff, and defendants excepted. Exceptions sustained.

This action was brought to recover the amount of certain subscriptions alleged to have been made by defendants.

As an answer and defense to plaintiff's claim, defendant Tower offered to prove the following: that Dr. Harriman, as a solicitor of subscriptions for the capital stock of plaintiff corporation, which was to be formed at some time after the subscription was made, asked Tower to subscribe; that, in the course of the conversation relative to the matter of subscribing, Tower said that if the subscribers were going to mortgage the property to be bought with the subscriptions his subscription would be merely nominal, but that if they would raise the full amount by subscription and not mortgage the property he would subscribe for 10 shares, or $500 worth; that Dr. Harriman thereupon asked him to subscribe with that understanding but he declined to do so that day; that when the doctor urged again that he should subscribe upon that understanding, Tower said that he would put down his name if it was understood between them that that was the condition of his subscription, and, upon this assurance from Dr. Harriman, he did subscribe at the time for that amount; that thereafter Dr. Harriman reported to the meeting of the subscribers, and that in consequence of that report the meeting voted "that there should be no mortgage on the property"; that thereafter and before anything was done by the subscribers or the corporation was organized, the subscribers voted "that the vote which we voted August 14, 1889, not to place a mortgage on the property be rescinded"; that thereafter the subscribers formed the corporation, and on August 1, 1890, the corporation placed a mortgage upon said property.

ALLEN, J. At the time when the defendant signed the subscription paper declared on, it was not a contract, for want of a contracting party on the other side; but it has now been established that a subscription of this sort becomes a contract with the corporation when the corporation has been organized, and in this way the objection of the want of a proper contracting party is fully avoided, provided everything goes on as contemplated without any interruption. Until the organization of the corporation, the subscription is a mere proposition or offer, which may be withdrawn, like any other unaccepted offer. Unless the signer is bound upon a contract he is not bound at all. It is open to him to withdraw. It is not on the ground that there was no sufficient consideration. The seal would do away with any doubt on that score. But it is on the ground that for the time being, and until the corporation is organized, the writing does not take effect as a contract because the contemplated party to the contract on the other side is not yet in existence, and for this reason, there being no contract, the whole undertaking is inchoate and incomplete; and, since there is no contract, the party may withdraw. *Music Hall Co. v. Curey*, 116 Mass. 471; *Phipps v. Jones*, 20 Pa. St. 260. In the present case there was evidence which would warrant a finding that the defendant thus withdrew before the time came when his subscription would have become a contract. Exceptions sustained.

GOVERNMENT REGULATION OF SECURITY ISSUES

Owing to the prevalence of misrepresentation and fraud in the marketing of corporate securities, both the states and the federal government have enacted laws designed to protect the investing public. Since these laws apply alike to both honest and dishonest promoters, incorporators, issuers, and brokers, everyone who undertakes the marketing of corporate securities must be aware of their existence and vigilant in complying with them. Violation may render the offenders not only civilly liable to the party or parties defrauded but also criminally liable. Ignorance of the existence of such statutes is no defense.

STATE BLUE SKY LAWS. Every state except Nevada has some type of legislation regulating the sale and issuance of corporate securities.[1] In enacting these laws the states had in mind the protection of the investing public. "Get-rich-quick" schemes were numerous, and great numbers of uninformed citizens were being defrauded by unscrupulous promoters, brokers, and agents. Often a corporation was overcapitalized and its stock was "watered," the incorporators themselves having put little or none of their own capital into the undertaking. "The sky was the limit" in the marketing of these spurious "securities," and so when the states began to enact laws to curb these excesses, people referred to them as "Blue Sky Laws."

Some of the state Blue Sky Laws are much more stringent than others. The more effective type of statute usually creates a special securities commission and requires that the securities of a corporation must be registered and approved by this commission before they may be legally marketed within the state. Failure to comply with the statute is made a criminal offense. Other state statutes merely require that dealers and brokers secure a license from the state before they may offer for sale the securities of the corporation. Still others prescribe no conditions precedent to the sale and issuance of securities, but simply make it illegal to employ "any device, scheme, or artifice to defraud, or to obtain money or property by means of any false or fraudulent pretense, representation, or promise." The enforcement of such statutes is generally left up to the Attorney General of the state. If, upon complaint and hearing, the Attorney General is of the opinion that the statute has been violated, he may issue a cease and desist order. Right to appeal from this order to the state courts is granted by such statutes.

Since the state Blue Sky Laws usually apply to foreign as well as domestic corporations, a corporation which desires to sell its stock in a

---

[1] No special legislation has been enacted by Congress for the District of Columbia; compliance with the applicable federal statutes satisfies the requirements there.

foreign jurisdiction usually must comply with the Blue Sky Laws of such jurisdiction.

FEDERAL REGULATION—SECURITIES & EXCHANGE COMMISSION.   The state Blue Sky Laws are of course not applicable to interstate marketing of corporate securities. To protect the public from unscrupulous promoters and dealers in interstate sales, Congress in 1933 enacted the Federal Securities Act and in 1934 the Securities Exchange Act. The Securities & Exchange Commission (S. E. C.) was created by the latter to administer and enforce the provisions of these acts.

The constitutional authority for the enactment of the Securities Acts is found in the commerce clause of the United States Constitution, which gives to the federal government exclusive jurisdiction over interstate and foreign commerce, and in the exclusive jurisdiction given the federal government over the establishment of post offices and the use of the mails. Thus, if corporate securities are offered for sale in interstate commerce or through the mails, such sales are regulated by the provisions of the Securities Acts of 1933 and 1934. One engaging in the marketing of securities should keep this in mind. The safe practice to follow is always to determine whether the federal statutes are applicable before a single security is sold. Unless the sale of the stock is to be made to the immediate incorporators, who are limited in number and who agree to take for investment and not for distribution, the chances are that the Acts do apply.

Very briefly, the basic requirements of the Securities Acts are as follows:

(1) In the absence of an exemption from the Securities Act of 1933, if the offering exceeds $300,000 the following must be prepared and filed with the S. E. C.:
  (a) A registration statement, including
  (b) A prospectus.
(2) If the offering is under $300,000 the following must be prepared and filed with the S. E. C.:
  (a) Form 1-A—Notification, and under certain conditions
  (b) An offering circular.

Registration with the S. E. C. does not imply that the Commission approves the issue. The whole purpose of requiring registration is to compel the corporation to file with the Commission detailed information concerning such matters as who the promoters, incorporators, directors, and officers are, what they gave in exchange for their holdings in the corporation, the nature of the business of the corporation, the price at which the proposed offering is to be sold, what the corporation plans to do with the money obtained from such sale, and many other pertinent data. When there is an applicable regulation the corporation is also required to file certain financial statements certified by independent accountants.

The Securities Acts apply to bonds and other corporate securities, as well as to stock.

The sale of securities in interstate commerce or through the mails without first complying with the requirements of the Federal Securities Acts is a serious matter. Likewise, filing untrue statements or failing to disclose some material fact can be in violation of the Acts. Such violations and infractions carry with them certain criminal penalties.

FINANCING THROUGH BORROWING

INTRODUCTION

The second source of funds to finance the business activities of corporations is borrowing, i.e. the use of credit. As we have already seen, the power to borrow money to carry out the purposes for which it was created was early recognized as one of the incidental powers of a private corporation and is included among the general powers of corporations enumerated in modern corporation statutes. Such power may, however, be limited by the articles of incorporation. As a general rule, authority to borrow money on behalf of the corporation is vested in the board of directors, but the state corporation statutes sometimes require the consent of the stockholders before certain types of loans may be negotiated by the corporation.

The legal relationship of a corporation to those who extend it credit is very different from its relationship to its stockholders. One who extends credit to a corporation does not thereby purchase any interest in the corporation or become entitled to any voice in the control of the corporation. He simply becomes entitled to receive interest on his loan and to have the principal repaid according to the terms of his contract with the corporation. This right is not conditioned in any way upon the financial success of the company. We shall soon see that stockholders have no right to a return on their shares of stock if there are no earnings out of which dividends may be legally paid. In the case of creditors, however, the existence of an annual profit or a surplus account is not a condition precedent to the payment of interest or principal. Failure on the part of the corporation to pay either interest or principal as agreed constitutes a breach of contract with the creditors, and gives them the right to proceed against the corporation.

Borrowing by corporations may be either long-term or short-term. In general, funds secured from long-term borrowing go into the fixed assets of the corporation; funds secured from short-term borrowing become a part of the current assets of the corporation, and may be used for purchase of raw materials and merchandise, payment of wages, and so on.

USE OF BONDS FOR LONG-TERM BORROWING

NATURE OF A BOND ISSUE. Long-term borrowing is usually accomplished by the issuance and sale of bonds. In the sale of bonds the issuing corporation obligates itself to pay the owner (original purchaser or subsequent holder) of the bond a definite rate of interest and to redeem or pay the bond (principal) upon a specified date. Many bond issues run for a long time, not maturing for 50, 75, or even 100 years from the date of their issue. They may be for any denomination but are generally for $500 or $1,000. Sometimes "baby bonds" of $100 are issued. In a large bond issue, involving millions of dollars, thousands of bonds are issued and sold to large numbers of purchasers. The marketing of such large issues is often handled by underwriters, i.e. investment bankers who underwrite the issue and market the bonds in return for a commission.

The technical arrangement which is generally used in the creation of a bond issue involves the drawing up of a deed of trust. Under its terms a trustee (usually a trust company) is named to accept the legal title to the security which the corporation gives to secure the payment of the interest and principal to the owners of the bonds. Under the deed of trust the purchasers of the bonds are the cestuis que trust or beneficiaries, i.e. the equitable owners. The trustee holds the legal title to the security given by the corporation, for the use and benefit of the bondholders. The deed of trust stands as security for the entire bond issue. In case of default on the part of the corporation, it is the trustee's duty to take all necessary legal steps to protect the interests of the bondholders.

TYPES OF BONDS. While legally all bonds and bond issues are essentially the same, in that they represent an obligation of the issuing corporation to pay the interest and principal to the owners of the bonds, certain types may be distinguished. Most bonds may be classified on the basis of the type of security given by the corporation for the protection of the bondholders. Upon that basis, the principal types of bonds are: (1) mortgage bonds—where the security is real property; (2) equipment bonds—usually where a railroad gives as security a mortgage or deed of trust on certain of its equipment, most commonly on its "rolling stock"; (3) collateral trust bonds—where collateral is pledged as security for the bond issue; (4) income bonds—where the "security" is merely the right to "first call" on the income of the corporation.

At times, corporations also issue unsecured bonds, called *debenture bonds*. While the holders of such bonds do not have "first claim" upon any specific assets of the issuing corporation, in effect the general credit of the corporation does stand behind such bonds.

There may be different issues of the foregoing types of bonds. For example, a "first mortgage bond" may be a senior bond or security, the holders of which would have first claim upon the assets given as security, while a "second mortgage bond" would in all probability be a junior bond, the holders of which would have no right to satisfy their claims from the security given by the corporation until the holders of the first mortgage bonds had first satisfied their claims.

ARE CORPORATION BONDS NEGOTIABLE?   Corporation bonds may or may not be negotiable, depending upon the wording of the bonds and the conditions under which they were issued.

UNIFORM COMMERCIAL CODE

Corporate bonds are classified by Article 8 of the U. C. C. as investment securities. Sec. 8–105 of the Code states that "Securities governed by this Article are negotiable instruments." The Code in Sec. 8–102 defines a security as "an instrument which is issued in bearer or registered form; and is of a type commonly dealt in upon securities exchanges or markets or commonly recognized in any area in which it is issued or dealt in as a medium for investment; and is either one of a class or series or by its terms is divisible into a class or series of instruments; and evidences a share, participation or other interest in property or in an enterprise or evidences an obligation of the issuer. A security is in "registered form" when it specifies a person entitled to the security or to the rights it evidences and when its transfer may be registered upon books maintained for that purpose by or on behalf of an issuer or the security so states.

A security is in "bearer form" when it runs to bearer according to its terms and not by reason of any indorsement.

Bonds are usually considered negotiable instruments under the Code irrespective of the terms stated thereon.

USE OF NOTE AND MORTGAGE FOR LONG–TERM BORROWING

A second method occasionally employed in long-term borrowing is the use of a note and mortgage or deed of trust on the corporation's real property. This method is practically confined to situations where relatively small amounts of capital are involved and usually where the corporation is able to borrow the money it needs from one lender. For example, if a corporation needs to borrow $50,000 and is able to secure the entire loan from a single bank, it may execute a note for the amount of the loan, and secure the note by giving a mortgage or deed of trust on a part or all of its real property.

METHODS OF SHORT–TERM BORROWING

The short-term borrowing of a corporation depends largely upon the type of business it is conducting. For instance, the retailer usually finances his purchases from wholesalers and jobbers through the use of trade acceptances, open accounts (accounts payable), or bank loans. The trust receipt is also used to a certain extent as in the purchase of automobiles, refrigerators, television sets, and a few other lines. Borrowers for short-term financing may also obtain credit through the use of pledge agreements, chattel mortgages, and conditional sales contracts.

REVIEW CASES

1. The Beaver Meadow Railroad and Coal Co. issued preferred stock, which was entitled to a preference over all other stock of the company in every future dividend of profits declared, until the holders were paid, from funds applicable to the payment of such dividends, 10 per cent per annum. The company was later merged with the Lehigh Valley Railroad Co., and the preferred stockholders received preferred stock of the Lehigh Valley Railroad Co. entitling them to the same rights and preferences. From Oct. 17, 1893, no dividends of any kind were declared until 1904, when the Lehigh Valley Railroad Co. declared a dividend of 10 per cent on the preferred stock and a dividend of 1 per cent on the common stock. The preferred stockholders filed a bill in equity to enjoin the payment of any dividend to common stockholders until the preferred stockholders had been paid at the rate of 10 per cent per annum from Oct. 17, 1893. Ruling? (Fidelity Trust Co. et al. v. Lehigh Valley Railroad Co., 215 Pa. 710, 64 A. 829)

2. The United States Cast Iron Pipe & Foundry Co. declared a dividend on its preferred stock out of a fund known as "Reserve for additional working capital." Under the articles of incorporation the preferred stock was entitled to non-cumulative dividends not exceeding 7 per cent a year, payable out of any and all surplus net profits; and the common stock was entitled to dividends out of the surplus net profits remaining after payment of the dividends on the preferred stock. The reserve fund had been accumulated from the surplus net profits for five earlier years, and $1,593,750 of it had been obtained by scaling down the dividends on preferred stock below 7 per cent in four of the five years. The proposed dividend amounted to $218,750. Bassett, one of the common stockholders, filed a bill in equity, contending that dividends on preferred stock for any fiscal year must be paid out of the profits earned during that year, and that profits accumulated in earlier years, when distributed, must be paid to the common stockholders to the exclusion of holders of preferred stock. The defendant corporation claimed that it was entitled to pay dividends on its preferred stock out of any and all surplus net profits, without regard to the year in which they were earned. Ruling? (Bassett v. United States Cast Iron Pipe & Foundry Co., 75 N. J. Eq. 539, 73 A. 514)

3. A number of citizens of Schuyler, Nebraska, undertook to form a corporation for the processing of chicory. Lednicky signed a subscription agreement to purchase five shares of stock, par value $50, in the proposed company. Articles of incorporation were obtained, and sufficient stock was sold and paid for to commence business. Lednicky agreed to pay for his five shares at the rate of $10 a month. After paying $80 he refused to continue payment, and the corporation sued for the balance. The defense was that the subscription agreement was not an enforceable contract. Holding? Nebraska Chicory Co. of Schuyler, Nebraska v. Lednicky, 79 Neb. 587, 113 N. W. 245)

4. Lawson purchased from Davis 100 shares of stock in the Household Finance Corp., but the company refused to transfer the stock on its books to Lawson because Davis had failed to comply with the following requirement in the charter: "Any holder desirous of selling stocks . . . shall give the president or treasurer written notice of the desire . . . and the corporation shall have a twenty-day option to buy such stocks." Lawson maintained that this provision was not legally binding, and asked the court to force the transfer of the stock. Judgment for whom? (Lawson v. Household Finance Corp., 147 A. 312)

5. McNeil owned 134 shares of stock in the First National Bank of Johnsville, and delivered it to his broker to secure a balance of $3,000 on account. McNeil had properly indorsed the certificate, and the broker, without McNeil's knowledge, through another broker caused the Tenth National Bank, an innocent party, to pay $45,135 for this and other securities. McNeil filed suit asking that the Tenth National Bank be enjoined from transferring the stock to its name. The lower court decreed that the stock be delivered to McNeil for $3,000 and interest. The case was appealed. Holding? (McNeil v. Tenth National Bank, 46 N. Y. 325)

Rights and Liabilities of Stockholders

47

RIGHTS OF STOCKHOLDERS

The principal rights of stockholders are as follows: (1) the right to vote, (2) the right to receive dividends, (3) the right to inspect the books and records of the corporation, and (4) preemptive rights.[1]

RIGHT TO VOTE

WHO MAY VOTE. Theoretically, all stockholders, regardless of the type of stock they hold, have a right to vote at the regular and special meetings of the stockholders for the election of directors and upon other matters presented for their consideration. However, the corporation statutes of most states expressly provide that the privilege of voting may be denied the holders of any class of stock by the inclusion of a provision to that effect in the articles of incorporation. If a stockholder has not been denied the right to vote by such a provision, the right may not be taken from him by the bylaws. Under the provisions of the charter the holders of preferred stock are usually denied the right to vote, but in some instances with the proviso that they are to be given such right in the event the corporation defaults in the payment of their dividends for a specified length of time.

NUMBER OF VOTES. At common law each stockholder was entitled to one vote, regardless of the number of shares he owned. At the present time, by statute, a stockholder is entitled to as many votes as he has shares with voting rights.

PROXY. Under the common law a stockholder could not vote his stock unless he was present at a meeting of the stockholders. Under modern

[1] The stockholders' right to share in the distribution of assets after dissolution is discussed in Chapter 50.

statutes, however, stockholders may vote by proxy. Since the relation between a stockholder and his proxy holder is that of principal and agent, the stockholder may revoke the proxy at any time he chooses to do so, unless the proxy has created an agency coupled with an interest.

VOTING TRUST.   At times some or all of the stockholders of a corporation enter into an agreement whereby they create a voting trust. The commonest reason for taking such action is to concentrate voting power in the hands of a trustee or trustees. Under the terms of the agreement setting up the trust the participating stockholders transfer to a trustee or trustees their shares of stock, and in exchange they receive trust certificates. While the trustee or trustees have the legal title to the stock, the stockholders are the equitable owners. The courts in some jurisdictions have held that voting trusts are against public policy and therefore void. In a majority of the states, however, the courts have held such agreements valid and enforceable where they have been formed for lawful objectives and do not violate the rights of minority stockholders. Many of the states now have statutes that regulate the creation of voting trusts. Where such statutes exist voting trusts are valid and enforceable if they are in conformity with the terms of the statute.

CUMULATIVE VOTING.   Most of the states have statutes which permit cumulative voting by stockholders in the election of directors. Cumulative voting was not recognized at common law. Its purpose is to improve the minority stockholders' chance of gaining representation on the board of directors. Where cumulative voting is provided for in the articles of incorporation, a stockholder is entitled to as many votes as he has shares of voting stock multiplied by the number of directors to be elected. For example, if five directors are to be elected and a stockholder has 100 shares of voting stock, he may cast 500 votes. He may distribute these votes among the candidates as he sees fit. In such a situation the minority stockholders frequently agree in advance to concentrate their votes on one candidate, or perhaps on two. They may thus be able to place one or two of their candidates on the board of directors and consequently gain a voice in the management of the corporation, which would otherwise have been beyond their reach.

Thompson et al. v. Blaisdell et al.
93 N. J. L. 31, 107 A. 405 (1919)

Application by Schenk S. Thompson and others (plaintiffs) against E. T. Blaisdell and others (defendants) for summary investigation of a corporate election. New election ordered.

This was a summary investigation of a corporate election under section 42 of the Corporation Act of 1896. The controversy turned on the right to vote 242 shares standing in the name of Albert Kumpel. This right was denied by the inspectors at the election. These shares, if voted, would have changed the result. Theodore Kumpel sought to vote them by virtue of a proxy from Albert Kumpel. It is not denied that Albert appeared as owner on the books of the company on the day of the election, or that the proxy was in proper form and properly executed. On the face of the papers Theodore was entitled to vote the shares.

Albert gave the proxy to Theodore on March 24th. On April 5th Theodore decided to buy the stock at Albert's request, and sent Albert a check for the purchase price. Albert signed a transfer, but Theodore did not register the transfer on the books of the company, and the stock still stood in Albert's name on May 13th, the day of the election. His reason seems to have been that there was a real or supposed right of preemption in the company, and he desired to avoid any question as to his title to the stock. It is now argued that the proxy was revoked by the sale to Theodore.

SWAYZE, J. Under the ruling of *Downing v. Potts*, 23 N. J. L. 66, and the St. Lawrence Steamboat Co. case, 44 N. J. L. 529, the action of the inspectors was erroneous, and the election ought to be set aside or the contesting party put in office. The incumbents rely, not on any defect in the record title to the stock or in the proxy, but on a situation disclosed by the facts of the case as established by evidence aliunde and not legally before the inspectors of election.

Stock is often sold while the transfer books are closed, and it would be a manifest injustice to deprive the vendee of the right to vote, which the Act is at some pains to secure him, because he has bought within 20 days next preceding the election. Section 36 secures each stockholder the right to vote; it does not disfranchise stock which has been sold within 20 days next preceding the election. Whether the vendee shall be disfranchised is thus made to depend on his own action or inaction. There is nothing in the language to prevent the vendee, by agreement with the vendor, from securing his right to vote by means of a proxy, although not yet registered as a stockholder. The law was long ago established in New York under similar legislation (*People v. Tibbets*, 4 Col. (N. Y.) 358), and has more recently been followed in *Re Argus Co.*, 138 N. Y. 557, 31 N. E. 388. This rule is in harmony with the principle that requires a trustee in case of a dry trust to give a proxy. Granting that the sale is a technical revocation of the proxy, it would be idle to require the former owner, now because a trustee of a dry trust for the unregistered vendee, to execute a new proxy, where both he and his vendee are content with the control of the voting power given by the title shown on the transfer books accompanied by the proxy. The rule is also in harmony with the policy that entitles every stockholder to the benefit of the vote of every other stockholder and intrusts the voting power to the beneficial owner. . . . A man may vote although not a bona fide owner of stock, and may vote by proxy. We see no reason why a vendor who is still registered as a stockholder cannot vote by proxy. The case is still stronger where the proxy is held by the vendee.

We are now dealing with technical legal rights. Those rights at the time of the election were with Theodore Kumpel. The inspectors could not go outside the face of the papers. We are dealing with a question of right and justice under the mandate of the statute, and the answer to the question depends on the beneficial title to the stock. If there was no right of preemption in the corporation, Theodore Kumpel was the beneficial owner of the stock as well as the person entitled to vote it on the face of the books and the proxy. If there was a right of preemption, the legal title was still in Albert, the sale had never been perfected, and the proxy had not been revoked. As the right of preemption seems to be a disputed question, we think we ought not now establish the title of the contestants and oust the incumbents. Instead of that we order a new election which, if necessary, may be conducted under the direction of a Supreme Court Commissioner. New election ordered.

RIGHT TO DIVIDENDS

NATURE OF DIVIDENDS.   Corporate dividends constitute a portion of the profits or net earnings of the corporation legally set apart for distribution among the stockholders according to their respective interests. Until a dividend has been properly declared and set aside by the corporation, the earnings of the corporation belong to the corporation, and stockholders have no claim upon them. But after a dividend has been validly declared, stockholders have a property interest in their proportionate shares of the dividend, and if the corporation later refuses to pay the dividend the stockholders may bring action against the corporation to recover same. The declaration of a dividend creates a debtor-creditor relationship between the corporation and the stockholders, the stockholders becoming general creditors of the corporation. If the corporation goes into bankruptcy before the dividend has been paid, the stockholders share equally along with the other general creditors of the corporation.

While the general rule is that a corporation may not revoke or rescind its action after it has declared a dividend to its stockholders, such revocation is possible if made prior to public notice of the declaration, or upon discovery that the declaration was illegal.

Dividends may be paid in money, stocks, bonds, or other property of the corporation. Most corporate dividends are paid in money. If a dividend has been legally declared and the corporation has insufficient cash on hand to pay the dividend, it may borrow the money with which to pay the dividend. The effect of paying a dividend in stock is to capitalize surplus. Stock dividends are not true dividends, since the relative positions of the stockholders have not been changed by the payment of the dividend. Stock dividends are not treated as income by the Bureau of Internal Revenue, and are not taxable as such.

HOW DIVIDENDS ARE DECLARED.   Dividends are declared by the board of directors. Even though a corporation has sufficient net profits or a large surplus out of which to pay a dividend, the general rule is that the stockholders may not compel the directors to declare a dividend, so long as the directors are acting in good faith. The declaration of a dividend usually rests in the sound discretion of the board of directors. The courts are reluctant to substitute their judgment for that of the board, and only where it can be shown that the board has acted arbitrarily, fraudulently, or unreasonably in refusing to declare a dividend will the courts grant relief by requiring a distribution of corporate earnings.

WHEN DIVIDENDS MAY BE DECLARED.   When the board of directors considers whether to declare a dividend, it must first determine whether the financial status of the corporation is such that.it may legally declare a dividend. If it finds that it may legally pay a dividend, it must then decide whether it would be wise from a business standpoint to do so. This second question is not a legal one, like the first, but one involving. the business judgment of the board of directors.

The courts have quite generally taken the position that a corporation carries on business for the purpose of earning a profit or "surplus," and that dividends may legally be paid only out of such surplus earnings. They have held conversely that dividends may not be paid out of capital. To permit the payment of dividends out of capital would be a fraud upon the creditors of the corporation. However, a "surplus" may be created in a number of different ways, and the courts do not treat all types alike. (1) An *earned surplus* is a surplus created in past years by not paying out all the net profits in dividends to the stockholders, but by retaining or "plowing back into the business" some of these profits. All the courts agree that a dividend may be paid out of an earned surplus. (2) A *paid-in* or *capital surplus* is created if the corporation sells the stock at a premium, i.e. above par, and allocates the amount above par to the "paid-in or capital surplus" account. Some courts have permitted the payment of dividends out of this account, and under certain circumstances it is permitted by statute. Such payment is permitted under the provisions of the Uniform Business Corporation Act. (3) A *revaluation surplus* is created by "marking up" certain of the corporation's assets, such as real property, inventory, and good will. The courts very generally agree that a *cash* dividend may not be paid out of a revaluation surplus, but some courts have permitted the payment of a *stock* dividend out of such a surplus account. (4) A *reduction surplus* is created by reducing the capital stock or "stated capital" of the corporation. Few courts permit the payment of dividends out of such an account.

The courts will not permit the payment of a dividend if the corporation is insolvent, or if the payment of the dividend will render the corporation insolvent. Nor will they permit the payment of a dividend if such payment will impair the capital of the corporation. Most courts further hold that a dividend may not be paid out of current profit if the capital of the corporation is impaired owing to deficits created during previous years.

Since most of the state corporation statutes· have provisions designed to regulate the payment of dividends, the local state statutes should be consulted.

WHO ARE ENTITLED TO DIVIDENDS. As between the corporation and the stockholders, the stockholders of record on the day the dividend is declared are entitled to the dividend, regardless of when it was earned. If the corporation closed its books prior to the declaration of the dividend, then the stockholders of record on the day the books were closed would be entitled to receive the dividend. In the absence of an agreement to the contrary, the same rule applies as between the seller (transferor) and the buyer (transferee) where the stock is sold after the books are closed and the dividend is declared, but before the dividend is paid. In other words the transferor would be entitled to the dividend. However, the parties may agree at the time of the sale that the transferee shall be entitled to the dividend. If the corporation is notified of this agreement, then the corporation is required to make payment to the transferee. But if the parties fail to notify the corporation of the agreement and the corporation pays the dividend to the transferor, it will not be liable to the transferee, since the transferor was the stockholder of record, rather, the transferor will have the legal duty of accounting to the transferee for the dividend.

It is not uncommon nowadays for a corporation, in declaring a dividend, not only to fix a future date for the payment of the dividend but also to provide that the dividend is payable to the stockholders of record as of some future specified date. For example, the following dividend notice was issued by a certain corporation: "The Board of Directors of the _____ Company on August 17, 1949, declared a quarterly dividend of fifty cents (50¢) per share on its $10 par value common stock, payable September 19, 1949, to stockholders of record as of the close of business August 26, 1949." While the courts have not all reached the same conclusion in regard to the legal effect of such a declaration, it appears that at least a majority of the courts have held that if stock is transferred after the declaration but before the designated record date (in the foregoing example, between August 17 and August 26, 1949), the transferee is entitled to the dividend. This point is frequently litigated, especially when large sums of money are involved.

Dodge v. Ford Motor Co.
204 Mich. 459, 170 N. W. 668 (1919)
Supreme Court of Michigan

This is an action by John F. Dodge and Horace E. Dodge (plaintiffs) against Ford Motor Company and others (defendants). Judgment for plaintiffs, and defendants appealed. Judgment affirmed in part and reversed in part.

The Ford Motor Company is a corporation, organized and existing under Act No. 232 of the Public Acts of 1903 of the State of Michigan.

The business of the company started to expand. The cars it manufactured met a public demand, and were profitably marketed, so that, in addition to regular quarterly dividends equal to 5 per cent monthly on the capital stock of $2,000,000, its board of directors declared and the company paid special dividends: December 13, 1911, $1,000,000; May 15, 1912, $2,000,000; July 11, 1912, $2,000,000; June 16, 1913, $10,000,000; May 14, 1914, $2,000,000; June 12, 1914, $2,000,000; July 6, 1914, $2,000,000; July 23, 1914, $2,000,000; August 23, 1914, $3,000,000; May 28, 1915, $10,000,000; October 13, 1915, $5,000,000, a total of $41,000,000 in special dividends. Sales and profits for several years were: Year ending Sept. 30, 1910, 18,664 cars, $4,521,509.51. Year ending Sept. 30, 1911, 34,466 cars, $6,275,031.07. Year ending Sept. 30, 1912, 68,544 cars, $13,057,312.24. Year ending Sept. 30, 1913, 168,304 cars, $25,046,767.43. Year ending Sept. 30, 1914, 248,307 cars, $30,338,454.63. Ten months ending July 31, 1915, 264,351 cars, $24,641,423.17. Three years ending July 31, 1916, 472,350 cars, $59,994,918.01.

The surplus above capital stock was, September 30, 1912, $14,745,095.67, and was increased year by year to $28,124,173.68, $48,827,032.07, $59,135,770.66. In July 31, 1916, it was $111,960,907.53. Originally, the car made by the Ford Motor Company sold for more than $900. From time to time, the selling price was lowered and the car itself improved until in the year ending July 31, 1916, it sold for $440. Up to July 31, 1916, it had sold 1,272,986 cars at a profit of $173,-895,416.06. As the cars in use multiplied, sales of parts and of repairs increased, so that, in the year ending July 31, 1916, the gross profits from repairs and parts was $3,915,778.94; sales being more than $600,000 for each of the months of May, June, and July. For the year beginning August 1, 1916, the price of the car was reduced $80 to $360.

No special dividend having been paid after October, 1915 (a special dividend of $2,000,000 was declared in November, 1916, before the filing of the answers), the plaintiffs, who together own 2,000 shares, or one-tenth of the entire capital stock of the Ford Motor Company, brought suit to have defendant continue to pay special dividends.

The record, and especially the testimony of Mr. Ford, convinces that he has to some extent the attitude towards shareholders of one who has dispensed and distributed to them large gains and that they should be content to take what he chooses to give. His testimony creates the impression, also, that he thinks the Ford Motor Company has made too much money, has had too large profits, and that, although large profits might be still earned, a sharing of them with the public, by reducing the price of the output of the company, ought to be undertaken.

A business corporation is organized and carried on primarily for the profit of the stockholders. The powers of the directors are to be employed for that end. The discretion of directors is to be exercised in the choice of means to attain that end, and does not extend to a change in the end itself, to the reduction of profits, or to the nondistribution of profits among stockholders in order to devote them to other purposes.

When plaintiffs made their complaint and demand for further dividends, the Ford Motor Company had concluded its most prosperous year of business. A refusal to declare and pay further dividends appears to be not an exercise of discretion on the part of the directors, but an arbitrary refusal to do what the circumstances required to be done.

In reaching this conclusion, we do not ignore, but recognize, the validity of the proposition that plaintiffs have from the beginning profited by, if they have not lately, officially, participated in, the general policy of expansion pursued by this corporation. We do not lose sight of the fact that it had been, upon an occasion, agreeable to the plaintiffs to increase the capital stock to $100,000,000 by a stock dividend of $98,000,000. These things go only to answer other contentions now made by plaintiffs, and do not and cannot operate to estop them to demand proper dividends upon the stock they own. It is obvious that an annual dividend of 60 per cent upon $2,000,000, or $1,200,000, is the equivalent of a very small dividend upon $100,000,000, or more.

The decree of the court below fixing and determining the specific amount to be distributed to stockholders is affirmed.

Richter & Co. v. Light
116 A. 600, 97 Conn. 364 (1922)

This was an action by Richter & Co. (plaintiff) against one Light (defendant). Judgment for plaintiff, and defendant appealed. Affirmed.

The complaint alleged that on October 21, 1919, the directors of Stanley Rule & Level Company declared a dividend on its capital stock, to be paid on January 1, 1920, to stockholders of record on December 26, 1919. On October 21, 1919, defendant was the owner of seventy shares of the capital stock of this corporation, which stood in his name on the corporation's books. On December 16, 17, and 19, 1919, defendant sold these shares to plaintiff, which was engaged in the business of buying and selling stocks and bonds, but the certificates were not delivered by defendant in time to be transferred to plaintiff on the books of the corporation, which were closed for transfer of stock from December 26, 1919, to January 1, 1920, and therefore the transfers to plaintiff were not actually made until after the latter date.

Defendant received all the dividends payable on these seventy shares of stock, on January 1, 1920, and refused to pay or account for them to plaintiff.

Defendant demurred to this complaint because (1) it appeared that the dividends which plaintiff sought to recover were declared before it bought defendant's stock, and there was no special agreement that they should belong to the transferee; (2) that when the dividends were declared they became thereby defendant's individual property, and the subsequent transfer of the stock to plaintiff carried with it no right to the dividends; and (3) that plaintiff was not a stockholder of record at the time fixed for the payment of the dividends, and it did not appear that the legal title to the stock had vested in it at that time.

BURPRE, J. The declaration of a dividend by the board of directors of a corporation severs from its assets a portion to be distributed among its stockholders in proportion to their respective holdings. Thereupon the share of each stockholder vests in him as an individual. It makes no difference when the assets were accumulated. Unless otherwise provided by statute, by the corporate charter, or by other governing instruments or contract, the authority to declare a dividend is in the board of directors only, and unless they act fraudulently, unreasonably, or with unjust discrimination, their decisions will not be interfered with by the courts. To determine whether and when a dividend shall be declared rests within their discretion; and if declared, they have the power to fix the amount, time, place, manner, and means of payment with only such limitation as reason and good faith with the stockholders may require. As they may determine and declare the amount of the dividend and its conditions and terms, they may prescribe the day when the division shall be made and take effect, and specify that it shall be paid to stockholders of record on its books on that day.

The power of the directors to declare a dividend which shall rest in the stockholders of record on the day when their resolution is passed, implies and includes the power to declare a dividend which shall rest in the stockholders of record on another day. Before the declaration, the assets of the corporation belong to the corporation, and the stockholders as individuals have no legal right to any share therein. It is the declaration of the dividend that sets apart a portion of the assets to be distributed as dividends and vests in each stockholder individually the legal title to his proportion of them. . . . We find no authority which tends to limit the power of the board of directors to fix the day when a part of the assets of the corporation shall be separated and vested in its stockholders as individuals.

We are satisfied by principle and by authority that the declaration of the dividends in question must be interpreted and given the effect which the directors evidently intended it to have; that is, that the dividends declared on October 21, 1919, belonged to the stockholders of record on December 26, 1919. Since on that day the defendant appeared to be the holder of these shares on the stock book of the corporation, and it does not appear that notice of the transfer of ownership had been given to the corporation, it was warranted in paying the dividends to the defendant. But on that day the plaintiff was in fact the owner of these shares, and its failure to have them transferred before the books of the corporation were closed was caused by the neglect of the defendant. The unrecorded transfer was good between the parties, and therefore the plaintiff had the right to the dividends as against the defendant. But for his neglect, the plaintiff would have appeared in that position on that day, and the corporation would have paid to him the subsequent dividends which the defendant took. He had made no stipulation or contract to reserve these dividends to himself. The plaintiff, according to the customs of corporations in declaring dividends, and the usage of dealers in stocks and bonds, was justified in believing that these dividends would belong to it, and therefore in paying a correspondingly increased price for the stock.

Judgment affirmed.

RIGHT TO INSPECT BOOKS AND RECORDS

At common law stockholders have the right to inspect the books and records of the corporation. However, the stockholder who wishes to assert this right must act in good faith. He is not entitled to make such an inspection out of idle curiosity or for improper purposes. Likewise, the inspection must be made at a proper time and place. In general, the inspection is considered to be for a proper purpose if it is made in order to advance the interests of the corporation or to protect the rights of the stockholder.

In a given case where a stockholder is entitled to inspect the books and records of the corporation he may do so with the aid of his attorney, accountant, or secretary. He may also take copies of the records which he is legally entitled to inspect.

Most states now have statutes regulating the right of stockholders to examine the books and records of a corporation. These statutes are not uniform. While some statutes seem to make the right of inspection absolute, others seem merely to enlarge the stockholders' rights of inspection under the common law. However, in those states wherein statutes have been enacted which seem to make the right of inspection absolute, the courts in interpreting the statutes refuse to issue a writ of mandamus requiring the corporation to permit inspection, unless it appears that the stockholder is acting in good faith.

Sanders v. Neely et al.

19 So. (2d) (Miss.) 424 (1944)

Mandamus by R. D. Sanders (plaintiff) against W. H. Neely and others, executive officers of the Standard Life Insurance Company of the South (defendants), to compel defendants to permit plaintiff, as a stockholder, to inspect the books and records of defendant corporation. Defendants' demurrer was sustained, and plaintiff appealed. Reversed and remanded.

The petition alleged in substance that defendant insurance company is a domestic corporation; that petitioner owned a substantial amount of the capital stock thereof; that he had asked the executive officers of the company to permit him to inspect its books and records "at such time and under such conditions as would not interfere with the operations or conduct of the affairs" thereof; that these requests had been made on several occasions shortly prior to the filing of the petition herein, and had in each instance been refused; and that plaintiff's purpose in making the request was "in order to ascertain and know how the affairs of the company were conducted and whether or not the capital of which he had contributed a share was being prudently and profitably employed, and in order that he might protect the business interests of the corporation and his interest as a stockholder."

McGHEE, J. The common law right of a stockholder to inspect the books and records of his corporation is stated in 13 *Am. Jur.* 480, as follows: "A stockholder in a corporation has in the very nature of things and upon principles of equity, good faith, and fair dealings, the right to know how the affairs of the company are conducted and whether the capital of which he had contributed a share is being prudently and profitably employed. In order to obtain this information he has . . . a common law right, at proper and seasonable times, to inspect all the books and records of the corporation." And it is not contended by counsel for the appellees herein that this is not an accurate statement of the rule, but it is stated by them, and correctly so, that this common law right can be exercised by the stockholder only in good faith and for a just, useful, or reasonable purpose germane to his interest as a stockholder; and that such right will not be enforced by the court for speculative purposes or to gratify idle curiosity and particularly when the purpose of the inspection is hostile to the corporation. In other words, the appellees contend that to this extent the right is not absolute but is a qualified one.

It may be conceded that such right as a stockholder may have in this state to inspect and examine the books and records of his corporation are governed by the common law since we have no statute providing therefor, and also that the same is qualified to the extent above stated. Nevertheless it will be seen that the allegation contained in the petition before us setting forth the purpose for which the inspection was devised has clearly brought the petitioner within the rule entitling him thereto, unless the defendants shall plead and prove as an affirmative defense in response to the petition that the stockholder in the instant case is actuated by bad motives or that the inspection is not desired in order to obtain information germane to his interest as a stockholder but is for speculative purposes or to gratify idle curiosity, or out of a spirit of hostility to the welfare of the corporation, since good motives and a proper purpose will be presumed and the converse thereof cannot be assumed by the court in passing upon the sufficiency of the petition herein if we follow the well-established rule in that behalf as stated in 13 *Am. Jur.* 488, where it is said: "It will not be presumed, however, when a request for inspection is made that the motive of the stockholder is an improper one or that his purpose is other than in the interest of the corporation, and if the motive or purpose is charged to be otherwise, the burden is on the officers refusing the request to establish it." Unless such a defensive showing is made by an affirmative plea and proof in support thereof, the proper exercise of judicial discretion of the court may appear just and reasonable.

Many of the states, if not a majority of them, have enacted statutes guaranteeing such right of inspection, and the only distinction between the common law right and that given by these statutes is that at common law the right is qualified to the extent hereinbefore mentioned as to the motives of the stockholders, etc., whereas under the statutes the motive is immaterial, the right being an absolute one.

The defendants' demurrer should have been overruled. Reversed and remanded.

PREEMPTIVE RIGHTS

STOCKHOLDERS' PREEMPTIVE RIGHTS IN NEW STOCK ISSUE. The articles of incorporation authorize the issuance of a specified amount of stock. After this original issue has been sold the corporation may not legally sell any more stock without first obtaining the consent of the state to do so. To obtain such consent the charter must be amended. The usual procedure is for the board of directors to adopt a resolution that such an amendment is desirable, after which the resolution must be approved by a certain number (usually the holders of a majority of the voting stock) of the stockholders at a regular or special meeting of the stockholders. When such new stock is authorized the stockholders of record are entitled to subscribe for or purchase the new stock in proportion to their interest in the old or original stock before the new stock may be offered for sale to outsiders. This right of a stockholder to subscribe to the new issue of stock is known as his *preemptive right.* Its purpose is to afford him the opportunity of maintaining the same relative voting position in the corporation (thereby securing to himself his proportional right to control corporate affairs) and the same relative share in its profits.

If there are no statutory provisions to the contrary, the preemptive rights of stockholders may be modified, or such rights may be denied them altogether, by the articles of incorporation, or by a provision to that effect in the amendment of the articles providing for the new issue of stock.

The courts have consistently held that preemptive rights do not apply (1) to treasury stock; (2) where the stock is issued for services or property other than cash; (3) in the case of a reorganization, merger, or combination. Some courts have held that such rights do not apply in the case of an employee stock purchase plan.

STOCKHOLDERS' PREEMPTIVE RIGHTS IN ORIGINAL ISSUE OF STOCK.   The general rule is that there are no preemptive rights in the original issue of stock of a corporation. No problem arises in this respect if all the authorized stock is issued immediately upon incorporation. But if only a part of the original stock is issued and the balance remains unissued for a time, have the original purchasers preemptive rights in the unissued stock? Some courts have held that under no circumstances do stockholders have a preemptive right in the original issue of stock. Other courts have held that, in the absence of a statutory provision to the contrary, stockholders are entitled to preemptive rights in the original stock where it has remained unissued for a considerable time. Some corporation statutes cover this question, but they are not uniform.

WHO ARE ENTITLED TO PREEMPTIVE RIGHTS.   Preemptive rights usually pertain only to holders of voting stock. Generally the voting stockholders of record at the time the charter was amended authorizing a new issue are entitled to preemptive rights in the new issue, but the statutes may specify some other time as a basis for the determination.

PREEMPTIVE RIGHTS ARE VALUABLE RIGHTS.   Preemptive rights are property rights. Since the stock is usually offered to the stockholders below the market price, and since they are privileged to sell their rights to outsiders if they themselves are not in a position to purchase additional stock, stock rights often have considerable value to the stockholder. Stockholders who are entitled to preemptive rights are notified of such rights and are given a certain time in which to exercise them. Failure to act is deemed to be a waiver of the rights.

Stokes v. Continental Trust Co. of the City of New York
186 N. Y. 285, 78 N. E. 1090 (1906)

This was a suit by William Stokes (plaintiff) against the Continental Trust Company of the City of New York (defendant). From an order of the Appellate Division reversing a judgment in favor of plaintiff, plaintiff appealed. Reversed and judgment of the trial court modified and affirmed.

This suit was brought by a stockholder to compel his corporation to issue to him at par such a proportion of an increase made in its capital stock as the number of shares held by him before such increase bore to the number of all the shares originally issued, and in case such additional shares could not be delivered to him, for his damages in the premises.

Defendant was a domestic banking corporation, organized in 1890, with a capital stock of $500,000, consisting of 5,000 shares of the par value of $100 each. Plaintiff was one of the original stockholders of the corporation, and at the time of this suit was a substantial holder of its stock. On January 29, 1902, defendant had a surplus of $1,048,450.94, which made the book value of the stock at that time $309.69 per share. On January 21, 1902, Blair & Co. made the following proposition to defendant: "If your stockholders at the special meeting to be called January 29, 1902, vote to increase your capital stock from $500,000 to $1,000,000, you may deliver the additional stock to us as soon as issued at $450 per share ($100 par value) for ourselves and associates, it being understood that we may nominate ten of the twenty-one trustees to be elected at the adjourned annual meeting of stockholders." The directors of defendant promptly met and duly authorized a special meeting on January 29, 1902, for the purpose of voting on the proposed increase of stock and the acceptance of the offer to purchase same. Upon due notice a meeting of the stockholders was held accordingly, more than a majority attending either in person or by proxy. A resolution to increase the stock was adopted by the vote of 4,197 shares, all that were cast. Plaintiff thereupon demanded from defendant the right to subscribe for 221 shares of the new stock at par, and offered to pay immediately for same, which demand was refused. A resolution directing the sale to Blair & Co. at $450 a share was then adopted. Plaintiff voted for the first resolution but against the last. On January 30, 1902, the stock was increased and on the same day was sold to Blair & Co. at the price named. By April, 1904 the stock was worth $700 per share.

The trial court found that plaintiff had the right to subscribe for such proportion of the increase as his holdings bore to all the stock before the increase was made; that the corporation had no power to deprive him of that right, and that he was entitled to recover the difference between the market value of 221 shares on January 30, 1902, and the par value thereof, or the sum of $99,450. The judgment entered accordingly was reversed by the Appellate Division, and plaintiff appealed to this court.

VANN, J. The question presented for decision is whether according to the facts found the plaintiff had a legal right to subscribe for and take the same number of shares of the new stock that he held of the old? The subject is not regulated by statute, and the question presented has never been directly passed upon by this court, and only to a limited extent has it been considered by courts in this state. In other jurisdictions the decisions support the claim of the plaintiff. In *Morris v. Stevens*, 178 Pa. 563, 36 A. 151, the court said "In general, the present holders of stock have a primary right to subscribe in proportion to their holdings for any new issue. . . ." The elementary writers are very clear and emphatic in laying down the same rule. 1 Cook on Corporations, p. 286, states: "Each stockholder, it has been held, has a right to the opportunity to subscribe for and take the new or increased stock in proportion to the old stock held by him, so that a vote at a stockholders' meeting, directing the new stock to be sold, without giving to each stockholder such an opportunity, is void as to any dissenting stockholder."

If the right claimed by the plaintiff was a right of property belonging to him as a stockholder, he could not be deprived of it by the joint action of the other stockholders, and of all the directors and officers of the corporation. What is the nature of the right acquired by a stockholder through the ownership of shares of stock? While he does not own and cannot dispose of any specific property of the corporation, yet he and his associates own the corporation itself, its charter, franchises, and all rights conferred thereby, including the right to increase stock. He has an inherent right to his proportionate share of any dividend declared, of any surplus arising upon dissolution, and he can prevent waste or misappropriation of the property of the corporation by those in control. Finally, he has the right to vote for directors and upon all propositions subject by law to the control of the stockholders, and this is his supreme right and main protection. Stockholders have no direct voice in transacting the corporate business, but through their right to vote they can select those whom the law invests with the power of management and control. The power to manage its affairs resides in the directors, who are its agents, but the power to elect directors resides in the stockholders. . . . Hence the power of the individual stockholder to vote in proportion to the number of his stocks is vital and cannot be cut off or curtailed by the action of all the other stockholders, even with the cooperation of the directors and officers.

[The judgment of the trial court was modified by reducing the amount of damages allowed to the plaintiff and affirmed.]

LIABILITIES OF STOCKHOLDERS

LIMITED LIABILITY

A major advantage of the corporation over the single proprietorship and the partnership is that the liability of the stockholders is limited to their investment in the shares of the corporation. This means that the stockholders are not liable out of their own estates for the debts and liabilities of the corporation, arising either in contract or in tort.

The principle of limited liability of the stockholder is, however, predicated upon certain conditions and assumptions, which are discussed in the following paragraphs. As will be pointed out, the holder of stock may have further liability if certain legal requirements have not been met.

LIABILITY ON UNPAID SUBSCRIPTIONS

A subscription to buy stock for a named consideration, when accepted by the corporation, is a valid contract with the corporation. Failure to pay for the stock according to the terms of the contract gives the corporation the right to bring action against the subscriber for the balance due under the contract. If and when the full amount is paid, the stockholder has no further liability, either to the corporation or to its creditors.

Where subscriptions are made payable upon call of the board of directors, stockholders are not in default until a valid call for payment is made. But if the subscription is payable immediately following the subscription, a call by the board of directors is not required in order to put a subscriber in default.

In case of insolvency of the corporation the stockholder may be held liable to the creditors of the corporation for any unpaid subscriptions. This is so because any unpaid subscription is an asset of the corporation. However, the other assets of the insolvent corporation must be exhausted before the creditors of the corporation may proceed against the stockholders to recover on the unpaid portions of their subscriptions.

LIABILITY ON WATERED STOCK

The corporation statutes generally provide that stock may be issued for cash, property other than cash, or services. If stock purports to be fully paid but was in fact issued to the stockholder for less than its full equivalent in cash, property, or services, the stock is overvalued. Such stock is known as *watered stock*. Is the stockholder to whom it was thus issued liable to the corporation and to creditors of the corporation for the difference between the par value (or, in the case of no-par stock, the stated value) of the stock and the consideration which he actually paid for the stock? As between the corporation and the stockholder, if the stockholder has paid all that he contracted to pay for the stock he has no further liability to the corporation. However, those who deal with the corporation and extend credit to it have a right to assume that full value was paid for the stock; if this was not the case, then if the corporation becomes insolvent the stockholder will be liable to the corporate creditors for the difference between the amount actually paid and the par or stated value of the stock.

Where stock has been paid for in cash, it is easy to determine whether it is fully paid and non-assessable. A more difficult problem rises where stock has been issued in return for property or services, as very frequently occurs in the organization of a corporation. Two tests have been applied by the courts in determining whether full value has been given for such stock; that is, whether it is fully paid. One of these tests is known as the *actual value test*, the other as the *good faith test*. In applying the actual value test an effort is made to determine the actual value of the property or services given in exchange for the stock; if it is found that the actual value of such property or services is less than the par or stated value of the stock, the stock is held to be not fully paid, and the stockholder would be liable for the difference to the creditors, under a *creditors' bill*, brought in case of the insolvency of the corporation. This rule is difficult to apply. Hence most courts apply the good faith test. If it is found that the directors acted in good faith and without fraud in evaluating the property or services exchanged for the stock, the value established by the directors cannot be challenged. In such case, if the good faith value placed upon the property or services was the equivalent of the par or stated value of the stock, the stock is fully paid and non-assessable, and the stockholder has no further liability either to the corporation or to the corporate creditors.

If the original owner sells and transfers watered stock and the purchaser (transferee) knows when he purchases the stock that it is not fully paid, he is liable both to the corporation and to the corporate creditors. But if he does not have such knowledge, he is not liable to either, since he is entitled to assume that the stock is fully paid and non-assessable.

Owners of no-par stock are liable only for the price they agreed to pay. Hence if the agreed price has been fully paid, the owners of such stock have no further liability.

After stock has been purchased from the corporation the holder of the stock may sell it at any price it will bring and he is willing to accept for it. In such case, neither the seller nor the buyer would be liable, either to the corporation or to its creditors, if the price paid for the stock were less than its par or nominal value.

LIABILITY TO RETURN DIVIDENDS ILLEGALLY RECEIVED

If dividends have been illegally declared and paid by the corporation, they may be recovered by the corporation from the stockholders. If the corporation fails or refuses to recover such dividends and afterwards becomes bankrupt, the creditors may recover them by filing a creditors' bill in equity.

Russell et al. v. Tennessee & Kentucky Tobacco Co. et al.
65 S. W. (2d) 256, 16 Tenn. App. 561 (1933)

This was a suit by S. R. Russell and another (plaintiffs) against the Tennessee & Kentucky Tobacco Co. and others (defendants). The Chancellor sustained the bill as a general creditors' bill, and defendants appealed. Decree affirmed.

This appeal involved the rights of the creditors of the Tennessee & Kentucky Tobacco Co., a corporation, to hold the stockholders of the corporation for their unpaid capital stock. The bill was filed on August 13, 1925, by S. R. Russell and R. F. Long, trustee for E. B. Long, based on a note of the corporation for $1,063.33, dated July 31, 1924, due eight months after date, payable to the order of Miss Mary Dunn, which plaintiffs alleged had been transferred to them by her for value. In the bill various other creditors of the corporation were made defendants. It was prayed that a receiver be appointed to take possession of all of the property of the corporation and that it be converted into money; that an accounting be had; and for general relief. More specifically stated, it is sought to hold the stockholders liable for $9,000 each for unpaid subscriptions to the capital stock of the Tennessee & Kentucky Tobacco Co.

The facts showed that the Tennessee & Kentucky Tobacco Co. was incorporated in March, 1918, with an authorized capital stock of $36,000. The original subscribers were R. T. Bohanan, H. T. Stratton, R. F. Long, and R. F. Long, trustee for E. B. Long. No money was ever paid to the corporation directly for these shares of stock. Each of the four stockholders subscribed for stock amounting to $9,000 par value. At the time of its organization the corporation had no property, no money, and no credit; but it purchased a warehouse for a sum of $22,000, of which $5,500 was furnished by the stockholders, and for the balance the corporation executed its three notes for $5,500 each, secured by a mortgage on the property and by the personal indorsement of the stockholders. R. T. Bohanan soon retired from the corporation as manager, and he was succeeded by S. R. Russell, who acquired Bohanan's stock. Russell testified that when he acquired Bohanan's stock he thought it was paid-up stock.

The facts further showed that the defendant stockholders loaned their credit to the corporation and that none of them ever had to pay anything by reason of their indorsements of the corporation's notes. The corporation did a successful business, at least until the warehouse was burned in 1920. Although the business was successful during those years no dividends were ever paid to the stockholders. The profits were allowed to remain in the business. It is claimed by the stockholders that the corporation could have paid dividends to an amount equal to twice the par value of the capital stock owned by the stockholders. They therefore contend that this should be treated as a full, though indirect, payment for their capital stock. The corporation finally became bankrupt in 1924.

DE WITT, J. The Tennessee & Kentucky Tobacco Co. was duly incorporated under the laws of Tennessee and it was duly organized with directors and officers and engaged in the business for which it was chartered and organized. It was not a sham organization. The charter of the corporation contained the following provision, taken from the general laws of the state: ". . . nor shall the transfer of stock by any stockholder relieve him from payment, unless the transferee has paid up all or any of the balance due on the said original subscription."

The rule is well settled that a corporation may treat as payment for stock any property which it is authorized to own and which is necessary to the operation of its business, provided that it is taken in good faith and at a fair valuation.

In the instant case it does appear that these defendants loaned their credit to the corporation, thereby enabling it to accumulate property in value to the extent of at least twice the value of the capital stock. It does not appear that this corporation was materially indebted at the time when it enjoyed this status, just before the fire occurred in 1920, which finally led to its insolvency. We are compelled to hold that the mere lending of credit, the indorsing of notes for the corporation, when the indorsers were not compelled to pay anything by reason of the indorsements, was not consideration for the issuance of shares of stock to the indorsers. In such case the stockholder paid nothing, he merely loaned his credit and the credit which he loaned was abated when the corporation paid the debt. . . . Our law contemplates that the corporation itself should receive for its capital stock land, money, or other property. We have no statute or reported decision in Tennessee to the effect that the mere lending of credit could be made in payment of a subscription to capital stock.

To allow a corporation thus to operate without receiving a dollar for its stock; even to earn profits and accumulate a surplus; finally to become insolvent, owing large sums for borrowed money; and then to absolve its stockholders from liability for capital stock subscribed and held by them, would be to sanction unsafe methods, ignore the law of liability of subscribers to stock, and grossly violate the rights of creditors. Our law and our public policy do not permit the doing of such things.

It appears that R. F. Long and R. F. Long, trustee, subscribed each for $9,000 worth of the stock at par value. The rule is that a trustee of stock who is recorded on the corporate books as a stockholder is, at common law, liable on such stock as though he were the absolute owner of the stock.

In behalf of S. R. Russell it is insisted that he is a bona fide purchaser and owner of his stock for value and without notice or knowledge that it had not been paid for by his vendor, Bohanan. If this is true, he cannot be held liable for the unpaid subscription. In Cook on Corporations, Vol. 2, sec. 418, the rule is stated that the transferee who buys stock supposing it to be fully paid is not liable for uncollected and unpaid parts of the subscription, even though the certificate is silent as to whether the par value of the stock had been paid or not. Russell testified that Bohanan transferred his stock certificate to him; that it recited on its face that it was fully paid up; that he understood that this was true; that the books had been kept by Bohanan; and that when he took them they showed that the stock had been paid up. There is no direct evidence to the contrary. In view of the absence of evidence tending to contradict the testimony of Russell, we are unable to find that he was not a bona fide purchaser and owner of the stock; and thus it was not error to decree that he is not liable for the price of the stock acquired by him from Bohanan.

REVIEW CASES

1. The Great Western Sugar Co., a corporation, was organized with one million shares of preferred and ten million shares of common stock, and in time accumulated surplus and undivided profits, including working capital, in excess of $39,000,000. From this sum of money, accumulated in prior years, the corporation paid dividends to common stockholders. Frazer, one of the preferred stockholders, brought suit, contending that this payment was out of capital assets of the corporation. Was Frazer correct? (People of Colorado ex rel. Frazer v. Great Western Sugar Co., 29 F.(2d) 810)

2. The Portland Mining Co., a corporation with three million shares of fully paid and non-assessable stock, acquired 704,000 shares of treasury stock from its stockholders. The board of directors authorized the sale of the treasury stock, and Stratton, one of the directors, bought 208,000 shares for himself. Crosby, one of the stockholders, maintained that he had a preemptive right to buy 28,641 of the shares issued to Stratton, and brought suit to enforce this alleged right. Holding? (Crosby v. Stratton, 17 Colo. App. 212, 68 P. 130)

3. Under the will of Charles Wuichet, deceased, his widow was to receive the entire income from a trust estate during her lifetime, and upon her death the estate was to pass to several named persons. The estate included certain shares of stock. On Jan. 31st the corporation declared dividends on this stock, to be paid in quarterly installments to stockholders of record as of Feb. 24th, May 25th, Aug. 25th, and Nov. 24th. Mrs. Wuichet died on March 19th. The executor of her estate claimed all the dividends. The trustee claimed the last three quarterly dividends for the trust estate. Judgment for whom? (In re Wuichet's Estate, 138 Ohio St. 97, 33 N. E.(2d) 15)

4. The Clifton Coal Co., a corporation, was organized with 1,200 shares, par value $100, with power to increase the shares to 2,000 by a majority vote of the stockholders. This increase was later voted, but the corporation was unable to sell the additional 800 shares. The corporation then issued $50,000 worth of bonds and was able to dispose of them by offering the buyers $50,000 worth of stock as a bonus; the remaining $30,000 worth of stock was given to the original stockholders of the corporation. The stock certificates bore the statement that the shares were "fully paid and non-assessable." Stutz and others, judgment creditors of the corporation, brought an action to compel an assessment upon the 800 shares. Holding? (Handley v. Stutz, 139 U. S. 417, 35 L. Ed. 227)

5. Sherman, to whom certain judgment creditors of the Oleum Development Co. had assigned their judgments, sued the stockholders to recover amounts alleged due on unpaid subscriptions to the capital stock of the corporation. The stock had a par value of $1 a share and was issued as fully paid-up stock, but in no instance was it actually fully paid for, and in some cases the corporation had received no more than 10¢ a share. These facts were fully known to the creditors when they extended credit to the corporation. Holding? (Sherman v. Harley et al., 178 Cal. 594, 174 P. 901)

Management and Operation of Corporations

48

The management and operation of a corporation involve both the determination of basic policies and the execution of those policies. Every corporation, under the local state statutes or codes, the articles of incorporation, and the bylaws, is provided with certain "machinery" for its management and operation, whereby authority for these purposes is distributed among the stockholders, the board of directors, the senior and junior officers, and other agents and employees. Some of these groups have responsibility for deciding upon the basic policies by which the operations of the corporation are governed; other groups are primarily concerned with putting such policies into effect. In other words, the functions of some groups or individuals are policy-determining; of others, administrative.

STOCKHOLDERS

POSITION IN CORPORATE MANAGEMENT AND CONTROL

Stockholders have no administrative functions to perform. What policy-determining authority they possess is derived from two sources: (1) their authority to elect the members of the board of directors; (2) the powers conferred on them or reserved to them by law, or the articles of incorporation, or the bylaws.

Under modern corporation law the authority to manage and control the *ordinary and usual operations* of a corporation is vested in the board of directors, and the stockholders therefore have no right to participate in the management of such operations. The principal control of the stockholders over the board of directors and the policies established by them exists through their authority to elect the members of the board of directors. If the stockholders are dissatisfied with the board of directors in its conduct of the affairs of the corporation, they are privileged to elect a new board of directors. However, this means of control is often largely theoretical. The state statutes usually require a simple majority vote for the election of directors, so that in a given case a very large minority of dissatisfied stockholders would be powerless to change the composition of the board of directors.

The stockholders' second source of influence upon the policies adopted by the corporation is the fact that certain *unusual and extraordinary acts,* or *fundamental changes* in the corporation, require stockholder approval. Authority to exercise this type of control is conferred upon them or reserved to them by law, the articles of incorporation, or the bylaws. Such authority is often conferred in the sections of the corporation statutes which make provision for amendment of the articles of incorporation and specify that such amendment requires the approval of the holders of two thirds, or in some states three fourths, of the voting stock of the corporation. Stockholder approval through the amending process is generally required to change the corporate name; to modify the corporate purpose; to change the duration of the corporate existence; to alter the financial structure of the corporation; or to change the provisions of the articles of incorporation concerning the powers of the corporation and of the board of directors. In addition, the courts quite generally hold that stockholder approval is required to sell all the assets of the corporation, or to effect a consolidation or merger, or to dissolve the corporation. Some states also have statutes concerning these matters.

The ownership of stock in a corporation does not create the relation of principal and agent between the corporation and the stockholder. Hence the stockholder has no authority to bind the corporation contractually. The corporation is not liable for the stockholder's torts.

Mimnaugh v. Atlantic City Electric Co.
70 A. (2d) 904, 7 N. J. Supr. 310 (1950)

This was an action by Winfield Mimnaugh (plaintiff) against Atlantic City Electric Company (defendant). Judgment for defendant, and plaintiff appealed. Affirmed.

On or about April 23, 1948, plaintiff became the owner of 100 shares of the stock of defendant corporation. Defendant was engaged in the business of manufacturing and selling electricity. The processes used in the manufacturing and generation of electricity produced two by-products, designated in the trade as "cinders" and "fly ash." For some period prior to December 21, 1948, defendant had a contract with the Atlantic City Construction Company for removal of these by-products. Under the terms of the contract the construction company neither received nor paid any consideration for the removal of the cinders, but was paid at the rate of $3.00 per hour for the removal of the fly ash.

On October 1, 1948, plaintiff retained one Samuel Morris, an attorney, to investigate this arrangement. A plan for the disposal of the cinders and fly ash was worked out which plaintiff thought would result in a saving for the corporation. He wrote to the president, giving him his suggestions and plan. After some consideration, plaintiff's plan was adopted by the corporation but there was no contract with plaintiff or any understanding that he was to receive any compensation for his plan and suggestions. It turned out that the adoption of plaintiff's plan resulted in a saving for the corporation. Plaintiff then demanded that defendant pay him for his plan and also a reasonable fee for his attorney, Mr. Morris. Defendant refused to pay him, and plaintiff filed this action.

HANEMAN, J. An individual stockholder has not, by reason of his relationship as such, the direction or management of the corporation, and cannot act for it. Vol. 5, Fletcher, *Cyc. Corp.*, Sec. 2098, p. 343. Nor is such a stockholder, ipso facto, an agent of the corporation. It follows that in the absence of an actual agency, the plaintiff is not entitled, as an implied agent of the defendant, to compensation.

Was plaintiff entitled to recover as a representative of other stockholders? To be entitled to compensation as such implied agent his action of relationship must be likened to that taken by a stockholder in commencing a derivative or representative suit. In reaching a conclusion on this subject it must be borne in mind that the business of a corporation is normally entrusted to its board of directors. If the board of directors exercise their judgment honestly and sincerely, in the absence of a purpose which is unlawful or against good morals, the courts of this state will not substitute their judgment for that of the board. In *Ellerman v. Chicago Junction Railway & Union Stockyards Co.*, 49 N. Y. Eq. 217, the court said: "Individual stockholders cannot question in judicial proceedings the corporate acts of directors if the same are within the powers of the corporation and in furtherance of its purposes, are not unlawful or against good morals, and are done in good faith and in the exercise of an honest judgment. Questions of policy of management . . . are left solely to the honest decision of the directors if their powers are without limitation and free from restraint. . . ."

A derivative action is brought not only for the benefit of the individual plaintiff stockholder but as well for the benefit of all stockholders of a similar class and of the corporation. In the case sub judice we have neither any allegation nor any proof that the officers and directors violated their duties as trustees nor that the disputed action violated the stockholders' contractual rights. The sole cause of complaint lies in the fact that the judgment of the officers was not infallible, and that had they sought further, a greater return could have been had by the corporation for a disposal of the by-products. Judgment affirmed.

STOCKHOLDERS' MEETINGS

Stockholders acting individually have no authority to influence the corporation's policies. Such authority as they possess must be exercised collectively, through action taken by a legally called and constituted stockholders' meeting.

Meetings of stockholders may be either *regular* or *special*. The regular meetings are sometimes referred to as "general" or "stated." Special meetings are often referred to as "call" meetings. The statute or bylaws usually provide that there must be one general or regular meeting each year, and further provide for the calling of special meetings when desirable.

Usually the charter or bylaws specify the method to be followed in calling stockholders' meetings. In the absence of such provision meetings may be called by the board of directors. To protect the stockholders against arbitrary action by the board of directors it is usually provided by statute or the bylaws that a stockholders' meeting may be called by the holders of a specified number of shares of voting stock.

Where the charter or bylaws prescribe the time and place for the regular meeting of the stockholders, formal notice need not be given, though as a practical matter such notice is customarily given. For special meetings, formal notice must be given. Such notice must state the day and hour of the meeting, the place of the meeting, and the business to be taken up at the meeting. Action on any matter not set out in the notice is invalid. Either the statute or the bylaws provide that the notice must be given a certain number of days (usually ten days) before the date on which the meeting is to be held.

The requirement of formal notice in the case of special meetings may be waived by the stockholders, in either of two ways. (1) The stockholders may sign a *waiver of notice*. This is especially convenient if there are relatively few stockholders and it is desired to hold a special meeting quickly. In such case, a meeting might be held on much shorter notification than is specified by the statute or bylaws if the stockholders sign a waiver of notice before or at the meeting. Some statutes even provide that such waiver notice may be signed after the meeting. (2) A stockholder or stockholders may waive notice of special meetings if they actually attend the meeting and participate in its deliberations and actions. They may not later attack the legality of any action taken at such a meeting on the ground that the meeting was not legally called.

Under the common law rule, if a meeting has been properly called, two or more stockholders will constitute a quorum, i.e. the number required to be present at a meeting in order to transact business. A majority of those present may take legal action. Today it is generally provided by statute or bylaws that in order to have a quorum present at a stockholders' meeting the holders of a majority of the voting stock must be represented, either in person or by proxy.

Asbury v. Mauney
173 N. C. 454, 92 S. E. 267 (1917)

This was an action by E. M. Asbury (plaintiff) against C. J. Mauney (defendant). Judgment for defendant, and plaintiff appealed. Affirmed.

This was an action to recover the sum of $93.66 which plaintiff alleged was due him on account of an agreement entered into by defendant, a stockholder of the E. M. Asbury Co. The E. M. Asbury Company was a corporation and the stockholders were Watkins, Mauney, Andrews, Asbury, McRae, and Spencer.

The corporation became insolvent and on September 16, 1909, the stockholders held a call meeting. In the notice sent to stockholders, calling the meeting, it was stated: "The object of the meeting is to fix a price on the stock of merchandise on hand with a view to closing out the business, which has been running at a loss to the stockholders for three years." At the meeting the stockholders fixed a price of 50 cents on the dollar on the merchandise, and appointed a committee of stockholders to sell it and pay the creditors as far as the proceeds from the sale would go. At the time this meeting was held the corporation was indebted to J. W. Ould & Co. and to the Hetch-Hirschler Co. in certain amounts for which plaintiff was personally liable, which amounts plaintiff afterward paid. He therefore brought this action to recover of defendant a proportionate part thereof, relying upon the following statement in the minutes of the special meeting of the stockholders:

"Moved by C. W. Andrews, seconded by C. J. Mauney, that after the stock of goods had been sold and the proceeds placed to the payment of notes, accounts, and claims against the said E. M. Asbury Co., all remaining unpaid bills and notes be paid by stockholders in proportion to the stock they owned."

Plaintiff contended that this was an agreement entered into by defendant and the other stockholders who were present, to pay the debts of the corporation; that the minutes signed by the secretary of the corporation was a sufficient memorandum thereof to satisfy the statute of frauds; and that, as he has paid certain debts of the corporation in existence at the time of the meeting of the stockholders, he was entitled to be subrogated to the rights of the creditors as against defendant. Judgment for defendant in the trial court, and plaintiff appealed.

ALLEN, J. In the first place, it does not appear that the stockholders entered into any agreement to pay the debts of the corporation. It is stated in the minutes that a motion to this effect was made and seconded, but it does not appear that it was voted upon or adopted.

Secondly, the stockholders' meeting of September 16th was a call meeting for a special purpose and at such meeting no action can be taken which will be binding upon the corporation unless every stockholder has notice, and if the meeting is called for a special purpose, business not embraced in the notice will be void unless all the members of the corporation are present and give their consent, or the action is thereafter ratified. 10 *Cyc.* 327.

In this case notice was given to all the stockholders but the notice did not suggest that any action would be taken or considered as to the imposition of personal liability upon the stockholders for the debts of the corporation, and the action of the stockholders, if they agreed to become personally liable, could not be corporate action, and would amount in any event to no more than a personal agreement between the stockholders. The agreement also, if made, was not the act of the corporation because it did not purport to deal with the property of the corporation or the conduct of its business, but simply undertook to determine the relationship between the stockholders themselves as to their liability for the debts of the corporation. Affirmed.

DIRECTORS

POSITION IN CORPORATE MANAGEMENT AND CONTROL

The management and control of the ordinary and usual business of a corporation is vested in its board of directors, generally by express provision of the corporation statute. While the board, as such, does not handle the day-to-day activities of the corporation, it does, within the scope of its authority, determine basic policies which control those activities. It is essentially a policy-determining body.

As we have seen, only in extraordinary situations are the directors required to obtain the approval of the stockholders. Consequently, it may be said that, with few exceptions, the board of directors has exclusive power and authority to exercise all the rights and powers vested in the corporation under the law and by its articles of incorporation. The directors, acting as a board, are the legally constituted agents of the corporation in dealing with outside persons. The board of directors has full capacity to contract, upon behalf of the corporation, within the confines of the law and the corporation's charter. It has the authority to exercise the express, implied, and incidental powers of the corporation. The board of directors has broad discretion in the exercise of its powers and only in extreme situations will the courts interfere with its exercise of this discretionary power.

The authority of the directors is conferred upon them as a board, and they can bind the corporation only by acting together as an official body. A majority of them, in their individual names, cannot act for the board itself and bind the corporation.[1] Official or legal action is taken by the board of directors by the adoption of resolutions.

[1] See *Mosell Realty Corporation v. Schofield*, below.

ELECTION, FILLING OF VACANCIES, AND COMPENSATION

The directors are elected by the stockholders, except that under the corporation statutes of some states the first board of directors is named in the articles of incorporation. The statutes usually provide that the directors shall be elected annually; but directors remain in office until their successors are chosen.

The statutes usually specify the minimum number of directors required; in some cases they also specify the maximum number permitted. Within these confines the charter or bylaws may determine the exact number for a given corporation. A minimum of three directors is usually required.

In the absence of specific requirements in the statutes, articles of incorporation, or bylaws, any person is eligible to serve on the board of directors. In most, but not all, of the states a director is required to be a stockholder of the corporation. Some statutes also require that at least one of the directors be a resident of the state of incorporation; but a number of the states make no such requirement.

A director may resign at will. Likewise, he may be removed by the stockholders for cause, such as fraud, bad faith, or neglect of duty. He may not usually be removed without cause without subjecting the corporation to an action for damages. Unless the board of directors is given authority to do so, it may not remove one of its own members.

Unless otherwise provided, vacancies on the board of directors must be filled by the stockholders at a regular or special meeting. However, it is not uncommon for the statutes to permit a corporation to include in its bylaws a provision establishing a method for filling vacancies on the board. Such a provision may give the board of directors authority to fill vacancies.

If the directors are given authority to fill vacancies this authority does not extend to the appointment of new directors in cases where the membership of the board is increased. Such new directors must be chosen by the stockholders unless the statute specifically gives to the board of directors the authority to make such appointments.

Directors seldom receive anything by way of compensation for their services. In fact, they have no legal right to vote themselves compensation unless they are authorized to do so by the articles of incorporation or bylaws. The stockholders may authorize the payment of compensation to the directors. Where compensation is provided for, it usually amounts to no more than a nominal sum or fee to the directors for attending meetings of the board of directors.

DIRECTORS' MEETINGS

The bylaws provide for the time and place of the regular or stated meetings of the board of directors. Such meetings may therefore be held without notice. Special meetings may also be called by the chairman of the board of directors or by the president. Notice of the time, place, and purposes of special meetings must be given to each director. However, if no formal written notice is given but the directors attend the meeting, they may sign a *waiver of notice*, before or at the meeting.

If the statutes, articles, or bylaws do not provide otherwise, meetings of the board of directors may be held outside the state of incorporation. A number of the state corporation statutes specifically provide that directors' meetings may be held "within or without the state." Some of the state statutes require that they be held within the state of incorporation.

A majority of the directors constitute a quorum, and, if not otherwise provided, a majority of the quorum may legally carry on business and take action that will bind the corporation. Directors may not act by proxy.

The chairman of the board of directors, or, if there is no chairman, the president of the corporation, usually presides over the meeting of the directors. In the absence of the president the vice president may preside. The secretary keeps minutes of all meetings of the board of directors. The minutes should show, among other things, the time and place of the meeting, the number and names of the directors who were present, and the resolutions voted upon and adopted.

Worley v. Dunkle

62 A. (2d) 699, 2 N. J. Super. 161 (1948)

This was a suit by Mary E. Worley (plaintiff) against Mae K. Dunkle et al. (defendants). Judgment for plaintiff.

In 1906 Bayard L. Dunkle caused the incorporation in New Jersey of the National Porcelain Company to engage in the manufacture of pottery, porcelain, and tile. In 1943 the corporate name of the company was changed to the National Ceramic Company, by which it is now known. The business operations continued under the management of Joseph A. Schermerhorn. On March 5, 1947, Mr. Dunkle died. By his will he nominated his widow, the present defendant, and the Broad Street National Bank as the representatives of his estate. Plaintiff is the daughter of the decedent by a former marriage, a stockholder of the company. Mr. Dunkle, at the time of his death, owned 1551 shares of the common stock of the corporation, of a total of slightly less than 2,000 shares issued and outstanding. It was to a large extent a one-man corporation. Dunkle was a director and he had named his daughter (plaintiff) a director, but she was never informed by Dunkle of this fact during his lifetime. He also made his wife (defendant) a stockholder and director. Indeed, it is not evident that after the death of Dunkle there were, on March 9, 1947, three surviving directors of the company, until Paul O. Abbe subsequently received the requisite stock to qualify him as a director.

Although Mr. Dunkle died on March 5, 1947, on Saturday, March 8, 1947, Mrs. Dunkle invited Mr. Schermerhorn, the general manager, Miss Hunt, an office secretary, and plaintiff to assemble at her home at a stated time on the following day, Sunday, March 9th. Thus congregated, Mrs. Dunkle announced that in accordance with her interpretation of the wishes of her late husband she would temporarily clench the offices previously occupied by him of president and treasurer of the corporation, at an annual salary of $12,000. No vote was taken, but Mrs. Dunkle directed Mr. Schermerhorn to insert such an entry in the minute book. Since the meeting was held on Sunday she directed him to make the record show that the meeting was held on Monday, March 10, 1947. On March 10th Mrs. Dunkle called Miss Hunt over the telephone and told her to instruct Mr. Schermerhorn to change the amount of her salary from $12,000 to $24,000 per year. This was obediently done. The records show that she was actually paid $15,018 in 1947 and $16,224 in 1948.

Plaintiff brought this suit for judicial inquiry and intervention in the matter of the defendant's acquisition of excessive sums of money from the funds of the corporation under the guise of a salary to which, it was alleged, she was not entitled.

JAYNES, J. It seems to me perfectly manifest that Mrs. Dunkle was not lawfully elected president and treasurer of the company and that neither an annual salary of $12,000 nor one of $24,000 was sanctioned at any lawfully organized body of the directors or stockholders. Pretending to be the majority stockholder and suppositional successor of her husband's interest in the company, she sought to establish herself in the corporate organization at an attractive salary. In that, she has legally failed. The meeting held at her home may not be considered as a lawfully called and held meeting of either the board of directors or of the stockholders.

I have resolved that a fair and reasonably adequate salary for the type of services actually rendered by Mrs. Dunkle for the corporation should be computed at the rate of $625 per month. She is directed to refund the excess received by her in 1947 and 1948, to the corporation. So ordered.

LIABILITIES OF DIRECTORS

One who accepts appointment to the board of directors of a corporation owes a duty to the corporation and the stockholders to attend the meetings of the board of directors and participate in the deliberations and the actions taken by the board. It is his responsibility to acquaint himself with the articles of incorporation and the bylaws of the corporation and to keep informed concerning the business activities of the corporation. His ignorance of such matters is usually no defense.

A fiduciary relationship exists between the directors, on the one hand, and the corporation and the stockholders, on the other. For that reason a director may not engage in any activity or transaction whereby he makes a secret profit at the expense of the corporation or the stockholders. If he does so and is discovered, the corporation may require him to account to it for the ill-gotten profits.

If a director has a personal interest in a proposed contract that is to be considered by the board of directors, he should not attend the meeting at which the matter is considered. Usually his personal interest in the proposed contract will disqualify him from voting upon it. If he does attend and cast his vote as a director, particularly if his vote was necessary to effect a contract, the contract will in all probability be held to be voidable at the election of the corporation. If he does not attend the meeting, and the other members pass favorably upon the contract, his personal interest in it will not prevent the corporation from being bound, assuming, of course, that the contract was fair and beneficial to the corporation and that no fraud existed. Under such circumstances, a director may, in his individual capacity, contract with the corporation.

To escape liability, directors must act in good faith. However, in carrying out their duties they are required to exercise only reasonable or ordinary care, skill, and diligence, such as a reasonably prudent and cautious man would have used in transacting his own business affairs. They are not liable for any loss resulting to the corporation from honest mistake or error of judgment, nor for the wrongful acts of the officers and agents whom they employ if they use due diligence in their appointment or employment. A director is clearly liable for his gross negligence where such negligence results in injury to the corporation. Likewise, he is liable for his fraudulent acts, such as the misuse of corporate funds. He is also liable if he knowingly exceeds his authority or knowingly commits an ultra vires act and the corporation is damaged. Directors are liable if they knowingly and wrongfully pay a dividend to the stockholders.

The various state corporation statutes contain sections covering the liability of directors and officers.

Responsibility for bringing action against directors for their wrongful acts lies with the corporation itself. However, if it fails or refuses to bring such action, owing to the fact that the directors are in control of the corporation, then a *derivative action* may be brought by one or more stockholders on behalf of the corporation. Such a suit is brought in equity.

Simon v. Socony-Vacuum Oil Co., Inc., et al.
38 N. Y. S. (2d) 270 (1942)

This was an action by Carl N. Simon (plaintiff) against Socony-Vacuum Oil Company, Inc., et al. (defendants). Judgment for defendants dismissing complaint on the merits.

This was a derivative stockholders' suit brought by plaintiff Simon, in behalf of the stockholders of defendant corporation, against the corporation and its directors, alleging breach by the directors of their duty to defendant corporation. The alleged breach of duty was in connection with certain transactions of defendant corporation in buying "distress" gasoline from small refiners in the Mid-Western areas, in accordance with a buying program participated in by defendant company and other large oil companies. These transactions were made the basis of an indictment charging an unlawful combination and conspiracy in restraint of trade and commerce by raising and fixing the price of gasoline, in violation of the Sherman Anti-Trust Act. Upon the trial the Socony-Vacuum Oil Co., Inc. was convicted by a jury and was fined. This suit was therefore brought for the purpose of recovering the amount of that fine from the directors of the corporation because of their alleged neglect of duty.

BENVENGA, J. That the defendant corporation participated in the unlawful buying program is not disputed. Nor is it questioned that defendants, as directors, participated therein in behalf of the corporation. But it is asserted that, in so doing, defendants did not violate any duty which they owed to the corporation; that they acted honestly and reasonably and for what they believed to be the best interest of the company. The evidence supports this conclusion. It does not show that defendants acted fraudulently, negligently, corruptly, or in bad faith. Nor does it show that they knew, or had reason to believe, that the buying program violated the Sherman Act. Neither does it show that they made personal profit or gained any personal advantage at the expense of the corporation or otherwise. Accordingly, defendants are entitled to the presumption or inference that their actions were fair and honest.

The question here presented is whether, under the circumstances, the defendants should be held personally liable to the corporation for damages resulting from participation in the buying program.

It is elementary that directors owe a corporation the duty to exercise reasonable care in managing its affairs; that is, the same degree of care which a business man of ordinary prudence generally exercises in the management of his own affairs. If the directors fail to use such care they are liable to the corporation. However, if the directors act in good faith and exercise reasonable care in the performance of their duties, they are not liable for mistakes and errors of judgment, either of law or fact. *Case v. Realty Securities Co.*, 206 N. Y. 649, 99 N. E. 1105.

Applying these principles, it would seem that defendants did not fail in their duty of reasonable care. At most, they made an honest and reasonable mistake or error of judgment or of law. But it is argued that defendants are liable because they committed acts prohibited by statute; that when the defendants, as directors, participated in the buying program in behalf of the defendant company, they failed in their duty to the corporation, even though they acted in good faith and with reasonable care.

The rule for which plaintiff contends is too broadly stated. Whether directors are personally liable depends upon the nature of the prohibited act; whether the statute is plain and unambiguous, and whether it contains a limitation or restriction on the powers of the corporation or the powers or duties of the directors themselves. Moreover, the rule is the same whether the act is ultra vires or prohibited by statute. Thus, in *Groaderick v. Marcus*, 272 N. Y. S. 455, the statute prohibited loans in excess of ten per cent of the capital and surplus of the bank. The statute is plain and unambiguous. It clearly lays down the rule governing the duty of directors in respect of loans. Therefore, when the directors made or participated in the making of the prohibited loans, there was no error or mistake of judgment, or any error or mistake of law of fact. On the contrary, in making the loans, the directors must have done so "with the knowledge of the extent and limitation of the powers of the corporations for which they act, and of their own authority as the agents of these corporations." In short the directors must have known when they made the loans that they were ultra vires and illegal. Obviously, no such knowledge can be imputed to the defendants when they, in behalf of the defendant corporation, entered into the buying programs which were later held to be in violation of law. Judgment is accordingly directed for the defendants dismissing the complaint on the merits.

OFFICERS

SELECTION, REMOVAL, AND COMPENSATION OF OFFICERS

The state corporation statutes or codes usually provide that every corporation shall have as officers a president, a secretary, and a treasurer, and may have such other officers as are provided for in the bylaws. The bylaws customarily provide that the corporation shall have certain named officers; in addition to a president, a secretary, and a treasurer, these usually include one or more vice presidents, an assistant secretary, and an assistant treasurer. Usually the statute or code permits the offices of secretary and treasurer to be held by the same person. In a large corporation there may be a chairman of the board of directors and several vice presidents, each heading some important department or division of the corporation, such as production, sales, labor relations, and so on.

The officers of a corporation are generally appointed by the board of directors. The statutes generally provide that the president shall be selected from among the directors but that the other officers need not be members of the board of directors. However, the fact that one is a member of the board of directors does not preclude his being named an officer, directors very commonly do serve as the officers of the corporation. The officers are selected by the board of directors at its annual meeting, usually for a one-year term.

An officer of a corporation may be removed by the board of directors whenever, in its judgment, the best interests of the corporation will be served thereby. However, such removal is without prejudice to the contract rights, if any, of the person removed.

An officer who is not also a director has the right to receive the salary the corporation contracted to pay him, or, if no definite salary was agreed upon, he is entitled to receive the reasonable value of his services. An officer who is also a director is not entitled to compensation for performing the ordinary and usual duties of the office, unless he has, prior to the performance of such services, contracted with the corporation for the payment of compensation. However, he may recover for any extraordinary services, such as legal services rendered at the request of the corporation.

The general rule is that the board of directors has the power to fix the salaries of the officers, unless the charter or bylaws provide otherwise. However, in fixing such salaries the directors must act in good faith. And the courts quite generally hold that an officer who is also a director may not vote on a resolution fixing his own salary. As a practical matter, confusion arising out of the problem of payment of compensation to officers may be avoided by placing in the bylaws a clear statement covering the matter.

Schulte v. Ideal Pure Foods Products Co.
208 Ia. 767, 226 N. W. 174 (1929)

This was an action by A. E. Schulte (plaintiff) against the Ideal Pure Foods Products Co. (defendant). Judgment for plaintiff, and defendant appealed. Reversed.

This action was to recover $3,499.44, as a balance of compensation due upon an alleged express oral contract of employment entered into between plaintiff and defendant.

One Strasburger owned a majority of the stock of defendant corporation. He died in December, 1922. His wife succeeded to his ownership of the shares of stock. The next largest stockholder was the wife of one Bennett. Plaintiff was in the employ of the corporation at the time of Strasburger's death. Bennett became general manager of the corporation when Strasburger died. Shortly after Strasburger's death plaintiff became a stockholder of the corporation. On January 1, 1923, a stockholders' meeting was held and a board of directors was elected, consisting of plaintiff and four other persons. There was a meeting of the new board of directors after the stockholders' meeting. At this meeting a resolution was adopted which provided, in part, as follows: "Resolved that Henry Bennett be continued as manager for the ensuing year, of the Ideal Foods Products Co., and that he, as such manager, is hereby delegated general powers to manage the business and affairs of the company, to hire employees and fix the pay and salaries thereof, including his salary, and the right to discharge such employees, to purchase goods for manufacturing purposes, to make or authorize sales thereof. . . ."

It was contended by plaintiff that under this resolution Bennett orally employed him to perform services as manager of the corporation, and this action was brought to recover the balance claimed to be due under the said oral contract of employment.

It appeared that Bennett fixed his own salary and withdrew large sums from the company.

The defense was that the corporation was not bound by the alleged contract because it was a wrongful attempt by the directors to pay one of its own number a large amount of the company's earnings under the guise of a salary, and that no such power was granted to the directors of the corporation or its manager by the stockholders, or allowed or permitted under the articles or bylaws.

FAVILLE, J. The defendant invokes the general rule that the directors of a corporation have no authority to vote compensation to themselves. We have recognized this general rule. In the recent case of *Bennett v. Klipto Loose Leaf Co.*, 201 Ia. 236, 207 N. W. 228, we reviewed the authorities recognizing the general rule that the directors of a corporation cannot legally vote themselves salaries or compensation for their services, unless specifically authorized to do so. This is especially true where it is shown that the salaries voted by the directors to themselves as officers are excessive. In the instant case, however, we do not have a situation where the directors voted salaries to themselves as officers of the corporation. The directors elected Bennett as manager of the corporation, and by resolution clothed him with power to engage employees and to fix and pay the salaries therefor.

The question of law presented by the defendant's motion for a directed verdict is, in last analysis, whether or not a board of directors has legal authority to delegate to a manager of a corporation power and authority to employ agents and employees to work for said corporation and to fix the salaries of such employees, when a party so employed is also a director of the corporation.

It is a well-established rule that the directors of a corporation are charged with the general management of the business affairs of a corporation. In a very broad and general way, it is a generally recognized rule that the board of directors of a corporation may delegate to agents of their own appointment the performance of acts which they themselves, as directors, can legally perform. This is especially true where the delegated acts are ministerial in character. The duties of the board of directors are often, if not usually, fixed by the articles of incorporation and the bylaws of the corporation. Such delegation of power is generally upheld, when it does not involve the exercise of the discretionary powers of the board of directors.

Under the record of this case we conclude that the board of directors of the defendant corporation are not shown to have been circumscribed by any limitation in the articles or bylaws of the corporation in the legal right to employ a manager and to delegate to that manager the power and authority to employ agents and employees and to fix the salaries of said employees. Did the fact, then, that the manager, under said resolution of authority, employed the plaintiff, who was at the time a director in the corporation, render the contract of employment invalid? It does not appear that the plaintiff, as a director, voted for the resolution delegating to Bennett the power to employ and fix the salaries of employees, but inasmuch as he (plaintiff) offered the resolution to the board of directors, we assume that he acquiesced affirmatively in its adoption. If the resolution was adopted in good faith and without fraud, could the manager, under the broad powers given him and while acting in good faith, employ a director of the company to render services for the corporation and fix his compensation for such service? We do not think it can be said, as a matter of law, that the employment of the plaintiff, although he was a director of the corporation, was invalid. Conceding the general rule that directors cannot fix their own salaries unless authorized so to do by the charter or bylaws of the corporation or by action of the stockholders, we do not think this rule is applicable under the facts of the instant case. The board of directors adopted a resolution empowering the manager to engage employees and to fix their salaries. There was no attempt to fix the salary of the plaintiff as a director. He was employed to render services entirely distinct and separate from his duties as a director. It is for compensation for such services that this action is brought. It is a customary thing for a board of directors to elect one of their own number as president or other officer or employee of the corporation and to fix the salary of such officer or employee. Such an act is not illegal unless made so by some provision of the rules governing the corporation. The contract of employment in such a case is not ipso facto illegal.

[NOTE: The judgment of the lower court was reversed for error in not giving the jury proper instructions concerning defendant's allegation that the adoption of the resolution of the board of directors was a scheme and collusion between Bennett and plaintiff to defraud the corporation.]

AUTHORITY AND LIABILITIES OF OFFICERS

The day-to-day operations of the business of a corporation are carried on by the officers of the corporation. Their authority is derived primarily from two sources. In the first place, the bylaws create certain offices and state what their duties shall be. In the second place, the board of directors delegate, by resolution, to the various officers of the corporation the power and authority to carry on the day-to-day work of the corporation. The board may not, however, delegate to the officers of the corporation any of its policy-determining functions, e.g. the authority to declare dividends. It goes without saying that the board of directors may not delegate to an officer the authority to perform an act which the board itself has no authority to perform.

While actually many of the policies adopted by the board of directors of a corporation originate with the officers, they do not become binding upon the corporation unless they first receive the stamp of approval of the board of directors.

The officers are the legal agents of the corporation. In this connection the principles of agency law apply. Briefly, in order to bind the corporation by his act or contract, an officer must have express, implied, or apparent authority to perform the act or enter into the contract upon behalf of the corporation. If he exceeds his authority the corporation is not bound, but as a general rule he will be personally bound.

The officers, like the directors, occupy a fiduciary relationship with the corporation and the stockholders. They are, therefore, not permitted to make a secret profit in connection with business transactions handled on behalf of the corporation, or in dealing with the corporation. If they do so they may be compelled to account for such profits to the corporation, either by a suit by the corporation itself or by a stockholders' suit on behalf of the corporation.

The officers of a corporation must use ordinary care and skill in the handling of corporate business. If they fail to do so they will be liable to the corporation for any losses suffered by the corporation. However, they are not liable for any losses suffered by the corporation resulting from a mistake or error of judgment while performing their discretionary authority. They are, of course, liable for their negligent, willful, and tortious acts if such acts result in damage to the corporation.

Mosell Realty Corporation v. Schofield
193 Va. 380, 22 S. E. 153 (1889)

This was an action by Dora Schofield, trading as Schofield & Herman (plaintiff) against the Mosell Realty Corporation (defendant), to recover for services as a broker in procuring a purchaser for defendant's real estate. Judgment for plaintiff, and defendant appealed. Reversed and final judgment entered for defendant.

The Mosell Realty Corporation owned a valuable piece of property in Norfolk, on which was located a moving picture theatre and four stores. This was the only property the corporation owned or had ever owned. The capital stock was distributed equally among Sol Kaplan, L. H. Goldman, and Leon Banks, who were its only directors. Kaplan was the president, Goldman the vice president, and Banks the secretary and treasurer.

In October, 1940, A. S. Herman, a salesman employed by Dora Schofield, obtained a prospective purchaser of the property. He knew that the property was owned by the Mosell Realty Corporation and that Sol Kaplan was its president. Accordingly, he called on Kaplan at the latter's place of business and inquired whether the property was for sale, and if so, at what price. Kaplan told Herman that the property was for sale at the price of $50,000 net to the owner, and authorized him to sell at that price.

Shortly thereafter Herman visited Kaplan with his prospect, one Joseph Silverberg, who wanted to buy the property but was willing to pay only $45,000. Kaplan stood out for a price of $50,000 net to the corporation and the deal failed. In 1941 Herman interested another purchaser in the property but no offer from him was obtained. No further negotiations for the sale of the property were had until the early summer of 1943, when Herman obtained two prospects for its purchase. Because of the lapse of time since his original authority, Herman returned to Kaplan and asked whether he (Herman) was still authorized to sell the property at the same price. Kaplan's reply was: "That is still all right. I will accept such an offer." On June 28, 1943, Herman obtained a written offer from D. Galanides to buy the property at the sum of $51,000. The offer was accompanied by a deposit of $500. Herman presented the offer and check to Kaplan who examined and approved them but requested that Herman hold them, saying that he (Kaplan) was leaving for New York that afternoon. Kaplan further said that upon his return "I will accept the offer." Herman called upon Kaplan upon the latter's return from New York. In the meantime Herman had obtained a written offer from Harry Kramer, accompanied by a deposit of $500 to purchase the property at $52,500. Herman presented both the Galanides and Kramer offers to Kaplan who refused to accept either, because he said that on his trip to New York he "happened to see Goldman" and that Goldman informed him that he (Goldman) was not willing to sell the property.

The plaintiff filed this action to recover for services as a broker in procuring a purchaser for the property. The defense was that the president (Kaplan) of the corporation lacked the necessary authority to enter into the contract.

EGGLESTON, J. Although the record discloses no formal resolution of the board of directors or stockholders authorizing Kaplan, its president, to sell this property, which, as has been said, was the corporation's principal asset, or to enter into the brokerage contract to effect such a sale, the defendant in error contends that such authority is sustainable on two theories: first, Kaplan, who was president of the corporation, had the implied or inherent authority to enter into the contract sued on; and, second, the directors of the corporation clothed him with the apparent authority to enter into the contract sued on, and hence they and the corporation are estopped to deny the lack of actual authority therefor. In our opinion, neither of these contentions can be sustained.

It is well settled that the inherent or implied authority of a corporate president is limited to acts within the ordinary course of its business and does not extend to extraordinary and unusual transactions such as the sale and purchase of real estate. As is stated in 13 *Am. Jur.*, Corporations, Sec. 939, "By virtue of his office alone, no executive officer or agent of a corporation has any authority to sell or make a contract for the sale of the real estate of the corporation. Thus, the secretary has no such power, nor has the president."

If a corporation president is without implied authority, by virtue of his office, to sell a part of the real estate of the corporation, a fortiori he is without implied power to negotiate a sale of the real estate which, as here, constitutes the corporation's principal asset. Neither do we think that the verdict and judgment here can be sustained under the principal that the corporation clothed its president with apparent authority to enter into the contract sued on and for that reason is estopped to deny that it actually authorized him to do so.

It is elementary that the authority of the directors is conferred upon them as a board, and they can bind the corporation only by acting together as an official body. A majority of them, in their individual names, cannot act for the board itself and bind the corporation. Reversed and a final judgment entered for the defendant corporation.

REVIEW CASES

1. A derivative stockholders' suit was brought against the directors of the Celanese Corporation of America to hold them individually liable for breaching their fiduciary duties to the corporation by negligently and improvidently embarking upon a radio advertising program costing $1,000,-000 a year. The most serious charge was that the directors were motivated by a non-corporate purpose in undertaking the radio program. It was alleged that the program was for the benefit of Miss Jean Tennyson, one of the singers on the program, who in private life was the wife of the president (also a director) of the corporation. The evidence showed that Miss Tennyson was an outstanding soprano, that she was paid less than the other artists on the program, and that no special effort was made to promote her. Judgment for whom? (Bayer et al. v. Beran et al., 49 N. Y. S.(2d) 2)

2. Connolly, owner of 60 shares of stock in the Mercantile Trust Co., was approached by Shannon, president of the corporation, who offered $1,400 per share for 50 shares of the stock. Connolly accepted the offer. Unknown to Connolly, Shannon had been negotiating a merger of the corporation with another bank, and had good reason to know that the merger would go through and increase the value of the stock to about $2,500 per share. After the merger Connolly brought suit asking for an accounting and a decree directing Shannon to pay the full value of the stock after the merger. He contended that a relationship of trust had existed between the parties which put Shannon under a duty to tell him of the prospective merger before the stock sale. Holding? (Connolly v. Shannon, 105 N. Y. Eq. 155, 147 A. 234)

3. The Columbia City Lumber Co., Inc., owed a debt to Lowe, who assigned his claim to Doernbecher. Doernbecher sued the corporation on the obligation, and judgment was ultimately rendered in his favor; but before judgment was rendered, three of the five directors of the corporation, without giving notice to the others, held a meeting and by a unanimous vote as-

signed all the property of the corporation for the benefit of creditors. Doernbecher attacked the assignment as invalid because of failure to give notice to the directors who did not attend. Was he correct in his contention? Ruling? (Doernbecher v. Columbia City Lumber Co., 21 Ore. 573, 28 P. 899)

4. The Indurated Concrete Corporation had four directors, including Abbott and Smith. Abbott and Smith rendered special services to the corporation, and they asked payment therefor at a meeting when one member of the board was absent. Abbott and Smith cast their votes for payment of the claims, but the other director present voted against allowing the claims. The claims were paid by the corporation. The next year a different board was elected to office, and this board filed suit in the name of the corporation against Abbott and Smith for the money paid them on the claims. Judgment for whom? (Indurated Concrete Corporation v. Abbott, 74 A.(2d) (Md.) 17)

5. The directors of the Metals & Chemical Corporation met and passed a resolution which empowered the president to borrow $100,000 for the corporation and to issue corporation notes containing a stipulation that they would be paid out of the first funds received by the corporation from the sale of stock. Drake and Walsh loaned $100,000 and received corporation notes containing said stipulation. The corporation sold more than $200,000 worth of stock but used the money for purposes other than payment of the notes. Drake and Walsh sued the board of directors, asking that they be held personally liable on the obligation. Holding? (Emmert v. Drake 224 F.(2d) 299)

Foreign Corporations

49

DOMESTIC AND FOREIGN CORPORATIONS DISTINGUISHED

A corporation is a *domestic corporation* in the state, jurisdiction, or country in which it secures its articles of incorporation, and a *foreign corporation* in all other states, jurisdictions, or countries. The laws applicable to domestic and foreign corporations vary in a number of important respects, and it is essential that those who have responsibility for the management and operation of the affairs of a corporation be familiar with the differences.

We have seen that a corporation is a "person" but not a "citizen" under the federal Constitution. It is held to be a "person" under the provision of the Fourteenth Amendment which reads: " . . . nor shall any state deprive any person of life, liberty, or property without due process of law; nor deny to any person within its jurisdiction the equal protection of the laws." Thus a domestic corporation, acting within the state of its creation, is as fully protected as to its "life, liberty, and property" as are natural persons. However, the Supreme Court has held that corporations are not "citizens" within the meaning of the provision of Article IV, Section II of the federal Constitution that "the citizens of each state shall be entitled to all the privileges and immunities of citizens of the several states." Corporations are therefore not protected by that section. Natural persons are citizens and, as such, may cross state boundary lines and carry on business in any other state. But corporations are "foreign" in every state or country other than that in which they received their articles of incorporation. While the Fourteenth Amendment does provide that no state shall "deny to any person within its jurisdiction the equal

1039

protection of the laws," this provision does not protect foreign corporations, since they are not "within the jurisdiction" of any state other than the state of their creation. However, if a corporation is admitted to carry on intrastate business within a "foreign" state, then it is held to be "within the jurisdiction" of that state, and as such it is fully protected by this provision of the Fourteenth Amendment.

Bezant et ux. v. Home Owners' Loan Corporation
98 P. (2d) 852, 55 Ariz. 85 (1940)

Action by the Home Owners' Loan Corporation (plaintiff) against Sam Bezant and Lenora Bezant (defendants). Judgment for plaintiff, and defendants appealed. Affirmed.

This was an action by Home Owners' Loan Corporation, a corporation organized under the laws of the United States, to foreclose on certain property owned by Sam Bezant and Lenora Bezant, his wife.

The facts were substantially agreed upon and the assignment of error dealt almost entirely with questions of law. The most important was that since admittedly plaintiff had failed to comply with the constitution and statutes of Arizona regulating foreign corporations, the mortgage and notes upon which the suit was brought were void.

Section 5, Const. of Arizona, Art. 14, provides: "No corporation organized outside the limits of this state shall be allowed to transact business within this state on more favorable conditions than are prescribed by law for similar corporations organized under the laws of this state; and no foreign corporation shall be permitted to transact business within this state unless said foreign corporation is by the laws of the country, state, or territory under which it is formed permitted to transact a like business in such country, state, or territory."

Section 658, R. S. 1928, provides: "No foreign corporation shall transact any business in this state until it shall have complied with the requirement of the preceding section, and every act done by said corporation prior thereto shall be void."

It was the contention of defendant that plaintiff corporation was a foreign corporation, and, since it had not complied with the constitution and statutes of the state of Arizona to do intrastate business within the state, its acts were void.

The issue was whether or not plaintiff was a "foreign corporation" within the state of Arizona.

LOCKWOOD, J. The question whether a corporation organized by and under the laws of the United States is a foreign corporation, within the meaning of the state statutes regulating foreign corporations, has been before the courts in a number of cases, and it has been held practically invariably that unless the statute of the state expressly defines foreign corporations in language such as will necessarily bring a corporation organized under the laws of the United States within its terms, such corporation is not a foreign one. Our constitution and statutes do not do this.

In *Commonwealth v. Texas & Pacific R. R. Co.*, 98 Pa. 90, the court said: "The general government in its relation to that of the several states cannot be considered a foreign government in the ordinary acceptation of that term. Within the sphere of its delegated powers its authority extends over all the states of which it is composed, and to that extent it may be said to be identified with the government of each. Hence a corporation created by the United States government cannot, with propriety, be called a foreign corporation. . . ."

Par. 2226 of the statutes of Arizona defines corporations which come under its provisions in the following language: "Any company *incorporated under the law of any other state, territory, or any foreign country,* which shall carry on, do, or transact any business enterprise, or occupation, in this state, shall, before entering upon, doing, or transacting such business, enterprise, or occupation, in this state. . . ."

The corporations which are required to perform the acts set forth in the foregoing section are those which are incorporated "under the laws of any other state, territory, or foreign country." Certainly the United States of America is neither another state, territory, nor a foreign country, so far as the state of Arizona is concerned. In *Steward v. Atlantic National Bank*, 27 F. (2d) 228, it was contended that a national bank was a foreign corporation, and since it had not complied with the provisions of the statute necessary for it to obtain a permit to do business, it could not maintain an action in our courts. The court said: "However important may be the general question, to what extent a state may have authority to impose regulations on a national bank seeking to carry on or transacting business in a state other than that named in its charter, that question is not here involved, for the reason that a national bank is not a foreign corporation within the terms of the constitutional and statutory provisions of Arizona referred to; nor is it an association incorporated under the laws of any other state or territory. We find nothing in the phraseology of the statutes which indicates an intention to classify national banks created by national law as foreign corporations. . . ." We are satisfied that it was not the intent of our legislature to classify a corporation such as the plaintiff herein as a foreign one. Judgment affirmed.

FOREIGN CORPORATIONS IN INTERSTATE BUSINESS

Under the commerce clause of the federal Constitution, Congress is given exclusive jurisdiction over "commerce between the several states" and over foreign commerce. Consequently, a state may not exclude a foreign corporation from engaging in interstate commerce within its territorial limits. Nor may it levy a tax or place a burden on interstate commerce, without the consent of Congress. The U. S. Supreme Court, in its opinion in the case of the *International Textbook Co. v. Pigg*, 217 U. S. 91, made the following statement concerning this matter: "It is the established rule of this court that a state may not, in any form or under any guise, directly burden the prosecution of interstate commerce."

A corporation may therefore engage in interstate commerce without first obtaining permission from the state or states in which such commerce is being carried on. For example, a New York corporation may engage in interstate commerce in every state in the Union without securing permission from the various states to do so. It may buy raw materials or any type of merchandise in another state or sell its own materials and products in any other state so long as such transactions are kept wholly within the realm of interstate commerce. If it buys materials or merchandise in another state, the transaction is interstate so long as the contract provides that the material or merchandise is to be shipped to the corporation's domicile. Likewise, a sale is interstate if the corporation ships the merchandise from its domicile into another state. It has been held that this is true even though the contract requires installation of the property, provided that the installation is to be made by the skilled employees of the corporation (seller). However, if the installation of the property sold is made by local unskilled labor the corporation is held to be doing intrastate business within the state of the purchaser.

Since Congress has jurisdiction over the mails a corporation may solicit business in another state by mail and the authorities of that state may not object so long as the sales or contracts to sell which result from such solicitation are consummated in the state in which the corporation received its charter. For example, mail order houses keep their transactions in other states wholly within the realm of interstate commerce. The customer's order is an offer, and a contract results only when the offer is accepted by the corporation at its home office (its domicile). The same situation exists when an agent of a corporation secures orders (offers) from the customers in another state and relays the orders to the corporation for acceptance or rejection. If the corporation accepts the offer (order) a contract comes into being. But the contract (sale) was consummated at the domicile of the corporation and not within the territorial limits of another state.

Dahnke-Walker Milling Co. v. Bondurant
257 U. S. 282, 42 S. Ct. 106 (1921)

This was an action by the Dahnke-Walker Milling Co. (plaintiff) against one Bondurant (defendant). Judgment for defendant, and plaintiff appealed. Reversed.

This was an action to recover damages for the breach of a contract for the sale and delivery of a crop of wheat estimated at 14,000 bushels. Plaintiff was a Tennessee corporation engaged in operating a flour and feed mill at Union City in that state. Defendant was a resident of Hickman, Kentucky, and extensively engaged in farming in that vicinity. They were the parties to the contract. It was made at Hickman, and the wheat was to be delivered and paid for there. But the delivery was to be on board the cars of a common carrier, and plaintiff intended to ship the wheat to its mill in Tennessee. A small part of the crop was delivered, but delivery of the rest was refused, although plaintiff was prepared and expecting to receive and pay for it. A payment advanced on the crop more than covered what was delivered. At the time for delivery wheat had come to be worth several cents per bushel more than the price fixed by the contract. The action was brought in a state court in Kentucky.

The defense was that plaintiff had not complied, as was the fact, with a statute of Kentucky (Sec. 571) prescribing the conditions on which corporations of other states might do business in that state, and that the contract was therefore not enforceable. To this plaintiff replied that the only business done by it in Kentucky consisted in purchasing wheat and other grain in that state for immediate shipment to its Tennessee mill and then shipping the same there; that the contract in question was made in the course of business and with the purpose of forwarding the wheat to the mill as soon as it was delivered on board the cars; and that this transaction was interstate commerce, and as to it the statute of Kentucky, whose application was invoked by defendant, was invalid because in conflict with the commerce clause of the Constitution of the United States.

MR. JUSTICE VAN DEVANTER. The commerce clause of the Constitution, Art. 1, sec. 8, clause 3, expressly commits to Congress and impliedly withholds from the several states the power to regulate commerce among the latter. Such commerce is not confined to transportation from one state to another, but comprehends all commercial intercourse between different states and all the component parts of that intercourse. Where goods in one state are transported into another for purpose of sale the commerce does not end with the transportation, but embraces as well the sale of the goods after they reach their destination and while they are in the *original package. Brown v. Maryland*, 12 Wheat. 419. On the same principle, where goods are purchased in one state for transportation to another the commerce includes the purchase quite as much as it does the transportation. *American Express Co. v. Iowa*, 196 U. S. 133. It was said in *Wealton v. Missouri*, 91 U. S. 275: "Commerce is a term of largest import. It comprehends intercourse for the purposes of trade in any and all its forms, including the transportation, purchase, sale, and exchange of commodities." In no case has the court made any distinction between buying and selling or between buying for transportation to another state and transporting for sale in another state.

A corporation of one state may go into another, without obtaining the leave and license of the latter, for all the legitimate purposes of such commerce; and any statute of the latter state which obstructs or lays a burden on the exercise of this privilege is void under the commerce clause. *Crutcher v. Kentucky*, 141 U. S. 47, *International Textbook Co. v. Pigg*, 217 U. S. 91.

There is no controversy about the facts bearing on the character of the transaction in question. It had been the practice of the plaintiff to go into Kentucky to purchase grain to be transported to and used in its mill in Tennessee. This contract was made in continuance of that practice, the plaintiff intending to forward the grain to its mill as soon as the delivery was made. In keeping with that purpose the delivery was to be on board the cars of a public carrier. Applying to these facts the principles before stated, we think the transportation was in interstate commerce. The state court, stressing the fact that the contract was made in Kentucky and was to be performed there, put aside the further facts that the delivery was to be on board cars and that the plaintiff, in continuance of its prior practice, was purchasing the grain for shipment to its mill in Tennessee. We think the facts so neglected had a material bearing and should have been considered. They showed that what otherwise seemed to be intrastate transportation was a part of interstate commerce. *Swift & Co. v. United States*, 196 U. S. 375.

We are of the opinion that the transportation was a part of interstate commerce, in which the plaintiff lawfully could engage without any permission from the state of Kentucky, and that the statute in question, which concededly imposed burdensome conditions, was as to that transaction invalid because repugnant to the commerce clause. Judgment reversed.

Mandel Bros., Inc. v. Henry A. O'Neil, Inc., et al.
69 F. (2d) 452 (1934)

This was an action by Mandel Bros., Inc. (plaintiff) against Henry A. O'Neil, Inc., and another (defendants). Judgment for defendants and plaintiff appealed. Affirmed.

Plaintiff was a corporation organized under the laws of the state of Delaware, with its principal office at Chicago. In the spring of 1930 plaintiff and defendant entered into a contract whereby plaintiff agreed to sell and defendant agreed to buy complete furnishings for a hotel owned by defendant in Belle Fourche, South Dakota. The furnishings included lighting fixtures, kitchen equipment and utensils, shades, room and lobby draperies, general furniture and many other items. Under the terms of the agreement the articles of merchandise were to be delivered at Belle Fourche, South Dakota, and were to be installed by and at the expense of the seller, to the end that, when the contract was fully executed, the hotel should be completely furnished and equipped. The purchase price aggregated $36,046.67 and a down payment of $5,000 was provided for in the contract. The down payment was paid by defendant and the sum of $7,015.59 was paid upon delivery. The balance of

$24,031.08 was covered by 18 notes each for $1,335.06. Defendant paid six of these notes but refused to pay the remaining notes, and plaintiff brought this action.

The defense was based upon the statutes of South Dakota which provided that a foreign corporation, as a condition of being permitted to do business in that state, must file in the office of the Secretary of State a duly certified copy of its articles of incorporation; must file with the Secretary of State a statement in writing by its president . . . , constituting the Secretary of State its agent for the service of process; and must file with the Secretary of State a duly sworn statement setting forth its name, the location of its office, or principal place of business within the state of South Dakota, and the names and addresses of its officers and of its agents who represented it in that state. Section 809 of the statutes provided that "Every contract made by or on behalf of any foreign corporation, subject to the provisions of this chapter, affecting the personal liability thereof or relating to property within this state, before it shall have complied with the provisions of this chapter, shall be wholly void, on its behalf and on the behalf of its assigns, but shall be enforceable against it or them." It was stipulated that the plaintiff, Mandel Bros., Inc. had not complied with the statute.

The trial court found that the business transactions set forth in the findings of fact were essentially intrastate in character and subject to the control and regulation of the State of South Dakota, and held for defendant. Plaintiff appealed.

VAN VALKENBURGH, C.J. Whether there is substantial evidence to support the findings makes necessary a consideration of what may constitute intrastate business within the meaning of the South Dakota statutes invoked. Merely soliciting orders for goods to be shipped in the course of interstate commerce does not constitute doing business in the state to which the goods are shipped and therefore does not subject such property to police regulation.

The test is whether the business done in the state of destination involves a "question of the delivery of property shipped in interstate commerce, or of the right to complete an interstate commerce transaction," or whether it concerns "merely the doing of a local act after interstate commerce had completely terminated." *Browning v. Waycross*, 34 S. Ct. 578, 233 U. S. 16.

The distinction between what is inherently intrastate and what is inherently and necessarily connected with interstate commerce is clearly pointed out by the Supreme Court in the cases cited, to which may be added *York Manufacturing Company v. Colley*, 247 U. S. 21, and the decision of this court in *Palmer v. Aeolian Company*, 46 F. (2d) 746. The York case involved the sale of an ice-making plant, which required the supervision of an expert in assembling and erecting it as necessary to complete delivery in interstate commerce. *Palmer v. Aeolian Company* concerned the manufacture and sale of a pipe organ, the installation of which required "not only the highest mechanical skill, but a thorough understanding of the methods employed by the manufacturer in the arrangement of mechanical and electrical connections." The installation was held to be inherently connected with interstate commerce.

In *General Railway Signal Company v. Virginia*, 246 U. S. 500, the contract was to furnish completed automatic railway signal systems. . . . It was held that, in the installation, local business was involved, separate and distinct from interstate commerce, and subject to the licensing power of the state. In all cases bearing upon the subject, the distinction is carefully drawn between situations requiring local work as essential to a complete delivery in interstate commerce, because of the peculiar nature of the subject matter of the contract, and those in which the local work done is inherently and intrinsically intrastate. In our judgment, the installation of these furnishings in the hotel at Belle Fourche, S. D., falls within the latter classification. The record convincingly shows that furnishings of the nature described may be, and generally are, put in place by work of men of no exceptional skill, and do not require expert supervision by employees of the seller to complete the transaction in interstate commerce. Judgment affirmed.

FOREIGN CORPORATIONS IN INTRASTATE BUSINESS

While the federal Constitution gives Congress exclusive control over interstate commerce, it reserves to the states the right to control and regulate intrastate commerce. For that reason a state may, subject to constitutional limitations, exclude a foreign corporation from doing intrastate business within its jurisdiction. However, it is not the policy of any of our states to prohibit foreign corporations from carrying on intrastate business within their boundaries. Such a policy would be economically unsound and undesirable. Consequently, as a matter of comity between the states, foreign corporations may be licensed to do intrastate business within the various states provided they conform to the requirements of admission established by statute and do not violate local law or public policy. The states have the right to revoke the license of a foreign corporation, and such revocation may take place without first showing cause.

The requirements for admission to carry on intrastate business usually include the following: (1) The corporation, in its application, must supply certain information, such as its name, state of incorporation, date of incorporation, nature of its business, names and addresses of its directors and officers, its authorized capital stock, and so on. (2) It must file a certified copy of its articles of incorporation with the Secretary of State. (3) It must designate an office within the state. (4) It must appoint a resident agent on whom legal service may be had, or name the Secretary of State as its agent upon whom process may be served. (5) It usually must make certain periodic reports. (6) It must pay certain fees and taxes. If a corporation complies with the requirements set out in the statute it will receive a *certificate of authority* to carry on intrastate business within the state.

The state statutes provide severe penalties for foreign corporations which carry on intrastate business without complying with the statutory requirements. The noncomplying corporation is usually denied the privilege of suing on its contracts (or for any other cause) in the state courts (while the corporation itself may be sued in such courts), and the corporation and its directors and officers may be fined. In some states the corporation's contracts are made absolutely void, and criminal penalties are assessed against the corporation and its directors and officers. In some instances the directors and officers may be imprisoned. The seriousness of such penalties should impress upon those who manage and control the business activities of a corporation the importance of being fully aware of the law applicable to foreign corporations.

While it is clear that a corporation must obtain a license to carry on intrastate business in another state, the problem of determining just what constitutes "doing business," in a given case, has at times proved perplexing for the courts. It has been difficult to lay down hard and fast rules that will cover every situation that may arise. However, a few general rules are universally recognized. It is clear that if a Georgia corporation, incorporated to carry on a manufacturing business, crosses over the state line and opens up a factory in Alabama, it will be "doing business" in that state. The courts also generally agree that a single or isolated transaction within another state is not sufficient to bring a corporation under the laws of that state. The business transacted must be substantial and continuous before the courts will hold that a corporation is "doing business" in another state. Likewise, the holding of corporate meetings, the transferring of corporate stock, the securing of legal counsel, or the doing of banking business in another state does not constitute interstate commerce.

Walden et al. v. Automobile Brokers, Inc.

160 P. (2d) 400, 195 Okla. 453 (1945)

This was an action by Automobile Brokers, Inc. (plaintiff) against Dewey H. Walden et al. (defendants). Judgment for plaintiff, and defendants appealed. Affirmed.

Defendant Dr. Walden was a practicing physician, living in Blackwell, Oklahoma. On June 18, 1942, he went to Wichita, Kansas, to plaintiff's place of business for the purpose of purchasing the automobile in question. At that time he signed a purchase agreement. He did not have the certificate of purchase required to be obtained from the federal government. Being a physician, he was advised that he was qualified to obtain the certificate, and he returned to his home in Blackwell, obtained the certificate, and on July 24, 1942, returned to Wichita and there executed a second agreement to purchase the automobile in question. Subsequently the salesman (Seifert) in charge of the sale drove the automobile from Wichita to Blackwell for the purpose of delivering it. When he arrived, defendant said that his wife was not satisfied with the transaction and desired to take a ride in the automobile. Seifert left the chattel mortgage and the note representing the mortgage transaction in defendant's office and took Mrs. Walden for a demonstration ride. He returned to the office of defendant, who then and there executed the note and chattel mortgage and delivered them to Seifert. Seifert delivered them to plaintiff's place of business, after which they were transferred to a finance company. Subsequent to the transfer it was discovered that there was inserted in the mortgage the following clause: "Mortgagor granted nine months' extension on any or all payments." The finance company demanded that plaintiff repurchase the paper and this was done. This action resulted.

PER CURIAM. The closely contested question of fact in the case at bar is whether or not the agent, Paul Seifert, inserted the clause by writing it in on a typewriter in the office of the defendant Walden, or whether it was placed there without the knowledge or consent of the plaintiff or Seifert, the agent of the plaintiff. The court found in favor of plaintiff and there is ample evidence to sustain the finding of the court in this respect.

It is first argued that the judgment cannot be sustained for the reason that the court erred in holding that the plaintiff was not doing business in the state of Oklahoma within the purview and meaning of 18o S. 1941, secs. 451–54, which, in effect, denies the right of a foreign corporation the use of the courts of this state and declares a contract made in violation of the terms of the enactment void as to the corporation where there is not a compliance with the provisions. We are of the opinion and hold that the court did not err in finding that the acts and conduct of the plaintiff did not constitute doing business within the state of Oklahoma. *Fuller v. Allen*, 46 Okla. 417, 148 P. 1008; *Metal Door and Trim Co. v. Hunt*, 170 Okla. 240, 39 P. (2d) 72. As stated in *Metal Door and Trim Co. v. Hunt*, supra, this court has followed the rule that in order to be doing business within the state of Oklahoma within the purview of said above sections there must be a series of acts showing an intention to do business in violation of the statutes and a single instance or transaction does not contravene the terms of the statutory enactment. Judgment affirmed.

Hastings v. Piper Aircraft Corporation
84 N. Y. S. (2d) 580 (1948)

This was an action by Dorothy Hastings, as administratrix of the goods, chattels, and credits of George C. Hastings, deceased (plaintiff) against the Piper Aircraft Corporation (defendant). The court denied defendant's motion to vacate service of summons and complaint, and defendant appealed. Order reversed and motion granted.

Plaintiff sued to recover damages for the wrongful death of her intestate in Florida, on May 26, 1947, as a result of the alleged negligence of defendant.

On December 18, 1947, summons and complaint in this action were allegedly served on defendant by leaving a copy of same with one Stanley M. Lambert at 120 Wall Street, in the city of New York. The person thus served was an employee of Frank Sheridan Jonas, Inc. Defendant appearing specially moved to vacate the service and for dismissal of the action on the ground that it is a foreign corporation not doing business in the state of New York and that the court had no jurisdiction over its person. The Special Term denied the motion, and defendant appealed from the order entered on such denial.

Defendant was a foreign corporation organized under the laws of Pennsylvania. It was engaged in the manufacture and sale of airplanes with its office and principal place of business in the City of Lock Haven, Pennsylvania. Defendant was not licensed to do business and had no employees soliciting business or otherwise working for it in the state of New York. The name of defendant, however, was listed in the telephone directory as having an export department at 120 Wall Street, in the city of New York. The Jonas Company maintained an office at that address. Defendant's name was carried on the building directory and on the outer office of the Jonas office as occupying the same quarters. It further appeared that a business letterhead listed the same address for the export department of defendant and its cable address as "Jonasnell, N. Y." There was no proof that showed that defendant arranged for the telephone or building listings or that the letterhead in question was prepared or printed by it. The Jonas company was an export company specializing in the foreign sale of products and articles of all descriptions made by American manufacturers. It was wholly independent of defendant, with which it had a contract as exclusive distributor of defendant's produce in specialized foreign territory. The Jonas company purchased airplanes from defendant by transactions completed in Pennsylvania. They were shipped and delivered to the purchaser in New York, packed for export. They were resold by the Jonas company to its own customers in the foreign territory assigned by defendant, on resale terms fixed by the Jonas company itself. Defendant did not exercise any supervision or control over the employees of the Jonas company, nor contribute to the maintenance of the offices or the salaries of its employees. Defendant maintained a substantial and active bank account with the Manufacturers Trust Company, in the city of New York. Defendant occasionally borrowed money from the bank. Defendant also retained a New York law firm as its general counsel.

GALLAHAN, J. Apart from the fact that Lambert, the employee of Jonas company, does not appear to be a person through whom service of process might be effected upon defendant, we think the proof fails to show that the defendant was present and doing business in the state of New York so as to be amenable to the service of process in this action.

A non-resident manufacturer, such as the defendant, does not conduct business in the jurisdictional sense in the absence of continuous and systematic solicitation within the state merely because it delivers or sends goods into the state to local buyers on sales transactions completed elsewhere. *Halzer v. Dodge Brothers*, 233 N. Y. 216, 135 N. E. 268. Nor does the maintenance of a deposit in a local bank by the non-resident defendant of itself constitute the doing of business by the depositor in this state. While borrowing of money from a local bank after negotiations conducted here by the officers or representatives of a foreign corporation is a transaction that constitutes the doing of business in New York as to the lender, we think that such transaction is not a jurisdictional conduct of business on the part of the borrowers and does not warrant a holding that the defendant is present within this jurisdiction, especially where the loan is intended for use in another state. And, finally, we fail to see how consultation with its attorneys in New York can fairly be said to bring the business of the defendant corporation into the state.

There is no precise test as to the nature or extent of the business that must be done to satisfy the requirements of doing business in the state. But in this case it is clear that the facts do not show that the defendant was "doing business" within the state of New York. Order reversed.

REVIEW CASES

1. The Connecticut General Life Insurance Co. was a Connecticut corporation, admitted to do business in California. It entered into contracts with other companies doing business in California to reinsure them against losses on policies sold by them to residents of California. All the reinsurance transactions took place in Connecticut; premiums were paid there, and when losses occurred, payments were issued there. California levied a tax on the insurance company's receipts on the reinsurance premiums. Payment was refused, and California sued to recover the tax. Did the State of California have the right to levy the tax? (Connecticut General Life Insurance Co. v. Johnson, 303 U. S. 77, 58 S. Ct. 436)

2. The U. S. Rubber Co., incorporated in New Jersey, contracted with Butler Bros. Shoe Corp., wholesale merchants of Denver, Colorado, to act as its agent in selling certain goods. The rubber company was to ship the goods, at agreed prices, from its warehouse in Chicago, to Butler Bros. as consignee; and Butler Bros. was to assume all the expenses and risks of receiving, storing, and selling the goods. After some months Butler Bros. defaulted in some of its payments, and U. S. Rubber Co. brought suit in Denver. The defense was that the rubber company had not qualified to do business in Colorado as a foreign corporation, and therefore had no right to sue in the courts of that state. Holding? (Butler Bros. Shoe Corp. v. U. S. Rubber Co., 156 F. 1)

3. Lichtenberg brought an action on contract in the District of Columbia against the Bullis School, Inc. The principal question at issue was whether

the school was doing business in the District of Columbia. The school was located and incorporated in Maryland, but it purchased food, equipment, and supplies in the District of Columbia. It had a bank account in the District of Columbia, advertised there for students, and was listed in the Washington telephone directory. Was the corporation doing business in the District of Columbia? (Lichtenberg v. Bullis School, Inc., 68 A.(2d) 586)

4. All States Theatres, Inc., a Michigan corporation, opened an office as a place of business in Talladega, Alabama, without obtaining a license to do business in Alabama. It planned to open a theatre in South Carolina, and it leased a building there and spent several thousand dollars in preparing it for use as a theatre. The Royal Insurance Co., Ltd. insured the risk of the theatre company against fire. The building burned, and the theatre company brought a suit in Alabama to recover under its fire policy. The insurance company contended that the theatre company had no standing in the courts of Alabama. Holding? (Royal Insurance Co., Ltd. v. All States Theatres, Inc., 242 Ala. 417, 6 So.(2d) 494)

5. Penn Collieries Co., a corporation organized in West Virginia, sued McKeever in New York for coal sold there. The defense was that the corporation was doing business in New York without permission to do so. The evidence showed that an agent of the corporation had an office in New York, but that this was the only sale ever made by the corporation in New York State. The coal had been sold originally in New Jersey, had been rejected by the purchaser in New York, and while there in a canal boat had been resold through a broker to McKeever. The corporation kept no books in New York, had no bank account there, and kept no goods there. Holding? (Penn Collieries Co. v. McKeever, 183 N. Y. 98, 75 N. E. 935)

Dissolution of Corporations

50

A corporation is dissolved when its corporate existence is terminated. However, a corporation is not ipso facto dissolved if it becomes insolvent, if it temporarily ceases to carry on business, or if it sells all of its assets. Broadly speaking, dissolution may be either voluntary or involuntary.

VOLUNTARY DISSOLUTION

A corporation may be voluntarily dissolved and its legal existence terminated (1) by the expiration of the time limit specified in its charter or (2) by the corporation's surrendering its charter to the state.

EXPIRATION OF TIME SPECIFIED IN CHARTER

While existing corporation statutes quite generally provide that corporations may be given perpetual existence, the incorporators may provide that the corporation is to exist for a specified number of years or until the happening of a named condition precedent. In such cases the corporation is automatically dissolved upon the expiration of the stated period or the happening of the stated condition as set forth in the articles of incorporation. Where a corporation is thus dissolved automatically, it is usually provided that the articles may be renewed.

SURRENDER OF CHARTER

The corporation statutes of the various states provide that the corporate existence of a corporation may be terminated by the voluntary surrender of its charter. The procedure for bringing about dissolution in this way varies somewhat from state to state. In general the statutes provide that the board of directors must adopt a resolution to the effect that "it is desirable that the X Corporation be dissolved," and that this resolution must be approved by the stockholders, usually by the holders of at least two thirds of the voting stock. Articles of dissolution are then prepared and executed in conformity with the applicable provisions of the statute, and are filed in the office of a designated state official, usually the Secretary of State.

INVOLUNTARY DISSOLUTION

Involuntary dissolution of a corporation may result from the forfeiture of its charter either (1) at the instance of the state or (2) at the instance of its stockholders or creditors.

Forfeiture of a corporate charter will be decreed by an equity court only in an extreme case. Whether or not a court will decree forfeiture is a matter of discretion upon the part of the court. If some other equity or law remedy, e.g. fine or injunction, will suffice, the courts often resort to such remedies instead of decreeing the forfeiture of the corporation's charter.

Where forfeiture of a corporation's charter has been decreed at the instance of the state, it has usually been decreed upon one of the following grounds: (1) misuser, (2) nonuser, (3) non-payment of taxes, and (4) failure to file certain reports required by the state statutes. Misuser has reference to the illegal use of corporate powers. Nonuser means either the prolonged failure of the corporation to organize and carry on business, or its discontinuance of operations without surrender of its charter to the state.

When a state proceeds against a corporation and demands that it surrender its charter, a quo warranto proceeding is brought by the Attorney General in the name of the state.

Until modern times courts of equity very generally held that, without statutory authority, they could not dissolve a corporation upon the petition of minority stockholders or of creditors. More recently the courts have been inclined to grant such relief to minority stockholders and to creditors, even without statutory authority, if the dissolution and winding up of the corporate business seem necessary to protect them. The courts will usually grant such relief if they find fraud on the part of the majority stockholders or gross mismanagement on the part of the directors and officers. The statutes in a number of states also grant to equity courts jurisdiction over such cases and authority to decree dissolution and forfeiture in proper cases.

State v. Dilbeck et al.
297 S. W. 1049 (Tex.) (1927)

This was a suit in the nature of a quo warranto by the Attorney General, in the name of the state (plaintiff) against W. D. Dilbeck, the Bankers' Life Insurance Co., and others (defendants). Judgment for defendants, and plaintiff appealed. Reversed.

The Texas Mutual Life Insurance Co. was organized by special act of the Texas Legislature on August 3, 1870. Its corporate office was in Galveston. It ceased to function in 1880, and nothing was heard of it from that time until 1925, when the individual defendants, claiming to have acquired the rights of the original incorporators, attempted its reorganization, changed its name to the Bankers' Life Insurance Co., and began to carry on business. In July and August, 1925, various persons claiming to be heirs of the original incorporators made assignments of such interests as they had inherited from their several ancestors. Under these assignments Dilbeck and the other individual defendants, on August 28, 1925, held a stockholders' meeting in Galveston and elected Dilbeck and three other directors of the corporation. These then met and passed a resolution changing the corporate name to Bankers' Life Insurance Co., and the principal office was moved from Galveston to Dallas. Certificate showing this action was filed with the Secretary of State. Immediately following, the corporation began to write life insurance. The corporation never did obtain a permit to write life insurance in the state of Texas.

The suit against the defendants was a proceeding in the nature of a quo warranto, having two purposes: (1) to call in question the right of the individual defendants to exercise the corporate rights, privileges, and franchises under which they were assuming to act, and (2) to oust or cancel the franchise or charter under which the Bankers' Life Insurance Co. was undertaking to act, if the individual defendants prevailed as against the first part of the action.

The contentions upon which the state rested its suit follow:

(1) That the individual defendants had not met the burden resting upon them to affirmatively show their right to exercise the corporate franchise, in that there was no showing that they had acquired the rights of the original incorporators, or any of them.

(2) That by failure to perform any corporate function for a period of 45 years, the right to exercise the corporate franchise had been lost by nonuser or abandonment; that, therefore, the state had the right to reclaim and have declared forfeited the franchise granted by the Act of 1870.

(3) That the corporation had violated the terms of its charter in failing to elect directors, and thereby committed an act entitling the state to the forfeiture.

(4) That in the attempted reorganization there had been no compliance with the present regulatory laws governing life insurance.

McCLENDON, C.J. The soundness of the state's second contention seems so plain to us as hardly to require more than its statement. As early as 1815, the Supreme Court of the United States said: "A private corporation created by the Legislature may lose its franchises by a misuser or a nonuser of them; and they may be resumed by the government under a judicial judgment upon a quo warranto to ascertain and enforce the forfeiture. This is the common law of the land, and is a tacit condition annexed to the creation of every such corporation." *Terrett v. Taylor*, 9 Cranch 43, 3 L. Ed. 650. The rule is given in *Corpus Juris* (Vol. 14A, p. 1104): "Whenever a corporation voluntarily and totally abandons the exercise of its franchises, and does or suffers to be done acts which destroy the end and objects for which it was incorporated, it is either ipso facto dissolved, or it has subjected itself to liability to be dissolved in judicial proceedings instituted for that purpose, as the case may be, under the particular statute under consideration."

In view of our holding upon the state's second contention, we find it unnecessary to decide the question involved in the first.

The state's third contention, that under the charter provision governing election of directors the right of forfeiture arose, we find unnecessary to decide. . . . The courts have been loath to declare a forfeiture merely for failure to comply with some charter requirement, in the absence of an affirmative declaration prescribing forfeiture.

We sustain the state's fourth contention that the corporation, although chartered prior to the statutes regulating insurance and creating the department of insurance, was subject to such regulation, and that it was necessary, before it could engage in the insurance business, to obtain the prescribed permit. Whether this failure would constitute ground for dissolution we do not decide as it is unnecessary under our above holding that the right arose from continued nonuser. Reversed.

EFFECT OF DISSOLUTION

Dissolution has the effect of terminating the corporation as a legal entity. Under the common law rules governing the dissolution of private corporations, when a corporation is dissolved it may no longer sue or be sued, enter into contracts, hold or convey property, or exercise any of its original corporate powers. However, under present-day corporation statutes, while dissolution is accomplished when the articles of dissolution are accepted by the state, the statutes usually provide that the dissolved corporation has a limited existence after dissolution for the purpose of winding up the corporation's business. During this period the corporation may not take on new business, but it may perform all acts required to liquidate and wind up its affairs, and in the course of such winding up it may sue and be sued in the corporate name.

The creditors of the corporation have first claim upon the assets of the corporation. After the claims of the creditors have been satisfied, any remaining assets belong to the stockholders of the corporation in accordance with their contracts with the corporation. If there are both common and preferred stockholders, the preferred stockholders usually have priority over the common stockholders in the distribution of assets.

Appendix

UNIFORM PARTNERSHIP ACT

PART I

PRELIMINARY PROVISIONS

Sec. 1. Name of Act. This act may be cited as Uniform Partnership Act.

Sec. 2. Definition of Terms. In this act, "Court" includes every court and judge having jurisdiction in the case.

"Business" includes every trade, occupation, or profession.

"Person" includes individuals, partnerships, corporations, and other associations.

"Bankrupt" includes bankrupt under the Federal Bankruptcy Act or insolvent under any state insolvent act.

"Conveyance" includes every assignment, lease, mortgage, or encumbrance.

"Real property" includes land and any interest or estate in land.

Sec. 3. Interpretation of "Knowledge" and "Notice." (1) A person has "knowledge" of a fact within the meaning of this act not only when he has actual knowledge thereof, but also when he has knowledge of such other facts as in the circumstances shows bad faith.

(2) A person has "notice" of a fact within the meaning of this act when the person who claims the benefit of the notice:

(a) States the fact to such person, or

(b) Delivers through the mail, or by other means of communication, a written statement of the fact to such person or to a proper person at his place of business or residence.

Sec. 4. Rules of Construction. (1) The rule that statutes in derogation of the common law are to be strictly construed shall have no application to this act.

(2) The law of estoppel shall apply under this act.

(3) The law of agency shall apply under this act.

(4) This act shall be so interpreted and construed as to effect its general purpose to make uniform the law of those states which enact it.

(5) This act shall not be construed so as to impair the obligations of any contract existing when the act goes into effect, nor to affect any action or proceedings begun or right accrued before this act takes effect.

Sec. 5. Rules for Cases Not Provided For in This Act. In any case not provided for in this act the rules of law and equity, including the law merchant, shall govern.

PART II

NATURE OF A PARTNERSHIP

Sec. 6. Partnership Defined. (1) A partnership is an association of two or more persons to carry on as co-owners a business for profit.

(2) But any association formed under any other statute of this state, or any statute adopted by authority, other than the authority of this state, is not a partnership under this act, unless such association would have been a partnership in this state prior to the adoption of this act; but this act shall apply to limited partnerships except in so far as the statutes relating to such partnerships are inconsistent herewith.

Sec. 7. Rules for Determining the Existence of a Partnership. In determining whether a partnership exists, these rules shall apply:

(1) Except as provided by section 16 persons who are not partners as to each other are not partners as to third persons.

(2) Joint tenancy, tenancy in common, tenancy by the entireties, joint property, common property, or part ownership does not of itself establish a partnership, whether such co-owners do or do not share any profits made by the use of the property.

(3) The sharing of gross returns does not of itself establish a partnership, whether or not the persons sharing them have a joint or common right or interest in any property from which the returns are derived.

(4) The receipt by a person of a share of the profits of a business is *prima facie* evidence that he is a partner in the business, but no such inference shall be drawn if such profits were received in payment:

(a) As a debt by installments or otherwise,

(b) As wages of an employee or rent to a landlord,

(c) As an annuity to a widow or representative of a deceased partner,

(d) As interest on a loan, though the amount of payment vary with the profits of the business,

(e) As the consideration for the sale of a good-will of a business or other property by installments or otherwise.

Sec. 8. Partnership Property. (1) All property originally brought into the partnership stock or subsequently acquired by purchase or otherwise, on account of the partnership, is partnership property.

(2) Unless the contrary intention appears, property acquired with partnership funds is partnership property.

(3) Any estate in real property may be acquired in the partnership name. Title so acquired can be conveyed only in the partnership name.

(4) A conveyance to a partnership in the partnership name, though without words of inheritance, passes the entire estate of the grantor unless a contrary intent appears.

PART III

RELATIONS OF PARTNERS TO PERSONS DEALING WITH THE PARTNERSHIP

Sec. 9. Partner Agent of Partnership as to Partnership Business. (1) Every partner is an agent of the partnership for the purpose of its business, and the act of every partner, including the execution in the partnership name of any instrument, for apparently carrying on in the usual way the business of the partnership of which he is a member, binds the partnership, unless the partner so acting has in fact no authority to act for the partnership in the particular matter, and the person with whom he is dealing has knowledge of the fact that he has no such authority.

(2) An act of a partner which is not apparently for the carrying on of the business of the partnership in the usual way does not bind the partnership unless authorized by the other partners.

(3) Unless authorized by the other partners or unless they have abandoned the business, one or more but less than all the partners have no authority to:

(a) Assign the partnership property in trust for creditors or on the assignee's promise to pay the debts of the partnership,

(b) Dispose of the good-will of the business,

(c) Do any other act which would make it impossible to carry on the ordinary business of a partnership,

(d) Confess a judgment,

(e) Submit a partnership claim or liability to arbitration or reference.

(4) No act of a partner in contravention of a restriction on authority shall bind the partnership to persons having knowledge of the restriction.

Sec. 10. Conveyance of Real Property of the Partnership. (1) Where title to real property is in the partnership name, any partner may convey title to such property by a conveyance executed in the partnership name; but the partnership may recover such property unless the partner's act binds the partnership under the provisions of paragraph (1) of section 9, or unless such property has been conveyed by the grantee or a person claiming through such grantee to a holder for value without knowledge that the partner, in making the conveyance, has exceeded his authority.

(2) Where title to real property is in the name of the partnership, a conveyance executed by a partner, in his own name, passes the equitable interest of the partnership, provided the act is one within the authority of the partner under the provisions of paragraph (1) of section 9.

(3) Where title to real property is in the name of one or more but not all the partners, and the record does not disclose the right of the partnership, the partners in whose name the title stands may convey title to such property, but the partnership may recover such property if the partners' act does not bind the partnership under the provisions of paragraph (1) of section 9, unless the purchaser or his assignee, is a holder for value, without knowledge.

(4) Where the title to real property is in the name of one or more or all the partners, or in a third person in trust for the partnership, a conveyance executed by a partner in the partnership name, or in his own name, passes the equitable interest of the partnership, provided the act is one within the authority of the partner under the provisions of paragraph (1) of section 9.

(5) Where the title to real property is in the names of all the partners a conveyance executed by all the partners passes all their rights in such property.

Sec. 11. Partnership Bound by Admission of Partner. An admission or representation made by any partner concerning partnership affairs within the scope of his authority as conferred by this act is evidence against the partnership.

Sec. 12. Partnership Charged with Knowledge of or Notice to Partner. Notice to any partner of any matter relating to partnership affairs, and the knowledge of the partner acting in the particular matter, acquired while a partner or then present to his mind, and the knowledge of any other partner who reasonably could and should have communicated it to the acting partner, operate as notice to or knowledge of the partnership, except in the case of a fraud on the partnership committed by or with the consent of that partner.

Sec. 13. Partnership Bound by Partner's Wrongful Act. Where, by any wrongful act or omission of any partner acting in the ordinary course of the business of the partnership or with the authority of his co-partners, loss or injury is caused to any person, not being a partner in the partnership, or any penalty is incurred, the partnership is liable therefor to the same extent as the partner so acting or omitting to act.

Sec. 14. Partnership Bound by Partner's Breach of Trust. The partnership is bound to make good the loss:

(a) Where one partner acting within the scope of his apparent authority receives money or property of a third person and misapplies it; and

(b) Where the partnership in the course of its business receives money or property of a third person and the money or property so received is misapplied by any partner while it is in the custody of the partnership.

Sec. 15. Nature of Partner's Liability. All partners are liable

(a) Jointly and severally for everything chargeable to the partnership under sections 13 and 14.

(b) Jointly for all other debts and obligations of the partnership; but any partner may enter into a separate obligation to perform a partnership contract.

Sec. 16. Partner by Estoppel. (1) When a person, by words spoken or written or by conduct, represents himself, or consents to another representing him to any one, as a partner in an existing partnership or with one or more persons not actual partners, he is liable to any such person to whom such representation has been made, who has, on the faith of such representation, given credit to the actual or apparent partnership, and if he has made such representation or consented to its being made in a public manner he is liable to such person, whether the representation has or has not been made or communicated to such person so giving credit by or with the knowledge of the apparent partner making the representation or consenting to its being made.

(*a*) When a partnership liability results, he is liable as though he were an actual member of the partnership.

(*b*) When no partnership liability results, he is liable jointly with the other persons, if any, so consenting to the contract or representation as to incur liability, otherwise separately.

(2) When a person has been thus represented to be a partner in an existing partnership, or with one or more persons not actual partners, he is an agent of the persons consenting to such representation to bind them to the same extent and in the same manner as though he were a partner in fact, with respect to persons who rely upon the representation. Where all the members of the existing partnership consent to the representation, a partnership act or obligation results; but in all other cases it is the joint act or obligation of the person acting and the persons consenting to the representation.

Sec. 17. Liability of Incoming Partner. A person admitted as a partner into an existing partnership is liable for all the obligations of the partnership arising before his admission as though he had been a partner when such obligations were incurred, except that this liability shall be satisfied only out of partnership property.

PART IV

RELATIONS OF PARTNERS TO ONE ANOTHER

Sec. 18. Rules Determining Rights and Duties of Partners. The rights and duties of the partners in relation to the partnership shall be determined, subject to any agreement between them, by the following rules:

(*a*) Each partner shall be repaid his contributions, whether by way of capital or advances to the partnership property and share equally in the profits and surplus remaining after all liabilities, including those to partners, are satisfied; and must contribute toward the losses, whether of capital or otherwise, sustained by the partnership according to his share in the profits.

(*b*) The partnership must indemnify every partner in respect of payments made and personal liabilities reasonably incurred by him in the ordinary and proper conduct of its business, or for the preservation of its business or property.

(*c*) A partner, who in aid of the partnership makes any payment or advance beyond the amount of capital which he agreed to contribute, shall be paid interest from the date of the payment or advance.

(*d*) A partner shall receive interest on the capital contributed by him only from the date when repayment should be made.

(*e*) All partners have equal rights in the management and conduct of the partnership business.

(*f*) No partner is entitled to remuneration for acting in the partnership business, except that a surviving partner is entitled to reasonable compensation for his services in winding up the partnership affairs.

(*g*) No person can become a member of a partnership without the consent of all the partners.

(*h*) Any difference arising as to ordinary matters connected with the partnership business may be decided by a majority of the partners; but no act in contravention of any agreement between the partners may be done rightfully without the consent of all the partners.

Sec. 19. Partnership Books. The partnership books shall be kept, subject to any agreement between the partners, at the principal place of business of the partnership, and every partner shall at all times have access to and may inspect and copy any of them.

Sec. 20. Duty of Partners to Render Information. Partners shall render on demand true and full information of all things affecting the partnership to any partner or the legal representative of any deceased partner or partner under legal disability.

Sec. 21. Partner Accountable as a Fiduciary. (1) Every partner must account to the partnership for any benefit, and hold as trustee for it any profits, derived by him without the consent of the other partners from any transaction connected with the formation, conduct, or liquidation of the partnership or from any use by him of its property.

(2) This section applies also to the representatives of a deceased partner engaged in the liquidation of the affairs of the partnership as the personal representatives of the last surviving partner.

Sec. 22. Right to an Account. Any partner shall have the right to a formal account as to partnership affairs:

(a) If he is wrongfully excluded from the partnership business or possession of its property by his co-partners,

(b) If the right exists under the terms of any agreement,

(c) As provided by section 21,

(d) Whenever other circumstances render it just and reasonable.

Sec. 23. Continuation of Partnership beyond Fixed Term. (1) When a partnership for a fixed term or particular undertaking is continued after the termination of such term or particular undertaking without any express agreement, the rights and duties of the partners remain the same as they were at such termination, so far as is consistent with a partnership at will.

(2) A continuation of the business by the partners or such of them as habitually acted therein during the term, without any settlement or liquidation of the partnership affairs, is *prima facie* evidence of a continuation of the partnership.

PART V

PROPERTY RIGHTS OF A PARTNER

Sec. 24. Extent of Property Rights of a Partner. The property rights of a partner are (1) his rights in specific partnership property, (2) his interest in the partnership, and (3) his right to participate in the management.

Sec. 25. Nature of a Partner's Right in Specific Partnership Property. (1) A partner is co-owner with his partners of specific partnership property holding as a tenant in partnership.

(2) The incidents of this tenancy are such that:

(a) A partner, subject to the provisions of this act and to any agreement between the partners, has an equal right with his partners to possess specific partnership property for partnership purposes; but he has no right to possess such property for any other purpose without the consent of his partners.

(b) A partner's right in specific partnership property is not assignable except in connection with the assignment of rights of all the partners in the same property.

(c) A partner's right in specific partnership property is not subject to attachment or execution, except on a claim against the partnership. When partnership property is attached for a partnership debt the partners, or any of them, or the representatives of a deceased partner, cannot claim any right under the homestead or exemption laws.

(d) On the death of a partner his right in specific partnership property vests in the surviving partner or partners, except where the deceased was the last surviving partner, when his right in such property vests in his legal representative. Such surviving partner or partners, or the legal representative of the last surviving partner, has no right to possess the partnership property for any but a partnership purpose.

(e) A partner's right in specific partnership property is not subject to dower, curtesy, or allowances to widows, heirs, or next of kin.

Sec. 26. Nature of Partner's Interest in the Partnership. A partner's interest in the partnership is his share of the profits and surplus, and the same is personal property.

Sec. 27. Assignment of Partner's Interest. (1) A conveyance by a partner of his interest in the partnership does not of itself dissolve the partnership, nor, as against the other partners in the absence of agreement, entitle the assignee, during the continuance of the partnership, to interfere in the management or administration of the partnership business or affairs, or to require any information or account of partnership transactions, or to inspect the partnership books; but it merely entitles the assignee to receive in accordance with his contract the profits to which the assigning partner would otherwise be entitled.

(2) In case of a dissolution of the partnership, the assignee is entitled to receive his assignor's interest and may require an account from the date only of the last account agreed to by all the partners.

Sec. 28. Partner's Interest Subject to Charging Order. (1) On due application to a competent court by any judgment creditor of a partner, the court which entered the judgment, order, or decree, or any other court, may charge the interest of the debtor partner with payment of the unsatisfied amount of such judgment debt with interest thereon; and may then or later appoint a receiver of his share of the profits, and of any other money due or to fall due to him in respect of the partnership, and make all other orders, directions, accounts and inquiries which the debtor partner might have made, or which the circumstances of the case may require.

(2) The interest charged may be redeemed at any time before foreclosure, or in case of a sale being directed by the court may be purchased without thereby causing a dissolution:

(*a*) With separate property, by any one or more of the partners, or

(*b*) With partnership property, by any one or more of the partners with the consent of all the partners whose interests are not so charged or sold.

(3) Nothing in this act shall be held to deprive a partner of his right, if any, under the exemption laws, as regards his interest in the partnership.

PART VI

DISSOLUTION AND WINDING UP

Sec. 29. Dissolution Defined. The dissolution of a partnership is the change in the relation of the partners caused by any partner ceasing to be associated in the carrying on as distinguished from the winding up of the business.

Sec. 30. Partnership Not Terminated by Dissolution. On dissolution the partnership is not terminated, but continues until the winding up of partnership affairs is completed.

Sec. 31. Causes of Dissolution. Dissolution is caused: (1) Without violation of the agreement between the partners,

(*a*) By the termination of the definite term or particular undertaking specified in the agreement,

(*b*) By the express will of any partner when no definite term or particular undertaking is specified,

(*c*) By the express will of all the partners who have not assigned their interests or suffered them to be charged for their separate debts, either before or after the termination of any specified term or particular undertaking,

(*d*) By the expulsion of any partner from the business *bona fide* in accordance with such a power conferred by the agreement between the partners;

(2) In contravention of the agreement between the partners, where the circumstances do not permit a dissolution under any other provision of this section, by the express will of any partner at any time;

(3) By any event which makes it unlawful for the business of the partnership to be carried on or for the members to carry it on in partnership;

(4) By the death of any partner;

(5) By the bankruptcy of any partner or the partnership;

(6) By decree of court under section 32.

Sec. 32. Dissolution by Decree of Court. (1) On application by or for a partner the court shall decree a dissolution whenever:

(*a*) A partner has been declared a lunatic in any judicial proceeding or is shown to be of unsound mind, (*b*) A partner becomes in any other way incapable of performing his part of the partnership contract,

(*c*) A partner has been guilty of such conduct as tends to affect prejudicially the carrying on of the business,

(*d*) A partner wilfully or persistently commits a breach of the partnership agreement, or otherwise so conducts himself in matters relating to the partnership business that it is not reasonably practicable to carry on the business in partnership with him,

(*e*) The business of the partnership can only be carried on at a loss,

(*f*) Other circumstances render a dissolution equitable.

(2) On the application of the purchaser of a partner's interest under sections 27 and 28:

(*a*) After the termination of the specified term or particular undertaking,

(*b*) At any time if the partnership was a partnership at will when the interest was assigned or when the charging order was issued.

Sec. 33. General Effect of Dissolution on Authority of Partner. Except so far as may be necessary to wind up partnership affairs or to complete transactions begun but not then finished, dissolution terminates all authority of any partner to act for the partnership,

(1) With respect to the partners,

(*a*) When the dissolution is not by the act, bankruptcy or death of a partner; or

(*b*) When the dissolution is by such act, bankruptcy or death of a partner, in cases where section 34 so requires.

(2) With respect to persons not partners, as declared in section 35.

Sec. 34. Right of Partner to Contribution from Co-partners after Dissolution. Where the dissolution is caused by the act, death or bankruptcy of a partner, each partner is liable to his co-partners for his share of any liability created by any partner acting for the partnership as if the partnership had not been dissolved unless

(*a*) The dissolution being by act of any partner, the partner acting for the partnership had knowledge of the dissolution, or

(*b*) The dissolution being by the death or bankruptcy of a partner, the partner acting for the partnership had knowledge or notice of the death or bankruptcy.

Sec. 35. Power of Partner to Bind Partnership to Third Persons after Dissolution. (1) After dissolution a partner can bind the partnership except as provided in paragraph (3),

(*a*) By any act appropriate for winding up partnership affairs or completing transactions unfinished at dissolution;

(*b*) By any transaction which would bind the partnership if dissolution had not taken·place, provided the other party to the transaction

(i) Had extended credit to the partnership prior to dissolution and had no knowledge or notice of the dissolution; or

(ii) Though he had not so extended credit, had nevertheless known of the partnership prior to dissolution, and, having no knowledge or notice of dissolution, the fact of dissolution had not been advertised in a newspaper of general circulation in the place (or in each place if more than one) at which the partnership business was regularly carried on.

(2) The liability of a partner under paragraph (1*b*) shall be satisfied out of partnership assets alone when such partner had been prior to dissolution

(*a*) Unknown as a partner to the person with whom the contract is made; and

(*b*) So far unknown and inactive in partnership affairs that the business reputation of the partnership could not be said to have been in any degree due to his connection with it.

(3) The partnership is in no case bound by any act of a partner after dissolution

(*a*) Where the partnership is dissolved because it is unlawful to carry on the business, unless the act is appropriate for winding up partnership affairs; or

(*b*) Where the partner has become bankrupt; or

(*c*) Where the partner has no authority to wind up partnership affairs; except by a transaction with one who

(I) Had extended credit to the partnership prior to dissolution and had no knowledge or notice of his want of authority; or

(II) Had not extended credit to the partnership prior to dissolution, and, having no knowledge or notice of his want of authority, the fact of his want of authority has not been advertised in the manner provided for advertising the fact of dissolution in paragraph (1*b*II).

(4) Nothing in this section shall affect the liability under section 16 of any person who after dissolution represents himself or consents to another representing him as a partner in a partnership engaged in carrying on business.

Sec. 36. Effect of Dissolution on Partner's Existing Liability. (1) The dissolution of the partnership does not of itself discharge the existing liability of any partner.

(2) A partner is discharged from any existing liability upon dissolution of the partnership by an agreement to that effect between himself, the partnership creditor and the person or partnership continuing the business; and such agreement may be inferred from the course of dealing between the creditor having knowledge of the dissolution and the person or partnership continuing the business.

(3) Where a person agrees to assume the existing obligations of a dissolved partnership, the partners whose obligations have been assumed shall be discharged from any liability to any creditor of the partnership who, knowing of the agreement, consents to a material alteration in the nature or time of payment of such obligations.

(4) The individual property of a deceased partner shall be liable for all obligations of the partnership incurred while he was a partner but subject to the prior payment of his separate debts.

Sec. 37. Right to Wind Up. Unless otherwise agreed the partners who have not wrongfully dissolved the partnership, or the legal representative of the last surviving partner, not bankrupt, has the right to wind up the partnership affairs; provided, however, that any partner, his legal representative, or his assignee, upon cause shown, may obtain winding up by the court.

Sec. 38. Rights of Partners to Application of Partnership Property. (1) When dissolution is caused in any way, except in contravention of the partnership agreement, each partner, as against his co-partners and all persons claiming through them in respect of their interests in the partnership, unless otherwise agreed, may have the partnership property applied to discharge its liabilities, and the surplus applied to pay in cash the net amount owing to the respective partners. But if dissolution is caused by expulsion of a partner, *bona fide* under the partnership agreement, and if the expelled partner is discharged from all partnership liabilities, either by payment or agreement under section 36 (2), he shall receive in cash only the net amount due him from the partnership.

(2) When dissolution is caused in contravention of the partnership agreement the rights of the partners shall be as follows:

(*a*) Each partner who has not caused dissolution wrongfully shall have,

(I) All the rights specified in paragraph (1) of this section, and

(II) The right, as against each partner who has caused the dissolution wrongfully, to damages for breach of the agreement.

(*b*) The partners who have not caused the dissolution wrongfully, if they all desire to continue the business in the same name, either by themselves or jointly with others, may do so, during the agreed term for the partnership and for that purpose may possess the partnership property, provided they secure the payment by bond approved by the court, or pay to any partner who has caused the dissolution wrongfully, the value of his interest in the partnership at the dissolution, less any damage recoverable under clause (2*a*II) of this section, and in like manner indemnify him against all present or future partnership liabilities.

(*c*) A partner who has caused the dissolution wrongfully shall have:

(I) If the business is not continued under the provisions of paragraph (2*b*) all the rights of a partner under paragraph (1), subject to clause (2*a*II), of this section,

(II) If the business is continued under paragraph (2*b*) of this section the right as against his co-partners and all claiming through them in respect of their interests in the partnership, to have the value of his interest in the partnership, less any damages caused to his co-partners by the dissolution, ascertained and paid to him in cash, or the payment secured by bond approved by the court, and to be released from all existing liabilities of the partnership; but in ascertaining the value of the partner's interest the value of the good-will of the business shall not be considered.

Sec. 39. Rights Where Partnership Is Dissolved for Fraud or Misrepresentation. Where a partnership contract is rescinded on the ground of the fraud or misrepresentation of one of the parties thereto, the party entitled to rescind is, without prejudice to any other right, entitled,

(*a*) To a lien on, or right of retention of, the surplus of the partnership property after satisfying the partnership liabilities to third persons for any sum of money paid by him for the purchase of an interest in the partnership and for any capital or advances contributed by him; and

(*b*) To stand, after all liabilities to third persons have been satisfied, in the place of the creditors of the partnership for any payments made by him in respect of the partnership liabilities; and

(*c*) To be indemnified by the person guilty of the fraud or making the representation against all debts and liabilities of the partnership.

Sec. 40. Rules for Distribution. In settling accounts between the partners after dissolution, the following rules shall be observed, subject to any agreement to the contrary:

(*a*) The assets of the partnership are:

(ı) The partnership property,

(ıı) The contributions of the partners necessary for the payment of all the liabilities specified in clause (*b*) of this paragraph.

(*b*) The liabilities of the partnership shall rank in order of payment, as follows:

(ı) Those owing to creditors other than partners,

(ıı) Those owing to partners other than for capital and profits,

(ııı) Those owing to partners in respect of capital,

(ıv) Those owing to partners in respect of profits.

(*c*) The assets shall be applied in the order of their declaration in clause (*a*) of this paragraph to the satisfaction of the liabilities.

(*d*) The partners shall contribute, as provided by section 18 (*a*) the amount necessary to satisfy the liabilities; but if any, but not all, of the partners are insolvent, or, not being subject to process, refuse to contribute, the other partners shall contribute their share of the liabilities, and, in the relative proportions in which they share the profits, the additional amount necessary to pay the liabilities.

(*e*) An assignee for the benefit of creditors or any person appointed by the court shall have the right to enforce the contributions specified in clause (*d*) of this paragraph.

(*f*) Any partner or his legal representative shall have the right to enforce the contributions specified in clause (*d*) of this paragraph, to the extent of the amount which he has paid in excess of his share of the liability.

(*g*) The individual property of a deceased partner shall be liable for the contributions specified in clause (*d*) of this paragraph.

(*h*) When partnership property and the individual properties of the partners are in possession of a court for distribution, partnership creditors shall have priority on partnership property and separate creditors on individual property, saving the rights of lien or secured creditors as heretofore.

(*i*) Where a partner has become bankrupt or his estate is insolvent the claims against his separate property shall rank in the following order:

(ı) Those owing to separate creditors,

(ıı) Those owing to partnership creditors,

(ııı) Those owing to partners by way of contribution.

Sec. 41. Liability of Persons Continuing the Business in Certain Cases. (1) When any new partner is admitted into an existing partnership, or when any partner retires and assigns (or the representative of the deceased partner assigns) his rights in partnership property to two or more of the partners, or to one or more of the partners and one or more third persons, if the business is continued without liquidation of the partnership affairs, creditors of the first or dissolved partnership are also creditors of the partnership so continuing the business.

(2) When all but one partner retire and assign (or the representative of a deceased partner assigns) their rights in partnership property to the remaining partner, who continues the business without liquidation of partnership affairs, either alone or with others, creditors of the dissolved partnership are also creditors of the person or partnership so continuing the business.

(3) When any partner retires or dies and the business of the dissolved partnership is continued as set forth in paragraphs (1) and (2) of this section, with the consent of the retired partners or the representative of the deceased partner, but without any assignment of his right in partnership property, rights of creditors of the dissolved partnership and of the creditors of the person or partnership continuing the business shall be as if such assignment had been made.

(4) When all the partners or their representatives assign their rights in partnership property to one or more third persons who promise to pay the debts and who continue the business of the dissolved partnership, creditors of the dissolved partnership are also creditors of the person or partnership continuing the business.

(5) When any partner wrongfully causes a dissolution and the remaining partners continue the business under the provisions of section 38 (2b), either alone or with others, and without liquidation of the partnership affairs, creditors of the dissolved partnership are also creditors of the person or partnership continuing the business.

(6) When a partner is expelled and the remaining partners continue the business either alone or with others, without liquidation of the partnership affairs, creditors of the dissolved partnership are also creditors of the person or partnership continuing the business.

(7) The liability of a third person becoming a partner in the partnership continuing the business, under this section, to the creditors of the dissolved partnership shall be satisfied out of partnership property only.

(8) When the business of a partnership after dissolution is continued under any conditions set forth in this section the creditors of the dissolved partnership, as against the separate creditors of the retiring or deceased partner or the representative of the deceased partner, have a prior right to any claim of the retired partner or the representative of the deceased partner against the person or partnership continuing the business, on account of the retired or deceased partner's interest in the dissolved partnership or on account of any consideration promised for such interest or for his right in partnership property.

(9) Nothing in this section shall be held to modify any right of creditors to set aside any assignment on the ground of fraud.

(10) The use by the person or partnership continuing the business of the partnership name, or the name of a deceased partner as part thereof, shall not of itself make the individual property of the deceased partner liable for any debts contracted by such person or partnership.

Sec. 42. Rights of Retiring or Estate of Deceased Partner When the Business Is Continued. When any partner retires or dies, and the business is continued under any of the conditions set forth in section 41 (1, 2, 3, 5, 6), or section 38 (2b), without any settlement of accounts as between him or his estate and the person or partnership continuing the business, unless otherwise agreed, he or his legal representative as against such persons or partnership may have the value of his interest at the date of dissolution ascertained, and shall receive as an ordinary creditor an amount equal to the value of his interest in the dissolved partnership with interest, or, at his option or at the option of his legal representative, in lieu of interest, the profits attributable to the use of his right in the property of the dissolved partnership; provided that the creditors of the dissolved partnership as against the separate creditors, or the representative of the retired or deceased partner, shall have priority on any claim arising under this section, as provided by section 41 (8) of this act.

Sec. 43. Accrual of Actions. The right to an account of his interest shall accrue to any partner, or his legal representative, as against the winding up partners or the surviving partners or the person or partnership continuing the business, at the date of dissolution, in the absence of any agreement to the contrary.

PART VII

MISCELLANEOUS PROVISIONS

Sec. 44. When Act Takes Effect. This act shall take effect on the .... day of .... one thousand nine hundred and ....

Sec. 45. Legislation Repealed. All acts or parts of acts inconsistent with this act are hereby repealed.

UNIFORM COMMERCIAL CODE

TITLE

AN ACT

To be known as the Uniform Commercial Code, Relating to Certain Commercial Transactions in or regarding Personal Property and Contracts and other Documents concerning them, including Sales, Commercial Paper, Bank Deposits and Collections, Letters of Credit, Bulk Transfers, Warehouse Receipts, Bills of Lading, other Documents of Title, Investment Securities, and Secured Transactions, including certain Sales of Accounts, Chattel Paper, and Contract Rights; Providing for Public Notice to Third Parties in Certain Circumstances; Regulating Procedure, Evidence and Damages in Certain Court Actions Involving such Transactions, Contracts or Documents; to Make Uniform the Law with Respect Thereto; and Repealing Inconsistent Legislation.

1962 OFFICIAL TEXT

CONTENTS

ARTICLE 1

GENERAL PROVISIONS

PART I

SHORT TITLE, CONSTRUCTION, APPLICATION AND SUBJECT MATTER OF THE ACT

ARTICLE 3

COMMERCIAL PAPER

PART I

SHORT TITLE, FORM AND INTERPRETATION

PART II

TRANSFER AND NEGOTIATION

PART III

RIGHTS OF A HOLDER

PART IV

LIABILITY OF PARTIES

PART V

PRESENTMENT, NOTICE OF DISHONOR AND PROTEST

PART VI

DISCHARGE

PART VII

ADVICE OF INTERNATIONAL SIGHT DRAFT

ARTICLE 7

WAREHOUSE RECEIPTS, BILLS OF LADING AND OTHER DOCUMENTS OF TITLE

PART I

GENERAL

PART II

WAREHOUSE RECEIPTS: SPECIAL PROVISIONS

PART III

BILLS OF LADING: SPECIAL PROVISIONS

PART II

VALIDITY OF SECURITY AGREEMENT AND RIGHTS
OF PARTIES THERETO

PART III

RIGHTS OF THIRD PARTIES; PERFECTED AND UNPERFECTED
SECURITY INTERESTS; RULES OF PRIORITY

ARTICLE I

GENERAL PROVISIONS

PART I

SHORT TITLE, CONSTRUCTION, APPLICATION AND SUBJECT MATTER OF THE ACT

Sec. 1—101. Short Title. This Act shall be known and may be cited as Uniform Commercial Code.

Sec. 1—102. Purposes; Rules of Construction; Variation by Agreement. (1) This Act shall be liberally construed and applied to promote its underlying purposes and policies.

(2) Underlying purposes and policies of this Act are

(a) to simplify, clarify and modernize the law governing commercial transactions;

(b) to permit the continued expansion of commercial practices through custom, usage and agreement of the parties;

(c) to make uniform the law among the various jurisdictions.

(3) The effect of provisions of this Act may be varied by agreement, except as otherwise provided in this Act and except that the obligations of good faith, diligence, reasonableness and care prescribed by this Act may not be disclaimed by agreement but the parties may by agreement determine the standards by which the performance of such obligations is to be measured if such standards are not manifestly unreasonable.

(4) The presence in certain provisions of this Act of the words "unless otherwise agreed" or words of similar import does not imply that the effect of other provisions may not be varied by agreement under subsection (3).

(5) In this Act unless the context otherwise requires

(a) words in the singular number include the plural, and in the plural include the singular;

(b) words of the masculine gender include the feminine and the neuter, and when the sense so indicates words of the neuter gender may refer to any gender.

Sec. 1—103. Supplementary General Principles of Law Applicable. Unless displaced by the particular provisions of this Act, the principles of law and equity, including the law merchant and the law relative to capacity to contract, principal and agent, estoppel, fraud, misrepresentation, duress, coercion, mistake, bankruptcy, or other validating or invalidating cause shall supplement its provisions.

Sec. 1—104. Construction Against Implicit Repeal. This Act being a general act intended as a unified coverage of its subject matter, no part of it shall be deemed to be impliedly repealed by subsequent legislation if such construction can reasonably be avoided.

Sec. 1—105. Territorial Application of the Act; Parties' Power to Choose Applicable Law. (1) Except as provided hereafter in this section, when a transaction bears a reasonable relation to this state and also to another state or nation the parties may agree that the law either of this state or of such other state or nation shall govern their rights and duties. Failing such agreement this Act applies to transactions bearing an appropriate relation to this state.

(2) Where one of the following provisions of this Act specifies the applicable law, that provision governs and a contrary agreement is effective only to the extent permitted by the law (including the conflict of laws rules) so specified:

Rights of creditors against sold goods. Section 2—402.

Applicability of the Article on Bank Deposits and Collections. Section 4—102.

Bulk transfers subject to the Article on Bulk Transfers. Section 6—102.

Applicability of the Article on Investment Securities. Section 8—106.

Policy and scope of the Article on Secured Transactions. Sections 9—102 and 9—103.

Sec. 1—106. Remedies to Be Liberally Administered. (1) The remedies provided by this Act shall be liberally administered to the end that the aggrieved party may be put in as good a position as if the other party had fully performed but neither consequential or special nor penal damages may be had except as specifically provided in this Act or by other rule of law.

(2) Any right or obligation declared by this Act is enforceable by action unless the provision declaring it specifies a different and limited effect.

Sec. 1—107. Waiver or Renunciation of Claim or Right After Breach. Any claim or right arising out of an alleged breach can be discharged in whole or in part without consideration by a written waiver or renunciation signed and delivered by the aggrieved party.

Sec. 1—108. Severability. If any provision or clause of this Act or application thereof to any person or circumstances is held invalid, such invalidity shall not affect other provisions or applications of the Act which can be given effect without the invalid provision or application, and to this end the provisions of this Act are declared to be severable.

Sec. 1—109. Section Captions. Section captions are parts of this Act.

PART II

GENERAL DEFINITIONS AND PRINCIPLES OF INTERPRETATION

Sec. 1—201. General Definitions. Subject to additional definitions contained in the subsequent Articles of this Act which are applicable to specific Articles or Parts thereof, and unless the context otherwise requires, in this Act:

(1) "Action" in the sense of a judicial proceeding includes recoupment, counterclaim, set-off, suit in equity and any other proceedings in which rights are determined.

(2) "Aggrieved party" means a party entitled to resort to a remedy.

(3) "Agreement" means the bargain of the parties in fact as found in their language or by implication from other circumstances including course of dealing or usage of trade or course of performance as provided in this Act (Sections 1—205 and 2—208). Whether an agreement has legal consequences is determined by the provisions of this Act, if applicable; otherwise by the law of contracts (Section 1—103). (Compare "Contract".)

(4) "Bank" means any person engaged in the business of banking.

(5) "Bearer" means the person in possession of an instrument, document of title, or security payable to bearer or indorsed in blank.

(6) "Bill of lading" means a document evidencing the receipt of goods for shipment issued by a person engaged in the business of transporting or forwarding goods, and includes an airbill. "Airbill" means a document serving for air transportation as a bill of lading does for marine or rail transportation, and includes an air consignment note or air waybill.

(7) "Branch" includes a separately incorporated foreign branch of a bank.

(8) "Burden of establishing" a fact means the burden of persuading the triers of fact that the existence of the fact is more probable than its non-existence.

(9) "Buyer in ordinary course of business" means a person who in good faith and without knowledge that the sale to him is in violation of the ownership rights or security interest of a third party in the goods buys in ordinary course from a person in the business of selling goods of that kind but does not include a pawnbroker. "Buying" may be for cash or by exchange of other property or on secured or unsecured credit and includes receiving goods or documents of title under a pre-existing contract for sale but does not include a transfer in bulk or as security for or in total or partial satisfaction of a money debt.

(10) "Conspicuous": A term or clause is conspicuous when it is so written that a reasonable person against whom it is to operate ought to have noticed it. A printed heading in capitals (as: NON-NEGOTIABLE BILL OF LADING) is conspicuous. Language in the body of a form is "conspicuous" if it is in larger or other contrasting type or color. But in a telegram any stated term is "conspicuous." Whether a term or clause is "conspicuous" or not is for decision by the court.

(11) "Contract" means the total legal obligation which results from the parties' agreement as affected by this Act and any other applicable rules of law. (Compare "Agreement.")

(12) "Creditor" includes a general creditor, a secured creditor, a lien creditor and any representative of creditors, including an assignee for the benefit of creditors, a trustee in bankruptcy, a receiver in equity and an executor or administrator of an insolvent debtor's or assignor's estate.

(13) "Defendant" includes a person in the position of defendant in a cross-action or counterclaim.

(14) "Delivery" with respect to instruments, documents of title, chattel paper or securities means voluntary transfer of possession.

(15) "Document of title" includes bill of lading, dock warrant, dock receipt, warehouse receipt or order for the delivery of goods, and also any other document which in the regular course of business or financing is treated as adequately evidencing that the person in possession of it is entitled to receive, hold and dispose of the document and the goods it covers. To be a document of title a document must purport to be issued by or addressed to a bailee and purport to cover goods in the bailee's possession which are either identified or are fungible portions of an identified mass.

(16) "Fault" means wrongful act, omission or breach.

(17) "Fungible" with respect to goods or securities means goods or securities of which any unit is, by nature or usage of trade, the equivalent of any other like unit. Goods which are not fungible shall be deemed fungible for the purposes of this Act to the extent that under a particular agreement or document unlike units are treated as equivalents.

(18) "Genuine" means free of forgery or counterfeiting.

(19) "Good faith" means honesty in fact in the conduct or transaction concerned.

(20) "Holder" means a person who is in possession of a document of title or an instrument or an investment security drawn, issued or indorsed to him or to his order or to bearer or in blank.

(21) To "honor" is to pay or to accept and pay, or where a credit so engages to purchase or discount a draft complying with the terms of the credit.

(22) "Insolvency proceedings" includes any assignment for the benefit of creditors or other proceedings intended to liquidate or rehabilitate the estate of the person involved.

(23) A person is "insolvent" who either has ceased to pay his debts in the ordinary course of business or cannot pay his debts as they become due or is insolvent within the meaning of the federal bankruptcy law.

(24) "Money" means a medium of exchange authorized or adopted by a domestic or foreign government as a part of its currency.

(25) A person has "notice" of a fact when

(a) he has actual knowledge of it; or

(b) he has received a notice or notification of it; or

(c) from all the facts and circumstances known to him at the time in question he has reason to know that it exists.

A person "knows" or has "knowledge" of a fact when he has actual knowledge of it. "Discover" or "learn" or a word or phrase of similar import refers to knowledge rather than to reason to know. The time and circumstances under which a notice or notification may cease to be effective are not determined by this Act.

(26) A person "notifies" or "gives" a notice or notification to another by taking such steps as may be reasonably required to inform the other in ordinary course whether or not such other actually comes to know of it. A person "receives" a notice or notification when

(a) it comes to his attention; or

(b) it is duly delivered at the place of business through which the contract was made or at any other place held out by him as the place for receipt of such communications.

(27) Notice, knowledge or a notice or notification received by an organization is effective for a particular transaction from the time when it is brought to the attention of the individual conducting that transaction, and in any event from the time when it would have been brought to his attention if the organization had exercised due diligence. An organization exercises due diligence if it maintains reasonable routines for communicating significant information to the person conducting the transaction and there is reasonable compliance with the routines. Due diligence does not require an individual acting for the organization to communicate information unless such

communication is part of his regular duties or unless he has reason to know of the transaction and that the transaction would be materially affected by the information.

(28) "Organization" includes a corporation, government or governmental subdivision or agency, business trust, estate, trust, partnership or association, two or more persons having a joint or common interest, or any other legal or commercial entity.

(29) "Party," as distinct from "third party," means a person who has engaged in a transaction or made an agreement within this Act.

(30) "Person" includes an individual or an organization (See Section 1—102).

(31) "Presumption" or "presumed" means that the trier of fact must find the existence of the fact presumed unless and until evidence is introduced which would support a finding of its nonexistence.

(32) "Purchase" includes taking by sale, discount, negotiation, mortgage, pledge, lien, issue or re-issue, gift or any other voluntary transaction creating an interest in property.

(33) "Purchaser" means a person who takes by purchase.

(34) "Remedy" means any remedial right to which an aggrieved party is entitled with or without resort to a tribunal.

(35) "Representative" includes an agent, an officer of a corporation or association, and a trustee, executor or administrator of an estate, or any other person empowered to act for another.

(36) "Rights" includes remedies.

(37) "Security interest" means an interest in personal property or fixtures which secures payment or performance of an obligation. The retention or reservation of title by a seller of goods notwithstanding shipment or delivery to the buyer (Section 2—401) is limited in effect to a reservation of a "security interest." The term also includes any interest of a buyer of accounts, chattel paper, or contract rights which is subject to Article 9. The special property interest of a buyer of goods on identification of such goods to a contract for sale under Section 2—401 is not a "security interest," but a buyer may also acquire a "security interest" by complying with Article 9. Unless a lease or consignment is intended as security, reservation of title thereunder is not a "security interest" but a consignment is in any event subject to the provisions on consignment sales (Section 2—326). Whether a lease is intended as security is to be determined by the facts of each case; however, (a) the inclusion of an option to purchase does not of itself make the lease one intended for security, and (b) an agreement that upon compliance with the terms of the lease the lessee shall become or has the option to become the owner of the property for no additional consideration or for a nominal consideration does make the lease one intended for security.

(38) "Send" in connection with any writing or notice means to deposit in the mail or deliver for transmission by any other usual means of communication with postage or cost of transmission provided for and properly addressed and in the case of an instrument to an address specified thereon or otherwise agreed, or if there be none to any address reasonable under the circumstances. The receipt of any writing or notice within the time at which it would have arrived if properly sent has the effect of a proper sending.

(39) "Signed" includes any symbol executed or adopted by a party with present intention to authenticate a writing.

(40) "Surety" includes guarantor.

(41) "Telegram" includes a message transmitted by radio, teletype, cable, any mechanical method of transmission, or the like.

(42) "Term" means that portion of an agreement which relates to a particular matter.

(43) "Unauthorized" signature or indorsement means one made without actual, implied or apparent authority and includes a forgery.

(44) "Value." Except as otherwise provided with respect to negotiable instruments

and bank collections (Sections 3—303, 4—208 and 4—209) a person gives "value" for rights if he acquires them

(*a*) in return for a binding commitment to extend credit or for the extension of immediately available credit whether or not drawn upon and whether or not a charge-back is provided for in the event of difficulties in collection; or

(*b*) as security for or in total or partial satisfaction of a pre-existing claim; or

(*c*) by accepting delivery pursuant to a pre-existing contract for purchase; or

(*d*) generally, in return for any consideration sufficient to support a simple contract.

(45) "Warehouse receipt" means a receipt issued by a person engaged in the business of storing goods for hire.

(46) "Written" or "writing" includes printing, typewriting or any other intentional reduction to tangible form.

Sec. 1—202. Prima Facie Evidence by Third Party Documents. A document in due form purporting to be a bill of lading, policy or certificate of insurance, official weigher's or inspector's certificate, consular invoice, or any other document authorized or required by the contract to be issued by a third party shall be prima facie evidence of its own authenticity and genuineness and of the facts stated in the document by the third party.

Sec. 1—203. Obligation of Good Faith. Every contract or duty within this Act imposes an obligation of good faith in its performance or enforcement.

Sec. 1—204. Time; Reasonable Time; "Seasonably." (1) Whenever this Act requires any action to be taken within a reasonable time, any time which is not manifestly unreasonable may be fixed by agreement.

(2) What is a reasonable time for taking any action depends on the nature, purpose and circumstances of such action.

(3) An action is taken "seasonably" when it is taken at or within the time agreed or if no time is agreed at or within a reasonable time.

Sec. 1—205. Course of Dealing and Usage of Trade. (1) A course of dealing is a sequence of previous conduct between the parties to a particular transaction which is fairly to be regarded as establishing a common basis of understanding for interpreting their expressions and other conduct.

(2) A usage of trade is any practice or method of dealing having such regularity of observance in a place, vocation or trade as to justify an expectation that it will be observed with respect to the transaction in question. The existence and scope of such a usage are to be proved as facts. If it is established that such a usage is embodied in a written trade code or similar writing the interpretation of the writing is for the court.

(3) A course of dealing between parties and any usage of trade in the vocation or trade in which they are engaged or of which they are or should be aware give particular meaning to and supplement or qualify terms of an agreement.

(4) The express terms of an agreement and an applicable course of dealing or usage of trade shall be construed wherever reasonable as consistent with each other; but when such construction is unreasonable express terms control both course of dealing and usage of trade and course of dealing controls usage of trade.

(5) An applicable usage of trade in the place where any part of performance is to occur shall be used in interpreting the agreement as to that part of the performance.

(6) Evidence of a relevant usage of trade offered by one party is not admissible unless and until he has given the other party such notice as the court finds sufficient to prevent unfair surprise to the latter.

Sec. 1—206. Statute of Frauds for Kinds of Personal Property Not Otherwise Covered. (1) Except in the cases described in subsection (2) of this section a contract for the sale of personal property is not enforceable by way of action or defense beyond five thousand dollars in amount or value of remedy unless there is some writing which indicates that a contract for sale has been made between the parties at a defined or stated price, reasonably identifies the subject matter, and is signed by the party against whom enforcement is sought or by his authorized agent.

(2) Subsection (1) of this section does not apply to contracts for the sale of goods (Section 2–201) nor of securities (Section 8–319) nor to security agreements (Section 9–203).

Sec. 1—207. Performance or Acceptance Under Reservation of Rights.   A party who with explicit reservation of rights performs or promises performance or assents to performance in a manner demanded or offered by the other party does not thereby prejudice the rights reserved. Such words as "without prejudice," "under protest" or the like are sufficient.

Sec. 1—208. Option to Accelerate at Will.   A term providing that one party or his successor in interest may accelerate payment or performance or require collateral or additional collateral "at will" or "when he deems himself insecure" or in words of similar import shall be construed to mean that he shall have power to do so only if he in good faith believes that the prospect of payment or performance is impaired. The burden of establishing lack of good faith is on the party against whom the power has been exercised.

ARTICLE II

SALES

PART I

SHORT TITLE, GENERAL CONSTRUCTION AND SUBJECT MATTER

Sec. 2—101. Short Title.   This Article shall be known and may be cited as Uniform Commercial Code—Sales.

Sec. 2—102. Scope; Certain Security and Other Transactions Excluded From This Article.   Unless the context otherwise requires, this Article applies to transactions in goods; it does not apply to any transaction which although in the form of an unconditional contract to sell or present sale is intended to operate only as a security transaction nor does this Article impair or repeal any statute regulating sales to consumers, farmers or other specified classes of buyers.

Sec. 2—103. Definitions and Index of Definitions.   (1) In this Article unless the context otherwise requires

(*a*) "Buyer" means a person who buys or contracts to buy goods.

(*b*) "Good faith" in the case of a merchant means honesty in fact and the observance of reasonable commercial standards of fair dealing in the trade.

(*c*) "Receipt" of goods means taking physical possession of them.

(*d*) "Seller" means a person who sells or contracts to sell goods.

(2) Other definitions applying to this Article or to specified Parts thereof, and the sections in which they appear are:

"Acceptance." Section 2–606.

"Banker's credit." Section 2–325.

"Between merchants." Section 2–104.

"Cancellation." Section 2–106(4).

"Commercial unit." Section 2–105.

"Confirmed credit." Section 2–325.

"Conforming to contract." Section 2–106.

"Contract for sale." Section 2–106.

"Cover." Section 2–712.

"Entrusting." Section 2–403.

"Financing agency." Section 2–104.

"Future goods." Section 2–105.

"Goods." Section 2—105.

"Identification." Section 2—501.

"Installment contract." Section 2—612.

"Letter of Credit." Section 2—325.

"Lot." Section 2—105.

"Merchant." Section 2—104.

"Overseas." Section 2—323.

"Person in position of seller." Section 2—707.

"Present sale." Section 2—106.

"Sale." Section 2—106.

"Sale on approval." Section 2—326.

"Sale or return." Section 2—326.

"Termination." Section 2—106.

(3) The following definitions in other Articles apply to this Article:

"Check." Section 3—104.

"Consignee." Section 7—102.

"Consignor." Section 7—102.

"Consumer goods." Section 9—109.

"Dishonor." Section 3—507.

"Draft." Section 3—104.

(4) In addition Article 1 contains general definitions and principles of construction and interpretation applicable throughout this Article.

Sec. 2—104. Definitions: "Merchant"; "Between Merchants"; "Financing Agency." (1) "Merchant" means a person who deals in goods of the kind or otherwise by his occupation holds himself out as having knowledge or skill peculiar to the practices or goods involved in the transaction or to whom such knowledge or skill may be attributed by his employment of an agent or broker or other intermediary who by his occupation holds himself out as having such knowledge or skill.

(2) "Financing agency" means a bank, finance company or other person who in the ordinary course of business makes advances against goods or documents of title or who by arrangement with either the seller or the buyer intervenes in ordinary course to make or collect payment due or claimed under the contract for sale, as by purchasing or paying the seller's draft or making advances against it or by merely taking it for collection whether or not documents of title accompany the draft. "Financing agency" includes also a bank or other person who similarly intervenes between persons who are in the position of seller and buyer in respect to the goods (Section 2—707).

(3) "Between merchants" means in any transaction with respect to which both parties are chargeable with the knowledge or skill of merchants.

Sec. 2—105. Definitions: Transferability; "Goods"; "Future" Goods; "Lot"; "Commercial Unit." (1) "Goods" means all things (including specially manufactured goods) which are movable at the time of identification to the contract for sale other than the money in which the price is to be paid, investment securities (Article 8) and things in action. "Goods" also includes the unborn young of animals and growing crops and other identified things attached to realty as described in the section on goods to be severed from realty (Section 2—107).

(2) Goods must be both existing and identified before any interest in them can pass. Goods which are not both existing and identified are "future" goods. A purported present sale of future goods or of any interest therein operates as a contract to sell.

(3) There may be a sale of a part interest in existing identified goods.

(4) An undivided share in an identified bulk of fungible goods is sufficiently identified to be sold although the quantity of the bulk is not determined. Any agreed proportion of such a bulk or any quantity thereof agreed upon by number, weight or other measure may to the extent of the seller's interest in the bulk be sold to the buyer who then becomes an owner in common.

(5) "Lot" means a parcel or a single article which is the subject matter of a separate sale or delivery, whether or not it is sufficient to perform the contract.

(6) "Commercial unit" means such a unit of goods as by commercial usage is a single whole for purposes of sale and division of which materially impairs its character or value on the market or in use. A commercial unit may be a single article (as a machine) or a set of articles (as a suite of furniture or an assortment of sizes) or a quantity (as a bale, gross, or carload) or any other unit treated in use or in the relevant market as a single whole.

Sec. 2—106. Definitions: "Contract"; "Agreement"; "Contract for Sale"; "Sale"; "Present Sale"; "Conforming" to Contract; "Termination"; "Cancellation." (1) In this Article unless the context otherwise requires "contract" and "agreement" are limited to those relating to the present or future sale of goods. "Contract for Sale" includes both a present sale of goods and a contract to sell goods at a future time. A "sale" consists in the passing of title from the seller to the buyer for a price (Section 2—401). A "present sale" means a sale which is accomplished by the making of the contract.

(2) Goods or conduct including any part of a performance are "conforming" or conform to the contract when they are in accordance with the obligations under the contract.

(3) "Termination" occurs when either party pursuant to a power created by agreement or law puts an end to the contract otherwise than for its breach. On "termination" all obligations which are still executory on both sides are discharged but any right based on prior breach or performance survives.

(4) "Cancellation" occurs when either party puts an end to the contract for breach by the other and its effect is the same as that of "termination" except that the cancelling party also retains any remedy for breach of the whole contract or any unperformed balance.

Sec. 2—107. Goods to Be Severed From Realty: Recording. (1) A contract for the sale of timber, minerals or the like or a structure or its materials to be removed from realty is a contract for the sale of goods within this Article if they are to be severed by the seller but until severance a purported present sale thereof which is not effective as a transfer of an interest in land is effective only as a contract to sell.

(2) A contract for the sale apart from the land of growing crops or other things attached to realty and capable of severance without material harm thereto but not described in subsection (1) is a contract for the sale of goods within this Article whether the subject matter is to be severed by the buyer or by the seller even though it forms part of the realty at the time of contracting, and the parties can by identification effect a present sale before severance.

(3) The provisions of this section are subject to any third party rights provided by the law relating to realty records, and the contract for sale may be executed and recorded as a document transferring an interest in land and shall then constitute notice to third parties of the buyer's rights under the contract for sale.

PART II

FORM, FORMATION AND READJUSTMENT OF CONTRACT

Sec. 2—201. Formal Requirements; Statute of Frauds. (1) Except as otherwise provided in this section a contract for the sale of goods for the price of $500 or more is not enforceable by way of action or defense unless there is some writing sufficient to indicate that a contract for sale has been made between the parties and signed by the party against whom enforcement is sought or by his authorized agent or broker. A writing is not insufficient because it omits or incorrectly states a term agreed upon but the contract is not enforceable under this paragraph beyond the quantity of goods shown in such writing.

(2) Between merchants if within a reasonable time a writing in confirmation of the contract and sufficient against the sender is received and the party receiving it

has reason to know its contents, it satisfies the requirements of subsection (1) against such party unless written notice of objection to its contents is given within ten days after it is received.

(3) A contract which does not satisfy the requirements of subsection (1) but which is valid in other respects is enforceable

(*a*) if the goods are to be specially manufactured for the buyer and are not suitable for sale to others in the ordinary course of the seller's business and the seller, before notice of repudiation is received and under circumstances which reasonably indicate that the goods are for the buyer, has made either a substantial beginning of their manufacture or commitments for their procurement; or

(*b*) if the party against whom enforcement is sought admits in his pleading, testimony or otherwise in court that a contract for sale was made, but the contract is not enforceable under this provision beyond the quantity of goods admitted; or

(*c*) with respect to goods for which payment has been made and accepted or which have been received and accepted (Sec. 2–606).

Sec. 2–202. Final Written Expression: Parol or Extrinsic Evidence. Terms with respect to which the confirmatory memoranda of the parties agree or which are otherwise set forth in a writing intended by the parties as a final expression of their agreement with respect to such terms as are included therein may not be contradicted by evidence of any prior agreement or of a contemporaneous oral agreement but may be explained or supplemented

(*a*) by course of dealing or usage of trade (Section 1–205) or by course of performance (Section 2–208); and

(*b*) by evidence of consistent additional terms unless the court finds the writing to have been intended also as a complete and exclusive statement of the terms of the agreement.

Sec. 2–203. Seals Inoperative. The affixing of a seal to a writing evidencing a contract for sale or an offer to buy or sell goods does not constitute the writing a sealed instrument and the law with respect to sealed instruments does not apply to such a contract or offer.

Sec. 2–204. Formation in General. (1) A contract for sale of goods may be made in any manner sufficient to show agreement, including conduct by both parties which recognizes the existence of such a contract.

(2) An agreement sufficient to constitute a contract for sale may be found even though the moment of its making is undetermined.

(3) Even though one or more terms are left open a contract for sale does not fail for indefiniteness if the parties have intended to make a contract and there is a reasonably certain basis for giving an appropriate remedy.

Sec. 2–205. Firm Offers. An offer by a merchant to buy or sell goods in a signed writing which by its terms gives assurance that it will be held open is not revocable, for lack of consideration, during the time stated or if no time is stated for a reasonable time, but in no event may such period of irrevocability exceed three months; but any such term of assurance on a form supplied by the offeree must be separately signed by the offeror.

Sec. 2–206. Offer and Acceptance in Formation of Contract. (1) Unless otherwise unambiguously indicated by the language or circumstances

(*a*) an offer to make a contract shall be construed as inviting acceptance in any manner and by any medium reasonable in the circumstances;

(*b*) an order or other offer to buy goods for prompt or current shipment shall be construed as inviting acceptance either by a prompt promise to ship or by the prompt or current shipment of conforming or non-conforming goods, but such a shipment of non-conforming goods does not constitute an acceptance if the seller seasonably notifies the buyer that the shipment is offered only as an accommodation to the buyer.

(2) Where the beginning of a requested performance is a reasonable mode of ac-

ceptance an offeror who is not notified of acceptance within a reasonable time may treat the offer as having lapsed before acceptance.

Sec. 2—207. Additional Terms in Acceptance or Confirmation. (1) A definite and seasonable expression of acceptance or a written confirmation which is sent within a reasonable time operates as an acceptance even though it states terms additional to or different from those offered or agreed upon, unless acceptance is expressly made conditional on assent to the additional or different terms.

(2) The additional terms are to be construed as proposals for addition to the contract. Between merchants such terms become part of the contract unless:

(a) the offer expressly limits acceptance to the terms of the offer;

(b) they materially alter it; or

(c) notification of objection to them has already been given or is given within a reasonable time after notice of them is received.

(3) Conduct by both parties which recognizes the existence of a contract is sufficient to establish a contract for sale although the writings of the parties do not otherwise establish a contract. In such case the terms of the particular contract consist of those terms on which the writings of the parties agree, together with any supplementary terms incorporated under any other provisions of this Act.

Sec. 2—208. Course of Performance or Practical Construction. (1) Where the contract for sale involves repeated occasions for performance by either party with knowledge of the nature of the performance and opportunity for objection to it by the other, any course of performance accepted or acquiesced in without objection shall be relevant to determine the meaning of the agreement.

(2) The express terms of the agreement and any such course of performance, as well as any course of dealing and usage of trade, shall be construed whenever reasonable as consistent with each other; but when such construction is unreasonable, express terms shall control course of performance and course of performance shall control both course of dealing and usage of trade (Section 1—205).

(3) Subject to the provisions of the next section on modification and waiver, such course of performance shall be relevant to show a waiver or modification of any term inconsistent with such course of performance.

Sec. 2—209. Modification, Rescission and Waiver. (1) An agreement modifying a contract within this Article needs no consideration to be binding.

(2) A signed agreement which excludes modification or rescission except by a signed writing cannot be otherwise modified or rescinded, but except as between merchants such a requirement on a form supplied by the merchant must be separately signed by the other party.

(3) The requirements of the statute of frauds section of this Article (Section 2—201) must be satisfied if the contract as modified is within its provisions.

(4) Although an attempt at modification or rescission does not satisfy the requirements of subsection (2) or (3) it can operate as a waiver.

(5) A party who has made a waiver affecting an executory portion of the contract may retract the waiver by reasonable notification received by the other party that strict performance will be required of any term waived, unless the retraction would be unjust in view of a material change of position in reliance on the waiver.

Sec. 2—210. Delegation of Performance; Assignment of Rights. (1) A party may perform his duty through a delegate unless otherwise agreed or unless the other party has a substantial interest in having his original promisor perform or control the acts required by the contract. No delegation of performance relieves the party delegating of any duty to perform or any liability for breach.

(2) Unless otherwise agreed all rights of either seller or buyer can be assigned except where the assignment would materially change the duty of the other party, or increase materially the burden or risk imposed on him by his contract, or impair materially his chance of obtaining return performance. A right to damages for breach

of the whole contract or a right arising out of the assignor's due performance of his entire obligation can be assigned despite agreement otherwise.

(3) Unless the circumstances indicate the contrary a prohibition of assignment of "the contract" is to be construed as barring only the delegation to the assignee of the assignor's performance.

(4) An assignment of "the contract" or of "all my rights under the contract" or an assignment in similar general terms is an assignment of rights and unless the language or the circumstances (as in an assignment for security) indicate the contrary, it is a delegation of performance of the duties of the assignor and its acceptance by the assignee constitutes a promise by him to perform those duties. This promise is enforceable by either the assignor or the other party to the original contract.

(5) The other party may treat any assignment which delegates performance as creating reasonable grounds for insecurity and may without prejudice to his rights against the assignor demand assurances from the assignee (Section 2–609).

PART III

GENERAL OBLIGATION AND CONSTRUCTION OF CONTRACT

Sec. 2–301. General Obligations of Parties. The obligation of the seller is to transfer and deliver and that of the buyer is to accept and pay in accordance with the contract.

Sec. 2–302. Unconscionable Contract or Clause. (1) If the court as a matter of law finds the contract or any clause of the contract to have been unconscionable at the time it was made the court may refuse to enforce the contract, or it may enforce the remainder of the contract without the unconscionable clause, or it may so limit the application of any unconscionable clauses as to avoid any unconscionable result.

(2) When it is claimed or appears to the court that the contract or any clause thereof may be unconscionable the parties shall be afforded a reasonable opportunity to present evidence as to its commercial setting, purpose and effect to aid the court in making the determination.

Sec. 2–303. Allocation or Division of Risks. Where this Article allocates a risk or a burden as between the parties "unless otherwise agreed," the agreement may not only shift the allocation but may also divide the risk or burden.

Sec. 2–304. Price Payable in Money, Goods, Realty, or Otherwise. (1) The price can be made payable in money or otherwise. If it is payable in whole or in part in goods each party is a seller of the goods which he is to transfer.

(2) Even though all or part of the price is payable in an interest in realty the transfer of the goods and the seller's obligations with reference to them are subject to this Article, but not the transfer of the interest in realty or the transferor's obligations in connection therewith.

Sec. 2–305. Open Price Term. (1) The parties if they so intend can conclude a contract for sale even though the price is not settled. In such a case the price is a reasonable price at the time for delivery if

(a) nothing is said as to price; or

(b) the price is left to be agreed by the parties and they fail to agree; or

(c) the price is to be fixed in terms of some agreed market or other standard as set or recorded by a third person or agency and it is not so set or recorded.

(2) A price to be fixed by the seller or by the buyer means a price for him to fix in good faith.

(3) When a price left to be fixed otherwise than by agreement of the parties fails to be fixed through fault of one party the other may at his option treat the contract as cancelled or himself fix a reasonable price.

(4) Where, however, the parties intend not to be bound unless the price be fixed or agreed and it is not fixed or agreed there is no contract. In such a case the buyer must return any goods already received or if unable so to do must pay their reason-

able value at the time of delivery and the seller must return any portion of the price paid on account.

Sec. 2—306. Output, Requirements and Exclusive Dealings. (1) A term which measures the quantity by the output of the seller or the requirements of the buyer means such actual output or requirements as may occur in good faith, except that no quantity unreasonably disproportionate to any stated estimate or in the absence of a stated estimate to any normal or otherwise comparable prior output or requirements may be tendered or demanded.

(2) A lawful agreement by either the seller or the buyer for exclusive dealing in the kind of goods concerned imposes unless otherwise agreed an obligation by the seller to use best efforts to supply the goods and by the buyer to use best efforts to promote their sale.

Sec. 2—307. Delivery in Single Lot or Several Lots. Unless otherwise agreed all goods called for by a contract for sale must be tendered in a single delivery and payment is due only on such tender but where the circumstances give either party the right to make or demand delivery in lots the price if it can be apportioned may be demanded for each lot.

Sec. 2—308. Absence of Specified Place for Delivery. Unless otherwise agreed

(a) the place for delivery of goods is the seller's place of business or if he has none his residence; but

(b) in a contract for sale of identified goods which to the knowledge of the parties at the time of contracting are in some other place, that place is the place for their delivery; and

(c) documents of title may be delivered through customary banking channels.

Sec. 2—309. Absence of Specific Time Provisions; Notice of Termination. (1) The time for shipment or delivery or any other action under a contract if not provided in this Article or agreed upon shall be a reasonable time.

(2) Where the contract provides for successive performances but is indefinite in duration it is valid for a reasonable time but unless otherwise agreed may be terminated at any time by either party.

(3) Termination of a contract by one party except on the happening of an agreed event requires that reasonable notification be received by the other party and an agreement dispensing with notification is invalid if its operation would be unconscionable.

Sec. 2—310. Open Time for Payment or Running of Credit; Authority to Ship Under Reservation. Unless otherwise agreed

(a) payment is due at the time and place at which the buyer is to receive the goods even though the place of shipment is the place of delivery; and

(b) if the seller is authorized to send the goods he may ship them under reservation, and may tender the documents of title, but the buyer may inspect the goods after their arrival before payment is due unless such inspection is inconsistent with the terms of the contract (Section 2—513); and

(c) if delivery is authorized and made by way of documents of title otherwise than by subsection (b) then payment is due at the time and place at which the buyer is to receive the documents regardless of where the goods are to be received; and

(d) where the seller is required or authorized to ship the goods on credit the credit period runs from the time of shipment but post-dating the invoice or delaying its dispatch will correspondingly delay the starting of the credit period.

Sec. 2—311. Options and Cooperation Respecting Performance. (1) An agreement for sale which is otherwise sufficiently definite (subsection (3) of Section 2—204) to be a contract is not made invalid by the fact that it leaves particulars of performance to be specified by one of the parties. Any such specification must be made in good faith and within limits set by commercial reasonableness.

(2) Unless otherwise agreed specifications relating to assortment of the goods are at the buyer's option and except as otherwise provided in subsections (1) (c) and

(3) of Section 2—319 specifications or arrangements relating to shipment are at the seller's option.

(3) Where such specification would materially affect the other party's performance but is not seasonably made or where one party's cooperation is necessary to the agreed performance of the other but is not seasonably forthcoming, the other party in addition to all other remedies

(*a*) is excused for any resulting delay in his own performance; and

(*b*) may also either proceed to perform in any reasonable manner or after the time for a material part of his own performance treat the failure to specify or to cooperate as a breach by failure to deliver or accept the goods.

Sec. 2—312. Warranty of Title and Against Infringement; Buyer's Obligation Against Infringement. (1) Subject to subsection (2) there is in a contract for sale a warranty by the seller that

(*a*) the title conveyed shall be good, and its transfer rightful; and

(*b*) the goods shall be delivered free from any security interest or other lien or encumbrance of which the buyer at the time of contracting has no knowledge.

(2) A warranty under subsection (1) will be excluded or modified only by specific language or by circumstances which give the buyer reason to know that the person selling does not claim title in himself or that he is purporting to sell only such right or title as he or a third person may have.

(3) Unless otherwise agreed a seller who is a merchant regularly dealing in goods of the kind warrants that the goods shall be delivered free of the rightful claim of any third person by way of infringement or the like but a buyer who furnishes specifications to the seller must hold the seller harmless against any such claim which arises out of compliance with the specifications.

Sec. 2—313. Express Warranties by Affirmation, Promise, Description, Sample. (1) Express warranties by the seller are created as follows:

(*a*) Any affirmation of fact or promise made by the seller to the buyer which relates to the goods and becomes part of the basis of the bargain creates an express warranty that the goods shall conform to the affirmation or promise.

(*b*) Any description of the goods which is made part of the basis of the bargain creates an express warranty that the goods shall conform to the description.

(*c*) Any sample or model which is made part of the basis of the bargain creates an express warranty that the whole of the goods shall conform to the sample or model.

(2) It is not necessary to the creation of an express warranty that the seller use formal words such as "warrant" or "guarantee" or that he have a specific intention to make a warranty, but an affirmation merely of the value of the goods or a statement purporting to be merely the seller's opinion or commendation of the goods does not create a warranty.

Sec. 2—314. Implied Warranty: Merchantability; Usage of Trade. (1) Unless excluded or modified (Section 2—316), a warranty that the goods shall be merchantable is implied in a contract for their sale if the seller is a merchant with respect to goods of that kind. Under this section the serving for value of food or drink to be consumed either on the premises or elsewhere is a sale.

(2) Goods to be merchantable must be at least such as

(*a*) pass without objection in the trade under the contract description; and

(*b*) in the case of fungible goods, are of fair average quality within the description; and

(*c*) are fit for the ordinary purposes for which such goods are used; and

(*d*) run, within the variations permitted by the agreement, of even kind, quality and quantity within each unit and among all units involved; and

(*e*) are adequately contained, packaged, and labeled as the agreement may require; and (*f*) conform to the promises or affirmations of fact made on the container or label if any.

(3) Unless excluded or modified (Section 2–316) other implied warranties may arise from course of dealing or usage of trade.

Sec. 2–315. Implied Warranty: Fitness for Particular Purpose.   Where the seller at the time of contracting has reason to know any particular purpose for which the goods are required and that the buyer is relying on the seller's skill or judgment to select or furnish suitable goods, there is unless excluded or modified under the next section an implied warranty that the goods shall be fit for such purpose.

Sec. 2–316. Exclusion or Modification of Warranties.   (1) Words or conduct relevant to the creation of an express warranty and words or conduct tending to negate or limit warranty shall be construed wherever reasonable as consistent with each other; but subject to the provisions of this Article on parol or extrinsic evidence (Section 2–202) negation or limitation is inoperative to the extent that such construction is unreasonable.

(2) Subject to subsection (3), to exclude or modify the implied warranty of merchantability or any part of it the language must mention merchantability and in case of a writing must be conspicuous, and to exclude or modify any implied warranty of fitness the exclusion must be by a writing and conspicuous. Language to exclude all implied warranties of fitness is sufficient if it states, for example, that "There are no warranties which extend beyond the description on the face hereof."

(3) Notwithstanding subsection (2)

(*a*) unless the circumstances indicate otherwise, all implied warranties are excluded by expressions like "as is," "with all faults" or other language which in common understanding calls the buyer's attention to the exclusion of warranties and makes plain that there is no implied warranty; and

(*b*) when the buyer before entering into the contract has examined the goods or the sample or model as fully as he desired or has refused to examine the goods there is no implied warranty with regard to defects which an examination ought in the circumstances to have revealed to him; and

(*c*) an implied warranty can also be excluded or modified by course of dealing or course of performance or usage of trade.

(4) Remedies for breach of warranty can be limited in accordance with the provisions of this Article on liquidation or limitation of damages and on contractual modification of remedy (Sections 2–718 and 2–719).

Sec. 2–317. Cumulation and Conflict of Warranties Express or Implied.   Warranties whether express or implied shall be construed as consistent with each other and as cumulative, but if such construction is unreasonable the intention of the parties shall determine which warranty is dominant. In ascertaining that intention the following rules apply:

(*a*) Exact or technical specifications displace an inconsistent sample or model or general language of description.

(*b*) A sample from an existing bulk displaces inconsistent general language of description.

(*c*) Express warranties displace inconsistent implied warranties other than an implied warranty of fitness for a particular purpose.

Sec. 2–318. Third Party Beneficiaries of Warranties Express or Implied.   A seller's warranty whether express or implied extends to any natural person who is in the family or household of his buyer or who is a guest in his home if it is reasonable to expect that such person may use, consume or be affected by the goods and who is injured in person by breach of the warranty. A seller may not exclude or limit the operation of this section.

Sec. 2–319. F.O.B. and F.A.S. Terms.   (1) Unless otherwise agreed the term F.O.B. (which means "free on board") at a named place, even though used only in connection with the stated price, is a delivery term under which (*a*) when the term is F.O.B. the place of shipment, the seller must at that place ship the goods in the manner provided in this Article (Section 2—504) and bear the expense and risk of putting them into the possession of the carrier; or

(*b*) when the term is F.O.B. the place of destination, the seller must at his own expense and risk transport the goods to that place and there tender delivery of them in the manner provided in this Article (Section 2—503);

(*c*) when under either (*a*) or (*b*) the term is also F.O.B. vessel, car or other vehicle, the seller must in addition at his own expense and risk load the goods on board. If the term is F.O.B. vessel the buyer must name the vessel and in an appropriate case the seller must comply with the provisions of this Article on the form of bill of lading (Section 2—323).

(2) Unless otherwise agreed the term F.A.S. vessel (which means "free alongside") at a named port, even though used only in connection with the stated price, is a delivery term under which the seller must

(*a*) at his own expense and risk deliver the goods alongside the vessel in the manner usual in that port or on a dock designated and provided by the buyer; and

(*b*) obtain and tender a receipt for the goods in exchange for which the carrier is under a duty to issue a bill of lading.

(3) Unless otherwise agreed in any case falling within subsection (1) (*a*) or (*c*) or subsection (2) the buyer must seasonably give any needed instructions for making delivery, including when the term is F.A.S. or F.O.B. the loading berth of the vessel and in an appropriate case its name and sailing date. The seller may treat the failure of needed instructions as a failure of cooperation under this Article (Section 2—311). He may also at his option move the goods in any reasonable manner preparatory to delivery or shipment.

(4) Under the term F.O.B. vessel or F.A.S. unless otherwise agreed the buyer must make payment against tender of the required documents and the seller may not tender nor the buyer demand delivery of the goods in substitution for the documents.

Sec. 2—320. C.I.F. and C. & F. Terms. (1) The term C.I.F. means that the price includes in a lump sum the cost of the goods and the insurance and freight to the named destination. The term C. & F. or C.F. means that the price so includes cost and freight to the named destination.

(2) Unless otherwise agreed and even though used only in connection with the stated price and destination, the term C.I.F. destination or its equivalent requires the seller at his own expense and risk to

(*a*) put the goods into the possession of a carrier at the port for shipment and obtain a negotiable bill or bills of lading covering the entire transportation to the named destination; and

(*b*) load the goods and obtain a receipt from the carrier (which may be contained in the bill of lading) showing that the freight has been paid or provided for; and

(*c*) obtain a policy or certificate of insurance, including any war risk insurance, of a kind and on terms then current at the port of shipment in the usual amount, in the currency of the contract, shown to cover the same goods covered by the bill of lading and providing for payment of loss to the order of the buyer or for the account of whom it may concern; but the seller may add to the price the amount of the premium for any such war risk insurance; and

(*d*) prepare an invoice of the goods and procure any other documents required to effect shipment or to comply with the contract; and

(*e*) forward and tender with commercial promptness all the documents in due form and with any indorsement necessary to perfect the buyer's rights.

(3) Unless otherwise agreed the term C. & F. or its equivalent has the same effect and imposes upon the seller the same obligations and risks as a C.I.F. term except the obligation as to insurance.

(4) Under the term C.I.F. or C. & F. unless otherwise agreed the buyer must make

payment against tender of the required documents and the seller may not tender nor the buyer demand delivery of the goods in substitution for the documents.

Sec. 2—321. C.I.F. or C. & F.: "Net Landed Weights"; "Payment on Arrival"; Warranty of Condition on Arrival. Under a contract containing a term C.I.F. or C. & F.

(1) Where the price is based on or is to be adjusted according to "net landed weights," "delivered weights," "out turn" quantity or quality or the like, unless otherwise agreed the seller must reasonably estimate the price. The payment due on tender of the documents called for by the contract is the amount so estimated, but after final adjustment of the price a settlement must be made with commercial promptness.

(2) An agreement described in subsection (1) or any warranty of quality or condition of the goods on arrival places upon the seller the risk of ordinary deterioration, shrinkage and the like in transportation but has no effect on the place or time of identification to the contract for sale or delivery or on the passing of the risk of loss.

(3) Unless otherwise agreed where the contract provides for payment on or after arrival of the goods the seller must before payment allow such preliminary inspection as is feasible; but if the goods are lost delivery of the documents and payment are due when the goods should have arrived.

Sec. 2—322. Delivery "Ex-Ship". (1) Unless otherwise agreed a term for delivery of goods "ex-ship" (which means from the carrying vessel) or in equivalent language is not restricted to a particular ship and requires delivery from a ship which has reached a place at the named port of destination where goods of the kind are usually discharged.

(2) Under such a term unless otherwise agreed

(a) the seller must discharge all liens arising out of the carriage and furnish the buyer with a direction which puts the carrier under a duty to deliver the goods; and

(b) the risk of loss does not pass to the buyer until the goods leave the ship's tackle or are otherwise properly unloaded.

Sec. 2—323. Form of Bill of Lading Required in Overseas Shipment; "Overseas." (1) Where the contract contemplates overseas shipment and contains a term C.I.F. or C. & F. or F.O.B. vessel, the seller unless otherwise agreed must obtain a negotiable bill of lading stating that the goods have been loaded on board or, in the case of a term C.I.F. or C. & F., received for shipment.

(2) Where in a case within subsection (1) a bill of lading has been issued in a set of parts, unless otherwise agreed if the documents are not to be sent from abroad the buyer may demand tender of the full set; otherwise only one part of the bill of lading need be tendered. Even if the agreement expressly requires a full set

(a) due tender of a single part is acceptable within the provisions of this Article on cure of improper delivery (subsection (1) of Section 2—508); and

(b) even though the full set is demanded, if the documents are sent from abroad the person tendering an incomplete set may nevertheless require payment upon furnishing an indemnity which the buyer in good faith deems adequate.

(3) A shipment by water or by air or a contract contemplating such shipment is "overseas" insofar as by usage of trade or agreement it is subject to the commercial, financing or shipping practices characteristic of international deep water commerce.

Sec. 2—324. "No Arrival, No Sale" Term. Under a term "no arrival, no sale" or terms of like meaning, unless otherwise agreed,

(a) the seller must properly ship conforming goods and if they arrive by any means he must tender them on arrival but he assumes no obligation that the goods will arrive unless he has caused the non-arrival; and

(b) where without fault of the seller the goods are in part lost or have so deteriorated as no longer to conform to the contract or arrive after the contract time, the buyer may proceed as if there had been casualty to identified goods (Section 2—613).

Sec. 2—325. "Letter of Credit" Term; "Confirmed Credit." (1) Failure of the buyer seasonably to furnish an agreed letter of credit is a breach of the contract for sale.

(2) The delivery to seller of a proper letter of credit suspends the buyer's obligation to pay. If the letter of credit is dishonored, the seller may on seasonable notification to the buyer require payment directly from him.

(3) Unless otherwise agreed the term "letter of credit" or "banker's credit" in a contract for sale means an irrevocable credit issued by a financing agency of good repute and, where the shipment is overseas, of good international repute. The term "confirmed credit" means that the credit must also carry the direct obligation of such an agency which does business in the seller's financial market.

Sec. 2—326. Sale on Approval and Sale or Return; Consignment Sales and Rights of Creditors. (1) Unless otherwise agreed, if delivered goods may be returned by the buyer even though they conform to the contract, the transaction is

(a) a "sale on approval" if the goods are delivered primarily for use, and

(b) a "sale or return" if the goods are delivered primarily for resale.

(2) Except as provided in subsection (3), goods held on approval are not subject to the claims of the buyer's creditors until acceptance; goods held on sale or return are subject to such claims while in the buyer's possession.

(3) Where goods are delivered to a person for sale and such person maintains a place of business at which he deals in goods of the kind involved, under a name other than the name of the person making delivery, then with respect to claims of creditors of the person conducting the business the goods are deemed to be on sale or return. The provisions of this subsection are applicable even though an agreement purports to reserve title to the person making delivery until payment or resale or uses such words as "on consignment" or "on memorandum." However, this subsection is not applicable if the person making delivery

(a) complies with an applicable law providing for a consignor's interest or the like to be evidenced by a sign, or

(b) establishes that the person conducting the business is generally known by his creditors to be substantially engaged in selling the goods of others, or

(c) complies with the filing provisions of the Article on Secured Transactions (Article 9).

(4) Any "or return" term of a contract for sale is to be treated as a separate contract for sale within the statute of frauds section of this Article (Section 2—201) and as contradicting the sale aspect of the contract within the provisions of this Article on parol or extrinsic evidence (Section 2—202).

Sec. 2—327. Special Incidents of Sale on Approval and Sale or Return. (1) Under a sale on approval unless otherwise agreed

(a) although the goods are identified to the contract the risk of loss and the title do not pass to the buyer until acceptance; and

(b) use of goods consistent with the purpose of trial is not acceptance but failure seasonably to notify the seller of election to return the goods is acceptance, and if the goods conform to the contract acceptance of any part is acceptance of the whole; and

(c) after due notification of election to return, is at the seller's risk and expense but a merchant buyer must follow any reasonable instructions.

(2) Under a sale or return unless otherwise agreed

(a) the option to return extends to the whole or any commercial unit of the goods while in substantially their original condition, but must be exercised seasonably; and

(b) the return is at the buyer's risk and expense.

Sec. 2—328. Sale by Auction. (1) In a sale by auction if goods are put up in lots each lot is the subject of a separate sale.

(2) A sale by auction is complete when the auctioneer so announces by the fall of the hammer or in other customary manner. Where a bid is made while the

hammer is falling in acceptance of a prior bid the auctioneer may in his discretion reopen the bidding or declare the goods sold under the bid on which the hammer was falling.

(3) Such a sale is with reserve unless the goods are in explicit terms put up without reserve. In an auction with reserve the auctioneer may withdraw the goods at any time until he announces completion of the sale. In an auction without reserve, after the auctioneer calls for bids on an article or lot, that article or lot cannot be withdrawn unless no bid is made within a reasonable time. In either case a bidder may retract his bid until the auctioneer's announcement of completion of the sale, but a bidder's retraction does not revive any previous bid.

(4) If the auctioneer knowingly receives a bid on the seller's behalf or the seller makes or procures such a bid, and notice has not been given that liberty for such bidding is reserved, the buyer may at his option avoid the sale or take the goods at the price of the last good faith bid prior to the completion of the sale. This subsection shall not apply to any bid at a forced sale.

PART IV

TITLE, CREDITORS AND GOOD FAITH PURCHASERS

Sec. 2—401. Passing of Title; Reservation for Security; Limited Application of This Section. Each provision of this Article with regard to the rights, obligations and remedies of the seller, the buyer, purchasers or other third parties applies irrespective of title to the goods except where the provision refers to such title. Insofar as situations are not covered by the other provisions of this Article and matters concerning title become material the following rules apply:

(1) Title to goods cannot pass under a contract for sale prior to their identification to the contract (Section 2—501), and unless otherwise explicitly agreed the buyer acquires by their identification a special property as limited by this Act. Any retention or reservation by the seller of the title (property) in goods shipped or delivered to the buyer is limited in effect to a reservation of a security interest. Subject to these provisions and to the provisions of the Article on Secured Transactions (Article 9), title to goods passes from the seller to the buyer in any manner and on any conditions explicitly agreed on by the parties.

(2) Unless otherwise explicitly agreed title passes to the buyer at the time and place at which the seller completes his performance with reference to the physical delivery of the goods, despite any reservation of a security interest and even though a document of title is to be delivered at a different time or place; and in particular and despite any reservation of a security interest by the bill of lading.

(a) if the contract requires or authorizes the seller to send the goods to the buyer but does not require him to deliver them at destination, title passes to the buyer at the time and place of shipment; but

(b) if the contract requires delivery at destination, title passes on tender there.

(3) Unless otherwise explicitly agreed where delivery is to be made without moving the goods,

(a) if the seller is to deliver a document of title, title passes at the time when and the place where he delivers such documents; or

(b) if the goods are at the time of contracting already identified and no documents are to be delivered, title passes at the time and place of contracting.

(4) A rejection or other refusal by the buyer to receive or retain the goods, whether or not justified, or a justified revocation of acceptance revests title to the goods in the seller. Such revesting occurs by operation of law and is not a "sale."

Sec. 2—402. Rights of Seller's Creditors Against Sold Goods. (1) Except as provided in subsections (2) and (3), rights of unsecured creditors of the seller with respect to goods which have been identified to a contract for sale are subject to the buyer's rights to recover the goods under this Article (Sections 2—502 and 2—716).

(2) A creditor of the seller may treat a sale or an identification of goods to a contract for sale as void if as against him a retention of possession by the seller is fraudulent under any rule of law of the state where the goods are situated, except that retention of possession in good faith and current course of trade by a merchant-seller for a commercially reasonable time after a sale or identification is not fraudulent.

(3) Nothing in this Article shall be deemed to impair the rights of creditors of the seller

(a) under the provisions of the Article on Secured Transactions (Article 9); or

(b) where identification to the contract or delivery is made not in current course of trade but in satisfaction of or as security for a preexisting claim for money, security or the like and is made under circumstances which under any rule of law of the state where the goods are situated would apart from this Article constitute the transaction a fraudulent transfer or voidable preference.

Sec. 2—403. Power to Transfer; Good Faith Purchase of Goods; "Entrusting." (1) A purchaser of goods acquires all title which his transferor had or had power to transfer except that a purchaser of a limited interest acquires rights only to the extent of the interest purchased. A person with voidable title has power to transfer a good title to a good faith purchaser for value. When goods have been delivered under a transaction of purchase the purchaser has such power even though

(a) the transferor was deceived as to the identity of the purchaser, or

(b) the delivery was in exchange for a check which is later dishonored, or

(c) it was agreed that the transaction was to be a "cash sale," or

(d) the delivery was procured through fraud punishable as larcenous under the criminal law.

(2) Any entrusting of possession of goods to a merchant who deals in goods of that kind gives him power to transfer all rights of the entruster to a buyer in ordinary course of business.

(3) "Entrusting" includes any delivery and any acquiescence in retention of possession regardless of any condition expressed between the parties to the delivery or acquiescence and regardless of whether the procurement of the entrusting or the possessor's disposition of the goods have been such as to be larcenous under the criminal law.

(4) The rights of other purchasers of goods and of lien creditors are governed by the Articles on Secured Transactions (Article 9), Bulk Transfers (Article 6) and Documents of Title (Article 7).

PART V

PERFORMANCE

Sec. 2—501. Insurable Interest in Goods; Manner of Identification of Goods. (1) The buyer obtains a special property and an insurable interest in goods by identification of existing goods as goods to which the contract refers even though the goods so identified are non-conforming and he has an option to return or reject them. Such identification can be made at any time and in any manner explicitly agreed to by the parties. In the absence of explicit agreement identification occurs.

(a) when the contract is made if it is for the sale of goods already existing and identified;

(b) if the contract is for the sale of future goods other than those described in paragraph (c), when goods are shipped, marked or otherwise designated by the seller as goods to which the contract refers;

(c) when the crops are planted or otherwise become growing crops or the young are conceived if the contract is for the sale of unborn young to be born within twelve months after contracting or for the sale of crops to be harvested within twelve months or the next normal harvest season after contracting which-ever is longer.

(2) The seller retains an insurable interest in goods so long as title to or any security interest in the goods remains in him and where the identification is by the seller alone he may until default or insolvency or notification to the buyer that the identification is final substitute other goods for those identified.

(3) Nothing in this section impairs any insurable interest recognized under any other statute or rule of law.

Sec. 2—502. Buyer's Right to Goods on Seller's Insolvency. (1) Subject to subsection (2) and even though the goods have not been shipped a buyer who has paid a part or all of the price of goods in which he has a special property under the provisions of the immediately preceding section may on making and keeping good a tender of any unpaid portion of their price recover them from the seller if the seller becomes insolvent within ten days after receipt of the first installment on their price.

(2) If the identification creating his special property has been made by the buyer he acquires the right to recover the goods only if they conform to the contract for sale.

Sec. 2—503. Manner of Seller's Tender of Delivery. (1) Tender of delivery requires that the seller put and hold conforming goods at the buyer's disposition and give the buyer any notification reasonably necessary to enable him to take delivery. The manner, time and place for tender are determined by the agreement and this Article, and in particular

(a) tender must be at a reasonable hour, and if it is of goods they must be kept available for the period reasonably necessary to enable the buyer to take pos-session; but

(b) unless otherwise agreed the buyer must furnish facilities reasonably suited to the receipt of the goods.

(2) Where the case is within the next section respecting shipment tender requires that the seller comply with its provisions.

(3) Where the seller is required to deliver at a particular destination tender re-quires that he comply with subsection (1) and also in any appropriate case tender documents as described in subsections (4) and (5) of this section.

(4) Where goods are in the possession of a bailee and are to be delivered without being moved

(a) tender requires that the seller either tender a negotiable document of title covering such goods or procure acknowledgment by the bailee of the buyer's right to possession of the goods; but

(b) tender to the buyer of a non-negotiable document of title or of a written direction to the bailee to deliver is sufficient tender unless the buyer seasonably objects, and receipt by the bailee of notification of the buyer's rights fixes those rights as against the bailee and all third persons; but risk of loss of the goods and of any failure by the bailee to honor the non-negotiable document of title or to obey the direction remains on the seller until the buyer has had a reasonable time to present the document or direction, and a refusal by the bailee to honor the document or to obey the direction defeats the tender.

(5) Where the contract requires the seller to deliver documents

(a) he must tender all such documents in correct form, except as provided in this Article with respect to bills of lading in a set (subsection (2) of Section 2—323); and

(b) tender through customary banking channels is sufficient and dishonor of a draft accompanying the documents constitutes nonacceptance or rejection.

Sec. 2—504. Shipment by Seller. Where the seller is required or authorized to send the goods to the buyer and the contract does not require him to deliver them at a particular destination, then unless otherwise agreed he must

(a) put the goods in the possession of such a carrier and make such a contract for their transportation as may be reasonable having regard to the nature of the goods and other circumstances of the case; and

(*b*) obtain and promptly deliver or tender in due form any document necessary to enable the buyer to obtain possession of the goods or otherwise required by the agreement or by usage of trade; and

(*c*) promptly notify the buyer of the shipment.

Failure to notify the buyer under paragraph (*c*) or to make a proper contract under paragraph (*a*) is a ground for rejection only if material delay or loss ensues.

Sec. 2—505. Seller's Shipment Under Reservation. (1) Where the seller has identified goods to the contract by or before shipment:

(*a*) his procurement of a negotiable bill of lading to his own order or otherwise reserves in him a security interest in the goods. His procurement of the bill to the order of a financing agency or of the buyer indicates in addition only the seller's expectation of transferring that interest to the person named.

(*b*) a non-negotiable bill of lading to himself or his nominee reserves possession of the goods as security but except in a case of conditional delivery (subsection (2) of Section 2—507) a non-negotiable bill of lading naming the buyer as consignee reserves no security interest even though the seller retains possession of the bill of lading.

(2) When shipment by the seller with reservation of a security interest is in violation of the contract for sale it constitutes an improper contract for transportation within the preceding section but impairs neither the rights given to the buyer by shipment and identification of the goods to the contract nor the seller's powers as a holder of a negotiable document.

Sec. 2—506. Rights of Financing Agency. (1) A financing agency by paying or purchasing for value a draft which relates to a shipment of goods acquires to the extent of the payment or purchase and in addition to its own rights under the draft and any document of title securing it any rights of the shipper in the goods including the right to stop delivery and the shipper's right to have the draft honored by the buyer.

(2) The right to reimbursement of a financing agency which has in good faith honored or purchased the draft under commitment to or authority from the buyer is not impaired by subsequent discovery of defects with reference to any relevant document which was apparently regular on its face.

Sec. 2—507. Effect of Seller's Tender; Delivery on Condition. (1) Tender of delivery is a condition to the buyer's duty to accept the goods and, unless otherwise agreed, to his duty to pay for them. Tender entitles the seller to acceptance of the goods and to payment according to the contract.

(2) Where payment is due and demanded on the delivery to the buyer of goods or documents of title, his right as against the seller to retain or dispose of them is conditional upon his making the payment due.

Sec. 2—508. Cure by Seller of Improper Tender or Delivery; Replacement. (1) Where any tender or delivery by the seller is rejected because non-conforming and the time for performance has not yet expired, the seller may seasonably notify the buyer of his intention to cure and may then within the contract time make a conforming delivery.

(2) Where the buyer rejects a non-conforming tender which the seller had reasonable grounds to believe would be acceptable with or without money allowance the seller may if he seasonably notifies the buyer have a further reasonable time to substitute a conforming tender.

Sec. 2—509. Risk of Loss in the Absence of Breach. (1) Where the contract requires or authorizes the seller to ship the goods by carrier

(*a*) if it does not require him to deliver them at a particular destination, the risk of loss passes to the buyer when the goods are duly delivered to the carrier even though the shipment is under reservation (Section 2—505); but (*b*) if it does require him to deliver them at a particular destination and the goods are there duly tendered while in the possession of the carrier, the risk of loss passes to the buyer when the goods are there duly so tenderd as to enable the buyer to take delivery.

(2) Where the goods are held by a bailee to be delivered without being moved, the risk of loss passes to the buyer

(*a*) on his receipt of a negotiable document of title covering the goods; or

(*b*) on acknowledgment by the bailee of the buyer's right to possession of the goods; or

(*c*) after his receipt of a non-negotiable document of title or other written direction to deliver, as provided in subsection (4) (*b*) of Section 2–503.

(3) In any case not within subsection (1) or (2), the risk of loss passes to the buyer on his receipt of the goods if the seller is a merchant; otherwise the risk passes to the buyer on tender of delivery.

(4) The provisions of this section are subject to contrary agreement of the parties and to the provisions of this Article on sale on approval (Section 2–327) and on effect of breach on risk of loss (Section 2–510).

Sec. 2–510. Effect of Breach on Risk of Loss. (1) Where a tender or delivery of goods so fails to conform to the contract as to give a right of rejection the risk of their loss remains on the seller until cure or acceptance.

(2) Where the buyer rightfully revokes acceptance he may to the extent of any deficiency in his effective insurance coverage treat the risk of loss as having rested on the seller from the beginning.

(3) Where the buyer as to conforming goods already identified to the contract for sale repudiates or is otherwise in breach before risk of their loss has passed to him, the seller may to the extent of any deficiency in his effective insurance coverage treat the risk of loss as resting on the buyer for a commercially reasonable time.

Sec. 2–511. Tender of Payment by Buyer; Payment by Check. (1) Unless otherwise agreed tender of payment is a condition to the seller's duty to tender and complete any delivery.

(2) Tender of payment is sufficient when made by any means or in any manner current in the ordinary course of business unless the seller demands payment in legal tender and gives any extension of time reasonably necessary to procure it.

(3) Subject to the provisions of this Act on the effect of an instrument on an obligation (Section 3–802), payment by check is conditional and is defeated as between the parties by dishonor of the check on due presentment.

Sec. 2–512. Payment by Buyer Before Inspection. (1) Where the contract requires payment before inspection non-conformity of the goods does not excuse the buyer from so making payment unless

(*a*) the non-conformity appears without inspection; or

(*b*) despite tender of the required documents the circumstances would justify injunction against honor under the provisions of this Act (Section 5–114).

(2) Payment pursuant to subsection (1) does not constitute an acceptance of goods or impair the buyer's right to inspect or any of his remedies.

Sec. 2–513. Buyer's Right to Inspection of Goods. (1) Unless otherwise agreed and subject to subsection (3), where goods are tendered or delivered or identified to the contract for sale, the buyer has a right before payment or acceptance to inspect them at any reasonable place and time and in any reasonable manner. When the seller is required or authorized to send the goods to the buyer, the inspection may be after their arrival.

(2) Expenses of inspection must be borne by the buyer but may be recovered from the seller if the goods do not conform and are rejected.

(3) Unless otherwise agreed and subject to the provisions of this Article on C.I.F. contracts (subsection (3) of Section 2–321), the buyer is not entitled to inspect the goods before payment of the price when the contract provides

(*a*) for delivery "C.O.D." or on other like terms; or

(*b*) for payment against documents of title, except where such payment is due only after the goods are to become available for inspection.

(4) A place or method of inspection fixed by the parties is presumed to be exclusive but unless otherwise expressly agreed it does not postpone identification or shift the place for delivery or for passing the risk of loss. If compliance becomes impossible, inspection shall be as provided in this section unless the place or method fixed was clearly intended as an indispensable condition failure of which avoids the contract.

Sec. 2—514. When Documents Deliverable on Acceptance; When on Payment. Unless otherwise agreed documents against which a draft is drawn are to be delivered to the drawee on acceptance of the draft if it is payable more than three days after presentment; otherwise, only on payment.

Sec. 2—515. Preserving Evidence of Goods in Dispute. In furtherance of the adjustment of any claim or dispute

(*a*) either party on reasonable notification to the other and for the purpose of ascertaining the facts and preserving evidence has the right to inspect, test and sample the goods including such of them as may be in the possession or control of the other; and

(*b*) the parties may agree to a third party inspection or survey to determine the conformity or condition of the goods and may agree that the findings shall be binding upon them in any subsequent litigation or adjustment.

PART VI

BREACH, REPUDIATION AND EXCUSE

Sec. 2—601. Buyer's Rights on Improper Delivery. Subject to the provisions of this Article on breach in installment contracts (Section 2—612) and unless otherwise agreed under the sections on contractual limitations of remedy (Sections 2—718 and 2—719), if the goods or the tender of delivery fail in any respect to conform to the contract, the buyer may

(*a*) reject the whole; or

(*b*) accept the whole; or

(*c*) accept any commercial unit or units and reject the rest.

Sec. 2—602. Manner and Effect of Rightful Rejection. (1) Rejection of goods must be within a reasonable time after their delivery or tender. It is ineffective unless the buyer seasonably notifies the seller.

(2) Subject to the provisions of the two following sections on rejected goods (Sections 2—603 and 2—604),

(*a*) after rejection any exercise of ownership by the buyer with respect to any commercial unit is wrongful as against the seller; and

(*b*) if the buyer has before rejection taken physical possession of goods in which he does not have a security interest under the provisions of this Article (subsection (3) of Section 2—711), he is under a duty after rejection to hold them with reasonable care at the seller's disposition for a time sufficient to permit the seller to remove them; but

(*c*) the buyer has no further obligations with regard to goods rightfully rejected.

(3) The seller's rights with respect to goods wrongfully rejected are governed by the provisions of this Article on Seller's remedies in general (Section 2—703).

Sec. 2—603. Merchant Buyer's Duties as to Rightfully Rejected Goods. (1) Subject to any security interest in the buyer (subsection (3) of Section 2—711), when the seller has no agent or place of business at the market of rejection a merchant buyer is under a duty after rejection of goods in his possession or control to follow any reasonable instructions received from the seller with respect to the goods and in the absence of such instructions to make reasonable efforts to sell them for the seller's account if they are perishable or threaten to decline in value speedily. Instructions are not reasonable if on demand indemnity for expenses is not forthcoming.

(2) When the buyer sells goods under subsection (1), he is entitled to reimbursement from the seller or out of the proceeds for reasonable expenses of caring for and selling them, and if the expenses include no selling commission then to such commission as is usual in the trade or if there is none to a reasonable sum not exceeding ten per cent on the gross proceeds.

(3) In complying with this section the buyer is held only to good faith and good faith conduct hereunder is neither acceptance nor conversion nor the basis of an action for damages.

Sec. 2—604. Buyer's Options as to Salvage of Rightfully Rejected Goods. Subject to the provisions of the immediately preceding section on perishables if the seller gives no instructions within a reasonable time after notification of rejection the buyer may store the rejected goods for the seller's account or reship them to him or resell them for the seller's account with reimbursement as provided in the preceding section. Such action is not acceptance or conversion.

Sec. 2—605. Waiver of Buyer's Objections by Failure to Particularize. (1) The buyer's failure to state in connection with rejection a particular defect which is ascertainable by reasonable inspection precludes him from relying on the unstated defect to justify rejection or to establish breach

(a) where the seller could have cured it if stated seasonably; or

(b) between merchants when the seller has after rejection made a request in writing for a full and final written statement of all defects on which the buyer proposes to rely.

(2) Payment against documents made without reservation of rights precludes recovery of the payment for defects apparent on the face of the documents.

Sec. 2—606. What Constitutes Acceptance of Goods. (1) Acceptance of goods occurs when the buyer

(a) after a reasonable opportunity to inspect the goods signifies to the seller that the goods are conforming or that he will take or retain them in spite of their nonconformity; or

(b) fails to make an effective rejection (subsection (1) of Section 2—602), but such acceptance does not occur until the buyer has had a reasonable opportunity to inspect them; or

(c) does any act inconsistent with the seller's ownership; but if such act is wrongful as against the seller it is an acceptance only if ratified by him.

(2) Acceptance of a part of any commercial unit is acceptance of that entire unit.

Sec. 2—607. Effect of Acceptance; Notice of Breach; Burden of Establishing Breach After Acceptance; Notice of Claim or Litigation to Person Answerable Over. (1) The buyer must pay at the contract rate for any goods accepted.

(2) Acceptance of goods by the buyer precludes rejection of the goods accepted and if made with knowledge of a non-conformity cannot be revoked because of it unless the acceptance was on the reasonable assumption that the non-conformity would be seasonably cured but acceptance does not of itself impair any other remedy provided by this Article for non-conformity.

(3) Where a tender has been accepted

(a) the buyer must within a reasonable time after he discovers or should have discovered any breach notify the seller of breach or be barred from any remedy; and

(b) if the claim is one for infringement or the like (subsection (3) of Section 2—312) and the buyer is sued as a result of such a breach he must so notify the seller within a reasonable time after he receives notice of the litigation or be barred from any remedy over for liability established by the litigation.

(4) The burden is on the buyer to establish any breach with respect to the goods accepted.

(5) Where the buyer is sued for breach of a warranty or other obligation for which his seller is answerable over

(a) he may give his seller written notice of the litigation. If the notice states that the seller may come in and defend and that if the seller does not do so he will be bound in any action against him by his buyer by any determination of fact common to the two litigations, then unless the seller after seasonable receipt of the notice does come in and defend he is so bound.

(b) if the claim is one for infringement or the like (subsection (3) of Section 2—312) the original seller may demand in writing that his buyer turn over to him control of the litigation including settlement or else be barred from any remedy over and if he also agrees to bear all expense and to satisfy any adverse judgment, then unless the buyer after seasonable receipt of the demand does turn over control the buyer is so barred.

(6) The provisions of subsections (3), (4) and (5) apply to any obligation of a buyer to hold the seller harmless against infringement or the like (subsection (3) of Section 2—312).

Sec. 2—608. Revocation of Acceptance in Whole or in Part. (1) The buyer may revoke his acceptance of a lot or commercial unit whose non-conformity substantially impairs its value to him if he has accepted it

(a) on the reasonable assumption that its non-conformity would be cured and it has not been seasonably cured; or

(b) without discovery of such non-conformity if his acceptance was reasonably induced either by the difficulty of discovery before acceptance or by the seller's assurances.

(2) Revocation of acceptance must occur within a reasonable time after the buyer discovers or should have discovered the ground for it and before any substantial change in condition of the goods which is not caused by their own defects. It is not effective until the buyer notifies the seller of it.

(3) A buyer who so revokes has the same rights and duties with regard to the goods involved as if he had rejected them.

Sec. 2—609. Right to Adequate Assurance of Performance. (1) A contract for sale imposes an obligation on each party that the other's expectation of receiving due performance will not be impaired. When reasonable grounds for insecurity arise with respect to the performance of either party the other may in writing demand adequate assurance of due performance and until he receives such assurance may if commercially reasonable suspend any performance for which he has not already received the agreed return.

(2) Between merchants the reasonableness of grounds for insecurity and the adequacy of any assurance offered shall be determined according to commercial standards.

(3) Acceptance of any improper delivery or payment does not prejudice the aggrieved party's right to demand adequate assurance of future performance.

(4) After receipt of a justified demand failure to provide within a reasonable time not exceeding thirty days such assurance of due performance as is adequate under the circumstances of the particular case is a repudiation of the contract.

Sec. 2—610. Anticipatory Repudiation. When either party repudiates the contract with respect to a performance not yet due the loss of which will substantially impair the value of the contract to the other, the aggrieved party may

(a) for a commercially reasonable time await performance by the repudiating party; or

(b) resort to any remedy for breach (Section 2—703 or Section 2—711), even though he has notified the repudiating party that he would await the latter's performance and has urged retraction; and (*c*) in either case suspend his own performance or proceed in accordance with the provisions of this Article on the seller's right to identify goods to the contract notwithstanding breach or to salvage unfinished goods (Section 2—704).

Sec. 2—611. Retraction of Anticipatory Repudiation. (1) Until the repudiating party's next performance is due he can retract his repudiation unless the aggrieved party has since the repudiation cancelled or materially changed his position or otherwise indicated that he considers the repudiation final.

(2) Retraction may be by any method which clearly indicates to the aggrieved party that the repudiating party intends to perform, but must include any assurance justifiably demanded under the provisions of this Article (Section 2—609).

(3) Retraction reinstates the repudiating party's rights under the contract with due excuse and allowance to the aggrieved party for any delay occasioned by the repudiation.

Sec. 2—612. "Installment Contract"; Breach. (1) An "installment contract" is one which requires or authorizes the delivery of goods in separate lots to be separately accepted, even though the contract contains a clause "each delivery is a separate contract" or its equivalent.

(2) The buyer may reject any installment which is non-conforming if the non-conformity substantially impairs the value of that installment and cannot be cured or if the non-conformity is a defect in the required documents; but if the non-conformity does not fall within subsection (3) and the seller gives adequate assurance of its cure the buyer must accept that installment.

(3) Whenever non-conformity or default with respect to one or more installments substantially impairs the value of the whole contract there is a breach of the whole. But the aggrieved party reinstates the contract if he accepts a non-conforming installment without seasonably notifying of cancellation or if he brings an action with respect only to past installments or demands performance as to future installments.

Sec. 2—613. Casualty to Identified Goods. Where the contract requires for its performance goods identified when the contract is made, and the goods suffer casualty without fault of either party before the risk of loss passes to the buyer, or in a proper case under a "no arrival, no sale" term (Section 2—324) then

(*a*) if the loss is total the contract is avoided; and

(*b*) if the loss is partial or the goods have so deteriorated as no longer to conform to the contract the buyer may nevertheless demand inspection and at his option either treat the contract as avoided or accept the goods with due allowance from the contract price for the deterioration or the deficiency in quantity but without further right against the seller.

Sec. 2—614. Substituted Performance. (1) Where without fault of either party the agreed berthing, loading, or unloading facilities fail or an agreed type of carrier becomes unavailable or the agreed manner of delivery otherwise becomes commercially impracticable but a commercially reasonable substitute is available, such substitute performance must be tendered and accepted.

(2) If the agreed means or manner of payment fails because of domestic or foreign governmental regulation, the seller may withhold or stop delivery unless the buyer provides a means or manner of payment which is commercially a substantial equivalent. If delivery has already been taken, payment by the means or in the manner provided by the regulation discharges the buyer's obligation unless the regulation is discriminatory, oppressive or predatory.

Sec. 2—615. Excuse by Failure of Presupposed Conditions. Except so far as a seller may have assumed a greater obligation and subject to the preceding section on substituted performance:

(*a*) Delay in delivery or non-delivery in whole or in part by a seller who complies with paragraphs (*b*) and (*c*) is not a breach of his duty under a contract for sale if performance as agreed has been made impracticable by the occurrence of a contingency the non-occurrence of which was a basic assumption on which the contract was made or by compliance in good faith with any applicable foreign or domestic governmental regulation or order whether or not it later proves to be invalid.

(*b*) Where the causes mentioned in paragraph (*a*) affect only a part of the seller's capacity to perform, he must allocate production and deliveries among his customers but may at his option include regular customers not then under contract as well as his own requirements for further manufacture. He may so allocate in any manner which is fair and reasonable.

(*c*) The seller must notify the buyer seasonably that there will be delay or non-delivery and, when allocation is required under paragraph (*b*), of the estimated quota thus made available for the buyer.

Sec. 2—616. Procedure on Notice Claiming Excuse. (1) Where the buyer receives notification of a material or indefinite delay or an allocation justified under the preceding section he may by written notification to the seller as to any delivery concerned, and where the prospective deficiency substantially impairs the value of the whole contract under the provisions of this Article relating to breach of installment contracts (Section 2—612), then also as to the whole,

(*a*) terminate and thereby discharge any unexecuted portion of the contract; or

(*b*) modify the contract by agreeing to take his available quota in substitution.

(2) If after receipt of such notification from the seller the buyer fails so to modify the contract within a reasonable time not exceeding thirty days the contract lapses with respect to any deliveries affected.

(3) The provisions of this section may not be negated by agreement except in so far as the seller has assumed a greater obligation under the preceding section.

PART VII

REMEDIES

Sec. 2—701. Remedies for Breach of Collateral Contracts Not Impaired. Remedies for breach of any obligation or promise collateral or ancillary to a contract for sale are not impaired by the provisions of this Article.

Sec. 2—702. Seller's Remedies on Discovery of Buyer's Insolvency. (1) Where the seller discovers the buyer to be insolvent he may refuse delivery except for cash including payment for all goods theretofore delivered under the contract, and stop delivery under this Article (Section 2—705).

(2) Where the seller discovers that the buyer has received goods on credit while insolvent he may reclaim the goods upon demand made within ten days after the receipt, but if misrepresentation of solvency has been made to the particular seller in writing within three months before delivery the ten day limitation does not apply. Except as provided in this subsection the seller may not base a right to reclaim goods on the buyer's fraudulent or innocent misrepresentation of solvency or of intent to pay.

(3) The seller's right to reclaim under subsection (2) is subject to the rights of a buyer in ordinary course or other good faith purchaser or lien creditor under this Article (Section 2—403). Successful reclamation of goods excludes all other remedies with respect to them.

Sec. 2—703. Seller's Remedies in General. Where the buyer wrongfully rejects or revokes acceptance of goods or fails to make a payment due on or before delivery or repudiates with respect to a part or the whole, then with respect to any goods directly affected and, if the breach is of the whole contract (Section 2—612), then also with respect to the whole undelivered balance, the aggrieved seller may

(*a*) withhold delivery of such goods;

(*b*) stop delivery by any bailee as hereafter provided (Section 2—705);

(*c*) proceed under the next section respecting goods still unidentified to the contract;

(*d*) resell and recover damages as hereafter provided (Section 2—706);

(*e*) recover damages for non-acceptance (Section 2—708) or in a proper case the price (Section 2—709);

(*f*) cancel.

Sec. 2—704. Seller's Right to Identify Goods to the Contract Notwithstanding Breach or to Salvage Unfinished Goods. (1) An aggrieved seller under the preceding section may

(*a*) identify to the contract conforming goods not already identified if at the time he learned of the breach they are in his possession or control;

(*b*) treat as the subject of resale goods which have demonstrably been intended for the particular contract even though those goods are unfinished.

(2) Where the goods are unfinished an aggrieved seller may in the exercise of reasonable commercial judgment for the purposes of avoiding loss and of effective realization either complete the manufacture and wholly identify the goods to the contract or cease manufacture and resell for scrap or salvage value or proceed in any other reasonable manner.

Sec. 2—705. Seller's Stoppage of Delivery in Transit or Otherwise. (1) The seller may stop delivery of goods in the possession of a carrier or other bailee when he discovers the buyer to be insolvent (Section 2—702) and may stop delivery of carload, truckload, planeload or larger shipments of express or freight when the buyer repudiates or fails to make a payment due before delivery or if for any other reason the seller has a right to withhold or reclaim the goods.

(2) As against such buyer the seller may stop delivery until

(*a*) receipt of the goods by the buyer; or

(*b*) acknowledgment to the buyer by any bailee of the goods except a carrier that the bailee holds the goods for the buyer; or

(*c*) such acknowledgment to the buyer by a carrier by reshipment or as warehouseman; or

(*d*) negotiation to the buyer of any negotiable document of title covering the goods.

(3) (*a*) To stop delivery the seller must so notify as to enable the bailee by reasonable diligence to prevent delivery of the goods.

(*b*) After such notification the bailee must hold and deliver the goods according to the directions of the seller but the seller is liable to the bailee for any ensuing charges or damages.

(*c*) If a negotiable document of title has been issued for goods the bailee is not obliged to obey a notification to stop until surrender of the document.

(*d*) A carrier who has issued a non-negotiable bill of lading is not obliged to obey a notification to stop received from a person other than the consignor.

Sec. 2—706. Seller's Resale Including Contract for Resale. (1) Under the conditions stated in Section 2—703 on seller's remedies, the seller may resell the goods concerned or the undelivered balance thereof. Where the resale is made in good faith and in a commercially reasonable manner the seller may recover the difference between the resale price and the contract price together with any incidental damages allowed under the provisions of this Article (Section 2—710), but less expenses saved in consequence of the buyer's breach.

(2) Except as otherwise provided in subsection (3) or unless otherwise agreed resale may be at public or private sale including sale by way of one or more contracts to sell or of identification to an existing contract of the seller. Sale may be as a unit or in parcels and at any time and place and on any terms but every aspect of the sale including the method, manner, time, place and terms must be commercially reasonable. The resale must be reasonably identified as referring to the broken contract, but it is not necessary that the goods be in existence or that any or all of them have been identified to the contract before the breach.

(3) Where the resale is at private sale the seller must give the buyer reasonable notification of his intention to resell.

(4) Where the resale is at public sale

(*a*) only identified goods can be sold except where there is a recognized market for a public sale of futures in goods of the kind; and

(*b*) it must be made at a usual place or market for public sale if one is reasonably available and except in the case of goods which are perishable or threaten to decline in value speedily the seller must give the buyer reasonable notice of the time and place of the resale; and

(*c*) if the goods are not to be within the view of those attending the sale the notification of sale must state the place where the goods are located and provide for their reasonable inspection by prospective bidders; and

(*d*) the seller may buy.

(5) A purchaser who buys in good faith at a resale takes the goods free of any rights of the original buyer even though the seller fails to comply with one or more of the requirements of this section.

(6) The seller is not accountable to the buyer for any profit made on any resale. A person in the position of a seller (Section 2—707) or a buyer who has rightfully rejected or justifiably revoked acceptance must account for any excess over the amount of his security interest, as hereinafter defined (subsection (3) of Section 2—711).

Sec. 2—707. "Person in the Position of a Seller." (1) A "person in the position of a seller" includes as against a principal an agent who has paid or become responsible for the price of goods on behalf of his principal or anyone who otherwise holds a security interest or other right in goods similar to that of a seller.

(2) A person in the position of a seller may as provided in this Article withhold or stop delivery (Section 2—705) and resell (Section 2—706) and recover incidental damages (Section 2—710).

Sec. 2—708. Seller's Damages for Non-acceptance or Repudiation. (1) Subject to subsection (2) and to the provisions of this Article with respect to proof of market price (Section 2—723), the measure of damages for non-acceptance or repudiation by the buyer is the difference between the market price at the time and place for tender and the unpaid contract price together with any incidental damages provided in this Article (Section 2—710), but less expenses saved in consequence of the buyer's breach.

(2) If the measure of damages provided in subsection (1) is inadequate to put the seller in as good a position as performance would have done then the measure of damages is the profit (including reasonable overhead) which the seller would have made from full performance by the buyer, together with any incidental damages provided in this Article (Section 2—710), due allowance for costs reasonably incurred and due credit for payments or proceeds or resale.

Sec. 2—709. Action for the Price. (1) When the buyer fails to pay the price as it becomes due the seller may recover, together with any incidental damages under the next section, the price

(*a*) of goods accepted or of conforming goods lost or damaged within a commercially reasonable time after risk of their loss has passed to the buyer; and

(*b*) of goods identified to the contract if the seller is unable after reasonable effort to resell them at a reasonable price or the circumstances reasonably indicate that such effort will be unavailing.

(2) Where the seller sues for the price he must hold for the buyer any goods which have been identified to the contract and are still in his control except that if resale becomes possible he may resell them at any time prior to the collection of the judgment. The net proceeds of any such resale must be credited to the buyer and payment of the judgment entitles him to any goods not resold.

(3) After the buyer has wrongfully rejected or revoked acceptance of the goods or has failed to make a payment due or has repudiated (Section 2—610), a seller

who is held not entitled to the price under this section shall nevertheless be awarded damages for non-acceptance under the preceding section.

Sec. 2—710. Seller's Incidental Damages. Incidental damages to an aggrieved seller include any commercially reasonable charges, expenses or commissions incurred in stopping delivery, in the transportation, care and custody of goods after the buyer's breach, in connection with return or resale of the goods or otherwise resulting from the breach.

Sec. 2—711. Buyer's Remedies in General; Buyer's Security Interest in Rejected Goods. (1) Where the seller fails to make delivery or repudiates or the buyer rightfully rejects or justifiably revokes acceptance then with respect to any goods involved, and with respect to the whole if the breach goes to the whole contract (Section 2—612), the buyer may cancel and whether or not he has done so may in addition to recovering so much of the price as has been paid

(*a*) "cover" and have damages under the next section as to all the goods affected whether or not they have been identified to the contract; or

(*b*) recover damages for non-delivery as provided in this Article (Section 2—713).

(2) Where the seller fails to deliver or repudiates the buyer may also

(*a*) if the goods have been identified recover them as provided in this Article (Section 2—502); or

(*b*) in a proper case obtain specific performance or replevy the goods as provided in this Article (Section 2—716).

(3) On rightful rejection or justifiable revocation of acceptance a buyer has a security interest in goods in his possession or control for any payments made on their price and any expenses reasonably incurred in their inspection, receipt, transportation, care and custody and may hold such goods and resell them in like manner as an aggrieved seller (Section 2—706).

Sec. 2—712. "Cover"; Buyer's Procurement of Substitute Goods. (1) After a breach within the preceding section the buyer may "cover" by making in good faith and without unreasonable delay any reasonable purchase of or contract to purchase goods in substitution for those due from the seller.

(2) The buyer may recover from the seller as damages the difference between the cost of cover and the contract price together with any incidental or consequential damages as hereinafter defined (Section 2—715), but less expenses saved in consequences of the seller's breach.

(3) Failure of the buyer to effect cover within this section does not bar him from any other remedy.

Sec. 2—713. Buyer's Damages for Non-Delivery or Repudiation. (1) Subject to the provisions of this Article with respect to proof of market price (Section 2—723), the measure of damages for non-delivery or repudiation by the seller is the difference between the market price at the time when the buyer learned of the breach and the contract price together with any incidental and consequential damages provided in this Article (Section 2—715), but less expenses saved in consequence of the seller's breach.

(2) Market price is to be determined as of the place for tender or, in cases of rejection after arrival or revocation of acceptance, as of the place of arrival.

Sec. 2—714. Buyer's Damages for Breach in Regard to Accepted Goods. (1) Where the buyer has accepted goods and given notification (subsection (3) of Section 2—607) he may recover as damages for any non-conformity of tender the loss resulting in the ordinary course of events from the seller's breach as determined in any manner which is reasonable.

(2) The measure of damages for breach of warranty is the difference at the time and place of acceptance between the value of the goods accepted and the value they would have had if they had been as warranted, unless special circumstances show proximate damages of a different amount.

(3) In a proper case any incidental and consequential damages under the next section may also be recovered.

Sec. 2—715. Buyer's Incidental and Consequential Damages. (1) Incidental damages resulting from the seller's breach include expenses reasonably incurred in inspection, receipt, transportation and care and custody of goods rightfully rejected, any commercially reasonable charges, expenses or commissions in connection with effecting cover and any other reasonable expense incident to the delay or other breach.

(2) Consequential damages resulting from the seller's breach include

(a) any loss resulting from general or particular requirements and needs of which the seller at the time of contracting had reason to know and which could not reasonably be prevented by cover or otherwise; and

(b) injury to person or property proximately resulting from any breach of warranty.

Sec. 2—716. Buyer's Right to Specific Performance or Replevin. (1) Specific performance may be decreed where the goods are unique or in other proper circumstances.

(2) The decree for specific performance may include such terms and conditions as to payment of the price, damages, or other relief as the court may deem just.

(3) The buyer has a right of replevin for goods identified to the contract if after reasonable effort he is unable to effect cover for such goods or the circumstances reasonably indicate that such effort will be unavailing or if the goods have been shipped under reservation and satisfaction of the security interest in them has been made or tendered.

Sec. 2—717. Deduction of Damages From the Price. The buyer on notifying the seller of his intention to do so may deduct all or any part of the damages resulting from any breach of the contract from any part of the price still due under the same contract.

Sec. 2—718. Liquidation or Limitation of Damages; Deposits. (1) Damages for breach by either party may be liquidated in the agreement but only at an amount which is reasonable in the light of the anticipated or actual harm caused by the breach, the difficulties of proof of loss, and the inconvenience or nonfeasibility of otherwise obtaining an adequate remedy. A term fixing unreasonably large liquidated damages is void as a penalty.

(2) Where the seller justifiably withholds delivery of goods because of the buyer's breach, the buyer is entitled to restitution of any amount by which the sum of his payments exceeds

(a) the amount to which the seller is entitled by virtue of terms liquidating the seller's damages in accordance with subsection (1), or

(b) in the absence of such terms, twenty per cent of the value of the total performance for which the buyer is obligated under the contract or $500, whichever is smaller.

(3) The buyer's right to restitution under subsection (2) is subject to offset to the extent that the seller establishes

(a) a right to recover damages under the provisions of this Article other than subsection (1), and

(b) the amount or value of any benefits received by the buyer directly or indirectly by reason of the contract.

(4) Where a seller has received payment in goods their reasonable value or the proceeds of their resale shall be treated as payments for the purposes of subsection (2); but if the seller has notice of the buyer's breach before reselling goods received in part performance, his resale is subject to the conditions laid down in this Article on resale by an aggrieved seller (Section 2—706).

Sec. 2—719. Contractual Modification or Limitation of Remedy. (1) Subject to the provisions of subsections (2) and (3) of this section and of the preceding section on liquidation and limitation of damages,

(a) the agreement may provide for remedies in addition to or in substitution for those provided in this Article and may limit or alter the measure of damages recoverable under this Article, as by limiting the buyer's remedies to return of the goods and repayment of the price or to repair and replacement of non-conforming goods or parts; and

(*b*) resort to a remedy as provided is optional unless the remedy is expressly agreed to be exclusive, in which case it is the sole remedy.

(2) Where circumstances cause an exclusive or limited remedy to fail of its essential purpose, remedy may be had as provided in this Act.

(3) Consequential damages may be limited or excluded unless the limitation or exclusion is unconscionable. Limitation of consequential damages for injury to the person in the case of consumer goods is prima facie unconscionable but limitation of damages where the loss is commercial is not.

Sec. 2—720. Effect of "Cancellation" or "Rescission" on Claims for Antecedent Breach. Unless the contrary intention clearly appears, expressions of "cancellation" or "rescission" of the contract or the like shall not be construed as a renunciation or discharge of any claim in damages for an antecedent breach.

Sec. 2—721. Remedies for Fraud. Remedies for material misrepresentation or fraud include all remedies available under this Article for non-fraudulent breach. Neither rescission or a claim for rescission of the contract for sale nor rejection or return of the goods shall bar or be deemed inconsistent with a claim for damages or other remedy.

Sec. 2—722. Who Can Sue Third Parties for Injury to Goods. Where a third party so deals with goods which have been identified to a contract for sale as to cause actionable injury to a party to that contract

(*a*) a right of action against the third party is in either party to the contract for sale who has title to or a security interest or a special property or an insurable interest in the goods; and if the goods have been destroyed or converted a right of action is also in the party who either bore the risk of loss under the contract for sale or has since the injury assumed that risk as against the other;

(*b*) if at the time of the injury the party plaintiff did not bear the risk of loss as against the other party to the contract for sale and there is no arrangement between them for disposition of the recovery, his suit or settlement is, subject to his own interest, as a fiduciary for the other party to the contract;

(*c*) either party may with the consent of the other sue for the benefit of whom it may concern.

Sec. 2—723. Proof of Market Price: Time and Place. (1) If an action based on anticipatory repudiation comes to trial before the time for performance with respect to some or all of the goods, any damages based on market price (Section 2—708 or Section 2—713) shall be determined according to the price of such goods prevailing at the time when the aggrieved party learned of the repudiation.

(2) If evidence of a price prevailing at the times or places described in this Article is not readily available the price prevailing within any reasonable time before or after the time described or at any other place which in commercial judgment or under usage of trade would serve as a reasonable substitute for the one described may be used, making any proper allowance for the cost of transporting the goods to or from such other place.

(3) Evidence of a relevant price prevailing at a time or place other than the one described in this Article offered by one party is not admissible unless and until he has given the other party such notice as the court finds sufficient to prevent unfair surprise.

Sec. 2—724. Admissibility of Market Quotations. Whenever the prevailing price or value of any goods regularly bought and sold in any established commodity market is in issue, reports in official publications or trade journals or in newspapers or periodicals of general circulation published as the reports of such market shall be admissible in evidence. The circumstances of the preparation of such a report may be shown to affect its weight but not its admissibility.

Sec. 2—725. Statute of Limitations in Contracts for Sale. (1) An action for breach of any contract for sale must be commenced within four years after the cause of action has accrued. By the original agreement the parties may reduce the period of limitation to not less than one year but may not extend it.

(2) A cause of action accrues when the breach occurs, regardless of the aggrieved party's lack of knowledge of the breach. A breach of warranty occurs when tender of delivery is made, except that where a warranty explicitly extends to future performance of the goods and discovery of the breach must await the time of such performance the cause of action accrues when the breach is or should have been discovered.

(3) Where an action commenced within the time limited by subsection (1) is so terminated as to leave available a remedy by another action for the same breach such other action may be commenced after the expiration of the time limited and within six months after the termination of the first action unless the termination resulted from voluntary discontinuance or from dismissal for failure or neglect to prosecute.

(4) This section does not alter the law on tolling of the statute of limitations nor does it apply to causes of action which have accrued before this Act becomes effective.

ARTICLE III

COMMERCIAL PAPER

PART I

SHORT TITLE, FORM AND INTERPRETATION

Sec. 3—101. Short Title. This Article shall be known and may be cited as Uniform Commercial Code—Commercial Paper.

Sec. 3—102. Definitions and Index of Definitions. (1) In this Article unless the context otherwise requires

(*a*) "Issue" means the first delivery of an instrument to a holder or a remitter.

(*b*) An "order" is a direction to pay and must be more than an authorization or request. It must identify the person to pay with reasonable certainty. It may be addressed to one or more such persons jointly or in the alternative but not in succession.

(*c*) A "promise" is an undertaking to pay and must be more than an acknowledgment of an obligation.

(*d*) "Secondary party" means a drawer or endorser.

(*e*) "Instrument" means a negotiable instrument.

(2) Other definitions applying to this Article and the sections in which they appear are:

"Acceptance." Section 3—410.

"Accommodation party." Section 3—415.

"Alteration." Section 3—407.

"Certificate of deposit." Section 3—104.

"Certification." Section 3—411.

"Check." Section 3—104.

"Definite time." Section 3—109.

"Dishonor." Section 3—507.

"Draft." Section 3—104.

"Holder in due course." Section 3—302.

"Negotiation." Section 3—202.

"Note." Section 3—104.
"Notice of dishonor." Section 3—508.
"On demand." Section 3—108.
"Presentment." Section 3—504.
"Protest." Section 3—509.
"Restrictive Indorsement." Section 3—205.
"Signature." Section 3—401.

(3) The following definitions in other Articles apply to this Article:
"Account." Section 4—104.
"Banking Day." Section 4—104.
"Clearing house." Section 4—104.
"Collecting bank." Section 4—105.
"Customer." Section 4—104.
"Depositary Bank." Section 4—105.
"Documentary Draft." Section 4—104.
"Intermediary Bank." Section 4—105.
"Item." Section 4—104.
"Midnight deadline." Section 4—104.
"Payor bank." Section 4—105.

(4) In addition Article 1 contains general definitions and principles of construction and interpretation applicable throughout this Article.

Sec. 3—103. Limitations on Scope of Article. (1) This Article does not apply to money, documents of title or investment securities.

(2) The provisions of this Article are subject to the provisions of the Article on Bank Deposits and Collections (Article 4) and Secured Transactions (Article 9).

Sec. 3—104. Form of Negotiable Instruments; "Draft"; "Check"; "Certificate of Deposit"; "Note." (1) Any writing to be a negotiable instrument within this Article must

(a) be signed by the maker or drawer; and

(b) contain an unconditional promise or order to pay a sum certain in money and no other promise, order, obligation or power given by the maker or drawer except as authorized by this Article; and

(c) be payable on demand or at a definite time; and

(d) be payable to order or to bearer.

(2) A writing which complies with the requirements of this section is

(a) a "draft" ("bill of exchange") if it is an order;

(b) a "check" if it is a draft drawn on a bank and payable on demand;

(c) a "certificate of deposit" if it is an acknowledgment by a bank of receipt of money with an engagement to repay it;

(d) a "note" if it is a promise other than a certificate of deposit.

(3) As used in other Articles of this Act, and as the context may require, the terms "draft," "check," "certificate of deposit" and "note" may refer to instruments which are not negotiable within this Article as well as to instruments which are so negotiable.

Sec. 3—105. When Promise or Order Unconditional. (1) A promise or order otherwise unconditional is not made conditional by the fact that the instrument

(a) is subject to implied or constructive conditions; or

(b) states its consideration, whether performed or promised, or the transaction which gave rise to the instrument, or that the promise or order is made or the instrument matures in accordance with or "as per" such transaction; or

(c) refers to or states that it arises out of a separate agreement or refers to a separate agreement for rights as to prepayment or acceleration; or

(d) states that it is drawn under a letter of credit; or

(e) states that it is secured, whether by mortgage, reservation of title or otherwise; or (*f*) indicates a particular account to be debited or any other fund or source from which reimbursement is expected; or

(*g*) is limited to payment out of a particular fund or the proceeds of a particular source, if the instrument is issued by a government or governmental agency or unit; or

(*h*) is limited to payment out of the entire assets of a partnership, unincorporated association, trust or estate by or on behalf of which the instrument is issued.

(2) A promise or order is not unconditional if the instrument

(*a*) states that it is subject to or governed by any other agreement; or

(*b*) states that it is to be paid only out of a particular fund or source except as provided in this section.

Sec. 3—106. Sum Certain. (1) The sum payable is a sum certain even though it is to be paid

(*a*) with stated interest or by stated installments; or

(*b*) with stated different rates of interest before and after default or a specified date; or

(*c*) with a stated discount or addition if paid before or after the date fixed for payment; or

(*d*) with exchange or less exchange, whether at a fixed rate or at the current rate; or

(*e*) with costs of collection or an attorney's fee or both upon default.

(2) Nothing in this section shall validate any term which is otherwise illegal.

Sec. 3—107. Money. (1) An instrument is payable in money if the medium of exchange in which it is payable is money at the time the instrument is made. An instrument payable in "currency" or "current funds" is payable in money.

(2) A promise or order to pay a sum stated in a foreign currency is for a sum certain in money and, unless a different medium of payment is specified in the instrument, may be satisfied by payment of that number of dollars which the stated foreign currency will purchase at the buying sight rate for that currency on the day on which the instrument is payable or, if payable on demand, on the day of demand. If such an instrument specifies a foreign currency as the medium of payment the instrument is payable in that currency.

Sec. 3—108. Payable on Demand. Instruments payable on demand include those payable at sight or on presentation and those in which no time for payment is stated.

Sec. 3—109. Definite Time. (1) An instrument is payable at a definite time if by its terms it is payable

(*a*) on or before a stated date or at a fixed period after a stated date; or

(*b*) at a fixed period after sight; or

(*c*) at a definite time subject to any acceleration; or

(*d*) at a definite time subject to extension at the option of the holder, or to extension to a further definite time at the option of the maker or acceptor or automatically upon or after a specified act or event.

(2) An instrument which by its terms is otherwise payable only upon an act or event uncertain as to time of occurrence is not payable at a definite time even though the act or event has occurred.

Sec. 3—110. Payable to Order. (1) An instrument is payable to order when by its terms it is payable to the order or assigns of any person therein specified with reasonable certainty, or to him or his order, or when it is conspicuously designated on its face as "exchange" or the like and names a payee. It may be payable to the order of

(*a*) the maker or drawer; or

(*b*) the drawee; or

(*c*) a payee who is not maker, drawer or drawee; or

(*d*) two or more payees together or in the alternative; or

(*e*) an estate, trust or fund, in which case it is payable to the order of the representative of such estate, trust or fund or his successors; or (*f*) an office, or an officer by his title as such in which case it is payable to the principal but the incumbent of the office or his successors may act as if he or they were the holder; or

(*g*) a partnership or unincorporated association, in which case it is payable to the partnership or association and may be indorsed or transferred by any person thereto authorized.

(2) An instrument not payable to order is not made so payable by such words as "payable upon return of this instrument properly indorsed."

(3) An instrument made payable both to order and to bearer is payable to order unless the bearer words are handwritten or typewritten.

Sec. 3—111. Payable to Bearer. An instrument is payable to bearer when by its terms it is payable to

(*a*) bearer or the order of bearer; or

(*b*) a specified person or bearer; or

(*c*) "cash" or the order of "cash," or any other indication which does not purport to designate a specific payee.

Sec. 3—112. Terms and Omissions Not Affecting Negotiability. (1) The negotiability of an instrument is not affected by

(*a*) the omission of a statement of any consideration or of the place where the instrument is drawn or payable; or

(*b*) a statement that collateral has been given to secure obligations either on the instrument or otherwise of an obligor on the instrument or that in the case of default on those obligations the holder may realize on or dispose of the collateral; or

(*c*) a promise or power to maintain or protect collateral or to give additional collateral; or

(*d*) a term authorizing a confession of judgment on the instrument if it is not paid when due; or

(*e*) a term purporting to waive the benefit of any law intended for the advantage or protection of any obligor; or

(*f*) a term in a draft providing that the payee by indorsing or cashing it acknowledges full satisfaction of an obligation of the drawer; or

(*g*) a statement in a draft drawn in a set of parts (Section 3—801) to the effect that the order is effective only if no other part has been honored.

(2) Nothing in this section shall validate any term which is otherwise illegal.

Sec. 3—113. Seal. An instrument otherwise negotiable is within this Article even though it is under a seal.

Sec. 3—114. Date, Antedating, Postdating. (1) The negotiability of an instrument is not affected by the fact that it is undated, antedated or postdated.

(2) Where an instrument is antedated or postdated the time when it is payable is determined by the stated date if the instrument is payable on demand or at a fixed period after date.

(3) Where the instrument or any signature thereon is dated, the date is presumed to be correct.

Sec. 3—115. Incomplete Instruments. (1) When a paper whose contents at the time of signing show that it is intended to become an instrument is signed while still incomplete in any necessary respect it cannot be enforced until completed, but when it is completed in accordance with authority given it is effective as completed.

(2) If the completion is unauthorized the rules as to material alteration apply (Section 3—407), even though the paper was not delivered by the maker or drawer; but the burden of establishing that any completion is unauthorized is on the party so asserting.

Sec. 3—116. Instruments Payable to Two or More Persons. An instrument payable to the order of two or more persons (*a*) if in the alternative is payable to any one of them and may be negotiated, discharged or enforced by any of them who has possession of it;

(*b*) if not in the alternative is payable to all of them and may be negotiated, discharged or enforced only by all of them.

Sec. 3—117. Instruments Payable With Words of Description. An instrument made payable to a named person with the addition of words describing him

(*a*) as agent or officer of a specified person is payable to his principal but the agent or officer may act as if he were the holder;

(*b*) as any other fiduciary for a specified person or purpose is payable to the payee and may be negotiated, discharged or enforced by him;

(*c*) in any other manner is payable to the payee unconditionally and the additional words are without effect on subsequent parties.

Sec. 3—118. Ambiguous Terms and Rules of Construction. The following rules apply to every instrument:

(*a*) Where there is doubt whether the instrument is a draft or a note the holder may treat it as either. A draft drawn on the drawer is effective as a note.

(*b*) Handwritten terms control typewritten and printed terms, and typewritten control printed.

(*c*) Words control figures except that if the words are ambiguous figures control.

(*d*) Unless otherwise specified a provision for interest means interest at the judgment rate at the place of payment from the date of the instrument, or if it is undated from the date of issue.

(*e*) Unless the instrument otherwise specifies two or more persons who sign as maker, acceptor or drawer or indorser and as a part of the same transaction are jointly and severally liable even though the instrument contains such words as "I promise to pay."

(*f*) Unless otherwise specified consent to extension authorizes a single extension for not longer than the original period. A consent to extension, expressed in the instrument, is binding on secondary parties and accommodation makers. A holder may not exercise his option to extend an instrument over the objection of a maker or acceptor or other party who in accordance with Section 3—604 tenders full payment when the instrument is due.

Sec. 3—119. Other Writings Affecting Instrument. (1) As between the obligor and his immediate obligee or any transferee the terms of an instrument may be modified or affected by any other written agreement executed as a part of the same transaction, except that a holder in due course is not affected by any limitation of his rights arising out of the separate written agreement if he had no notice of the limitation when he took the instrument.

(2) A separate agreement does not affect the negotiability of an instrument.

Sec. 3—120. Instruments "Payable Through" Bank. An instrument which states that it is "payable through" a bank or the like designates that bank as a collecting bank to make presentment but does not of itself authorize the bank to pay the instrument.

Sec. 3—121. Instruments Payable at Bank. Note: *If this Act is introduced in the Congress of the United States this section should be omitted. (States to select either alternative)*

Alternative A A note or acceptance which states that it is payable at a bank is the equivalent of a draft drawn on the bank payable when it falls due out of any funds of the maker or acceptor in current account or otherwise available for such payment.

Alternative B A note or acceptance which states that it is payable at a bank is not of itself an order or authorization to the bank to pay it.

Sec. 3—122. Accrual of Cause of Action. (1) A cause of action against a maker or an acceptor accrues

(*a*) in the case of a time instrument on the day after maturity;

(*b*) in the case of a demand instrument upon its date or, if no date is stated, on the date of issue.

(2) A cause of action against the obligor of a demand or time certificate of deposit accrues upon demand, but demand on a time certificate may not be made until on or after the date of maturity.

(3) A cause of action against a drawer of a draft or an indorser of any instrument accrues upon demand following dishonor of the instrument. Notice of dishonor is a demand.

(4) Unless an instrument provides otherwise, interest runs at the rate provided by law for a judgment

(a) in the case of a maker, acceptor or other primary obligor of a demand instrument, from the date of demand;

(b) in all other cases from the date of accrual of the cause of action.

PART II

TRANSFER AND NEGOTIATION

Sec. 3—201. Transfer: Right to Indorsement. (1) Transfer of an instrument vests in the transferee such rights as the transferor has therein, except that a transferee who has himself been a party to any fraud or illegality affecting the instrument or who as a prior holder had notice of a defense. or claim against it cannot improve his position by taking from a later holder in due course.

(2) A transfer of a security interest in an instrument vests the foregoing rights in the transferee to the extent of the interest transferred.

(3) Unless otherwise agreed any transfer for value of an instrument not then payable to bearer gives the transferee the specifically enforceable right to have the unqualified indorsement of the transferor. Negotiation takes effect only when the indorsement is made and until that time there is no presumption that the transferee is the owner.

Sec. 3—202. Negotiation. (1) Negotiation is the transfer of an instrument in such form that the transferee becomes a holder. If the instrument is payable to order it is negotiated by delivery with any necessary indorsement; if payable to bearer it is negotiated by delivery.

(2) An indorsement must be written by or on behalf of the holder and on the instrument or on a paper so firmly affixed thereto as to become a part thereof.

(3) An indorsement is effective for negotiation only when it conveys the entire instrument or any unpaid residue. If it purports to be of less it operates only as a partial assignment.

(4) Words of assignment, condition, waiver, guaranty, limitation or disclaimer of liability and the like accompanying an indorsement do not affect its character as an indorsement.

Sec. 3—203. Wrong or Misspelled Name. Where an instrument is made payable to a person under a misspelled name or one other than his own he may indorse in that name or his own or both; but signature in both names may be required by a person paying or giving value for the instrument.

Sec. 3—204. Special Indorsement; Blank Indorsement. (1) A special indorsement specifies the person to whom or to whose order it makes the instrument payable. Any instrument specially indorsed becomes payable to the order of the special indorsee and may be further negotiated only by his indorsement.

(2) An indorsement in blank specifies no particular indorsee and may consist of a mere signature. An instrument payable to order and indorsed in blank becomes payable to bearer and may be negotiated by delivery alone until specially indorsed.

(3) The holder may convert a blank indorsement into a special indorsement by writing over the signature of the indorser in blank any contract consistent with the character of the indorsement.

Sec. 3—205. Restrictive Indorsements. An indorsement is restrictive which either

(a) is conditional; or

(*b*) purports to prohibit further transfer of the instrument; or

(*c*) includes the words "for collection," "for deposit," "pay any bank," or like terms signifying a purpose of deposit or collection; or

(*d*) otherwise states that it is for the benefit or use of the indorser or of another person.

Sec. 3—206. Effect of Restrictive Indorsement. (1) No restrictive indorsement prevents further transfer or negotiation of the instrument.

(2) An intermediary bank, or a payor bank which is not the depository bank, is neither given notice nor otherwise affected by a restrictive indorsement of any person except the bank's immediate transferor or the person presenting for payment.

(3) Except for an intermediary bank, any transferee under an indorsement which is conditional or includes the words "for collection," "for deposit," "pay any bank," or like terms (subparagraphs (*a*) and (*c*) of Section 3—205) must pay or apply any value given by him for or on the security of the instrument consistently with the indorsement and to the extent that he does so he becomes a holder for value. In addition such transferee is a holder in due course if he otherwise complies with the requirements of Section 3—302 on what constitutes a holder in due course.

(4) The first taker under an indorsement for the benefit of the indorser or another person (subparagraph (*d*) of Section 3—205) must pay or apply any value given by him for or on the security of the instrument consistently with the indorsement and to the extent that he does so he becomes a holder for value. In addition such taker is a holder in due course if he otherwise complies with the requirements of Section 3—302 on what constitutes a holder in due course. A later holder for value is neither given notice nor otherwise affected by such restrictive indorsement unless he has knowledge that a fiduciary or other person has negotiated the instrument in any transaction for his own benefit or otherwise in breach of duty (subsection (2) of Section 3—304).

Sec. 3—207. Negotiation Effective Although It May Be Rescinded. (1) Negotiation is effective to transfer the instrument although the negotiation is

(*a*) made by an infant, a corporation exceeding its powers, or any other person without capacity; or

(*b*) obtained by fraud, duress or mistake of any kind; or

(*c*) part of an illegal transaction; or

(*d*) made in breach of duty.

(2) Except as against a subsequent holder in due course such negotiation is in an appropriate case subject to rescission, the declaration of a constructive trust or any other remedy permitted by law.

Sec. 3—208. Reacquisition. Where an instrument is returned to or reacquired by a prior party he may cancel any indorsement which is not necessary to his title and reissue or further negotiate the instrument, but any intervening party is discharged as against the reacquiring party and subsequent holders not in due course and if his indorsement has been cancelled is discharged as against subsequent holders in due course as well.

PART III

RIGHTS OF A HOLDER

Sec. 3—301. Rights of a Holder. The holder of an instrument whether or not he is the owner may transfer or negotiate it and, except as otherwise provided in Section 3—603 on payment or satisfaction, discharge it or enforce payment in his own name.

Sec. 3—302. Holder in Due Course. (1) A holder in due course is a holder who takes the instrument

(*a*) for value; and

(*b*) in good faith; and

(*c*) without notice that it is overdue or has been dishonored or of any defense against or claim to it on the part of any person.

(2) A payee may be a holder in due course.

(3) A holder does not become a holder in due course of an instrument:

(*a*) by purchase of it at judicial sale or by taking it under legal process; or

(*b*) by acquiring it in taking over an estate; or

(*c*) by purchasing it as part of a bulk transaction not in regular course of business of the transferor.

(4) A purchaser of a limited interest can be a holder in due course only to the extent of the interest purchased.

Sec. 3—303. Taking for Value. A holder takes the instrument for value

(*a*) to the extent that the agreed consideration has been performed or that he acquires a security interest in or a lien on the instrument otherwise than by legal process; or

(*b*) when he takes the instrument in payment of or as security for an antecedent claim against any person whether or not the claim is due; or

(*c*) when he gives a negotiable instrument for it or makes an irrevocable commitment to a third person.

Sec. 3—304. Notice to Purchaser. (1) The purchaser has notice of a claim or defense if

(*a*) the instrument is so incomplete, bears such visible evidence of forgery or alteration, or is otherwise so irregular as to call into question its validity, terms or ownership or to create an ambiguity as to the party to pay; or

(*b*) the purchaser has notice that the obligation of any party is voidable in whole or in part, or that all parties have been discharged.

(2) The purchaser has notice of a claim against the instrument when he has knowledge that a fiduciary has negotiated the instrument in payment of or as security for his own debt or in any transaction for his own benefit or otherwise in breach of duty.

(3) The purchaser has notice that an instrument is overdue if he has reason to know

(*a*) that any part of the principal amount is overdue or that there is an uncured default in payment of another instrument of the same series; or

(*b*) that acceleration of the instrument has been made; or

(*c*) that he is taking a demand instrument after demand has been made or more than a reasonable length of time after its issue. A reasonable time for a check drawn and payable within the states and territories of the United States and the District of Columbia is presumed to be thirty days.

(4) Knowledge of the following facts does not of itself give the purchaser notice of a defense or claim

(*a*) that the instrument is antedated or postdated;

(*b*) that it was issued or negotiated in return for an executory promise or accompanied by a separate agreement, unless the purchaser has notice that a defense or claim has arisen from the terms thereof;

(*c*) that any party has signed for accommodation;

(*d*) that an incomplete instrument has been completed, unless the purchaser has notice of any improper completion;

(*e*) that any person negotiating the instrument is or was a fiduciary;

(*f*) that there has been default in payment of interest on the instrument or in payment of any other instrument, except one of the same series.

(5) The filing or recording of a document does not of itself constitute notice within the provisions of this Article to a person who would otherwise be a holder in due course.

(6) To be effective notice must be received at such time and in such manner as to give a reasonable opportunity to act on it.

Sec. 3—305. Rights of a Holder in Due Course. To the extent that a holder is a holder in due course he takes the instrument free from

(1) all claims to it on the part of any person; and

(2) all defenses of any party to the instrument with whom the holder has not dealt except

(*a*) infancy, to the extent that it is a defense to a simple contract; and

(*b*) such other incapacity, or duress, or illegality of the transaction, as renders the obligation of the party a nullity; and

(*c*) such misrepresentation as has induced the party to sign the instrument with neither knowledge nor reasonable opportunity to obtain knowledge of its character or its essential terms; and

(*d*) discharge in insolvency proceedings; and

(*e*) any other discharge of which the holder has notice when he takes the instrument.

Sec. 3—306. Rights of One Not Holder in Due Course. Unless he has the rights of a holder in due course any person takes the instrument subject to

(*a*) all valid claims to it on the part of any person; and

(*b*) all defenses of any party which would be available in an action on a simple contract; and

(*c*) the defenses of want or failure of consideration, non-performance of any condition precedent, non-delivery, or delivery for a special purpose (Section 3—408); and

(*d*) the defense that he or a person through whom he holds the instrument acquired it by theft, or that payment or satisfaction to such holder would be inconsistent with the terms of a restrictive indorsement. The claim of any third person to the instrument is not otherwise available as a defense to any party liable thereon unless the third person himself defends the action for such party.

Sec. 3—307. Burden of Establishing Signatures, Defenses and Due Course. (1) Unless specifically denied in the pleadings each signature on an instrument is admitted. When the effectiveness of a signature is put in issue

(*a*) the burden of establishing it is on the party claiming under the signature; but

(*b*) the signature is presumed to be genuine or authorized except where the action is to enforce the obligation of a purported signer who has died or become incompetent before proof is required.

(2) When signatures are admitted or established, production of the instrument entitles a holder to recover on it unless the defendant establishes a defense.

(3) After it is shown that a defense exists a person claiming the rights of a holder in due course has the burden of establishing that he or some person under whom he claims is in all respects a holder in due course.

PART IV

LIABILITY OF PARTIES

Sec. 3—401. Signature. (1) No person is liable on an instrument unless his signature appears thereon.

(2) A signature is made by the use of any name, including any trade or assumed name, upon an instrument, or by any word or mark used in lieu of a written signature.

Sec. 3—402. Signature in Ambiguous Capacity. Unless the instrument clearly indicates that a signature is made in some other capacity it is an indorsement.

Sec. 3—403. Signature by Authorized Representative. (1) A signature may be made by an agent or other representative, and his authority to make it may be established as in other cases of representation. No particular form of appointment is necessary to establish such authority.

(2) An authorized representative who signs his own name to an instrument

(*a*) is personally obligated if the instrument neither names the person represented nor shows that the representative signed in a representative capacity;

(*b*) except as otherwise established between the immediate parties, is personally obligated if the instrument names the person represented but does not show that the representative signed in a representative capacity, or if the instrument does not name the person represented but does show that the representative signed in a representative capacity.

(3) Except as otherwise established the name of an organization preceded or followed by the name and office of an authorized individual is a signature made in a representative capacity.

Sec. 3—404. Unauthorized Signatures. (1) Any unauthorized signature is wholly inoperative as that of the person whose name is signed unless he ratifies it or is precluded from denying it; but it operates as the signature of the unauthorized signer in favor of any person who in good faith pays the instrument or takes it for value.

(2) Any unauthorized signature may be ratified for all purposes of this Article. Such ratification does not of itself affect any rights of the person ratifying against the actual signer.

Sec. 3—405. Impostors; Signature in Name of Payee. (1) An indorsement by any person in the name of a named payee is effective if

(*a*) an impostor by use of the mails or otherwise has induced the maker or drawer to issue the instrument to him or his confederate in the name of the payee; or

(*b*) a person signing as or on behalf of a maker or drawer intends the payee to have no interest in the instrument; or

(*c*) an agent or employee of the maker or drawer has supplied him with the name of the payee intending the latter to have no such interest.

(2) Nothing in this section shall affect the criminal or civil liability of the person so indorsing.

Sec. 3—406. Negligence Contributing to Alteration or Unauthorized Signature. Any person who by his negligence substantially contributes to a material alteration of the instrument or to the making of an unauthorized signature is precluded from asserting the alteration or lack of authority against a holder in due course or against a drawee or other payor who pays the instrument in good faith and in accordance with the reasonable commercial standards of the drawee's or payor's business.

Sec. 3—407. Alteration. (1) Any alteration of an instrument is material which changes the contract of any party thereto in any respect, including any such change in

(*a*) the number of relations of the parties; or

(*b*) an incomplete instrument, by completing it otherwise than as authorized; or

(*c*) the writing as signed, by adding to it or by removing any part of it.

(2) As against any person other than a subsequent holder in due course

(*a*) alteration by the holder which is both fraudulent and material discharges any party whose contract is thereby changed unless that party assents or is precluded from asserting the defense;

(*b*) no other alteration discharges any party and the instrument may be enforced according to its original tenor, or as to incomplete instruments according to the authority given.

(3) A subsequent holder in due course may in all cases enforce the instrument according to its original tenor, and when an incomplete instrument has been completed, he may enforce it as completed.

Sec. 3—408. Consideration. Want or failure of consideration is a defense as against any person not having the rights of a holder in due course (Section 3–305), except that no consideration is necessary for an instrument or obligation thereon given in payment of or as security for an antecedent obligation of any kind. Nothing in this section shall be taken to displace any statute outside this Act under which a promise is enforceable notwithstanding lack or failure of consideration. Partial failure of consideration is a defense pro tanto whether or not the failure is in an ascertained or liquidated amount.

Sec. 3—409. Draft Not an Assignment. (1) A check or other draft does not of itself operate as an assignment of any funds in the hands of the drawee available for its payment, and the drawee is not liable on the instrument until he accepts it.

(2) Nothing in this section shall affect any liability in contract, tort or otherwise arising from any letter of credit or other obligation or representation which is not an acceptance.

Sec. 3—410. Definition and Operation of Acceptance. (1) Acceptance is the drawee's signed engagement to honor the draft as presented. It must be written on the draft, and may consist of his signature alone. It becomes operative when completed by delivery or notification.

(2) A draft may be accepted although it has not been signed by the drawer or is otherwise incomplete or is overdue or has been dishonored.

(3) Where the draft is payable at a fixed period after sight and the acceptor fails to date his acceptance the holder may complete it by supplying a date in good faith.

Sec. 3—411. Certification of a Check. (1) Certification of a check is acceptance. Where a holder procures certification the drawer and all prior indorsers are discharged.

(2) Unless otherwise agreed a bank has no obligation to certify a check.

(3) A bank may certify a check before returning it for lack of proper indorsement. If it does so the drawer is discharged.

Sec. 3—412. Acceptance Varying Draft. (1) Where the drawee's proffered acceptance in any manner varies the draft as presented the holder may refuse the acceptance and treat the draft as dishonored in which case the drawee is entitled to have his acceptance cancelled.

(2) The terms of the draft are not varied by an acceptance to pay at any particular bank or place in the United States, unless the acceptance states that the draft is to be paid only at such bank or place.

(3) Where the holder assents to an acceptance varying the terms of the draft each drawer and indorser who does not affirmatively assent is discharged.

Sec. 3—413. Contract of Maker, Drawer and Acceptor. (1) The maker or acceptor engages that he will pay the instrument according to its tenor at the time of his engagement or as completed pursuant to Section 3—115 on incomplete instruments.

(2) The drawer engages that upon dishonor of the draft and any necessary notice of dishonor or protest he will pay the amount of the draft to the holder or to any indorser who takes it up. The drawer may disclaim this liability by drawing without recourse.

(3) By making, drawing or accepting the party admits as against all subsequent parties including the drawee the existence of the payee and his then capacity to indorse.

Sec. 3—414. Contract of Indorser; Order of Liability. (1) Unless the indorsement otherwise specifies (as by such words as "without recourse") every indorser engages that upon dishonor and any necessary notice of dishonor and protest he will pay the instrument according to its tenor at the time of his indorsement to the holder or to any subsequent indorser who takes it up, even though the indorser who takes it up was not obligated to do so.

(2) Unless they otherwise agree indorsers are liable to one another in the order in which they indorse, which is presumed to be the order in which their signatures appear on the instrument.

Sec. 3—415. Contract of Accommodation Party. (1) An accommodation party is one who signs the instrument in any capacity for the purpose of lending his name to another party to it.

(2) When the instrument has been taken for value before it is due the accom-

modation party is liable in the capacity in which he has signed even though the taker knows of the accommodation.

(3) As against a holder in due course and without notice of the accommodation oral proof of the accommodation is not admissible to give the accommodation party the benefit of discharges dependent on his character as such. In other cases the accommodation character may be shown by oral proof.

(4) An indorsement which shows that it is not in the chain of title is notice of its accommodation character.

(5) An accommodation party is not liable to the party accommodated, and if he pays the instrument has a right of recourse on the instrument against such party.

Sec. 3—416. Contract of Guarantor. (1) "Payment guaranteed" or equivalent words added to a signature mean that the signer engages that if the instrument is not paid when due he will pay it according to its tenor without resort by the holder to any other party.

(2) "Collection guaranteed" or equivalent words added to a signature mean that the signer engages that if the instrument is not paid when due he will pay it according to its tenor, but only after the holder has reduced his claim against the maker or acceptor to judgment and execution has been returned unsatisfied, or after the maker or acceptor has become insolvent or it is otherwise apparent that it is useless to proceed against him.

(3) Words of guaranty which do not otherwise specify guarantee payment.

(4) No words of guaranty added to the signature of a sole maker or acceptor affect his liability on the instrument. Such words added to the signature of one of two or more makers or acceptors create a presumption that the signature is for the accommodation of the others.

(5) When words of guaranty are used presentment, notice of dishonor and protest are not necessary to charge the user.

(6) Any guaranty written on the instrument is enforceable notwithstanding any statute of frauds.

Sec. 3—417. Warranties on Presentment and Transfer. (1) Any person who obtains payment or acceptance and any prior transferor warrants to a person who in good faith pays or accepts that

(a) he has a good title to the instrument or is authorized to obtain payment or acceptance on behalf of one who has a good title; and

(b) he has no knowledge that the signature of the maker or drawer is unauthorized, except that this warranty is not given by a holder in due course acting in good faith

(i) to a maker with respect to the maker's own signature; or

(ii) to a drawer with respect to the drawer's own signature, whether or not the drawer is also the drawee; or

(iii) to an acceptor of a draft if the holder in due course took the draft after the acceptance or obtained the acceptance without knowledge that the drawer's signature was unauthorized; and

(c) the instrument has not been materially altered, except that this warranty is not given by a holder in due course acting in good faith

(i) to the maker of a note; or

(ii) to the drawer of a draft whether or not the drawer is also the drawee; or

(iii) to the acceptor of a draft with respect to an alteration made prior to the acceptance if the holder in due course took the draft after the acceptance, even though the acceptance provided "payable as originally drawn" or equivalent terms; or

(iv) to the acceptor of a draft with respect to an alteration made after the acceptance.

(2) Any person who transfers an instrument and receives consideration warrants to

his transferee and if the transfer is by indorsement to any subsequent holder who takes the instrument in good faith that

(*a*) he has a good title to the instrument or is authorized to obtain payment or acceptance on behalf of one who has a good title and the transfer is otherwise rightful; and

(*b*) all signatures are genuine or authorized; and

(*c*) the instrument has not been materially altered; and

(*d*) no defense of any party is good against him; and

(*e*) he has no knowledge of any insolvency proceeding instituted with respect to the maker or acceptor or the drawer of an unaccepted instrument.

(3) By transferring "without recourse" the transferor limits the obligation stated in subsection (2) (*d*) to a warranty that he has no knowledge of such a defense.

(4) A selling agent or broker who does not disclose the fact that he is acting only as such gives the warranties provided in this section, but if he makes such disclosure warrants only his good faith and authority.

Sec. 3—418. Finality of Payment or Acceptance. Except for recovery of bank payments as provided in the Article on Bank Deposits and Collections (Article 4) and except for liability for breach of warranty on presentment under the preceding section, payment or acceptance of any instrument is final in favor of a holder in due course, or a person who has in good faith changed his position in reliance on the payment.

Sec. 3—419. Conversion of Instrument; Innocent Representative. (1) An instrument is converted when

(*a*) a drawee to whom it is delivered for acceptance refuses to return it on demand; or

(*b*) any person to whom it is delivered for payment refuses on demand either to pay or to return it; or

(*c*) it is paid on a forged indorsement.

(2) In an action against a drawee under subsection (1) the measure of the drawee's liability is the face amount of the instrument. In any other action under subsection (1) the measure of liability is presumed to be the face amount of the instrument.

(3) Subject to the provisions of this Act concerning restrictive indorsements a representative, including a depositary or collecting bank, who has in good faith and in accordance with the reasonable commercial standards applicable to the business of such representative dealt with an instrument or its proceeds on behalf of one who was not the true owner is not liable in conversion or otherwise to the true owner beyond the amount of any proceeds remaining in his hands.

(4) An intermediary bank or payor bank which is not a depositary bank is not liable in conversion solely by reason of the fact that proceeds of an item indorsed restrictively (Sections 3—205 and 3—206) are not paid or applied consistently with the restrictive indorsement of an indorser other than its immediate transferor.

PART V

PRESENTMENT, NOTICE OF DISHONOR AND PROTEST

Sec. 3—501. When Presentment, Notice of Dishonor, and Protest Necessary or Permissible. (1) Unless excused (Section 3—511) presentment is necessary to charge secondary parties as follows:

(*a*) presentment for acceptance is necessary to charge the drawer and indorsers of a draft where the draft so provides, or is payable elsewhere than at the residence or place of business of the drawee, or its date of payment depends upon such presentment. The holder may at his option present for acceptance any other draft payable at a stated date;

(*b*) presentment for payment is necessary to charge any indorser;

(*c*) in the case of any drawer, the acceptor of a draft payable at a bank or the maker of a note payable at a bank, presentment for payment is necessary, but failure to make presentment discharges such drawer, acceptor or maker only as stated in Section 3—502(1) (*b*).

(2) Unless excused (Section 3—511)

(*a*) notice of any dishonor is necessary to charge any indorser;

(*b*) in the case of any drawer, the acceptor of a draft payable at a bank or the maker of a note payable at a bank, notice of any dishonor is necessary, but failure to give such notice discharges such drawer, acceptor or maker only as stated in Section 3—502(1) (*b*).

(3) Unless excused (Section 3—511 protest of any dishonor is necessary to charge the drawer and indorsers of any draft which on its face appears to be drawn or payable outside of the states and territories of the United States and the District of Columbia. The holder may at his option make protest of any dishonor of any other instrument and in the case of a foreign draft may on insolvency of the acceptor before maturity make protest for better security.

(4) Notwithstanding any provision of this section, neither presentment nor notice of dishonor nor protest is necessary to charge an indorser who has indorsed an instrument after maturity.

Sec. 3—502. Unexcused Delay; Discharge. (1) Where without excuse any necessary presentment or notice of dishonor is delayed beyond the time when it is due

(*a*) any indorser is discharged; and

(*b*) any drawer or the acceptor of a draft payable at a bank or the maker of a note payable at a bank who because the drawee or payor bank becomes insolvent during the delay is deprived of funds maintained with the drawee or payor bank to cover the instrument may discharge his liability by written assignment to the holder of his rights against the drawee or payor bank in respect of such funds, but such drawer, acceptor or maker is not otherwise discharged.

(2) Where without excuse a necessary protest is delayed beyond the time when it is due any drawer or indorser is discharged.

Sec. 3—503. Time of Presentment. (1) Unless a different time is expressed in the instrument the time for any presentment is determined as follows:

(*a*) where an instrument is payable at or a fixed period after a stated date any presentment for acceptance must be made on or before the date it is payable;

(*b*) where an instrument is payable after sight it must either be presented for acceptance or negotiated within a reasonable time after date or issue whichever is later;

(*c*) where an instrument shows the date on which it is payable presentment for payment is due on that date;

(*d*) where an instrument is accelerated presentment for payment is due within a reasonable time after the acceleration;

(*e*) with respect to the liability of any secondary party presentment for acceptance or payment of any other instrument is due within a reasonable time after such party becomes liable thereon.

(2) A reasonable time for presentment is determined by the nature of the instrument, any usage of banking or trade and the facts of the particular case. In the case of an uncertified check which is drawn and payable within the United States and which is not a draft drawn by a bank the following are presumed to be reasonable periods within which to present for payment or to initiate bank collection:

(*a*) with respect to the liability of the drawer, thirty days after date or issue whichever is later; and

(*b*) with respect to the liability of an indorser, seven days after his indorsement.

(3) Where any presentment is due on a day which is not a full business day for either the person making presentment or the party to pay or accept, presentment is due on the next following day which is a full business day for both parties.

(4) Presentment to be sufficient must be made at a reasonable hour, and if at a bank during its banking day.

Sec. 3—504. How Presentment Made. (1) Presentment is a demand for acceptance or payment made upon the maker, acceptor, drawee or other payor by or on behalf of the holder.

(2) Presentment may be made

(a) by mail, in which event the time of presentment is determined by the time of receipt of the mail; or

(b) through a clearing house; or

(c) at the place of acceptance or payment specified in the instrument or if there be none at the place of business or residence of the party to accept or pay. If neither the party to accept or pay nor anyone authorized to act for him is present or accessible at such place presentment is excused.

(3) It may be made

(a) to any one of two or more makers, acceptors, drawees or other payors; or

(b) to any person who has authority to make or refuse the acceptance or payment.

(4) A draft accepted or a note made payable at a bank in the United States must be presented at such bank.

(5) In the cases described in Section 4—210 presentment may be made in the manner and with the result stated in that section.

Sec. 3—505. Rights of Party to Whom Presentment Is Made. (1) The party to whom presentment is made may without dishonor require

(a) exhibition of the instrument; and

(b) reasonable identification of the person making presentment and evidence of his authority to make it if made for another; and

(c) that the instrument be produced for acceptance or payment at a place specified in it, or if there be none at any place reasonable in the circumstances; and

(d) a signed receipt on the instrument for any partial or full payment and its surrender upon full payment.

(2) Failure to comply with any such requirement invalidates the presentment but the person presenting has a reasonable time in which to comply and the time for acceptance or payment runs from the time of compliance.

Sec. 3—506. Time Allowed for Acceptance or Payment. (1) Acceptance may be deferred without dishonor until the close of the next business day following presentment. The holder may also in a good faith effort to obtain acceptance and without either dishonor of the instrument or discharge of secondary parties allow postponement of acceptance for an additional business day.

(2) Except as a longer time is allowed in the case of documentary drafts drawn under a letter of credit, and unless an earlier time is agreed to by the party to pay, payment of an instrument may be deferred without dishonor pending reasonable examination to determine whether it is properly payable, but payment must be made in any event before the close of business on the day of presentment.

Sec. 3—507. Dishonor; Holder's Right of Recourse; Term Allowing Re-Presentment. (1) An instrument is dishonored when

(a) a necessary or optional presentment is duly made and due acceptance or payment is refused or cannot be obtained within the prescribed time or in case of bank collections the instrument is seasonably returned by the midnight deadline (Section 4—301); or

(b) presentment is excused and the instrument is not duly accepted or paid.

(2) Subject to any necessary notice of dishonor and protest, the holder has upon dishonor an immediate right of recourse against the drawers and indorsers.

(3) Return of an instrument for lack of proper indorsement is not dishonor.

(4) A term in a draft or an indorsement thereof allowing a stated time for re-presentment in the event of any dishonor of the draft by nonacceptance if a time draft or by nonpayment if a sight draft gives the holder as against any secondary party bound by the term an option to waive the dishonor without affecting the

liability of the secondary party and he may present again up to the end of the stated time.

Sec. 3—508. Notice of Dishonor. (1) Notice of dishonor may be given to any person who may be liable on the instrument by or on behalf of the holder or any party who has himself received notice, or any other party who can be compelled to pay the instrument. In addition an agent or bank in whose hands the instrument is dishonored may give notice to his principal or customer or to another agent or bank from which the instrument was received.

(2) Any necessary notice must be given by a bank before its midnight deadline and by any other person before midnight of the third business day after dishonor or receipt of notice of dishonor.

(3) Notice may be given in any reasonable manner. It may be oral or written and in any terms which identify the instrument and state that it has been dishonored. A misdescription which does not mislead the party notified does not vitiate the notice. Sending the instrument bearing a stamp, ticket or writing stating that acceptance or payment has been refused or sending a notice of debit with respect to the instrument is sufficient.

(4) Written notice is given when sent although it is not received.

(5) Notice to one partner is notice to each although the firm has been dissolved.

(6) When any party is in insolvency proceedings instituted after the issue of the instrument notice may be given either to the party or to the representative of his estate.

(7) When any party is dead or incompetent notice may be sent to his last known address or given to his personal representative.

(8) Notice operates for the benefit of all parties who have rights on the instrument against the party notified.

Sec. 3—509. Protest; Noting for Protest. (1) A protest is a certificate of dishonor made under the hand and seal of a United States consul or vice consul or a notary public or other person authorized to certify dishonor by the law of the place where dishonor occurs. It may be made upon information satisfactory to such person.

(2) The protest must identify the instrument and certify either that due presentment has been made or the reason why it is excused and that the instrument has been dishonored by nonacceptance or nonpayment.

(3) The protest may also certify that notice of dishonor has been given to all parties or to specified parties.

(4) Subject to subsection (5) any necessary protest is due by the time that notice of dishonor is due.

(5) If, before protest is due, an instrument has been noted for protest by the officer to make protest, the protest may be made at any time thereafter as of the date of the noting.

Sec. 3—510. Evidence of Dishonor and Notice of Dishonor. The following are admissible as evidence and create a presumption of dishonor and of any notice of dishonor therein shown:

(a) a document regular in form as provided in the preceding section which purports to be a protest;

(b) the purported stamp or writing of the drawee, payor bank or presenting bank on the instrument or accompanying it stating that acceptance or payment has been refused for reasons consistent with dishonor;

(c) any book or record of the drawee, payor bank, or any collecting bank kept in the usual course of business which shows dishonor, even though there is no evidence of who made the entry.

Sec. 3—511. Waived or Excused Presentment, Protest or Notice of Dishonor or Delay Therein. (1) Delay in presentment, protest or notice of dishonor is excused when the party is without notice that it is due or when the delay is caused by circumstances beyond his control and he exercises reasonable diligence after the cause of the delay ceases to operate.

(2) Presentment or notice or protest as the case may be is entirely excused when

(a) the party to be charged has waived it expressly or by implication either before or after it is due; or

(b) such party has himself dishonored the instrument or has countermanded payment or otherwise has no reason to expect or right to require that the instrument be accepted or paid; or

(c) by reasonable diligence the presentment or protest cannot be made or the notice given.

(3) Presentment is also entirely excused when

(a) the maker, acceptor or drawee of any instrument except a documentary draft is dead or in insolvency proceedings instituted after the issue of the instrument; or

(b) acceptance or payment is refused but not for want of proper presentment.

(4) Where a draft has been dishonored by nonacceptance a later presentment for payment and any notice of dishonor and protest for nonpayment are excused unless in the meantime the instrument has been accepted.

(5) A waiver of protest is also a waiver of presentment and of notice of dishonor even though protest is not required.

(6) Where a waiver of presentment or notice or protest is embodied in the instrument itself it is binding upon all parties; but where it is written above the signature of an indorser it binds him only.

PART VI

DISCHARGE

Sec. 3—601. Discharge of Parties. (1) The extent of the discharge of any party from liability on an instrument is governed by the sections on

(a) payment or satisfaction (Section 3—603); or

(b) tender of payment (Section 3—604); or

(c) cancellation or renunciation (Section 3—605); or

(d) impairment of right of recourse or of collateral (Section 3—606); or

(e) reacquisition of the instrument by a prior party (Section 3—208); or

(f) fraudulent and material alteration (Section 3—407); or

(g) certification of a check (Section 3—411); or

(h) acceptance varying a draft (Section 3—412); or

(i) unexcused delay in presentment or notice of dishonor or protest (Section 3—502).

(2) Any party is also discharged from his liability on an instrument to another party by any other act or agreement with such party which would discharge his simple contract for the payment of money.

(3) The liability of all parties is discharged when any party who has himself no right of action or recourse on the instrument

(a) reacquires the instrument in his own right; or

(b) is discharged under any provision of this Article, except as otherwise provided with respect to discharge for impairment of recourse or of collateral (Section 3—606).

Sec. 3—602. Effect of Discharge Against Holder in Due Course. No discharge of any party provided by this Article is effective against a subsequent holder in due course unless he has notice thereof when he takes the instrument.

Sec. 3—603. Payment or Satisfaction. (1) The liability of any party is discharged to the extent of his payment or satisfaction to the holder even though it is made with knowledge of a claim of another person to the instrument unless prior to such payment or satisfaction the person making the claim either supplies indemnity deemed adequate by the party seeking the discharge or enjoins payment or satisfaction by order of a court of competent jurisdiction in an action in which the adverse claimant and the holder are parties. This subsection does not, however, result in the discharge of the liability

(a) of a party who in bad faith pays or satisfies a holder who acquired the instrument by theft or who (unless having the rights of a holder in due course) holds through one who so acquired it; or

(b) of a party (other than an intermediary bank or a payor bank which is not a depositary bank) who pays or satisfies the holder of an instrument which has been restrictively indorsed in a manner not consistent with the terms of such restrictive indorsement.

(2) Payment or satisfaction may be made with the consent of the holder by any person including a stranger to the instrument. Surrender of the instrument to such a person gives him the rights of a transferee (Section 3—201).

Sec. 3—604. Tender of Payment. (1) Any party making tender of full payment to a holder when or after it is due is discharged to the extent of all subsequent liability for interest, costs and attorney's fees.

(2) The holder's refusal of such tender wholly discharges any party who has a right of recourse against the party making the tender.

(3) Where the maker or acceptor of an instrument payable otherwise than on demand is able and ready to pay at every place of payment specified in the instrument when it is due, it is equivalent to tender.

Sec. 3—605. Cancellation and Renunciation. (1) The holder of an instrument may even without consideration discharge any party

(a) in any manner apparent on the face of the instrument or the indorsement, as by intentionally cancelling the instrument or the party's signature by destruction or mutilation, or by striking out the party's signature; or

(b) by renouncing his rights by a writing signed and delivered or by surrender of the instrument to the party to be discharged.

(2) Neither cancellation nor renunciation without surrender of the instrument affects the title thereto.

Sec. 3—606. Impairment of Recourse or of Collateral. (1) The holder discharges any party to the instrument to the extent that without such party's consent the holder

(a) without express reservation of rights releases or agrees not to sue any person against whom the party has to the knowledge of the holder a right of recourse or agrees to suspend the right to enforce against such person the instrument or collateral or otherwise discharges such person, except that failure or delay in effecting any required presentment, protest or notice of dishonor with respect to any such person does not discharge any party as to whom presentment, protest or notice of dishonor is effective or unnecessary; or

(b) unjustifiably impairs any collateral for the instrument given by or on behalf of the party or any person against whom he has a right of recourse.

(2) By express reservation of rights against a party with a right of recourse the holder preserves

(a) all his rights against such party as of the time when the instrument was originally due; and

(b) the right of the party to pay the instrument as of that time; and

(c) all rights of such party to recourse against others.

PART VII

ADVICE OF INTERNATIONAL SIGHT DRAFT

Sec. 3—701. Letter of Advice of International Sight Draft. (1) A "letter of advice" is a drawer's communication to the drawee that a described draft has been drawn.

(2) Unless otherwise agreed when a bank receives from another bank a letter of

advice of an international sight draft the drawee bank may immediately debit the drawer's account and stop the running of interest pro tanto. Such a debit and any resulting credit to any account covering outstanding drafts leaves in the drawer full power to stop payment or otherwise dispose of the amount and creates no trust or interest in favor of the holder.

(3) Unless otherwise agreed and except where a draft is drawn under a credit issued by the drawee, the drawee of an international sight draft owes the drawer no duty to pay an unadvised draft if it does so and the draft is genuine, may appropriately debit the drawer's account.

PART VIII

MISCELLANEOUS

Sec. 3—801. Drafts in a Set. (1) Where a draft is drawn in a set of parts, each of which is numbered and expressed to be an order only if no other part has been honored, the whole of the parts constitutes one draft but a taker of any part may become a holder in due course of the draft.

(2) Any person who negotiates, indorses or accepts a single part of a draft drawn in a set thereby becomes liable to any holder in due course of that part as if it were the whole set, but as between different holders in due course to whom different parts have been negotiated the holder whose title first accrues has all rights to the draft and its proceeds.

(3) As against the drawee the first presented part of a draft drawn in a set is the part entitled to payment, or if a time draft to acceptance and payment. Acceptance of any subsequently presented part renders the drawee liable thereon under subsection (2). With respect both to a holder and to the drawer payment of a subsequently presented part of a draft payable at sight has the same effect as payment of a check notwithstanding an effective stop order (Section 4—407).

(4) Except as otherwise provided in this section, where any part of a draft in a set is discharged by payment or otherwise the whole draft is discharged.

Sec. 3—802. Effect of Instrument on Obligation for Which It Is Given. (1) Unless otherwise agreed where an instrument is taken for an underlying obligation

(a) the obligation is pro tanto discharged if a bank is drawer, maker or acceptor of the instrument and there is no recourse on the instrument against the underlying obligor; and

(b) in any other case the obligation is suspended pro tanto until the instrument is due or if it is payable on demand until its presentment. If the instrument is dishonored action may be maintained on either the instrument or the obligation; discharge of the underlying obligor on the instrument also discharges him on the obligation.

(2) The taking in good faith of a check which is not postdated does not of itself so extend the time on the original obligation as to discharge a surety.

Sec. 3—803. Notice to Third Party. Where a defendant is sued for breach of an obligation for which a third person is answerable over under this Article he may give the third person written notice of the litigation, and the person notified may then give similar notice to any other person who is answerable over to him under this Article. If the notice states that the person notified may come in and defend and that if the person notified does not do so he will in any action against him by the person giving the notice be bound by any determination of fact common to the two litigations, then unless after seasonable receipt of the notice the person notified does come in and defend he is so bound.

Sec. 3—804. Lost, Destroyed or Stolen Instruments. The owner of an instrument which is lost, whether by destruction, theft or otherwise, may maintain an action in his own name and recover from any party liable thereon upon due proof of his ownership, the facts which prevent his production of the instrument and its terms. The court may require security indemnifying the defendant against loss by reason of further claims on the instrument.

Sec. 3—805. Instruments Not Payable to Order or to Bearer. This Article applies to any instrument whose terms do not preclude transfer and which is otherwise negotiable within this Article but which is not payable to order or to bearer, except that there can be no holder in due course of such an instrument.

ARTICLE IV

BANK DEPOSITS AND COLLECTIONS

PART I

GENERAL PROVISIONS AND DEFINITIONS

Sec. 4—101. Short Title. This Article shall be known and may be cited as Uniform Commercial Code—Bank Deposits and Collections.

Sec. 4—102. Applicability. (1) To the extent that items within this Article are also within the scope of Articles 3 and 8, they are subject to the provisions of those Articles. In the event of conflict the provisions of this Article govern those of Article 3 but the provisions of Article 8 govern those of this Article.

(2) The liability of a bank for action or nonaction with respect to any item handled by it for purposes of presentment, payment or collection is governed by the law of the place where the bank is located. In the case of action or nonaction by or at a branch or separate office of a bank, its liability is governed by the law of the place where the branch or separate office is located.

Sec. 4—103. Variation by Agreement; Measure of Damages; Certain Action Constituting Ordinary Care. (1) The effect of the provisions of this Article may be varied by agreement except that no agreement can disclaim a bank's responsibility for its own lack of good faith or failure to exercise ordinary care or can limit the measure of damages for such lack or failure; but the parties may by agreement determine the standards by which such responsibility is to be measured if such standards are not manifestly unreasonable.

(2) Federal Reserve regulations and operating letters, clearing house rules, and the like, have the effect of agreements under subsection (1), whether or not specifically assented to by all parties interested in items handled.

(3) Action or non-action approved by this Article or pursuant to Federal Reserve regulations or operating letters constitutes the exercise of ordinary care and, in the absence of special instructions, action or non-action consistent with clearing house rules and the like or with a general banking usage not disapproved by this Article, prima facie constitutes the exercise of ordinary care.

(4) The specification or approval of certain procedures by this Article does not constitute disapproval of other procedures which may be reasonable under the circumstances.

(5) The measure of damages for failure to exercise ordinary care in handling an item is the amount of the item reduced by an amount which could not have been realized by the use of ordinary care, and where there is bad faith it includes other damages, if any, suffered by the party as a proximate consequence.

Sec. 4—104. Definitions and Index of Definitions. (1) In this Article unless the context otherwise requires

(*a*) "Account" means any account with a bank and includes a checking, time, interest or savings account;

(*b*) "Afternoon" means the period of a day between noon and midnight;

(*c*) "Banking day" means that part of any day on which a bank is open to the public for carrying on substantially all of its banking functions;

(*d*) "Clearing house" means any association of banks or other payors regularly clearing items;

(*e*) "Customer" means any person having an account with a bank or for whom a bank has agreed to collect items and includes a bank carrying an account with another bank;

(*f*) "Documentary draft" means any negotiable or non-negotiable draft with accompanying documents, securities or other papers to be delivered against honor of the draft;

(*g*) "Item" means any instrument for the payment of money even though it is not negotiable but does not include money;

(*h*) "Midnight deadline" with respect to a bank is midnight on its next banking day following the banking day on which it receives the relevant item or notice or from which the time for taking action commences to run, whichever is later;

(*i*) "Properly payable" includes the availability of funds for payment at the time of decision to pay or dishonor;

(*j*) "Settle" means to pay in cash, by clearing house settlement, in a charge or credit or by remittance, or otherwise as instructed. A settlement may be either provisional or final;

(*k*) "Suspends payments" with respect to a bank means that it has been closed by order of the supervisory authorities, that a public officer has been appointed to take it over or that it ceases or refuses to make payments in the ordinary course of business.

(2) Other definitions applying to this Article and the sections in which they appear are:

"Collecting bank"	Section 4—105.
"Depositary bank"	Section 4—105.
"Intermediary bank"	Section 4—105.
"Payor bank"	Section 4—105.
"Presenting bank"	Section 4—105.
"Remitting bank"	Section 4—105.

(3) The following definitions in other Articles apply to this Article:

"Acceptance"	Section 3—410.
"Certificate of deposit"	Section 3—104.
"Certification"	Section 3—411.
"Check"	Section 3—104.
"Draft"	Section 3—104.
"Holder in due course"	Section 3—302.
"Notice of dishonor"	Section 3—508.
"Presentment"	Section 3—504.
"Protest"	Section 3—509.
"Secondary party"	Section 3—102.

(4) In addition Article 1 contains general definitions and principles of construction and interpretation applicable throughout this Article.

Sec. 4—105. "Depositary Bank"; "Intermediary Bank"; "Collecting Bank"; "Payor Bank"; "Presenting Bank"; "Remitting Bank". In this Article unless the context otherwise requires:

(*a*) "Depositary bank" means the first bank to which an item is transferred for collection even though it is also the payor bank;

(*b*) "Payor bank" means a bank by which an item is payable as drawn or accepted;

(*c*) "Intermediary bank" means any bank to which an item is transferred in course of collection except the depositary or payor bank;

(*d*) "Collecting bank" means any bank handling the item for collection except the payor bank;

(*e*) "Presenting bank" means any bank presenting an item except a payor bank;

(*f*) "Remitting bank" means any payor or intermediary bank remitting for an item.

Sec. 4—106. Separate Office of a Bank. A branch or separate office of a bank [maintaining its own deposit ledgers] is a separate bank for the purpose of computing the time within which and determining the place at or to which action may be taken or notices or orders shall be given under this Article and under Article 3.

Note: *The brackets are to make it optional with the several states whether to require a branch to maintain its own deposit ledgers in order to be considered to be a separate bank for certain purposes under Article 4. In some states "maintaining its own deposit ledgers" is a satisfactory test. In others branch banking practices are such that this test would not be suitable.*

Sec. 4—107. Time of Receipt of Items. (1) For the purpose of allowing time to process items, prove balances and make the necessary entries on its books to determine its position for the day, a bank may fix an afternoon hour of two P.M. or later as a cut-off hour for the handling of money and items and the making of entries on its books.

(2) Any item or deposit of money received on any day after a cut-off hour so fixed or after the close of the banking day may be treated as being received at the opening of the next banking day.

Sec. 4—108. Delays. (1) Unless otherwise instructed, a collecting bank in a good faith effort to secure payment may, in the case of specific items and with or without the approval of any person involved, waive, modify or extend time limits imposed or permitted by this Act for a period not in excess of an additional banking day without discharge of secondary parties and without liability to its transferor or any prior party.

(2) Delay by a collecting bank or payor bank beyond time limits prescribed or permitted by this Act or by instructions is excused if caused by interruption of communication facilities, suspension of payments by another bank, war, emergency conditions or other circumstances beyond the control of the bank provided it exercises such diligence as the circumstances require.

Sec. 4—109. Process of Posting. The "process of posting" means the usual procedure followed by a payor bank in determining to pay an item and in recording the payment including one or more of the following or other steps as determined by the bank:

(*a*) verification of any signature;

(*b*) ascertaining that sufficient funds are available;

(*c*) affixing a "paid" or other stamp;

(*d*) entering a charge or entry to a customer's account;

(*e*) correcting or reversing an entry or erroneous action with respect to the item.

PART II

COLLECTION OF ITEMS: DEPOSITARY AND COLLECTING BANKS

Sec. 4—201. Presumption and Duration of Agency Status of Collecting Banks and Provisional Status of Credits; Applicability of Article; Item Indorsed "Pay Any Bank." (1) Unless a contrary intent clearly appears and prior to the time that a settlement given by a collecting bank for an item is or becomes final (subsection (3) of Section 4—211 and Sections 4—212 and 4—213) the bank is an agent or subagent of the owner of the item and any settlement given for the item is provisional. This provision applies regardless of the form of indorsement or lack of indorsement and even though credit given for the item is subject to immediate withdrawal as of right or is in fact withdrawn; but the continuance of ownership of an item by its owner and any rights of the owner to proceeds of the item are subject to rights of a collecting bank such as those resulting from outstanding advances on the item and valid rights of setoff. When an item is handled by banks for purposes of presentment, payment and collection, the relevant provisions of this Article apply even though action of parties clearly establishes that a particular bank has purchased the item and is the owner of it.

(2) After an item has been indorsed with the words "pay any bank" or the like, only a bank may acquire the rights of a holder

    (*a*) until the item has been returned to the customer initiating collection; or

    (*b*) until the item has been specially indorsed by a bank to a person who is not a bank.

Sec. 4—202. Responsibility for Collection; When Action Seasonable. (1) A collecting bank must use ordinary care in

    (*a*) presenting an item or sending it for presentment; and

    (*b*) sending notice of dishonor or non-payment or returning an item other than a documentary draft to the bank's transferor [or directly to the depositary bank under subsection (2) of Section 4—212] (*see note to Section 4—212*) after learning that the item has not been paid or accepted, as the case may be; and

    (*c*) settling for an item when the bank receives final settlement; and

    (*d*) making or providing for any necessary protest; and

    (*e*) notifying its transferor of any loss or delay in transit within a reasonable time after discovery thereof.

(2) A collecting bank taking proper action before its midnight deadline following receipt of an item, notice or payment acts seasonably; taking proper action within a reasonably longer time may be seasonable but the bank has the burden of so establishing.

(3) Subject to subsection (1) (*a*), a bank is not liable for the insolvency, neglect, misconduct, mistake or default of another bank or person or for loss or destruction of an item in transit or in the possession of others.

Sec. 4—203. Effect of Instructions. Subject to the provisions of Article 3 concerning conversion of instruments (Section 3—419) and the provisions of both Article 3 and this Article concerning resrtictive indorsements only a collecting bank's transferor can give instructions which affect the bank or constitute notice to it and a collecting bank is not liable to prior parties for any action taken pursuant to such instructions or in accordance with any agreement with its transferor.

Sec. 4—204. Methods of Sending and Presenting; Sending Direct to Payor Bank. (1) A collecting bank must send items by reasonably prompt method taking into consideration any relevant instructions, the nature of the item, the number of such items on hand, and the cost of collection involved and the method generally used by it or others to present such items.

(2) A collecting bank may send

    (*a*) any item direct to the payor bank;

    (*b*) any item to any non-bank payor if authorized by its transferor; and

    (*c*) any item other than documentary drafts to any non-bank payor, if authorized by Federal Reserve regulation or operating letter, clearing house rule or the like.

(3) Presentment may be made by a presenting bank at a place where the payor bank has requested that presentment be made.

Sec. 4—205. Supplying Missing Indorsement; No Notice From Prior Indorsement. (1) A depositary bank which has taken an item for collection may supply any indorsement of the customer which is necessary to title unless the item contains the words "payee's indorsement required" or the like. In the absence of such a requirement a statement placed on the item by the depositary bank to the effect that the item was deposited by a customer or credited to his account is effective as the customer's indorsement.

(2) An intermediary bank, or payor bank which is not a depositary bank, is neither given notice nor otherwise affected by a restrictive indorsement of any person except the bank's immediate transferor.

Sec. 4—206. Transfer Between Banks. Any agreed method which identifies the transferor bank is sufficient for the item's further transfer to another bank.

Sec. 4—207. Warranties of Customer and Collecting Bank on Transfer or Presentment of

Items; Time for Claims. (1) Each customer or collecting bank who obtains payment or acceptance of an item and each prior customer and collecting bank warrants to the payor bank or other payor who in good faith pays or-accepts the item that

(*a*) he has a good title to the item or is authorized to obtain payment or acceptance on behalf of one who has a good title; and

(*b*) he has no knowledge that the signature of the maker or drawer is unauthorized, except that this warranty is not given by any customer or collecting bank that is a holder in due course and acts in good faith

(*i*) to a maker with respect to the maker's own signature; or

(*ii*) to a drawer with respect to the drawer's own signature, whether or not the drawer is also the drawee; or

(*iii*) to an acceptor of an item if the holder in due course took the item after the acceptance or obtained the acceptance without knowledge that the drawer's signature was unauthorized; and

(*c*) the item has not been materially altered, except that this warranty is not given by any customer or collecting bank that is a holder in due course and acts in good faith

(*i*) to the maker of a note; or

(*ii*) to the drawer of a draft whether or not the drawer is also the drawee; or

(*iii*) to the acceptor of an item with respect to an alteration made prior to the acceptance if the holder in due course took the item after the acceptance, even though the acceptance provided "payable as originally drawn" or equivalent terms; or

(*iv*) to the acceptor of an item with respect to an alteration made after the acceptance.

(2) Each customer and collecting bank who transfers an item and receives a settlement or other consideration for it warrants to his transferee and to any subsequent collecting bank who takes the item in good faith that

(*a*) he has a good title to the item or is authorized to obtain payment or acceptance on behalf of one who has a good title and the transfer is otherwise rightful; and

(*b*) all signatures are genuine or authorized; and

(*c*) the item has not been materially altered; and

(*d*) no defense of any party is good against him; and

(*e*) he has no knowledge of any insolvency proceeding instituted with respect to the maker or acceptor or the drawer of an unaccepted item.

In addition each customer and collecting bank so transferring an item and receiving a settlement or other consideration engages that upon dishonor and any necessary notice of dishonor and protest he will take up the item.

(3) The warranties and the engagement to honor set forth in the two preceding subsections arise notwithstanding the absence of indorsement or words of guaranty or warranty in the transfer or presentment and a collecting bank remains liable for their breach despite remittance to its transferor. Damages for breach of such warranties or engagement to honor shall not exceed the consideration received by the customer or collecting bank responsible plus finance charges and expenses related to the item, if any.

(4) Unless a claim for breach of warranty under this section is made within a reasonable time after the person claiming learns of the breach, the person liable is discharged to the extent of any loss caused by the delay in making claim.

Sec. 4—208. Security Interest of Collecting Bank in Items, Accompanying Documents and Proceeds. (1) A bank has a security interest in an item and any accompanying documents or the proceeds of either

(*a*) in case of an item deposited in an account to the extent to which credit given for the item has been withdrawn or applied;

(*b*) in case of an item for which it has given credit available for withdrawal as of right, to the extent of the credit given whether or not the credit is drawn upon and whether or not there is a right of charge-back; or

(*c*) if it makes an advance on or against the item.

(2) When credit which has been given for several items received at one time or pursuant to a single agreement is withdrawn or applied in part the security interest remains upon all the items, any accompanying documents or the proceeds of either. For the purpose of this section, credits first given are first withdrawn.

(3) Receipt by a collecting bank of a final settlement for an item is a realization on its security interest in the item, accompanying documents and proceeds. To the extent and so long as the bank does not receive final settlement for the item or give up possession of the item or accompanying documents for purposes other than collection, the security interest continues and is subject to the provisions of Article 9 except that

(*a*) no security agreement is necessary to make the security interest enforceable (subsection (1) (*b*) of Section 9—203); and

(*b*) no filing is required to perfect the security interest; and

(*c*) the security interest has priority over conflicting perfected security interests in the item, accompanying documents or proceeds.

Sec. 4—209. When Bank Gives Value for Purposes of Holder in Due Course. For purposes of determining its status as a holder in due course, the bank has given value to the extent that it has a security interest in an item provided that the bank otherwise complies with the requirements of Section 3—302 on what constitutes a holder in due course.

Sec. 4—210. Presentment by Notice of Item Not Payable by, Through or at a Bank; Liability of Secondary Parties. (1) Unless otherwise instructed, a collecting bank may present an item not payable by, through or at a bank by sending to the party to accept or pay a written notice that the bank holds the item for acceptance or payment. The notice must be sent in time to be received on or before the day when presentment is due and the bank must meet any requirement of the party to accept or pay under Section 3—505 by the close of the bank's next banking day after it knows of the requirement.

(2) Where presentment is made by notice and neither honor nor request for compliance with a requirement under Section 3—505 is received by the close of business on the day after maturity or in the case of demand items by the close of business on the third banking day after notice was sent, the presenting bank may treat the item as dishonored and charge any secondary party by sending him notice of the facts.

Sec. 4—211. Media of Remittance; Provisional and Final Settlement in Remittance Cases. (1) A collecting bank may take in settlement of an item

(*a*) a check of the remitting bank or of another bank on any bank except the remitting bank; or

(*b*) a cashier's check or similar primary obligation of a remitting bank which is a member of or clears through a member of the same clearing house or group as the collecting bank; or

(*c*) appropriate authority to charge an account of the remitting bank or of another bank with the collecting bank; or

(*d*) if the item is drawn upon or payable by a person other than a bank, a cashier's check, certified check or other bank check or obligation.

(2) If before its midnight deadline the collecting bank properly dishonors a remittance check or authorization to charge on itself or presents or forwards for collection a remittance instrument of or on another bank which is of a kind approved by subsection (1) or has not been authorized by it, the collecting bank is not liable to prior parties in the event of the dishonor of such check, instrument or authorization.

(3) A settlement for an item by means of a remittance instrument or authorization

to charge is or becomes a final settlement as to both the person making and the person receiving the settlement

(*a*) if the remittance instrument or authorization to charge is of a kind approved by subsection (1) or has not been authorized by the person receiving the settlement and in either case the person receiving the settlement acts seasonably before its midnight deadline in presenting, forwarding for collection or paying the instrument or authorization,—at the time the remittance instrument or authorization is finally paid by the payor by which it is payable;

(*b*) if the person receiving the settlement has authorized remittance by a non-bank check or obligation or by a cashier's check or similar primary obligation of or a check upon the payor or other remitting bank which is not of a kind approved by subsection (1) (*b*),—at the time of the receipt of such remittance check or obligation; or

(*c*) if in a case not covered by subparagraphs (*a*) or (*b*) the person receiving the settlement fails to seasonably present, forward for collection, pay or return a remittance instrument or authorization to it to charge before its midnight deadline,—at such midnight deadline.

Sec. 4—212. Right of Charge-Back or Refund. (1) If a collecting bank has made provisional settlement with its customer for an item and itself fails by reason of dishonor, suspension of payments by a bank or otherwise to receive a settlement for the item which is or becomes final, the bank may revoke the settlement given by it, charge back the amount of any credit given for the item to its customer's account or obtain refund from its customer whether or not is is able to return the items if by its midnight deadline or within a longer reasonable time after it learns the facts it returns the item or sends notification of the facts. These rights to revoke, charge-back and obtain refund terminate if and when a settlement for the item received by the bank is or becomes final (subsection (3) of Section 4—211 and subsections (2) and (3) of Section 4—213).

[(2) Within the time and manner prescribed by this section and Section 4—301, an intermediary or payor bank, as the case may be, may return an unpaid item directly to the depositary bank and may send for collection a draft on the depositary bank and obtain reimbursement. In such case, if the depositary bank has received provisional settlement for the item, it must reimburse the bank drawing the draft and any provisional credits for the item between banks shall become and remain final.]

Note: *Direct returns is recognized as an innovation that is not yet established bank practice, and therefore, Paragraph 2 has been bracketed. Some lawyers have doubts whether it should be included in legislation or left to development by agreement.*

(3) A depositary bank which is also the payor may charge-back the amount of an item to its customer's account or obtain refund in accordance with the section governing return of an item received by a payor bank for credit on its books (Section 4—301).

(4) The right to charge-back is not affected by

(*a*) prior use of the credit given for the item; or

(*b*) failure by any bank to exercise ordinary care with respect to the item but any bank so failing remains liable.

(5) A failure to charge-back or claim refund does not affect other rights of the bank against the customer or any other party.

(6) If credit is given in dollars as the equivalent of the value of an item payable in a foreign currency the dollar amount of any charge-back or refund shall be calculated on the basis of the buying sight rate for the foreign currency prevailing on the day when the person entitled to the charge-back or refund learns that it will not receive payment in ordinary course.

Sec. 4—213. Final Payment of Item by Payor Bank; When Provisional Debits and Credits Become Final; When Certain Credits Become Available for Withdrawal. (1) An item is finally paid by a payor bank when the bank has done any of the following, whichever happens first:

(a) paid the item in cash; or

(b) settled for the item without reserving a right to revoke the settlement and without having such right under statute, clearing house rule or agreement; or

(c) completed the process of posting the item to the indicated account of the drawer, maker or other person to be charged therewith; or

(d) made a provisional settlement for the item and failed to revoke the settlement in the time and manner permitted by statute, clearing house rule or agreement.

Upon a final payment under subparagraphs (b), (c) or (d) the payor bank shall be accountable for the amount of the item.

(2) If provisional settlement for an item between the presenting and payor banks is made through a clearing house or by debits or credits in an account between them, then to the extent that provisional debits or credits for the item are entered in accounts between the presenting and payor banks or between the presenting and successive prior collecting banks seriatim, they become final upon final payment of the item by the payor bank.

(3) If a collecting bank receives a settlement for an item which is or becomes final (subsection (3) of Section 4—211, subsection (2) of Section 4—213) the bank is accountable to its customer for the amount of the item and any provisional credit given for the item in an account with its customer becomes final.

(4) Subject to any right of the bank to apply the credit to an obligation of the customer, credit given by a bank for an item in an account with its customer becomes available for withdrawal as of right

(a) in any case where the bank has received a provisional settlement for the item,—when such settlement becomes final and the bank has had a reasonable time to learn that the settlement is final;

(b) in any case where the bank is both a depositary bank and a payor bank and the item is finally paid,—at the opening of the bank's second banking day following receipt of the item.

(5) A deposit of money in a bank is final when made but, subject to any right of the bank to apply the deposit to an obligation of the customer, the deposit becomes available for withdrawal as of right at the opening of the bank's next banking day following receipt of the deposit.

Sec. 4—214. Insolvency and Preference. (1) Any item in or coming into the possession of a payor or collecting bank which suspends payment and which item is not finally paid shall be returned by the receiver, trustee or agent in charge of the closed bank to the presenting bank or the closed bank's customer.

(2) If a payor bank finally pays an item and suspends payments without making a settlement for the item with its customer or the presenting bank which settlement is or becomes final, the owner of the item has a preferred claim against the payor bank.

(3) If a payor bank gives or a collecting bank gives or receives a provisional settlement for an item and thereafter suspends payments, the suspension does not prevent or interfere with the settlement becoming final if such finality occurs automatically upon the lapse of certain time or the happening of certain events (subsection (3) of Section 4—211, subsections (1) (d), (2) and (3) of Section 4—213).

(4) If a collecting bank receives from subsequent parties settlement for an item which settlement is or becomes final and suspends payments without making a settlement for the item with its customer which is or becomes final, the owner of the item has a preferred claim against such collecting bank.

PART III

COLLECTION OF ITEMS: PAYOR BANKS

Sec. 4—301. Deferred Posting; Recovery of Payment by Return of Items; Time of Dishonor.
(1) Where an authorized settlement for a demand item (other than a documentary draft) received by a payor bank otherwise than for immediate payment over the counter has been made before midnight of the banking day of receipt the payor bank may revoke the settlement and recover any payment if before it has made final payment (subsection (1) of Section 4—213) and before its midnight deadline it

(a) returns the item; or

(b) sends written notice of dishonor or nonpayment if the item is held for protest or is otherwise unavailable for return.

(2) If a demand item is received by a payor bank for credit on its books it may return such item or send notice of dishonor and may revoke any credit given or recover the amount thereof withdrawn by its customer, if it acts within the time limit and in the manner specified in the preceding subsection.

(3) Unless previous notice of dishonor has been sent an item is dishonored at the time when for purposes of dishonor it is returned or notice sent in accordance with this section.

(4) An item is returned:

(a) as to an item received through a clearing house, when it is delivered to the presenting or last collecting bank or to the clearing house or is sent or delivered in accordance with its rules; or

(b) in all other cases, when it is sent or delivered to the bank's customer or transferor or pursuant to his instructions.

Sec. 4—302. Payor Bank's Responsibility for Late Return of Item. In the absence of a valid defense such as breach of a presentment warranty (subsection (1) of Section 4—207), settlement effected or the like, if an item is presented on and received by a payor bank the bank is accountable for the amount of

(a) a demand item other than a documentary draft whether properly payable or not if the bank, in any case where it is not also the depositary bank, retains the item beyond midnight of the banking day of receipt without settling for it or, regardless of whether it is also the depositary bank, does not pay or return the item or send notice of dishonor until after its midnight deadline; or

(b) any other properly payable item unless within the time allowed for acceptance or payment of that item the bank either accepts or pays the item or returns it and accompanying documents.

Sec. 4—303. When Items Subject to Notice, Stop-Order, Legal Process or Setoff; Order in Which Items May Be Charged or Certified. (1) Any knowledge, notice or stop-order received by, legal process served upon or setoff exercised by a payor bank, whether or not effective under other rules of law to terminate, suspend or modify the bank's right or duty to pay an item or to charge its customer's account for the item, comes too late to so terminate, suspend or modify such right or duty if the knowledge, notice, stop-order or legal process is received or served and a reasonable time for the bank to act thereon expires or the setoff is exercised after the bank has done any of the following:

(a) accepted or certified the item;

(b) paid the item in cash;

(c) settled for the item without reserving a right to revoke the settlement and without having such right under statute, clearing house rule or agreement;

(d) completed the process of posting the item to the indicated account of the drawer, maker or other person to be charged therewith or otherwise has evidenced by examination of such indicated account and by action its decision to pay the item; or (*e*) become accountable for the amount of the item under subsection (1) (*d*) of Section 4—213 and Section 4—302 dealing with the payor bank's responsibility for late return of items.

(2) Subject to the provisions of subsection (1) items may be accepted, paid, certified or charged to the indicated account of its customer in any order convenient to the bank.

PART IV

RELATIONSHIP BETWEEN PAYOR BANK AND ITS CUSTOMER

Sec. 4—401. When Bank May Charge Customer's Account. (1) As against its customer, a bank may charge against his account any item which is otherwise properly payable from that account even though the charge creates an overdraft.

(2) A bank which in good faith makes payment to a holder may charge the indicated account of its customer according to

(*a*) the original tenor of his altered item; or

(*b*) the tenor of his completed item, even though the bank knows the item has been completed unless the bank has notice that the completion was improper.

Sec. 4—402. Bank's Liability to Customer for Wrongful Dishonor. A payor bank is liable to its customer for damages proximately caused by the wrongful dishonor of an item. When the dishonor occurs through mistake liability is limited to actual damages proved. If so proximately caused and proved damages may include damages for an arrest or prosecution of the customer or other consequential damages. Whether any consequential damages are proximately caused by the wrongful dishonor is a question of fact to be determined in each case.

Sec. 4—403. Customer's Right to Stop Payment; Burden of Proof of Loss. (1) A customer may by order to his bank stop payment of any item payable for his account but the order must be received at such time and in such manner as to afford the bank a reasonable opportunity to act on it prior to any action by the bank with respect to the item described in Section 4—303.

(2) An oral order is binding upon the bank only for fourteen calendar days unless confirmed in writing within that period. A written order is effective for only six months unless renewed in writing.

(3) The burden of establishing the fact and amount of loss resulting from the payment of an item contrary to a binding stop payment order is on the customer.

Sec. 4—404. Bank Not Obligated to Pay Check More Than Six Months Old. A bank is under no obligation to a customer having a checking account to pay a check, other than a certified check, which is presented more than six months after its date, but it may charge its customer's account for a payment made thereafter in good faith.

Sec. 4—405. Death or Incompetence of Customer. (1) A payor or collecting bank's authority to accept, pay or collect an item or to account for proceeds of its collection if otherwise effective is not rendered ineffective by incompetence of a customer of either bank existing at the time the item is issued or its collection is undertaken if the bank does not know of an adjudication of incompetence. Neither death nor incompetence of a customer revokes such authority to accept, pay, collect or account until the bank knows of the fact of death or of an adjudication of incompetence and has reasonable opportunity to act on it.

(2) Even with knowledge a bank may for ten days after the date of death pay or certify checks drawn on or prior to that date unless ordered to stop payment by a person claiming an interest in the account.

Sec. 4—406. Customer's Duty to Discover and Report Unauthorized Signature or Alteration. (1) When a bank sends to its customer a statement of account accompanied by items paid in good faith in support of the debit entries or holds the statement and items pursuant to a request or instructions of its customer or otherwise in a reasonable manner makes the statement and items available to the customer, the customer must exercise reasonable care and promptness to examine the statement and items to discover his unauthorized signature or any alteration on an item and must notify the bank promptly after discovery thereof.

(2) If the bank establishes that the customer failed with respect to an item to comply with the duties imposed on the customer by subsection (1) the customer is precluded from asserting against the bank

(a) his unauthorized signature or any alteration on the item if the bank also establishes that it suffered a loss by reason of such failure; and

(b) an unauthorized signature or alteration by the same wrongdoer on any other item paid in good faith by the bank after the first item and statement was available to the customer for a reasonable period not exceeding fourteen calendar days and before the bank receives notification from the customer of any such un-authorized signature or alteration.

(3) The preclusion under subsection (2) does not apply if the customer establishes lack of ordinary care on the part of the bank in paying the item(s).

(4) Without regard to care or lack of care of either the customer or the bank a customer who does not within one year from the time the statement and items are made available to the customer (subsection (1)) discover and report his unauthorized signature or any alteration on the face or back of the item or does not within three years from that time discover and report any unauthorized indorsement is precluded from asserting against the bank such unauthorized signature or indorsement or such alteration.

(5) If under this section a payor bank has a valid defense against a claim of a customer upon or resulting from payment of an item and waives or fails upon request to assert the defense the bank may not assert against any collecting bank or other prior party presenting or transferring the item a claim based upon the unauthorized signature or alteration giving rise to the customer's claim.

Sec. 4—407. Payor Bank's Right to Subrogation on Improper Payment. If a payor bank has paid an item over the stop payment order of the drawer or maker or otherwise under circumstances giving a basis for objection by the drawer or maker, to prevent unjust enrichment and only to the extent necessary to prevent loss to the bank by reason of its payment of the item, the payor bank shall be subrogated to the rights

(a) of any holder in due course on the item against the drawer or maker; and

(b) of the payee or any other holder of the item against the drawer or maker either on the item or under the transaction out of which the item arose; and

(c) of the drawer or maker against the payee or any other holder of the item with respect to the transaction out of which the item arose.

PART V

COLLECTION OF DOCUMENTARY DRAFTS

Sec. 4—501. Handling of Documentary Drafts; Duty to Send for Presentment and to Notify Customer of Dishonor. A bank which takes a documentary draft for collection must present or send the draft and accompanying documents for presentment and upon learning that the draft has not been paid or accepted in due course must seasonably notify its customer of such fact even though it may have discounted or bought the draft or extended credit available for withdrawal as of right.

Sec. 4—502. Presentment of "On Arrival" Drafts. When a draft or the relevant instructions require presentment "on arrival," "when goods arrive" or the like, the collecting bank need not present until in its judgment a reasonable time for arrival of the goods has expired. Refusal to pay or accept because the goods have not arrived is not dishonor; the bank must notify its transferor of such refusal but need not present the draft again until it is instructed to do so or learns of the arrival of the goods.

Sec. 4—503. Responsibility of Presenting Bank for Documents and Goods; Report of Reasons

for Dishonor; Referee in Case of Need. Unless otherwise instructed and except as provided in Article 5 a bank presenting a documentary draft

(*a*) must deliver the documents to the drawee on acceptance of the draft if it is payable more than three days after presentment; otherwise, only on payment; and

(*b*) upon dishonor, either in the case of presentment for acceptance or presentment for payment, may seek and follow instructions from any referee in case of need designated in the draft or if the presenting bank does not choose to utilize his services it must use diligence and good faith to ascertain the reason for dishonor, must notify its transferor of the dishonor and of the results of its effort to ascertain the reasons therefor and must request instructions.

But the presenting bank is under no obligation with respect to goods represented by the documents except to follow any reasonable instructions seasonably received; it has a right to reimbursement for any expense incurred in following instructions and to prepayment of or indemnity for such expenses.

Sec. 4—504. Privilege of Presenting Bank to Deal With Goods; Security Interest for Expenses. (1) A presenting bank which, following the dishonor of a documentary draft, has seasonably requested instructions but does not receive them within a reasonable time may store, sell, or otherwise deal with the goods in any reasonable manner.

(2) For its reasonable expenses incurred by action under subsection (1) the presenting bank has a lien upon the goods or their proceeds, which may be foreclosed in the same manner as an unpaid seller's lien.

ARTICLE V

LETTERS OF CREDIT

Sec. 5—101. Short Title. This Article shall be known and may be cited as Uniform Commercial Code—Letters of Credit.

Sec. 5—102. Scope. (1) This Article applies

(*a*) to a credit issued by a bank if the credit requires a documentary draft or a documentary demand for payment; and

(*b*) to a credit issued by a person other than a bank if the credit requires that the draft or demand for payment be accompanied by a document of title; and

(*c*) to a credit issued by a bank or other person if the credit is not within subparagraphs (*a*) or (*b*) but conspicuously states that it is a letter of credit or is conspicuously so entitled.

(2) Unless the engagement meets the requirements of subsection (1), this Article does not apply to engagements to make advances or to honor drafts or demands for payment, to authorities to pay or purchase, to guarantees or to general agreements.

(3) This Article deals with some but not all of the rules and concepts of letters of credit as such rules or concepts have developed prior to this act or may hereafter develop. The fact that this Article states a rule does not by itself require, imply or negate application of the same or a converse rule to a situation not provided for or to a person not specified by this Article.

Sec. 5—103. Definitions. (1) In this Article unless the context otherwise requires

(*a*) "Credit" or "letter of credit" means an engagement by a bank or other person made at the request of a customer and of a kind within the scope of this Article (Section 5—102) that the issuer will honor drafts or other demands for payment upon compliance with the conditions specified in the credit. A credit may be either revocable or irrevocable. The engagement may be either an agreement to honor or a statement that the bank or other person is authorized to honor.

(*b*) A "documentary draft" or a "documentary demand for payment" is one honor of which is conditioned upon the presentation of a document or documents. "Document" means any paper including document of title, security, invoice, certificate, notice of default and the like.

(c) An "issuer" is a bank or other person issuing a credit.

(d) A "beneficiary" of a credit is a person who is entitled under its terms to draw or demand payment.

(e) An "advising bank" is a bank which gives notification of the issuance of a credit by another bank.

(f) A "confirming bank" is a bank which engages either that it will itself honor a credit already issued by another bank or that such a credit will be honored by the issuer or a third bank.

(g) A "customer" is a buyer or other person who causes an issuer to issue a credit. The term also includes a bank which procures issuance or confirmation on behalf of that bank's customer.

(2) Other definitions applying to this Article and the sections in which they appear are:

"Notation of Credit."	Section 5—108.
"Presenter."	Section 5—112 (3).

(3) Definitions in other Articles applying to this Article and the sections in which they appear are:

"Accept" or "Acceptance."	Section 3—410.
"Contract for sale."	Section 2—106.
"Draft."	Section 3—104.
"Holder in due course."	Section 3—302.
"Midnight deadline."	Section 4—104.
"Security."	Section 8—102.

(4) In addition, Article 1 contains general definitions and principles of construction and interpretation applicable throughout this Article.

Sec. 5—104. Formal Requirements; Signing. (1) Except as otherwise required in subsection (1) (c) of Section 5—102 on scope, no particular form of phrasing is required for a credit. A credit must be in writing and signed by the issuer and a confirmation must be in writing and signed by the confirming bank. A modification of the terms of a credit or confirmation must be signed by the issuer or confirming bank.

(2) A telegram may be a sufficient signed writing if it identifies its sender by an authorized authentication. The authentication may be in code and the authorized naming of the issuer in an advice of credit is a sufficient signing.

Sec. 5—105. Consideration. No consideration is necessary to establish a credit or to enlarge or otherwise modify its terms.

Sec. 5—106. Time and Effect of Establishment of Credit. (1) Unless otherwise agreed a credit is established

(a) as regards the customer as soon as a letter of credit is sent to him or the letter of credit or an authorized written advice of its issuance is sent to the beneficiary; and

(b) as regards the beneficiary when he receives a letter of credit or an authorized written advice of its issuance.

(2) Unless otherwise agreed once an irrevocable credit is established as regards the customer it can be modified or revoked only with the consent of the customer and once it is established as regards the beneficiary it can be modified or revoked only with his consent.

(3) Unless otherwise agreed after a revocable credit is established it may be modified or revoked by the issuer without notice to or consent from the customer or beneficiary.

(4) Notwithstanding any modification or revocation of a revocable credit any person authorized to honor or negotiate under the terms of the original credit is entitled to reimbursement for or honor of any draft or demand for payment duly honored or negotiated before receipt of notice of the modification or revocation and the issuer in turn is entitled to reimbursement from its customer.

Sec. 5—107. Advice of Credit; Confirmation; Error in Statement of Terms. (1) Unless otherwise specified an advising bank by advising a credit issued by another bank does not assume any obligation to honor drafts drawn or demands for payment made under the credit but it does assume obligation for the accuracy of its own statement.

(2) A confirming bank by confirming a credit becomes directly obligated on the credit to the extent of its confirmation as though it were its issuer and acquires the rights of an issuer.

(3) Even though an advising bank incorrectly advises the terms of a credit it has been authorized to advise the credit is established as against the issuer to the extent of its original terms.

(4) Unless otherwise specified the customer bears as against the issuer all risks of transmission and reasonable translation or interpretation of any message relating to a credit.

Sec. 5—108. "Notation Credit"; Exhaustion of Credit. (1) A credit which specifies that any person purchasing or paying drafts drawn or demands for payment made under it must note the amount of the draft or demand on the letter or advice of credit is a "notation credit."

(2) Under a notation credit

(a) a person paying the beneficiary or purchasing a draft or demand for payment from him acquires a right to honor only if the appropriate notation is made and by transferring or forwarding for honor the documents under the credit such a person warrants to the issuer that the notation has been made; and

(b) unless the credit or a signed statement that an appropriate notation has been made accompanies the draft or demand for payment the issuer may delay honor until evidence of notation has been procured which is satisfactory to it but its obligation and that of its customer continue for a reasonable time not exceeding thirty days to obtain such evidence.

(3) If the credit is not a notation credit

(a) the issuer may honor complying drafts or demands for payment presented to it in the order in which they are presented and is discharged pro tanto by honor of any such draft or demand;

(b) as between competing good faith purchasers of complying drafts or demands the person first purchasing has priority over a subsequent purchaser even though the later purchased draft or demand has been first honored.

Sec. 5—109. Issuer's Obligation to Its Customer. (1) An issuer's obligation to its customer includes good faith and observance of any general banking usage but unless otherwise agreed does not include liability or responsibility

(a) for performance of the underlying contract for sale or other transaction between the customer and the beneficiary; or

(b) for any act or omission of any person other than itself or its own branch or for loss or destruction of a draft, demand or document in transit or in the possession of others; or

(c) based on knowledge or lack of knowledge of any usage of any particular trade.

(2) An issuer must examine documents with care so as to ascertain that on their face they appear to comply with the terms of the credit but unless otherwise agreed assumes no liability or responsibility for the genuineness, falsification or effect of any document which appears on such examination to be regular on its face.

(3) A non-bank issuer is not bound by any banking usage of which it has no knowledge.

Sec. 5—110. Availability of Credit in Portions; Presenter's Reservation of Lien or Claim. (1) Unless otherwise specified a credit may be used in portions in the discretion of the beneficiary.

(2) Unless otherwise specified a person by presenting a documentary draft or demand for payment under a credit relinquishes upon its honor all claims to the

documents and a person by transferring such draft or demand or causing such presentment authorizes such relinquishment. An explicit reservation of claim makes the draft or demand non-complying.

Sec. 5—111. Warranties on Transfer and Presentment. (1) Unless otherwise agreed the beneficiary by transferring or presenting a documentary draft or demand for payment warrants to all interested parties that the necessary conditions of the credit have been complied with. This is in addition to any warranties arising under Articles 3, 4, 7 and 8.

(2) Unless otherwise agreed a negotiating, advising, confirming, collecting or issuing bank presenting or transferring a draft or demand for payment under a credit warrants only the matters warranted by a collecting bank under Article 4 and any such bank transferring a document warrants only the matters warranted by an intermediary under Articles 7 and 8.

Sec. 5—112. Time Allowed for Honor or Rejection; Withholding Honor or Rejection by Consent; "Presenter." (1) A bank to which a documentary draft or demand for payment is presented under a credit may without dishonor of the draft, demand or credit

(a) defer honor until the close of the third banking day following receipt of the documents; and

(b) further defer honor if the presenter has expressly or impliedly consented thereto.

Failure to honor within the time here specified constitutes dishonor of the draft or demand and of the credit [except as otherwise provided in subsection (4) of Section 5—114 on conditional payment].

Note: *The bracketed language in the last sentence of subsection (1) should be included only if the optional provisions of Sections 5—114(4) and (5) are included.*

(2) Upon dishonor the bank may unless otherwise instructed fulfill its duty to return the draft or demand and the documents by holding them at the disposal of the presenter and sending him an advice to that effect.

(3) "Presenter" means any person presenting a draft or demand for payment for honor under a credit even though that person is a confirming bank or other correspondent which is acting under an issuer's authorization.

Sec. 5—113. Indemnities. (1) A bank seeking to obtain (whether for itself or another) honor, negotiation or reimbursement under a credit may give an indemnity to induce such honor, negotiation or reimbursement.

(2) An indemnity agreement inducing honor, negotiation or reimbursement

(a) unless otherwise explicitly agreed applies to defects in the documents but not in the goods; and

(b) unless a longer time is explicitly agreed expires at the end of ten business days following receipt of the documents by the ultimate customer unless notice of objection is sent before such expiration date. The ultimate customer may send notice of objection to the person from whom he received the documents and any bank receiving such notice is under a duty to send notice to its transferor before its midnight deadline.

Sec. 5—114. Issuer's Duty and Privilege to Honor; Right to Reimbursement. (1) An issuer must honor a draft or demand for payment which complies with the terms of the relevant credit regardless of whether the goods or documents conform to the underlying contract for sale or other contract between the customer and the beneficiary. The issuer is not excused from honor of such a draft or demand by reason of an additional general term that all documents must be satisfactory to the issuer, but an issuer may require that specified documents must be satisfactory to it.

(2) Unless otherwise agreed when documents appear on their face to comply with the terms of a credit but a required document does not in fact conform to the warranties made on negotiation or transfer of a document of title (Section 7—507) or of a security (Section 8—306) or is forged or fraudulent or there is fraud in the transaction

(*a*) the issuer must honor the draft or demand for payment if honor is demanded by a negotiating bank or other holder of the draft or demand which has taken the draft or demand under the credit and under circumstances which would make it a holder in due course (Section 3—302) and in an appropriate case would make it a person to whom a document of title has been duly negotiated (Section 7—502) or a bona fide purchaser of a security (Section 8—302); and

(*b*) in all other cases as against its customer, an issuer acting in good faith may honor the draft or demand for payment despite notification from the customer of fraud, forgery or other defect not apparent on the face of the documents but a court of appropriate jurisdiction may enjoin such honor.

(3) Unless otherwise agreed an issuer which has duly honored a draft or demand for payment is entitled to immediate reimbursement of any payment made under the credit and to be put in effectively available funds not later than the day before maturity of any acceptance made under the credit.

[(4) When a credit provides for payment by the issuer on receipt of notice that the required documents are in the possession of a correspondent or other agent of the issuer

(*a*) any payment made on receipt of such notice is conditional; and

(*b*) the issuer may reject documents which do not comply with the credit if it does so within three banking days following its receipt of the documents; and

(*c*) in the event of such rejection, the issuer is entitled by charge-back or otherwise to return of the payment made.]

[(5) In the case covered by subsection (4) failure to reject documents within the time specified in subparagraph (*b*) constitutes acceptance of the documents and makes the payment final in favor of the beneficiary.]

Note: *Subsections (4) and (5) are bracketed as optional. If they are included the bracketed language in the last sentence of Section 5—112(1) should also be included.*

Sec. 5—115. Remedy for Improper Dishonor or Anticipatory Repudiation. (1) When an issuer wrongfully dishonors a draft or demand for payment presented under a credit the person entitled to honor has with respect to any documents the rights of a person in the position of a seller (Section 2—707) and may recover from the issuer the face amount of the draft or demand together with incidental damages under Section 2—710 on seller's incidental damages and interest but less any amount realized by resale or other use or disposition of the subject matter of the transaction. In the event no resale or other utilization is made the documents, goods or other subject matter involved in the transaction must be turned over to the issuer on payment of judgment.

(2) When an issuer wrongfully cancels or otherwise repudiates a credit before presentment of a draft or demand for payment drawn under it the beneficiary has the rights of a seller after anticipatory repudiation by the buyer under Section 2—610 if he learns of the repudiation in time reasonably to avoid procurement of the required documents. Otherwise the beneficiary has an immediate right of action for wrongful dishonor.

Sec. 5—116. Transfer and Assignment. (1) The right to draw under a credit can be transferred or assigned only when the credit is expressly designated as transferable or assignable.

(2) Even though the credit specifically states that it is nontransferable or nonassignable the beneficiary may before performance of the conditions of the credit assign his right to proceeds. Such an assignment is an assignment of a contract right under Article 9 on Secured Transactions and is governed by that Article except that

(*a*) the assignment is ineffective until the letter of credit or advice of credit is delivered to the assignee which delivery constitutes perfection of the security interest under Article 9; and

(*b*) the issuer may honor drafts or demands for payment drawn under the credit until it receives a notification of the assignment signed by the beneficiary which reasonably identifies the credit involved in the assignment and contains a request to pay the assignee; and

(c) after what reasonably appears to be such a notification has been received the issuer may without dishonor refuse to accept or pay even to a person otherwise entitled to honor until the letter of credit or advice of credit is exhibited to the issuer.

(3) Except where the beneficiary has effectively assigned his right to draw or his right to proceeds, nothing in this section limits his right to transfer or negotiate drafts or demands drawn under the credit.

Sec. 5—117. Insolvency of Bank Holding Funds for Documentary Credit. (1) Where an issuer or an advising or confirming bank or a bank which has for a customer procured issuance of a credit by another bank becomes insolvent before final payment under the credit and the credit is one to which this Article is made applicable by paragraphs (a) or (b) of Section 5—102(1) on scope, the receipt or allocation of funds or collateral to secure or meet obligations under the credit shall have the following results:

(a) to the extent of any funds or collateral turned over after or before the insolvency as indemnity against or specifically for the purpose of payment of drafts or demands for payment drawn under the designated credit, the drafts or demands are entitled to payment in preference over depositors or other general creditors of the issuer or bank; and

(b) on expiration of the credit or surrender of the beneficiary's rights under it unused any person who has given such funds or collateral is similarly entitled to return thereof; and

(c) a charge to a general or current account with a bank if specifically consented to for the purpose of indemnity against or payment of drafts or demands for payment drawn under the designated credit falls under the same rules as if the funds had been drawn out in cash and then turned over with specific instructions.

(2) After honor or reimbursement under this section the customer or other person for whose account the insolvent bank has acted is entitled to receive the documents involved.

ARTICLE VI

BULK TRANSFERS

Sec. 6—101. Short Title. This Article shall be known and may be cited as Uniform Commercial Code—Bulk Transfers.

Sec. 6—102. "Bulk Transfer"; Transfers of Equipment; Enterprises Subject to This Article; Bulk Transfers Subject to This Article. (1) A "bulk transfer" is any transfer in bulk and not in the ordinary course of the transferor's business of a major part of the materials, supplies, merchandise or other inventory (Section 9—109) of an enterprise subject to this Article.

(2) A transfer of a substantial part of the equipment (Section 9—109) of such an enterprise is a bulk transfer if it is made in connection with a bulk transfer of inventory, but not otherwise.

(3) The enterprises subject to this Article are all those whose principal business is the sale of merchandise from stock, including those who manufacture what they sell.

(4) Except as limited by the following section all bulk transfers of goods located within this state are subject to this Article.

Sec. 6—103. Transfers Excepted From This Article. The following transfers are not subject to this Article:

(1) Those made to give security for the performance of an obligation;

(2) General assignments for the benefit of all the creditors of the transferor, and subsequent transfers by this assignee thereunder;

(3) Transfers in settlement or realization of a lien or other security interest;

(4) Sales by executors, administrators, receivers, trustees in bankruptcy, or any public officer under judicial process;

(5) Sales made in the course of judicial or administrative proceedings for the dissolution or reorganization of a corporation and of which notice is sent to the creditors of the corporation pursuant to order of the court or administrative agency;

(6) Transfers to a person maintaining a known place of business in this State who becomes bound to pay the debts of the transferor in full and gives public notice of that fact, and who is solvent after becoming so bound;

(7) A transfer to a new business enterprise organized to take over and continue the business, if public notice of the transaction is given and the new enterprise assumes the debts of the transferor and he receives nothing from the transaction except an interest in the new enterprise junior to the claims of creditors;

(8) Transfers of property which is exempt from execution.

Public notice under subsection (6) or subsection (7) may be given by publishing once a week for two consecutive weeks in a newspaper of general circulation where the transferor had its principal place of business in this state an advertisement including the names and addresses of the transferor and transferee and the effective date of the transfer.

Sec. 6—104. Schedule of Property, List of Creditors. (1) Except as provided with respect to auction sales (Section 6—108), a bulk transfer subject to this Article is ineffective against any creditor of the transferor unless:

(a) The transferee requires the transferor to furnish a list of his existing creditors prepared as stated in this section; and

(b) The parties prepare a schedule of the property transferred sufficient to identify it; and

(c) The transferee preserves the list and schedule for six months next following the transfer and permits inspection of either or both and copying therefrom at all reasonable hours by any creditor of the transferor, or files the list and schedule in (*a public office to be here identified*).

(2) The list of creditors must be signed and sworn to or affirmed by the transferor or his agent. It must contain the names and business addresses of all creditors of the transferor, with the amounts when known, and also the names of all persons who are known to the transferor to assert claims against him even though such claims are disputed. If the transferor is the obligor of an outstanding issue of bonds, debentures or the like as to which there is an indenture trustee, the list of creditors need include only the name and address of the indenture trustee and the aggregate outstanding principal amount of the issue.

(3) Responsibility for the completeness and accuracy of the list of creditors rests on the transferor, and the transfer is not rendered ineffective by errors or omissions therein unless the transferee is shown to have had knowledge.

Sec. 6—105. Notice to Creditors. In addition to the requirements of the preceding section, any bulk transfer subject to this Article except one made by auction sale (Section 6—108) is ineffective against any creditor of the transferor unless at least ten days before he takes possession of the goods or pays for them, whichever happens first, the transferee gives notice of the transfer in the manner and to the persons hereafter provided (Section 6—107).

[**Sec. 6—106. Application of the Proceeds.** In addition to the requirements of the two preceding sections:

(1) Upon every bulk transfer subject to this Article for which new consideration becomes payable except those made by sale at auction it is the duty of the transferee to assure that such consideration is applied so far as necessary to pay those debts of the transferor which are either shown on the list furnished by the transferor (Section

6—104) or filed in writing in the place stated in the notice (Section 6—107) within thirty days after the mailing of such notice. This duty of the transferee runs to all the holders of such debts, and may be enforced by any of them for the benefit of all.

(2) If any of said debts are in dispute the necessary sum may be withheld from distribution until the dispute is settled or adjudicated.

(3) If the consideration payable is not enough to pay all of the said debts in full distribution shall be made pro rata.]

Note: *This section is bracketed to indicate division of opinion as to whether or not it is a wise provision, and to suggest that this is a point on which state enactments may differ without serious damage to the principle of uniformity.*

In any state where this section is omitted, the following parts of sections, also bracketed in the text, should also be omitted, namely:

Section 6—107(2)(e).
 6—108(3)(c).
 6—109(2).

In any state where this section is enacted, these other provisions should be also.

[(4) The transferee may within ten days after he takes possession of the goods pay the consideration into the (specify court) in the county where the transferor had its principal place of business in this state and thereafter may discharge his duty under this section by giving notice by registered or certified mail to all the persons to whom the duty runs that the consideration has been paid into that court and that they should file their claims there. On motion of any interested party, the court may order the distribution of the consideration to the persons entitled to it.]

Note: *Optional subsection (4) is recommended for those states which do not have a general statute providing for payment of money into court.*

Sec. 6—107. The Notice. (1) The notice to creditors (Section 6—105) shall state:

(*a*) that a bulk transfer is about to be made; and

(*b*) the names and business addresses of the transferor and transferee, and all other business names and addresses used by the transferor within three years last past so far as known to the transferee; and

(*c*) whether or not all the debts of the transferor are to be paid in full as they fall due as a result of the transaction, and if so, the address to which creditors should send their bills.

(2) If the debts of the transferor are not to be paid in full as they fall due or if the transferee is in doubt on that point then the notice shall state further:

(*a*) the location and general description of the property to be transferred and the estimated total of the transferor's debts;

(*b*) the address where the schedule of property and list of creditors (Section 6—104) may be inspected;

(*c*) whether the transfer is to pay existing debts and if so the amount of such debts and to whom owing;

(*d*) whether the transfer is for new consideration and if so the amount of such consideration and the time and place of payment; [and]

[(*e*) if for new consideration the time and place where creditors of the transferor are to file their claims.]

(3) The notice in any case shall be delivered personally or sent by registered or certified mail to all the persons shown on the list of creditors furnished by the transferor (Section 6—104) and to all other persons who are known to the transferee to hold or assert claims against the transferor.

Sec. 6—108. Auction Sales; "Auctioneer." (1) A bulk transfer is subject to this Article even though it is by sale of auction, but only in the manner and with the results stated in this section.

(2) The transferor shall furnish a list of his creditors and assist in the preparation of a schedule of the property to be sold, both prepared as before stated (Section 6—104).

(3) The person or persons other than the transferor who direct, control or are responsible for the auction are collectively called the "auctioneer." The auctioneer shall:

(*a*) receive and retain the list of creditors and prepare and retain the schedule of property for the period stated in this Article (Section 6—104);

(*b*) give notice of the auction personally or by registered or certified mail at least ten days before it occurs to all persons shown on the list of creditors and to all other persons who are known to him to hold or assert claims against the transferor; [and]

[(*c*) assure that the net proceeds of the auction are applied as provided in this Article (Section 6—106).]

(4) Failure of the auctioneer to perform any of these duties does not affect the validity of the sale or the title of the purchasers, but if the auctioneer knows that the auction constitutes a bulk transfer such failure renders the auctioneer liable to the creditors of the transferor as a class for the sums owing to them from the transferor up to but not exceeding the net proceeds of the auction. If the auctioneer consists of several persons their liability is joint and several.

Sec. 6—109. What Creditors Protected; [Credit for Payment to Particular Creditors]. (1) The creditors of the transferor mentioned in this Article are those holding claims based on transactions or events occurring before the bulk transfer, but creditors who become such after notice to creditors is given (Sections 6—105 and 6—107) are not entitled to notice.

[(2) Against the aggregate obligation imposed by the provisions of this Article concerning the application of the proceeds (Section 6—106 and subsection (3) (*c*) of 6—108) the transferee or auctioneer is entitled to credit for sums paid to particular creditors of the transferor, not exceeding the sums believed in good faith at the time of the payment to be properly payable to such creditors.]

Sec. 6—110. Subsequent Transfers. When the title of a transferee to property is subject to a defect by reason of his non-compliance with the requirements of this Article, then:

(1) a purchaser of any of such property from such transferee who pays no value or who takes with notice of such non-compliance takes subject to such defect, but

(2) a purchaser for value in good faith and without such notice takes free of such defect.

Sec. 6—111. Limitation of Actions and Levies. No action under this Article shall be brought nor levy made more than six months after the date on which the transferee took possession of the goods unless the transfer has been concealed. If the transfer has been concealed, actions may be brought or levies made within six months after its discovery.

ARTICLE VII

WAREHOUSE RECEIPTS, BILLS OF LADING AND OTHER DOCUMENTS OF TITLE

PART I

GENERAL

Sec. 7—101. Short Title. This Article shall be known and may be cited as Uniform Commercial Code—Documents of Title.

Sec. 7—102. Definitions and Index of Definitions. (1) In this Article, unless the context otherwise requires:

(*a*) "Bailee" means the person who by a warehouse receipt, bill of lading or other document of title acknowledges possession of goods and contracts to deliver them.

(*b*) "Consignee" means the person named in a bill to whom or to whose order the bill promises delivery.

(*c*) "Consignor" means the person named in a bill as the person from whom the goods have been received for shipment.

(*d*) "Delivery order" means a written order to deliver goods directed to a warehouseman, carrier or other person who in the ordinary course of business issues warehouse receipts or bills of lading.

(*e*) "Document" means document of title as defined in the general definitions in Article 1 (Section 1–201).

(*f*) "Goods" means all things which are treated as movable for the purposes of a contract of storage or transportation.

(*g*) "Issuer" means a bailee who issues a document except that in relation to an unaccepted delivery order it means the person who orders the possessor of goods to deliver. Issuer includes any person for whom an agent or employee purports to act in issuing a document if the agent or employee has real or apparent authority to issue documents, notwithstanding that the issuer received no goods or that the goods were misdescribed or that in any other respect the agent or employee violated his instructions.

(*h*) "Warehouseman" is a person engaged in the business of storing goods for hire.

(2) Other definitions applying to this Article or to specified Parts thereof, and the sections in which they appear are:

"Duly negotiate." Section 7–501.

"Person entitled under the document." Section 7–403(4).

(3) Definitions in other Articles applying to this Article and the sections in which they appear are:

"Contract for sale." Section 2–106.

"Overseas." Section 2–323.

"Receipt" of goods. Section 2–103.

(4) In addition Article 1 contains general definitions and principles of construction and interpretation applicable throughout this Article.

Sec. 7–103. Relation of Article to Treaty, Statute, Tariff, Classification or Regulation. To the extent that any treaty or statute of the United States, regulatory statute of this State or tariff, classification or regulation filed or issued pursuant thereto is applicable, the provisions of this Article are subject thereto.

Sec. 7–104. Negotiable and Non-Negotiable Warehouse Receipt, Bill of Lading or Other Document of Title. (1) A warehouse receipt, bill of lading or other document of title is negotiable

(*a*) if by its terms the goods are to be delivered to bearer or to the order of a named person; or

(*b*) where recognized in overseas trade, if it runs to a named person or assigns.

(2) Any other document is non-negotiable. A bill of lading in which it is stated that the goods are consigned to a named person is not made negotiable by a provision that the goods are to be delivered only against a written order signed by the same or another named person.

Sec. 7–105. Construction Against Negative Implication. The omission from either Part 2 or Part 3 of this Article of a provision corresponding to a provision made in the other Part does not imply that a corresponding rule of law is not applicable.

PART II

WAREHOUSE RECEIPTS: SPECIAL PROVISIONS

Sec. 7–201. Who May Issue a Warehouse Receipt; Storage Under Government Bond. (1) A warehouse receipt may be issued by any warehouseman.

(2) Where goods including distilled spirits and agricultural commodities are

stored under a statute requiring a bond against withdrawal or a license for the issuance of receipts in the nature of warehouse receipts, a receipt issued for the goods has like effect as a warehouse receipt even though issued by a person who is the owner of the goods and is not a warehouseman.

Sec. 7—202. Form of Warehouse Receipt; Essential Terms; Optional Terms. (1) A warehouse receipt need not be in any particular form.

(2) Unless a warehouse receipt embodies within its written or printed terms each of the following, the warehouseman is liable for damages caused by the omission to a person injured thereby:

(*a*) the location of the warehouse where the goods are stored;

(*b*) the date of issue of the receipt;

(*c*) the consecutive number of the receipt;

(*d*) a statement whether the goods received will be delivered to the bearer, to a specified person, or to a specified person or his order;

(*e*) the rate of storage and handling charges, except that where goods are stored under a field warehousing arrangement a statement of that fact is sufficient on a non-negotiable receipt;

(*f*) a description of the goods or of the packages containing them;

(*g*) the signature of the warehouseman, which may be made by his authorized agent;

(*h*) if the receipt is issued for goods of which the warehouseman is owner, either solely or jointly or in common with others, the fact of such ownership; and

(*i*) a statement of the amount of advances made and of liabilities incurred for which the warehouseman claims a lien or security interest (Section 7—209). If the precise amount of such advances made or of such liabilities incurred is, at the time of the issue of the receipt, unknown to the warehouseman or to his agent who issues it, a statement of the fact that advances have been made or liabilities incurred and the purpose thereof is sufficient.

(3) A warehouseman may insert in his receipt any other terms which are not contrary to the provisions of this Act and do not impair his obligation of delivery (Section 7—403) or his duty of care (Section 7—204). Any contrary provisions shall be ineffective.

Sec. 7—203. Liability for Non-Receipt or Misdescription. A party to or purchaser for value in good faith of a document of title other than a bill of lading relying in either case upon the description therein of the goods may recover from the issuer damages caused by the non-receipt or misdescription of the goods, except to the extent that the document conspicuously indicates that the issuer does not know whether any part or all of the goods in fact were received or conform to the description, as where the description is in terms of marks or labels or kind, quantity or condition, or the receipt or description is qualified by "contents, condition and quality unknown," "said to contain" or the like, if such indication be true, or the party or purchaser otherwise has notice.

Sec. 7—204. Duty of Care; Contractual Limitation of Warehouseman's Liability. (1) A warehouseman is liable for damages for loss of or injury to the goods caused by his failure to exercise such care in regard to them as a reasonably careful man would exercise under like circumstances but unless otherwise agreed he is not liable for damages which could not have been avoided by the exercise of such care.

(2) Damages may be limited by a term in the warehouse receipt or storage agreement limiting the amount of liability in case of loss or damage, and setting forth a specific liability per article or item, or value per unit of weight, beyond which the warehouseman shall not be liable; provided, however, that such liability may on written request of the bailor at the time of signing such storage agreement or within a reasonable time after receipt of the warehouse receipt be increased on part or all of the goods thereunder, in which event increased rates may be charged based on such increased valuation, but that no such increase shall be permitted contrary to

a lawful limitation of liability contained in the warehouseman's tariff, if any. No such limitation is effective with respect to the warehouseman's liability for conversion to his own use.

(3) Reasonable provisions as to the time and manner of presenting claims and instituting actions based on the bailment may be included in the warehouse receipt or tariff.

(4) This section does not impair or repeal.

Note: *Insert in subsection (4) a reference to any statute which imposes a higher responsibility upon the warehouseman or invalidates contractual limitations which would be permissible under this Article.*

Sec. 7—205. Title Under Warehouse Receipt Defeated in Certain Cases. A buyer in the ordinary course of business of fungible goods sold and delivered by a warehouseman who is also in the business of buying and selling such goods takes free of any claim under a warehouse receipt even though it has been duly negotiated.

Sec. 7—206. Termination of Storage at Warehouseman's Option. (1) A warehouseman may on notifying the person on whose account the goods are held and any other person known to claim an interest in the goods require payment of any charges and removal of the goods from the warehouse at the termination of the period of storage fixed by the document, or, if no period is fixed, within a stated period not less than thirty days after the notification. If the goods are not removed before the date specified in the notification, the warehouseman may sell them in accordance with the provisions of the section on enforcement of a warehouseman's lien (Section 7—210).

(2) If a warehouseman in good faith believes that the goods are about to deteriorate or decline in value to less than the amount of his lien within the time prescribed in subsection (1) for notification, advertisement and sale, the warehouseman may specify in the notification any reasonable shorter time for removal of the goods and in case the goods are not removed may sell them at public sale held not less than one week after a single advertisement or posting.

(3) If as a result of a quality or condition of the goods of which the warehouseman had no notice at the time of deposit the goods are a hazard to other property or to the warehouse or to persons, the warehouseman may sell the goods at public or private sale without advertisement on reasonable notification to all persons known to claim an interest in the goods. If the warehouseman after a reasonable effort is unable to sell the goods he may dispose of them in any lawful manner and shall incur no liability by reason of such disposition.

(4) The warehouseman must deliver the goods to any person entitled to them under this Article upon due demand made at any time prior to sale or other disposition under this section.

(5) The warehouseman may satisfy his lien from the proceeds of any sale or disposition under this section but must hold the balance for delivery on the demand of any person to whom he would have been bound to deliver the goods.

Sec. 7—207. Goods Must Be Kept Separate; Fungible Goods. (1) Unless the warehouse receipt otherwise provides, a warehouseman must keep separate the goods covered by each receipt so as to permit at all times identification and delivery of those goods except that different lots of fungible goods may be commingled.

(2) Fungible goods so commingled are owned in common by the persons entitled thereto and the warehouseman is severally liable to each owner for that owner's share. Where because of overissue a mass of fungible goods is insufficient to meet all the receipts which the warehouseman has issued against it, the persons entitled include all holders to whom overissued receipts have been duly negotiated.

Sec. 7—208. Altered Warehouse Receipts. Where a blank in a negotiable warehouse receipt has been filled in without authority, a purchaser for value and without notice of the want of authority may treat the insertion as authorized. Any other unauthorized alteration leaves any receipt enforceable against the issuer according to its original tenor.

Sec. 7—209. Lien of Warehouseman. (1) A warehouseman has a lien against the bailor on the goods covered by a warehouse receipt or on the proceeds thereof in his possession for charges for storage or transportation (including demurrage and terminal charges), insurance, labor, or charges present or future in relation to the goods, and for expenses necessary for preservation of the goods or reasonably incurred in their sale pursuant to law. If the person on whose account the goods are held is liable for like charges or expenses in relation to other goods whenever deposited and it is stated in the receipt that a lien is claimed for charges and expenses in relation to other goods, the warehouseman also has a lien against him for such charges and expenses whether or not the other goods have been delivered by the warehouseman. But against a person to whom a negotiable warehouse receipt is duly negotiated a warehouseman's lien is limited to charges in an amount or at a rate specified on the receipt or if no charges are so specified then to a reasonable charge for storage of the goods covered by the receipt subsequent to the date of the receipt.

(2) The warehouseman may also reserve a security interest against the bailor for a maximum amount specified on the receipt for charges other than those specified in subsection (1), such as for money advanced and interest. Such a security interest is governed by the Article on Secured Transactions (Article 9).

(3) A warehouseman's lien for charges and expenses under subsection (1) or a security interest under subsection (2) is also effective against any person who so entrusted the bailor with possession of the goods that a pledge of them by him to a good faith purchaser for value would have been valid but is not effective against a person as to whom the document confers no right in the goods covered by it under Section 7—503.

(4) A warehouseman loses his lien on any goods which he voluntarily delivers or which he unjustifiably refuses to deliver.

Sec. 7—210. Enforcement of Warehouseman's Lien. (1) Except as provided in subsection (2), a warehouseman's lien may be enforced by public or private sale of the goods in block or in parcels, at any time or place and on any terms which are commercially reasonable, after notifying all persons known to claim an interest in the goods. Such notification must include a statement of the amount due, the nature of the proposed sale and the time and place of any public sale. The fact that a better price could have been obtained by a sale at a different time or in a different method from that selected by the warehouseman is not of itself sufficient to establish that the sale was not made in a commercially reasonable manner. If the warehouseman either sells the goods in the usual manner in any recognized market therefor, or if he sells at the price current in such market at the time of his sale, or if he has otherwise sold in conformity with commercially reasonable practices among dealers in the type of goods sold, he has sold in a commercially reasonable manner. A sale of more goods than apparently necessary to be offered to insure satisfaction of the obligation is not commercially reasonable except in cases covered by the preceding sentence.

(2) A warehouseman's lien on goods other than goods stored by a merchant in the course of his business may be enforced only as follows:

(a) All persons known to claim an interest in the goods must be notified.

(b) The notification must be delivered in person or sent by registered or certified letter to the last known address of any person to be notified.

(c) The notification must include an itemized statement of the claim, a description of the goods subject to the lien, a demand for payment within a specified time not less than ten days after receipt of the notification, and a conspicuous statement that unless the claim is paid within that time the goods will be advertised for sale and sold by auction at a specified time and place.

(d) The sale must conform to the terms of the notification.

(e) The sale must be held at the nearest suitable place to that where the goods are held or stored.

(f) After the expiration of the time given in the notification, an advertisement of the sale must be published once a week for two weeks consecutively in a newspaper of general circulation where the sale is to be held The advertisement must include a description of the goods, the name of the person on whose account they are being held, and the time and place of the sale. The sale must take place at least fifteen days after the first publication. If there is no newspaper of general circulation where the sale is to be held, the advertisement must be posted at least ten days before the sale in not less than six conspicuous places in the neighborhood of the proposed sale.

(3) Before any sale pursuant to this section any person claiming a right in the goods may pay the amount necessary to satisfy the lien and the reasonable expenses incurred under this section. In that event the goods must not be sold, but must be retained by the warehouseman subject to the terms of the receipt and this Article.

(4) The warehouseman may buy at any public sale pursuant to this section.

(5) A purchaser in good faith of goods sold to enforce a warehouseman's lien takes the goods free of any rights of persons against whom the lien was valid, despite noncompliance by the warehouseman with the requirements of this section.

(6) The warehouseman may satisfy his lien from the proceeds of any sale pursuant to this section but must hold the balance, if any, for delivery on demand to any person to whom he would have been bound to deliver the goods.

(7) The rights provided by this section shall be in addition to all other rights allowed by law to a creditor against his debtor.

(8) Where a lien is on goods stored by a merchant in the course of his business the lien may be enforced in accordance with either subsection (1) or (2).

(9) The warehouseman is liable for damages caused by failure to comply with the requirements for sale under this section and in case of willful violation is liable for conversion.

PART III

BILLS OF LADING: SPECIAL PROVISIONS

Sec. 7—301. Liability for Non-Receipt or Misdescription; "Said to Contain"; "Shipper's Load and Count"; Improper Handling. (1) A consignee of a non-negotiable bill who has given value in good faith or a holder to whom a negotiable bill has been duly negotiated relying in either case upon the description therein of the goods, or upon the date therein shown, may recover from the issuer damages caused by the misdating of the bill or the non-receipt or misdescription of the goods, except to the extent that the document indicates that the issuer does not know whether any part or all of the goods in fact were received or conform to the description, as where the description is in terms of marks or labels or kind, quantity, or condition or the receipt or description is qualified by "contents or condition of contents of packages unknown," "said to contain," "shipper's weight, load and count" or the like, if such indication be true.

(2) When goods are loaded by an issuer who is a common carrier, the issuer must count the packages of goods if package freight and ascertain the kind and quantity if bulk freight. In such cases "shipper's weight, load and count" or other words indicating that the description was made by the shipper are ineffective except as to freight concealed by packages.

(3) When bulk freight is loaded by a shipper who makes available to the issuer adequate facilities for weighing such freight, an issuer who is a common carrier must ascertain the kind and quantity within a reasonable time after receiving the written request of the shipper to do so. In such cases "shipper's weight" or other words of like purport are ineffective.

(4) The issuer may by inserting in the bill the words "shipper's weight, load and count" or other words of like purport indicate that the goods were loaded by the shipper; and if such statement be true the issuer shall not be liable for damages caused by the improper loading. But their omission does not imply liability for such damages.

(5) The shipper shall be deemed to have guaranteed to the issuer the accuracy at the time of shipment of the description, marks, labels, number, kind, quantity, condition and weight, as furnished by him; and the shipper shall indemnify the issuer against damage caused by inaccuracies in such particulars. The right of the issuer to such indemnity shall in no way limit his responsibility and liability under the contract of carriage to any person other than the shipper.

Sec. 7—302. Through Bills of Lading and Similar Documents. (1) The issuer of a through bill of lading or other document embodying an undertaking to be performed in part by persons acting as its agents or by connecting carriers is liable to anyone entitled to recover on the document for any breach by such other persons or by a connecting carrier of its obligation under the document but to the extent that the bill covers an undertaking to be performed overseas or in territory not contiguous to the continental United States or an undertaking including matters other than transportation this liability may be varied by agreement of the parties.

(2) Where goods covered by a through bill of lading or other document embodying an undertaking to be performed in part by persons other than the issuer are received by any such person, he is subject with respect to his own performance while the goods are in his possession to the obligation of the issuer. His obligation is discharged by delivery of the goods to another such person pursuant to the document, and does not include liability for breach by any other such persons or by the issuer.

(3) The issuer of such through bill of lading or other document shall be entitled to recover from the connecting carrier or such other person in possession of the goods when the breach of the obligation under the document occurred, the amount it may be required to pay to anyone entitled to recover on the document therefor, as may be evidenced by any receipt, judgment, or transcript thereof, and the amount of any expense reasonably incurred by it in defending any action brought by anyone entitled to recover on the document therefor.

Sec. 7—303. Diversion; Reconsignment; Change of Instructions. (1) Unless the bill of lading otherwise provides, the carrier may deliver the goods to a person or destination other than that stated in the bill or may otherwise dispose of the goods on instructions from

(*a*) the holder of a negotiable bill; or

(*b*) the consignor on a non-negotiable bill notwithstanding contrary instructions from the consignee; or

(*c*) the consignee on a non-negotiable bill in the absence of contrary instructions from the consignor, if the goods have arrived at the billed destination or if the consignee is in possession of the bill; or

(*d*) the consignee on a non-negotiable bill if he is entitled as against the consignor to dispose of them.

(2) Unless such instructions are noted on a negotiable bill of lading, a person to whom the bill is duly negotiated can hold the bailee according to the original terms.

Sec. 7—304. Bills of Lading in a Set. (1) Except where customary in overseas transportation, a bill of lading must not be issued in a set of parts. The issuer is liable for damages caused by violation of this subsection.

(2) Where a bill of lading is lawfully drawn in a set of parts, each of which is numbered and expressed to be valid only if the goods have not been delivered against any other part, the whole of the parts constitute one bill.

(3) Where a bill of lading is lawfully issued in a set of parts and different parts are negotiated to different persons, the title of the holder to whom the first due

negotiation is made prevails as to both the document and the goods even though any later holder may have received the goods from the carrier in good faith and discharged the carrier's obligation by surrender of his part.

(4) Any person who negotiates or transfers a single part of a bill of lading drawn in a set is liable to holders of that part as if it were the whole set.

(5) The bailee is obliged to deliver in accordance with Part 4 of this Article against the first presented part of a bill of lading lawfully drawn in a set. Such delivery discharges the bailee's obligation on the whole bill.

Sec. 7—305. Destination Bills. (1) Instead of issuing a bill of lading to the consignor at the place of shipment a carrier may at the request of the consignor procure the bill to be issued at destination or at any other place designated in the request.

(2) Upon request of anyone entitled as against the carrier to control the goods while in transit and on surrender of any outstanding bill of lading or other receipt covering such goods, the issuer may procure a substitute bill to be issued at any place designated in the request.

Sec. 7—306. Altered Bills of Lading. An unauthorized alteration or filling in of a blank in a bill of lading leaves the bill enforceable according to its original tenor.

Sec. 7—307. Lien of Carrier. (1) A carrier has a lien on the goods covered by a bill of lading for charges subsequent to the date of its receipt of the goods for storage or transportation (including demurrage and terminal charges) and for expenses necessary for preservation of the goods incident to their transportation or reasonably incurred in their sale pursuant to law. But against a purchaser for value of a negotiable bill of lading a carrier's lien is limited to charges stated in the bill or the applicable tariffs, or if no charges are stated then to a reasonable charge.

(2) A lien for charges and expenses under subsection (1) on goods which the carrier was required by law to receive for transportation is effective against the consignor or any person entitled to the goods unless the carrier had notice that the consignor lacked authority to subject the goods to such charges and expenses. Any other lien under subsection (1) is effective against the consignor and any person who permitted the bailor to have control or possession of the goods unless the carrier had notice that the bailor lacked such authority.

(3) A carrier loses his lien on any goods which he voluntarily delivers or which he unjustifiably refuses to deliver.

Sec. 7—308. Enforcement of Carrier's Lien. (1) A carrier's lien may be enforced by public or private sale of the goods, in bloc or in parcels, at any time or place and on any terms which are commercially reasonable, after notifying all persons known to claim an interest in the goods. Such notification must include a statement of the amount due, the nature of the proposed sale and the time and place of any public sale. The fact that a better price could have been obtained by a sale at a different time or in a different method from that selected by the carrier is not of itself sufficient to establish that the sale was not made in a commercially reasonable manner. If the carrier either sells the goods in the usual manner in any recognized market therefor or if he sells at the price current in such market at the time of his sale or if he has otherwise sold in conformity with commercially reasonable practices among dealers in the type of goods sold he has sold in a commercially reasonable manner. A sale of more goods than apparently necessary to be offered to ensure satisfaction of the obligation is not commercially reasonable except in cases covered by the preceding sentence.

(2) Before any sale pursuant to this section any person claiming a right in the goods may pay the amount necessary to satisfy the lien and the reasonable expenses incurred under this section. In that event the goods must not be sold, but must be retained by the carrier subject to the terms of the bill and this Article.

(3) The carrier may buy at any public sale pursuant to this section.

(4) A purchaser in good faith of goods sold to enforce a carrier's lien takes the

goods free of any rights of persons against whom the lien was valid, despite non-compliance by the carrier with the requirements of this section.

(5) The carrier may satisfy his lien from the proceeds of any sale pursuant to this section but must hold the balance, if any, for delivery on demand to any person to whom he would have been bound to deliver the goods.

(6) The rights provided by this section shall be in addition to all other rights allowed by law to a creditor against his debtor.

(7) A carrier's lien may be enforced in accordance with either subsection (1) or the procedure set forth in subsection (2) of Section 7—210.

(8) The carrier is liable for damages caused by failure to comply with the requirements for sale under this section and in case of willful violation is liable for conversion.

Sec. 7—309. Duty of Care; Contractual Limitation of Carrier's Liability. (1) A carrier who issues a bill of lading whether negotiable or non-negotiable must exercise the degree of care in relation to the goods which a reasonably careful man would exercise under like circumstances. This subsection does not repeal or change any law or rule of law which imposes liability upon a common carrier for damages not caused by its negligence.

(2) Damages may be limited by a provision that the carrier's liability shall not exceed a value stated in the document if the carrier's rates are dependent upon value and the consignor by the carrier's tariff is afforded an opportunity to declare a higher value or a value as lawfully provided in the tariff, or where no tariff is filed he is otherwise advised of such opportunity; but no such limitation is effective with respect to the carrier's liability for conversion to its own use.

(3) Reasonable provisions as to the time and manner of presenting claims and instituting actions based on the shipment may be included in a bill of lading or tariff.

PART IV

WAREHOUSE RECEIPTS AND BILLS OF LADING: GENERAL OBLIGATIONS

Sec. 7—401. Irregularities in Issue of Receipt or Bill or Conduct of Issuer. The obligations imposed by this Article on an issuer apply to a document of title regardless of the fact that

(a) the document may not comply with the requirements of this Article or of any other law or regulation regarding its issue, form or content; or

(b) the issuer may have violated laws regulating the conduct of his business; or

(c) the goods covered by the document were owned by the bailee at the time the document was issued; or

(d) the person issuing the document does not come within the definition of warehouseman if it purports to be a warehouse receipt.

Sec. 7—402. Duplicate Receipt or Bill; Overissue. Neither a duplicate nor any other document of title purporting to cover goods already represented by an outstanding document of the same issuer confers any right in the goods, except as provided in the case of bills in a set, overissue of documents for fungible goods and substitutes for lost, stolen or destroyed documents. But the issuer is liable for damages caused by his overissue or failure to identify a duplicate document as such by conspicuous notation on its face.

Sec. 7—403. Obligation of Warehouseman or Carrier to Deliver; Excuse. (1) The bailee must deliver the goods to a person entitled under the document who complies with subsections (2) and (3), unless and to the extent that the bailee establishes any of the following:

(a) delivery of the goods to a person whose receipt was rightful as against the claimant;

(*b*) damage to or delay, loss or destruction of the goods for which the bailee is not liable [, but the burden of establishing negligence in such cases is on the person entitled under the document];

Note: *The brackets in (1) (b) indicate that State enactments may differ on this point without serious damage to the principle of uniformity.*

(*c*) previous sale or other disposition of the goods in lawful enforcement of a lien or on warehouseman's lawful termination of storage;

(*d*) the exercise by a seller of his right to stop delivery pursuant to the provisions of the Article on Sales (Section 2—705);

(*e*) a diversion, reconsignment or other disposition pursuant to the provisions of this Article (Section 7—303) or tariff regulating such right;

(*f*) release, satisfaction or any other fact affording a personal defense against the claimant;

(*g*) any other lawful excuse.

(2) A person claiming goods covered by a document of title must satisfy the bailee's lien where the bailee so requests or where the bailee is prohibited by law from delivering the goods until the charges are paid.

(3) Unless the person claiming is one against whom the document confers no right under Sec. 7—503 (1), he must surrender for cancellation or notation of partial deliveries any outstanding negotiable document covering the goods, and the bailee must cancel the document or conspicuously note the partial delivery thereon or be liable to any person to whom the document is duly negotiated.

(4) "Person entitled under the document" means holder in the case of a negotiable document, or the person to whom delivery is to be made by the terms of or pursuant to written instructions under a non-negotiable document.

Sec. 7—404. No Liability for Good Faith Delivery Pursuant to Receipt or Bill. A bailee who in good faith including observance of reasonable commercial standards has received goods and delivered or otherwise disposed of them according to the terms of the document of title or pursuant to this Article is not liable therefor. This rule applies even though the person from whom he received the goods had no authority to procure the document or to dispose of the goods and even though the person to whom he delivered the goods had no authority to receive them.

PART V

WAREHOUSE RECEIPTS AND BILLS OF LADING: NEGOTIATION AND TRANSFER

Sec. 7—501. Form of Negotiation and Requirements of "Due Negotiation." (1) A negotiable document of title running to the order of a named person is negotiated by his indorsement and delivery. After his indorsement in blank or to bearer any person can negotiate it by delivery alone.

(2) (*a*) A negotiable document of title is also negotiated by delivery alone when by its original terms it runs to bearer.

(*b*) When a document running to the order of a named person is delivered to him the effect is the same as if the document had been negotiated.

(3) Negotiation of a negotiable document of title after it has been indorsed to a specified person requires indorsement by the special indorsee as well as delivery.

(4) A negotiable document of title is "duly negotiated" when it is negotiated in the manner stated in this section to a holder who purchases it in good faith without notice of any defense against or claim to it on the part of any person and for value, unless it is established that the negotiation is not in the regular course of business or financing or involves receiving the document in settlement or payment of a money obligation.

(5) Indorsement of a non-negotiable document neither makes it negotiable nor adds to the transferee's rights.

(6) The naming in a negotiable bill of a person to be notified of the arrival of the goods does not limit the negotiability of the bill nor constitute notice to a purchaser thereof of any interest of such person in the goods.

Sec. 7—502. Rights Acquired by Due Negotiation. (1) Subject to the following section and to the provisions of Section 7—205 on fungible goods, a holder to whom a negotiable document of title has been duly negotiated acquires thereby:

(a) title to the document;

(b) title to the goods;

(c) all rights accruing under the law of agency or estoppel, including rights to goods delivered to the bailee after the document was issued; and

(d) the direct obligation of the issuer to hold or deliver the goods according to the terms of the document free of any defense or claim by him except those arising under the terms of the document or under this Article. In the case of a delivery order the bailee's obligation accrues only upon acceptance and the obligation acquired by the holder is that the issuer and any indorser will procure the acceptance of the bailee.

(2) Subject to the following section, title and rights so acquired are not defeated by any stoppage of the goods represented by the document or by surrender of such goods by the bailee, and are not impaired even though the negotiation or any prior negotiation constituted a breach of duty or even though any person has been deprived of possession of the document by misrepresentation, fraud, accident, mistake, duress, loss, theft or conversion, or even though a previous sale or other transfer of the goods or document has been made to a third person.

Sec. 7—503. Document of Title to Goods Defeated in Certain Cases. (1) A document of title confers no right in goods against a person who before issuance of the document had a legal interest or a perfected security interest in them and who neither

(a) delivered or entrusted them or any document of title covering them to the bailor or his nominee with actual or apparent authority to ship, store or sell or with power to obtain delivery under this Article (Section 7—403) or with power of disposition under this Act (Sections 2—403 and 9—307) or other statute or rule of law; nor

(b) acquiesced in the procurement by the bailor or his nominee of any document of title.

(2) Title to goods based upon an unaccepted delivery order is subject to the rights of anyone to whom a negotiable warehouse receipt or bill of lading covering the goods has been duly negotiated. Such a title may be defeated under the next section to the same extent as the rights of the issuer or a transferee from the issuer.

(3) Title to goods based upon a bill of lading issued to a freight forwarder is subject to the rights of anyone to whom a bill issued by the freight forwarder is duly negotiated; but delivery by the carrier in accordance with Part 4 of this Article pursuant to its own bill of lading discharges the carrier's obligation to deliver.

Sec. 7—504. Rights Acquired in the Absence of Due Negotiation; Effect of Diversion; Seller's Stoppage of Delivery. (1) A transferee of a document, whether negotiable or non-negotiable, to whom the document has been delivered but not duly negotiated, acquires the title and rights which his transferor had or had actual authority to convey.

(2) In the case of a non-negotiable document, until but not after the bailee receives notification of the transfer, the rights of the transferee may be defeated

(a) by those creditors of the transferor who could treat the sale as void under Section 2—402; or

(b) by a buyer from the transferor in ordinary course of business if the bailee has delivered the goods to the buyer or received notification of his rights; or

(c) as against the bailee by good faith dealings of the bailee with the transferor.

(3) A diversion or other change of shipping instructions by the consignor in a non-negotiable bill of lading which causes the bailee not to deliver to the consignee defeats the consignee's title to the goods if they have been delivered to a buyer in ordinary course of business and in any event defeats the consignee's rights against the bailee.

(4) Delivery pursuant to a non-negotiable document may be stopped by a seller under Section 2—705, and subject to the requirement of due notification there provided. A bailee honoring the seller's instructions is entitled to be indemnified by the seller against any resulting loss or expense.

Sec. 7—505. Indorser Not a Guarantor for Other Parties. The indorsement of a document of title issued by a bailee does not make the indorser liable for any default by the bailee or by previous indorsers.

Sec. 7—506. Delivery Without Indorsement: Right to Compel Indorsement. The transferee of a negotiable document of title has a specifically enforceable right to have his transferor supply any necessary indorsement but the transfer becomes a negotiation only as of the time the indorsement is supplied.

Sec. 7—507. Warranties on Negotiation or Transfer of Receipt or Bill. Where a person negotiates or transfers a document of title for value otherwise than as a mere intermediary under the next following section, then unless otherwise agreed he warrants to his immediate purchaser only in addition to any warranty made in selling the goods

(a) that the document is genuine; and

(b) that he has no knowledge of any fact which would impair its validity or worth; and

(c) that his negotiation or transfer is rightful and fully effective with respect to the title to the document and the goods it represents.

Sec. 7—508. Warranties of Collecting Bank as to Documents. A collecting bank or other intermediary known to be entrusted with documents on behalf of another or with collection of a draft or other claim against delivery of documents warrants by such delivery of the documents only its own good faith and authority. This rule applies even though the intermediary has purchased or made advances against the claim or draft to be collected.

Sec. 7—509. Receipt or Bill: When Adequate Compliance With Commercial Contract. The question whether a document is adequate to fulfill the obligations of a contract for sale or the conditions of a credit is governed by the Articles on Sales (Article 2) and on Letters of Credit (Article 5).

PART VI

WAREHOUSE RECEIPTS AND BILLS OF LADING: MISCELLANEOUS PROVISIONS

Sec. 7—601. Lost and Missing Documents. (1) If a document has been lost, stolen or destroyed, a court may order delivery of the goods or issuance of a substitute document and the bailee may without liability to any person comply with such order. If the document was negotiable the claimant must post security approved by the court to indemnify any person who may suffer loss as a result of non-surrender of the document. If the document was not negotiable, such security may be required at the discretion of the court. The court may also in its discretion order payment of the bailee's reasonable costs and counsel fees.

(2) A bailee who without court order delivers goods to a person claiming under a missing negotiable document is liable to any person injured thereby, and if the delivery is not in good faith becomes liable for conversion. Delivery in good faith is not conversion if made in accordance with a filed classification or tariff or, where no classification or tariff is filed, if the claimant posts security with the bailee in an amount at least double the value of the goods at the time of posting to indemnify any

person injured by the delivery who files a notice of claim within one year after the delivery.

Sec. 7—602. Attachment of Goods Covered by a Negotiable Document. Except where the document was originally issued upon delivery of the goods by a person who had no power to dispose of them, no lien attaches by virtue of any judicial process to goods in the possession of a bailee for which a negotiable document of title is outstanding unless the document be first surrendered to the bailee or its negotiation enjoined, and the bailee shall not be compelled to deliver the goods pursuant to process until the document is surrendered to him or impounded by the court. One who purchases the document for value without notice of the process or injunction takes free of the lien imposed by judicial process.

Sec. 7—603. Conflicting Claims; Interpleader. If more than one person claims title or possession of the goods, the bailee is excused from delivery until he has had a reasonable time to ascertain the validity of the adverse claims or to bring an action to compel all claimants to interplead and may compel such interpleader, either in defending an action for non-delivery of the goods, or by original action, whichever is appropriate.

ARTICLE VIII

INVESTMENT SECURITIES

PART I

SHORT TITLE AND GENERAL MATTERS

Sec. 8—101. Short Title. This Article shall be known and may be cited as Uniform Commercial Code—Investment Securities.

Sec. 8—102. Definitions and Index of Definitions. (1) In this Article unless the context otherwise requires

(*a*) A "security" is an instrument which

(*i*) is issued in bearer or registered form; and

(*ii*) is of a type commonly dealt in upon securities exchanges or markets or commonly recognized in any area in which it is issued or dealt in as a medium for investment; and

(*iii*) is either one of a class or series or by its terms is divisible into a class or series of instruments; and

(*iv*) evidences a share, participation or other interest in property or in an enterprise or evidences an obligation of the issuer.

(*b*) A writing which is a security is governed by this Article and not by Uniform Commercial Code—Commercial Paper even though it also meets the requirements of that Article. This Article does not apply to money.

(*c*) A security is in "registered form" when it specifies a person entitled to the security or to the rights it evidences and when its transfer may be registered upon books maintained for that purpose by or on behalf of an issuer or the security so states.

(*d*) A security is in "bearer form" when it runs to bearer according to its terms and not by reason of any indorsement.

(2) A "subsequent purchaser" is a person who takes other than by original issue.

(3) A "clearing corporation" is a corporation all of the capital stock of which is held by or for a national securities exchange or association registered under a statute of the United States such as the Securities Exchange Act of 1934.

(4) A "custodian bank" is any bank or trust company which is supervised and examined by state or federal authority having supervision over banks and which is acting as custodian for a clearing corporation.

(5) Other definitions applying to this Article or to specified Parts thereof and the sections in which they appear are:

"Adverse claim."	Section 8—301.
"Bona fide purchaser."	Section 8—302.
"Broker."	Section 8—303.
"Guarantee of the signature."	Section 8—402.
"Intermediary bank."	Section 4—105.
"Issuer."	Section 8—201.
"Overissue."	Section 8—104.

(6) In addition Article 1 contains general definitions and principles of construction and interpretation applicable throughout this Article.

Sec. 8—103. Issuer's Lien. A lien upon a security in favor of an issuer thereof is valid against a purchaser only if the right of the issuer to such lien is noted conspicuously on the security.

Sec. 8—104. Effect of Overissue; "Overissue." (1) The provisions of this Article which validate a security or compel its issue or reissue do not apply to the extent that validation, issue or reissue would result in overissue; but

(a) if an identical security which does not constitute an overissue is reasonably available for purchase, the person entitled to issue or validation may compel the issuer to purchase and deliver such a security to him against surrender of the security, if any, which he holds; or

(b) if a security is not so available for purchase, the person entitled to issue or validation may recover from the issuer the price he or the last purchaser for value paid for it with interest from the date of his demand.

(2) "Overissue" means the issue of securities in excess of the amount which the issuer has corporate power to issue.

Sec. 8—105. Securities Negotiable; Presumptions. (1) Securities governed by this Article are negotiable instruments.

(2) In any action on a security

(a) unless specifically denied in the pleadings, each signature on the security or in a necessary indorsement is admitted;

(b) when the effectiveness of a signature is put in issue the burden of establishing it is on the party claiming under the signature but the signature is presumed to be genuine or authorized;

(c) when signatures are admitted or established production of the instrument entitles a holder to recover on it unless the defendant establishes a defense or a defect going to the validity of the security; and

(d) after it is shown that a defense or defect exists the plaintiff has the burden of establishing that he or some person under whom he claims is a person against whom the defense or defect is ineffective (Section 8—202).

Sec. 8—106. Applicability. The validity of a security and the rights and duties of the issuer with respect to registration of transfer are governed by the law (including the conflict of laws rules) of the jurisdiction of organization of the issuer.

Sec. 8—107. Securities Deliverable; Action for Price. (1) Unless otherwise agreed and subject to any applicable law or regulation respecting short sales, a person obligated to deliver securities may deliver any security of the specified issue in bearer form or registered in the name of the transferee or indorsed to him or in blank.

(2) When the buyer fails to pay the price as it comes due under a contract of sale the seller may recover the price

(a) of securities accepted by the buyer; and

(b) of other securities if efforts at their resale would be unduly burdensome or if there is no readily available market for their resale.

PART II

ISSUE—ISSUER

Sec. 8—201. "Issuer." (1) With respect to obligations on or defenses to a security "issuer" includes a person who

(a) places or authorizes the placing of his name on a security (otherwise than as authenticating trustee, registrar, transfer agent or the like) to evidence that it represents a share, participation or other interest in his property or in an enterprise or to evidence his duty to perform an obligation evidenced by the security; or

(b) directly or indirectly creates fractional interests in his rights or property which fractional interests are evidenced by securities; or

(c) becomes responsible for or in place of any other person described as an issuer in this section.

(2) With respect to obligations on or defenses to a security a guarantor is an issuer to the extent of his guaranty whether or not his obligation is noted on the security.

(3) With respect to registration of transfer (Part 4 of this Article) "issuer" means a person on whose behalf transfer books are maintained.

Sec. 8—202. Issuer's Responsibility and Defenses; Notice of Defect or Defense. (1) Even against a purchaser for value and without notice, the terms of a security include those stated on the security and those made part of the security by reference to another instrument, indenture or document or to a constitution, statute, ordinance, rule, regulation, order or the like to the extent that the terms so referred to do not conflict with the stated terms. Such a reference does not of itself charge a purchaser for value with notice of a defect going to the validity of the security even though the security expressly states that a person accepting it admits such notice.

(2) (a) A security other than one issued by a government or governmental agency or unit even though issued with a defect going to its validity is valid in the hands of a purchaser for value and without notice of the particular defect unless the defect involves a violation of constitutional provisions in which case the security is valid in the hands of a subsequent purchaser for value and without notice of the defect.

(b) The rule of subparagraph (a) applies to an issuer which is a government or governmental agency or unit only if either there has been substantial compliance with the legal requirements governing the issue or the issuer has received a substantial consideration for the issue as a whole or for the particular security and a stated purpose of the issue is one for which the issuer has power to borrow money or issue the security.

(3) Except as otherwise provided in the case of certain unauthorized signatures on issue (Section 8—205), lack of genuineness of a security is a complete defense even against a purchaser for value and without notice.

(4) All other defenses of the issuer including nondelivery and conditional delivery of the security are ineffective against a purchaser for value who has taken without notice of the particular defense.

(5) Nothing in this section shall be construed to affect the right of a party to a "when, as and if issued" or a "when distributed" contract to cancel the contract in the event of a material change in the character of the security which is the subject of the contract or in the plan or arrangement pursuant to which such security is to be issued or distributed.

Sec. 8—203. Staleness as Notice of Defects or Defenses. (1) After an act or event which creates a right to immediate performance of the principal obligation evidenced by the security or which sets a date on or after which the security is to be presented or surrendered for redemption or exchange, a purchaser is charged with notice of any defect in its issue or defense of the issuer (*a*) if the act or event is one requiring the payment of money or the delivery of securities or both on presentation or surrender of the security and such funds or securities are available on the date set for payment or exchange and he takes the security more than one year after that date; and

(*b*) if the act or event is not covered by paragraph (*a*) and he takes the security more than two years after the date set for surrender or presentation or the date on which such performance became due.

(2) A call which has been revoked is not within subsection (1).

Sec. 8—204. Effect of Issuer's Restrictions on Transfer.   Unless noted conspicuously on the security a restriction on transfer imposed by the issuer even though otherwise lawful is ineffective except against a person with actual knowledge of it.

Sec. 8—205. Effect of Unauthorized Signature on Issue.   An unauthorized signature placed on a security prior to or in the course of issue is ineffective except that the signature is effective in favor of a purchaser for value and without notice of the lack of authority if the signing has been done by

(*a*) an authenticating trustee, registrar, transfer agent or other person entrusted by the issuer with the signing of the security or of similar securities or their immediate preparation for signing; or

(*b*) an employee of the issuer or of any of the foregoing entrusted with responsible handling of the security.

Sec. 8—206. Completion or Alteration of Instrument.   (1) Where a security contains the signatures necessary to its issue or transfer but is incomplete in any other respect

(*a*) any person may complete it by filling in the blanks as authorized; and

(*b*) even though the blanks are incorrectly filled in, the security as completed is enforceable by a purchaser who took it for value and without notice of such incorrectness.

(2) A complete security which has been improperly altered even though fraudulently remains enforceable but only according to its original terms.

Sec. 8—207. Rights of Issuer With Respect to Registered Owners.   (1) Prior to due presentment for registration of transfer of a security in registered form the issuer or indenture trustee may treat the registered owner as the person exclusively entitled to vote, to receive notifications and otherwise to exercise all the rights and powers of an owner.

(2) Nothing in this Article shall be construed to affect the liability of the registered owner of a security for calls, assessments or the like.

Sec. 8—208. Effect of Signature of Authenticating Trustee, Registrar or Transfer Agent.

(1) A person placing his signature upon a security as authenticating trustee, registrar, transfer agent or the like warrants to a purchaser for value without notice of the particular defect that

(*a*) the security is genuine; and

(*b*) his own participation in the issue of the security is within his capacity and within the scope of the authorization received by him from the issuer; and

(*c*) he has reasonable grounds to believe that the security is in the form and within the amount the issuer is authorized to issue.

(2) Unless otherwise agreed, a person by so placing his signature does not assume responsibility for the validity of the security in other respects.

PART III

PURCHASE

Sec. 8—301. Rights Acquired by Purchaser; "Adverse Claim"; Title Acquired by Bona Fide Purchaser.   (1) Upon delivery of a security the purchaser acquires the rights in the security which his transferor had or had actual authority to convey except that a purchaser who has himself been a party to any fraud or illegality affecting the security or who as a prior holder had notice of an adverse claim cannot improve his position by taking from a later bona fide purchaser. "Adverse claim" includes a claim that a transfer was or would be wrongful or that a particular adverse person is the owner of or has an interest in the security.

(2) A bona fide purchaser in addition to acquiring the rights of a purchaser also acquires the security free of any adverse claim.

(3) A purchaser of a limited interest acquires rights only to the extent of the interest purchased.

Sec. 8—302. "Bona Fide Purchaser." A "bona fide purchaser" is a purchaser for value in good faith and without notice of any adverse claim who takes delivery of a security in bearer form or of one in registered form issued to him or indorsed to him or in blank.

Sec. 8—303. "Broker." "Broker" means a person engaged for all or part of his time in the business of buying and selling securities, who in the transaction concerned acts for, or buys a security from or sells a security to a customer. Nothing in this Article determines the capacity in which a person acts for purposes of any other statute or rule to which such person is subject.

Sec. 8—304. Notice to Purchaser of Adverse Claims. (1) A purchaser (including a broker for the seller or buyer but excluding an intermediary bank) of a security is charged with notice of adverse claims if

(a) the security whether in bearer or registered form has been indorsed "for collection" or "for surrender" or for some other purpose not involving transfer; or

(b) the security is in bearer form and has on it an unambiguous statement that it is the property of a person other than the transferor. The mere writing of a name on a security is not such a statement.

(2) The fact that the purchaser (including a broker for the seller or buyer) has notice that the security is held for a third person or is registered in the name of or indorsed by a fiduciary does not create a duty of inquiry into the rightfulness of the transfer or constitute notice of adverse claims. If, however, the purchaser (excluding an intermediary bank) has knowledge that the proceeds are being used or that the transaction is for the individual benefit of the fiduciary or otherwise in breach of duty, the purchaser is charged with notice of adverse claims.

Sec. 8—305. Staleness as Notice of Adverse Claims. An act or event which creates a right to immediate performance of the principal obligation evidenced by the security or which sets a date on or after which the security is to be presented or surrendered for redemption or exchange does not of itself constitute any notice of adverse claims except in the case of a purchase

(a) after one year from any date set for such presentment or surrender for redemption or exchange; or

(b) after six months from any date set for payment of money against presentation or surrender of the security if funds are available for payment on that date.

Sec. 8—306. Warranties on Presentment and Transfer. (1) A person who presents a security for registration of transfer or for payment or exchange warrants to the issuer that he is entitled to the registration, payment or exchange. But a purchaser for value without notice of adverse claims who receives a new, reissued or re-registered security on registration of transfer warrants only that he has no knowledge of any unauthorized signature (Section 8—311) in a necessary indorsement.

(2) A person by transferring a security to a purchaser for value warrants only that

(a) his transfer is effective and rightful; and

(b) the security is genuine and has not been materially altered; and

(c) he knows no fact which might impair the validity of the security.

(3) Where a security is delivered by an intermediary known to be entrusted with delivery of the security on behalf of another or with collection of a draft or other claim against such delivery, the intermediary by such delivery warrants only his

own good faith and authority even though he has purchased or made advances against the claim to be collected against the delivery.

(4) A pledgee or other holder for security who redelivers the security received, or after payment and on order of the debtor delivers that security to a third person makes only the warranties of an intermediary under subsection (3).

(5) A broker gives to his customer and to the issuer and a purchaser the warranties provided in this section and has the rights and privileges of a purchaser under this section. The warranties of and in favor of the broker acting as an agent are in addition to applicable warranties given by and in favor of his customer.

Sec. 8—307. Effect of Delivery Without Indorsement; Right to Compel Indorsement. Where a security in registered form has been delivered to a purchaser without a necessary indorsement he may become a bona fide purchaser only as of the time the indorsement is supplied, but against the transferor the transfer is complete upon delivery and the purchaser has a specifically enforceable right to have any necessary indorsement supplied.

Sec. 8—308. Indorsement, How Made; Special Indorsement; Indorser Not a Guarantor; Partial Assignment. (1) An indorsement of a security in registered form is made when an appropriate person signs on it or on a separate document an assignment or transfer of the security or a power to assign or transfer it or when the signature of such person is written without more upon the back of the security.

(2) An indorsement may be in a blank or special. An indorsement in blank includes an indorsement to bearer. A special indorsement specifies the person to whom the security is to be transferred, or who has power to transfer it. A holder may convert a blank indorsement into a special indorsement.

(3) "An appropriate person" in subsection (1) means

(a) the person specified by the security or by special indorsement to be entitled to the security; or

(b) where the person so specified is described as a fiduciary but is no longer serving in the described capacity,—either that person or his successor; or

(c) where the security or indorsement so specifies more than one person as fiduciaries and one or more are no longer serving in the described capacity,—the remaining fiduciary or fiduciaries, whether or not a successor has been appointed or qualified; or

(d) where the person so specified is an individual and is without capacity to act by virtue of death, incompetence, infancy or otherwise,—his executor, administrator, guardian or like fiduciary; or

(e) where the security or indorsement so specifies more than one person as tenants by the entirety or with right of survivorship and by reason of death all cannot sign,—the survivor or survivors; or

(f) a person having power to sign under applicable law or controlling instrument; or

(g) to the extent that any of the foregoing persons may act through an agent,—his authorized agent.

(4) Unless otherwise agreed the indorser by his indorsement assumes no obligation that the security will be honored by the issuer.

(5) An indorsement purporting to be only of part of a security representing units intended by the issuer to be separately transferable is effective to the extent of the indorsement.

(6) Whether the person signing is appropriate is determined as of the date of signing and an indorsement by such a person does not become unauthorized for the purposes of this Article by virtue of any subsequent change of circumstances.

(7) Failure of a fiduciary to comply with a controlling instrument or with the law of the state having jurisdiction of the fiduciary relationship, including any law requiring the fiduciary to obtain court approval of the transfer, does not render his indorsement unauthorized for the purposes of the Article.

Sec. 8—309. **Effect of Indorsement Without Delivery.** An indorsement of a security whether special or in blank does not constitute a transfer until delivery of the security on which it appears or if the indorsement is on a separate document until delivery of both the document and the security.

Sec. 8—310. **Indorsement of Security in Bearer Form.** An indorsement of a security in bearer form may give notice of adverse claims (Section 8—304) but does not otherwise affect any right to registration the holder may possess.

Sec. 8—311. **Effect of Unauthorized Indorsement.** Unless the owner has ratified an unauthorized indorsement or is otherwise precluded from asserting its ineffectiveness

(*a*) he may assert its ineffectiveness against the issuer or any purchaser other than a purchaser for value and without notice of adverse claims who has in good faith received a new, reissued or re-registered security on registration of transfer; and

(*b*) an issuer who registers the transfer of a security upon the unauthorized indorsement is subject to liability for improper registration (Section 8—404).

Sec. 8—312. **Effect of Guaranteeing Signature or Indorsement.** (1) Any person guaranteeing a signature of an indorser of a security warrants that at the time of signing

(*a*) the signature was genuine; and

(*b*) the signer was an appropriate person to indorse (Section 8—308); and

(*c*) the signor had legal capacity to sign.

But the guarantor does not otherwise warrant the rightfulness of the particular transfer.

(2) Any person may guarantee an indorsement of a security and by so doing warrants not only the signature (subsection 1) but also the rightfulness of the particular transfer in all respects. But no issuer may require a guarantee of indorsement as a condition to registration of transfer.

(3) The foregoing warranties are made to any person taking or dealing with the security in reliance on the guarantee and the guarantor is liable to such person for any loss resulting from breach of the warranties.

Sec. 8—313. **When Delivery to the Purchaser Occurs; Purchaser's Broker as Holder.** (1) Delivery to a purchaser occurs when

(*a*) he or a person designated by him acquires possession of a security; or

(*b*) his broker acquires possession of a security specially indorsed to or issued in the name of the purchaser; or

(*c*) his broker sends him confirmation of the purchase and also by book entry or otherwise identifies a specific security in the broker's possession as belonging to the purchaser; or

(*d*) with respect to an identified security to be delivered while still in the possession of a third person when that person acknowledges that he holds for the purchaser;

(*e*) appropriate entries on the books of a clearing corporation are made under Section 8—320.

(2) The purchaser is the owner of a security held for him by his broker, but is not the holder except as specified in subparagraphs (*b*), (*c*) and (*e*) of subsection (1). Where a security is part of a fungible bulk the purchaser is the owner of a proportionate property interest in the fungible bulk.

(3) Notice of an adverse claim received by the broker or by the purchaser after the broker takes delivery as a holder for value is not effective either as to the broker or as to the purchaser. However, as between the broker and the purchaser the purchaser may demand delivery of an equivalent security as to which no notice of an adverse claim has been received.

Sec. 8—314. **Duty to Deliver, When Completed.** (1) Unless otherwise agreed where a sale of a security is made on an exchange or otherwise through brokers

(*a*) the selling customer fulfills his duty to deliver when he places such a security in the possession of the selling broker or of a person designated by the broker or if requested causes an acknowledgment to be made to the selling broker that it is held for him; and

(*b*) the selling broker including a correspondent broker acting for a selling customer fulfills his duty to deliver by placing the security or a like security in the possession of the buying broker or a person designated by him or by effecting clearance of the sale in accordance with the rules of the exchange on which the transaction took place.

(2) Except as otherwise provided in this section and unless otherwise agreed, a transferor's duty to deliver a security under a contract of purchase is not fulfilled until he places the security in form to be negotiated by the purchaser in the possession of the purchaser or of a person designated by him or at the purchaser's request causes an acknowledgment to be made to the purchaser that it is held for him. Unless made on an exchange a sale to a broker purchasing for his own account is within this subsection and not within subsection (1).

Sec. 8—315. Action Against Purchaser Based Upon Wrongful Transfer. (1) Any person against whom the transfer of a security is wrongful for any reason, including his incapacity, may against anyone except a bona fide purchaser reclaim possession of the security or obtain possession of any new security evidencing all or part of the same rights or have damages.

(2) If the transfer is wrongful because of an unauthorized indorsement, the owner may also reclaim or obtain possession of the security or new security even from a bona fide purchaser if the ineffectiveness of the purported indorsement can be asserted against him under the provisions of this Article on unauthorized indorsements (Section 8—311).

(3) The right to obtain or reclaim possession of a security may be specifically enforced and its transfer enjoined and the security impounded pending the litigation.

Sec. 8—316. Purchaser's Right to Requisites for Registration of Transfer on Books. Unless otherwise agreed the transferor must on due demand supply his purchaser with any proof of his authority to transfer or with any other requisite which may be necessary to obtain registration of the transfer of the security but if the transfer is not for value a transferor need not do so unless the purchaser furnishes the necessary expenses. Failure to comply with a demand made within a reasonable time gives the purchaser the right to reject or rescind the transfer.

Sec. 8—317. Attachment or Levy Upon Security. (1) No attachment or levy upon a security or any share or other interest evidenced thereby which is outstanding shall be valid until the security is actually seized by the officer making the attachment or levy but a security which has been surrendered to the issuer may be attached or levied upon at the source.

(2) A creditor whose debtor is the owner of a security shall be entitled to such aid from courts of appropriate jurisdiction, by injunction or otherwise, in reaching such security or in satisfying the claim by means thereof as is allowed at law or in equity in regard to property which cannot readily be attached or levied upon by ordinary legal process.

Sec. 8—318. No Conversion by Good Faith Delivery. An agent or bailee who in good faith (including observance of reasonable commercial standards if he is in the business of buying, selling or otherwise dealing with securities) has received securities and sold, pledged or delivered them according to the instructions of his principal is not liable for conversion or for participation in breach of fiduciary duty although the principal had no right to dispose of them.

Sec. 8—319. Statute of Frauds. A contract for the sale of securities is not enforceable by way of action or defense unless

(*a*) there is some writing signed by the party against whom enforcement is sought or by his authorized agent or broker sufficient to indicate that a contract has been made for sale of a stated quantity of described securities at a defined or stated price; or (*b*) delivery of the security has been accepted or payment has been made but the contract is enforceable under this provision only to the extent of such delivery or payment; or

(*c*) within a reasonable time a writing in confirmation of the sale or purchase and sufficient against the sender under paragraph (*a*) has been received by the party against whom enforcement is sought and he has failed to send written objection to its contents within ten days after its receipt; or

(*d*) the party against whom enforcement is sought admits in his pleading, testimony or otherwise in court that a contract was made for sale of a stated quantity of described securities at a defined or stated price.

Sec. 8—320. Transfer or Pledge within a Central Depository System. (1) If a security

(*a*) is in the custody of a clearing corporation or of a custodian bank or a nominee of either subject to the instructions of the clearing corporation; and

(*b*) is in bearer form or indorsed in blank by an appropriate person or registered in the name of the clearing corporation or custodian bank or a nominee of either; and

(*c*) is shown on the account of a transferor or pledgor on the books of the clearing corporation;

then, in addition to other methods, a transfer or pledge of the security or any interest therein may be effected by the making of appropriate entries on the books of the clearing corporation reducing the account of the transferor or pledgor and increasing the account of the transferee or pledgee by the amount of the obligation or the number of shares or rights transferred or pledged.

(2) Under this section entries may be with respect to like securities or interests therein as a part of a fungible bulk and may refer merely to a quantity of a particular security without reference to the name of the registered owner, certificate or bond number or the like and, in appropriate cases, may be on a net basis taking into account other transfers or pledges of the same security.

(3) A transfer or pledge under this section has the effect of a delivery of a security in bearer form or duly indorsed in blank (Section 8—301) representing the amount of the obligation or the number of shares or rights transferred or pledged. If a pledge or the creation of a security interest is intended, the making of entries has the effect of a taking of delivery by the pledgee or a secured party (Sections 9—304 and 9—305). A transferee or pledgee under this section is a holder.

(4) A transfer or pledge under this section does not constitute a registration of transfer under Part 4 of this Article.

(5) That entries made on the books of the clearing corporation as provided in subsection (1) are not appropriate does not affect the validity or effect of the entries nor the liabilities or obligations of the clearing corporation to any person adversely affected thereby.

PART IV

REGISTRATION

Sec. 8—401. Duty of Issuer to Register Transfer. (1) Where a security in registered form is presented to the issuer with a request to register transfer, the issuer is under a duty to register the transfer as requested if

(*a*) the security is indorsed by the appropriate person or persons (Section 8—308); and

(*b*) reasonable assurance is given that those indorsements are genuine and effective (Section 8—402); and

(*c*) the issuer has no duty to inquire into adverse claims or has discharged any such duty (Section 8—403); and

(*d*) any applicable law relating to the collection of taxes has been complied with; and (*e*) the transfer is in fact rightful or is to a bone fide purchaser.

(2) Where an issuer is under a duty to register a transfer of a security the issuer is also liable to the person presenting it for registration or his principal for loss resulting from any unreasonable delay in registration or from failure or refusal to register the transfer.

Sec. 8—402. Assurance that Indorsements Are Effective. (1) The issuer may require the following assurance that each necessary indorsement (Section 8—308) is genuine and effective

(*a*) in all cases, a guarantee of the signature (subsection (1) of Section 8—312) of the person indorsing; and

(*b*) where the indorsement is by an agent, appropriate assurance of authority to sign;

(*c*) where the indorsement is by a fiduciary, appropriate evidence of appointment or incumbency;

(*d*) where there is more than one fiduciary, reasonable assurance that all who are required to sign have done so;

(*e*) where the indorsement is by a person not covered by any of the foregoing, assurance appropriate to the case corresponding as nearly as may be to the foregoing.

(2) A "guarantee of the signature" in subsection (1) means a guarantee signed by or on behalf of a person reasonably believed by the issuer to be responsible. The issuer may adopt standards with respect to responsibility provided such standards are not manifestly unreasonable.

(3) "Appropriate evidence of appointment or incumbency" in subsection (1) means

(*a*) in the case of a fiduciary appointed or qualified by a court, a certificate issued by or under the direction or supervision of that court or an officer thereof and dated within sixty days before the date of presentation for transfer; or

(*b*) in any other case, a copy of a document showing the appointment or a certificate issued by or on behalf of a person reasonably believed by the issuer to be responsible or, in the absence of such a document or certificate, other evidence reasonably deemed by the issuer to be appropriate. The issuer may adopt standards with respect to such evidence provided such standards are not manifestly unreasonable. The issuer is not charged with notice of the contents of any document obtained pursuant to this paragraph (*b*) except to the extent that the contents relate directly to the appointment or incumbency.

(4) The issuer may elect to require reasonable assurance beyond that specified in this section but if it does so and for a purpose other than that specified in subsection 3(*b*) both requires and obtains a copy of a will, trust, indenture, articles of co-partnership, by-laws or other controlling instrument it is charged with notice of all matters contained therein affecting the transfer.

Sec. 8—403. Limited Duty of Inquiry. (1) An issuer to whom a security is presented for registration is under a duty to inquire into adverse claims if

(*a*) a written notification of an adverse claim is received at a time and in a manner which affords the issuer a reasonable opportunity to act on it prior to the issuance of a new, reissued or re-registered security and the notification identifies the claimant, the registered owner and the issue of which the security is a part and provides an address for communications directed to the claimant; or

(*b*) the issuer is charged with notice of an adverse claim from a controlling instrument which it has elected to require under subsection (4) of Section 8—402.

(2) The issuer may discharge any duty of inquiry by any reasonable means, including notifying an adverse claimant by registered or certified mail at the address furnished by him or if there be no such address at his residence or regular place of business that the security has been presented for registration of transfer by a

named person, and that the transfer will be registered unless within thirty days from the date of mailing the notification, either

(*a*) an appropriate restraining order, injunction or other process issues from a court of competent jurisdiction; or

(*b*) an indemnity bond sufficient in the issuer's judgment to protect the issuer and any transfer agent, registrar or other agent of the issuer involved, from any loss which it or they may suffer by complying with the adverse claim is filed with the issuer.

(3) Unless an issuer is charged with notice of an adverse claim from a controlling instrument which it has elected to require under subsection (4) of Section 8—402 or receives notification of an adverse claim under subsection (1) of this section, where a security presented for registration is indorsed by the appropriate person or persons the issuer is under no duty to inquire into adverse claims. In particular

(*a*) an issuer registering a security in the name of a person who is a fiduciary or who is described as a fiduciary is not bound to inquire into the existence, extent, or correct description of the fiduciary relationship and thereafter the issuer may assume without inquiry that the newly registered owner continues to be the fiduciary until the issuer receives written notice that the fiduciary is no longer acting as such with respect to the particular security;

(*b*) an issuer registering transfer on an indorsement by a fiduciary is not bound to inquire whether the transfer is made in compliance with a controlling instrument or with the law of the state having jurisdiction of the fiduciary relationship, including any law requiring the fiduciary to obtain court approval of the transfer; and

(*c*) the issuer is not charged with notice of the contents of any court record or file or other recorded or unrecorded document even though the document is in its possession and even though the transfer is made on the indorsement of a fiduciary to the fiduciary himself or to his nominee.

Sec. 8—404. Liability and Non-Liability for Registration. (1) Except as otherwise provided in any law relating to the collection of taxes, the issuer is not liable to the owner or any other person suffering loss as a result of the registration of a transfer of a security if

(*a*) there were on or with the security the necessary indorsements (Section 8—308); and

(*b*) the issuer had no duty to inquire into adverse claims or has discharged any such duty (Section 8—403).

(2) Where an issuer has registered a transfer of a security to a person not entitled to it the issuer on demand must deliver a like security to the true owner unless

(*a*) the registration was pursuant to subsection (1); or

(*b*) the owner is precluded from asserting any claim for registering the transfer under subsection (1) of the following section; or

(*c*) such delivery would result in overissue, in which case the issuer's liability is governed by Section 8—104.

Sec. 8—405. Lost, Destroyed and Stolen Securities. (1) Where a security has been lost, apparently destroyed or wrongfully taken and the owner fails to notify the issuer of that fact within a reasonable time after he has notice of it and the issuer registers a transfer of the security before receiving such a notification, the owner is precluded from asserting against the issuer any claim for registering the transfer under the preceding section or any claim to a new security under this section.

(2) Where the owner of a security claims that the security has been lost, destroyed or wrongfully taken, the issuer must issue a new security in place of the original security if the owner

(*a*) so requests before the issuer has notice that the security has been acquired by a bona fide purchaser; and (*b*) files with the issuer a sufficient indemnity bond; and

(*c*) satisfies any other reasonable requirements imposed by the issuer.

(3) If, after the issue of the new security, a bona fide purchaser of the original security presents it for registration of transfer, the issuer must register the transfer unless registration would result in overissue, in which event the issuer's liability is governed by Section 8—104. In addition to any rights on the indemnity bond, the issuer may recover the new security from the person to whom it was issued or any person taking under him except a bona fide purchaser.

Sec. 8—406. Duty of Authenticating Trustee, Transfer Agent or Registrar. (1) Where a person acts as authenticating trustee, transfer agent, registrar, or other agent for an issuer in the registration of transfers of its securities or in the issue of new securities or in the cancellation of surrendered securities

(*a*) he is under a duty to the issuer to exercise good faith and due diligence in performing his functions; and

(*b*) he has with regard to the particular functions he performs the same obligation to the holder or owner of the security and has the same rights and privileges as the issuer has in regard to those functions.

(2) Notice to an authenticating trustee, transfer agent, registrar or other such agent is notice to the issuer with respect to the functions performed by the agent.

ARTICLE IX

SECURED TRANSACTIONS; SALES OF ACCOUNTS, CONTRACT RIGHTS AND CHATTEL PAPER

PART I

SHORT TITLE, APPLICABILITY AND DEFINITIONS

Sec. 9—101. Short Title. This Article shall be known and may be cited as Uniform Commercial Code—Secured Transactions.

Sec. 9—102. Policy and Scope of Article. (1) Except as otherwise provided in Section 9—103 on multiple state transactions and in Section 9—104 on excluded transactions, this Article applies so far as concerns any personal property and fixtures within the jurisdiction of this state

(*a*) to any transaction (regardless of its form) which is intended to create a security interest in personal property or fixtures including goods, documents, instruments, general intangibles, chattel paper, accounts or contract rights; and also

(*b*) to any sale of accounts, contract rights or chattel paper.

(2) This Article applies to security interests created by contract including pledge, assignment, chattel mortgage, chattel trust, trust deed, factor's lien, equipment trust, conditional sale, trust receipt, other lien or title retention contract and lease or consignment intended as security. This Article does not apply to statutory liens except as provided in Section 9—310.

(3) The application of this Article to a security interest in a secured obligation is not affected by the fact that the obligation is itself secured by a transaction or interest to which this Article does not apply.

Note: *The adoption of this Article should be accompanied by the repeal of existing statutes dealing with conditional sales, trust receipts, factor's liens where the factor is given a non-possessory lien, chattel mortgages, crop mortgages, mortgages on railroad equipment, assignment of accounts and generally statutes regulating security interests in personal property.*

Where the state has a retail installment selling act or small loan act, that legislation should be carefully examined to determine what changes in those acts are needed to conform them to this Article. This Article primarily sets out rule defining rights of a secured party against persons dealing with the debtor; it does not prescribe regulations and controls which may be necessary to curb abuses arising in the small loan business or in the financing of consumer purchases on credit. Accordingly there is no intention to repeal existing regulatory acts in those fields. See Section 9—203(2) and the Note thereto.

Sec. 9—103. Accounts, Contract Rights, General Intangibles and Equipment Relating to Another Jurisdiction; and Incoming Goods Already Subject to a Security Interest. (1) If the office where the assignor of accounts or contract rights keeps his records concerning them is in this state, the validity and perfection of a security interest therein and the possibility and effect of proper filing is governed by this Article; otherwise by the law (including the conflict of laws rules) of the jurisdiction where such office is located.

(2) If the chief place of business of a debtor is in this state, this Article governs the validity and perfection of a security interest and the possibility and effect of proper filing with regard to general intangibles or with regard to goods of a type which are normally used in more than one jurisdiction (such as automotive equipment, rolling stock, airplanes, road building equipment, commercial harvesting equipment, construction machinery and the like) if such goods are classified as equipment or classified as inventory by reason of their being leased by the debtor to others. Otherwise, the law (including the conflict of laws rules) of the jurisdiction where such chief place of business is located shall govern. If the chief place of business is located in a jurisdiction which does not provide for perfection of the security interest by filing or recording in that jurisdiction, then the security interest may be perfected by filing in this state. [For the purpose of determining the validity and perfection of a security interest in an airplane, the chief place of business of a debtor who is a foreign air carrier under the Federal Aviation Act of 1958, as amended, is the designated office of the agent upon whom service of process may be made on behalf of the debtor.]

(3) If personal property other than that governed by subsections (1) and (2) is already subject to a security interest when it is brought into this state, the validity of the security interest in this state is to be determined by the law (including the conflict of laws rules) of the jurisdiction where the property was when the security interest attached. However, if the parties to the transaction understood at the time that the security interest attached that the property would be kept in this state and it was brought into this state within 30 days after the security interest attached for purposes other than transportation through this state, then the validity of the security interest in this state is to be determined by the law of this state. If the security interest was already perfected under the law of the jurisdiction where the property was when the security interest attached and before being brought into this state, the security interest continues perfected in this state for four months and also thereafter if within the four month period it is perfected in this state. The security interest may also be perfected in this state after the expiration of the four month period; in such case perfection dates from the time of perfection in this state. If the security interest was not perfected under the law of the jurisdiction where the property was when the security interest attached and before being brought into this state, it may be perfected in this state; in such case perfection dates from the time of perfection in this state.

(4) Notwithstanding subsections (2) and (3), if personal property is covered by a certificate of title issued under a statute of this state or any other jurisdiction which requires indication on a certificate of title of any security interest in the property as a condition of perfection, then the perfection is governed by the law of the jurisdiction which issued the certificate.

[(5) Notwithstanding subsection (1) and Section 9—302, if the office where the assignor of accounts or contract rights keeps his records concerning them is not located in a jurisdiction which is a part of the United States, its territories or possessions, and the accounts or contract rights are within the jurisdiction of this state or the transaction which creates the security interest otherwise bears an appropriate relation to this state, this Article governs the validity and perfection of the security interest and the security interest may only be perfected by notification to the account debtor.]

Note: *The last sentence of subsection (2) and subsection (5) are bracketed to indicate optional enactment. In states engaging in financing of airplanes of foreign carriers and of international open accounts receivable, bracketed language will be of value. In other states not engaging in financing of this type, the bracketed language may not be considered necessary.*

Sec. 9—104. Transactions Excluded From Article.   This Article does not apply

(*a*) to a security interest subject to any statute of the United States such as the Ship Mortgage Act, 1920, to the extent that such statute governs the rights of parties to and third parties affected by transactions in particular types of property; or

(*b*) to a landlord's lien; or

(*c*) to a lien given by statute or other rule of law for services or materials except as provided in Section 9—310 on priority of such liens; or

(*d*) to a transfer of a claim for wages, salary or other compensation of an employee; or

(*e*) to an equipment trust covering railway rolling stock; or

(*f*) to a sale of accounts, contract rights or chattel paper as part of a sale of the business out of which they arose, or an assignment of accounts, contract rights or chattel paper which is for the purpose of collection only, or a transfer of a contract right to an assignee who is also to do the performance under the contract; or

(*g*) to a transfer of an interest or claim in or under any policy of insurance; or

(*h*) to a right represented by a judgment; or

(*i*) to any right of set-off; or

(*j*) except to the extent that provision is made for fixtures in Section 9—313, to the creation or transfer of an interest in or lien on real estate, including a lease or rents thereunder; or

(*k*) to a transfer in whole or in part of any of the following: any claim arising out of tort; any deposit, savings passbook or like account maintained with a bank, savings and loan association, credit union or like organization.

Sec. 9—105. Definitions and Index of Definitions.   (1) In this Article unless the context otherwise requires:

(*a*) "Account debtor" means the person who is obligated on an account, chattel paper, contract right or general intangible;

(*b*) "Chattel paper" means a writing or writings which evidence both a monetary obligation and a security interest in or a lease of specific goods. When a transaction is evidenced both by such a security agreement or a lease and by an instrument or a series of instruments, the group of writings taken together constitutes chattel paper;

(*c*) "Collateral" means the property subject to a security interest, and includes accounts, contract rights and chattel paper which have been sold;

(*d*) "Debtor" means the person who owes payment or other performance of the obligation secured, whether or not he owns or has rights in the collateral, and includes the seller of accounts, contract rights or chattel paper. Where the debtor and the owner of the collateral are not the same person, the term "debtor" means the owner of the collateral in any provision of the Article dealing with the collateral, the obligor in any provision dealing with the obligation, and may include both where the context so requires;

(*e*) "Document" means document of title as defined in the general definitions of Article 1 (Section 1—201);

(*f*) "Goods" includes all things which are movable at the time the security interest attaches or which are fixtures (Section 9–313), but does not include money, documents, instruments, accounts, chattel paper, general intangibles, contract rights and other things in action. "Goods" also include the unborn young of animals and growing crops;

(*g*) "Instrument" means a negotiable instrument (defined in Section 3–104), or a security (defined in Section 8–102) or any other writing which evidences a right to the payment of money and is not itself a security agreement or lease and is of a type which is in ordinary course of business transferred by delivery with any necessary indorsement or assignment;

(*h*) "Security agreement" means an agreement which creates or provides for a security interest;

(*i*) "Secured party" means a lender, seller or other person in whose favor there is a security interest, including a person to whom accounts, contract rights or chattel paper have been sold. When the holders of obligations issued under an indenture of trust, equipment trust agreement or the like are represented by a trustee or other person, the representative is the secured party.

(2) Other definitions applying to this Article and the sections in which they appear are:

"Account."	Section 9–106.
"Consumer goods."	Section 9–109(1).
"Contract right."	Section 9–106.
"Equipment."	Section 9–109(2).
"Farm products."	Section 9–109(3).
"General intangibles."	Section 9–106.
"Inventory."	Section 9–109(4).
"Lien creditor."	Section 9–301(3).
"Proceeds."	Section 9–306(1).
"Purchase money security interest."	Section 9–107.

(3) The following definitions in other Articles apply to this Article:

"Check."	Section 3–104.
"Contract for sale."	Section 2–106.
"Holder in due course."	Section 3–302.
"Note."	Section 3–104.
"Sale."	Section 2–106.

(4) In addition Article 1 contains general definitions and principles of construction and interpretation applicable throughout this Article.

Sec. 9–106. Definitions: "Account"; "Contract Right"; "General Intangibles." "Account" means any right to payment for goods sold or leased or for services rendered which is not evidenced by an instrument or chattel paper. "Contract right" means any right to payment under a contract not yet earned by performance and not evidenced by an instrument or chattel paper. "General intangibles" means any personal property (including things in action) other than goods, accounts, contract rights, chattel paper, documents and instruments.

Sec. 9–107. Definitions: "Purchase Money Security Interest." A security interest is a "purchase money security interest" to the extent that it is

(*a*) taken or retained by the seller of the collateral to secure all or part of its price; or

(*b*) taken by a person who by making advances or incurring an obligation gives value to enable the debtor to acquire rights in or the use of collateral if such value is in fact so used.

Sec. 9–108. When After-Acquired Collateral Not Security for Antecedent Debt. Where a secured party makes an advance, incurs an obligation, releases a perfected security interest, or otherwise gives new value which is to be secured in whole or in part by after-acquired property his security interest in the after-acquired collateral shall be deemed to be taken for new value and not as security for an antecedent debt if the debtor acquires his rights in such collateral either in the ordinary course of his business or under a contract of purchase made pursuant to the security agreement within a reasonable time after new value is given.

Sec. 9—109. Classification of Goods: "Consumer Goods"; "Equipment"; "Farm Products"; "Inventory." Goods are

(1) "consumer goods" if they are used or bought for use primarily for personal, family or household purposes;

(2) "equipment" if they are used or bought for use primarily in business (including farming or a profession) or by a debtor who is a non-profit organization or a governmental subdivision or agency or if the goods are not included in the definitions of inventory, farm products or consumer goods;

(3) "farm products" if they are crops or livestock or supplies used or produced in farming operations or if they are products of crops or livestock in their unmanufactured states (such as ginned cotton, wool-clip, maple syrup, milk and eggs), and if they are in the possession of a debtor engaged in raising, fattening, grazing or other farming operations. If goods are farm products they are neither equipment nor inventory;

(4) "inventory" if they are held by a person who holds them for sale or lease or to be furnished under contracts of service or if he has so furnished them, or if they are raw materials, work in process or materials used or consumed in a business. Inventory of a person is not to be classified as his equipment.

Sec. 9—110. Sufficiency of Description. For the purposes of this Article any description of personal property or real estate is sufficient whether or not it is specific if it reasonably identifies what is described.

Sec. 9—111. Applicability of Bulk Transfer Laws. The creation of a security interest is not a bulk transfer under Article 6 (see Section 6—103).

Sec. 9—112. Where Collateral Is Not Owned by Debtor. Unless otherwise agreed, when a secured party knows that collateral is owned by a person who is not the debtor, the owner of the collateral is entitled to receive from the secured party any surplus under Section 9—502(2) or under Section 9—504(1), and is not liable for the debt or for any deficiency after resale, and he has the same right as the debtor

(a) to receive statements under Section 9—208;

(b) to receive notice of and to object to a secured party's proposal to retain the collateral in satisfaction of the indebtedness under Section 9—505;

(c) to redeem the collateral under Section 9—506;

(d) to obtain injunctive or other relief under Section 9—507(1); and

(e) to recover losses caused to him under Section 9—208(2).

Sec. 9—113. Security Interests Arising Under Article on Sales. A security interest arising solely under the Article on Sales (Article 2) is subject to the provisions of this Article except that to the extent that and so long as the debtor does not have or does not lawfully obtain possession of the goods

(a) no security agreement is necessary to make the security interest enforceable; and

(b) no filing is required to perfect the security interest; and

(c) the rights of the secured party on default by the debtor are governed by the Article on Sales (Article 2).

PART II

VALIDITY OF SECURITY AGREEMENT AND RIGHTS OF PARTIES THERETO

Sec. 9—201. General Validity of Security Agreement. Except as otherwise provided by this Act a security agreement is effective according to its terms between the parties, against purchasers of the collateral and against creditors. Nothing in this Article validates any charge or practice illegal under any statute or regulation thereunder governing usuary, small loans, retail installment sales, or the like, or extends the application of any such statute or regulation to any transaction not otherwise subject thereto.

Sec. 9—202. Title to Collateral Immaterial. Each provision of this Article with regard to rights, obligations and remedies applies whether title to collateral is in the secured party or in the debtor.

Sec. 9—203. Enforceability of Security Interest; Proceeds, Formal Requisites. (1) Subject to the provisions of Section 4—208 on the security interest of a collecting bank and Section 9—113 on a security interest arising under the Article on Sales, a security interest is not enforceable against the debtor or third parties unless

(*a*) the collateral is in the possession of the secured party; or

(*b*) the debtor has signed a security agreement which contains a description of the collateral and in addition, when the security interest covers crops or oil, gas or minerals to be extracted or timber to be cut, a description of the land concerned. In describing collateral, the word "proceeds" is sufficient without further description to cover proceeds of any character.

(2) A transaction, although subject to this Article, is also subject to . . . . ,* and in the case of conflict between the provisions of this Article and any such statue, the provisions of such statute control. Failure to comply with any applicable statute has only the effect which is specified therein.

Note: *At * subsection (2) insert reference to any local statute regulating small loans, retail installment sales and the like.*

The foregoing subsection (2) is designed to make it clear that certain transactions, although subject to this article, must also comply with other applicable legislation.

This Article is designed to regulate all the "security" aspects of transactions within its scope. There is, however, much regulatory legislation, particularly in the consumer field, which supplements this Article and should not be repealed by its enactment. Examples are small loan acts, retail installment selling acts and the like. Such acts may provide for licensing and rate regulation and may prescribe particular forms of contract. Such provisions should remain in force despite the enactment of this Article. On the other hand if a Retail Installment Selling Act contains provisions on filing, rights on default, etc., such provisions should be repealed as inconsistent with this Article.

Sec. 9—204. When Security Interest Attaches; After-Acquired Property; Future Advances. (1) A security interest cannot attach until there is agreement (subsection (3) of Section 1—201) that it attach and value is given and the debtor has rights in the collateral. It attaches as soon as all of the events in the preceding sentence have taken place unless explicit agreement postpones the time of attaching.

(2) For the purposes of this section the debtor has no rights

(*a*) in crops until they are planted or otherwise become growing crops, in the young of livestock until they are conceived;

(*b*) in fish until caught, in oil, gas or minerals until they are extracted, in timber until it is cut;

(*c*) in a contract right until the contract has been made;

(*d*) in an account until it comes into existence.

(3) Except as provided in subsection (4) a security agreement may provide that collateral, whenever acquired, shall secure all obligations covered by the security agreement.

(4) No security interest attaches under an after-acquired property clause

(*a*) to crops which become such more than one year after the security agreement is executed except that a security interest in crops which is given in conjunction with a lease or a land purchase or improvement transaction evidenced by a contract, mortgage or deed of trust may if so agreed attach to crops to be grown on the land concerned during the period of such real estate transaction;

(*b*) to consumer goods other than accessions (Section 9–314) when given as additional security unless the debtor acquires rights in them within ten days after the secured party gives value.

(5) Obligations covered by a security agreement may include future advances or other value whether or not the advances or value are given pursuant to commitment.

Sec. 9—205. Use of Disposition of Collateral Without Accounting Permissible. A security interest is not invalid or fraudulent against creditors by reason of liberty in the debtor to use, commingle or dispose of all or part of the collateral (including returned or repossessed goods) or to collect or compromise accounts, contract rights or chattel paper, or to accept the return of goods or make repossessions, or to use, commingle or dispose of proceeds, or by reason of the failure of the secured party to require the debtor to account for proceeds or replace collateral. This section does not relax the requirements of possession where perfection of a security interest depends upon possession of the collateral by the secured party or by a bailee.

Sec. 9—206. Agreement Not to Assert Defenses Against Assignee; Modification of Sales Warranties Where Security Agreement Exists. (1) Subject to any statute or decision which establishes a different rule for buyers or lessees of consumer goods, an agreement by a buyer or lessee that he will not assert against an assignee any claim or defense which he may have against the seller or lessor is enforceable by an assignee who takes his assignment for value, in good faith and without notice of a claim or defense, except as to defenses of a type which may be asserted against a holder in due course of a negotiable instrument under the Article on Commercial Paper (Article 3). A buyer who as part of one transaction signs both a negotiable instrument and a security agreement makes such an agreement.

(2) When a seller retains a purchase money security interest in goods the Article on Sales (Article 2) governs the sale and any disclaimer, limitation or modification of the seller's warranties.

Sec. 9—207. Rights and Duties When Collateral Is in Secured Party's Possession. (1) A secured party must use reasonable care in the custody and preservation of collateral in his possession. In the case of an instrument or chattel paper reasonable care includes taking necessary steps to preserve rights against prior parties unless otherwise agreed.

(2) Unless otherwise agreed, when collateral is in the secured party's possession

(*a*) reasonable expenses (including the cost of any insurance and payment of taxes or other charges) incurred in the custody, preservation, use or operation of the collateral are chargeable to the debtor and are secured by the collateral;

(*b*) the risk of accidental loss or damage is on the debtor to the extent of any deficiency in any effective insurance coverage;

(*c*) the secured party may hold as additional security any increase or profits (except money) received from the collateral, but money so received, unless remitted to the debtor, shall be applied in reduction of the secured obligation;

(*d*) the secured party must keep the collateral identifiable but fungible collateral may be commingled;

(*e*) the secured party may repledge the collateral upon terms which do not impair the debtor's right to redeem it.

(3) A secured party is liable for any loss caused by his failure to meet any obligation imposed by the preceding subsections but does not lose his security interest.

(4) A secured party may use or operate the collateral for the purpose of preserving the collateral or its value or pursuant to the order of a court of appropriate jurisdiction or, except in the case of consumer goods, in the manner and to the extent provided in the security agreement.

Sec. 9—208. Request for Statement of Account or List of Collateral. (1) A debtor may sign a statement indicating what he believes to be the aggregate amount of unpaid indebtedness as of a specified date and may send it to the secured party with a request that the statement be approved or corrected and returned to the debtor.

When the security agreement or any other record kept by the secured party identifies the collateral a debtor may similarly request the secured party to approve or correct a list of the collateral.

(2) The secured party must comply with such a request within two weeks after receipt by sending a written correction or approval. If the secured party claims a security interest in all of a particular type of collateral owned by the debtor he may indicate that fact in his reply and need not approve or correct an itemized list of such collateral. If the secured party without reasonable excuse fails to comply he is liable for any loss caused to the debtor thereby; and if the debtor has properly included in his request a good faith statement of the obligation or a list of the collateral or both the secured party may claim a security interest only as shown in the statement against persons misled by his failure to comply. If he no longer has an interest in the obligation or collateral at the time the request is received he must disclose the name and address of any successor in interest known to him and he is liable for any loss caused to the debtor as a result of failure to disclose. A successor in interest is not subject to this section until a request is received by him.

(3) A debtor is entitled to such a statement once every six months without charge. The secured party may require payment of a charge not exceeding $10 for each additional statement furnished.

PART III

RIGHTS OF THIRD PARTIES; PERFECTED AND UNPERFECTED SECURITY INTERESTS; RULES OF PRIORITY

Sec. 9—301. Persons Who Take Priority Over Unperfected Security Interests; "Lien Creditor."
(1) Except as otherwise provided in subsection (2), an unperfected security interest is subordinate to the rights of

(a) persons entitled to priority under Section 9—312;

(b) a person who becomes a lien creditor without knowledge of the security interest and before it is perfected;

(c) in the case of goods, instruments, documents, and chattel paper, a person who is not a secured party and who is a transferee in bulk or other buyer not in ordinary course of business to the extent that he gives value and receives delivery of the collateral without knowledge of the security interest and before it is perfected;

(d) in the case of accounts, contract rights, and general intangibles, a person who is not a secured party and who is a transferee to the extent that he gives value without knowledge of the security interest and before it is perfected.

(2) If the secured party files with respect to a purchase money security interest before or within ten days after the collateral comes into possession of the debtor, he takes priority over the rights of a transferee in bulk or of a lien creditor which arise between the time the security interest attaches and the time of filing.

(3) A "lien creditor" means a creditor who has acquired a lien on the property involved by attachment, levy or the like and includes an assignee for benefit of creditors from the time of assignment, and a trustee in bankruptcy from the date of the filing of the petition or a receiver in equity from the time of appointment. Unless all the creditors represented had knowledge of the security interest such a representative of creditors is a lien creditor without knowledge even though he personally has knowledge of the security interest.

Sec. 9—302. When Filing Is Required to Perfect Security Interest; Security Interests to Which Filing Provisions of This Article Do Not Apply. (1) A financing statement must be filed to perfect all security interests except the following:

(a) a security interest in collateral in possession of the secured party under Section 9—305;

(b) a security interest temporarily perfected in instruments or documents without delivery under Section 9–304 or in proceeds for a 10 day period under Section 9–306;

(c) a purchase money security interest in farm equipment having a purchase price not in excess of $2500; but filing is required for a fixture under Section 9–313 or for a motor vehicle required to be licensed;

(d) a purchase money security interest in consumer goods; but filing is required for a fixture under Section 9–313 or for a motor vehicle required to be licensed;

(e) an assignment of accounts or contract rights which does not alone or in conjunction with other assignments to the same assignee transfer a significant part of the outstanding accounts or contract rights of the assignor;

(f) a security interest of a collecting bank (Section 4–208) or arising under the Article on Sales (see Section 9–113) or covered in subsection (3) of this section.

(2) If a secured party assigns a perfected security interest, no filing under this Article is required in order to continue the perfected status of the security interest against creditors of and transferees from the original debtor.

(3) The filing provisions of this Article do not apply to a security interest in property subject to a statute

(a) of the United States which provides for a national registration or filing of all security interests in such property; or

Note: *States to select either Alternative A or Alternative B.*

Alternative A—

(b) of this state which provides for central filing of, or which requires indication on a certificate of title of, such security interests in such property.

Alternative B—

(b) of this state which provides for central filing of security interests in such property, or in a motor vehicle which is not inventory held for sale for which a certificate of title is required under the statutes of this state if a notation of such a security interest can be indicated by a public official on a certificate or a duplicate thereof.

(4) A security interest in property covered by a statute described in subsection (3) can be perfected only by registration or filing under that statute or by indication of the security interest on a certificate of title or a duplicate thereof by a public official.

Sec. 9–303. When Security Interest Is Perfected; Continuity of Perfection. (1) A security interest is perfected when it has attached and when all of the applicable steps required for perfection have been taken. Such steps are specified in Sections 9–302, 9–304, 9–305 and 9–306. If such steps are taken before the security interest attaches, it is perfected at the time when it attaches.

(2) If a security interest is originally perfected in any way permitted under this Article and is subsequently perfected in some other way under this Article, without an intermediate period when it was unperfected, the security interest shall be deemed to be perfected continuously for the purposes of this Article.

Sec. 9–304. Perfection of Security Interest in Instruments, Documents, and Goods Covered by Documents; Perfection by Permissive Filing; Temporary Perfection Without Filing or Transfer of Possession. (1) A security interest in chattel paper or negotiable documents may be perfected by filing. A security interest in instruments (other than instruments which constitute part of chattel paper) can be perfected only by the secured party's taking possession, except as provided in subsections (4) and (5).

(2) During the period that goods are in the possession of the issuer of a negotiable document therefor, a security interest in the goods is perfected by perfecting a security interest in the document, and any security interest in the goods otherwise perfected during such period is subject thereto.

(3) A security interest in goods in the possession of a bailee other than one who has issued a negotiable document therefor is perfected by issuance of a document

in the name of the secured party or by the bailee's receipt of notification of the secured party's interest or by filing as to the goods.

(4) A security interest in instruments or negotiable documents is perfected without filing or the taking of possession for a period of 21 days from the time it attaches to the extent that it arises for new value given under a written security agreement.

(5) A security interest remains perfected for a period of 21 days without filing where a secured party having a perfected security interest in an instrument, a negotiable document or goods in possession of a bailee other than one who has issued a negotiable document therefor

    (*a*) makes available to the debtor the goods or documents representing the goods for the purpose of ultimate sale or exchange or for the purpose of loading, unloading, storing, shipping, transshipping, manufacturing, processing or otherwise dealing with them in a manner preliminary to their sale or exchange; or

    (*b*) delivers the instrument to the debtor for the purpose of ultimate sale or exchange or of presentation, collection, renewal or registration of transfer.

(6) After the 21 day period in subsections (4) and (5) perfection depends upon compliance with applicable provisions of this Article.

Sec. 9–305. When Possession by Secured Party Perfects Security Interest Without Filing. A security interest in letters of credit and advices of credit (subsection (2) (*a*) of Section 5—116), goods, instruments, negotiable documents or chattel paper may be perfected by the secured party's taking possession of the collateral. If such collateral other than goods covered by a negotiable document is held by a bailee, the secured party is deemed to have possession from the time the bailee receives notification of the secured party's interest. A security interest is perfected by possession from the time possession is taken without relation back and continues only so long as possession is retained, unless otherwise specified in this Article. The security interest may be otherwise perfected as provided in this Article before or after the period of possession by the secured party.

Sec. 9—306. "Proceeds"; Secured Party's Rights on Disposition of Collateral. (1) "Proceeds" includes whatever is received when collateral or proceeds is sold, exchanged, collected or otherwise disposed of. The term also includes the account arising when the right to payment is earned under a contract right. Money, checks and the like are "cash proceeds." All other proceeds are "non-cash proceeds."

(2) Except where this Article otherwise provides, a security interest continues in collateral notwithstanding sale, exchange or other disposition thereof by the debtor unless his action was authorized by the secured party in the security agreement or otherwise, and also continues in any identifiable proceeds including collections received by the debtor.

(3) The security interest in proceeds is a continuously perfected security interest if the interest in the original collateral was perfected but it ceases to be a perfected security interest and becomes unperfected ten days after receipt of the proceeds by the debtor unless

    (*a*) a filed financing statement covering the original collateral also covers proceeds; or

    (*b*) the security interest in the proceeds is perfected before the expiration of the ten day period.

(4) In the event of insolvency proceedings instituted by or against a debtor, a secured party with a perfected security interest in proceeds has a perfected security interest

    (*a*) in identifiable non-cash proceeds;

    (*b*) in identifiable cash proceeds in the form of money which is not commingled with other money or deposited in a bank account prior to the insolvency proceedings;

    (*c*) in identifiable cash proceeds in the form of checks and the like which are not deposited in a bank account prior to the insolvency proceedings; and (*d*) in all cash and bank accounts of the debtor, if other cash proceeds have been commingled or deposited in a bank account, but the perfected security interest under this paragraph (*d*) is

(*i*) subject to any right of set-off; and

(*ii*) limited to an amount not greater than the amount of any cash proceeds received by debtor within ten days before the institution of the insolvency proceedings and commingled or deposited in a bank account prior to the insolvency proceedings less the amount of cash proceeds received by the debtor and paid over to the secured party during the ten day period.

(5) If a sale of goods results in an account or chattel paper which is transferred by the seller to a secured party, and if the goods are returned to or are repossessed by the seller or the secured party, the following rules determine priorities:

(*a*) If the goods were collateral at the time of sale for an indebtedness of the seller which is still unpaid, the original security interest attaches again to the goods and continues as a perfected security interest if it was perfected at the time when the goods were sold. If the security interest was originally perfected by a filing which is still effective, nothing further is required to continue the prefected status; in any other case, the secured party must take possession of the returned or repossessed goods or must file.

(*b*) An unpaid transferee of the chattel paper has a security interest in the goods against the transferor. Such security interest is prior to a security interest asserted under paragraph (*a*) to the extent that the transferee of the chattel paper was entitled to priority under Section 9—308.

(*c*) An unpaid transferee of the account has a security interest in the goods against the transferor. Such security interest is subordinate to a security interest asserted under paragraph (*a*).

(*d*) A security interest of an unpaid transferee asserted under paragraph (*b*) or (*c*) must be perfected for protection against creditors of the transferor and purchasers of the returned or repossessed goods.

Sec. 9—307. Protection of Buyers of Goods. (1) A buyer in ordinary course of business (subsection (9) of Section 1—201) other than a person buying farm products from a person engaged in farming operations takes free of a security interest created by his seller even though the security interest is perfected and even though the buyer knows of its existence.

(2) In the case of consumer goods and in the case of farm equipment having an original purchase price not in excess of $2500 (other than fixtures, see Section 9—313), a buyer takes free of a security interest even though perfected if he buys without knowledge of the security interest, for value and for his own personal, family or household purposes or his own farming operations unless prior to the purchase the secured party has filed a financing statement covering such goods.

Sec. 9—308. Purchase of Chattel Paper and Non-Negotiable Instruments. A purchaser of chattel paper or a non-negotiable instrument who gives new value and takes possession of it in the ordinary course of his business and without knowledge that the specific paper or instrument is subject to a security interest has priority over a security interest which is perfected under Section 9—304 (permissive filing and temporary perfection). A purchaser of chattel paper who gives new value and takes possession of it in the ordinary course of his business has priority over a security interest in chattel paper which is claimed merely as proceeds of inventory subject to a security interest (Section 9—306), even though he knows that the specific paper is subject to the security interest.

Sec. 9—309. Protection of Purchasers of Instruments and Documents. Nothing in this Article limits the rights of a holder in due course of a negotiable instrument (Section 3—302) or a holder to whom a negotiable document of title has been duly negotiated (Section 7—501) or a bona fide purchaser of a security (Section 8—301) and such holders or purchasers take priority over an earlier security interest even though perfected. Filing under this Article does not constitute notice of the security interest to such holders or purchasers.

Sec. 9—310. Priority of Certain Liens Arising by Operation of Law. When a person in the ordinary course of his business furnishes services or materials with respect to goods subject to a security interest, a lien upon goods in the possession of such person given by statute or rule of laws for such materials or services takes priority over a perfected security interest unless the lien is statutory and the statute expressly provides otherwise.

Sec. 9—311. Alienability of Debtor's Rights: Judicial Process. The debtor's rights in collateral may be voluntarily or involuntarily transferred (by way of sale, creation of a security interest, attachment, levy, garnishment or other judicial process) notwithstanding a provision in the security agreement prohibiting any transfer or making the transfer constitute a default.

Sec. 9—312. Priorities Among Conflicting Security Interests in the Same Collateral. (1) The rules of priority stated in the following sections shall govern where applicable: Section 4—208 with respect to the security interest of collecting banks in items being collected, accompanying documents and proceeds; Section 9—301 on certain priorities; Section 9—304 on goods covered by documents; Section 9—306 on proceeds and repossessions; Section 9—307 on buyers of goods; Section 9—308 on possessory against non-possessory interests in chattel paper or non-negotiable instruments; Section 9—309 on security interests in negotiable instruments, documents or securities; Section 9—310 on priorities between perfected security interests and liens by operation of law; Section 9—313 on security interests in fixtures as against interests in real estate; Section 9—314 on security interests in accessions as against interest in goods; Section 9—315 on conflicting security interests where goods lose their identity or become part of a product; and Section 9—316 on contractual subordination.

(2) A perfected security interest in crops for new value given to enable the debtor to produce the crops during the production season and given not more than three months before the crops become growing crops by planting or otherwise takes priority over an earlier perfected security interest to the extent that such earlier interest secures obligations due more than six months before the crops become growing crops by planting or otherwise, even though the person giving new value had knowledge of the earlier security interest.

(3) A purchase money security interest in inventory collateral has priority over a conflicting security interest in the same collateral if

(a) the purchase money security interest is perfected at the time the debtor receives possession of the collateral; and

(b) any secured party whose security interest is known to the holder of the purchase money security interest or who, prior to the date of the filing made by the holder of the purchase money security interest, had filed a financing statement covering the same items or type of inventory, has received notification of the purchase money security interest before the debtor receives possession of the collateral covered by the purchase money security interest; and

(c) such notification states that the person giving the notice has or expects to acquire a purchase money security interest in inventory of the debtor, describing such inventory by item or type.

(4) A purchase money security interest in collateral other than inventory has priority over a conflicting security interest in the same collateral if the purchase money security interest is perfected at the time the debtor receives possession of the collateral or within ten days thereafter.

(5) In all cases not governed by other rules stated in this section (including cases of purchase money security interests which do not qualify for the special priorities set forth in subsections (3) and (4) of this section), priority between conflicting security interests in the same collateral shall be determined as follows:

(a) in the order of filing if both are perfected by filing, regardless of which security interest attached first under Section 9—204(1) and whether it attached before or after filing;

(b) in the order of perfection unless both are perfected by filing, regardless of which security interest attached first under Section 9—204(1) and, in the case of a filed security interest, whether it attached before or after filing; and

(c) in the order of attachment under Section 9—204(1) so long as neither is perfected.

(6) For the purpose of the priority rules of the immediately preceding subsection, a continuously perfected security interest shall be treated at all times as if perfected by filing if it was originally so perfected and it shall be treated at all times as if perfected otherwise than by filing if it was originally perfected otherwise than by filing.

Sec. 9—313. Priority of Security Interests in Fixtures. (1) The rules of this section do not apply to goods incorporated into a structure in the manner of lumber, bricks, tile, cement, glass, metal work and the like and no security interest in them exists under this Article unless the structure remains personal property under applicable law. The law of this state other than this Act determines whether and when other goods become fixtures. This Act does not prevent creation of an encumbrance upon fixtures or real estate pursuant to the law applicable to real estate.

(2) A security interest which attaches to goods before they become fixtures takes priority as to the goods over the claims of all persons who have an interest in the real estate except as stated in subsection (4).

(3) A security interest which attaches to goods after they become fixtures is valid against all persons subsequently acquiring interests in the real estate except as stated in subsection (4) but is invalid against any person with an interest in the real estate at the time the security interest attaches to the goods who has not in writing consented to the security interest or disclaimed an interest in the goods as fixtures.

(4) The security interests described in subsections (2) and (3) do not take priority over

(a) a subsequent purchaser for value of any interest in the real estate; or

(b) a creditor with a lien on the real estate subsequently obtained by judicial proceedings; or

(c) a creditor with a prior encumbrance of record on the real estate to the extent that he makes subsequent advances

if the subsequent purchase is made, the lien by judicial proceedings is obtained, or the subsequent advance under the prior encumbrance is made or contracted for without knowledge of the security interest and before it is perfected. A purchaser of the real estate at a foreclosure sale other than an encumbrancer purchasing at his own foreclosure sale is a subsequent purchaser within this section.

(5) When under subsections (2) or (3) and (4) a secured party has priority over the claims of all persons who have interests in the real estate, he may, on default, subject to the provisions of Part 5, remove his collateral from the real estate but he must reimburse any encumbrancer or owner of the real estate who is not the debtor and who has not otherwise agreed for the cost of repair of any physical injury, but not for any diminution in value of the real estate caused by the absence of the goods removed or by any necessity for replacing them. A person entitled to reimbursement may refuse permission to remove until the secured party gives adequate security for the performance of this obligation.

Sec. 9—314. Accessions. (1) A security interest in goods which attaches before they are installed in or affixed to other goods takes priority as to the goods installed or affixed (called in this section "accessions") over the claims of all persons to the whole except as stated in subsection (3) and subject to Section 9—315(1).

(2) A security interest which attaches to goods after they become part of a whole is valid against all persons subsequently acquiring interests in the whole except as

stated in subsection (3) but is invalid against any person with an interest in the whole at the time the security interest attaches to the goods who has not in writing consented to the security interest or disclaimed an interest in the goods as part of the whole.

(3) The security interests described in subsections (1) and (2) do not take priority over

(*a*) a subsequent purchaser for value of any interest in the whole; or

(*b*) a creditor with a lien on the whole subsequently obtained by judicial proceedings; or

(*c*) a creditor with a prior perfected security interest in the whole to the extent that he makes subsequent advances

if the subsequent purchase is made, the lien by judicial proceedings obtained or the subsequent advance under the prior perfected security interest is made or contracted for without knowledge of the security interest and before it is perfected. A purchaser of the whole at a foreclosure sale other than the holder of a perfected security interest purchasing at his own foreclosure sale is a subsequent purchaser within this section.

(4) When under subsections (1) or (2) and (3) a secured party has an interest in accessions which has priority over the claims of all persons who have interests in the whole, he may on default subject to the provisions of Part 5 remove his collateral from the whole but he must reimburse any encumbrancer or owner of the whole who is not the debtor and who has not otherwise agreed for the cost of repair of any physical injury but not for any diminution in value of the whole caused by the absence of the goods removed or by any necessity for replacing them. A person entitled to reimbursement may refuse permission to remove until the secured party gives adequate security for the performance of this obligation.

Sec. 9—315. Priority When Goods Are Commingled or Processed. (1) If a security interest in goods was perfected and subsequently the goods or a part thereof have become part of a product or mass, the security interest continues in the product or mass if

(*a*) the goods are so manufactured, processed, assembled or commingled that their identity is lost in the product or mass; or

(*b*) a financing statement covering the original goods also covers the product into which the goods have been manufactured, processed or assembled.

In a case to which paragraph (*b*) applies, no separate security interest in that part of the original goods which has been manufactured, processed or assembled into the product may be claimed under Section 9—314.

(2) When under subsection (1) more than one security interest attaches to the product or mass, they rank equally according to the ratio that the cost of the goods to which each interest originally attached bears to the cost of the total product or mass.

Sec. 9—316. Priority Subject to Subordination. Nothing in this Article prevents subordination by agreement by any person entitled to priority.

Sec. 9—317. Secured Party Not Obligated on Contract of Debtor. The mere existence of a security interest or authority given to the debtor to dispose of or use collateral does not impose contract or tort liability upon the secured party for the debtor's acts or omissions.

Sec. 9—318. Defenses Against Assignee; Modification of Contract After Notification of Assignment; Term Prohibiting Assignment Ineffective; Identification and Proof of Assignment. (1) Unless an account debtor has made an enforceable agreement not to assert defenses or claims arising out of a sale as provided in Section 9—206 the rights of an assignee are subject to

(*a*) all the terms of the contract between the account debtor and assignor and any defense or claim arising therefrom; and (*b*) any other defense or claim of the account debtor against the assignor which accrues before the account debtor receives notification of the assignment.

(2) So far as the right to payment under an assigned contract right has not already become an account, and notwithstanding notification of the assignment, any modification of or substitution for the contract made in good faith and in accordance with reasonable commercial standards is effective against an assignee unless the account debtor has otherwise agreed but the assignee acquires corresponding rights under the modified or substituted contract. The assignment may provide that such modification or substitution is a breach by the assignor.

(3) The account debtor is authorized to pay the assignor until the account debtor receives notification that the account has been assigned and that payment is to be made to the assignee. A notification which does not reasonably identify the rights assigned is ineffective. If requested by the account debtor, the assignee must seasonably furnish reasonable proof that the assignment has been made and unless he does so the account debtor may pay the assignor.

(4) A term in any contract between an account debtor and an assignor which prohibits assignment of an account or contract right to which they are parties is ineffective.

PART IV

FILING

Sec. 9—401. Place of Filing; Erroneous Filing; Removal of Collateral.
First Alternative Subsection (1)

(1) The proper place to file in order to perfect a security interest is as follows:

(*a*) when the collateral is goods which at the time the security interest attaches are or are to become fixtures, then in the office where a mortgage on the real estate concerned would be filed or recorded;

(*b*) in all other cases, in the office of the [Secretary of State].

Second Alternative Subsection (1)

(1) The proper place to file in order to perfect a security interest is as follows:

(*a*) when the collateral is equipment used in farming operations, or farm products, or accounts, contract rights or general intangibles arising from or relating to the sale of farm products by a farmer, or consumer goods, then in the office of the .... in the county of the debtor's residence or if the debtor is not a resident of this state then in the office of the .... in the county where the goods are kept, and in addition when the collateral is crops in the office of the .... in the county where the land on which the crops are growing or to be grown is located;

(*b*) when the collateral is goods which at the time the security interest attaches are or are to become fixtures, then in the office where a mortgage on the real estate concerned would be filed or recorded;

(*c*) in all other cases, in the office of the [Secretary of State].

Third Alternative Subsection (1)

(1) The proper place to file in order to perfect a security interest is as follows:

(*a*) when the collateral is equipment used in farming operations, or farm products, or accounts, contract rights or general intangibles arising from or relating to the sale of farm products by a farmer, or consumer goods, then in the office of the .... in the county of the debtor's residence or if the debtor is not a resident of this state then in the office of the .... in the county where the goods are kept, and in addition when the collateral is crops in the office of the .... in the county where the land on which the crops are growing or to be grown is located;

(*b*) when the collateral is goods which at the time the security interest attaches are or are to become fixtures, then in the office where a mortgage on the real estate concerned would be filed or recorded;

(c) in all other cases, in the office of the [Secretary of State] and in addition, if the debtor has a place of business in only one county of this state, also in the office of .... of such county, or, if the debtor has no place of business in this state, but resides in the state, also in the office of .... of the county in which he resides.

Note: *One of the three alternatives should be selected as subsection (1).*

(2) A filing which is made in good faith in an improper place or not in all of the places required by this section is nevertheless effective with regard to any collateral as to which the filing complied with the requirements of this Article and is also effective with regard to collateral covered by the financing statement against any person who has knowledge of the contents of such financing statement.

(3) A filing which is made in the proper place in this state continues effective even though the debtor's residence or place of business or the location of the collateral or its use, whichever controlled the original filing, is thereafter changed.

Alternative Subsection (3)

[(3) A filing which is made in the proper county continues effective for four months after a change to another county of the debtor's residence or place of business or the location of the collateral, whichever controlled the original filing. It becomes ineffective thereafter unless a copy of the financing statement signed by the secured party is filed in the new county within said period. The security interest may also be perfected in the new county after the expiration of the four-month period; in such case perfection dates from the time of perfection in the new county. A change in the use of the collateral does not impair the effectiveness of the original filing.]

(4) If collateral is brought into this state from another jurisdiction, the rules stated in Section 9–103 determine whether filing is necessary in this state.

Sec. 9—402. Formal Requisites of Financing Statement; Amendments. (1) A financing statement is sufficient if it is signed by the debtor and the secured party, gives an address of the secured party from which information concerning the security interest may be obtained, gives a mailing address of the debtor and contains a statement indicating the types, or describing the items, of collateral. A financing statement may be filed before a security agreement is made or a security interest otherwise attaches. When the financing statement covers crops growing or to be grown or goods which are or are to become fixtures, the statement must also contain a description of the real estate concerned. A copy of the security agreement is sufficient as a financing statement if it contains the above information and is signed by both parties.

(2) A financing statement which otherwise complies with subsection (1) is sufficient although it is signed only by the secured party when it is filed to perfect a security interest in

(a) collateral already subject to a security interest in another jurisdiction when it is brought into this state. Such a financing statement must state that the collateral was brought into this state under such circumstances.

(b) proceeds under Section 9–306 if the security interest in the original collateral was perfected. Such a financing statement must describe the original collateral.

(3) A form substantially as follows is sufficient to comply with subsection (1):

Name of debtor (or assignor) ....

Address ....

Name of secured party (or assignee) ....

Address ....

1. This financing statement covers the following types (or items) of property:
(Describe) ....

2. (If collateral is crops) The above described crops are growing or are to be grown on:

(Describe Real Estate) ....

3. (If collateral is goods which are or are to become fixtures) The above described goods are affixed or to be affixed to:

(Describe Real Estate) ....

4. (If proceeds or products of collateral are claimed) Proceeds—Products of the collateral are also covered.

Signature of Debtor (or Assignor) ....

Signature of Secured Party (or Assignee) ....

(4) The term "financing statement" as used in this Article means the original financing statement and any amendments but if any amendment adds collateral, it is effective as to the added collateral only from the filing date of the amendment.

(5) A financing statement substantially complying with the requirements of this section is effective even though it contains minor errors which are not seriously misleading.

Sec. 9—403. What Constitutes Filing; Duration of Filing; Effect of Lapsed Filing; Duties of Filing Officer. (1) Presentation for filing of a financing statement and tender of the filing fee or acceptance of the statement by the filing officer constitutes filing under this Article.

(2) A filed financing statement which states a maturity date of the obligation secured of five years or less is effective until such maturity date and thereafter for a period of sixty days. Any other filed financing statement is effective for a period of five years from the date of filing. The effectiveness of a filed financing statement lapses on the expiration of such sixty day period after a stated maturity date or on the expiration of such five year period, as the case may be, unless a continuation statement is filed prior to the lapse. Upon such lapse the security interest becomes unperfected. A filed financing statement which states that the obligation secured is payable on demand is effective for five years from the date of filing.

(3) A continuation statement may be filed by the secured party (i) within six months before and sixty days after a stated maturity date of five years or less, and (ii) otherwise within six months prior to the expiration of the five year period specified in subsection (2). Any such continuation statement must be signed by the secured party, identify the original statement by file number and state that the original statement is still effective. Upon timely filing of the continuation statement, the effectiveness of the original statement is continued for five years after the last date to which the filing was effective whereupon it lapses in the same manner as provided in subsection (2) unless another continuation statement is filed prior to such lapse. Succeeding continuation statements may be filed in the same manner to continue the effectiveness of the original statement. Unless a statute on disposition of public records provides otherwise, the filing officer may remove a lapsed statement from the files and destroy it.

(4) A filing officer shall mark each statement with a consecutive file number and with the date and hour of filing and shall hold the statement for public inspection. In addition the filing officer shall index the statements according to the name of the debtor and shall note in the index the file number and the address of the debtor given in the statement.

(5) The uniform fee for filing, indexing and furnishing filing data for an original or a continuation statement shall be $ ......

Sec. 9—404. Termination Statement. (1) Whenever there is no outstanding secured obligation and no commitment to make advances, incur obligations or otherwise give value, the secured party must on written demand by the debtor send the debtor a statement that he no longer claims a security interest under the financing statement, which shall be identified by file number. A termination statement signed by a person other than the secured party of record must include or be accompanied by the assignment or a statement by the secured party of record that he has assigned the security interest to the signer of the termination statement. The uniform fee for filing and indexing such an assignment or statement thereof shall be $..... If the affected secured party fails to send such a termination statement within ten days after proper demand therefor he shall be liable to the debtor for one hundred dollars, and in addition for any loss caused to the debtor by such failure.

(2) On presentation to the filing officer of such a termination statement he must note it in the index. The filing officer shall remove from the files, mark "terminated" and send or deliver to the secured party the financing statement and any continuation statement, statement of assignment or statement of release pertaining thereto.

(3) The uniform fee for filing and indexing a termination statement including sending or delivering the financing statement shall be $......

Sec. 9—405. Assignment of Security Interest; Duties of Filing Officer; Fees. (1) A financing statement may disclose an assignment of a security interest in the collateral described in the statement by indication in the statement of the name and address of the assignee or by an assignment itself or a copy thereof on the face or back of the statement. Either the original secured party or the assignee may sign this statement as the secured party. On presentation to the filing officer of such a financing statement the filing officer shall mark the same as provided in Section 9—403(4). The uniform fee for filing, indexing and furnishing filing data for a financing statement so indicating an assignment shall be $......

(2) A secured party may assign of record all or a part of his rights under a financing statement by the filing of a separate written statement of assignment signed by the secured party of record and setting forth the name of the secured party of record and the debtor, the file number and the date of filing of the financing statement and the name and address of the assignee and containing a description of the collateral assigned. A copy of the assignment is sufficient as a separate statement if it complies with the preceding sentence. On presentation to the filing officer of such a separate statement, the filing officer shall mark such separate statement with the date and hour of the filing. He shall note the assignment on the index of the financing statement. The uniform fee for filing, indexing and furnishing filing data about such a separate statement of assignment shall be $......

(3) After the disclosure or filing of an assignment under this section, the assignee is the secured party of record.

Sec. 9—406. Release of Collateral; Duties of Filing Officer; Fees. A secured party of record may by his signed statement release all or a part of any collateral described in a filed financing statement. The statement of release is sufficient if it contains a description of the collateral being released, the name and address of the debtor, the name and address of the secured party, and the file number of the financing statement. Upon presentation of such a statement to the filing officer he shall mark the statement with the hour and date of filing and shall note the same upon the margin of the index of the filing of the financing statement. The uniform fee for filing and noting such a statement of release shall be $......

[**Sec. 9—407. Information From Filing Officer.** [(1) If the person filing any financing statement, termination statement, statement of assignment, or statement of release, furnishes the filing officer a copy thereof, the filing officer shall upon request note upon the copy the file number and date and hour of the filing of the original and deliver or send the copy to such person.

(2) Upon request of any person, the filing officer shall issue his certificate showing whether there is on file on the date and hour stated therein, any presently effective financing statement naming a particular debtor and any statement of assignment thereof and if there is, giving the date and hour of filing of each such statement and the names and addresses of each secured party therein. The uniform fee for such a certificate shall be $...... plus $...... for each financing statement and for each statement of assignment reported therein. Upon request the filing officer shall furnish

a copy of any filed financing statement or statement of assignment for a uniform fee of $ . . . . . . per page.]

Note: *This new section is proposed as an optional provision to require filing officers to furnish certificates. Local law and practices should be consulted with regard to the advisability of adoption.*

PART V

DEFAULT

Sec. 9—501. Default; Procedure When Security Agreement Covers Both Real and Personal Property. (1) When a debtor is in default under a security agreement, a secured party has the rights and remedies provided in this Part and except as limited by subsection (3) those provided in the security agreement. He may reduce his claim to judgment, foreclose or otherwise enforce the security interest by any available judicial procedure. If the collateral is documents the secured party may proceed either as to the documents or as to the goods covered thereby. A secured party in possession has the rights, remedies and duties provided in Section 9—207. The rights and remedies referred to in this subsection are cumulative.

(2) After default, the debtor has the rights and remedies provided in this Part, those provided in the security agreement and those provided in Section 9—207.

(3) To the extent that they give rights to the debtor and impose duties on the secured party, the rules stated in the subsections referred to below may not be waived or varied except as provided with respect to compulsory disposition of collateral (subsection (1) of Section 9—505) and with respect to redemption of collateral (Section 9—506) but the parties may by agreement determine the standards by which the fulfillment of these rights and duties is to be measured if such standards are not manifestly unreasonable:

(*a*) subsection (2) of Section 9—502 and subsection (2) of Section 9—504 insofar as they require accounting for surplus proceeds of collateral;

(*b*) subsection (3) of Section 9—504 and subsection (1) of Section 9—505 which deal with disposition of collateral;

(*c*) subsection (2) of Section 9—505 which deals with acceptance of collateral as discharge of obligation;

(*d*) Section 9—506 which deals with redemption of collateral; and

(*e*) subsection (1) of Section 9—507 which deals with the secured party's liability for failure to comply with this Part.

(4) If the security agreement covers both real and personal property, the secured party may proceed under this Part as to the personal property or he may proceed as to both the real and the personal property in accordance with his rights and remedies in respect of the real property in which case the provisions of this Part do not apply.

(5) When a secured party has reduced his claim to judgment the lien of any levy which may be made upon his collateral by virtue of any execution based upon the judgment shall relate back to the date of the perfection of the security interest in such collateral. A judicial sale, pursuant to such execution, is a foreclosure of the security interest by judicial procedure within the meaning of this section, and the secured party may purchase at the sale and thereafter hold the collateral free of any other requirements of this Article.

Sec. 9—502. Collection Rights of Secured Party. (1) When so agreed and in any event on default the secured party is entitled to notify an account debtor or the obligor on an instrument to make payment to him whether or not the assignor was theretofore making collections on the collateral, and also to take control of any proceeds to which he is entitled under Section 9—306.

(2) A secured party who by agreement is entitled to charge back uncollected col-

lateral or otherwise to full or limited recourse against the debtor and who undertakes to collect from the account debtors or obligors must proceed in a commercially reasonable manner and may deduct his reasonable expenses of realization from the collections. If the security agreement secures an indebtedness, the secured party must account to the debtor for any surplus, and unless otherwise agreed, the debtor is liable for any deficiency. But, if the underlying transaction was a sale of accounts, contract rights, or chattel paper, the debtor is entitled to any surplus or is liable for any deficiency only if the security agreement so provides.

Sec. 9—503. Secured Party's Right to Take Possession After Default. Unless otherwise agreed a secured party has on default the right to take possession of the collateral. In taking possession a secured party may proceed without judicial process if this can be done without breach of the peace or may proceed by action. If the security agreement so provides the secured party may require the debtor to assemble the collateral and make it available to the secured party at a place to be designated by the secured party which is reasonably convenient to both parties. Without removal a secured party may render equipment unusable, and may dispose of collateral on the debtor's premises under Section 9—504.

Sec. 9—504. Secured Party's Right to Dispose of Collateral After Default; Effect of Disposition. (1) A secured party after default may sell, lease or otherwise dispose of any or all of the collateral in its then condition or following any commercially reasonable preparation or processing. Any sale of goods is subject to the Article on Sales (Article 2). The proceeds of disposition shall be applied in the order following to

(*a*) the reasonable expenses of retaking, holding, preparing for sale, selling and the like and, to the extent provided for in the agreement and not prohibited by law, the reasonable attorneys' fees and legal expenses incurred by the secured party;

(*b*) the satisfaction of indebtedness secured by the security interest under which the disposition is made;

(*c*) the satisfaction of indebtedness secured by any subordinate security interest in the collateral if written notification of demand therefor is received before distribution of the proceeds is completed. If requested by the secured party, the holder of a subordinate security interest must seasonably furnish reasonable proof of his interest, and unless he does so, the secured party need not comply with his demand.

(2) If the security interest secures an indebtedness, the secured party must account to the debtor for any surplus, and, unless otherwise agreed, the debtor is liable for any deficiency. But if the underlying transaction was a sale of accounts, contract rights, or chattel paper, the debtor is entitled to any surplus or is liable for any deficiency only if the security agreement so provides.

(3) Disposition of the collateral may be by public or private proceedings and may be made by way of one or more contracts. Sale or other disposition may be as a unit or in parcels and at any time and place and on any terms but every aspect of the disposition including the method, manner, time, place and terms must be commercially reasonable. Unless collateral is perishable or threatens to decline speedily in value or is of a type customarily sold on a recognized market, reasonable notification of the time and place of any public sale or reasonable notification of the time after which any private sale or other intended disposition is to be made shall be sent by the secured party to the debtor, and except in the case of consumer goods to any other person who has a security interest in the collateral and who has duly filed a financing statement indexed in the name of the debtor in this state or who is known by the secured party to have a security interest in the collateral. The secured party may buy at any public sale and if the collateral is of a type customarily sold in a recognized market or is of a type which is the subject of widely distributed standard price quotations he may buy at private sale.

(4) When collateral is disposed of by a secured party after default, the disposition transfers to a purchaser for value all of the debtor's rights therein, discharges the security interest under which it is made and any security interest or lien subordinate thereto. The purchaser takes free of all such rights and interests even though the secured party fails to comply with the requirements of this Part or of any judicial proceedings

(a) in the case of a public sale, if the purchaser has no knowledge of any defects in the sale and if he does not buy in collusion with the secured party, other bidders or the person conducting the sale; or

(b) in any other case, if the purchaser acts in good faith.

(5) A person who is liable to a secured party under a guaranty, indorsement, repurchase agreement or the like and who receives a transfer of collateral from the secured party or is subrogated to his rights has thereafter the rights and duties of the secured party. Such a transfer of collateral is not a sale or disposition of the collateral under this Article.

Sec. 9—505. Compulsory Disposition of Collateral; Acceptance of the Collateral as Discharge of Obligation. (1) If the debtor has paid sixty per cent of the cash price in the case of a purchase money security interest in consumer goods or sixty per cent of the loan in the case of another security interest in consumer goods, and has not signed after default a statement renouncing or modifying his rights under this Part a secured party who has taken possession of collateral must dispose of it under Section 9—504 and if he fails to do so within ninety days after he takes possession the debtor at his option may recover in conversion or under Section 9—507(1) on secured party's liability.

(2) In any other case involving consumer goods or any other collateral a secured party in possession may, after default, propose to retain the collateral in satisfaction of the obligation. Written notice of such proposal shall be sent to the debtor and except in the case of consumer goods to any other secured party who has a security interest in the collateral and who has duly filed a financing statement indexed in the name of the debtor in this state or is known by the secured party in possession to have a security interest in it. If the debtor or other person entitled to receive notification objects in writing within thirty days from the receipt of the notification or if any other secured party objects in writing within thirty days after the secured party obtains possession the secured party must dispose of the collateral under Section 9—504. In the absence of such written objection the secured party may retain the collateral in satisfaction of the debtor's obligation.

Sec. 9—506. Debtor's Right to Redeem Collateral. At any time before the secured party has disposed of collateral or entered into a contract for its disposition under Section 9—504 or before the obligation has been discharged under Section 9—505(2) the debtor or any other secured party may unless otherwise agreed in writing after default redeem the collateral by tendering fulfillment of all obligations secured by the collateral as well as the expenses reasonably incurred by the secured party in retaking, holding and preparing the collateral for disposition, in arranging for the sale, and to the extent provided in the agreement and not prohibited by law, his reasonable attorneys' fees and legal expenses.

Sec. 9—507. Secured Party's Liability for Failure to Comply With This Part. (1) If it is established that the secured party is not proceeding in accordance with the provisions of this Part disposition may be ordered or restrained on appropriate terms and conditions. If the disposition has occurred the debtor or any person entitled to notification or whose security interest has been made known to the secured party prior to the disposition has a right to recover from the secured party any loss caused by a failure to comply with the provisions of this Part. If the collateral is consumer goods, the debtor has a right to recover in any event an amount not less than the credit service charge plus ten per cent of the principal amount of the debt or the time price differential plus ten per cent of the cash price.

(2) The fact that a better price could have been obtained by a sale at a different time or in a different method from that selected by the secured party is not of itself sufficient to establish that the sale was not made in a commercially reasonable manner. If the secured party either sells the collateral in the usual manner in any recognized market therefor or if he sells at the price current in such market at the time of his sale or if he has otherwise sold in conformity with reasonable commercial practices among dealers in the type of property sold he has sold in a commercially reasonable manner. The principles stated in the two preceding sentences with respect to sales also apply as may be appropriate to other types of disposition. A disposition which has been approved in any judicial proceeding or by any bona fide creditors' committee or representative of creditors shall conclusively be deemed to be commercially reasonable, but this sentence does not indicate that any such approval must be obtained in any case nor does it indicate that any disposition not so approved is not commercially reasonable.

ARTICLE X

EFFECTIVE DATE AND REPEALER

Sec. 10—101. Effective Date. This Act shall become effective at midnight on December 31st following its enactment. It applies to transactions entered into and events occurring after that date.

Sec. 10—102. Specific Repealer; Provision for Transition. (1) The following acts and all other acts and parts of acts inconsistent herewith are hereby repealed:

(Here should follow the acts to be specifically repealed including the following:
Uniform Negotiable Instruments Act
Uniform Warehouse Receipts Act
Uniform Sales Act
Uniform Bills of Lading Act
Uniform Stock Transfer Act
Uniform Conditional Sales Act
Uniform Trust Receipts Act
Also any acts regulating:
Bank collections
Bulk sales
Chattel mortgages
Conditional sales
Factor's lien acts
Farm storage of grain and similar acts
Assignment of accounts receivable)

(2) Transactions validly entered into before the effective date specified in Section 10—101 and the rights, duties and interests flowing from them remain valid thereafter and may be terminated, completed, consummated or enforced as required or permitted by any statute or other law amended or repealed by this Act as though such repeal or amendment had not occurred.

Note

Subsection (1) should be separately prepared for each state. The foregoing is a list of statutes to be checked.

Sec. 10—103. General Repealer. Except as provided in the following section, all acts and parts of acts inconsistent with this Act are hereby repealed.

Sec. 10—104. Laws Not Repealed. [(1)] The Article on Documents of Title (Article 7) does not repeal or modify any laws prescribing the form or contents of documents of title or the services or facilities to be afforded by bailees, or otherwise regulating bailees' businesses in respects not specifically dealt with herein; but the fact that such laws are violated does not affect the status of a document of title which otherwise complies with the definition of a document of title (Section 1—201).

[(2) This Act does not repeal ....,*
cited as the Uniform Act for the Simplification of Fiduciary Security Transfers, and if in any respect there is any inconsistency between that Act and the Article of this Act on investment securities (Article 8) the provisions of the former Act shall control.]

Note: *At * in subsection (2) insert the statutory reference to the Uniform Act for the Simplification of Fiduciary Security Transfers if such Act has previously been enacted. If it has not been enacted, omit subsection (2).*

PERMANENT EDITORIAL BOARD'S 1966 OFFICIAL RECOMMENDATIONS FOR AMENDMENT OF THE UNIFORM COMMERCIAL CODE

Sec. 2—702. Seller's Remedies on Discovery of Buyer's Insolvency. (1) Where the seller discovers the buyer to be insolvent he may refuse delivery except for cash including payment for all goods theretofore delivered under the contract, and stop delivery under this Article (Section 2—705).

(2) Where the seller discovers that the buyer has received goods on credit while insolvent he may reclaim the goods upon demand made within ten days after the receipt, but if misrepresentation of solvency has been made to the particular seller in writing within three months before delivery the ten day limitation does not apply. Except as provided in this subsection the seller may not base a right to reclaim goods on the buyer's fraudulent or innocent misrepresentation of solvency or of intent to pay.

(3) The seller's right to reclaim under subsection (2) is subject to the rights of a buyer in ordinary course or other good faith purchaser under this Article (Section 2—403). Successful reclamation of goods excludes all other remedies with respect to them.

Sec. 3—501. When Presentment, Notice of Dishonor, and Protest Necessary or Permissible. (1) Unless excused (Section 3—511) presentment is necessary to charge secondary parties as follows:

(*a*) presentment for acceptance is necessary to charge the drawer and indorsers of a draft where the draft so provides, or is payable elsewhere than at the residence or place of business of the drawee, or its date of payment depends upon such presentment. The holder may at his option present for acceptance any other draft payable at a stated date;

(*b*) presentment for payment is necessary to charge any indorser;

(*c*) in the case of any drawer, the acceptor of a draft payable at a bank or the maker of a note payable at a bank, presentment for payment is necessary, but failure to make presentment discharges such drawer, acceptor or maker only as stated in Section 3—502(1) (*b*).

(2) Unless excused (Section 3—511)

(*a*) notice of any dishonor is necessary to charge any indorser;

(*b*) in the case of any drawer, the acceptor of a draft payable at a bank or the maker of a note payable at a bank, notice of any dishonor is necessary, but failure to give such notice discharges such drawer, acceptor or maker only as stated in Section 3—502(1)(*b*).

(3) Unless excused (Section 3—511) protest of any dishonor is necessary to charge the drawer and indorsers of any draft which on its face appears to be drawn or payable outside of the states, territories, dependencies and possessions of the United

States, the District of Columbia and the Commonwealth of Puerto Rico. The holder may at his option make protest of any dishonor of any other instrument and in the case of a foreign draft may on insolvency of the acceptor before maturity make protest for better security.

(4) Notwithstanding any provision of this section, neither presentment nor notice of dishonor nor protest is necessary to charge an indorser who has indorsed an instrument after maturity.

Sec. 7—209. Lien of Warehouseman. (1) A warehouseman has a lien against the bailor on the goods covered by a warehouse receipt or on the proceeds thereof in his possession for charges for storage or transportation (including demurrage and terminal charges), insurance, labor, or charges present or future in relation to the goods, and for expenses necessary for preservation of the goods or reasonably incurred in their sale pursuant to law. If the person on whose account the goods are held is liable for like charges or expenses in relation to other goods whenever deposited and it is stated in the receipt that a lien is claimed for charges and expenses in relation to other goods, the warehouseman also has a lien against him for such charges and expenses whether or not the other goods have been delivered by the warehouseman. But against a person to whom a negotiable warehouse receipt is duly negotiated with a warehouseman's lien is limited to charges in an amount or at a rate specified on the receipt or if no charges are so specified then to a reasonable charge for storage of the goods covered by the receipt subsequent to the date of the receipt.

(2) The warehouseman may also reserve a security interest against the bailor for a maximum amount specified on the receipt for charges other than those specified in subsection (1), such as for money advanced and interest. Such a security interest is governed by the Article on Secured Transactions (Article 9).

(3) (a) A warehouseman's lien for charges and expenses under subsection (1) or a security interest under subsection (2) is also effective against any person who so entrusted the bailor with possession of the goods that a pledge of them by him to a good faith purchaser for value would have been valid but is not effective against a person as to whom the document confers no right in the goods covered by it under Section 7—503.

(b) A warehouseman's lien on household goods for charges and expenses in relation to the goods under subsection (1) is also effective against all persons if the depositor was the legal possessor of the goods at the time of deposit. "Household goods" means furniture, furnishings and personal effects used by the depositor in a dwelling.

(4) A warehouseman loses his lien on any goods which he voluntarily delivers or which he unjustifiably refuses to deliver.

PERMANENT EDITORIAL BOARD'S 1966 OFFICIAL RECOMMENDATIONS FOR OPTIONAL AMENDMENT OF THE UNIFORM COMMERCIAL CODE

Sec. 1—209. Subordinated Obligations. An obligation may be issued as subordinated to payment of another obligation of the person obligated, or a creditor may subordinate his right to payment of an obligation by agreement with either the person obligated or another creditor of the person obligated. Such a subordination does not create a security interest as against either the common debtor or a subordinated creditor. This section shall be construed as declaring the law as it existed prior to the enactment of this section and not as modifying it.

Note: *This new section is proposed as an optional provision to make it clear that a subordination agreement does not create a security interest unless so intended.*

Sec. 2—318. Third Party Beneficiaries of Warranties Express or Implied.

Note: *If this Act is introduced in the Congress of the United States this section should be omitted. (States to select one alternative.)*

Alternative A A seller's warranty whether express or implied extends to any natural person who is in the family or household of his buyer or who is a guest in his home if it is reasonable to expect that such person may use, consume or be affected by the goods and who is injured in person by breach of the warranty. A seller may not exclude or limit the operation of this section.

Alternative B A seller's warranty whether express or implied extends to any natural person who may reasonably be expected to use, consume or be affected by the goods and who is injured in person by breach of the warranty. A seller may not exclude or limit the operation of this section.

Alternative C A seller's warranty whether express or implied extends to any person who may reasonably be expected to use, consume or be affected by the goods and who is injured by breach of the warranty. A seller may not exclude or limit the operation of this section with respect to injury to the person of an individual to whom the warranty extends.

Sec. 9—105. Definitions and Index of Definitions. (1) In this Article unless the context otherwise requires:

(*a*) "Account debtor" means the person who is obligated on an account, chattel paper, contract right or general intangible;

(*b*) "Chattel paper" means a writing or writings which evidence both a monetary obligation and a security interest in or a lease of specific goods; a charter or other contract involving the use or hire of a vessel is not chattel paper. When a transaction is evidenced both by such a security agreement or a lease and by an instrument or a series of instruments, the group of writings taken together constitutes chattel paper;

(*c*) "Collateral" means the property subject to a security interest, and includes accounts, contract rights and chattel paper which have been sold;

(*d*) "Debtor" means the person who owes payment or other performance of the obligation secured, whether or not he owns or has rights in the collateral, and includes the seller of accounts, contract rights or chattel paper. Where the debtor and the owner of the collateral are not the same person, the term "debtor" means the owner of the collateral in any provision of the Article dealing with the collateral, the obligor in any provision dealing with the obligation, and may include both where the context so requires;

(*e*) "Document" means document of title as defined in the general definitions of Article 1 (Section 1—201);

(*f*) "Goods" includes all things which are movable at the time the security interest attaches or which are fixtures (Section 9—313), but does not include money, documents, instruments, accounts, chattel paper, general intangibles, contract rights and other things in action. "Goods" also include the unborn young of animals and growing crops;

(*g*) "Instrument" means a negotiable instrument (defined in Section 3—104), or a security (defined in Section 8—102) or any other writing which evidences a right to the payment of money and is not itself a security agreement or lease and is of a type which is in ordinary course of business transferred by delivery with any necessary indorsement or assignment;

(*h*) "Security agreement" means an agreement which creates or provides for a security interest;

(*i*) "Secured party" means a lender, seller or other person in whose favor there is a security interest, including a person to whom accounts, contract rights or chattel paper have been sold. When the holders of obligations issued under an indenture of trust, equipment trust agreement or the like are represented by a trustee or other person, the representative is the secured party.

(2) Other definitions applying to this Article and the sections in which they appear are:

"Account." Section 9—106.

"Consumer goods." Section 9—109(1).

"Contract right." Section 9—106.

"Equipment." Section 9—109(2).

"Farm products." Section 9—109(3).

"General intangibles." Section 9—106.

"Inventory." Section 9—109(4).

"Lien creditor." Section 9—301(3).

"Proceeds." Section 9—306(1).

"Purchase money security interest." Section 9—107.

(3) The following definitions in other Articles apply to this Article:

"Check." Section 3—104.

"Contract for sale." Section 2—106.

"Holder in due course." Section 3—302.

"Note." Section 3—104.

"Sale." Section 2—106.

(4) In addition Article 1 contains general definitions and principles of construction and interpretation applicable throughout this Article.

Sec. 9—106. Definitions: "Account"; "Contract Rights"; "General Intangibles." "Account" means any right to payment for goods sold or leased or for services rendered which is not evidenced by an instrument or chattel paper. "Contract right" means any right to payment under a contract not yet earned by performance and not evidenced by an instrument or chattel paper. "General intangibles" means any personal property (including things in action) other than goods, accounts, contract rights, chattel paper, documents and instruments. All rights earned or unearned under a charter or other contract involving the use or hire of a vessel and all rights incident to the charter or contract are contract rights and neither accounts nor general intangibles.

1972 OFFICIAL TEXT—ARTICLE IX—
SECURED TRANSACTIONS AND
RELATED SECTIONS

AMENDMENTS TO OTHER ARTICLES OF
UNIFORM COMMERCIAL CODE
CONFORMING TO REVISED ARTICLE IX*

AMENDMENTS TO ARTICLE I

Sec. 1—105. Territorial Application of the Act; Parties' Power to Choose Applicable Law.
(1) Except as provided hereafter in this section, when a transaction bears a reasonable relation to this state and also to another state or nation the parties may agree that the law either of this state or of such other state or nation shall govern their

* These amendments to articles other than Article 9 show additions by underlining and deletions by brackets, on the assumption that the draftsman of the amendatory bill in a particular state will deal specifically with only these few sections of these articles.

rights and duties. Failing such agreement this Act applies to transactions bearing an appropriate relation to this state.

(2) Where one of the following provisions of this Act specifies the applicable law, that provision governs and a contrary agreement is effective only to the extent permitted by the law (including the conflict of laws rules) so specified:

Rights of creditors against sold goods. Section 2—402.

Applicability of the Article on Bank Deposits and Collections. Section 4—102.

Bulk transfers subject to the Article on Bulk Transfers. Section 6—102.

Applicability of the Article on Investment Securities. Section 8—106.

[Policy and scope of the Article on Secured Transactions. Sections 9—102 and 9—103.]

Perfection provisions of the Article on Secured Transactions, Section 9—103.

Sec. 1—201. General Definitions.

* * * * *

(9) "Buyer in ordinary course of business" means a person who in good faith and without knowledge that the sale to him is in violation of the ownership rights or security interest of a third party in the goods buys in ordinary course from a person in the business of selling goods of that kind but does not include a pawnbroker. *All persons who sell minerals or the like (including oil and gas) at wellhead or minehead shall be deemed to be persons in the business of selling goods of that kind.* "Buying" may be for cash or by exchange of other property or on secured or unsecured credit and includes receiving goods or documents of title under a pre-existing contract for sale but does not include a transfer in bulk or as security for or in total or partial satisfaction of a money debt.

* * * * *

(37) "Security interest" means an interest in personal property or fixtures which secures payment or performance of an obligation. The retention or reservation of title by a seller of goods notwithstanding shipment or delivery to the buyer (Section 2—401) is limited in effect to a reservation of a "security interest." The term also includes any interest of a buyer of accounts [,] *or* chattel paper [, or contract rights] which is subject to Article 9. The special property interest of a buyer of goods on identification of such goods to a contract for sale under Section 2—401 is not a "security interest," but a buyer may also acquire a "security interest" by complying with Article 9. Unless a lease or consignment is intended as security, reservation of title thereunder is not a "security interest" but a consignment is in any event subject to the provisions on consignment sales (Section 2—326). Whether a lease is intended as security is to be determined by the facts of each case; however, (*a*) the inclusion of an option to purchase does not of itself make the lease one intended for security, and (*b*) an agreement that upon compliance with the terms of the lease the lessee shall become or has the option to become the owner of the property for no additional consideration or for a nominal consideration does make the lease one intended for security.

AMENDMENT TO ARTICLE II

Sec. 2—107. Goods to Be Severed From Realty: Recording. (1) A contract for the sale of [timber,] minerals or the like (*including oil and gas*) or a structure or its materials to be removed from realty is a contract for the sale of goods within this Article if they are to be severed by the seller but until severance a purported present sale thereof which is not effective as a transfer of an interest in land is effective only as a contract to sell.

(2) A contract for the sale apart from the land of growing crops or other things attached to realty and capable of severance without material harm thereto but not

described in subsection (1) *or of timber to be cut* is a contract for the sale of goods within this Article whether the subject matter is to be severed by the buyer or by the seller even though it forms part of the realty at the time of contracting, and the parties can by identification effect a present sale before severance.

(3) The provisions of this section are subject to any third party rights provided by the law relating to realty records, and the contract for sale may be executed and recorded as a document transferring an interest in land and shall then constitute notice to third parties of the buyer's rights under the contract for sale.

AMENDMENT TO ARTICLE V

Sec. 5—116. Transfer and Assignment. (1) The right to draw under a credit can be transferred or assigned only when the credit is expressly designated as transferable or assignable.

(2) Even though the credit specifically states that it is nontransferable or nonassignable the beneficiary may before performance of the conditions of the credit assign his right to proceeds. Such an assignment is an assignment of [a contract right] *an account* under Article 9 on Secured Transactions and is governed by that Article except that

(a) the assignment is ineffective until the letter of credit or advice of credit is delivered to the assignee which delivery constitutes perfection of the security interest under Article 9; and

(b) the issuer may honor drafts or demands for payment drawn under the credit until it receives a notification of the assignment signed by the beneficiary which reasonably identifies the credit involved in the assignment and contains a request to pay the assignee; and

(c) after what reasonably appears to be such a notification has been received the issuer may without dishonor refuse to accept or pay even to a person otherwise entitled to honor until the letter of credit or advice of credit is exhibited to the issuer.

(3) Except where the beneficiary has effectively assigned his right to draw or his right to proceeds, nothing in this section limits his right to transfer or negotiate drafts or demands drawn under the credit.

REVISED ARTICLE IX OF THE UNIFORM COMMERCIAL CODE.**

ARTICLE IX

SECURED TRANSACTIONS; SALES OF ACCOUNTS AND CHATTEL PAPER

PART I

SHORT TITLE, APPLICABILITY AND DEFINITIONS

Sec. 9—101. Short Title. This Article shall be known and may be cited as Uniform Commercial Code—Secured Transactions.

Sec. 9—102. Policy and Subject Matter of Article. (1) Except as otherwise provided in Section 9—104 on excluded transactions, this Article applies

(a) to any transaction (regardless of its form) which is intended to create a security interest in personal property or fixtures including goods, documents, instruments, general intangibles, chattel paper or accounts; and also

** The revised text of Article 9 is set forth without showing additions and deletions, on the assumption that the draftsman of the amendatory bill in a particular state will provide that existing Article 9 be stricken and the revised Article 9 substituted.

(*b*) to any sale of accounts or chattel paper.

(2) This Article applies to security interests created by contract including pledge, assignment, chattel mortgage, chattel trust, trust deed, factor's lien, equipment trust, conditional sale, trust receipt, other lien or title retention contract and lease or consignment intended as security. This Article does not apply to statutory liens except as provided in Section 9–310.

(3) The application of this Article to a security interest in a secured obligation is not affected by the fact that the obligation is itself secured by a transaction or interest to which this Article does not apply.

Note: *The adoption of this Article should be accompanied by the repeal of existing statutes dealing with conditional sales, trust receipts, factor's liens where the factor is given a non-possessory lien, chattel mortgages, crop mortgages, mortgages on railroad equipment, assignment of accounts and generally statutes regulating security interests in personal property.*

Where the state has a retail installment selling act or small loan act, that legislation should be carefully examined to determine what changes in those acts are needed to conform them to this Article. This Article primarily sets out rules defining rights of a secured party against persons dealing with the debtor; it does not prescribe regulations and controls which may be necessary to curb abuses arising in the small loan business or in the financing of consumer purchases on credit. Accordingly there is no intention to repeal existing regulatory acts in those fields by enactment or re-enactment of Article 9. See Section 9–203(4) and the Note thereto.

Sec. 9—103. Perfection of Security Interests in Multiple State Transactions. (1) Documents, instruments and ordinary goods.

(*a*) This subsection applies to documents and instruments and to goods other than those covered by a certificate of title described in subsection (2), mobile goods described in subsection (3), and minerals described in subsection (5).

(*b*) Except as otherwise provided in this subsection, perfection and the effect of perfection or non-perfection of a security interest in collateral are governed by the law of the jurisdiction where the collateral is when the last event occurs on which is based the assertion that the security interest is perfected or unperfected.

(*c*) If the parties to a transaction creating a purchase money security interest in goods in one jurisdiction understand at the time that the security interest attaches that the goods will be kept in another jurisdiction, then the law of the other jurisdiction governs the perfection and the effect of perfection or non-perfection of the security interest from the time it attaches until thirty days after the debtor receives possession of the goods and thereafter if the goods are taken to the other jurisdiction before the end of the thirty-day period.

(*d*) When collateral is brought into and kept in this state while subject to a security interest perfected under the law of the jurisdiction from which the collateral was removed, the security interest remains perfected, but if action is required by Part 3 of this Article to perfect the security interest,

(*i*) if the action is not taken before the expiration of the period of perfection in the other jurisdiction or the end of four months after the collateral is brought into this state, whichever period first expires, the security interest becomes unperfected at the end of that period and is thereafter deemed to have been unperfected as against a person who became a purchaser after removal;

(*ii*) if the action is taken before the expiration of the period specified in subparagraph (*i*), the security interest continues perfected thereafter;

(*iii*) for the purpose of priority over a buyer of consumer goods (subsection (2) of Section 9–307), the period of the effectiveness of a filing in the jurisdiction from which the collateral is removed is governed by the rules with respect to perfection in subparagraphs (*i*) and (*ii*).

(2) Certificate of title.

(*a*) This subsection applies to goods covered by a certificate of title issued under a statute of this state or of another jurisdiction under the law of which indication of a security interest on the certificate is required as a condition of perfection.

(*b*) Except as otherwise provided in this subsection, perfection and the effect of perfection or non-perfection of the security interest are governed by the law (including the conflict of laws rules) of the jurisdiction issuing the certificate until four months after the goods are removed from that jurisdiction and thereafter until the goods are registered in another jurisdiction, but in any event not beyond surrender of the certificate. After the expiration of that period, the goods are not covered by the certificate of title within the meaning of this section.

(*c*) Except with respect to the rights of a buyer described in the next paragraph, a security interest, perfected in another jurisdiction otherwise than by notation on a certificate of title, in goods brought into this state and thereafter covered by a certificate of title issued by this state is subject to the rules stated in paragraph (*d*) of subsection (1).

(*d*) If goods are brought into this state while a security interest therein is perfected in any manner under the law of the jurisdiction from which the goods are removed and a certificate of title is issued by this state and the certificate does not show that the goods are subject to the security interest or that they may be subject to security interests not shown on the certificate, the security interest is subordinate to the rights of a buyer of the goods who is not in the business of selling goods of that kind to the extent that he gives value and receives delivery of the goods after issuance of the certificate and without knowledge of the security interest.

(3) Accounts, general intangibles and mobile goods.

(*a*) This subsection applies to accounts (other than an account described in subsection (5) on minerals) and general intangibles and to goods which are mobile and which are of a type normally used in more than one jurisdiction, such as motor vehicles, trailers, rolling stock, airplanes, shipping containers, road building and construction machinery and commercial harvesting machinery and the like, if the goods are equipment or are inventory leased or held for lease by the debtor to others, and are not covered by a certificate of title described in subsection (2).

(*b*) The law (including the conflict of laws rules) of the jurisdiction in which the debtor is located governs the perfection and the effect of perfection or non-perfection of the security interest.

(*c*) If, however, the debtor is located in a jurisdiction which is not a part of the United States, and which does not provide for perfection of the security interest by filing or recording in that jurisdiction, the law of the jurisdiction in the United States in which the debtor has its major executive office in the United States governs the perfection and the effect of perfection or non-perfection of the security interest through filing. In the alternative, if the debtor is located in a jurisdiction which is not a part of the United States or Canada and the collateral is accounts or general intangibles for money due or to become due, the security interest may be perfected by notification to the account debtor. As used in this paragraph, "United States" includes its territories and possessions and the Commonwealth of Puerto Rico.

(*d*) A debtor shall be deemed located at his place of business if he has one, at his chief executive office if he has more than one place of business, otherwise at his residence. If, however, the debtor is a foreign air carrier under the Federal Aviation Act of 1958, as amended, it shall be deemed located at the designated office of the agent upon whom service of process may be made on behalf of the foreign air carrier.

(*e*) A security interest perfected under the law of the jurisdiction of the location of the debtor is perfected until the expiration of four months after a change of the debtor's location to another jurisdiction, or until perfection would have ceased by the law of the first jurisdiction, whichever period first expires. Unless perfected in the new jurisdiction before the end of that period, it becomes unperfected thereafter and is deemed to have been unperfected as against a person who became a purchaser after the change.

(4) Chattel paper.

The rules stated for goods in subsection (1) apply to a possessory security interest in chattel paper. The rules stated for accounts in subsection (3) apply to a non-possessory security interest in chattel paper, but the security interest may not be perfected by notification to the account debtor.

(5) Minerals.

Perfection and the effect of perfection or non-perfection of a security interest which is created by a debtor who has an interest in minerals or the like (including oil and gas) before extraction and which attaches thereto as extracted, or which attaches to an account resulting from the sale thereof at the wellhead or minehead are governed by the law (including the conflict of laws rules) of the jurisdiction wherein the wellhead or minehead is located.

Sec. 9—104. Transactions Excluded From Article. This Article does not apply

(*a*) to a security interest subject to any statute of the United States to the extent that such statute governs the rights of parties to and third parties affected by transactions in particular types of property; or

(*b*) to a landlord's lien; or

(*c*) to a lien given by statute or other rule of law for services or materials except as provided in Section 9—310 on priority of such liens; or

(*d*) to a transfer of a claim for wages, salary or other compensation of an employee; or

(*e*) to a transfer by a government or governmental subdivision or agency; or

(*f*) to a sale of accounts or chattel paper as part of a sale of the business out of which they arose, or an assignment of accounts or chattel paper which is for the purpose of collection only, or a transfer of a right to payment under a contract to an assignee who is also to do the performance under the contract or a transfer of a single account to an assignee in whole or partial satisfaction of a preexisting indebtedness; or

(*g*) to a transfer of an interest in or claim in or under any policy of insurance, except as provided with respect to proceeds (Section 9—306) and priorities in proceeds (Section 9—312); or

(*h*) to a right represented by a judgment (other than a judgment taken on a right to payment which was collateral); or

(*i*) to any right of set-off; or

(*j*) except to the extent that provision is made for fixtures in Section 9—313, to the creation or transfer of an interest in or lien on real estate, including a lease or rents thereunder; or

(*k*) to a transfer in whole or in part of any claim arising out of tort; or

(*l*) to a transfer of an interest in any deposit account (subsection (1) of Section 9—105), except as provided with respect to proceeds (Section 9—306) and priorities in proceeds (Section 9—312).

Sec. 9—105. Definitions and Index of Definitions. (1) In this Article unless the context otherwise requires:

(*a*) "Account debtor" means the person who is obligated on an account, chattel paper or general intangible;

(*b*) "Chattel paper" means a writing or writings which evidence both a monetary obligation and a security interest in or a lease of specific goods, but a charter or other contract involving the use or hire of a vessel is not chattel paper. When a transaction is evidenced both by such a security agreement or a lease and by an instrument or a series of instruments, the group of writings taken together constitutes chattel paper;

(*c*) "Collateral" means the property subject to a security interest, and includes accounts and chattel paper which have been sold;

(*d*) "Debtor" means the person who owes payment or other performance of the obligation secured, whether or not he owns or has rights in the collateral, and includes the seller of accounts or chattel paper. Where the debtor and the owner of the collateral are not the same person, the term "debtor" means the owner of the collateral in any provision of the Article dealing with the collateral, the obligor in any provision dealing with the obligation, and may include both where the context so requires;

(*e*) "Deposit account" means a demand, time, savings, passbook or like account maintained with a bank, savings and loan association, credit union or like organization, other than an account evidenced by a certificate of deposit;

(*f*) "Document" means document of title as defined in the general definitions of Article 1 (Section 1–201), and a receipt of the kind described in subsection (2) of Section 7–201;

(*g*) "Encumbrance" includes real estate mortgages and other liens on real estate and all other rights in real estate that are not ownership interests;

(*h*) "Goods" includes all things which are movable at the time the security interest attaches or which are fixtures (Section 9–313), but does not include money, documents, instruments, accounts, chattel paper, general intangibles, or minerals or the like (including oil and gas) before extraction. "Goods" also includes standing timber which is to be cut and removed under a conveyance or contract for sale, the unborn young of animals, and growing crops;

(*i*) "Instrument" means a negotiable instrument (defined in Section 3–104), or a security (defined in Section 8–102) or any other writing which evidences a right to the payment of money and is not itself a security agreement or lease and is of a type which is in ordinary course of business transferred by delivery with any necessary indorsement or assignment;

(*j*) "Mortgage" means a consensual interest created by a real estate mortgage, a trust deed on real estate, or the like;

(*k*) An advance is made "pursuant to commitment" if the secured party has bound himself to make it, whether or not a subsequent event of default or other event not within his control has relieved or may relieve him from his obligation;

(*l*) "Security agreement" means an agreement which creates or provides for a security interest;

(*m*) "Secured party" means a lender, seller or other person in whose favor there is a security interest, including a person to whom accounts or chattel paper have been sold. When the holders of obligations issued under an indenture of trust, equipment trust agreement or the like are represented by a trustee or other person, the representative is the secured party;

(*n*) "Transmitting utility" means any person primarily engaged in the railroad, street railway or trolley bus business, the electric or electronics communications transmission business, the transmission of goods by pipeline, or the transmission or the production and transmission of electricity, steam, gas or water, or the provision of sewer service.

(2) Other definitions applying to this Article and the sections in which they appear are:

"Account."	Section 9–106.
"Attach."	Section 9–203.
"Construction mortgage."	Section 9–313(1).
"Consumer goods."	Section 9–109(1).
"Equipment."	Section 9–109(2).
"Farm products."	Section 9–109(3).
"Fixture."	Section 9–313(1).
"Fixture filing."	Section 9–313(1).

"General intangibles."   Section 9—106.
"Inventory."   Section 9—109(4).
"Lien creditor."   Section 9—301(3).
"Proceeds."   Section 9—306(1).
"Purchase money security interest."   Section 9—107.
"United States."   Section 9—103.

(3) The following definitions in other Articles apply to this Article:

"Check."   Section 3—104.
"Contract for sale."   Section 2—106.
"Holder in due course."   Section 3—302.
"Note."   Section 3—104.
"Sale."   Section 2—106.

(4) In addition Article 1 contains general definitions and principles of construction and interpretation applicable throughout this Article.

Sec. 9—106. Definitions: "Account"; "General Intangibles." "Account" means any right to payment for goods sold or leased or for services rendered which is not evidenced by an instrument or chattel paper, whether or not it has been earned by performance. "General intangibles" means any personal property (including things in action) other than goods, accounts, chattel paper, documents, instruments, and money. All rights to payment earned or unearned under a charter or other contract involving the use or hire of a vessel and all rights incident to the charter or contract are accounts.

Sec. 9—107. Definitions: "Purchase Money Security Interest." A security interest is a "purchase money security interest" to the extent that it is

(a) taken or retained by the seller of the collateral to secure all or part of its price; or

(b) taken by a person who by making advances or incurring an obligation gives value to enable the debtor to acquire rights in or the use of collateral if such value is in fact so used.

Sec. 9—108. When After-Acquired Collateral Not Security for Antecedent Debt. Where a secured party makes an advance, incurs an obligation, releases a perfected security interest, or otherwise gives new value which is to be secured in whole or in part by after-acquired property his security interest in the after-acquired collateral shall be deemed to be taken for new value and not as security for an antecedent debt if the debtor acquires his rights in such collateral either in the ordinary course of his business or under a contract of purchase made pursuant to the security agreement within a reasonable time after new value is given.

Sec. 9—109. Classification of Goods; "Consumer Goods"; "Equipment"; "Farm Products"; "Inventory." Goods are

(1) "consumer goods" if they are used or bought for use primarily for personal, family or household purposes;

(2) "equipment" if they are used or bought for use primarily in business (including farming or a profession) or by a debtor who is a non-profit organization or a governmental subdivision or agency or if the goods are not included in the definitions of inventory, farm products or consumer goods;

(3) "farm products" if they are crops or livestock or supplies used or produced in farming operations or if they are products of crops or livestock in their un-manufactured states (such as ginned cotton, wool-clip, maple syrup, milk and eggs), and if they are in the possession of a debtor engaged in raising, fattening, grazing or other farming operations. If goods are farm products they are neither equipment nor inventory;

(4) "inventory" if they are held by a person who holds them for sale or lease or to be furnished under contracts of service or if he has so furnished them, or if they are raw materials, work in process or materials used or consumed in a business. Inventory of a person is not to be classified as his equipment.

Sec. 9—110. Sufficiency of Description. For the purposes of this Article any description of personal property or real estate is sufficient whether or not it is specific if it reasonably identifies what is described.

Sec. 9—111. Applicability of Bulk Transfer Laws. The creation of a security interest is not a bulk transfer under Article 6 (see Section 6—103).

Sec. 9—112. Where Collateral Is Not Owned by Debtor. Unless otherwise agreed, when a secured party knows that collateral is owned by a person who is not the debtor, the owner of the collateral is entitled to receive from the secured party any surplus under Section 9—502(2) or under Section 9—504(1), and is not liable for the debt or for any deficiency after resale, and he has the same right as the debtor

(*a*) to receive statements under Section 9—208;

(*b*) to receive notice of and to object to a secured party's proposal to retain the collateral in satisfaction of the indebtedness under Section 9—505;

(*c*) to redeem the collateral under Section 9—506;

(*d*) to obtain injunctive or other relief under Section 9—507(1); and

(*e*) to recover losses caused to him under Section 9—208(2).

Sec. 9—113. Security Interests Arising Under Article on Sales. A security interest arising solely under the Article on Sales (Article 2) is subject to the provisions of this Article except that to the extent that and so long as the debtor does not have or does not lawfully obtain possession of the goods

(*a*) no security agreement is necessary to make the security interest enforceable; and

(*b*) no filing is required to perfect the security interest; and

(*c*) the rights of the secured party on default by the debtor are governed by the Article on Sales (Article 2).

Sec. 9—114. Consignment. (1) A person who delivers goods under a consignment which is not a security interest and who would be required to file under this Article by paragraph (3) (*c*) of Section 2—326 has priority over a secured party who is or becomes a creditor of the consignee and who would have a perfected security interest in the goods if they were the property of the consignee, and also has priority with respect to identifiable cash proceeds received on or before delivery of the goods to a buyer, if

(*a*) the consignor complies with the filing provision of the Article on Sales with respect to consignments (paragraph (3) (*c*) of Section 2—326) before the consignee receives possession of the goods; and

(*b*) the consignor gives notification in writing to the holder of the security interest if the holder has filed a financing statement covering the same types of goods before the date of the filing made by the consignor; and

(*c*) the holder of the security interest receives the notification within five years before the consignee receives possession of the goods; and

(*d*) the notification states that the consignor expects to deliver goods on consignment to the consignee, describing the goods by item or type.

(2) In the case of a consignment which is not a security interest and in which the requirements of the preceding subsection have not been met, a person who delivers goods to another is subordinate to a person who would have a perfected security interest in the goods if they were the property of the debtor.

PART II

VALIDITY OF SECURITY AGREEMENT AND RIGHTS OF PARTIES THERETO

Sec. 9—201. General Validity of Security Agreement. Except as otherwise provided by this Act a security agreement is effective according to its terms between the parties, against purchasers of the collateral and against creditors. Nothing in this Article validates any charge or practice illegal under any statute or regulation thereunder governing usury, small loans, retail installment sales, or the like, or extends the application of any such statute or regulation to any transaction not otherwise subject thereto.

Sec. 9—202. Title to Collateral Immaterial. Each provision of this Article with regard to rights, obligations and remedies applies whether title to collateral is in the secured party or in the debtor.

Sec. 9—203. Attachment and Enforceability of Security Interest; Proceeds; Formal Requisites. (1) Subject to the provisions of Section 4—208 on the security interest of a collecting bank and Section 9—113 on a security interest arising under the Article on Sales, a security interest is not enforceable against the debtor or third parties with respect to the collateral and does not attach unless

(*a*) the collateral is in the possession of the secured party pursuant to agreement, or the debtor has signed a security agreement which contains a description of the collateral and in addition, when the security interest covers crops growing or to be grown or timber to be cut, a description of the land concerned; and

(*b*) value has been given; and

(*c*) the debtor has rights in the collateral.

(2) A security interest attaches when it becomes enforceable against the debtor with respect to the collateral. Attachment occurs as soon as all of the events specified in subsection (1) have taken place unless explicit agreement postpones the time of attaching.

(3) Unless otherwise agreed a security agreement gives the secured party the rights to proceeds provided by Section 9—306.

(4) A transaction, although subject to this Article, is also subject to ....*, and in the case of conflict between the provisions of this Article and any such statute, the provisions of such statute control. Failure to comply with any applicable statute has only the effect which is specified therein.

Note: *At * in subsection (4) insert reference to any local statute regulating small loans, retail installment sales and the like.*

The foregoing subsection (4) is designed to make it clear that certain transactions, although subject to this Article, must also comply with other applicable legislation.

This Article is designed to regulate all the "security" aspects of transactions within its scope. There is, however, much regulatory legislation, particularly in the consumer field, which supplements this Article and should not be repealed by its enactment. Examples are small loan acts, retail installment selling acts and the like. Such acts may provide for licensing and rate regulation and may prescribe particular forms of contract. Such provisions should remain in force despite the enactment of this Article. On the other hand if a retail installment selling act contains provisions on filing, rights on default, etc., such provisions should be repealed as inconsistent with this Article except that inconsistent provisions as to deficiencies, penalties, etc., in the Uniform Consumer Credit Code and other recent related legislation should remain because those statutes were drafted after the substantial enactment of the Article and with the intention of modifying certain provisions of this Article as to consumer credit.

Sec. 9—204. After-Acquired Property; Future Advances. (1) Except as provided in subsection (2), a security agreement may provide that any or all obligations covered by the security agreement are to be secured by after-acquired collateral.

(2) No security interest attaches under an after-acquired property clause to consumer goods other than accessions (Section 9—314) when given as additional security unless the debtor acquires rights in them within ten days after the secured party gives value.

(3) Obligations covered by a security agreement may include future advances or other value whether or not the advances or value are given pursuant to commitment (subsection (1) of Section 9—105).

Sec. 9—205. Use or Disposition of Collateral Without Accounting Permissible. A security interest is not invalid or fraudulent against creditors by reason of liberty in the debtor to use, commingle or dispose of all or part of the collateral (including returned or repossessed goods) or to collect or compromise accounts or chattel paper, or to accept the return of goods or make repossessions, or to use, commingle or dispose of proceeds, or by reason of the failure of the secured party to require the debtor to account for proceeds or replace collateral. This section does not relax the requirements of possession where perfection of a security interest depends upon possession of the collateral by the secured party or by a bailee.

Sec. 9—206. Agreement Not to Assert Defenses Against Assignee; Modification of Sales Warranties Where Security Agreement Exists. (1) Subject to any statute or decision which establishes a different rule for buyers or lessees of consumer goods, an agreement by a buyer or lessee that he will not assert against an assignee any claim or defense which he may have against the seller or lessor is enforceable by an assignee who takes his assignment for value, in good faith and without notice of a claim or defense, except as to defenses of a type which may be asserted against a holder in due course of a negotiable instrument under the Article on Commercial Paper (Article 3). A buyer who as part of one transaction signs both a negotiable instrument and a security agreement makes such an agreement.

(2) When a seller retains a purchase money security interest in goods the Article on Sales (Article 2) governs the sale and any disclaimer, limitation or modification of the seller's warranties.

Sec. 9—207. Rights and Duties When Collateral Is in Secured Party's Possession. (1) A secured party must use reasonable care in the custody and preservation of collateral in his possession. In the case of an instrument or chattel paper reasonable care includes taking necessary steps to preserve rights against prior parties unless otherwise agreed.

(2) Unless otherwise agreed, when collateral is in the secured party's possession

(a) reasonable expenses (including the cost of any insurance and payment of taxes or other charges) incurred in the custody, preservation, use or operation of the collateral are chargeable to the debtor and are secured by the collateral;

(b) the risk of accidental loss or damage is on the debtor to the extent of any deficiency in any effective insurance coverage;

(c) the secured party may hold as additional security any increase or profits (except money) received from the collateral, but money so received, unless remitted to the debtor, shall be applied in reduction of the secured obligation;

(d) the secured party must keep the collateral identifiable but fungible collateral may be commingled;

(e) the secured party may repledge the collateral upon terms which do not impair the debtor's right to redeem it.

(3) A secured party is liable for any loss caused by his failure to meet any obligation imposed by the preceding subsections but does not lose his security interest.

(4) A secured party may use or operate the collateral for the purpose of preserving the collateral or its value or pursuant to the order of a court of appropriate jurisdiction or, except in the case of consumer goods, in the manner and to the extent provided in the security agreement.

Sec. 9—208. Request for Statement of Account or List of Collateral. (1) A debtor may sign a statement indicating what he believes to be the aggregate amount of unpaid indebtedness as of a specified date and may send it to the secured party with a request that the statement be approved or corrected and returned to the debtor. When the security agreement or any other record kept by the secured party identifies the collateral a debtor may similarly request the secured party to approve or correct a list of the collateral.

(2) The secured party must comply with such a request within two weeks after receipt by sending a written correction or approval. If the secured party claims a security interest in all of a particular type of collateral owned by the debtor he may indicate that fact in his reply and need not approve or correct an itemized list of such collateral. If the secured party without reasonable excuse fails to comply he

is liable for any loss caused to the debtor thereby; and if the debtor has properly included in his request a good faith statement of the obligation or a list of the collateral or both the secured party may claim a security interest only as shown in the statement against persons misled by his failure to comply. If he no longer has an interest in the obligation or collateral at the time the request is received he must disclose the name and address of any successor in interest known to him and he is liable for any loss caused to the debtor as a result of failure to disclose. A successor in interest is not subject to this section until a request is received by him.

(3) A debtor is entitled to such a statement once every six months without charge. The secured party may require payment of a charge not exceeding $10 for each additional statement furnished.

PART III

RIGHTS OF THIRD PARTIES; PERFECTED AND UNPERFECTED SECURITY INTERESTS; RULES OF PRIORITY

Sec. 9—301. Persons Who Take Priority Over Unperfected Security Interests; Rights of "Lien Creditor." (1) Except as otherwise provided in subsection (2), an unperfected security interest is subordinate to the rights of

(a) persons entitled to priority under Section 9—312;

(b) a person who becomes a lien creditor before the security interest is perfected;

(c) in the case of goods, instruments, documents, and chattel paper, a person who is not a secured party and who is a transferee in bulk or other buyer not in ordinary course of business or is a buyer of farm products in ordinary course of business, to the extent that he gives value and receives delivery of the collateral without knowledge of the security interest and before it is perfected;

(d) in the case of accounts and general intangibles, a person who is not a secured party and who is a transferee to the extent that he gives value without knowledge of the security interest and before it is perfected.

(2) If the secured party files with respect to a purchase money security interest before or within ten days after the debtor receives possession of the collateral, he takes priority over the rights of a transferee in bulk or of a lien creditor which arise between the time the security interest attaches and the time of filing.

(3) A "lien creditor" means a creditor who has acquired a lien on the property involved by attachment, levy or the like and includes an assignee for benefit of creditors from the time of assignment, and a trustee in bankruptcy from the date of the filing of the petition or a receiver in equity from the time of appointment.

(4) A person who becomes a lien creditor while a security interest is perfected takes subject to the security interest only to the extent that it secures advances made before he becomes a lien creditor or within 45 days thereafter or made without knowledge of the lien or pursuant to a commitment entered into without knowledge of the lien.

Sec. 9—302. When Filing Is Required to Perfect Security Interest; Security Interests to Which Filing Provisions of This Article Do Not Apply. (1) A financing statement must be filed to perfect all security interests except the following:

(a) a security interest in collateral in possession of the secured party under Section 9—305;

(b) a security interest temporarily perfected in instruments or documents without delivery under Section 9—304 or in proceeds for a 10 day period under Section 9—306;

(c) a security interest created by an assignment of a beneficial interest in a trust or a decedent's estate;

(d) a purchase money security interest in consumer goods; but filing is required for a motor vehicle required to be registered; and fixture filing is required for priority over conflicting interests in fixtures to the extent provided in Section 9—313;

(e) an assignment of accounts which does not alone or in conjunction with other assignments to the same assignee transfer a significant part of the outstanding accounts of the assignor;

(f) a security interest of a collecting bank (Section 4—208) or arising under the Article on Sales (see Section 9—113) or covered in subsection (3) of this section;

(g) an assignment for the benefit of all the creditors of the transferor, and subsequent transfers by the assignee thereunder.

(2) If a secured party assigns a perfected security interest, no filing under this Article is required in order to continue the perfected status of the security interest against creditors of and transferees from the original debtor.

(3) The filing of a financing statement otherwise required by this Article is not necessary or effective to perfect a security interest in property subject to

(a) a statute or treaty of the United States which provides for a national or international registration or a national or international certificate of title or which specifies a place of filing different from that specified in this Article for filing of the security interest; or

(b) the following statutes of this state; [list any certificate of title statute covering automobiles, trailers, mobile homes, boats, farm tractors, or the like, and any central filing statute*.]; but during any period in which collateral is inventory held for sale by a person who is in the business of selling goods of that kind, the filing provisions of this Article (Part 4) apply to a security interest in that collateral created by him as debtor; or

* **Note:** *It is recommended that the provisions of certificate of title acts for perfection of security interests by notation on the certificates should be amended to exclude coverage of inventory held for sale.*

(c) a certificate of title statute of another jurisdiction under the law of which indication of a security interest on the certificate is required as a condition of perfection (subsection (2) of Section 9—103).

(4) Compliance with a statute or treaty described in subsection (3) is equivalent to the filing of a financing statement under this Article, and a security interest in property subject to the statute or treaty can be perfected only by compliance therewith except as provided in Section 9—103 on multiple state transactions. Duration and renewal of perfection of a security interest perfected by compliance with the statute or treaty are governed by the provisions of the statute or treaty; in other respects the security interest is subject to this Article.

Sec. 9—303. When Security Interest Is Perfected; Continuity of Perfection.   (1) A security interest is perfected when it has attached and when all of the applicable steps required for perfection have been taken. Such steps are specified in Sections 9—302, 9—304, 9—305 and 9—306. If such steps are taken before the security interest attaches, it is perfected at the time when it attaches.

(2) If a security interest is originally perfected in any way permitted under this Article and is subsequently perfected in some other way under this Article, without an intermediate period when it was unperfected, the security interest shall be deemed to be perfected continuously for the purposes of this Article.

Sec. 9—304. Perfection of Security Interest in Instruments, Documents, and Goods Covered by Documents; Perfection by Permissive Filing; Temporary Perfection Without Filing or Transfer of Possession.   (1) A security interest in chattel paper or negotiable documents may be perfected by filing. A security interest in money or instruments (other than instruments which constitute part of chattel paper) can be perfected only by the secured party's taking possession, except as provided in subsections (4) and (5) of this section and subsections (2) and (3) of Section 9—306 on proceeds.

(2) During the period that goods are in the possession of the issuer of a negotiable document therefor, a security interest in the goods is perfected by perfecting a

security interest in the document, and any security interest in the goods otherwise perfected during such period is subject thereto.

(3) A security interest in goods in the possession of a bailee other than one who has issued a negotiable document therefor is perfected by issuance of a document in the name of the secured party or by the bailee's receipt of notification of the secured party's interest or by filing as to the goods.

(4) A security interest in instruments or negotiable documents is perfected without filing or the taking of possession for a period of 21 days from the time it attaches to the extent that it arises for new value given under a written security agreement.

(5) A security interest remains perfected for a period of 21 days without filing where a secured party having a perfected security interest in an instrument, a negotiable document or goods in possession of a bailee other than one who has issued a negotiable document therefor

(a) makes available to the debtor the goods or documents representing the goods for the purpose of ultimate sale or exchange or for the purpose of loading, unloading, storing, shipping, transshipping, manufacturing, processing or otherwise dealing with them in a manner preliminary to their sale or exchange, but priority between conflicting security interests in the goods is subject to subsection (3) of Section 9–312; or

(b) delivers the instrument to the debtor for the purpose of ultimate sale or exchange or of presentation, collection, renewal or registration of transfer.

(6) After the 21 day period in subsections (4) and (5) perfection depends upon compliance with applicable provisions of this Article.

Sec. 9–305. When Possession by Secured Party Perfects Security Interest Without Filing. A security interest in letters of credit and advices of credit (subsection (2)(a) of Section 5–116), goods, instruments, money, negotiable documents or chattel paper may be perfected by the secured party's taking possession of the collateral. If such collateral other than goods covered by a negotiable document is held by a bailee, the secured party is deemed to have possession from the time the bailee receives notification of the secured party's interest. A security interest is perfected by possession from the time possession is taken without relation back and continues only so long as possession is retained, unless otherwise specified in this Article. The security interest may be otherwise perfected as provided in this Article before or after the period of possession by the secured party.

Sec. 9–306. "Proceeds"; Secured Party's Rights on Disposition of Collateral. (1) "Proceeds" includes whatever is received upon the sale, exchange, collection or other disposition of collateral or proceeds. Insurance payable by reason of loss or damage to the collateral is proceeds, except to the extent that it is payable to a person other than a party to the security agreement. Money, checks, deposit accounts, and the like are "cash proceeds." All other proceeds are "non-cash proceeds."

(2) Except where this Article otherwise provides, a security interest continues in collateral notwithstanding sale, exchange or other disposition thereof unless the disposition was authorized by the secured party in the security agreement or otherwise, and also continues in any identifiable proceeds including collections received by the debtor.

(3) The security interest in proceeds is a continuously perfected security interest if the interest in the original collateral was perfected but it ceases to be a perfected security interest and becomes unperfected ten days after receipt of the proceeds by the debtor unless

(a) a filed financing statement covers the original collateral and the proceeds are collateral in which a security interest may be perfected by filing in the office or offices where the financing statement has been filed and, if the proceeds are acquired with cash proceeds, the description of collateral in the financing statement indicates the types of property constituting the proceeds; or (*b*) a filed financing statement covers the original collateral and the proceeds are identifiable cash proceeds; or

(*c*) the security interest in the proceeds is perfected before the expiration of the ten day period.

Except as provided in this section, a security interest in proceeds can be perfected only by the methods or under the circumstances permitted in this Article for original collateral of the same type.

(4) In the event of insolvency proceedings instituted by or against a debtor, a secured party with a perfected security interest in proceeds has a perfected security interest only in the following proceeds:

(*a*) in identifiable non-cash proceeds and in separate deposit accounts containing only proceeds;

(*b*) in identifiable cash proceeds in the form of money which is neither commingled with other money nor deposited in a deposit account prior to the insolvency proceedings;

(*c*) in identifiable cash proceeds in the form of checks and the like which are not deposited in a deposit account prior to the insolvency proceedings; and

(*d*) in all cash and deposit accounts of the debtor in which proceeds have been commingled with other funds, but the perfected security interest under this paragraph (*d*) is

(*i*) subject to any right to set-off; and

(*ii*) limited to an amount not greater than the amount of any cash proceeds received by the debtor within ten days before the institution of the insolvency proceedings less the sum of (I) the payments to the secured party on account of cash proceeds received by the debtor during such period and (II) the cash proceeds received by the debtor during such period to which the secured party is entitled under paragraphs (*a*) through (*c*) of this subsection (4).

(5) If a sale of goods results in an account or chattel paper which is transferred by the seller to a secured party, and if the goods are returned to or are repossessed by the seller or the secured party, the following rules determine priorities:

(*a*) If the goods were collateral at the time of sale, for an indebtedness of the seller which is still unpaid, the original security interest attaches again to the goods and continues as a perfected security interest if it was perfected at the time when the goods were sold. If the security interest was originally perfected by a filing which is still effective, nothing further is required to continue the perfected status; in any other case, the secured party must take possession of the returned or repossessed goods or must file.

(*b*) An unpaid transferee of the chattel paper has a security interest in the goods against the transferor. Such security interest is prior to a security interest asserted under paragraph (*a*) to the extent that the transferee of the chattel paper was entitled to priority under Section 9–308.

(*c*) An unpaid transferee of the account has a security interest in the goods against the transferor. Such security interest is subordinate to a security interest asserted under paragraph (*a*).

(*d*) A security interest of an unpaid transferee asserted under paragraph (*b*) or (*c*) must be perfected for protection against creditors of the transferor and purchasers of the returned or repossessed goods.

Sec. 9–307. Protection of Buyers of Goods. (1) A buyer in ordinary course of business (subsection (9) of Section 1–201) other than a person buying farm products from a person engaged in farming operations takes free of a security interest created by his seller even though the security interest is perfected and even though the buyer knows of its existence.

(2) In the case of consumer goods, a buyer takes free of a security interest even though perfected if he buys without knowledge of the security interest, for value

and for his own personal, family or household purposes unless prior to the purchase the secured party has filed a financing statement covering such goods.

(3) A buyer other than a buyer in ordinary course of business (subsection (1) of this section) takes free of a security interest to the extent that it secures future advances made after the secured party acquires knowledge of the purchase, or more than 45 days after the purchase, whichever first occurs, unless made pursuant to a commitment entered into without knowledge of the purchase and before the expiration of the 45 day period.

Sec. 9—308. **Purchase of Chattel Paper and Instruments.** A purchaser of chattel paper or an instrument who gives new value and takes possession of it in the ordinary course of his business has priority over a security interest in the chattel paper or instrument

(a) which is perfected under Section 9—304 (permissive filing and temporary perfection) or under Section 9—306 (perfection as to proceeds) if he acts without knowledge that the specific paper or instrument is subject to a security interest; or

(b) which is claimed merely as proceeds of inventory subject to a security interest (Section 9—306) even though he knows that the specific paper or instrument is subject to the security interest.

Sec. 9—309. **Protection of Purchasers of Instruments and Documents.** Nothing in this Article limits the rights of a holder in due course of a negotiable instrument (Section 3—302) or a holder to whom a negotiable document of title has been duly negotiated (Section 7—501) or a bona fide purchaser of a security (Section 8—301) and such holders or purchasers take priority over an earlier security interest even though perfected. Filing under this Article does not constitute notice of the security interest to such holders or purchasers.

Sec. 9—310. **Priority of Certain Liens Arising by Operation of Law.** When a person in the ordinary course of his business furnishes services or materials with respect to goods subject to a security interest, a lien upon goods in the possession of such person given by statute or rule of law for such materials or services takes priority over a perfected security interest unless the lien is statutory and the statute expressly provides otherwise.

Sec. 9—311. **Alienability of Debtor's Rights: Judicial Process.** The debtor's rights in collateral may be voluntarily or involuntarily transferred (by way of sale, creation of a security interest, attachment, levy, garnishment or other judicial process) notwithstanding a provision in the security agreement prohibiting any transfer or making the transfer constitute a default.

Sec. 9—312. **Priorities Among Conflicting Security Interests in the Same Collateral.** (1) The rules of priority stated in other sections of this Part and in the following sections shall govern when applicable: Section 4—208 with respect to the security interests of collecting banks in items being collected, accompanying documents and proceeds; Section 9—103 on security interests related to other jurisdictions; Section 9—114 on consignments.

(2) A perfected security interest in crops for new value given to enable the debtor to produce the crops during the production season and given not more than three months before the crops become growing crops by planting or otherwise takes priority over an earlier perfected security interest to the extent that such earlier interest secures obligations due more than six months before the crops become growing crops by planting or otherwise, even though the person giving new value had knowledge of the earlier security interest.

(3) A perfected purchase money security interest in inventory has priority over a conflicting security interest in the same inventory and also has priority in identifiable cash proceeds received on or before the delivery of the inventory to a buyer if

(a) the purchase money security interest is perfected at the time the debtor receives possession of the inventory; and

(b) the purchase money secured party gives notification in writing to the holder of the conflicting security interest if the holder had filed a financing statement covering the same types of inventory (*i*) before the date of the filing made by the purchase money secured party, or (*ii*) before the beginning of the 21 day period where the purchase money security interest is temporarily perfected without filing or possession (subsection (5) of Section 9–304); and

(*c*) the holder of the conflicting security interest receives the notification within five years before the debtor receives possession of the inventory; and

(*d*) the notification states that the person giving the notice has or expects to acquire a purchase money security interest in inventory of the debtor, describing such inventory by item or type.

(4) A purchase money security interest in collateral other than inventory has priority over a conflicting security interest in the same collateral or its proceeds if the purchase money security interest is perfected at the time the debtor receives possession of the collateral or within ten days thereafter.

(5) In all cases not governed by other rules stated in this section (including cases of purchase money security interests which do not qualify for the special priorities set forth in subsections (3) and (4) of this section), priority between conflicting security interests in the same collateral shall be determined according to the following rules:

(*a*) Conflicting security interests rank according to priority in time of filing or perfection. Priority dates from the time a filing is first made covering the collateral or the time the security interest is first perfected, whichever is earlier, provided that there is no period thereafter when there is neither filing nor perfection.

(*b*) So long as conflicting security interests are unperfected, the first to attach has priority.

(6) For the purposes of subsection (5) a date of filing or perfection as to collateral is also a date of filing or perfection as to proceeds.

(7) If future advances are made while a security interest is perfected by filing or the taking of possession, the security interest has the same priority for the purposes of subsection (5) with respect to the future advances as it does with respect to the first advance. If a commitment is made before or while the security interest is so perfected, the security interest has the same priority with respect to advances made pursuant thereto. In other cases a perfected security interest has priority from the date the advance is made.

Sec. 9–313. Priority of Security Interests in Fixtures. (1) In this section and in the provisions of Part 4 of this Article referring to fixture filing, unless the context otherwise requires

(*a*) goods are "fixtures" when they become so related to particular real estate that an interest in them arises under real estate law;

(*b*) a "fixture filing" is the filing in the office where a mortgage on the real estate would be filed or recorded of a financing statement covering goods which are or are to become fixtures and conforming to the requirements of subsection (5) of Section 9–402;

(*c*) a mortgage is a "construction mortgage" to the extent that it secures an obligation incurred for the construction of an improvement on land including the acquisition cost of the land, if the recorded writing so indicates.

(2) A security interest under this Article may be created in goods which are fixtures or may continue in goods which become fixtures, but no security interest exists under this Article in ordinary building materials incorporated into an improvement on land.

(3) This Article does not prevent creation of an encumbrance upon fixtures pursuant to real estate law.

(4) A perfected security interest in fixtures has priority over the conflicting interest of an encumbrancer or owner of the real estate where

(*a*) the security interest is a purchase money security interest, the interest of the encumbrancer or owner arises before the goods become fixtures, the security interest is perfected by a fixing filing before the goods become fixtures or within ten days thereafter, and the debtor has an interest of record in the real estate or is in possession of the real estate; or

(*b*) the security interest is perfected by a fixture filing before the interest of the encumbrancer or owner is of record, the security interest has priority over any conflicting interest of a predecessor in title of the encumbrancer or owner, and the debtor has an interest of record in the real estate or is in possession of the real estate; or

(*c*) the fixtures are readily removable factory or office machines or readily removable replacements of domestic appliances which are consumer goods, and before the goods become fixtures the security interest is perfected by any method permitted by this Article; or

(*d*) the conflicting interest is a lien on the real estate obtained by legal or equitable proceedings after the security interest was perfected by any method permitted by this Article.

(5) A security interest in fixtures, whether or not perfected, has priority over the conflicting interest of an encumbrancer or owner of the real estate where

(*a*) the encumbrancer or owner has consented in writing to the security interest or has disclaimed an interest in the goods as fixtures; or

(*b*) the debtor has a right to remove the goods as against the encumbrancer or owner. If the debtor's right terminates, the priority of the security interest continues for a reasonable time.

(6) Notwithstanding paragraph (*a*) of subsection (4) but otherwise subject to subsections (4) and (5), a security interest in fixtures is subordinate to a construction mortgage recorded before the goods become fixtures if the goods become fixtures before the completion of the construction. To the extent that it is given to refinance a construction mortgage, a mortgage has this priority to the same extent as the construction mortgage.

(7) In cases not within the preceding subsections, a security interest in fixtures is subordinate to the conflicting interest of an encumbrancer or owner of the related real estate who is not the debtor.

(8) When the secured party has priority over all owners and encumbrancers of the real estate, he may, on default, subject to the provisions of Part 5, remove his collateral from the real estate but he must reimburse any encumbrancer or owner of the real estate who is not the debtor and who has not otherwise agreed for the cost of repair of any physical injury, but not for any diminution in value of the real estate caused by the absence of the goods removed or by any necessity of replacing them. A person entitled to reimbursement may refuse permission to remove until the secured party gives adequate security for the performance of this obligation.

Sec. 9—314. Accessions. (1) A security interest in goods which attaches before they are installed in or affixed to other goods takes priority as to the goods installed or affixed (called in this section "accessions") over the claims of all persons to the whole except as stated in subsection (3) and subject to Section 9—315(1).

(2) A security interest which attaches to goods after they become part of a whole is valid against all persons subsequently acquiring interests in the whole except as stated in subsection (3) but is invalid against any person with an interest in the whole at the time the security interest attaches to the goods who has not in writing consented to the security interest or disclaimed an interest in the goods as part of the whole.

(3) The security interests described in subsections (1) and (2) do not take priority over

(*a*) a subsequent purchaser for value of any interest in the whole; or

(*b*) a creditor with a lien on the whole subsequently obtained by judicial proceedings; or (*c*) a creditor with a prior perfected security interest in the whole to the extent that he makes subsequent advances

if the subsequent purchase is made, the lien by judicial proceedings obtained or the subsequent advance under the prior perfected security interest is made or contracted for without knowledge of the security interest and before it is perfected. A purchaser of the whole at a foreclosure sale other than the holder of a perfected security interest purchasing at his own foreclosure sale is a subsequent purchaser within this section.

(4) When under subsections (1) or (2) and (3) a secured party has an interest in accessions which has priority over the claims of all persons who have interests in the whole, he may on default subject to the provisions of Part 5 remove his collateral from the whole but he must reimburse any encumbrancer or owner of the whole who is not the debtor and who has not otherwise agreed for the cost of repair of any physical injury but not for any diminution in value of the whole caused by the absence of the goods removed or by any necessity for replacing them. A person entitled to reimbursement may refuse permission to remove until the secured party gives adequate security for the performance of this obligation.

Sec. 9–315. Priority When Goods Are Commingled or Processed. (1) If a security interest in goods was perfected and subsequently the goods or a part thereof have become part of a product or mass, the security interest continues in the product or mass if

(*a*) the goods are so manufactured, processed, assembled or commingled that their identity is lost in the product or mass; or

(*b*) a financing statement covering the original goods also covers the product into which the goods have been manufactured, processed or assembled.

In a case to which paragraph (*b*) applies, no separate security interest in that part of the original goods which has been manufactured, processed or assembled into the product may be claimed under Section 9–314.

(2) When under subsection (1) more than one security interest attaches to the product or mass, they rank equally according to the ratio that the cost of the goods to which each interest originally attached bears to the cost of the total product or mass.

Sec. 9–316. Priority Subject to Subordination. Nothing in this Article prevents subordination by agreement by any person entitled to priority.

Sec. 9–317. Secured Party Not Obligated on Contract of Debtor. The mere existence of a security interest or authority given to the debtor to dispose of or use collateral does not impose contract or tort liability upon the secured party for the debtor's acts or omissions.

Sec. 9–318. Defense Against Assignee; Modification of Contract After Notification of Assignment; Term Prohibiting Assignment Ineffective; Identification and Proof of Assignment. (1) Unless an account debtor has made an enforceable agreement not to assert defenses or claims arising out of a sale as provided in Section 9–206 the rights of an assignee are subject to

(*a*) all the terms of the contract between the account debtor and assignor and any defense or claim arising therefrom; and

(*b*) any other defense or claim of the account debtor against the assignor which accrues before the account debtor receives notification of the assignment.

(2) So far as the right to payment or a part thereof under an assigned contract has not been fully earned by performance, and notwithstanding notification of the assignment, any modification of or substitution for the contract made in good faith and in accordance with reasonable commercial standards is effective against an assignee unless the account debtor has otherwise agreed but the assignee acquires corresponding rights under the modified or substituted contract. The assignment may provide that such modification or substitution is a breach by the assignor.

(3) The account debtor is authorized to pay the assignor until the account debtor

receives notification that the amount due or to become due has been assigned and that payment is to be made to the assignee. A notification which does not reasonably identify the rights assigned is ineffective. If requested by the account debtor, the assignee must seasonably furnish reasonable proof that the assignment has been made and unless he does so the account debtor may pay the assignor.

(4) A term in any contract between an account debtor and an assignor is ineffective if it prohibits assignment of an account or prohibits creation of a security interest in a general intangible for money due or to become due or requires the account debtor's consent to such assignment or security interest.

PART IV

FILING

Sec. 9—401. Place of Filing; Erroneous Filing; Removal of Collateral.
First Alternative Subsection (1)
(1) The proper place to file in order to perfect a security interest is as follows:

(a) when the collateral is timber to be cut or is minerals or the like (including oil and gas) or accounts subject to subsection (5) of Section 9—103, or when the financing statement is filed as a fixture filing (Section 9—313) and the collateral is goods which are or are to become fixtures, then in the office where a mortgage on the real estate would be filed or recorded;

(b) in all other cases, in the office of the [Secretary of State].
Second Alternative Subsection (1)
(1) The proper place to file in order to perfect a security interest is as follows:

(a) when the collateral is equipment used in farming operations, or farm products, or accounts or general intangibles arising from or relating to the sale of farm products by a farmer, or consumer goods, then in the office of the ....
in the county of the debtor's residence or if the debtor is not a resident of this state then in the office of the .... in the county where the goods are kept, and in addition when the collateral is crops growing or to be grown in the office of the .... in the county where the land is located;

(b) when the collateral is timber to be cut or is minerals or the like (including oil and gas) or accounts subject to subsection (5) of Section 9—103, or when the financing statement is filed as a fixture filing (Section 9—313) and the collateral is goods which are or are to become fixtures, then in the office where a mortgage on the real estate would be filed or recorded;

(c) in all other cases, in the office of the [Secretary of State].
Third Alternative Subsection (1)
(1) The proper place to file in order to perfect a security interest is as follows:

(a) when the collateral is equipment used in farming operations, or farm products, or accounts or general intangibles arising from or relating to the sale of farm products by a farmer, or consumer goods, then in the office of the ....
in the county of the debtor's residence or if the debtor is not a resident of this state then in the office of the .... in the county where the goods are kept, and in addition when the collateral is crops growing or to be grown in the office of the .... in the county where the land is located;

(b) when the collateral is timber to be cut or is minerals or the like (including oil and gas) or accounts subject to subsection (5) of Section 9—103, or when the financing statement is filed as a fixture filing (Section 9—313) and the collateral is goods which are or are to become fixtures, then in the office where a mortgage on the real estate would be filed or recorded;

(c) in all other cases, in the office of the [Secretary of State] and in addition, if the debtor has a place of business in only one county of this state, also in the office of .... of such county, or, if the debtor has no place of business in this state, but resides in the state, also in the office of .... of the county in which he resides.

Note: *One of the three alternatives should be selected as subsection (1).*

(2) A filing which is made in good faith in an improper place or not in all of the places required by this section is nevertheless effective with regard to any collateral as to which the filing complied with the requirements of this Article and is also effective with regard to collateral covered by the financing statement against any person who has knowledge of the contents of such financing statement.

(3) A filing which is made in the proper place in this state continues effective even though the debtor's residence or place of business or the location of the collateral or its use, whichever controlled the original filing, is thereafter changed.

Alternative Subsection (3)

[(3) A filing which is made in the proper county continues effective for four months after a change to another county of the debtor's residence or place of business or the location of the collateral, whichever controlled the original filing. It becomes ineffective thereafter unless a copy of the financing statement signed by the secured party is filed in the new county within said period. The security interest may also be perfected in the new county after the expiration of the four-month period; in such case perfection dates from the time of perfection in the new county. A change in the use of the collateral does not impair the effectiveness of the original filing.]

(4) The rules stated in Section 9—103 determine whether filing is necessary in this state.

(5) Notwithstanding the preceding subsections, and subject to subsection (3) of Section 9—302, the proper place to file in order to perfect a security interest in collateral, including fixtures, of a transmitting utility in the office of the [Secretary of State]. This filing constitutes a fixture filing (Section 9—313) as to the collateral described therein which is or is to become fixtures.

(6) For the purposes of this section, the residence of an organization is its place of business if it has one or its chief executive office if it has more than one place of business.

Note: *Subsection (6) should be used only if the state chooses the Second or Third Alternative Subsection (1).*

Sec. 9—402. Formal Requisites of Financing Statement; Amendments; Mortgage as Financing Statement. (1) A financing statement is sufficient if it gives the names of the debtor and the secured party, is signed by the debtor, gives an address of the secured party from which information concerning the security interest may be obtained, gives a mailing address of the debtor and contains a statement indicating the types, or describing the items, of collateral. A financing statement may be filed before a security agreement is made or a security interest otherwise attaches. When the financing statement covers crops growing or to be grown, the statement must also contain a description of the real estate concerned. When the financing statement covers timber to be cut or covers minerals or the like (including oil and gas) or accounts subject to subsection (5) of Section 9—103, or when the financing statement is filed as a fixture filing (Section 9—313) and the collateral is goods which are or are to become fixtures, the statement must also comply with subsection (5). A copy of the security agreement is sufficient as a financing statement if it contains the above information and is signed by the debtor. A carbon, photographic or other reproduction of a security agreement or a financing statement is sufficient as a financing statement if the security agreement so provides or if the original has been filed in this state.

(2) A financing statement which otherwise complies with subsection (1) is sufficient when it is signed by the secured party instead of the debtor if it is filed to perfect a security interest in

(*a*) collateral already subject to a security interest in another jurisdiction when it is brought into this state, or when the debtor's location is changed to this state.

Such a financing statement must state that the collateral was brought into this state or that the debtor's location was changed to this state under such circumstances; or

(*b*) proceeds under Section 9–306 if the security interest in the original collateral was perfected. Such a financing statement must describe the original collateral; or

(*c*) collateral as to which the filing has lapsed; or

(*d*) collateral acquired after a change of name, identity or corporate structure of the debtor (subsection (7)).

(3) A form substantially as follows is sufficient to comply with subsection (1):

Name of debtor (or assignor) ....

Address ....

Name of secured party (or assignee) ....

Address ....

1. This financing statement covers the following types (or items) of property:
   (Describe) ....

2. (If collateral is crops) The above described crops are growing or are to be grown on:
   (Describe Real Estate) ....

3. (If applicable) The above goods are to become fixtures on*

* Where appropriate substitute either "The above timber is standing on . . . ." or "The above minerals or the like (including oil and gas) or accounts will be financed at the wellhead or minehead of the well or mine located on . . . ."

   (Describe Real Estate) ....
   and this financing statement is to be filed [for record] in the real estate records. (If the debtor does not have an interest of record) The name of a record owner is ....

4. (If products of collateral are claimed) Products of the collateral are also covered.

   (*use*   ....
   whichever   Signature of Debtor
   is   (or Assignor)
   applicable)   ....
                        Signature of Secured Party
                        (or Assignee)

(4) A financing statement may be amended by filing a writing signed by both the debtor and the secured party. An amendment does not extend the period of effectiveness of a financing statement. If any amendment adds collateral, it is effective as to the added collateral only from the filing date of the amendment. In this Article, unless the context otherwise requires, the term "financing statement" means the original financing statement and any amendments.

(5) A financing statement covering timber to be cut or covering minerals or the like (including oil and gas) or accounts subject to subsection (5) of Section 9–103, or a financing statement filed as a fixture filing (Section 9–313) where the debtor is not a transmitting utility, must show that it covers this type of collateral, must recite that it is to be filed [for record] in the real estate records, and the financing statement must contain a description of the real estate [sufficient if it were contained in a mortgage of the real estate to give constructive notice of the mortgage under the law of this state]. If the debtor does not have an interest of record in the real estate, the financing statement must show the name of a record owner.

(6) A mortgage is effective as a financing statement filed as a fixture filing from the date of its recording if

(*a*) the goods are described in the mortgage by item or type; and

(*b*) the goods are or are to become fixtures related to the real estate described in the mortgage; and (*c*) the mortgage complies with the requirements for a financing statement in this section other than a recital that it is to be filed in the real estate records; and

(*d*) the mortgage is duly recorded.

No fee with reference to the financing statement is required other than the regular recording and satisfaction fees with respect to the mortgage.

(7) A financing statement sufficiently shows the name of the debtor if it gives the individual, partnership or corporate name of the debtor, whether or not it adds other trade names or names of partners. Where the debtor so changes his name or in the case of an organization its name, identity or corporate structure that a filed financing statement becomes seriously misleading, the filing is not effective to perfect a security interest in collateral acquired by the debtor more than four months after the change, unless a new appropriate financing statement is filed before the expiration of that time. A filed financing statement remains effective with respect to collateral transferred by the debtor even though the secured party knows of or consents to the transfer.

(8) A financing statement substantially complying with the requirements of this section is effective even though it contains minor errors which are not seriously misleading.

Note: *Language in brackets is optional.*

Note: *Where the state has any special recording system for real estate other than the usual grantor-grantee index (as, for instance, a tract system or a title registration or Torrens system) local adaptations of subsection (5) and Section 9–403(7) may be necessary. See Mass. Gen. Laws Chapter 106, Section 9–409.*

Sec. 9—403. What Constitutes Filing; Duration of Filing; Effect of Lapsed Filing; Duties of Filing Officer. (1) Presentation for filing of a financing statement and tender of the filing fee or acceptance of the statement by the filing officer constitutes filing under this Article.

(2) Except as provided in subsection (6) a filed financing statement is effective for a period of five years from the date of filing. The effectiveness of a filed financing statement lapses on the expiration of the five year period unless a continuation statement is filed prior to the lapse. If a security interest perfected by filing exists at the time insolvency proceedings are commenced by or against the debtor, the security interest remains perfected until termination of the insolvency proceedings and thereafter for a period of sixty days or until expiration of the five year period, whichever occurs later. Upon lapse the security interest becomes unperfected, unless it is perfected without filing. If the security interest becomes unperfected upon lapse, it is deemed to have been unperfected as against a person who became a purchaser or lien creditor before lapse.

(3) A continuation statement may be filed by the secured party within six months prior to the expiration of the five year period specified in subsection (2). Any such continuation statement must be signed by the secured party, identify the original statement by file number and state that the original statement is still effective. A continuation statement signed by a person other than the secured party of record must be accompanied by a separate written statement of assignment signed by the secured party of record and complying with subsection (2) of Section 9–405, including payment of the required fee. Upon timely filing of the continuation statement, the effectiveness of the original statement is continued for five years after the last date to which the filing was effective whereupon it lapses in the same manner as provided in subsection (2) unless another continuation statement is filed prior to such lapse. Succeeding continuation statements may be filed in the same manner to continue the effectiveness of the original statement. Unless a statute on disposition of public records provides otherwise, the filing officer may remove a lapsed statement from the files and destroy it immediately if he has retained a microfilm or other photographic record, or in other cases after one year after the lapse. The filing officer shall so arrange matters by physical annexation of financing statements to

continuation statements or other related filings, or by other means, that if he physically destroys the financing statements of a period more than five years past, those which have been continued by a continuation statement or which are still effective under subsection (6) shall be retained.

(4) Except as provided in subsection (7) a filing officer shall mark each statement with a file number and with the date and hour of filing and shall hold the statement or a microfilm or other photographic copy thereof for public inspection. In addition the filing officer shall index the statement according to the name of the debtor and shall note in the index the file number and the address of the debtor given in the statement.

(5) The uniform fee for filing and indexing and for stamping a copy furnished by the secured party to show the date and place of filing for an original financing statement or for a continuation statement shall be $.............. if the statement is in the standard form prescribed by the [Secretary of State] and otherwise shall be $.............., plus in each case, if the financing statement is subject to subsection (5) of Section 9–402, $............... The uniform fee for each name more than one required to be indexed shall be $.............. The secured party may at his option show a trade name for any person and an extra uniform indexing fee of $.............. shall be paid with respect thereto.

(6) If the debtor is a transmitting utility (subsection (5) of Section 9–401) and a filed financing statement so states, it is effective until a termination statement is filed. A real estate mortgage which is effective as a fixture filing under subsection (6) of Section 9–402 remains effective as a fixture filing until the mortgage is released or satisfied of record or its effectiveness otherwise terminates as to the real estate.

(7) When a financing statement covers timber to be cut or covers minerals or the like (including oil and gas) or accounts subject to subsection (5) of Section 9–103, or is filed as a fixture filing, [it shall be filed for record and] the filing officer shall index it under the names of the debtor and any owner of record shown on the financing statement in the same fashion as if they were the mortgagors in a mortgage of the real estate described, and, to the extent that the law of this state provides for indexing of mortgages under the name of the mortgagee, under the name of the secured party as if he were the mortgagee thereunder, or where indexing is by description in the same fashion as if the financing statement were a mortgage of the real estate described.

Note: *In states in which writings will not appear in the real estate records and indices unless actually recorded the bracketed language in subsection (7) should be used.*

Sec. 9–404. Termination Statement. (1) If a financing statement covering consumer goods is filed on or after ...., then within one month or within ten days following written demand by the debtor after there is no outstanding secured obligation and no commitment to make advances, incur obligations or otherwise give value, the secured party must file with each filing officer with whom the financing statement was filed, a termination statement to the effect that he no longer claims a security interest under the financing statement, which shall be identified by file number. In other cases whenever there is no outstanding secured obligation and no commitment to make advances, incur obligations or otherwise give value, the secured party must on written demand by the debtor send the debtor, for each filing officer with whom the financing statement was filed, a termination statement to the effect that he no longer claims a security interest under the financing statement, which shall be identified by file number. A termination statement signed by a person other than the secured party of record must be accompanied by a separate written statement of assignment signed by the secured party of record and complying with subsection (2) of Section 9–405, including payment of the required fee. If the affected secured party fails to file such a termination statement as required by this subsection, or to send such a termination statement within ten days after proper demand therefor, he shall be liable to the debtor for one hundred dollars, and in addition for any loss caused to the debtor by such failure.

(2) On presentation to the filing officer of such a termination statement he must note it in the index. If he has received the termination statement in duplicate, he shall return one copy of the termination statement to the secured party stamped to show the time of receipt thereof. If the filing officer has a microfilm or other photographic record of the financing statement, and of any related continuation statement, statement of assignment and statement of release, he may remove the originals from the files at any time after receipt of the termination statement, or if he has no such record, he may remove them from the files at any time after one year after receipt of the termination statement.

(3) If the termination statement is in the standard form prescribed by the [Secretary of State], the uniform fee for filing and indexing the termination statement shall be $.......... and otherwise shall be $.........., plus in each case an additional fee of $......... for each name more than one against which the termination statement is required to be indexed.

Note: *The date to be inserted should be the effective date of the revised Article 9.*

Sec. 9—405. **Assignment of Security Interest; Duties of Filing Officer; Fees.** (1) A financing statement may disclose an assignment of a security interest in the collateral described in the financing statement by indication in the financing statement of the name and address of the assignee or by an assignment itself or a copy thereof on the face or back of the statement. On presentation to the filing officer of such a financing statement the filing officer shall mark the same as provided in Section 9—403(4). The uniform fee for filing, indexing and furnishing filing data for a financing statement so indicating an assignment shall be $......... if the statement is in the standard form prescribed by the [Secretary of State] and otherwise shall be $........., plus in each case an additional fee of $......... for each name more than one against which the financing statement is required to be indexed.

(2) A secured party may assign of record all or part of his rights under a financing statement by the filing in the place where the original financing statement was filed of a separate written statement of assignment signed by the secured party of record and setting forth the name of the secured party of record and the debtor, the file number and the date of filing of the financing statement and the name and address of the assignee and containing a description of the collateral assigned. A copy of the assignment is sufficient as a separate statement if it complies with the preceding sentence. On presentation to the filing officer of such a separate statement, the filing officer shall mark such separate statement with the date and hour of the filing. He shall note the assignment on the index of the financing statement, or in the case of a fixture filing, or a filing covering timber to be cut, or covering minerals or the like (including oil and gas) or accounts subject to subsection (5) of Section 9—103, he shall index the assignment under the name of the assignor as grantor and, to the extent that the law of this state provides for indexing the assignment of a mortgage under the name of the assignee, he shall index the assignment of the financing statement under the name of the assignee. The uniform fee for filing, indexing and furnishing filing data about such a separate statement of assignment shall be $......... if the statement is in the standard form prescribed by the [Secretary of State] and otherwise shall be $........., plus in each case an additional fee of $......... for each name more than one against which the statement of assignment is required to be indexed. Notwithstanding the provisions of this subsection, an assignment of record of a security interest in a fixture contained in a mortgage effective as a fixture filing (subsection (6) of Section 9—402) may be made only by an assignment of the mortgage in the manner provided by the law of the state other than this Act.

(3) After the disclosure or filing of an assignment under this section, the assignee is the secured party of record.

Sec. 9—406. Release of Collateral; Duties of Filing Officer; Fees. A secured party of record may by his signed statement release all or a part of any collateral described in a filed financing statement. The statement of release is sufficient if it contains a description of the collateral being released, the name and address of the debtor, the name and address of the secured party, and the file number of the financing statement. A statement of release signed by a person other than the secured party of record must be accompanied by a separate written statement of assignment signed by the secured party of record and complying with subsection (2) of Section 9—405, including payment of the required fee. Upon presentation of such a statement of release to the filing officer he shall mark the statement with the hour and date of filing and shall note the same upon the margin of the index of the filing of the financing statement. The uniform fee for filing and noting such a statement of release shall be $.......... if the statement is in the standard form prescribed by the [Secretary of State] and otherwise shall be $.........., plus in each case an additional fee of $.......... for each name more than one against which the statement of release is required to be indexed.

[**Sec. 9—407. Information From Filing Officer.**] [(1) If the person filing any financing statement, termination statement, statement of assignment, or statement of release, furnishes the filing officer a copy thereof, the filing officer shall upon request note upon the copy the file number and date and hour of the filing of the original and deliver or send the copy to such person.]

[(2) Upon request of any person, the filing officer shall issue his certificate showing whether there is on file on the date and hour stated therein, any presently effective financing statement naming a particular debtor and any statement of assignment thereof and if there is, giving the date and hour of filing of each such statement and the names and addresses of each secured party therein. The uniform fee for such a certificate shall be $.......... if the request for the certificate is in the standard form prescribed by the [Secretary of State] and otherwise shall be $.......... Upon request the filing officer shall furnish a copy of any filed financing statement or statement of assignment for a uniform fee of $.......... per page.]

Note: *This section is proposed as an optional provision to require filing officers to furnish certificates. Local law and practices should be consulted with regard to the advisability of adoption.*

Sec. 9—408. Financing Statements Covering Consigned or Leased Goods. A consignor or lessor of goods may file a financing statement using the terms "consignor," "consignee," "lessor," "lessee" or the like instead of the terms specified in Section 9—402. The provisions of this Part shall apply as appropriate to such a financing statement but its filing shall not of itself be a factor in determining whether or not the consignment or lease is intended as security (Section 1—201 (37)). However, if it is determined for other reasons that the consignment or lease is so intended, a security interest of the consignor or lessor which attaches to the consigned or leased goods is perfected by such filing.

PART V

DEFAULT

Sec. 9—501. Default; Procedure When Security Agreement Covers Both Real and Personal Property. (1) When a debtor is in default under a security agreement, a secured party has the rights and remedies provided in this Part and except as limited by subsection (3) those provided in the security agreement. He may reduce his claim to judgment, foreclose or otherwise enforce the security interest by any available judicial procedure. If the collateral is documents the secured party may proceed either as to the documents or as to the goods covered thereby. A secured party in possession has the rights, remedies and duties provided in Section 9—207. The rights and remedies referred to in this subsection are cumulative.

(2) After default, the debtor has the rights and remedies provided in this Part, those provided in the security agreement and those provided in Section 9—207.

(3) To the extent that they give rights to the debtor and impose duties on the secured party, the rules stated in the subsections referred to below may not be waived or varied except as provided with respect to compulsory disposition of collateral (subsection (3) of Section 9—504 and Section 9—505) and with respect to redemption of collateral (Section 9—506) but the parties may by agreement determine the standards by which the fulfillment of these rights and duties is to be measured if such standards are not manifestly unreasonable:

(a) subsection (2) of Section 9—502 and subsection (2) of Section 9—504 insofar as they require accounting for surplus proceeds of collateral;

(b) subsection (3) of Section 9—504 and subsection (1) of Section 9—505 which deal with disposition of collateral;

(c) subsection (2) of Section 9—505 which deals with acceptance of collateral as discharge of obligation;

(d) Section 9—506 which deals with redemption of collateral; and

(e) subsection (1) of Section 9—507 which deals with the secured party's liability for failure to comply with this Part.

(4) If the security agreement covers both real and personal property, the secured party may proceed under this Part as to the personal property or he may proceed as to both the real and the personal property in accordance with his rights and remedies in respect of the real property in which case the provisions of this Part do not apply.

(5) When a secured party has reduced his claim to judgment the lien of any levy which may be made upon his collateral by virtue of any execution based upon the judgment shall relate back to the date of the perfection of the security interest in such collateral. A judicial sale, pursuant to such execution, is a foreclosure of the security interest by judicial procedure within the meaning of this section, and the secured party may purchase at the sale and thereafter hold the collateral free of any other requirements of this Article.

Sec. 9—502. Collection Rights of Secured Party. (1) When so agreed and in any event on default the secured party is entitled to notify an account debtor or the obligor on an instrument to make payment to him whether or not the assignor was theretofore making collections on the collateral, and also to take control of any proceeds to which he is entitled under Section 9—306.

(2) A secured party who by agreement is entitled to charge back uncollected collateral or otherwise to full or limited recourse against the debtor and who undertakes to collect from the account debtors or obligors must proceed in a commercially reasonable manner and may deduct his reasonable expenses of realization from the collections. If the security agreement secures an indebtedness, the secured party must account to the debtor for any surplus, and unless otherwise agreed, the debtor is liable for any deficiency. But, if the underlying transaction was a sale of accounts or chattel paper, the debtor is entitled to any surplus or is liable for any deficiency only if the security agreement so provides.

Sec. 9—503. Secured Party's Right to Take Possession After Default. Unless otherwise agreed a secured party has on default the right to take possession of the collateral. In taking possession a secured party may proceed without judicial process if this can be done without breach of the peace or may proceed by action. If the security agreement so provides the secured party may require the debtor to assemble the collateral and make it available to the secured party at a place to be designated by the secured party which is reasonably convenient to both parties. Without removal a secured party may render equipment unusable, and may dispose of collateral on the debtor's premises under Section 9—504.

Sec. 9—504. Secured Party's Right to Dispose of Collateral After Default; Effect of Disposition. (1) A secured party after default may sell, lease or otherwise dispose of any or all of the collateral in its then condition or following any commercially reasonable preparation or processing. Any sale of goods is subject to the Article on Sales (Article 2). The proceeds of disposition shall be applied in the order following to

(a) the reasonable expenses of retaking, holding, preparing for sale or lease, selling, leasing and the like and, to the extent provided for in the agreement and not prohibited by law, the reasonable attorneys' fees and legal expenses incurred by the secured party;

(b) the satisfaction of indebtedness secured by the security interest under which the disposition is made;

(c) the satisfaction of indebtedness secured by any subordinate security interest in the collateral if written notification of demand therefor is received before distribution of the proceeds is completed. If requested by the secured party, the holder of a subordinate security interest must seasonably furnish reasonable proof of his interest, and unless he does so, the secured party need not comply with his demand.

(2) If the security interest secures an indebtedness, the secured party must account to the debtor for any surplus, and, unless otherwise agreed, the debtor is liable for any deficiency. But if the underlying transaction was a sale of accounts or chattel paper, the debtor is entitled to any surplus or is liable for any deficiency only if the security agreement so provides.

(3) Disposition of the collateral may be by public or private proceedings and may be made by way of one or more contracts. Sale or other disposition may be as a unit or in parcels and at any time and place and on any terms but every aspect of the disposition including the method, manner, time, place and terms must be commercially reasonable. Unless collateral is perishable or threatens to decline speedily in value or is of a type customarily sold on a recognized market, reasonable notification of the time and place of any public sale or reasonable notification of the time after which any private sale or other intended disposition is to be made shall be sent by the secured party to the debtor, if he has not signed after default a statement renouncing or modifying his right to notification of sale. In the case of consumer goods no other notification need be sent. In other cases notification shall be sent to any other secured party from whom the secured party has received (before sending his notification to the debtor or before the debtor's renunciation of his rights) written notice of a claim of an interest in the collateral. The secured party may buy at any public sale and if the collateral is of a type customarily sold in a recognized market or is of a type which is the subject of widely distributed standard price quotations he may buy at private sale.

(4) When collateral is disposed of by a secured party after default, the disposition transfers to a purchaser for value all of the debtor's rights therein, discharges the security interest under which it is made and any security interest or lien subordinate thereto. The purchaser takes free of all such rights and interests even though the secured party fails to comply with the requirements of this Part or of any judicial proceedings

(a) in the case of a public sale, if the purchaser has no knowledge of any defects in the sale and if he does not buy in collusion with the secured party, other bidders or the person conducting the sale; or

(b) in any other case, if the purchaser acts in good faith.

(5) A person who is liable to a secured party under a guaranty, indorsement, repurchase agreement or the like and who receives a transfer of collateral from the

secured party or is subrogated to his rights has thereafter the rights and duties of the secured party. Such a transfer of collateral is not a sale or disposition of the collateral under this Article.

Sec. 9—505. Compulsory Disposition of Collateral; Acceptance of the Collateral as Discharge of Obligation. (1) If the debtor has paid sixty per cent of the cash price in the case of a purchase money security interest in consumer goods or sixty per cent of the loan in the case of another security interest in consumer goods, and has not signed after default a statement renouncing or modifying his rights under this Part a secured party who has taken possession of collateral must dispose of it under Section 9—504 and if he fails to do so within ninety days after he takes possession the debtor at his option may recover in conversion or under Section 9—507(1) on secured party's liability.

(2) In any other case involving consumer goods or any other collateral a secured party in possession may, after default, propose to retain the collateral in satisfaction of the obligation. Written notice of such proposal shall be sent to the debtor if he has not signed after default a statement renouncing or modifying his rights under this subsection. In the case of consumer goods no other notice need be given. In other cases notice shall be sent to any other secured party from whom the secured party has received (before sending his notice to the debtor or before the debtor's renunciation of his rights) written notice of a claim of an interest in the collateral. If the secured party receives objection in writing from a person entitled to receive notification within twenty-one days after the notice was sent, the secured party must dispose of the collateral under Section 9—504. In the absence of such written objection the secured party may retain the collateral in satisfaction of the debtor's obligation.

Sec. 9—506. Debtor's Right to Redeem Collateral. At any time before the secured party has disposed of collateral or entered into a contract for its disposition under Section 9—504 or before the obligation has been discharged under Section 9—505(2) the debtor or any other secured party may unless otherwise agreed in writing after default redeem the collateral by tendering fulfillment of all obligations secured by the collateral as well as the expenses reasonably incurred by the secured party in retaking, holding and preparing the collateral for disposition, in arranging for the sale, and to the extent provided in the agreement and not prohibited by law, his reasonable attorneys' fees and legal expenses.

Sec. 9—507. Secured Party's Liability for Failure to Comply With This Part. (1) If it is established that the secured party is not proceeding in accordance with the provisions of this Part disposition may be ordered or restrained on appropriate terms and conditions. If the disposition has occurred the debtor or any person entitled to notification or whose security interest has been made known to the secured party prior to the disposition has a right to recover from the secured party any loss caused by a failure to comply with the provisions of this Part. If the collateral is consumer goods, the debtor has a right to recover in any event an amount not less than the credit service charge plus ten per cent of the principal amount of the debt or the time price differential plus ten per cent of the cash price.

(2) The fact that a better price could have been obtained by a sale at a different time or in a different method from that selected by the secured party is not of itself sufficient to establish that the sale was not made in a commercially reasonable manner. If the secured party either sells the collateral in the usual manner in any recognized market therefor or if he sells at the price current in such market at the time of his sale or if he has otherwise sold in conformity with reasonable commercial practices among dealers in the type of property sold he has sold in a commercially reasonable manner. The principles stated in the two proceding sentences with respect to sales also apply as may be appropriate to other types of disposition. A disposition which has been approved in any judicial proceeding or by any bona fide creditors' com-

mittee or representative of creditors shall conclusively be deemed to be commercially reasonable, but this sentence does not indicate that any such approval must be obtained in any case nor does it indicate that any disposition not so approved is not commercially reasonable.

ARTICLE XI

EFFECTIVE DATE AND TRANSITION PROVISIONS

Sec. 11—101. Effective Date. This Act shall become effective at 12:01 A.M. on ...., 19.....

Sec. 11—102. Preservation of Old Transition Provision. The provisions of [here insert reference to the original transition provision in the particular state] shall continue to apply to [the new U.C.C.] and for this purpose the [old U.C.C. and new U.C.C.] shall be considered one continuous statute.

Sec. 11—103. Transition to [New Code]—General Rule. Transactions validly entered into after [effective date of old U.C.C.] and before [effective date of new U.C.C.], and which were subject to the provisions of [old U.C.C.] and which would be subject to this Act as amended if they had been entered into after the effective date of [new U.C.C.] and the rights, duties and interests flowing from such transactions remain valid after the latter date and may be terminated, completed, consummated or enforced as required or permitted by the [new U.C.C.]. Security interests arising out of such transactions which are perfected when [new U.C.C.] becomes effective shall remain perfected until they lapse as provided in [new U.C.C.], and may be continued as permitted by [new U.C.C.], except as stated in Section 11—105.

Sec. 11—104. Transition Provision on Change of Requirement of Filing. A security interest for the perfection of which filing or the taking of possession was required under [old U.C.C.] and which attached prior to the effective date of [new U.C.C.] but was not perfected shall be deemed perfected on the effective date of [new U.C.C.] if [new U.C.C.] permits perfection without filing or authorizes filing in the office or offices where a prior ineffective filing was made.

Sec. 11—105. Transition Provision on Change of Place of Filing. (1) A financing statement filed prior to [effective date of new U.C.C.] which shall not have lapsed prior to [the effective date of new U.C.C.] shall remain effective for the period provided in the [old Code], but not less than five years after the filing.

(2) With respect to any collateral acquired by the debtor subsequent to the effective date of [new U.C.C.], any effective financing statement or continuation statement described in this section shall apply only if the filing or filings are in the office or offices that would be appropriate to perfect the security interests in the new collateral under [new U.C.C.].

(3) The effectiveness of any financing statement or continuation statement filed prior to [effective date of new U.C.C.] may be continued by a continuation statement as permitted by [new U.C.C.], except that if [new U.C.C.] requires a filing in an office where there was no previous financing statement, a new financing statement conforming to Section 11—106 shall be filed in that office.

(4) If the record of a mortgage of real estate would have been effective as a fixture filing of goods described therein if [new U.C.C.] had been in effect on the date of recording the mortgage, the mortgage shall be deemed effective as a fixture filing as to such goods under subsection (6) of Section 9—402 of the [new U.C.C.] on the effective date of [new U.C.C.].

Sec. 11—106. Required Refilings. (1) If a security interest is perfected or has priority when this Act takes effect as to all persons or as to certain persons without any filing or recording, and if the filing of a financing statement would be required for the perfection or priority of the security interest against those persons under [new U.C.C.], the perfection and priority rights of the security interest continue until 3 years after the effective date of [new U.C.C.]. The perfection will then lapse unless a financing statement is filed as provided in subsection (4) or unless the security interest is perfected otherwise than by filing.

(2) If a security interest is perfected when [new U.C.C.] takes effect under a law other than [U.C.C.] which requires no further filing, refiling or recording to continue its perfection, perfection continues until and will lapse 3 years after [new U.C.C.] takes effect, unless a financing statement is filed as provided in subsection (4) or unless the security interest is perfected otherwise than by filing, or unless under subsection (3) of Section 9—302 the other law continues to govern filing.

(3) If a security interest is perfected by a filing, refiling or recording under a law repealed by this Act which required further filing, refiling or recording to continue its perfection, perfection continues and will lapse on the date provided by the law so repealed for such further filing, refiling or recording unless a financing statement is filed as provided in subsection (4) or unless the security interest is perfected otherwise than by filing.

(4) A financing statement may be filed within six months before the perfection of a security interest would otherwise lapse. Any such financing statement may be signed by either the debtor or the secured party. It must identify the security agreement, statement or notice (however denominated in any statute or other law repealed or modified by this Act), state the office where and the date when the last filing, refiling or recording, if any, was made with respect thereto, and the filing number, if any, or book and page, if any, of recording and further state that the security agreement, statement or notice, however denominated, in another filing office under the [U.C.C.] or under any statute or other law repealed or modified by this Act is still effective. Section 9—401 and Section 9—103 determine the proper place to file such a financing statement. Except as specified in this subsection, the provisions of Section 9—403(3) for continuation statements apply to such a financing statement.

Sec. 11—107. Transition Provisions as to Priorities. Except as otherwise provided in [Article 11], [old U.C.C.] shall apply to any questions of priority if the positions of the parties were fixed prior to the effective date of [new U.C.C.]. In other cases questions of priority shall be determined by [new U.C.C.].

Sec. 11—108. Presumption that Rule of Law Continues Unchanged. Unless a change in law has clearly been made, the provisions of [new U.C.C.] shall be deemed declaratory of the meaning of the [old U.C.C.].

CASE INDEX

SUBJECT INDEX

Abandoned property, 496
Acceleration clause, 750-751
Acceptance
  additional terms, 629
  agreements for later writing, 138-140
  banker's, 736
  of bilateral offer, 132-136
  communication, 132-138
  in contracts, 120-142
  of goods, 277-278, 714-717
  how made, 128-132
  and presentment, 824-829
  response to offer, 124-126, 628
  terms unqualified, 120-124
  trade, 737-739
  of unilateral offer, 136-138
  who may accept, 126-128
Acceptor, 734
Accession, and title, 493-494
Accommodation parties, 818-821,
  832
Account, common law action, 11-12
Accountings, 15
  to partner, 897-898, 925
  to principal by agent, 400-403
Actions, 11-12
Act of God, 515
Administrative law, 24-26
Administrator of estate, 15, 259, 295-296,
  543-544, 560
Adultery, 30
Adverse possession, 557-560
Advertisement, contract offer, 95
Age misrepresentation, by infant, 173-
  176
Agency, 371-469. *See also* Agent;
  Principal
  capacity of parties, 376-379, 456-460
  and corporation, 978
  coupled with an interest, 463-466
  creation, 379-385
  dual, 388
  gratuitous, 379-380
  nature, 371-379
  operation of law in, 382-385
  among partners, 906
  ratification of contract, 380-381
  termination, 456-459
  at will, 456-457
Agent. *See also* Agency; Principal
  authority, 416-421
  and authorized contracts, 437-442
  duties, 387-403
  and principal, 372-373, 387-409,
    837-850
  purchasing, 417-418
  sales, 416-417
  and third party, 421, 437-454
  and unauthorized contracts, 443-447
  who may be, 377-379
Agreements. *See also* Contracts
  against competition, 252-253
  completion within year, 269-272
  composition, 215
  illegal, 229-231
  limiting liability, 247-248
  lobbying, 242-246
  in restraint of trade, 251-255
  Sunday, 248-251

  usurious, 235-238
  wagering, 238-242
Alien
  and contract, 180-181
  as partner, 875
Alimony, 4
Allonge, 760, 770
Alteration
  of contract, 341-343
  of negotiable instrument, 793, 812
    855-857
Ambassadors, 53
American system of law, 19-49
Anglo-Saxon law, 9-10, 73
Antitrust legislation, 52, 253-255
Appeal, writ, 66-67
Appellate jurisdiction, 20 n, 56-57
Appropriation, and title, 498-499
Architect approval of building, 305-306
Arguments to jury, 65
Arson, 29, 30
Assault, 29
Assembly, unlawful, 30
Assent
  and duress, 156-158
  and fraud, 150-156
  genuineness, 143-160
  and innocent misrepresentation, 148-
    150
  mistake in, 143-148
  and undue influence, 158-160
Assignee, legal position, 291-293
Assignment
  of duties, 293-295
  of errors, 67
  of money claims, 284
  nature, 282-283
  vs negotiation, 739
  notice, 289-291
  by operation of law, 295-296
  partial, 284-289
  of personal rights, 283
  rights assignable, 283-289
  vs sublease, 578-579
  of wages, 283-284
Assignor, legal position, 291-293
Assumpsit, 11, 185
Attestation clause, 536
Attorney
  at law, 4-5, 373
  in fact, 373
  prosecuting, 56
Auction sales, contract offer, 96
Automobile accident cases, 55
Automobile damage, and bailment, 503

Bail bond, 613
Bailee, 501, 507-511
Bailment, 501-517
  actual, 502
  classification, 507-517
  constructive, 502
  creation, 503-507
  extraordinary, 507, 514-517
  nature, 501-503
  ordinary, 507-514
Bailor, 501, 511-514
Bank, drawee and drawer, 837-850
Bank draft, 736